Child Development

Second Edition

Child Development

Second Edition

A. Christine Harris, Ph. D.

Cosumnes River College

West Publishing Company
Minneapolis/St. Paul   New York   Los Angeles   San Francisco

Dedication: To my best brother Steve

Copy Editor: Benjamin Shriver
Composition: Parkwood Composition
Illustrations: Precision Graphics; Barbara Barnett
Index: Teresa Casey

Cover Photo: © Comstock

Student Study Guide

A study guide has been developed to assist students in mastering the concepts presented in this text. It reinforces chapter material presenting it in a concise format with review questions. An examination copy is available to instructors by contacting West Publishing Company. Students can purchse the study guide from their local bookstore under the title Study Guide to Accompany Child Development, Second Edition, prepared by Ann Le Cheminant Rothschild.

West's Commitment to the Environment

In 1906, West Publishing Company began recycling materials left over from the production of books. This began a tradition of efficient and responsible use of re-sources. Today, up to 95 percent of our legal books and 70 percent of our college and school texts are printed on recycled, acid-free stock. West also recycles nearly 22 million pounds of scrap paper annually—the equivalent of 181,717 trees. Since the 1960s, West has devised ways to capture and recycle waste inks, solvents, oils, and vapors created in the printing process. We also recycle plastics of all kinds, wood, glass, corrugated cardboard, and batteries, and have eliminated the use of styrofoam book packaging. We at West are proud of the longevity and the scope of our commitment to the environment.

Production, Prepress, Printing and Binding by West Publishing Company.

COPYRIGHT © 1986 by   WEST PUBLISHING COMPANY
COPYRIGHT © 1993 by   WEST PUBLISHING COMPANY
                                610 Opperman Drive
                                P.O. Box 64526
                                St. Paul, MN 55164–0526

Library of Congress Cataloging-in-Publication Data

Harris, A. Christine.
   Child development / A. Christine Harris.—2nd ed. p.   cm.
   Includes bibliographical references and index.
   ISBN 0–314–00961–2
   1. Child development.   I. Title.
RJ131.H287   1993
305.23′1—dc20
                                                                92-28570
                                                                CIP ∞

Contents in Brief

Contents

■ PART 2: Infancy and Toddlerhood   163

● Chapter 5: Physical Development in Infancy and Toddlerhood   165

Toward Effective Parenting
Superbaby Syndrome—Pushed Too
Far, Too Fast   271

● **Chapter 7: Social and Emotional Development in
                        Infancy and Toddlerhood   277**

A Closer Look
Jimmy   297

■ PART 3: The Preschool Years   335

● Chapter 8: Physical Development During the Preschool Years   337

● **Chapter 10: Social and Emotional Development During
                the Preschool Years   421**

● Chapter 12: Cognitive Development During the School Years   521

■ PART 5: Adolescence   633

● Chapter 14: Physical Development During Adolescence   635

Preface

Developmental psychology is a dynamic, rapidly changing discipline. There is much more to talk about today than there was in 1986—much of what we know has changed, much is new, yet some aspects of child development stay the same. *Child Development, Second Edition* reflects the dynamics of the field it represents—many aspects of the second edition have changed, much is new, but some features remain the same.

Our Goals for this Edition

Our goal is still to serve the needs of both students and instructors. Those with a professional interest in child development will find the contents comprehensive, current, well-researched, extensively documented, and interesting. Students will discover that the text is well-organized, succinct, easy to understand, engaging, and relevant. A balance is achieved between the scientific and practical sides of child development: a research-and-theory-based framework organizes knowledge, examples and behavioral illustrations tie that knowledge to the real world of children, and numerous suggestions, recommendations and guidelines provide solutions to practical problems.

Organization

The text continues to take a chronological look at development from conception through adolescence. This logical, step-by-step coverage of development proceeds in the text as it does in real life. A topical focus within the chronological framework permits an examination of physical, cognitive, and social/emotional development for each age group.

Readers can also sequence the chapters by topic:

Introduction	Chapter 1 (Introduction)
The Foundations of Life	Chapter 2 (Genetics and Conception)
	Chapter 3 (Prenatal Development)
	Chapter 4 (Birth and the Newborn)
Physical Development	Chapter 5 (Infancy & Toddlerhood)
	Chapter 8 (Preschool Years)
	Chapter 11 (School Years)
	Chapter 14 (Adolescence)
Cognitive Development	Chapter 6 (Infancy & Toddlerhood)
	Chapter 9 (Preschool Years)
	Chapter 12 (School Years)
	Chapter 15 (Adolescence)
Social and Emotional Development	Chapter 7 (Infancy & Toddlerhood)
	Chapter 10 (Preschool Years)
	Chapter 13 (School Years)
	Chapter 16 (Adolescence)

Contents

Each of the five major chronological periods of development—prenatal, infancy and toddlerhood, preschool age, school age, and adolescence—is given comparable coverage. In addition to bringing the information in each chapter up-to-date, this edition has been *extensively* revised and expanded. The theoretical approach material has been integrated into each chapter instead of being concentrated in a single chapter. A special effort has been made to include topics that have been neglected or overlooked by other texts.

New/Updated Topics

Chapter 1: Interdisciplinary themes in child development; Qualitative and quantitative aspects of change; Identification of developmental themes; Evaluating research findings; Ethical guidelines in research.

Chapter 2: Incomplete dominance; Genetic foundations of temperament and personality; Genetic counseling; Autism; Prenatal diagnostic procedures; Causes and treatments of infertility; Biomedical ethics; Sex-preselection; Comparison of birth control effectiveness.

Chapter 3: Preventing stillbirth; Fasting and premature labor; VDTs and occupational hazards and pregnancy; Spouse abuse and pregnancy; Prenatal learning; Teratogens and prenatal development (especially drug use); Exercise during pregnancy.

Chapter 4: Infanticide that masquerades as SIDS; Curbing infant mortality; The Shaken Baby syndrome; New C-section guidelines; Assisting the birth; Preventing prematurity; Newborn pain sensitivity; Color transmitting mechanisms of the newborn eye; Fetal surgery.

Chapter 5: Cultural differences in infant motor behavior; Infant sleeping arrangements, worldwide; Predictors of prehension; Hib conjugate vaccine; Fetal/infant brain development; SIDS; The risks of second-hand smoke on development.

Chapter 6: NeoPiagetian views on cognitive development; Earliest memories; HOME Inventory; Information Processing view of cognitive development; The Superbaby Syndrome; The psychometric approach to measuring infant intelligence; Sex differences in social play; Early conversation skills.

Chapter 7: The development of specific emotions; Acquiring emotional display rules; Organizational theories of emotional development; The emotional climate of the family; The development of self control; Self awareness; Selecting high quality daycare; Physical/emotional neglect; Development aspects of empathy; Factors that influence attachment.

Chapter 8: Health education; The impact of dietary sugar on behavior.

Chapter 9: Raising good readers; The process of attention; Stuttering; Bilingualism/multilingualism.

Chapter 10: China's one child policy; The building blocks of social skills; Things parents should avoid saying to their children; Nonsexist childrearing; Parental mood and child behavior; The impact of TV; Prosocial behavior; Recognizing emotions in others; Early friendships; Peer relationships; Self concept and self esteem; Sex stereotypes and sexual identity; The aftermath of divorce; Psychological maltreatment.

Chapter 11: The hazards of "noisy" toys; Protecting children from people who "love" them; Bulletproof vests for children; Anticipatory coping; Obesity; Molestation, incest and sexual assault; Hyperactivity; Learning disabilities; Drug and alcohol use by school children; Type A behavior.

Chapter 12: Myelogenetic cycles in the brain; Constructing a cognitive map; Comparing Japanese and American school systems; Female-only schools to bolster girls' academic achievement; Setting the tone for homework at home; Cultural assessments of the 5-to-7 shift; Factors influencing the accuracy of IQ test scores; Creativity; Alternatives to traditional IQ testing; The development of ideas about fairness and justice; Basic school skills.

Chapter 13: Lesbian mothers; Children whose parents served in Desert Storm; Children of alcoholics; Promoting child mental health; Married couples with absent partners; Homeless children; Facilitating school success.

Chapter 14: The consequences of parent treatment: aggression, competence, dependence/independence; Home drug tests; Pregnancy simulation–the Empathy Belly; Talking to children about sex; Cultural attitudes about menstruation; Infectious mononucleosis; Smokeless tobacco; SADD and driving contracts; Behavior change as a function of AIDS; Death rate updates for adolescents; Eating disorders; Acquaintance (date) rape; Teen drug use; Drug education and resistance programs; Teen pregnancy—incidence, complications, prevention.

Chapter 15: Adolescent skinheads; Helping children develop critical thinking skills; Social cognition; Working and going to high school; Teen values and thinking about society.

Chapter 16: Hate motivated violence/"wilding"; Teens and mental hospitals; Acknowledging anger; Achievement motivation; Adolescent suicide.

Special Features

These features have been designed to stimulate interest in child development by focusing on applications:

- **In Touch** boxes appear in the margin of the text to help the reader obtain information or assistance for specific behaviors or conditions. They include the name of the agency or organization, the mailing address, and a telephone number when available. Sometimes a brief description is included to clarify the agency's focus.
- **Toward Effective Parenting** features (at the end of chapters 2–16) present current and practical information for today's parents and caregivers. Some topics include "Superbaby Syndrome—Pushed Too Far Too Fast" (Chapter 6), "Selecting High Quality Daycare" (Chapter 7), and "Talking to Your Children about Sex" (Chapter 14).
- **Issue** boxes are found throughout the text, providing both sides of a specific issue that is of high interest today. The issues allow for discussion and encourage critical thinking for students. Some issues include "Beverage or Drug: The Confusion Over Mixing Alcohol with Pregnancy" (Chapter 3); "Home Drug Tests: Is Spying a Parental Right?" (Chapter 14); and "Adolescent Skinheads and Hate Motivated Violence" (Chapter 15).
- **A Closer Look** (one or more in each chapter) offers a closer look at specific topics related to the chapter material. Some topics include "Infertility Firsts" (Chapter 2); "Being Different: A Personal Story of Birth Defects" (Chapter 3); and "The Nonadult Children of Alcoholics" (Chapter 13).

- **Observational Exercises** found at the end of chapters 2–16 offer suggestions for applying chapter information in an interactive or observational setting.

Learning Aids

The following elements help students better organize, understand, and remember the chapter contents.

A running glossary provides definitions of key terms in the margin of the text pages. This aids comprehension and provides an easy reference for students.

The complete glossary (back of the book) has been expanded to include terms that will assist the progress of ESL and other language-limited students.

Concept summaries, interspersed throughout each chapter, provide a framework for organizing and remembering key chapter material.

A **point-by-point chapter summary** appears in narrative form at the end of each chapter. These summaries provide at-a-glance content reminders.

Lists of **recommended readings** follow each chapter so the student can follow up on topics they found useful or thought-provoking.

An extensive illustration program emphasizes and expands on chapter topics.

The **reference section** contains over 1700 citations, most from the 1980s and 1990s.

Supplementary Materials

The package of educational supplements adds to the usefulness of *Child Development, Second Edition.*

Instructor's Manual and Test Bank by the text author provides chapter overviews, learning objectives, lists of key terms, both detailed and brief outlines, film and AV suggestions, discussion/essay questions to stimulate critical thinking, and teaching aids.

WESTEST 3.0, a computerized testing system.

Understanding Children Through Observation by Ann Sherrill Richarz, (Washington State University), focuses on learning about children through active and objective observation.

Study Guide by Ann Le Cheminant Rothschild (Consumnes River College) includes review aids like learning objectives, chapter summaries, practice tests (multiple choice, sentence completion, and essay questions) and lists of key terms.

Child Development Videotapes

Acknowledgments

I would like to express my sincerest thanks to all of those people who offered suggestions and support on this edition.

The comments of the academic reviewers were invaluable in shaping the contents and organization of the new edition:

C.Berkeley Adams
Jamestown Community College

Peggy Apple
San Antonio College

Robert C. Barnes
Harden-Simmons University

Tillie Byler
Glendale Community College

Richard Comstock
Monroe Community College

Louella Fong
Western Kentucky University

Kathleen McCormick
Ocean County College

Margie McMahan
Cameron University

Marie Murphy
Curry College

Karen Nemeth
Jacksonville State University

Robert Stewart
Oakland University

Kathy Watson
Arizona Western College

West Educational Publishing deserves its reputation as one of the best publishing companies in the business. They select their titles carefully; but more importantly, they select their staff carefully. Clyde Perlee, Editor-in-Chief, sets the tone. He doesn't demand excellence, he *inspires* it. Theresa O'Dell, Senior Developmental Editor, nurtures with skill, grace, and tact. Kent Baird, Administrative Editor, is a gem. I am sure there is no one on the planet more efficient, hard-working, dedicated, or well-organized. I was grateful for Ben Shriver's good-natured spirit and his incredible attention to detail.

Ann Rothschild has done a wonderful job preparing the Study Guide and John Davis gave a clean, professional look to the pages of the Instructor's Manual and Test Bank. My colleagues in the Humanities and Social Sciences at Cosumnes River College never fail to provide support, good cheer, stimulating conversation . . . and chocolate!

Finally, my family is invaluable to me. Through these two editions, I have watched my children, Heather and Wendy, grow from little girls to fine young women. They are strong, bright, and independent and I am extremely proud of both of them. My husband, Bob is one-in-a-million. I depend on him for so much, and he never lets me down. With thanks to them, my work gets done.

PART 1
Foundations and Beginnings

Chapter 1: Introduction
Studying and Understanding Child Behavior
The Nature of Change
Finding the Answers: Research in Child Development
Ethics and Child Research

Chapter 2: Genetics and Conception
The Beginning of Human Life
Forces Affecting Development
Choosing to Conceive: The Social and Psychological Implications
    of Conception
After Deciding to Have a Child
After Deciding Not to Have a Child

Chapter 3: Prenatal Development
Historical Perspectives
Stages of Prenatal Development
Influences on Prenatal Development

Chapter 4: Birth and the Newborn
Keeping Babies Healthy: Medical Care Before Birth
Keeping Babies Healthy: Estimating a Due Date
Keeping Babies Healthy: The Birth Setting
Labor and Birth
Evaluating the Newborn
Characteristics of the Newborn
Adapting to Life Outside the Womb
Maternal Adjustments to Birth

Introduction

● **Studying and Understanding Child Behavior**

Child development is the scientific study of how and why children change over time. Researchers who investigate child development are called *developmental psychologists* or *developmentalists*. Typically, the time span of interest in this field extends from conception to young adulthood. Traditionally, the work of developmental psychologists is to describe, explain, predict, and through behavioral intervention, to modify behavior.

When developmental psychologists *describe* behavior they pinpoint *how* behavior changes or stays the same. How do children make new friends? How do older siblings affect younger ones? How do children learn their native language? What is the process that leads to each outcome? By describing the behavior they see, developmental psychologists are able to represent the kinds of activities and actions children engage in.

Once the behavioral process has been described and facts have been gathered, the next major task is to explain *why* that behavior occurs. Why are teens more likely to receive information about sexuality from their peers than from their parents? Why do some children overeat? Why do children misbehave? Explanation is provided by the theories of development. *Theories* offer general principles about behavior by building on past findings. Theories can also provide a framework for *predicting* future behavior. If a scientist knows what behaviors happened in the past, he or she can predict under what circumstances the behavior will be likely to reappear in the future. For example, research tells us that seventh and eighth graders will often model the behavior of their friends even if their parents are likely to disapprove (Hartup, 1983). In that way, if the peers smoke, drink alcohol, or are delinquent, it would

child development
the scientific study of how and why growth and change occur in the preadult years

developmental psychologists
scientists who study changes in growth and behavior in the preadult years

theory
a set of statements designed to explain or predict behavior

3

be reasonable to predict that the child will be inclined to experiment with those behaviors, too. Accurate prediction is a challenging aspect of child development. The major developmental theories are highlighted in Table 1–1. Each of these theories will be presented in more detail as they are encountered in the following chapters.

The Focus of the Research: Basic vs. Applied

Different researchers have different objectives in conducting research in child development. Investigators who conduct what is called *basic re-*

■ **Table 1–1** *Major Theories in Child Development*

THEORY	VIEW OF CHILD DEVELOPMENT	METHOD OF STUDY	APPLICATION
Biological maturation theory (Gesell)	Behavior is predetermined and unfolds as the child matures	Questionnaires and naturalistic observation	Child rearing advice
Psychoanalytic theory (Freud, Erikson)	Each stage of development is qualitatively different from the last	Clinical method	Child rearing advice; treatment of children with emotional problems
Behaviorism and social learning theory (Watson, Skinner, Bandura)	New behaviors are acquired due to reinforcement and modeling; old behaviors are extinguished by punishment	Laboratory experiment	Behavior modification to eliminate undesirable behavior and increase the likelihood of desirable, adaptive responses
Ecological theory (Barker, Bronfenbrenner)	The environmental context can influence child behavior	Naturalistic observation	Design environments to enhance growth and positive change
Ethological theory (Bowlby, Ainsworth, Harlow)	Behavior patterns are built in the organism for survival and for purposes of adaptation	Naturalistic observation/ field research and follow-up laboratory experimentation	Help parents and infants form secure attachments
Cognitive-developmental theory (Piaget, Kohlberg)	Children adapt their thinking as they pass through a series of qualitatively different stages	Naturalistic observations; clinical interview	Improvement of educational techniques and strategies; IQ assessment
Information processing (Atkinson, Shiffrin, Chomsky, Craik)	There is a quantitative increase in knowledge as information processing systems become more efficient	Laboratory experiment	Improving learning and problem solving strategies
Social Cognition (Damon, Kohlberg, Flavell, Hoffman)	Children actively think about their world; social understanding changes as children progress through qualitatively different stages	Naturalistic observation; clinical interview; laboratory experimentation	Helping children solve interpersonal problems

Adapted from: Laura E. Berk, *Child Development*, 2d Ed. © 1991 Allyn & Bacon. Reprinted with permission.

■ ● ▲   CONCEPT SUMMARY

The focus of developmental psychology:

- To *describe* behavior—pinpointing how behavior changes or remains constant
- To *explain* behavior—using theory to explain why behavior occurs
- To *predict* behavior—explaining the circumstances under which a behavior will reappear
- To *modify* behavior—changing behavior by offering training, advice, or treatment

---

search in developmental psychology consider the pursuit of scientific knowledge to be a good and useful activity in itself. They attempt to find out as much as they can about child behavior by identifying the processes and factors that influence it. Those who conduct *applied research*, on the other hand, study development in order to solve practical problems. Whereas basic researchers might study variables that influence excessive weight gain in children, the applied scientist would investigate techniques for preventing obesity or treating the overweight child. In that way the applied scientist attempts to *modify* development by offering training, advice, or treatment. Thus, developmental psychologists not only enrich our understanding of child development but attempt to improve the quality of life for children, their families, and society.

basic research
research designed to accumulate information about a particular behavior or issue

applied research
research designed to solve practical problems

Interdisciplinary Themes in Child Development

To carry out the goals of explanation, description, prediction, and modification, information about development from a variety of academic disciplines must be used. This book includes research from the fields of psychology, medicine, law, sociology, genetics, anthropology, education, history, and biology. Some common themes regarding characteristics of children will emerge:

 At all ages, each child is *competent*.
At all ages, each child is *complex*.
At all ages, each child is *unique*.
At all ages, each child is *vulnerable*.

The child is *competent* since all children are capable of a wide range of sensory, cognitive, and social responses even before birth. The child is *complex* because all human behavior is multidetermined, intricate, and

■ **Figure 1–1**

(upper left) All children are vulnerable.
(upper right) All children are complex.
(lower left) All children are unique.
(lower right) All children are competent.
(Here, a 2 year old washes herself along
with her dishes. A great way to conserve
water!)

difficult to analyze. The child is *unique* because he or she brings to the world a genetic organization, personality, and set of predispositions that is unlike anyone else's, even if the child is an identical twin. And the child is *vulnerable* because at all ages, children need love, good care, and guidance to protect them and keep them from harm. A knowledge of child development helps us understand our own development and that of the people around us. Ideally, as professionals or as parents, the more we understand about child growth and behavior, the better we will be at guiding, directing, and encouraging children in their growth.

Studying the Whole Child: Aspects of Development

A comprehensive understanding of child development requires an examination of growth and change in every aspect of behavior. This is most efficiently accomplished by separating physical development and cognitive development from social and emotional development. The chapters on *physical development* focus on changes in height, weight, body proportions, internal systems, and sensory capabilities as well as health and safety issues.

The chapters on *cognitive development* describe changes in the way the child can process and understand the world. As development takes place in memory, language, reasoning, problem solving, and concept formation, the child's behavior undergoes predictable changes. Finally, the child is a social creature influenced by his or her own personality and the people and events of the surrounding culture. These topics are covered in the chapters dealing with *social and emotional development.* Many physical, cognitive, and social/emotional topics are distinct, but at times a great deal of overlap among subject areas can be seen.

Studying the Whole Child: From Conception Through Adolescence

Although development is a continuous process, in this text it will be divided into five periods for the purposes of discussion:

1. *The prenatal period*—Conception to birth
2. *Infancy and toddlerhood*—Birth to age 3
3. *The preschool period*—Ages 3 to 6
4. *Middle childhood/the school years*—Ages 6 to 12
5. *Adolescence*—Age 12 to adulthood

● The Nature of Change

Both the type and amount of behavior displayed by the child can change over time (Appelbaum & McCall, 1983). *Quantitative change* involves increases or decreases in the *amount* of activity or process. A 3 year old has cut more teeth than a 2 year old, for example. They also tend to weigh more and sleep less. Sometimes change is *qualitative* and results in a new *type* of activity, process, or function. Children make qualitative changes in their ability to think and reason between the ages of 6 and 12. A young child links together the noncausal attributes of an object into causal relationships. Such children will assert, for example, that the sun shines because it is big. It's not until they are able to think *differently* about cause and effect that they realize that the perceived size of the sun has nothing to do with its light-emitting properties. At this point, they can understand that the sun shines because it is a fiery ball of hot gasses, not because it's big.

Some change has both qualitative and quantitative elements. In terms of friendship patterns, young children prefer same-sex friends, while older children tend to have both same- and other-sex friends. Thus, as a child grows older, he or she not only makes more friends (quantitative change) but also makes changes in the types of friends selected (qualitative change).

quantitative change
variation in amount

qualitative change
variation in type

A Closer Look

Some Surprises of New Parenthood

Babies change people's worlds, sometimes predictably, sometimes not. In response to her own experience of parenthood, Ellen Galinsky (1981) polled professionals and new parents about their expectations and their actual experiences with new parenthood. Here are these participants' Seven Revelations about New Parenthood:

1. I never realized how little I knew about babies.
2. I never realized how smart my own parents were and what it took to raise me.
3. I never thought I'd be so protective of my baby.
4. I never thought I'd miss my old job.
5. I never thought I'd put my marriage second.
6. I never thought I'd get so caught up in my baby.
7. I never thought that, by being a parent, I'd grow so much as a person.

Source: Galinsky, E. (1981). *Between Generations: The Six Stages of Parenthood.* New York: Times Books.

Change can be abrupt or gradual. The process of growing to final adult height takes place imperceptibly over the course of about 18 to 20 years. When a child loses a tooth, however, the change is immediately apparent. Most of the time, developmental psychologists compare groups of children in order to pinpoint growth and change. It might be interesting for a newspaper to note, for example, that by age 16, half the males in the United States will have had sexual intercourse. But what about the other half? Do they wait years before they get involved? Or is it just a matter of weeks or months? Statistics like this tell us little about the pattern of change for each individual and how those individual patterns compare.

■ **Figure 1–2**

Quantitative change: The body proportions of a 1 year old and a 2 year old. In 12 short months, the child acquires a neck, has broader shoulders, has lost baby fat, and has longer arms and legs.

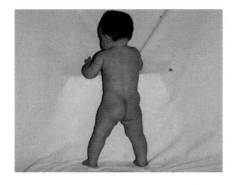
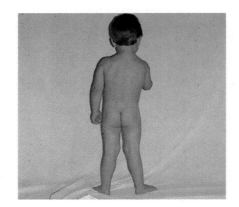

■ ● ▲   CONCEPT SUMMARY

The dimensions of change:

● quantitative (amount) vs. qualitative (type)

● abrupt vs. gradual

Influences on Child Development: What Makes Change Occur?

Each child is endowed with a certain genetic potential inherited from the parents. Although the genes set the limits for any particular behavior, it is the environment that determines just where within those limits the behavior will be expressed. Major environmental influences include:

Culture—the impact of American values and socialization

Race—the behavior of Asian, black, white, or Hispanic youth may vary or be similar

Social class—the influence of wealth, poverty, or middle-class status

Ethnicity—the impact of a common language, religion, or national origin

Key people in the child's life—parents, peers, relatives, heroes, and others who exert a powerful influence

The media—information and attitudes conveyed to children on TV, over the radio, and through books, magazines, newspapers, records, tapes, and CDs

Unpredictable life events—the unexpected turns life sometimes takes— sudden wealth or poverty, the loss or gain of a parent, sudden disability, and other factors that can alter the course of the child's life

■ **Figure 1–3**

Life in the country is very different from life in the city.

cohort effect
differences between groups of
individuals that are attributable to
differential socialization (also called
the historical context of development)

The historical context of development—called a *cohort effect* in research, since the times in which people live affect their development. War, depression, natural disaster, social movements, or conservative/liberal politics can set the tone for growth.

In light of these behavioral influences, once again, some themes in development emerge:

- The child's behavior is *organized, not random.*
- The child is both *active and passive;* both *initiator and receiver.*
- The child engages in a *behavior exchange* with his or her surroundings. The child is influenced but also influences other people and events.
- Children develop in *remarkably similar ways* throughout the world.
- There are *many paths to normal development.*
- In many cases, it is *difficult to distinguish normal from abnormal* behavior.
- The *"average" child does not exist;* average is a statistical concept, not a human one.
- Measured change *between* groups of children *may not accurately reflect changes among* individual children. (For example, although *most* children in the United States walk by 15 months of age, *some* individual children have progressed to running at 15 months, while others are still crawling.)

● Finding the Answers: Research in Child Development

Fundamental to all research—in child development and all other scientific endeavors in the West—is a set of time-honored procedures known collectively as the *scientific method.* (For purposes of discussion, let's say we're interested in researching the following question: Should teachers and principals be permitted to spank their pupils for misbehaving?) The scientific method is an impartial, systematic procedure for examining such questions about child development—or any other observable phenomenon. It involves five steps:

scientific method
specific procedures and assumptions
that guide the conduct of scientific
investigations

1. *Observe carefully.* Observations of adult/child interactions, plus our own experiences, our discussions with others, and reports of previous research can all yield questions deserving of investigation. Whether or not teachers should spank pupils is one such larger question about the comparative effectiveness of particular disciplinary techniques that could be investigated.

hypothesis
predicted outcomes of experiments
based on the results of related
studies, theories, and real-life
experiences

2. *Develop a hypothesis.* A *hypothesis* is a specific prediction about a behavior that can be tested. If a researcher's reading or observations suggest that spanking is not beneficial, that person might hypothesize that spanking is not the most effective method of disciplining school-age children.

3. *Test the hypothesis.* Once a researcher has formed a testable hypothesis, he or she gathers data through various research procedures to support or refute it. In child development, the most common data-gathering techniques are naturalistic observation, laboratory experimentation, field experimentation, interviews, and case studies. These methods are described in detail below.
4. *Draw conclusions based on test results.* In this stage, the investigator analyzes the collected data to discern its meaning.
5. *Make findings available so others can analyze the methods and conclusions by reproducing or replicating research.*

replication
repeating an experiment to verify its results

Research Procedures

We turn now to a survey of the data-gathering techniques used most frequently in child development research. To illustrate how these methods work, we'll apply each in turn to this sample hypothesis: *Spanking in schools is ineffective in diminishing disruptive classroom behavior.*

Naturalistic Observation

One way to test a hypothesis is to observe the behavior of people in natural settings. Researchers can engage in *naturalistic observation* of child behavior in classrooms, homes, clinics, hospitals, playgrounds, churches, or camps. However, naturalistic observation is only valid if the children are not aware that they are being studied. Otherwise, they

naturalistic observation
a research method in which subjects' naturally occurring behavior is observed in their usual surroundings and subjects are unaware of the presence of the investigator

---

■ ● ▲ CONCEPT SUMMARY

Steps in the scientific method: *ways to study children*

1. Observe behavior to clarify the research question.
2. Develop a hypothesis, or testable prediction.
3. Test the hypothesis using one of the following procedures:
   - naturalistic observation
   - laboratory experimentation
   - field experimentation
   - interviews
   - case studies

   Incorporate cross-sectional, longitudinal, and cross-cultural principles where appropriate.

   Observe ethical guidelines at all times.
4. Analyze data and draw conclusions.
5. Make findings available to others for application or replication.

---

may act differently from usual simply because they know they are under observation.

To test our hypothesis about the effectiveness of spanking, we might observe the behavior of children in two types of classrooms—ones in which teachers spanked children for misbehaving and ones in which no spanking occurred. We would then carefully note the incidence and types of disruptive behavior (i.e., hitting, talking out of turn, name calling, and so on) that ensued in each classroom.

ADVANTAGES AND DISADVANTAGES OF NATURALISTIC TECHNIQUES. One advantage of naturalistic observation is that it focuses on real behavior performed in real environments. Nothing is artificial or contrived about this particular procedure. However, although realism is highly desirable in research, there are some drawbacks to the use of naturalistic observation. First, it is difficult to identify the variable(s) responsible for causing the observed behavior. In our example, children might behave well in school to avoid being spanked. But they might also behave well because they like their teacher, enjoy learning, or have interesting work to do—regardless of the presence or absence of the threat of spanking. Thus, classroom behavior in this case may or may not have anything to do with the particular disciplinary strategy used, and naturalistic observation here will offer no clue to the mystery.

Another drawback of naturalistic observation is that by its nature it prohibits the exploration of children's feelings and ideas. Since the researchers must remain hidden for the research to be valid, they must limit their activities strictly to observing and taking notes. This method also raises ethical questions about whether it is all right to study people (children) without their consent.

A final disadvantage of naturalistic observation is that it does not readily permit researchers to answer motivational questions. For example, an investigator observing the behavior of children on a school playground may see that one child is not participating with the others. Simply by observing, this researcher really couldn't answer the obvious question ("Why not?") because he or she would have no access to information that might help eliminate alternative explanations. For example, the child might feel rejected by his or her peers, or might be tired or grumpy. Or the child might simply prefer seclusion for the moment or need time to consider something alone.

Laboratory Experimentation

In *laboratory experiments*, scientific researchers control certain of their subjects' experiences. A researcher who is interested in how children respond to different forms of discipline can examine just that aspect of a group of children's behavior by changing certain factors, called *variables*. For example, one of the variables might be whether the children were spanked or not. Half of the children tested could be *randomly as-*

---

laboratory experiment
a research method in which subjects are studied in a controlled environment

variable
qualities or characteristics of people or events that scientists measure or manipulate in experiments

random assignment
using random procedures such as flipping a coin to assign subjects to a particular group in an experiment, thereby eliminating a source of potential bias

independent variables
the factors in an experiment that are manipulated by the experimenter

dependent variables
the subject's responses to the independent variables

signed to a group that would receive spanking as a punishment for misbehavior. The other half would then receive no spanking for misbehavior. The variable or variables under the control of the experimenter—in this case, whether the child is to be spanked or not—are called *independent variables.* The subjects' responses in an experiment are called the *dependent variables.* In this case, we might wonder whether spanking (independent variable) has any effect on the frequency of behaviors that the supervising adults disapprove of (dependent variables).

WHEN RANDOM ASSIGNMENT IS NOT POSSIBLE. Sometimes random assignment cannot be used. If a researcher is interested in studying the effect of emotional abuse on development, for example, children could not ethically be assigned to an "abuse" group while others receive no abuse just to study the outcomes. In the same way, the effects of parent–child separation can *only* be assessed under naturally occurring circumstances, not under artificial ones. Without random assignment, the conclusions that can be drawn by these studies are limited. Cause and effect cannot be inferred because other factors are present in the design and may be responsible for the outcome. For example, if children who are emotionally abused have lower self esteem than nonabused children, did the abuse produce low self-esteem (low esteem as outcome) or did low self-esteem result in abuse (low esteem as cause)? Either conclusion is possible. Such research is called *correlational* because it only helps us discover which variables are related to the outcomes rather than exactly which specific causal role each of the variables plays.

ADVANTAGES AND DISADVANTAGES OF LABORATORY EXPERIMENTATION. Unlike testing performed in the "real world," laboratory research is not affected by such extraneous factors as barking dogs, recess bells, or other distractions. It is much easier to pinpoint the causes of the behavior in question when the influence of other such variables has been eliminated or held constant. In fact, a clear advantage of laboratory research is the precision and *control* it affords the researcher.

Another advantage is that laboratory researchers can extract a large and varied amount of information from subjects unavailable to them in natural settings. Thus, in a lab experiment the investigator can measure and record physiological responses such as heart rate, observe such minute behavior as eye pupil size changes, and stop and interview subjects at any time during the process. Finally, since experimental procedures must be carefully designed and specified, any particular study can be repeated (*replicated*) by other investigators in the future. Thus, the findings of the original study may be verified or disproven by any who might challenge them. For all these reasons, most developmental psychologists rely on laboratory experimentation for testing hypotheses about child behavior.

■ Figure 1–4

Children from all age groups may be asked to come into the laboratory so their reactions can be recorded.

correlational research
a research method that indicates whether two variables are related to one another

control
in experimental research, the ability to exclude potentially confounding variables from influencing the outcome of the study

Ironically, the conclusions of laboratory research studies may be limited by the very factors that lend precision and effectiveness to the technique. The laboratory is an artificial environment. The behavior observed there may or may not reflect naturally occurring responses. Also, most children, except young babies, know that they are participating in a study when they are in a laboratory and may behave differently than they would, for example, in a classroom or on a playground. Although researchers in child development try to provide realistic settings that elicit spontaneous behavior from their young subjects, they must be cautious in assuming that the findings of laboratory research apply to nonlaboratory settings.

Field Experimentation

field experiment
a research method in which subjects are assigned to treatment or control groups in the natural environment instead of in the laboratory setting

The *field experiment* represents a compromise between the rigor of a laboratory setting and the realism of a natural environment. Here, investigators can introduce variables into a real-life setting and record subjects' responses. For example, researchers would work with school district officials to test disciplinary effectiveness in the classroom by randomly assigning children to classes, training teachers in such techniques as spanking and *time out,* and keeping a record of student misbehavior. Alternatively, researchers can use naturalistic observation and laboratory research in combination either by lab testing observations from natural environments or by applying laboratory findings in real-life settings.

Perhaps caregivers have noticed that some babies respond to strangers by crying, turning, or trying to escape. Researchers can test this real-life observation in the laboratory by observing the responses of a variety of babies of different ages to a variety of strangers. In fact, research that has tested these variables has found that *fear of strangers* (or *stranger anxiety*), is most prevalent in children 8 to 12 months old. Furthermore, "angry" looking strangers who approach closely are those who provoke the most anxiety in children, particularly if the stranger tries to hold the child. These laboratory findings can be usefully applied, for example, in setting the timing of medical treatment for children. If children are ill or have to undergo some operative procedure when they are very young, it might be best where possible to postpone treatment until their stranger anxiety subsides and they can thus be more comfortable with the many different people who will be looking after them in the hospital.

The Interview Method

interview
a research method in which the investigator asks specific questions pertaining to a particular hypothesis

In *interviews,* researchers ask subjects questions about a particular subject or issue. Interviews vary in style—from telephone surveys to written questionnaires to face-to-face conversations—but in all such situations individuals can be questioned specifically about the question at hand, in our example, disciplinary strategies. Survey research designed to investigate the use of disciplinary strategies might ask such questions as "Have you ever spanked a child for misbehaving? If so, what behavior(s) prompted this response?" or "Do you ever use anything besides your hand when spanking—for example, a belt or a paddle?" The kinds of responses called for in interviews also vary—they might be descriptive, yes/no, or ratings derived from a particular scale.

ADVANTAGES AND DISADVANTAGES OF THE INTERVIEW/SURVEY METHOD. Interviews are useful when behavior is difficult to observe or manipulate or when a large number of persons must be questioned. On the negative side, however, it is difficult to know whether respondents are being truthful or remember facts accurately when they answer interview questions. Even "memorable" events, such as when mothers weaned their babies or when a child's first tooth appeared, are easily forgotten or not quite remembered accurately. In addition, individuals may interpret questions differently within their personal frames of reference. For example, when asked "Were you spanked as a child?", a person who recalls only receiving such punishment as an adolescent might truthfully answer no. Likewise, in answer to a question about preferred punishment measures, those who consider discipline to be "love" and not "punishment" might respond that they never punish their children even though they discipline them. Finally, questions that are ambiguous or use language that is too sophisticated for the subject are likely to yield varied results. Responses like those above could invalidate the results of an interviewer's study or lead researchers to incorrect conclusions.

■ **Figure 1–5**

Testing a child for learning disabilities.

The Case-Study Method

case study research
a research method in which a single subject or a small number of cases is studied extensively

Case-study research is the extensive investigation into the behavior of a single person. Although the case-study method is most often used in clinical work, virtually any question about behavior can be explored through case study. A researcher might address the issue of disciplinary effectiveness by questioning, observing, and describing the behavior of a selected individual. Case studies have provided us with some of our richest and most detailed accounts of human behavior. However, they also draw criticism, since the conclusions they yield about the behavior of one person may not necessarily apply to others.

Cross-Sectional Research

cross sectional research
research that involves comparing the behavior of groups of individuals of various ages to determine whether age-related differences exist

The research methods described so far—naturalistic observation, laboratory experimentation, field experimentation, interviews, and case studies—can be used with children of the same age. But all five can also be used to collect data on children of different ages. Two research techniques have been specifically designed for this purpose: cross-sectional studies and longitudinal studies. Let's look at the cross-sectional technique first.

The essential element in *cross-sectional research* lies in the composition of the groups of people under study. If researchers want to know, for example, how vocabulary, speech skills, height, weight, IQ, or play change with age, they can study groups of say, 4-, 8-, and 12-year-olds and compare their behaviors. If we wanted to extend our research on disciplinary strategies, for example, we might test whether the likelihood of using spanking changes with the age of the child. By studying groups of 3-, 6-, 9-, 12- and 15-year-olds, for example, we might find that 3-year-olds get spanked frequently for their misbehavior, while 12- and 15-year-olds are more likely to have their privileges withheld than to be spanked.

"tabula rasa"
John Locke's notion of the child-as-a-blank-slate

"noble savage"
Jean-Jacques Rousseau's notion of the child-as-uncivilized-potential

baby biographies
records kept by laypersons about the growth and development of their children

SELECTING RESEARCH PARTICIPANTS: THE REPRESENTATIVE SAMPLE. Cross-sectional research is infinitely flexible—one can use it to investigate almost any question by selecting any number of children within any age group. It is important, however, that the children who participate in the study constitute a representative sample of their peers. A *representative sample* is one that reflects the relevant characteristics—such as gender, race, IQ, ethnicity, social class, and birth order—of a chosen segment of the child population, since such variables can affect the conclusions reached in the developmental research.

representative sample
a research sample in which every individual in the total population in question has an equal chance of being included in the study.

ADVANTAGES AND DISADVANTAGES OF CROSS-SECTIONAL RESEARCH. One advantage of cross-sectional research is that it permits the collection of a large amount of information in a relatively short time period. A problem, though, is that significant historical events or

A Closer Look

We've Come a Long Way, Baby

Using the tools of science and the knowledge that can come from experience, the Western world has learned a lot more about babies during the past 200 years than we have over the past 2000.

It wasn't until the seventeenth century that parents began to take children very seriously, if not lovingly. Prior to that time the infant mortality rates were so high that parents resisted investing much care or money in a child who wasn't expected to live very long. Many infants during the Middle Ages were sold as slaves or servants or given to monasteries or nunneries. Parents who could afford it sent their infants away to live with wet nurses until they were old enough either to be sent away to school or put to work.

In the seventeenth century "Spare the rod and spoil the child" was the watchword of the day. John Locke's philosophy prevailed, which described the child's mind as a "tabula rasa" or blank slate. Parents didn't become emotionally close to their child—fearing that such contact would "soften" or "weaken" their resolve. Instead, when parents or teachers tried to "write on the child's mental slate" they most often choose the type of training that was accompanied by physical punishment administered by a cane or rod.

A major turning point in the history of child development came during the 18th century with the teachings of Jean-Jacques Rousseau. Rousseau, in contrast with the philosophy of John Locke a century before, saw the child as a "noble savage." He argued that children needed to grow and unfold in an atmosphere of freedom and encouragement. This change in the attitude toward children and childhood led to a growing fascination with the growth and development of young children. The medical specialty of pediatrics was established, slowing the mortality of young infants. And societies for the prevention of cruelty to children were established.

During the nineteenth century, scholars like Charles Darwin chronicled the day-by-day activities of their young children in "baby biographies." Child psychology was invented in 1879 to study and understand the physical, cognitive, social, and emotional capabilities of children and infants. In the United States, G. Stanley Hall was the first developmental psychologist, a professional dedicated to the serious investigation of growth and change in the young child. In 1890, pioneering psychologist William James felt that infants are unsensing, unresponsive, unlearning organisms. James' ideas about infant awareness remained prominent until the early 1960s.

After years of work and preparation, psychology has now developed research tools, methods, and theories sophisticated enough to examine even subtle aspects of child behavior. High-speed computers allow for data analysis in minutes, rather than hours and years. They also permit visual graphics and predictions based on the values of specific variables. Videotape equipment permits a permanent visual and auditory record of the child that can be stored indefinitely and reexamined. Fiber-optic cameras make accessible the inaccessible recesses of the infant's being or even the prenatal environment. With these tools, the agenda of the behavioral scientist is set: if public engineers could clean up the physical environment and save kid's lives that way, and the pediatrician can safeguard the physical health of the child, then the developmental scientist should be able to find out about the causes of behavior and set forth recommendations for treatment and prevention.

Adapted from: Trotter, R. J. (1987, May). "You've Come a Long Way, Baby." *Psychology Today*, pp. 34–45 changes in the participants' lifestyles or attitudes can affect the results of the study. For example, do 12 year olds play differently from 3 year olds because they are 9 years older or because they are being raised differently? Such complications, called cohort effects, sometimes make the results of cross-sectional studies difficult to interpret.

Longitudinal Research

longitudinal research
long-term studies of an individual or group of individuals designed to monitor changes that take place over time

The *longitudinal method* is an alternative to cross-sectional research. In longitudinal research, rather than studying groups of people of different ages, developmentalists study the same individuals over an extended period of time. The famous Berkeley Growth Study initiated in the early 1930s by Dr. Nancy Bayley (1935, 1949, 1965, 1968, 1970) is a longitudinal study of changes in children's IQs from infancy to adulthood. Lewis Terman (Terman & Oden, 1959) was interested in a similar issue when he published his longitudinal study of high-IQ individuals called "Scientists and Nonscientists in a Group of 800 Gifted Men" (Terman, 1954). Our interest in disciplinary practices might encourage us to study children who were spanked in school and those who were not over a period of years to see if we could attribute any differences between groups to the type of punishment used.

ADVANTAGES AND DISADVANTAGES OF LONGITUDINAL RESEARCH. Ongoing longitudinal studies provide a wealth of information about individual growth and change over time. No other research technique is so sensitive to individual differences and the long-term impact of variables on development. But where such studies outlive their initiators and are carried on by second- or third-generation scientists, the new researchers have been known to lose sight of the methods and even the purpose of the original research. Also, some experimental methods become obsolete over time as newer and more effective techniques are developed. When this happens, a longitudinal study might be rendered invalid. For example, longitudinal research has been conducted on premature infants to determine the effect of early birth on later growth and development. Before the invention of the PET scan—an activity-related X-ray-like procedure that shows blood-flow patterns in the brain—the brain hemorrhages that can lead to mental retardation and that are not uncommon in premature infants could only be verified through surgery or spinal tap. Now, with newer nonsurgical X-ray procedures, we can document the existence of these "bleeds" and study their effects on behavior more accurately and reliably than before, thus calling into question the validity of some of the earlier research in this area.

attrition
a decrease in the original number of subjects due to factors beyond the investigator's control, such as illness, relocation, or lack of motivation

A major disadvantage of longitudinal research is *attrition*. Attrition refers to the tendency of some individuals to drop out before the end of the study. Some become bored with the project; others move out of the area; still others find it inconvenient to continue. Illness and death also take their toll in subject populations. Useful longitudinal research requires persistent investigators and cooperative participants.

Cross-Cultural Studies

Sometimes the variable of interest is not age but culture. Children of different cultures are compared to determine whether social factors—such as childrearing techniques, lifestyles, family organization, or economic patterns and activities—influence child development or behavior. Such studies fall into the category of *cross-cultural research*.

THE IMPORTANCE OF OBJECTIVITY. Despite the expense and time involved, cross-cultural research is becoming more common as investigators attempt to extend their observations past the cultural boundaries of middle-class Western society and to discover universal trends in development applicable to all children.. One critical aspect of cross-cultural research is *objectivity*. Investigators have to be particularly careful about preventing their own culturally influenced ideas, feelings, perspectives, and interpretations from affecting the research. Consider a study that asks children to manipulate quantities of colored candies to display their knowledge of arithmetic. Middle-class American children might do well, but if children of other cultures score poorly, what do we conclude? It's possible that they were not taught quantitative skills at the same time as the American children. It's also possible that they simply failed to understand what was asked of them. Or they might have been reflecting a cultural prohibition against "playing with food" in their society, which using candies violated. This particular experimental situation, then, might not provide an accurate test of children's math skills. A score of 0 may have little to do with a child's ability to count or calculate and much more to do with his or her ability to interpret instructions or adherence to social norms.

■ **Figure 1–6**

A handsomely dressed Ifugao boy from the Philippines.

cross-cultural research
a research method that attempts to compare the activities/behaviors of one culture with another/others

objectivity
impartiality, lack of bias

Evaluating Research Findings

Conclusions about child development should not be accepted uncritically. As you have occasion to read through the studies cited throughout this book, use the following guidelines to help evaluate the researcher's use of the scientific method.

Clarity	Can you understand what was done and what was found?
Importance of findings	How does the study help advance our knowledge or solve practical problems?
Promotion of new ideas	What new insights does this research provide? Does it help us examine familiar issues in a new way?

Consistency	Does this study support or refute other findings? *Why* does it conform to or conflict with other evidence?
Replicability	Can/would these same results be replicated if the research were done again?
Choice of subjects	Was a representative sample chosen? Was random assignment used?
Appropriateness of method	Was the research method chosen the best one to answer the question posed?

Adapted from: Bee, 1989, p. 30.

● Ethics and Child Research

ethics
acceptable standards of conduct or a code of responsible behavior

Whenever we experiment with human subjects and attempt to examine, manipulate, and control behavior, ethical questions arise. Was it ethical, for example, in a now well-known experiment, to condition a child to fear a white rat just to see if such responses can be acquired (Watson & Raynor, 1920)? Should babies be left in unfamiliar settings with unfamiliar people so we can see if they will cry without their mothers (Ainsworth & Bell, 1970)? Should babies be raised in isolated environments and deprived of all normal motor experiences so we can see whether or not they will ever be able to walk (Dennis, 1935)? Is it appropriate to punish retarded children in experiments with painful electric shocks (Lovaas & Simmons, 1969)? Although the quest for knowledge is an important goal of science, the end does not necessarily justify the means. All experimentation must reflect a balance between the needs of the scientific community and the rights of the subjects involved.

Both the American Psychological Association (1968) and the Society for Research in Child Development (1975) have had a longstanding commitment to the protection of child subjects and their parents. In 1989 the United Nations Convention on the Rights of the Child was adopted by the UN General Assembly to provide global guarantees to children. From these sources, guidelines have been developed to protect the participants of developmental research. These guidelines contain the following provisions:

1. THE RIGHT TO THE TRUTH
   Children and their parents should be told the full and truthful purpose of the study. Research procedures should be described in detail, especially those that might affect participants' willingness to respond.

informed consent
a full disclosure of the research aims and procedures prior to agreeing to participate

2. THE RIGHT TO INFORMED CONSENT
   After the description of the study, the child's parents should provide informed consent, preferably in writing.

3. THE RIGHT TO FREE CHOICE
   Children and their parents are free to choose whether or not they will participate in the research project. They are also free to withdraw at any time, receiving full compensation.
4. THE RIGHT TO FULL PROTECTION AGAINST HARM
   No research technique may be used that will harm the child either physically or psychologically.
5. THE RIGHT TO INFORMATION
   All child participants and their parents have the right to receive information about the outcome of the study.
6. THE RIGHT TO CONFIDENTIALITY
   Participants have the right to expect that any personal information gathered during the course of the investigation will remain confidential.

free choice
a decision made without coercion or constraint

confidentiality
to maintain documents/information in strict secrecy; nondisclosure of personally identifying information

A child's vulnerability to risks from research does not simply decline linearly as the child grows older. Instead, age is but one of many factors that should be considered to safeguard the rights of child research participants (Thompson, 1990).

In most institutions and settings that conduct research in child development, ethical standards are enforced by ethics committees, which carefully review research proposals before any data are collected. When such a committee rejects a proposal, it usually urges the investigator to develop some other procedure for testing stated hypothesis. This screening process, along with the growing tendency to educate the general population of their rights as research subjects, is helping to ensure that high ethical standards are maintained in scientific investigation.

Of course, ethical issues are involved in the treatment of children as well as in the conduct of scientific investigations. Is it ethical, for example, for parents to spank their children knowing that spanking may injure the child? Is it ethical for the parents of a child with Down's syndrome to withhold vital treatment such as heart surgery knowing that without such treatment, the child will die? Is abortion ethical? In contrast to scientific investigations, parenting issues like these are not governed by universally agreed-upon rules. However, the pros and cons of some of these and similar issues are examined by developmental psychologists and are discussed in subsequent chapters.

● Chapter Summary

- Developmental psychologists, or developmentalists, study changes in child behavior over time. Their goals are to describe, explain, predict, and to modify behavior (if necessary).
- One objective of developmental research is to find out as much as possible about child behavior by conducting basic research. Another objective is to use the findings of applied research to solve practical

problems. Many disciplines contribute basic and applied research findings of interest to developmentalists. Conclusions from across the disciplines show children to be competent, complex, unique, and vulnerable.

● The *whole* child is studied by examining three behavioral domains: physical/physiological, cognitive, and social/emotional. Quantitative and qualitative changes in behavior are assessed by comparing different age groups: prebirth/prenatal, infancy, preschool, school age, and adolescent. For each age group, change can be influenced by genetics, culture, race, social class, ethnicity, key people in the child's life, the media, unpredictable life events, and the historical context of development.

● All research questions are answered using the scientific method. After careful observation, a hypothesis is formulated and data are gathered using naturalistic observation, laboratory experimentation, field experimentation, the interview method, or case-study techniques. These five procedures can be modified to compare different age groups (cross-sectional research), to study the same children over time (longitudinal research), or to examine the impact of different cultures on behavior (cross-cultural research). Unique advantages and disadvantages are associated with each approach. Research findings should not be accepted uncritically.

● No matter which research procedure is used, scientists are expected to protect the child participants and their families by maintaining high ethical standards in their investigations.

● Observational Exercise

Careful observation forms the foundation for understanding child behavior. Observation is watching with a purpose—to see what children do and then to think about why they do it. Most observation takes place at a distance; it is not possible to observe children and work with them at the same time. It takes time and practice to become skilled at both making and recording observations. Isaksen (1986) suggests keeping the following observation principles in mind:

1. *Be objective.* Your observation must reflect what the child did, not what you *think* of what he or she did, or what you think it means, or what you think he or she should have done.
2. *Focus on the "what" and "how" of behavior.* In describing child behavior or quoting speech, include *what* was said or done as well as the *manner* in which the speech or activity was performed. If the child made a statement, was it done quietly, quickly, or while whining or laughing? In this way, the context for the behavior can be appreciated.

3. *Use specific detail.* To give an accurate picture of the child, describe the behavior in detail. Instead of concluding that a child was bored during a story time, for example, describe the behavior: "The child stared unblinking out the window"; "The child pulled at a thread on her jacket." Rather than interpreting a behavior ("Clint had a good time") describe *how* he acted, *what* he was doing, and *the manner* in which he behaved. Since all behavior is complex and multidetermined, premature conclusions or preconceived ideas bias the observation process.

4. *Use quotes and context notes.* Report what the child or children say along with what they do. Quote the language they use rather than your interpretation of their language. For example, it's one thing to say a child spoke with an angry voice; it's quite another to quote what the child said, to describe what events preceded and followed the event, and to convey the child's body language, look, and facial expression. Whoever reads the observation, needs to be able to see *all* of the child's behavior at any given moment, not just a sample.

Now, practice your observational skills by doing a series of sample observations. Create "running behavior records" by using a time sampling approach. Follow the example below.

Setting Description:

Time	Overt Behavior	Comments
3.02 p.m.	P picks up the doll in the corner of the room and walks slowly toward D, who is sitting quietly on a towel near the wash basin leafing through a book. P stretches out her arm. "See," P says. D looks up, and smiles. P sits down on the towel next to D.	Is P fond of D? Are they friends?

● Recommended Readings

Damon, W. (1989). *Child development: Today and tomorrow.* San Francisco: Jossey-Bass.

Hall, E. (1987). *Growing and changing: What the experts say.* New York: Random House.

Irwin, D. M., & Bushnell, M. M. (1980). *Observational strategies for child study.* New York: Holt, Rinehart & Winston.

Kagan, J. (1984). *The nature of the child.* New York: Basic Books.

Genetics and Conception

● The Beginning of Human Life

Human life begins when two reproductive cells, or *gametes*, unite. These are the female *ovum* and the male *sperm cell*, also called a *spermatozoan*. Gametes contain *chromosomes*, which in turn carry *genes*. Together the chromosomes and genes comprise the genetic material, which biochemically dictates the development of an individual. Each gamete contains half the genetic material necessary for a human being. Sexual intercourse is the usual means by which the ovum and spermatozoa come together.

Fertilization

Immature sperm cells, or *spermatogonia*, are present in the male's testes at birth. After a boy passes through adolescence, hormones cause about 200 million spermatogonia to mature into spermatozoa each day throughout his adulthood. Mature sperm are stored in the testes. Sperm are among the *smallest* cells of the adult body. About 600 sperm could be lined up, head to tail, within the space of the following inch (_____) (Mange, 1990). When ejaculation occurs, the sperm are carried out of the penis in a substance called *semen* and into the female's body. The sperm are ejaculated in blobs of semen. Apparently, this is nature's way of ensuring that the sperm are deposited in concentrated masses. The semen then liquifies, freeing 250 to 500 million sperm that begin migrating toward the woman's uterus.

Immature ova, or *oocytes,* are present in the female's ovaries from birth. After a girl reaches puberty, hormones stimulate the oocytes to ripen into ova. As the largest cell in the adult human body, three or

gametes
male and female reproductive cells. Each carries half the number of chromosomes found in the other cells of the human body

ovum (ova, pl.)
female gamete or reproductive cell

sperm cell (spermatozoa, pl.)
male gametes or reproductive cells

chromosomes
thread-like microscopic bodies found in the nucleus of every human cell. Chromosomes carry the genes transmitted from parents to offspring that determine an individual's inherited characteristics

gene (s)
the basic units of heredity carried by the chromosomes; each gene is a section of the genetic code

testes (testis, sing.)
male gonad inside the scrotum that produces sperm and male sex hormones

uterus
a pear-shaped organ in the female's pelvis that provides a place for the fetus to develop (also called the womb)

25

■ **Figure 2–1**

A cut-away view of the left ovary, left Fallopian tube, uterus and vagina. (a) The solid-ball stage achieved after about three days of development. (b) The implanted zygote.

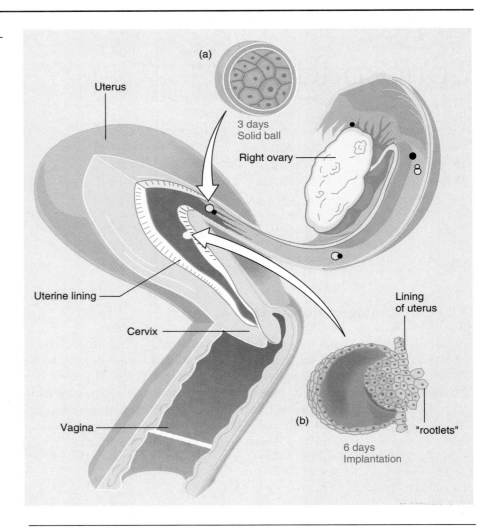

ovary (ovaries, pl.)
female gonad in the pelvis that produces ova and female sex hormones

ovulate
release of a mature ovum from the ovary

Fallopian tubes
tubes providing a conduit between each ovary and the uterus

fertilization
when the genetic material from the egg and sperm merge to form a zygote; also called conception

multiple ovulation
releasing more than one ovum during a cycle thus allowing for the possibility of twins or multiple conception

fraternal twins two eggs
twins formed from two separate zygotes; also called dizygotic twins

identical twins
twins formed from a single zygote that spontaneously duplicates itself and separates; also called monozygotic twins one egg

four ova could fit within the space created by this period (.) From puberty until menopause, each month one of the woman's ovaries releases an egg (or *ovulates*) which travels from the *ovary* down one of the *Fallopian tubes* toward the uterus. If the ovum meets and is penetrated by one of the sperm released into the vagina during intercourse, it is said to be *fertilized, and conception* has occurred. In short, a child begins to develop. Although only one ovum is usually released during the woman's monthly cycle, *multiple ovulation*—the release of two or more ova— is possible. And if more than one ovum is fertilized, multiple births become possible. *Fraternal twins* are the result of the simultaneous fertilization of two ova. *Identical twins* result when a single fertilized ovum spontaneously duplicates, forming two *zygotes* which will each develop into a baby.

become pregnant

The ovum and sperm generally meet in the Fallopian tube. Although it is believed that the egg releases some sort of chemical "attractant," the exact process by which the sperm finds the egg is still under investigation (Booth, 1991). The process of fertilization, which occurs when a sperm penetrates the egg's protective membrane, represents the merging of the father's and the mother's genetic material. The cell formed by the egg and sperm is called a zygote. Because each gamete carries half the necessary chromosomes, the zygote contains the full complement of chromosomes necessary for a human being. More than one sperm is prevented from fertilizing the egg by a chemical change that takes place in the ovum's outside wall. Timing is crucial if conception is to take place. The egg is generally released between the 10th and 14th day of the woman's menstrual cycle and can live about 24 hours before degenerating. The individual sperm have a functional lifespan of about 48 hours (Edlin, 1990). Since the sperm outnumber the egg by about 500 million to one, the odds obviously favor conception.

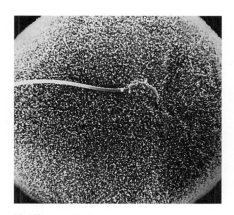

■ **Figure 2–2**

The moment of fertilization.

Implantation

As the zygote floats from the Fallopian tube to the uterus, *cell division and specialization* begin. The zygote cleaves into two cells, then into four, continuing to divide by a process known as *mitosis* until it resembles the clustered seeds of a berry. During this time the cells also prepare to form the specialized tissues of the baby's body.

About 7 to 10 days after conception, the zygote settles into the wall of the mother's uterus. This process, called *implantation,* may cause some slight bleeding or "spotting," which may be mistaken for the start of the woman's monthly menstrual period. After implantation, the woman's body mobilizes to nurture the developing life, which is now called an *embryo.*

zygote
the one-celled organism that results from the union of the egg and the sperm

cell division
the process of chromosome duplication that produces new cells

cell specialization
the process whereby body cells assume responsibility for the development of specific organs and systems

mitosis
the process of chromosome duplication and cell division that creates new cells, each containing the same 46 chromosomes

implantation
occurs when the zygote burrows into the lining of the uterus where it can be nourished and protected until birth

embryo
the developing child 2–8 weeks after conception. Basic body structures and systems are formed during this period.

■ ● ▲   CONCEPT SUMMARY

From Gamete to Embryo

Fertilization/Conception   Implantation

Ovum ——————↘
                      Zygote ——————→ Embryo
Sperm ——————↗

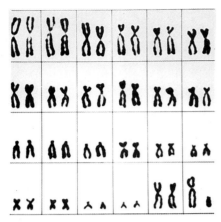

■ Figure 2–3

A karyotype, or geneticist's sorting, of human chromosomes. In this photo, both the XX and XY form of the 23rd chromosome are shown on the lower right.

genetics
the passing of genes and the inherited characteristics they specify from one generation to the next

sex chromosomes
the chromosomes that determine, among other things, the sex of the developing child.

XX
sex chromosome configuration for a normal human female

XY
sex chromosome configuration for a normal human male

TDF (testes determining factor) gene
sections of DNA within the Y chromosome that instruct the development of the testes and hence the formation of a male

● Forces Affecting Development

From the moment of conception, development is guided by two interrelated forces: genetics and the environment. Very simply, the biochemical information contained in the child's genes, the units of specific genetic information on the chromosomes, provides a basic blueprint for human growth. Aspects of that genetic growth potential may be modified by the environment. The impact of environmental factors on prenatal growth is discussed in Chapter 3; this chapter focuses primarily on the role of genetics in development.

Genetics and Development

Genes are bound together on the chromosomes contained in the ovum and sperm. At conception, 23 chromosomes in the ovum combine with the 23 in the sperm to form 23 pairs of chromosomes, or 46 single chromosomes (Figure 2–3). The number of chromosomes resulting from the union of two gametes provides the first clue about the developing life—the species to which it belongs. Forty-six chromosomes must be present to form a normal human being; if more or less than 46 chromosomes exist, then abnormalities in development occur. Purely genetic factors account for 20–25% of all human malformations (Brent & Beckman, 1990).

Sex Determination

The sex of the organism is also determined at conception. The chromosomes in the 23rd pair are called *sex chromosomes*, because they differ in males and females. The two types of chromosomes, which differ in shape, are designated X and Y chromosomes. All female ova carry a single X sex chromosome, but the males produce two types of sperm—some bearing an X sex chromosome and some bearing a Y sex chromosome. When an X-bearing sperm fertilizes the ovum, creating an XX zygote, the result is a female child. When a Y-bearing sperm fertilizes the ovum, creating an XY zygote, a male child is conceived. Although each parent contributes 50% of the genetic material needed for conception, the father, not the mother, determines the sex of the child.[1] Apparently, the whole Y chromosome is not needed to produce a male child, just a part of it. In 1987 David Page made a remarkable discovery: a single gene on the Y chromosome seemed to trigger the development of testes in the male and thus to differentiate that embryo from the female. The precise location of this gene, designated TDF (testes determining factor) was pinpointed; in 1990 another TDF gene was located.

[1]Although the sex of the baby is determined by the father's sperm, the acid/alkaline balance of the mother's vagina (among other things) affects the viability of the sperm.

DIFFERENTIAL MORTALITY OF THE SEXES Boys outnumber girls at conception by 120 to 100 and at birth by 106 to 100 (James, 1987). By middle childhood, however, the ratio of boys to girls in the general population is roughly equal. Why are male babies more likely to be miscarried or to die during infancy? The genes responsible for activating the body's immune system are also located on the X sex chromosome. Since females have two X sex chromosomes and males only one, females have more natural protection against illness and disease. Also, besides being more resistant to disease, girls are more neurologically mature than boys from conception until about age 14. Thus, more females than males survive the prenatal period and infancy because their nervous systems are more responsive, their bodies are more mature, and their immune systems are more efficient at any given time during development.

Variations in Development Caused by Errors in Cell Division

SEX CHROMOSOME ABNORMALITIES Zygotes are either XY males or XX females more than 99% of the time. In rare cases, however, the ova or sperm carry an abnormal number of X or Y chromosomes owing to an error during *meiosis,* the specialized cell-division process that forms eggs and sperm. During normal meiosis, one duplication of the original cell's genetic material occurs for every two cell divisions. The result is four gametes, each containing 23 chromosomes, or half the full complement for a human being. In order for cell division to take place during meiosis, the chromosomal material must make a carbon copy of itself. The original 23 pairs of chromosomes then migrate toward one end of the cell while the duplicated pairs migrate toward the opposite end. The term *alignment* refers to the appearance of the chromosomes during this process. They actually seem to line up right before the cell divides.

The vast majority of the time, meiosis works perfectly: chromosomes duplicate and align and cells divide as they should. But if, for reasons not entirely understood, the sex chromosomes align improperly, a female might produce a no-X ovum and an XX ovum, while a male may produce a no-X sperm and an XX sperm or a no-Y sperm and a YY sperm. In the rare cases where such abnormal sex cells have been fertilized, variations in development occur (Table 2–1).

AUTOSOME ABNORMALITIES: DOWN'S SYNDROME Chromosome pairs other than the sex chromosomes are called *autosomes.* When portions of an autosome spontaneously misalign, cross-over, or "break" during meiosis, the result is a gamete with an abnormal number of chromosomes. These abnormalities manifest themselves in complex ways during development. For example, children with an extra 21st chromosome are said to have *Down's syndrome.* These children have 47 chromosomes instead of the usual 46. The likelihood of Down's syndrome increases

meiosis
the special process of chromosome duplication and cell division that produces ova and sperm, each containing different combinations of genetic material on 23 chromosomes

autosomes
twenty two pairs of chromosomes in the nucleus of the cell that do not include the sex chromosomes

viability
the baby's ability to survive outside the womb if born

Down's syndrome
a chromosomal abnormality caused by the presence of an extra (47th) chromosome; formerly called Mongolism

■ **Figure 2–4**

Meiosis, or reduction division, to form new spermatogonia.

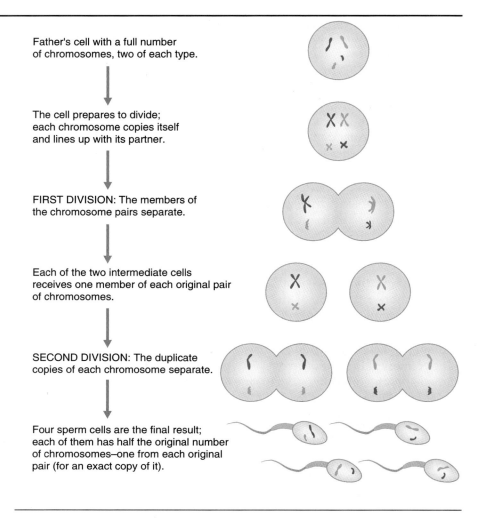

Father's cell with a full number of chromosomes, two of each type.

The cell prepares to divide; each chromosome copies itself and lines up with its partner.

FIRST DIVISION: The members of the chromosome pairs separate.

Each of the two intermediate cells receives one member of each original pair of chromosomes.

SECOND DIVISION: The duplicate copies of each chromosome separate.

Four sperm cells are the final result; each of them has half the original number of chromosomes—one from each original pair (for an exact copy of it).

amniocentesis
a prenatal diagnostic procedure whereby amniotic fluid is withdrawn from the womb so the fetal cells can be examined for specified genetic, metabolic, and chromosomal abnormalities.

hCG (human chorionic gonadotropin)
the hormone secreted soon after implantation; it is detected in pregnancy tests to confirm conception

with the age of the parents, especially the mother. Apparently, the genetic material in older ova is more apt to divide improperly than that in young ova, since it has been exposed to environmental variables such as diet, pollution, stress, radiation, or drug use for a relatively longer period of time (Smith & Warren, 1985). Similar processes affect the genetic material in the sperm of older fathers. Prenatal diagnosis of Down's syndrome can be confirmed by amniocentesis or by a blood test developed in 1987 that measures the levels of alpha-fetoprotein and two hormones, estriol and hCG, in the mother's bloodstream (Canick et al., 1988).

Down's syndrome affects 1 or 2 babies of every 100 born in the United States (Times Wire Service, 1987). More than 5000 Down's babies are born annually. Babies with Down's syndrome are easy to recognize at

■ **Table 2–1** *Sex Chromosome Abnormalities*

TOO LITTLE CHROMOSOMAL MATERIAL

XO—Turner's syndrome
    Number of chromosomes: 45
    Formed by: union of normal X-bearing sperm with O-ovum (no sex chromo-
        somes)
        union of normal ovum with O-sperm (no sex chromosomes)
    Characteristics: small, underdeveloped female; infertile; no spontaneous men-
        struation
YO—Unnamed (lethal condition)
    Humans cannot survive without at least one X sex chromosome (holds
        genes important to autoimmune functioning)
    Formed by: union of normal Y-bearing sperm with O-ovum

TOO MUCH CHROMOSOMAL MATERIAL

XXX—Trisomy X
    Number of chromosomes: 47
    Formed by: union of normal X-bearing sperm with XX ovum
        union of normal ovum with XX sperm
    Characteristics: variable; generally normal female, may have fertility compli-
        cations
XXY—Klinefelter's syndrome
    Number of chromosomes: 47
    Formed by: union of normally Y-bearing sperm with XX ovum
    Characteristics: small, underdeveloped male; infertile; may have some femi-
        nized structures (breast development, rounded body contours)
XYY—Supermale syndrome
    Number of chromosomes: 47
    Formed by: union of normal ovum with YY sperm
    Characteristics: Large male with precocious sexual maturation; may have fer-
        tility problems and mental retardation

birth (Table 2–2). In the past, congenital heart problems, the incidence of leukemia (15–20 times higher than normal), and susceptibility to infection prevented most Down's babies from living much beyond infancy. Today, antibiotics and advanced surgical and medical treatments are available to help correct these conditions, and Down's syndrome individuals survive until their 30s and 40s and sometimes beyond.

Mental retardation is commonly associated with Down's syndrome. However, the fear that all Down's babies will be severely retarded is unfounded. Just as in the nonaffected population, people with Down's syndrome exhibit a wide range of mental ability: some are only minimally affected, others have moderate difficulties, and some are severely retarded. It is impossible to predict before birth the specific capabilities and limitations of any particular child with Down's syndrome. Even

In Touch

NATIONAL DOWN'S SYNDROME
  SOCIETY
666 Broadway
New York, NY 10012
1-800-221-4602

(left) The relationship of Down's syndrome to maternal age. (right) A boy with Down's syndrome.

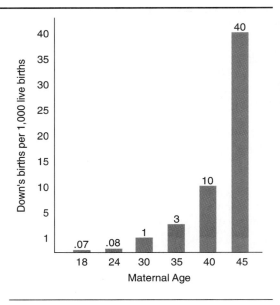

after birth, intelligence as measured by IQ tests is hard to assess accurately, since the typically oversized tongue in those with the syndrome makes coherent speech difficult and the typically stubby fingers can hamper motor ability. These physical limitations may mask mental ability. Surgery to reduce tongue size or restructure facial features has not been shown to have any functional benefits but may help the child be more accepted socially (Katz & Kravetz, 1989). More often than not, Down's individuals are capable of learning and understanding a variety of concepts if people will taken the time to teach them at their level.

■ ● ▲   CONCEPT SUMMARY

Developmental Outcomes Influenced by Genetics:

● Sex determination

● Sex chromosome abnormalities (see Table 2.1)

● Autosome abnormalities (especially Down's syndrome)

● Physical characteristics, intelligence, medical conditions, temperament and personality traits, and other psychological predispositions inherited from parents

■ **Table 2–2** *The Most Accurate Clinical Symptoms for Diagnosing Down's Syndrome*

SYMPTOM	PERCENT SHOWING SYMPTOM
Physical characteristics	
Abundant neck skin	94
Mouth corners turned downward	84
General hypotonia (limpness)	82
Flat face	80
At least one malformed ear	78
Epicanthus in at least one eye (fold of skin on eyelid giving an Asian appearance)	76
Gap between first and second toes	67
Protruding tongue	63
Head circumference at birth (not exceeding 32 cm)	43
Simian crease in at least one hand (unbroken "lifeline")	42
OTHER SIGNS IN LESS THAN 40% OF THE CASES	
Behavioral Signs	
Absent Moro reflex	
Small size at birth ("small for date")	
Slow in developing basic motor skills	
Internal complications	
Heart malformations	
Obstructed bowel	
Faulty immune system	
Premature aging after age 40	

Source: Selikowitz, 1990.

Variations in Development Caused by Genetic Messages

The information contained in the individual genes on each chromosome serves as a biochemical blueprint for constructing a living organism of a specific species and certain sex. The size of our blood vessels, the shape of our hearts, and the number of bones in our wrist are all determined by our genes. Such genetic information varies little from person to person. But the genes also carry instructions for the physical characteristics we inherit from our parents, such as eye color, blood type, and the shapes of our noses. These characteristics are responsible for variations in appearance. Genes also influence nonphysical processes of development such as personality development and intelligence. As with most genetic determinants, of course, the environment in which the child lives plays a major role in the final manifestation of the trait.

DNA (deoxyribonucleic acid)
the chemical molecule that makes up
the genes

genetic code
the biochemical message created by
the arrangement of the 4 bases of the
DNA molecule

heredity
the tendency of individuals to
develop the traits and characteristics
possessed by their ancestors

In 1953 Francis Crick and James Watson discovered that genetic messages are contained in the *DNA*, deoxyribonucleic acid, which makes up the hundreds of thousands of genes bound together on the chromosomes in the nucleus of the fertilized ovum. DNA is a relatively simple molecule composed of four organic components or bases: adenine (A), guanine (G), cytosine (C), and thymine (T). DNA takes the shape of a double helix, a long flexible ladder twisted about itself (Figure 2–6). Each rung of the ladder is one of the four organic bases and its complement (A always joins with T and T with A; C must join with G and G with C). The bases are held in place by sugar-phosphate supports, which may spiral as pictured or in the opposite direction. The vertical order of the base pairs determines the genetic code, or message. The code is divided into sections, called genes. The genes order the building of certain proteins which are associated with the appearance of particular traits. The gene for eye color, for example, directs the formation of proteins affecting eye color.

PATTERNS OF GENETIC TRANSMISSION Scientists are learning to decode genetic messages contained in DNA and to identify the gene or genes ultimately responsible for the expression of certain traits or characteristics. *Heredity*, or *genetic transmission*, is the process by which genetic traits are passed from one generation to the next. This process takes place in accordance with specific laws or principles. Without an understanding of them, one might consider heredity to be entirely haphazard and unpredictable. For example, the children born to a blue-eyed man and a brown-eyed woman all have green eyes. How can that be? A couple has two intellectually "normal" children and a third who is men-

■ **Figure 2–6**

The double helix design of DNA showing the base pairs that form the rungs of the DNA "ladder".

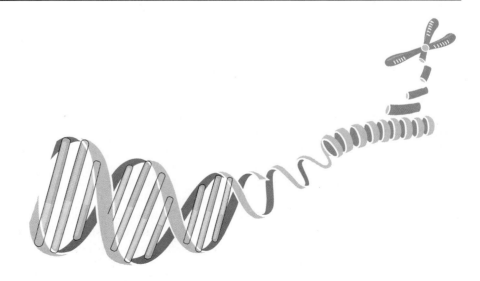

■ **Figure 2–7**

Generational similarities and differences. Notice how the eyes, ears, and noses of the ancestors in the pictures on the walls match with those of the current generations.

principles of dominant and recessive inheritance
laws of heredity governing dominant and recessive traits discovered by Gregor Mendel in 1865

allele
each gene in a gene pair; has a dominant or a recessive form

tally retarded. They are told the third child's condition is an inherited trait, yet neither can recall any such children on either side of the family. These cases, bewildering to the lay person, are accounted for by the normal action of the laws of heredity.

The *laws of heredity* were first discovered in 1865 by an Austrian monk named Gregor Mendel. Like many scientists, Mendel received no recognition for his work at the time. The significance of his findings simply were not understood. Slowly, though, Mendel's *principles of dominant and recessive inheritance* clarified the transmission of traits by single genes.

Dominant-Recessive Inheritance. Like chromosomes, genes exist in pairs. For each gene at a certain locus on a given chromosome, there is a similar gene at the same spot on the pair's corresponding chromosome. Each gene in a pair is called an *allele*. Alleles can take one of two forms: dominant or recessive. Where a *dominant allele* is present, the trait it represents is expressed even when the other gene in the pair is recessive. The traits represented by *recessive alleles* are expressed only when both genes of the pair are recessive for that trait—that is, when no dominant

■ **Figure 2–8**

Chromosome pair with alleles indicated.

Gene A$_1$
Allele contributed
by the mother

Gene A$_2$
Allele contributed
by the father

Chromosome pair

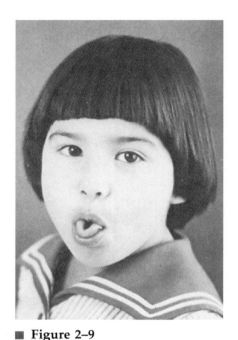

■ **Figure 2–9**

A person with genetic tongue-rolling ability. Can you roll your tongue like the child in this picture?

allele is present in the pair. Actually, it is the traits themselves, not the genes or alleles, that are dominant or recessive, but the terms dominant and recessive gene are commonly used. Two other terms are important in understanding the laws of heredity. When both alleles are alike (both dominant or both recessive), the person is said to be *homozygous* for that gene or trait. When two alleles are different, the person is said to be *heterozygous.*

Geneticists use letter symbols to diagram combinations of dominant and recessive alleles. A capital letter (usually the first letter of the name of the trait) represents the dominant allele; the lowercase form of the same letter represents the recessive allele. Let's take tongue rolling as an example. The ability to roll one's tongue, shown in Figure 2–9, is a genetic trait. Since a single gene governs tongue rolling, *T* can represent the dominant allele and *t*, the recessive allele.

Here we need to introduce a few more terms. *Genotype* describes the alleles present at a specific locus. Three genotypes are possible in dominant–recessive inheritance: two dominant alleles, two recessive alleles, or one of each. *Phenotype* refers to the characteristic or trait expressed by the genotype. So the ability to roll one's tongue is the *phenotype* for the person whose *genotype* is *TT* (homozygous dominant) or *Tt* (heterozygous). Thus, phenotype refers to appearance or behavior while genotype refers to the configuration of the alleles in the gene. If you can roll your tongue like the person in Figure 2–3, your genotype is either *TT* or *Tt*. Phenotypically, if you are *tt* (homozygous recessive), you have no inherited tongue-rolling ability. The expression of this trait is governed by the dominant allele, and therefore we call tongue-rolling ability a *dominant trait.*

Recessive traits are expressed only if both alleles are recessive. *Albinism* is an example of a recessive trait. Albinism occurs when individuals lack an enzyme needed to form melanin, the substance that pigments the skin, eyes, and hair. Albinism is the condition, or phenotype, ex-

■ **Figure 2–10**

Albino siblings.

pressed in people who are homozygous for the recessive allele (*aa*). Normal pigmentation owing to the presence of melanin is the phenotype for the other possible gene combinations (*AA* or *Aa*). Where recessive traits are concerned, certain individuals are "carriers." A *carrier* is one who appears normal but whose genotype is heterozygous for the recessive trait. Since the recessive gene is present in the carrier despite the fact that the trait is unexpressed, that person can transmit the trait to offspring. Using albinism as an example, let's see how carrier transmission of an unexpressed trait might occur.

When both parents are carriers of albinism (*Aa*), both are normally pigmented but half of the gametes of each parent carry the dominant allele (*A*), and half carry the recessive allele (*a*). Using the laws of probability, geneticists can project probable outcomes in gene combinations. The proportions of expected genotypes and phenotypes in offspring from their pairing are indicated in Figure 2–11. Statistically, this couple has one chance in four of conceiving a child with albinism. Stated another way, one-fourth (25%) of their children are expected to have albinism and to lack normal pigmentation even though neither parent is an albino.

Let's look at another pairing. Will the union of an albino parent and a normally pigmented parent always produce children with albinism? No. Remember, the genotype of the "normal" parent may be either *AA* (homozygous dominant) or heterozygous *Aa* (carrier). On the other hand, the albino parent's genotype *must* be homozygous recessive (*aa*)

homozygous
the condition that exists when the alleles of a gene pair are identical

heterozygous
the condition that exists when the alleles of a gene pair differ from one another

genotype
the characteristics that an individual has inherited, as prescribed by his or her genes, that may or may not be expressed

phenotype
the observable characteristics an individual has inherited

dominant trait
inherited characteristics that are expressed with relative frequency in the general population

recessive trait
inherited characteristics that are rarely expressed in the general population

carrier
individuals who possess recessive genes for particular traits but who do not manifest the traits themselves

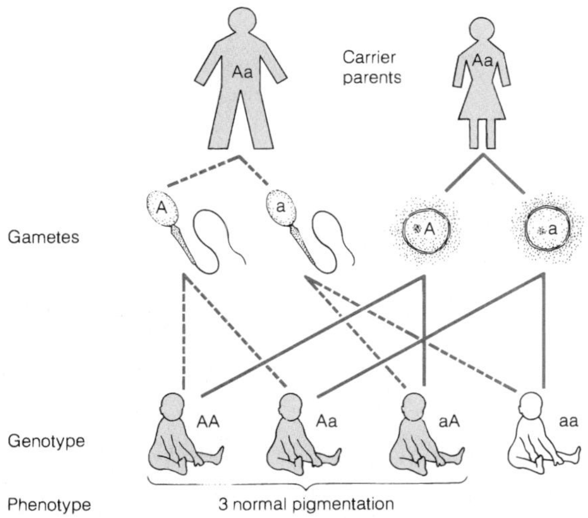

■ **Figure 2–11**

Genotypes and phenotypes for the offspring of carriers of albinism.

or the trait would not be expressed. The proportion of expected geno-types and phenotypes of these two pairings is given in Figure 2–12. As you can see, the ratios of expected albino offspring from each union vary greatly. Surprisingly, the couple in Figure 2–13 cannot conceive a

■ **Figure 2–12**

Genotypes and phenotypes for the offspring of a carrier and an albino parent.

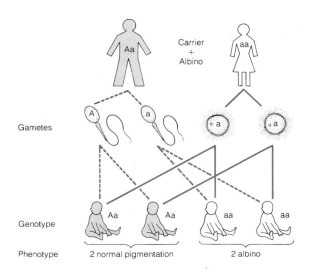

■ **Figure 2–13**

Genotypes and phenotypes for the offspring of an albino parent and a parent who is homozygous dominant for albinism.

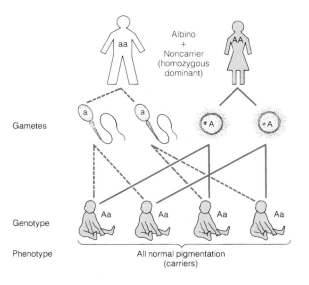

single child with albinism even though one parent is albino. However, all their children would be carriers of the trait (that is, they would all have heterozygous genotypes). In contrast, fully 50% of the other couple's children would be expected to have albinism, and the other 50% would be carriers of the trait. The only pairing that would inevitably produce children with albinism would be that of two albino parents (*aa* plus *aa*). In that case, there would be no allele variation, since the only possible combination would be *aa* for all offspring.

Polygenic Inheritance Sometimes inherited traits are influenced by several gene pairs rather than just one. Such traits are called *polygenic traits.* Eye color and skin pigmentation are both polygenic traits. The exact color of the eye's iris and the amount of pigment in the skin depends on the amount of melanin present. A single gene determines whether or not melanin will be produced, and other genes interact to regulate the *quantity* of melanin in the system. When the dominant allele for eye color is present, the eyes can be green, hazel, or shades of brown. Blue eyes are produced by a pair of recessive alleles. Despite their apparent lack of brown pigment, blue eyes contain melanin in the interior coating of the eyes; only the eyes of albinos are without melanin. Like brown eyes, blue eyes come in a variety of shades (even lavender), suggesting polygenic influence.

The genetic mechanism for skin pigmentation is similar to that for eye color. One gene governs the presence or absence of melanin and apparently four additional pairs of alleles are responsible for the range of pigmentation possible—from white through black (in skin areas not exposed to the sun). One would expect first-generation children of interracial marriages to inherit intermediate pigmentation, having one allele for darker pigmentation and one allele for lighter pigmentation. After considerable interracial blending, it is possible for two parents of intermediate pigmentation to have a normal child with very dark or very light pigmentation owing to the random assortment of the involved genes during meiosis. See Table 2–3 for examples of other dominant and recessive human traits.

Incomplete Dominance Sometimes in the heterozygous condition, the properties of the dominant gene do not completely dominate. Instead, an intermediate condition results. For example, in males, baldness (*B*) is dominant over having a full head of hair (*b*). But boys whose genotype is *Bb* rarely become completely bald. They usually lose *some* of their hair but not all. Similarly, curly hair (*H*) is dominant over straight hair (*h*). But the *Hh* genotype usually produces hair that looks more *wavy* than either curly or straight.

X-linked Inheritance Genes on the sex chromosomes are inherited differently from genes on the other chromosomes. This special pattern of

HERMAN®

"He's got his grandfather's nose."

polygenic traits
traits produced by the interaction of several genes

incomplete dominance
a condition where the heterozygous form does not express the dominant trait but an intermediate condition, part way between dominant and recessive expression

■ **Table 2–3** *Some Dominant and Recessive Human Traits*

TRAIT	DOMINANT	RECESSIVE
Eye characteristics	Brown, hazel, or green	Blue or gray
	Astigmatism and farsightedness	Normal
	Normal	Nearsightedness (a less common form is dominant)
	Normal	Red-green color blindness (sex-linked)
	Long lashes	Short lashes
	Tendency to cataracts	Normal
Nose	High convex bridge	Straight or concave bridge
	Narrow bridge	Broad bridge
	Straight tip	Upturned tip
	Flaring nostrils	Narrow nostrils
Ears	Free earlobe	Attached earlobe
Other facial traits	Full lips	Thin lips
	Normal	Recessive chin
	Dimpled chin	Undimpled chin
	Dimpled cheeks	Undimpled cheeks
	High cheekbones	Normal
	Freckled	Nonfreckled
Hair	Dark	Blond
	Nonred	Red
	Kinky	Curly
	Curly	Straight
	Baldness (males)	Normal
	Normal	Baldness (females)
	White forelock	Normal
	Premature grayness	Normal
	Abundant hair on body	Sparse
	Heavy, bushy eyebrows	Normal
Heads, fingers, toes	Index finger longer than ring finger (in males)	Index finger longer than ring finger (in females)
	Second toe longer than big toe	Second toe shorter than big toe
	Hypermobility of thumb	Normal
	Right-handedness	Left-handedness
Other	Dark skin color	Light skin color
	A, B, AB blood groups	Group O
	Tendency to varicose veins	Normal
	Normal	Phenylketonuria
	Normal	Tendency to schizophrenia
	Normal	Congenital deafness
	Normal	Tendency to diabetes mellitus
	Normal	Hemophilia (sex-linked)
	Normal	Albinism

Source: Russell, 1990.

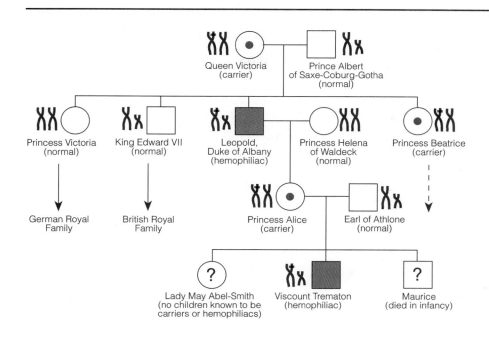

Tracing the genetic transmission of hemophilia carried by Queen Victoria of England through the British Royal line.

inheritance is called *X-linked inheritance*. Color blindness is an example of an X-linked trait. The most common type of color blindness is caused by a recessive X-linked gene that affects the function of the red/green sensitive structures within the eye. This recessive gene, located on the X sex chromosome, is contributed by the mother at conception. Female children usually have a dominant allele on their other X chromosome to offset the effects of any recessive allele contributed by their mothers, but male children do not. Most of the genes of the X chromosome have no corresponding alleles on the Y. Therefore, almost all genes on the X chromosome will be expressed in males (even those that are recessive). Hemophilia, or the "Bleeder's Disease", is an example of an X-linked condition. More than 3,500 inherited diseases have been identified. For a summary of other common genetic diseases and conditions, see Table 2–4.

x-linked inheritance
inherited characteristics influenced by genes carried on the X or Y sex chromosomes; also called sex-linked inheritance

Genetic Counseling

- A couple gives birth to a child with a troublesome illness, disease, or physical condition
- A history of muscular dystrophy exists in the family
- A woman with sickle cell anemia wants to begin a family with a man unaffected by sickle cell disease

■ **Table 2–4** *Some Common Genetic Diseases and Conditions*

NAME	DESCRIPTION OF EFFECTS	INCIDENCE	PRENATAL DIAGNOSIS?	TREATMENT
Alpha thalassemia	Severe anemia caused by abnormal blood cells. Nearly all infants die or are stillborn	Infants of Malaysian, African, or Southeast Asian families are at risk	Amniocentesis, CVS (chorionic villus sampling)	Periodic transfusions
Anencephaly	Absence of the majority of brain tissue; infants die at or shortly after birth	1/1,000 live births	Ultrasound, amniocentesis	No treatment; condition is fatal
Cleft lip/cleft palate	The upper lip or bony palate are not completely formed	1/700 live births; about 5,000 births per year	Not at this time	Plastic surgery
Club foot	Foot twisted in and down	1/400 live births; 9,000 births per year; twice as common in boys	Possibly MRI (magnetic resonance imaging)	Surgery
Cooley's anemia	Severe anemia resulting in muscle weakness, fatigue, and susceptibility to illness. Usually fatal by adolescence or young adulthood	Infants of Mediterranean descent are at risk	Amniocentesis, CVS	Periodic transfusions
Cystic fibrosis	Mucous is overproduced and collects in the lungs and digestive tract. Growth is adversely affected and most do not live past their 20s.	1/1,000 live births	Amniocentesis, CVS	Daily physical therapy to loosen and expel mucous; possible genetic engineering
Diabetes	Pancreas doesn't produce enough insulin to metabolize sugar	Up to 5 million American adults have diabetes	Not at this time	Administration of insulin; dietary restrictions
Fragile-X syndrome	The most common form of inherited mental retardation. Considered one of the main causes of autism	1/1,200 males; 1/2,000 females	Amniocentesis, CVS	None at this time
(Congenital) heart defects	Malformation of the heart in various degrees of severity	1 in 175 live births; over 20,000 cases anually	Ultrasound, MRI	Surgery
Hemophilia	Excessive bleeding due to lack of blood clotting; may lead to crippling arthritis in adulthood	1/10,000 families with a history of hemophilia	Amniocentesis, CVS	Blood transfusions containing "clotting factor"
Huntington's chorea	Progressive deterioration of brain and nervous system during middle age	Extremely rare	Not at this time	None; the disorder is fatal
Hydrocephalus	Excessive accumulation of fluid around the brain that may cause brain damage	1/500 live births	Ultrasound; other imaging techniques	Surgery (shunting) to redirect fluid
Muscular dystrophy, Duchenne type	Progressive muscle deterioration usually accompanied by mild retardation; respiratory failure and death usually occur in young adulthood	1/7,000 live male births	Amniocentesis, CVS	None; programs of intellectual stimulation try to maintain cognitive functioning

■ **Table 2–4** *(continued)*

NAME	DESCRIPTION OF EFFECTS	INCIDENCE	PRENATAL DIAGNOSIS?	TREATMENT
PKU (Phenylketonuria)	Inability to metabolize a specific protein (phenyl-alenine); accumulation of unmetabolized protein prevents brain development	Infants of North European ancestry are at highest risk; 1 in 10,000 live births annually	Blood test 2 days after birth	No phenylalenine in diet
Polycystic kidney disease	Enlarged kidneys leading to respiratory problems and heart failure	1/1,000 live births	Aminiocentesis	Kidney transplant surgery
Polydactyly	More than 10 fingers or toes	More than 9,000 cases per year	Ultrasound, MRI	Surgery
Rh disease	Blood disease that causes the destruction of red blood cells	7,000 cases per year	Amniocentesis, CVS	Blood transfusion
Sickle cell disease	Body produces deformed red blood cells that can't carry sufficient oxygen and can clog the vessels causing pain, slowed growth, and susceptibility to infection	1 in 500 births of infants of African descent	Amniocentesis	Blood transfusions and antibiotics
Spina bifida	Incompletely formed neural tube; spinal cord protrudes in pouch on back; may be accompanied by muscle weakness and/or mental retardation	6,200 cases per year	Ultrasound; also amniocentesis if tube is leaking spinal fluid	Surgery to close spinal tube and to redirect fluid away from brain; physical therapy
Tay-Sachs disease	Inability to metabolize fats causes body to store excess fat in brain cells, disrupting brain functioning and usually resulting in death before the age of 5	1 in 3,000 births to Eastern European Jews	Amniocentesis, CVS	None at this time

In each of these cases, the people involved may be curious about the possibility of giving birth to an afflicted child or having yet another child who has the particular disease or disability. These are the types of questions a genetic counselor is trained to answer. A *genetic counselor* can try to determine the *cause* of a particular condition or outcome (genetic, chromosomal, or environmental) and the likelihood of transmitting it to an unborn child. After the probable risks are calculated of having a baby with muscular dystrophy, for example, the parents can weigh the pro and cons of going ahead with conception. It is important for couples to remember that probability statistics are not cumulative. Two parents heterozygous for muscular dystrophy in its recessive form

genetic counseling
advice to potential parents based on principles of human genetics regarding the probability of genetic problems in offspring; conducted by a professional called a genetic counselor

in vitro **fertilization**
a technology to improve the chances
of fertilization by having the ovum
and sperm meet in a *petri* (laboratory
dish); the conceptus (if formed) is
then implanted back into the host
mother

have one chance in four of giving birth to a child with the disease *each
time they conceive:*

$$Mm(\text{mom}) \times Mm(\text{dad}) = MM, Mm, mM, mm$$

♀
		M	m
♂	M	*MM*	*Mm*
	m	*mM*	*mm*

mm = 1 chance in 4.

That does *not* mean that the couple will have one affected child out of
four births. It's possible (but unlikely) that the heterozygous couple
could have four completely normal children or four children with muscular dystrophy or any other combination (Table 2–5). Chance has no
memory. The statistical likelihood is the same for each conception regardless of how many previous children had been born with the disease
or had been born disease-free (Massarik, 1981).

If statistical probability makes regular conception seem too risky,
there are other options for the couple. They can adopt or they can attempt nontraditional conception (artificial insemination, in vitro fertilization, ovum transfer, etc.). These methods could allow the fertilized
egg to be screened for signs of genetic disease or could eliminate the
impact of the affected partner's genes altogether (Pullen, 1984). In the
very near future, the troublesome gene may even be modified through
genetic engineering.

■●▲   **CONCEPT SUMMARY**

Patterns of Genetic Transmission

● Dominant/recessive inheritance—one gene/one trait
  Principles of expression:
      dominant traits—the presence of at least one dominant allele
      recessive traits—the presence of two recessive alleles

● Polygenic inheritance—several genes/one trait

● Incomplete dominance—the heterozygous condition for a dominant
  trait produces an outcome that is a compromise between the homozygous dominant condition and the homozygous recessive condition

● X-linked inheritance—The expression of traits by genes on the sex
  chromosomes (23rd pair)

■ **Table 2–5** *Conceivable (but unlikely) Birth Outcomes for Two Parents Who Are Both Carriers of Muscular Dystrophy, Genotype* **Mm**

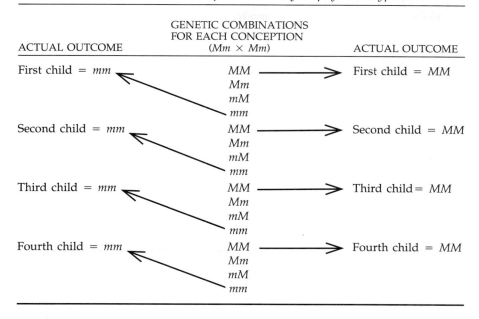

ACTUAL OUTCOME	GENETIC COMBINATIONS FOR EACH CONCEPTION (*Mm* × *Mm*)	ACTUAL OUTCOME
First child = *mm*	*MM* *Mm* *mM* *mm*	First child = *MM*
Second child = *mm*	*MM* *Mm* *mM* *mm*	Second child = *MM*
Third child = *mm*	*MM* *Mm* *mM* *mm*	Third child = *MM*
Fourth child = *mm*	*MM* *Mm* *mM* *mm*	Fourth child = *MM*

Genetic Engineering

Under ordinary circumstances, genetic traits are passed from generation to generation through the natural action of the laws of heredity. But in 1972, scientists made a major discovery. They found they could alter the genes of animals by adding to or removing part of the DNA containing the genetic code associated with a particular characteristic. The technique of transferring genes from one organism to another is called *genetic engineering.* In one study, scientists experimented with the genes controlling growth by injecting rat genes into a developing mouse egg. The result—SuperMouse(!), a mouse that grew larger than its noninjected counterparts, since its growth was directed by the genes of a larger organism.

Does this mean that giraffe genes might be injected into potential basketball players or that "designer genes" will be given to future interior decorators? Certainly not. But the field of genetic engineering holds great promise. Slowly but surely, scientists have identified the genes associated with various genetic diseases. Two genes for sex-determination have been identified since 1987; the gene for cystic fibrosis (CF) was identified in 1989; in 1991 a gene associated with inherited deafness was isolated. Today, scientists report that they have been able to use a normal copy of the CF gene to override the effects of the defective one.

genetic engineering
the intentional manipulation of genes to produce specific outcomes

It is important to keep in mind, however, that genes are complex structures. Manipulating them to produce a subtle effect might be profoundly difficult. Let's consider the possibility of adding growth hormone to human embryos. If tall children are designed, then logically one might add genes from tall individuals to developing egg cells with the intention of allowing the growth hormone gene to work longer or more effectively. The trick would be to induce a few inches of growth without bringing about gigantism. In fact, any form of gene manipulation would be like trying to place a golf ball on a very small green—overshooting the mark would be as bad as undershooting it (Bains, 1987).

Another complication is that genes may not function in isolation. A change in one gene might affect others and start a whole chain of events with positive or negative results. Also, if we start favoring certain traits, we might reduce the variation in the total gene pool available to human beings. Decreasing gene variety could compromise our survival potential as a species. In general, a species without adequate gene variety is less able to evolve further and is at greater risk of extinction as conditions change than a species with great variety.

■ **Table 2–6**   *Advances in Gene Research*

KEY SCIENTIFIC ADVANCES THAT HAVE MADE HUMAN
GENE THERAPY A POSSIBILITY.

1865   Gregor Mendel postulates the existence of specific inherited factors, later called genes.

1953   Francis Crick and James Watson determine the structure of DNA, the substance of which genes are made.

1966   Scientists establish the complete genetic code, which is the information carried by the DNA molecule that determines physical traits and other human characteristics.

1970   Discovery of retroviruses, the best current vehicle for inserting genes into cells.

1972   Scientists create recombinant DNA molecules.

1973   Researchers learn to make large quantities of human genes, from which proteins such as insulin or growth hormone are manufactured.

1982   Researchers perform successful gene therapy in fruit flies, correcting an eye color defect. Experiments show that the normal gene can be transmitted to subsequent generations. In the same year, "supermice" are born and grow to twice their normal weight after researchers inject the cloned gene for rat growth hormone into fertilized mice eggs.

1985   Viruses are used to transfer genes into mice bone marrow cells, which in turn make substantial amounts of protein from the added gene.

1986   First gene therapy experiments in monkeys in progress at the National Institutes of Health.

1987   The first modification of specific genes tied to specific functions.

Sources: © 1986, Los Angeles Times. Reprinted by permission. Russell (1990).

Finally, the implications of genetic engineering raise ethical and social questions about what constitutes a *defective gene* or an undesirable trait (Yanchinski, 1989). For example, all might agree that debilitating conditions such as muscular dystrophy or other genetic conditions should be eradicated. But what about traits like dark skin, curly hair, or even short legs? Could new "races" of people be created who, for example, could work more effectively at menial tasks because their need to socialize has been engineered out? And who would have access to genetic engineering technology? Could minors and others be engineered against their will? Could we engineer violence out of criminals in lieu of lengthy incarceration or other therapy? And what would become of the human mishaps of such technology? These are just a few of the issues that might result from the full-scale implementation of genetic engineering.

Environmental Modification of Genetic Traits

Does one inevitably become the person prescribed in the genes? With regard to some traits, such as blood type, the answer is *yes:* genetic instructions are carried out fully and precisely. But in most other cases, gene expression is modified by the environment. Trying to determine how much of our behavior is guided by our genes and how much is influenced by the environment is one of the oldest controversies in the field of psychology: the *nature/nurture controversy*. While developmentalists agree that both heredity (nature) and the environment (nurture) are essential to development, the question at issue is, What is the relative contribution of each? Studies of twins can be helpful in untangling the nature/nurture question. Two types of twins exist: identical, or monozygotic, twins and fraternal, or dizygotic, twins.

nature/nurture controversy
the debate within psychology over the relative influence on behavior of nature (genetics) and nurture (the environment)

Monozygotic (Identical) Twins

Identical twins are the only humans who are not genetically unique. *Identical,* or *monozygotic,* twins develop from one zygote that spontaneously duplicates and forms two embryos. They share the same or very similar genes (similar in that in some cases gene expression is only partial), resemble each other, are the same sex, and share other inherited characteristics. Still, identical twins may exhibit differences in appearance, health, and personality owing to the impact of the environment. Monozygotic twinning is coincidental and in most cases not influenced by heredity, although families sometimes report high frequencies of monozygotic twins. Some identical twins share almost uncanny similarities and claim to be able to sense and perceive the emotions and thoughts of each other.

When the zygote fails to separate after spontaneous duplication, *cojoined* or *Siamese twins* result. The first Siamese twins to gain significant

monozygotic twins
identical twins

cojoined (Siamese) twins
monozygotic twins that do not separate fully when the zygote from which they are formed spontaneously duplicates

In Touch

NATIONAL ORGANIZATION OF
   MOTHERS OF TWINS CLUBS,
   INC.
12404 Princess Jeanne NE
Albuquerque, NM 87112-4640
1-505-275-0955

attention were found in Siam (now Thailand) by a British merchant. Chang and Eng, born in 1811, were joined at the chest by a band of cartilage and were never separated although such surgery was feasible even then. They were exhibited in Europe and America by circus owner P. T. Barnum, married two sisters, and had six and five children, respectively. Chang and Eng died in 1874, just hours apart.

Cojoined twins are extremely rare, occurring once in every 50,000 to 80,000 deliveries (Edmonds et al., 1982). The most common sites of connection are the chest, lower back, or head (craniopagus twins). If each twin develops fully and no vital organs are shared, separation is possible. The first craniopagus twins to survive separation are Lisa and Elisa Hansen of Ogden, Utah, who were born in 1977 and separated at 18 months of age in 1979. (See the accompanying feature about them and other cojoined twins.)

Dizygotic (Fraternal) Twins

dizygotic twins
fraternal twins

Dizygotic twins are produced when two eggs are ovulated at the same time and both are fertilized. This outcome may be due to outside agents such as fertility drugs or to the natural action of the woman's menstrual cycle influenced by her genes. Adult dizygotic twins or people with a dizygotic twin for a parent are more likely to have dizygotic twins themselves. The popular idea that such twins "skip a generation" is a myth. Both fathers and mothers can pass this tendency to their offspring. Moreover, for reasons not fully understood, the likelihood of dizygotic twins increases with maternal age.

Eighty percent of twins born are dizygotic. Such twins are no more alike genetically than are brothers or sisters born at different times to

■ **Figure 2–15**

(left) Lisa and Elisa Hansen, 9 months, were born joined at the tops of their heads. (right) At age 5, the Hansen twins underwent their last surgery to repair the site of joinage.

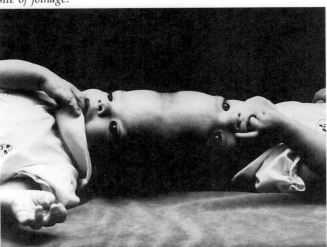

the same parents. But the common name *fraternal twins,* suggesting brothers only, is a misnomer. Dizygotic twins can just as easily be two females, or a male and a female. Interestingly, the incidence of natural two-egg twins is higher among blacks than among other groups, occurring once in 70 live births to black females, compared with once in 86 live births for white females and once in 300 live births for Chinese females.

Multiple Births

Multiple fetuses are formed either by multiple ovulation or by the spontaneous duplication (or reduplication) of the zygote or by both processes. The babies can all be fraternal twins or they may be combinations of fraternal twins and monozygotic twins and triplets. The highest number of babies medically recorded as coming from one pregnancy is nine (nonuplets) (Guiness Book of World Records, 1991). Sadly, the survival rate of multiple fetuses is low and their complication rates high (Campbell, 1991). Sometimes the number of fetuses is surgically reduced to permit more favorable outcomes for the ones remaining in utero (Boulot et al., 1990). Still, no more than six twins from any single pregnancy have ever survived.

Twin Concordance

Since monozygotic twins share the same genotype, any differences between them must be due to environmental factors. (Dizygotic twins, on the other hand, are not genetically identical, so both heredity and environment can be involved in trait expression.) The degree of similarity between twin pairs with respect to a particular trait is called *concordance* and is usually expressed in percentages. A high concordance rate between monozygotic twins would indicate a strong hereditary influence. A concordance rate that is about equivalent for monozygotic and dizygotic twins would reveal an outcome attributable to the environment.

■ **Figure 2–16**

Identical triplets.

concordance
the degree of similarity shared by twins on certain measurable traits

---

■●▲   CONCEPT SUMMARY

Genetic Influence Can be Understood Through:

● Genetic counseling

● Genetic engineering

● Studying twin concordance

A Closer Look

The Body Double

Identical (monozygotic) twins evoke a sense of awe and mystery. We don't expect to see human clones, but when they exist, in the form of identical twins, it seems we cannot help but stare.

Cojoined twins are more remarkable still. Formed by the same process as their monozygotic counterparts, the zygotes of cojoined twins didn't separate fully after duplicating. The result is that these babies have the same birthdates *and* are born at the same time since part of each is shared by the other.

Lisa and Elisa Hansen were born in 1978 in Ogden, Utah, joined at the tops of their heads. At 18 months of age, they were separated by a historic surgery that involved cutting the skulls apart, separating the blood vessels and covering the exposed surfaces of the girls' brains. Follow-up plastic surgeries restructured the tops of their heads and reconstructed their skulls. The girls are now in their teens and, by all accounts, have adapted amazingly well.

Prior to their separation, the Hansen twins learned to cooperate to get what they wanted. They first learned to move by rolling over together. And when they would crawl, they would either both move sideways or one would crawl forward while the other crawled backward. They were walking, by bending at the waist, and talking at the time of their separation.

Yvonne and Yvette McCarther are the oldest living unseparated craniopagus (joined at the head) twins. They, too, have made remarkable adaptations throughout their lives to cope with their condition. Born in 1949 in Los Angeles, California, their mother, Willie, was told that they would be hopelessly retarded and should be institutionalized. A separation was thought to be

Yvonne and Yvette working on an English assignment.

impossible at the time. Faced with a $40,000 hospital bill for the birth and care of the twins, Willie struggled desperately to keep her girls out of the circus sideshow. In the end, a saddened Mrs. McCarther capitulated and signed a contract with the Clyde Beatty circus. So in the tradition of Chang and Eng, Siamese twins of Barnum and Bailey circus fame, the McCarther twins went on exhibit to pay their debts. They were a huge success.

Today, despite their experiences, Yvonne and Yvette are without a trace of self-pity, complaint, or despair. They were raised in a large family that was too poor to pamper them, so they learned to take care of themselves at an early age. They did not attend public school, even though both were physically and mentally able, because nobody ever suggested it. The school system sent voluntary tutors to their home, so the twins learned to read and write. They don't regard themselves as handicapped or deformed, but merely as different. Others are sometimes less open-minded.

"People can't help themselves," said Yvette. "They're just so . . . surprised when they see us. But once they get over that, people are usually nice and also curious. They also want to ask us a bunch of questions."

There is almost no question the twins won't answer, although they say they've heard some pretty crazy ones in their time and a few they resent, too.

"One of my favorites," said Yvette, exasperated, "is 'How do you take a bath?' Now how do people think I take a bath? I climb into the tub like everybody else!"

The girls underscore their separateness mainly in small ways. The most notable is their constant use of single pronouns ("I went to the movies last night"; "I got up early today") even when they are referring to two. Wherever the twins go, they both carry large identical handbags, complete with identical sets of everything from family photos to vitamins. Although they both smoke the same brand of cigarettes, each carries her own pack and lighter. Both wear watches ("I wouldn't want her always grabbing at my arm to see what time it is").

Yvonne and Yvette have rejected an operation to separate them, opting instead to attend college, plan for marriage, and work as a permanent twosome.

Regarding their experiences at Compton Community College, Yvonne explains, "I just *love* it here! I can't believe I waited so long to sign up." "Me either," said Yvette. "I'm going to summer school, too," she added with a pleased grin. "Me, too," said her twin.

Source: © 1987 *Los Angeles Times*, May 3, 1987, II, 1:8. "Siamese Adopted Twins: College Opens Outside World" by Bella Stumbo. Reprinted by permission.

The McCarther twins in a college writing class.

PHYSICAL AND PHYSIOLOGICAL TRAITS In height, weight, physical appearance, and other biological measures such as heart rate, respiration rate, and blood pressure, monozygotic twins are more similar than dizygotic twins (Mange, 1990). (See Table 2–7.) Even though body height is strongly influenced by heredity, height may still be modified by the environment (Figure 2–17). Weight seems to be more easily affected by environmental factors like the amount and quality of food eaten and the opportunity for exercise. The rate of physical maturation is similar among monozygotic twins as measured by the age of first menstruation, the pattern of bone ossification, and age-related changes such as graying, wrinkling, loss of teeth, tendency toward obesity, visual acuity, the development of certain cancers, and even time of death (Stunkard et al., 1986).

■ **Table 2–7** *Concordance Rates for Physical Traits in Twins and Siblings*

TRAIT	MONOZYGOTIC TWINS	DIZYGOTIC TWINS	SIBS	MONOZYGOTIC TWINS REARED APART
Stature (difference in centimeters)	1.7	4.4	4.5	1.8
Weight (difference in pounds)	4.1	10.0	10.4	9.9
Age of first menstruation (difference in months)	2.8	12.0	12.9	—

Source: Winchester and Mertens, 1983.

Handedness is genetically influenced, although it doesn't follow any of the patterns of inheritance described earlier. Cratty (1979) found that if both parents are left-handed, there is a 40% chance their children will be left-handed, too. If only one parent is left-handed, the likelihood falls to 17%, and if both parents are right-handed, only 2% of the children will be left-handed. These figures remind us that right-handedness is the dominant mode. Even when both parents are *left*-handed, their children will be *right*-handed more than 60% of the time (Segal, 1989).

■ **Figure 2–17**

Environmental alteration of genetic potential for stature in identical twins. The twin at right appears to be farther from the camera, but in fact she's sitting right by her sister. The smaller twin probably experienced infection, poor nutrition, or injury that permanently affected her growth.

■●▲ CONCEPT SUMMARY

Twins and Multiple Fetuses

- Monozygotic or identical twins
  HOW FORMED? One zygote spontaneously duplicates and then separates and both zygotes implant. The occurrence is coincidental, although genetics may influence family likelihood.

- Cojoined or Siamese twins
  HOW FORMED? From a zygote that has spontaneously duplicated but has failed to separate completely. Occurrence is coincidental.

- Dizygotic or fraternal twins
  HOW FORMED? Through multiple ovulation influenced by genetics or fertility medications.

- Multiple fetuses
  HOW FORMED? Through multiple ovulation, zygote duplication, or some combination of the two processes. Occurrence is primarily influenced by fertility medications.

INTELLIGENCE Intelligence as measured by IQ tests is more similar among those with close genetic bonds than those genetically dissimilar (Bouchard, 1981). In a classic study summarizing 52 separate investigations, Erlenmeyer-Kimling and Jarvik (1963) found that in monozygotic twins (who have identical genes) IQ scores differed by only a few points. The twins' pattern of test performance was also very similar. Both twins might score much higher in mathematics than on vocabulary, for example, and both might display similar increases or decreases in IQ scores at the same age. Dizygotic twins score more like siblings reared together than like monozygotic twins. This is understandable, since dizygotic twins share no more genes than two offspring born to the same parents (Edlin, 1990).

Studies of adoptive families indicate that both heredity and environment influence IQ. Even if they were adopted in their first year of life, by adolescence the adopted child's intellectual performance more closely resembles the biological parents' level of schooling than the adoptive parents' IQ (Scarr & Weinberg, 1983). In a similar study, adopted children scored higher on intelligence tests than their biological mothers but lower that their adoptive parents (Horn, 1983). IQ is malleable but there appears to be a limit on the extent to which genetic potential can be enhanced by the environment (Scarr & Kidd, 1983).

IQ (intelligence quotient)
a formula originally based on measured mental age divided by chronological age times 100 (MA/CA $\times$ 100 = IQ)

personality (also called temperament)
distinctive traits, characteristics and behaviors of an individual

TEMPERAMENT AND PERSONALITY Personality traits are predictable patterns of behavior expressed in a variety of situations. Shyness, optimism, and selfishness are all personality traits. Investigators are interested in determining which traits are inborn and which are a consequence of environmental factors like imitation, reward, and parental expectation. Studies of identical twins have shown striking similarities in habits (like smoking and nail biting), behaviors (sitting position, holding a telephone, and the like), and attitudes (fondness for jewelry, antisocial behavior leading to military discharge, interest in old movies) even among twins who were separated for decades (Holden, 1980; Centerwall & Robinette, 1989). Genetic predispositions to behave in similar ways are also intensified by the environment: the most amazing similarities of all were found among identical twins who were treated the same by their parents (Scarr, 1968). In some cases, the twin behaviors were so predictable, it was like watching one brain control two bodies.

Other traits seem to have a genetic foundation, because they are apparent in the behavior of newborns and remain stable over time. These traits include:

Trait	Range of Behaviors
stress reaction	feels vulnerable and sensitive vs. feels invulnerable and rarely gets feelings hurt
conventionalism	follows rules and obeys authorities vs. deviates from rules and disobeys authorities
leadership	likes to be the center of attention and a leader vs. doesn't gravitate to leadership positions
sociability	extroverted, outgoing, enjoys people vs. reserved, withdrawn
activity level	busy, seeks a lot of stimulation from the environment vs. sedate, content to watch
reactivity	irritable, provoked by the slightest disturbance vs. calm and placid even under trying circumstances
contact seeking	enjoys physical contact, soothed when held vs. resists physical contact, soothed by music, motion, etc.
shyness	anxious, dislikes things and people that aren't familiar ("behavioral inhibition") vs. bold, comfortable with unfamiliar situations, people
mood quality	positive, happy, generally smiling vs. negative, complaining/fussing, frequent crying
rhythmicity	eats, sleeps, cries at about the same time each day vs. irregular, unpredictable cycles of activity
adaptability	adapts to change easily vs. distressed by new events

A Closer Look

Triumphing over Timidity

Shyness can be a blessing to the person who enjoys time away from the limelight. But it can be a burden for those who feel trapped and inhibited by their shyness. Children who feel extremely inhibited can be helped by easygoing, nurturant parents who protect them from stress and help them cope with their fears (Kagan et al., 1987).

Shyness is not necessarily a barrier to success. Some shy people who have become famous performers, artists, and celebrities (Asher, 1987) include

T. S. Eliot	Johnny Carson
Beethoven	Carol Burnett
Jimmy Carter	Michael Jackson
Barbara Walters	

Apparently, it is possible for the shy person to become relatively extroverted in public while remaining introverted in private.

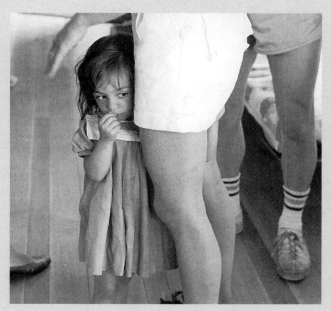

When you're shy, it's nice to have a leg to stand by.

distractibility	singleminded vs. willing to compromise
intensity of reaction	laughs or cries loudly vs. laughs or cries less intensely
absorption	imaginative vs. little sense of imagination
outlook on life	optimistic vs. pessimistic
persistence	keeps trying even after failure vs. gives up easily
attention span	moves quickly from task to task vs. persists with one task or activity for a long time
fearfulness	high fear of personal death or misfortune to loved ones vs. low fear of personal death or misfortune to loved ones

Sources: Kagan et al., 1988; Rose & Ditto, 1983; Tellegen et al., 1988

Although these response tendencies may be apparent at birth, child rearing practices can modify them as the child grows older. Moody, impulsive children can learn to become more persistent or more positive through practice or training. As with intelligence, there seem to be defined parameters that limit environmental modification of personality traits. Fussy, reserved children can't be magically transformed into happy, outgoing ones; they *can* be helped to become less fussy or they can learn to appreciate their own unique personalities.

MEDICAL AND BEHAVIORAL PROBLEMS Genetics influences the likelihood of developing certain medical or behavioral problems. Routine medical examinations include family histories, which provide valuable clues about genetic predispositions toward such health complications as high blood pressure, heart problems, stroke, and even cancer (Table 2–8). Although susceptibility to medical problems may be influenced by one's genes, personal habits such as diet, exercise, health care, drug use, and the immediate environment can modify ultimate outcomes.

Schizophrenia Schizophrenia is a severe mental disturbance. People diagnosed as schizophrenic usually require hospitalization, since they confuse reality and fantasy, have thought disturbances and emotional disorders, and are unable to cope with day-to-day living. For a long time, investigators thought that schizophrenia was caused by the stress of impending adulthood, since the disorder is more commonly diagnosed in young adults than in other age groups. Recent research suggests, however, that stress at *any* time in the person's life can result in schizophrenic behavior (Davison & Neale, 1982).

Schizophrenia has a genetic link since identical twins and children born to schizophrenic mothers have a greater tendency to develop schiz-

schizophrenia
a serious psychological disturbance marked by fluctuations in mood, unusual behavior, and disordered thinking and social reactions

■ **Table 2–8** *Twin Concordance (Percent of Similarity) for Certain Medical Problems*

TRAIT	MONOZYGOTIC TWINS	DIZYGOTIC TWINS
Measles	95	87
Site of cancer (when both have cancer)	95	58
Down's syndrome (Mongolism)	89	6
Rickets	88	22
Schizophrenia	86	15
Diabetes mellitus	84	37
Epilepsy	72	15
Tuberculosis	65	25
Cancer	61	44
Cleft lip	33	5
Clubfoot	32	3

Source: Winchester and Mertens, 1983.

ophrenia than fraternal twins and children born to mothers not labelled as schizophrenic (Hans & Marcus, 1987; Farmer et al., 1987). What may be transmitted is a tendency to overreact to stress, to use ineffective coping strategies, to develop a helpless-dependent personality style, or to select unhealthy environments over healthy ones. Under stressful situations, the brains of some individuals oversecrete serotonin, a chemical substance necessary for normal brain function (Sedvall, 1981). Too much serotonin interferes with information processing and transmission. It is possible that the tendency to overproduce serotonin has some genetic basis, but the specific mechanisms responsible for the high concordance rate for schizophrenia are not known at this time.

Autism *Autism* is a severe mental disorder similar to schizophrenia except that the diagnosis is usually made by age 2 or 3 (see Chapter 10). One of the main diagnostic symptoms is that the child is unresponsive to others and has extremely poor or nonexistant language skills. The high concordance rate for autism (96%) among identical twins strongly suggests that presence of a hereditary factor.

■ **Figure 2–18**

An autistic girl in a special day class.

Mood disorders The tendency to develop extreme *depression* or to alternate between depression and an agitated, excited state called *mania* (called a *bipolar disorder* or *manic-depressive behavior*) seems to have a hereditary basis. Severe depression and bipolar disorders run in families. Identical twins have a concordance rate of 70% for depression. The brains of severely depressed persons seem to have a greater sensitivity to the neurotransmitter *acetylcholine* than the brains of people without a history of depression (Leonard, 1990).

autism
a schizophrenic-like condition beginning in infancy or early childhood marked by social isolation, repetitive movements, and communication difficulties.

mood disorders
psychological disturbances that affect emotional states

Alcoholism Whether *alcoholism* is a disease or not has been the cause of considerable recent debate (Fingarette, 1988). Again, as with autism, schizophrenia, and depression, one does not inherit the disease of alcoholism per se but the predisposition to behave in ways that can lead to alcohol abuse. Marc Schuckit (1987) found a higher concordance rate for alcoholism among identical twins than fraternal twins. The study also determined that genetics was a more influential factor than the environment in the development of alcoholic behavior. Even when biological children of alcoholics are adopted by nonalcoholics shortly after birth, they *still* are at higher risk for alcoholism. Furthermore, the likelihood of alcoholism later developing in a child of a nonalcoholic who is adopted by an alcoholic adult is not as great as one would expect if the environment were the determining factor.

The quest for elusive biochemical mechanisms continues. As we increase our knowledge of gene/environment interaction, we simultaneously improve our ability to offer treatment and guidance and to plan preventive action.

● Choosing to Conceive: The Social and Psychological Implications of Conception

Genetics is a biological approach to understanding child development. However, many of the outcomes influenced by the genes have important social and psychological implications. For example, conception is a biological event that occurs when two gametes unite. But the product of conception is a human baby, a baby whose birth will dramatically and irreversibly alter many other lives. For this reason, today's young adults are giving more attention than any other generation to the pros and cons of parenthood. For these young people, having children is an option, not an inevitability. Many factors may influence a couple's decision to have a child, including cost, genetic history, parental age, religion, and psychological and emotional needs. Although couples are decision makers in most families, 25% of all babies are born to single women (Associated Press, 1989). Presumably, the same factors influence decisions in either case. However, comparative research on the topic has not been conducted.

The Cost of Having and Raising Children

Costs involved in raising children have increased steadily since we first started measuring them, especially if the children go to college. According to the Health Insurance Association of America, the tab for a normal pregnancy in 1990 plus delivery and hospital charges averaged $4334 (C-section, $7186). Beyond that, *Cosmopolitan* magazine (August, 1989) estimates that a couple can expect to spend 30% of their income on one child, 40–45% on two children, and 50% on 3. Of course, in cases where a child has special medical or educational needs, expenses are even higher. While it's not exactly "cheaper by the dozen," childrearing costs do decline per individual when there is more than one child, partly because families share space, facilities, equipment, and clothing (U.S. Bureau of the Census, 1983, p. 460).

In addition to the financial costs of childrearing, children require the spending of less measurable commodities, such as time, love, patience, energy, and attention, just to name a few. On the emotional side, people who decide to be parents must be prepared to commit themselves to parenting in general and to caring for a particular child on a day-to-day basis.

Genetic History

Sometimes a decision to have a child is influenced by the couple's genetic history. If hereditary disease or defects exist in either parent, the couple may wish to know the likelihood of passing on these defects to children, especially if the problems are lethal or severely debilitating.

As mentioned previously, through *genetic counseling*, they can learn the statistical probability of conceiving a child with a certain genetic, chromosomal, or metabolic disorder. If the risk is perceived to be high, the couple may decide against biological parenthood. If the risk is interpreted as low to moderate, the couple may opt for conception and gamble that the fetus will be problem-free.

Fortunately, parents who take that risk no longer have to wait until the birth of their baby to learn the outcome of their decision. Fetal health can be assessed by various methods during the prenatal period, including the familiar amniocentesis and ultrasound (Table 2–9). If a defect is present, parents are faced with the choice of preparing for the birth of a child with a disability or aborting the fetus (Fava et al., 1982).

Parental Age

Because she must act as a host for the developing baby, the age of the mother is an important consideration. If a woman is under age 17 when she conceives, her body may not be able to concentrate fully on the baby, since she herself is still growing and developing. Infant mortality rates, low birthweights, and other complications are high in this group. Although the likelihood of Down's syndrome is relatively low among mothers under 29 years old (1 of every 1,000 pregnancies, Edlin, 1990), the incidence of problems due to poor nutrition, drug involvement, and stress are high.

infant mortality
likelihood of a baby dying in the first year of life

According to available data, the woman's body is best suited for pregnancy between the ages of 20 and 35 (Crooks & Baur, 1990). A woman in her 20s is fully mature and in optimum physical condition, since chronic maladies such as hypertension or heart disease are rare during these years. A woman is most fertile between the ages of 20 and 24; after that her fertility declines gradually, dropping to about 50% among those over age 40. The problem is the quality of the egg, not the quality of the womb. A mother who conceives prior to age 35 avoids many complications, including increased likelihood of Down's syndrome in her baby. Other factors whose likelihood increases after the mother passes age 35 are complications of labor and delivery, a higher cesarean-section rate, and an increased incidence of dizygotic twinning, low birthweight, and birth defects (especially mental retardation), particularly in the first pregnancy. Women who are anxious about the health of their unborn babies are usually calmed by participating in an ultrasound examination. Mothers who are able to watch their preborn babies move and register facial expressions suffer less anxiety than other women, have fewer obstetrical complications, and have babies who weigh more and are more alert at birth (Field, 1985).

Is the father's age important? Probably less than the mother's, since he does not carry or bear the child. Nevertheless, the father does contribute 50 percent of the genetic material necessary for conception. We

■ **Table 2–9**   *Prenatal Diagnostic Procedures*

WHEN PERFORMED	PROCEDURE
	Fetal Behavior
7th month–birth	*"Counting kicks"*—A simple procedure that involves monitoring fetal movement. At least 10 "kicks" should be felt within a 2-hour period (the best time to count is between 7–10 p.m., when the baby is most active). This procedure prevents stillbirth (Piacquadio, 1988).
	Fetal Tissue Sampling
16 weeks (the feasibility of early amniocentesis at 11–14 weeks is currently being investigated.	*Amniocentesis*—About ½ ounce of amniotic fluid is withdrawn by a needle inserted into the mother's abdomen and uterus. Ultrasound guides needle placement to avoid poking the baby. The fluid contains fetal cells and products of metabolism that can be analyzed to reveal more than 100 different disorders. The results take between 1 and 4 weeks to obtain but are 99% accurate. Amniocentesis is the most commonly used diagnostic technique.
9–12 weeks	*Chorionic villus sampling (CVS)*—Involves sampling from a layer of tissue called the chorion, which lines the placenta. The tissue is sampled where the uterus joins the placenta. This test provides the same information as amniocentesis, only earlier in the pregnancy. Currently, the sampling device is inserted through the cervix. Insertion through the abdomen (like amniocentesis) is under investigation. Risk of limb defects (missing fingernails or missing or short fingers & toes) is under investigation.
17th week on	*Percutaneous umbilical blood sampling (PUBS)*—Developed in France in 1983, the procedure involves sampling fetal blood from a vein in the umbilical cord. Ultrasound equipment guides the needle. The blood can be typed and examined for signs of anemia, sickle cell disease, and other blood disorders. PUBS is a safer technique than fetoscopy for obtaining a blood sample.
anytime	*Percutaneous skin biopsy*—Sampling fetal skin cells for evidence of serious skin abnormalities.
anytime	*Other organ biopsies*—If problems are suspected, sometimes tissue is sampled directly from the organs themselves to confirm a diagnosis.
	Fetal Visualization
anytime	*Ultrasound*—Uses high frequency, inaudible sound waves to produce a picture of the uterus, placenta, and baby. Ultrasound is primarily used to monitor fetal growth, diagnose multiple fetuses, establish gestational age, locate the placenta, and, in some cases, screen for Down's syndrome (Benacerraf, 1987).

■ **Table 2–9** *(continued)*

WHEN PERFORMED	PROCEDURE
anytime	*Fetoscopy*—Inserted through the mother's abdomen, the fetoscope carries a fiber optic lens that transmits a continuous picture of the baby and the womb. The image is much clearer than ultrasound, but the risk of miscarriage and other complications is high so fetoscopy is rarely used.
anytime	*Magnetic Resonance Imaging (MRI)*—Provides a remarkably clear and detailed picture of internal structures through the use of directed magnetic energy. The impact of MRI on fetal development is being evaluated.
after 1st trimester	*X rays*—X ray use has largely been replaced in pregnancy by ultrasound visualization. Nevertheless, x-rays may still be used to diagnose certain specific disorders.
16–18 weeks	*Maternal AFP screening*—AFP (alphafetoprotein) is a substance naturally produced during pregnancy. The level of AFP in the mother's bloodstream can help detect a neural tube closure defect (like anencephaly and spina bifida) or to identify trisomy-21 Down's syndrome.*

*The cause of spina bifida and anencephaly in most cases is unknown. One baby in every 1,000 born in the United States has a neural tube defect (Morton, 1989).

Source: American Academy of Pediatrics: Committee on Genetics, 1989. Reproduced by permission of *Pediatrics*, vol. 84, p. 741, © 1989.

know that some males produce viable sperm well into their 60s and 70s. However, the quality and quantity of the sperm can change as the male's reproductive system ages. About one-quarter of all chromosomal abnormalities have been linked to division errors in the genetic material contributed by the father (Stene et al., 1981). The likelihood of such errors increases with paternal age, especially after the father passes age 55 (Mange, 1990). Since there is some decline in male fertility after age 45 owing to decreased sperm production, the best time for men to father children is between the ages of 20 and 45 to ensure maximum fertility and to minimize chromosomal error (Schwartz et al., 1981).

Midlife Motherhood

Despite the impact of age on the parents' reproductive systems, more and more babies are being born to "older" parents. The birthrate among women over 30 more than doubled between 1970 and 1979 and has been steadily increasing ever since (U.S. Bureau of the Census, 1983). Most of these parents consider the potential difficulties of conception after age 30 or 35 to be offset by significant benefits (Frankel & Wise,

■ Figure 2–19

Dad and baby.

1982). For example, women who have babies late in life may value their pregnancies more than younger women and may be more patient, involved, and knowledgeable about children (Gullo, 1988). Many of these women have careers to which they can return and have had enough time with their husbands to establish firm, stable relationships. Some ''older'' mothers even claim that seeing the world through the eyes of a young child keeps them young.

In terms of relative complications, the medical establishment is more concerned about mothers having babies in their early teens than with later-life pregnancies. Older women who obtain good prenatal care and are of normal weight and already have a few children can anticipate a good pregnancy (Hibbard, 1988). With the availability of amniocentesis and other prenatal diagnostic tools, much of the guesswork is eliminated from late-life conception.

Parental Needs

Some factors that influence a decision to become a parent are uniquely personal. Some couples are concerned about the impact of a child on their career priorities, their time, their relationship with each other, and their obligations to their own parents. Research suggests the prospective parents' childhood experiences affect their decision to have children. People who had unhappy family experiences and whose parents were unhappy are more likely to forego parenthood than those who grew up in happy families who are knowledgeable about and interested in children (Feldman, 1981).

According to Elizabeth Whelen (1975), having a baby to keep a boyfriend, save a marriage, please a parent, prove sexual prowess, or get money, tax refunds, or attention may be strategies with positive short-term consequences but they have a negative long-term impact. Commitment and desire on the part of the parents are an important component of long-term satisfaction with the parent's role.

Even after the prospective couple weighs the pros and cons of having children and assesses their psychological needs and current state of health, they might still have difficulty reaching a final decision because they do not have access to many relevant facts. First, it is hard to know in advance how one will adapt to the role of parents. Some might find parenting the most rewarding and exhilarating experiences of their lives, but others might be left irritated, tired, frustrated, and unfulfilled by parenthood. Second, owing to the complexities of genetic inheritance, it is *impossible* to predict the characteristics of the prospective child. A child's coloring, features, temperament, personality, intelligence, and other qualities remain a mystery until after birth. Even the sex of the child, statistically speaking, is a 50/50 proposition, though people who decide to have amniocentesis or CVB can know the sex of the child—if they choose to be told.

▶▶   I S S U E   ◀◀

A Matter of Death and Life: Gifts of Life That Trigger Debate over Medical Ethics

Few issues are as volatile as those that deal with the unborn or newborn baby.

In 1987, Brenda and Michael Winner of Arcadia, California, learned that they were about to give birth to an anencephalic baby. Missing most of the brain, anencephalic babies usually stop breathing and die within a day or two after birth. About 3,500 such babies are born each year. Since abortion was not an option for the Winners, they decided Brenda would carry the baby to term and let doctors use its organs for transplants after it died (Finke, 1987).

This decision sparked a flurry of concerns:

● Is it ethical to give birth for the sole purpose of "harvesting" organs?
● Might death be unnecessarily "hastened" or treatment foregone because of the handicapped status of the infant?
● Whose rights are more important—those of the anencephalic baby, those of its parents, or those of potential organ recipients and their parents?

The Winners' only hope was that their baby's organs could give life to other infants who, unlike their own child, truly had a chance for survival.

———————————

In 1987 at the age of 15, Anissa Ayala was diagnosed with leukemia. A nationwide search for bone marrow donors was conducted after it was found that neither the parents nor Anissa's older brother had the right tissue type. No suitable match was found.

In a desperate attempt to save the life of their daughter, Anissa's father had his vasectomy reversed and the couple conceived a child to serve as a bone marrow donor. When the pregnancy was 6 months along, Anissa's mother underwent amniocentesis to see if the baby's tissues were compatible with Anissa's (they were). In June of 1991 the transplant took place. Thirteen-month old Marissa had bone marrow withdrawn from her hip and injected into the body of her leukemic older sister.

While this against-all-odds story seems to have had a fairy tale ending, how will the parents feel about Marissa (the baby) if the older sister's leukemia isn't cured and she dies anyway? How would the family have felt about the baby if she *hadn't* been the right tissue type? And finally, how will all of this affect the baby and her feelings about herself?

———————————

While there are some in our society who believe that every human life has equal worth, the above cases are apparent contradictions. How can every new life have equal value when some newborns are donors and some recipients or when some babies must die so others can live?

Starting a new life—twice. Bone marrow recipient Anissa Ayala weds Bryan Espinosa a year after her sister, Marissa (pictured), was a marrow donor. Doctors say Anissa's recovery has been remarkable.

pronatalist
literally, "in favor of birth"; an
attitude that supports parenthood

One more factor complicating the parenting decision is the utter ir-reversibility of childbirth. The stork has a no-return policy. Children don't come with trade-in allowances, 30-day trial periods, or warranties against defective parts. From a consumer-marketing perspective, decid-ing to have a child is like making an irrevocable commitment to buy an unseen product. The "buyers" have no way of knowing if they will be satisfied until after delivery, and by then, of course, it is too late. People can sell their businesses, fire their employees, divorce their spouses, or move away from troublesome neighbors and relatives, but they cannot easily extricate themselves from their children.

Finally, prevailing pronatalist forces in society can affect a couple's decision. As of this writing, seven major pharmaceutical companies in the United States are developing fertility-enhancing medications while only one was pursuing a new direction in birth control, Norplant, re-leased in 1990. The federal government encourages parenthood by giv-ing tax advantages and other considerations to couples with children. Some religious, moral, and cultural traditions urge their members to have children as part of their traditional duties (Harris et al., 1980). While attitudes toward childless couples are becoming more positive, American society still encourages parenthood for its married and adult members (Crooks & Baur, 1990).

Whatever the outcome, decisions about parenthood are uniquely per-sonal. Parenthood and nonparenthood are equally difficult and respon-sible choices. Pressuring people to forego having children or making them feel guilty about the children they have is just as oppressive and unfair as forcing them into parenthood. No one alternative is best or more desirable, since each person's situation is different from all others. In the final analysis, one's individual freedom to choose is pitted against the common good. For the most part, research indicates that babies who are planned for and wanted are happier, better adjusted, get along better with their parents, have higher self-esteem, and less likely to be abused, depressed, delinquent, or drug dependent than their unplanned coun-terparts (David, 1989).

■●▲   CONCEPT SUMMARY

Factors that Influence the Decision to Have a Child:

- The cost of having and raising children
- Both partners' genetic histories
- Both partners' ages
- Both partners' psychological and emotional needs
- Social and cultural pressures

● After Deciding to Have a Child

Having intercourse may seem like the logical next step after deciding to become a parent. However, the medical profession recommends that other factors be considered first (Willson et al., 1991). A thorough physical examination prior to conception, for example, can verify each partner's good health. The period prior to pregnancy is also a good time to eliminate habits that might be detrimental to a developing child (like smoking, drinking, and drug use), improve nutrition, shed extra pounds, and check for protection against rubella and Hepatitis B. The at-risk woman should decide about taking the AIDS antibody test to see if she is infected (San Francisco AIDS Foundation, 1988). The impact of each of these factors on prenatal development is discussed in Chapter 3.

If the woman has been taking oral contraceptives, she may be advised to discontinue their use for a few months before trying to become pregnant, giving her body time to resume the natural regulation of her menstrual cycle. Former users of the pill frequently take longer to conceive than women who use other forms of contraception, since ovulation is suppressed by pill use (Rosenfield, 1982). When conception does occur, the likelihood of dizygotic twins is doubled in women who have used the pill if they become pregnant within the first two months after stopping oral contraceptives.

Planning intercourse around ovulation increases the likelihood of pregnancy. The most practical method of estimating the time of ovulation is by using an over-the-counter kit like First Response or by recording the basal body temperature each morning immediately after waking. (Basal body temperature drops slightly just before ovulation). On the average 6 to 9 months are necessary for conception to occur. Twenty to 35% of normal couples require as long as a year or a year and a half to conceive (Page, 1989). Since delay is normal and stress can postpone pregnancy by interfering with ovulation, couples are advised to relax and enjoy "trying."

Infertility

Over the past two decades, *primary infertility* in the United States has increased by 50%. About 2.4 million couples who want to be parents are unable to conceive. Interestingly, *secondary infertility,* when a couple already has one or two children but find it impossible to conceive again, is even more common than primary infertility (Beck & Quade, 1989). Several factors are responsible for the high infertility rates. First, more couples are delaying parenthood until their late 20s and 30s, past their peak fertile periods. Second, sexually transmitted disease exists in epidemic proportions among couples of childbearing age. Infections can leave scar tissue that can block tubes or interfere with implantation of

primary infertility
where the couple has never been able to conceive

secondary infertility
where the couple has been able to conceive, but is unsuccessful in subsequent attempts

ovulation. When infectious microorganisms are still present in the reproductive tract, the ovum, sperm, and/or fertilized egg can be attacked and killed. And third, alcohol, cigarette, and illicit drug use are widespread and impair fertility (Phipps et al., 1987). Smokers of 20 cigarettes a day experience only 72% of the fertility of nonsmokers. Other specific causes of infertility for men and women include:

Women	Men
lack of ovulation	low sperm count
hormone deficiencies	hormone deficiencies
lack of regular ovulation	poor sperm motility
endometriosis/fibroid tumors	varicocele
hot tub/spa bathing after intercourse	hot tub/spa bathing before intercourse
previous IUD use	tight clothing (jeans, pants, etc.)
antibodies in cervical mucous that kill sperm	undescended testicles
environmental toxins	environmental toxins

Although in the past the woman was usually considered responsible for infertility, researchers now estimate that 40–50% of organic fertility problems involve the man, and in 15–20% of the cases, the cause is shared or unknown (Hudson et al., 1987).

Infertility is a psychologically painful experience. Medication, hormone treatments, surgery, abstinence from drugs (especially cigarettes), basal body temperature measurement, loose clothing, and habit management will restore fertility 70% of the time (Polakoff, 1990). Couples are even encouraged to substitute egg whites for their normal vaginal lubricant since egg whites contain pure protein and facilitate the swimming action of the sperm (Schaffir, 1991).

If one partner continues to be infertile, there are still options if genetic relatedness is desired. *Artificial insemination* involves introducing semen from well-investigated, healthy sperm donors into the female's vagina or with a newer technique, directly into the Fallopian tubes (Pratt et al., 1991). The donor's characteristics are matched as closely as possible with those of the infertile male. Artificial insemination results in pregnancy 60–70% of the time (Ghazi et al., 1991).

Some women with blocked Fallopian tubes attempt to conceive by *in vitro fertilization*, a procedure that produces so-called *test-tube babies*. In vitro fertilization involves surgically removing the mother's ovum/ova and fertilizing it with her husband's sperm in a laboratory dish. After a few days, the zygote(s) is reintroduced into the mother's body and implanted into her uterus or frozen and stored for later use (special procedures prevent freezer burn!). Embryo defects and implantation failures are responsible for an 80% failure rate with this technique (Bolton et al., 1991).

artificial insemination
a birth technology where sperm are introduced into the vagina by a medical procedure rather than by sexual intercourse

test-tube babies
babies conceived by means of *in vitro* fertilization

A Closer Look

Infertility Firsts

First artificial insemination	Performed in 1790 in Europe Performed in 1890 in the United States
First test-tube baby	Louise Joy Brown (5 lb, 12 oz), delivered by cesarean section in Oldham, England, on July 25, 1978 Elizabeth Jordan Carr (5 lb, 12 oz), delivered by cesarean section in Norfolk, Virginia, on December 28, 1981
First birth from a frozen embryo	Zoe (last name unknown), 5 lb 13 oz, delivered by cesarean section in Melbourne, Australia, on March 18, 1984 A boy (name not released), 9 lb 8 oz, delivered by cesarean section in Santa Barbara, California, on June 4, 1986
First frozen embryo sibling	A sibling of "a boy" (above), born in Santa Barbara, California, on October 23, 1989, by the same procedure
First test-tube quintuplets	Alan, Brett, Connor, Douglas, and Edward were born in London, England, on April 26, 1985.
First surrogate mother of her own grandchildren	Test-tube triplets (2 boys and 1 girl) born in Johannesburg, South Africa on October 2, 1987 to Mrs. Pat Anthony of Tzaneen in Eastern Transvaal who served as a surrogate mother for her 25 year old daughter.
First embryo transfer/ovum	A child (name, sex, and birthweight of child unreleased) in Long Beach, California, in January (date unreleased) of 1984

Another medical breakthrough in infertility research involves a procedure called *embryo transfer*, whereby a woman achieves pregnancy by receiving a donated fertilized ovum. This method has the advantage of involving natural fertilization rather than in vitro fertilization. The ovum donor is inseminated with sperm from the prospective father, and four days later the fertilized ovum is washed from the donor's womb.

embryo transfer
a birth technology where an embryo is transferred from one organism to another as a remedy for infertility

surrogate motherhood
an arrangement in which a fertile woman agrees to have a baby for an infertile couple; the surrogate may or may not be genetically related to the child

GIFT (gamete intra-fallopian transfer)
a birth technology in which the sex cells or gametes are introduced into the woman's fallopian tubes instead of her vagina

frozen embryo
the process of lowering the temperature of an embryo so it can be preserved until it is time to be implanted

If all is well, it is transferred to the womb of the infertile woman, where it implants and matures. "Test-tube" babies have no increased risk of abnormal development (Moran, et al., 1989). When *surrogate motherhood* is chosen, a woman agrees to be artificially inseminated by a man's sperm and to relinquish the baby at birth to the sperm-donor and his wife. The couple then adopts the baby as their own.

The newest infertility breakthrough is a technique called *GIFT*, gamete intrafallopian transfer. It involves taking a man's sperm and a woman's ova (more than one has to be used to ensure conception) and placing them together in the woman's Fallopian tube. It is used primarily when the sperm are viable but for some reason, have trouble reaching the ovum. GIFT also results in a high rate of multiple births (Edwards & Craft, 1990). ZIFT is a recent modification of GIFT. In ZIFT, the *zygote* is placed into the woman's fallopian tube to reduce multiple birth outcomes.

Although the infertility options mentioned above may produce a baby for an otherwise infertile couple, all involve ethical questions and all have been involved in interesting court cases. So far, the courts have decided that a person can be awarded custody of a frozen zygote after a divorce and that a surrogate mother must do what she contracted to do and does not have the option of keeping the baby for herself. In another case twins were conceived by the surrogate mother. When the boy and girl were born, the judge decided the adopting couple only had to take one child and not both because that's all they agreed to do (the other baby was kept and raised by the surrogate mother and her husband). In the famous Baby M Case, *(Elizabeth and William Stern v. MaryBeth Whitehead),* the court had to decide if a woman could change

■ ● ▲   CONCEPT SUMMARY

Options for Infertile Couples Who Desire Biological Relatedness to Their Child:

- artificial insemination
- in vitro fertilization
- embryo transfer
- surrogate motherhood
- GIFT (gamete intrafallopian transfer)
- ZIFT (zygote intrafallopian transfer)

her mind and keep the baby she agreed to bear for another couple. The controversial decision was that Whitehead had to relinquish custody of Baby Melissa (Sara) but, through appeal, was given visitation rights as any "divorced" parent would have. The Vatican condemned all forms of medically-assisted conception in 1987. In 1991 France's supreme court outlawed surrogate motherhood, stating it violates a woman's body and undermines the practice of adoption. While the courts, medical ethicians, and the Church contemplate these issues, research on reversing infertility continues.

● After Deciding Not to Have a Child

Pregnancy can be prevented by sexual abstinence, contraception, or sterilization. If a couple is having unprotected intercourse, they are planning a family. Statistics indicate that 60% to 80% of fertile couples who do not use contraception conceive within a year whether or not they want to have children (Kleinman, 1980). If a sexually active couple has decided not to have children or if they are uncertain about children in their future, they are advised to consider contraception or sterilization.

■ **Figure 2–20**

Mary Beth Whitehead, surrogate mother.

Contraception

Contraceptive techniques are available for use both by males and females. Next to sterilization, the pill is the most popular birth control method in the United States. The newest contraceptive device, Norplant, is implanted under the skin of a woman's arm and provides a timed release dosage of progestin to prevent pregnancy. Table 2–10 summarizes the effectiveness of the various contraceptive techniques as well as their advantages and disadvantages.

■ **Table 2–10** *Effectiveness of Various Contraceptive Methods*

	% EFFECTIVENESS	# OF PREGNANCIES OUT OF 100 WOMEN USERS
Norplant implant	99.7%	<1
Tubal ligation	99.6%	<1
IUD	99.2%	<1
Oral contraceptives	97.0%	3
Condom	88.0%	12
Diaphragm	82.0%	18
Vaginal sponge	72.0%	28

Source: *Studies in Family Planning* magazine, 1991.

Sterilization

Sterilization is for individuals who desire permanent protection against conception. Voluntary sterilization is 10 times more common than it was a decade ago.

Male Sterilization

Vasectomy prevents conception by eliminating sperm for the semen. Each vas deferens, or sperm-carrying tube, is cut and sealed in a procedure usually performed in a physician's office. With a failure/infection rate of less than 1%, vasectomy is a safe and highly effective means of sterilization (Kjersgaard et al., 1989). It does not change physical appearance, diminish sex drive, or interfere with erection or ejaculation. In fact, many men report that sex is improved after vasectomy. (Apparently, the operation made a "vas deferens" in their lives!) Surgeons can attempt to reconnect the parts of the severed vas in an effort to restore fertility. Pregnancy results in about 29–85% of those cases (Hatcher, 1988). Each year, over 400,000 men in the United States opt for vasectomy (McCarthy, 1987).

Female Sterilization

Since it is usually done in the hospital, female sterilization is more expensive and requires more recovery time than male sterilization. However, it is just as effective (Kjersgaard et al., 1989). *Tubal ligation* procedures involve cutting and closing the Fallopian tubes to prevent the egg

sterilization
a surgical procedure designed to render a male or female incapable of reproducing

vasectomy
a male sterilization procedure

tubal ligation
a female sterilization procedure

■ **Figure 2–21**

Sterilization procedures for females and males.

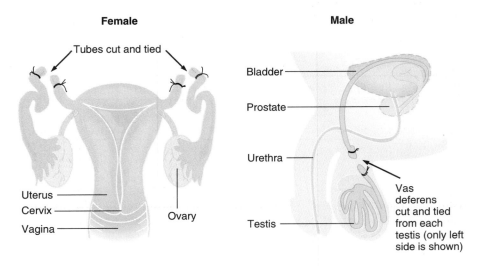

from contacting sperm and becoming fertilized. The tubes can be rejoined if the middle third was involved and if only a small portion of the tube was removed. Fertility is restored in 40–75% of these cases (Hatcher, 1988). About 700,000 American women have tubal ligation each year (McCarthy, 1987). Hysterectomy, the surgical removal of the uterus, is usually not performed for purposes of sterilization unless the procedure is indicated by other findings.

Can You Pick the Sex of Your Baby?

TOWARD EFFECTIVE PARENTING

If couples plan only one child, fathers tend to want a boy, while mothers prefer a girl (Gilroy & Steinbacher, 1991). For a first child, however, couples still traditionally want a boy.

Although the sex of the baby is determined by the father's sperm, the acid/alkaline balance of the mother's vagina affects the viability of the sperm. In a controversial 1989 publication, Drs. Shettles and Rorvik advised women to douche with baking soda to create an alkaline environment that favors Y-bearing sperm and thus the conception of a baby boy. An acidic environment created by a vinegar douche supposedly favors the conception of a baby girl. These techniques have not been overwhelmingly successful in producing the intended results (Schaffir, 1991).

A more sophisticated sperm selection technique called *sperm-washing* is carried out by laboratory technicians. It involves placing sperm in an albumen (egg white) solution. The lighter, Y-bearing sperm* float to the top and can be siphoned off and introduced into the vagina via artificial insemination or used in an in vitro process. This procedure would favor the conception of male babies. Other similar techniques have been less successful in retrieving X-bearing sperm.

In a less direct manipulation of the vaginal environment, Israeli scientists contend that dietary changes in the mother 2 months prior to conception influence the sex of the child-to-be. If a female child is desired, a woman should eat foods high in calcium and magnesium; for a male child, potassium and sodium rich foods should be selected. They claim a success rate of 80%.

The results of the parents' efforts can be assessed by amniocentesis or by CVS (chorionic villus sampling). The use of these diagnostic tools has raised ethical and moral questions. Should prenatal tests be reserved for diagnosing disease? (The sex of the baby is not a disease). Should health plans or the government pay for nonmedical applications of these procedures? If the baby was the "wrong sex," should parents be permitted to seek abortion so they can "try again"? Are we buying into a technology that favors male

---

*The Y-bearing sperm are lighter because the Y sex chromosome is smaller than the X sex chromosome.

(continued on next page)

babies and allows large numbers of female babies to fall victim to genocide? (In 1986 of the 8,000 abortions in Bombay, India, only 1 was of a male). In the United States couples are also electing to abort female babies (Steinbacher, 1986).

sex-preselection
an attempt to influence the sex of the unborn child

If its sex is the *only* measure of a baby's worth, then sex preselection is a must. It would be tragic if any child was a disappointment *just* because of her or his sex.

● Chapter Summary

● Human life begins when the chromosomes from the female ovum merge with the chromosomes of the male sperm during conception (fertilization). The pregnancy is established when implantation takes place.

Forty-six chromosomes (23 pairs) must be present to form human life. The 23rd pair of chromosomes determines the sex of the developing child: *XX* for a normal female, *XY* for a normal male. More boys than girls are conceived and born, but spontaneous abortion (miscarriage) and infant mortality rates are higher for boys than for girls.

● Errors in cell division can produce an abnormal number of chromosomes at various locations. Sex chromosome disorders occur but such problems are rare. The most common chromosome disorder, Down's syndrome, occurs when the child has 3 chromosomes at the 21st position. Children with Down's syndrome share some distinguishing physical characteristics.

● Genetic messages are coded in the DNA that makes up each gene. Traits expressed by genes may be transmitted according to dominant–recessive, polygenic, incomplete dominance, or X-linked patterns of inheritance.

● The likelihood of transmitting a particular genetic trait can be determined through genetic counseling. The DNA in the genes may be artificially manipulated by a process known as genetic engineering.

● Twins and multiple births are possible through the influence of fertility drugs, by natural multiple ovulation, and/or because of spontaneous duplication by the zygote.

● The action of most genes is influenced by the environment. Studies of twin concordance (the degree to which identical twins share certain characteristics) can assess the relative impact of heredity vs. environmental factors. If identical twins brought up under different circumstances share a trait, then that trait must be strongly influenced by heredity.

● Factors that appear to have a genetic basis include height, weight, pattern of maturation and other age-related changes, handedness, intelligence, certain personality traits, and susceptibility to health complications, schizophrenia, autism, mood disorders, and alcoholism.

- Although conception is a biological event, it has important social and psychological implications. Cost, genetic history, parental age, social-cultural attitudes, and the personal needs of the involved parties can influence the decision to have a child.
- Sometimes couples who wish to conceive are unsuccessful because one or both partners are infertile. Currently, many options are available to the infertile couple.
- Contraception is recommended for sexually active people who are undecided about the role of children in their lives. Sterilization provides permanent (often irreversible) protection against conception.

● Observational Exercise

Try to trace the pattern of several inherited characteristics through your family. For example, you might focus on easily observable traits such as left- or right-handedness, eye color, dimples (yes or no), natural hair color, or ear lobes (attached or unattached). For each trait, you might draw a "family tree" so that inheritance patterns become more clear. A family tree for eye color might look like the accompanying diagram. You might even think about inheritance possibilities for the generation after yours.

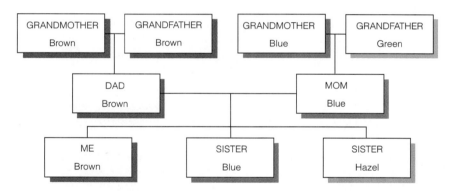

● Recommended Readings

Kitzinger, S. (1988). *Your baby, your way—Making pregnancy decisions and birth plans.* New York: Pantheon.

Menning, B. E. (1988). *Infertility: A guide for the childless couple (2nd ed.).* Englewood Cliffs, N.J.: Prentice-Hall.

Morris, M. (1988). *Last-chance children.* New York: Columbia University Press.

Rothman, B. K. (1989). *Recreating motherhood: Ideology and technology in a patriarchal society.* New York: W. W. Norton.

Tannenhaus, N. (1988). *Preconceptions.* Chicago: Contemporary Press.

Prenatal Development

This chapter focuses on prenatal development and the remarkable changes that take place as the product of conception develops into a full-fledged baby and prepares for life outside the womb. In this chapter, we will examine the *nurture* side of the nature/nurture controversy—that is, the environmental factors that influence growth.

The word *prenatal* literally means "before birth." *Embryologists* are the scientists who study prenatal development. The field of *embryology* involves a careful assessment of the growth sequence from conception to birth, identifying factors that can enhance or interfere with growth.

embryology
the branch of biology that focuses on change and development during the prenatal period

● Historical Perspectives

Before prenatal development was studied scientifically, there was considerable speculation about how life developed before birth. More than 2,000 years ago, Aristotle observed the development of a chick embryo, and from what he could see without a microscope, he inferred that human babies originate in an "admixture of male seminal fluid and menstrual blood" (Flanagan, 1962, p. 10). Five hundred years later, in the second century A.D., the Greek physician Galen proposed a theory that was to last for 1,500 years. Galen thought miniature, preformed babies existed in female "semen." Contact with the male allowed the tiny baby to be released and to grow to proper size. Individuals who supported this point of view were called *Ovists*. In 1677, using his newly perfected microscope, Anton van Leeuwenhoek discovered male sperm, creating confusion and controversy. A faction emerged that opposed Galen's original speculations, arguing that the male sperm, not the female ovum, contained the ready-made baby. These individuals, known as the *Homunculists*, even drew pictures to illustrate their views.

■ **Figure 3–1**

Early scientists and philosophers believed a tiny pre-formed baby exists inside each sperm cell. The ovum provided the nourishment for the embryo.

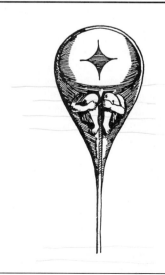

germinal stage/period of the ovum
the first period of prenatal development, extending from conception to implantation (about 10–14 days)

period of the embryo
the second period of prenatal development during which immature versions of all major body organs and systems develop; extends from the second gestational week to the end of the 8th gestational week

period of the fetus
the period of prenatal development that extends from the 9th gestational week until birth. During this time, the child prepares for life outside the womb

uterine cavity
the space inside the body of the uterus designed for the developing child

(cell) differentiation
see cell specialization

blastocyst
multicelled organism formed from the union of the egg and the sperm that implants on the uterine wall

placenta
the organ that develops at the site of implantation; the mother's blood circulates through the placenta and passes oxygen and nutrients to the baby

umbilical cord
the tubelike structure that connects the embryo/fetus (at the navel) with the placenta

amnion (or bag of waters; also amniotic sac)
the membrane that contains the amniotic fluid that cushions the developing child

Advances in modern science ended the feud between the Ovists and the Homunculists. The role of the egg and sperm in development was finally recognized in 1839 when Matthias Schleiden and Theodor Schwann discovered that life is assembled, step by step, out of growing cells. This last century has been a productive one for the science of embryology (Moore, 1988). In 1930, a mature human egg was first observed being released from the ovary. In 1944, the union of egg and sperm was seen for the first time. The details of development in the first 6 months were discovered in the 1950s. Today, a tiny camera can be inserted into the womb to videotape or photograph every aspect of fetal life and behavior.

In recent years, much more has been learned about prenatal growth. For ease of presentation, development in the prenatal period is divided into three stages: the *germinal stage*, or the *period of the ovum*; the *period of the embryo*; and the *period of the fetus*. Although prenatal development is a continuous process, each stage of our discussion highlights certain milestones in the development of the baby and the individual's preparation for birth (O'Rahilly & Muller, 1987).

● Stages of Prenatal Development

The Period of the Ovum, or the Germinal Stage

Chapter 2 covered the sequences of events leading to fertilization and implantation. The period of the ovum, or the germinal stage, begins once a zygote has been formed and ends with implantation, the attachment of the developing organism to the uterine wall. It takes the zygote about 72 hours to travel from the Fallopian tube to the uterus, where it spends the next 4 or 5 days floating in the uterine cavity before it implants or attaches to the uterus. Since the cells don't grow much larger before they divide, the original size of the zygote is maintained. The organism starts out as a compact ball of cells. Four or 5 days after fertilization, the cells begin to *differentiate*. A hollow fluid-filled ball is formed as some cells become the outer cell wall and other cells form an inner cell mass. This hollow ball is called a *blastocyst*. The outer layer of cells will become the placenta and its lining, the chorion; the umbilical cord; the amnion, or "bag of waters"; and the yolk sac, a temporary structure that produces nourishment for the baby until the baby's circulatory system is established. The baby then develops out of the inner cell mass called the *embryonic disk*.

The germinal stage lasts approximately 7 to 10 days. This is a surprisingly long time when one considers that the fertilized egg has to travel only 7 or 8 inches at most and is aided by the movement of cilia lining the tube, the force of gravity, and uterine contractions. Within this period, the developing child grows from 1 cell to more than 100.

Detecting Pregnancy

Once implantation occurs, the mother's body automatically initiates chemical and physical changes to support the new life. Despite all the activity and change in her system, the woman may not feel, look, or act any differently and may not even suspect she is pregnant. However fetal health and well-being depend on the early recognition of pregnancy, so sexually active women need to know the signs (Table 3–1). The presence in the woman's blood or urine of human chorionic gonadotropin *(hCG)*, a hormone released early in pregnancy, confirms pregnancy. A *hydatiform mole* in the uterus also causes hCG to be released, but such growths

■ **Table 3–1**   *The Signs and Symptoms of Pregnancy*

SIGNS OF PREGNANCY	USEFULNESS IN DIAGNOSING PREGNANCY	OTHER EXPLANATIONS FOR SIGNS BESIDES PREGNANCY
Presumptive Signs		
Missed menstrual period	Provide valuable evidence but are never proof	Emotional upset
Fatigue		Changes in climate or altitude
Nausea		Metabolic disease
Breast tenderness/"tingling sensations"		Age
		Illness
Discoloration of the vagina and cervix (from pink to purplish)		
Increased frequency of urination		
Increased vaginal secretions		
Probable Signs		
Fetal movement ("quickening")	More conclusive than presumptive signs but may be caused by other conditions	Indigestion
Softening of uterus		Imagination
Changes in size and shape of uterus		Bowel action
		Abdominal/pelvic masses
Uterine contractions		
Feeling "fetal parts" during pelvic examination		
The presence of hCG in maternal urine or blood		
Positive signs		
The birth of a baby	Unequivocal proof of pregnancy	None
X-ray, ultrasound, or MRI picture of baby (after 9 and 16 weeks gestation, respectively)		
Fetal heart sounds (heard distinctly after 20 weeks gestation)		

Source: Sandberg, 1978.

are rare. Laboratory tests performed by trained technicians to detect the hCG are about 97% accurate. The accuracy of *home pregnancy tests* range between 70 and 95% depending on the particular test and whether directions are followed fully (Asch et al., 1988). They do have the advantage of offering private results within 9 or 10 days of conception.

The Period of the Embryo

After implantation, the developing baby is called an *embryo*, and the next 6 weeks are referred to as the *period of the embryo*. During this time, the embryo's major body systems and organs develop by a process known as *morphogenesis* or *organogenesis*. Precisely coded genetic instructions direct the formation of three distinct layers of tissue within the embryonic disk—the *ectoderm*, the *mesoderm*, and the *endoderm*—each with a different function. Nails, teeth, the outer layer of skin, the skin's glands and sensory cells, and the nervous system (brain, spinal cord, and peripheral nerves) form from the ectoderm. From the mesoderm develop the muscles, bones, sex organs, and excretory and circulatory systems. The endoderm is responsible for forming the digestive system, salivary glands, respiratory system, and such vital organs as the liver and the pancreas. The whole process of morphogenesis is truly remarkable. Nature repeats this perfectly timed drama literally thousands of times each day and in more than 90% of the cases the result is a well-formed human being (Johnson, 1989).

As each organ or system develops, there is a time called a *critical period* when it grows most rapidly. If faulty genetic instructions or a harmful environment interferes with growth during a critical period, the development of the organ or system could be permanently affected (Bornstein, 1989). Figure 3–2 gives examples of critical periods in prenatal development. For instance, you can see that a cleft palate would result from developmental interference occurring sometime between the sixth and ninth gestational week. Ironically, the most vulnerable periods of a baby's growth take place *before* many women have discovered they're pregnant.

Important structures that support the pregnancy also develop during the period of the embryo. The *amniotic sac*, a protective membrane in which the fetus grows, begins as a tiny vesicle that becomes a small sac and completely surrounds the embryo as it enlarges. Amniotic fluid that fills this sac increases in volume as pregnancy continues. At the time of birth, about 1000 ml (or a little over a quart) of fluid is present. *Amniotic fluid* protects the baby from injury and heat loss and allows for free movement within the uterus. As mentioned in Chapter 2, some of the fluid may be withdrawn for analysis during *amniocentesis*.

The *placenta* forms at the site of implantation from both fetal and maternal tissue. Although not at all attractive, the placenta is extremely functional: It permits the exchange of nutrients and waste products be-

morphogenesis
the development of the body systems and organs during the period of the embryo (also called organogenesis)

critical period
a specific time in an organism's life when it is susceptible to the influence of certain stimuli and after which those same stimuli have little or no effect

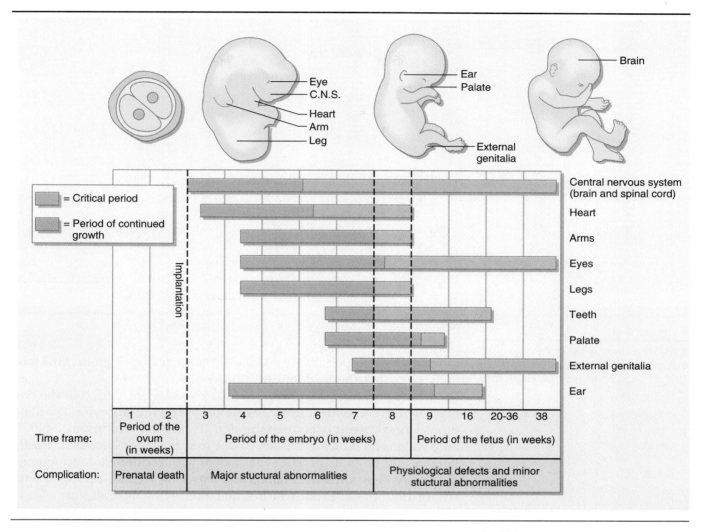

■ **Figure 3–2**

Critical/Sensitive Periods during Prenatal Development.

tween the mother's and baby's systems and produces hormones needed to maintain pregnancy (Moore, 1988). Initially, the placenta was thought to act as a barrier, screening out harmful substances present in the mother's system. We now know the placenta's protective capacity is limited. The *chorion* is a protective layer of tissue that lines the placenta. This tissue may be sampled for diagnosis if *CVS (Chorionic villus sampling)* is performed.

The *umbilical cord* extends from the placenta to the navel of the developing child and transports blood to and from the fetus. The cord blood contains oxygen and nutrients necessary for fetal growth. The cord often has a knotted or twisted appearance because the vessels within it are longer than the cord itself. Excessive twisting is rare, since continuous pressure within the blood vessels keeps the cord taut. Some-

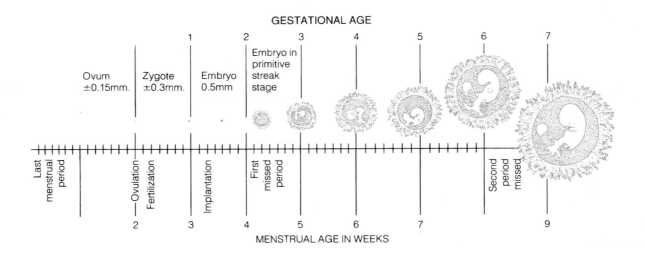

GESTATIONAL AGE

MENSTRUAL AGE IN WEEKS

■ Figure 3–3

A size comparison of the ovum and developing embryo between ovulation and the eighth gestational week (actual size).

■ Figure 3–4

This fertilized cell is called a zygote. This zygote is about 1 week old, is ready for implantation, and is about the size of a printed period.

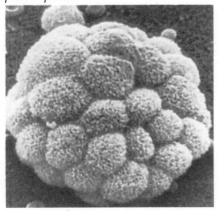

times the cord (especially a long one) becomes wrapped around the fetal body parts, but this seldom causes difficulty.

The baby dramatically increases in size during the period of the embryo. By the end of the eighth gestational week, the embryo is 2 million times larger than it was at conception (Figure 3–3) (Johnson, 1989). It only weighs an ounce and is about one inch long, but it looks distinctly human. Although its proportions change with continued development, the embryo has arms with hands and legs with feet, all equipped with sets of tiny digits. Facial features and the sex of the child are clearly distinguishable. The heart has been beating since the fourth gestational week and primitive digestive processes have been established. The baby even reacts to touch by reflex movement.

Due to morphogenesis and the rapid growth taking place, the developing child is particularly vulnerable to injury during the period of the embryo. *Miscarriage,* or the explusion of an embryo that cannot survive outside the womb, is more likely now than later in pregnancy. Some estimates are that the miscarriage rate may be as high as 70–80% for human embryos (Moore, 1989). Most of the time, the woman doesn't even realize it or report it to her doctor. Chromosome abnormalities, a poor implantation site, a lack of oxygen or nourishment as the result of faulty development of the placenta or umbilical cord or uterine infection, or physiological or structural problems in the mother are the most common causes of miscarriage (Brent & Beckman, 1990). In addition, exposure to environmental factors such as drugs and sexually transmitted disease can significantly affect development owing to the rapid and complex nature of growth during this period (Goldsmith, 1985).

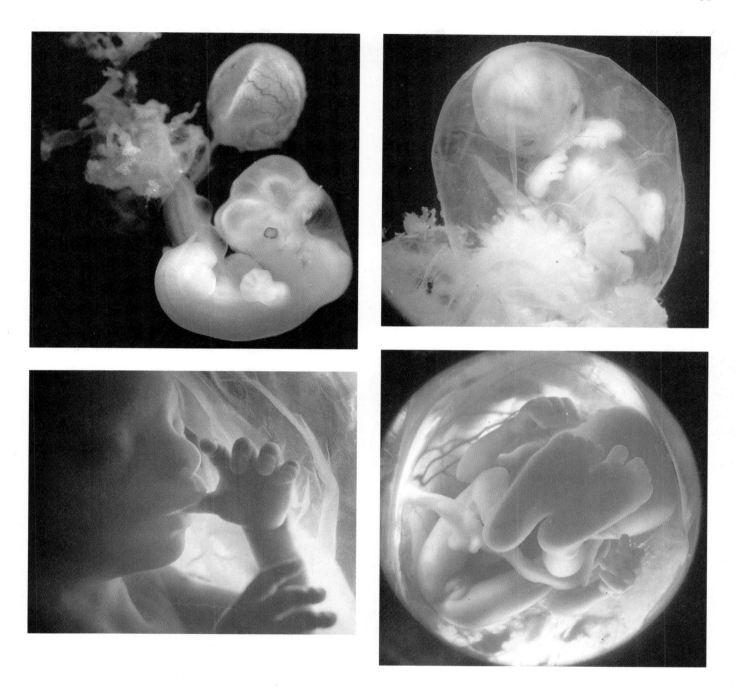

■ Figure 3–5

(upper left) The 5-week old embryo is curved, not straight. Notice the developing brain, the eye, the hand plate and the long tail. The yolk sac (a temporary organ) is still visible. (upper right) Development at 8 weeks marks the end of the period of the embryo. All major organs and systems have been established and now must develop to sustain life outside the womb. (lower left)

This 4½ month old infant measures just over 7 inches. Many reflex behaviors have been established already—like this one, sucking. (lower right) The 5 month old girl looks like she's ready to jump on the camera. Notice the detail that wasn't present at other gestational stages. She measures about 10 inches long.

2 things in each month

■ **Table 3–2**   *The Development of the Embryo and the Fetus*

1 MONTH

During the first month, the embryo grows 10,000 times larger than the zygote. By the end of this period, it is between ¼- to ½-inch in length. Blood is circulating through tiny veins and arteries as the heart beats 65 times per minute. The nervous system, digestive tract, and kidneys are forming. The umbilical cord transports nourishment-rich blood to the embryo in exchange for waste. Physical sex is not yet apparent.

2 MONTHS

The embryo is about 1-inch long now and weighs only ¹⁄₁₃ of an ounce. The head with facial features developed is one-half the total body length. Hands and fingers are present as well as knees, ankles, and toes. The liver is producing blood cells, and the digestive tract is secreting juices to break down food the embryo receives. The kidneys are already removing waste products from the bloodstream. The skin of the embryo is so sensitive that it will react by flexing its trunk and moving its head and arms if its skin is stimulated.

3 MONTHS

This begins the period of the fetus—the time when the immature organs and structures develop and the baby prepares for birth. Fingernails and toenails have been added to the organism which now weighs an ounce and measures 3 inches in length. Also present are closed eyelids, vocal cords, and lips. The sex of the fetus is easily distinguished. The fetus may breathe in and/or swallow amniotic fluid and may urinate occasionally. Immature egg or sperm cells are beginning to form in the reproductive system. More reflex behaviors are appearing. The fetus will now squint if its eyelids are touched, make a fist if its palm is rubbed, suck if its lip is touched, and fan its toes if the sole of its foot is stroked.

4 MONTHS

The mother may now be aware of movements by the fetus as it kicks and thumps in the uterus. This event is known as quickening or feeling life. The fetus is now 8–10 inches in length and weighs about 6 ounces. The head is now one-fourth of the total body length, a proportion that will remain until birth.

5 MONTHS

As the fetus grows larger, it becomes more active, and there is more force behind its movements. The fetus is now about 12 inches long and weighs between 12 and 16 ounces. Coarse hair may appear at the eyelids, eyebrows and scalp, and a soft downy hair called *lanugo* is formed that usually disappears before a full-term birth. The fetal heartbeat (along with other uterine and intestinal sounds) may be heard by placing an ear against the mother's abdomen. Although the baby has a definite sleep–wake pattern and seems to prefer some positions in the uterus more than others, it would have little or no chance for survival on its own should birth occur at this point.

6 MONTHS

The probabilities for survival are a little better now, especially if the infant weighs at least 2 pounds. Most babies weigh about a pound and a half now and measure 14 inches in length. Fat is being deposited under the fetus' skin to give it a more rounded appearance; the eyes open and close, and the head can orient in all directions. Muscle strength has improved, and the child is capable of crying.

7 MONTHS

Survival chances are good at this point since most fetuses weigh between 3 and 5 pounds. The greatest threat to survival is lung immaturity. Most reflex response patterns have been established: Crying, breathing, swallowing and sucking are all apparent in the child's behavior. The lanugo may begin to disappear around this time.

8 MONTHS

The 18–20-inch-long fetus is fast outgrowing its living quarters. Its movements are restricted because of the cramped conditions. The fetus now weighs between 5 and 7 pounds and continues to put on fat to help regulate temperature outside the womb.

9 MONTHS (CALLED THE FINISHING PERIOD)

Growth rate slows considerably now as the baby readies for birth. Organ systems operate more efficiently; heart rate increases; the reddish color of the skin fades; and the skin is covered with a creamy substance called *vernix* designed to protect it. If the infant is born on or near its projected due date, it will have been in the womb for approximately 266 days, the amount of time necessary for humans to develop normally.

The Period of the Fetus — to grow already have everything you need

The period of the fetus extends from the ninth gestational week to birth. During this time, the body systems developed within the first 8 weeks of life are improved and perfected (O'Rahilly & Muller, 1987). From now until birth, the baby will grow in size; organ systems will mature; muscle, bone, and nervous system tissue will be refined; and anatomical detail (hair, fingernails, eyelashes, and so forth) will be added as the baby prepares for life outside the womb. For a month-by-month record of prenatal development, see Table 3–2.

The mother first feels that baby move between the 14th and 20th weeks of pregnancy. This event is called *quickening*. It marks the first direct contact between the mother and the baby. In reality, the baby has been moving for some time. As the baby grows and the uterus becomes more crowded, the mother can feel stronger and more frequent movement. Individual differences between children are already apparent as some babies are more active in the womb than others and may maintain a higher activity level after birth. As a minimum, babies in their seventh gestational month and older should "kick" at least 10 times in any 2 hour period. Doctors have found that "counting kicks" is a good way to prevent stillbirth or late miscarriage (Friend, 1988). In addition to whole body movement, the fetus also practices sucking, swallowing, blinking, breathing, and urinating in preparation for birth. Prenatal

quickening
when fetal movements can be felt by the mother

■ **Figure 3–6**

Prenatal brain development.

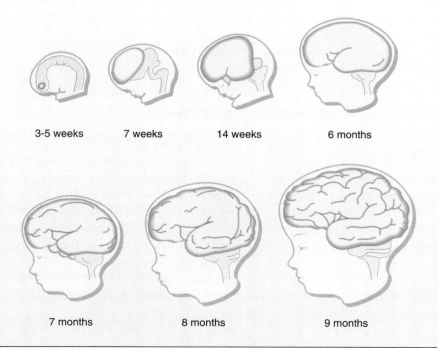

| 3-5 weeks | 7 weeks | 14 weeks | 6 months |

| 7 months | 8 months | 9 months |

■ ● ▲   CONCEPT SUMMARY

Stages of Prenatal Development

- *The germinal stage/period of the ovum* (fertilization to day 7–10)—minimal size increases due to duplication of cells; blastocyst forms, cells prepare for morphogenesis, implantation occurs, hCG is released.

- *The period of the embryo* (week 2 through week 8)—major organs and systems form through morphogenesis; critical periods exist where organs or systems grow most rapidly; structures to support the pregnancy form; embryo dramatically increases in size.

- *Period of the fetus* (week 9 to birth)—body systems are improved and perfected; baby prepares for life outside the womb; anatomical detail is added.

---

learning is addressed in an accompanying Toward Effective Parenting feature.

Human prenatal development is completed about 266 days after fertilization. Babies born before this time are termed *premature* and may not be ready for life outside the womb. Today the minimum age for *viability*, or the ability to survive outside the womb, is 24 weeks gestation. Less developed infants are given little or no chance of survival (Moore, 1989).

● Influences on Prenatal Development

The development described so far is initiated and sustained by precise biological mechanisms. This development seems quite independent of its surrounding environment, but is it? Would babies develop as well in big test tubes or incubators as they would in their mother's bodies? Does the prenatal environment affect fetal growth and development? The relationship between the mother and her developing child is a reciprocal one. Changes in the mother's system accommodate the baby. Some women report feeling better, happier, and more energetic during pregnancy. Others find it uncomfortable to cope with the emotional disequilibrium sometimes created by hormonal changes, and an additional 20 or 30 pounds creates some discomfort as well.

Throughout pregnancy, the baby is uniquely dependent on her mother. The mother does more than carry the child during pregnancy; her body provides the setting for development and mediates the effects of the events in the outside world. For example, the mother's habits, state of personal and psychological health, and behavior all affect her developing child. Mothers who are well-nourished, healthy, physically fit, and well-rested tend to have healthier babies and fewer complications than mothers who are poorly nourished, exhausted or ill (Moore, 1988). Prenatal development is also enhanced if mothers avoid pollutants, toxins, radiation, stress, and drug use during pregnancy. Let's look at how and why these factors affect development.

Teratology

Teratology is the study of environmental factors that affect prenatal growth and cause birth defects (Moore, 1989). As with embryology, people have long been interested in what causes *congenital* problems. More than 2000 years ago, the Greek physician Hippocrates described cases of cojoined or Siamese twins, congenital absence of limbs, and other defects. He speculated that the anomalies were caused by the diet or habits of the mothers (Needham, 1934). Another theory focused on the supernatural. Some people assumed that babies with birth defects were born to couples as punishment for their misdeeds. (Interestingly, this explanation is still believed by some today). Often the affected baby was killed or abandoned and the parents were either banished to protect the population from evil influence or punished to help them atone for their sins. Deformed babies who survived—for example, the fictionalized Hunchback of Notre Dame—were shunned by society and regarded with fear and suspicion.

congenital malformations
physical abnormalities present at birth

As scientists began to understand the principles of inheritance, a new theory arose: that all congenital malformations were due to the action of genes. This explanation has some basis in fact. Of all congenital disorders, 20–25% are caused by faulty genes and chromosomes (Brent & Beckman, 1990). However, even fetuses with "good genes" are vulnerable to certain environmental factors that can adversely affect growth. Environmental factors that have a negative effect on prenatal development are called *teratogens*.

teratogens
any nongenetic influence that can potentially complicate fetal development

Principles of Teratology

In 1973 *fetal alcohol syndrome (FAS)* was identified by K.L. Jones and colleagues. FAS is a collection of fetal symptoms associated with the use of alcohol during pregnancy. Some babies born to drinking mothers are affected, while others are not. What makes the difference? As with inheritance, the effects of specific teratogens seem random and unpredictable until one understands the basic principles of teratology.

fetal alcohol syndrome (FAS)
a congenital disorder in the infant associated with maternal ingestion of alcohol during pregnancy

Teratogens themselves produce quite predictable outcomes. Teratogenic chemicals, hormones, or microorganisms always affect the same organs or systems whenever they are introduced into the prenatal environment. For example, prenatal syphilis always affects the baby's central nervous system and the drug streptomycin always affects fetal hearing. Thus, variation in the outcome of pregnancy is not produced by the specific teratogen. Rather, variation in pregnancy outcome is attributable to individual genetics, interactions with other substances, and to the timing, dose, and duration of the exposure to the specific teratogen (Brent & Beckman, 1990). It is perhaps most accurate to refer to certain environmental agents as having *teratogenic potential*, since most pregnant women are exposed to some of these factors and most have normal, healthy babies in spite of exposure. For a summary of the factors that modify the impact of teratogens on development, see Table 3–3.

Research teratologists are continually identifying factors that may be harmful during prenatal development. By isolating these variables, they are able to develop guidelines for behavior to prevent damage. With the positive goal of prevention in mind, we turn now to the specific classes of known teratogens.

Specific Teratogens

Six classes of teratogens have been identified that account for 10% or fewer of all congenital malformations (Brent & Beckman, 1990):

- disease or illness in the mother
- prescription and social drugs
- nutritional deficits and inconsistencies
- stress and emotional factors
- radiation exposure
- chemicals, toxins, and pollutants

In the following subsections, we discuss the potential harm these teratogens can cause and give specific recommendations for avoiding complications in pregnancy.

Disease or Illness in the Mother

Maternal illness and disease might exist prior to pregnancy or develop during pregnancy. *Hypertension* (high blood pressure) and *diabetes* are the most significant risk factors in this category. Gestational diabetes encourages significant increases in fetal birth weight (10–12 pound newborns are not uncommon). Fifty percent of these large babies are obese by age 8 (Botta et al., 1990). A type of hypertension called *eclampsia* occurs later in pregnancy when the mother's system has difficulty ridding itself of fetal waste. Each of these pregnancies has to be carefully monitored for the sake of both the mother and the baby.

Rubella, chicken pox, mumps, and measles are all caused by viruses that cross the placenta and infect the baby. The effects of these infections depend more on when during the pregnancy the mother becomes ill rather than on how sick the disease makes the mother. Fetal death and severe birth defects may occur if these viruses are present during the

eclampsia
formerly called toxemia of pregnancy; a condition characterized by high blood pressure, water retention, and excess protein in the urine

rubella
formerly called German measles; an infection that is particularly teratogenic to the unborn

■ **Table 3–3** *Factors That Modify the Effects of Specific Teratogens*

FACTORS	CONDITIONS INCREASING THE CHANCES THAT SPECIFIC TERATOGENS WILL CAUSE BIRTH DEFECTS
Genetics	The fetus is genetically predisposed to certain problems.
	The fetus is XY (male).
Timing	The exposure occurs early in the pregnancy.
	The exposure coincides with critical periods of organ/system development.
Duration	Exposure occurs over a relatively long period of time.
Dose/level	The dose or exposure level is relatively high.
Interactive effects	Other teratogens are also present.

first trimester; later, mental retardation, cataracts, blindness/deafness, and heart problems may result. The only treatment is prevention through maternal vaccination or natural immunity. A vaccine for chicken pox is pending. Exposed or susceptible women can receive immune globulin VZIG from their physicians, which contains antibodies against chickenpox (Gause, 1988).

Lesser known but equally devastating diseases for the fetus are *cytomegalic inclusion disease* caused by cytomegalovirus, *fifth disease,* and *Lyme disease.* Spread by direct contact between people, cytomegalic inclusion disease causes no visible symptoms in the mother but results in death or mental retardation for her unborn baby. Since no treatment or vaccination exists, physicians recommend that pregnant women wash their hands after contact with others. Children in day care may bring home the virus and infect their pregnant mothers (Hibbard, 1988). Fifth disease, or erythema infectiosum, can cause a dangerous form of anemia in the fetus any time during pregnancy (Rodis et al., 1990). Infected children should be avoided since no vaccine is currently available. Lyme disease is spread by the bite of the deer tick and can cause stillbirth, prematurity, and heart defects. The risk is highest during peak tick season (May to October) in California (especially the California/Oregon border), Wisconsin, New York, Maine, Connecticut, and New Jersey. Prompt treatment with antibiotics reduces the risk to the fetus (Morton, 1989b).

Another disease without noticeable symptoms is *toxoplasmosis.* Infected animals (usually cats) may pass the parasite when they defecate; it may also be present in the raw meat eaten by humans or animals. The toxoplasmosis parasite damages the baby's nervous system. Since no vaccine or effective treatment is available, the pregnant woman should avoid eating raw meat, as well as contact with stray cats, changing the cat litter, or gardening in soil where cats dig (Frenkel, 1990).

Sexually transmitted diseases are found in epidemic proportions among women who are pregnant. *Genital herpes, chlamydia, syphilis,* and

toxoplasmosis
a disease with serious teratogenic potential caused by a protozoan that may be found in raw or undercooked meat

A Closer Look

Pregnancy Healthlines—Current Information about Teratogens is Just a Phone Call Away

A network of resource centers have been established throughout the country to answer the questions of anxious mothers about the impact of potential teratogens on pregnancy.

Some women medicate themselves before they know they're pregnant. Others are unaware of the risks of certain medications, habits, and lifestyles. Physicians should prescribe medications during pregnancy only when absolutely necessary, at the lowest dosage level possible, and only for a specified period of time (Ericson, 1987). But too many physicians adopt new therapies that have questionable benefits, unknown risks, and provide little or no follow-up for their patients.

While no medication is absolutely safe, understanding how medications can affect the fetus can help women make more informed choices. The calls are taken by specially trained health professionals, and the service is generally free.

ARIZONA — Arizona Teratogen Information Network
Tuscon, AZ
602-626-6016
1-800-362-0101 (in Arizona)

CALIFORNIA — California Teratogen Registry
San Diego, CA
619-294-3584
1-800-532-3749 (in California)

CONNECTICUT — Connecticut Pregnancy Exposure Information Service
Farmington, CT
203-674-2676
1-800-325-5391 (in Connecticut)

FLORIDA — Teratogen Program
Miami, FL
305-547-6006

IOWA — Iowa Teratogen Information Service
Iowa City, IA
319-356-2674

MARYLAND — FDA Adverse Drug Effects Branch
Rockville, MD
301-443-6410

MASSACHUSETTS — Pregnancy/Environmental Hotline
Brighton, MA
617-787-4957
1-800-322-5014 (in Massachusetts)

NEW JERSEY — Teratology Service Network
Camden, NJ
609-757-7869

NEW YORK — Pregnancy Hotline
New York, NY
212-230-1111

PENNSYLVANIA — Pregnancy Hotline
Philadelphia, PA
215-829-KIDS

TEXAS	Genetic Screening and Counseling Service Denton, TX 817-383-3561	WASHINGTON	Drug Information Service Seattle, WA 206-543-3373
	Teratogen Identification Program Houston, TX 713-792-4592	WASHINGTON, DC	Reproductive Toxicology Center Washington, DC 202-293-5137 (for members only, call for information on joining)
UTAH	Pregnancy Risk Line Salt Lake City, UT 801-583-2229 (in Utah and Montana only)	WISCONSIN	Teratology Hotline Milwaukee, WI 414-931-4172
VERMONT	Vermont Teratogen Information Network Burlington, VT 802-658-4310	CANADA	Motherisk Toronto, Ontario, Canada 416-598-5781

Excerpted from: Vogt, B.L. (1987) Pregnancy healthlines. *Childbirth Educator*, Winter/1987, 51–53.

AIDS are among the most damaging to the unborn. Cesarean section can spare the baby contact with herpes and chlamydia and the resulting blindness or pneumonia they may cause. These microorganisms are present in the woman's vagina and are transmitted to the baby during birth. Syphilis and AIDS both cross the placenta and attack the baby directly. Syphilis can be treated by antibiotic medication; there is no effective treatment for AIDS. Spread by sexual contact or the mother's IV drug use, newborns in 1990 were more likely than *any* other high risk population (including gay and bisexual men) to be exposed to AIDS (Crowley et al., 1990). Forty percent of those infants who become contaminated with AIDS do so during the birth process as they come into contact with HIV-positive blood from their own mother's system (Henrion, 1988). More than 35% of infected babies receive the virus prenatally. As of this writing, AIDS is fatal. Newborns can be screened for the presence of the HIV virus. Babies who have the infection are given medication to halt the disease's progress (Rogers, 1989). Sexually transmitted disease can be prevented by sexual abstinence, by limiting sexual contact, and by the use of latex condoms along with spermicides containing nonoxynol-9 or other proven chemical agents.

The Rh factor is a protein substance in the blood. If the mother is Rh negative (the RH factor is missing) and the baby is RH positive (the Rh factor is present), a *blood incompatibility* exists. Since the mother's body

In Touch

THE HERPES RESOURCE CENTER
260 Sheridan Ave.
Palo Alto, CA 94306
415-328-7710

AIDS HOTLINE
1-800-FOR-AIDS
(Atlanta area 404-329-1295)

blood (Rh) incompatibility
a condition that exists when the mother's blood contains the protein substance, Rh, and the baby's blood does not and vice versa

perceives the blood-incompatible baby to be a "foreign object," it begins to produce antibodies that will attack the baby in much the same way as an organ transplant recipient's body may reject the new liver or heart. The antibody buildup during the first pregnancy is slow and so that first baby is seldom affected. However, the antibodies remain in the mother's system. If a subsequent pregnancy involves an Rh incompatibility, the second and later babies may experience birth defects or even death (Treichel, 1987). To prevent her body from making antibodies that will attack an Rh positive fetus, the mother is given a Rhogam vaccine within three days of childbirth, stillbirth, miscarriage, or abortion.

Risks from disease during pregnancy can be substantially minimized through changes in behavior, immunization, and adequate/immediate prenatal care, as well as through routine maintenance of good health. Any woman—pregnant or not—who eats a well balanced diet, avoiding excessive salt, sugar, and fat, who avoids handling soiled cat litter and eating raw meat, who practices good hygiene, who maintains her optimum body weight, who is drug-free, who gets plenty of rest and exercise, and who avoids contact with sick individuals is less likely to contract infectious diseases or to develop chronic health problems. The fundamental principles of health, then, are an important prerequisite for disease prevention.

Drug Use

PRESCRIPTION DRUGS AND MEDICATIONS Drugs are available to treat almost any disease, illness or condition. In certain circumstances, some medications may be essential to the mother's or the baby's health and well-being, but others are elective. In the later case, the suspected risks of medication should always be weighed against the potential benefits. In some cases drugs prescribed specifically for pregnant women have had disastrous effects on fetal development.

Women are advised to forego elective drug treatment before and during pregnancy in favor of "natural" remedies for the sake of the conception. Laxatives, tranquilizers, diet pills, headache and cold remedies, antacids, and even aspirin can have complicating effects. The antinausea medication *Bendectin* was taken off the market because it resulted in birth defects when prescribed for pregnant women (Saunders & Saunders, 1990). The antiacne drug *accutane* had such a devastating influence on prenatal development that many physicians require their female patients to be on birth control pills before they will prescribe it (Kizer et al., 1990). An excellent source of information about the effects of various prescription and nonprescription drugs on prenatal development is the *Physician's Desk Reference*, available at the reference desk of most libraries. See Table 3–4 for information on over-the-counter products used prenatally.

■ **Table 3–4**   *Is It Safe? Over-the-Counter Products Used Prenatally*

DRUG PRODUCT	INGREDIENTS FOR WHICH STUDIES DOCUMENT ADVERSE EFFECTS	INGREDIENTS FOR WHICH STUDIES FIND NO ADVERSE EFFECTS	INGREDIENTS FOR WHICH NO STUDIES ARE PUBLISHED
Actifed	pseudoephedrine hydrochloride	pseudoephedrine hydrochloride	triprolidine hydrochloride
Afrin			oxymetazoline hydrochloride, sorbitol, glycine, sodium hydroxide, aminoacetic acid, phenylmercuric acetate
Akla-Seltzer Pain Reliever and Antacid	aspirin	aspirin	sodium bicarbonate, citric acid
Alka-Seltzer Plus	aspirin	aspirin	chlorpheniramine maleate, phenylpropanolamine bitartrate
Anacin	aspirin, caffeine	aspirin, caffeine	
Anbesol	iodine, alcohol		phenol, benzocaine
aspirin	aspirin	aspirin	
Asthma Nefrin	epinephrine hydrochloride		chlorobutanol
BC Powder	aspirin, salicylamide, caffeine	aspirin, caffeine	potassium chloride
Betadine	povidone-iodine		
BiCozene Creme			benzocaine, resorcinol
Black Draught			senna, anise, clove, peppermint, cinnamon
Bufferin	aspirin		magnesium carbonate, aluminum glycinate
Chloraseptic Spray			phenol, sodium phenolate
Chlor-Trimeton			chlorpheniramine maleate
Chooz			magnesium trisilicate calcium carbonate
Colace			dioctyl sodium sulfosuccinate
Comtrex	acetaminophen	acetaminophen	dextromethorphan hydrobromide, chlorpheniramine maleate, phenylpropanolamine hydrochloride
Contac			chlorpheniramine maleate, phenylpropanolamine hydrochloride
Coricidin D	aspirin	aspirin	chlorpheniramine maleate, phenylpropanolamine hydrochloride
Correctol			dioctyl sodium sulfosuccinate, yellow phenolphthalein
CoTylenol	pseudoephedrine hydrochloride, acetaminophen	acetaminophen	chlorpheniramine maleate, dextromethorphan hydrobromide
Creomulsion			creosote, ipecac, white pine, menthol, cascara, wild cherry, beechwood
Desitin			zinc oxide, talc, petrolatum, lanolin, cod liver oil

(continued on next page)

■ **Table 3–4**   *(continued)*

DRUG PRODUCT	INGREDIENTS FOR WHICH STUDIES DOCUMENT ADVERSE EFFECTS	INGREDIENTS FOR WHICH STUDIES FIND NO ADVERSE EFFECTS	INGREDIENTS FOR WHICH NO STUDIES ARE PUBLISHED
Dicarbosil			calcium carbonate, peppermint oil
Di-Gel			aluminum hydroxide, magnesium hydroxide, magnesium carbonate, simethicone
Dramamine		dimenhydrinate	
Dristan	phenylephrine hydrochloride, aspirin, caffeine	aspirin, caffeine	chlorpheniramine maleate
Excedrin	aspirin, caffeine, acetaminophen	aspirin, caffeine, acetaminophen	
Excedrin PM	pyrilamine maleate, acetaminophen	pyrilamine maleate, acetaminophen	
Ex-lax			yellow phenolphthalein
FDS	methylene chloride		isopropanol, myristate, mineral oil, lanolin
Feen-A-Mint			yellow phenolphthalein
Fleet Enema			sodium biphosphate, sodium phosphate, senna
Gaviscon			magnesium carbonate, aluminum hydroxide
Gelusil			aluminum hydroxide, magnesium hydroxide, simethicone
Haley's M-O			magnesium hydroxide, mineral oil
Halls Mentho-Lyptus Cough Drops			menthol, eucalyptus oil
Kaopectate			kaolin, pectin
Maalox	magnesium sulfate	magnesium sulfate	aluminum hydroxide, magnesium hydroxide
Metamucil			psyllium hydrophilic mucilloid
milk of magnesia			magnesium hydroxide, peppermint oil
Mylanta			magnesium hydroxide, aluminum hydroxide, simethicone
Neo-Synephrine II	xylometazoline hydrochloride		benzalkonium chloride, thimerosal
Norforms			methylbenzethonium chloride
Novahistine Cough & Cold Formula	pseudoephedrine hydrochloride	pseudoephedrine hydrochloride	chlorpheniramine maleate, dextromethorphan hydrobromide
Nyquil	acetaminophen, ephedrine sulfate, alcohol	acetaminophen, doxylamine succinate, ephedrine sulfate	dextromethorphan hydrobromide
Parapectolin	paregoric		pectin, kaolin
Pepto-Bismol	bismuth subsalicylate	bismuth subsalicylate	
Percogesic	acetaminophen	acetaminophen	phenyltoloxamine citrate

(continued on next page)

■ **Table 3–4**   (continued)

DRUG PRODUCT	INGREDIENTS FOR WHICH STUDIES DOCUMENT ADVERSE EFFECTS	INGREDIENTS FOR WHICH STUDIES FIND NO ADVERSE EFFECTS	INGREDIENTS FOR WHICH NO STUDIES ARE PUBLISHED
Peri-Colace			casanthranol, dioctyl sodium solfosuccinate
pHisoDerm			entsulfon sodium, petrolatum, lanolin, sodium benzoate, octoxynol-1, methylcellulose, lactic acid
Preparation H			shark liver oil, live yeast extract, phenylmercuric nitrate
Primatene Mist	epinephrine bitartrate		
Pristeen			cetyl octonate, isopropanol myristate
Privine Nose Drops			naphazoline hydrochloride, benzalkonium chloride
Riopan			magaldrate
Robitussin			guaifenesin
Robitussin DM			dextromethorphan hydrobromide guaifenesin
Rolaids			dihydroxyaluminum sodium carbonate
Sine-Off	aspirin	aspirin	chlorpheniramine maleate, phenylpropanolamine hydrochloride
Sinutab	acetaminophen	acetaminophen	phenylpropanolamine hydrochloride, phenyltoloxamine citrate
Sudafed	pseudoephedrine hydrochloride	pseudoephedrine hydrochloride	
Summer's Eve			sodium citrate, citric acid, zinc sulfate, allantoin
Tegrin			coal tar extract, allantoin
Triaminic Syrup	pyrilamine maleate	pyrilamine maleate	phenylpropanolamine hydrochloride, chlorpheniramine maleate
Tums			calcium carbonate, peppermint oil
Tylenol	acetaminophen	acetaminophen	
Vagisil			benzocaine, resorcinol
Vatronol	methyl salicylate ephedrine sulfate	ephedrine sulfate	menthol, eucalyptol, camphor
Vicks Formula 44	alcohol	doxylamine succinate	dextromethorphan hydrobromide, sodium citrate
Vicks Vaporub			camphor, menthol, turpentine spirits, eucalyptus oil, cedar leaf oil, nutmeg oil, thymol
Visine			tetrahydrozaline hydrochloride, benzalkonium chloride, disodium edetate

This chart shows over-the-counter preparations used by women in the University of Florida study, the ingredients of those preparations, and the studies about the ingredients that were found in a review of the literature. Findings of different studies often conflict as to whether a preparation causes adverse effects on the fetus.

Source: Brackbill, Y., McManus, K., Woodward, L. *Medication and Maternity: Infant Exposure and Maternal Information.* University of Michigan Press, 1985. Used with permission.

HORMONE USE Women should plan their pregnancies so that they will discontinue birth control pill use well in advance of becoming pregnant. Inadvertently taking birth control pills after conception can alter the hormonal balance of the fetal environment.

Steroids have devastating consequences for fertility for both men and women. Women may stop ovulating, and men's testes shrink and their sperm count drops under the influence of steroids (Whaley & Wong, 1988). When steroids are taken during pregnancy, the baby—whether male or female—may be masculinized.

ILLEGAL DRUGS Cocaine, "crack" (alkaloidal cocaine), "crank" (methamphetamine), heroin, morphine, and other addictive drugs rapidly cross the placenta, and consequently fetal addiction accompanies maternal addiction. Ten percent of babies born are exposed to cocaine in utero (Matera et al., 1990). Sixty percent of crack-using mothers receive no prenatal care (Cherukuri et al., 1988). Low birth weight and prematurity are complications due to the reduction in the flow of nutrients and oxygen to the baby. Perhaps the greatest threat to survival, however, is the stress caused by drug withdrawal (Chasnoff, 1991). Withdrawal symptoms are seen in 60–90% of infants born to drug-addicted mothers. These symptoms include irritability, a high-pitched cry, tremors, poor feeding, fever, and constant yawning, sneezing, and crying. Even with treatment, mortality of addicted newborns is high (Larin, 1982). The risk of *sudden infant death syndrome (SIDS)* is 50 times higher among cocaine exposed babies than nonexposed babies (it strikes one of every seven cocaine babies) (Gingras et al., 1990).

Cocaine-babies who survive are often distracted and easily overstimulated due to neurological impairment, and they exhibit growth retardation, limb reduction defects, intercranial hemorrhage as well as malformations of the urinary tract, intestinal tract, and the genitals (Jones, 1991). The drug reduces the size of the blood vessels and restricts nutrient flow to the baby before birth. About one-third of mothers have difficulty interacting with their cocaine-exposed babies after birth. In these cases, the baby's behavior at one month gets worse rather than better. Preliminary data suggest that showing mothers how to handle their babies does improve the outcome (Adler, 1989a). Infant-sized waterbeds seem to help ease withdrawal symptoms both in the hospital and at home (Oro & Dixon, 1988).

Leonard Nelson and colleagues (1987) suggest that maternal drug use during pregnancy may predispose infants to the development of *strabismus* (crossed eyes) and other disorders of the eye muscles. Twenty-five percent of the infants born to mothers who took methadone, tranquilizers, heroin, marijuana, amphetamines, or antidepressants during pregnancy had the disorder. In the general population, strabismus affects only 3–5% of infants.

cocaine
a white, crystalline alkaloid obtained from coca leaves

drug withdrawal
the physical reaction that accompanies the cessation or interruption of drug use by a drug addicted person

sudden infant death syndrome (SIDS)
the sudden death of an apparently healthy infant, usually 0–6 months of age. Also called crib death

growth retardation
preventing the organism from growing or developing to their genetic potential

■ **Figure 3–7**

This cocaine-exposed newborn is struggling to survive drug exposure, birth, and drug withdrawal.

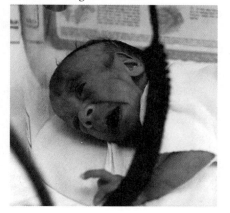

A longitudinal study begun in 1978 compared the long-term effects of prenatal exposure to marijuana and tobacco smoking (Fried, 1989). At 1 month of age, babies whose mothers smoked marijuana had symptoms similar to mild narcotic withdrawal. Dosage-related deficits in mental, motor, and language scores were apparent by age 1 year among the offspring of regular cigarette smokers. Cognitive and language deficits were noted by age 3 in the marijuana-exposed infants, but were not as pronounced as those experienced by the babies of cigarette users. Apparently, there are persistent effects of prenatal exposure to tobacco cigarettes and marijuana, but the marijuana effects are not as readily determined. While THC (tetrahydrocannabinol), the active ingredient in marijuana, is passed into human breastmilk, no effects of the drug on infant behavior have been noted (American Academy of Pediatrics: Committee on Drugs, 1989; Perez-Reyes & Wall, 1982).

A variety of problems arise in attempts to assess the impact of illegal drugs on pregnancy. Impurities exist and dosage levels vary. For example, heroin, cocaine, and PCP are often mixed or cut with other drug and nondrug substances, and the amount of THC, the active ingredient in marijuana, varies from batch to batch. Also, users of illegal drugs often take a variety of drugs, smoke and abuse alcohol, receive little or no prenatal care, are poorly nourished, or have illnesses and other health-related problems (Kreek, 1982). Thus, it becomes difficult to separate the effect of the drug itself from those of other factors. Contrary to popular belief, drug abuse during pregnancy is not confined to urban minority populations. In one Florida study, no significant difference in drug use during pregnancy was found between indigent women at public centers and upper-income women seeing private physicians (*Washington Post*, September 18, 1989).

CIGARETTE SMOKING About 30% of all U.S. women in their childbearing years smoke cigarettes (Chatterjee et al., 1988). Although cigarette smoking does not seem to cause major structural damage to the fetus, smoking can affect fetal health and complicate delivery. Smoking reduced the size of the blood vessels both in the mother's system and in the placenta; therefore, less oxygen and fewer nutrients are circulated to the baby than is normal and more waste is accumulated (Schwartz-Bickenbach et al., 1987). The baby of a smoker simply cannot grow as well as if the mother did not smoke. Babies born to mothers who smoked after the 16th week of pregnancy are more likely to be premature and weigh an average of one-half pound less than babies born to nonsmokers (MacArthur & Knox, 1988). They are also more likely to experience life-threatening complications after birth, including an increased likelihood of sudden infant death syndrome. Passive smoking, the third leading cause of preventable illness and death in 1991, may also affect fetal health in similar ways (Spitzer et al., 1990).

In Touch

> 1-800-COCAINE
>
> National hotline for cocaine information

THC (tetrahydrocannabinol)
the active ingredient in marijuana

passive smoking
inhaling tobacco smoke as a function of being in a smoke-filled environment

A Closer Look

Being Different—A Personal Story of Birth Defects

I am the daughter whose presence on the delivery table would have devastated most mothers. Imagine the scenario:

"Mrs. Smith," the doctor says, "you have a baby girl."

"Is she pretty?" Mrs. Smith asks. "Can I hold her?"

The doctor stammers. "Mrs. Smith, your baby is missing most of her legs."

The doctor gives the mother a tiny infant whose right leg is missing from the point just above the place where the knee might have been and whose left leg has a knee with only a small, underdeveloped portion of a lower calf extending from it.

This is what my body resembled at birth—and still does. Yet I would not choose any other life.

My story begins between the 26th and 60th day after I was conceived. On approximately the 28th day, we develop limb buds; this was true in my case. Usually the entire limb is developed by the 56th day; in my case the development was hindered. The agent that caused this was most likely the drug Thalidomide. Thalidomide was a sedative drug used by thousands of pregnant women in Europe to help them sleep. Thalidomide was being tested in clinical trials in the United States. After over 8,000 cases of birth defects were reported, Thalidomide was withdrawn from the world market in 1962.

The results of this chemical have been described as "monstrosities." And there were monumental lawsuits brought by parents. In addition, a number of abortions were also performed on women who were informed of the possibilities.

My mother vaguely remembers being given a drug while on a trip to Germany because she was experiencing nausea and restlessness from her pregnancy. For my parents, abortion was not an option even if they had been aware of my condition. They believe it was God's decision, and they were content with that decision. For this same reason they did not pursue any legal action. For them, a lawsuit never would have addressed this issue.

This belief has led me to accept—even prefer—things for what they are. Many people find this difficult to believe. They feel lucky that amniocentesis is available to screen out babies born with less severe deformities than mine. The thought frightens me.

Amniocentesis could never have told my mother that I would have artistic talent, a high intellectual capacity, a sharp wit, and an outgoing personality. The last thing amniocentesis would tell her is that I could be physically attractive.

My point is that we demean the value of an individual's worth by adhering to a medical label such as "disabled." What is worse, most medical professionals aren't even aware of the attitude they may convey to prospective parents—that a disabled life is not worth living.

Most people do not believe me when the subject comes up and I tell them that I have artificial limbs. Unless I were to wear miniskirts, which I don't, my physical differences would not be apparent. I limp, but not as much as people think I should.

I take off my legs to go swimming. On the surface, I suddenly appear very disabled, but I can actually swim much better than most people. I have learned to live with this frequent discrepancy between the image I have of myself and the one

Some investigators claim that prenatal exposure to maternal smoking can affect a child's school performance and social abilities. Recent research confirms that children whose mothers smoked during pregnancy tend to have attention deficits, lower IQ scores, and social and intellectual problems in school (Naeye & Peters, 1984). Regarding more subtle effects, Stjernfeldt and associates (1986) found that a mother smoking 10 or more cigarettes a day during pregnancy raises that child's risk of developing a childhood cancer. Passive smoking after birth may be related to later cancers, but the conclusions are considered tentative (Pershagen, 1989). Women whose mothers smoked while pregnant may be less fertile than women whose mothers were nonsmokers (Weinberg et al., 1989). Some indication also suggests that children who live in smoking households experience more respiratory difficulties than children who are free from smoke exposure.

Given the accumulated evidence, pregnant women are advised not to smoke past the 16th week of pregnancy and to avoid passive smoking. Those pregnant mothers who are unable to quite smoking are urged to reduce their cigarette consumption to below 10 per day.

ALCOHOL USE The earliest documentation of the effects of alcohol consumption in pregnancy was written by the second-century Roman physician Soranus of Ephesus. He warned, "When conception has taken place, one must beware of every excess . . . for the seed is easily evacuated through fright . . . by the administration of drugs . . . (and) through drunkenness" (Danis et al., 1981 p. 6). Research has substantiated these early observations: Babies born to alcoholic mothers tend to be smaller than normal and more likely to have facial alterations, mild to moderate mental retardation, and behavioral disorders, such as irritability, sleeping problems, short attention span, feeding problems, learning difficulties, and hyperactivity (Church & Gerkin, 1988). It is this collection of characteristics that comprises the fetal alcohol syndrome (FAS), mentioned earlier. There is also some suggestion that sus-

■ **Figure 3–8**

An ad by the American Cancer Society to discourage smoking during pregnancy.

Some People Commit Child Abuse Before Their Child Is Even Born.

According to the surgeon general, smoking by a pregnant woman may result in a child's premature birth, low birth weight and fetal injury. If that's not child abuse, then what is?

AMERICAN CANCER SOCIETY®

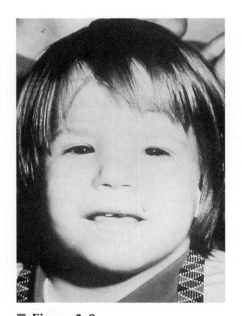

■ **Figure 3–9**

A child with the facial characteristics that reflect Fetal Alcohol Syndrome (FAS).

■ **Figure 3–10**

Alcohol conversion table.

1/2 ounce absolute alcohol (ethanol) =

12 ounces beer   4 ounces wine
(4% alcohol)   (12% alcohol)

1 ounce   1-1/4 ounces
100-proof liquor   80-proof liquor
(50% alcohol)   (40% alcohol)

ceptibility to hearing impairment may be part of FAS. FAS babies are more likely to have repeat respiratory infections resulting in otitis media (or middle ear infection) due to Eustachian tube dysfunction. Perhaps the resulting hearing impairment contributes to the speech, language, and learning difficulties often manifested by FAS children.

In the United States, the likelihood of alcohol-related birth defects is quite high (Tittmar, 1990). Most of the *2.25 million* alcoholic women in the United States are of childbearing age (U.S. Bureau of the Census, 1991). According to available statistics, 44% of chronic alcoholics have affected children: 50% of these children will be mentally retarded and 30% will have physical malformations. Anatomical abnormalities are a clear risk in infants whose mothers drink more than 6 drinks per day (Ernhart et al., 1987). We know that mothers who are heavy drinkers are more likely to smoke cigarettes and to use psychoactive drugs than lighter drinkers. The risk of FAS-related birth defects increases if mothers both smoke and drink or take other drugs. The critical period for alcohol teratogenicity is around the time of conception (Ernhart et al., 1987).

While heavy alcohol consumption during pregnancy can be detrimental to the developing child, moderate or periodic drinking in the first trimester is linked to developmental problems as well. In 1978, Hanson and colleagues identified a less severe form of FAS they labelled *fetal alcohol effects (FAE)*. When woman drink as little as 1 or 2 ounces of alcohol per day for the first 3 months of pregnancy, FAE is present in 11% of the births. Figure 3–10 is a chart for calculating the percentage of alcohol in beer, wine, and distilled liquor. J. M. Graham Jr. and his colleagues (1988) found that 4 years after birth, 80% of offspring classified as having fetal alcohol effects at birth were less attentive, less obedient, and more fidgety than children of nondrinkers. Significantly lower IQs were also noted (Streissguth et al., 1989). Small amounts of alcohol have also been associated with physical and behavioral complications, although they are less severe than FAS (Day et al., 1990).

One out of every 525 live births has some of the symptoms of FAS or FAE. FAS is the third most common recognizable cause of mental retardation, rivaled only by Down's syndrome and neural tube closure defects (problems with the tube that encloses the spinal cord) (Abel, 1988). Such statistics prompted the passage of a Federal law requiring retail liquor stores, bars, and restaurants to display warning signs against drinking during pregnancy and for beer, wine, and liquor manufacturers to put warning labels on their products. Women who eliminate or reduce alcohol intake during pregnancy report feeling more attached to their babies than women who continue to drink at an unmodified level (Condon & Hilton, 1988). Since a pregnant woman never drinks alone, abstaining from alcohol is recommended during pregnancy, especially in the first trimester. A screening test for FAS/FAE risk has been developed that assesses levels of AFP (alphafetopro-

▶▶   I S S U E   ◀◀

Beverage or Drug? The Confusion over Mixing Alcohol with Pregnancy

A newspaper columnist wrote the following:
Six months ago when I said in this column that for pregnant women "no drinking is the only safe course," I received a variety of responses. The more disturbing ones came from physicians who said generally, "That might be well and good but patients don't want that kind of answer." Physicians were told, "My husband won't like that at all" and "Can't I at least have some wine with my meals?" One doctor said if he pushed the no drinking idea too hard, he might become known in the community as "hard-nosed" on drinking and that would harm his credibility with patients in general (and ultimately his practice). Some angry laypeople insisted there wasn't enough "hard evidence" for that kind of alarmist reaction. Lastly, people in the liquor industry cautioned me verbally and in writing that "two drinks a day was a safe limit."

Since that time the Surgeon General of the United States published a statement recommending that pregnant women drink no alcoholic beverages because of the risks of fetal alcohol syndrome. Well, now that we have the Surgeon General's report, the issue should be settled. But is it?

I think not. The fact that my column prompted a controversy at all is indicative of our national preoccupation with drinking. We seem to think that drinking alcohol is not only a custom, or even a social norm, but it is actually a necessity, like health care, cars, or television. This attitude was graphically demonstrated several years ago when the fetal alcohol syndrome was first announced. A panel of experts from the field of addiction was answering questions for the media. A number of good questions were asked. One reporter in the press gallery repeated the same question in different ways, "Just how much can a pregnant woman drink without harming the fetus?" The panelists answered his question several times.

When the same reporter raised his hand again, one of the panelists, slightly irritated, said, "Asking the same question over and over won't change the facts. Until further scientific evidence proves otherwise, the only absolutely safe amount is zero drinking during pregnancy."

The finality of this answer really irritated the reporter. "Now you listen to me," he responded angrily. "I know you are scientists but you are not exact enough for me. The point is this: my wife is four months pregnant. Today is our anniversary. In the trunk of my car, I have a bottle of vintage wine. I was on my way home to celebrate our anniversary and to drink that wine. And unless you 'scientists' (he added this with a sneer) can come up with some real evidence that makes sense, my wife and I are going to drink that wine tonight." With that he hastily gathered his notes and stormed out of the room.

The audience and the panel were stunned. Was the reporter dramatizing a national norm? Maybe his actions were saying, "Life is an alcohol deficiency. You can't expect my wife and I to go on the wagon for 9 months on the mere chance that if she didn't, it might harm our baby."

Regardless of how we feel about the reporter's remarks, the Surgeon General's statement is clear and the research backs it up: Drinking during pregnancy is not worth the risk. Also, if you want your baby to have a right to make his/her own choice about drinking or not drinking, then abstaining is the only choice. Remember, a pregnant woman never drinks alone.

Source: © 1981, Los Angeles Times Syndicate. Reprinted with permission.

fetal alcohol effects (FAE)
a less severe form of FAS

neural tube closure defects
malformations in the development of
the spinal column that lead to
congenital defects like anencephaly or
spina bifida

tein), HPL (human placental lactogen), and SP-1 (specific beta-1-glycodprotein) (Halmesmaki et al., 1987).

CAFFEINE CONSUMPTION Although no evidence has been found linking caffeine consumption and birth defects in human babies, low birth weight is more likely in women who consume three or more cups of coffee per day or their equivalent in caffeine (Narod et al., 1991). Table 3–5 contains caffeine sources. Babies who are chronically exposed to

---

■ **Table 3–5**   *How Much Caffeine?*

BEVERAGE/FOOD	AVERAGE MG OF CAFFEINE
Coffee (5 oz)	
Brewed, drip method	115
Brewed, percolator	80
Instant	65
Decaffeinated, instant	2
Tea (5 oz)	
Brewed, imported brands	60
Brewed, major U.S. brands	40
Instant	30
Iced (12 oz)	70
Soft Drinks (12 oz)	
TAB	46.8
Coca-Cola	45.6
Diet Coke	45.6
Dr. Pepper	39.6
Pepsi-Cola	38.4
Diet Pepsi	36
Mountain Dew	54
Cocoa (5 oz)	4
Milk Chocolate (1 oz)	5–10
Bittersweet Chocolate (1 oz)	20–30
Chocolate Cake (average slice)	20–30

All such averages are widely variable. For example, loose tea has more caffeine than tea bags. Also, the dosage of caffeine per cup of tea increases an average 20 mg for every extra minute you brew it. Brewed coffee will have similar variations in caffeine content.

NONPRESCRIPTION DRUG	MG CAFFEINE ONE TABLET
Weight control aids	100–200
Alertness tablets	100–200
Analgesic/pain relief products	30–65
Diuretics	100–200
Cold/allergy remedies	16–30

Source: *American Baby*, October, 1985, p. 45.

high levels of caffeine prior to birth experience withdrawal after delivery. The jitteriness, irritability, and vomiting subsides after the caffeine leaves the baby's system (McGowan et al., 1988). The long-term effects of chronic caffeine exposure during pregnancy is unknown at this time. Physicians recommend limiting caffeine intake during pregnancy to the equivalent of two cups of coffee per day.

DRUG-USE GUIDELINES All drugs and medicines should be considered potentially harmful to the unborn. As a result of its unique dependency on the mother, the fetus is forced to consume substances not intended for its use or in too high a concentration for its body size. What a pregnant woman does to her own body is her own business. But her right to impose on a fetus, who cannot resist her drug use, is questionable at best. Obviously, the safest course of action during pregnancy is to avoid all drugs and medications not absolutely essential for health maintenance.

■ ●▲   CONCEPT SUMMARY

Teratogens and Their Effects

FACTOR	COMPLICATIONS DURING PREGNANCY	RECOMMENDATION
AIDS	Fatal after birth	Avoid contact with infected persons, needles
Alcohol	Low birthweight; mental retardation; learning difficulties; facial alterations	Plan pregnancy; stop using
Birth control pill use/ steroid use	Fetal masculinization	Plan pregnancy; stop using
Caffeine	Low birthweight	Limit to 2 cups of coffee/ day or equivalent
Calorie deficits	Low birthweight; prematurity; learning difficulties	300 extra calories per day
Chemical hazards (home or workplace)	Variable	Avoid exposure
Chicken pox	Birth defects	Treatment with VZIG or acyclovir (antiviral)
Crack/cocaine	Nervous system defects; eye defects; learning deficits; SIDS	Plan pregnancy; stop using
Cytomegalic inclusion disease	Fetal death or mental retardation	Avoid contact with public
Diagnostic X rays to maternal pelvis	Increased chance of childhood cancers	Avoid injury

(continued on next page)

■ ● ▲   CONCEPT SUMMARY

FACTOR	COMPLICATIONS DURING PREGNANCY	RECOMMENDATION
Electric blankets	Miscarriage; cancer	Avoid use
Fifth disease	Fetal anemia	Avoid contact with infected persons
Genital herpes/warts; chlamydia	Birth defects	Avoid contact with infected persons; use latex condoms
High and persistent stress	Miscarriage/childbirth complications	Planned pregnancy; stress management techniques
Hyperthermia	Birth defects	Avoid raising temperature to 101°F or above
Lyme disease	Stillbirth, prematurity, heart defects	Avoid contact with deer tick; receive prompt treatment
Marijuana	Deficits in language acquisition; cognitive skills	Plan pregnancy; stop using
Maternal diabetes	Increases in fetal birth weight	Good prenatal care
Maternal hypertension	High blood pressure	Good prenatal care
Nicotine (tobacco)	Low birthweight; SIDS; learning problems	Plan pregnancy; stop using
Physical or psychological stress at the workplace	Miscarriage; prematurity	Quit work; reassignment; follow doctor's orders
Prescription drug use	Variable	Consult PDR; use "natural remedies"
Protein deficits	Low birthweight; prematurity; learning difficulties	Sufficient protein
Rh/blood incompatibility	Fetal death or birth defects for later pregnancies	Rhogam treatment; blood transfusions
Rubella, mumps, measles	Fetal death, severe birth defects	Maternal inoculation or natural immunity
Strenuous exercise	Prematurity	Avoid strenuous exercise
Syphilis	Fetal death or birth defects	Avoid contact with infected persons; antibiotic treatment
Toxoplasmosis	Nervous system damage in fetus	Avoid contact with microorganism
Unprotected sexual intercourse—last weeks of pregnancy	Prematurity	Use latex condoms
Video display terminals (more than 20 hrs/wk)	Increased chance of miscarriage	Limit/avoid VDT use
Vitamin excesses (especially A, B_6, C, D & K)	Birth defects	Vitamins in proper dosages/vitamins from natural sources

Nutrition During Pregnancy

In the sixteenth and seventeenth centuries, midwives believed that labor began when the baby needed more food than the womb provided (Heslin, 1983/1984). The growing fetus is absolutely dependent on the mother for its nutritional needs. It takes about 80,000 calories to produce a full-term infant, or about 300 extra calories a day throughout pregnancy (Whitney & Cataldo, 1987). The food the mother eats provides the very substance from which fetal organs and tissues form. In addition, adequate nutrition is required to support the dramatic changes occurring in the mother's system with pregnancy. A whole new organ—the placenta—plus uterine muscles, blood vessels, and mammary gland tissue proliferate, while blood volume and fluid retention increase (Table 3–6). Thus, deficiencies or inconsistencies in the mother's diet can affect her developing baby and the environment in which she develops, or both. The fetus has preferential access to the circulating nutrients, and he may partially deplete the mother's nutrient reserves if her diet is inadequate, although the mother will not "lose a tooth" for each pregnancy to make up for calcium deficiencies, for example. But neither of these mechanisms ensure fetal well-being and normal prenatal development in the face of dietary deficiencies. Women who are young, poor, sick, undereducated, and who smoke run the greatest risk of gaining too little during pregnancy. Pregnant women are discouraged from skipping meals and from fasting. Fasting can provoke uterine contractions and bring about premature labor and delivery (Ogburn & Brenner, 1981). The baby is hungry even when the mother is not.

How does a woman know if her diet is adequate during pregnancy? Adequate nutrition is reflected in the pattern of fetal growth (Whaley & Wong, 1988). Babies who are well nourished grow according to established prenatal guidelines. The baby's nutritional requirements are actually greatest during the last trimester when the baby triples in weight gain as the lungs, muscles, brain, and bones are growing rapidly. And, despite occasional or frequent discomforts, the woman's system should function well during pregnancy. Unusual difficulties signal problems, nutritional or otherwise.

Dieting to lose weight during pregnancy is unequivocally discouraged, as the baby will be malnourished and suffer from growth retardation or any of a number of more serious complications. Low birth weight is consistently related to breakfast skipping during pregnancy (Heslin, 1983/1984). Although the pregnant women is not "eating for two", she does have to ensure that the fetus has sufficient and balanced nutrition. Weight loss programs are best undertaken *prior to conception* or *after breastfeeding has ceased.*

PREGNANCY CRAVINGS We have all heard about pregnancy cravings and about expectant women who eat unusual combinations of food or

cravings
an intense desire or longing

■ **Table 3–6** *Distribution of Weight Gain During Pregnancy (in Pounds)*

SOURCE	POUNDS	COMMENT
Increase in size of mother's breasts (1.5 lb. each)	3	Hormones from the placenta prepare the breasts for lactation (milk production). The breasts lose much of their fat and gain in mammary gland tissue and in increased blood supply. (If the woman ever wanted to be naturally voluptuous in her life, this is the time.) Colostrum, a clear, yellowish fluid may be secreted after the third or fourth months.
Placenta	1	The lining of the uterus (the endometrium) takes part in forming this (disposable) organ.
Infant at birth	7.5	The average American newborn weighs between 7 and 7.5 pounds at birth
Increase in size of mother's uterus and surrounding muscles	2.5	The uterus grows in weight from 3 ounces to more than 2 pounds and in capacity from 2 milliliters to more than 4 liters. The uterus grows to four times its original length. The average nonpregnant uterus is the approximate size and shape of a pear.
Increase in mother's blood volume to supply the placenta	4	The blood vessels supplying the uterus elongate and become larger in diameter. The amount of circulating blood increases by 25–40%.
Increase in maternal fat storage	4	Concentrations of fats and cholesterols are increased by 40–60% above prepregnancy levels. This surplus is presumably required for fetal development and lactation. Fat metabolism in the mother and fetus is poorly understood.
Extra fluid retained between body cells (interstitial fluid)	2.5	The precise reason for increased extracellular fluids is unclear. Edema (weight gain due to increased water retention) also exists during pregnancy.
Amniotic fluid surrounding the infant	2	The placenta, membranes, cord, and fetus all play a role in the absorption and formation of amniotic fluid. Fluid is completely replaced every three to four hours.
Total weight gain essential for fetal development (for both obese and nonobese mothers)*	26.5	

*Any additional weight gain is fluid and fat retained by the mother. Weight gain is concentrated in the last two trimesters of pregnancy (about 3 pounds of essential weight is added in the first trimester and about 10–11 pounds of essential weight in each of the other trimesters).

Source: Whitney & Cataldo, 1987; Sandberg, 1978.

nonfood items. Do these urges signal a need for some missing nutritional substance or are they more psychological than physiological in nature? It is unlikely that the craved foods supply a unique combination of nutrients available through no other source, especially if the woman's diet is adequate and supplemented with iron and folic acid (Whitney & Cataldo, 1987). Furthermore, cravings aren't restricted to pregnant women. Males, nonpregnant females, and children report irrepressible urges to consume certain foods. For example, think about the last time you were hungry for some type of food. Since the only specific messages the brain can interpret are the body's needs for water, possibly salt, and food in general, it is more likely that, with the exception of cravings for pickles and other salty items, pregnancy cravings are psychological.

One class of behaviors may reflect physiological needs, however. *Pica* is the habit of eating nonfood substances such as paint, starch, clay, and ice (as many as eight trays a day). These cravings often reflect iron deficiency, and the pica behavior disappears once iron is given (Whitney & Cataldo, 1987). If that painted door starts to make your mouth water, consult your physician about the possibility of a dietary iron supplement.

CALORIE AND PROTEIN DEFICITS Too few calories or insufficient protein can have detrimental effects on fetal growth. The population most at risk are the young, the poor, and others who voluntarily restrict their diets (Naeye, 1981). The impact on pregnancy of these deficits is influenced by their timing and severity. Poor nutrition early in the pregnancy may prevent the zygote from implanting or render the uterine environment unfavorable, causing miscarriage (Weathersbee, 1980). If the zygote is implanted and retained, poor nutrition during the period of the embryo can interfere with basic development and can be associated with profound defects, especially when nutritional deficits are severe. Poor nutrition 18–20 weeks after conception and extending through the first 2 years of life can affect brain growth and nervous system sophistication during a critical period of development. By the age of 2 the child's brain has attained 75% of its adult size and is 2 times heavier than at birth (Sinclair, 1989). Poor nutrition during this period might result in structural changes, slowing down the transmission of nervous system impulses, interfering with the processing of information, and resulting in retardation.

Infant mortality, prematurity, and low birth weight are likely complications in pregnancy when prenatal nutrition is poor (Leader et al., 1981). Although a small baby passes through the mother's pelvic region more readily than a larger one, there is no guarantee that the mother will have an easier time giving birth to a low birth weight baby than to one of average size. In fact, quite the opposite is true, since longer labors are associated with inadequate maternal nutrition (Whaley & Wong, 1988).

Children exposed to poor prenatal nutrition have more trouble learning than well-nourished children. Intellectual impairment is most pronounced in children whose mothers have a history of dietary deficiencies, especially severe ones, and whose continued poor health, lack of education, or emotional instability make them unable or unwilling to provide their infants with the stimulation needed for normal intellectual

catch-up growth
development that "makes up for" existing deficiencies in growth

growth. Thus, deficits begun prenatally are compounded by poor nutrition and inadequate infant care after birth.

Sometimes, if introduced soon after birth, adequate nutrition can stimulate *catch-up growth*. Previously poorly nourished babies now on good diets can achieve normal physical stature 3 to 5 years after birth. Adequate nutrition may also facilitate brain development during its critical phase of growth during infancy. And additional sources of social and intellectual stimulation, such as relatives, infant care centers, and babysitters, can counteract the effects of poor parental responsiveness and an impoverished environment provided such stimulation occurs during the first 2 years of life.

Preventing protein and calorie deficits is the wisest course of action. When pregnancies at risk for poor nutrition are supplemented with additional protein, calories, and vitamins (especially iron, calcium, vitamin C, magnesium, phosphorus, thiamin, riboflavin, niacin, vitamin B6, and vitamin B12), birth weight increases and mortality and delivery problems drop (Rush et al., 1988). After birth, infants from nutrition-supplemented pregnancies exhibited more rapid learning and longer episodes of play with toys than infants from nonsupplemented pregnancies.

VITAMIN DEFICIENCIES AND EXCESSES Certain vitamins in excessive concentrations in the bloodstream can be as detrimental as none at all. For example, too much vitamin A can cause birth defects, while in laboratory animals, vitamin A deficiency just as surely interferes with fetal growth and increases the likelihood of miscarriage and the rate of infection (Kizer et al., 1990). Excessive amounts of vitamins B6, C, D, and K should also be avoided.

Vitamins are best obtained from foods, not pills. Vitamins found in foods are more readily digested, and the risk of vitamin overdose is significantly reduced due to natural safeguards. For example, one would need to consume literally bushels of carrots to overdose on vitamin A, a task that would be physically impossible to accomplish at one sitting. A pregnant woman using a vitamin supplement should follow label directions and her doctor's advice.

CALORIE EXCESSES Calorie excesses affect the mother by promoting unwanted weight gain and putting additional strains on her heart, kidneys, legs and back. If, as a consequence of overnutrition, her blood pressure increases, the mother could be endangering her health and the well-being of her baby by increasing the likelihood of eclampsia (Andolsek, 1990).

ARTIFICIAL SWEETENERS NutraSweet and Equal both contain the substance *aspartame*. When ingested, aspartame breaks down into three harmless substances that occur naturally in many foods (Jimenez, 1989).

As with all substances, moderate use of artificial sweeteners may be prudent during pregnancy.

GUIDELINES FOR NUTRITION The woman's body should be in the best nutritional condition possible when she begins her pregnancy. The mother's nutrition prior to pregnancy is important for the future health of her infant. It's never too early nor too late to begin good nutritional habits. Women with a lifetime of good eating habits have fewer problems and complications with their pregnancies than those who have been poorly nourished or have dietary imbalances. The following guidelines contain specific dietary suggestions for pregnancy:

1. Diets should be balanced throughout pregnancy and supplemented with folic acid and iron according to doctor's specifications.
2. Foods with high fat, sugar, or calorie content should be avoided.
3. Labor and delivery complications are more likely in women who drink more than four cups of coffee per day or their caffeine equivalent.
4. Pregnant women should avoid mature beef liver. Synthetic hormones are given to many animals to fatten them up and speed maturation. Such hormones concentrate in the liver of mature animals and may be unsafe when consumed during pregnancy.
5. Dietary bulk and fluid intake should be increased to encourage more efficient body function in the mother.

Stress and Emotional Factors

Most expectant parents react to pregnancy with a variety of emotions ranging from fear to anxiety to joy and exhilaration. In fact, no one seems to escape from these emotional highs and lows. Do the emotions of the parents affect the developing child?

THE MOTHER'S EMOTIONS Before pregnancy was studied scientifically, people generally believed that any unusual shock or fright in the life of the mother produced a corresponding birthmark, physical defect, or personality disorder in her child. For example, before the discovery of the disease *neurofibromatosis*, the condition of the famous "Elephant Man" was attributed to the fact that his mother, while pregnant, was knocked down by a circus elephant (Needham, 1934). For some time, the celebrated Siamese twins Chang and Eng were forbidden to tour parts of Europe for fear that their presence would somehow increase the incidence of cojoined births and other complications. To date, however, there is no good evidence that a *single, dramatic experience* in the mother's life will by itself be responsible for prenatal problems (Chalmers, 1982).

However, diagnosed emotional disorders continuing into pregnancy and conditions causing persistent tensions can have profound effects on pregnancy. In an early study Sameroff and Zax (1973) found that women with severe or chronic personality disorders such as schizophrenia were more likely to experience complications during pregnancy and delivery than women without such disturbances. And, of course, the impact of psychiatric disturbance on the unborn is likely to be compounded where medication is in use to reduce symptoms in the mother.

In addition to severe or chronic emotional problems, acute stress brought about by changes in or reactions to daily living can also affect pregnancy (Table 3–7). High and persistent maternal anxiety has been associated with miscarriage, nausea during pregnancy, and childbirth complications, as well as with feeding and sleep problems in newborns and irritability during infancy (Blomberg, 1980). Stress can also interfere with the mother's ability to care for her newborn.

The mechanisms responsible for stress-related effects are not entirely clear (Blomberg, 1980). Stress increases the production of adrenal hormones in the mother's system, and these cross the placenta, altering the fetal environment and increasing fetal heart rate and activity level. In the mother, the presence of adrenal hormones causes increased heart rate, uterine contractions, and reduced blood flow owing to vessel constriction. In addition, mothers under considerable stress are more likely to neglect their nutritional needs, to smoke excessively or abuse alcohol or other drugs, to be excessively concerned about increased fetal movement, and to behave carelessly so as to provoke abortion. Any or all of these factors may be responsible for the effects of stress on pregnancy.

■ **Table 3–7**   *Some Stress-Producing Factors During Pregnancy*

PHYSICAL STRESSES

Chronic respiratory illness
Standing for prolonged periods
Carrying heavy loads

SITUATIONAL STRESSES

Excessive fears about fetal health or well-being (teratophobia)
Financial concerns
Marital problems
Out of wedlock conception
Unplanned pregnancy; unwanted baby
Moving
Reduced contact with family
Tensions involving people outside one's family
Wanting an abortion, but feeling forced to keep the pregnancy
Job and career stresses
Excessive concerns about one's ability to parent
Negative attitudes toward pregnancy

Source: Blomberg, 1980; Mowbray et al., 1982.

THE FATHER'S EMOTIONS The father's emotional state affects the fetus both directly and indirectly. The father's mood may influence the emotional state of the mother and therefore the environment of the developing child. Fathers who are mature, flexible, supportive, and loving can minimize the stresses, strains and emotional disequilibrium often associated with pregnancy (Mobray et al., 1982). Conversely, fathers who are immature, irresponsible, hostile, or nonsupportive can provoke and intensify negative emotions in their partners. Women who are abused by their partners cannot expect the violence to end if they become pregnant. Abusive partners may regard the pregnancy as a threat that results in loss of attention and personal power. Battered women are 4 times more likely to have a low birth weight baby and 2 times more likely than the general population to miscarry (March of Dimes, 1988).

Although in pregnancy the focus is typically on the mother, both parents can make a special effort to recognize and respect each other's needs during this unique period. Problems are usually minimized when parents regard each other as partners in the process and outcome and receive special help if they can't resolve their differences. People who are constantly faced with crises and stress sometimes adopt maladaptive ways of dealing with their challenges. Mismanagement of anxiety and a habit of poor decision making can only have negative effects on a pregnancy—for example, a couple with marriage problems deciding to have a baby to salvage the failing relationship. Stress-management problems during pregnancy might be a clue that more serious problems exist in the family. Until the parents learn effective coping strategies, the stresses of child rearing will only add to the existing emotional burden.

STRESS-REDUCTION GUIDELINES Counselors and other health care professionals can help couples cope with stress by discovering the source of the problem, identifying coping resources and adjustment goals, and developing a plan of action for achieving the goals. From the parents' point of view, becoming involved in a support group or even talking with friends can help. Where problems seem overwhelming, counseling by a mental health professional, psychologist, or psychiatrist may be appropriate. Clearly, though, as the foregoing sections suggest, psychoactive medications, like any other drugs, should be avoided wherever possible owing to their teratogenic potential for the baby.

The best course of action is to prevent or minimize the stress factors under the mother's control. Perhaps most important is the mother's true desire to have the baby, which suggests that ideally each pregnancy should be planned. A couple contemplating pregnancy needs to give careful consideration to the financial implications of a new child and the baby's potential impact on the family's lifestyle and interrelationships. A couple might reconsider the decision to buy a new home, to

■ **Figure 3–11**

Yoga or other exercise can help women manage stress during pregnancy.

move, or even to begin an exciting new career or an educational program, in light of the commitment to have a baby. And they need to recognize that even positive change, agreed to and expected, involves new adaptations that can cause stress.

Radiation Exposure

Where diagnostic X rays are necessary during pregnancy, the site determines the risk to the baby. Multiple X rays, whether 2 or 3 or 20 or 30, pose no appreciable danger to the fetus as long as the intensity is 5 rads or lower, the site is the mother's skull, chest, arms, legs, or upper gastrointestinal tract, and the rest of the mother's body is protected by an X ray–repellent drape. X rays directed at the mother's uterus or pelvis increase the likelihood that the baby (babies) prenatally exposed to radiation will develop cancer in childhood (E. B. Harvey et al., 1985). High levels of radiation are not used to treat cancer during pregnancy because of their potentially harmful effect on the baby and the risk that the mother will develop radiation sickness (R. L. Brent, 1989).

sonography (sonogram)
the use of high-intensity sound waves to project a visual image of the developing fetus; also called ultrasound

Sonography is an apparently safe alternative to X rays if we need to look at the fetus in utero. Sonograms involve high-intensity inaudible sound waves that create images by bounding off structures in the uterus. Ultrasound is primarily used to assess fetal maturity and to guide needle placement during amniocentesis and other diagnostic procedures. No complications have been associated with this procedure (American Academy of Pediatrics, Committee on Genetics, 1989).

If dental X rays are necessary during pregnancy, radiation shields should be used to protect the developing embryo from even this limited radiation exposure (Whaley & Wong, 1988). It's worth noting as an aside, that pregnancy does not cause or aggravate tooth decay. Dental problems during pregnancy are most often due to gum irritation caused by increased blood volume.

Pregnant women are advised to limit their use of video display terminals (VDTs) to 20 hours a week or less, particularly during the first 3 months of pregnancy to reduce the risk of miscarriage (Goldhaber et al., 1988). It is not clear whether radiation from the terminal, job-related stress, poor working conditions, or some combination of factors is responsible for the outcome.

Exposure to microwave radiation below the maximum permissible levels presents no measurable risk to prenatal development (Brent, 1989).

The low-frequency radiation emitted by electric blankets may be implicated in miscarriage and cancer. Currently, the FDA is working with blanket manufacturers to reduce their emissions (*Sacramento Bee*, November 16, 1990, p. A24). Pregnant women are advised to unplug their electric blankets or to avoid their use.

■ **Table 3–8** *Is Your Workplace Suspect?*
The following may pose a risk for you or your unborn baby:

SUBSTANCE	INDUSTRY/WORKER	SUBSTANCE	INDUSTRY/WORKER
Anesthetic gases	Operating-room personnel	Mercury	Dental and laboratory workers
Cadmium	Glass manufacturing		Drug manufacturing
Carbon disulfide	Laundry and dry cleaning	Pesticides	Pesticide manufacturing and applying
Infectious diseases	Health-care professionals		Spouses of the above
	Day-care workers		Farm workers
	Schoolteachers		Having your house exterminated
	Social workers	Tetrachloroethylene	Laundry and dry cleaning
	Animal handlers	Vinyl chloride	Manufacture of rubber and plastics
	Meat workers	X rays	Anyone who works in a lab or operating room, including nurses, doctors, technicians, anesthetists
Lead	Smelting		
	Printing		
	Battery manufacturing		
	Glassmaking		
	Painting		
Lead in paints and clays	Artists		
	Ceramicists		
	Potters		

Source: *American Baby*, March, 1991, p. 48.

Chemicals, Toxins, and Pollutants

Environmental pollution can pose significant hazards to the growth and development of the unborn child. Lead exposure (from plumbing or leaded gasoline), methylmercury poisoning, and use of pesticides and herbicides are suspected of causing neuromuscular disorders (such as mental retardation and epilepsy) and miscarriage (Paul & Himmelstein, 1988). Prenatal lead exposure suppresses intelligence test scores of affected babies through age 4 and perhaps beyond (Dietrich et al., 1991). Most chemical exposure during pregnancy occurs in industrial settings or at home. Table 3–8 summarizes the types of hazards encountered in certain lines of work. Paternal exposure to organic solvents before conception may have adverse effects on the offspring (Taskinen, 1990).

lead exposure
the inadvertent intake (usually ingestion or transdermal exposure) of lead, a potentially toxic heavy-metal

Other Maternal Habits and Behaviors

As a matter of course, good prenatal education promotes adequate nutrition, attention to stress reduction, and careful avoidance of possible teratogens, including chemicals and radiation. However, the effects of a number of other factors—specifically hyperthermia, exercise, employment, and sexual intercourse—also need mention.

hyperthermia
a condition that causes an increase in body temperature

HYPERTHERMIA Hyperthermia, or significant increases in maternal body temperature, can be caused by illness with fever or hot tub/spa bathing. Birth defects have been noted in fetuses exposed to maternal temperatures of 101°F and above for 24 hours, especially during the first trimester of pregnancy. Such defects include growth deficiency, lack of muscle tone, mental retardation, and certain facial deformities (B. B. Little et. al., 1991). A doctor should be consulted when a pregnant woman has a fever.

Medical advice is also necessary regarding hot tub/spa use. It takes ten minutes for a tub heated to 106°F to increase the mother's body temperature to 102°F. The safest course of action during pregnancy, of course, is to avoid hot tubs and spas altogether or to bathe in moderately cool tubs (under 100°F). The risk of hyperthermia from bath tub bathing is low, since heat is disbursed and even water that is initially hot cools down too quickly to substantially overheat the mother.

EXERCISE Exercise improves circulation, lowers blood pressure, increases respiratory efficiency, and improves bowel function. For all these reasons and more, regular exercise should be a matter of routine during pregnancy. Ancient tribal lore suggests if the labor is difficult, the woman hasn't gathered enough wood. Still, some precautions are necessary: pregnant women should not exercise too strenuously or indulge in activities that jar the uterus—jumping rope, for example. Even activities that require sustained balance can be hazardous as the pregnancy proceeds and balance and coordination becomes more difficult. The idea here is to protect against the danger of falling.

Rowing, using stationery exercise bicycles, and aerobic jogging in supervised programs at intensities of 50–85% of maximum sustain cardiovascular tone in a physically fit woman during pregnancy (Clapp, 1989). Swimming is one of the best exercises for pregnant women. It avoids the rising body temperature (hyperthermia) that accompanies other forms of exertion, it makes the woman feel light and buoyant by taking the strain off her back and legs, and it frees the woman from fears of falling. In addition, unlike other exercises, swimming does *not* move blood away from her uterus and into her muscles since immersion in water causes the woman's blood volume to expand (McMurray & Katz, 1990).

EMPLOYMENT Most women can work during a low risk pregnancy if they wish. Among other things, work can provide satisfaction, stimulation, and contact with others. It can also help reduce stress that might be caused by financial insecurity. Some women work until the day they deliver because they feel fine, can perform work-related duties satisfactorily, and their physicians approve since no pregnancy-related complications exist. Other women may have to work part-time or take an extended leave of absence to integrate pregnancy and work. Physicians

■ **Figure 3–12**

(a) Swimming is excellent exercise during pregnancy. (b) Couples at a LaMaze class

will advise against continued employment in jobs that are physically strenuous, that require prolonged standing or heavy lifting, or that are judged to be dangerous or unhealthy, so as to safeguard the health of the baby (A. D. McDonald et al., 1988; Taskinen, 1990).

SEXUAL INTERCOURSE Some couples are reluctant to have sexual intercourse during pregnancy for fear of harming the baby or interrupting the pregnancy. Recent evidence suggests that sexual intercourse does not cause amniotic fluid infection unless the amniotic sac is leaking or ruptured (J. L. Mills et al., 1981). Thus, couples need not avoid coitus if the membranes are intact. Those concerned about infection are advised to use latex condoms. If physical discomfort exists, intercourse positions can be modified. Noncoital sexual activity is also an option (Crooks & Baur, 1990).

The rate of premature labor increases among couples who have intercourse in the last weeks of pregnancy. The semen contains a hormone that has been identified as one of the stimulants of the onset of labor. Some couples may be advised to abstain from intercourse entirely during that period; other couples can reduce risks by using latex condoms.

Contrary to popular opinion, female orgasm does not initiate labor (J. R. Mills et al., 1981). Labor beginning during or after intercourse is coincidental, since it is hormonal action, not sex, that initiates the birth process.

The bulk of scientific evidence suggests that as long as intercourse is rewarding and satisfying for the partners, and as long as there is no vaginal bleeding, preterm labor, evidence of ruptured membranes, discomfort, cramping, and/or indication that more than one fetus is present (which would put added stress on the cervix), there is no reason to stop having sex during pregnancy. Women who have a history of miscarriage are sometimes advised to avoid intercourse during pregnancy. Since the medical reasons for chronic miscarriage are unclear, this recommendation is designed to improve the woman's psychological outlook and to limit alternative explanations if the baby is not carried to term.

Physically, pregnancy tends to elevate sexual interest, anticipation, and fantasy in 80% of expectant females, as a function of increased blood flow to the pelvic region. Thus, experiencing orgasm becomes easier during pregnancy (Crooks & Baur, 1990). Psychologically, sex during pregnancy is highly desirable. The need for love, security, and appreciation is often accentuated during pregnancy for both partners. Furthermore, because relationship difficulties during pregnancy can be compounded and intensified later, it is important at this time to nourish the relationship. The happiest, most well-adjusted couples have active, satisfying sexual relations. Couples who are content, mutually supportive, and well adjusted and who have a firm foundation of closeness and trust can more effectively cope with the responsibilities and challenges of raising a child than couples without such positive interpersonal feelings.

TOWARD EFFECTIVE PARENTING

Can Learning Take Place Before Birth?

Some parents are making a point of talking to and playing music for their babies even before they are born. Apparently, parents want to initiate the bonding process prenatally, stimulate learning by "exercising brain cells," and/or get a head start on exposing their baby to culture. Does it work?

Scientific and anecdotal evidence suggests that babies seem to "recognize" the sound of their parent's voices or music played prenatally by becoming alert and attentive. When women read Dr. Seuss's *The Cat in the Hat* aloud three times daily during their last 8 weeks of pregnancy, their babies seemed to recognize the familiar cadence after birth (deCasper, 1989). Babies seemed more relaxed and had slower heart rates when the story was read for them again.

In a study of self-proclaimed soap opera "addicts" in England, Peter Hepper (1989) found that babies suddenly stopped crying when the show's theme began playing. In addition, these same babies adopted a "quiet alert" state throughout the program. The soap opera theme and the program itself generated little interest in babies whose mothers were nonviewers.

Do responsive babies actually recognize the theme song from hearing it in utero? Or are babies actually reacting to their mother's relaxed state during viewing time? When pregnant women watch TV, they typically sit or lay and put up their feet. Relaxation lowers their blood pressure and heart rate since different adrenal hormones are secreted during relaxation than during more active states. It may well be that the music was the cue that the unborn baby would receive a dose of relaxation hormones, too. Now after birth, babies can produce their own calming adrenal hormones in response to the show's theme and settle themselves down.

"Baby tapes" can be purchased to stimulate the child's prebirth intellect. The tapes consist of a series of sound patterns that are basically a variation of the mother's heartbeat. Advocates of the Prelearning Program distributed by Firstlearning Corp. in Santa Barbara, California, claim that children who listen to the tapes in utero are born more alert, talk sooner, and learn faster than unexposed babies. While scientific investigations have not yet been conducted, the parents' mere *expectation* that their child will be a precocious learner might be a valuable and positive outcome since positive expectations can provide a self-fulfilling prophecy for success.

But what if it all works too well? One father laments, "I was having nightmares about our child being an (unteachable) brat. Now (that my wife is wearing and playing the prenatal tapes), I'm having other nightmares. What if this kid comes out and starts bossing us around and correcting our spelling!" (Smith, 1990).

● Chapter Summary

● Scientists called embryologists study prenatal development, the growth and change that takes place before birth. Although interest in prenatal development has existed since the time of Aristotle, the major scientific discoveries in the field of embryology have been made in the last 65 years.

● Prenatal development is divided into three stages. The first, the period of the ovum, or the germinal stage, begins with fertilization and ends with implantation 7 to 10 days later. During the period of the embryo (week 2 through week 8), major body systems and organs develop through morphogenesis. The placenta, umbilical cord, amniotic sac, and other support structures form during this time. The baby dramatically increases in size during the period of the embryo. The last period of prenatal development, the period of the fetus, extends from the 9th gestational week to birth. During this time, body systems developed during the period of the embryo are perfected and the fetus readies itself for life outside the womb.

● Environmental factors that can have a negative impact on prenatal development are called teratogens. Specific teratogens include disease or illness in the mother; prescription, over-the-counter, and social drug use (including illicit drugs like cocaine and marijuana and legal drugs like alcohol, caffeine, and tobacco products); poor nutrition; stress and emotional factors; radiation exposure; chemicals, toxins and pollutants; hyperthermia; and strenuous exercise. Most women

with low risk pregnancies can work during pregnancy if they wish. Sexual intercourse is safe throughout pregnancy provided there is only one fetus and there is no bleeding, amniotic fluid loss, pain, discomfort, cramping, or history of miscarriage. Couples in their last weeks of pregnancy may wish to abstain or use latex condoms to help prevent premature labor.
- Positive pregnancy outcomes are maximized when the mother takes precautions to ensure her own and her developing child's well-being.

Observational Exercise

Invite several pregnant women to class to be part of a panel discussion on pregnancy. Develop a line of questions that would help students understand more about each woman's personal experience of pregnancy. For example:

1. When did you first discover you were pregnant? What was your reaction?
2. (If she is with a partner) What was his reaction to the pregnancy?
3. Was the pregnancy planned?
4. What symptoms have you experienced?
5. Have any of your habits or behaviors changed now that you are pregnant?
6. Have you felt movement yet? What did it feel like?
7. What plans have you made for the birth? Where will it take place? Do you have a doctor or a midwife?
8. What do you think will be the greatest challenges of new parenthood?
9. (If other children are present) How is this pregnancy different from or similar to your other pregnancies?
10. If there was anything you could change about this pregnancy, what would it be?

It might be interesting to compare the responses of different women on similar questions: a younger mother with an older mother; a mother experiencing her first pregnancy with one who has other children; a single mother with a married woman; a woman who planned her pregnancy with one who did not.

Recommended Readings

The Boston Women's Health Collective. (1984). *The new our bodies, ourselves: A book by and for women.* New York: Simon & Schuster.

David, H. et al. (1987). *Born unwanted: Developmental effects of denied abortion.* New York: Springer Publishing Co.

Heinowitz, J. (1982) *Pregnant fathers.* Englewood Cliffs, NJ: Prentice-Hall.

Kitzinger, S. (1985). *Birth over 30.* New York: Penguin Books.

Nilsson, L. (1977). *A child is born.* New York: Dell.

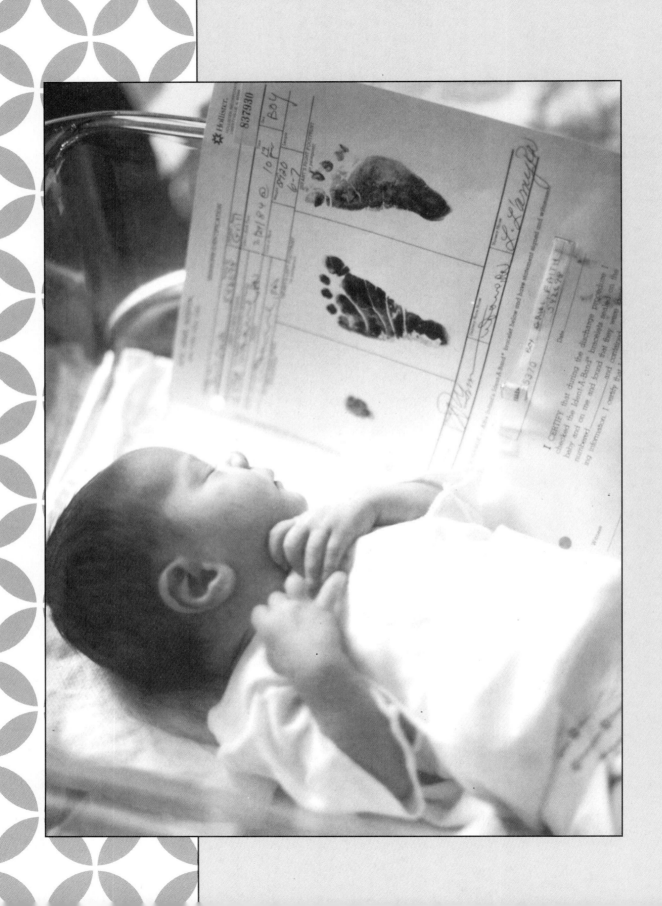

Birth and the Newborn

● Keeping Babies Healthy: Medical Care Before Birth

Prenatal medical care is recommended for women after pregnancy has been confirmed. Since such care can be costly, some people are tempted to forego the expense and "let nature take its course." But being pregnant without medical supervision is like learning to drive a car without training. It can be done, but it is not recommended under any circumstances. Medical supervision greatly reduces any risk of injury or complications, since the physician can provide guidance and interpret potential danger signs. With little or no prenatal care, infants are 3 times more likely to die.

Some pregnancies are designated as *high risk pregnancies*. This term focuses attention on a group of patients who require especially close supervision and extensive care during pregnancy because their potential for complications is significantly greater than average. Specifically, high risk pregnancies are those involving twins or multiple fetuses or any disease, condition, or abnormality that threatens the growth or survival of the fetus. Women with previous pregnancy or delivery complications are also considered to have high risk pregnancies.

A variety of diagnostic tests are used to evaluate the maturity and health status of the high risk fetus. These include ultrasound, amniocentesis, CVS, PUBS, fetoscopy, and maternal AFP screening, each described in Chapter 2. The outcome of these tests can reassure worried parents and enable medical personnel to assess the risks to the fetus should quick delivery become necessary. Sometimes these diagnostic procedures turn up problems or deficiencies in fetal development that can be corrected by altering maternal diet or administering medicine to the baby via the mother. A more direct method of treating development problems before the baby is born is fetal surgery, covered in the accompanying feature.

high risk pregnancies
pregnancies that require close medical supervision to safeguard the health of the mother and/or the baby

ultrasound
see sonography

fetoscopy
a prenatal diagnostic procedure where fiberoptic imaging is used to view the developing child within the uterus

fetal surgery
operating on the developing child prior to birth to correct conditions that could result in serious impairment or even death

119

● Keeping Babies Healthy: Estimating a Due Date

Since much planning and anticipation are usually associated with the birth of a baby, most parents want to know the expected due date. Human babies require 266 days to complete the prenatal phase of development. Since the precise moment of conception is usually difficult to determine, however, the expected delivery date is usually calculated from the first day of the woman's last menstrual cycle. The practitioner may either count forward 280 days from the first day of the last menstrual period (weekends and holidays included!) or count backward 3 months from the first day of the menstrual period, adding 7 days, and if necessary, adjusting the year. No matter which method is used, the projected due date is only an estimate. Only 4% of babies are born "on time"; however, 85% of all women deliver within 2 weeks of the expected date, either "early" or "late." The remaining 11% of births are classified as premature or postmature (Whaley & Wong, 1988).

Why bother calculating a due date at all if it's going to be wrong 96% of the time? Despite its inaccuracy, even an estimated due date benefits the expectant parents and the medical staff. As the pregnancy goes on, having a due date to look forward to can be reassuring. Without a specific end date, it can feel as if the pregnancy might go on forever. From the point of view of the medical staff, the due date serves as a reference point for estimating the stages of development and guiding treatment decisions. A baby born sooner than expected might require special attention, and a baby born significantly past due might be artificially hastened along to prevent any complications stemming from possible deterioration of the placenta. (The placenta is a temporary organ designed to function well for the duration of normal gestation, but not much beyond that). Without a due date, either of these critical situations might be overlooked.

● Keeping Babies Healthy: The Birth Setting

Within certain limits, parents can choose the setting in which their babies will be born. Currently, the options include a traditional hospital maternity ward, a hospital-based birth center, a free-standing birth center, and homebirth. Birth centers are becoming increasingly popular in the United States; homebirth is still more common in Europe than in America (Tew, 1985). Weighing the pros and cons of each option can help prospective parents decide which setting is best for them and their child.

Traditional Hospital Delivery

The hospital maternity unit has been the traditional setting for childbirth for the last 50 or so years. Hospitals have personnel and emergency medical equipment ready for newborns in distress and mothers experiencing difficulty. Thus, they are the best choice where there is concern over the possibility of obstetrical emergency. Perhaps as a consequence, hospitals tend to be more expensive and less personal than the other options. Parents sometimes feel left out of the decision-making process and alienated by routine hospital procedures that might be unnecessary—such as the chemical induction of labor and episiotomy. Prospective parents are advised to discuss the details of hospital delivery with their chosen physician.

Birth Centers

Some hospitals have *birthing rooms* or *alternative birth centers (ABCs)* on premises, which serve as alternatives to traditional labor and delivery facilities. ABCs and birthing rooms look more like bedrooms in a private home than units in a hospital facility (Figure 4–1). They are designed to be an alternative to home birth for individuals with low risk pregnancies who wish to actively participate in delivery and share the birth experience with offspring, friends, and relatives. They also cost 35–47% less than a hospital birth (*New England Journal of Medicine*, April 1990). Although these suites are generally small and the number of births they accommodate is limited, birthing rooms soften the clinical atmosphere of the hospital and are generally less expensive than traditional hospital maternity care. The staff generally minimizes intervention but monitors the birth closely so that mother and child can be moved to a surgical suite or neonatal intensive care unit should serious problems arise.

Free-Standing Birth Clinics

In some areas, independent birthing clinics are located near and associated with local hospitals. A more personalized kind of atmosphere pervades these settings, too, but clinics also tend to limit their clients to those with low risk pregnancies to help ensure safety and minimize complications. A certified nurse midwife or a physician may attend the birth.

Homebirth

In homebirth the expectant parents remain at home and a practitioner comes in to attend the birth. Homebirth is an option in uncomplicated pregnancies and is usually supervised by a midwife (either a man or a woman) who is specially trained in homebirth procedures. To reduce the risk of complications, midwives screen prospective homebirth candidates extensively. They are also much more likely than physicians to implement natural or nondrug remedies to combat pain, prevent tearing, or stimulate labor.

■ **Figure 4–1**

A homelike atmosphere is created in hospital alternative birth centers for low risk pregnancies.

In Touch

NATIONAL ASSOCIATION OF
PARENTS AND PROFESSIONALS
FOR SAFE ALTERNATIVES IN
CHILDBIRTH (NAPSAC)
PO Box 267
Marble Hill, MO 63764

Assists parents in finding alternatives
in childbirth both within and outside
the hospital

homebirth
giving birth at home or in familiar surroundings rather than in a medical facility

midwife
(also called a certified nurse-midwife) a nurse with special training and licensing who monitors pregnancy and oversees delivery, often in a home setting

Homebirth benefits those who choose it in a number of ways. The surroundings, of course, are completely familiar and the atmosphere more relaxed than in a hospital setting. Compared to hospitalization, the cost is minuscule. There is less risk of infection, since people are generally immune to their own home bacteria. In addition, the father, siblings, and others can all participate freely, having immediate and sustained contact with the newborn. The major drawback to homebirth is the need to transfer the laboring woman to emergency facilities should complications arise.

Childbirth Preparation

Physical and psychological preparation for childbirth are important components of prenatal care. The classic book on prepared childbirth is *Childbirth without Fear* published in 1933 by Grantly Dick-Read, a British physician. After his book appeared, other practitioners contributed to reducing the pain of birth. Fernand Lamaze, a French physician (1890–1957) believed that labor pain could be reduced if the woman could learn to voluntarily relax her abdominal muscles, breathe to increase oxygen intake, and focus attention away from the pain. His book, optimistically titled *Painless Childbirth*, was published in 1956.

prepared childbirth
a term coined by Grantly Dick-Read to refer to instruction given to prospective parents about the birth process and about pain management

The term *prepared childbirth* has come to mean special classes instructing prospective parents in the physiology of pregnancy and birth and in exercises and breathing techniques designed to facilitate delivery and reduce pain. In prepared childbirth, the use of pain-killing medication is optional but not routine. Advocates feel it is advantageous for the mother to stay alert so she can participate fully in the birth and interact immediately with her newborn. The Lamaze method trains a "labor coach" who can provide assistance and emotional support during the birth experience. The presence of another caring person, such as the father, a parent, or a friend, reduces the likelihood of complications, shortens the duration of labor, reduces the level of pain reported by the mother, and increases the mother's satisfaction with the birth experience (Sosa et al., 1980). Sometimes parents want their existing children to attend the birth for a variety of reasons. Birth is an incredible event, but depending on the age and personality of the child, what is stupendous for an adult may leave a child *just plain scared*. Weigh the pros and cons carefully before inviting children to the birth setting.

cesarean section (C-section)
a surgical procedure in which a baby is delivered through an incision in the abdominal and uterine walls.

Sometimes women take childbirth training and anticipate a vaginal birth only to deliver by cesarean section—that is, by surgical removal of the fetus from the womb. Mothers in this situation often feel cheated, resentful, and sometimes guilty about letting their coaches down. However, cesarean section is performed because vaginal delivery is judged too risky for the mother, the baby, or both. To avoid feeling disappointed and inadequate, couples need to prepare for the realistic pos-

■ ● ▲   **CONCEPT SUMMARY**

Planning for Birth

- Select a birth attendant (physician or midwife)
- Receive regular prenatal care
- Select a birth setting
- Attend classes in prepared childbirth, child development, and other useful subjects
- Report any of the following symptoms to the practitioner for evaluation: severe or frequent headache, chills, fever, vaginal bleeding, drainage from the vagina, burning during urination, swelling of the face or extremities, any problem with vision (blurred vision, double vision), pain (especially abdominal)

---

sibility of cesarean section birth, especially since they are increasingly common.

Actually, adequate childbirth preparation involves more than attending classes that focus on labor and delivery. Consider the following comments.

> Before our first child was born, I hadn't given much thought as to what our lives would be like after the birth, which occupied most of my attention. If I thought at all about it, I guess I had a subconscious picture of myself in a *Woman's Day* ad—one of those slightly out of focus pictures of a beautiful young mother in a pastel dressing gown nursing her baby in a pose of peaceful fulfillment. I must have imagined she took care of her baby in her spare time. Was I surprised! I was totally unprepared for being almost solely responsible for the care of my newborn. Why did I waste 9 months thinking about a birth that lasted only 20 minutes instead of how to live with a dependent human being for another 20 years? (Pantell et al., 1977, pp. 4–5)

And another point of view:

> I believe the notion that the labor coach should be the dominant role of men during pregnancy and birth has outlived its usefulness and should be retired. Quite simply, we must stop training men to be labor coaches and start concentrating on helping them prepare to be fathers (May, 1989, p. 30).

Unfortunately, human beings are not born with the ability to parent. Caring for a child is a learned skill, not an instinctive or genetically endowed one. Training or preparation can come from a variety of sources—for example, babysitting, observing parents with younger siblings, talking with other parents, reading books on caretaking issues, and formal course work. A good childbirth education class will deal with delivery not as an end in itself, but as the beginning of a new phase of family life.

● Labor and Birth

After all the gaining, training, and waiting, the time for birth arrives. Before actual labor starts, some preparatory events usually occur. Two or more weeks before delivery, the fetus usually descends into the mother's pelvis in preparation for birth. This process is called lightening, settling, or dropping. Optimally, the baby is positioned head down, facing the mother's spine. False labor pains (irregular contractions) often accompany lightening. For women who have had two or more previous deliveries, lightening may not occur until early labor (Kitzinger, 1981).

The cervix is the entry to the uterus. During pregnancy, a mucous plug seals the cervical canal. A few hours to a few days before the onset of labor, the plug may be discharged, accompanied by some slight bleeding called the *bloody show* (J. R. Scott et al., 1990). This event indicates that cervical dilatation, or expansion, is starting. The cervix is slowly opening to allow the baby to pass out of the uterus. Also, just prior to labor, the balance of hormones changes in the mother's system. This change may precipitate the loss of 2–5 pounds, nausea, or vomiting. She may also feel sensations of pressure or heaviness in the pelvis as the baby prepares for birth. Another sign that labor is imminent is a feeling of excess energy. If the woman fails to recognize this burst of energy as a signal that labor will soon begin, she might deplete her newfound energy by excess activity and enter labor exhausted. Normal labor can involve all or some of these signals. The order of their appearance is variable.

lightening (also called settling, dropping)
the settling of the fetus into the mother's pelvis in preparation for birth enters the birth canal

mucous plug
mucous secretions and blood vessels that accumulate at the mouth of the cervix to help protect the uterus from contamination holds amniotic sac up

bloody show
the loss of the mucous plug usually during labor

dilatation
the opening or dilating of the cervix to allow the baby to pass into the birth canal

■ **Figure 4–2**

(a) The cervix and uterus in a nonpregnant female. (b) Cervical changes during pregnancy.

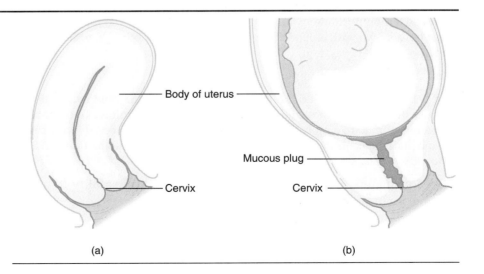

Body of uterus

Mucous plug

Cervix

Cervix

(a)   (b)

A Closer Look

Born Twice

On June 15, 1989, Blake Schultz was surgically removed from his mother's womb—and then put back again! No, this wasn't some bizarre version of peek-a-boo. Blake was partially removed from the womb to have surgery to repair a hernia, or hole, in his diaphragm. If unrepaired, the hole would have allowed his abdominal organs to push into the chest cavity, preventing his lungs from developing normally. This condition, occurring in about 1 of every 2500 fetuses, is usually fatal.

During the operation, doctors cut into his mother's uterus and pulled out the baby's arm, attaching wires to monitor his heart rate and oxygen intake. After his organs were returned to their normal positions and the hole was sealed, Blake was tucked back into the womb and the incision was closed. In this way, he could continue to develop naturally and avoid compounding the trauma of surgery with the shock of birth. He was born (for keeps) about six weeks later.

Fetal surgery is still experimental. In theory, the earlier developmental problems (like Blake's) can be detected and treated, the better the outcome. Treating a baby's problem in the womb prevents further damage from occuring. However, the procedures are not without considerable risk (Ohlendorf-Moffat, 1991). Blake was the *first* baby to survive diaphragmatic hernia repair (as of this writing, there are now *two* survivors).

Other operations (to drain excess water from the fetal brain, kidneys, or bladder; or, rarely, to remove an ailing twin) also have high mortality rates. The risk of internal infection, permanent disability, and premature labor are common complications. Doctors and parents deal with uncertainty as they try to make the best choice for the child—to wait until birth, to operate now, or, for some, to terminate the pregnancy.

While surgeons perfect their techniques, another line of research holds even greater promise—gene therapy. Once surgeons figure out how to pinpoint and replace defective DNA responsible for life-threatening problems, infant mortality and complications rates should improve dramatically.

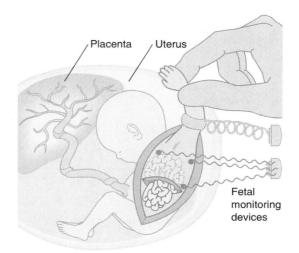

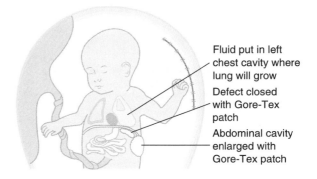

The procedure for a successful operation on a fetus with a hole (hernia) in the diaphragm. After the baby was accessed, surgeons repositioned the organs, patched the diaphragm, and used another patch to make room for the repositioned organs. Fluid was put into the left lung cavity to "save room" for the growth of the shunted lung. This defect occurs in about 1 in 2500 fetuses; it is usually fatal.

The Stages of Labor

The First Stage of Labor

Braxton-Hicks contractions
uterine contractions that may persist through the pregnancy without dilating the cervix; also called false labor pains or false labor

Sometimes labor is preceded by irregular and painless muscle contractions in the uterus called Braxton-Hicks contractions. When these are replaced by regular and usually painful contractions, the first stage of labor has begun. These contractions gradually increase in frequency, duration, and intensity. The function of the contractions is to open, or dilate, the cervix to 4 inches (10 cm.) across to allow the baby's head to pass into the birth canal. This process occurs more rapidly if the amniotic sac has been ruptured or if the mother is able to walk around while in labor (Andolsek, 1990). Even then, the first stage of labor is typically the longest, lasting an average of 10–13 hours with the first birth once dilatation begins. First-stage labor in second and subsequent deliveries is usually shorter than in first births.

During the course of labor, fetal movement is restricted by the confines of the mother's pelvis. To monitor the baby's well-being during labor, hospital personnel often use electronic devices to record fetal heart rate. Normal fetal heart rate ranges between 120 and 160 beats per minute. The fetal heart typically decelerates as a contraction begins and

■ **Figure 4–3**

Cervical dilatation and the position of the baby.

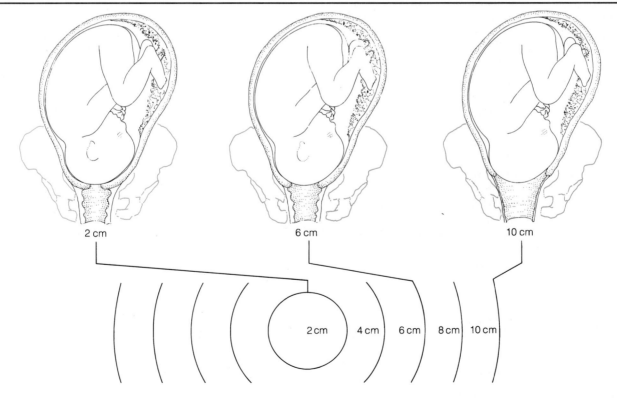

2 cm   6 cm   10 cm

2 cm   4 cm   6 cm   8 cm   10 cm

recovers as it ends. Abnormal heart rate patterns can indicate that the fetus is in distress.

The Second Stage of Labor

The second stage of labor begins after the cervix is completely dilated. A period called *transition* bridges the first and second stages, and at this time frequent and intense contractions maintain dilatation and force the

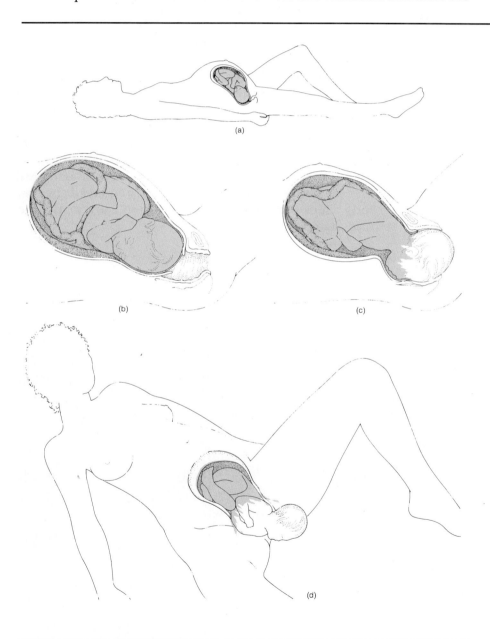

■ **Figure 4–4**

Stages of birth. (a) The baby's position before labor begins and the cervix is not dilated. (b) During labor the cervix dilates and the head descends. (c) The cervix is fully dilated and the head emerges into the birth canal. (d) The birth of the head and shoulders.

baby from the uterus. Now involuntary uterine contractions are reinforced by the mother's own pushing or bearing down with her abdominal wall and diaphragm. To progress, the laboring woman must coordinate her voluntary pushing with the involuntary contractions. As labor progresses, the baby's scalp may become visible momentarily at the vaginal opening, only to recede again between contractions. The appearance of the scalp is called *crowning.*

Ninety-five percent of babies are born head first and face down. The remaining 5% are positioned with the bottom and/or feet or a shoulder presenting first. The *breech*, or bottom-first presentation, is the most common of the three. The birth attendant will try to manually rotate a baby out of one of these positions to facilitate the birth. Where the presentation is normal, the birth attendant usually gently rotates the baby's face when it comes out and makes breathing easier by clearing the mouth and nose of mucous and fluids. Some babies emerge from the birth canal crying (and breathing), while others begin to cry after suctioning and still others must be gently encouraged to breathe by additional stimulation (stroking the sole of the baby's foot or massaging the baby's back). After the head, one shoulder, and an arm emerge, the rest of the baby's body slides out easily. The birth of the baby marks the end of the second stage of labor.

The Third Stage of Labor

After the baby is delivered and the umbilical cord stops pulsating, the birth attendant clamps and severs the cord in a painless procedure that

breech (breech presentation)
a position in the mother's uterus where the baby lies with its bottom and/or feet toward the cervix rather than with its head down

■ **Figure 4–5**

A baby just moments away from birth.

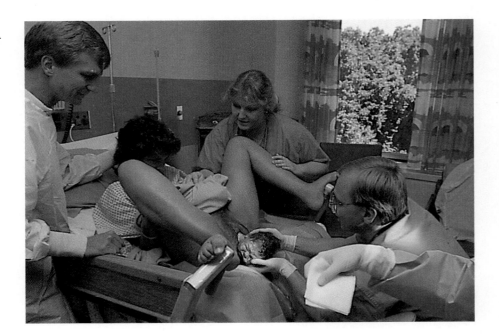

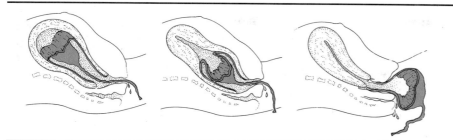

■ **Figure 4–6**

Expulsion of the afterbirth.

officially frees the baby from the mother. The sudden shrinkage of the uterus with the baby gone means that there is less room inside for the placenta. The placenta now becomes bunched up (twice as thick as it was at the onset of labor) and starts pulling away from the uterine surface. Generally, contractions stop after the baby is born, but they usually begin again to help expel the separated placenta and remaining supportive tissues, collectively called the *afterbirth*. The delivery of the afterbirth lasts between 5 and 30 minutes, and with it labor ends. Contractions may continue for a while after that, however. Postpartum contractions, or afterpains, are usually more prolonged and intense in women who have given birth before or who have just delivered large babies (J. R. Scott et al., 1990).

The third stage of labor poses the greatest risk for the mother. When the placenta detaches from the uterus, supporting blood vessels are torn. Normally the placenta separates completely and the uterus contracts uniformly to constrict the torn vessels and stop their blood flow. But if only partial separation occurs, or if placental fragments remain attached, third-stage bleeding or *postpartum hemorrhage*, may occur. Skillful obstetrical procedures can prevent excessive blood loss and complications.

afterbirth
the placenta and other membranes present in the uterus to support the baby; delivered during the third stage of labor

postpartum contractions (afterpains)
uterine contractions that persist after the baby is born

postpartum hemorrhage (third stage bleeding)
bleeding that occurs after the delivery of a baby if fragments of the placenta remain in the uterus

Assisting the Birth

Cesarean Section

In the recent past, the rules were: (1) once a woman had a cesarean section (C-section), all her subsequent babies had to be delivered surgically, and (2) only three C-sections to a customer. Nowadays, (1) women who have low, horizontal "bikini" incisions can have safe vaginal deliveries with later pregnancies 50–80% of the time (Meehan et al., 1989). Horizontal incisions are more resistant to tearing than vertical incisions. The National Institutes of Health and the American College of Obstetricians and Gynecologists have recommended encouraging vaginal birth after cesarean section (VBAC) since 1982 (McClain, 1990). (2) Repeat C-sections are generally considered to be safe (Ethel Kennedy, wife of Robert F. Kennedy, had all 11 of her children via cesarean surgery).

■ **Figure 4–7**

The placenta and umbilical cord.

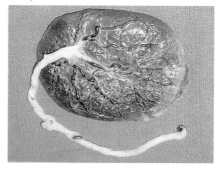

The cesarean section rate has tripled in the last 10 years to almost 25% and could exceed 40% by the year 2000 (Sperling, 1987). C-section is becoming increasingly common because of its low complication rates and because of the increased reliance on epidural anesthesia (which slows down the pushing stage) and because sexually transmitted diseases like herpes and chlamydia are found in epidemic proportions in the pregnant and nonpregnant population. Another possible explanation for the rising C-section rate is to protect hospitals and doctors against malpractice suits where the outcome of a vaginal delivery is poor, to increase hospital revenues (it costs more to give birth by cesarean section than to deliver vaginally), and to have control over scheduling (vaginal birth is unpredictable). However, among women who are given continuous emotional support from a trained companion, the C-section rate drops to 8%. Apparently, the support helps reduce some of the pain and anxiety that may disturb the process of labor.

The recovery time required after cesarean section is somewhat longer than for a vaginal delivery, but there is great individual variation (Andolsek, 1990). Cesarean section involves major surgery, and both the uterus and the abdominal wall must heal for recovery to be complete. With vaginal birth, the mother might have an *episiotomy* or sustain a laceration of the vagina during the birth process. These incisions are minor compared with the C-section incision.

episiotomy
a surgical incision made at the base of the vagina during childbirth to prevent tearing

Induced Birth

Sometimes the birth process is artificially induced or aided by the synthetic hormone pitocin. Such a birth is termed an *induced birth*. It is required if membranes have ruptured but labor has failed to begin, if the baby is overdue by more than two weeks, if the labor is prolonged or irregular, if the mother is beginning to tire, or if certain medical conditions (like hypertension or diabetes) exist. Pitocin speeds the activation process so that uterine contractions become forceful very soon and the whole birth process is accelerated. Induced labor is not without its risks. In 1979 pitocin was relabeled by the FDA for use only when medically necessary for the safety of the mother or the baby (Lieberman, 1990). Most often however, the mother's system spontaneously initiates labor. Considerable debate still exists as to what actually causes labor to begin, although the mother's uterus is thought to become more responsive to the natural oxytocin produced by the pituitary gland.

induced birth
an artificially initiated birth

Medication

The childbirth education movement of the 1960s and 1970s stressed drug-free deliveries. In the 1990s, that trend has been somewhat reversed. Pain-killing medication (analgesia) may be given to reduce the pain of labor. Analgesics are not given in labor until the cervix is dilated to 3 or 4 cm, so that the progress of labor is not slowed or stopped.

Analgesics are also not given if delivery is expected in an hour, so that the infant and mother may not become lethargic and less responsive due to the medication.

Unlike analgesics, regional anesthetics completely eliminate labor pain by preventing nervous system pain impulses from reaching the brain. Examples of obstetric anesthesia include spinal blocks, epidural anesthesia, and caudal blocks. (Figure 4–8) These procedures are becoming more commonly used since they are more effective in blocking pain than analgesics (C. L. Olson et al., 1991). One note of caution, however. There are no magic bullets. *All* regional anesthetics reach the fetal blood stream and consequently, the fetal brain within seconds or minutes of administration to the mother. Each drug carries its own specific risks (Sanders-Phillips et al., 1988).

regional anesthetics
a substance that produces the loss of physical sensation in certain body regions without the accompanying loss of consciousness

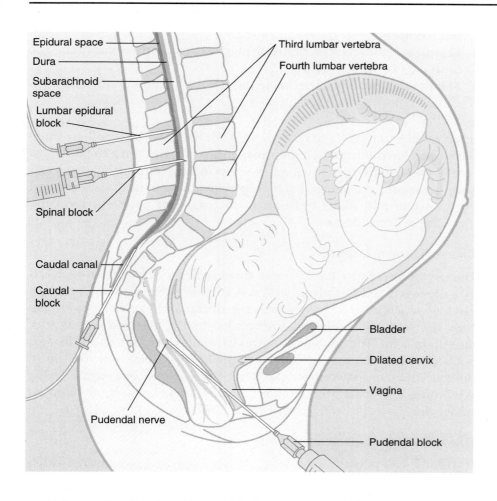

Epidural space
Dura
Subarachnoid space
Lumbar epidural block
Spinal block
Caudal canal
Caudal block
Pudendal nerve
Third lumbar vertebra
Fourth lumbar vertebra
Bladder
Dilated cervix
Vagina
Pudendal block

■ **Figure 4–8**

Common sites for the administration of regional anesthesia during labor and delivery. Lumbar, spinal and caudal blocks numb the woman in varying degrees from the waist down. A pudendal block accessed through the vagina numbs the perineum in preparation for the episiotomy.

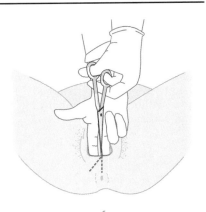

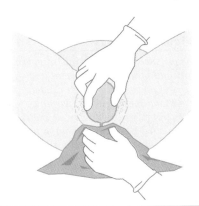

■ Figure 4–9

The episiotomy incision. It can be vertical or transverse.

■ Figure 4–10

By taking advantage of gravity, a birthing bar can shorten labor for the average birth.

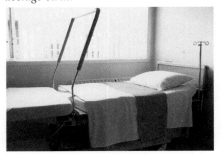

Episiotomy

An *episiotomy* is a surgical incision that extends the size of the vaginal opening. It is performed to avoid a tear when the baby is too large, when the vaginal tissue is unyielding, when there is fetal distress, when the mother is tiring, or when second stage progress is not being made (Lieberman, 1989). Episiotomy rates vary widely, ranging from 10% in some parts of the country and among some physicians to 75% in others. Because of the pain and numbness associated with healing, many women try to avoid episiotomy by:

1. Selecting a physician who is used to delivering without an episiotomy
2. Doing Kegel exercises (exercises that tone the muscles of the pelvic floor)
3. Practicing birth positions (like sitting or squatting) that may make birth easier
4. Learning how to override the "urge to push" that forces the baby out too soon
5. Learning techniques of perineal massage to prepare the tissue for birth
6. Maintaining healthy, stretchable tissue through good nutrition

Underwater Birth

In an attempt to lessen childbirth pain for the laboring mother, some physicians have encouraged their patients to give birth in a tub of warm water. These underwater deliveries are primarily experimental but can have successful outcomes if the baby's breathing reflex is suppressed by the water and if the birth attendant has clear access to the baby (Seaward & Sonnedecker, 1990).

Forceps/Vacuum Extraction

The use of forceps to aid babies in distress has virtually been replaced by a process called *vacuum extraction*. A suction cup placed on the baby's head is attached to a chain which the doctor pulls to help guide the baby out. If the vacuum pressure applied by the machine is too great, the cup falls off. The advantage of this procedure over the use of forceps is that forceps may tear or cut the vaginal wall if there is a tight fit in the birth canal or may bruise or cut the baby's scalp (Combs et al., 1990). A vacuum cup spares the mother but may cause bruising or bleeding under the baby's scalp (Hanigan et al., 1990).

Positioning the Mother During Birth

Currently, the majority of women in developed nations recline when they give birth. This convention exists not because it is the best position for the mother and child but because it provides the best view for the

■ ● ▲   CONCEPT SUMMARY

Labor and Delivery

● Physical events that may precede labor: lightening, Braxton-Hicks contractions, loss of mucous plug, maternal weight loss, feeling energetic

● Stages of labor
  – 1st stage—initiated by regular painful contractions that dilate the cervix to 4 inches (10 cm)
  – 2nd stage—(transition)—contractions which force the baby from the uterus—baby is born during this stage
  – 3rd stage—umbilical cord is severed and placenta and afterbirth are delivered; surgical repair to the mother if necessary

● Alternative to vaginal birth—birth by cesarean section

● The birth procedure may or may not include: induction by pitocin, pain-killing medication, an episiotomy, forceps/vacuum extraction, an obstetric chair or birthing bed.

---

doctor! When women who have given birth before get off their backs and use obstetric chairs or special motorized beds during childbirth, they significantly reduce the length of labor by augmenting the force of gravity, experience less perineal tearing, and improve blood flow to the baby by reducing pressure on a major abdominal vein (R. Olson et al., 1990). The chair was found to be much more comfortable than the traditional "stirrups". Mothers who give birth in obstetric chairs may be at some higher risk for blood loss, although more follow-up on this question is needed (Stewart & Spiby, 1989).

forceps
curved metal instruments designed to fit around the baby's head to assist with the birth; the use of forceps is largely outdated

vacuum extraction
helping the baby out of the birth canal by the use of suction device that fits on the baby's skull

● Evaluating the Newborn

Whatever the birth method, vaginal or surgical, it is urgent that the baby be evaluated immediately following delivery. Newborns can have trouble adapting to life on their own. To determine the baby's status rapidly and accurately, almost all hospitals use the scale known as the Apgar scoring system after its developer, pediatrician Dr. Virginia Apgar.

The Apgar Scoring System

One minute after delivery and again 5 minutes later, the birth attendant, delivery room nurse, or anesthesiologist rates each of five infant vital

Apgar scale
an assessment device used to evaluate the health-status of the just born baby

signs—heart rate, respiratory effort, muscle tone, reflex irritability, and color—on a scale from 0 to 2. These signs and their possible ratings make up the *Apgar scale* (Table 4–1). The Apgar score can total from 0 to 10 each time testing takes place. Babies with an Apgar score of 7–10 immediately after birth are in good condition. Ninety percent of all normal babies score within this range: they are breathing well, crying, pink in color, and active (Apgar & Beck, 1973). Babies who score between 4 and 6 need help breathing and might require supplemental oxygen. A newborn with a score of 0, 1, 2, or 3 is generally limp, unresponsive, pale, not breathing, and possibly without a heartbeat. Emergency procedures are initiated. It may take several minutes before an infant with one of these scores is ready to breathe alone.

Both the 1-minute and 5-minute Apgar scores are recorded in the hospital record. Consistently high scores indicate the baby has stabilized and is functioning well; improvement in the second score shows that intervention has paid off and the baby is in better condition. Consistently low Apgar scores or a significant drop in the second score indicates that additional care is needed. Apgar scores (especially the second) are related to infant survival, neurological status, and later performance on standardized tests. However, the Apgar score is not a good predictor of the child's later intelligence or health, since many other factors intervene after birth.

A more thorough examination of the newborn is conducted a few hours after birth. At that time, screening tests for specific medical disorders like sickle cell disease, PKU, and/or hypothyroidism will be conducted. Umbilical cord blood and blood gases will be analyzed as markers of fetal well-being. Other aspects of the baby's behavior (such as alertness, ability to quiet, hand–mouth activity, and responses to stress) will be assessed by the Brazelton Newborn Assessment Scale (BNAS)

■ **Table 4–1**   *The Apgar Scoring System*

SIGN	SCORE		
	0	1	2
Heart rate	Absent	Slow (less than 100 beats/minute)	Over 100
Respiratory effort	Absent	Slow, irregular	Good, crying
Muscle tone	Flaccid	Some flexion of extremities	Active motion
Reflex irritability	No response	Cry	Vigorous cry
Color	Blue, pale	Body pink, extremities blue	Completely pink

Source: Apgar, 1953.

devised by the renowned pediatrician Dr. T. Berry Brazelton in 1973. The BNAS may help familiarize parents with their infants (Tedder, 1991).

Birth Injury and Trauma

Fewer than 1% of otherwise healthy infants are injured or traumatized by the birth process. Some injuries have long-term consequences; others do not. The following subsections describe the most common problems among the small population of newborns that sustain them.

Skeletal Fractures

If the baby's shoulder becomes trapped during delivery, fractures of the baby's collarbone (clavicle) and upper arm bone (humerus) can occur (Carlan et al., 1991). Skull fractures may occur but other bones are rarely injured. When fractures are not associated with other injuries, the baby usually recovers well.

Brain Injury

Brain injury to the baby is usually associated with difficult or complicated labor involving a shorter than normal bony pelvis, breech delivery or other unusual fetal positions, early detachment of the placenta, constriction of the umbilical cord, and manipulation of the fetus by the attendant. Brain injured infants may be drowsy and pale, and may vomit, have convulsions and a weak cry, and fail to feed.

The outcome of brain injury is variable. Some infants do not survive; others recover but are mentally retarded and have assorted neurological and physical problems such as cerebral palsy (Freeman & Nelson, 1988). Fortunately, many of these babies improve with time.

cerebral palsy
damage to the brain before or during birth that results in lack of voluntary muscular control

Breathing Difficulties

Respiratory distress is a relatively common complication of birth (see the discussion of respiratory distress syndrome in the following section on Prematurity). Postmature infants, anxious to begin life on their own, may begin to breathe in the womb during labor. When these babies inhale meconium or the tarry fetal waste material in the amniotic fluid, they develop *meconium aspiration syndrome,* a condition that may cause infection and interfere with breathing by coating the lungs (Seo et al., 1990). Current techniques are successful in clearing the baby's lungs 96% of the time (Wiswell, 1990).

respiratory distress/respiratory distress syndrome (RDS)
breathing complications experienced by newborns

meconium aspiration syndrome
a collection of symptoms associated with the fetus's inhalation of meconium present in the amniotic fluid at birth

Jaundice

About 50% of all full-term newborns have some degree of *jaundice,* usually on the third or fourth day of life (P. Rosenthal et al., 1989). Jaundice, caused by an accumulation of a substance called bilirubin due to liver

jaundice
a condition caused by the build up of bilirubin in the baby's bloodstream

---

■ ●▲　　CONCEPT SUMMARY

The Newborn Will be Evaluated:

- by the APGAR scoring system at 1 minute and then 5 minutes after birth
- for fractures
- for brain injury
- for breathing difficulties
- for signs of jaundice that may appear in 3–4 days
- for birthmarks
- on length, weight, and head circumference
- for birth status (premature, full-term, SGA, LGA, or postmature)
- by testing their reflexes
- by noting their sex
- for any other irregularities or difficulties

---

immaturity, may make the skin and the whites of the eyes look yellow. If the level of bilirubin is not controlled, it can accumulate in the brain tissue and cause permanent damage (Scheidt et al., 1991). Neonatal jaundice is more common, prolonged, and severe in premature infants. Controlled exposure to fluorescent light, or in severe cases drugs or blood transfusion, can help rid the infant's system of excess bilirubin.

Circumcision

circumcision
the surgical removal of the foreskin of the penis

Parents of a male child must decide whether or not to have their baby circumcised. Circumcision is the surgical removal of the foreskin of the penis. Usually performed on the second or third day after birth, the procedure usually involves cutting and requires that the infant be restrained. Until recently most physicians felt that newborns felt little if any pain and if they did, they wouldn't remember it anyway. Now a local anesthetic like lidocaine is used during the procedure (Fontaine & Toffler, 1991).

The circumcision rate among newborn males in the United States has fallen from more than 80% in 1982 to near 50% in 1989. Two factors are primarily responsible. First, with the possible exception of preventing urinary tract infections and penile cancer in men with poor hygiene habits, the American Academy of Pediatrics (1989) contends that there is no medical advantage to routine circumcision. Contrary to popular belief, cleaning the uncircumcised penis is not difficult, painful, or time consuming. When a boy is 4 years old, he can be taught to pull back the foreskin himself. Training in good hygiene takes less time than instruction in thorough tooth brushing (E. Wallerstein, 1980). Second, since 1987 medical insurers like Community Mutual (formerly Blue Cross and Blue Shield) will no longer pay for a surgery that they now consider to be primarily cosmetic. While Moslems and Jews will continue to practice circumcision as a religious rite, the pros and cons of circumcision for nonreligious reasons should be carefully considered.

● Characteristics of the Newborn

General Appearance

The newborn is a compact creature with a disproportionately large head, representing one-quarter of total body size. The arms, legs, and neck are short, the hands and feet appear to be perfect miniatures, and the shoulders seem quite narrow. The nose is flat and the chin is small, presumably to make nursing easier.

First-time parents should be warned that their babies might not be beautiful right after birth (Figure 4–11). Being squeezed through a narrow passageway and pounded by contractions that exert as much as 30 pounds of force is no picnic. Newborns are often bruised, scraped, and swollen. Their heads may be temporarily molded or misshapen, since their skulls have to adapt to the size and shape of the mother's pelvis (Figure 4–12). Babies delivered by cesarean section often look less battered, but they must cope with anesthesia and special procedures.

molded head
a newborn head that is temporarily misshapen due to pressures on the fetal skull during birth

The parents may not automatically recognize the baby as their own, and might feel disappointed at their lack of initial "family feeling." But there is rarely any obvious family resemblance between newborns and their families. In fact, new babies look more like each other than they look like members of their own families. As the infant recovers from the birth process and begins to mature, however, her distinct appearance as an individual becomes apparent.

The Skin

The skin of the newborn is usually covered by a white creamy substance called vernix. The *vernix* is composed of dead skin, oil from the oil-bearing glands of the skin, and lanugo. Vernix forms between the 25th and 28th gestational week to protect the skin and its developing glands and sensory cells. It is not necessary to remove the vernix after birth, for the substance is absorbed by the newborn's skin in the first 24 hours

vernix
a creamy white protective substance that covers some of the skin surface of newborn babies

lanugo
temporary downy hair found on the shoulders, forehead, and neck of some newborns

■ Figure 4–11

A normal newborn.

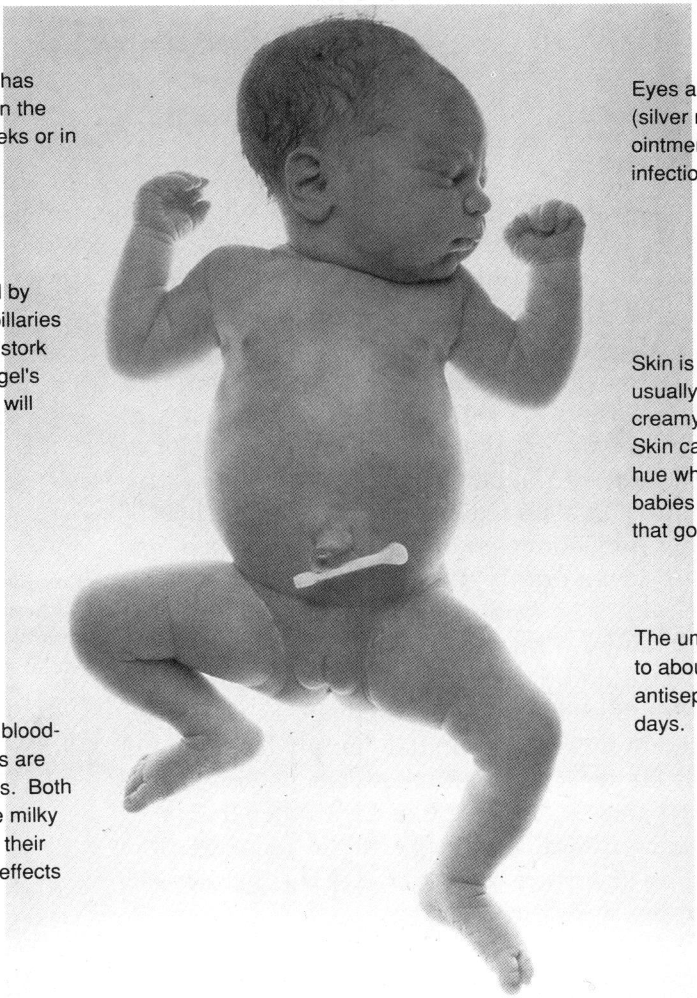

Headfirst vaginal delivery causes temporary head molding. The forehead is flattened and slopes toward a rounded apex at the back of the head. The scalp may be somewhat swollen or have ridges. These changes disappear in a few days.

One in every two babies has tiny, yellow-white cysts on the nose, forehead, and cheeks or in the mouth.

Eyes are treated with medication (silver nitrate or an antibiotic ointment) to prevent gonococcal infection.

Dull pink patches caused by localized dilated skin capillaries may occur on the neck ("stork bite"), mid-forehead ("angel's kiss"), or eyelids. These will fade with age.

Skin is bright pink or red and usually covered by a white creamy substance called vernix. Skin can darken to a purplish hue when the baby cries. Many babies will have red blotches that go away in a few days.

The umbilical cord is shortened to about an inch and treated with antiseptic. It will fall off in 7-10 days.

Thick, white (sometimes blood-tinged) vaginal secretions are common in female babies. Both sexes may secrete some milky fluid ("witch's milk") from their brests. These hormonal effects may last several days.

Footprints and/or fingerprints may be taken. The baby is usually weighed and measured.

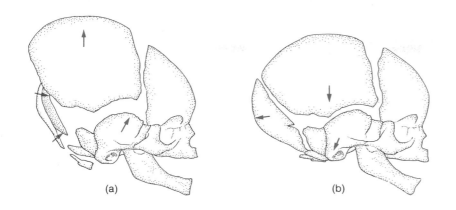

(a)   (b)

■ **Figure 4–12**

(a) Molding of the bones of the baby's head during passage through the birth canal. (b) By the third day following birth, the bones return to their normal position.

of life, providing beneficial lubrication (J. R. Scott et al., 1990). Without vernix, the newborn's skin is pale and thin. Blood in the vessels close to the surface gives the infant's skin a pinkish cast (this is true even in the case of babies who will be darkly pigmented later on).

About 40% of all babies have some sort of birthmark, or hemangioma, on their skin. The most common types are strawberry marks and port-wine stains. *Strawberry marks* are patches of red, raised tissue caused by spontaneous overgrowth of blood vessels in a particular area. Strawberry marks are twice as common in girls as in boys and occur in about 3% of all live births. They often grow rapidly during the first 6 months of life (though most never get larger than 2 inches in diameter), stop enlarging thereafter, and usually disappear without treatment. Seventy percent are completely gone by age 7 (Whaley & Wong, 1988).

Port-wine stains, like the one on Mikhail Gorbachev's head, are much more common than strawberry marks. This birthmark is flat, red or purplish in color, and made up of enlarged or malformed skin-surface blood vessels. Such a mark may be less than 1 inch in diameter or large enough to cover an arm, a shoulder, or part of the face. Unlike other birthmarks, port-wine stains seldom disappear with age. Tunable laser treatment of port-wine stain hemangiomas erases the stain completely in about six sessions without disfiguring scars (Begley & Robins, 1989).

hemangioma (birthmark)
patches of discolored skin caused by the overaccumulation of blood vessels in the skin's surface

The External Genitals

The birth attendant identifies the baby's sex by examining its genitals. In both males and females, genitals and breast tissue may be enlarged, because high levels of the female hormone estrogen are secreted by the placenta and absorbed by the baby prior to birth. Vaginal secretions (sometimes blood-tinged) are common in female babies and are no cause for alarm. Both females and males may secrete some fluid from their breasts.

A Closer Look

A Chinese Horoscope

The Chinese believe that the year of a person's birth affects their personality and compatibility with others. All persons born during that year are believed to be similarly affected. The years, Rat, Ox, Tiger, and so on, follow 12-year cycles. The following was compiled by Toy Len Chang. See how well your birth year horoscope matches your own personality.

RAT   Years: 1900–1912–1924–1936–1948–
             1960–1972–1984–1996

             Resourceful, successful, charming,
             ambitious
             Quick to anger, fussy, pennypinching,
             but generous to those loved, tends
             to make friendships short
             + Good for matrimony with dragon,
             monkey, or ox year people
             – Avoid mating with horse year
             people

OX   Years: 1901–1913–1925–1937–1949–
             1961–1973–1985–1997

             Hardworking, patient, mentally alert,
             dexterous, soft spoken
             Inspires confidence in others
             Stubborn, hot-tempered, hates failures
             + Good for matrimony with snake,
             cock, or rat year people
             – Avoid mating with horse, dog, or
             ram year people

TIGER   Years: 1902–1914–1926–1938–1950–
             1962–1974–1986–1998

             Courageous, dignified, sympathetic,
             deep thinker, sensitive
             Cannot make up mind quickly, short
             tempered, selfish

             + Good for matrimony with horse,
             dragon, or dog year people
             – Avoid mating with snake or
             monkey year people

RABBIT   Years: 1903–1915–1927–1939–1951–
             1963–1975–1987–1999

             Financially lucky, born gambler,
             talented, generally liked
             Sheds tears easily, somewhat pedantic,
             timid, prone to gossip.
             + Good for matrimony with ram,
             boar, or dog year people
             – Avoid mating with cock, rat, or
             dragon year people

DRAGON   Years: 1904–1916–1928–1940–1952–
             1964–1976–1988–2000

             Aggressive, brave, born leader,
             sensitive, energetic, most eccentric
             of the cycle
             Excitable, short tempered, verbose,
             healthy
             + Good for matrimony with rat,
             snake, monkey, or cock year people
             – Avoid mating with ox, rabbit, or
             dog year people

SNAKE   Years: 1905–1917–1929–1941–1953–
             1965–1977–1989–2001

             Attractive, possesses much wisdom,
             compassionate, financially fortunate
             Tends to be vain, hates to fail, prefers
             to rely on own judgment
             + Good for matrimony with ox, cock,
             or rat year people
             – Avoid mating with monkey, tiger,
             or boar year people

HORSE   Years: 1906–1918–1930–1942–1954–1966–1978–1990–2002

Inventive, big thinker, popular, usually successful, cheerful

Impatient, strong-willed, cannot stick to project and follow thru

+ Good for matrimony with tiger, dog, or ram year people

− Avoid mating with ox, rabbit, or rat year people

RAM   Years: 1907–1919–1931–1943–1955–1967–1979–1991–2003

Wise, gentle, talented in the arts, deeply religious, has pity for unfortunate ones

Shy, pessimistic, must be guided

+ Good for matrimony with rabbit, boar, or horse year people

− Avoid mating with rat, ox or dog year people

MONKEY   Years: 1908–1920–1932–1944–1956–1968–1980–1992–2004

Skillful with money, extremely active, cheerful, good memory. Can succeed in life, popular

Hot-blooded, talkative, impatient, showy, erratic

+ Good for matrimony with rat or dragon year people

− Avoid mating with snake, boar, or tiger year people

COCK   Years: 1909–1921–1933–1945–1957–1969–1981–1993–2005

Capable, deep thinker, brave, idealistic, devoted to work

Often tactless, selfish, takes on more than can accomplish, loner

+ Good for matrimony with ox, snake, or dragon year people

− Avoid mating with rat, cock, or rabbit year people

DOG   Years: 1910–1922–1934–1946–1958–1970–1982–1994–2006

Honest, loyal, chivalrous, devoted with deep sense of duty, good in business

Stubborn, critical, a bit selfish, cares little for social life

+ Good for matrimony with horse, tiger, or rabbit year people

− Avoid mating with ox, cock, or ram year people

BOAR   Years: 1911–1923–1935–1947–1959–1971–1983–1995–2007

Loyal, affectionate, kind, courageous, honest, retains friendships for life, shy

Quick-tempered, impulsive, dogmatic, single-minded

+ Good for matrimony with rabbit or ram year people

− Avoid mating with monkey, boar, or snake year people

Size

The average American newborn weighs 7 to 7.5 pounds and measures between 19 and 21 inches long. Newborn males are usually longer and heavier than females, but there is great individual variation. Low birth weight (due to SGA or prematurity) is the singlemost important determinant of the baby's survival and healthy development.

Head circumference averages 35 centimeters among newborns and is carefully monitored through the first 2 years of life. Deviations in head circumference can alert the medical staff to potential developmental problems.

head circumference
the distance around the head at the eyebrows

intrauterine growth retardation
see growth retardation

[handwritten: less than 5.5 lbs]

Two size-related terms applied to newborns are *small for gestational age (SGA)* and *large for gestational age (LGA)*. (*Small for date* and *intrauterine growth retardation* are synonyms for SGA). An SGA baby is any infant who is below the third percentile for weight, length, and head circumference (97% of all babies have height, weight, and head measurements larger than the SGA baby). The incidence of SGA in the United States is about 7%. Poor maternal weight gain, eclampsia, and smoking are the most important risk factors (Tenovuo et al., 1988). These babies seldom weigh more than 2500 grams (5.5 pounds) at birth and may be at risk for a variety of problems (Martorell, 1989). Interestingly, SGA babies don't differ from term babies in temperament or personality (Riese, 1988).

The infant who is large for gestational age is one born at term who weighs more than 3800 grams (8.3 pounds). Oversized infants are at increased risk for trauma or injury during vaginal delivery. Maternal diabetes, Rh incompatibility, and some fetal heart problems are associated with excessive birth weight. The largest surviving infant was born on May 24, 1982, to Mrs. Christina Samane of South Africa. The baby weighed 22 pounds and 8 ounces at birth, more than three times as much as an average newborn! (*The Guiness Book*, 1989).

A normal newborn loses 5–10% of its birth weight owing to loss of fluid and lack of nourishment during the birth process. Not only plump infants lose weight; those who can least afford it do, too. Weight loss is often more significant in the smaller infant because it accounts for a greater percentage of total body weight. With adequate care, however, infants are back to birth weight in 8 to 10 days.

Timing of the Birth

Prematurity

premature (preterm)
a baby born who has developed for less than 37 gestational weeks and weighs less than 5½ lbs.

An infant's weight may be appropriate for the gestational age but the baby may be born too soon. A premature, or preterm, infant is one who weighs less than 2500 grams (5 pounds 8 ounces) and has developed in utero for fewer than 37 weeks. Six to twelve percent of all infants born in the United States and 90% of all low birth weight infants are premature (Andolsek, 1990). A disproportionately large number of low birth weight babies are born to black women (Murray and Bernfield, 1988). The likelihood of complications and infant mortality is directly related to the baby's birth weight: the more the baby weighs at birth, the greater the chances for survival and uncomplicated growth. More than half of the children who weigh under 2.2 pounds (1000 grams) at birth do not survive and those who do are likely to sustain permanent physical and cognitive disabilities (Koops et al., 1982; Mazur et al., 1988).

Premature babies may encounter problems because they are not ready for life on their own. The most common complication of prematurity is

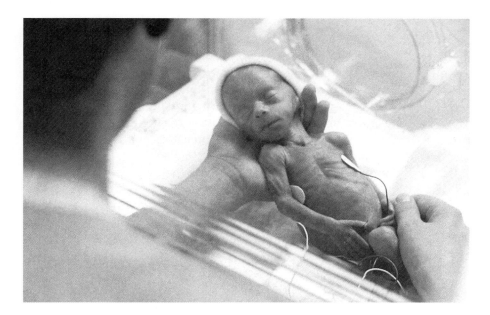

A premature baby. The stocking cap helps keep its head warm.

hyaline membrane disease, or *respiratory distress syndrome (RDS)*, due to lungs which aren't efficient in transferring oxygen to the baby's bloodstream. Fourteen percent of premature infants are affected by this condition (Hack et al., 1989). Drugs can be given to the mother to help mature the baby's lungs before birth and therefore prevent respiratory problems. After birth, infants can be given a surfactant supplement (surfactant keeps the baby's lungs inflated). Bovine surfactant replacement therapy helps babies breathe on their own faster and reduces the incidence of chronic lung disease (M. S. Dunn et al., 1991).

In an effort to facilitate breathing, massive amounts of oxygen were pumped into the incubators of premature babies in the 1940s and 1950s. The result was not helpful but disastrous—many of these babies were going home blind after developing a condition called retinopathy of prematurity (ROP). Their retinas were just too immature to cope with the high levels of raw oxygen. ROP is still with us and a new cause is suspected—high intensity hospital lights. Doctors know that light waves can damage the retina (that is why baby's eyes are shielded before they are placed under the powerful lamps used to treat jaundice). Intensive care nursery lights are 5–10 times brighter than they were 30 years ago and infants are exposed to them 24 hours a day. The work of Penny Glass (1990) suggests that the incidence of ROP can be decreased by 20% if premature babies wear eyeshades or if their incubators are shaded by light filters.

Another relatively common complication of prematurity is interventricular hemorrhage, or the accumulation of blood in the "spaces," or ventricles, of the brain (Korones, 1981). This happens because the pre-

retinopathy of prematurity (ROP) permanent damage to the immature retina of the newborn eye by prolonged exposure to intense light or oxygen

interventricular hemorrhage bleeding into the spaces or the ventricles of the brain

■ **Figure 4–14**

David, age 4, lost his vision to retinopathy of prematurity (ROP).

mature baby's blood vessels are thin and may collapse or break. X rays of the fetal head can alert the medical staff to this sort of blood accumulation. Premature infants are also more vulnerable to infection (especially pneumonia) than full-term infants and are less able to regulate their own body temperature. The reflexes that help them survive, like sucking, coughing, swallowing, spitting up and sneezing, are weak and caregivers must be alert to the real possibility of choking or suffocation. Giving premature babies pacifiers to suck on can strengthen the sucking response and help them gain weight faster (Hack et al., 1989).

Clearly, prematurity should be avoided whenever possible. Drugs called tocolytics are available that can halt premature labor if it is detected soon enough and allow babies to continue growing. The following conditions are associated with premature birth (Mason, 1986), and specific suggestions for prevention are given.

Cause

1. Chronic or severe illness in the mother such as high blood pressure, heart or liver disease, hepatitis, diabetes, viral or bacterial infections and breathing problems.

2. Younger (under 18) and older (over 40) mothers are at risk. The babies of teenage mothers are particularly vulnerable to prematurity.

3. Poor nutrition and dehydration.

4. Twins or multiple fetuses put more pressure on the cervix than a single baby does.

Prevention

1. Specific disease may not be preventable but 1 hour of rest 3 times a day can significantly reduce high blood pressure (Hoble, 1982).

2. Plan pregnancy to take place between age 20 and 35.

3. Fasting or even a reduced diet can provoke uterine contractions. This association was discovered by accident when it was observed that pregnant Jewish women close to term who observe the traditional Yom Kippur day of fasting are more likely to go into labor the next day than those who had not fasted (the "Yom Kippur Syndrome", Ogburn & Brenner, 1981).

4. Rest; suture cervix.

5. High levels of physical stress (especially if it is prolonged).
6. High levels of emotional stress (especially if it is prolonged).

5. Stop lifting, standing for prolonged periods of time, etc.
6. Keep drastic change to a minimum (like moving). Transfer out of a stressful job or temporarily stop working.

7. Structural problems with the uterus or cervix. (A cervix that does not close completely is called an *incompetent cervix*.)
8. Bleeding after 12 weeks gestation.
9. Alcohol use.
10. Cigarette smoking.
11. Intercourse without condoms.

7. Surgically close cervix.

8. Avoid physical/emotional stress.
9. Avoid alcohol completely.
10. Don't smoke.
11. The semen contains a hormone identified as one of the possible stimulants of the onset of labor. Use latex condoms.

12. Intercourse that jars the cervix.
13. Poor prenatal care.

14. Fatigue.

15. Urinary tract infection (UTI).

12. Be gentle. Avoid deep penetration. Try "outercourse."
13. Have regular medical checkups while pregnant.
14. Decrease activities that lead to fatigue (even exercise, housework, etc.).
15. Report the first sign of possible infection (frequent or burning urination). Urinary tract bacteria release an enzyme important in the manufacture of one of three substances that stimulate uterine contractions. UTI can be safely treated with antibiotics.

16. Previous premature births.

17. Previous miscarriages.

16. Monitor subsequent pregnancies carefully.
17. Monitor subsequent pregnancies carefully.

Sometimes what seems to be prematurity is solely the result of a miscalculated due date. Premature inducement of labor or cesarean section based on wrong due dates are themselves causes of prematurity. But the spontaneous onset of premature labor can be provoked by many of the same factors implicated in SGA births. In about half of the cases, however, the cause of prematurity is not known (Andolsek, 1990).

Parents of premature babies are sometimes shocked by the appearance of their offspring. Compared with full-term babies, the preterm infant looks sickly and frail (Figure 4–13). The skin may be loose and sagging, for there may not have been time for layers of insulating fat to form before birth. The baby might also be generously coated with downy (sometimes pigmented) hair called *lanugo* on the face, neck, and shoulders. Lanugo is less abundant on the full-term infant, but in either case, it is shed within 2 weeks after birth. If the baby is a boy, his testicles may not have descended into the scrotum yet, a condition that usually corrects itself within a few weeks or months (Crooks & Baur, 1990).

Premature babies are often whisked out of the delivery room for prompt care as anxious parents look on. When the parents do have a chance to glimpse at their baby, they might find her literally covered with monitoring devices and specialized equipment. This can be a very unsettling sight to the parents; few things are more worrisome than having a baby in distress. And, since hospitals routinely keep premature babies in intensive care until they reach a certain body weight, the parents usually have to go home to an empty nursery after the birth—not an easy thing to do and not at all what they had expected.

Sometimes it's even hard to love premature babies at first because they come early and catch everyone by surprise. Parents and relatives of premature infants are advised to redirect into positive action the energy they might be inclined to use to worry, cry, or feel depressed or resentful—specifically, by spending as much time in the hospital as possible with the baby. Many hospital nurseries encourage parents to visit any time of the day or night and to stay as long as they wish. Parents of premature infants should realize that in addition to needing expert medical attention, their infants need to be held, cuddled, rocked, touched, and talked to. Auditory and touch stimulation are important to the growth and well-being of the premature infant. The more stimulation preterm babies have, the stronger and healthier they become, especially if such attention is actively continued at home (Bower, 1985). Hospitals even have little waterbeds and maternal heartbeat simulators for preemies to help recreate the womb environment (Barnard & Bee, 1983). Visits have a positive effect on parents, too. Parents will come to know their infant, they'll note progress and observe procedures, and they'll be heartened by the care and concern of the medical staff.

In general, once babies are released from the hospital, their progress is directly related to the overall quality of their environment. Premature babies who are well-nourished, well-loved, and have parents who are stable, drug-free, and responsible have the best prognosis (Kopp, 1983).

In Touch

PARENT CARE
University of Utah
50 North Medical Drive
Room 2A210
Salt Lake City, UT 84132

Support for parents caring for high
  risk infants

PARENT CARE, INC
101 1/2 South Union
Alexandria, VA 22314

Support for families with newborns in
  intensive care

MARCH OF DIMES BIRTH
  DEFECTS FOUNDATION
Community Services
1275 Mamaroneck Ave.
White Plains, NY 10605
914-997-4464

Information on infant health and
  congenital conditions

► ►　　I S S U E　　◄ ◄

How Much Is This Tiny Life Worth?

In an age of escalating medical costs and dramatic advances in medical technology, Americans find themselves caught in an ironic dilemma. Modern medicine can save thousands of babies who would have succumbed to cancers, diseased organs, or the complications of prematurity, but the American health system cannot afford to pay the bill. With only so much money to go around, some touchy questions need to be posed: Who will be saved among those who need expensive treatment, and How much are we willing to spend?

Some would say: "Spend money on health care as long as you save a life." Others might counter that the saved child should be able to give something back to society. If the infant rescued by medical technology would be severely limited, the money might be better spent elsewhere.

Consider this case: Erik weighed 1¾ pounds at birth, as much as seven sticks of butter. Statistics on extremely low birthweight babies show that a substantial percentage are mentally retarded and/or physically handicapped. Erik is having trouble breathing. Should the state pay Erik's medical costs if his parents can't? COST: $200,000.

And this: Evan's delivery was uncomplicated but he was born addicted to cocaine because of his mother's habit. He is going to need intensive care just to get through drug withdrawal. He is also going to need an immediate liver transplant. COST: $200,000.

If only one could survive, who's the best risk? Erik or Evan?

Parents want doctors to do everything within their power—all they want to be able to do is bring their baby home and then to live life one day at a time. Maybe neither child should receive heroic treatment because of the real possibility of long-term health problems that will cost taxpayers literally millions. In 1987 the state of Oregon prioritized its medical services for those without health insurance. At the top of its list are acute illnesses, immunizations, cataract surgery, pregnancy testing, and prenatal care. At the bottom are liver, heart, bone marrow, and pancreas transplants and cosmetic surgery (D. Robinson, 1989). The reasoning goes something like this: Why spend $200,000 on *one* child on the *chance* the child may recover when you can, say, inoculate *40,000* kids against measles and *know* they will be protected. These are tough choices.

It ends up that *both* Erik and Evan beat the odds. Both are healthy and strong. Both are at grade level in school and both are reasonably well adjusted. If there's any reminder of their difficult beginnings, it's that both boys are a little shorter than their peers. "That's OK," quipped Evan when asked about his size. "I'm faster than all them guys and cuter, too. Besides, a lot of good people are a little on the small side."

A lot, indeed. It's difficult to make rational decisions about rationing medical care.

Postmaturity

Some infants seem reluctant to leave the womb (perhaps they have heard about our air pollution or the rising national debt!) If the birth weight is over 3800 grams and the gestational age is greater than 42 weeks, the infant is considered *postmature*. Some risks of postmaturity

postmaturity
an infant born weighing more than 3800 grams and more than 2 weeks past due

include an increased likelihood of fetal injury during vaginal delivery owing to the larger than average size, dehydration, and complications related to reduced placental function (McLean et al., 1991).

● Adapting to Life Outside the Womb

Dramatic changes take place within the body of the newborn to enable him to survive on his own. The baby's lungs must begin to breathe air efficiently, since oxygen no longer circulates to him through the blood of the umbilical cord. And the baby's blood must circulate to the lungs for the first time to pick up needed oxygen. Also, the gastrointestinal system must prepare to accept nutrition from the mouth rather than from the umbilical cord. Digestive enzymes begin to be manufactured to break down food into usable products, and waste must be channeled out of the body, since the umbilical cord is no longer present to do the job. The first waste material evacuated from the large intestine of the newborn is *meconium,* the tarry, greenish-black substance that accumulates before birth. Meconium is composed of swallowed amniotic fluid, mucous, cell by-products, bile, and intestinal secretions. After a few days, when the meconium has been completely eliminated, the newborn's stools take on their more characteristic appearance.

Part of the shock of birth for the newborn includes a sudden and dramatic change in body temperature. The temperature of the amniotic fluid in the fetal environment is at least 20 degrees higher than that of most delivery rooms, which are cooled for the comfort of the staff. With the help of heat lamps, blankets, clothing, and incubators, full-term babies can regulate their own body temperature. But premature and SGA babies have particular difficulty regulating body heat, since they usually lack the insulating fat that helps generate and maintain body weight (J. R. Scott et al., 1990).

In his book, *Birth without Violence (1975),* Dr. Frederick Leboyer, a French physician, has suggested that shock to the newborn can be minimized by dimming delivery room lights, raising room temperatures, speaking in hushed tones, allowing the birth to proceed at its own pace, and immersing the newborn in a warm bath (Figure 4–15). Babies born under such circumstances breathe well, cry less, and seem more alert and attentive than babies born under more traditional circumstances. No significant long-term benefits of these gentle birth procedures have been verified, however (Maziade et al., 1986).

In addition to minimizing temperature loss and approximating the fluid environment of the womb, the warm bath that Leboyer recommends is intended to reduce the shock of gravity's pull that the baby feels for the first time at birth. Fetal movement is assisted by the weightless buoyancy provided by the amniotic fluid. But outside the womb, the infant must struggle with gravity plus his own neuromuscular immaturity, so movement becomes more difficult and unpredictable.

gentle birth procedures (Leboyer method)
a birth designed to accommodate the newborn's needs rather than the needs of the medical staff (i.e., higher room temperature, no harsh lighting, etc.)

■ **Figure 4–15**

The Leboyer bathing procedure.

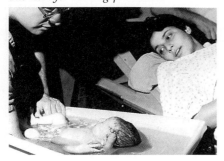

■ ●▲   CONCEPT SUMMARY

Adaptations Baby Must Make After Birth

Before Birth	After Birth
Oxygen circulated through bloodstream via the umbilical cord	Baby's lungs must provide CO_2/O_2 exchange
Nutrients were circulated to the baby through the bloodstream via the umbilical cord	Nutrients must be ingested by the baby and processed by the digestive tract
Some waste products circulated out of the baby's body via the umbilical cord; others just accumulated in the bladder and bowel	Baby's intestinal tract needs to channel waste out of the body
Mother's body and amniotic fluid kept the baby's body temperature stable	With the help of the environment, the baby regulates his own body temperature

What Can The Baby Do?

Reflexes: The Foundations of Behavior

The behavior of the newborn is based on reflexes—inborn involuntary behaviors controlled by the spinal cord and midbrain. The normal full-term newborn can display more than 70 reflex behaviors. Some reflexes have survival value; the ability to suck, blink, breathe, root, sneeze, cough, yawn, swallow, spit up, and withdraw from a painful object are examples. In evaluating some of the other reflexes of newborns, we can gain important information about the maturity and function of the newborn's neuromuscular system. With regard to many reflexes, their absence indicates more about development than their presence.

Several reflexes appear as early as the eighth or ninth gestational week, while others develop between that time and the time of birth. Thus, motor behavior at birth is basically a continuation of prenatal activity. All the reflexes present at birth can best be elicited after the 2nd day of life when the infant is rested. Infants who are hungry, tired, overstimulated, or uncomfortable may not respond in the expected manner. Behavioral state also influences the infant's responsiveness (Parmelee & Sigman, 1983). Because they are developmentally younger, premature infants both develop and lose these reflexes later than term babies. The major reflexes present at birth are discussed in Table 4–2.

■ **Figure 4–16**

The rooting reflex. When the baby's cheek is stroked, the head turns in the direction of the stimulation.

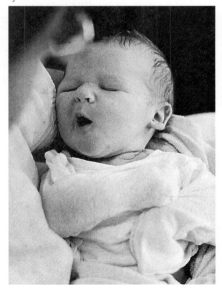

Know 2

■ Table 4–2 ✱ *Newborn Reflexes*

NAME	DESCRIPTION	FIRST APPEARS (GESTATIONAL WEEK)	CLINICAL SIGNIFICANCE
Asymmetrical tonic neck reflex	Fencing position	24th–28th	Replaced by symmetrical positioning of both sides of body
Babinski	Big toe is flexed and toes fan when sole is stroked	16th–24th	Used in diagnosing maturity of neuromuscular system
Crossed-extensor	When on its back, with one leg extended and that foot stimulated, baby will extend and withdraw other leg	24th	Absence indicates spinal cord or peripheral nerve damage
Deep tendon	Action of the tendon of some muscle groups	birth	Diagnoses motor disturbance and maturity of nervous system
Galant's	Baby flexes trunk toward stimulation	24th	Spinal cord function
Moro	Similar to startle reflex	28th	Absence associated with mental retardation, brain damage, and certain fractures
Neck-righting	Body orients in same direction as the head	34th–36th	Diagnosis of prematurity vs. SGA status
Placing reaction	When held upright and top of foot is stimulated, infant flexes knee to place foot on top of perceived surface	36th	Absence indicates spinal cord injury
Plantar grasp	Toes are flexed when sole of foot is pressed	16th–24th	Absence suggests spinal cord injury
Positive supportive	Attempts to support weight with legs when held upright and feet are pressed against a solid surface	32th–36th	Persistant absence indicates motor dysfunction in lower limbs
Stepping	Infant "walks" when supported and feet are placed on solid surface	34th	Absence associated with neuromuscular complications
Tonic-labyrinthine	Infant extends legs when placed on back and flexes legs when placed on stomach	unclear	Persistant absence is associated with cerebral palsy
Traction	Arms and trunk flex when pulled to sitting position	32nd–36th	Absence signals central nervous system damage
Withdrawal	Hip, knee, and ankle are flexed when sole of foot is stimulated	unclear	Absence means nerve damage

✱ **reflexes**
automatic, inborn behaviors that generally have survival value

Behavioral States

In addition to reflexes, the other basic behaviors, or states, are sleeping, drowsiness, alertness, and crying. P. H. Wolff first described the states of the newborn in 1959. He outlined seven descriptive categories: regular sleep, irregular sleep, periodic sleep, drowsiness, alert activity, waking activity, and crying. More recently Prechtl (1974) consolidated

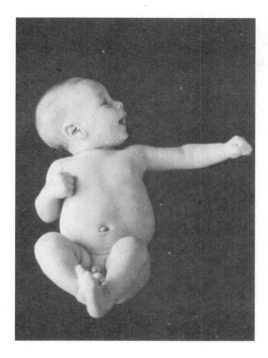 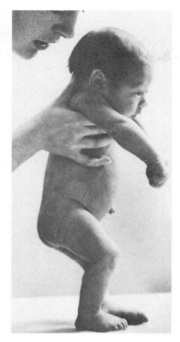 

■ **Figure 4–17**

(left) The asymmetrical tonic-neck reflex (ATNR) or "fencing position." (center) The positive supporting reaction. (right) The Moro reflex.

these original categories into six stages, each differentiated by a distinct mode of brain activity (Table 4–3).

The *behavioral state,* or orientation of the newborn, is a critical consideration in infant behavior for three reasons. First, the baby responds to stimuli differently in different states. Second, observing infant states over a period of time gives some indication of the pattern and organization of newborn behavior. And third, the behavioral state has important implications for infant/caregiver interactions. By coming to understand their infant's behavioral states, parents can better time feedings, respond to vocalizations and startles, and adjust other parenting behavior to facilitate interaction (Whaley & Wong, 1988).

Most infants are alert in the first few hours following birth. Babies who have gestated longer are more visually alert, less irritable, and more likely to display less rather than more large-muscle activity when being washed or diapered (Ricciuti & Breitmayer, 1988). During the first 3 days of life, state fluctuates significantly and rapidly. This 3-day pattern is different from anything that happens prenatally or at any time after 3 days of age. Apparently, the newborn is responding to the birth process and adapting to life outside the womb. State becomes stabilized in the 4th day after birth.

Although newborns spend more of their time asleep, state 3—the quiet-alert state—is the optimal period for reciprocal parent/child interactions. In this state the infant visually scans the environment and is more responsive to external stimuli than when asleep, crying, or

behavioral states
the sleep-wake orientation of the newborn

■ **Table 4–3** *Newborn Behavioral States*

STATE	DURATION PER DAY	IMPLICATIONS FOR PARENTING
Quiet sleep Closed eyes Regular breathing No movement (some sudden body jerks)	4/5 hours 20–30 minutes per sleep cycle	External stimuli do not wake infant
Active/Irregular sleep Closed eyes Irregular breathing Slight muscular twitching	12–15 hours 20–45 minutes per sleep cycle	May be more sensitive to external stimuli Periodic groaning or crying is usual; not a sign of pain or discomfort
Drowsiness Eyes may be open Irregular breathing Active body movements	Variable	Most stimuli arouse infant Pick infant up rather than leave in crib
Active awake/alert Responds to the environment Active body movements Stares at close-range objects	2–3 hours	Satisfy infant's needs for food, comfort, stimulation Place objects 8–10 inches from infant's view
Fussing/crying Eyes open or closed May begin with whimpering and slight body movement Progresses to strong, angry cry and thrashing of extremities	Variable	Remove intense external stimuli Rock or swaddle to decrease crying

drowsy. Caregivers need to act quickly, however, since this state is, on the average, the shortest in duration.

The newborn is awake and active in stage 6, kicking, waving, and squirming. Babies are interesting to observe in this state but difficult to interact with, because their movement interferes with their ability to sustain attention. When babies are drowsy, fussy, or in a transitional stage, not even food or play is successful in attracting their attention. Infants can be comforted by being rocked (fast tempo is *not* better than slow), sucking on a pacifier, being wrapped snugly (swaddled), being walked, listening to a continuous, rhythmic sound (like a heartbeat, music, or the like), or being taken for a ride in the car (in their carseat). Crying tends to peak in the late afternoon and evening. Persistent crying increases until the child is 6–8 weeks old and then tapers off by 4 months (St. James-Roberts, 1989). In general, the more parents carry their infants, the less they cry.

Sensory Capabilities

The newborn's senses are actively transmitting information about the way the environment feels, looks, sounds, tastes, and smells. Although

■ ● ▲ CONCEPT SUMMARY

What Can the Newborn Do?

- They can display more than 70 involuntary reflex behaviors
- They can engage in basic behavioral states: crying, drowsy, asleep, and awake/alert
- They can accept and interpret information about the environment via their senses

---

all senses are operational at birth, some are much more mature than others.

TOUCH At birth all parts of the infant's body are sensitive to touch, but the face, hands, and soles of the feet are especially so. Touch is essential for normal infant growth and development. As I've mentioned, touching (cuddling, patting, and so on) can also help calm distressed infants.

PAIN Normal full-term infants respond to painful stimuli from the time of delivery. A pinprick consistently elicits limb retraction, crying, and/or grimacing in newborns. Incredibly, until very recently, infants received *no* anesthesia during surgery, even when organ transplants and lengthy heart procedures were being performed. Physicians felt that newborns were relatively insensitive to pain and that pain medications were too risky to use with young patients. In 1987, the American Academy of Pediatrics recommended changes in some surgical procedures and the use of local anesthetics to reduce the stress and pain infants suffer during medical procedures (Anand et al., 1987).

HEARING Once the fluid has drained from their ears, infants probably have the auditory acuity of adults (Whaley & Wong, 1988). Newborns usually quiet themselves to low-frequency sounds (whispers, lullabies, metronomes, music, and heartbeats) and become alert and active to high-frequency sounds. They are also most sensitive to sounds within the 1000–3000 Hz range—the primary frequency of human speech.

Babies only a few hours old will orient to the direction of a sound by changing their gaze and posture. By the time babies are 3 days old, they can tell the difference between their mother's voice and a stranger's voice and prefer to listen to a tape recording of their mother reading a story as opposed to another female reading the same material. Apparently, the more familiar voice is more interesting to them (DeCasper & Fifer, 1980).

In Touch

AMERICAN FOUNDATION FOR
  THE BLIND
15 West 16th Street
New York, New York 10011
212-620-2000

Publishes materials about visual
  handicaps. Recently developed a
  "Reach out and teach" course for
  parents of blind infants; also
  available *An Orientation of Mobility
  Primer for Families and Young
  Children*

NATIONAL ASSOCIATION OF THE
  DEAF
141 Fifth Ave.
New York, NY 10010

In the past, hearing impairment was difficult if not impossible to detect in very young babies. In the first few weeks of life most babies with normal hearing will respond by startling or crying to a loud clap or noise (3–6 feet away) or by interrupting their sucking momentarily when there is a sound or when someone starts talking to them. If there is cause for concern, infants as young as 5 weeks old can have their hearing assessed by the Brain Stem Auditory Evoked Response test. This test measures how well the baby hears by studying the sound waves that pass from the auditory nerve to the brain stem. Some infants with immature nervous systems may be overstimulated by sound and other sensory input.

SMELL Newborns react to strong odors by turning their heads, but they are capable of making rather subtle olfactory discriminations. Even infants with no nursing experience are preferentially attracted to the breast odors of a lactating woman over the smell of bottled formula (Makin & Porter, 1989). In addition, breastfed infants as young as 6 days old can distinguish the odor of their mother's breast milk from that of the breast milk of other nursing mothers (Macfarlane, 1975). Newborns can also tell where smells are coming from and accurately turn their heads away from noxious odors (Riesner et al., 1976).

TASTE Newborns demonstrate a preference for sweet-tasting liquid. By puckering, turning away, and crying, they show a dislike of sour and bitter liquids (Whaley & Wong, 1988). There is obvious survival value in rejecting bad tasting food or drink.

VISION Visual stimulation is necessary for the development of the visual system. The eye is structurally incomplete at birth and the muscles that control eye movement are immature. Tear glands usually do not begin to function until the infant is 2 to 4 weeks old. The infant's pupils reflexively prevent too much light from entering the eye and damaging the retina. Blinking occurs with little provocation. The newborn can focus their visual attention for 4 to 10 seconds on a high-contrast or moving object at least one-quarter of an inch in size, in the center of their visual field, and 8 inches away (Haith, 1986). Fixation increases as the newborn becomes less distractable. Newborns are very nearsighted. While mom or dad might be able to see an object 600 feet away, their newborn would have to be within 20 feet of that same object in order to see it!

Evidence to date suggests that newborns can distinguish among pure reds, greens, and yellows if the stimulus size is large enough (R. J. Adams, 1989). Apparently, it takes about 2 months for the mechanisms that transmit and interpret information about color to begin to operate efficiently (Banks & Bennett, 1988).

High contrast, close objects attract infant attention.

It was once thought that newborns have no sense of direction—that they made eye contact with things in the environment only by accident. Careful observation now suggests that newborns use their vision to locate stimuli in the environment. They make purposeful and directionally appropriate eye movements toward stimuli, but the process is slow and precise (Kreminitzer et al., 1979).

Newborns prefer patterned or high-contrast stimuli. They are fascinated by black and white contrast and by geometric design. Big pictures of animals or pastel Jacks and Jills evoke very little interest. Babies also seem to prefer looking at three-dimensional objects over two-dimensional objects and prefer curved lines over straight lines (Fantz et al., 1975). The newborn scans primarily along the horizontal axis. Thus, babies are more apt to show visual preference for interesting elements organized horizontally than in another pattern.

Since the human face is a stimulus the newborn sees frequently, developmentalists are interested in just when the infant is able to discriminate familiar from unfamiliar faces. Newborns find the human face interesting and attend to the high-contrast facial areas—eyes, hairlines, skin, chin and garment borders of the real face. Newborns 12–101 hours old can recognize their mother's face on the basis of visual cues alone (Bushnell et al., 1989). If the mother is breastfeeding, maternal face recognition is adaptive since she is also the primary food source. As more and more fathers become primary caregivers, I would hope studies would focus on *paternal* face recognition as well.

■●▲   CONCEPT SUMMARY

Sensory Capabilities

● *Touch:* The infant's entire body is touch sensitive

● *Pain:* Sensitivity to pain exists from birth

● *Hearing:* Excellent acuity, orients in the direction of the sound, especially if the sound is a human voice, can distinguish mother's voice (primary caregiver) from the voice of a stranger by 3 days of age

● *Smell:* Reacts to strong smells; orients to the direction a smell is coming from; by day 6 can distinguish the odor of mother's breastmilk

● *Taste:* Prefers sweet tastes and rejects bad tasting substances

● *Vision:* Pupil responds to light intensity; can focus momentarily; can distinguish pure colors among large sized stimuli; can use vision to locate environmental stimuli; movement, patterns, high contrast stimuli, and the human face attract the newborn's visual attention; can use visual cues to recognize mother's face

● Maternal Adjustments to Birth

Physical Adjustments

rooming-in
the practice of keeping the mother and the baby in a single room after delivery

Mothers and infants used to be routinely separated after hospital delivery. Now, depending on the birth setting chosen and whether or not "rooming in" is available, mothers and their infants can have sustained and extended contact provided they are both well enough to tolerate it. Because of careful screening procedures, women who give birth in birth centers experience few complications and are generally discharged within 24 hours of the birth. Women who give birth at home have the easiest transition of all since their permanent living quarters served as the ward, recovery room, and labor and delivery suite.

Physically, a woman's body requires from 1 to 2 years to recover fully from pregnancy. Directly following the birth, mothers may experience pain and discomfort, especially if they had stitches. Vaginal bleeding will persist for weeks after delivery. Since breastfeeding does not prevent ovulation, new parents need to use some type of reliable contraception once sexual relations are resumed to avoid closely spaced pregnancies.

Psychological Adjustments

It is difficult to predict a woman's emotional orientation after childbirth. Western society expects new mothers to feel content and fulfilled by the childbirth experience. Some mothers are genuinely elated, but others have more conflicting and negative emotions that can affect their behavior in varying degrees. *Postpartum depression* describes negative emotions that appear within 2 weeks after childbirth. (A more severely debilitating reaction is called *postpartum psychosis*.) Women experiencing postpartum depression may feel unhappy, vulnerable, and moody, and sometimes cry for no apparent reason. They might also be less than enthusiastic about the new baby and, often, feel helpless and out of control. Women who have postpartum psychosis feel all these same symptoms in an exaggerated way, have lost touch with reality and may hallucinate (Affonso & Domino, 1984). Interestingly, this constellation of emotions is not limited to women who were emotionally tentative about childrearing during pregnancy, but can affect even those most enthusiastic about the prospect of a new baby. In one study 62% of *fathers* reported having similar feelings (Ferketich & Mercer, 1989).

Postpartum depression is very common: 50 to 80% of all new mothers experience these feelings to some extent (J. R. Scott et al., 1990). Many factors have been cited as responsible: depression during pregnancy, fatigue, drug side-effects, hormonal changes, dietary deficiencies, milk production, poor postnatal nutrition, separation from the newborn or other family members, lack of attention from the hospital staff or one's family, concerns about one's parenting abilities, feelings of insecurity,

postpartum depression
hormonally influenced feelings of loss and sadness after the delivery; also called the baby blues

In Touch

DEPRESSION AFTER PREGNANCY
PO Box 1282
Morrisville, PA 19067
215-295-3994

■●▲ CONCEPT SUMMARY

Maternal Adjustment Following Birth

1. Physical adjustments:
   - Pain and discomfort following delivery—the degree of which varies from woman to woman and from delivery to delivery
   - Vaginal bleeding, which can occur for some weeks after delivery
   - Lactation (milk-production) and breastfeeding

   Psychological adjustments:
   - Emotions ranging from highly positive to very negative (postpartum depression/postpartum psychosis)
   - Learning and applying skills for caring for baby
   - Developing an attachment to the infant
   - Identifying with the role of mother
   - Making the transition from couple or single parent to family

In Touch

MOTHERING SEMINARS INC (MSI)
PO Box 712
Columbia, MD 21045
301-730-6255
301-381-5195

sexual abstinence or a change in sexual feelings, general discontent, perceived parental care during childhood, and worries about one's health or the health of the baby (Gotlib et al., 1991). Support and understanding are effective antidotes to postpartum depression. Medication is rarely necessary. Postpartum depression is generally short-lived—only about 10% of the women continue to feel depressed 6 weeks after delivery but some continue to experience psychological problems for up to 4 years after childbirth (Kumar & Robson, 1984).

TOWARD EFFECTIVE PARENTING

Transitions Following Childbirth

Although the mother carries and bears the child, she may not be alone in having to adapt and adjust to the new baby. First-time parents suddenly find themselves cast as mother and father, not just man and woman, with a new person to relate to both individually and together. In short, the couple becomes a family. For families with other children, all must find a way of permanently incorporating a brand new person into what may have been a stable unit. These shifts represent major physical and psychological adjustments for everyone (Belsky, 1985). While having a baby neither improves a bad marriage nor ruins a good one, the lives of the people involved will never be the same once the baby is born. The following guidelines can help to facilitate the complex transition.

1. *The first thoughts should be for the immediate family.* Usually the mother has been separated from her partner and her other children since the delivery. Young children, especially, may be worried about her health and well-being and concerned about whether she still cares for them. They will need emotional reassurance and will probably have a lot of pressing questions. Immature, baby-like behavior from older children is a common, though temporary, response to the birth of a new sibling, and it's often a signal the child needs extra loving attention.

2. *Parents shouldn't expect a comfortable routine to develop quickly.* Adjusting to the needs and patterns of a new baby takes time. The baby's habits probably won't fit into the established routine. Expecting disruptions to the old order can make them easier to endure. Deciding ahead of time who's responsible for certain chores (laundry, bathing the baby, and so on) also helps people adapt with less confusion.

3. *New mothers shouldn't try to do too much.* Women usually need rest to compensate for the strain of delivery and nighttime feedings that interrupt sleep. Housecleaning and entertaining should be secondary both to the parent's needs and those of the older siblings. It's a good idea for the mother to sleep when the baby sleeps or when the older children take their naps.

4. *Advice from well meaning friends and relatives should be accepted cautiously.* New parents often receive a lot of advice—sometimes the advice is

inconsistent, conflicting with other opinions and makes parents feel uncomfortable. For their own peace of mind, parents need to settle on safe and effective methods that they find comfortable.

5. *Parents should expect to feel a bit inexperienced and clumsy around the new baby.* No matter how many children parents have, most have to become reacquainted with the daily tasks involved in caring for a newborn. Popular mythology aside, childcare is a learned, not an inherited, skill. It improves with practice and can get "rusty" from disuse.

6. *Parents should be aware of the possibility of postpartum depression.* If parents are aware of postpartum depression and its symptoms ahead of time, they won't be overly concerned (or surprised) if it occurs.

7. *Resource people can be helpful to new parents.* Parents are benefited by having trustworthy, knowledgeable people with whom to consult when problems, issues, or questions arise. The family physician or nurse practitioner can be a resource person; many others can play that role, also.

8. *Understand something about baby's propensity to cry.* Crying is the only means the infant has of signalling her needs and wants. With practice, parents will learn to distinguish the meaning of the baby's cries (for instance, hungry, cold, lonely). Parents should be assured that responding to a baby's cries does not constitute "spoiling" the infant since the infant's needs are all appropriate and should be attended to. Responding promptly to infants when they cry actually *limits* their need to cry since they learn to trust the parents to anticipate their needs.

9. *Avoid feeding babies whenever they cry.* Babies do cry when they are hungry and they generally quiet down and are soothed by feeding. But feeding a baby *every time* she cries leads the child to falsely assume that all its needs are food related in some way. This habit could lead to overeating and excessive weight gain. It also means that nonfood-related needs go unmet.

10. *Babies need time to themselves just like everyone else.* Parents shouldn't feel obligated to hold, carry, or play with the child whenever she is awake.

11. *Find a responsible, trustworthy babysitter so you can go out without the baby if you wish.*

12. *Monitor the behavior of pets around the baby.* Pets that are treated like part of the family before the baby arrives become accustomed to considerable care and attention. Parents can be sensitive to the pet's continued need for attention while remaining alert for signs of hostility or jealousy.

13. *Encourage others in the family to get to know the new baby.* Parents can encourage other children in the family to become acquainted with the new baby without forcing contact where siblings are reluctant. Supervise, and instruct children on how to safely hold, pick up, cuddle, and play with babies and praise their efforts.

14. *Infants are social creatures.* When babies are awake, they are happiest around the family. They can also learn to nap in the more social regions of the house by learning to tune out noise just like older children and adults do.

15. *Babies, even identical twins, are unique human beings.* Parents shouldn't expect the new baby to resemble her siblings in temperament, appear-

(continued)

ance, or behavior. After all, the baby is a unique individual. Even identical twins have different personalities.

16. *Help the baby establish a routine.* Once established, the baby's routine (like that of the other family members) should be respected. For example, it's disruptive to wake the baby up from a scheduled (and needed) nap just because a friend or relative is visiting and wants to see the baby. It's nice for people to be interested in the newborn, but it's easier for adults to wait until the baby is ready to see them than for the baby to have to conform to the social needs of other adults.

17. *Babies don't need a lot of toys or fancy clothes to feel welcome and loved.* What babies need most is human contact. Holding, rocking, cuddling, and talking to the baby are the best ways for parents to express affection and to let the baby know she has an important place in the family.

● Chapter Summary

● Prenatal medical care improves pregnancy outcomes by monitoring the health of the mother and the baby. A due date is estimated to help parents plan for the arrival of the baby and to help the medical staff provide appropriate care.

● The birth typically takes place in one of three settings: a hospital, a birth center (located on or near hospital grounds), or in the parents' home.

● Childbirth preparation usually involves training in techniques of breathing and pain control and instruction in the physiology of labor and the birth process.

● The onset of labor may be preceded by lightening, painless and erratic contractions, the loss of the mucous plug, maternal weight loss, and feelings of excess energy. Labor begins when muscle contractions become regular and cervical dilatation begins. Labor is three-stage process: the first stage ends when the cervix is fully dilated; the second stage culminates with the birth of the baby; the third stage involves the expulsion of the afterbirth and surgical repair (if necessary) for the mother.

● When normal vaginal delivery poses too great a risk for the mother or the baby, a surgical delivery, called cesarean section, is performed.

● Sometimes a vaginal delivery is accompanied by pitocin to induce labor, pain-killing medication for the mother, an episiotomy, submersion in water during labor, the use of forceps or vacuum extraction, and/or repositioning of the mother in an obstetric chair or a birthing bed to assist the progress of labor.

- The physical well-being of the newborn is first assessed by the Apgar scoring system, which evaluates five infant vital signs: heart rate, muscle tone, reflex irritability, respiratory effort, and color.
- Most babies are in good condition after the birth. A small percentage of newborns sustain fractures, brain injury, have trouble breathing, or are jaundiced.
- Circumcision is an elective procedure performed on about 50% of newborn males in the United States. A local anesthetic is used to reduce the pain.
- The average American newborn weighs 7 to 7½ pounds and is between 19 and 21 inches long. Newborns may have molded heads, be covered with vernix or lanugo, or have a birthmark.
- A newborn's size at birth may be determined as average, large for gestational age (more than 8.3 pounds) or small for gestational age (below the 3rd percentile for length, weight, and head circumference). The newborn will also receive one of three gestational age designations: full-term (born within two weeks of the due date, either early or late), premature (weighing less than 5.5 pounds and gestating less than 37 weeks), or postmature (weighing over 8.3 pounds or gestating more than 42 weeks). Premature babies are considered to be at risk since they are less well developed than full-term or postmature babies. The more premature the baby is, the more difficult it will be adjusting to life outside the womb. Most premature births can be prevented by medication, good prenatal care, and habit change on the part of the mother.
- The newborn's physical adjustments to life outside the womb involve taking oxygen into the lungs, redirecting the circulatory system, digesting food taken by mouth, eliminating waste through the intestinal system, and the self-regulation of body temperature.
- Newborns come equipped with a set of automatic behaviors called reflexes. Many reflexes have survival value, since they help protect the baby from harm and ensure proper physiological functioning. Medical personnal use reflexes to assess the development of the brain and nervous system and to judge physical maturity.
- In addition to reflexes, the other basic behaviors or behavioral states displayed by newborns include sleeping, crying, drowsiness, and alertness/wakefulness.
- The senses of touch, hearing, smell, taste, and vision are operational at birth and actively transmit messages about the outside world to the newborn's brain. Of all the senses, touch and hearing are probably the best developed, while vision is the least well developed. The newborn is able to recognize his or her mother (or the primary caregiver) by sight, smell, and sound within a few days of birth. Pain sensitivity exists from birth.
- The mother makes both physical and psychological adjustments following the birth of her child. Although each pregnancy and birth are unique, first-time mothers/parents may have more difficulty adjusting to a new baby because of their lack of experience.

● Observational Exercise

Conduct a follow-up interview with women who have recently given birth to gain first-hand information about their experiences.

QUESTIONS ABOUT LABOR AND DELIVERY

1. When did your labor begin and how long did it last?
2. Where did you have the baby?
3. Was labor anything like you imagined it to be?
   (or for mothers with other children) Was this labor anything like your previous labors?
4. What care and attention did you receive as the labor progressed?
5. Were drugs given to you during the process?
6. Did you have an episiotomy?
7. Was the birth considered normal or were there complications?
8. What happened immediately after the baby was born? Did you get to hold and touch your baby?
9. Would you go through all this again? Why or why not?

Take time to observe interactions between the mother and her newborn. Does she seem comfortable with the baby? Is she loving and tender? Does she attempt to "make conversation" with the baby? Is she responsive? (If other children are present) how does the mother coordinate interactions between herself, the existing children, and the newborn?

● Recommended Readings

Bettelheim, B. (1987) *The good enough parent.* New York: Knopf.

Bing, E. (1983). *Dear Elisabeth Bing: We've had our baby.* New York: Pocket Books.

Eisenberg, Eisenberg-Murkoff, H., & Eisenberg-Hathaway, S. (1988). *What to expect when you're expecting.* New York: Workman.

Gresh, S. (1980). *Becoming a father: A handbook for expectant fathers.* NY: Butterick.

Hales, D., & Creasy, R. K. (1982). *New hope for problem pregnancies: Helping babies before they're born.* New York: Harper & Row.

Jason, J., & van der Meer, A. (1989). *Parenting your premature baby.* New York: Holt.

Jiminez, S. L. M. (1982). *The other side of pregnancy.* Englewood Cliffs, NJ: Prentice-Hall. (This book focuses on miscarriage.)

LaLeche League (1991) *The womanly art of breastfeeding* (5th ed.). Franklin Park, IL: LaLeche League.

Leach, P. (1983). *Babyhood* (2nd ed). New York: Knopf.

Lubic, R. W., & Hawes, G. R. (1987). *Childbearing: A book of choices.* New York: McGraw-Hill.

PART 2
Infancy and Toddlerhood

Physical Development in Infancy and Toddlerhood

● Growth

At birth, the average North American newborn weighs between 7 and 7.5 pounds and measures 19–21 inches in length. In everyday terms the newborn baby weighs less than a gallon of milk and is about as long as the distance from your elbow to your fingertips. As tiny as they seem, however, full-term newborns are almost *one-third* their adult height.

Height

Children grow faster during their first year of life than in any subsequent period until the onset of puberty. While the child's genes dictate her ultimate size, shape, and proportions, genetic instructions can be modified by such environmental factors as poor nutrition, illness, poor medical care, and stress. Children who experienced intrauterine growth retardation (because their mothers were small or because adverse conditions existed) tend to grow particularly rapidly in favorable environments. Under normal circumstances, infants will increase their length by 10 or 12 inches in their first 12 months of life (Sinclair, 1989). So when we say that the child grows a foot by her first birthday, we don't mean just another place to put a shoe! By age 1, the infant will stand about as high as a kitchen table. Height at 2 years is about 50% of mature adult height! (Post et al., 1981).

Weight

Along with rapid change in height comes impressive weight gain. In the first few months of life, infants can be expected to gain an ounce a day. At this rate, birth weight is doubled by 4 months of age, tripled by the end of the first year, and quadrupled by age 2 (Bogin, 1988). Thus, the infant who weighs 7 pounds at birth can be expected to weigh 21 pounds by age 1, almost the equivalent of three gallons of milk. Compared to term babies, low birth weight babies will generally remain smaller throughout the first 5 years of life (Binkin et al., 1988).

Much of the weight gain in the first 9 months of life is fat. Fat provides insulation and is a source of calories if food intake is temporarily reduced or interrupted. Normal infant plumpness should not be confused with obesity, which is unhealthy during infancy. After 9 months, fat production slows down as other body systems account for a larger percentage of total weight gain. After infants start walking, they actually lose fat rather than gain it. In general babies gain weight in spurts rather than in an even, continuous fashion. And weight gain slows down after the first birthday because growth rate begins to decelerate and appetite decreases.

Principles of Growth

Two principles of growth guide all physical development both before and after birth. The *cephalocaudal principle* of growth directs the development from the head downward. Since the brain is the master organ of the child's body, early, rapid head growth is essential for normal development. Proportionately, the feet are the smallest part of the child's body—in keeping with the cephalocaudal principle, since they are the part farthest from the brain.

The *proximodistal principle* of growth encourages development from the central part of the body outward. Children will be able to control their head movements before they can efficiently use their arms. And they will use their hands as a whole unit for grasping before they can use their thumbs and forefingers in opposition. The growth of boys and girls is remarkably similar during infancy.

Body Proportions

During the first year, the infant looks compact and cute. The head is disproportionately large, the trunk is long, the abdomen protrudes, and the legs are bowed and relatively short, not much longer than the head. The pot-bellied look is normal and has nothing to do with overfeeding or malnutrition in healthy babies. The infant's liver is relatively large at this age, and the immature abdominal muscles lack the strength to hold in the abdominal contents. The bowed appearance of the legs results from uterine confinement and disappears by about 3 months of age as muscle strength increases. Bowing that persists or worsens is often a sign of vitamin D deficiency or deficient calcium utilization (Whitney & Cataldo, 1987).

cephalocaudal principle
a pattern of growth that proceeds from the head downward (literally, "from head to tail")

Proximodistal principle
growth that proceeds from the spine to the extremities (literally, "from near to far")

■ **Figure 5–1**

Typical infant physique.

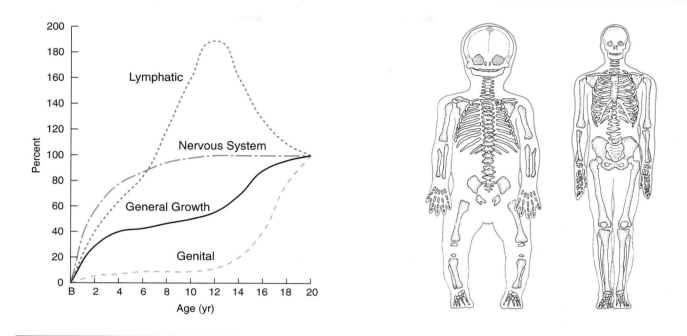

■ **Figures 5–2 and 5–3**

(left) Differential growth rates of the lymphatic system, nervous system, and genital tissues in relation to whole-body development. (right) Newborn and adult skeletons are shown at the same height to illustrate the differences between the skeletal development at birth and at maturity.

The Foundations of Obesity

Although fat infants are often considered cute and cuddly, infant obesity might have important implications for long-term health and psychological well-being. Three factors contribute to infant obesity: genetics, overfeeding, and a low metabolic rate.

Infants can inherit a predisposition to be heavy. The chances of being a fat adult are 7% if neither parent is fat; 40% if there is one fat parent, and 80% if there are two (Bouchard, 1991). (Infants are encouraged to choose their parents wisely!) In addition, overnourished infants often prefer sweet, high-calorie foods and ignore internal cues that they are full. They may also be less active than other infants. In 1975 Mayer found activity level, not the amount of calories consumed, to be the most accurate predictor of weight gain in infants. Fat babies were placid and quiet and tended to eat moderate amounts; thinner babies were loud and intense and ate the most. Fatter babies also have lower metabolic rates (they burn fewer calories for energy than infants with higher metabolic rates) (Bouchard, 1991). It may be better to increase physical activity than reduce food intake to control the weight of low metabolic rate babies. A child who eats 100 extra calories per day will put on 10 extra pounds a year. This may seem like a trivial increase, but consider the cumulative effects. By the time an infant with these habits reaches adolescence, she could weigh 100 pounds more than normal. About 85%

obesity
extremely fat

(genetic) predispositions
a tendency to inherit the traits, characteristics or behaviors of one's ancestors

■ Figure 5–4

Do fat babies become fat adults?

of all obese infants (infants who are 20% heavier than the norm for their particular height, body structure, and genetic predisposition) are at risk for becoming obese adults.

Overnutrition is a preventable cause of obesity. When caregivers are aware of their infant's food requirements, understand the relationship between food intake and weight gain, know about food value, and avoid using food as bribes or reinforcers, they can avoid overfeeding or having children develop preferences for sweets over other foods and eating less nutritious meals after a high-calorie snack. Fat babies won't necessarily become fat adults, but they may be healthier and better nourished if the poor eating and exercise habits that are so hard to break never get started.

Internal Organs and Systems

The Brain

neuron(s)
nerve cells

Nervous system tissue grows faster than any other tissue or organ in the baby's body during the first 3 years of life. Apparently, breast milk does much to support this growth. Low birth weight babies who are breast-fed have higher mental index scores than babies who are bottle-fed (Morley et al., 1988). Most of the *neurons* or nerve cells in the fetal brain develop between the 2nd and the 5th gestational months at the staggering rate of 250,000 per minute! (W.M. Cowan, 1979). Not surprisingly, the baby's brain has already attained 25% of its adult growth by birth. Once present, the brain cells must migrate to their correct location and develop the characteristics of their particular cell type.

After birth, each brain cell forms up to 15,000 connections with other neurons. To speed the transmission of nerve impulses throughout the brain and body, nerve fibers must be *myelinated* or insulated with a fatty coating. Myelinization is not complete until age 6 (Sinclair, 1989). But does the human brain really need 100,000,000,000 (one hundred billion) cells with 1.5×10^{40} interconnections (15,000,000,000,000,000,000,000,000,-000,000,000,000) to function efficiently? The answer is no. By about age 2 an interesting reversal of development takes place—unneeded brain cells begin to die off and redundant interconnections start to disintegrate (Kolb, 1989). Cell death is a process that continues in the brain throughout adult life but at a greatly slowed place in the mature brain.

myelinate/myelinization
the process of coating nerve fibers with a fatty covering called the myelin sheath that speeds up nervous system transmission

BRAIN DEVELOPMENT AND BEHAVIOR At birth the two most advanced areas of the brain are the midbrain and the hindbrain. The *midbrain* controls attention, arousal, waking, elimination of body wastes, and habituation, or the process of becoming accustomed to familiar stimuli. The *hindbrain* is even more primitive. It regulates body temperature, heart rate, breathing, blood pressure, sucking, and muscle tone. Nervous system pathways that transmit messages from the senses to the brain

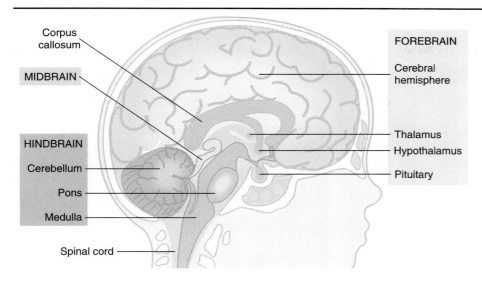

Corpus callosum

MIDBRAIN

HINDBRAIN

Cerebellum

Pons

Medulla

Spinal cord

FOREBRAIN

Cerebral hemisphere

Thalamus

Hypothalamus

Pituitary

■ **Figure 5–5**

The three main divisions of the human brain: the hindbrain, the midbrain, and the forebrain.

are myelinated before the *motor,* or response output, pathways. This helps babies know what's going on around them but prevents them from reacting in a very sophisticated fashion. For example, a 2-month-old baby with normal vision has no trouble seeing the rattle held before the face, but has a difficult time reaching for it. Between 3 and 6 months of age, control of the brain is switched from the lower brain centers (the midbrain and the hindbrain) to the cortex, or outer layer of the brain (Kalat, 1981). With the cortex in charge, behavior becomes more voluntary and less reflexive, making higher level intellectual and motor activity possible (Rakic, 1988).

The environment has a profound impact on brain development. A well-balanced diet is necessary to nourish and sustain brain growth. But the brain also hungers for sensory stimulation and affection (Parmelee & Sigman, 1983). Babies need things to touch, taste, smell, see, and listen to. They also need to interact with other humans who will hold, cuddle, and love them. Brain cell groups need to practice their particular skills to develop fully. But no matter how stimulating the environment may be, a baby who does not receive physical affection will not thrive. Researchers speculate that the stress of neglect interferes with the process of brain and body growth (L.I. Gardner, 1972).

Bone

At birth, babies have soft bones composed mostly of *cartilage.* Cartilage facilitates birth by giving babies tremendous flexibility compared with mature adults. Through a process known as *ossification,* minerals are

cartilage
the soft, mineral-laden tissue that hardens into bone

ossification
the process of replacing cartilage with bony tissue

■ Figure 5–6

All young babies have extremely flexible bodies.

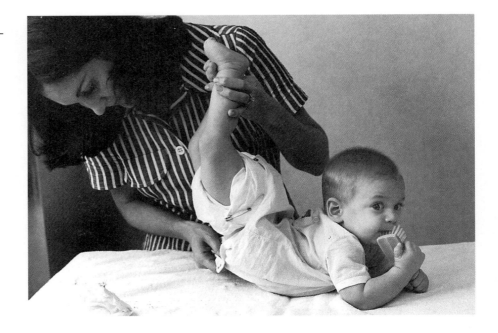

fontanels/soft spots
areas of cartilage between the bones of the baby's skull

■ Figure 5–7

The fontanels or "soft spots" of the infant's skull. The frontal fontanel closes between 18 and 24 months."

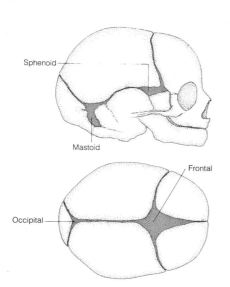

deposited in the cartilage that harden it into bone. Ossification begins prenatally but is not completed until the end of adolescence. Ossification closes the *fontanels,* or soft spots, between the bones of the baby's skull by age 2. The exact timing of fontanel closure is highly variable and unrelated to sex, race, size at birth, or postnatal growth rate (Kataria et al., 1988). The other major skeletal changes during this period are elongation of the trunk followed by leg and arm growth. Clearly, ossification, along with nerve and muscle changes, helps the baby progress in motor development. The skeleton must be able to support the baby's weight before the child can sit, crawl, stand, or walk.

The ossification rate, which is determined by distinguishing bone from cartilage in X rays, is a reliable indicator of the level of physical maturity. Ossification proceeds more rapidly in girls than boys and more rapidly in blacks than whites (Bogin, 1988). At birth, girls are about 4 weeks ahead of boys in skeletal maturity, and it is not until adolescence that the ossification rate of all children equals out.

Muscle

Babies are born with a complete set of immature muscles. Although no new muscle tissue is added after birth, existing muscle fibers change in size and composition. The proportion of protein and salt in the muscle tissue increases, while the amount of water decreases, improving the infant's strength and stamina (Sinclair, 1989). Muscles increase in size through exercise and hormone action according to the cephalocaudal principle. Within each muscle group, the muscle mass becomes responsive before the individual muscles. The first muscles to develop are

A Closer Look

Getting Away with Murder

It's easy to kill a child and bury the secret.

Deep in the boot heel of rural Missouri, no one knows why Dante Mosby died. The last months of the boy's short life were spent in hospitals where doctors suspected child abuse and called authorities. But when the 19-month-old toddler died, the acting coroner saw no need to autopsy or investigate further. "Natural causes, exact cause unknown," he wrote on the death certificate. Then the case was closed.

Today, almost seven years after the boy's death, Dr. Mary Case, the St. Louis medical examiner, is continuing her crusade to dig up the child's body and to search for clues to a crime. "The truth was buried with that boy," said Gary Stangler, director of Missouri's Department of Social Services, which went to court seeking authority to exhume the body.

The Dante Mosby case is not unique. Often, the death of a child can go overlooked and almost forgotten (Lundstrom & Sharpe, 1991).

Throughout America, poorly trained coroners and shoddy death investigations are helping mothers and fathers get away with murder. Children are frequently buried without anyone knowing why they died.

"I believe all kinds of homicides are being missed," said Dr. Mary Case. "Children are being killed and just buried."

Dr. Ronald Reeves of Tallahassee, Florida, said he believes child-abuse deaths are "grossly underestimated." "Children are expendable items that can be killed and disposed of," said Reeves, a former medical examiner now specializing in children's deaths.

Three children are known to die of child abuse every day, but at least three more child-abuse deaths each day are believed to go undetected, according to pathologists, prosecutors, and child welfare advocates interviewed in 32 states.

These are the children whose deaths are incorrectly labeled accidental, undetermined, or due to natural causes—sometimes as sudden infant death syndrome. These are the children no one bothered to autopsy.

However disturbing an autopsy might be, especially to a grieving family, experts agree the procedure is a key to detecting child abuse. But a computer study of all death certificates nationwide in 1987—the latest year available from the federal government—found that autopsies on children are conducted almost by whim. Whether dead children are autopsied appears to depend more on where they lived than on the circumstances of their deaths.

The 49,569 death certificates for children under age 9 revealed:

1. Overall autopsy rates for children varied widely from state to state, ranging from 23% in Tennessee to 67% in Rhode Island. (Tennessee's poor performance may reflect poor bookkeeping: Officials there did not completely fill out nearly half of the death certificates. The next lowest rate was 29% in Mississippi).

2. The South consistently had the nation's lowest autopsy rates. Some counties in southern states saw no need to autopsy any children at all. In Arkansas, officials in 30 of 75 counties autopsied no children in 1987—yet 72 children died in those counties. Often rural areas rely on elected coroners—ranging from the local funeral director to janitors, bus drivers, and coal miners. They may be unqualified to recognize child abuse or make complicated diagnoses and being paid as little as $1200 a year to be on call 24-hours a day, 7 days a week, makes the job of coroner one to moonlight at, at best.

3. Another reason for a low autopsy rate is lack of funds. Counties often do not set aside enough

(continued on next page)

(continued from previous page)

funds to perform all the autopsies necessary. One official in Cumberland County, Pennsylvania, said that suspicious deaths are particularly unlikely to be investigated during the last 2 or 3 months of the year because their county is "always out of money by then." Worse still, some coroners will simply look the other way, stating they don't want to get involved and they don't want to testify.

Here is a listing of state by state autopsy rates:

Rhode Island	67.3	Pennsylvania	45.5
Vermont	61.3	Texas	45.4
New Hampshire	59.1	New Jersey	45.0
Washington	59.0	Utah	44.4
Nebraska	58.4	Maryland	43.8
Colorado	58.0	Kansas	43.7
Massachusetts	57.8	Louisiana	41.5
Minnesota	57.4	Wyoming	41.1
Alaska	56.7	Connecticut	40.8
Wisconsin	55.6	Arizona	40.7
Illinois	54.8	So. Carolina	40.5
Montana	53.9	Hawaii	39.4
California	53.8	No. Carolina	39.2
Iowa	52.6	Oklahoma	38.9
Oregon	52.1	Maine	38.6
Delaware	50.7	Alabama	38.5
Washington, D.C.	50.7	South Dakota	37.7
Idaho	50.3	Indiana	37.5
Ohio	50.2	West Virginia	37.5
Michigan	50.0	Georgia	37.1
Missouri	50.0	Virginia	35.6
North Dakota	49.7	Kentucky	35.4
Florida	48.8	Arkansas	31.4
New York	48.8	Mississippi	28.8
New Mexico	45.9	Tennessee	23.1

Of the 7,422 child deaths in the United States that most experts would call suspicious, 531 were not autopsied. These were children whose deaths were labeled, among other things, sudden infant death syndrome, undetermined, or asphyxiation. Yet no autopsy supported those findings. Experts fear undetected murders are most likely slipping into these kinds of categories.

For example, in Utah a coroner declared 3-year-old Michael Benjamin Barrie had died of an aneurysm in December 1986. Months later, after the body was exhumed, an autopsy proved the boy had been suffocated and 11 ribs had been broken. Steven Ray Allen, the mother's boyfriend, was convicted of second-degree murder.

Across the nation, almost 1 out of every 12 deaths diagnosed as SIDS was not autopsied—a flagrant violation of accepted medical procedure. A finding of SIDS means that every other cause of death should have been ruled out through autopsy, according to the National Institutes of Health, the nation's leading biomedical research center. Eerily, SIDS is also the most common alibi used by parents who murder a child.

Without a thorough investigation of children's deaths, others may be in danger. Many times, murdered children had siblings—brothers and sisters who remain in the custody of a killer. When the hospital notified Coroner Sue Townsend about an 11-month-old baby who had died of SIDS, she didn't like it. Skeptical of any SIDS victim over 6 months, she picked up the body and then rushed with police to the child's home. Her fears were confirmed. Inside, the baby's identical twin was near death, so malnourished he was suffering from rickets. The baby, who weighed less than 13 pounds, was quickly removed from the home and hospitalized. Four years later, he thrives with his adoptive parents.

Requiring autopsies on all child victims is a start. Experts say that death-scene investigations are as important as autopsies because they can prove the homicide by revealing inconsistencies in the parents' stories. Changes in state laws that restrict release of information about children, as well as the formation of death-review committees can do much to curb the rash of child abuse that is masquerading as misfortune, bad luck, and happenstance.

Until changes occur, it's still easy to kill a child and bury the secret.

Source: Excerpted from "Some parents are getting away with murder" by Marjie Lundstrom and Rochelle Sharpe (The Sacramento Bee, April 21, 1991). Used with permission.

those in the neck and back. Thus, head control is the first motor skill accomplished by the infant. Later, muscles in the legs and arms mature to permit locomotion, directed reaching, and object manipulation.

locomotion
movement from place to place

Digestion

Starting shortly after birth and continuing during infancy, digestion is facilitated by "friendly" intestinal bacteria, increased stomach capacity, and salivation (Bogin, 1988). Nevertheless, digestive processes are still immature by age 2. The immaturity of the digestive system is apparent in the appearance of the stools—many foods pass only partially digested and the stools are often colored by the food the child consumes. (Variation in the child's diet makes for more interesting diaper changing!) The digestion of most fibrous foods improves between 12 and 24 months.

Spitting up is also associated with an immature digestive system. The infant usually outgrows this tendency by 6 or 7 months of age. If spitting up persists, it could indicate inadequate bubbling or burping after feeding.

Immune Protection

The newborn begins life protected from infection by antibodies received prenatally. If the newborn is breast-fed, antibodies continue to be passed from mother to child. Shortly after birth, the infant's own immature immune system slowly begins producing antibodies. It takes the entire first year of life for the infant to even approach antibody levels similar to those of an older child or adult (Whaley & Wong, 1988). Thus, compared to bottle-fed babies, breast-fed babies have more natural protection against gastrointestinal and respiratory infections as well as common viral illnesses such as chickenpox, mumps, measles, and polio—that is, if such antibodies are present in the mother's system. Bottle-fed babies, who must rely on prenatal transfer and their own immune systems, may be sick more often during infancy than breast-fed babies.

inoculation
see immunization

Artificial immunization through inoculation protects the child from illness after immunity from maternal transfer disappears. The United States lags behind most industrialized nations in preventing diseases of childhood. One fourth of the preschoolers and one third of all poor American children under age 5 are not immunized (*Newsweek*, October 8, 1990, p. 48). Table 5–1 is the immunization schedule recommended by the American Academy of Pediatrics. In addition, a vaccine for chronic ear infection is currently being tested (Kent & Jones, 1988).

Breathing

Lung capacity increases during infancy, and respiration rate therefore decreases without affecting the transfer of oxygen. Infants are still

■ **Table 5–1**   *American Academy of Pediatrics Infant Immunization Schedule*

AGE	INOCULATION	COMMENTS
2 months	Polio DTP Hib	Infants receive the oral polio vaccine that contains live but weakened polio virus. Rarely, the vaccine itself causes polio (5 times in the US since 1989)
4 months	Polio DTP Hib	*Hib* stands for *Haemophilus B* an organism that causes dangerous forms of meningitis (an infection in the lining around the brain) and croup. One in 200 children develops a serious Hib infection before age 5. The infection rate is higher among children in day care and some settings require Hib inoculations of their families.
6 months	DTP Hib MMR*	DTP stands for *diphtheria, tetanus,* and *pertussis* (or whooping cough). If the child has already had seizures, doctors and parents should consider giving the child DT-only shots because of the rare but serious complications that can stem from the pertussis vaccination
12 months	MMR**	MMR stands for *measles, mumps,* and *rubella* (also called German measles or 3-day measles). The vaccine doesn't work well in children who have a viral infection (such as a cold) when they get the shot
15 months	Hib*** Polio MMR	
15–18 months	DTP	
4–6 years	Polio DTP****	
11–12 years	MMR	
14–16 years	Diphtheria booster	

*In measles-emergency areas, only
**In measles areas with intermittent outbreaks
***Depending on the vaccine type, one shot at 12 months may replace the 6- and 15-months shots
****Adults are advised to get a tetanus booster every 10 years.

"stomach breathers," however, since respiratory movements are abdominal.

Infant lung tissue is sensitive to irritation. Babies of smoking parents have a higher incidence of bronchitis, pneumonia, and colds during their first year of life than infants of nonsmoking parents (Malloy et al., 1988). They are also more likely to develop asthma than babies of nonsmokers. If only one parent smokes, the incidence figures are halfway between those for smoking and nonsmoking parents. Exposure to 25 "smoker years" (two parents smoking for 12.5 years of a child's life) doubles the child's long-term risk of lung cancer (Janerich et al., 1990). In light of all this evidence, it's not surprising that a California Supreme Court judge ruled that a mother awarded custody of her 5-year-old son stop smoking in his presence (*Newsweek*, August 27, 1990, p. 66).

Circulation

The heart grows less rapidly than the rest of the body, but it is still large in relation to the infant's chest cavity. Blood pressure changes during this period because the left ventricle becomes increasingly able to pump blood into circulation. As blood pressure decreases and the heart becomes stronger and more efficient, the baby's stamina and endurance increase.

Temperature Regulation

During the first 2 years of life, the ability of the baby's skin to contract and shiver in response to cold increases. Muscle activity during shivering generates heat that is transferred throughout the body. Also, the capillaries in the skin's surface become more responsive to ambient temperature, constricting to conserve heat in cold environments and dilating to release heat when it is hot. Children between 18 and 24 months of age rarely have difficulty maintaining body temperature.

Colic

Unrelenting, inconsolable crying, tightened abdominal muscles, and spitting up (normally around the same time each day) that is not caused by any of the usual sources of discomfort is called *colic* (Arnott, 1990). Colic may begin as soon as the baby's 2nd or 3rd week but generally ends when the baby is 3 months old or so. About 1 million American babies are affected annually. Babies who develop colic may be particularly sensitive to external and internal stimuli (Hewson et al., 1987). As they age, their stimulation threshold increases. Cow antibodies (called immunoglobulinG or IgG) may also be implicated. The antibodies can remain in the mother's breast milk for as long as a week after she drinks cow's milk. When these same women switch to a dairy-free diet, the colic subsides in about 10 days (Maugh, 1991). Maternal stress (especially from working outside the home) has been offered as a cause of infant colic. But the incidence of colic remains steady at about 20% even as more and more women enter the work force (Shukat & Haines, 1986).

Calming or quieting strategies for the colicky (or crying) baby include rocking, carrying baby in a front-sling baby carrier, taking her for a ride in the car (in her carseat), offering something to suck, swaddling (wrap-

colic
a sudden severe attack of abdominal pain

immunoglobulin/IgG
cow antibodies present in human breastmilk if the mother eats dairy products

■ **Figure 5–8**

An angry, colicky baby.

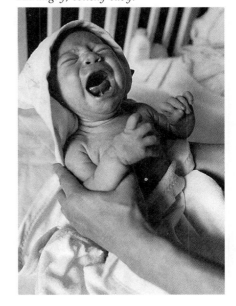

►► **I S S U E** ◄◄

When to Call the Doctor

When the child's behavior changes or when the child has sustained an injury, it's important to consult with the physician to see if treatment is needed. Parents sometimes worry about "bothering" the doctor. Consultation is not a bother for doctors, it's their job. It's always better to call and be told that the child will be fine than to avoid calling and have the child's situation worsen. Here are some guidelines.

Colds

Call the doctor if:

1. The cold lasts more than a week
2. Unusual symptoms appear
3. The child has a fever of over 101 degrees (100 degrees in a newborn)

Coughs

Call the doctor if:

1. The coughing is persistent
2. Nightime coughing sounds like barking (a possible sign of croup)

Cuts

The child may need stitches if:

1. Bleeding persists despite pressure
2. The skin must be held together to stop the bleeding

If possible, call the doctor: otherwise, go to the emergency room.

Dehydration

(For infants) Call the doctor if:

1. The child doesn't urinate for 8 hours *and* vomits or has diarrhea
2. The child vomits repeatedly over a brief period of time

(For older children) Call the doctor if:

1. The child doesn't urinate for 8–12 hours
2. The child won't/doesn't drink fluids
3. The child has been vomiting or has diarrhea
4. The child has "sunken" eyes or "doughy" skin that doesn't return to normal when pressed
5. The child is unusually lethargic or irritable

Fever

Call the doctor if:

1. The fever reaches 100 for a newborn; 101 for an infant

Call the doctor immediately if:

1. The child has a fever *and* has breathing difficulty
2. The child has a fever *and* pain on urination
3. The child has a fever *and* is having seizures
4. The child has a fever *and* is refusing liquids

Head Injuries

Call the doctor if:

1. The child is 12 months old or younger and hits his head
2. The child injures his eye

Call the doctor immediately if:

1. The child has lost consciousness
2. The child is vomiting
3. The child is having trouble breathing
4. The child is exhibiting unusual behavior

Vomiting

Check to see if the child has swallowed a toxic substance or a poison.

If so or if you're not sure, call the Poison Control Center immediately.

Call the doctor if:

1. The vomiting continues for a few hours

THESE CONDITIONS ARE MEDICAL EMERGENCIES. CALL THE DOCTOR IMMEDIATELY:

1. Breathing difficulties
2. High fever

3. Blood in urine
4. Prolonged diarrhea or vomiting
5. Unusual lethargy or listlessness
6. An unusual rash
7. Food refusal (refuses to eat for 3 or 4 feedings)
8. Serious injury

From: "Calling the Doctor," *Newsweek*, Special Issue: How Kids Grow, Summer, 1991. © 1991 Newsweek, Inc. All rights reserved. Reprinted by permission.

---

ping snugly in a lightweight blanket), and massaging (see Schnieder, *Infant Massage*, Bantam, 1982).

Teething

Teething is the eruption of the 20 deciduous, or baby, teeth, plus their replacement by 32 permanent teeth beginning around age 6 or 7. The term also is used to describe the discomfort the whole process sometimes causes. The timing of the first tooth's eruption varies considerably. One baby out of every 1500 is born with one erupted tooth, whereas some normal babies don't get their first tooth until they are 15 months old (Whaley & Wong, 1988).

For most children, teeth emerge between 6 and 7 months. The two bottom front teeth are usually the first to appear, followed by the two top front teeth. These deciduous teeth had begun to form during the third month of gestation. A full set of 20 baby teeth is usually present by the time the child is 2.5 or 3. Baby teeth are lost in order of their appearance except in cases of injury.

Most children have a little gum soreness and tenderness when teething owing to the rupturing of blood vessels and the displacement of tissue. As a result, the child may resist eating and be a little cranky. However, high fever, convulsions, vomiting, diarrhea, and earaches are *never* normal signs of teething. Parents should avoid coating the baby's pacifier with honey in an attempt to sooth them since honey may cause botulism (Center for Disease Control, 1978).

BABY BOTTLE TOOTH DECAY (BBTD) Baby bottle tooth decay is a characteristic pattern of tooth decay that occurs because liquid from a baby bottle pools around the infant's teeth and gums, encouraging the growth of bacteria that erode the tooth enamel (Druerd et al., 1989). Compared with breast-fed babies, babies who fall asleep with bottles, especially bottles filled with sugary liquid such as juice, are more likely to develop this pattern of decay. BBTD may be more pronounced in babies who have a genetic predisposition to develop cavities because of weak enamel or other structural tooth problems. Dietary fluoride supplements

Poison Control Center
any of several regionalized offices specializing in prompt information about the toxicity of specific substances and in the treatment of poison ingestion

teething
cutting teeth; growing or developing teeth

baby bottle tooth decay (BBTD)
tooth decay that occurs in some bottlefed infants

■ **Figure 5–9**

Emerging teeth. This baby has 2 + ¼ + ⅛(?) teeth.

■ ● ▲   CONCEPT SUMMARY

Summary of Physical Growth

- *Height*—adds 10–12 inches by first birthday; 50% of adult height by age 2

- *Weight*—birthweight doubled by 4 months, tripled by 1 year, quadrupled by year 2; some infants are obese

- *Brain*—fastest growing organ; redundant cells/connections begin to die off by age 2

- *Skeleton*—ossification continues; soft spots (fontanels) close by age 2

- *Musculature*—change in size and composition leads to more strength, stamina

- *Digestion*—food only partially digested; spitting up likely

- *Immune system*—child slowly produces own antibodies; receives supplemental antibodies through inoculation and breast milk

- *Respiratory system*—lung capacity increases; lungs sensitive to irritation

- *Circulatory system*—heart becomes stronger, more efficient; blood pressure decreases

- *Temperature regulation*—efficient by age 1½ to 2

- *Teething*—Teeth erupt between 6 months and 3 years.

---

to prevent tooth decay are recommended for all children not drinking fluoridated water (Alley et al., 1988).

● Motor Development

The normal child masters an impressive list of motor accomplishments during infancy and toddlerhood. Although he may begin life unable to lift up his chin, the infant does not remain helpless for long. Motor development follows a well-established sequence that parallels the cephalocaudal and proximodistal development of the nervous system (Lou, 1982). Some motor skills like grasping and walking have their foundation in reflex equivalents that were present at birth. As the brain matures and the cortex assumes more and more control, the reflex behaviors are replaced by voluntary, purposeful versions of those same activities.

Gross Motor Development: Locomotion

Locomotor development—which eventually results in the ability to crawl, walk, and run—involves maturation in head control, posture, sitting, kneeling, crawling, creeping, standing, and walking. Through locomotor activity, infants gain control over the large body muscles that will enable them to move about their environment. Although creeping and crawling are essential to perceptual development, the major locomotor achievement during infancy is walking (J. C. Clark et al., 1988). Most children walk alone by 14.5 months, but their gait is unsteady and awkward. Toes are pointed inward or outward, feet are placed far apart, and arms are held out to improve balance. By 18 months, most infants can run, but they fall frequently. Toddlers with walking experience have a more narrowed stance and recover fairly easily if their balance is threatened. They can turn, stop, or pick up a toy when walking, and tend to walk in a straighter line than less experienced walkers. By the way, barefoot walking promotes the development of strong feet, ankle, and leg muscles (Seder, 1980). The overuse of walkers—seats on frames with wheels—may damage the child's hip sockets (Ridenour, 1982).

Walking is preceded by an orderly sequence of developmental events. Before infants can walk, they must be able to stand and support their weight with their legs. And in order to stand, they must have sufficient trunk control to sit. Sitting requires head and arm control. Head control is no easy task, given the size and weight of the infant's disproportionately large skull. More than 60 years ago, Mary Shirley (1933) identified the sequence of development that leads to walking.

Although the sequence of development is invariant, the age at which the motor skills are accomplished may vary owing to the individual child's motivation, heredity, health, neurological maturity or "readiness," and the level of environmental stimulation. Parents of premature, SGA, and retarded infants should expect delays in development, since their infants were less mature at birth than full-term babies (Gorga et al., 1991). Some infants skip some locomotor behaviors altogether or spend a relatively longer or shorter time than others practicing certain activities. Also, because of improved nutrition, children born today generally accomplish these locomotor tasks a little earlier than the Depression-era children whom Shirley studied (Beardslee et al., 1982). The Denver Developmental Screening Test (Frankenburg et al., 1975) provides updated norms for the ages at which 25%, 50%, 75%, and 90% of American children can accomplish each motor task. Babies of African descent mature at a faster rate than nonAfrican babies and pass each motor skill sooner (Super, 1981).

It is important that the behavior of children from other cultures not be applied to these Denver Developmental Test norms. Due to differences in cultural expectations and child rearing practices, babies from other cultures may not develop at the same rate or engage in the same

■ **Figure 5–10**

The toddling gait of the young walker.

readiness
Arnold Gesell's term describing the physical maturation that prepares the child to make advances in motor development

■ Figure 5–11

The progression of gross motor development (Adapted from Frankenburg, 1978).

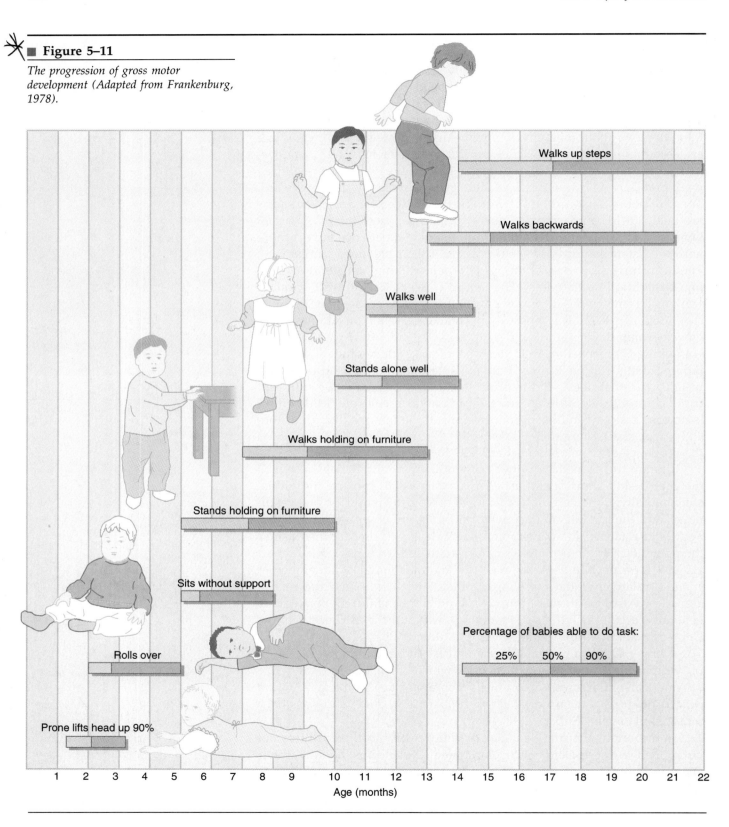

behaviors as Western children. For example, just because children from other cultures don't play peek-a-boo at a certain age doesn't necessarily indicate a neurological deficit or abnormally slow development; likewise, motor superiority is not assured if they are "early" (V. Miller et al., 1984).

Considerable social pressure is placed on American parents to report precocious motor development in their babies. The reasoning goes something like this: If baby Jenny walks sooner than baby Janis and they're both the same age, then Jenny must be the superior baby and Jenny's mom and dad must be better parents. In reality, is there anything Janis's parents could have done to encourage Janis to walk earlier? Probably not. In a classic investigation Gesell and Thompson (1934) studied pairs of monozygotic and dizygotic twins and found that giving one twin in each pair practice in block-handling tasks did not affect their performance—both the experienced and the inexperienced twin did equally well when tested. Thirty-eight years later, R. S. Wilson (1972) found that progress in motor development was almost identical among 261 pairs of monozygotic and dizygotic twins. Since the rate of locomotor development appears to be influenced by maturation (supporting Gesell's notion of readiness), any "pushing" on the part of the parent is likely to result in frustration for the child, *not* in accelerated development.

prehension
skills involved in grasping or holding objects

voluntary grasping
grasping that is planned and purposeful, not reflexive

Fine Motor Development: Directed Reaching and Grasping

As part of their proximodistal development during infancy, children reach and grasp reflexively and then intentionally. At first babies move their arms toward objects but make no attempt to grasp them, since their hands are fisted rather than open. By 4 months of age their hands are predominately open and they can extend an arm in the general direction of an object, but usually do not grasp it. The child looks back and forth from the hand to the object, focusing attention first on one, then the other. In another month or so, visually guided reach develops. By the time they are 5 or 5.5 months old, children can keep their eyes on a target and reach for it directly. When sound is associated with an object, a 7–7.5 month old infant will reach toward the sounding object even in the dark, indicating that visual cues are not necessary for guided hand placement if auditory clues are present (Perris & Clifton, 1988). The capacity to time and coordinate movements to catch a suspended moving object is a skill possessed by 8–9 month old infants (vonHofsten, 1983).

Prehension is the ability to grasp objects between the fingers and opposing thumb. Grasping that occurs in the first 2 or 3 months of life is primarily reflexive. Voluntary grasping does not begin until approximately 3 months of age when the baby's hands are predominately open

■ **Figure 5–12**

The infant pincer grasp.

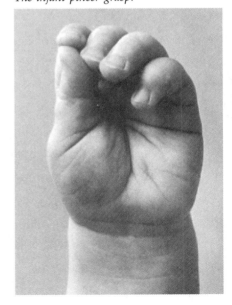

■ Figure 5–13

Milestones in infant locomotor development.

Age (mo)	Age (wk)	HEAD CONTROL	SITTING POSITION	ROLLING OVER AND CRAWLING	STANDING ERECT	STEPS TO FIRST STEPS
		When lifted from supine position the normal newborn shows a complete lack of head control. As the infant's neuromuscular system matures, control becomes greater.	The average term infant doubles his weight between birth and 5 months. During this period, signs of maturation, such as head control and a straightening back, are seen in the sitting position.	The righting response is composed of a series of reflexes developing along the body axis from head to buttocks. As time passes, the activity becomes purposeful and is accompanied by leg and arm activity that produces movement.	Here is shown the development of control over antigravity muscles used to assume an erect posture.	By supporting an infant in an erect posture, development of posture, balance, and effort to take steps may be observed.
1	4	1–4 WEEKS There is complete head lag when pulled to sitting position.	First 4 WEEKS The back is uniformly rounded—there is absence of head control. 4–6 WEEKS There is a rounded back and the head is held up intermittently. 8–12 WEEKS The back is still rounded. Baby is now raising head well, but tends to bob forward. Knees are flexed. Can sit for 10–15 minutes if propped.	Makes crawling or swimming movements when on stomach. Moves arms and legs together on one side of the body.		
2	8	8–10 WEEKS At this stage, head lag is still apparent, but not complete.				Up to 14 WEEKS From birth to about 14 weeks, posture in supported position is generally limp. Some infants rest no weight on their feet.
3	12			Up to 14 WEEKS The newborn infant is unable to turn from back to stomach. Turning the head does not affect the rest of the body.	Up to 14 WEEKS The newborn exhibits distinctly passive response to efforts to pull him upward past a sitting position.	
4	16	16–20 WEEKS Now there is only slight or no head lag when pulled up. Turns head in all directions.	16–20 WEEKS The back is much straighter. Baby holds head erect without wobble. Birth weight is nearly doubled. Can sit for 30 minutes if well supported.	Rolls from stomach to back. Pushes with hands and flexes knees when on stomach.	16–24 WEEKS As development begins in the lower extremities, the infant exhibits an urge to push upward. He raises the buttocks, but cannot sustain this position.	18–24 WEEKS Head is more in line with body plane; upper and lower limbs are less lame. Mechanisms controlling posture appear to advance more rapidly than those governing progressive movements. Stamps foot, support most of weight in standing position.
5	20			26–28 WEEKS The infant turns his face to the side and toward the back. The shoulder raises and the spine curves. Legs and arms are carried toward the side. A complete roll is accomplished (back to stomach). Crawls (lies on stomach and pulls self ahead with arms.)		
6	24	24–28 WEEKS at this point, baby lifts head spontaneously from supine position.	Sits with slight support; pulls self to sitting position. Sits well-balanced on a chair.			
7	28					

Age (mo)	Age (wk)	HEAD CONTROL	SITTING POSITION	ROLLING OVER AND CRAWLING	STANDING ERECT	STEPS TO FIRST STEPS
		When lifted from supine position the normal newborn shows a complete lack of head control. As the infant's neuromuscular system matures, control becomes greater.	The average term infant doubles his weight between birth and 5 months. During this period, signs of maturation, such as head control and a straightening back, are seen in the sitting position.	The righting response is composed of a series of reflexes developing along the body axis from head to buttocks. As time passes, the activity becomes purposeful and is accompanied by leg and arm activity that produces movement.	Here is shown the development of control over antigravity muscles used to assume an erect posture.	By supporting an infant in an erect posture, development of posture, balance, and effort to take steps may be observed.
7	28			Rocks in crawling position. Creeps (moving forward on hands and knees) unsteady at first. Pivots from side to side on stomach.		
8	32		Sits alone steadily and briefly. Pushes self into sitting position. Sits alone steadily; bounces.			26–30 WEEKS Postural adjustment is much the same as in previous phase, but up and down movements and stamping may be seen. Some stepping movements may be observed. Supports weight well when leaning on furniture. Pulls self up on furniture.
9	36		Sits alone for long periods of time.	34–38 WEEKS Early rolling appears more involuntary than deliberate. Spinal extension is still the major initial movement. If near the edge of a bed or table, the infant shows no awareness of it. He might roll off. Creeping and crawling well coordinated.	36–44 WEEKS As capacity increases, the infant extends his lower extremities and attains a somewhat erect posture. However, a vertical position usually cannot be achieved.	Walks around furniture (cruises). Pulls self to feet when helped. Stands alone briefly.
10	40		Lowers self to sit.			40–48 WEEKS Stepping and postural adjustment are more evidently deliberate at about 36 weeks. Some support is needed. Walks holding on to two hands. Cruising continues. Pulls self to stand. Lifts one foot when standing.
11	44					
12	48			48–52 WEEKS The infant begins to use the act of rolling to complete some deliberate performance. He may flex the legs and raise the abdomen in order to creep or push into a sitting position. He shows some tendency towards adjusting to his whereabouts. Prefers to crawl.		Stands by self. Walks around small objects when someone holds one hand.
13	52				48–52 WEEKS Erect, vertical position is finally accomplished. Movements are made with effort.	Loses balance with sudden stops. Jumps in place; falls forward often.
15						Walks side ways and backwards. Pushes furniture when walking; pulls pull toy. Runs awkwardly and falls often.
18						

rather than closed. Early reaching and grasping is guided by sight, but by 5 months of age a baby must actually touch an object before trying to grasp it (Bower, 1981).

Prehension progresses from involving the whole hand as a single unit (hand grasp, 5–7 months), to using the palm and middle fingers (palmar grasp, 9–10 months) to using the thumb and forefinger in precise opposition (pincer grasp, 9–15 months) (Hohlstein, 1982) (Figure 5–14). Most infants relentlessly practice their pincer grasp, picking up anything from food and toys to lint and crawling insects. The acquisition of posture is actually a more accurate predictor of prehension than is age (Fontaine & le Bonniec, 1988). Apparently, postural acquisition may help restructure infant reaching and grasping.

At 5 months, both hands are used together to improve efficiency. By 8–10 months, babies can perform two activities simultaneously such as supporting their weight on one arm while reaching with the other. Letting go of an object and hand-to-hand transfer are complex behaviors learned by the age of 7 months (Hohlstein, 1982). The earliest signs of hand preference appear around 6 months or so, when the child uses one hand as an "active hand" and the other as a "passive hand." Like most adults, most babies prefer their right hands (McCormick & Maurer, 1988). Before this time, the child uses the left hand, the right hand, or both hands together. Even then, handedness is not established until the child enters school.

Like locomotor skills, the development of directed reaching and prehension are influenced both by genetics and the environment. Bower

hand preference
see handedness

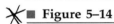

■ Figure 5–14

Milestones in fine motor development.

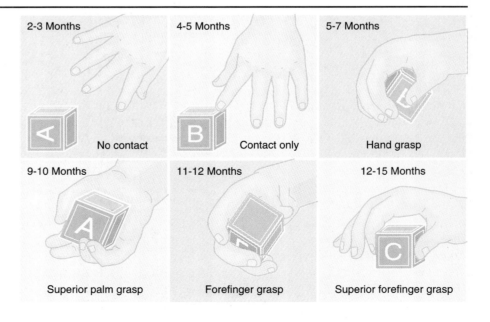

2-3 Months	4-5 Months	5-7 Months
No contact	Contact only	Hand grasp
9-10 Months	11-12 Months	12-15 Months
Superior palm grasp	Forefinger grasp	Superior forefinger grasp

Infants will reflexively grasp anything, even if they can't yet drive.

(1981) reports that blind babies attempt to reach and grasp early in life in response to environmental sounds. But since the sound does not tell the infant how far away the object is, the blind baby's grasping efforts are unsuccessful, and reaching soon stops. It is possible to make special alterations in the environment, however, to encourage normal development in handicapped infants.

● Sensory Perception

Like adults, infants receive information about their environments from their senses. From birth to age 3, rapid and dramatic changes take place in the infant's sensory systems, so by the end of infancy the incoming sensations have changed both quantitatively and qualitatively. The process of recognizing, combining, and interpreting those sensations is called *perception.*

   The scientific study of the sensory and perceptual capabilities of infants is a challenging task. Infants are limited in the types of responses they can provide. For example, they cannot describe what they see; nor can they reach or point to stimuli with any accuracy or walk or crawl like adults or older children. Also, what may be sweet or loud or bright to an older child may not be regarded in the same way by an infant, since subjective judgments of stimulus intensity can change with age. To help discover more about the infant's capabilities, researchers focus on behaviors the baby can perform with some consistency and predictability. General activity level may be one indication of attention—children may stop what they are doing, for instance, to look at or listen to a particular stimulus. More reliably, changes in the infant's heart rate, breathing rate, or physiological functions may indicate the infant's sensitivity to particular environmental events.

perception
the process of interpreting sensory input

Visual Perception

In the first few weeks of life, infants actively use their visual systems by scanning the environment for objects, tracking sound and movement, and switching attention to new objects. In order for infants to make full use of their visual capabilities, they must be awake and alert and the lighting must not be too bright (Haith, 1986). Infants stay awake for longer periods of time as they grow older. They achieve greater control over head movements and improve their focusing, refine their tracking skills, and lengthen their attention spans. Thus, the time they spend scanning the environment increases from 5% at birth to 35% by age 2. By the time the baby is 6 months old, she can see 800 times more clearly than at one month of age. In another year, visual acuity approaches adult levels.

The first 3 years of life appear to be a critical period for the development of binocular vision, or using both eyes together (Bertenthal & Campos, 1987). When crossed eyes and other visual defects are corrected by age 3, children have better vision than children whose surgeries were delayed.

What do babies like to look at? One- to 2-month-old infants seem predisposed to search for edges, corners, and areas of contrasting color in their surroundings and to scan these objects intently by tracking from edge to corner, edge to edge, and corner to corner (Bronson, 1990). In one interesting study of visual discrimination, investigators wanted to find out when infants assemble the edges, boundaries and details into unified perceptions. Fagan (1977) repeatedly showed infants a green square until it lost its novelty and infants looked at it only briefly. He then showed infants a green circle or a blue square to determine if the babies were fixating on color, shape, or the compound figure. Infants who looked only briefly at the green circle were thought to be respond-

■ Figure 5–16

Newborns prefer to scan edges and boundaries. Shown at left is the way one newborn scanned a triangle. Within a month or so, they are scanning features of the human face as well. (Sources: a. Kessen, 1967 and b. Haurer & Salapatek, 1975)

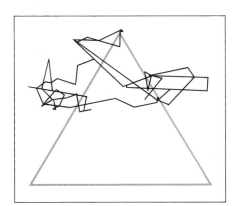

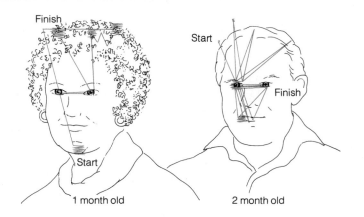

1 month old   2 month old

ing to color, not shape, since they treated the green circle and the green square similarly. Likewise, if the blue square attracted little attention, then shape, not color, was presumed to be the important dimension. But if the infant gazed longer at either the green circle or the blue square, the infant must be remembering the green square as a compound stimulus, and thus, regarding any other figure as novel by comparison. The results indicated that before 5 months of age infants tend to focus on one characteristic of an object, such as shape or color, while after that time infants perceive the compound figure as well. Even though infants can distinguish all primary colors by 4 months of age, they, like adults, prefer red and blue (Teller & Bornstein, 1987). Infants also like to look at things they've never seen before (Fantz, 1964).

The human face is the infant's favorite visual stimulus (Dannemiller & Stephens, 1988). When 1-month-old babies scan faces, they tend to focus on the outer edges. These young infants can recognize their mother's face (or the face of their primary caregiver) apparently by recognizing her chin and her unique hairline.

By the time babies are 5–7 weeks old, they spend less time looking at contours and significantly more time looking at the eyes of a face. Apparently, by that time the eyes have become a meaningful stimulus to the infants, since eye contact is important in the development of emotional bonds (Haith, 1986). Babies seem to prefer eyes that are open to closed eyes and are most responsive when they can see *both* eyes instead of just one. By age 5 months, infants are able to perceive faces as distinctive units rather than collections of unrelated features, since they can distinguish faces they have seen before from faces they have not. Year-old babies are more sophisticated still, preferring attractive faces to unattractive ones probably because attractive faces are more curved and less angular (Langlois et al., 1990). Infants prefer curved lines over straight. This shift from the perception of parts to the perception of patterns is similar for both objects and faces (Teller & Bornstein, 1987).

Depth Perception

Depth perception involves the ability to recognize uneven surfaces or drop-offs. Depth perception is adaptive, since it prevents us from routinely falling down stairs or walking out of the upper floors of high-rise buildings. It also lets us judge distance and perceive the world in three dimensions. The ability to perceive depth develops quite early. The classic study of infant depth perception was conducted in 1960 by Eleanor Gibson and Richard Walk. They constructed a "visual cliff" using a sheet of glass over a painted surface to give the illusion of a drop off. Infants 6 to 14 months old were placed on the apparatus to see if they could be coaxed onto the cliff side by their mothers. Since only 3 babies out of the 36 tested crawled off the wooden platform onto the "deep side," the experiment supported the notion that crawling infants can perceive depth. In another study, Campos and colleagues (1970) placed

depth perception
an awareness of the distance between oneself and an object

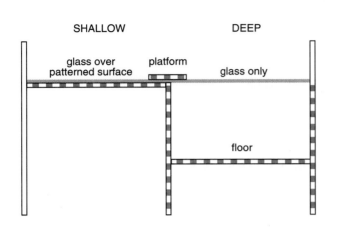

■ Figure 5–17

(left) The visual cliff. (right) A baby testing his depth perception on the visual cliff apparatus.

precrawling infants on the deep and shallow sides of the visual cliff and measured changes in their heart rates. If infants can perceive depth, their heart rates should decelerate when placed on the deep side, because vital signs slow down when attention is directed at an object (though they accelerate when the stimulus changes initially). Campos concluded from measured heart rate changes that infants as young as 1.5 months perceive depth.

The perception of depth should be distinguished from depth avoidance. Scarr and Salapatek (1970) found that 2- to 8-month-old infants distinguished between deep and shallow surfaces but showed no fear or avoidance of depth. It was only after crawling or walking infants spent considerable time exploring their environments and becoming aware of edges and surfaces that fear of depth developed. Thus, although infants may be able to recognize depth, fear of a drop-off and cliff avoidance apparently have to be learned through experience (Bremner, 1989).

Object Constancy

When babies start to crawl, they are able to experience the world from an entirely new vantage point. As they move about unaided, they encounter tables, chairs, doors, and other objects and perhaps for the first time really pay attention to their size, shape, and location. Crawling gives a sense of dimensionality to objects that walking can't provide: Through crawling one becomes aware of the *underside* of things. All of this experience in the environment is vital to the development of object constancy.

Infants who have *object constancy* have learned that the color, shape, and size of people or objects remain the same despite changes in dis-

object constancy
the realization that the actual size, shape, or color of an object is not affected by viewing angle, lighting, or distance.

■ ● ▲   CONCEPT SUMMARY

Major Developments in Vision During the First Year

- *Birth*
  - Pupil adjusts to light intensity (pupillary reflex) and the child blinks
  - If head is rotated to one side, the eyes follow slowly (doll's eye reflex)
  - Can focus momentarily on moving object 8–10 inches away

- *4 weeks (1 month)*
  - Very interested in the human face
  - Can distinguish mother's face from that of a stranger
  - Tear glands begin to function

- *6–12 weeks (1½–3 months)*
  - Has peripheral vision to 180 degrees
  - Both eyes are working well together (binocular vision)
  - Eyes move together to focus on close objects (convergence)
  - Doll's eye reflex disappears
  - Focuses on edges and corners

- *12–20 weeks (3–5 months)*
  - Responds to familiar objects and people
  - Looks at hands while sitting or lying on back (an action called hand regard)
  - Focuses on mirror image of self

- *20–28 weeks (5–7 months)*
  - Develops eye-hand coordination (grasping well established)
  - Can move objects from hand to hand
  - Prefers more complex visual stimuli
  - Pats image of self in the mirror
  - Prefers reds and blues
  - Adjusts posture to see an object
  - Visual acuity (sharpness) is 800 times better than it was at 1 month of age

- *28–44 weeks (7–11 months)*
  - Can focus on very small objects
  - Likes to look at new things
  - Depth perception becoming apparent

- *44–52 weeks (11–13 months)*
  - Can follow rapidly moving objects

tance and viewing angle, which alter the size and shape of images on the retina. Size and color constancy are present between 4 and 6 months (Dannemiller, 1989). By this time infants know that color remains the same despite changes in light intensity and that people at a distance haven't really shrunk in size or become more massive as they approach. Shape constancy appears between 8 and 10 months (McKenzie et al., 1980). Besides playing other roles, shape constancy enables the infant to perceive the primary caregiver's face as a constant stimulus no matter what the viewing angle.

Hearing

As I mentioned in the last chapter, infants are born with the ability to discriminate between low- and high-frequency sounds, to get used to sounds and filter them out, and to attempt to locate sound sources. Sound localization improves as the infant's head size changes (Clifton et al., 1988). Very young infants not only hear well but can interpret what they hear. Four- to 6-month-old infants can discriminate between very similar sounds such as *bah* and *pah* and prefer their mothers' voices over those of female strangers saying the same words (De Casper & Fifer, 1980). Between 3 and 6 months of age, babies can imitate a variety of low- and high-pitched tones. Thus, early social growth and language development seem intimately related.

Babies not only attend to the sound of a human voice, they synchronize their body movements to the patterns of adult speech as early as the first day of life. This synchronization is called the *language dance* (Penman et al., 1983b). Infants a few months old will attempt to imitate movements of adult models as they speak. Babies can also stop an activity such as feeding or playing to listen and respond to voices by making head and body movements, smiling, raising eyebrows, opening eyes, and changing facial expressions.

As perception and memory develop, infants expect certain objects to be associated with certain sounds. Thus, they become distressed if a familiar object (a squeeze toy, for example) is associated with an unexpected sound (say, a dog barking) (Lyons-Ruth, 1977). Four-month-old babies also display distress by increasing body movement and crying when recordings of their mothers' voices come from the side of the room opposite to where the mothers are standing.

Eighty to 85% of congenitally deaf children are born to hearing parents, so most parents have no reason to suspect their babies can't hear (Clarkson, 1989). Every child occasionally fails to respond to a sound. Sometimes they are intentionally ignoring the speaker or are absorbed in play. But because early detection of hearing loss is crucial, parents should be vigilant to some signs of potential hearing loss and should report their concerns to their pediatrician (Brody, 1989):

sound localization
the ability to pinpoint the source of a sound in the environment

language dance
the tendency of the baby to synchronize his or her movements to the sound and pattern of human speech directed toward them

A Closer Look

Keeping Baby Safe

Safeguard the baby's life by keeping the environment free from hazards.

Carseats

Use *safety approved* carseats *correctly every time* the child is transported in the car. Most states have laws requiring carseat use since they can prevent 71% of infant deaths and 66% of infant hospitalizations when used correctly (Department of Transportation, 1987).

Toys

Select toys without sharp edges, removable pieces, or small decorations that might be swallowed.

Hanging crib toys that are not designed for actual handling by infants (like mobiles or decorative ropes) may be pulled down by babies and have caused strangulation. Remove such toys by the time the child is 5 months old and replace with a baby gym or play center.

Plants

Many homes and gardens contain plants that are toxic when ingested. To avoid accidents, rid the home of these plants:

Mild (the juice of these plants may contain oxalate crystals which may cause pain and irritation of the mouth, lips, and tongue)

arrowhead vine	nephthytis
begonia	philodendron
caladium	virginia creeper
calla lily	pothos
chinese evergreen	rhubarb leaf
devil's ivy	schefflera
dieffenbachia	spathiphyllum

dumbcane	split leaf
jack-in-the-pulpit	umbrella tree
marble queen pothos	

Minor toxicity (ingestion may cause vomiting or diarrhea; eating small portions may not cause any symptoms)

acacia	hyacinth
agapanthus	hydrangea
aloe vera	iris
amaryllis	juniper
belladonna	mother-in-law tongue
birch tree	naked lady
boxwood	pansy
cedar	pyracantha
century plant	ranunculus
chrysanthemum	redwood tree
creeping charlie	snake plant
crown of thorns	strawberry
daffodil	sweet pea
daisy	sweet william
eucalyptus globulus	umbrella plant
gladiola	violas
holly	

Major toxicity (ingestion, especially in large amounts, can cause serious effects to major body organs like the heart, liver, and kidneys. Call the Poison Control Center at once

apple tree	licorice plant
apricot tree	lily of the valley
azalea	lobelia
black acacia	lupine
black locust	mock orange
camphor tree	morning glory
carnation	mountain laurel
castor beans	nightshade
cherry tree	oak tree

(continued on next page)

(continued from previous page)

china berry	oleander
coffee tree plant	ornamental pepper
cyclamen	ornamental plum tree
daphne	peach tree
delphinium	photinia arbutifolia
elderberry	potato plant
english ivy	pregnant onion
euonymus	privet
four-o-clocks	rhododendron
foxglove	rosary beads
california geranium	toyon
ivy	vinca
jequerity bean	wisteria
jimson weed	yellow jessamine
lantana camara	yew

Medical Equipment

It may be helpful to have a digital thermometer on hand to check the child's temperature and an otoscope to detect the earliest signs of ear infection.

First Aid Supplies, Cleaning Products, Cosmetics, Haircare Items, Medicines, and Vitamins

All these items are potential poisons. Keep them in a locked chest or a child-proofed cabinet. Keep the number of the Poison Control Center by the phone just in case. Alcohol and tobacco are toxic to children, too.

Supervision

Never leave a child alone around heat sources, open windows, water, stairs or steps, outside, on a high surface (even if the child is strapped onto a changing table or in an infant seat). The risk of injury is great.

Crib

A crib needs to provide a safe, inescapable sleeping environment.

The spaces between the bars should be no more than 2⅜ inches (keeps baby from squeezing through or trapping her head).

Make sure a lead-free paint was used.

Make sure there is no room between the crib and the mattress itself (Bumper pads help here).

Extra blankets, pillows, and animals are a suffocation hazard for babies under 4 months of age.

When the baby can stand, remove the bumper pad and stuffed toys. Babies can use them to boost themselves out.

Make sure the side rails cannot be accidentally released.

There should be 26 inches from the top of the side rail to the top of the mattress when the mattress is in its lowest position.

Stop using the crib when the child reaches 35 inches in height.

Appliances

Unplug all appliances when not in use. Unplug and store all fans (their edges are sharp even when they're not moving).

Cover unused outlets with small plug caps.

Fireplaces and Other Heat Sources

Keep them screened.

Keep matches and lighters out of reach.

Tubs and Showers

Lower the hot water heater setting to 120°F to avoid serious burns that could occur at higher temperatures.

Cover the knobs with a soft guard to avoid bumps and burns.

Place nonslip strips on the tub bottom to make it less slippery.

Miscellaneous

Buy safe equipment and know how to use it.

Make it difficult for baby to pull something down by avoiding the use of table cloths and runners and turning all handles away from baby.

Keep loose plastic bags locked up. Tie into knots before discarding.

Sources: *Sunset New Western Garden Book,* Lane Publishing, 1986; Kretschmer & Wright, 1990.

1. The child *consistently* fails to respond to speech or quiet sounds, especially after 6 to 9 months of age. (By themselves whispers, jangling keys, clapping hands may not test hearing adequately. Some children may react normally only because they can hear within a limited range.)
2. The infant turns only one ear in the direction of a sound (a clue to one-ear hearing loss).
3. The child *consistently* cannot recognize certain sounds or locate the origin of sounds.
4. The child frequently acts stubborn, has trouble learning, or is inattentive, irritable, or withdrawn.

The Other Senses

Touch is probably the best developed sense of infants. All parts of their bodies have been touch sensitive since the 8th gestational month (Haith,

---

■ ●▲   CONCEPT SUMMARY

Major Developments in Hearing During the First Year

- *Birth*
  - Startles when noise is sounded
  - Orients to the sound of a human voice
  - Low-pitched sounds like a lullaby or heartbeat have a quieting effect
- *8–12 weeks (2–3 months)*
  - Turns head to the side when sound is made at ear level
- *12–16 weeks (3–4 months)*
  - Localizes sound in environment by turning head and looking for the sound source
- *16–24 weeks (4–6 months)*
  - Can localize sound made above or below the head by turning head to the side and looking up or down
- *24–32 weeks (6–8 months)*
  - Responds to own name
- *32–52 weeks (8–13 months)*
  - Responds to some words as though their meaning is understood (e.g., "no" and the names of family members and familiar objects)
  - Controls response in reaction to sound (e.g., listens for the sound to occur twice before behaving)

1986). By 12 months of age, infants can recognize an object by the way it feels and can use touch to distinguish between familiar and unfamiliar objects in the dark (Gottfried & Rose, 1980). Newborn infants mouth objects to determine whether they are hard or soft (Rochat, 1987). (Table 5.3) For reasons not fully understood, females tend to be more touch-sensitive than males.

Pain is also experienced by the infant. Babies become pain sensitive in the first 5 days of life and judging from their crying, grimacing, withdrawing, and elevated heart rates and blood pressure, circumcision, procedures to obtain blood samples, and surgery are painful experiences for the infant (Arand & Hickey, 1987). The American Academy of Pediatrics now recommends the use of local pain killers and other safe medications for infant pain relief. Sucrose (sugar) has shown promise in reducing infant pain. Babies given an oral dose of sugar solution (about the equivalent of 1 tsp of table sugar) before being circumcised or having blood drawn cried less than infants given water or nothing (Blass et al., 1991).

During infancy, the senses of smell and taste gradually become more acute. As noted in the last chapter, the newborns' sense of smell is already helping them identify their primary caregiver. One-week-old breast-fed babies awaken more quickly to the smell of fabric worn inside their mothers' bras than to the smell of fabric worn by other nursing mothers. Female babies are particularly sensitive to the breast odors of lactating women (Makin & Porter, 1989). The sense of smell also adds to the infant's enjoyment of food. Infants prefer sweet-tasting liquids. The sweeter the liquid, the harder babies suck (Haith, 1986). They can also discriminate the three nonsweet tastes, bitter, sour, and salty (Rosenstein & Oster, 1988). And—like older children and adults—if the food tastes bad, the infant won't eat it.

● Infant Routines

Sleep

Sleep is vital to the human organism. It is restorative and may be involved in protein synthesis, memory storage, and other biochemical processes. No one can do without sleep, and infants require more sleep than older children or mature adults. The pineal gland may be the master switch of sleep (Kocaard, 1991). In the first month of life, newborns can be expected to sleep 17 to 20 hours per day (Berg & Berg, 1979). By the time babies are a year old, they have spent more than half their lives asleep!

Sleep is not continuous but a series of long or short naps. It's difficult to predict how long infants will nap. Since babies' brains are so immature, accidental "storms" or nerve impulses may occur and wake the

pineal gland
the gland within the brain that may influence sleep and wakefulness

baby up (Parmalee & Stern, 1972). Well-nourished babies sleep better than malnourished ones (Pairano et al., 1988). Breast-fed and smaller babies usually sleep for longer periods of time than larger or bottle-fed babies (Ogra et al., 1982). Breast milk is highly digestible and is absorbed more quickly than formula; smaller babies may have a smaller stomach capacity and may get hungry sooner. However, young infants are seldom awake for longer than 2 hours at a time.

Temperament is another factor that may be related to infant sleep patterns. Infants who are less fussy, more adaptable, and "easier" sleep longer than more difficult babies (Weissbluth & Liu, 1983). Within the first year the child's sleep/wake pattern becomes adapted to the outside environment, so babies increasingly concentrate their sleep during the nighttime hours. By 6 months of age or so, most are sleeping through the night—much to their parents' delight—and are taking both morning and afternoon naps. Joanne Cuthbertson and Susanna Schevill claim that healthy infants can be taught to sleep through the night as early as 6 weeks of age. Their training procedure is detailed in their book *Helping Your Child Sleep Through the Night* (Doubleday, 1989).

By 18 months the only regular daytime sleep is usually a nap after lunch. At this age 10 or 12 hours of nighttime sleep is required. Babies who receive sufficient sleep are active when awake and are growing normally. Babies who lack sufficient sleep are irritable, infection prone, and hard to wake in the morning. These same babies often lack appetite and show less intellectual ability than well-rested infants (Lowrey, 1978). Each baby sleeps according to her unique biological needs, so variation in sleep patterns is common.

Infants exhibit two types of sleep: quiet (NREM) sleep and active (REM) sleep. In *quiet (NREM or non-REM)* sleep, the baby is still, very relaxed, and breathing slowly and regularly. Blood pressure, heart rate, digestion, and brain activity are slowed. In *active (REM)* sleep, the baby's facial muscles may twitch and the child may vocalize. The eyes may dart back and forth under their closed eyelids. These movements, which are easy to see, are called *rapid eye movements,* or REMs. In REM sleep, internal body activity is similar to that during waking. In adults and children, REM sleep is associated with dreaming. As yet there is no way of determining if infants dream during REM sleep, since they cannot report their experiences. Episodes of active and quiet sleep alternate throughout the sleep period.

rapid eye movements (REMs) darting movements made by the eyes during sleep, but especially during dreaming

One interesting pattern is the change that takes place in the proportion of time spent in REM and NREM sleep with development. Newborn infants spend about 50% of the sleep time in REM. They also cycle into REM sleep from almost any sleeping or waking state. In contrast, mature adults spend only 20–23% of their sleep time in REM sleep and usually cycle into quiet, or NREM, sleep from a drowsy or waking state (Thoman & Whitney, 1989). Apparently, one function of REM sleep is to help infants make developmental progress. REM sleep may help

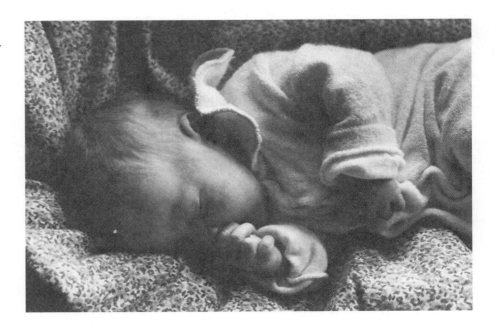

stimulate the development of the nervous system at a time when babies spend little time awake and thus receive little outside stimulation. As the infant becomes more alert and aware, increased environmental stimulation may reduce the need for large amounts of REM sleep (Boismier, 1977).

In most of the world's cultures, babies and young children sleep in the same bed as their parents. In the United States, however, such arrangements are rare. Sharing sleep has the advantage of easy access to the child and relaxed breastfeeding. The baby may sleep better since she's become accustomed to the sound of breathing, heartbeat, and human warmth in the womb. There are drawbacks, however. Parents need to make adjustments for intimacy; parents who are light sleepers will get little rest; and the child will have to be weaned into her own bed eventually (D. L. Davis, 1989). Whether parents choose to share their bed or not is less important overall than the relationship established between the baby and her parents.

Sleep Problems

Sleep problems may begin between the age of 1 and 2. Many toddlers are reluctant to go to bed. They may dawdle, invent excuses, or get up after being put to bed. This behavior is often due to their growing need to exert control over all aspect of their lives. They also seem worried that they are "missing out on something," especially if older siblings get to stay up later. Many toddlers find bedtime easier to accept if a bedtime routine or bedtime ritual is established. Repeating a sequence of quiet activities each night that culminates in going to bed (e.g., bath, story, potty, toothbrushing, good night kisses), allows the child to wind down and ease into bedtime rather than being abruptly wrenched from some favorite activity and forced to sleep. Caregivers should minimize stimulation in the hour prior to bedtime, since excitement and stress interfere with the child's ability to relax and fall asleep.

"Insomnia" is observed during infancy. Night terrors, inconsistent limit setting by the parents, and the anticipation of nighttime feeding can be responsible (Ferber, 1987).

Of all the sleep-related disorders of infancy, *sudden infant death syndrome (SIDS)* is the most baffling, unpredictable, and difficult to prevent. Sudden infant death syndrome is so named because it primarily affects babies in their first year of life who are apparently healthy but die suddenly, usually in their sleep. SIDS is the leading cause of infant death, affecting 6,000–7,000 babies in the United States annually (Shelov, 1989). The peak age for SIDS is 10–12 weeks (2.5 to 3 months). More than half the deaths occur by 3 months of age; 90% by 6 months of age.

Although scientists have ruled out suffocation by blankets or bedclothes, poisoning, disease, and choking from vomiting as possible causes of SIDS, actual causal factors are difficult to identify. Characteristics of the pregnancy, the family, and the infant have been associated with the likelihood of SIDS (Table 5.2). Some investigators advocate home use of respiratory monitors for infants at risk for SIDS, especially those who are "near miss" cases rescued just after they quit breathing. But home monitors are expensive and difficult to use, and the stress they can cause parents and siblings may be more devastating than the risk of SIDS (S. Phipps et al., 1989).

The loss of a child is always traumatic, but a SIDS death is particularly difficult because it is sudden, unexpected, and unexplained. A few comments seem appropriate:

1. The person who discovers the dead child may be the most profoundly affected. The mother, father, siblings, or sitter may feel responsible, try and fail to revive the child, and not know where to turn for help.
2. The family needs a great deal of support as they grieve their loss and attempt to cope. The incidence of divorce is high among couples who have lost a child to SIDS.
3. Good prenatal care and a drug-free pregnancy do not eliminate the risk of SIDS.
4. The grieving family should avoid making hasty or irreversible decisions (like selling the house, having surgery so they never have another child, or getting pregnant to "replace" the dead child). These actions are ways of avoiding the issue and do not help parents resolve the conflicts produced by the child's death.
5. SIDS has been with us for a long time. A possible account can be found in the Bible, in 1 Kings 3:19.

In Touch

SIDS ALLIANCE
10500 Little Patuxent Parkway
Suite 420
Columbia, MD 21044
800-221-7437
in Maryland 301-964-8000

Provides referrals to local support
  groups and information about SIDS.

NATIONAL SUDDEN INFANT
  DEATH FOUNDATION, INC.
2 Metro Plaza
Suite 104
8200 Professional Place
Landover, MD 20785

6. SIDS cannot always be confirmed by autopsy; neither can it always
   unerringly be ruled out. Thus, distinguishing between infanticide
   and SIDS may be a difficult task (see accompanying feature).

■ **Table 5–2**   *Risk Factors for SIDS*

CHARACTERISTICS OF THE PREGNANCY

Mom less than 20 years old

Dad less than 20 years old

Little or no prenatal care

Smoked cigarettes, took drugs (especially cocaine) or both (Gingras et al., 1990)

Diagnosed illness present (e.g., anemia, urinary tract infection)

CHARACTERISTICS OF THE INFANT

Male

Black

Premature

Small for gestational age (less than 7 lbs at birth)

Low Apgar score

Bottle-fed

Sibling died of SIDS less than a year before

Lags behind peers in length, weight, head circumference, and in the size of major
body organs

2–6 months old

Sinus tachycardia (abnormal heart rhythm), faster heart rate

Is a twin, triplet, etc.

After death

Elevated levels of the hormone T-3 (regulates automatic functions like breathing
and heart rate)

Lungs contain abnormal surfactant (more lyso-PC and sphingomyelin and less
phosphatidylcholine than normal)

Intrathoracic petechiae present (hemorrhages in the lungs caused by upper airway
obstruction?)

2½ times the normal amount of fetal hemoglobin in the blood (Guilian, et al.,
1987)

Pineal gland malfunction (possible) (Kocaard, 1991)

MISCELLANEOUS FACTORS

Prevalence higher during the *winter months*

Infants and mothers *not* sleeping in physical contact (co-sleeping infants and
mothers show synchronized arousal) (Mckenna et al., 1990)

Important note: Not all SIDS infants have all these symptoms; infants in groups not listed
(females, term babies, etc.) are not exempt from the risk of SIDS.

A Closer Look

Curbing Infant Mortality

Surviving the first year of life is an important milestone for infants. Yet nations with fewer resources than the United States are doing a better job of promoting infant survival. Worldwide, the United States ranks 20th among industrialized nations (Wegman, 1990). Right now babies in Singapore in Malaysia have a better chance of surviving their first year than American babies (see table). The infant mortality rate for black American babies is *double* that for white babies. The infant mortality rate for white, Hispanic, and Asian Americans ranks with Britain and Austria. Black America ranks with Cuba. Even though some states do a better job than some nations of

the world, the United States is at an all time low in ensuring the health and survival of its most vulnerable citizens. About 40,000 American infants die each year before reaching their first birthday.

Two factors account for the majority of infant deaths: birth defects and low birth weight. Both factors can be caused by genetics or may be spontaneous or induced by teratogen exposure. Low birth weight is associated with being single, receiving no prenatal care, and being black (Giblin et al., 1988). Sudden infant death syndrome claims a lot of lives as does pediatric AIDS, cocaine exposure, child abuse and neglect (leads to nonorganic failure-to-thrive). The *shaken baby syndrome* is a newly recognized cause of infant

(continued on next page)

Infant Mortality Rates, Worldwide, Developed Countries, 1988

NUMBER OF DEATHS PER 1,000 LIVE BIRTHS WITHIN THE FIRST 12 MONTHS OF LIFE				INFANT MORTALITY BY STATE—LOWEST RATES		INFANT MORTALITY BY STATE—HIGHEST RATES	
Japan	4.8	Austria	8.1	Vermont	6.8	Delaware	11.8
Finland	5.3	U.S. whites	8.5	Hawaii	7.2	Alabama	12.1
Sweden	5.8	Britain	9.0	Minnesota	7.8	Mississippi	12.3
Netherlands	6.8	Australia	9.2	Maine	7.9	So. Carolina	12.3
Switzerland	6.8	Ireland	9.2	Massachusetts	7.9	No. Carolina	12.5
Singapore*	7.0	Italy	9.5	Utah	8.0	Georgia	12.6
Canada	7.2	Israel	10.0	Kansas	8.0	Washington, DC	23.2
Hong Kong*	7.4	All U.S.	10.0	Rhode Island	8.2		
West Germany	7.5	Czechoslovakia	11.9	New Hampshire	8.3		
Denmark	7.6	China	12.0	Wisconsin	8.4		
France	7.7	Nigeria	13.8	Nevada	8.4		
Norway	8.0	U.S. blacks	17.6	Oregon	8.6		
				California	8.6		

*Singapore and Hong Kong are not defined as "developed" by the United Nations but have better infant mortality than the United States and so were included

(continued from previous page)
death brought about by shaking the baby by the arms or shoulders so she will stop crying. Parents mistakenly think the shaking will frighten the baby without causing harm. One-third of shaken babies die; one-third recover fully; but one-third are left with permanent disabilities like learning disability, blindness, or cerebral palsy (Dykes, 1986). Sadly, there are still American babies who die because they don't get their inoculations, because their environment contains hazards, or because they get pneumonia or diarrhea and their parents can't afford treatment.

The one thing that America doesn't have that is ensured in countries with lower infant mortality rates is accessible, affordable prenatal and postnatal medical care (American Academy of Pediatrics, Task Force on Infant Mortality, 1986). Twenty percent of all pregnant women in the United States fail to receive early prenatal care

(C. A. Miller, 1987). Most of this group is young (under 19), using illicit drugs, and have had previous pregnancies (Giblin et al., 1988). Medical consultation prior to birth makes it easier to influence nutritional decisions and monitor drug use and maternal habits. No pregnant woman in Scandinavia or Japan needs to ask how or where she will receive prenatal care or who will pay for it.

Beyond medical care for expectant women is the goal of ensuring that every baby is a wanted baby. When women carry babies they don't want, they don't take their pregnancies seriously and infant mortality rates soar. Better health education and effective, affordable contraception/sterilization can help women and their partners plan their families and have healthy babies. It can cost as little as $500 for prenatal care or as much as $500,000 to rescue a baby born at risk. Which is the better investment?

Feeding

During infancy, feeding serves three important functions. First, it provides adequate nutrition so the infant can grow as her genes direct. Nutrition affects the number of cells produced and the functional capability of those cells. Second, it provides contact with others and social stimulation. And third, it encourages muscle development and coordination as children learn to feed themselves. For the first 3 or 4 months of life, human milk or infant formula is the only food the baby requires or is physiologically prepared to handle. The decision to breast- or bottle-feed is a personal one. Both methods can provide adequate nutrition and intimacy. And both methods require the learning of new skills. Let's consider the advantages and disadvantages of breast-feeding and bottle-feeding.

Breast-feeding

prolactin
a hormone released by the woman's body after childbirth that stimulates milk production

acinar cells
milk-producing cells of the mammary glands

One of the nicest things about breast-feeding is that women come equipped with all the accoutrements necessary for the task—there's nothing to buy or try. Also, milk is automatically produced and released by the mother's body in response to stimulation. Three hormones are primarily responsible: progesterone, prolactin, and oxytocin (Glasier & McNeilly, 1990). Progesterone levels fall dramatically at delivery and are kept low by *prolactin*, which acts on the special acinar cells of the mammary glands to stimulate milk production. Prolactin is first produced by the pituitary gland after the placenta is delivered. Later, when the infant begins to suck at the breast, nerves in the nipple trigger the release of both prolactin and *oxytocin,* another pituitary hormone. Oxytocin causes the milk-storage sites in the mammary glands to contract, forcing milk through the nipple so the baby can feed. This action is called the let-down or ejection reflex. Oxytocin also causes the uterus to contract. The nursing mother may feel some slight tugging or cramping in her lower pelvis as the uterus returns to its nonpregnant size.

As early as the fourth month of pregnancy, the mammary glands prepare for milk production by secreting colostrum, a thin, yellowish fluid rich in protein and antibodies. The newborn benefits from colostrum intake and the mother's system benefits from breast-feeding. Colostrum is replaced by milk 3 to 4 days after childbirth. Milk production will continue for months, even years, as long as the breasts are emptied regularly and pregnancy, poor diet, caffeine, antihistamines, smoking, birth control pills, or fatigue do not interfere. Normal breast milk looks like skim milk.

■ **Figure 5–19**

A mother breast-feeding her infant.

ADVANTAGES Breast-feeding benefits both the nursing mother and her baby in many ways (Ogra et al., 1982). For the mother the advantages are these:

1. Breast-feeding promotes faster healing (the release of oxytocin during nursing encourages uterine contractions, which encourage healing).
2. It reduces the incidence of breast cancer before menopause by 50%.
3. Breast milk requires no preparation.
4. Breast milk is readily available.
5. Breast-feeding is less expensive than bottle-feeding.
6. Feedings force the mother to slow down and relax.
7. Night feedings can be done with a minimum of disturbance.
8. Breast milk does not stain the baby's clothes.
9. Nursing helps metabolize the fat deposits on the mother's body that were laid down during pregnancy. Thus, nursing mothers may lose weight faster than mothers who bottle-feed.

The advantages of breast-feeding for the infant are these:

1. Breast milk is sterile.
2. Breast milk is always the correct temperature.
3. Breast milk is easily digested.
4. Immunoglobulin protects the baby from bacterial infection (such as intestinal diseases).
5. Antibodies continue to be passed to protect against common viral illnesses.
6. Colostrum and breast milk have a laxative effect.
7. Breast milk provides more absorbable iron than formula to help infants fight infection.

mammary glands
specialized milk-producing glands within the woman's breasts

oxytocin
a hormone that causes the milk storage glands in the breasts to release their milk; it also causes the uterus to contract and heal after childbirth

ejection (let down reflex)
the automatic action caused by the release of oxytocin in a woman's body

colostrum
the first fluid produced by the breasts before actual milk production begins; also called first milk

8. Colic, spitting up, and allergic reactions are less common.
9. Breast-feeding promotes better jaw development (Westover et al., 1989).
10. Breast milk provides more of the substances needed for proper growth in their proper proportions than commercial formula, especially for the low birth weight infant (Ziemer & George, 1990).
11. Feedings require physical contact.

MYTHS ABOUT BREAST-FEEDING Misconceptions about breast-feeding abound. The most common of these myths are listed below:

- *Myth 1: Breast-feeding is the only way to get really close to the baby.* Parents can achieve the same feeling of closeness by holding the baby during bottle-feeding. The quality of the infant/parent interaction, *not* the feeding method, is the most important issue.
- *Myth 2: Women can't get pregnant while breast-feeding.* In fact, 50% of all breast-feeding women begin ovulating by the fourth week after delivery. By the time most women have recovered enough from childbirth to resume sexual relations, they are also fertile. To avoid having closely spaced babies, the couple needs to use some reliable method of birth control.
- *Myth 3: Breast-feeding causes sagging breasts.* Pregnancy is more likely to cause sagging breasts than is breast-feeding. Support and exercise to strengthen the chest muscles can be helpful under both circumstances.
- *Myth 4: Breast-feeding makes a woman's breasts smaller than before she was pregnant.* Fluctuations in breast size are more often due to patterns of exercise, weight gain, and nutritional habits than to breast-feeding per se. Thus, breast size may increase, decrease, or stay the same after breast-feeding.
- *Myth 5: Only women with large breasts can breast-feed.* The mammary gland structure of all breasts is the same. As long as poor nutrition, structural problems, illness, drug use, or fatigue don't interfere, the mammary glands will produce enough milk to replace what the infant uses.
- *Myth 6: Breast-feeding women have to avoid many foods that cause stomach upset in babies.* Generally, what's good for the mother is probably fine for the baby.
- *Myth 7: Drinking beer increases the nursing mother's milk supply.* This myth is based on the belief that the yeast in beer stimulates milk production and that drinking beer helps the mother relax and facilitates the let-down reflex. The *truth* is that yeast in beer has no effect on milk production and that beer actually *impedes* the let-down reflex in many women. In addition, the alcohol is passed to nursing babies, making them sleepy, listless, and inattentive.

Since 1982, breast-feeding has remained the most common method of feeding in the United States with 62% of all women who give birth choosing to breast-feed (Popper and Culley, 1989). Breast-feeding is particularly common among older, white, married, higher income, educated women who also take courses in prepared childbirth and who room-in with their babies after birth ((Kurinij et al., 1988; Yamauchi & Yamanouchi, 1990). Twenty-five percent of mothers without outside jobs and 10% of employed mothers were still breast-feeding 6 months later.

The most important factors in breast-feeding success are desire and commitment on the part of the mother, early attempts at breast-feeding, especially within the first hour of life, and support from others (Macey, 1986). If pacifiers are introduced too soon, they render sucking less effective and may result in breast refusal (Newman, 1990). Contrary to popular opinion, women don't instinctively know how to breast-feed. *Like parenting, breast-feeding is a skill that must be learned.* Women who have been successful at breast-feeding can be the most helpful to the inexperienced mother. These women might be family members, friends, pediatric nurses, or women in organizations such as La Leche League. A good resource is *The Complete Book of Breastfeeding* by M. Eiger and Sally Wendkos Olds (1987).

Most women who choose not to breast-feed do so because they feel it's socially inappropriate or because they have persistent uncertainties or worries about the process. A small percentage of women are physiologically unable to breast-feed, either because of structural problems in the breasts or because the quality or quantity of the breast milk is poor.

Some factors make it difficult or potentially risky to breast-feed. Babies who are premature, mentally retarded, or have cleft palates may be unable to stimulate the breasts sufficiently to encourage milk production because of poor sucking reflexes. In fact, premature babies may require up to 35 weeks to breast-feed successfully (Weaver & Anderson, 1988). That time frame may be reduced by giving the premature baby a pacifier shortly after birth to strengthen the sucking reflex. Babies who have galactosemia lack the enzyme needed to metabolize milk sugar (lactose) and cannot tolerate lactose either in breast milk or commercial formula.

Debilitating illness in the mother—such as active tuberculosis, severe breast infection, advanced cancer, or severe heart disease—prevent the mother from breast-feeding her infant. The AIDS virus has been found in the breast milk of infected women and can be transmitted to the baby (Steihm & Vink, 1991). Similarly, drugs and other chemicals can be transmitted to the baby via the breast milk. The pediatrician should approve all medications taken by the mother, especially drugs used to treat postpartum depression. It's in the baby's best interest for nursing mothers to avoid *all* nonessential drugs and medications (Table 5.3).

In Touch

LA LECHE LEAGUE
9616 Minneapolis Ave.
Box 1209
Franklin Park, IL 60131-8209
800-LA-LECHE

Information and encouragement for the breastfeeding woman, including a bimonthly newsletter of shared experiences

---

■ **Table 5–3**   *Drugs Found in Breast Milk and Their Effects on Infant Behavior*

Alcohol	— Lethargy, drowsiness, delayed development of motor skills
Amphetamine	— Irritability, poor sleep patterns
Cocaine	— Cocaine intoxication
Heroin	— Heroin intoxication
Marijuana	— No effect noted
Nicotine	— Shock, vomiting, diarrhea, increased heart rate, restlessness; decreases in milk production

For a complete listing of chemical substances and their effects, see the American Academy of Pediatric's Committee on Drugs report entitled, "Transfer of Drugs and Other Chemicals into Human Milk." *Pediatrics*, 1989 84(5), 924–936.

Bottle-Feeding

Bottle-feeding offers a psychologically satisfying, nutritious alternative to breast-feeding. As with breast-feeding, this option also has many advantages and disadvantages.

ADVANTAGES

1. Everyone can feed the baby using formula or expressed breast milk.
2. There's no breast discomfort or sore nipples.
3. The mother has more freedom since anyone can feed the baby.
4. Bottle-fed babies do not have to be fed as often as breast-fed babies (breast-fed babies eat every 2–3 hours; bottlefed babies every 3–4 hours).
5. Bottle-fed babies sleep through the night sooner than breast-fed babies.
6. Bottle-feeding reduces the risk of anemia in infants (A.F. Mills, 1990).

DISADVANTAGES

1. Formula forms large, rubbery curds in the baby's stomach that are difficult for her to digest.
2. Formula contains no immune protection.
3. It takes time to purchase and mix the formula and to sterilize the equipment.
4. Bottle-feeding is more costly than breast-feeding.
5. Caregivers may be tempted to "prop the bottle" rather than to hold the baby during feeding.

When properly prepared, commercial infant formulas approximate the nutritional quality of breast milk. Since quality control standards are rigorous, few problems have arisen since commercial formula was first produced. Since infants can detect the calorie value of milk or formula by 6 weeks of age, they will compensate by eating more of a dilute formula or less of a concentrated formula (Adler, 1989b). Commercial nipples are available that help the baby duplicate the sucking motion used in breast-feeding. As long as the water used for dilution is safe to drink, sterilization is not necessary unless feedings for several days are made up in advance. Care must be taken not to scald the baby when warming the formula (this is particularly likely when a microwave oven is used since it creates "hot spots" in the infant formula.) Microwaving may also destroy some of the essential nutrients in formula and some of the nutrients and antibodies found in breast milk (Sigman et al., 1989).

Sometimes busy caregivers are tempted to prop the bottle on a blanket, toy, or towel, but this is not a good idea. Young infants are not able to push a bottle away when they are finished drinking, and they could inhale formula while sleeping, choking themselves or even drowning.

■●▲ CONCEPT SUMMARY

Factors to Consider When Comparing Breast Feeding and Bottle Feeding

- Nutritional value to infant
- Expense
- Convenience/preparation time
- Availability
- Quality of infant–parent interaction
- Ease of digestion
- Allergic-potential
- Number of feedings required per day
- Potential for overnutrition/obesity
- Potential for undernutrition/nutrition-related deficits
- Family/social support for feeding method
- Cultural support for feeding method
- Employment-related considerations
- Physical impact on mother
- Personal preference

Infants who suck from propped bottles also tend to get more ear infections and cavities than those who do not since formula can drip into the outer ear if the child is lying flat or remain pooled around the gums and teeth while the child sleeps. Babies need to be held during bottle-feeding to help establish close, affectionate ties between the infant and her parents. The baby should be held at a 45 degree angle when drinking from the bottle or breast.

Parents should be assured that "being a good parent" is not dependent on the feeding method chosen. Parents should choose the feeding method that makes them feel most comfortable (Table 5.4). With few exceptions, when the parents are relaxed and happy, the infant will be relaxed and happy, too, regardless of whether he is fed by bottle or breast.

Weaning

Weaning is the gradual transition from breast- or bottle-feeding to drinking from a glass or cup and eating solid food. In the United States, most infants are weaned between 6 and 12 months of age, although sometimes weaning occurs as late as age 2 or older (Whaley & Wong, 1988). If the infant is consuming more than 32 ounces of formula per day or is nursing vigorously every 3 or 4 hours and still seems dissatisfied, she is physiologically ready for solid food (American Academy of Pediatrics, 1958). Change should be introduced slowly, and alternative sucking sources such as pacifiers and teething toys should be provided if they seem necessary. Many infants gradually wean themselves, especially if there is an older sibling present to imitate and if parents encourage drinking from a cup.

New parents should be warned that the transition from bottle or breast to cup can be a messy business. It is also potentially traumatic since the child is required to give up a major source of oral pleasure. Therefore, parents should try to avoid weaning their infants during times of change or family stress. Moving, hospitalization, vacation, divorce, or any change in routine can increase the baby's need to be comforted by sucking. Babies sometimes start thumb or finger sucking during or after weaning. They usually exhibit this behavior when they are tired, sick, or hungry, and if it occurs at all it seems to reach a peak by 18 to 20 months (Whaley & Wong, 1988). Thumb sucking can push the baby teeth forward somewhat, but dental displacement or jaw malalignment is usually not a danger unless thumb sucking continues after the permanent teeth erupt.

Parents who object to thumb or finger sucking can give the baby a pacifier to suck. They can also use habit-reversal strategies with older children, like having the child clench her fists and count to 20 whenever she feels tempted to suck her thumb (Christensen & Matthew, 1987). Discouraging thumb or finger sucking by the use of physical punishment, restraints, or bitter liquids painted on the fingers is inappropriate

weaning
the baby's transition from breast- or bottle-feeding to eating solid food and drinking from a cup

■ **Figure 5–20**

Making the transition from bottle to cup is a hit-and-miss arrangement at first.

■ **Table 5–4**   *General Recommendations for Infant Feeding*

BUBBLING (BURPING)

Some babies swallow a lot of air while feeding, and others swallow very little. In the early weeks, babies should be bubbled (burped) after every ounce of fluid they ingest to prevent regurgitation and pain due to stomach distension.

RIGHT-SIDE POSITION AFTER FEEDING

When the infant is placed on his or her right side after feeding, the fluid can flow to the lower end of the stomach and any swallowed air can rise above the fluid to escape through the esophagus so that upset and discomfort are prevented (see figure) (Bakwin, 1965). Caregivers can place a pillow behind the infant's back to help maintain this position.

SUPPLEMENTS

Fluoride is essential for building sound teeth and preventing tooth decay. Formula for bottle-fed babies should be prepared with clean fluoridated tap water.* The American Academy of Pediatrics (1979) recommends a daily fluoride supplement for both breast-fed and formula-fed infants. Fluoride from the water the mother drinks is not transmitted to the breast milk (Ogra et al., 1982).

Neither cow's milk nor human milk is a rich source of iron. Babies of well-nourished mothers are born with iron reserves that last for five or six months; premature babies have reserves that last two or three months. Nevertheless, as a protection against anemia, the American Academy of Pediatrics (1976) recommends an iron supplement for all infants during the first year of life.

ENCOURAGING QUALITY INTERACTIONS

Feedings should not be hurried. Where feedings are too short, babies might fail to get enough to eat and may thus become hungry again soon, or they might swallow a lot of air or even choke on the formula. Also, tensions that the caregiver communicates can suppress the baby's appetite, resulting in fussiness. Ideally, whoever is doing the feeding should set aside sufficient time to keep the pace relaxed and unhurried (usually at least a half hour is needed) and should minimize other distractions. All babies need to be held and cuddled during feeding. It is important that the caregiver establish eye contact so the baby can become familiar with his or her features and important to initiate touching and talking. Feeding is a wonderful opportunity for children and parents to get to know each other better and to come to feel more comfortable during interactions. (If you're lucky, your baby may stop feeding long enough to smile at you!)

SCHEDULED VERSUS DEMAND FEEDING

The needs of infants are relatively straightforward. When awake, they need food, stimulation, and someone to attend to hygiene. At other times, they need to sleep to make developmental progress—for example, a pituitary growth hormone is released during sleep. The patterning and timing of these events is determined by each baby's unique physical and psychological needs, but they can be influenced by caregivers.

In a demand feeding schedule, infants are fed whenever they are hungry (usually every 2 to 5 hours). A healthy infant is able to signal the caregiver by crying when hungry and stopping feeding when full.** More variation is introduced into infant care with demand feeding. Initially, it is difficult to predict when the infant will need to be fed, but, with time, all infants settle into a predictable pattern. Because demand feeding seems to meet the baby's needs most effectively, most health care workers advocate this approach.

Although generally popular at one time, strictly scheduled feeding times are usually only found in institutional settings, such as hospital nurseries, orphanages, and daycare centers, where time and personnel are limited. In the strict-scheduling approach, infants are typically fed every four hours.

Some time between the first and sixth month, most babies give up middle-of-the-night feeding and take their daily food in about five feedings, usually early morning, mid-morning, early afternoon, early evening, and late evening. By the time children are a year old, they have usually adapted to having three meals a day, sometimes supplemented with milk at naptime or before bed.

*Caregivers may feel that they are protecting their children by using bottled water in formula preparation. However, unless the bottled water contains trace elements and minerals, it may actually be less beneficial than tap water.

**The challenge here is to discriminate "hunger cries" from cries that signal other needs. It's neither necessary nor advisable to feed infants every time they cry or seem fussy.

Source: Whaley, L. and Wong, D. *Essentials of Pediatric Nursing*, 3rd ed., 1989, Mosby-Year Book, Inc., St. Louis. Used with permission.

during infancy. In fact, making an issue of thumb sucking usually prolongs and intensifies it.

Solid Food

Solid food is introduced to provide a new source of calories and iron, to facilitate adequate chewing, and to help the infant establish eating preference through exposure to various tastes and textures. Rice cereal is usually the baby's first solid food because it is high in iron, is easily digested, and has a low allergic potential. Any food can trigger an allergic reaction, however. The most common are eggs, wheat, chocolate, strawberries, and fish (Eden, 1989). Infants seem to accept solid food best between 2.5 and 6 months of age (Whitney & Cataldo, 1987).

The objective in infant nutrition is to create a well-balanced diet to meet the baby's nutritional needs. Remember that infant growth needs are vastly different from the health maintenance needs of an adult. Low-fat, skim milk, low-cholesterol, low-sugar, and low-salt diets designed for adult weight control and heart disease prevention can retard the growth and development of babies who actually *need* fat, whole milk, calories, and sugar to grow properly (Hegsted, 1990). In fact, compared to breast milk, weaning foods (even liver and whole eggs) are extremely deficient in essential long-chain polyunsaturated fatty acids (Jackson & Gibson, 1989). When nutritional deficits occur in the United States, they most commonly involve iron deficiency anemia and reduced levels of vitamin A, vitamin C and riboflavin (vitamin B_2). Three-fifths of American households receiving food stamps contain children. The average dollar amount of food stamps received by those families has not increased since 1980 (*Newsweek,* October 8, 1990, p. 48).

In Third World countries, babies may have a lot to eat and still be malnourished. Protein–calorie deficiencies pose the most serious threat to infant health. Most of these deficiencies occur because of early weaning and a trend away from breast-feeding. Prepared formula is seen as a status symbol in underdeveloped nations. However, poor hygiene, overdilution and no refrigeration make formula a poor substitute for breast milk. Ironically, "progress" is costing the lives of millions of Third World babies each year—lives that could be saved if mothers would breast-feed.

Even when infants are breast-fed, if they are weaned onto a protein-deficient diet, they can develop *kwashiorkor*. The disease leaves the child inactive, susceptible to illness, and weak. Fluid fills the child's abdomen, producing a bloated appearance. The disease can result in permanent damage or death. The treatment for kwashiorkor is a protein-rich diet. This condition is rare in the United States.

SELF-FEEDING As babies grow older, they become more and more interested in feeding themselves. The development of the pincer grasp aids in finger feeding. Bite-sized foods can be introduced when the child

---

■ ● ▲   CONCEPT SUMMARY

Developmental Milestones Associated with Feeding During the First Year

● *Birth*
  - Sucking, rooting, and swallowing reflexes present
  - Cries when hungry; falls asleep when full

● *1 month*
  - Tongue thrust reflex is strong when spoon is placed in the child's mouth

● *3–4 months*
  - Can take food from a spoon—tongue thrust fading

● *4–5 months*
  - Can move lips to the rim of a cup

● *5–6 months*
  - Can use fingers in self-feeding

● *6–7 months*
  - Bites and chews
  - May hold own bottle but may also prefer to be fed

● *7–9 months*
  - Displays food preferences (refuses food by keeping lips closed, turning head)
  - Can hold a spoon but cannot use it in feeding
  - May drink from a cup with help
  - May be able to drink from a straw

● *9–12 months*
  - Prefers finger feeding
  - Holds own bottle and drinks from it
  - Holds a cup and spills liquid while drinking
  - Uses a spoon with much spilling

---

is 6–7 months old. By this time, some teeth are erupting and the child can make chewing motions with his jaw. By about 9 months, developments in reaching and eye-hand coordination permit children to hold a spoon, attempt to fill it, and direct it toward the mouth. By this same time, most children can sit in a high chair.

EATING RITUALS Toddlers are comfortable with pattern and predictability in their lives. Often they rigidly insist on the same utensils and dishes ("their baby cup" or "their Raggedy Ann plate") and may become quite concerned when the family members don't sit in their accustomed places. Because toddlers cannot relate to the world in a more mature, less rigid fashion, it is probably a good idea to maintain the mealtime routine so as not to upset their sense of order and interfere with eating. When toddlers complain that the peas were placed in the wrong spot or point out some other earthshaking problem, they are not criticizing so much as trying to understand how things are done and verbalizing their expectations.

FOOD REFUSAL Parents accustomed to an infant who eagerly consumes meals might become concerned when, at 18 months or so, the child begins to pick, fuss, or refuse food altogether. Two factors may be operating here. First, growth between 12 and 24 months is not as rapid as in the first year of life. Since less food is required by the baby's system, appetite is decreased. Second, an increasing sense of independence might also be expressing itself through self-assertiveness: The child says "No" to eating or to certain foods as a way of exercising choice and achieving a measure of self-control. Sometimes offering a limited selection of foods can avert a confrontation.

Toilet Training

Toilet training is an important experience in the life of the toddler. During the toilet training process, the child is asked to conform to societal norms regarding bowel and bladder control. Parents are often eager to toilet train, since getting rid of diapers really simplifies childcare. However, the rate of physical maturation, not the needs of the parents, should determine when toilet training is initiated. For toilet training to be successful, the child must have passed certain developmental milestones (Hauck, 1991):

1. *Involuntary bowel and bladder control must be replaced by voluntary control.* At birth, reflex action controls urination and elimination. Stretching the bladder to a certain point or impacting the bowel triggers the *gastrocolic reflex*, which spontaneously empties the system. This reflex gradually diminishes as myelinization aids information flow—the muscles of the bowel and bladder become more responsive to signals from the brain and the brain is better able to interpret signals that the bladder or bowel is full. Voluntary control of the anal and urethral sphincters is achieved between 18 and 24 months. Boys, premature, and small-for-gestational-age babies often require a little more time than full-term girls since they are less physically mature at birth. Some children with neurological impairment may never

achieve voluntary control. Toilet training should not begin before the child is physically capable of cooperating.

2. *The child must be able to physically sense that the bladder and/or bowel are full.* The child must be able to recognize and interpret signals that urination or a bowel movement is about to occur.

3. *The child must be able to tell caregivers when the bladder or bowel is full.* The child must approach the caregivers and express her needs verbally or nonverbally.

4. *The child must have appropriate motor skills.* The child must be able to walk to the bathroom, pull down clothing, and sit down on the potty. Cleaning up remains the adult's responsibility during infancy.

Once the child seems ready and the necessary equipment is on hand, the training may begin. A helpful source with an optimistic title is *Toilet Training in Less Than a Day* by Nathan Azrin and Richard Foxx (Simon & Schuster, 1980). Azrin and Foxx use modeling to teach the child specific behaviors (the imitative model is a doll) and positive reinforcement to reward the child's effort. Vicki Lansky's *Toilet Training* (Bantam, 1984) is another useful resource for parents.

The parent's mood and level of patience are important to the training. Forcing a disinterested or resistant child to stay on the toilet for prolonged periods of time is unproductive. Punishing or scolding the child when "accidents" occur is actually counterproductive and associated with *more* wetting and soiling, not less. Often accidents are as much the parent's fault as the child's. Changes in the child's routine, traveling, extra liquid to drink, stress, illness, restrictive clothing that can't easily be removed, or an insensitivity to the child's verbal or behavioral cues can result in wetting or soiling. Parents need to be sensitive, patient, and considerate of their children at this time.

Because of its greater predictability and regularity, bowel control is usually accomplished before bladder control. Most children will be bowel trained and will stay clean during the day by the time they are 2 or 2.5. Nighttime control may take another year or more. Routine toileting and the avoidance of liquids an hour before bedtime will help children stay dry. However, 50% of boys have not achieved complete nighttime bladder control by age 5 (Whaley & Wong, 1988).

Freud (1938/1973) suggested that the child's personality is influenced by the specific experiences of the first 2 years of life. He believed that early (before age 1.5 or 2), harsh, or inconsistent toilet training produces "anal type personalities"—individuals who constantly worry about constipation and diarrhea, have difficulty relaxing, and are unusually neat, clean, and precise. There have been no studies that have established a causal link between toilet training and later personality characteristics or emotional problems, although some controversy remains (Fisher & Greenberg, 1977).

■ **Table 5–5** *Summary of Growth and Development during the First Year*

AGE (months)	PHYSICAL DEVELOPMENT	GROSS MOTOR BEHAVIOR	FINE MOTOR BEHAVIOR
1	Gains ⅓ to ½ pound weekly (5–7 oz) for the first 6 months Grows 1 inch per month for the first 6 months Head circumference increases ½ inch per month for the first 6 months Behavior primarily reflexive Most infants are nose breathers	At birth, knees are flexed under abdomen when placed on stomach Later, pelvis is high but knees not under abdomen when on stomach Drags head from side to side when lying down Head follows body (head-lag) when infant is pulled to a sitting position Back rounded when infant is in a sitting position Holds head momentarily in midline when sitting When held in a standing position, knees flex and body limp at the hips	Strong grasp reflex Hands primarily closed
2	Posterior fontanel closed Crawling reflex disappears	Body less flexed when lying on stomach—hips are flat, knees are extended, arms are flexed Less head lag when pulled to a sitting position Can hold head up when in a sitting position, but head bobs forward When on stomach, can lift head 45 degrees from table	Grasp reflex fading Hands more open than closed
3	Reflexes fading	Head lag slight when pulled to a sitting position Holds head more erect when sitting, but head still bobs forward Can raise head and shoulders 45–90 degrees from the table when on stomach; bears weight on forearms Knees and pelvis less flexed when held in a standing position; able to bear a tiny bit of own weight Begins to study own hands (hand regard)	Grasp reflex absent Will hold an object but not reach for it Hands kept loosely open Pulls at blankets, clothing
4	Drooling begins Moro, tonic-neck, and rooting reflex have disappeared	Almost no head lag when pulled to a sitting position Balance head well when sitting	Reaches for objects but overshoots the mark Grasps objects with two hands

(continued on next page)

■ Table 5–5 *(continued)*

AGE (months)	PHYSICAL DEVELOPMENT	GROSS MOTOR BEHAVIOR	FINE MOTOR BEHAVIOR
4 *(cont.)*		Back less rounded when sitting Can roll from back to side when lying down Can raise head and chest 90 degrees from table when on stomach	Reaches for objects but overshoots the mark Grasps objects with two hands Can use hands to place objects into mouth Plays with rattle, shakes it, cannot pick it up again if it is dropped
5	First teeth may begin to appear Growth rate may begin to decline	No head lag when pulled to a sitting position When sitting, can hold head upright and steady Back is straight when in a sitting position Can roll from stomach to back when lying down Puts feet to mouth when lying on back	Uses palmar grasp to grasp objects voluntarily Uses both hands when grasping Can hold one object while looking at another Plays with toes
6	Birth weight has doubled Gains 1/5 to 1/3 pound (3–5 oz.) each week Grows 1/2 inch taller each month for the next 6 months Teething may begin Chewing and biting can occur	When on stomach, can lift chest and upper abdomen off table; weight is borne on the hands Lifts head before pulled to a sitting position Sits with a straight back in a high chair Roll from back to abdomen when lying down Can bear almost all his/her body weight when held in a standing position	Can re-grasp dropped object Grasps and manipulates small objects Holds bottle Grasps feet and pulls to mouth Drops one toy when given another
7	Upper front teeth begin to erupt	When lying down, spontaneously lifts head from table When lying down, can bear weight on one hand Can sit alone momentarily When held in a standing position, bears full weight on feet When held in a standing position, actively bounces	Transfers objects from hand to hand Favors one hand in grasping Can bang toy/object on a table Rakes at small objects with fingers
8	Regular patterns in bowel and bladder elimination appear	Sits unsupported Adjusts posture to reach an object May stand holding on to furniture	Pincer grasp beginning Releases objects easily Rings bell purposefully Can hold two objects while looking at a third Reaches out for toys out of reach Can secure an object by pulling on its string

■ **Table 5–5** *(continued)*

AGE (months)	PHYSICAL DEVELOPMENT	GROSS MOTOR BEHAVIOR	FINE MOTOR BEHAVIOR
9	Eruption of upper teeth on each side of front teeth	Can crawl (may crawl backwards at first) Can sit on the floor for 10 minutes Recovers balance when leans forward Cannot recover balance when leans sideways Pulls self to standing position Can stand and hold onto furniture	Dominant hand emerging Can use pincer grasp, just not terribly efficiently Can hold 2 toys and grasp a third Caompres two toys by bringing them together
10	Few basic reflexes remain	Crawls by pulling self forward with hands Can go from a laying to a sitting position Can pull self to a standing position Easily recovers balance when sitting While standing, lifts one foot to take a step	Can grasp toys/objects by their handle Crude release of object appears
11	Eruption of lower teeth beside two middle lower incisors	Creeps with abdomen off floor Can reach toward the back when sitting to grasp an object Cruises (walks holding onto furniture) Can also walk with both hands held	Can hold a crayon to mark a paper Examines objects more thoroughly (i.e., finds clapper in bell, etc) Has an efficient pincer grasp Drops an object deliberately just to pick it up Can put one object after another into a container (sequential play) Can manipulate objects (i.e., remove object from tight enclosure)
12	Birth weight has tripled Height at birth has increased by 50% Head and chest circumference are equal (usually around 18½ inches) 6–8 teeth are present Anterior fontanel almost closed Babinski reflex disappears Lumbar (lower back) curve develops	Walks with one hand held Cruises well May attempt to stand alone Can sit from a standing position without help	Tries to build a two-block tower but fails Tries to insert a pellet into a narrow neck bottle, but fails Can turn the pages in a book, many at a time

Health Education

TOWARD EFFECTIVE PARENTING

In the first 4 years of life, information about sexuality and health is gathered from interactions within the family. *How* parents respond to children's questions and actions is as important as *what* is said. At this point, parents are setting the tone for further discussion. When parents act embarrassed or are critical of the child, children may learn to suppress or redirect their inquiries (Mattis, 1988). Parents of infants and toddlers should also be encouraged to use the correct terms for body parts. The words *penis, scrotum, vagina,* and *breasts* are preferred over nicknames that convey silliness and immaturity.

Toddlers and young preschoolers are not prepared for long, detailed answers. Simple, brief, and positive responses are best. If parents do not know the answers or need more information, they can say so, promising to get back to the child as soon as they find out. The local library is a good resource for material on human sexuality written with the child in mind. (Parents sometimes say they "don't know" to avoid answering questions or participating in discussion. Children will soon discover their parents' reluctance and discomfort and may become uncomfortable with their own sexuality as a consequence).

Sometimes it's important just to understand *what* the child is asking. The classic story on this theme involves a child who asked "where he came from". After the parent sweated through an uncomfortable (and in their mind, premature) recounting of the facts of life, the child still wasn't satisfied. "No," explained the child with exasperation, "that's not it. I mean did I come from *Cleveland* or not."

More on the topic of sexuality and sex education is included at the end of Chapter 14.

● **Chapter Summary**

● During the first year of life, growth in height and weight is unparalleled except during the prenatal period and adolescence. By the first birthday, infants grow half again as tall as they were at birth and triple their birth weight. Body proportions change and skills are acquired according to the cephalocaudal and proximodistal principles of development.

● Internal organs and systems grow impressively during infancy. Genetics, overfeeding, and a low activity/low metabolic rate can contribute to infant obesity. The brain and the nervous system grow more rapidly than any other system or tissue. Unneeded brain cells and redundant interconnections begin to disintegrate by age 2. The infant's skeleton continues to ossify. Muscles increase in size and strength but the digestive system remains immature. The infant's own immune system is supplemented by maternal antibody transfer (if breast-fed) and artificial immunization through inoculation. Lung capacity increases during this time as does endurance and stamina. Children between 18 and 24 months of age can regulate their own body temperature.

- Colic may develop in the baby's second or third week of life. First teeth generally emerge between 6 and 7 months of age. Care should be taken to prevent baby bottle tooth decay syndrome.

- Progress in motor development depends on maturation, motivation, and experience. Walking is the major gross motor accomplishment; reaching and grasping are examples of fine motor skills acquired during infancy.

- Improvements are made in the area of perception through maturation of the sensory systems. Infants refine their visual tracking skills, lengthen their attention spans, develop binocular vision, spend considerable time making eye contact, and develop depth perception and size, shape and color constancy. Sound localization and sound discrimination both improve. Infants synchronize their body movements to the sound of adult speech in a pattern known as the language dance. Caregivers should be alert to the signs of hearing loss. Touch plays an important role in object recognition during infancy. Smell and taste become more acute during this time.

- Sleep requirements decrease with age. The sleep/wake pattern begins with a series of long and short naps which are eventually consolidated into a pattern of continuous nighttime sleep accompanied by one or two daytime naps. Infant size, temperament, and feeding method influence sleep patterns. Both REM and NREM sleep can be observed from birth. In the United States parents and infants are more likely to sleep apart than together. Predictable rituals make bedtime easier for infants to accept. "Insomnia" and night terrors can disturb infant sleep.

- While most infants begin life being breast-fed, the majority are switched to bottled formula by the time they are 6 months old. A variety of physical, psychological, and social factors influence choice of feeding method and both methods have advantages and disadvantages. Propping the bottle or microwaving its contents should be avoided, however. Weaning usually occurs between 6 and 12 months of age. It may be accompanied by thumb or finger sucking.

- Infant formula or breast milk must be replaced by solid food high in nutritional quality. Infants are most comfortable with predictability in their feeding routines and may both refuse food and insist on self-feeding during this time.

- Toilet training can begin after the child has acquired voluntary control over bowel and bladder functions.

● Observational Exercise

During the first few years of life, the infant/toddler acquires a great many motor and perceptual skills. You can assess the skill level of any particular child by playing some perceptual/motor "games" with the child and observing whether he or she can perform the tasks at hand. Use the questions and tasks listed below as a guide and record the child's responses under the correct headings.

Select an infant between 12 and 18 months of age. If the child is uncomfortable with you, ask the child's parent or caregiver to work with the child instead of you. Be sure that you perform the testing in a room free of distractions, since babies are naturally curious and their attention is easily captured by other stimuli. Let the child attempt each task several times before you make a determination as to skill level. Discontinue testing if the child seems tired, hungry, uncomfortable, or bored. You can do the testing over a period of several days.

Locomotor Development	*Not Yet*	*Sometimes*	*Always*	*Comments*
1. Stands alone. (Can the infant stand, either with support or alone?)	_____	_____	_____	_____
2. Walks when held by hand. (Can the infant take steps when held by the hand?)	_____	_____	_____	_____
3. Walks alone.	_____	_____	_____	_____
4. Climbs stairs. (Can the infant climb upstairs? Can he or she climb back down?)	_____	_____	_____	_____

Reaching and Grasping				
1. Picks up large toy. (Place a large toy in your hand and present it close to the child. Does the child reach and grasp the toy?)	_____	_____	_____	_____
2. Picks up small snacks. (Place in your hand several raisins, Cheerios, or other finger foods that the child enjoys. Does the child reach and pick up the snacks?)	_____	_____	_____	_____
3. Uses cup. (Hand the child a cup so he or she can grasp the handle with the preferred hand. Can the child grasp it and hold it? Does the child attempt to drink from it?)	_____	_____	_____	_____

Locomotor Development	Not Yet	Sometimes	Always	Comments
4. Drops blocks into container. (Drop several blocks into a container as the child watches. Now give the child a block and see if he or she drops it into the container when it is held within reach.)	___	___	___	_____
5. Grasps moving object. (Slowly swing an object on a string in front of the child. Does he or she attempt to reach for and grasp the object?)	___	___	___	_____

Perceptual Skills

	Not Yet	Sometimes	Always	Comments
1. Orients to unseen noise. (Have someone close a door or make a noise behind the child. Does the child appear to have heard the sound? Does he or she move head/body to look for the source?)	___	___	___	_____
2. Tracking moving objects. (Stand in front of the child and move the toy on the string so it encircles the child. Can he or she track its movement?)	___	___	___	_____
3. Response to pictures. (Show the child a large picture of an animal, a toy, and a family member. Record the responses to each. Which one provokes the most smiling and sustained looking?)	___	___	___	_____

In general, what do you observe in the area of this child's physical development?

● Recommended Readings

Adebonojo, F., & Sherman, W., with Jones, L. C. (1985). *How a baby grows: A parent's guide to nutrition.* New York: Arbor.

Ames, L. B., Ilg, F. L., & Haber, C. C. (1982). *Your one-year-old: The fun-loving, fussy 12–24 month old.* New York: Delacorte.

Evans, J. & Ilfield, E. (1982). *Good beginnings: Parenting in the early years.* Ypsilanti, MI: High/Scope Press.

Kitzinger, S. (1989). *The crying baby.* New York: Viking Press.

Sammons, W. A. H. (1989). *Self-calmed baby: A revolutionary new approach to parenting your infant.* Boston: Little, Brown & Co.

Tanner, J. M. (1978). *The fetus into man: Physical growth from conception to maturity.* Cambridge, MA: Harvard University Press.

Cognitive Development in Infancy and Toddlerhood

Cognitive Development

Paralleling the remarkable physical development that takes place during infancy is an equally astounding change in the child's capacity to understand and relate to the world. The newborn begins life without much voluntary control over movement, vocalization, or mental processes. By the time the child is 2, he can use language to express feelings, needs, and perceptions; solve problems by applying several solutions; think about things that happened in the past and those that may begin in the future; and remember people, places, and events. The growth and change in mental capacity that begin in infancy and end in adolescence together are called *cognitive development*. Cognitive abilities are those that require thinking and learning, such as memory, problem solving, imagining, classification, concept formation, and language acquisition. The concept of intelligence combines several cognitive functions into an integrated system.

Four major theoretical perspectives have been proposed to explain how children gather and process information about their world: the cognitive theory of Jean Piaget, NeoPiagetian views of cognitive development, the information processing approach, and the psychometric approach.

Piaget's Theory of Cognitive Development

Jean Piaget believed that two interrelated processes—organization and adaptation—contributed to the development of cognition. Both children and adults organize their thoughts into understandable units or schemes, identifying some thoughts as more important than others and connecting related ideas. In a fundamental way, organization involves

cognitive development
age-related changes in the child's ability to think, remember, solve problems, and make decisions

organization
Piaget's term for the process of synthesizing and analyzing perceptions and thoughts

adaptation
Piaget's term for the cognitive process of adjusting one's thinking to accept ideas or information; adaptation takes two forms, accommodation and assimilation

assimilation
Piaget's term for the inclusion of new information into already existing mental categories or schema

scheme(s)/schema
Piaget's term for general ways of thinking about, interacting with, or comprehending different aspects of the environment. Piaget believed children develop specific schemes or mental categories of information about specific objects or experiences and that these schemes are retained in memory

accommodation
Piaget's term for the process of shifting or enlarging mental categories or modes of thinking to encompass new information

equilibration
Piaget's term for the mental balance achieved through the assimilation and accommodation of conflicting experiences and perceptions

object permanence
the knowledge that objects in the environment have a permanent existence independent of one's interaction with them

the way infants and children (as well as adults) perceive and process information: They analyze key features of an object to determine whether it is something new or familiar, and whether it has recognizable features such as paws, wings, a shiny surface, and so forth.

At the same time, people *adapt* their thinking to new ideas and new experiences. The process of adaptation itself occurs through one of two processes: assimilation or accommodation. In *assimilation*, new information is simply added to the existing cognitive structure. Infants with a well-developed *scheme* for sucking may suck on new objects such as thumbs, rattles, or blocks in the same general way that they suck on pacifiers and nipples. However, when the existing cognitive structure itself is modified by new learning, *accommodation* has taken place. For example, infants who have developed the ability to extend an arm to reach a toy learn to vary the degree of extension to accommodate toys that are close or farther away. In this way accommodation makes reaching more efficient. Accommodation and assimilation work together to produce changes in the child's perceptions of the world and his reactions to it. When a balance is reached between the processes of accommodation and assimilation, equilibration has occurred. Piaget believed that every time equilibration takes place, the child has acquired new knowledge.

Piaget observed that children between birth and age 2 gather knowledge about the world through sensory input and motor activity. Infants listen to, touch, taste, smell, and look at objects and people in their environment. They also explore through movement. It was for these reasons that Piaget called the first phase of cognitive development the *sensorimotor period*. Sensorimotor development is complete when, by age 3 or so, the child can:

1. Integrate information from the senses. When a child first sees a bell, for example, and hears its tinkling sound, he does not associate the object with the sound. Later the child will understand that the sound is produced by the bell.
2. Recognize that objects and people continue to exist even when they are not perceived (an ability called *object permanence*).
3. Imitate the behavior of others.
4. Plan and carry out actions with an intended purpose (A. Baldwin, 1968).

In the following sections the development of each of these cognitive accomplishments is traced through the six stages of the sensorimotor period.

The Sensorimotor Period

STAGE 1: MODIFICATION OF REFLEXES (FIRST MONTH) In the first 4 weeks of life, infants practice the reflex behaviors they were born with, primarily sucking, grasping, and crying. As infants repeat reflex responses, they become more and more efficient in their use. For example, young children can use sucking to discriminate between objects that provide food and those that do not. Thus, in this first stage, reflex responses are modified as a function of the child's experiences.

STAGE 2: PRIMARY CIRCULAR REACTIONS (1–4 MONTHS) Between 1 and 4 months of age, reflex behaviors are gradually replaced by more deliberate actions. Infants in this stage begin to coordinate sensory input and motor output (actions) such as vision and hand control. Thus, they can repeat useful or interesting behaviors and abandon those that are no longer gratifying or helpful. If the 1–4 month old infant wants to suck his thumb, he does not have to wait until the thumb accidentally touches the mouth. Instead, the infant can *deliberately* direct a hand to the mouth and commence sucking. Consider Piaget's description of this behavior in his young son, Laurent (Piaget, 1936/1963):

> *Observation 62.* At 0;2(4) (0 years, 2 months, 4 days) Laurent by chance discovers his right index finger and looks at it briefly. At 0;2(11) he inspects for a moment his open right hand, perceived by chance. At 0;2(17) he follows its spontaneous movement for a moment, then examines it several times while it searches for his nose or rubs his eye. . . At 0;2(21) he holds his two fists in the air and looks at the left one, after which he slowly brings it toward his face and rubs his nose with it, then his eye. A moment later the left hand again approaches his face; he looks at it and touches his nose. (Note the shift from passive to active). He recommences and laughs 5 or 6 times in succession while moving the left hand to his face. He seems to laugh before the hand moves, but looking has no influence on its movement. He laughs beforehand but begins to smile again on seeing the hand. Then he rubs his nose. At a given moment he turns his head to the left but looking has no effect on the direction. The next day, same reaction. At 0;2(23) he looks at his right hand, then at his clasped hands (at length). At 0;2(24) at last it may be stated that looking acts on the orientation of the hands which tend to remain in the visual field (pp. 96–97).

Piaget believes that such *primary circular reactions* imply the existence of memory, the primary component of cognition. During this stage, actions that causes pleasurable reactions tend to be repeated. The child may derive pleasure from sucking on objects placed in the mouth, for example, and recalling that experience may make deliberate efforts to suck on objects not for food but for enjoyment. Piaget labeled these reactions *primary* because their focus is on the infant's own actions and the pleasure they derive rather than on some external goal (P.A. Cowan, 1978). Although 1–2 month old infants may enjoy sucking, they actually learn more about objects by mouthing them (Pecheux, et al., 1988).

Object Permanence If a 1–4 month old infant drops a rattle, he will stare momentarily at the hand that held it and then focus on something else

primary circular reactions
according to Piaget, simple repetitive acts that involve the child's body such as kicking or thumb sucking; these behaviors are characteristics of Piaget's second stage of the sensorimotor period

A Closer Look

The People Behind the Scenes: Jean Piaget (1896–1980)

Jean Piaget was born in the village of Neuchatel, Switzerland, on August 9, 1896. His parents encouraged his intellectual curiosity and his father taught him to think systematically. Such instruction was not lost on a boy so young. By age 10, Piaget had published his first scientific paper describing a rare albino sparrow he had sighted. The article was so brilliant that it prompted officials of the Geneva Museum of Natural History to offer Piaget the job as curator of the museum. Imagine their surprise when they found out their choice for curator was a 10 year old boy! The offer was quickly withdrawn.

Piaget's interest in zoology continued throughout his teen years. After school he would assist the director of Neuchatel's Museum of Natural History, who taught him a great deal about mollusks. By the age of 15, Piaget had published several papers on mollusks and was recognized among Swiss scientists for his expertise. He noticed that when large mollusks were taken from lakes and placed into small ponds, they underwent structural changes that permitted them to survive in the quiet waters. Piaget interpreted these changes to mean that the mollusks's genetic inheritance enabled them to adapt, within certain limits, to varied environments. This remarkable insight was later applied to humans as Piaget wondered whether children made similar adaptations.

At the age of 22, after earning a doctorate in the Natural Sciences in 1918 from the University of Neuchatel, Piaget found his interests turning more and more toward philosophy and psychology. He traveled to Zurich and took a job with Joseph Bleuler, a well-known psychoanalyst who was a contemporary of Sigmund Freud. There he learned

Jean Piaget, Swiss psychologist, 1896–1980

how to conduct a clinical interview, a technique that would profoundly influence his later work with children.

After a year of study with Bleuler, Piaget found himself in Paris at the laboratory of Alfred Binet, who was in the process of creating the first standardized test of intelligence, the Binet-Simon Intelligence Scale. Piaget's job was to ask children of different ages questions which were being considered for inclusion on the test. Piaget was supposed to determine the age at which most children could correctly answer each question. But in the process of establishing these age norms, he became more intrigued by the *wrong* answers children gave, noting that children of similar ages made similar types of mistakes. For example, preschoolers feel they have more pennies when the coins are spread out than when they are stacked up. School age children, however, focus on quantity (the relevant factor) and ignore the area covered by the coins. They know that five pennies are five pennies, whether stacked up, spread out, or turned sideways.

Influenced by his training in biology, Piaget reasoned that the children's maturational state, as dictated by their genes, must play a role in cognitive development. Further, he concluded that age-related changes in mental abilities have survival value because they improve reasoning, problem-solving, and comprehension skills. According to Piaget, the older children (who were more often correct) were able to *adapt* their thought processes to improve their understanding of the questions being asked (like the mollusks adapted to the change in their environment). He concluded that older children don't simply know more than younger ones; they actually think differently about problems.

Much of Piaget's knowledge about how children acquire information about their world came from careful observations of his own three children, Jacqueline, Lucienne, and Laurent. In 1921 Jean Piaget was appointed Director of Research at the Rousseau Institute in Geneva. Piaget spent the rest of his life trying to understand the age-relevant patterns he discovered in children's cognitive development. In his 60-year career, he published over 40 books and over 200 articles. By the time of his death on September 16, 1980, Piaget's work had attained worldwide attention. He is recognized today as the father of cognitive psychology.

if the toy does not reappear. Object permanence does not exist at this stage. Out of sight is truly out of mind, since objects not seen or touched are regarded as nonexistent.

Imitation *Pseudoimitation* occurs during the stage of primary circular reactions. In pseudoimitation, the adult initiates the imitation, not the child. If an adult interrupts a baby's vocal play by repeating the same sounds the baby has been making, the baby may resume vocal play and reinitiate the primary circular reaction. For example, the baby may be saying what sounds like *goo,* may listen to an adult make the same sound, and may continue saying *goo* after the adult has spoken. Piaget feels at this stage the baby does not distinguish between its own sounds and those of adults, and so the adult sounds represent a continuation rather than an interruption of the primary circular activity. Pseudoimitation may also explain why one infant will begin to cry after another one does, a common phenomenon in newborn nurseries (Simner, 1971). Young babies who cry may assume that they themselves made the noise and so may produce cries in order to be consistent with their perception of their own behavior.

pseudoimitation
an adult interrupts the child's vocal play to imitate its sound and the baby continues its vocalizations in turn after the adult

STAGE 3: SECONDARY CIRCULAR REACTIONS (4–8 MONTHS) *Secondary circular reactions* are elaborations of primary circular behaviors; their effect is to make interesting activities last. In this stage, although babies still engage in pleasurable repetitive activities, they are no longer focused on their own bodies. Instead, children at stage 3 are concerned with external objects and events. Actions with this focus are called sec-

secondary circular reactions
behaviors characteristic of the third sensorimotor stage, whereby the infant repeats an action to produce responses from objects or people (i.e., squeezing a toy to hear it squeak or laughing with an adult during play)

■ Figure 6–1

Repetetive arm wavings are an example of a secondary circular reaction.

ondary circular reactions because they mark the beginning of *intentional goal-related activity*. In this stage the child learns the association between a random event and an outcome and then repeats the behavior to prolong interesting events. For example, speaking of his daughter, Piaget writes,

> At 0;3(5) Lucienne shakes her bassinet by moving her legs violently (bending and unbending them, etc.) which makes the cloth dolls swing from the hood. Lucienne looks at them, smiling, and recommences at once. These movements appear simply to be the concomitants of joy.... The next day...I present the dolls: Lucienne immediately moves, shakes her legs, but this time without smiling. Her interest is intense and sustained...
>
> 0;3(8)...a chance movement disturbs the dolls: Lucienne...looks at them...and shakes herself with regularity. She stares at the dolls, barely smiles and moves her legs vigorously and thoroughly...
>
> 0;3(16) as soon as I suspended the dolls she immediately shakes them, without smiling, with precise and rhythmical movements with quite an interval between shakes, as though she were studying the phenomenon. Success gradually causes her to smile (Piaget, 1952, pp. 157–158).

Lucienne noticed that the dolls moved when she shook her legs, so she repeated her movements, intently watching the doll's reaction. Lucienne's attention was focused on the dolls. While children in the stage of primary circular reactions would repeatedly shake their legs because that activity was fun, children performing secondary circular reactions would shake their legs to make dolls move or would pull a blanket to bring toys closer.

Although infants can formulate strategies to achieve external goals, they sometimes have difficulty keeping the goal in mind. An interpreter of Piaget notes:

> Lucienne as a five-month-old reaches across the crib to pick up a toy. Piaget places a hand in her path which obscures her view. She pushes the hand aside, but in the process becomes involved in playing with the hand or with new objects coming into view as a result of her actions (P.A. Cowan, 1978, p. 92).

Object Permanence The stage 3 infant will follow the trajectory of the object as it disappears but once it disappears will abandon the search. The infant is making some progress toward object permanence, however, since he can recognize objects from partial images. If a toy is partially covered by a cloth, for example, the child may remove the cloth and find the toy. A toy that is completely covered encourages no investigation.

Imitation Four to 6 month old infants deliberately imitate the actions and sounds made by others, as long as the behaviors are not too complex or too novel. The baby who can bang a spoon on a tray can also bang a spoon on a pan or a toy drum if he has seen that behavior demonstrated.

STAGE 4: COORDINATION OF MEANS AND ENDS (8–12 MONTHS)

According to Piaget, the remarkable accomplishment of this stage is the child's ability to *differentiate schemes of means (e.g., grasping, reaching, moving, and the like) from schemes of ends (e.g., toys)*. In the previous stage, Lucienne pushed Piaget's hand aside but became distracted and forgot about the toy she was reaching for. By stage 4 she can usually remove his hand and return to her goal. For the first time, assimilation and accommodation appear to operate independently. Lucienne's accommodation to the barrier was not assimilated to her activities of reaching the goal; she remained undistracted (Cowan, 1978). Conversely, her assimilative focus on obtaining the object did not prevent her from accommodating the barrier.

Stage 4 infants seem to have an actual purpose in mind when they attempt to find appropriate actions to accomplish their goals. If an infant's mother closes a toy box that he cannot open, the child may bang on the box to get the mother's attention or place her hand on the box and wait. Babies at this stage are beginning to see that objects and other people can have an effect on the world, but their notions of causality are still very limited. They still consider themselves to be the initiators of all activity.

Object Permanence For the first time, at stage 4 the infant seems to have a meaningful representation of a permanent object. If children in this stage see a toy hidden behind a screen or under a cover, they will retrieve it. Eight to 12 month old children love "peek-a-boo" and other games in which people and things appear and reappear. However, if an object is moved sequentially from one hiding place to another, the infant will search only under the first cover. This has been called the *A, not B, phenomenon*. Although the infant has some mental representation of the object, memory is still tied to the act of searching for the object.

■ **Figure 6–2**

Object permanence can be demonstrated by infants 8–12 months old.

Piaget (1970) thought babies in this stage know what they are looking for and where to begin, but they cannot yet grasp the significance of the displacement or recall the sequence of events. More recent research indicates that infants have a longer and more extensive memory for object placement than previously believed. Infants as young as 8 months old can search in two different locations for an object and are surprised when an object is retrieved from behind a screen where they did not see it placed (Baillargeon & Graber, 1988).

The infant's level of locomotor skill may affect object permanence performance. Infants with more locomotor experience are more likely to employ spatial search strategies than infants with limited movement skills (Kermoian & Campos, 1988).

Imitation Along with object permanence, stage 4 children develop two important imitative skills. First, they imitate movements they have made but never seen.

> Piaget's daughter, in the last half of her first year, is sitting quietly, when he approaches and sticks out his tongue. She laughs and immediately imitates the action. (P.A. Cowan, 1978, p. 92)

Second, 8–12 month old infants can copy new sounds and gestures. This ability clearly makes them seem more attentive and responsive to the world around them.

tertiary circular reactions
Piaget's term for the repetition of certain behaviors that vary each time they are performed (i.e., hitting a drum with a toy and then with a stick). These behaviors characterize the fifth sensorimotor stage.

trial-and-error experimentation
learning, usually without a guide, by making mistakes until the correct solution is discovered

"little scientist"
Piaget's term for the active "hypothesis testing" during the trial-and-error experimentation stage

STAGE 5: TERTIARY CIRCULAR REACTIONS (12–18 MONTHS) Between 12 and 18 months, the child operates in the stage of *tertiary circular reactions*. Like other circular reactions, behaviors at this stage display the child's growing understanding of cause-and-effect relationships. This time, however, the child employs a rather sophisticated problem-solving skill, *trial-and-error experimentation*, to bring about certain outcomes. By varying their actions to see effects, stage 5 children become "little scientists" who gather important information about how things happen.

> Laurent. . .grasps a succession of objects. A celluloid swan, a box, etc., stretches out his arm and lets them fall. He distinctly varies the position of the fall. . . . He lets (an object fall two or three times. . .in the same place as though to study the spatial relation; then he modifies the situation. (Piaget, 1937/1954, p. 269)

Piaget characterizes children in this stage as miniature scientists whose mobility and curiosity motivate them to explore the effects of varied actions. Now the child who wants a toy from a closed toy box will not just shout to get attention or place the mother's hand on the toy box and wait. He will also look at the mother, push her toward the box, place a hand on hers, slap her hand against the toy box lid, and so forth. With each new strategy, the child learns more about the relationship between cause and effect—between his actions and the results.

Children at this age sometimes seem mischievous when they dust the furniture with a dirty diaper, play with Mother's make-up, or place the dog's bowl on their heads. In most cases these activities are experiments to find out what will happen in each case. If their hair becomes wet and messy from the dog bowl, for example, they might gradually modify their actions, playing with the bowl only when it is empty or avoiding contact with it altogether. Since stage 5 children have little appreciation of danger, they must be carefully supervised. The same curiosity that draws them to investigate Mother's make-up also encourages children to poke at electrical outlets or take aspirin or vitamin tablets in quantity.

Object Permanence Object permanence advances in this stage. Infants are able to track visual displacements and will search for the object under the last cover. However, if infants cannot see some of the moves, they get lost:

> In this substage, when Jacqueline's toy parrot is hidden at A and then moved beyond a screen at B, she correctly looks for her toy parrot at B. However, when Piaget puts a ring in his hand and places his hand behind the screen, leaving the ring there, Jacqueline actively searches the hand and does not think of looking behind the screen. (Piaget 1937/1954, p. 79)

Imitation Imitation becomes more precise during stage 5. Infants will attempt to make sounds and gestures exactly like the model. They may also perform rituals in association with certain objects.

> For example, one morning a sixteen–month–old child sees a stuffed animal which he usually takes to bed with him; he lies down immediately, sucks his thumb and closes his eyes. In the fifth sensorimotor stage, the ritual may be repeated every time the child approaches the object. (P.A. Cowan, 1978, p. 98–99)

The rituals are self-imitations of behaviors performed by the child at another time. The object used in the ritual seems to serve as a cue that releases a succession of responses that help the child learn more about the functional qualities of the object.

STAGE 6: INVENTING NEW MEANS THROUGH MENTAL COMBINATIONS (18–24 MONTHS) In the sixth and final stage of the sensorimotor period, the child can represent the external world in terms of mental images and memories. Because the child can now *"think,"* he no longer has to go through the process of trial and error. Children at the end of the sensorimotor period can "imagine" and invent solutions by making new mental combinations of schemes. They can also save time and effort by discarding solutions that do not seem appropriate or useful. Piaget notes:

> I put the chain back into the box, an empty matchbox, and reduce the opening to 3mm. It is understood that Lucienne is not aware of the func-

tioning of the opening and closing of the matchbox and has not seen me prepare the experiment. She only possesses the two preceding (schemes): turning the box over in order to empty it of its contents, and sliding her finger into the slit to make the chain come out. It is of course this last procedure that she tries first. She puts her finger inside and gropes to reach the chain, but fails completely. A pause follows during which Lucienne manifests a very curious reaction bearing witness not only to the fact that she tries to think out the situation and to represent to herself through mental combination the operation to be performed, but also to the role played by the imitation in the genesis of representations. Lucienne mimics the widening of the slit.

> She looks at the slit with great attention; then, several times in succession, she opens and shuts her mouth, at first slightly, then wider and wider!...The attempt at representation which she thus furnishes is expressed plastically, that is to say, due to inability to think out the situation in words of clear visual images she uses a simple motor indication as "signifier" or symbol. Lucienne, by opening her mouth thus expresses, or even reflects her desire to enlarge the opening of the box. This (scheme) of imitation, with which she is familiar, constitutes for her the means of thinking out the situation. (Piaget, 1952, pp. 337–338)

It's important to point out that although mental representation, or the ability to think, is the crowning achievement of the sensorimotor period, the infant's mental images are based on sensations and motor activities and are quite different from mental symbols based on spoken language that come with the next cognitive period. For example, the sensorimotor child might move a little child out of the way before opening a door to avoid knocking her over but cannot begin to understand more complex cause-and-effect relationships, such as why the sun rises and sets.

Object Permanence Just as the infant can mentally conceptualize and follow a series of events in his mind that lead to problem solving, he can also track down an object hidden almost anywhere, even if some of the moves were not visible. Observing his other daughter, Piaget writes

> At 1:6(8) Jacqueline throws a ball under a sofa. But instead of bending down at once and searching for it on the floor, she looks at the place, realizes that the ball must have crossed under the sofa, and sets out to go behind it. But there is a table at her right, and the sofa is backed against a bed on the left; therefore, she begins by turning her back on the place where the ball disappeared...goes around the table, and finally arrives behind the sofa at the right place (Piaget, 1937/1954, p. 23).

cognitive map
a mental representation of a physical location

deferred imitation
copying a behavior sometime after it was observed

This example also indicates that the child can construct a *cognitive map* to help locate objects in space by finding alternative routes to a goal (Tolman, 1948).

Imitation *Deferred imitation* involves imitating actions seen in the past but not immediately copied.

At 1;4 (1 year, 4 months) Jacqueline had a visit from a little boy of 1;6 whom she used to see from time to time, and who, in the course of the afternoon, got into a terrible temper. He screamed as he tried to get out of his playpen and pushed it backwards, stamping his feet. J stood watching him in amazement, never having witnessed such a scene before. The next day, she herself screamed in her playpen and tried to move it, stamping her foot lightly several times in succession. The imitation of the whole scene was most striking. Had it been immediate, (the imitation) would naturally not have involved representation, but coming as it did after an interval of more than 12 hours, it must have involved some representative or pre-representative element (Piaget, 1951, p. 63)

Piaget felt this ability develops around 18 months of age. More contemporary research places the capacity for deferred imitation at about 14 months (Meltzoff, 1988). Interestingly, children can defer imitation of both live and symbolic models, so it is not uncommon to begin to influence the child's behavior at this time. Jean Mandler (1988) has suggested that infants create concepts *at the same time* that they develop a sensorimotor representation of objects.

The Preoperational Period of Cognitive Development

By age 2 the child has entered a new phase of cognitive development, a phase Piaget calls the *preoperational period*. He chose that term because the child has acquired some symbols such as words and numbers but cannot use mental operations to manipulate or transform these symbols. For example, most 3 year olds can recite the numbers from 1 to 10 but they cannot count out 10 candies or 10 buttons. This type of thinking is also called preconceptual or prelogical.

The main difference between sensorimotor and preoperational thought is that the sensorimotor child is primarily action oriented, concentrating on concrete goals, while the preoperational child is more concerned with the process of goal attainment and how behavior is organized than on the goal itself. The entire preoperational period extends from ages 2 to 7, cutting across infancy (0 to 2 years), toddlerhood (2 to 3 years) and the preschool period (3 to 6). Since preoperational thought is more typical of the preschooler than the infant, a detailed description of this phase of cognitive development appears in Chapter 9.

NeoPiagetian Views of Cognitive Development

Piaget presumes an evenness of development as children pass from stage to stage. When children develop a scheme, they should be able to apply that scheme to all similar situations. Building on the work of Heinz Werner (1948) and Lev Vygotsky (1962), NeoPiagetian theorists led by Jerome Bruner (1973), Jerome Kagan (1971), and Robert Ende (et al., 1976) observe that not all the infant's abilities have advanced to the

■●▲   CONCEPT SUMMARY

Three Dimensions of Piaget's Theory of Sensorimotor Development

STAGE	FOCUS	IMITATION SKILLS	OBJECT PERMANENCE
Reflexes (0–1 month)	Elaboration of reflexes	Lacking	Lacking
Primary circular reactions (1–4 months)	Producing interesting effects involving own body	Pseudoimitation	Looks where object was last
Secondary circular reactions (4–8 months)	Producing interesting effects involving objects in the environment	Imitation of familiar patterns	Uncovers partially hidden object; follows the trajectory of a hidden object—no search initiated
Coordination of some means and ends (8–12 months)	Child has a purpose in mind when he initiates actions to accomplish his goals	Imitation of somewhat novel patterns	Uncovers hidden object but may only search in first hiding place, not subsequent ones (A, not B, phenomenon)

same extent at the same time. Some abilities have progressed to a higher level and some have not. Thus, it's not the child's behavior that has changed from stage to stage but the child's *capacity* to perform at a higher level. Through reward and punishment, the environment determines whether or not this new capacity is revealed. Thus, the child must *learn* how to extend his schemes to a wide variety of situations.

NeoPiagetians have found that changes in capacity are supported by corresponding changes in the brain's performance (Kagan, 1982). The NeoPiagetian levels extend to age 3, while for Piaget, sensorimotor de-

STAGE	FOCUS	IMITATION SKILLS	OBJECT PERMANENCE
Tertiary circular reactions (12–18 months)	Trial and error experimentation; can consider several solutions but must apply each to see if it is successful or not	Imitation of novel patterns	Uncovers hidden object; searches under last cover rather than stopping with first location
Invention of new means through mental combinations (18–24 months)	Insight without trial and error	Deferred imitation	Uncovers object hidden through invisible displacement

velopment is accomplished by age 2. Table 6–1 shows how the four sensorimotor levels of the NeoPiagetians compare with Piaget's original formulations. There is considerable debate on the adequacy of Piaget's concepts to explain cognitive growth (see Halford, 1989, and Commentary published in *Human Development*, Vol. 32, No. 6).

Sensorimotor Levels

LEVEL 1: SINGLE ACTIONS (2–7 MONTHS) As reflex actions are replaced by voluntary behaviors, the child can control single voluntary actions by 3 months of age. The child can vocalize, for example, and he can reach. But he can't yet reach *while* he's vocalizing.

Level 1—single actions corresponds with Piaget's stage of primary circular reactions.

LEVEL 2: RELATIONS OF ACTIONS (6–12 MONTHS) By about 6 months of age, the child can perform two actions simultaneously. He can cry *while* he reaches and suck *while* he plays. In this way the child engages in a sensorimotor *relation of actions*.

A variation of this theme occurs when one action is used to produce another. Such means-end relationships are also discussed by Piaget. For example, the child learns that if he squeezes a certain toy, it will squeak or if he cries loudly, someone will attend to him. In order to engage in

■ **Table 6–1** *Piaget's Sensorimotor Stages Compared with NeoPiagetian Sensorimotor Levels*

PIAGET'S STAGES	NEOPIAGETIAN SENSORIMOTOR LEVELS	APPROXIMATE AGES
Reflexes		
Primary circular reactions	Level 1 Single actions	2 to 7 months
Secondary circular reactions		
Coordindation of secondary circular reactions	Level 2 Relations of actions	6 to 12 months
Tertiary circular reactions	Level 3 Systems of actions	10 to 20 months
The beginnings of representational thought	Level 4 Single representations	18 to 36 months

Source: From *Human Development* by Fischer and Lazerson. © 1984 by Kurt W. Fischer and Arlyne Lazerson. Reprinted by permission of W. H. Freeman and Company.

these activities, the child must be able to remember how two actions fit together. Otherwise, he might need to summon his mother, for example, and not know how to do that. Another thing the child learns at this level is that the environment is responsive—that action produces reaction and that those activities can be repeated.

LEVEL 3: SYSTEMS OF ACTIONS (10–20 MONTHS) When the child is about 10 months old, he can begin to progress to the level of coordinating systems of actions. Now, instead of being limited to performing two activities at once (looking while grasping), he can integrate several activities together (looking, vocalizing, moving, while grasping). All of this behavior flows smoothly because the child can remember the relationship between each behavior and its outcome.

LEVEL 4: SINGLE REPRESENTATIONS (18–36 MONTHS) In this final stage, children can use items for their intended purpose or they can use that same item to represent something completely different. For example, a child can use a box for storing his toys or he can pretend that same box is a car. Using one object *as if* it were something else is the hallmark of symbolic thought.

The Information Processing Approach to Cognitive Development

information processing approach
a general theoretical approach to the study of cognition that views the human mind as a complex, symbol manipulating system through which information flows, is processed/examined, and then is utilized, dismissed, or stored as memory

The stage theories of Piaget and the NeoPiagetians describe the types of changes that take place in the infant's ability to interact with the world. In order to understand the mental processes that support this change, we must turn to the information processing approach. This approach does not offer a single unified theory but instead focuses on the operations of attention, perception, and memory to explain the inner workings of the child's mind. Researchers in this area tend to assume the human mind is analogous to a computer where the hardware (brain, nervous system, and senses) and software (problem-solving "programs" and strategies) improve over time.

Attention: Getting Information Into the System

Attention involves focusing on aspects of the environment. As children grow older, they become better at deliberately focusing their attention and resisting distraction (Ruff & Lawson, 1990). How do we know what attracts a child's attention? Visual preference can be monitored by a camera that records the infant's eye movements as she scans the environment (Banks and Salapatek, 1983). Attention can also be measured by monitoring infants' heart rates or the rate at which they suck a pacifier while they are exposed to a picture, sound, or smell. Heart rate deceleration and an increased rate of sucking are signs of interest. If the heart rate stays the same or if sucking slows, the baby is bored. From this line of research, we can conclude that babies are interested in human faces, sounds, and smells; curved lines; three-dimensional objects; and complex patterns. Information that is too complex, however, is of little interest. Children look away, cry, wander off, or go to sleep when they feel overwhelmed (D.R. Anderson et al., 1981).

When several stimuli simultaneously compete for the child's attention, how does she choose between them? Children under 6 years of age are more attentive to the visual aspects of their environment (D.S. Hayes et al., 1981). Young children literally *watch* TV, paying far more

■ **Figure 6–3**

Hi, baby.

attention to movement, color, and appearance than to the music or storyline. Infants and preschoolers learn most efficiently without distraction (background conversation or music) and when they can focus on one task at a time (Higgins & Turnure, 1984). Compared to other babies, the infants of depressed women focus attention on more objects for shorter periods of time. This difference may be due to differences in depressed and nondepressed mother's involvement in their child's play (Breznitz & Friedman, 1988).

SELECTIVE ATTENTION Besides selecting a stimulus and attending to it, a child must be able to focus on the relevant aspects of the task and ignore irrelevant ones. This process, known as *selective attention,* is usually measured by having a child wear a set of headphones through which two different messages are presented. The child is then asked to focus on one message or the other and to be prepared to report what they hear (Cherry, 1981). Older children are more efficient at maintaining the concentration needed to selectively attend. Until the age of 11 or 12, children process both relevant and irrelevant information. After age 12, the child processes much more relevant than irrelevant information.

Strategies for Improving Attention As children learn to maintain focus for longer and longer periods of time and to filter out irrelevance, they also become more skilled in applying strategies to make information gathering more efficient. If the task is to decide which two stimuli in Figure 6–3 are identical, children have to scan and compare the images. Children age 4 and younger are unsystematic, comparing only one or two windows at random and often drawing incorrect conclusions. Four to 9 year olds are much more systematic and planful, comparing each pair of windows until they find a difference (Vurpillot, 1968). Although most children develop more deliberate, selective, sustained, and planful changes in attention, some children, mostly boys, experience attention-related problems that interfere with learning. Attention-deficit disorders (ADD) are discussed in Chapters 12 and 13.

Examining and Storing Information: The Role of Memory

The system that holds and stores information from the senses is called *memory.* In 1968 Atkinson and Shiffrin proposed a *store model of memory* that posits the existence of three stores of stages in which information can be retained and processed—the sensory store, the short-term memory store, and the long-term memory store. The store system is thought to be present at birth in all humans with a capacity and efficiency that is modified with development. Information enters the system at the sensory store and if not incidental, is transferred to short-term memory. Although short-term memory has a limited capacity, information can

store model of memory
Atkinson and Shiffrin's (1968) notion that memory exists in stages and information is passed along through each stage, processed, stored, or forgotten

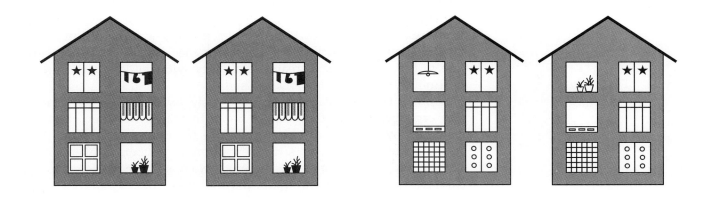

■ **Figure 6–4**

Older children are more adept at comparing the essential features of elements than younger children.

be held here briefly, forgotten, or transferred to long-term memory for permanent storage.

SHORT-TERM STORAGE CAPACITY How much "room" exists in a young child's short-term memory? A child might be asked to listen to and repeat a series of numbers in sequence: 3–7, 3–4–5, 2–6–7–1, and so forth. Adults can repeat about eight numbers in a series, 12 year olds can repeat six or seven, and 5 year olds can repeat four. Thus, short-term memory capacity seems to improve over time (Pascual-Leone, 1980).

MEMORY STRATEGIES As more space is being created in memory, children are also employing more efficient strategies for organizing and retaining incoming information. One of the simplest strategies is to *rehearse* or repeat (either out loud or "in one's head") the information to be remembered. Children as young as 3 will name an object but will rehearse only when told to do so and may repeat the material only once for mastery (Naus, 1982). By age 10 almost all children spontaneously rehearse, perhaps because they have had enough time to master the strategy.

Another memory strategy is to organize or combine the single pieces of information into units of meaning. For example, the string 741776 would overtax the short-term memory of most young children. But an older child or adult could organize that whole string into a single unit of meaning—the original date of U.S. independence: 7(July)–4–1776. One "chunk" of information takes up far less memory space than six individual numbers. Similarly, when children are shown a picture of a kitchen and asked to remember as many items as they can, older children will group common items into categories—such as food, furniture, appliances. Younger children group items haphazardly if at all (Kee & Bell, 1981). Four to 10 month olds can better remember objects presented together that go together (cookies and a lollipop—both snacks) than two unrelated items (a lion and M&Ms). They can also be helped to organize if prompted by an instruction to sort items into groups of things that "go together" or "are alike." The performance differences are probably due to the older child's greater familiarity with the language and opportunity to practice classification skills.

Younger children may not be consciously aware that they are sorting and organizing since they cannot name the categories they choose or explain why they organized as they did (Bjorklund & Zeman, 1983). Although older children's strategies are more deliberate, even 11 and 12 year olds fail to organize material when items have few obvious characteristics in common (Bjorklund & Hack, 1982).

How old must a baby be to show evidence of information in long-term storage? By 5 months of age, babies can recognize a pattern they have seen up to 2 weeks after it was first presented (Rovee-Collier et al., 1989). Three-day-old babies can tell familiar sounds from unfamiliar ones (L. R. Brody et al., 1984). Amazingly, infants born 5 weeks premature can study pictures and patterns thoroughly enough to recognize differences between them and other similar shapes. Apparently, as long as sensory information can enter the infant's system, he can organize and process it in some rudimentary way, although repeated exposure does help improve retention in children as young as 2 years (Fivush & Hamond, 1989). The accompanying feature focuses on remembering early experiences as adults.

There is a qualitative change that takes place in infant memory in the first year of life: Babies aren't able to consciously remember the past until they are 6 or 7 months old (Kail, 1984). John Flavell (1985) argues that the memory system of adults and older children involves conscious feelings of familiarity ("I have seen that before" or "I remember that as though it were yesterday"). Such feelings apparently are not present yet in young children. Rovee-Collier (1984) trained 2–3 month olds to move a mobile by kicking the leg that was attached to a ribbon tied to the mobile. Infants remembered the association without prompting for 1 week. Twenty-one days after the training, the infant needed to be "reminded" of the kicking responses she learned by seeing the mobile and watching it move briefly (Hill et al., 1988). No such cuing is needed for older infants. Infants over 7 months of age will search for lost or removed objects on their own or for items they recalled being in one drawer, for example, but were moved elsewhere (Ashmead & Perlmutter, 1980). Why does it take 7–9 months for infant memory to assume a conscious or purposeful nature? Perhaps conscious memory depends on the maturation of specific brain structures or, as Piaget suggested, the development of knowledge categories called schema must precede any attempt to act on that knowledge (Schacter & Moscovitch, 1984).

infantile amnesia
Freud's term for the apparent "forgetting" of experiences that occurred during infancy

A Closer Look

Remembering Infancy

Think back. Think way, way back. What's the earliest memory you have of your childhood?

Do you remember the second grade (age 7 or 8)?

Who was your teacher?

Who were your best friends?

Do you remember your first day in kindergarten (age 5 or 6)?

Were you excited or scared?

Do you remember what your life was like before you were in school (age 4 or younger?)

When adults are asked to recall their earliest memories, they can remember events that occurred when they were 3 or 3 1/2 but generally no younger (White & Pillemer, 1979). Over the years, researchers have tried to explain why we cannot recall earlier (even prenatal) experiences.

Freud (1905/1953) suggested that we have the ability to remember *all* of life experiences if we truly *want* to. He felt that our earliest memories focus on the sexual pleasure derived from sucking and mouthing objects (oral stage birth–1 year) and from retaining or expelling feces (1–3 years). As such, they are too raw and socially unacceptable to recall or discuss. Driven by pressure from the superego (the moral conscience), such memories are repressed or pushed into the unconscious mind where they remain hidden. Freud labeled the adult's inability to access early memories *infantile amnesia.* The problem with this explanation is that even after extensive psychoanalysis, patients *still* cannot recall memories from infancy (White & Pillemer, 1979). (Are the memories really *that* bad or are they just not there?)

Brain researchers point out that the hippocampus plays a crucial role in memory formation. Damage to the hippocampus results in an inability to transfer new memories to long-term storage (Kolb, 1989). As a consequence, every moment exists in isolation, without any tie to the past or the future. Interestingly, the hippocampus isn't mature enough to tie memories to specific events so they can be stored and recalled until the child is 2½ or 3 years of age (Kolb, 1989).

Recall also depends on an organizational scheme. Some information is simply easier to remember than others. Highly memorable information is usually unique or novel, tied to other things we know, deliberately processed into memory, or easy to "find." If young children do remember events as infants or toddlers, they tend to recall important life events, like being adopted, a memorable trip, a death, or the birth of a sibling. These autobiographical events "stand out" in memory because they are novel and emotionally charged. Children get better at storing and accessing daily memories as their vocabularies grow and they acquire more conceptual labels for events, for instance birthdays, life with grandma, or fun at the park. (White & Pillemer, 1979).

So, if you look back into your memory bank and find you remember little or nothing about your infancy, don't worry. You're not alone.

■●▲ CONCEPT SUMMARY

Infant Attention and Memory Systems

Attention

- Interested in human faces, human voices, human smells
- Interested in curved rather than straight lines
- Interested in three-dimensional rather than two-dimensional objects
- If visual information is too complex, infant becomes frustrated or loses interest
- Visual stimuli attract more attention than auditory, taste, or olfactory stimuli
- Very distractable—short attention span

Memory

- Capacity improves with age
- Doesn't spontaneously rehearse information to remember it better
- Can't consciously remember until 6 or 7 months old
- Object permanence skills depend on memory functions

The Origins of Cause-and-Effect Reasoning

Peter White (1988) suggests that causal processing first occurs around 3 months of age when infants begin to notice the sequential actions of objects (one ball striking another, pushing on a toy to make it squeak). Observation then leads to action. Three to 8 month old children can remember what they saw and then act with the *intention* of effecting a specific outcome. If a toy has wheels, for example, they will push the toy or spin the wheels with their hands. Even very young babies understand that the closer the bottle is to their mouth, the sooner they will be fed. They will often pull at the caregiver's arms or push the hand that is holding the bottle closer to their mouth to facilitate meal delivery.

Causal reasoning during infancy is hampered by cognitive immaturity and lack of experience. Using the principle of contiguity, young infants will associate the loud, sudden thunder of an electrical storm with the house going dark in an electrical power outage. Infants may then cry and display other signs of discomfort when they hear thunder again both because the thunder startles them and because they might anticipate another power loss. Thus, causality is easy for the infant to understand if one action consistently produces a specific reaction; it becomes much more difficult when one event (thunder) may or may not be linked to an inevitable outcome (sudden darkness).

The Psychometric Approach: Assessing Cognition by Measuring Infant Intelligence

Psychometrics is the science involved with measuring human characteristics. It is more concerned with outcomes and results and less concerned with the processes people use to arrive at those outcomes. In the 1940s in the United States, scientists and the general population became interested in the measurement and prediction of intelligence. The number of adoptions in this country had increased dramatically because of World War II, and prospective parents wanted to know if their adopted sons and daughters had normal capabilities (Brooks and Weintraub, 1976). As a consequence, two infant intelligence scales were developed by prominent psychologists: The Bayley Scales of Infant Development (Bayley, 1949) and the Gesell Developmental Schedules (Gesell & Ames, 1937).

The Gesell Developmental Schedules can evaluate the behavior of children between 1 month and 6 years of age. Four developmental areas are assessed: motor (movement, sitting, balance), adaptation (alertness, exploration, intelligence), language (sounds, gestures, facial expressions), and social behavior (feeding, self-care skills). In each of the areas, the child's behavior is compared with that of age-mates. The Bayley scales are more widely used than the Gesell schedules. The Bayley scales focus on the infant's mental capacity (as measured by memory, perception, senses, learning, language use, and problem-solving ability) and psychomotor development (as measured by gross and fine motor skills and coordination scores). (See Table 6–2.) The child who scores the same as his age mates on the Mental Development Index or on the Psychomotor Development Index would receive a score of 100 (called a developmental quotient). The score would be higher if the child were more advanced than his peers; it would be lower if he were more delayed.

The measurement of infant intelligence has always been controversial. What constitutes intelligent behavior in babies? College students were asked to identify traits they felt characterized intelligent behavior in 6-month-old and 2-year-old children (Siegler & Richards, 1982). Here are the five choices listed most frequently:

psychometrics
using tests or assessment devices to measure behavior

intelligence
measurable abilities that represent accumulated knowledge or experience (i.e., the ability to cope with the environment, to judge, comprehend and reason, to understand and deal with people, symbols and objects, to act with purpose and effectiveness)

■ **Table 6–2** *Selected Items from the Bayley Mental Scale*

AGE IN MONTHS	ITEM
0.1	Responds to sound of bell
1.6	Turns eyes to light
2.0	Visually recognizes mother
2.8	Simple play with rattle
3.8	Inspects own hands
4.4	Eye-hand coordination in reaching
5.0	Reaches persistently
6.2	Playful response to mirror
7.9	Says "da-da" or equivalent
8.1	Uncovers toy
9.1	Responds to verbal request
9.7	Stirs with spoon in imitation
10.1	Inhibits on command
11.3	Pushes car along
12.0	Turns pages of a book
12.5	Imitates words
13.8	Builds tower of 2 cubes
14.3	Puts 9 cubes in cup
14.6	Uses gestures to make wants known

6 Month Olds	2 Year Olds
1. Recognition of objects and people	1. Verbal ability
2. Motor coordination	2. Learning ability
3. Alertness	3. Awareness of people and the environment.
4. Awareness of the environment	4. Motor coordination
5. Verbalization	5. Curiosity

Even if we agree that these traits are associated with intelligence, how do we measure them? Is a 2 year old curious or merely verbal if he asks a lot of questions about his environment? Is it possible to be curious without asking questions? Children are notorious for "not performing" for others. If a baby can stack blocks at home but refuses to stack them when being tested on motor coordination, do we give him credit for the activity even though it can't be demonstrated on demand? And finally, what do the results of any infant IQ test mean? Since infant IQ test scores are not reliably predictive of IQ scores in childhood and adolescence, most infant intelligence tests are used only to identify infants who are progressing poorly (Fagan, 1985). If IQ prediction is needed, the baby's reactions to visual novelty and repetition in habituation paradigms and measures of looking behavior are more useful than scores from traditional infant intelligence tests, particularly for highlighting perceptual–cognitive deficits (Bornstein & Sigman, 1986; G. Ross, 1989; Slater et al., 1989). Four-month-old babies who habituated fastest tended to have parents who take an active role in handing them toys, naming objects, and pointing things out to them (Bornstein, 1985). Infant's habituation test scores are also correlated with later infant IQ scores (Rose & Wallace, 1985). Slower habituation and reduced attention is displayed by high risk, preterm babies (Rose et al., 1988).

Bradley and Caldwell's HOME (Home Observation for Measurement of the Environment) Inventory is a systematic assessment of the social, cognitive, and emotional aspects of the child's home environment. Information about six categories is collected by interview and observation:

HOME Categories

1. Emotional and verbal responsivity of mother
2. Avoidance of restriction and punishment
3. Organization of physical and temporal environment
4. Provision of appropriate play materials
5. Maternal involvement with child
6. Opportunities for variety in daily stimulation

Scores on the HOME Inventory at 6 months of age are predictive of infant IQ at age 3. Infant boy's IQ scores are influenced by an organized environment where encouragement is given to play with a variety of toys and materials. For infant girls, a responsive mother and a varied and nonpunitive environment are highly related to IQ scores (Bee et al., 1982).

Play as a Measure of Intelligence

When children play they engage in spontaneous self-expressive behavior that gives them pleasure. Play is not wasted time but rather time spent building new knowledge from previous experience. In infancy, play and cognitive development are intimately related: Children learn to play and they play to learn. The following are some long-range developmental functions of play:

1. Developing coordination through muscle development (throwing, drawing, running, jumping)
2. Understanding events that take place in life (death, divorce) and learning to solve emotional problems
3. Acting out roles they see enacted around them (Mommy, teacher, firefighter, soldier)
4. Learning social skills such as cooperation, sharing, self-control, and the like

When children under 1 year of age are in a free play situation surrounded by toys, they spend most of their time touching and mouthing each object (Zelazo & Leonard, 1983). By age 1, young children are able to generate ideas about objects and events and so their play changes dramatically. By 13.5 months of age, children play with two toys at once but pay little attention to the toy's intended purpose. For example, a plate may be used as a "lid" for a truck, or blocks and dolls may be banged together. A noticeable change in the focus of play takes place when the child's behavior is cued by the toy rather than randomly associated with it. A 15.5 month old will be more likely to "talk" into a toy telephone than bang it or stack it, and to drive a truck than to throw it or mouth it. Where do children learn about the functional features of play things? Most likely by watching older children and TV models "play" or by having toy-specific play demonstrated for them by adults (Zelazo & Kearsley, 1980).

For the most part, sensorimotor play is *solitary play*—babies play alone with their toys. Parents or caregivers might be part of a play time when they initiate a game of peek-a-boo or provide a model for imitation. And when other children are present, *parallel play* might occur. In parallel play, children play side by side, sometimes at the same activities, as in the sandbox or with blocks, but do not interact. The children are not being unfriendly or antisocial; they just have difficulty concentrating on any needs but their own. The toddler's egocentrism encourages him to grab at other children's toys and fight to get what he wants. The concepts of ownership and sharing are still fairly ambiguous at this stage.

A Closer Look

Play During the First Year— Suggested Activities and Toys

AGE	TYPE OF STIMULATION	SUGGESTED TOYS
Birth–1 month	**Visual Stimulation**	
	Look at the infant at close range	Nursery mobiles
	Hang bright, shiny objects within 8–10 in. of baby's face and in the midline of his body	Unbreakable mirrors
		See-through crib bumpers
		Contrasting color sheets
	Auditory Stimulation	
	Talk to/sing to infant in soft voice	Music box
	Play something that makes music/produces sounds	Radio/stereo
		Television
		Metronome
		Musical mobiles
		Clock
	Tactile Stimulation	
	Hold, cuddle, caress	Stuffed animals
	Keep infant warm	Soft mobiles
	Wrap in soft clothing/swaddle	Soft or furry quilt
	Motion Stimulation	
	Rock infant/place in cradle	Rocking crib/cradle
	Use carriage/stroller for walks	Weighted toys
		Suction toys
2–3 months	**Visual Stimulation**	
	Take infant to various rooms while doing chores	(same as above)
	Place in infant seat for vertical view of the world	
	Auditory Stimulation	
	Include infant at family gatherings	(same as above)
	Expose to sounds other than those at home	
	Tactile Stimulation	
	Comb hair with soft brush	Baby brush
	Motion Stimulation	
	Use baby swing	Baby swing
	Take in car for rides	Car seat
	Exercise body	Mobile that's interesting to play with (10+ wks.)

AGE	TYPE OF STIMULATION	SUGGESTED TOYS
4–6 months	**Visual Stimulation**	
	Place infant in front of mirror	Mirror
	Place infant in front of TV when family watches	Television
	Give brightly colored toys to hold	Bright, soft toys
	Auditory Stimulation	
	Repeat sounds infant makes	
	Laugh when infant laughs	
	Call the baby by name	
	Place rattle or bell in hand and show how to shake it	Rattle, bell toy
	Tactile Stimulation	
	Offer squeeze toys of various textures	Squeeze toys
	Allow to splash in bath	
	Place unclothed on soft, furry rug and move extremities	Furry rug
	Motion Stimulation	
	Use swing or stroller	
	Bounce infant in lap while holding baby in standing position	
	Help baby roll over	
	Support baby while sitting (let baby lean forward to balance self)	
6–9 months	**Visual Stimulation**	
	Give large, bright toys with moveable parts and noise makers	Appropriate toy
	Play peek-a-boo	Pop-up toys
	Make funny faces to encourage imitation	
	Give infant paper to tear/crumple	
	Give a ball	Ball (too large to swallow
	Give ball of yarn to pull apart	or choke on)
	Auditory Stimulation	
	Call infant by name	
	Repeat simple words/speak clearly	
	Name the parts of baby's body, people, and foods	
	Tell the infant what you're doing	
	Use simple commands	
	Use "No" only when necessary	
	Show how to clap hands	
	Show how to bang a drum	Drum/pots and pans
	Tactile Stimulation	
	Let infant play with fabrics of different textures	Busy box for crib
	Let infant feel foods of different sizes, textures	
	Let infant "catch" running water	
	Give wad of sticky tape to play with	
	Motion Stimulation	
	Place infant on floor/carpet to roll over, crawl, etc.	
	Hold upright to bear weight and bounce	
	Pick up, say "Up"	
	Put down, say "Down"	
	Place toys out of reach—encourage infant to get them	
	Play pat-a-cake	

(continued on next page)

AGE	TYPE OF STIMULATION	SUGGESTED TOYS
9–12 months	**Visual Stimulation**	
	Show infant pictures in books	Picture books
	Play ball by rolling it	Large ball
	Demonstrate how to throw the ball	
	Demonstrate building a two-block tower	Large blocks
		Nested boxes/cups
		Strings of big beads
		Simple take-apart toys
	Auditory Stimulation	
	Read simple nursery rhymes	Appropriate books
	Point and name objects	
	Imitate the sounds of animals	See-and-say toys
	Tactile Stimulation	
	Give finger foods of different textures	Teething toys
	Let infant "squash" foods	Sponge toys
	Let infant feel cold (ice) and warm (not hot) objects	Floating toys
	Let infant feel a breeze	Fan blowing
		Books with texture and objects like fur and zippers
	Motion Stimulation	
	Give large push–pull toys	Push–pull toys
	Place furniture in a circle to encourage cruising	Push–ride toys
	Turn baby in different positions	

Source: Whaley, L. F., & Wong, D. L. (1988). *Essentials of Pediatric Nursing*, 3rd ed., Mosby.

In Touch

INFANT DEVELOPMENT EDUCATION ASSOCIATION
Service Headquarters
PO Drawer 13320
San Antonio, TX 78213-3320

This organization publishes materials describing methods for enhancing infant sensory growth and development

Stimulation is an essential feature of play. It is not enough to place a mobile over the child's crib or toys in the playpen. Optimally, physical, social, and cognitive growth through play involves interpersonal contact. Infants need to be *played with* in addition to being allowed to play. Sex differences begin to emerge in infant–parent social play. Fathers try to engage 4 month old boys and girls into play by touching them more when they look away. Mothers try to encourage interaction with male babies but are involved in a more reciprocal style with female children—when the girl baby looks away, the mother looks away, too (Roggman & Peery, 1989). When adults imitate the behavior of 2 year olds, toddlers imitate back, initiating social games while looking at the adult's face (Eckerman & Stein, 1990).

While the stimulation of play is important, parents of premature babies have a difficult time judging where understimulation stops and overstimulation begins. Parents of preemies tend to play with their babies 10–15% less than parents of full-term infants perhaps because preemies make less eye contact, have trouble holding their heads up, and

■ Figure 6–5

A 9 month old child offering a ball to her 11 month old playmate.

usually need more prompting before they will even respond (Field et al., 1986).

Educational stimulation such as picture books and stories can be introduced at any time during infancy. Reading to infants provides visual and auditory stimulation and indicates that reading is a valued activity. It can also accelerate language development by prompting answers to what, when, and where questions and by encouraging the use of more phrases and longer sentences (Whitehurst et al., 1988). If the child is held during the reading session, tactile stimulation is also provided. Table 6–3 is a list of recommended books for infants and toddlers.

■●▲ CONCEPT SUMMARY

Developmental Aspects of Play Behavior

- Under 12 months of age—mouths and touches play objects
- 12–15 months—plays with two objects at once but does not pay attention to intended purpose of objects
- 15½ months—the beginnings of toy-specific play
- Play during infancy is usually either *solitary* (playing alone) or *parallel* (playing beside other children without interacting)
- Play things and play setting need to be *safe* and *well supervised*

Parents not actively involved in the child's play activities should provide supervision and safe play things to prevent accident or injury. Toys should be sturdy, too large to swallow or insert in an ear or nose, and free of sharp edges, loose pieces, or points. Some age-appropriate toys are suggested in Table 6-4. Caregivers need not spend a fortune on toys to provide play things for their children. Some of the best toys are sturdy plastic cups and bowls, shoe boxes, discarded gift wrapping, and other items readily available in most homes and easily replaced.

■ **Table 6–3** *Recommended Picture and Storybooks for Infants and Toddlers*

These books are particularly good for reading to young children (age 6 and under). Books marked by a (*) hold special appeal for children under 2 years old and listings with a (#) are of especially high literary and/or artistic quality.

* Wood, Audrey. *Quick as a Cricket*. Child's Play.

*# Wood, Don, and Audrey Wood. *The Little Mouse, the Red Ripe Strawberry, and the Hungry Bear*. Child's Play.

* Wood, Don, and Audrey Wood. *Piggies*. Harcourt Brace Jovanovich.

* Wood, Audrey. *The Napping House*. Harcourt Brace Jovanovich.

* Brown, Margaret Wise. *Goodnight Moon*. HarperCollins.

Sendak, Maurice. *In the Night Kitchen*. HarperCollins.

Mayer, Mercer. *There's a Nightmare in My Closet*. Dial Books for Young Readers.

Hoban, Russell. *Bread and Jam for Frances*. Harper and Row.

Lobel, Arnold. *Ming Lo Moves the Mountain*. Greenwillow.

Lobel, Arnold. *Mouse Soup*. HarperCollins.

\# Cendrars, Blaise (translation by Marcia Brown). *Shadow*. Macmillan.

Seuss, Dr. *The Lorax*. Random House.

* Numeroff, Laura Joffe. *If You Gave a Mouse a Cookie*. HarperCollins.

*# Williams, Vera B. *"More, More, More" Said the Baby*. Greenwillow.

Minarik, Else Holmelund. *Little Bear*. HarperCollins.

Viorst, Judith. *Alexander and the Terrible, Horrible, No Good, Very Bad Day*. HarperCollins.

MacDonald, Golden. *The Little Island*. Doubleday.

Macaulay, David. *Why the Chicken Crossed the Road*. Houghton Mifflin.

Noble, Trinka Hakes. *The Day Jimmy's Boa Ate the Wash*. Puffin.

\# Van Allsburg, Chris. *Two Bad Ants*. Houghton Mifflin.

\# Van Allsburg, Chris. *Jumanjii*. Houghton Mifflin.

OUT OF PRINT

\# Mayer, Mercer. *One Monster after Another*. Golden Press.

Hurd, Edith Thatcher. *Wilkie's World*. Faber and Faber.

\# Goodman, Robert B. *Urashima Taro*. Island Heitage.

Maxley, Susan. *Gardener George Goes to Town*. Harper and Row.

List compiled by Mary K. Marsh, Michael Marsh, and Beverly S. Marsh

■ **Table 6–4**   *Age-Appropriate Toys and Sources of Stimulation for Infants and Toddlers*

1 MONTH	2 MONTHS	3 MONTHS
Pacifiers	Music boxes	Rattles (ring or dumbbell shaped)
Lullabies	Mobiles, dangle toys for crib	Music
Tape recordings of heartbeats	Your smile	
Rocking chairs		
Small, textured clutch toys		
Mobiles		
Large, bright pictures		
Your face close by		
4 MONTHS	**5 MONTHS**	**6 MONTHS**
Crib or playpen gyms	Suction toys	Household objects to bang and throw—e.g., cups, spoons, pot lids, plastic containers
Bells tied to crib	Toys to kick	Teething rings
Plastic disks on chains	Interlocking plastic rings	Squeaky, clutch toys
7 MONTHS	**8 MONTHS**	**9 MONTHS**
Floating bath toys	Nested cups	Toys tied to high chair
Kitchen objects	Roly-poly toys	Mirror (unbreakable)
String	Space to creep in	Jack-in-the-box
Soft rubber squeeze toys	Toys to bang together	
Small, soft, washable toys to clutch	Big soft blocks	
10 MONTHS	**11–12 MONTHS**	
Pegboards	Stacking disks	
Cardboard or cloth books	Large crayons	
Push-and-pull toys without handles	Small items to place inside containers	
	Personal drinking cups	
	Bright, medium-sized balls	

	18 MONTHS	2–3 YEARS
Gross motor play:	Large hollow wooden blocks	Sand boxes
	Low slides	Large blocks, cardboard boxes
	Low swings with arms and back	Interlocking block trains
	Large riding toys (cars, fire engines, etc.)	
	Rocking chairs	
	Small table and chairs	

(continued on next page)

■ **Table 6–4**   *(continued)*

	18 MONTHS	2–3 YEARS
Creative play:	Nesting blocks Hammer boards Toys with shaped openings to receive different shaped blocks Wrist bells	Large beads to string Braided strings with rigid tips to lace Wooden puzzles Finger paints Clay Colored construction paper Blunt scissors
Dramatic play:	Wooden trains Sand toys (pail, shoven, seive) Stuffed toys	Strong vehicles (car, truck, etc.) Toy telephone Housekeeping toys (mixer, iron, broom) Carriage, doll bed, and high chair Washable doll to bathe Baby doll
Quiet play:	Fingerpaints Clay	Wooden shoe to lace Paint Large crayons Cloth or cardboard books Cloth boards to lace with string Toys for water play (sponge, soap, rotary beater, sieve)

Source: Whaley & Wong, 1982.

From Memory to Behavior Change: The Infant's Ability to Learn

While most of the very young infant's behavior consists of automatic reflex responses, even young babies can acquire new behaviors through the process of learning. *Learning* is defined as a relatively permanent change in behavior that occurs as a result of experience. The phrase "relatively permanent" rules out temporary behavior changes resulting from illness, medication, or fatigue. Learning provides evidence of memory because without a memory of the event, the infant could not perform the new behavior. Babies, like children and adults, have auditory, visual, olfactory, tactile, and taste components to learning.

According to Arnold Gesell's biological-maturation theory (Gesell et al., 1974), learning and maturation are intimately tied. Maturation involves genetically determined patterns of growth. Sometimes perfor-

learning
relatively permanent changes in behavior resulting from specific experiences and/or instruction rather than from genetics or inherited characteristics

biological maturation theory
Gesell's theory which suggests that development proceeds as the nervous system matures

mance based on learning depends on maturation; maturation, however, is independent of learning. Gesell's theory asserts that development is "profoundly and inseparably bound up with the growth of the nervous system" (p. 18). According to this theory, a child does not *learn* to crawl, he *matures* to crawl. Development will not proceed until the child's nervous system, musculature, and skeletal system is "ready," or sufficiently well developed, to send and receive essential nerve impulses and to process incoming information. Thus, an infant may actually understand the concept of walking, but will not be able to apply that knowledge until his skeleton can bear his weight.

Mechanisms of Basic Learning

The principles that govern the learning of new responses are the same for both children and adults. Basic learning mechanisms include habituation, classical conditioning, and operant conditioning. Facial interest and other emotional behaviors in 1 year olds distinguish learners from nonlearners under all circumstances (Sullivan & Lewis, 1988).

HABITUATION *Habituation* involves responding less to a particular stimulus after repeated presentations. With visual habituation, infants spend progressively less time looking at an object that they have seen before, because it loses its novelty and becomes boring. Through habituation the child learns to differentiate between routine, predictable events, and new, unexpected stimuli in order to direct more attention to the latter. If habituation did not occur, children would devote as much attention to the inconsequential hum of the heater or air conditioner as to the sound of their mother's voice. Habituation also helps children become accustomed to routine environmental noises such as telephone conversations, noise from the television, and traffic sounds so they can sleep peacefully. The baby who spends some of his sleep time in the kitchen or family room gets used to sounds that might otherwise be disturbing or startling. Parents who take a "Shh!! The baby's sleeping!" approach to naptime are actually training their child to require a quiet sleep environment and to be sensitive to even low-intensity noise.

Peter Kaplan (1990) found that the older children are, the more rapidly they tend to habituate. Rapid habituation is also related to a high Apgar score, absence of medication at birth, good central nervous system functioning, high socioeconomic status, high IQ, and good performance on learning tasks. Rapid habituators tend to stay in free-exploration situations for relatively shorter periods of time and take less time to explore new toys than slower habituators (Pecheux & Lecuyer, 1983).

CLASSICAL CONDITIONING Through conditioning, or training, the child forms an association between two events or stimuli. In *classical condi-*

habituation
a simple type of learning whereby a particular stimulus becomes so familiar to the organism that it ceases to elicit any physiological response

classical conditioning
the process by which a subject learns to associate a neutral stimulus (such as a tone) with a meaningful stimulus that evokes a reflex response (such as food). After the subject receives training, the neutral stimulus alone will evoke the same response as the meaningful stimulus

tioning a reflex or automatic response such as blinking, startle, or heart rate is associated with a previously neutral stimulus (one that causes no predictable reaction). The most famous example of classical conditioning comes from the work of Ivan Pavlov (1849–1936). In early studies of the digestive system, Pavlov discovered that food placed in a dog's mouth automatically and consistently caused salivation. He called the food an unconditioned stimulus (UCS) and salivation the unconditional response (UCR). Other stimuli, such as a blinking light or the sound of a buzzer, had no reliable effect on the dog's behavior.

UCS   ————————————→   UCR

food   salivation

Pavlov found, however, that if a light, called here a conditioned stimulus (CS), was lashed just before the dog was fed, the dog would learn to associate the light with the food and when the light was on would salivate in anticipation of being fed.

CS

light

UCS   ————————————→   UCR

food   salivation

Thus, through conditioning, a previously neutral stimulus such as a light came to produce a salivation response by itself without the presence of the food.

CS   ————————————→   CR

light   salivation

In Pavlov's terminology, after learning takes place the light is called the *conditioned stimulus,* and salivation, the *conditioned response.*

Since few of us are interested in training children to drool, let's look at some other examples of classical conditioning. In individuals with normal sensitivity, pain in consistently produced by an injeciton from a needle.

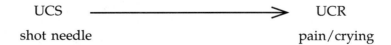

UCS   ————————————→   UCR

shot needle   pain/crying

Children who receive injections from doctors or nurses may come to associate previously neutral stimuli (such as the "surgical green uniform," a white laboratory coat, or a stethoscope around the neck) with the painful shot.

CS

lab coat, etc.

UCS ——————————————————▶ UCR

shot needle   pain/crying

Thus, the child may cry at the sight of the nurse or the doctor in anticipation of receiving an injeciton.

CS ——————————————————▶ CR

lab coat, etc.   pain/crying

Thus, phobias and other fears can be classically conditioned by pairing one event with the other.

Newborns have been classically conditioned to suck or blink when a tone is sounded or to show changes in heart rate or pupil dilation (Little et al., 1984). The infant's ability to learn through classical conditioning greatly improves with age since some newborns are not responsive to some CS-UCS combinations. Infants as young as 6 or 7 months old have learned to associate sweet and sour tastes with the color of the cup the food came in. After the training trials, nearly all infants reached for the cup whose color was associated with the sweet applesauce and avoided the colored cup associated with the sour applesauce (Reardon & Bushnell, 1988). Infants will also make anticipatory sucking movements when they see the nipple, indicating that conditioning has taken place.

OPERANT CONDITIONING Compared with classical conditioning, infants learn readily by *operant conditioning*. Operant conditioning is also a form of learning by association, but in operant conditioning, the association is between a behavior and the consequences of that behavior. The key term in operant conditioning is *reinforcement:* Behavior that is reinforced by some reward, such as a smile, food treat, or the absence of punishment, will be more likely to recur in the future. Operant conditioning can be used to teach new skills or to maintain existing behaviors. During training, behaviors that approximate the final desired responses are reinforced. This procedure is called *shaping.* If a caregiver wanted to teach an infant to say the word "drink," for example, the sequence of reinforced responses to the cue, "Say, drink" might include:

1. any verbalization
2. an approximation of the "d" sound

operant conditioning
Skinner's term for learning that results from past reinforcement or punishment

3. a more complex sound such as "dree" or "drik"
4. a word that sounds like "drink"

The idea is to encourage progress toward the goal by selective use of reinforcement.

The frequency of sucking in newborns, and of smiling, babbling, and motor movements in older infants, has been increased through operant conditioning (Myslivecek et al., 1987). In a classic study, infants learned to quickly turn their heads to the side when they received a sugary liquid for doing so (Siqueland & Lipsitt, 1966). Through studies of operant conditioning, research can discover infant preferences. Some early studies suggested that infants find music reinforcing because they keep sucking as long as the music is played and stop as soon as it is turned off (Butterfield & Siperstein, 1972). Similarly, adult attention must be rewarding since babies smile more when they are picked up, cuddled, and smiled back at by adults. It must take longer for babies to show an interest in the value of money since infants promised lottery pay-offs don't show any appreciable change in sucking, looking, or smiling! (Maybe they've just learned to be skeptical!)

Punishment (or the delivery of an unpleasant consequence) is another factor that affects which responses will be repeated and which ones will not. When a child's behavior is punished (through deprivation of attention, time-out, loss of a privilege, and the like), the punished behavior should *be less likely* to be repeated in the future. Reward and punishment can affect the incidence of both "good" and "bad" behaviors; ideally, good behaviors should be rewarded and bad punished. But occasionally, good behaviors are punished and bad behaviors rewarded.

LEARNING THROUGH IMITATION New behaviors can also be acquired through the process of *imitation* or watching and copying the behavior of others. Although Piaget felt that young infants were not capable of imitating behaviors they cannot see themselves performing, most contemporary researchers have found otherwise. In 1977 Meltzoff and Moore demonstrated that 12–20 day old infants can imitate an adult who wriggles his fingers, purses his lips, sticks out his tongue, and opens his mouth. Babies 1–3 days old can imitate the tongue thrust and open mouth movements (Meltzoff & Moore, 1983, 1989) and 3 day old babies can also copy happy, sad, and surprised facial expressions (Field et al., 1982). The critics claim that some of these findings cannot be replicated, that the infant had to be prompted repeatedly (except for the tongue protrusion), that some responses were imperfect and accompanied by other actions that were not part of the behavior demonstrated, and that young babies' imitation is reflexive or accidental and shows no conscious choice or awareness of process. Nevertheless, infants *can* imitate and that ability improves dramatically over the first 2 years of life (P. L. Harris, 1983).

■ **Figure 6–6**

A young infant imitating an adult's facial expressions.

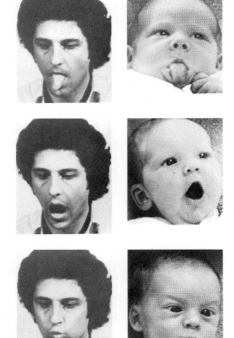

In all of the preceding studies, the adult model was in the same room as the baby and positioned only a few feet away. Can infants learn by watching televised models? When the TV is on, it competes for the infant's visual attention. Six month old babies spend about half their time looking at children's TV programs and about half their time looking elsewhere (Hollenbeck & Slaby, 1979). It takes about 3 years for children to imitate televised models as much as they imitate live models (McCall et al., 1977).

■ ● ▲   CONCEPT SUMMARY

Mechanisms of Basic Learning

Habituation

- Getting used to a familiar stimulus
- Habituation occurs more quickly with age

Classical conditioning

- Learning by associating a neutral stimulus with an unconditioned stimulus to produce a learned (conditioned) response
- Ability to learn by classical conditioning improves with age

Operant conditioning

- Learning by consequences—if reinforcement/reward follows a behavior, the behavior is more likely to be repeated; if punishment follows a behavior, the behavior is less likely to be repeated
- Ideally, desirable behaviors should be reinforced and undesirable behaviors should be punished
- Sometimes desirable behaviors are punished and undesirable behaviors are reinforced

Learning through Imitation

- Involves watching, remembering, and copying a behavior performed by another
- 1–3 day old babies can imitate simple behaviors (like tongue thrust)
- By age 3, children can imitate televised models

● Language Development

One of the milestone accomplishments in cognitive development is the ability to think using mental representations of language and to communicate using sounds and words. The groundwork for this process is laid during infancy and toddlerhood, when the child begins to acquire words that stand for people, objects, and events. To use language, the child must understand the rules that govern spoken language and be able to produce understandable speech. Except in cases of accelerated development, these abilities gradually unfold between the second and third years of life.

Language Comprehension vs. Language Production

Children learn to understand their native language long before they can speak it (K. Roberts, 1983). Although it has long been assumed that at all stages of language development children understand much more than they can say, recent evidence suggests that language production becomes coordinated with comprehension during the course of language acquisition (Clark & Hecht, 1983). One way children may demonstrate comprehension is through their behavior. A 22 month old child may raise her arms when asked "Do you want up?" and may begin to suck her thumb when a parent says "Are you sleepy?" Each of these responses indicates that the child understands the question asked and is responding affirmatively. Acredolo and Goodwyn (1988) have identified five classes of symbolic gestures used by the 1–2 year old child. These gestures may form part of a spontaneous pantomime or may be responses to an adult question or statement (Table 6–5).

There's also some evidence that 15 month old infants can comprehend the names associated with basic animals (Roberts & Cuff, 1989). Huttenlocher and Smiley (1987) found that mothers facilitate their infants' understanding by providing gestural cues along with verbal instruction and that infants' object names approximate adult name categories. For example, the mother might point at the stuffed animals while she says "Go get your bear." When the gesture was eliminated, the intonation flat, and the context ambiguous, 10–12 month old infants were less successful in locating certain objects or performing certain actions (Fernald, 1989). Of course, in some circumstances, gesture alone makes the message perfectly clear.

Prelinguistic Communication

Spoken language develops out of the young infant's cries and undifferentiated sounds. The pattern of language acquisition is similar for chil-

■ **Table 6–5** *Symbolic Gestures Shown by 17-Month-Olds*

CATEGORY	EXAMPLE	AGE FIRST USED
Naming attribute	"Flower": child sniffs "Dog": child pants "Airplane": child holds out arms	13.47 months
Making request	"Go out": child makes knob-turning gesture without touching doorknob "Nurse": child pats mother's chest "Food": child smacks lips	12.88 months
Naming event	"Hot": child blows or waves hand "Many": child waves hand back and forth "Big": child raises arms	12.40 months
Naming object	"I don't know": child opens palms	14.12 months
Replying	"Baseball game": child claps	13 months

Source: Papalia and Olds, *Child Development*, Fifth Edition. © 1990. (Adapted from Acredolo & Goodwyn, 1988, p. 454.) Used with permission.

dren the world over, regardless of culture or native dialect (Lenneberg, 1967). Let's examine the sequence of stages leading to language acquisition.

Crying

The first vocalizations that have meaning to adult caregivers are cries. Crying is a reflex ability present from birth. Congenital problems are sometimes detected by the way babies cry. When babies have chromosomal damage (like Down's syndrome), brain damage, or birth complications, they cry differently than unaffected infants do (M. Roberts, 1987). Eventual victims of SIDS reportedly cry differently from healthy babies. Normal newborns learn to use crying as a signal by varying the intensity, duration, and pattern of their cries. In 1969 Peter Wolff tape-recorded newborn cries and played them to new mothers to see if different cries provoked different responses. He found that mothers attended to the child most quickly and appeared most anxious when the cry was a *pain cry*—loud and long with a long pause between cries. For example, the infant might cry intensely for 5 seconds and then pause for 3 seconds to breathe before the next 5-second cry. The mothers acknowledged *hunger cries* (shorter, less intense, but more rhythmic cries) but in a more relaxed manner. Helping parents understand and cope with infant crying facilitates attachment and positive parent/child relations (St. James-Roberts, 1989). Parents become more adept at translating baby's cries with practice and apparently use other noncry cues to guide their caregiving (Gustafson & Harris, 1990).

coos/cooing
the infant's first noncry vocalizations

Cooing

As they cry, breathe, and swallow, infants inadvertently practice the vowel and consonant sounds that will become the syllables and words of later speech. Noncrying vocalizations are called *coos*. Cooing usually appears by 7–8 weeks of age when crying begins to taper off (St. James-Roberts, 1989). Early cooing sounds are primarily vowels. *I* and *e* sounds are produced when the infant is agitated or uncomfortable; *a, o,* and *u* are more often produced in a relaxed state and are probably expressions of pleasure or interest since they are often uttered at the sight of a human face or after a meal (Menyuk, 1977). The first consonants, such as *h, l,* and *g,* are associated with gasping and crying.

Almost all babies, regardless of their native language, will say *mama* or *nana* in the first few months after birth. A hungry baby who is crying rhythmically may make anticipatory sucking movement with the lips and tongue. The result is an expression that sounds like *mama* or *nana* but actually has no meaning to the child.

babbling
an early stage of language development during which the infant repeats a combination of sounds such as *bebebe*

Babbling

Some time between 3 and 6 months of age infants begin to babble. *Babbling* involves the repetition of consonant/vowel combinations, such as *gagaga* or *meme*. In the early stages, babbling is vocal play most often produced when the child is alone and content. Infants all over the world regardless of their native language use the same sounds when they begin to babble. Retarded babies produce well-formed babbles but at a lower rate than nonretarded infants (Oller & Siebert, 1988). Later, the sounds produced during babbling specify objects and people in the environment: *mama* for mother and *baba* for drink or bottle, for example, or some other combination depending on the infant's culture and native language. As sounds acquire meaning, infants begin to practice speech sounds common to their culture while other sounds fall from use. Babbling becomes less common after the child can produce real words. Even then the child under age 2 may lapse into babbling when excited or engaged in imaginative play (Zinobar & Martlew, 1985).

The pattern of language acquisition for babies who are hearing impaired has been studied in some detail. Hans Furth (1964) was one of the first to note that deaf infants cry, coo, and babble just like hearing infants, suggesting an innate predisposition for these behaviors. However, at some point deaf infants stop vocalizing altogether or may produce only limited babbling sounds. One explanation is that they lose interest in vocalizing because they cannot hear the sounds made by themselves or others. In a different application Locke and Pearson (1990) reports that a 20 month old infant, mute since age 5 months because of a tracheostomy, produced only one-tenth of the syllable sounds of normal infants. At 22 months, this same infant produced only a few different words, perhaps because her muteness prevented her from discovering the usefulness of vocabulary. It may also be that without specific input from the environment, deaf infants cannot perfect the speech sounds they produce into recognizable words and phrases. Infants who are deaf can be taught to communicate by signing. These babies progress just as quickly, learn just as much, and make errors identical to those made by infants who communicate verbally (Schlesinger & Meadow, 1972).

Imitation of Sounds

The baby is able to imitate the sound of others, first by accident (*lallation*) and then intentionally (*echolalia*) between 7 and 10 months of age. Although children are acquiring and perfecting the speech sounds of their language, they do not yet know the meaning of their vocalizations.

Another type of imitation involves practicing the patterns of pause, inflection, and intonation used in conversational speech. *Expressive jargon* is the term used to describe a string of utterances that sounds like a sentence but in fact contains no recognizable words. By 12 months of age, children may apply the stress and intonation patterns of their language to their babbling. Adults will commonly ask an infant, "What did you say?" in response to a string of expressive jargon (Sachs, 1985).

expressive jargon
the apparently meaningless sounds infants make that sound like meaningful words and sentences

Linguistic Communication

First Words and Early Sentences

Once children know the sounds and patterns of their native language, they are ready to attach meaning to their speech. First words are generally spoken around the time of the child's first birthday. Seven percent of all children talk before 8 months of age, whereas 2% do not attempt to use words until after age 2. Usually, these words consist of one or two duplicated syllables, such as *baba* or *dada*. The consonants *p, b, v, d, t, m,* and *n* and the vowels *o* (as in *drop*) and *e* (as in *week*) are the most common sounds.

Children talk about familiar objects and people and about actions and experiences that are important to them (Mervus, 1983). Typical first words include names of important people (Mom, Dad, baby); food (juice, milk, cookie); body parts (eye, ear, nose); clothing (shoe, sock, hat); animals (dog, cat, Max); household items (clock; fan); and vehicles (car, boat, truck) (K. Nelson, 1973, 1981). Abstract ideas (such as space, love, justice) and static objects (carpet, wall, sky) are seldom if ever named. Almost one-fourth of the words in the child's vocabulary describe some action (bye-bye, up, and give). Referential language can be distinguished from expressive language as the child acquires more and more words (Nelson, 1981).

holophrase
the use of a single word to convey a complete thought; a single-word sentence

grammar
a language skill concerned with the rules by which words are arranged (syntax) as well as the meanings of the words (number, person, case, gender, and tense)

telegraphic speech
an abbreviated pattern of early speech that consists primarily of nouns, verbs, and a few adjectives

HOLOPHRASES Some early words are not words at all but have significance because their meaning is shared by caregiver and child. For example, *ba* might refer to bottle. And even though *ba* is not an actual English word, both the baby and the caregiver know what *ba* is. Another characteristic of some early words is a function of their use. Single words that are used to express complete thoughts are called *holophrases*. Words used as holophrases take on different meaning depending upon the context and intonation. For example, "Car?" might mean "Is that a car?" or "Where is the car?" whereas "Car!" might mean "Let's go for a drive " or "Wow, look at that car!" When caregivers expand the one-word sentences by filling in the missing words, children hear the words that will eventually be added to their vocabularies and are reinforced for attempting to communicate their thoughts. The reciprocal nature of language development is underscored by the fact that caregivers actually change the content of their speech just before infants begin to say their first words (West & Rheingold, 1978). Parents begin to speak very distinctly to their 9–10 month old infant, correcting grammatical errors common to adult speech and using more auxiliary verbs such as *is* and *were*. Thus, a baby influences her parent's speech and vice versa.

Individual differences in children and variations in caregiving styles influence the size of the child's vocabulary at any particular age. Many 1 year olds can say one or two words and by 18 months of age (6 short months later) have vocabularies between three and fifty words (deVilliers & deVilliers, 1978). Responsive mothers who talk frequently to their children encourage the most vocabulary progress (S. L. Olson et al., 1986). Also, by about 18 months of age "grammar" spontaneously emerges.

TELEGRAPHIC SPEECH Children indicate an understanding of grammar, or the rules that govern word order and usage, when they begin to form single sentences by combining two or more words. "All gone," "Baby up," "Mama go bye-bye" are examples of the type of communication called *telegraphic speech*. These sentences are abbreviated versions of adult messages. They are composed primarily of nouns, verbs, and a few adjectives, and attempt to communicate an idea or a message. Words singled out for repetition and practice are called *pivot words. More* and *my* are common pivot words as in *more milk, more up,* and *my dog, my spoon*. The words associated with pivot words (e.g., *milk, up, dog,* and *spoon*) are called *X-words*. Children at this stage also compress the speech they imitate by reducing it to its vital elements. If you ask a child between the ages of 2 and 3 to repeat a single sentence like "Where did the doggie go?" the result is likely to be "Where doggy go?" or more simply "Doggie go?" (S. L. Olson et al., 1986). Table 6–6 offers an interesting comparison of a single child's speech abilities at 18 and 27 months of age.

■ **Table 6–6** *Beyond Two Words*

EVE AT 18 MONTHS	EVE AT 27 MONTHS*
More grapejuice.	This not better.
Door.	See, this one better but this not better.
Right down.	There some cream.
Mommy soup.	Put in your coffee.
Eating.	I go get pencil n' write.
Mommy celery?	Put my pencil in there.
No celery.	Don't stand on my ice cubes.
Oh drop celery.	They was in the refrigerator, cooking.
Open toy box.	I put them in the refrigerator to freeze.
Oh horsie stuck.	An' I want to take off my hat.
Mommy read.	That why Jacky comed.
No mommy read.	We're going to make a blue house.
Write a paper.	You come help us.
Write a pencil.	You make a blue one for me.
My pencil.	How 'bout another eggnog instead of cheese sandwich?
Mommy.	I have a fingernail.
Mommy head?	And you have a fingernail.
Look at dollie.	Just like Mommy has, and David has, and Sara has.
Head.	What is that on the table?
What doing, Mommy?	
Drink juice.	

*Eve was a precocious speaker. Most children do not progress this rapidly.

Source: de Villiers & de Villiers, *Language Acquisition.* (Harvard University Press, 1979). Used with permission.

Telegraphic speech is rich in meaning. Interestingly, the telegraphic sentences of children speaking very different languages, such as English, German, Russian, Finnish, Turkish and Luo (spoken in Kenya), convey similar types of messages (Slobin, 1981). Most of the statements are action oriented and assertive—for example, "fire burn," "give ball," and "more milk."

Semantics, or the aspect of language development based on understanding word meaning, is slowest to develop. Children classify objects, people, and events into categories based on a comparison of their similarities and differences. Because their experience is limited and they tend to focus on one aspect of an object at a time, misclassification often occurs. *Overextension* is a type of misclassification that involves a broader meaning for a word than its conventional use (Clark & Clark, 1977). For example, a child who knows a ball is round may focus on that single aspect and call other round objects—such as a donut, the moon, a balloon—balls also. They may also assume that *dancing* in-

semantics
the language skill involved with learning word meaning

volves any foot movement fancier than simple walking or running and a *purse* is any container with a handle or shoulder strap, including sewing boxes and brief cases. Overextensions can be reduced by having adults use the correct label, correcting the child's speech and demonstrating the important attributes that make an object a member of a particular category (Mervis & Mervis, 1988). *Underextensions* are words that are narrowly defined by a child. Children may think the name Jeremy can apply only to their own brother and not to other children or adults and especially not to animals.

Between 2 and 2.5 years of age, children begin to indicate past and ongoing activity by changing word endings. "I walks over" connotes present, while "We camed home" indicates a past happening. As you can see, the rules of grammar have been overgeneralized. Young children still egocentrically cling to their linguistic forms, showing less concern for grammatical correctness than for the accuracy of the statement.

> CHILD: My teacher holded the rabbits and we petted them.
> MOTHER: Did you say your teacher held the baby rabbits?
> CHILD: Yes.
> MOTHER: What did you say she did?
> CHILD: She holded the baby rabbits.
> MOTHER: Did you say she held them tightly?
> CHILD: No, she holded them loosely.
>   (Bellugi, 1970)

Early conversation skills probably develop from the turn-taking routines incorporated into many social games (Bruner, 1977). The game of peek-a-boo, for example, involves a verbal prompt ("Peek-a-boo!") and a response by the child (child covers her face with her hands and then uncovers). Caregivers will frequently speak and pause, waiting for some response from the child. A blink, movement, smile, or attempt to speak may prompt the parent to speak and wait again. What the listener hears, then, is not a real dialogue but a *pseudodialogue* (Schaffer, 1978).

pseudodialogue
a prompted dialogue where the speaker responds to looks and other nonverbal signals as though they were words

> MOTHER: Aren't you my cutie?
> (Pause)
> IMAGINED RESPONSE FROM BABY: Yes.
> (Pause)
> MOTHER: You sure are!

This prompting pays off. The shift from primarily overlapping speech to primarily alternating speech occurs when the child is between 12 and 18 weeks old (Ginsburg & Kilbourne, 1988). The infant vocalizes during pauses, taking turns with the speaker. A typical infant conversation goes something like this:

> BABY: (Looks at a toy top.)
> MOTHER: Do you like that?
> BABY: Da!

MOTHER: Yes, it's a nice toy, isn't it?
BABY: Da! Da!

Sometimes several communication exchanges take place. Golinkoff (1983) offers an example of a 14 month old boy who wants his mother to hand him the sponge on the kitchen counter.

JORDAN: (Vocalizes repeatedly until his mother turns around.)
MOTHER: (Turns around to look at him.)
JORDAN: (Points to one of the objects on the counter)
MOTHER: Do you want this? (Holding up the milk container)
JORDAN: (Shakes head "no"; continues to point; two more offer–
         rejection pairs.)
MOTHER: This? (Picking up the sponge)
JORDAN: (Leans back in high chair, puts arms down, tension
         leaves body.)
MOTHER: (Hands Jordan the sponge)
              (p. 58–59)

When conversation breakdowns occur with 15–21 month old infants, they are usually repaired by an adult initiating a clarifying question. Breakdowns occur more frequently with secondary caregivers (usually the father) than with primary caregivers (usually the mother) but both caregivers can be equally successful at getting the conversation back on track (Tomasello et al., 1990).

The vocalizations of children with Down's syndrome are as frequent and varied as those of unaffected infants. However, infants with Down's syndrome do not learn to take turns, because they do not incorporate pauses into their speech. Thus, the speech of Down's syndrome babies and their caregivers is more likely to be in unison than one after the other. Down's children are more verbal when their mothers are more responsive (Mahoney, 1988).

Infants who hear two or more languages spoken in the home can distinguish between the languages by 5 months of age (Bahrick & Pickens, 1988). Thus, bi/multilingualism does not confuse young children since they have the capacity to recognize which language they are learning. If a critical period for language learning does exist in infancy, then acquiring a second or third language would be easiest for the child while she is learning the native language.

bi/multilingualism
fluency in two (bi) or more than 2 (multi) languages

Theories of Language Acquisition

Children's use of speech and the orderly progress of their behavior are fairly easy to observe and describe. A more challenging task involves explaining how and why the child develops language. The theories that have been proposed to account for language acquisition can be classified

■ Figure 6–7

Is this child's naming ability due to learning, genetics, or both?

in accordance with the relative influence they ascribe to heredity versus the environment. B. F. Skinner (1957) and other behaviorists believe language is learned, while theorists such as Chomsky and Piaget argue that we are born with the inclination to learn our native language. The issue of language acquisition continues to be one of the most hotly debated topics in psychology. Let's examine the arguments on both sides.

The Environmental Position (Nurture)

Will children speak their native language even if they don't hear that language spoken around them? The behaviorists believe that several features of the child's environment play an important role in language development. Children born in Romania and adopted by U.S. families end up speaking *English* not Romanian. Do such children learn Romanian more readily because their brains are somehow organized to do so? Apparently, they don't learn Romanian any more rapidly than motivated children from other cultures.

Hearing the language spoken seems to be a critical component in the acquisition of spoken language. In addition to becoming familiar with words and word order, the "melody" of the language also becomes apparent to the listener. When adults speak to babies, they exaggerate the pitch, intonation, pause, and inflection of "normal" language. Babies seem to prefer this "baby talk" or infant-directed speech over "adult talk," even though it is not yet clear what they like better about baby talk (Cooper & Aslin, 1990).

B. F. Skinner (1957) suggests that language is learned through *selective reinforcement.* Sounds that approximate intelligible speech are praised or given attention and thus become more prominent in the child's vocabulary. According to the behaviorists' view, children will learn to speak early and well if caregivers reward the sounds and speech patterns that form the basis of their native language. *Imitation* is another aspect of the environment's influence on language acquisition. Bandura (1977) and others believe that much of what children know about their native language they learn by observing and imitating the speech around them, often without reinforcement. The deaf babies of deaf parents babble with their hands, childishly imitating the sign language their parents use to communicate (Petitto et al., 1991). Hearing infants learn words, phrases, and speech patterns directly by imitation and use them during communication. Thus, children can be expected to learn their native language and to speak well or poorly based on the quality of the imitative model.

Primary caregivers are the most likely models for speech. Mothers adjust their speech style according to the behavioral "feedback" given by their prelinguistic infants, shifting from emotion-oriented speech to communicative speech and back again (Penman et al., 1983a). Television can also serve as a model for the acquisition of language. In an extensive

■●▲ CONCEPT SUMMARY

Developmental Milestones in Language Acquisition—First 2½ Years

● *1 month*

Responds to human voice; begins to coo; produces different cries to signal different basic needs

● *2 months*

Coos; makes throaty sounds; "talks" to family members

● *3 months*

Babbles and coos; "talks" when spoken to

● *4 months*

Cooing changes pitch and volume; talks to objects and faces; "talking" varies with moods; consonant sounds appear: *h, n, k, f, p, b*

● *5 months*

Makes vowel sounds; consonant sounds increase in frequency; makes attempts to imitate sounds

● *6 months*

Combines vowel and consonant sounds into syllables (*ki; bee*); varies pitch and rate of speech; "talks" to toys and mirror image of self; calls for help

● *7 months*

Repeats syllables (*kiki; beebee*); "talks" with adult-like intonations when others are talking

● *8 months*

Shouts for attention; shows emotion through speech; responds to "no, no," "bye-bye"; may label object with sound (meows for kitty; barks for dog)

● *9 months*

Says some words meaningfully (such as *ma-ma; da-da*); "talking" increases; intonation becomes patterned

(continued on next page)

■ ● ▲ CONCEPT SUMMARY

Developmental Milestones in Language Acquisition—First 2½ Years *(continued)*

- *10 months*

  One word "sentences" ("No," "Hi"); combines consonants; understands and responds to own name; associates action with a word (waves to "bye-bye"; raises arms to "up"); understands some simple commands (such as "Come here")

- *11 months*

  Says two or three words with meaning; uses jargon; continues to imitate intonation and expression; recognizes a word as a symbol for an object

- *12 months (1 year)*

  Says three words with meaning; enjoys expressive jargon ("jabbering") in short sentences; can't speak and walk at the same time; comprehends the meaning of a word before speaking; understands more complex commands ("Go get your shoes"); may have one word for a whole class of objects (*doggie* means all furry animals)

- *15 months*

  Combines two or three words in a sentence; points to desired object; responds with "No" to all requests

- *18 months (1½ years)*

  Imitates adult words; uses short phrases with adjectives and nouns; economy of speech (few words needed to express needs); follows directions; points to some objects while speaking

- *24 months (2 years)*

  Combines three or four words into a short sentence; refers to self by using pronouns ("I," "me"); names familiar objects; vocalizes needs for food, drink, "potty"; understands and obeys simple commands

- *30 months (2½ years)*

  Uses plural form of some words; talks constantly; telegraphic pattern to speech; talks in a monologue; knows first and last name; knows at least one color review, Mabel Rice (1983) suggests that children learn about word meaning by viewing attention-getting, content-redundant TV dialogues. They also incorporate verbal routines from television into their playtime activities. Thus, television programs could be designed to promote language acquisition in children age 2 and older.

Critics of the environmental perspective point to the enormous task adults face in tutoring children in language instruction, a task that *no* parent seems to undertake.

The Genetic Position (Nature)

The contrasting view emphasizes the importance of genetics and of brain organization and structure in language acquisition. According to this perspective, language is a product of the forces of heredity, maturation, and the environment. Children do not learn language because they are reinforced; they learn language because they are born with a capacity to do so and because language is essential to human survival and adaptation. Thus linguist Noam Chomsky (1968) states that humans have an innate capacity to learn language because their brains are organized to process language information. Chomsky calls the brain mechanism that understands language and aids in speech production the *language acquisition device (LAD)*. Basically, the LAD helps infants process the language they hear into understandable units and analyze the content of speech so they can produce grammatically correct sentences (Chomsky, 1968).

The best evidence for Chomsky's position comes from the fact that children all over the world acquire language skills at about the same age and in about the same way regardless of their culture or native tongue. The organizational framework for language is so powerful that it overrides the impact of most environments. Deaf babies babble as much as hearing infants do until 6 months of age, when babbling becomes more of an imitation of spoken speech sounds. The Kaluli of Papua, New Guinea, and the people of Western Samoa do not play social games with their infants nor spend much time communicating with them. Yet the babies of these two cultures learn to speak their native language at about the same time as children from more interactive cultures do (Schieffelin & Ochs, 1983). Also, the brains of all normal humans contain a network of specialized cells involved in language production and comprehension. For most of us, these cells are situated in the left hemisphere of the brain. However, the acquisition of language is such an integral part of human function that if the speech centers in the left hemisphere are damaged or destroyed in a child of 2 or 3 or younger, speech function will be "assumed" by cells in the other hemisphere. Normal verbal communication skills generally result.

More evidence of the importance of genetic organization for language acquisition comes from accounts of children who were not exposed to

■ Figure 6–8

Sometimes babies don't want to wait for their turn to talk.

language acquisition device (LAD)
Chomsky's term for the hypothetical mechanism that accounts for the infant's inborn ability to learn language

feral children
children who were lost in the wild and survived but did not learn the ways of civilization

language in early childhood. About 60 recorded cases of *feral children* exist. These are children who were abandoned in the wild, somehow survived, and later returned to human society. Some of these children acquired some linguistic skills, but their ability to use language remained consistently poor (Reich, 1986). Genie was a girl who spent almost 12 years (from age 20 months to 13.5 years of age) locked in a closet by her parents. No one spoke to her and she was severely beaten if she made any sounds at all. After she was discovered, she was able to learn words and to understand speech but was slow to respond, unable to use intonation appropriately, and unable to use pronouns (Curtiss, 1977). These cases suggest that there may be a critical period of language acquisition, a time during which children are sensitive to spoken language and able to learn it easily and readily. While feral and severely neglected children acquire some language, their linguistic ability remains compromised and true language competence is never achieved. Had these children been discovered earlier and exposed to their native language, it is conceivable that no language deficits would exist.

Weighing the Nature/Nurture Evidence

Neither reinforcement, imitation, the survival value of verbal communication, nor the LAD alone can account for all the complexities of language acquisition. For one thing, even with consistent reinforcement, children learn speech at different rates. If children talked because they were reinforced, there would not be periods of slow development followed by periods of rapid expansion of speech. In addition, grammar is acquired despite the caregiver's tendency to reward the "truth" or meaning of the child's statement and not its grammatical accuracy. For example, when the child says "He a girl" (expressing the opinion that the mother is a girl), adults generally agree. However, a child's grammatically perfect statement, " 'Sesame Street' comes on Saturday" may be disapproved if the program is aired on another day (R. Brown et al., 1969).

Similarly, it is unlikely that imitation is the total explanation for language development, since children make up novel utterances that they could not possibly have heard. Parents usually do not say, "All gone drink" when they have finished their milk or "Daddy sleepy-time" when they are ready for bed.

An interactionist position with regard to language acquisition seems reasonable—humans are biologically prepared to learn to speak, and learning takes place within the context of spoken language. Still, because each organism seems primed to produce language (even sign language in the case of congenitally deaf children), Chomsky's position may prove to be the most useful.

■●▲ CONCEPT SUMMARY

The Nature vs. Nurture Debate over Language Acquisition

NATURE	NURTURE
Born with a capacity to learn language	Sounds that are reinforced are more prominent in the child's speech
Language learning is necessary for survival	Children always learn the language they hear spoken around them, not the language of another (even their native) culture
Regardless of native language, all children acquire language at about the same age and in about the same way	Deaf babies imitate the sign language of their parents with their hands
Deaf babies cry, coo, and babble	Hearing infants born to deaf parents learn to speak by imitating other spoken language sources
Parents are not observed "teaching" their children language or grammar	
Feral children and neglected children never acquire true language competence	
Children make up novel utterances they couldn't have possibly heard	

Factors Affecting Language Development

Poor Speech Development

Deafness and mental retardation are the two major physical problems affecting speech acquisition. Deafness and retardation may be caused by genetic or prenatal factors or may result from accident, injury, or illness after birth. Physicians need to be particularly alert to the common causes of speech problems (hearing impairment, learning disability, mental retardation, and autism) so that prompt treatment and retraining can begin (D. A. Allen et al., 1988).

Sometimes children learn very little language because no one speaks to them or they are not required to communicate with words. A neglected child who receives little attention from parents may also be isolated from others who could provide care and could model speech. Some children are not told the names of people and objects around them when they ask. Ignoring the child's questions or relying on general statements like, "Get that," "Go over there," or "Hold this" does not encourage precise speech. In some families children are offered objects, food, and care if they simply point or whine. Sometimes an older sibling serves as a self-appointed "manager" for the little one, saying "She wants a drink" or "He doesn't want to go to bed now." In these instances, language does not develop since there is no need to learn to communicate.

The activity level of the child may also influence language acquisition, with an active child using fewer words than one who is less active. Although the capacity for language development is similar in both, the active child may be too busy "doing" to verbalize.

On the average, males acquire language a little later than female children, probably because they are less physiologically mature at birth and perhaps because they are talked to less by parents. Also, premature and low birth weight babies tend to show delays in perceptual abilities and expressive language even though their mothers show higher responsiveness to lower level behaviors (Landry et al., 1988, 1989). Abused/maltreated 31-month-old infants speak in shorter sentences, express less relevant speech, and are less descriptive about their own activities and feelings than nonmaltreated toddlers (Coster et al., 1989).

Promoting Language Development

Here are a few suggestions for promoting language development:

1. *Talk to the baby even though she might not understand everything you say.* This provides children with exposure to their language.
2. *Create opportunities for the child to participate in a dialogue.* If the child makes a statement, "I want my cup," before complying the mother might say, "This cup?" or "Your bear cup?" to permit the child to respond.
3. *Use "protodirectives."* A protodirective involves telling the baby to do something she is already doing. For example, if a child is about to pick up her pillow, the caregiver might say, "Pick up your pillow" (Menyuk, 1984). This style of discourse gives children the opportunity to hear the description of their behavior as well as to comment if they choose.
4. *Modify your speech when talking to young children.* Use shorter sentences, a simplified vocabulary and sentence structure, more attention-getting expressions (such as "Look" or "Hey"), more repetition, a slow pace, and exaggerated pronunciation to provide a clear model for the child to imitate.
5. *Provide information for the child.* As the child grows older, adults can add more information to the content of their speech talking *to* infants rather than simply talking *with* them (Elias et al., 1988). When children hear more about their world, they have more to say.

6. *Reinforce the child's efforts to communicate.* Listening, eye contact, smiling, physical affection, and words such as *good* and *yes* all provide positive feedback. When children first learn to speak, their language is filled with mispronunciation and misuse. Rewarding reasonable facsimiles of proper speech will encourage effort and practice.
7. *Don't use baby talk, slang, or swear words unless you want the child to incorporate those words into her speech.* Remember, children can't discriminate between "proper" and "improper" words since they're just learning the language.
8. *Use polite speech (the use of "please," "thank you," and so forth) around the child if you want these words to be included in her vocabulary.*
9. *Encourage hearing children to use speech rather than gesture or nonspeech sounds to communicate.*

Superbaby Syndrome—Pushed Too Far, Too Fast

TOWARD EFFECTIVE PARENTING

So far Marie has had swimming lessons, instruction in French, has her own computer, plays the flute, and has art on Tuesday and exercise class on Thursdays. At age 3 Marie is one of a growing population of children whose parents feel early academic and social exposure will help her achieve later on. Years ago people thought that precociousness was dangerous. The

A Suzuki violin school for toddlers and young children. Here a 3-year-old practices his craft.

superbaby syndrome
the stress and malcontent experienced by children pushed to behave more maturely than their years

motto was, "Early ripe, early rot." Today the idea is, "Early ripe, early rich" as parents become concerned about their child's place in a competitive market. This trend is most noticeable among young upwardly mobile parents who may plan 50 and 60 hour weeks for the children to help them "get ahead." Some public school systems are responding to parents' demands and are allowing children to enter school at age 4. Enrollment in some academically-oriented private preschools requires toddlers to pass a formidable "entrance exam" before being considered.

While some children thrive at the opportunities to develop at a precocious rate, others flounder. The most vocal proponent for slowing the pace is psychologist David Elkind, President of the National Association for the Education of Young Children. His book *Miseducation: Preschoolers at Risk* (Knopf, 1987) suggests that quicker isn't necessarily better for some young children. He warns that these children are at increased risk for stress and educational burnout, characteristics Elkind calls the *superbaby syndrome.*

Is there evidence of stress and burnout in young children as a function of academic/enrichment overstimulation? Researchers have watched some hurried babies develop into bored and unmotivated second and third graders (Seal, 1987). It's possible that some could miss the faster pace of learning, but more likely these kids are tired of the constant demands to do, achieve, and never let down. The American Academy of Pediatrics (AAP) has noticed more and more evidence of stress-linked psychosomatic illness and behavioral problems in overstimulated children. The pressured child may develop headaches, stomachaches, sleep disturbances, and chest pain—symptoms that were unheard of until recently among toddlers and young preschoolers who were otherwise disease and illness free. In February, 1988, the AAP drafted guidelines to help pediatricians recognize and deal with the problems experienced by "superbabies." Since these children want to comply and they want to please, they internalize the pressure and stress and psychosomatic symptoms result.

Here are some suggestions for providing enrichment experiences for the young child while avoiding the superbaby syndrome:

- Guide but don't push. Your insistence may create stress. If you want your child to take French but he's not interested, maybe *you* should take French yourself.
- Take your cues from the baby. If he seems happy and pleased in the activity, fine. If he seems disturbed and disinterested, consider something else. No one likes everything.
- Balance rigor and academics with play and enjoyment. Don't be afraid to let the child just have *fun.*
- When the child is old enough, let him have some say in the activities he participates in. Giving children a choice between 2 or 3 alternatives lets them assert their preference within a framework the parent finds suitable.
- Parents don't need to schedule baby's every waking hour to be a good parent. Include an appropriate balance of scheduled and unscheduled activity. *Free time* is an important concept even in toddlerhood.

- Appreciate the effort even though the outcome is not quite what you envisioned. If the child is not the best Suzuki violinist, it's OK. He is still a worthwhile and wonderful child.
- Have realistic expectations for your child.
- Consider stressing the enjoyment and benefits of the task rather than a competitive motive. It's probably healthier to appreciate the task than to worry about beating someone else.

Chapter Summary

- Cognitive development involves growth and change in the child's mental capacity.
- According to Jean Piaget, the child adapts his thinking to new ideas and experiences. The first stage in Piaget's theory of cognitive development is called the sensorimotor period. During this period, children between birth and age 2 gather knowledge about the world through sensory input and motor activity. The major cognitive accomplishments of the first 2 years include the development of object permanence, imitation, the ability to plan and carry out purposeful behavior, and the ability to integrate information from the senses.
- The NeoPiagetians have taken issue with Piaget's view that all children have the same cognitive capacities at the same time. The NeoPiagetians note an unevenness in development, suggest that children must learn how to adapt their knowledge, and see parallels between cognitive change and brain growth. They have suggested their own stage-theory model of sensorimotor development.
- The information processing theorists feel that an understanding of the mechanisms of attention, memory, and organizational strategies are vital to the appreciation of cognitive development.
- Psychometrics is the approach concerned with the measurement of infant intelligence. Infant intelligence scales and the HOME Inventory can be used for IQ assessment but are more accurate in highlighting delayed development.
- Play behavior provides a wealth of information about children's social skills, motor development, and cognitive functioning.
- New responses are acquired through learning. The mechanisms of learning include habituation, classical conditioning, operant conditioning, and learning through imitation.
- Language acquisition is a milestone cognitive accomplishment. Throughout development, children can understand much more than

they can say. The development of spoken language follows a pre-dictable sequence of stages regardless of culture or native dialect. Conversation skills emerge out of turn-taking play and pseudodia-logues.

● Behavioral theorists account for language acquisition in terms of learning, while other rival theorists stress the importance of genetic organization and brain structure.

● Language acquisition may be affected by deafness/hearing loss, men-tal retardation, neglect, lack of motivation, lack of practice opportu-nities, activity level, lack of an opportunity to hear spoken language, lack of an opportunity to hear precise/appropriate speech, and the child's sex. Parents and other adults can help promote language de-velopment by negating or minimizing the effects of these variables.

● Observational Exercise

One of the cognitive concepts that develops during infancy is object permanence. Infants learn through maturation and experience that ob-jects and people continue to exist even if they are not visible at the moment. Object permanence can be observed in the 10–12 month infant.

Procedure: Have the child and his or her familiar caregiver sit on the floor with you. Show the child a brightly colored object such as a ball or an interesting toy. While the infant is watching, hide the object under a blanket or towel so that part is still visible.

1. What is the baby's reaction when the object partially disappears? Does the infant search for the object? Reveal the object and partially hide it again. Record the baby's response.
2. Now hide the object completely and note the infant's reactions. Does the baby ignore the object when it disappears completely?
3. Now you're going to hide the object twice. Display the toy and hide it under the original blanket. Then hide it a second time under a blanket 3 or 4 feet away from the infant. Does the baby search under the first cover? Under the second? What is its reaction when it fails to find the object under the first blanket?

● Recommended Readings

Beadle, M. (1971). *A child's mind: How children learn during the critical years from birth to age 5.* New York: Doubleday-Anchor.

Elkind, D. (1987). *Miseducation: Preschoolers at risk.* New York: Knopf.

Evans, J., & Ilfeld, E. (1982). *Good beginnings: Parenting in the early years.* Ypsilanti, MI: High/Scope Press.

Kaye, K. (1984). *The mental and social life of babies: How parents create persons.* Chicago: University of Chicago Press.

White, B. L. (1985). *The first three years of life* (rev. ed.). Englewood Cliffs, NJ: Prentice-Hall.

Social and Emotional Development in Infancy and Toddlerhood

CHAPTER

7

● Emotional Development

Displays of emotion communicate needs and feelings and regulate social distance (smiling encourages approach, frowning/staring keeps people away). Do infants display recognizable emotions? Based on facial, vocal, and gestural cues, infants display interest, distress, and disgust as newborns (Johnson et al., 1983). Within a few weeks, happiness can be observed followed by surprise, anger, and sadness (3–4 months) and then fear (5–7 months) (Campos et al., 1983). Complex emotions like guilt, envy, pride, shame, and contempt are not seen until the second year of life (Izard, 1982; Heckhausen, 1988). The course of the baby's emotional development is influenced by the mother's specific behavior as well as the baby's gender and birth status (Malatesta et al., 1989).

Do babies actually experience the feelings their emotions suggest? Infant emotions do seem tied to specific experience. When inoculated, younger babies display distress, while babies over 2 months of age show anger. Similarly, expressions of anger could be reliably evoked by removing a cookie just before it was to be placed in the baby's mouth (Izard et al., 1983).

The Development of Specific Emotions

Happiness

The infant's first smiles are not planned but reflexive. Early spontaneous *reflex smiles* can be elicited by stroking the baby's cheek or lips. Smiling also occurs when infants are comfortable or experiencing REM sleep (Field et al., 1987). (The theory that early smiles are due to "gas" in the infant's system is full of hot air!)

Social smiles, or responses to external events, appear between 3 and 8 weeks of age. Although almost anything can elicit a smile during this period, infants seem to prefer a high-pitched human voice. Within the first 6 months of life, a combination of a human face, voice, and movement most reliably elicits a smile. By the time they are 5 or 6 months old, infants begin to discriminate between familiar and unfamiliar individuals, smiling at people they recognize and withholding smiles from strangers (Jones & Raag, 1989).

Laughter is a more intense expression than smiling. Laughter generally occurs between 12 and 16 weeks of age and is first elicited by a combination of auditory and physical stimulation (caregiver says, suddenly, "Whatcha doing, huh?" and then tickles or rubs the baby who generally squeals delightedly) (Johnson et al., 1983). As the baby grows older, the types of stimuli that elicit laughter change (Table 7–1). Increasingly, laughter becomes a social event. Ninety-five percent of the laughing that 3–5 year olds do is in the presence of other children or adults (Bainum et al., 1984).

While the onset of both smiling and laughing are genetically determined, cognitive growth accounts for changes in expressions of happiness with age. As infants memories develop, they "remember" events they have seen before. Infants smile if the stimulus is perceived as pleasurable or familiar and are sober until they are able to comprehend a novel stimulus. And, of course, infants can become bored with often-presented stimuli, needing something new to again elicit laughter or smiling (Kagan et al., 1978).

Anger

During the first 2 months of life, infants express anger when forcibly restrained or hurt (Stenberg et al., 1983). By 12 months of age, anger is sometimes observed in response to frustration or during brief separa-

---

■ **Table 7–1** *Laughter-Eliciting Stimuli*

AGE	STIMULI
4–6 months	Laughter and vocal stimuli Stimuli can be less vigorous to elicit same response
6–12 months	Social games like peek-a-boo; playing tug-of-war with a cloth
12 months and older	Elements of discrepency (mother sucking her thumb or placing a pan on her head) Laughter in response to activities infants themselves create (push a toy and laughing when it squeeks) Laughing in anticipation of an event (when mother moves her finger before she begins tickling baby)

tions from the primary caregiver. The level of angry outbursts rises steadily after 7 months of age and peaks by about age 2 (Izard et al., 1987).

Hitting and temper tantrums are common expressions of anger in infancy and toddlerhood. The tantrum may involve wild, undirected activity such as screaming, kicking, throwing oneself on the floor, or holding one's breath. Tantrums are a natural consequence of development—the child needs self-expression but is not mature or controlled enough to find a more acceptable outlet. They occur most frequently when the child is ill, tired, overstimulated, under pressure to behave in a prescribed manner, or confronted by an unrealistic request, a difficult decision, or an overly restrictive environment. In a Swedish longitudinal study, adult Type A behavior (irritability, hurry, competitiveness, and the intense need for work achievement) were tied to the child's liveliness, sociability, and poor appetite in the first 6 years of life (MacEnvoy et al., 1988).

temper tantrums
an outburst or fit of uncontrollable rage

Type A behavior
a pattern of impatience, hostility, and intense striving

Probably the best approach to managing tantrums is for parents to make it clear that they disapprove of the tantrum and then to ignore it. For example, the mother might say, "I'll be in the bedroom. When you stop screaming, you can come, too." Tantrums rarely last more than a few minutes after the caregiver leaves. Once the toddler's behavior is under control and she has rejoined the parent, interaction may proceed as though the event never occurred. Other tantrum management strategies are best avoided, since they have the potential to produce negative effects. For example, the parent who quickly grants the child's wishes when the tantrum starts is actually rewarding the behavior, ensuring that it will be displayed more frequently in the future. And parents who mimic their child's behavior by screaming just as loudly or biting back are hardly helping the child develop more mature ways of coping with frustration. Also, since children tend to model their parent's emotionality, such an outburst from a parent could encourage the child to increase the intensity and duration of the child's tantrum rather than reduce it.

Sometimes when children hold their breath and pass out, the parent is not sure if the child had a tantrum or a seizure. Unlike breath holding, seizure activity is unprovoked and not accompanied by crying. The child in seizure slumps to the floor unconscious before turning blue, and after the incident, is groggy and has no memory of the event. The child who passes out after voluntary breath holding is almost always crying, turns blue before losing consciousness, and is alert and active after the incident (Whaley & Wong, 1988). Suspected seizures should immediately be reported to a physician.

Sadness

Sadness can be expressed in response to pain or separation, but it is a far less common reaction than anger in those circumstances (Izard et

Happiness: *Mouth forms smile, cheeks lifted, twinkle in the eyes.*

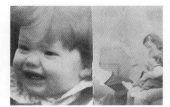

Interest: *Brows raised or knit, mouth may be softly rounded, lips may be pursed.*

Anger: *Brows drawn together and downward, eyes fixed, mouth squarish.*

Disgust: *Nose wrinkled, upper lip raised, tongue pushed outward.*

Sadness: *Inner corners of brows raised, mouth corners drawn down.*

Surprise: *Brows raised, eyes widened, mouth rounded in oval shape.*

Fear: *Brows level, drawn in and up, eyelids lifted, mouth retracted.*

Distress: *Eyes tightly closed, mouth squared and angular.*

■ **Figure 7–1**

Infant facial expressions of emotion:

startle reflex
a sudden surprise or fright that causes the baby to jump

fear of strangers (stranger anxiety)
a fear of unfamiliar others or changes in familiar settings and people first displayed by infants around 7–8 months of age

al., 1987). More significantly, prolonged separation from the primary caregiver without the benefit of warm, nurturant substitute care leads to sadness in infants that mimics severe depression (Gaensbauer, 1980).

Fear and Anxiety

FEAR OF STRANGERS, OR STRANGER ANXIETY Of all the negative emotions of infancy, fear has aroused the most interest. At first, what passes for a fear reaction is the *startle reflex,* provoked when something unexpected, sudden, or loud occurs (Marks, 1987). Infants are seemingly fearless in the first 6 months of their lives, interacting indiscriminately with people and situations. Then, between 6 and 8 months, infants become more wary, reacting to unfamiliar people differently than they react to familiar ones. Whether or not the baby manifests a *fear of strangers* (or *stranger anxiety*) is mediated by the setting, the identity and behavior of the stranger, and the maturational level of the child (Table 7–2). Most infants do not demonstrate an intensely emotional reaction to strangers unless they are alone and the stranger does not retreat. If the mother is holding the infant when the stranger appears, the infant usually does not cry and may even be inclined to smile. Also, infants who are raised in group-care situations (like a kibbutz) or who have older preschool siblings may be less likely to show stranger anxiety than only children or infants raised with a limited number of primary caregivers (Bird,

■ **Table 7–2** *Some Variables That Affect the Child's Reactions to Strangers*

FACTORS RESULTING IN MINIMAL REACTIONS TO STRANGERS	FACTORS RESULTING IN INTENSE REACTIONS TO STRANGERS
Characteristics of Stranger	
Female	Male
Friendly, active, offers toy	Quiet, passive
Context	
Mother or primary caregiver present	Primary caregiver absent
Child is held by or touching primary caregiver	Child is some distance from primary caregiver
Stranger remains distant	Stranger is close to child (or is in physical contact)
Familiar setting (e.g., home)	Unfamiliar setting (e.g., laboratory)
Alone but holding a familiar object (e.g., a blanket or favorite toy)	
Mother responds to stranger in relaxed manner	Mother responds to stranger in anxious manner

Source: Adapted from Smart & Smart, 1978.

1980). If the stranger is a child or another infant, the baby tends to show a mildly positive reaction rather than fear (Bigelow et al., 1990).

Stranger anxiety is of interest for several reasons. Developmentally, it is one indication of strong, healthy parent–child attachments. Fear of strangers is adaptive, since it encourages rejection of unfamiliar others who may be hostile or nonnurturant. It also indicates that infants can, through repeated exposure and the use of memory, come to appreciate the stable features of their world. But stranger anxiety can create stress for parents who do not understand why this behavior occurs. The parents may feel frustrated or embarrassed when the child rejects adoring out-of-town grandparents or the new babysitter. This rejection is normal and understandable—strangers are strangers to the child despite their emotional significance to others.

SEPARATION PROTEST OR SEPARATION ANXIETY At about the same time that stranger anxiety appears, attached children may become concerned whenever their caregiver departs for any length of time and express their concern by crying, searching, and rejecting alternative care. This reaction called *separation protest* or *separation anxiety* seems to reach a peak by age 18 months regardless of the child's native culture.

According to Jerome Kagan (1979), children react to separation with distress because they are faced with discrepant or unfamiliar events that

separation protest (separation anxiety)
a child's verbal or nonverbal expression of distress at the departure of his or her attachment figure

■ **Figure 7–2**

Even though it's grandpa, it's still separation anxiety if he's not that familiar to the infant.

they cannot understand or correct. When mother leaves, a major source of the child's pleasure and contentment is lost. The emotional significance of this departure is underscored by the fact that the child cannot even take comfort in the fact that she will return. Object permanence, the knowledge that things and people continue to exist even when physically absent, does not develop until the child is 10 months old. By age 2, separation protest subsides, since the infant is better able to recognize the permanence of objects and to tolerate frustration. The learning that supports these changes is a function of experience and brain maturation.

Infant separation distress is related to the mother's caregiving style, particularly her responsiveness to the baby's physical and emotional needs. Parents often assume that prompt response to the baby's cries will reinforce crying and produce a whining, overly demanding infant who cannot tolerate separation. Just the opposite is true. Prompt, appropriate response to the baby's signals will increase the child's confidence in the mother's accessibility and responsiveness. The more confidence and trust the child has in the mother, the more easily she will accept brief separation. Instead of crying when the mother leaves, the confident child will greet her happily when she returns. The anxious baby, who may not trust the mother to return or be accessible, cries when she leaves and may cry and avoid her when she returns as well, preferring to be held by strangers (Main et al., 1985).

Another aspect of parent responsiveness involves physical contact and affection. Contrary to popular belief, infants who are held, rocked, and cuddled by affectionate parents during their first year are less likely to object to being put down and are more likely to move off and explore the environment during their second year than infants who receive less physical contact (Ainsworth, 1982).

■ ● ▲   CONCEPT SUMMARY

The Expression of Infant Emotions

Emotion	Appearance	Elicited by
● *Happiness*		
Reflex smiles	Birth	Physical stimulation of the face REM sleep
Social smiles	3–8 wks	Human face and voice; movement Familiar person
Laughter	12–16 wks	Sudden auditory and physical stimulation (like tickling)
	3–5 years	Presence of other children/ adults
● *Anger*		
Outbursts	0–2 months	Forcible restraint Pain
	2–12 months	Frustration Separation from caregiver
Temper tantrums	Infancy	Illness, fatigue, overstimulation, frustration, unwanted restriction
● *Sadness*		
Crying	Infancy	Prolonged separation from primary caregiver without adequate substitute (Occasionally) pain
● *Fear/anxiety*		
Startle reflex	Birth	Unexpected, sudden, or loud event
Fear of strangers	6–8 months	Unfamiliar person in strange setting; close proximity; no caregiver present
Separation protest	10–24 months	Separation from attachment figure
● *Surprise*	3–4 months	Unexpected circumstances
● *Disgust*	Birth	Unpleasant taste/smell

To minimize separation distress, children who are adopted should be placed before they are 6 months of age. After that time, children may require weeks, sometimes months, to adjust. Parents can also encourage early attachment to others outside the immediate family to minimize the stress of temporary separation. The child who has repeated contact with a substitute caregiver will feel more comfortable and less frightened when left alone in his or her care. Although multiple attachments are best for the child who periodically receives substitute care, such attachments may be threatening to parents who fear their relationship with the child will be undermined. Parents need to know that their child does not have to love them less to love another person more. In fact, a child with strong multiple attachments may feel more secure and self-confident than a child with fewer or weaker emotional ties.[†]

The clingy, dependent behavior sometimes prompted by separation distress is normal and even expected. The child is confirming her emotional ties to the parents and expressing her displeasure in being left behind. If the child's increased needs to be rocked, held, or cuddled are satisfied, the dependent behavior will gradually diminish as the child is reassured of the continued love of the parents. On the other hand, if the child's behavior is ignored or punished, dependent behavior may increase and insecurity may result.

Acquiring Emotional Display Rules

emotional display rules
learned guidelines for the expression of emotion

As children display emotions, they also learn how and under what circumstances emotions may be expressed. Within the first few months of life, infants are socialized to suppress certain emotions, particularly negative ones (Malatesta et al., 1986). When interacting with their infants, mothers imitate their baby's interest, happiness, and surprise but not their anger, fear, or sadness. Babies are ignored, rebuked ("Stop that screaming!"), or threatened ("If you don't stop that, I'll put you down") in an effort to suppress certain emotions deemed undesirable or poorly timed (Malatesta & Haviland, 1982). It's not until children are 10–12 years old, however, that they become adept at regulating their own emotional displays.

[†]When our oldest daughter Heather began to talk I was horrified to discover she was calling Grace, the babysitter "Mom" and me "Chris." I knew she loved Grace, and I did too, but somehow I thought the name "Mom" should be reserved for me. Although Grace was careful to point out that she did not encourage this labeling and shared my distress, I began to feel a little insecure about my role. (After all, I pouted, how good a mom could I be if my first and only child did not even acknowledge my status!) Finally, the explanation for Heather's behavior became clear. She was imitating the behavior of those around her. Heather heard Grace's children call Grace "Mom" and she heard Grace and Bob (Heather's father) call me "Chris," not "Mom." When I realized my fears were unfounded, I felt both foolish and relieved. In most circumstances children's behavior is remarkably rational if we take the time to look for the causes!

Recognizing and Responding to Other's Emotions

Infants are responsive to vocal emotion before they are able to interpret facial expressions that convey emotion. Infants hear emotional overtones in their caregiver's voice. But if mother speaks in a monotone, without any feeling or emotion, the 6 week old infant does not react to the mother as the familiar person she is. The mother becomes a stranger to her own infant when the emotional quality of her voice is absent (Mehler et al., 1978).

Infants rely on the emotional cues in their mother's voices to know how to respond to strangers and new toys. If mothers react in a calm, happy way, the baby shows more interest than fear in both situations (Boccia & Campos, 1983; Svejda & Campos, 1982). By 8 or 9 months of age, infants are reading both faces and voices and are actively seeking out information about other people's feelings to help them appraise an uncertain situation (a behavior called *social referencing* (Walker-Andrews, 1986; Walden & Ogan, 1988). As children become more mobile and exploration increases, both bold and wary infants are more likely to reference their mothers when new stimuli are presented or changes occur (Hornik & Gunnar, 1988).

social referencing
looking for clues about how other people are perceiving/feeling about certain circumstances

Empathy

Empathy involves the ability to understand the feelings of others and to imagine oneself in another's place (Hoffman, 1984). Empathy has its roots in infancy. Newborns cry when they hear other babies cry, indicating some predisposition to experience the emotions of others. Yet true empathy depends on cognitive development—a child must see herself as separate from others and be able to take another's perspective to realize that another person, not she herself, is experiencing distress (Thompson, 1987). During the second year of life, infants no longer cry in response to tears from another. Instead, they withhold crying and attempt to give comfort by touching, hugging, or offering a toy to the distressed child.

empathy
sharing emotions with another by imagining what they must be feeling or going through

Theories of Emotional Development

How do emotions originate and what factors account for the observed sequence of emotional development? Several theoretical perspectives offer explanations.

Learning Theory/Behaviorism

According to the behaviorists, emotions like all other behaviors are learned. In a classic experiment, John B. Watson and Rosalie Raynor (1920) associated a loud, fear-eliciting sound with a white rat, thus classically conditioning a 9 month old baby named Albert to fear the rat

learning theory/behaviorism
a theoretical perspective founded by John B. Watson that maintains that most behavior is learned or conditioned rather than inborn

rather than remain passive to it. In the 1950s and 1960s, careful reward and punishment was discovered to influence the rate of smiling, crying, or vocalizing in infants (Brackbill, 1958; Elzel & Gewirtz, 1967). A few years later, Albert Bandura (1969) emphasized that babies could imitate other's emotions.

Learning theory can help explain why infants approach, avoid, or display certain emotions. But it cannot explain why some emotions, like fear of strangers, appears in most infants at around 8 months of age *without* any prior negative conditioning. Thus, learning theory can explain how emotions can be modified, but it does not explain where emotions come from nor why they appear at certain ages.

Ethological Theory

ethological theory
a theory interested in understanding the evolutionary origins of behavior and its adaptive value or significance for survival

Ethologists are interested in the genetic origins of behaviors and how behaviors help organisms adapt to new situations. In 1872 Charles Darwin noted that some facial expressions of emotions (for example, smiles and frowns) are used in similar ways by all the world's people and have counterparts in primates as well. Contemporary psychologist Carroll Izard (1990) feels that infant emotions are genetically preprogrammed and expressed as they are needed. For example, disgust helps infants stay away from potentially harmful substances or experiences, whereas fear encourages caution and protects against injury while avoiding pain. Izard's timetable of emotions agrees with that of other researchers (Table 7–3).

■ **Table 7–3**   *Izard's Timetable for Infant Emotions*

EXPRESSION OF FUNDAMENTAL EMOTIONS	APPROXIMATE TIME OF EMERGENCE
Interest	Present at birth
Neonatal smile* (a half-smile that appears spontaneously and for no apparent reason)	
Startle response*	
Distress* (in response to pain)	
Disgust	
Social smile	4–6 weeks
Anger	3–4 months
Surprise	
Sadness	
Fear	5–7 months
Shame/Shyness/Self-awareness	6–8 months
Contempt	2nd year of life
Guilt	

*The neonatal smile, the startle response, and distress in response to pain are precursors of the social smile and the emotions of surprise and sadness, which appear later. Izard has no evidence that they are related to inner feelings when they are seen in the first few weeks of life.

(Trotter, 1983)

(1979) have each proposed separate organizational models, they all emphasize that emotion plays a central organizing function—facilitating self-awareness, encouraging exploration or caution, and promoting bonding and attachment. Thus, a reciprocal relationship is hypothesized to exist between cognition and emotion—emotions allow for cognitive growth while cognitive development sets the stage for more complex emotional expression (Lewis et al., 1984). Organizational theorists agree with the cognitivists since they feel emotional responsiveness is a function of how an infant interprets or perceives a situation. They agree with the ethologists that some emotions are universal, have a genetic foundation, and are goal-directed and adaptive. And they agree with the behaviorists in asserting that learning and the environment can create significant changes in emotional responsiveness. As infants mature, they can control their emotions by ignoring the situation, crawling (or walking) away, or repeating comforting thoughts to themselves (*Daddy will be back soon*) (Campos et al., 1983).

organizational theories
an approach that suggests that emotions play a central role in behavior by influencing cognition and encouraging exploration, attachment, and withdrawal from harm.

● Temperament and Personality

As I mentioned in Chapter 2, some differences in the response patterns of babies are apparent from birth. Researchers define temperament as individual differences in the type, intensity, and duration of emotional reactions (Thomas & Chess, 1977). Temperament influences the development of personality and social relations.

In 1956 Alexander Thomas and Stella Chess initiated a longitudinal study of newborns in the New York area. After more than 20 years of careful observation, nine dimensions of temperament emerged (Table 7–4), which clustered into three different temperament types:

The easy child (about 40% of the original sample): Playful, cheerful, and generally happy, this child adapts well to new situations and establishes routines easily.

The slow-to-warm-up child (about 15% of the original sample): Tends to withdraw from new situations and needs time to adjust to change. Is inactive, somewhat negative, but mild in response intensity.

The difficult child (about 10% of the original sample): Cries a great deal, is generally negative, and reacts with intensity. This child has irregular habits and patterns and adjusts poorly to new situations.

Note that only 65% of all children could be classified as easy, slow to warm up, or difficult. Thirty-five percent did not fit any one pattern but displayed a blend of styles and traits. Difficult infants have been studied most extensively, but difficult temperament does not necessarily predict later behavioral problems (Daniels et al., 1984).

Thomas and Chess's (1970, 1977) findings on infant temperament helped dispel the myth that "good families/good environments" consistently produce "good babies." The best outcomes result when par-

■ **Table 7–4** *Nine temperament types identified by Thomas and Chess and how they are expressed in children at 2 months and 10 years of age. Plus (+) indicates high levels of characteristic; minus (−) indicates low levels.*

TEMPERAMENTAL QUALITY	AT 2 MONTHS	AT 10 YEARS
1. ACTIVITY LEVEL (Proportion of active periods to inactive ones)	+ Moves often in sleep. Wriggles when diaper is changed. − Does not move when being dressed or during sleep.	Plays ball and engages in other sports. Cannot sit still long enough to do homework. Likes solitary sedentary activity (like reading). Eats very slowly.
2. RHYTHMICITY (Regularity of functions, such as hunger, excretion, sleep and wakefulness)	+ Has been on a four-hour feeding schedule since birth. Regular bowel movements. − Awake at a different time each morning. Size of feedings varies.	Eats only at mealtimes. Sleeps the same amount of time each night. Food intake varies. Falls asleep at a different time each night.
3. APPROACH OR WITHDRAWAL (Initial reaction to any new stimulation)	+ Smiles and licks washcloth. Has always liked bottle. − Rejected cereal the first time. Cries when strangers appear.	Went to camp happily. Loved to ski the first time. Severely homesick at camp during first days. Does not like new activities.
4. ADAPTABILITY (Ease with which the child adapts to changes in the environment)	+ Was passive during first bath; now enjoys bathing. Smiles at nurse. − Still startled by sudden, sharp noise. Resists diapering.	Likes camp, although homesick during first days. Learns enthusiastically. Does not adjust well to new school or new teacher; comes home late for dinner even when punished.
5. INTENSITY OF REACTION (Energy level of responses)	+ Cries when diapers are wet. Rejects food vigorously when satisfied. − Does not cry when diapers are wet. Whimpers instead of crying when hungry.	Tears up an entire page of homework if one mistake is made. Slams door of room when teased by younger brother. When a mistake is made in a model airplane; corrects it quietly. Does not comment when reprimanded.
6. THRESHOLD OF RESPONSIVENESS (Intensity of stimulation required to produce reaction)	+ Stops sucking on bottle when approached. − Is not startled by loud noise. Takes bottle and breast equally well.	Rejects fatty foods. Adjusts shower until water is at exactly the right temperature. Never complains when sick. Eats all foods.
7. QUALITY OF MOOD (Proportion of happy, friendly to unhappy, unfriendly behavior)	+ Smacks lips when first tasting new food. Smiles at parents. − Fusses after nursing. Cries when stroller is rocked.	Enjoys new accomplishments. Laughs aloud when reading a funny passage. Cries when he cannot solve a homework problem. Very "weepy" if he does not get enough sleep.
8. DISTRACTIBILITY (Degree to which extraneous stimulation disrupts ongoing behavior)	+ Will stop crying for food if rocked. Stops fussing if given pacifier when diaper is being changed. − Will not stop crying when diaper is changed. Fusses after eating, even if rocked.	Needs absolute silence for homework. Has a hard time choosing a shirt in a store because they all appeal to him. Can read a book while television set is at high volume. Does chores on schedule.

■ **Table 7-4** *(continued)*

TEMPERAMENTAL QUALITY	AT 2 MONTHS	AT 10 YEARS
9. ATTENTION SPAN AND PERSISTENCE (Length of time activities are maintained and tolerance for difficulty and distraction)	+ If soiled, continues to cry until changed. Repeatedly rejects water if he wants milk. − Cries when awakened but stops almost immediately. Objects only mildly if cereal precedes bottle.	Reads for two hours before sleeping. Does homework carefully. Gets up frequently from homework for a snack. Never finishes a book.

Source: Adapted from Thomas, Chess, and Birch, "The Origin of Personality." © 1970 by Scientific American, Inc. All rights reserved.

enting styles complement infant temperament; the worst outcomes involve conflict. Some parents and some babies mesh well and meet each others needs and expectations and others don't (Thomas et al., 1970). A difficult baby may thrive with a patient, low-key mother, but an easy baby might suffer from low levels of interactions and stimulation. In fact, temperament influences parent–child interactions in two ways: Infants solicit certain reactions *from* others; they also react *to* others as a function of their own style and disposition. Thus, infants and parents either experience harmony and achieve a "good fit" or experience discord due to a "poor fit."

One of the most important things a parent can do is to accept his or her child's basic temperament. Trying to mold a resistant child will inevitably lead to conflict. Instead, let the child set the pace and offer guidance, limitations, and encouragement as he sets forth. Of all characteristics, parents appreciate good mood and adaptability most (Hubert, 1989).

The Origins of Temperament

Infants seem to inherit a predisposition or a tendency to respond to certain situations in certain ways. The most compelling support for this position comes from studies of identical (monozygotic) and fraternal (dizygotic) twins (Goldsmith, 1983). Results indicate that twins who share common genes react similarly 55% of the time. Siblings (who share no genes in common) are no more alike in temperament than two strangers selected at random. Contrary to popular opinion, prematurity and very low birth weight are not associated with difficult temperament any more than full-term status (Goldstein & Bracey, 1988).

Can the environment influence emotional responsiveness? To a certain degree it can. The environment can probably emphasize or deemphasize a certain trait but may not be able to promote or eliminate a particular temperament style. In other words, the difficult child can be encouraged to be less "difficult," but he will never become "easy."

■ ●▲   CONCEPT SUMMARY

Temperament and Personality

● Accounts for some individual differences in emotional behavior

● Three basic temperament types (easy, difficult, and slow-to-warm-up)

● Best infant–parent interactions when child's temperament pleases parent or fits with parent's expectations

● Some traits may have genetic basis

● Traits may be modified by the environment but probably not eliminated

● Some traits remain stable over time

The Stability of Temperament

Some infants show stable ways of responding as they age. The fussy, tearful infant may become the fussy, tearful toddler (Kagan et al., 1987a). However, the temperament of most infants changes between age 1 and the preschool years. What is responsible for this change? Most likely the child's environment, particularly his mother, and the child rearing experiences she provides (Koniak-Griffin & Rummell, 1988). Overall, sociabililty, distractibility, shyness, activity level, and irritability show the most stability over the period of infancy and into childhood (Worobey & Blajda, 1989). Activity level declines across birth position: Early-borns are rated as more active than later-borns (Eaton et al., 1989).

● Self-Awareness

self-awareness
recognizing the existence of the self

At what point does the infant understand that he has a unique identity separate from others? Evidence of an emerging sense of self was given in an experiment by Michael Lewis and Jeanne Brooks-Gunn (1979). Babies were permitted to look in a mirror to see how they behaved. Then, while pretending to wipe the baby's face with a cloth, the experimenter put a dot of red lipstick on the baby's nose and allowed the baby to look in the mirror once again. Babies who recognized that the red spot was on *their* nose would touch their own nose; those who did not would reach for the nose on the face in the mirror. None of the children studied under 12 months of age touched their noses. It's not until children are 15–18 months old that they have some kind of schema for their own face and touch the lipstick spot on their own nose rather than on the nose in the mirror. At this age, children can also distinguish self from others in photographs. They can point to themselves in pictures and by 18–24 months can state their own name and the name of their reflection in the mirror if asked (Harter, 1983). Shadow self-recognition follows mirror self-recognition and doesn't typically occur until age 3 (Cameron & Gallup, 1988).

The *self-concept* or evaluation of the self does not emerge until the preschool years (age 3–6) when the child develops symbolic thought and acquires language. Emotional responses to wrongdoing follow physical self-recognition and self-description in the sequence of behaviors associated with the development of self-concept and self-awareness (Stipek et al., 1990).

self-concept
a person's perception of him or herself as an individual with specific characteristics and behaviors

symbolic thought
thinking in which words and images represent actions and objects

● Social Development

Attachment

An attachment is an enduring emotional tie that develops between the infant and other significant people. When an infant is attached to others, she will display pleasure in their presence, seek their comfort when distressed, miss them when they are gone, and greet them happily when they return (Maccoby, 1980). Parents form attachments to infants and infants to parents through a process of familiarization and reciprocal interactions. For most babies and caregivers, bonding is an easy, natural process that develops over time. Some parents form love relationships with their infants before birth, while others require more time to develop a strong sense of commitment and caring. Since attachment plays an important role in parent–child relationships and in the emotional development of the child, we will examine attachment from both the parents' and the child's perspective and will identify the variables that affect the quality of the outcome in both cases.

attachment (bond)
an affectionate emotional tie between two people, a person and an animal, or a person and an object that endures over time

The Parents' Attachment to the Infant

Forming an attachment to the newborn is one of the first tasks parents face. Attachments or emotional bonds are crucial to infant survival and well-being. Bonds help ensure that the child will be nurtured and protected. But sometimes parents who expect to feel intense love for and unity with their newborn are puzzled and ashamed to find that their feelings are neutral. Such feelings are not unusual, however, since attachment is generally a gradual process based on experience and learning, not instincts. Parents must *learn* to appreciate the baby's positive and unique qualities; timing and duration of the interaction and the parent's perceptions of the infant can also influence attachment.

sensitive period
see critical period

TIMING AND DURATION OF THE INTERACTION Marshall Klaus and John Kennell's *Maternal–Infant Bonding* (1976) changed the course of pediatric practice. Prior to 1976 no special effort was made to acquaint mother and baby after birth. In fact, in standard hospital procedure the mother was allowed only a glimpse of the infant before the latter was whisked away to the nursery. Klaus and Kennell's research, based mainly on animal studies, suggested that a *sensitive period* existed during the first few hours of life when close physical contact with the mother was essential to the baby's normal emotional development. Hormone activity in the mother was presumed to facilitate the bonding process. Parents who were denied early contact such as holding, touching, or nursing their newborn in the delivery room were made to feel disadvantaged because they missed out on a supposedly crucial phase of their child's emotional development.

Recently, the impact of early parent–child contact has been questioned (Lamb, 1982; Myers, 1984). While early contact may be emotionally satisfying, it is certainly not critical, since fathers, adoptive parents, and mothers who deliver by cesarean section under general anesthesia develop close ties to their infants. Moreover, in some studies cited by Klaus and Kennell, infants received both early and extended contact, so it is impossible to tell which factor was responsible for any reported effects.

While immediate, close, and/or prolonged physical contact with the infant certainly cannot hurt, it may be naive to consider such experiences sufficient for the development of attachment (Svejda et al., 1980). For some parents, contact with the infant at birth might initiate a sense of commitment to the baby. But establishing enduring affectionate ties is a complex process influenced by the parents' perceptions of their infant, the reward value of the interactions, and even social and economic situations that may or may not complicate the parents' lives.

PARENTS' PERCEPTIONS OF THE INFANT One early influence on parent–infant attachment is the parents' combined expectations of their unborn child and of the birth process. The parents often imagine that the newborn will have a certain appearance, temperament, and behavior pattern and expect that the birth will proceed in an uneventful manner. At birth, such expectations might be confirmed, but they might also be proven completely wrong (Zeanah et al., 1985). Where expectations are met the attachment process will be facilitated; however, if the parents expect a child who requires little attention but find themselves parents to an active child from a troublesome birth, they might experience emotional conflict unless they can adjust their parenting style to fit the baby's needs (Sroufe, 1983). To avoid disappointment, parents should probably hope only for a healthy baby and a birth that is as uncomplicated as possible. Signs of poor parent/child adaptation are summarized in

■ **Table 7-5**   *Signs in Parent of Poor Parent/Child Adaptation*

Disappointment over sex of baby

Does not hold, touch, or examine the newborn

Disgusted by normal infant behavior and habits (drooling, sucking sounds, dirty diapers, etc.)

Speaks of the infant as ugly and unattractive

Doesn't make eye contact with the baby

Doesn't talk to or play with the baby

Concerned that child has a defect even though this possibility has been ruled out

Cannot find any physical or psychological attribute to admire in the child

Doesn't hold baby warmly (holds away from the body)

Picks up baby without warning

Jiggles baby and interacts roughly

Cannot discriminate between signs of hunger, fatigue, etc., in the baby

Thinks the infant judges him or her

Thinks that the infant doesn't love him or her

Source: Schmidt & Eldridge, 1986

Table 7–5. These signs can have important implications for the quality and quantity of care the infant receives.

The birth of a child with special needs may be unexpected and traumatic. Moreover, in such an event parents might be so preoccupied with their own feelings of shock, disappointment, or guilt that they have little or no energy to turn toward their infant. They might also consciously avoid contact to prevent becoming attached to the child, especially if survival seems unlikely. However, whether the child is premature, has Down's syndrome, or is critically ill, the infant with special needs can also benefit from affectionate care. In fact, it is important for the child that the family's psychological orientation to the special needs infant be the same as it would be toward any other birth. If the family has the personal resources to care for the special child, an at-risk child can attach and be attached to as readily as any other child (Rode et al., 1981). Skin-to-skin contact at visitations may help mothers attach to very low birth weight babies and help babies cry less by the time they are 6 months old (Whitelaw et al., 1988).

In a review of the literature, Sally Rogers (1988) found that some disabled children are challenging to interact with since they provide fewer readable cues, demonstrate less positive affect and more negative affect, and have more trouble synchronizing turn-taking than their nondisabled counterparts. While mothers of craniofacially disfigured babies may rate their parental satisfaction and life satisfaction higher than

special needs child
a child who requires some special assistance to function up to their personal potential

■ **Figure 7–5**

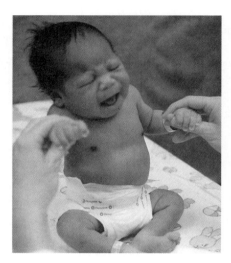
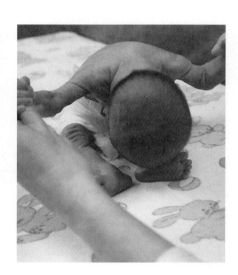

(upper) The full term baby cuddles and is responsive . . . The preemie stiffens, squirms and pushes away. (lower) The full term baby can sit with support and hold his head up . . . The preemie appears limp, has no head control, and cannot make eye contact.

mothers of nondisfigured babies, they actually behave in a consistently less nurturant way toward their infants (Barden et al., 1989).

OTHER VARIABLES

The Mother's Mood The mother's mood is important to the success of maternal attachment since babies tend to imitate their mother's moods. Mothers who were happy and pleased with their babies had happier babies, enjoyed a more pleasant and cooperative relationship with the baby's father, and formed attachments to the infant more easily than mothers who were disappointed with their babies (Jones & Raag, 1989). When mothers are sad, babies are sad, too, expressing more anger and spending less time playing than babies whose mothers exhibit more positive moods (Termine & Izard, 1988). Maternal depression has a profoundly disruptive effect on parent–child relations. Depressed mothers are slower to respond to infant vocalizations, fail to modify their behavior to correspond with the behavior of the infant, and do not modulate their voices when talking to the baby (Bettes, 1988). In addition, depressed mothers and their infants matched negative behavior states more often than positive behavior states (Field et al., 1990). Where at-

A Closer Look

Jimmy

Dear Abby:

This letter has taken me two and a half years to write. It is in response to someone who asked you if she would acknowledge the birth of a friend's baby who had been diagnosed as having Down's syndrome. Thank you, Abby, for saying, "Yes, the mother of such a child needs all the support and cheering up she can get."

I read that column the day I came home from the hospital with little Jimmy, my newborn Down's syndrome baby. But there is so much more that most people need to know, and as one who has had the experience, may I say it:

Please keep in mind that what happened to Jimmy was tragic, but the child himself is not a tragedy, and neither is his birth. He is as much a loving member of our family as our other children, so do send a card, note, or gift to acknowledge his birth.

Here are a few suggestions that will help you feel more comfortable when talking to the parents of a Down's baby:

1. Please don't ask if insanity runs in our family. Down's syndrome is a chromosome defect and is rarely heredity. Furthermore, a Down's child is retarded, which is vastly different from insane.

2. Don't hesitate to ask how he is getting along. Some people avoid mentioning the child (as though he had died) because they think the situation is too horrible even to discuss.

3. When the child seems to be progressing, please don't say he seems "normal" and maybe won't be retarded after all! New parents need to face up to the facts regarding their special child before they themselves can accept him as he is. By denying his limitations, you encourage false hope and convey the message that you really don't accept or love him.

4. About one-third of all Down's children are born with heart defects. Our Jimmy required open-heart surgery. He survived the operation and is much improved. We thank God for that, so please don't say it might have been a "blessing" if he had died. And don't express surprise that they "would bother" to operate on such a child.

5. Please believe the parents when they say that their special child is a very worthwhile little person, and they are actually glad to have him. While Down's syndrome is nothing to wish for, it can be accepted, and is not nearly as catastrophic as it seems the first few weeks.

6. In the beginning, the parents need to talk about their feelings. Don't argue. Listen. Let them weep, and weep with them. And when they can finally smile about their baby, you smile, too.

7. Don't refer to the child as "that poor little thing." It hurts me to see people look upon my child with pity and know they wish he had never been born. He's not repulsive in the least, and I can honestly say that much good has already come from our little treasure. Our other children (the eldest is 9 years old) have learned understanding and compassion because of their little brother. We told them the truth immediately, and they have loved him from the day they first saw him.

I cannot imagine life without Jimmy. He is the sunshine of our lives.

People don't mean to be insensitive or cruel—they just don't know how to handle the birth of an exceptional child.

Jimmy's Mother

tachment problems appeared, prolonged maternal depression, marital stress, disagreement in child-rearing philosophies, competition with the father for care of the newborn, and withdrawal of the father were the most common explanations (Siegel et al., 1980; Cox et al., 1989). Apparently, postpartum depression puts women at greater risk for later depression and all the child behavior problems that accompany it (Philips & O'Hara, 1991).

Flexibility and Caregiving Training from Parents When mothers recalled their own parents as warm and loving *or* were able to forgive or understand unsatisfactory attachment experiences, they were more likely to become securely attached to their own babies (Main et al., 1985). These data are reassuring since they indicate that one needn't come from a secure relationship with one's parents to be able to provide warm, consistent parenting for one's own child.

Infant Behavior

Full-term infants come equipped with behaviors that attract the parent's attention and facilitate attachment.

gazing
to look steadily; to fix one's attention

GAZING Newborns can focus on objects 8–10 inches from their eyes. Because the mother's face is that distance away during breast- or bottle-feeding and the human face is an attractive stimulus for the newborn, an infant spends a great deal of time gazing at the mother's face, particularly her hairline, eyes, and mouth. This behavior is usually interpreted as a sign of recognition or interest. Infant gazing often prompts a variety of responses from the caregiver, including looking, exaggerated facial expressions, vocalizations, moving closer, and social games such as tickling and peek-a-boo. The pattern of infant–parent gaze is not based on interpersonal synchrony but on the way each individual organizes his or her own behavior (Messer & Vietze, 1988).

Between birth and 3 months of age, the child's ability to visually fixate and follow a slowly moving object becomes perfected. Infants often watch their mothers move from place to place, another behavior that parents interpret as a sign of interest. When infants of 3 or 4 months gain control over their head movements, they can track motion more easily and can regulate the amount of eye contact they give and receive by turning toward or away from the caregiver.

SMILING Smiling is another important social signal. Infants between birth and 8 weeks of age will smile spontaneously and indiscriminately at a variety of stimuli. Once babies begin to smile, the time parents spend with them increases remarkably. Between 2 and 3 months of age the baby can initiate the *greeting response*. Babies in this period will open their eyes wide, form their open mouth into a distinctive shape, coo,

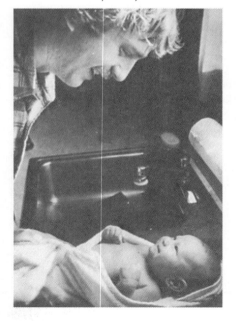

■ **Figure 7–6**

The social smile of an infant.

and sometimes smile at the sight of a face or a familiar person (Hubley & Trevarthen, 1979). The frequency of infant smiling can also be increased when parents imitate the behavior of their babies (vocalizations, lip movements, eye movements, and the like.) When mothers exhibit the same behavior as their baby, the baby is amused and smiles (Moran et al., 1987). In 17–19 month old infants, smiling also increased in the presence of any attentive human (Jones & Raag, 1989). Infants who save their smiles for people they know can make caregivers feel very special. In fact, the greeting response is one of the first elements of an infant–parent social interaction. Fifty percent of the time, infants and young children actually being such interactions by crying, gesturing to, or greeting the adult (Bell, 1974).

Parents and other adults demonstrate a greeting response similar to baby's by raising their eyebrows, opening their mouth and eyes wide, moving their head back slightly, vocalizing, and smiling. When parents, even first-time mothers, talk to their babies, they speak baby talk, slurring and creating words, exaggerating pitch, and selecting short, simple, repetitive statements (Fernald & Simon, 1984).

■ **Figure 7–7**

The greeting response.

CRYING AND OTHER VOCALIZATIONS Newborn cries most often reflect hunger, anger, or pain. Most adult caregivers are able to distinguish among these motivations and act accordingly. Developmentally, the number of crying episodes are more frequent in late afternoon and early evening. Crying gradually increases from birth to 6–8 weeks and then declines rapidly (St. James-Roberts, 1989). Babies with colic and/or difficult temperaments cry more than babies without colic or with easier temperaments. Babies who are easily soothed are often liked best (Newton, 1983). Carrying may both prevent and soothe a crying infant in the first 3 months of life (St. James-Roberts, 1989).

Infants make noises that sound like gurgles, coos, and laughter as they struggle to control their swallowing, breathing, and facial muscles. Babies can respond to others with gurgles and coos by the end of the first month. Laughter or chuckling develops between 12 and 16 weeks and is initially a response to tickling, pat-a-cake, or other tactile stimulation. As with smiling, laughter takes on a purposeful quality when the baby laughs during an interaction with a caregiver or to bring about a desired response. Laughter and smiling are usually interpreted as signs of pleasure.

CLINGING/GRASPING The newborn's grasp reflex causes her to clutch anything placed in the hand. New babies will grasp the caregiver's finger as readily as they will grasp a toy. The indiscriminate nature of early grasping does not seem to bother parents, who tend to interpret the action as a signal that the baby wants them close. As development proceeds and grasping comes under voluntary control, the baby can choose to grasp, let go of, and even push away.

greeting response
a characteristic pattern of facial expressions that infants display when they are pleased to see someone they know

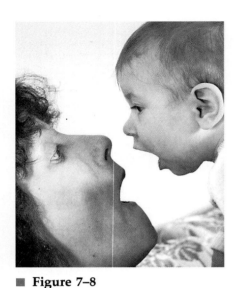

■ **Figure 7–8**

Sharing a moment of synchrony.

synchrony
carefully coordinated interactions
between an infant and another person
in which each is attuned to the
other's verbal and nonverbal cues

SYNCHRONY An important element in the development of attachment to infants is *synchrony*, the meshing of infant and parent behaviors into a smooth reciprocal exchange (Belsky & Rovine, 1987). Synchrony may have a neurophysiological basis, as infants who are more socially responsive and attentive (i.e., more mature) mesh more readily with mothers who interpret infant signals accurately and screen out redundant stimuli for their babies (Penman et al., 1983). These mother/infant pairs also experience less disengagement, or asynchrony, than other pairs (Isabella et al., 1989). The following behavioral "dialogue" is an example of synchrony:

> While talking and looking at me the mother turned her head and gazed at the infant's face. He was gazing at the ceiling, but out of the corner of his eye he saw her head turn toward him and turned to gaze back at her. This had happened before, but now he broke rhythm and stopped sucking. He let go of the nipple and the suction around it broke as he eased into the faintest suggestion of a smile. The mother abruptly stopped talking, and as she watched his face begin to transform, her eyes opened a little wider and her eyebrows raised a bit. His eyes locked onto hers, and together they held motionless for an instant. The infant did not return to sucking and his mother held frozen her slight expression of anticipation. This silent and almost motionless instant continued to hang until the mother suddenly shattered it by saying "Hey!" and simultaneously opening her eyes wider, raising her eyebrows further, and throwing her head up and toward the infant. Almost simultaneously, the baby's eyes widened. His head tilted up and, as his smile broadened, the nipple fell out of his mouth. Now she said, "Well, hello. . .hello. . . heeelllooo!!" so that her pitch rose and the "hellos" became longer and more stressed on each successive repetition. With each phrase, the baby expressed more pleasure, and his body resonated almost like a balloon being pumped up, filling a little more with each breath.
>
> The mother then paused and her face relaxed. They watched each other expectantly for a moment. The shared excitement between them ebbed, but before it faded completely, the baby suddenly took an initiative and intervened to rescue it. His head lurched forward, his hands jerked up, and a fuller smile blossomed. His mother was jolted into motion. She moved forward, mouth open and eyes alight, and said, "ooooh. . .ya wanna play, do ya. . .yeah?. . .I didn't know if you were still hungry. . . .no. . .nooooo. . .no I didn't." (Stern, 1977, p. 3)

You can imagine how emotionally satisfying such a well-synchronized pattern of exchange between infant and caregiver can be. Keep in mind that synchrony develops only after long hours of patience and practice. Early parent/infant interactions can be very frustrating since parents might misinterpret or ignore infant cues. Premature infants pose a special challenge. Because of their immaturity, they may be unable to sustain eye contact, cuddle, or be easily comforted. Parents of premies may find themselves frustrated as their efforts to interact with their babies are disrupted by the child's lack of responsiveness. These parents frequently feel incompetent and unloved by their infants.

The Infant's Attachment to the Parents

In most families, as the parents bond with the baby, the baby prepares to form a reciprocal attachment with the caregivers. Infant-initiated attachments tend to take longer to complete, however, since babies cannot make progress in attachment until they have passed certain maturational milestones. The development of attachment in the infant follows a predictable pattern, which we can break down into four overlapping stages. Although most research focuses on the mother as the primary caregiver and the infant's attachment to her, the sex of the caregiver does not alter the process, provided the baby's needs are met (Lamb, 1977).

PHASES OF ATTACHMENT

1. **The Preattachment Phase (Birth to 6 Weeks)** In the first phase, the infant responds indiscriminately to anyone who offers appropriate and timely stimulation. Infants begin to study the attributes of people around them and to respond by smiling, gazing, and vocalizing. Although infants prefer their own mother's smell and voice to that of strangers, they are only beginning to distinguish her from others. For the most part, the infant is pleasantly responsive to all.

■ **Figure 7–9**

Attachment.

2. The Attachment-in-the-Making Phase (6 Weeks to 6–8 Months) The infant begins to show a more marked preference for the primary caregiver (usually the mother) by smiling more freely at her, visually tracking her movements, and looking at her when there is a choice. During this time, the baby will cry when separated from the mother but separation from *any* human at this time causes distress.

Before infants can become attached to a particular person they must have repeated contact with that person and be able to distinguish that person from everyone else. The quality of the exclusive attachment is influenced by the satisfaction the interaction brings (Stern, 1977). Babies are more likely to become strongly attached to caregivers who are warm, responsive, predictable, and careful during handling, and who gratify their needs, including that for stimulation (Londerville & Main, 1981).

3. The Phase of Clear-Cut, Specific Attachment (6–8 Months to 18–24 Months) By the time infants are 6–8 months old, their preference for the primary caregiver is pronounced. They smile when the mother comes into view, reach up to be held, track her movements, call for her, crawl after her, and climb onto her lap, thus acting more deliberately to maintain her attention and sustain her presence. The caregiver is no longer a replaceable person. The baby knows whom she wants and no one else will satisfy as well.

4. Forming a Reciprocal Partnership (18 Months to 24 Months) As cognitive and language development takes place, children actively attempt to influence the mother's goals and behaviors rather than simply adjusting their behavior to suit hers. Language helps the baby state her needs and negotiate a plan that is mutually acceptable. As time goes on, the baby can appreciate the factors that influence the mother's disappearance and return. Babies who are given advance notice of their mother's departure ("I'm going to the store now"), and explicit instructions about what to do in the meantime ("Put together this puzzle while I'm gone") accept their mother's absence better than children whose mothers just slipped out without a word (Adams & Passman, 1981).

paternal engrossment
the father's fascination with and commitment to his infant

MULTIPLE ATTACHMENTS: THE ROLE OF THE FATHER *Paternal engrossment* refers to the father's sense of absorption and interest in the infant (Greenberg and Morris, 1974). Fathers who observe their child's birth or who hold and cuddle their infants soon after delivery spend more time than others in caring for and playing with their babies when the family returns home, especially when the father is more highly educated and the baby is a male (Toney, 1983). Fathers touch, look at, talk to, and kiss their newborns just as much as mothers do and are just as sensitive to the baby's cries, coughs, and sneezes during feedings and to their babblings (Parke, 1981). The more time fathers spend with their infants, the more competence they ascribe to their babies (for example, great verbal abilities and sensory perception) and the better able they are to meet their baby's needs (Ninio & Rinott, 1988). Infants drink just as much milk when their father feeds them as when mother does.

Despite these and other similarities, however, father–infant interactions differ from mother–infant interactions. While mothers are more likely to play soft, imitative talking and rhyming games with the infant, fathers are more likely to engage the baby in active physical play such as wrestling, "horsey," and poking games, especially if the baby is a male (Snow et al., 1983). The emotional ties fostered by this interaction style appear just as early and are apparently just as strong as the mother–infant bonds. At least 25% of infants develop initial attachment to both parents simultaneously, especially when infant-care tasks are shared from the beginning.

With the exception of father's tendency toward rough-and-tumble play with infants, especially sons, the behavior of mothers and fathers who are primary caregivers is remarkably similar (Parke & Tinsley, 1981). Both males and females in the role of primary caregiver spend

---

■●▲ CONCEPT SUMMARY

Infant Behavior That Attracts the Parents' Attention and Facilitates Attachment

- Looking at parents
- Following parents' movement
- Smiling at the sight of a human face
- Responding positively to mother's familiar smell
- Reaching up to be held
- Preferring to look at a familiar person over an unfamiliar one
- Crying
- Infant vocalizations (gurgles, coos, laughter)
- Grasping
- Infant movement that is interpreted as nonverbal responses of pleasure (e.g., kicking when spoken to)
- Calling for the parent
- Creeping or crawling after parent
- Climbing up onto parent's lap

---

less time smiling, laughing, imitating, and baby-talking than secondary caregivers. Fathers who display less traditionally masculine gender roles maintain their highly involved play style while at the same time increasing their attentiveness to the baby's physical needs (Hwang, 1986). As more and more fathers choose to become actively involved in childcare, the task of fathering takes on new depth and significance in child development. It's important to underscore the fact that no evidence exists that cites the mothers as better physically, emotionally, or psychologically prepared to parent than fathers.

ATTACHMENTS TO INANIMATE OBJECTS AND PETS Although babies usually form attachments to others of the same species, they can become attached to blankets, favorite toys, and pets. The attachment object seems to satisfy some of the baby's comfort and security needs. For example, in one early study, babies attached to blankets explored and played more freely and expressed less distress during their mother's absence than babies not attached to blankets (Passman & Weisberg, 1975). Attachment to inanimate objects is not unusual during infancy;

PEANUTS

more than half of children under age 2.5 display such attachments, especially if they also suck their thumbs or fingers (Mahalski, 1983).

Children's attachments to inanimate objects can create problems for parents, though. Keeping the blanket or toy clean, taking care not to lose it, and finding a suitable replacement when it is in shreds can pose a challenge even to the most resourceful. Desperate parents report stealing into their child's bedroom at night to wash and return the object, only to have their child complain the next day that the blanket or toy smells "funny" (i.e., clean). Also, social pressure may come to bear on parents of children who insist on clutching their threadbare, ragged, soiled (and often fragrant!) object in public. (However, not many parents have been ousted from public places because of the condition of their child's blanket!)

Children will abandon their attachment object when it is no longer needed. The parent who feels the need to "wean" the child from the blanket or toy might do so gradually rather than abruptly. For example, access could be limited to when the child is at home, but not at the store or in the restaurant. Throwing the object away or hiding it (and then sometimes lying about its whereabouts) shows disrespect for the child's property and needs and undermines the child's faith and trust in her parents.

Theories of Attachment

A variety of theories attempt to explain why infant–parent attachment occurs. Let's look at the major theories in turn.

Psychoanalytic Theory

Freud (1938) felt that the infant's relationship with the mother was "unique and unparalleled." He and his followers considered the pleasure the infant derived from feeding to be the basis for the development of a "primary object relation" with the other. Although it does seem reasonable to assume that an infant will attach to the person who takes care of her physical needs, the data suggest that feeding is not the most important variable in attachment formation. In a classic study of monkey behavior, Harry Harlow (Harlow & Zimmerman, 1959) separated infant rhesus monkeys from their mothers 6 to 12 hours after birth and raised them with two substitute, or surrogate, mothers. One of the "mothers" was made with wire mesh; the other was made of the same wire mesh wrapped with terry cloth. Some of the baby monkeys were fed from the "cloth mother" and some from the "wire mother." Harlow found that baby monkeys spent significantly more time on the cloth surrogate whether or not she was the one that provided nourishment. He concluded that the cloth mother provided *contact comfort*, an attachment quality more important from a caregiver than feeding.

psychoanalytic theory
a theoretical position originated by Sigmund Freud that emphasizes the role of unconscious motives and of early childhood experience

contact comfort
Harry Harlow's term for the security and satisfaction derived from stimuli that satisfy the infant's tactile needs

■ **Figure 7–10**

Feeding alone does not cause attachment. This young monkey clings to its cloth surrogate mother even though feeding comes from its wire surrogate mother.

Learning Theory/Behaviorism

Learning theorists emphasize the responsiveness of the mother. They see attachment as developing through a series of mutually reinforcing behaviors (Gewirtz, 1969; Maccoby, 1980). For example, the baby smiles and the mother interprets the smile as a sign of interest and smiles back; the baby responds by smiling and vocalizing; the mother imitates the vocalization, touches the child, and so forth. Obviously, attachment would not develop to an unresponsive adult. Learning theory also asserts that the infant may become attached to adults who satisfy certain basic needs (hunger, need for stimulation) since such behavior is reinforcing.

One major difficulty that learning theory has, however, is explaining why attachment is maintained over long periods of time when attachment figures are absent and cannot provide reinforcement. Learning theory would predict that such bonds would weaken over time, but they do not. Sometimes, in fact, the intensity of emotional ties *increases* through separation. Learning theory ignores the child's ability to represent the absent person symbolically in memory and, thus, to hold an image of the absent one in mind when they cannot have actual physical contact.

Ethological Theory

The ethological view is the most widely accepted explanation of attachment. For ethologists, attachment is based on inherited patterns of behavior that facilitate survival: Infants who stay close to their mothers are more likely to survive (Bowlby, 1958). Sucking, clinging, gazing, smiling, crying, and other reflex behaviors attract caregiver attention and encourage close contact, thereby protecting the baby from danger and ensuring her survival. In addition, adults may be biologically pro-

 Figure 7–11

"Babyness".

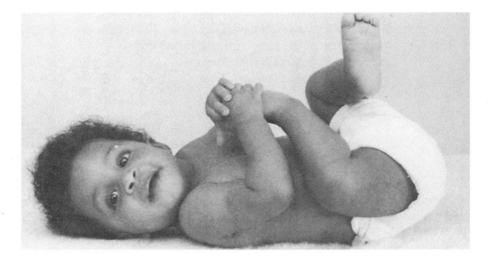

■●▲ CONCEPT SUMMARY

Theoretical Explanations for Attachment

Theory	Weaknesses of Theory
Psychoanalytic theory ● Infants attach to person to feeds them	● Contact comfort more important than feeding in forming attachments
Learning theory/Behaviorism ● Attachment develops to responsive adults (those that provide reinforcing consequences)	● Separation often *increases* attachment rather than decreasing it
Ethological theory ● Attachment behavior facilitates infant survival ● Adults are genetically organized to respond favorably to "baby characteristics"	

grammed to respond in a nurturant way to "baby characteristics" or *babyness* such as a relatively large head and forehead, eyes below the midpoint of the head, and cheeks that are round and protruding (Lorenz, 1971; Fullard & Reiling, 1976).

babyness
Lorenz's term for the collection of endearing physical characteristics of infants that persuade people to care for them because "they're so cute"

Assessing the Quality of Infant–Parent Attachment

In 1969 Mary Ainsworth and Barbara Wittig devised a procedure called the *Strange Situation* that has been used to assess the quality of infant–parent attachment in 1–2 year olds. This research procedure is carried out as follows:

1. The mother brings the infant into a laboratory playroom and puts her down on the floor next to a large assortment of attractive toys, and then goes to sit in a chair (3 minutes).
2. A female stranger enters the room, sits down and begins to talk with the mother (3 minutes).
3. The stranger then tries to engage the infant in play, while the mother quietly leaves the room (3 minutes or less*).

   a. While the mother is gone, the reactions of the stranger and the infant are observed.

*Time is shortened if the baby is distressed and lengthened if the baby needs extra time to be comforted or reinvolved in play.

4. The mother returns and her reunion with the infant is observed (3 minutes or more).
5. With the stranger gone, the mother again leaves the room for a few minutes (3 minutes or less).
6. The mother returns once more (3 minutes).

Based on their observations, Ainsworth and her colleagues (1969; 1978) were able to identify three distinct patterns of attachment in American middle class babies:

secure attachment
according to Ainsworth, the most common form of attachment, whereby the child feels comfort when the parent is present, experiences moderate levels of stress when the parent leaves, and quickly and happily reestablishes contact when the parent returns

1. Sixty-five percent of the children were identified as *securely attached.* Using their mothers as a safe base, these children explored the toys and their environment, gravitating back to their mothers when they felt the need. Some securely attached children showed distress at separation, while others did not. Many securely attached parents negotiated a peaceful separation from their babies. All secure infants greeted their mothers happily when they returned or stayed close to the mother during play. All securely attached babies were clearly more interested in their mothers than in the stranger.

insecure/avoidance attachment
according to Ainsworth, children who do not miss parents when they leave and actually avoid them when they return

2. Twenty-five percent of the sample, called *insecure/avoidant children,* rarely cried when their mothers left the room. When the mothers returned, these infants either ignored them or turned away without establishing contact, ignoring the mothers in the same way they ignored the stranger. Interestingly, the presence of the stranger may have been a comfort to some babies who disliked being alone. When avoidant babies were picked up by their mothers, they did not cuddle, cling, *or* resist.

ambivalent attachment
in Ainsworth's scheme, children who display a blend of contact-seeking and contact-resisting behavior

3. A few children in the sample (15%) were characterized as *ambivalently attached.* These infants became extremely upset when their mothers left the room, but took no comfort in their return, squirming to get down or pushing the mother away. These infants show a mix of contact-seeking and angry, contact-resisting behavior.

disorganized/disoriented attachment
either use contradictory approach-avoidance strategies or lack a consistent attachment strategy with their parent

Main and Solomon (1989) propose a fourth attachment category, *disorganized/disoriented.* Children in this category display contradictory strategies (strong avoidance followed by proximity seeking, for example) or seemed dazed and lacked a coherent strategy (or both). About 13% of Main and Solomon's middle-class sample could be classified as disorganized/disoriented.

Attachment status stabilizes between 12.5 and 19.5 months of age (Thompson & Lamb, 1984). Attachment status in premature and seriously ill newborns cannot be reliably predicted from days of neonatal intensive care, parental visiting patterns, birth weight, Bayley Developmental scores, or gestational age at birth (Rode et al., 1982). Instead, high risk babies seem resilient in forming attachments, responding more to the quality of the parent–infant interactions over time.

Caregiver Style and Attachment

Caregiver style influences the security of attachment. Mothers of securely attached infants tend to be more gentle, more sensitive, and more available than mothers of ambivalent or avoidant babies (Kiser et al., 1986). The securely attached infants behaved as though they trusted their mothers and had confidence in them to meet their needs. In one study, maternal sensitivity predicted the quality of infant–parent attachment 94% of the time (Smith & Pederson, 1988). Interestingly, it's not necessarily harder for mothers to form secure attachments to difficult children than to easy children (Vaughn et al., 1989).

Mothers of insecure/avoidant babies, on the other hand, seemed to dislike close physical contact, withheld their emotions, were angrier, more negative, and more depressed than other mothers (Zaslow et al., 1988). Some mothers of avoidant babies lacked good parenting skills. More often, however, poor parent–child relations are due to stress-induced attention problems. Mothers who live with high levels of stress are distracted and not in synchrony with the cues offered by their child's behavior (Wahler & Dumas, 1989).

Many ambivalent babies may have been difficult newborns who cried a lot, were generally negative and withdrawn, were unable to adapt easily, and were more likely to be abused or neglected (Waters, et al., 1980; Schneider-Rosen, et al., 1985). When family conditions change (e.g., increased stress), the quality of the attachment may change, too, and infants may become more insecure or ambivalent (Vaughn et al., 1989). These same insecure/ambivalent children may become the preschoolers who display aggressive and disruptive behavior at school in an attempt to attract the attention of an unresponsive adult (Moses, 1989).

Attachment and Social Development

The quality of infant–parent attachment has implications for later social development. Joffe & Vaughn (1982) found that by age 2 securely attached infants tend to respond more positively toward unfamiliar people than infants who are less securely attached. Securely attached infants are also more likely to explore their environments and to develop a nonantagonistic relationship with an older sibling (Teti & Ablard, 1989). At age 3.5, children identified as securely attached during infancy are more likely to be identified as peer leaders and to be actively involved in their surroundings, because they demonstrate greater personal competence than others and gain peer approval. Other long-term differences between securely attached and insecurely attached infants are summarized in Table 7–6.

■ **Table 7–6**   *Some Differences Between Securely and Insecurely Attached Children*

Sociability with peers. Up through age 5 or 6 (the latest ages studied), securely attached children show consistently higher rates of social behaviors and greater popularity with peers.

Self-esteem. Securely attached children have higher self-esteem at age 4 to 5.

Flexibility and resourcefulness. Securely attached children rate higher in these aspects of "ego resiliency" at age 4 and 5.

Dependency. Insecurely attached children show more clinging attention seeking from a teacher as well as "negative attention seeking" (getting attention by being "bad") in preschool years.

Tantrums and aggressive behavior. Insecurely attached children show more of this behavior.

Compliance and good deportment. Securely attached children are easier to manage in the classroom and at home. They require less discipline.

Empathy. Secure children show more empathy toward other children and toward adults. They also do not show pleasure on seeing others' distress, which is fairly common among avoidant children.

Behavior problems. At age 6, behavior problems are more common among boys who were insecurely attached as infants; no such pattern has been found for girls.

Self-recognition. At age 2, insecurely attached children show earlier and more complete self-recognition (in a mirror test), suggesting that individuation and attachment may be somewhat reciprocal processes at this age.

Sociability with a strange adult. As preschoolers, securely attached children show faster and smoother interaction with a strange adult.

Problem solving. Securely attached toddlers show longer attention spans in free play. They are more confident in attempting solutions to tasks involving tool use, and they use the mother more effectively as a source of assistance.

Symbolic play. At age 18 to 30 months, secure children show more mature and complex play.

Source: From *The Developing Child*, Fifth Ed. by Helen Bee. © 1989 by Harper & Row, Publishers, Inc. Reprinted by permission of HarperCollins Publishers.

Reactions to Separation

Employed Mothers

Since 1987 more women with 1 year old infants have chosen to work outside the home than to stay home with their babies (Bureau of Labor Statistics, 1987). Thus, the *majority* of young infants in the United States now receive alternative care. Lay and professional people alike have asked if day care weakens the infant's attachment to the mother and if it affects aspects of the infant's behavior or development adversely. After studying dozens of infants between 3 and 29 months of age in various settings, researchers have concluded that the impact of day care on attachment and child development is contingent on several factors (Belsky, 1988; Clarke-Stewart, 1988; Sroufe, 1988):

No Undesirable Effects of Day Care:	Complications Stemming From Day Care:
Child securely attached to caregiver*	Insecure/ambivalent attachment
Child from stable family	Child from unstable family
High quality daycare	Poor quality daycare
Good fit between mother's personality and baby's temperament	Poor fit between mother's personality and baby's temperament
Mother sensitive, responsive to baby	Mother less responsive, unresponsive
Child (especially boys) receives less than 35 hours of day care per week	Child (especially boys) receives more than 35 hours of day care per week
Low family stress	High family stress
High marital satisfaction	Low marital satisfaction
Mother is warm, accepting, and positive	Mother is not warm or accepting or positive
Placement in day care: prior to 6 months of age between 12 and 18 months after 2.5 years of age	Placement in day care: between 6 and 12 months of age
Mom prefers employment	Mom ambivalent or negative about employment

*Secure attachment is the most important of these factors.

In the final analysis, day care can be not only an acceptable experience, but enriching and stimulating, where the quality of care is optimal, when infants and their working mothers have warm, synchronous relationships, when family stress is minimal, and when children are placed in day care prior to 6 months of age (Clarke-Stewart, 1989; Hoffman, 1989). High quality day care has even been found to have a positive long-term effect on children's social competence, happiness, and assertiveness (Vandell et al., 1988). For some guidelines in selecting high quality day care for young children, see the Toward Effective Parenting feature at the end of this chapter.

Separation of Days or Weeks

Infants receiving short-term hospital care or who are placed with unfamiliar caregivers for a few days to a few weeks often seem distressed and unsettled after being reunited with their parents. They often display a curious combination of approach and avoidant behavior. Also, in these circumstances attention-seeking behavior such as tantrums, hitting, or

■ **Figure 7–12**

A three-year-old girl being dropped off at day care.

biting might become more frequent. All of this is usually upsetting to parents who have been anticipating a joyous reunion and a happy re-establishment of routine. Instead, they find a child who is both angry and hostile about being abandoned and having her routine disrupted (Ainsworth, 1982). Here are some suggestions for preventing or minimizing such reactions:

1. Having someone familiar stay with the child can be a tremendous comfort to a baby who is hurting, scared, or confused. If the baby is in the hospital, policy generally permits 24-hour access to the child.
2. If possible, avoid hospitalization between 6 months and 4 years of age. Younger children have more adverse reactions to hospitalization than older ones. Day-care procedures are less traumatic than inpatient surgery when minor treatment is required.
3. If hospitalization is necessary and the parent can't be with the child on a continuous basis, leave something that reminds the child of the parent. A soft article of clothing (a sweater, a knitted scarf) might be best since it is soft to the touch and carries the parent's scent.
4. In the hospital, keep visitors to a minimum since the child needs to rest in order to heal. Too much commotion and too many people may be distressing rather than enjoyable.
5. Prolonged and/or repeated hospitalization or institutional placement increases the chances of problems later on.
6. Children who return to stable families after separation lower their risk of problem behaviors.
7. Be sure to let any special attachment items (such as pillows, pacifiers, stuffed toys, blankets, and the like) accompany the child during the separation.

Most of the negative effects that arise after brief separation (like sleep disturbance, aggression, or incontinence) subside within 6 months (Yap, 1988). Accommodations for families are sometimes available near primary-treatment hospitals or clinics. For example, Ronald McDonald House is a nationwide chain of shelters for families of critically ill children. In operation since the late 1970s, these houses allow parents to stay close to their children for the duration of the treatment. They are funded by donations from parents and contributions from the McDonald Foundation.

Separation of Weeks or Months

When an infant between 8 months and 3 years of age is left by the mother for several weeks to several months, a predictable pattern of behavior emerges. In observing children placed in foster care, John Bowlby (1973, 1980) found that their reactions to separation fell into three sequential phases: protest, despair, and detachment. During the *protest* phase, the child shows acute distress and often searches for mother—behaviors that reflect separation distress. After a variable period of time, protest gives way to *despair*, the second phase. The despairing child is quiet and withdrawn. This phase suggests a period of mourning, grief, and acknowledgement of loss. *Detachment* follows despair. During detachment, the child becomes more active and interested in the environment and begins to smile, talk, and socialize again. Such a child will accept care from a variety of caregivers and displays little interest when placed with someone new. On the surface, the child seems to have adjusted and returned to normal, having working through the initial shock and depression. In actuality, a striking change has occurred in the child's orientation to her primary caregiver—the child has completely lost interest in the mother as a person. The child is no longer excited by visits from the mother and is distant and apathetic in her presence. Although the child has an avid interest in the gifts mother brings, *she* is no longer the special person she once was to the child. In some cases the attachment relationship that was originally established may reappear with time.

Does this fundamental change in parent–infant relations affect the child's later behavior? One long-term consequence of deprivation or disrupted attachment in infancy seems to be difficulty in establishing or maintaining interpersonal relations in adulthood (Ainsworth, 1973). Psychoanalytic theorists speculate that chronic loneliness in adulthood could have its roots in insecure or unfulfilled attachment in infancy and childhood (Hojat, 1987). Two factors may be responsible for this outcome: first, individuals with prolonged separation experiences may be reluctant to trust others to care for them since that trust was violated by the separation; second, an attitude of mistrust may create a lack of attachment opportunities and thus provide little practice in learning to love or care for others.

It is important to note that an infant's reaction to long-term separation depends on factors like the characteristics of the alternative care and the child's personality. Under certain conditions, temporary separation from parents in the context of a positive environment can actually be helpful in the development of social assurance and independence (Lamb, 1978). Negative reactions are more likely among children who are emotionally vulnerable to stress and deprivation (Rutter, 1983).

Permanent Separation: Death and Loss

There is very little research on the reactions of infants and toddlers to death and other permanent loss (Sroufe, 1986). We do know that the child should be told of the loss in language she can understand and should be placed in the care of others who are familiar and nurturant. A child may respond to the caregiver's continued absence by yearning for that person and refusing to allow others to take over the caregiving role ("Only my momma can hug me"), by asking questions and talking incessantly about the missing person, and by insisting on repeating activities enjoyed with the dead parent (e.g., walks, reading favorite books). The child might also become concerned that the remaining parent or substitute caregiver will disappear and may react more intensely than normal to brief separations from that person.

Reversing the Negative Effects of Separation

Early separation from one or both parents can lead to psychiatric or behavioral disturbance for the child, particularly if the family is experiencing stress and the separation exceeds 4 consecutive weeks (Rutter, 1983). Fortunately, the negative effects of separation aren't necessarily permanent. In a remarkable account of trauma and separation, Anna Freud (Sigmund Freud's daughter) and Sophie Dann (1951) describe the behavior of six 3–4 year olds who were found together in the Nazi concentration camp at Tereszin, orphaned since infancy. Freud and Dann established a refuge for concentration camp survivors at Bulldogs Bank, England, in 1945.

When the children first arrived at the refuge, they were wild, uncontrolled, and extremely hostile toward adults. Toward each other, however, they were kind, generous, and caring. The children would comfort each other and share their food and clothing even if it meant being hungry or cold themselves. The children were each other's constant companions, resisting separation even on a temporary basis.

Over time they warmed to the adults who were caring for them and learned to interact with others outside their own group. As adults, these children were effective and competent, showing virtually no signs of maladjustment, deficiency, or disengagement (Hartup, 1983). Apparently, the orphan's strong mutual attachments helped insulate them from the loss of their families and the horror of the concentration camp by substituting for the attention they had originally invested in their parents.

An equally remarkable report of early separation trauma comes from an American "Foundling Home" in the late 1930s. Harold Skeels (1942) assessed the status of 25 orphans age 1–2 years and found them to be in good health but severely developmentally delayed. He arranged to have 13 of the most profoundly retarded infants transferred to an institute for retarded women where each child would be placed in the care of a "foster mother." By the time the transferred infants were 3–4 years old, they had achieved nearly normal intellectual status and surpassed their counterparts who stayed in the orphanage in all aspects of development. (The children who stayed at the Home actually *lost* IQ points). Apparently, the attention, devotion, and stimulation provided by the retarded foster mothers was responsible for this incredible reversal since babies left in the orphanage received very little in the way of affection or human interaction. Eventually, 11 of the 13 transferred children were adopted, compared to 8 of 12 of the children who remained in the orphanage. As adults, all of the transferred individuals (including the two who had not been adopted) were self-supporting, half had completed high school, and four had taken college coursework. No such independence or academic prowess was found among the adult foundling home residents (Skeels, 1966).

Taken together these two studies offer hope of reversing the trauma of parent–child separation in the first 2 years of life. When orphaned infants are permitted immediate and sustained contact with other children or adults, the stress of separation is reduced as new attachments are formed.

The Consequences of Insecure Attachment: Detachment, Neglect, Abuse

A mismatch between the parents' skill and the baby's needs can interfere with the development of attachment. Stress, emotional problems, and lack of experience or knowledge may prevent parents from accurately interpreting the baby's cues or deriving pleasure from interactions with their infant. Children with special needs may pose additional challenges. For example, blind, retarded, or premature babies have difficulty playing an active role in parent–infant interactions, ignoring parents' attempts to establish eye contact, smiling less, and not showing mutual gaze (Blanchard & Meyers, 1983). After several weeks or months of trying to provoke an appropriate response, parents may conclude their child is rejecting them or that the baby is moody, depressed, or difficult and the quality of care they provide may diminish. The child may react in turn by avoiding contact with the parent or turning away or crying when held. If this negative cycle continues and the parent's attachment does not develop fully, neglect or abuse may result. Reports of child abuse and neglect have been increasing steadily in the past decade.

Physical or Emotional Neglect

The neglected child is deprived of the physical, medical, and/or emotional care necessary for growth (Wolock & Horowitz, 1984). Babies are allowed to starve, freeze, or burn to death by their parents or sustain injuries or death because the parents won't supervise or provide for the child. Neglectful parents are apathetic, irresponsible, and apparently unable to create a warm, safe, nurturant environment for their children (Casey et al., 1984).

neglect
failure to provide proper attention or support

EMOTIONAL NEGLECT: NONORGANIC FAILURE TO THRIVE Emotional neglect involves withholding love, affection, and positive attention from the child. Parents who neglect their child's emotional needs often resent their babies, have trouble feeding them, and were neglected themselves as infants (Altemeir et al., 1985). The parents may have difficulty relating to their infant because they were disappointed by her appearance or behavior, or because their interactions with the child are frustrating

■ ● ▲   CONCEPT SUMMARY

Characteristics of Nonorganic Failure to Thrive (NOFTT)

- Developmental delays (language, motor skills, etc.)
- Severe physical growth retardation
- Resists social contact
- Resists physical contact
- No eye contact
- Shows no signs of contentment when cuddled or hugged
- Never display fear of strangers
- May refuse food

■ **Figure 7–13**

A 5-year-old child who weighs 13 pounds. She did not thrive because her parents failed to give her the attention she needed.

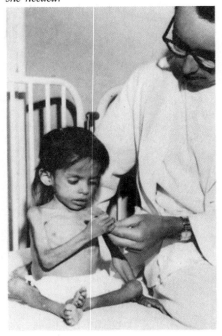

and nonreinforcing. Lack of synchrony is usually apparent. The mother may report that the baby seems uninterested in her and dissatisfied by her attempts to offer care. Typically, these mothers have trouble perceiving and assessing their infant's needs. For example, they may be unable to distinguish hunger cries from cries indicating pain or general unhappiness. Since they usually do not know what behavior to anticipate as their child develops, they cannot provide appropriate stimulation (Newton, 1983). Hospitalization is often necessary to stabilize the infant's poor health. When parents continue to be insecurely attached to their infants, the rehospitalization rate is higher than if a secure attachment was formed (Rinich et al., 1989).

Emotional neglect results in *nonorganic failure to thrive (NOFTT),* a condition marked by severe growth retardation and developmental delays (Singer, 1986). Failure-to-thrive children also display a characteristic posture and social orientation. They resist contact with others by stiffening their bodies and becoming rigid or by becoming limp and floppy. They also do not mold to the holder's body, do not maintain eye contact, and do not show signs of contentment or satisfaction when they are finally cuddled or cared for. They don't fear strangers at the time when stranger avoidance is normal (Whaley & Wong, 1988). Some researchers suggest that an infantile form of anorexia nervosa (an eating disorder involving food refusal) may be responsible for the NOFTT seen in neglected babies (Chatoor, 1989).

PHYSICAL ABUSE Although not as common as neglect, physical abuse involves actively rather than passively hurting a child. The *battered child syndrome,* first identified in 1962, describes a vicious cycle of abuse in families and alerted professionals to be wary of "accidental" injuries, especially where scars and X rays indicated a history of trauma (Kempe & Helfer, 1980). Children, especially boys and special-needs and unwanted children, between the ages of 3 months and 3 years are particularly vulnerable. There are 2,000 deaths per year from physical abuse and tens of thousands of children who suffer lasting damage from abuse (Straus & Gelles, 1986). What kinds of people physically torture, maim, or kill their own child? The characteristics of abusive parents include:

■ **Figure 7–14**

A victim of child abuse.

1. They are isolated—have no social support system.
2. They have persistent negative moods (depressed, lonely, unhappy).
3. They are under stress (have marital problems, are under- or unemployed, and so forth).
4. Ten percent of abusive parents are mentally ill or criminally insane (thus in 90% of abusers, there is no mental illness or criminal personality).
5. These parents feel powerless to control their lives.
6. They believe in the appropriateness of physical punishment for children, even infants.
7. They were mistreated/rejected by their own parents.
8. They do not know how to be good parents.
9. They have unrealistic expectations about children:

   - feel children can raise themselves
   - feel children exist to satisfy their parent's needs, not vice versa
   - are ignorant of normal child development
   - feel children are little adults in terms of their capabilities (i.e., they should always stay neat and clean; should help; shouldn't wet the bed, and on and on)

10. Such parents report being more annoyed and less sympathetic when their babies cry.
11. They misread their baby's cries (e.g., feed them when they are in pain) (Kropp & Haynes, 1987).
12. Many have at least 4 children.
13. Sixty percent of these parents are from low-income families (economic deprivation seems to lead single-parent mothers to be abusive; income is unrelated to abuse in single-father homes—Gelles, 1989).

nonorganic failure to thrive (NOFTT)
a collection of symptoms associated with significantly delayed growth in children caused by emotional deprivation and neglect rather than direct physical abuse

battered child syndrome
the cycle of abuse that leads ⅓ of those who were abused to abuse others

Both men and women are implicated in physical abuse. Young parents (under 25 years of age) are no more likely than older parents (over age 25) to abuse their children, but when they do, the abuse is generally more severe.

A child who survives abusive assaults is likely to grow into a very hostile and aggressive individual. Abuse never corrects the child's behavior, as discipline can, since it is usually harsh, inconsistent, and not specifically tied to the child's behavior. Such treatment is related to later

■●▲ CONCEPT SUMMARY

Some Long Terms Consequences of Physical Abuse

- Delinquency
- Resistance to authority
- Aggressive/hostile behavior
- Depression
- Roughly 1 abuse victim in 3 will later abuse their own children
- Low self-esteem

delinquency, resistance to authority, and continued aggression. Thus, abuse produces the very behavior it is sometimes initiated to suppress. Abuse is most traumatic if the nonabusive parent is unsupportive of the child, if the child has suffered repeated abuse, or if the child is removed from the home (Bryer et al., 1987). Two-thirds of abused children grow up to take good care of their own children but one-third become abusive themselves (Kaufman & Zigler, 1987). This means that repeating the cycle of abuse is not inevitable for those experiencing abuse as children, but some risk does exist.

Preventing Abuse Most abusive parents are not malicious or mentally ill. They are normal individuals pushed beyond their ability to cope. In their own way they love their children and regret their actions but they cannot control their behavior. Ruth and Henry Kempe (1978) believe that 80% of abusive parents can be taught nonviolent ways of reacting to their children. The following recommendations can be helpful in breaking the cycle of abuse:

1. All people who come in contact with children must be alert to the physical and behavioral signs of abuse and neglect (Table 7–7).
2. An around-the-clock crisis nursery or "relief parents" can provide a place for parents who are losing control to drop off their children for a few hours.
3. Government subsidized day care to take the financial strain off parents who must work but cannot afford day care.
4. Providing information about child development.
5. Making family planning services affordable and readily available so every child is a wanted child.
6. Providing training in nonviolent child-management strategies.
7. Offering individual and family therapy to those who may require long-term help.

■ **Table 7–7** *Symptoms of Abuse and Neglect*

These symptoms should be interpreted as warning signs. They signal the need for additional investigation or attention. They do not automatically indicate abuse or neglect.

SYMPTOMS OF ABUSE	SYMPTOMS OF NEGLECT
Evidence of repeated injury	Clothing inappropriate for weather
New injuries before previous ones have healed	Torn, tattered, unwashed clothing
	Poor skin hygiene
Frequent complaints of abdominal pain	Rejection by other children because of body odor
Evidence of bruises	
Bruises of different ages	Need for glasses, dental work, hearing aid, or other health services
Welts	
Wounds, cuts, or punctures	Lack of proper nourishment
Scalding liquid burns with well-defined parameters	Consistent tiredness or sleepiness in class
Caustic burns	Consistent, very early school arrival
Frostbite	Frequent absenteeism or chronic tardiness
Cigarette burns	
	Tendency to hang around school after dismissal

Source: W. H. Berdine and A. E. Blackhurst, *An Introduction to Special Education*, Second Ed. © 1985 by William H. Berdine and A. Edward Blackhurst. Reprinted by permission of HarperCollins Publishers.

8. Actively working toward reducing the acceptance of physical punishment in particular and violence in general.
9. Because premature infants are at risk for abuse, reducing the incidence of prematurity by providing good prenatal care for all pregnant women.
10. Banning the use of corporeal punishment in schools.

● **Children in Families**

Infants' social and emotional growth is influenced not only by their parents, but also by their place in the family and the existence of any sisters or brothers. In this section, we will consider the effects of the family context.

Sibling Relationships

More than 80% of American children have siblings or age peers who live within the same family (cousins, stepchildren, or others). Since siblings share a unique relationship by virtue of their common genetic and

■ Figure 7–15

"James, watch this!"

socialization

the process through which the beliefs, attitudes, and behavioral expectations of the culture are transmitted

social background, sibling relationships are among the most enduring and influential in people's lives (Hay, 1985). These relationships are not necessarily happy ones, however. Personality differences between siblings as well as the number, sex, spacing, and birth order of siblings can influence their interactions and affect each child's development. Children between the ages of 2 and 10 seem most susceptible to sibling influence.

Even very young siblings can provide attention, companionship, and comfort for each other (Banks & Kahn, 1982). Infants who have a brother or sister present with them at nursery school are less distressed than other children without siblings when parents drop them off (Dunn, 1985). Babies generally begin interacting with older siblings after they are 6 months old and by the time they have their first birthday spend as much time with brothers and sisters and with the primary caregiver (Dunn & Kendrick, 1982). Younger siblings frequently imitate the behavior of older siblings. By age 2 the younger ones have learned to reciprocate the loving, comforting, teasing, and annoying offered by older brothers and sisters (Dunn, 1983).

Socialization

Parents play an important role in helping children control their behavior and behave in ways society considers acceptable. This process is known as *socialization*. One means of socializing the child, *discipline*, involves instructing or guiding the child to make more appropriate choices. The issue of discipline becomes more important as the baby's mobility increases. By the child's second year, the child is able to comply with parent requests/instructions and so discipline begins in earnest (Maccoby & Martin, 1983). Most discipline is related to exploration and play activities; biological functions such as eating, toileting, and sleeping; or issues such as sexual curiosity, dependency, and aggression (Lunde & Lunde, 1980). Early on, parents do well to create a safe environment for the baby by removing breakable objects, locking any cabinets, and blocking stairways rather than imposing verbal prohibitions that a child may or may not understand.

The emotional climate of the family, *warm vs. hostile*, sets the tone for socialization practices. Warmth involves the open expressing of caring and affection for the child, being responsive to the child's needs, sensitive to the child's feelings, and enthusiastic about the child's activities (Maccoby, 1980). Hostile parents are emotionally cold, rejecting, and distant. Not surprisingly, the child is more responsive to warm parents than hostile parents, thus increasing the effectiveness of discipline in loving, caring homes. In general parents most successful in training competent, responsive children (Swick & Hassell, 1990):

1. Enjoy their children
2. Talk to children at a level they can understand
3. Value their child's ability to learn and explore more than they value a clean or tidy house
4. Set reasonable limits on their child's behavior
5. Encourage safety but are not overly restrictive or overly protective
6. Are busy and happy as parents and adults

Reinforcement and *punishment* form the foundation of any child guidance program. A reinforcer is anything the child finds pleasant or satisfying. Reinforcement can be tangible (e.g., money, candy, a hug) or intangible (e.g., love, or feelings of satisfaction). Punishment is anything the child finds unpleasant or aversive. There are tangible punishments (like spanking) and intangible ones (like guilt, shame, feelings of incompetence). Reinforcement strengthens and punishment weakens the behavior they follow because they teach the child about the consequences of his actions.

Child Guidance Strategies: Reward and Punishment

PUNISHMENT Where toddlers are concerned, guidance usually involves saying, "No" when they do something they are not supposed to do. Even though toddler's understanding is limited, it is a good practice to give a short, firm, immediate explanation for the prohibition ("You'll get hurt" or "It will break" or some such), to remove the child from the area, and to provide the child with something safe to play with. Delayed, long, gentle reprimands are less effective in promoting compliance (Pfiffner & O'Leary, 1989). As children gain more and more responsibility over their behavior, they can begin to face the logical consequences of their actions ("If you spill your milk on purpose, I won't refill your glass and you might be thirsty.") Some parents use physical punishment when they discipline—for instance, following "no" with a slap or a spank. The pros and cons of physical punishment are addressed in the accompanying issue.

The child's reaction to imminent punishment can actually affect the caregiver's response. Children who are defiant or who ignore the punishing adult are more likely to receive severe punishment. On the other hand, children who act remorseful or who try to make up for their misdeeds are often not punished at all and may even be subtly rewarded by caregivers (Sawin et al., 1975).

REWARD/REINFORCEMENT In many homes children do not receive attention until their behavior needs correction. Tantruming, aggression, or defiance all attract the parent's attention and provoke harsh words, time out, or other punishing responses, whereas appropriate and desir-

▶ ▶   **I S S U E**   ◀ ◀

Should Parents Spank Their Children?

American parents have spanked their children since colonial times. Even today, over 80% of parents report spanking their children at home when they misbehave. However, most professionals contend that spanking is not a good idea, for these reasons:

1. *Spanking can lead to child abuse.* Physical punishment can hurt a child if it is carried out with excessive force when parents are angry or out of control. Even though the majority of parents do not intend to harm their child during spanking, many do.

2. *Spanking provides an aggressive model.* The adult who spanks a child is condoning the use of force and aggression in interpersonal interactions. Children who are spanked by parents are more likely to hit peers, playmates, and later their own partners and children than children whose parents do not use physical punishment in discipline.

3. *Spanking can lower the child's self-esteem.* A spanking may humiliate a child or confuse him if it is used unconsistently. A spanked child often feels angry at the punisher for striking him and may be reluctant to trust a person who can be so volatile.

4. *Spanking trains the child to avoid the punisher.* Many parents warn, "Don't let me catch you doing that again." The child is all too willing to comply with that demand. For example, a child who is spanked for hitting (an interesting paradox in itself) may simply become more discreet about when, where, and even whom they hit. Although they may not hit in the presence of the spanking adult, they may hit freely outside the home or when parents are not watching.

5. *Spanking loses its effectiveness when applied inconsistently or excessively.* Spanking a child to stop

A toddler being spanked with a kitchen spoon.

a dangerous behavior (like running into the street) can be effective if it is immediate and sufficiently novel to attract the child's attention. However, children who are spanked for every minor misdeed will come to ignore the spankings and do whatever they please. "After all," they might conclude, "if I get spanked for everything, I may as well do what I want."

Currently, 41 states have laws forbidding the use of spanking (corporeal punishment) in schools, foster homes, and group care facilities. The exceptions are Alabama, Idaho, Indiana, Michigan, Mississippi, Ohio, South Carolina, Tennessee, and Wyoming (Lipsitt, 1987).

able behavior such as cooperation or quiet play appears to go unnoticed. Consider the following exchange between a parent and a toddler:

CHILD: Momma, drink.
MOTHER: [No answer]

CHILD: Momma, want drink.
MOTHER: Uh, huh.
CHILD: Drink, peez.
MOTHER: Just a minute.
CHILD: [after several minutes] Drink, drink, drink. . .
MOTHER: [No answer]
CHILD: [more intensely] Drink! Drink!
MOTHER: In a second.
CHILD: [Screams, cries, hits, etc.]
MOTHER: [shouting] Is that really necessary? I told you I'd get
           it, didn't I? [Handing the child a drink]. I don't know
           why you have to act like this!

Well, we do. The mother ignored all the child's reasonable requests, even the one using "peez" (please). Since the child received a drink only after screaming and crying, that is the approach he will more likely take the next time he is thirsty. It was the screaming and crying that were reinforced, not the patient, polite asking.

Caregivers who conscientiously reinforce desirable behavior report an increased incidence of pleasant, cooperative behavior from their children. It really doesn't take much effort to say, "You're playing so nicely!" or "That's really good!" or "Thanks for helping me," or to give a pat or a hug. When children learn that they can consistently get the attention they need by behaving nicely or doing what's expected of them, they won't need to misbehave for attention. Parents who can "catch their children being good" don't end up having to spend so much time "catching their children being bad."

The key to positive child guidance is the use of *effective* discipline. For guidelines to help improve disciplinary effectiveness, see the accompanying feature.

The Development of Self-Control

At first, the environment provides feedback about acceptable/unacceptable actions. The child behaves in a trial-and-error fashion, receiving both positive and negative reinforcement for his actions. Once memory develops the child is able to internalize these prescriptions and apply them to himself. *Self-regulation,* or *self-control,* develops as children become increasingly self-aware and have more efficient memories and improved understanding of the world around them. A child who has had an encounter with the stove, for example, may say "Hot, hot" whenever he ventures by it. By reminding himself of his previous experience, the child can avoid future distress, embarrassment, or even injury. Children whose mothers rely on physical punishment are less likely to develop self-control than toddlers whose mothers "babyproof" their environments (Power & Chapieski, 1986). When physical punishment is used, children don't *need* to learn to regulate their own behavior—they simply rely on the environment to do that for them.

A Closer Look

Strategies to Improve the Effectiveness of Discipline

Timing

In order for discipline to change behavior, it has be to clearly associated with a particular action. Initiate discipline as soon as the child misbehaves. When delays are necessary (to avoid embarrassing the child or because you are on the phone), verbally disapprove of the behavior and state that the disciplinary action will be implemented. Then, when the delay is over, remind the child of her behavior, and institute the appropriate action. ("When I was on the phone with grandma you hit Teri. We don't hit. Hitting can hurt. . . .''

Flexibility

Choose disciplinary strategies that are appropriate to the child's temperament and the severity of the misbehavior. Severe physical punishment can injure the child, can indicate the parent is out of control, and will prove no more effective over time than more moderate strategies.

Consistency

Consistency is one of the most important features of effective discipline but is also one of the hardest to achieve. Discipline is consistent if it is applied each and every time the specific behavior occurs. Behavior that is disciplined erratically persists longer than behavior that is not punished at all, because the message to the child about the parent's expectations is less clear.

Rationale

Discipline is more effective if the child knows *why* she is being punished. Short, concrete explanations are best for younger children. ("You

The development of self-regulation involves a predictable sequence of events (Kopp, 1982):

1. **PHASE 1: NEUROPHYSIOLOGICAL MODULATION (BIRTH TO 2–3 MONTHS)** Infants can sooth themselves by sucking or relying on some other inborn behavior. When overstimulated, however, such strategies may have limited effectiveness.

2. **PHASE 2: SENSORIMOTOR MODULATION (2–3 MONTHS TO 9–12 MONTHS)** Children can't yet plan to carry out purposeful activities but are aware that their actions can influence the world around them.

3. **PHASE 3: CONTROL (9–12 MONTHS AND OLDER)** Babies can consciously choose to obey or defy caregivers, indicating they are aware of environmental demands. Learning is still situation-specific: Avoiding one dangerous situation (hot stoves) does not automatically generalize to other similar hazards (hot curling irons or fireplaces).

have to go to your room because you threw a rock and rocks can hurt.")

Empathy

Discipline that comes from a warm, nurturant adult is more effective than that delivered by someone cold and aloof. Follow discipline by indicating a concern for the child's feelings: "I know you are angry because you can't play any longer. But you need to remember to be careful with other people's toys and property."

Unity

All caregivers need to share an agreed-upon approach. Without such a plan, children can become confused and alliances or hostilities can form between a child and one parent.

Commitment

Threatened punishment is only effective as the caregiver carries out the threat. If the threatened punishment is never delivered, the child's behavior is actually rewarded, since she has escaped an undesirable consequence.

Behavior orientation.

The focus of the discipline should be the child's behavior and not the child per se. Statements like "You're a bad girl" and "Nice boys don't do that" can have a destructive impact. It's more effective and accurate to say to the child, "I don't like your behavior" than to say, "I don't like you."

Privacy

Administer discipline in private, especially to older children, to respect their self-esteem and to avoid public humiliation.

Termination

Once the discipline is administered, consider the incident over. The child now has a "clean slate." Avoid bringing up the incident later or lecturing the child about it.

4. PHASE 4: SELF-CONTROL AND PROGRESSION TO SELF-REGULATION (18–24 MONTHS AND OLDER) The child now remembers the rules even though he may not choose to comply with them. True self-regulation is not possible until around age 3 when the child can delay gratification and isn't so apt to "forget" a rule or be impulsive (i.e., being so caught up in a game of chase that they forget to avoid the radiator) (Power & Chapieski, 1986). Erik Erikson's psychosocial theory (1963) suggests that the child ultimately needs to achieve a balance between self-control and control by others.

psychosocial theory
a stage level approach to development advanced by Erik Erikson that emphasizes the importance of social interaction and the environment in shaping behavior

● **Outside the Family**

Peer Interactions

Babies begin to visually recognize the presence of peers by 2 months of age. If in close proximity to each other, 3–4 month olds will touch. When

■ Figure 7–16

Even babies notice and are interested in each other, or at least in each other's ears.

babies become mobile, they will crawl after each other and by the time they are a year old, social play is possible (Ross, 1982). Toddlers watch preschoolers more often than same age peers but use more language and imitation in their play with other toddlers (Rothstein-Fisch & Howes, 1988).

As they are with siblings, toddlers are capable of both positive and negative exchanges with peers—cooperating and sharing on some occasions and hitting and grabbing on others. Peer interaction is more likely when children are already familiar with each other, when no toys or only large toys are present, when the setting is familiar, and when only one or two other infants are present rather than a large group (Hay, 1985). Conflicts between mutual friends occur just as frequently and were just as lengthy as conflicts between neutral associates but were less intense and resulted more frequently in equal or partially equal outcomes (Hartup et al., 1988).

Pretend play becomes possible as children acquire knowledge about people and are able to perceive the nature of other people's relatedness to the world (Hobson, 1990). Play is more sophisticated with mothers than with peers (Turkheimer et al., 1989).

 ■ ● ▲   CONCEPT SUMMARY

Summary of Infant Social Behavior

● *0–1 Month*
Watches parent's face intently as she or he talks to infant

- *2 Months*
  Social smile in response to various stimuli

- *3 Months*
  Much interest in surroundings
  Stops crying when parent enters room
  Recognizes familiar faces and objects, such as feeding bottle
  Aware of strange situations

- *4 Months*
  Demands attention by fussing; becomes bored if left alone
  Enjoys social interaction with people
  Anticipates feeding when sees bottle
  Shows excitement with whole body, squeals, breathes heavily
  Shows interest in strange stimuli

- *5 Months*
  Smiles at mirror image
  Pats bottle with both hands
  More enthusiastically playful, but may have rapid mood swings
  Able to discriminate strangers from family
  Vocalizes displeasure when an object is taken away

- *6 Months*
  Recognizes parents; begins to fear strangers
  Holds arms out to be picked up
  Has definite likes and dislikes
  Beginning of imitation (cough, protrusion of tongue)
  Excites on hearing footsteps
  Laughs when head is hidden in a towel
  Briefly searches for a dropped object (object permanence beginning)

- *7 Months*
  Increasing fear of strangers; shows signs of fretfulness when mother
    disappears
  Imitates simple acts and noises
  Tries to attract attention by coughing or snorting
  Plays peek–a–boo
  Demonstrates dislike of food by keeping lips closed
  Exhibits oral aggressiveness in biting and mouthing
  Demonstrates expectation in response to repetition of stimuli

- *8 Months*
  Increasing anxiety over loss of parent, particularly mother, and fear
    of strangers
  Responds to word "no"
  Dislikes dressing, diaper change

(continued on next page)

Summary of Infant Social Behavior *(continued)*

- *9 Months*
  Parent (mother) is increasingly important for own sake
  Increased interest in pleasing mother
  Begins to show fears of going to bed and being left alone
  Puts arm in front of face to avoid having face washed

- *10 Months*
  Inhibits behavior to verbal command of "no-no" or own name
  Imitates facial expressions, waves bye-bye
  Extends toy to another person but will not release it
  Looks around a corner or under a pillow for an object
  Repeats actions that attract attention and are laughed at
  Pulls clothes of another to attract attention
  Plays interactive games, such as pat-a-cake
  Reacts to adult anger, cries when scolded
  Demonstrates independence in dressing, feeding, locomotive skills,
      and testing parents
  Looks at and follows pictures in a book

- *11 Months*
  Experiences joy and satisfaction when a task is mastered
  Reacts to restrictions with frustration

- *12 Months*
  Rolls ball to another on request
  Anticipates body gestures when a familiar nursery rhyme or story is
      being told (for example, holds toes or feet in response to "This little
      piggy went to market")
  Plays game up-down, "so-big," or peek-a-boo, by covering face
  Shakes head for "no"

- *13 Months*
  Shows emotions such as jealousy, affection (may give hug or kiss on
      request), anger, fear
  Enjoys familiar surroundings and will explore away from mother
  Fearful of strange situation, clings to mother
  May develop habit of "security blanket" or favorite toy
  Unceasing determination to practice locomotor skills

- *15 Months*
  Tolerates some separation from mother
  Less likely to fear strangers
  Begins to imitate parents, such as cleaning house (sweeping, dusting,
      folding clothes)
  Feeds self using cup with little spilling

May discard bottle
Manages spoon but rotates it near mouth
Kisses and hugs parents, may kiss pictures in a book
Expresses emotions, has temper tantrums

- *18 Months*
  Great imitator ("domestic mimicry")
  Manages spoon well
  Takes off gloves, socks, and shoes and unzips
  Temper tantrums may be more evident
  Beginning awareness of ownership ("my toy")
  May develop dependency on transitional objects, such as "security blanket"

- *24 Months (2 years)*
  Stage of parallel play
  May have imaginary playmate
  Has sustained attention span
  Temper tantrums decreasing
  Pulls people to show them something
  Increased independence from mother
  Dresses self in simple clothing

- *30 Months (2½ years)*
  Separates more easily from mother
  In play, helps put things away, can carry breakable objects, pushes with good steering
  Begins to notice sex differences; knows own sex
  May attend to toilet needs without help except for wiping

- *36 Months (3 years)*
  Dresses self almost completely if helped with back buttons and told which shoe is right or left
  Buttons and unbuttons accessible buttons
  Pulls on shoes
  Has increased attention span
  Feeds self completely
  Pours from a bottle or pitcher
  Can prepare simple meals, such as cold cereal and milk
  Can help to set table, dry dishes without breaking any
  Likes to "help" entertain by passing around food
  May have fears, especially of dark and going to bed
  Knows own sex and appropriate sex of others
  In play, parallel and associative phase; begins to learn simple games and meaning of rules, but follows them according to self-interpretation; speaks to doll, animal, truck, and so on; begins to

(continued on next page)

Summary of Infant Social Behavior *(continued)*

work out social interaction through play; able to share toys, although expresses idea of "mine" frequently

Attempts to please parents and conform to their expectations

Is less jealous of younger sibling; may be opportune time for birth of additional sibling

Is aware of family relationships and sex role functions

Boys tend to identify more with father or other male figure

Has increased ability to separate easily and comfortably from parents for short periods

Source: Whaley & Wong, 1982.

TOWARD EFFECTIVE PARENTING

alternative care
child care provided by someone other than the child's parents

Selecting High Quality Childcare

Selecting appropriate alternative care is one of the most important decisions parents will make in behalf of their children. Generally, two types of alternative care are available to families with young children. *Homecare* is provided in the home of a substitute caregiver who is often a mother with children of her own. Homecare providers must be licensed by the state, but licensing requirements vary widely throughout the country. *Childcare centers* are established settings where children are cared for in a group while away from home. Accreditation guidelines have been established by the National Academy of Early Childhood Programs.

The following guidelines can help parents evaluate particular settings:

Is the substitute caregiver/staff

- well trained in child development
- responsible and mature
- experienced
- flexible
- energetic
- warm and loving
- respectful toward children
- supportive and encouraging toward children
- sensitive to the child's needs
- cognizant of individual differences among children
- able to shift caregiver practices as the child grows
- well trained in emergency first aid and CPR
- happy with their work
- stable (in terms of job turnover)
- hygenic (do they wash hands before and after contacting each child, after diaper changes, and so forth)

Is the physical setting

- clean and well maintained
- in compliance with safety codes
  - smoke detectors
  - fire extinguishers
  - covers on electrical outlets
  - marked emergency exits
- big enough to handle the children present, or is it crowded
- well-lit
- structurally sound
- appropriately warmed and cooled
- equipped with age-appropriate toys and games
- equipped with age-appropriate furniture
- equipped to handle injured or sick children
- equipped with outdoor equipment that is surrounded with sand or mulch to pad falls
- attractive and pleasing
- equipped with adequate restroom, rest, and kitchen facilities
- fenced

Is the child's day

- filled with more than unstructured play and TV watching
- planned around both group and individual activities
- scheduled to provide flexibility and choice
- varied and interesting, including quiet activities, art, imaginative play, small muscle skills, and large muscle skills
- filled with praise and encouragement
- filled with age-appropriate activities
- properly supervised

Are the policies and procedures

- clearly articulated
- reasonable and well considered
- applied consistently, without bias or discrimination
- open to discussion or modification
- designed to promote trust and openness
- careful to condemn physical punishment or other harsh treatment
- designed to encourage parent involvement and participation
- protective of the children

● Chapter Summary

- Within the first few months of life, infants are able to display basic emotions (i.e., happiness, anger, sadness, fear, surprise, and disgust) and to experience the feelings these emotions suggest. Infants attend to vocal and visual emotional cues in others. They also learn how and under what circumstances emotions may be expressed.

- Learning theorists, ethologists, and cognitive developmentalists offer theories about the origins and function of infant emotions. An organizational model of emotional development is also presented.
- Temperament—or individual differences in the type, intensity, and duration of emotional reactions—influences the development of social relationships and personality. Genetic predispositions to respond may be modified by the environment. Some traits remain stable throughout infancy and early childhood.
- Self-awareness emerges between 15 and 18 months of age. The self-concept does not begin develop until age 3 or 4.
- Attachments, or close emotional ties, are formed between infants and parents during the first year of life. The process is a reciprocal one that follows a predictable pattern. Several factors influence the depth and stability of infant–parent and parent–infant attachments. By age 2.5 attachments may have generalized to include inanimate objects and/or pets.
- The mechanisms of feeding (psychoanalytic theory), reinforcement (learning theory/behaviorism), and survival (ethological theory) have all been proposed to account for the development of attachment.
- Attachments can be identified as secure, insecure/avoidance, ambivalent, or disorganized/disoriented. The quality of attachment influences caregiving style and later social development.
- How infants adjust to separations of hours, days, weeks, or longer depends on several factors including the infant's temperament, the quality of the infant–parent relationship, and the alternative care arrangements. When infants are orphaned, new attachments reduce the stress of the loss.
- If a secure infant–parent attachment does not exist, infants are at risk for neglect and abuse.
- The quality of sibling interactions during infancy varies as a function of individual needs and temperament styles of the involved children as well as the emotional tone and stability of the family.
- Socialization begins during infancy as caregivers train the child to behave in ways society considers acceptable. True self-control isn't possible until the child is 3 years of age or older.
- Infants can recognize their peers and engage in social play.

Observational Exercise

Like adults, babies employ different strategies to gain the attention of people around them. These strategies sometimes reflect the child's basic temperament, but are often maintained because they are successful.

Procedure: Observe two different 12–18 month old infants on different occasions.

1. What behaviors on the part of the children prompt adult attention?
2. What does each baby seem to need?
3. Does any shared interaction take place when the caregiver attends to the child?
4. Why do you think the baby uses the particular attention-getting strategies you observe?

● Recommended Readings

Balter, L. (1988). *Who's in control? Dr. Balter's guide to discipline without combat.* New York: Simon & Schuster.

Bank, S. P., & Kahn, M. D. (1982). *The sibling bond.* New York: Basic Books.

Brazelton, T. B. (1983). *Infants and mothers: Differences in development* (rev. ed.). New York: Delta/Seymour Lawrence.

Brazelton, T. B. (1981). *On becoming a family: The growth of attachment.* New York: Delacorte.

Kempe, R. S., & Kempe, C. H. (1985). *Child abuse* (8th ed.). Cambridge, MA: Harvard Univ. Press.

O'Shea, J. S. (Ed.). (1988). *Under three: A comprehensive guide to caring for your baby and toddler.* New York: Van Nostrand Reinhold.

Scarr, S. (1984). *Mother care/other care.* New York: Basic Books.

Stern, D. (1985). *The first relationship* (4th ed.). Cambridge, MA: Harvard Univ. Press.

PART 3
The Preschool Years

335

Physical Development During the Preschool Years

● **Physical Growth**

Height and Weight

Compared with the rapid growth that took place during infancy, the growth rate during the preschool years is slower and steadier. While the average infant gains about 14 pounds in the first year of life, the average preschooler can be expected to gain 5–6 pounds annually until age 6. By age 3 the typical boy weighs about 32 pounds, or as much as three large sacks of potatoes. Muscle and bone growth account for most of the weight gain during this period. The child actually loses body fat during the preschool years. Until adolescence, boys outweigh girls their age by about a pound, although diet, exercise, illness, stress, and the amount and type of food consumed all interact with genetics to influence the amount of weight an individual gains (Lowrey, 1978).

Gain in height also decelerates during the preschool years. The average 1 year old stands about as tall as a kitchen table; the 3 year old can rest his chin on the table's surface. Throughout the preschool period children grow 2–3 inches in height per year. By age 3 the average boy is 38 inches tall. By age 6 that same child probably measures 48 inches and weighs 48 pounds. Girls tend to be slightly shorter than boys until around age 11, when girls on average have become taller than boys.

Variation in Physical Growth

Many children's heights and weights vary from these norms. Variation may be expected (taller children come from taller parents) or it may be a sign of developmental difficulties (underweight as a function of chronic illness, malnutrition, or low birth weight). Gary Coleman was

chronic illness
persistent health problems
malnutrition
a condition resulting from a lack of nutrients in the body tissues
low birth weight
either a premature or small-for-date designation that is associated with a weight at birth of less than seven pounds

■ **Figure 8–1**

Actor Gary Coleman.

neurosensory impairment
nervous system damage that affects
sensation

metabolic rate
the rate at which the body converts
food into energy

■ **Figure 8–2**

Typical body proportions of a preschooler.

born with a serious kidney disorder that significantly affected his
growth. He went on to become a TV star even though by age 15 he was
only as tall as the average 8 year old.

Low birth weight (especially below 1000 grams [2.2 lbs]) can represent
a major threat to developmental progress (Lefebvre et al., 1988). The
extent of the developmental delays are difficult to predict until the child
is of school age, but growth retardation, neurosensory impairment,
learning deficits, and health complications are common (Astbury et al.,
1990). In one British study, mothers who realized their low birth weight
infants were less advanced as preschoolers than other children tried to
compensate for their children's developmental delays by providing
more explanation during a drawing test (Parkinson et al., 1986).

Body Proportions

Proximodistal growth is centered in the preschooler's legs and trunk.
During this period, the stomach flattens and the child becomes taller
and more slender. Although the 3 year old still looks rather squat and
compact, by age 5 or 6 boys and girls, with their long arms, long legs,
and long torsos, are definitely proportioned more like children than
babies. Preschoolers also have more mobility than infants, in part because they are no longer top heavy and their center of gravity is lower,
making balance easier.

Internal Systems and Tissues

Growth Rate and Activity Level

Body systems slow down and stabilize during early childhood. Fevers
during illness are not as high as they were in infancy, since by age 5
normal body temperature has stabilized at 98.6°F. (The average normal
body temperature of a 1 year old is 99.7°F.) (Whaley & Wong, 1988).
The child's metabolic rate, heart rate, respiration rate, and blood pressure are all slower than they were during infancy.

Activity level also decreases in the preschool years. The caregiver can
expect less fidgeting and wriggling in the preschooler than in the infant,
and less flitting from task to task (Prior et al., 1983). Preschool-age children tend to concentrate their efforts on one project for increasingly
longer periods of time and seem more concerned about satisfactory
completion (They are sometimes even interested in cleaning up, especially if cleanup is made fun). A normally active preschooler is busy,
curious, and industrious. It is ironic that preschoolers have so much
energy while the adults who supervise them often have so little!

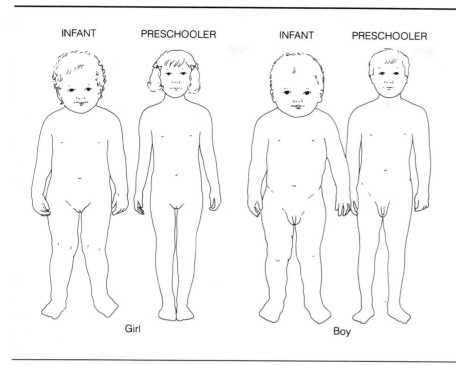

INFANT   PRESCHOOLER   INFANT   PRESCHOOLER

Girl

Boy

■ **Figure 8–3**

A comparison of the body proportions of infants and preschoolers.

The Brain

Since the brain influences every aspect of development, it grows faster and achieves relative maturity sooner than any other part of the body. By age 2 the child's brain has attained 75% of its adult weight, but by age 5 the brain is nearly 90% of its full weight (Lowrey, 1978). Some new brain cells are added and the size of existing cells and the complexity of their interconnections increases during the preschool period (Harmon, 1984). New capillaries branch from the existing vessels in the brain to nourish these cells. The brain does not grow linearly, but in spurts at 3–10 months, 2–4 years, 10–12 years and 14–16 years of age (Kolb, 1989). These growth spurts together with the dominant growth periods for interhemisphere development overlap with the timing for Piaget's stages of cognitive development (Thatcher et al., 1987).

Sex differences in head circumference originally described by Nancy Bayley in the Berkeley Growth study in the 1920s continue to exist, with boys having larger head circumferences than girls (Clifton et al., 1988). Mylenization, the process of insulating the nervous system with fat, is more nearly complete in the 6 year old than in the 3 year old. School readiness is, in part, dependent on brain development since a more complex brain can support more sophisticated learning.

In Touch

HUMAN GROWTH FOUNDATION
4720 Montgomery Lane
Bethesda, MD 20814
1–800–451–6434

Provides support for growth–retarded children and their families

auditory cortex
the portion of the brain that is involved in interpreting auditory inputs; located in the temporal lobe

left hemisphere
the half of the brain on the left hand side of the person's body that influences speech and right side body movement, among other things

motor cortex
the portion of the brain involved in sending messages out to the muscles of the body to initiate movement; located in the frontal lobes

frontal lobes
located in the anterior portion of each hemisphere, areas of tissue that play a role in directing muscle movement and in higher order mental processes such as reasoning, problem solving and the acquisition of knowledge

hemisphere lateralization
the process in which the two hemispheres of the brain acquire primary control over specific functions such as spoken language and handedness

ORGANIZATIONAL CHANGES WITHIN THE BRAIN Organizational changes take place during the preschool years to improve brain effectiveness and function. *Specialization* occurs as specific areas of the brain begin to respond most strongly to particular stimuli. Incoming speech sounds, for example, are directed to a group of cells called Wernicke's area in the auditory cortex of the left hemisphere. Voluntary movement (like turning one's head or clenching one's fist) produces the greatest neural activity in the motor cortex located in the frontal lobes.

Another change in brain functioning is *hemisphere lateralization*. Structurally, the brain is divided into two halves, or hemispheres. Lateralization implies that each hemisphere supervises different functions and processes information differently (Kisbourne, 1982). The left hemisphere generally processes information in a linear fashion or item by item, as when one person is listening to another person reading a spelling list. The right hemisphere is more concerned with the perception of patterns of relationships among items, as when a person is counting by 2s. Depending on the type of information, then, either the left hemisphere or the right hemisphere will become active.

Lateralization also influences behavior. Preschool children begin to perform certain activities with one side of their body more than the other. The best example of a lateralized behavior is hand preference. Up to 90% of all children are right-handed. In terms of the way the brain is organized, this implies that the *left* hemisphere controls the dominant *right* hand. Since right-hand preference is the dominant mode, parents might be concerned if their child is left-handed. But forcing a left-handed child to use the right hand could create more problems than it solves. Children suffer less emotional upset and perform better in tasks that require fine motor coordination if they use their preferred hand. There is no relationship between handedness and intelligence, verbal ability, or reading ability (McManus et al., 1988; Xeromeritou, 1989). Left-handed scissors, left-handed desks, and other accommodations can help improve the functioning of the left-handed child. Some even argue that left-handers have a functional advantage in certain tasks, as in sports or the arts.

A right-handed child may also display other right-sided preferences but not necessarily. A right-handed child may kick the ball with his right foot and hold the telephone to his right ear, but a few have mixed or crossed lateral preferences (left-footed, but right-eyed, for example) and still others perform tasks equally well with both hands, feet, eyes, or ears. One type of lateral preference pattern does not seem to be better or more adaptive than another.

Body Fat, Muscles and Bones

One reason preschoolers look slender is that they have less body fat than they did during infancy. By 5.5 years of age, the body-fat layer is

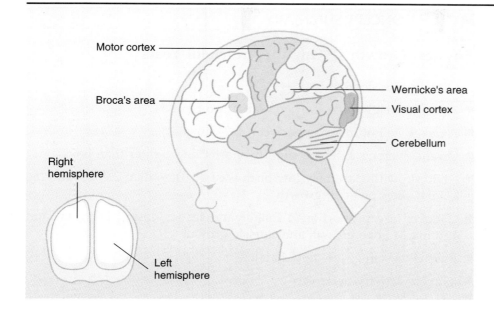

The left and right hemispheres and regions of the cortex.

half as thick as it was at age 9 months. Sex differences are apparent, too. On the average, boys have more muscle and bone than girls, probably owing to the action of the male hormone testosterone, and girls have more fat than boys. Individual differences create considerable variation. Muscle tissue growth slows down gradually during childhood, lagging behind the growth of other tissue until adolescence.

■ **Figure 8–5**

A preschooler with a full set of teeth.

The younger the child, the more cartilage there is in the skeletal system and the less securely muscles and ligaments are attached to bones. While preschoolers can move well and play vigorously, their muscles and bones are more prone to damage by overuse, pull, infection, and poor nutrition than those of older children. Shoes that fit, good posture, and chairs and desks designed for children encourage optimum bone/muscle development.

The preschooler usually has a full set of 20 baby teeth by age 2.5 or 3, which means that feeding restrictions can be lifted, since the child can crunch, bite, chew, or grind just about anything. Throughout this period, the child's jaw elongates to accommodate the permanent teeth, which begin to erupt by age 6 or 7. In the process, the preschooler loses the "baby face" look of infancy.

Tooth decay is a significant health problem among American children. About 40% of all 3 year olds have cavities, and that percentage continues to rise until the late teens (Whaley & Wong, 1988). Persistent strong mouth odors in children often indicate throat infection or tooth

■ ● ▲   CONCEPT SUMMARY

Physical Growth During the Preschool Years

- Growth rate slows
- Average weight increase per year is 5–6 pounds
- Average height increase per year is 2–3 inches
- On the average, girls are slightly shorter and lighter than boys
- Children with extremely low birth weights (less than 2.2 lbs) still lag behind their peers in growth
- Children are proportioned longer and leaner, losing body fat and gaining in bone growth and muscle growth
- Internal systems slow and stabilize
- Aimless activity decreases
- The brain is still the fastest growing organ
- A full set of baby teeth is present by age 2.5 or 3
- Bladder control improves
- The stomach is half its adult capacity
- The reproductive tract grows little if at all

decay. In almost all cases, dental problems associated with tooth decay can be prevented with proper care.

Breathing

By age 3, the respiratory system has matured to permit adult-like chest and abdominal breathing movements. (Remember, infants are "stomach breathers.") The air passageways are relatively small throughout early childhood and the tonsils and adenoids are at their maximum size owing to the prominence of the lymphatic system.

lymphatic system
the tissues in the body that screen out harmful substances and produce lymphocytes to aid in infection control

Bladder Control

The bladder is larger than it was in infancy, so the child can go for longer periods without trips to the bathroom. Although most bed wetters are dry by age 6, one in five still have occasional or frequent "accidents" and 10–15% of boys this age still wet the bed at night (Butler et al., 1986). Sound sleep patterns, or a small bladder may be a cause, but emotional or disease factors can also affect urinary continence. Wetting is more common when children sleep away from home or when they are coping with trauma, such as death or divorce.

urinary continence
the ability to control one's bladder and urination

Digestion

The stomach of the 4–6 year old has less than half the capacity of the adult stomach. It is also straighter and more upright than that of the infant or older child, so it empties readily in either direction. The lining of the digestive tract is easily irritated by too much fiber or seasoning, so caretakers should be knowledgeable about suitable food preparation.

In this age group, stomachache and intestinal disorders are commonly caused by viruses and bacteria and are accompanied by vomiting, diarrhea, low-grade fever, and abdominal pain. Since dehydration can be a life-threatening consequence of fluid loss, a physician should also be consulted when young children experience extensive vomiting and diarrhea.

The Reproductive System

The reproductive system grows little if at all until adolescence. The pineal gland appears to be responsible for this outcome by secreting large amounts of the substance *melatonin* during childhood and very small amounts during adolescence (Schmeck, 1984).

melatonin
a substance secreted by the pineal gland that plays a role in sexual maturation

● Motor Development

Large-muscle activity, or *gross motor skills*, continue to follow the cephalocaudal principle of development. While infants concentrated on their arms and trunks, rolling over and pushing or pulling, preschoolers focus primarily on their legs, running, climbing, jumping and kicking. Small-muscle, or *fine motor*, growth proceeds according to the proximodistal principle (development from "near to far"). Whole-arm activities such as banging or throwing are now accompanied by more precise skills—for example, cutting with scissors or drawing with a crayon. Preschoolers seem to enjoy the motor activities they engage in and derive a sense of satisfaction as they master physical tasks.

gross motor skills
physical skills that require large-muscle movement such as running, climbing and jumping

fine motor skills
physical skills that require small muscle coordination such as drawing, sewing, or playing a musical instrument

Gross Motor Activity

As preschoolers grow taller, they become steadier on their feet owing to a lowering of the center of gravity. True running develops between the ages of 2 and 3 after a period of "fast walking." Stopping and changing direction are mastered between 4.5 and 5. Most children can stop more efficiently once they are able to swing their arms to counterbalance the swinging, twisting motion of their legs (Wickstrom, 1977).

Jumping down is easier than jumping across and jumping across is easier than jumping up. Most children can broad jump a few feet by the time they are 5. Hopping is more complex since it involves balance and single-leg strength. Jumping and hopping skills can be practiced

■ Figure 8–6

Gross motor play on the playground.

manual dexterity
skill in using the hands

through various playground activities (hop scotch, jump rope, leap frog).

During the preschool period, throwing skills improve. Children learn to use their elbows and shoulders in throwing rather than their bodies, to relax their arms, and to improve velocity and accuracy by stepping as they throw (Williams, 1983). Catching progresses from passive acceptance to stepping toward and grabbing the thrown object. Preschoolers' reaction times are slower than those of older children because the nervous system is less mature. At this age, catching skills can be safely practiced with a balloon or a spongy ball. Generally, the younger the child, the larger the ball required, since at this age children use their whole bodies and arms to catch rather than their hands, fingers, and wrists.

Table 8–1 summarizes the gross motor behaviors of typical 3, 4, and 5 year olds. Most 5 year olds can ride a tricycle, swing a swing, and climb a ladder. Some can even swim, skate, and ride a two-wheel bicycle. The range of variation is due to differences in maturation rates, motivation levels, nutrition quality, and the opportunity to practice (Malina, 1982).

Children who were premature or SGA at birth may still lag behind their age peers at this stage in accomplishing some gross motor tasks (Crowe et al., 1988). Parents who note marked discrepancies between the child's expected and actual behavior should consult a health care practitioner.

Fine Motor Activity

Fine motor skills are more difficult for preschoolers than gross motor skills, because they require more precise muscle control, careful judgment, and more patience. Trying to lace a show, cut with scissors, or button buttons can be a frustrating ordeal for preschoolers, particularly if their fingers are short and stubby. Parents can minimize frustration by selecting toys, clothing, and utensils that match the child's skill level and by offering plenty of opportunities for practice and mastery. Between the ages of 2 and 6, girls tend to be more skilled at tasks that require manual dexterity, while boys perform better at gross motor tasks (Lindner, 1988).

Drawing

One of the major fine motor accomplishments during the preschool years is the refinement of drawing skills. The progression from scribbling to drawing recognizable pictures occurs in a series of distinct stages (Trautner et al., 1989). At first, scribbling occurs spontaneously and the placement of scribbles on the page seems random. During the *placement stage,* the 15 month old scribbles in a particular region or area.

■ **Table 8–1** *Gross Motor Development During the Preschool Years*

ACTIVITY	3 YEAR OLD	4 YEAR OLD	5 YEAR OLD
Walking and running	Walks a line without watching feet Walks backward Runs with little control over stops, starts, turns Runs "flatfooted" Most cannot gallop	Heel-toe walk Runs with control over starts, stops Speed increases Longer strides than 3 year old Early gallop is a run-and-leap step	Walks backward with heel–toe pattern Speed increases Longer strides than 4 year old Running is well established 78% can gallop Can stop and start at will
Stepping and climbing	Goes up stairs, alternating feet May come downstairs using both feet on a step Hops 1–3 times on one foot	Walks downstairs alternating feet 7–9 hops on one foot Can climb stairs without holding the rail Can climb a large ladder, alternating feet Can descend a large ladder, alternating feet	Hops well on either leg 10+ hops on one foot 79% become proficient at hopping 32% can climb a rope with the bottom free 37% can climb a pole 70% can climb a rope ladder with the bottom free
Balance	Stands on one foot for a few seconds Balance beam walking pattern: no foot alternation Can walk 7.4 feet forward on a 3-inch beam; 3.9 feet backward	Balance beam walking pattern: shuffles, alternating feet Can walk 8.8 feet forward on a 3-inch balance beam; 5.8 feet backward Balances on one foot for 5 or more seconds	Balance beam walking pattern: alternating feet Can walk 11 feet forward on a 3-inch balance beam; 8.1 feet backward Balances on alternative feet with eyes closed
Skipping	Can skip on one foot and walk on the other	14% can skip Stiff movement Excessive arm use Flat-footed skip	72% can skip Fluid movement More efficient use of arms Most skip on balls of feet
Jumping	Jumps off bottom step Jumps in place 42% are proficient at jumping Lands without knees bent Can jump from a height of 28 inches 68% can hurdle-jump 3.5 inches	Assumes more of a crouch when jumping 72% are proficient at jumping Standing broad jump: 8–10 inches Running broad jump: 23-33 inches 90% hurdle-jump 5 inches; 51% hurdle 9.5 inches	Jumps from a height of 12 in, lands on toes Standing broad jump: 15–18 inches Running broad jump: 28–35 inches 90% can hurdle 8 inches; 68% can hurdle 21.5 inches Jumps rope
Throwing	Throws ball overhand Catches ball with arms fully extended Catch successful about 33% of time	Throws ball overhand Reliably catches ball thrown at 5 feet	Throws and catches ball Uses hands more than arms to catch ball
Other	May try to dance, but balance may not be adequate; rides tricycle	Climbs a jungle gym	Rollerskates with good balance

Source: Corbin, C. *A Textbook of Motor Development*, 2d ed. © 1980 Wm. C. Brown Communications, Inc. Dubuque, Iowa. All rights reserved. Reprinted by permission.

■ **Figure 8–7**

(left) Tying one's shoes requires fine motor skills (thank goodness for velcro!) (right) Playing with **legos.**

For example, the scribble pattern might be confined to the center, the lower half, or the diagonal of the page. The scribble is not just exercise but a task involving color selection, form, placement, and sometimes a representational pattern like an airplane flying across the sky or a rabbit going hop (Tarr, 1990). These patterns are interpretable only by the child (Winner, 1986).

By age 3, children hold a crayon with their fingers rather than their fists and are capable of more precise movement. During the *shape stage,* the child can approximate some geometric figures, such as a circle, rectangle, or an oval and can draw other free-form shapes, such as a cross. When the child begins to draw these simple forms together as a structured design, she has entered the *design stage.* Designs can be simple or complex and may or may not represent something to the child.

Between the ages of 4 and 5, most children enter the last stage of drawing development, the *pictorial stage.* In this stage, designs are readily recognizable as familiar objects, such as houses, people, and trees, but may be placed in novel and creative arrangements. Young children truly have "fun with art," losing themselves in the medium and worrying less about precise artistic renderings than self-expression (H. Gardner, 1980). Cows may be green and dogs pink because "the child felt like it" or because all the "good" colors were gone when they were ready to create their picture. "Tell me about your picture" is a productive entree to encouraging children to talk about their art. Drawing is

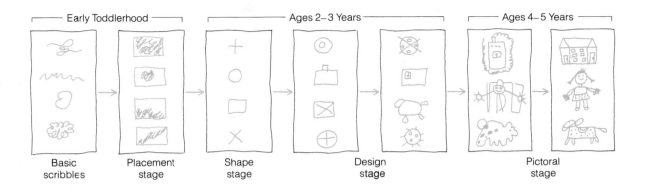

Early Toddlerhood		Ages 2–3 Years			Ages 4–5 Years	
Basic scribbles	Placement stage	Shape stage	Design stage		Pictoral stage	

■ **Figure 8–8**

The stages in the development of drawing.

more than just child's play. The fine motor skills and eye/hand coordination practiced through drawing form the foundation for the more serious tasks of printing, writing, and making numbers. Drawing also may be an outlet for expressing thoughts and feelings.

Throughout the preschool period, the child's artistic renderings are limited by relatively immature fine motor skills. A child who draws a human that looks like a tadpole (head and legs) will often describe many more body parts than actually appear in the drawing (N. Freeman, 1980). Either the child doesn't know how to coordinate the drawing of the "missing" body parts or she is content to use a pictorial shorthand to represent humans. Girls are developmentally able or willing to include more detail in their drawings than boys (E.V. Brown, 1990). When preschool children draw two objects together, they will often misrepresent the relative size of the objects. If we lived in the world the preschooler draws, people and animals would dwarf houses and buildings and sometimes each other! The difficulty occurs because preschoolers have trouble attending to two stimuli simultaneously. Interestingly, if children draw people first, other objects are scaled more accurately (Silk & Thomas, 1988). Also, sometimes preschoolers will represent significant objects or people as larger—pretty flowers and nice people may take up more space than dead flowers and nasty people (G.V. Thomas et al., 1989). Overestimation of the relative size of objects decreases as children grow older. Depth is represented (if at all) by placing more distant elements toward the top of the picture and closer elements toward the bottom (Ingram & Butterworth, 1989).

In addition to drawing, other fine motor accomplishments of the preschool period are listed in Table 8–2.

■ **Figure 8–9**

A 4 year-old girl coloring in a coloring book.

■ **Table 8–2** *Fine Motor Activity During the Preschool Years*

AGE (IN YEARS)	3 YEAR OLD	4 YEAR OLD	5 YEAR OLD
Dressing	Undresses self Helps dress self Undoes buttons on sides and front of clothing	Dresses and undresses self except for tying bows, closing zippers, and putting on boots Buttons Laces shoes but cannot tie them Can distinguish front from back	Dresses self without assistance Ties shoelaces
Self-care	Feeds self Washes hands May brush own teeth	Brushes teeth alone	Washes self without splashing clothes
Writing and drawing	Recognizes and draws a circle Scribbles Copies a cross Names what he has drawn Cannot draw a stick figure; but can draw a circle with facial features	Copies a square Traces a diamond Traces a cross Adds 3 parts to stick figure Form and meaning in drawings are apparent to adults Combines 2 simple geometric forms	Copies a diamond Copies a triangle Prints a few letters, numbers or words Prints his first name Adds 6 parts to a stick figure Differentiates parts of the drawing Draws lifelike representations Knows that right and left exist but cannot differentiate between them Has a definite hand preference
Play	Builds a tower of 9–10 blocks Builds a bridge with 3 blocks Pours fluid from a pitcher, with occasional spills Places pellets into narrow-necked bottle Begins to use scissors Strings large beads	Uses scissors successfully to cut out pictures with outlines Surveys a puzzle before placing the pieces Has poor space perception Builds a bridge with 5 blocks Notices missing parts—requests to fix Builds complicated structures, vertically and laterally Likes water play	Uses scissors, simple tools, & pencils well Folds paper diagonally Does simple puzzles easily and quickly Builds complex 3-dimensional structures Disassembles and reassembles some objects Uses hammer to hit nail on head Likes water play

● Sensory Perception

Paralleling the growth in other systems, the sensory systems continue to develop and perfect the quality of input sent to the brain for interpretation. Since the preschooler relies most heavily on vision and hear-

A Closer Look

The Art of Grief

Jenny was 4 when her infant brother died of sudden infant death syndrome. She was sad that he had died and she missed him, but her biggest problem was her fear of the night. She was afraid that if she went to sleep, she would die, too.

Five year old Susan didn't want to go to sleep either. All she knew about her grandmother's death was that she was sleeping with the angels. Susan was afraid if she went to sleep she'd end up like her grandmother—with the angels, yes, but still forever asleep.

Grief is hard for anyone at any age to handle. But coping with loss can be especially hard for children. In addition to normal grieving, children face special problems unique to early childhood. Children are rarely told the physical details of death. While that is usually done to protect them, lack of knowledge increases the mysteriousness of death for children and enhances their fear of the unknown. Children don't have access to the same type of logic and reasoning abilities as older children or adults. They don't accept the finality of death. They know it's something different than life but they still may think the dead person will come walking through the door at any time. It doesn't pacify them to know, for example, that the doctor did everything possible. A child will always reason that the doctor could have done more or even that *they themselves* could have saved the loved one. After his father's death, a 7 year old named Adam began destroying things at home and disrupting the classroom. Adam was told that God took his father up to live with him. Adam didn't want to live with God, he wanted to live with his mother. He figured if God took his father because he was good, the way to avoid the same fate was to be so bad that God wouldn't want him.

An older child drew herself in black, showing the emptiness she felt after a death. The orange and red lines, the fiery part, represent the anger she felt. She negated the anger inside herself, but drew it on the outside as a kind of protective shield.

Many young children cannot find words to express their fears and feelings. Art gives grieving children a means to express themselves. The pictures they draw or the sculptures they make can reveal thoughts, anxieties, and even misconceptions that the child cannot articulate. Children may show

(continued on next page)

(continued from previous page)

anger through their brushstrokes or the colors they choose or may hit and punch the clay to vent their feelings. Since children communicate their feelings through actions and play, art is an ideal medium: It's tangible, safe, and even fun.

Children have elaborate imaginations. Many times, what they imagine is worse than the truth. One boy drew a picture of his grandmother in her casket without legs. He thought that the reason he couldn't see his grandmother's legs in her casket was because someone cut them off! Children benefit from timely and accurate information about the death event or ceremony. They also benefit from knowing that others have suffered as they do and that they can make and create through their art even in the wake of their pain and confusion.

Excerpted from: Smith, L. "The Art of Grief." *The Sacramento Bee,* October 13, 1990 S1,7. Used with permission.

This drawing represents what a child remembers most about a funeral. She drew the gravesite, putting the casket and herself beside it on the green grass.

ing for information about the world, these two systems will be considered in the most detail.

Visual Perception

Visual development continues throughout the preschool period. The *fovea* is the area of the retina where vision is the sharpest. Since the fovea is not completely developed until the age of 6 or 7, something less than 20/20 vision can be expected in the preschool years. Children younger than 6 are normally *farsighted,* since the eyeball is shorter and shallower than it will be at maturity (Lowrey, 1978). Because farsightedness makes it difficult to focus on close material, *large print is necessary* for the beginning reader to avoid eyestrain (Whaley & Wong, 1988). Most educators recommend that children receive a thorough visual examination before entering school. The examination should test for nearsightedness and eyestrain and assess visual acuity by letter recognition as well as *binocular vision,* the working together of both eyes.

Preschoolers can not only see more clearly than infants but their ability to make sense of their visual environment has also improved. By age 5 or 6, preschool children are as skilled as adults at coordinating the senses of touch, vision, and hearing. With maturity, shifts occur in perceptual preference. Three and 4 year olds prefer to explore unfamiliar objects by touch, while 5 and 6 year olds rely on vision. During problem solving, 3 and 4 year olds pay more attention to the color and

perceptual preference
the sensory system that the child relies on most for information about the world

size of the object, while 6 year olds (like adults) focus more on the shape. The senses of vision and touch won't be fully integrated until the school years. Older children also consider objects and tasks more slowly and more systematically than younger ones and learn to avoid environmental distractions. At this time in their development, preschoolers literally "can't talk and chew gum at the same time." If they try to do two things simultaneously (like getting dressed and watching TV or eating and talking), one task will surely interrupt the other because their level of distractibility is so high.

Patterns perception and form discrimination also improve with age. A 2 year old is just as likely to look at pictures that are upside down as right side up. With repeated exposure, forms gain meaning and become recognizable, even if their placement or orientation is slightly changed. The shape-constancy skills that children use to recognize stability in their physical environments is a hindrance when they are learning to discriminate the letters of the alphabet. For example, although a face turned to the left and a face turned to the right are still faces, the letter *b* is not the same as the letter *d*.

The child's ability to process information at a distance and to separate out meaningful objects from the whole configuration improves during early childhood (Gottfried & Gilman, 1985). For example, 2 and 3 year old children have a great deal of difficulty locating their caregivers in a crowd of adults. Their visual scanning abilities are inefficient and they look about aimlessly without any systematic search strategy. By age 6, because their memories have improved and they are able to focus on pertinent details, children have an easier time recognizing their parents in a crowd. By this time, too, the preschooler has a larger vocabulary and can actually use language to enhance visual memory. If they can label an image as a "belt" or a "diamond" then they have the label *plus* the form to store in memory.

A small number of children have perceptual disabilities. Prenatal influences account for half of all cases of blindness in children (Astbury et al., 1990). After birth, injury and disease are the primary causes of visual handicaps. Blind children are born with the same potential for movement as sighted children. They may not be motivated to explore, however, because they remain generally unaware of interesting toys and other objects in their environment. Caregivers can encourage blind children to be mobile in some environments and to make maximum use of all their senses.

Hearing

The sense of hearing is well developed in early childhood, and young children can easily distinguish the phonemes, or speech sounds, that make up spoken language. Good hearing is especially important during infancy and the preschool years because of its role in language acqui-

■ Figure 8–10

Reading together is a good quiet-time activity.

pattern perception
the ability to recognize designs or arrangements

form discrimination
the ability to tell one shape or object from another

In Touch

AMERICAN PRINTING HOUSE FOR
  THE BLIND
1839 Frankfort Ave.
Louisville, KY 40206
502–895–2405

Prints large-type reading material and
  recreational materials; provides
  recorded materials and educational
  aids for the blind and visually
  impaired

phonemes
the smallest unit of speech sounds
that can be discerned auditorally

A Closer Look

How Much Noise Is Too Much?

Hearing should be safeguarded at all ages. Parents may inadvertently expose children to sound/noise levels that are damaging.

SOURCE	DECIBELS (dBs)*	DANGER LEVEL
Speech	60 dB	—
City traffic	75 dB	—
Noisy restaurant	80 dB	—
Chain saws, jackhammers, factory noise, subway noise	85–90 dB	8 hours
Live concert (especially rock), radio earphones, power mower	110+ dB	30 minutes
Snowmobile	115 dB	15 minutes
Crowd noise at a stadium	120 dB	Almost immediately
Jet noise, gunshot blast	140 dB	Threshold of pain

*Sound intensity is measured in decibels (dB), a unit of loudness named after Alexander Graham Bell

Source: Adapted from Lefton & Valvatue, 1988, p. 221.

decibel(s)
a unit of measuring sound intensity

In Touch

ALEXANDER GRAHAM BELL
  ASSOCIATION FOR THE DEAF
3417 Volta Place
Washington, DC 20007

sition. Infants and preschoolers have more ear infections than older children because in them the Eustachian tubes, which connect the middle ears to the throat, are wider, shorter, and more horizontal than at maturity. Bacteria are easily trapped within the immature Eustachian tubes of the younger child and transferred to the middle ears. A vaccine to prevent childhood ear infection is currently being tested. Suspected ear infections should immediately be reported to the child's physician.

Taste, Touch, and Smell

Touch is highly developed at birth and continues to provide important information about the world. The senses of taste and smell are fully developed by the preschool years. If anything, the preschooler's sense of taste is sharper than that of adults, owing to the presence of extra taste buds in the throat and inside the cheeks.

■●▲   CONCEPT SUMMARY

Sensory Perception During the Preschool Years

Vision

- Farsightedness is normal
- Large print facilitates reading, but most preschool children are not fluent readers, even with large print
- Are beginning to coordinate the senses of touch, vision, and hearing
- Can focus on one visual task at a time
- Still make mistakes trying to discriminate similar forms (e.g., *d* and *b*)
- Scanning abilities improve

Hearing

- Is well developed
- Can easily distinguish speech sounds
- Ear infections are common; untreated infections can lead to hearing loss

Taste, touch and smell

- Are fully developed

● Preschool Routines

Sleep

Most preschoolers need 11–13 hours of sleep per day to grow well and to feel alert, rested, and energetic. Individual children can get by with as little as 8 hours of sleep; others do best when permitted as many as 14 hours. The child of this age who goes to bed between 7 and 8 at night will usually sleep without awakening until morning. Maintaining a consistent bedtime ritual, avoiding scary or disturbing TV programs, and reducing activity prior to bedtime help preschoolers fall asleep and stay asleep. Letting the child take a blanket, stuffed toy, or other object along to bed really helps ease the transition between waking and sleep.

■ **Figure 8–11**

No matter what kind of trouble they've been into that day, sleeping preschoolers always look like angels.

The object gives comfort in two ways: It makes the child feel as though he is not alone, and since the object is associated with sleeping, the child feels relaxed and tired in its presence.

Up to age 3 children usually take an afternoon nap for about an hour. Naps can be discontinued once the child begins to resist going to bed in the daytime and demonstrate the ability to function well until bedtime without additional rest.

Sometimes preschoolers will experience sleepwalking, sleeptalking, nightmares, and/or night terrors. Sleeptalking is harmless, but the sleepwalking child needs to be protected from injury. Lock windows and doors and guide the child back into bed. There is no need to wake the sleepwalker and there is no evidence that the sleepwalking child is unconsciously trying to escape the family. This tendency runs in families, is outgrown with age, and is not associated with emotional disturbance. Nightmares *could* be an indication that the child is experiencing too much stress if the bad dreams are persistent, have repetitive themes, and cause sleep avoidance. Night terrors resemble nightmares in that the child is in a state of panic but he is not really awake since the episode occurs during quiet, NREM sleep, not REM sleep, and is not associated with an underlying problem.

Nutrition

The child's appetite during the preschool years fluctuates as a function of the slowed but steady growth rate. Some days parents may run out of milk every 6 hours as the preschooler consumes everything in sight; other days serving the preschooler may be like trying to please the human equivalent of Morris the Cat. Fortunately, neither extreme persists

A Closer Look

Millions of Kids are Hungry

Economic hard times exempt no one. As the number of unemployed and homeless increase, one more grim statistic appears: Childhood hunger in America appears to be worse than many feared. A report conducted by the Washington-based Food Research and Action Center and released in April, 1991 indicated that *one in eight children under 12 years old* (5.5 million kids or 11% of all children) goes hungry each day. In addition, another 6 million more children (or 12% of all children) are underfed because their families cannot afford enough to eat (Howard & Carlo, 1991).

Taken together, those statistics suggest that *23% of America's children* under age 12 are either going hungry or receiving too little food to meet their needs. It's hard to reconcile that level of childhood poverty and hunger with the image of America as the land of plenty. And while we might encourage adults to return to school to develop job skills, children are the most innocent of victims—too young to provide for themselves and too powerless to demand care.

for long. As long as children are not given empty-calorie snacks between meals, they will consume enough nutritious food at mealtime to meet their biological needs. Other causes of appetite decline include overstimulation or stress at mealtime, illness, fatigue, tooth decay, irregular schedules, and unappetizing food.

The preschool child needs 1400–1800 kcalories per day, or about 40 kcalories per pound of body weight (Whitney & Cataldo, 1987). Protein and specific vitamins and minerals are key requirements in the child's diet. Protein helps build new tissue and plays an especially important role in brain growth and nervous system development. Sufficient dietary calcium and phosphorus are essential, too, since minerals are being deposited in the child's bones and teeth in increasing quantities. The child's supply of calcium and phosphorus is best provided by milk. Kcalories can be distributed among three meals and a nutritious midmorning, midafternoon, and evening snack. Contrary to popular belief, high dietary sugar consumption by normal preschoolers does not have an adverse impact on their ability to learn, attention to task, or activity level (Roshon & Hagen, 1989).

In terms of quantity, preschoolers eat a little more than toddlers, or about half of adult serving. Whenever possible, children should have their meals with the family. Mealtime encourages social interaction, language development, and the acquisition of feeding skills and customs.

kcalorie (pronounced calorie) a unit of food energy; stands for kilocalorie

■ **Figure 8–12**

Three-year-olds eating lunch at day care.

■ **Figure 8–13**

A carseat for a preschool age child.

● Health and Safety

Part of caring for the preschool-age child involves keeping her healthy and safe. Modern immunization practices protect inoculated children against red measles, tuberculosis, rubella (German measles), mumps, whooping cough, tetanus, diphtheria, polio, and meningitis. Despite their effectiveness, one-third of all preschool children in the United States lack full immune protection, causing periodic epidemics of preventable illness (U.S. Bureau of the Census, 1983).

Treatment and survival rates have improved for seriously ill children since 1977 (American Cancer Society, 1988). New medications and surgical procedures have provided hope to families of children with cancer (bone cancer, lymphoma, Hodgkin's disease, and leukemia), multiple sclerosis, muscular dystrophy, and diseased hearts, lungs, and livers.

Fortunately, the majority of children's illnesses involve colds and the flu. Because of their immature lungs and immune systems, preschool-age children will experience an average of 7–8 colds and upper respiratory illnesses per year. By the time they are 6 years olds, they will get sick fewer than 6 times a year and the infections will be milder and shorter-lived than when they were babies (Denny & Clyde, 1983). Good hygiene (washing hands), discouraging shared drinking cups and wash-cloths and the like, good nutrition, and sufficient sleep can greatly reduce the incidence of disease and illness.

Accidents

Today in the United States, accidents are the leading cause of preventable injury and death among children. Three factors influence the likelihood of a child having an accident: the amount and quality of adult supervision, the level of safety in the play area, and the child's activity level. Children who are highly active, more impulsive, play in unsafe areas, and have little or no adult supervision (sometimes because they are from single-parent families) are at risk for serious injury (Wadsworth et al., 1983; Nyman, 1987). Ironically, two-thirds of all serious accidents occur in the home or in a car. Boys are involved in twice as many accidents at age 5 as girls (U.S. Census Bureau, 1983). Compared to children who are accident-free, children who have had one accident requiring hospital admission are twice as likely to have another accident by the time they are 5 years old (Eminson et al., 1986). Because of our culture's expectations, many boys are more daring and curious than girls and are encouraged to become independent at an earlier age.

Motor Vehicle Accidents

Pedestrian accidents account for the majority of injuries and fatalities to children between the ages of 2 and 5. Children are hit while crossing

---

■ **Table 8–3** *Guidelines for Preventing Injury due to Motor-Vehicle Accidents*

Always use a well-constructed safety seat or car restraint.

Supervise children playing outside.

Do not allow children to play on curbs, behind parked cars, or in the street.

Do not permit children to play in a pile of leaves, in piles of snow, or in large cardboard containers.

Supervise all skating and tricycle and bicycle riding.

Lock fences and doors if children are in yard unsupervised.

Teach children to look for cars before crossing, recognize the color and meaning of traffic lights, and look for crossing guards and obey traffic officers. But always accompany children when they cross streets, however well-drilled in safety they may be.

Do not place a carriage or stroller behind a parked car.

Do not place an infant carrier on top of a parked car.

For outdoor play, fence the yard or place small children in a playpen.

Retrieve objects that find their way into the street for children.

Do not allow children to move about inside a car while it is in motion.

Do not hold a child in your lap while driving or as a passenger.

Adapted from Whaley & Wong, 1988.

the street, darting into the street from behind parked cars, and playing in the street (Table 8–3). Cars can be deadly to children who are passengers, too. Seatbelts and approved child carseats are the most effective means of reducing all types of passenger accidents. Educating children in the importance of seatbelts produces more compliance and saves more lives than punishing their parents with fines or court appearances (Bowman et al., 1987). When preschool teachers reward seatbelt use with stickers, children are also more likely to buckle-up (Roberts & Broadbent, 1989). Children should not be left unattended in parked cars even for short periods of time. An unsupervised child can disengage the hand brake or put the car into gear, can risk heat stroke or hyperthermia on hot days, or can be abducted.

Drowning

The peak age for drowning is 2; moreover, more children between the ages of 1 and 5 years old drown than any other age group except 15–19 year olds. It does not take much water for a child to drown. An unattended child and a bathtub, wading pond, or swimming pool, a running faucet, a bucket of water, a rain puddle, or even a toilet bowl can be a lethal combination. Four to 7 minutes after breathing stops, brain damage due to oxygen deprivation begins. Even cold-water near-drowning, when hypothermia takes place, places the child at risk for long-term complications such as memory and attention deficits, speech problems, and slower than normal cognitive processing (Cruikshank et al., 1988). Almost all drownings are preventable by adequate adult supervision

In Touch

AMERICAN ACADEMY OF
  PEDIATRICS
Division of Health Education
141 Northwest Point Road
Elk Grove, IL 60007

Offers help in selecting safe car
  seats and restraints

NATIONAL DROWNING
  PREVENTION COALITION
1875 Belcher Road North
Clearwater, FL 34624
1–800–456–7372
In Florida: 813–725–3627

Provides information to help promote
  water safety and reduce in-home
  accidents

hypothermia
a condition in which the body
temperature is cooler than normal

combined with swimming and water-safety instruction and approved life vests or jackets for nonswimmers. Mouth-to-mouth resuscitation and CPR (cardiopulmonary resuscitation) are invaluable skills that often make the difference between life and death and between full recovery and lifelong complications for a child.

Burns

Burns are profoundly traumatic injuries. Not only do survivors of burn-related incidents have to endure painful physical treatment, but they also have to cope with the psychological effect of appearance changes and distorted self-perceptions, especially when the face has been burned. The burns most often suffered by children under the age of 2 are caused by scalding. Toddlers can spill hot liquid on themselves as they reach for a coffee cup or a pan handle or pull a placemat or table cloth.

The most serious nonfatal burns are caused when children's clothing catches on fire through contact with fireplaces, ashtrays, heaters, or candles. Parents should teach their children to *stop, drop, and roll* to extinguish clothing fires and minimize the severity of the burn. Any sizeable burn should receive prompt medical attention to prevent fatal complications such as shock and infection. *Never* apply butter (it raises the skin temperature rather than lowering it) or ice (which can cause shock) to a burn. Immediately flood the burn with cool water and call the doctor.

Another common cause of serious injuries and fatalities is house fires. Prevention includes adequate supervision, functional smoke alarms, fire-safety instruction (including the stop/drop/roll technique), careful handling of cigarettes, and fire drills to familiarize children with escape routes.

As the ozone layer of the atmosphere becomes compromised, the threat of skin cancer or skin damage from sunburn becomes increasingly high for light- to medium-skinned children. Each time a child is sunburned, she is 10 times more likely to get skin cancer later in life. Parents should *always* apply a protective waterproof sunscreen and provide hats, visors, and light, long-sleeved clothing for further protection.

Poisoning

Prevention of accidental poisoning primarily consists of careful supervision and limiting the child's access to potentially toxic substances. Unattended children will eat or drink anything, no matter how it tastes or what its label says. Childproof caps are required by law but if the cap is not replaced correctly, it is easily removed.

Plants can be poisonous when touched or ingested. Parents need to become familiar with dangerous plants in their area, to replace problem plants in their yard and home, and to teach children to recognize poison

shock
a serious weakening of the body caused by a severe physical or psychological injury

A Closer Look

Fast Aid

Parents and caregivers can help their children by knowing what to do in a medical emergency. Here are some guidelines for the first few crucial minutes after a crisis.

Urgent care or the emergency room?

Urgent care facilities are appropriate for illnesses and conditions that are readily diagnosed and treated. When the child's doctor is not available, the urgent-care facility can handle:

- simple infections (sore throats, earaches)
- minor broken bones
- cuts that require only a few stitches

Emergency room treatment is recommended when there is:

- a serious breathing problem
- a seizure that doesn't stop
- a major injury (such as a fracture that has broken through the skin)
- a striking degree of lethargy or limpness

Drive or wait for emergency transportation?

Dialing 911 is the quickest access to help. Most of the time, emergency help is on the scene within 10 minutes. Before then, a dispatch technician can be giving emergency advice over the phone. Parents who race to the hospital with their child in the car can't tend to their child if he vomits, goes into shock, stops breathing, or needs other emergency care at the moment. Parents have also gotten into automobile accidents and experienced heart attacks and strokes while driving the stricken child to emergency care.

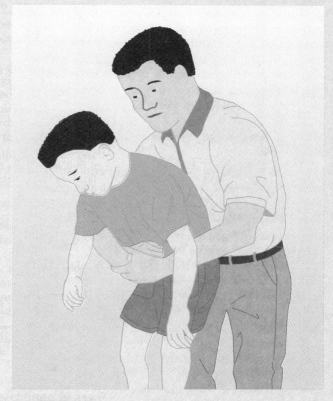

Heimlich maneuver with child standing (maneuver clears obstructed airway).

Where should the first aid kits be?

Each family should have two first aid kits—one at home and one in the car. Keep them out of the reach of small children. Restock them after each use.

(continued on next page)

(continued from previous page)

What if you're not there?

Remember that only a parent can give consent to treat a minor child. Grandparents, stepparents, and babysitters may not. To avoid delays in treatment and increased suffering by the child, give medical power of attorney to a friend, relative, or childcare provider. It doesn't have to be formal but it does have to be signed and dated. Give a copy of the medical history for each child, including allergies, regularly taken medications, immunizations and blood type, and health insurance information to anyone who looks after your child.

Mouth-to-mouth seal with older child (child not breathing, has heartbeat).

Other general recommendations in emergency situations:

1. *Take a course in first aid* to help you respond with confidence. Get a CPR card (the American Red Cross's CPR course takes only 4 hours). At the very least, familiarize yourself with first aid procedures (the phone book's information section is often a good source of information).

2. *Stay calm.* Your stress can greatly increase the child's fear and panic. Stay as controlled as possible so you can tend to the child. Be reassuring to him no matter how serious the situation. You can "freak out" later if you still feel the need.

3. *Don't move the child if there is a chance of serious injury.* Concentrate instead on immediate life-saving procedures—help with breathing, apply direct pressure if there is bleeding, and so forth. If the child *must* be moved, support the head and neck and move in a straight-line direction by pulling under the arms.

4. *Give clear information.* If you tend to do poorly under pressure, have information about your child's allergies, medications, birthdate, and so on a piece of paper where you can get it at a moment's notice. Clear, accurate information will help the emergency personnel or the doctor give the best treatment.

5. *Be at your child's side whenever possible.* Most emergency vehicles let parents ride along. Most hospitals encourage parents to be at the child's bedside or alongside wherever treatment is being given. The child's pain, confusion, and fear can be lessened by the presence of a loving, calm, and reassuring adult.

---

cardiopulmonary resuscitation (CPR) a lifesaving technique involving the administration of artificial breathing and heart stimulation

ivy, oak, and sumac and to avoid putting any plant in their mouth. Parents should have the number of the regional Poison Information Center within easy access.

Parents have always had to contend with insect stings and bites (which are particularly problematic for the allergic child). A relatively new outdoor threat is Lyme disease, caused by the bite of the deer tick. Save any tick responsible for a bite and take it to the physician right away. Bites can be avoided by staying on trails in wooded areas and wearing light, long-sleeved, and long-legged clothing. Ticks are most active between May and September.

■●▲   CONCEPT SUMMARY

Keeping Preschoolers Healthy

- Allow them to receive 11–13 hours of nighttime sleep
- Permit a nap, if needed
- Avoid disturbing TV programs and scary stories
- Protect the sleepwalking child from injury
- Investigate the causes of nightmares (stress, fear?)
- Plan meals that provide 1400–1800 kcal of high quality nutrition per day
- Sufficient dietary protein, calcium, and phosphorus are essential
- Keep to the child's inoculation schedule
- Prevent the incidence of illness and disease by good hygiene, limiting contact with others who are infected, good nutrition, and adequate sleep
- Provide good supervision while children play
- Provide a safe play environment

Falls

Falls occur frequently but usually are of little consequence in infancy and early childhood (Ivan et al., 1983). Bumps, scrapes, and bruises are common when children fall on level surfaces. Falls from furniture, playground equipment, fences, and trees can result in more serious injuries such as dislocated or broken bones. Head injuries are the most potentially serious consequences of falls. Immediate medical attention is necessary if one or more of the following symptoms are present after a fall or blow to the head:

1. unusual drowsiness
2. severe or persistent vomiting
3. double vision
4. slurred speech
5. convulsions
6. bleeding from areas other than the scalp (ears, eyes, etc.)
7. pale, sweaty, or weak appearance
8. black eyes or blackness behind the ears
9. fluid draining from the nose
10. slow or irregular breathing or heart rate
11. unequal pupil size (unless this is normal for the child)

In Touch

NATIONAL HEAD INJURY
  FOUNDATION
333 Turnpike Road
Southborough, MA 01772

AMERICAN RED CROSS NATIONAL
  HEADQUARTERS
17th and D Streets, NW
Washington, DC 20006

Local chapters offer first aid courses

TOWARD EFFECTIVE PARENTING

Parenting the Special Needs Child

The special needs child experiences conditions that place some limitation on his or her ability to function. Whether the condition is physical or mental, congenital or traumatic, internal or external, parents can greatly facilitate their child's adjustment by applying the following guidelines:

1. Special needs children need access to medical and technological advances that can improve their ability to function. Surgery, medications, hearing aids, and wheelchair-accessible facilities are all examples of innovations that make it easier for the child to learn, socialize, and live an effective daily life.

2. Special needs children need the same loving attention, good food, medical attention, rest, and exercise that help other children grow and thrive.

3. Special needs children also need the same contact with children and adults that other children receive. Sheltering or protecting these children from others because they are "different" or because parents fear their child will be ridiculed or criticized is misplaced concern. Normal development requires broad experiences that build self-reliance and understanding.

4. Like other children, special needs children are better equipped to cope with life's challenges if they are encouraged to be self-reliant, confident, and assertive. Children who are passive and dependent may lack in self-esteem, problem solving skills, and determination to strive and achieve.

5. Special needs children are much more similar to other children than they are different. *Everyone* makes adaptations in order to lead more productive and comfortable lives—one child may use crutches, another relies on reading glasses, and a third would rather take the elevator than climb the stairs. In a real sense, everyone is handicapped in one way or another, the only differences are that some conditions are more obvious and more debilitating than others. Different is not necessarily inferior, it's just different.

6. Know about your special child's condition so you can help educate the public and dispel myths. For example, blind children are not also deaf and mute and Down's syndrome is *not* contagious. Welcome questions so *you* can provide the information; teach your child to welcome questions about the condition so he or she can feel more empowered and in control.

"Everybody's Different/Nobody's Perfect" is a particularly helpful publication available through the Muscular Dystrophy Association, 810 Seventh Ave., New York, New York 10010. Although it speaks specifically about MD, it makes helpful statements that can be generalized to other conditions.

● **Chapter Summary**

● Growth rate during the preschool years is slower and steadier than in infancy, with muscles and bones accounting for most of the weight gained. The child becomes taller and more slender during this period, and internal systems stabilize. Genetics, low birth weight, malnutrition, and chronic illness account for most of the variation in growth.

- Aimless activity decreases as the child's attention span improves.
- The brain and nervous system are still growing at a rapid rate. Organizational changes in the brain include specialization and lateralization. Hand preference may be established.
- A full set of 20 baby teeth are usually present by age 2.5 or 3.
- The reproductive system grows little if at all.
- Gross and fine motor skills continue to develop according to the cephalocaudal and proximodistal principles of growth. Preschoolers refine and improve the motor skills established in infancy while adding new behaviors. Fine motor skills such as drawing or stringing beads are more difficult for the preschooler to master because of the precision they demand.
- The sensory systems are well developed by the end of the preschool period. The senses won't be fully integrated until the school years.
- Children under age 6 are normally farsighted because of the immature shape of their eyeball. The ability to visually discriminate items and to accurately identify them improves with age.
- Untreated middle ear infections place children at risk for hearing loss.
- Taste, touch, and smell are highly developed.
- Most preschool children need 11–13 hours of sleep to function efficiently. Naps will probably be abandoned during this time. Preschoolers may resist going to bed or experience sleepwalking, sleeptalking, nightmares, and/or night terrors.
- Appetite fluctuates as a function of the child's slowed growth rate. Balanced nutrition is still vital to meeting the child's developmental needs. Preschoolers often require nutritious snacks to tide them over until mealtime.
- Accidents, especially motor vehicle accidents, are the leading cause of preventable injury and death among preschool age children. Careful supervision and area/vehicle safety can reduce risks. Most serious accidents occur at home or in a car.

● Observational Exercise

Some of the most obvious changes in children during the preschool period involve height, weight, and motor skills. Students can come to appreciate the magnitude of change that occurs between the ages of 3 and 6 by noting differences in physical growth and motor development in two children.

Procedure: Measure and observe the behavior of a 3 year old child and a 6 year old child. The children should be of the same sex. (You must obtain the parents' permission.)

1. *Measure each child.* Have the children wear as little clothing as possible when being measured. Swimsuits, leotards, or underclothes work nicely. Remove all bulky clothing such as sweaters, and measure height, weight, and leg length with shoes removed. Record your observations:

	3 year old	6 year old
a. Head circumference (at eyebrow level)		
b. Height		
c. Weight		
d. Length of arms (shoulder to fingertips)		
e. Length of legs (waist to floor)		
f. Waist size (at the navel)		

What overall changes in growth and physical proportions take place between the ages of 3 and 6?

2. Compare the large- and small-muscle skills of the 3 and 6 year old. Record your observations:

Large-muscle skills	3 year old	6 year old
Hops on one foot		
Hops on two feet		
Jumps over a pillow with two feet		
Walks on tiptoes		
Skips		
Balances on one foot		
Walks toe-to-heel on a 5-foot chalk or tape line		
Catches a large balloon (note whether hands or arms are used)		
Walks down stairs using alternate feet		

Small-muscle skills
Picks up five pennies from a flat surface
Draws a circle
Draws a square
Cuts out a large paper triangle with scissors
Copies the letter in his or her name
Traces a straight line with a crayon.

Note: Test children in a safe area, free from traffic and clutter that may cause them to trip. Carefully supervise them while they jump or descend stairs to prevent accidents. Children should use their preferred hand for cutting, drawing, and tracing. Keep in mind as you observe that a great deal of individual variation in behavior is to be expected.

● Recommended Readings

Buscaglia, L. (Ed.). (1983). *The disabled and their parents: A counseling challenge* (rev. ed.). New York: Holt.

Endres, J. B. & Rockwell, R. E. (1980). *Food, nutrition, and the young child.* St. Louis, MO: Mosby.

Ferber, R. (1986). *Solving your child's sleep problems.* New York: Simon & Schuster.

Gazzaniga, M. (1985). *The social brain.* New York: Basic Books.

Skinner, L. (1979). *Motor development in the preschool years.* Springfield IL: Charles C. Thomas.

Cognitive Development During the Preschool Years

● Cognitive Development

Between birth and age 2, the child comes to understand the world by acting upon it. During the preschool years, sensorimotor actions become more internalized as the child becomes capable of *symbolic thought*. Symbolic thought allows the child to begin to make comparisons in her mind using mental imagery, memory, and language to represent concrete objects and events. For example, preschoolers learn to "count in their heads" without using their fingers. They learn to use words and concepts to aid in their thinking. Children can think about and tell others about the elephant they saw at the zoo without actually having to see the elephant each time they refer to it. The preschool child's ability to remember and use mental images at a later time makes pretend play possible. Using symbolic thought, the child can separate objects from events. The preschooler now recognizes that the high chair is not part of the eating process but is something to sit on during eating. They can also detach thought from action, realizing they don't have to do everything they think about. Thus, the ability to use symbols and symbolic representation is the cornerstone of all cognitive development during the preschool years.

Piaget's Theory of Cognitive Development

The shift from motor activity to symbolic thought marks the beginning of the *preoperational stage* of cognitive development. This stage lasts from age 2 to age 6 or 7. Two distinct levels of preoperational thought appear within this stage. The first level spans age 2–4; the second, between 4 and 6 (Kenny, 1983). A brain growth spurt permits the more sophisticated cognitive approach of the 4–6 year old (Fischer & Pipp, 1984).

preoperational stage
the stage of cognitive development that follows the sensorimotor stage in Piaget's scheme. The preoperational child has some mental concepts but hasn't acquired the means or operations by which to manipulate and transform them

Between ages 2 and 4 the child can apply a familiar action pattern to something outside herself. As an infant, the child could pretend that she was eating. Now she can pretend her *doll* is eating or that her bear is naughty or is a teacher, and so forth. As the child progresses to the second level, she can imagine relationships between two representations: One doll is the worker doll while the other is the boss doll (Watson, 1981). Besides understanding social relationships (husband–wife, mother–child), the preschooler can also understand contingencies—situations in which one factor depends on another. For example, the weight of the bucket is contingent on how much sand is in it; whether or not mother is home depends on how close it is to 3:00 p.m., and so on.

Limitations of Preoperational Thought

Although symbolic thought provides greater cognitive flexibility than sensorimotor actions, the preschool child is prevented from thinking logically by other characteristics of preoperational thought—notably, centration and egocentrism.

centration
the tendency of the preoperational child to focus attention on one aspect of a situation or object while excluding all others

CENTRATION *Centration* is the tendency of the preoperational child to focus attention on one aspect of a situation and to ignore all others (Inhelder, 1960). Centration prevents the child from understanding that a change in the appearance or configuration of an object does not affect certain attributes of that object. For example, preschool children believe that a tall, slender glass holds more than a short, wide cup even when the amount of liquid in each is the same. They are also convinced that they have more money if their 10 pennies are spread out rather than stacked up. Why do children make these errors in judgment? In both situations, the child is focusing on only one dimension of the configuration, considering the height of the glass but ignoring the width, or noting the surface area covered by the pennies but disregarding the number of pennies. Since preschoolers center on a single piece of visual information at a time, we say that their judgments are dominated by appearance, or are *perception bound*. Furthermore, to the young child, appearance is the most salient clue. Since 10 loose pennies *look* like more than 10 stacked pennies to the child, there must be more pennies in the former configuration than in the latter. Figure 9–2 illustrates the difficulties preschoolers have in understanding apparent transformations in *conservation tasks*, tasks devised by Piaget to test children's ability to understand transformation.

perception bound
making judgments based on one's perception of an object or situation while ignoring other relevant cues. A characteristic of preoperational thought

conservation tasks
tasks originally devised by Piaget to assess children's skill in understanding apparent transformations

Although they have learned to distinguish between themselves and other objects, preschool children do not understand that they are not the center of it all but a person among people with one viewpoint among many. Centration makes it impossible for them to understand other people's points of view or to imagine what it would be like to be another person. For example, consider this exchange (Phillips, 1969, p. 61):

INTERVIEWER: Do you have a brother?
CHILD: Yes.
INTERVIEWER: What's his name?
CHILD: Jim.
INTERVIEWER: Does Jim have a brother?
CHILD: No.

Piaget and Inhelder's (1969) *Three Mountain Task* provides an interesting demonstration of centration in early childhood (Fig. 9–1). When asked to select the view that the doll sees, young preschoolers select random pictures, apparently not realizing that position can change one's perspective. Somewhat older children choose the picture that represents their point of view, not the doll's. When 4–5.5 year olds are asked to generate *their own* view of the scene before generating the view for the observer, the percentage of self-centered and random errors in perspective taking are reduced (Gollin & Sharps, 1987).

Children age 2 or 3 think that if they know a secret or a fact, their caregiver knows it, too. Although centration is not relinquished until age 9 or 10, when children understand that other people's perceptions, feelings, wishes, and motives can differ from their own, they can assess another's knowledge when they have perceptual access to the same information. For example, if asked "What did Mike see in the box?" they can answer if they looked in the box as well (Ruffman & Olson, 1989).

Transformations involve the process of change from one stage to another. Centration makes it difficult for the preoperational child to understand transformation or to use language to describe it. These children

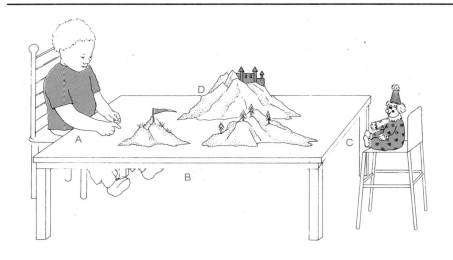

■ **Figure 9–1**

Piaget's Three Mountain Task.

tend to focus on the static, tangible aspects of a situation and to disregard the actions involved, thus orienting toward *states, not transformations.* For example, a preoperational child will agree that two equally spaced rows of buttons contain the same number. But when the space between the buttons in the bottom row is increased, the child will think there are more buttons in that row than in the other. Piaget describes the child's mental images at this stage as a series of separate and unrelated images. Preschoolers focus on the state or end result and not on the transformation, while adults view the sequence as a continuous, related action.

EGOCENTRISM Centration encourages egocentrism. *Egocentrism* is the condition whereby the individual—in this case, the preschooler—experiences every event in reference to herself. Children in this stage may assume, for example, that rain falls to keep them indoors, or the night comes to make them sleep. Young preschoolers may play hide-and-seek by covering their eyes with their hands. Apparently, they assume that if *they* cannot see others, others cannot see them.

Preschoolers also tend to believe in animism and finalism and engage in magical thinking. *Animism* refers to the child's tendency to attribute lifelike qualities to inanimate objects. Like other living creatures, preschoolers assume that kickballs and planets move of their own free will. One child explained that the clouds move very slowly "because they haven't any legs or paws" (Piaget, 1945/1951, p. 251). Older siblings soon discover that the surest way to upset little brother or sister is to "torture" their possessions. Young children react vigorously to assaults on their dolls and stuffed toys because they endow the toys with real feelings like their own and assume that the objects are actually suffering. They also recognize that the attack represents harm to them by harming their property.

Animism is responsible for some of children's most charming beliefs—faith in the Easter Bunny, for instance. But the phenomenon also forms the foundation of some of the preschooler's most serious fears. Children might be afraid that vacuum cleaners will inhale them, for example, or that bathtub drains might swallow them. They assume that demons and monsters on television are utterly real and housed behind the glass screen (and what if someone let them out??!!). Toward the end of this period, at about age 5 or 6, children begin to understand the distinction between animate and inanimate objects but still make some errors. They reason that a bird is alive because it flies, a bike is not alive because we make it move, but a stream is alive because it flows all the time (Piaget, 1929/1976).

Finalism is the belief that all movement accomplishes some purpose. For example, a child might believe that the moon rises high in the sky so we can see it, and that the clouds come to bring rain or to make the sky pretty. According to Piaget (1929/1976), children believe that the movements of objects are goal-directed because their own movements are.

egocentrism
the orientation that takes into account one's own point of view and excludes other's perspectives

animism
the belief that inanimate objects are alive and therefore have emotions, feelings and motives. A characteristic of preoperational thought

finalism
a preoperational notion that all movement is purposeful or is performed for some function

Since preschoolers believe themselves to be the center of the universe, they feel they can alter reality by their thoughts or wishes. Such a belief is called *magical thinking*. Through magical thinking children become totally absorbed in play, because they are convinced they have become the person, thing, or event they imagined themselves to be. With this orientation, it's no wonder that children in this age range behave with such conviction and authority.

magical thinking
the preoperational belief that reality can be altered by thoughts or wishes

Children in this stage assume that reactions of other people to events and circumstances are identical to their own. For example, they assume everyone likes corn flakes, hot dogs, and sandboxes and hates broccoli, wet dogs, and mushroom soup. Children characterized by egocentrism also expect others to be able to visualize what they have in mind. When preschoolers say something like, "I gave it to him" and are asked "Gave what to whom?" they become exasperated with the listener because they expect the listener to be intuitively aware of the exchange.

Although egocentrism implies self-centeredness and a narrow world view, it does not suggest selfishness. Preoperational children are capable of displaying great concern and empathy for others. They try to give comfort and consolation and will even give up something of their own to help a person in need. A young child who places her own special blanket around the shoulders of a sick parent or sibling is being supremely unselfish. At the same time, their egocentrism guides them to assume that their special comforts give comfort to others.

IRREVERSIBILITY Another limitation of preoperational thought is *irreversibility*. Children at this stage cannot play back actions in their imaginations in order to reconstruct the original. Interestingly, if children move the buttons in the bottom row of Figure 9–2 into their original positions, they will say that the rows once again contain the same number—not because they now understand that action and outcome are somehow related but because their perception that the two rows are the same length has been satisfied.

irreversibility
the inability of the preoperational child to reverse their thinking to undo transformations

CONCRETENESS A final characteristic of preschoolers' cognitive development is the static quality, or *concreteness*, of their language. Young children tend to describe tangible and observable aspects of the environment, disregarding subtleties and abstractions. Thus, the preoperational child can understand the word *cold* to describe ice cream but not an emotionally inexpressive person.

concreteness
a characteristic of preoperational thought whereby children can understand specific examples and situations they can observe and experience but have difficulty with the abstract

● Reasoning and Concept Formation

Concatenative Thought

Egocentrism and centration both affect the preschool child's ability to reason and to solve everyday problems. When attempting to explain

■ **Figure 9–2**

Centration.

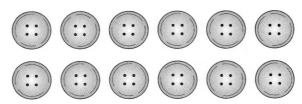

When the buttons are spaced equally, a child will agree that both rows have the same number of buttons.

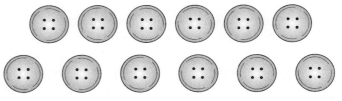

When the bottom row of buttons is spaced father apart, a child will think there are more buttons in that row.

cause and effect, preschoolers assume that the observable characteristics of an object have something to do with the outcome. Consider this exchange between Piaget and a preschool-age child:

> PIAGET: The sun does not fall down. Why?
> CHILD: Because it is hot.
> PIAGET: The sun stops there. How?
> CHILD: Because it is yellow.
> PIAGET: And the moon, how does it stop there?
> CHILD: Same as the sun, because it is lying down on the sky. Because it is very high up, because there is (no more) sun, because it is up very high. (Piaget, 1924/1964, p. 229)

In this example, the child connects unrelated ideas to explain why the sun and the moon do not fall from the sky. During the preoperational period, children also juxtapose cause and effect in their statements. A boy may say, for instance, that he's had a bath because he's clean or he fell from his bicycle because he broke his arm (Piaget, 1924/ 1964). All of these inappropriate links are examples of *concatenative thinking*—thinking that focuses on superficial attributes of an object or situation in an effort to understand causality or that transposes cause and effect.

Transductive Reasoning

Transductive reasoning also leads to illogical conclusions, since it involves reasoning from one particular instance to another particular instance

concatenative thinking
thinking characteristic of the preoperational period whereby the child assumes, wrongly, that a causal relationship exists between certain objects and situations

transductive reasoning
a type of reasoning used by children in the preoperational stage whereby generalizations are made from one specific instance to another specific instance

A Closer Look

Fishing for Ice??

The limitations of preschool logic make for some very interesting perceptions. In May, 1986, *American Baby Magazine* printed these observations submitted by parents:

> As four-year-old Donnie watched his father and uncle get all their fishing tackle ready for the next day, he asked, "Where are you going, Daddy?" His father replied, "We're going ice fishing tomorrow morning." After pondering this for a moment, Donnie asked, "But why do you want to catch ice?"

> Early in my second pregnancy, I thought it would be a good idea to begin preparing our four-year old Kyle for the birth of a brother or a sister.
> "Kyle," I said, "when a family decides to have a new baby, do you know what happens next?"
> "Yes," he replied confidently. "They go to the grocery store!"

> "No, Kyle," I tried to explain. "People don't buy babies at the grocery store."
> "Yes, they do," he quickly corrected. "I see them all the time in people's shopping carts."

> Jamie, age 5, was quite concerned to learn that his best friend had been grounded for misbehaving. He wasn't quite sure what grounded was and didn't know if his friend deserved such punishment. Finally, at dinner, he stopped eating and blurted out, "But, Mom, do they have to *bury* him?"

> In his first days in kindergarten, 5 year old Patrick received an abundance of gold stars for accomplishments. As time went on, however, the stars diminished in number until they stopped. When his visiting grandmother asked why he wasn't getting any more gold stars, he replied, "Oh, I just want to be a normal child."

without reference to the general. A preschool child may argue that A is like B so B is like A. Thus, if such a child were bitten by one black dog, she would assume that other black dogs will bite her, too. Transduction can sometimes yield a correct conclusion, but the overgeneralization resulting from this type of reasoning often leads to stubborn, rigid behavior. Using transduction, the child who learns from a doctor's visit that "needles hurt" will anticipate that all visits to the doctor will result in pain or discomfort. Reminding the child of pleasant visits to the doctor or of the benefits of inoculation will do little to change the child's frame of reference in such a case.

The child's perception of cause and effect is influenced by transductive as well as concatenative reasoning. The child usually infers cause and effect if two events are related in time. For example, if the child hears a loud clap of thunder during an electrical storm and the lights go out, she will erroneously assume that the thunder caused the power outage. In another example, a mother accidentally falls into a swimming pool with her clothes on while her young children are watching. From that time on, the children refer to the outfit the mother was wearing as "the clothes that pushed you in" because they consider the clothes responsible for the mother's fall.

Preschool children also believe that the details surrounding a given event must be precisely recreated if the event is to occur again. For example, a child who first saw a rainbow at preschool would consider it necessary to be at preschool to see another rainbow. Likewise, a child who is always served one wedge of a waffle at a time would have trouble believing that a whole (round) waffle was indeed a waffle. It couldn't be a waffle, she would reason; the shape isn't right.

Children can make causal inferences about sequences of events when they are between 3 and 4 years of age if they are provided with choices (e.g., "Did the hammer, the pin, or the light bulb cause the wet cup to break?") (das Gupta & Bryant, 1989). Foreshadowing this ability, there is an increase in the spontaneous use of *if* and *because* expressions between 3 and 4 years of age (Byrnes & Duff, 1988). Preschoolers understand that psychological states (like happy, upset, serious) exist and that such states can cause behavior. It's not clear that 2–6 year olds are aware that both people and situations are causal factors, too (Miller & Aloise, 1989).

With maturity the child becomes capable of logical thought based on inductive and deductive reasoning. *Inductive reasoning* proceeds from specific to general ("If I walk upright and humans walk upright, I must be human"). *Deductive reasoning* moves from general to specific ("If mammals are warm-blooded and dogs are mammals, then dogs are warm-blooded"). Between the ages of 4 and 5 children demonstrate knowledge of *certainty* by using terms like "I think" "I know" or "I am sure" accurately (Moore & Davidge, 1989). By age 4 children realize that saying "I know..." is a more reliable indicator of a particular fact or outcome than is saying "I think" or "I guess" (Moore et al., 1989).

Concept Formation

concept
an abstract idea based on grouping objects according to a common theme

According to Piaget, concept formation is one of the most important cognitive achievements of childhood. *Concepts* are cognitive categories that help children—and adults—organize information and acquire new knowledge. The concept *car*, for example, encompasses identifying information about the appearance (shiny, smooth, four tires) and the actions (loud, fast, smokey) of cars. Children learn that cars come in a variety of shapes and sizes and that other objects such as motorcycles and trucks might share similar characteristics but still are not classified as cars. Children acquire some basic concepts such as *dog, house,* and *toy* relatively early. Other more abstract concepts, such as *number,* distance, and space, require more time.

Identity Constancy

Preschoolers aged 3–4 years have not yet attained *identity constancy*, or the understanding that features of individuals, like their sex, age, or species, are permanent and unaffected by appearance. When Robert deVries (1969) placed a dog mask on the head of a cat named Maynard, young preschoolers incorrectly identified the cat as a dog. By the time children are 5 or 6 years old, they understand that Maynard is a cat no matter what changes take place in its appearance.

Numbers

Four and 5 year olds can count relatively easily from 0 to 10, especially if they have been regularly watching educational TV programs such as *Sesame Street*. But 4 and 5 year olds often have difficulty answering if, for example, six is more or less than three, and counting out seven straws may be too hard for them. At this stage, children lack a mature concept of numbers as separate values.

Young preschoolers also have yet to develop a sense of one-to-one correspondence. When 4 or 5 year olds are shown two rows of objects varying in number—for instance, six bottles and twelve glasses—and are asked to match the number of glasses with the number of bottles most are unable to do so. Instead of placing one glass next to each bottle and removing six of the glasses, children of this age lengthen the rows of bottles so that each set of objects appears to cover equal space. If the row of bottles is already longer than that of the glasses, preoperational children assume that there are more bottles than glasses. When the sets are small, however, even 3–4 year olds do better on tasks involving one-to-one correspondence (Sophian, 1988).

one-to-one correspondence matching each number with a single item when counting

Five and 6 year olds have an intermediate understanding of one-to-one correspondence. They can arrange bottles and glasses so there are six of each, with one glass corresponding to one bottle. But when the experimenter duplicates the configuration in Figure 9–3, adding extra glasses but compressing the glass line's length, the children revert back to believing that there are now more bottles than glasses. By the time children are 6 or 7 years old, one-to-one correspondence is complete and they are able to match glasses to bottles without being distracted by the length of the rows. Children can understand relational terms like *some* or *most* before they can understand the meaning of *all* or *none* (Badzinski et al., 1989).

Size Discrimination

What do 2 year olds know about the size of things? Preschoolers' knowledge of size is related both to their age and whether the object was familiar or unfamiliar (Sera et al., 1988). Two year olds had accurate knowledge of the typical sizes of shoes, but 4 year olds could skillfully estimate ordinary shoe, button, and plate sizes.

■ Figure 9–3

When bottles and glasses are lined up one-to-one (top), the preoperational child will agree that they are the same in number. When the glasses are close together and the bottles are spread out, the child will say that there are more bottles than glasses.

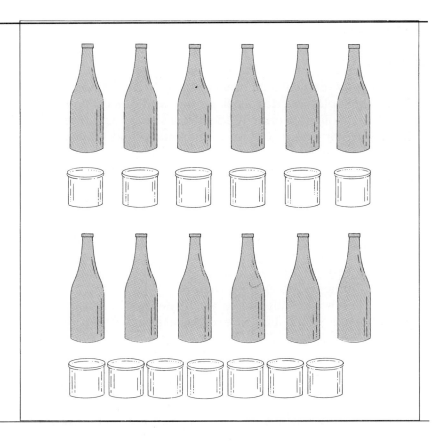

Age, Time, Weight, Space, Distance and Speed

Adults use concepts of age, time, weight, distance, and space to organize much of their experience. It's important for adults to know how long ago things happened and how old, how far, and how big objects are. According to Piaget, the first three essential ingredients in the development of concepts of time, distance, and speed are these:

1. The ability to represent and remember the order of events
2. The ability to conceptualize intervals between events
3. The ability to avoid confusing concepts of time and space (P. A. Cowan, 1978, p. 127)

Preoperational children have difficulty with all three. Thus, it's no surprise that preschool children have trouble understanding the passage of time and the occurrence of change. For them, life is static; the way things are now is the way they have always been. A child who looks through the family album, for example, might see a picture of her parents as children. "That's not you, Dad", the child might argue, "You're a dad, not a kid". Another child might hear her mother tell of the good times she had as a child—riding ponies, playing in the snow, and swimming in the summer. "Gee, Mom," the child might reply, "Too bad you're not my best friend now. We would have fun." A gradual change such as aging is difficult for the preschooler to comprehend, since it occurs slowly and is barely noticeable. Instead of realizing that the person in the album is the parent at a younger age, the preschool child tends to disregard the passage of time and to assume that the parent and the child in the picture are two different individuals.

The concept of age involves an understanding of both time and number. Two to 3 year olds may be able to tell you how old they are and may even be able to hold up the right number of fingers, but they don't understand what the numbers two or three represent and they can't comprehend how long a year lasts. Furthermore, preschool children become distracted by concrete dimensions such as size, and often assume that bigger people are also older and/or heavier (C. Smith et al., 1985). Often, too, preschoolers—and older children as well, as the following quote illustrates—do not understand that birth order is related to age (Piaget, 1959/1969, p. 209):

ADULT: How old are you?
DOUR: Seven and a half.
ADULT: Have you any brothers or sisters?
DOUR: No.
ADULT: Any friends?
DOUR: Yes. Gerald.
ADULT: Is he younger or older than you?
DOUR: A little older, he's twelve years old.
ADULT: How much older is he than you?
DOUR: Five years.
ADULT: Was he born before or after you?
DOUR: I don't know.
ADULT: But think about it. Haven't you just told me his age?
        Was he born before or after you?
DOUR: He didn't tell me.
ADULT: But is there no way of finding out whether he was born
        before you or after you?
DOUR: I could ask him.

While intervals of time involve duration (how long), intervals of space involve distance (how far or how high). Until about age 10, preschool children have trouble understanding that length is unaffected by the direction of movement (the drive from A to B covers the same distance as the drive from B to A along the same route), that size is unaffected by the amount of movement (a short ruler and a long one yield the same measurements of a room even though the one ruler will be moved more often), and that longer intervals don't necessarily imply longer distances (a half-hour shopping trip might cover five miles while another half-hour trip might cover ten). Since preschoolers can understand principles of distance (1. The straight route between 2 points is always the shortest, and 2. If the two routes are the same up to a point and then only one route continues, that route is the longest), they must conceive of distance as intervals of a fixed length (Bartsch & Wellman, 1988).

Speed is one variable that preschoolers (and some adult commuters) fail to consider at all, probably because distance is a more concrete concept that is easier to measure. Also, terms that imply temporal sequencing—such as *before* and *after*—are used ambiguously until children are 7 or 8 years old (Piaget & Inhelder, 1967/1969).

Constructing a Cognitive Map

Preschool children are better able to represent space in their minds and to read maps than previously assumed (Uttal & Wellman, 1989). When 4–7 year old children learn a map before entering a playhouse, they are able to trace a route through it more quickly than those who had not been exposed to the map. Older children performed significantly better than younger children.

Conservation Skills

The ability to perform Piagetian conservation tasks increases dramatically for children between kindergarten and Grade 1 (Gulko et al., 1988). However, conservation of substance, quantity, and weight were always more difficult among the children being studied than conservation of area and easier than conservation of volume.

Classification

classification
sorting objects into categories or classes

Simple *classification* involves sorting objects into categories on the basis of some common feature such as color, size, or shape (Piaget & Inhelder, 1959/1969). For the most part, classification skills are incomplete through age 4 even when objects share a close family resemblance (e.g., bears and big dogs) but improve with age (Alexander & Enns, 1988). When children are given an assortment of geometric shapes and asked to "put together the ones that are alike," they are inconsistent in the ability to focus on a single dimension and exclude other characteristics. Color is selected over shape and composition (as in the case of modern paintings) by 3, 4, and 5 year olds. Over time color loses influence and shape becomes the most prominent classification cue (Harrison, 1990). Piaget (1959/1969) indicated that children under age 7 are rarely able to sort multicolored shapes correctly. More recent findings suggest that after age 4 classification skills improve significantly. Young children do tend to focus on single attributes when making classifications, while second graders can focus on multiple attributes of an object (Ward et al., 1989). For example, when preschoolers are asked, "What makes a vibble a vibble?", they might say "All vibbles have long noses," while the older child might indicate vibbles have long noses, short fur, and a white ring around their necks.

NO SIMILARITY

The child made no response, or the response seemed random, or the child made a design with no apparent recognition of similar form. For example:

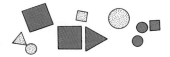

INCOMPLETE SIMILARITY

The child sorted some by shape, color, or size, but others randomly. For example:

COMPLETE SIMILARITY

The child sorted all thirty-two shapes by one category, or by two categories. For example:

SERIATION *Seriation* is a classification skill that involves ordering objects in a series or sequence according to some dimension. Four and five year olds who are given a pile of sticks can pick out the largest and smallest sticks from the pile but cannot arrange them in order from smallest to largest, a mental operation called *transitivity* (Piaget and Inhelder, 1948/1956). Rather, they usually alternate between large and small sticks in their arrangements, for they cannot see a relationship between more than two elements at one time or between the individual parts and the whole (Blevins-Knabe, 1987). Ordinarily, children don't develop the ability to order events in a sequence until after age 7, when they enter the stage of concrete operations, unless they have had practice manipulating and ordering objects.

CLASS INCLUSION *Class inclusion* is a more complicated classification skill. It involves the understanding that one item can be a member of

seriation
arranging items in a logical sequence (i.e., tallest to shortest; lightest to darkest)

transitivity
Piaget and Inhelder's term for *seriation*

class inclusion
the concept that one item can belong to several subsets or classes

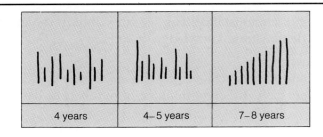

| 4 years | 4–5 years | 7–8 years |

■ **Figure 9–5**

Between the ages of 4 and 6 children have difficulty reordering a series. After age 7 they are able to correctly solve the seriation problem.

■●▲ **CONCEPT SUMMARY**

Characteristics of Preoperational Thought (Ages 2 to 6/7)

● *Level 1—Ages 2–4*
   – Can apply action patterns outside the self

● *Level 2—Ages 4–6/7*
   – Can imagine relationships between two entities
   – Can understand contingencies

● *Symbolic Thought*
   Using mental imagery, language, and memory to represent concrete objects and events

● *Centration*
   Focusing attention on one aspect of the situation while ignoring all others. Centration is manifested through
   – problems in understanding transformations

● *Egocentrism*
   Representing experiences in reference to the self. Egocentrism is manifested through
   – animism
   – finalism
   – magical thinking
   – difficulty in taking the perspective of others

● *Irreversibility*
   Inability to reconstruct the steps in an outcome, from the product to the beginning

● *Concreteness*
   Focusing on the tangible, observable aspects of people and objects

● *Reasoning*
   – Preschoolers presume cause and effect if two events or attributes are closely associated (concatenative thinking).
   – They make generalizations from one particular instance to another (transductive reasoning).
   – They can understand cause if they are provided with choices.
   – Preschoolers assume that occurrences are associated only with a specific set of circumstances (e.g., it rains only in the mountains).
   – They can demonstrate knowledge of certainty.

● *Concept Formation*
   – Identity constancy is achieved by the end of the preschool period.
   – Preschoolers have difficulty thinking of numbers as having specific values.

- Older preschoolers have an intermediate understanding of one-to-one correspondence. They do best if they deal with small sets of items.
- They can estimate the typical size of some common objects.
- They have difficulty understanding the passage of time and gradual change.
- They don't understand the concept of age.
- They don't understand that length or distance is unaffected by the direction of movement or the amount of time that has passed.
- They can use cognitive maps to help them represent space in their minds.
- Conservation skills improve.

● *Classification Skills*
- Preschoolers can sort objects easiest if they share a common appearance or if they can focus on color.
- They cannot consistently order objects according to some dimension (i.e., largest to smallest) even though they can identify the end points of classification.
- Preschoolers have difficulty understanding the relationship of parts to a whole or that one item might belong to several subsets. Training can aid the acquisition of class inclusion skills.

several subsets. A preschool child who is given pictures of chairs, tables, and beds might be able to name all the items correctly but when given a subset of three chairs and a table and asked, "Are there more chairs or more furniture?" will usually respond "More chairs." This problem also involves part–whole relationships—a notion which calls for the understanding that each item is an element of some greater whole. When asked if she is an Episcopalian like her parents, one child might reply, "No, I'm a girl." Another child might say, "No, I'm Spanish." Both these children may be having difficult with word meaning, but they are also having trouble recognizing that a person can have many identities, all equally valid. Three and 4 year olds who have had some practice working through class inclusion or part/whole problems and who have received training from adult observers on these problems do better than children without such experiences (Callanan, 1989). Of all the concepts preschoolers must master classification, time sequencing, seriation, and language comprehension are the areas in which most kindergarten children are weakest. Class inclusion is considerably easier than other concrete operational tasks (Chapman & Lindenberger, 1989).

Updating Piaget

Recent research suggests that under optimal conditions, the preoperational child's mind is much more organized and capable than Piaget originally thought it was (Flavell, 1985). When preschoolers are confronted with tasks that contain familiar rather than unfamiliar elements and limited rather than extensive information, some of their egocentrism, centration, and illogic disappears. For example, children don't attribute lifelike qualities to everything in their environment (animism), just to those capable of self-movement (like trucks and airplanes). When asked, however, children don't even feel that trucks and planes are alive. They just have little or no information about the characteristics and properties of the objects in question (Dolgin & Behrend, 1984).

Other nonegocentric responses can be demonstrated by children as young as 2 years of age. When showing a picture to an adult, the 2 year old child will turn it so it's facing the adult direction, thus taking into account the adult's perspective. Four year olds will adjust their speech when talking with younger children, using short, simple, attention-getting words and phrases to make sure they are understood. Such adjustment would not be possible if the child were strongly egocentric.

Centration may not always be a characteristic of preschoolers' thinking since children as young as 3 can evaluate the differences in the height and width of cookies to determine which a hungry child would judge most desirable (Cuneo, 1980). Rephrasing the more-furniture-or-more-chairs class inclusion problems can help preschoolers avoid misleading cues. For example, when a collection of soldiers was called an army, thus emphasizing the whole group, children can make more accurate comparisons (Markman, 1979). In addition when 3–4 year old children can work with concrete "picture stories" they made fewer errors in basic object transformations. Gelman and colleagues (1980) found that, when the middle card was missing, 80% of 3 year olds and 90% of 4 year olds could select the correct card to complete the sequence going from right to left or from left to right.

■ **Figure 9–6**

Stimuli used by Gelman et al. (1980) to see whether preschool children can understand object transformation. One sequence involves a cup breaking and then repairing that cup with glue.

Training in memory skills, offering adult instruction to point out errors, and being able to watch more cognitively capable peers solve Piagetian tasks improves performance in most children, particularly 4–5 year olds (D. Field, 1981; Russell et al., 1990). Apparently, when some capacity for logic exists, the child will be able to comprehend better than the child who demonstrates no understanding of logical operations at all.

Alternatives to Piaget: Information Processing Theory

Although Piaget's work on cognitive development is more thorough and comprehensive than that of other investigators, his is not the only interpretation of the process. The *information-processing model of cognitive development* traces the path of information into and out of memory. In this view, to solve problems and remember things, children and adults focus attention on specific sensory inputs (sensory memory), translate those inputs into meaningful patterns (short-term memory), act on the information, and retain selected material for future reference (long-term memory). According to this viewpoint, younger children do not think as logically or as well as older ones because their memory storage capacity isn't as great and because they organize and gain access to information in a qualitatively different fashion.

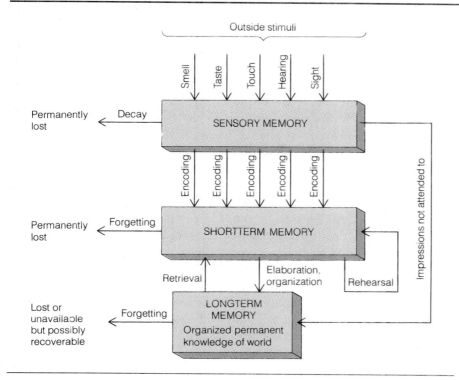

■ **Figure 9–7**

According to information processing theorists, memory functions through a succession of storehouses.

Attention

The process of *attention* is not as refined during the preschool years as it will be by the time the child is 9 or 10. Basically, the environment determines what captures the preschooler's attention. The 2–6 year old focuses on the brightest, loudest, or strongest stimulus, is easily distracted and has trouble distinguishing relevant information from irrelevant information (Fishbein, 1984). Preschoolers use a type of feature encoding/integration process when they scan. Before they can perceive the whole image, they register its features (brightness, size, color, and so on) and then integrate the features into a single image (Thompson & Massaro, 1989). According to Heinbuck and Hershberger (1989) 3 year olds are visual explorers who scan their world impulsively. In contrast, 6 year olds are searchers, investigating their visual environments in a more systematic, planful way. If a young preschooler is told to go find their shoes and the first one or two places they search yields nothing, they usually abandon the effort and sit down and do a puzzle or watch TV instead. The 6 year old is not stymied as easily. When the shoes aren't where they are "supposed" to be, they can think about and search in less obvious places and are successful more often than not.

feature encoding
remembering significant aspects of stimuli

Memory

At all ages, children can remember, but the amount and type of information remembered changes with age. Infants can remember sensorimotor events like how to grasp their blanket and how to move their arms to agitate the bathwater. By age 2, children can remember completed past events. They can remember they left their bear in the TV room, had macaroni yesterday for lunch, and saw Aunt June during a visit, but they can't correctly sequence their memories over time. By 3 years of age, children are beginning to discover the existence of their memory and to employ strategies to improve recall (Gopnik & Graf, 1988). When asked to remember which covered cup contains a toy, 3 year olds would stare at the cup or touch the cup; 2 year olds used no such strategy. Older preschool children find that telling someone else ("Mom, my skates are in the garage") or associating one item with another in memory *(The boy ate vanilla ice cream; the girl had candy)* aids memory. By the time children are 7 years of age, their understanding of *metamemory* and their reliance on memory enhancement strategies is more evident (Lange & Guttentag, 1990). Memory researcher John R. Anderson (Anderson & Milson, 1989) suggests memory uses experience to predict which knowledge will be needed from the past. Memory strategies such as rehearsal thus attempt to manipulate the statistics of the prediction to produce the best solution or outcome. *Rehearsing—*repeating or going over information—is not spontaneously initiated by preschoolers but does help them remember. Children who actively talked with their mothers about the displays as they walked through a

metamemory
an awareness and understanding of one's own thought processes; also called metacognition

museum had better memories of what they saw than children who merely asked questions about what they saw (Nelson, 1989). *Autobiographical memory*, or memory of specific events in one's own life, seems to begin around age 3 or 4 (rarely before age 3) and slowly increases until age 8 (K. Nelson, 1989).

Remembering in sequence becomes possible by the time children are 4 or 5. Although they can recall a series of items (e.g., clothes on a clothesline or a row of toys), they still have trouble fixing sequential events in time (A. L. Brown et al., 1983). In addition, a strong primacy effect operates such that if a preschooler experiences a sequence of related activities, he remembers more from the first activity than from subsequent ones (J. A. Hudson, 1990). Memory improvements during the preschool period are all related to changes in cognitive capacity. Since children can hold symbolic images in their mind and better comprehend functional relationships in the real world, they can also make better use of their memories. The rate of forgetting in preschoolers is due more to their neurological maturation than to their specific chronological age (Merriman et al., 1988).

primacy effect
in memory tasks, a better memory for items at the beginning of the list than at the middle or the end

At all ages people can recognize more than they can recall. *Recognition* involves realizing something is familiar and has been encountered before; *recall* involves naming objects from memory. To test recognition, preschoolers are shown a collection of items and then those items are mixed with others not seen. They are then asked to point to those items seen before and those that are new. Two year olds can separate familiar from unfamiliar items 80% of the time, while the recognition accuracy rate of 4 year olds approaches 90% (Rose & Wallace, 1985). Recall is a different story. When asked to name all the items on the tray from memory, children were correct only 20% of the time. In all cases, memory for unique or novel events or items is better than for the familiar or mundane (Fivush et al., 1983). Similarly, memory for activities is better than memory for objects (e.g., what did you *do* in the playhouse is recalled more accurately than what did you *see* in the playhouse) (D. C. Jones et al., 1988).

recognition
noticing that a stimulus is familiar
recall
to remember without cues or prompts

Learning to Learn

While much learning is spontaneous, efficient learning requires the acquisition of strategies for acquiring knowledge. Three to 5 year olds are more effective in promoting transfer of learning across problems if they are prompted to look for similarities between the situations (Brown & Kane, 1988). Parenting style has an impact on learning, too. Compared to authoritarian and permissive parents, authoritative parents are more effective in tutoring their own 3 year old children because they are more likely to adjust their teaching methods based on the child's success or failure. The rigidity of authoritarian parents and the lack of structure and direction of permissive parents undercuts their effectiveness as tutors (Pratt et al., 1988).

■●▲   CONCEPT SUMMARY

The Information Processing Approach to Cognitive Development

● *Attention*
  – Preschoolers on the strongest stimulus (brightest, loudest).
  – They are easily distracted by irrelevant information.
  – Older preschoolers can use more sophisticated scanning techniques.
  – Older preschoolers can remember the goal and continue the search.

● *Memory*
  – Preschoolers can use strategies to improve recall.
  – Rehearsing is not spontaneously used by preschoolers but can help them remember.
  – Autobiographical memory begins in the preschool period.
  – Remembering in sequence is possible by age 4 or 5.
  – Recognition tasks are easier than recall tasks.
  – Memory for tasks is better than memory for objects.

● *Learning to Learn*
  – Some transfer of learning strategies can take place across situations.

The Psychometric Approach: Measuring Cognitive Development

Measuring reasoning and problem solving in preschoolers involves specifically constructed *intelligence tests*. These instruments assess performance (motor) skills plus verbal skills. The verbal component of such a test might ask the young subject to define certain words, suggest the appropriate actions for certain situations, count forwards or backwards, and explain how two items are alike. The motor-ability component might involve maze tracing, bead stringing, the placing of pictures in temporal sequence, and puzzle assembly.

The two most commonly used tests of children's intelligence are the Stanford-Binet Intelligence Scale and the Wechsler Preschool and Primary Scale of Intelligence (WPPSI). The Stanford-Binet can be used with 3–8 year olds; the WPPSI is administered to children between 4 and 6½. Although IQ at age 6 is a moderately reliable predictor of adult intelligence test scores, IQ becomes more stable and less changeable with increasing age (Bornstein & Sigman, 1986). Conversely, the same factors that could influence infant test scores can also affect the perfor-

A Closer Look

Play it Safe

Even the smartest kids behave like children when they play. Each year more than 100,000 children get hurt by their toys and an even larger number are injured or killed when they play with guns, knives, or fireworks. Close supervision can help prevent accidents, but why have dangerous toys around? Here are some guidelines for buying safe toys:

1. *Pay attention to age labeling.* A toy labeled "For ages 3 and over" means that it is likely to have parts that can injure children under 3. A close inspection may persuade you that your 2 year old could use this toy safely; however, you might also be convinced that the label is accurate.

2. *Inspect toys carefully.* Small children have an amazing ability to take things apart. They also fall down a lot and can land on their toys. Watch for sharp edges and points that could poke them; test buttons, bells and decorations to make sure they won't come off or pull apart. Squeeze toys should not contain squeakers or whistles that can be pulled out. Take the crib gym down as soon as the child is able to get up on hands and knees—children can get tangled up in the crib strings or injure their necks on the gym bar. (Crib toys with strings longer than 12 inches or any toy with elastic can be hazardous to young children).

3. *Pay attention to size.* The Federal Government has determined that the smallest part of any toy for children under age 3 should not be shorter than 2 1/4 inches long or 1 1/4 inches in diameter. Any part smaller than these standards poses a potential choking hazard.

length: _____ 2¼" _____

diameter: _____ 1¼" _____

4. *Riding toys require special precautions.* When children have toys with wheels, they need a safe place to play and they need to be protected from injury due to falls. Keeping children away from traffic is an important first step. Requiring the child to wear a helmet is another must. Falls from bicycles, tricycles, wagons, "hot wheels," skates, and skateboards are all major causes of head trauma. A child old enough to ride is old enough to wear a helmet. Treat helmets like seat belts—nothing happens until the safety gear is in place. (Remember that you need to wear a helmet, too, if you bike or skate, and any passenger needs a helmet on as well).

5. *Some toys place children at risk for drowning or electric shock.* Any toy that needs to be filled with water and afterwards emptied puts a small child too near a water source for safety. Drownings can happen in a matter of seconds and young children usually don't cry out and thrash as older drowning victims do. Toys that require electrical energy should be avoided altogether. Children should be discouraged from playing with or near electrical outlets.

6. *Some toys are safe in one form but not in another.* Balloons are the biggest culprit. Inflated balloons are pretty to look at and fun. When popped or deflated, pieces of balloon material lodge easily in the child's throat causing breathing difficulties and even suffocation.

7. *Some toys are so dangerous they should never be given to children:* darts, lawn darts, air rifles, projectiles, and guns are prime examples.

Data source: Consumer Product Safety Commission.

mance of preschoolers: lack of interest, fright, fatigue, hunger, and illness. Thus, test scores can reflect variables other than intelligence per se. Bilingual children and children from disadvantaged homes, for example, often achieve low scores on standardized intelligence tests not because they lack intelligence but because they lack the verbal skills in formal English necessary for understanding and responding to the test items. Clearly, great caution is necessary among those whose business it is to interpret IQ test scores. During the preschool years, intelligence tests are used primarily to diagnose specific learning deficits rather than to determine the level of intelligence. The NAEYC (National Association for Education of Young Children) recommends that standardized test results be used in conjunction with other types of assessments and only to *improve* outcomes for children (NAEYC Position Statement on Standardized Testing of Young Children 3 through 8 Years of Age, 1988).

What types of children tend to score high on standardized tests of intelligence? Children who are active, assertive, curious, and self-motivated learn from their environments and do well both in school and on IQ tests (Stevens & Bakeman, 1985). Alison Clarke-Stewart (1977) found that children fitting this description usually have parents who are warm, loving, and sensitive, who accept their child's behavior, and who value learning and education highly. Parents of high-scoring children also encourage exploration, creativity, self-expression, and independence in their children through reading, teaching, and playing (see Table 9–1 for age appropriate toy suggestions). These same parents favor reasoning over physical punishment for discipline.

One particular factor in a child's home life has a measurable impact on IQ scores: the extent of the father's availability. Father absence prior to age 5 is associated with relatively low school achievement and test scores for boys, particularly in mathematics (Radin, 1981). Similar effects are noted for girls who lose their fathers after the age of 9. Children whose fathers are absent or unavailable can improve in performance if their mothers spend a lot of time with them, encouraging risk taking and independence, and if they have contact with a father substitute or other appropriate male role model (Radin, 1981). The child will be less affected by the father's death or absence if the mother copes well, is financially secure, and has a reliable support system.

● Language Development

By age 2 the child's ability to use language changes suddenly and dramatically. The 2 year old talks constantly, even when alone. The rapid acceleration of language functions corresponds to developmental changes in the brain called *myelagenetic cycles* (Yakovlev & Lecours, 1967). During each of three cycles myelin forms in a different area of the brain. In the first cycle, beginning before birth and ending in infancy,

myelagenetic cycles
a series of changes in the myelination of specific brain structures

■ **Table 9–1** *Age Appropriate Toys—Birth to 6 Years*

AGE	DEVELOPMENTAL NEEDS	APPROPRIATE TOYS

Birth–6 months	sees face and objects
	follows an object with eyes
	puts objects in mouth
	reaches and grasps for things
		mobile (remove when your
		    child can reach it)
		teething ring
		small stuffed animal
		    (washable)

3–6 months	learns cause and effect
	transfers object from one hand
	    to the other
	bangs toys together
	grasps with finger and thumb
	sits with support and then
	    alone
	pokes at objects
	can begin to entertain self
	likes textures, sounds, color
	    and visual activity
		activity ring
		teething ring
		bath toys
		
		rattle
		crib gym (remove at 5
		    months)
		activity center
		
		musical/noise toys

6–9 months	can push buttons with finger
	
	can do basic stacking
	likes color
	pulls apart and puts back
	    together
	throws small objects
	
	crawls and explores
	
	sees self and smiles
	loves bath
		activity center
		thick bright books with big
		    pictures
		stacking toy
		colored blocks
		two-part toy
		
		suctioned rattle (to attach to
		    high chair)
		small rubber ball (4") to push
		    and see over
		mirror toy
		floating toys, plastic funnel,
		    bottle, beater (for suds)
		rag doll

9–12 months	can put items in order of size
	    (pre-math skill)
	learns up/down, inside/out
	classifies (puts same items
	    together)
	can open and shut
	takes first steps
		stacking toy—rings on spindle
		
		nesting toy
		sorting toy, blocks
		
		activity center/book
		push toy to encourage
		    walking

1–2 years	imitates sounds and actions
	    (prelanguage and memory)
	listens to music and stories
	asks identification of items
	by 18 months can turn pages
	begins using words and
	    mimics inflection
		play telephone
		
		music making toy
		picture books
		
		your talk is better than talking
		    doll

(continued on next page)

■ **Table 9–1** *(continued)*

AGE	DEVELOPMENTAL NEEDS	APPROPRIATE TOYS
	walks and explores	push and pull toy (little wagon)
	can seat self	ride-on toy, chair
	carries and hugs favorite toys	small soft animal
	stacks toys	pots and pans and box
	can go up and down 3 stairs and jump 12"	small slide, little two-step stool
	when 2, can run and kick ball	big ball
	develops large muscles	pounding pegboard
	needs finger manipulation	big stringing beads, screw top bottle
	begins pretend play (tending dolls, pushing cars)	picture books, blocks, sturdy dolls and vehicles
	puts items in and out	toy box, shelves, basket
	reconstructs from memory	simple puzzle
	begins pouring, measuring	shovel, pail, funnel and sieve for water/sand
2–3 years	advances in pouring and measuring	cooking items
	learns mechanical skills	sturdy record player, magnets, "jewelry" kits (big beads, etc.)
	refines listening	songs, nursery rhymes
	enjoys simple stories	story books
	loves language	important to read aloud to children until they can read comfortably (age 7–8)
	classifies	good blocks—variety of shapes and sizes
	manipulates better	large crayons/markers, easel for drawing
	plays imaginatively, makes houses	dolls (for boys, too), old clothes/hats, puppets, small gym set for multi-use
3–4 years	imitates parent of same gender (ages 3–6)	toys to play house, store, doctor
	begins small muscle coordination (girls have better fine motor skills and wrist rotation for turning knobs, dressing and brushing teeth at this age)	small tools, cooking equipment drawing equipment (big pad of paper, liquid paints and wide brushes—small watercolor sets too frustrating) modeling clay
	begins to cut	safety scissors, paste and colored paper

■ **Table 9–1** *(continued)*

AGE	DEVELOPMENTAL NEEDS	APPROPRIATE TOYS
	begins group play	houses, forts from boxes, sheets
	continues big muscle development	tricycle, wheelbarrow, small rake, jungle gym
	gains leg strength, balances	small ball to throw/catch
4–5 years	builds complex structures	Lincoln Logs
	wants highly realistic miniature toys (ages 4–7)	dollhouse, cars, fire station
	needs hand-eye coordination	Spirograph, carroms, big needlepoint
		big ball to bounce
	needs foot-eye coordination	sidewalk games
	begins math/science concepts	simple board games with counting (dice or numbered cards)
	by age 5, can tell long story accurately and add fantasy	short fiction and nonfiction in area of interest (dinosaurs)
	asks how things work and meaning of words	
5–6 years	has lots of energy	ball game items
	likes complex projects (continues for days)	simple model boat, house
	likes cutting, pasting and folding	paper dolls, activity books, easy origami
	counts to 30s	Cribbage, games with adding/subtracting

Source: Kathleen P. O'Beirne, *Family* magazine (November 1986) and *Pass It On! How to Thrive in the Military Lifestyle.* (Lifescape Enterprises, 1991) pp. 393–399. © Kathleen P. O'Beirne. Used with permission.

the brain stem and limbic system are myelinated. This change is associated with the development of babbling. The second cycle, responsible for language development in infancy and the preschool period, begins around birth and ends when the child is 3.5 or 4.5 years old. During the third cycle, myelin forms in the association areas of the cortex or the brain's surface. This process permits the acceleration of intellectual growth and although it begins at birth it is not completed until age 15 or so. By the time the child is 6 or 7, he can use "everyday" speech as well as most adults.

association areas
areas in the cortex that are not affiliated with specific lobes; thought to process and store information

Language as a Reflection of Cognitive Capacity

Children's cognitive development is reflected in the language they use. They demonstrate their egocentrism by their frequent use of *I*, *me*, and *my,* by continually emphasizing their particular points of view, and by endless self-reporting ("I am coloring" and "I am eating my crackers"). Preschoolers tend to assume a narrow perspective (their own) and are constrained against comprehending the perspective of another. For example, a child on a talk show was asked what he would do to help humanity. "I'd make a cookie-cleaner-upper," the child replied. "Because so many people like cookies?" the host probed. "No, because Cookie's my parakeet" (Linkletter, 1957, p. 131). It's not that children don't see the need to focus outside themselves. It's just at this age, they don't know how.

Children in this age group also create original words and modify the meaning of existing words to serve their own unique purposes. For example, my daughter called all disapproved words (such as *shut up* or *stupid*) *SBY words.* Another child called all heavy children *donut people.*

The preoperational child also tends to use words that stand for tangible, concrete objects and to interpret speech literally. With this orientation, it is difficult for a child of this age to understand abstract concepts such as *masculinity* or *fairness* or to comprehend slang expressions or other figures of speech. For example, the child who overhears an adult reporting that his spouse is "tied up at the office" may wonder what being bound and gagged has to do with making a living. After a birthday, another child was asked whether her new wristwatch tells time. "No" said the child with exasperation in her voice "you have to *look* at it." A particularly entertaining example of the literal-mindedness of preschool aged children comes from the classroom. A group of kindergartners were learning about patriotic music and were asked to illustrate the song, "America the Beautiful." In one child's drawing, the teacher easily recognized the flag, map of the country, purple mountains, and even the shining seas. "This is nice," said the teacher pointing to a figure that looked like a jet covered with red and yellow balls. "Can you tell me what this is?" "That's the fruited plane," explained the 5 year old. (Other examples of the concrete nature of young childrens' speech may be found in the feature on page 373.)

Some of the most charming examples of children's speech occur when they try to explain or describe events around them but they don't know or can't find the right words. Consider the effort of the child trying to identify a particular relative but having some word-finding problems. "Oh, you know," the child said, "she's the lady-grandpa." A child once visited a chicken farm only to see a peacock on the grounds displaying its feathers. "Look!" the child said with wonder, "that chicken's in bloom!"

Vocabulary Growth, Sentence Length, and Grammar

By age 2, children have a vocabulary of about 50 words. These words are primarily nouns like *cookie, Grandma,* and *doggie* and pivot words like *here, all-gone,* and *go* (Corrigan, 1983). Between the ages of 3 and 5,

A Closer Look

Read to Me, Daddy!

Traditionally, mothers have been the ones who read stories to the little ones. Today, many fathers read to their children and may take special delight in reading a story where the focus is on dads. Here are a few titles.

Just Like Daddy by Frank Asch (Ages 2–4 years)
One of Frank Asch's Bear Books, this is the story of a boy bear who eats breakfast, gets dressed, and tries to do everything just like Daddy. In the end he succeeds in catching a big fish—just like Mommy did!

Gone Fishing by Earlene Long (Ages 2–4)
Written in simple phrases and with charming drawings, this book attempts to teach the concepts *big* and *little*. Father and son go fishing, catch a big fish and a little fish, and then take them home to show Mom.

Horton Hatches the Egg by Dr. Seuss (Ages 3–6 years)
A long-time favorite about a male elephant who hatches a bird's egg.

Bea and Mr. Jones by Amy Schwartz (Ages 4–6 years)
A hilarious story about a father and daughter who trade places. He goes to kindergarten, plays games, and stuns the teacher and kids with his abilities. She goes to the office, gives her secretary the day off, laughs at the boss's jokes and is a big success.

Father Bear Comes Home by Else Holmelund Minarik (Ages 4–7 years)
An "I can Read" book that is part of the charming Little Bear series. Contains four touching stories about Father Bear's return from his long fishing trip.

Where the River Begins by Thomas Locker (Ages 4–7)
Two boys, Josh and Aaron, set off on a camping trip with their grandfather to find the beginning of a river. The illustrations are reproductions of oil paintings.

A good story can leave a preschooler spellbound.

vocabulary growth accelerates dramatically. During this time, 50 new words per month are added to the child's vocabulary, particularly if the child lives in a language-rich environment. Programs like *Sesame Street* are well suited to preschooler's vocabulary development (Rice et al., 1990). At age 6, the average child knows between 8,000 and 14,000 words (Rescorla, 1984). Compared with the vocabulary of the younger child, that of the older child contains a greater percentage of abstract words such as *love, happy,* and *wish,* although the concept of the word as a unit of speech precedes comprehension of the word itself (Levine & Carey, 1982).

As vocabulary grows, sentence length increases (Dromi, 1984). Single words that function like complete sentences are called *holophrases.* With changes in intonation and infection, a single word can have several different meanings (e.g., "Mine," could mean "Is that mine?", "Give it to me!", "I want that!" or possibly something else). The ability to use single cognitive representations permits the formation of telegraphic sentences such as "Baby up" and "Where Daddy?" which are typical of the 18–24 month old child. The speech is called *telegraphic* because its content is compressed, like a telegram. Sentence length is extended to three words by age 2 or 3 ("I go outside"), to four or five words by age 4, and to six or eight words by age 5 or 6 (Miller & Chapman, 1981). Thus, while the 2 year old will speak of "kitty," the 3–4 year old will refer to "that fluffy kitten" or "Krista's little kitty," and the 5–6 year old will describe the "yellow striped kitty who lives by the school" (deVilliers & deVilliers, 1978). Fathers use language to place demands on their children and in so doing, raise performance. Mothers provide more linguistic support for their preschool children, tuning their language to the child's particular needs (McLaughlin et al., 1983).

Learning grammatical rules, like the simple past tense, requires the child to engage in several processes at once. They first have to be able to break up the flow of spoken language into words and to understanding the meaning of the words. The child then has to be able to distinguish between events that occur now and those that occurred before. Finally, the child needs to identify the general rule for expressing the past tense (adding "-ed") by listening to the speech of others and then adding "-ed" to the ends of appropriate words (Karmiloff-Smith, 1984). As this process implies, the transmission of rules of grammar is implicit rather than explicit and is guided by two sets of rules all humans inherit for processing speech:

1. *Visual scanning rule*—scan the environment to provide the best possible visual experience (Haith, 1980)

operating principles
rules for improving the
comprehension of oral language

2. *Operating principles*—listen to language in order to maximize comprehension (Slobin, 1981):
   a. Pay attention to the ends of words
   b. Pay attention to the order of words and word segments
   c. Avoid exceptions to language rules

Profanity

Much to their parents' dismay, preschool children sometimes incorporate taboo or "dirty" words into their vocabularies. Whatever their source, the words are usually chosen for their shock value and the re-action they bring from caregivers. A child might loudly announce at Thanksgiving dinner that Uncle Wayne has a winkie (a penis) or tell a neighbor that she can't talk anymore because she has to go home and pick her nose. Such language might cause parents to fear that their 3–4 year old is becoming a moral degenerate before their very eyes. But the repeated use of bad words really means that the child is engaging in behavior that he finds exciting because it causes unexpected and some-times funny reactions in listeners. Preschoolers also delight in whisper-ing about body parts, urine, and feces. When the child is by himself, this behavior is better ignored. In a group of 4–5 year olds, forbidden activities have "contagious quality" and need to be stopped.

Questions and Negatives

By age 3 children can ask questions that contain special verb forms such as *can, have,* or *did,* but they still do not get the word order quite right when asking a question (e.g., "Why I can't stay up?")

Three year olds ask so many *who, what, when, where,* and *why* ques-tions that they seem destined to major in journalism. When asked *when* questions, 3–5 year olds have a strong tendency to give "After . . ." responses (L. A. French, 1989). The meaning of *why?* still escapes them and they respond as though *why?* meant *what?* or *where?* For example, an adult might ask, "Why did you do that?" and the child might re-spond, "Yes, I did." The adult might counter, "Why did you hit. . .?" and "On her head" might be the answer. This exchange reflects the fact that questions about causation *(why),* manner *(how),* and time *(when)* involve more difficult concepts than those about location *(where),* objects *(what)* and agents *(who)* (Byrnes and Duff, 1988). Even young children attempt to express causality in their speech. There is a significant in-crease in the spontaneous use of *if* and *because* expressions between 3 and 4 years of age (Byrnes & Duff, 1988).

Bliss (1987) found that a developmental pattern was reflected in the use of negatives. The word *no* is first used to indicate nonexistence, as in "no drink" when the cup is empty. Then it signifies rejection of an offer, as in "No shoe" when the child does not want to put on shoes. Finally, *no* indicates denial of a statement, as when the caregiver points to a picture and says, "Look at the girl" and the child corrects the speaker by saying, "No, look at the *baby."*

By age 3, most children have acquired adult rules for forming nega-tives, as in the use of *didn't* and *can't* ("He can't play," "I didn't like the movie"). Some of the details still escape them, however, such as rules for the use of double negatives ("Nobody didn't come") and the need to include the auxiliary verb in contractions ("I not going").

Common Speech Errors: Overregularization

As children progress from the rote production of speech to an awareness and application of rules for combining words, they tend to make some interesting linguistic errors. For example, very young children may have memorized the irregular forms of some words such as "baby goes" or "two feet" and thus produced speech that is grammatically correct. As they become aware of the "rule" for forming the irregular past tense of verbs or the plural form of a noun, however, they often use *overregularization*—"baby goed," for example, or "two feets"—until they learn the irregular exceptions. By the time most children are 4–5 years old, they are using irregular noun and verb forms correctly (R. Berman, 1984).

Voice and Word Order

Children under 7 years of age hardly ever use the passive voice and have difficulty imitating such constructions (Lempert, 1984). Preschoolers focus on order and sequence when trying to understand language. When they hear a passive sentence such as "The boy was hit by the ball" they misinterpret it and assume that the boy did the hitting. For the same reason, young children are confused by such constructions as "You can have some dessert after you eat your peas" or "Before we go to the store, I want you to put your toys away". Since preschoolers assume that events are performed in the order spoken, they would probably interpret these sentences to mean that they would expect dessert before eating their vegetables and can go to the store before they clean up (Kavanaugh, 1979). To be sure that children understand, adults need to use such constructions as "Let's have lunch first and then we'll swim" or "If you get on your pajamas, we'll read a story."

Other subtle forms of syntax can be sources of confusion, too. When 5–6 year olds read the sentence, "John told Bill to shovel the snow" they correctly conclude that John made the request and Bill will do the work. However, children interpret the sentence "John promised Bill to shovel the snow" as identical to the first. In 1969 Carol Chomsky suggested that children make mistakes like this because they use the *minimum distance principle (MDP)* in interpreting such constructions. They rely on the order of the subjects in the sentence, and assume that the phrase following the second subject is somehow related to that subject. The MDP continues to influence children's interpretations of language until they are 9 or 10 years old. Children's greater awareness of word order helps them become better readers later in school (Warren-Leubecker & Carter, 1988).

syntax
grammatical rules for putting words together in a sentence or phrase

minimum distance principle (MDP)
the idea that children make mistakes in inferring causality from sentence constructions because they assume that a phrase that follows a subject is somehow related to it

Comparatives

Before the age of 6 or 7, children have difficulty making accurate comparisons (Bishop & Bowine, 1985). They use concepts such as *big* and *little*, *near* and *far*, and *heavy* and *light* ambiguously because they have difficulty judging relationships. They may see a task as hard or an object as heavy because it's hard or heavy for *them*. They might also confuse terms that are similar in meaning, missing subtle differences in usage. Thus, preschoolers may accuse Daddy of being fat when they actually mean he's tall, and they may argue that they're big when they actually wish to convey a sense of personal importance. In a classic study of children's understanding of the concepts of *more* or *less*, Donaldson and Balfour (1968) showed 3, 4, and 5 year olds two toy apple trees, one with more apples on its branches than the other. When asked which tree had more apples, most children correctly pointed to the tree with the greater number of apples. But when asked which tree had *fewer* apples, most pointed to the same tree. Taken one at a time, tangible comparatives *(taller, greener)* are easier for the preschooler to use than intangible ones *(smarter, hungrier)* (Gitterman & Johnston, 1983). Children as old as 7 may still confuse the concepts *more* and *less*, and thus may have difficulty understanding the process of subtraction.

Coordination of Ideas

With maturity and practice, children learn that they can express more than one idea in a single sentence and can use sentence structure to elaborate ideas. Four and 5 year olds use relative clauses marked by the word *that*—"She is the girl that I like," "There's the toy that I want"—but children do not usually use *who* and *which* in relative clauses until age 6 or so (Clark & Hecht, 1983). *Embedding,* or inserting a relative clause into a main one, is a complex construction that may not appear until a child reaches school age. In fact, adding a clause next to a noun—for example, "Here's the dress that I want for church"—is a more common construction than interrupting the main clause with a relative one—"The dress that I want for church is over there".

embedding
inserting a relative clause into a sentence with a main clause

As early as age 3, children can link two ideas together with a conjunction to form a *coordinate sentence:* "I jumped up and fell down" or "I want a drink and he wants a sandwich." The other conjunctions or coordinators 3 year olds use are *because, when, and,* and *but:* "I'll see you when I get home"; "I ate it because I was hungry." Conditional terms such as *if* and *so,* and terms reflecting temporal sequence such as *before, after,* and *until* are less common in the speech of young children (Clark & Hecht, 1983).

coordinate sentence
any sentence where a conjunction (and, but, etc.) ties together two ideas

Tag questions, or requests for confirmation—"My dog's cute, *isn't she?*"—begin to appear in the speech of some 4–4.5 year old children

tag question
a clause that requests confirmation from the listener. For example, in the sentence, "It's a nice day, isn't it" the last portion is the tag question

■●▲   CONCEPT SUMMARY

Language Development During the Preschool Years

- *Development*
  - The 6–7 year old can use "everyday speech" as well as an adult.
  - Brain growth underlies progress in language acquisition.
  - Egocentrism is manifested by frequent use of personal pronouns and self-references.
  - Preschoolers have difficulty understanding abstract concepts; interpret speech literally.
  - Vocabulary growth accelerates (50 new words per month between the ages of 3 and 5).
  - Sentence length increases from three words at age 2–3 to six to eight words by age 5 or 6.
  - Original words and taboo words may appear in the preschooler's vocabulary.
  - Preschoolers can form questions, but have difficulty answering *why, when,* and *how* questions.
  - Preschoolers use negatives in a developmental pattern (*no* first means nonexistence; later it means rejection of an offer and denial of a statement).
  - They use "overregularized" forms of words until they learn the exceptions (*deer–deers*).
  - They have difficulty using and understanding sentences in the passive voice.
  - They have difficulty making accurate comparisons.
  - Preschoolers can express more than one idea in a single sentence.
  - They use tag questions to make requests.

  Most speech difficulties (articulation problems, stuttering, delayed language) disappear with practice and maturity.

- *Conversation Skills*
  - Children as young as 2 years of age use attention-getting devices in their speech to maximize being heard and understood.
  - Preschoolers can adjust their speech, using simpler speech with younger individuals, more sophisticated speech with older children and adults.
  - Conversation with 2 year olds involves them repeating speech during their turn; by age 3, children can add to the conversation.
  - Conversation intrusions usually contain relevant information by age 3.
  - Preschoolers have difficulty judging whether their own messages are clear or not.

(Bellugi, 1970). The presence of these tag questions is one indication that the child's understanding of grammar is growing more complete. In some tag questions, children have to match pronouns to nouns: "My teacher is nice, isn't she?" In other cases, they need to pay attention to the verb in each clause: "He can go, can't he?" Such statements as "Him and me are playing" or "She don't listen" are common in the language of 3–5 year olds, indicating the rules about verbs and personal pronouns either haven't been learned yet or are being overgeneralized. Other sources of difficulty for the preschool child are *have* used as an auxiliary verb ("I have finished my breakfast"), *if* and *so* as conjunctions ("I can turn the channel if you want"), and verbs used as nouns ("Running is fun").

Speech Difficulties

Articulation

Although preschoolers know a great many words, they sometimes have difficulty pronouncing them correctly. But articulation problems involving mispronunciation generally disappear as children gain better control over their lips, tongue, jaws, larynx, and breathing.

While still in the error-making stage, though, it's common for preschoolers to simplify by altering the initial consonant combinations. For example, when words begin with double consonants—say, *st*, *dr*, or *sm*—young children often drop the first consonant sound, and *steak* become "take" and *smell* becomes "mell." The beginning letters of a word may also be transposed, producing a different sound. At our house, waffles were called "awfuls." (Personally, I never thought they were that bad!)

Sometimes both consonants are replaced by an entirely different sound. Thus, *frog* might become "wog." And sometimes all the consonants in the word are replaced by the same letters, as when dolly is called "doddie." Preschool children have certain speech preferences often beginning words with the consonants *b*, *g*, and *d* (perhaps because these sounds require less effort to form). *L* and *th* sounds are difficult to say, even for the 7 year old.

Other factors can be involved in mispronunciation, however. A child who has the potential to articulate well could be misled by a poor model. This same child might also fail to remember the appropriate word or might try to make sense out of a concept he doesn't fully understand by substituting actual but inappropriate words. Children's renditions of songs are often filled with inaccuracies—for example, "I came from Alabama with a *band-aid* on my knee." Before preschoolers are aware of word boundaries, they try to segment by phrase to change unfamiliar words to familiar ones (Chaney, 1989). Here is one kindergartner's "translation" of the end of the Pledge of Allegiance: ". . . and

■ Figure 9–8

A deaf child with his teacher.

stuttering
speech with frequent, involuntary
repetitions of sounds or syllables

to the Republic for Richard Stands. One naked individual with Liberty and Justice for all'' (Baughman, 1963, p. 173).

Children make more speech errors when they are tired or excited. On an interview program, one 4 year old boy got very excited when he was asked what animal he would like to be: ''I want to be an octopus so I could grab all the bad boys and girls and spank them with my testicles'' (Linkletter, 1957).

Stuttering

Learning to speak with precision is a complicated process. As I've mentioned, almost all children experience some speech dysfluencies as they are learning language. *Stuttering* involves hesitations or repetitions of sounds or words in speech. The first word, sound, or syllable may be repeated by the stutterer (''Ccccccome on!; lets-lets-lets-go'')

Stuttering may have a sex-linked genetic component since it runs in families and has a higher incidence among identical twins than fraternal twins and among boys than girls (3:1) (Homzie & Lindsay, 1984). Stuttering usually manifests itself by age 8 and is often accompanied by problems with attention, reading, or writing. Young stutterers are not delayed in receptive language skills (comprehension), however (Byrd & Cooper, 1989). By age 18, four-fifths of the childhood stutterers are fluent speakers. Speech therapy can help improve the child's fluency and self-esteem.

Delayed Language

Some children are slower than their peers in saying words and coming to understand the rules of sentence formation. In some cases, children do not have the chance to practice speaking enough because they are ignored or neglected or because others do all the talking for them. But some children simply proceed at a slower rate of development. Speech specialists can help caregivers understand the reasons for speech delay and, where necessary, provide instruction and remediation.

Private Speech

Twenty to 60% of the words preschoolers utter are not directed at anyone in particular (Berk, 1986). Such *private speech* is normal and helpful to young children who may talk for fun as they play, or talk to guide their own activities, to help them remember, or to provide emotional release.

Social Aspects of Language

Unlike private speech, social speech *is* intended for others to hear and understand. But it's not enough for the child to know what he wants to say to another person, he must also know *how* to express himself. Even infants seem to acknowledge that rules for communication, or *pragmatics,* exist (Kaye, 1982). One simple pragmatic function involves using language to initiate and sustain conversation. Judith Becker (1988a) found that children as young as age 2 maximize the likelihood of being understood by addressing the listener when they are physically close, interacting together, or looking at each other. By the time they are 3–5 years old, preschoolers also use attention-getting gestures or verbalizations such as "Hey!" or "Guess what?" They can also ask questions, give commands, and talk about what the listener is doing to prompt a response.

pragmatics
rules for language usage

Even very young children may adjust their speech to the demands of the situation and the competencies of their listeners. For instance, if a request is complicated or its solution difficult (for example, if the child is asking about a toy that is hard to find), 2 year olds use longer messages than if the request is more straightforward (Becker, 1988b). And 4 year olds have been reported to adjust their speech for their audience, talking to 2 year olds differently than they do to their own age peers or to adults.

CHILD (AGE 4) TO ADULT:　You're supposed to put one of these persons in, see? Then one goes with the other little girl. And then the little girl has marbles. . ."

SAME CHILD TO
YOUNGER CHILD (AGE 2):　Watch, Perry. Watch this. He's backing in here. Now he drives up. Look, Perry. Look here Perry. Put the men in here. Now I'll do it.

It's interesting to note that 4 year olds make the same speech modifications as adults when they address younger children. For the younger child, both adults and 4 year olds rely on shorter sentences, less complex grammar, and more attention-getting devices to facilitate communication. These findings contradict Piaget's (1926) belief that children younger than age 7 are too egocentric to accommodate any other point of view than their own. It may be that sensitivity to others develops earlier than Piaget first supposed.

Children learn one set of skills to begin conversations and another set to sustain them. The caregiver may speak, pause, and speak again, accepting smiles, movement, or sounds as the baby's contribution to the dialogue. Turn taking is also practiced in social games like peek-a-boo or pushing a ball back and forth. Conversational turn-taking involves repeating the adult's words when the child is age 2:

MOTHER: It fits in the puzzle somewhere.
ADAM: Puzzle? Puzzle somewhere?
MOTHER: Turn it around.

■ Figure 9–9

There's lots to talk about if you're a preschooler. "Hey, thanks for remembering the Beer Nuts" is probably not part of this conversation!

ADAM: Turn it around.
MOTHER: No, the other way.
ADAM: Other way?
MOTHER: I guess you have to turn it around.
ADAM: Guess around. Turn round. (Slobin, 1975, p. 438)

By the time children are 3 years old, they can elaborate on a topic and carry on a conversation for at least one turn.

ADULT: Let's get ready for the park.
CHILD: The park has a big slide. I'm going to the park.

Sometimes children want to break into an existing conversation that is not addressed to them. To do so they must (a) understand the topic being discussed, (b) plan what to say, and (c) discover a point of entry. The fine art of intrusion is learned more quickly by later-born children than by first borns who usually have uninterrupted conversational access to those around them. By the time the child is 3, their intrusions contain not only new and conversation-relevant information but are also likely to lead to a response (Dunn & Shatz, 1989). Boys tend to use more initiators and attention-getting phrases than girls; girls use more facilitating phrases and reinforcers (Austin et al., 1987). (see Table 9–2)

Children also take feedback into account and change their messages according to the listener's reactions. The younger the children, the more they benefit from clear, explicit feedback. Saying something like, "Now think carefully. What is it you really need me to do?" is more effective than a puzzled look or a nonspecific statement like "What?" or "I don't understand" in helping children communicate effectively (D. L. Rogers et al., 1987).

■ **Table 9–2**   *Development of Social Speech*

AGE	CHARACTERISTICS OF SPEECH

2½	Beginnings of conversation:
	    Speech is increasingly relevant to others' remarks.
	    Need for clarity is being recognized.

3	Breakthrough in attention to communication:
	    Child seeks ways to clarify and correct misunderstandings.
	    Pronunciation and grammar sharply improve.
	    Speech with children the same age expands dramatically.
	    Use of language as instrument of control increases.

4	Knowledge of fundamentals of conversation:
	    Child is able to shift speech according to listener's knowledge.
	    Literal definitions are no longer a sure guide to meaning.
	    Collaborative suggestions have become common.
	    Disputes can be resolved with words.

5	Good control of elements of conversation.

Source: E. B. Bolles, *So Much to Say*, 1982, p. 93. Used with permission.

As children's speech skills improve, so do their listening skills. Part of the communication process involves listening to the message one receives to make sure it is clear. Young children may not be aware that a message is unclear or that the information is inadequate until they try to apply it. When first graders were given only partial instructions for playing a game, Markman (1977) found they didn't realize some crucial information was missing until they attempted to play. Third graders caught on more readily.

Judging the adequacy of one's *own* messages is still beyond the skill of preschoolers. In fact, children at this age have difficulty in judging whether messages are clear or unclear and have trouble restating a question to conform to specific instructions. In an early study children were told if they asked a puppet for some candy, she would give them some (Bates, 1976). The child was then told to ask again "very nicely." Few of the 3 year olds had the pragmatic skill to include polite words like *please* or *may I* and basically restated their requests, showing that they did not understand the convention called "asking nicely." It's not until age 6 or 7 that their cognitive abilities allow children to be spontaneously polite and self-effacing. At *that* age they understand the need to be polite and have the skill to make a "nice request."

Bilingualism

Four and one-half million school children in the United States speak a native language other than English at home (Hakuta, 1986). Children

A Closer Look

Parlez-Vous. . .?

In the global marketplace of the twenty-first century, even Americans will need to know a foreign language. What better time to introduce a child to the pleasures of French, Spanish, German, or Japanese than between the ages of 2 and 6 when they are primed for language learning?

Advocates of multicultural language skills encourage instruction to begin early, to permit children to express themselves without worrying about tenses and so forth, and to be fun. Currently, several elementary schools around the nation use "total immersion" or "partial immersion" to help children learn a foreign language. In total immersion programs (93 U.S. schools have adopted this approach), all classes are taught in the second language from kindergarten through the second grade. English is phased in gradually; by the 6th grade, half the classes are taught in English and half in the second language. Partial immersion begins at the 50/50 point and stays there. In these programs, reading and language arts are always taught in English.

Some parents worry that children in total or partial immersion programs might lose ground academically since they have to learn both the new language and the new subject matter simultaneously. The total immersion program in Gates County, North Carolina, compared the national achievement test scores of its immersion students with those attending regular nonimmersion classes. Reassuringly, immersion students scored at or above the national average. Foreign language proficiency doesn't seem to be just a passing fad. Publishers are even redesigning textbooks to support a multilingual approach to learning.

As colleges reinstitute their foreign language requirements and high schools move toward required course work in multiculturalism, children could only be advantaged by early exposure to foreign language.

can become bilingual through the simultaneous acquisition of both languages or the sequential acquisition of the second language after mastering the first. When two languages are learned simultaneously, three stages of language acquisition can be identified. First, the child learns a word in one language or the other but not in both. Language switching occurs during this stage. Garcia (1983) observed that 3 and 4 year old children speaking in Spanish or Filipino substitute English words such as *doctor*, *Santa Claus* or *cookie* for those same words in their native languages. While language switching may be a function of learning two languages simultaneously, it may also be due to mixed input by parents so the child is actually imitating a model rather than creating novel speech (Genesee, 1989). Next, one set of grammatical rules is applied to both sets of vocabulary. Finally, by about age 7, the child can keep the two languages separate while maintaining fluency in each. When two languages are learned sequentially (the second after the first), fluency in the second language is achieved in about one year (Reich, 1986).

Does bilingualism affect language learning or cognitive development? Researchers find that, when the effects of socioeconomic status are eliminated from studies, bilingual children perform better than monolinguals on both verbal and nonverbal tests and bilingual children express more ideas when asked to tell a story. Bilingual children also outperform monolinguals on tests of analytic reasoning and concept formation (Diaz, 1983). When children are around age 4, they become aware of the concept of the "word" as a unit of speech. This understanding promotes the development of both bilingualism and literacy (Bialystok, 1986).

Some children are unable to speak English when they begin school in the United States. Today's bilingual education programs seek to maintain the child's first language and promote respect for their parent culture while introducing English as children are ready for it (Hakuta, 1986). Placing non-English speaking children into English-only classrooms (an approach called *immersion*) risks semilingualism—inadequate proficiency in both languages for several years. (Proficiency in the child's native language declines if speaking and writing skills are not taught and practiced).

immersion
the language training technique that involves the exclusive use of the nonnative language

Given the distinct cognitive advantages of bilingualism, one goal of American education could be broadened to encourage *all* children to master a second language in elementary school. In this way, the school system could provide support for a multicultural, multinational learning environment where all children, not just limited English speakers, are working to broaden their linguistic skills (O'Malley, 1982). Children acquire a second language most quickly when they are young and when they spend time communicating naturally with native speakers.

● Moral Development

Moral development involves the gradual internalization of society's standards of right and wrong. Because the development of moral concepts and the pattern of moral reasoning closely parallel cognitive development as described by Piaget, moral development is usually examined in light of cognitive theory.

moral development
the development of attitudes and beliefs that help children determine whether behaviors are right or wrong

Piaget's Theory of Moral Development

Piaget used two methods to study the development of moral judgment. The first involved questioning children about the rules of games (Piaget, 1935/1965). To discover whether children understood and abided by the rules of a game and if they were willing to change the rules, Piaget

■ **Figure 9–10**

According to Piaget, children between the ages of 3 and 5 believe that rules of a game come from an outside authority and are absolute.

observed pairs of boys playing marbles, a popular and exclusively male pastime at the time of his investigations.

Piaget identified two stages of moral development within the preschool period: the *egocentric stage* (also called the stage of *moral realism* or the stage of *heteronomous morality*—age 3–6) and the *incipient cooperation stage* (ages 6–10). Until age 3, boys played randomly with marbles and showed no understanding of rules. Between the ages of 3 and 6, children believe the rules come from an external authority such as parents or God and are absolute and unchangeable. But because they cannot understand the rules of play, egocentric children usually play their own version of the game, sometimes with others and sometimes by themselves, ignoring, changing, or adding rules to suit their purposes. If they do play with others, preschool children play to win, but they consider it possible for everyone to win.

By the time children are 6 or 7 years old, they are most likely to define a set of acceptable rules and to play cooperatively with a partner. This is the incipient cooperation stage. Now the rules are perceived as invariant—everyone must follow the same ones. However, an observer might notice a slightly different version of the rules each time the game is played. The explanation is that despite their respect for the rules, children's knowledge of the details may be vague and their conception of the rules may vary from game to game (Piaget, 1935/1965).

To find out more about the development of moral reasoning, Piaget asked children questions about two versions of a moralistic story. The stories described a conflict between a person's intentions and the amount of damage done. The stories Piaget told were these (Piaget, 1929/1976):

A little boy named John is in his room. He is called to dinner. He goes into the dining room. But behind the door there is a chair, and on the

■ **Table 9–3**   *(continued)*

	PRO	CON
Stage 6: Universal-ethical-principles orientation Following self-chosen ethical principles. Particular laws or social agreements are usually valid because they rest on such principles. When laws violate these principles, you must act in accordance with the principles, which are universal: giving equal rights to all and respecting the dignity of human beings as individual persons.	This is a situation which forces him to choose between stealing and letting his wife die. In a situation where the choice must be made, it is morally right to steal. He has to act in terms of the principle of preserving and respecting life.	Heinz is faced with the decision of whether to consider the other people who need the drug just as badly as his wife. Heinz ought to act not according to his particular feelings toward his wife but considering the value of all the lives involved.

Source: Kohlberg, 1969, pp. 379–380.

According to Kohlberg's scheme, preschoolers reason within the *preconventional level of morality*. They rely on avoiding punishment and are concerned about satisfying their personal needs. Because centration dominates their thinking, preschoolers judge each fact separately rather than taking all facts into consideration, thus confusing the overall picture. The following are examples of preoperational responses for avoiding punishment:

PRO: Heinz should steal the drug because if you let your wife die, you'll get into trouble.

CON: Heinz should not steal the drug because he will get into trouble for stealing. (Rest, 1983)

In the second stage of preconventional moral reasoning, children make deals that are advantageous to them. Although they seem to have some notion of fairness, to them fair exchanges are equal exchanges:

PRO: Heinz should steal the drug to save his wife. He'd go to jail but he'd still have his wife.

CON: He should not steal. The druggist is in business to make money. Taking the drug would take the druggist's profits. Maybe Heinz's friends could help raise more money.

When children can internalize rules, take the role of others, and make moral judgments based on abstract rather than concrete principles, then they can advance to higher stages of moral reasoning. Recent research (Walker, 1989) supports Kohlberg's stage model theory.

Criticisms of Kohlberg's Theory

Kohlberg's theory of moral development has been criticized on several grounds. For one, researchers have had difficulties in using Kohlberg's

situation bound
being unable to generalize from one situation to a similar other situation; assuming each situation is unique

scheme to identify a particular child's level of moral reasoning. Independent observers agree on their identifications less than 75% of the time. This difficulty in reaching consensus might be partly due to the possibility that moral judgments are more situation-bound than Kohlberg assumed: A child might apply preconventional reasoning to resolve one dilemma, but use another kind of reasoning in the very next instance because the situation demands it (Kurtines & Grief, 1974). In addition, Elliot Turiel (1978) has suggested that Kohlberg doesn't distinguish between moral prohibitions such as "Don't tell lies" and social rules such as the rules of games or etiquette. Hypothetical and real-life moral dilemmas elicit different moral reactions from children (Walker, 1989). For example, most children tested by Turiel said that some moral infractions such as stealing are wrong whether or not a country has an explicit law against them or punishes those who perform them. But these same children believed that if the participants could agree, it was fair to change the rules of a game. Television viewing can also influence children's moral judgment. In kindergartners, tolerance for moral transgression is associated more with total viewing time than with any particular type of program content (Rosenkoetter et al., 1990). Apparently the more young TV viewers see program characters "getting away with" questionable behavior or actually succeeding even though they do something wrong, the more acceptable their behaviors become.

Freud's Psychoanalytic Theory of Moral Development

Psychoanalytic theory suggests that the first emotions associated with moral development are usually fear and anxiety at the thought of losing a parent's love for having done something wrong (Freud 1938/1973). A child who has internalized standards of moral conduct and whose behavior is controlled by a knowledge of right and wrong is said to have developed a conscience. Freud felt that identifying with the same-sex parent (through the resolution of the Oedipal or Electra complex, see Chapter 10) was absolutely essential for the formation of a conscience. A child who can take the role of the parent can better understand the logic behind established standards and the disappointment that parents feel when the child's behavior doesn't live up to their expectations. Thus, the child follows moral rules because she fears losing the parent's love and feels guilty about transgressions.

conscience
a mental faculty which encourages one to distinguish right from wrong and to choose to do right

Although there is little current support for the psychoanalytic mechanisms that motivate the development of the conscience, Freud was correct in assuming that guilt plays an important role in moral judgment (M. L. Hoffman, 1979). School-age children may be more sensitive to feeling guilty than preschoolers, however.

■●▲   CONCEPT SUMMARY

Comparing Theories of Moral Development

- *The cognitive approach: Moral decision making advances with developments in cognition.*

  - *Jean Piaget*
    - The *egocentric stage* of moral development (ages 3–5). Standardized rules cannot be understood so the child makes up his or her own rules, changing them arbitrarily as play continues.
    - The *incipient cooperation stage* of moral development (ages 5–9). The child realizes that rules are invariant and applies them consistently throughout play, although he or she may change the rules associated with any particular game from time to time. The child focuses on the consequences of the behavior, not on the person's intentions.

  - *Lawrence Kohlberg*
    The preconventional level of morality.
    - *Stage 1—makes decisions to avoid punishment; focuses on self and need satisfaction; judges each fact separately, usually without considering the whole situation*
    - *Stage 2—follows rules if they benefit the user, sees only equal exchanges as fair exchanges*

- *The psychoanalytic approach: The child learns standards of moral conduct by identifying with the same-sex parent. The child follows these standards out of fear of losing the parent's love and feels guilty about transgressions.*

  - *Sigmund Freud*
    - Child identifies with same-sex parent through the resolution of the Electra/Oedipus complex. The child develops a conscience when she can internalize standards of right & wrong.

  - *Erik Erikson*
    - *Stage of initiative vs. shame/guilt*
      Success comes from planning and carrying out activities; oppression stems from too much parent intervention in the child's activities. Guilt is produced when the child wants to deviate from the parent's plans.

- *The learning theory approach: The child learns social standards through modeling, specific instruction, reinforcement/punishment, and identification with the parent.*

  - The parents are the child's main agent of socialization. The tone set by the parents influences the effectiveness of the moral instruction.

Erikson's Contribution to Understanding Moral Development

As one of Freud's disciples, Erik Erikson also discussed the role of guilt in the moral decision making of the preschool-age child (Erikson, 1963). But unlike Freud, Erikson believed that society played a profound role in personality development. Thus, his *psychosocial* theory emphasized people's (children's and adults) relationships with their social environments. According to Erikson, the 3–6 year olds psychosocial development focuses on making plans and setting goals. Organizing a backyard picnic lunch, planning the construction of a play fort, and arranging one's collection of bears so everyone can watch a favorite TV program are all examples of the activities that might be initiated by preschool age children. When preschoolers are permitted to initiate and plan some of their own behaviors, they are given the opportunity to create their own success. When parents intrude excessively into the child's plans or are overly restrictive, children feel oppressed, controlled, and guilty for wanting to deviate for their parent's schedule of activities.

Environmental Influences: Can Preschoolers be Taught Moral Values?

■ Figure 9–12

Identification encourages children to imitate the behavior and values of others.

In contrast to Piaget and Kohlberg, learning theorists suggest that parents and other socializing agents influence children's moral development through identification, modeling, reinforcement, and punishment. Parents stress the importance of certain social virtues such as truthfulness, cleanliness, honesty, fairness, and punctuality and attempt to encourage the internalization of these values through reward and punishment. Both *modeling* and *identification* with the parent are powerful factors in the development of moral behavior. For example, children are much more likely to display helpful, cooperative behavior if they have seen their parents behave in helpful, cooperative ways. This is especially true if the parents are warm and nurturant people. Children are more likely to identify with and imitate caring, loving parents.

Children can also learn to resist temptation through modeling and specific moral instruction (Bredemeier et al., 1986). Fourth grade boys who were told not to peek at a movie being shown behind a screen were more likely to obey if they hadn't see an adult leave his chair to peek. Encouraging preschool children to behave with maturity (in accordance with their abilities) and to assume some responsibility for others can stimulate their moral development by giving them practice (Baumrind, 1971).

Raising Good Readers

Whether taught using phonics or the whole-language approach, reading is the cornerstone of learning. Raising good readers takes time, not money. The only skill parents need to help their child become a reader is to know how to read themselves. Beyond that, a few suggestions:

1. *Draw your child's attention to written language at the earliest possible age.* Start reading books to your children as soon as they are able to be cradled in your lap. In this way they can look at the pictures and study the symbols on each page. They will also come to understand the basic format of the book: It tells a story, each page contains information, and the images and symbols have meaning. Sometimes young children don't want to proceed from the front to the back of the book in an orderly fashion. Let the young child decide "what" to read; narrate the pictures or pick up the story where they choose.

2. *Involve your children in a way that gradually lets them take over.* Once a child is familiar with a story, leave out key words for her to fill in. Let the child "read" the pictures or make up her own text. Encourage children to point to the existing printed words as they speak.

3. *Teach by example.* Because behavior speaks louder than words, parents must model whatever behaviors they want their children to value. If you don't wear your seat belt, why should they? By the same token, if you push your child to read but don't read yourself, your urgings will fall on deaf ears. Read *anything* in front of your children (books, the newspaper, magazines, even the racing form or the TV Guide!), but *read!* (And smile a lot as you do!)

3. *Not all children take to reading in the same way.* Some children will read the classics; others, the comics. Everyone has his or her own taste in literature (or quasi-literature!). Respect your child's individuality by allowing him to read appropriate materials of his own choosing. Just be glad the child is reading *anything*.

4. *Make a place for reading in the day's schedule of events.* Establish a time and place for reading at home. Maybe before bed; maybe before dinner; maybe after a nice bath. Turn the TV and the stereo off and open a book.

5. *Take advantage of your local library and librarian.* Parents can spend a fortune purchasing books for their children. And while it's nice to have books "around," visits to the lending library can provide much the same stimulation with an ever-changing selection. For the younger child, most libraries and children's book stores offer story hours and other special events. Most librarians are valuable resources for selecting age-appropriate books for your child. For older children, the library can teach valuable lessons about responsibility.

6. *Offer an incentive for reading.* Yes, reading should be its own reward, but for some children, it's not. Perhaps the child might want to join a reading club (often based in libraries and children's bookstores) where children get rewards for the number of books they have completed. Maybe a special chart can be hung on the refrigerator where special privileges are earned

(continued on next page)

for books/pages read. Perhaps part of the child's allowance can be tied to pages read or books completed. Perhaps reading can be the "summer job" of older children who earn extra money by reading. Some might worry about the child's motivation when outside incentives are used. The trick is always balance. Give children a reason to read, but don't make the money, status, or privilege *so* attractive that that's the *only* reason they're reading.

7. *Continue to read to your children even after they are proficient readers themselves.* Reading together is a great way to share time. Try reading something just a little beyond their current level. The benefits are many fold: you get to share an activity with your children, you may get to read a book you always wanted to read or to introduce to children, and they see how warm, fun, and entertaining reading can be as a family activity.

8. *Above all, make reading fun.* When something is boring, tedious, or non-reinforcing, we call it work, not fun. Let reading be an outlet—exercise for the brain and the imagination. Let children select stories that interest *them*, whether they are "good literature" or not. Praise their efforts—"You're such a good reader" or "I really like the books you pick for yourself. Good job!" Balance reading with their other activities to produce well-rounded children.

Source: Hammill, R. "The Reading Wars." © *Newsweek*, Special Issue Fall/Winter, 1990, p. 8–14. Reprinted with permission.

● Chapter Summary

- In Piaget's scheme, the 2–7 year old child enters the preoperational stage of cognitive development and is capable of using symbolic thought or mental imagry. The child's ability to think logically and to solve problems are affected by her egocentrism (an inability to take another person's perspective), her centration (the tendency to focus on one aspect of a situation, ignoring all others), her concreteness (an emphasis on the tangible rather than the abstract), and the irreversibility of her thinking (an inability to reconstruct the original after making changes).

- Preschoolers are able to form concepts or build cognitive categories to help them organize and understand new information. Children acquire some understanding of identity constancy, class inclusion, numbers, size, and time during this age period and are able to make some use of a cognitive map. Concepts of distance and speed, sorting and classifying objects, ordering objects in a series, and time sequencing are abilities that appear late in the preschool period.

- The information processing theorists note improvements in attention span, scanning ability, memory capacity, the organization of memory, and the application of learning strategies.

- Intelligence tests like the Stanford-Binet and the Wechsler Preschool and Primary Scale of Intelligence (WPPSI) are used to measure reasoning, motor abilities, and problem solving skills.

- Myelinization of brain areas during the preschool period encourages dramatic changes in language development. While inconsistencies and difficulties in speech as common throughout this period, by age 6 or 7, the child has acquired "everyday language skills" comparable to most adults.
- In addition to acquiring the rudiments of their native language, preschool age children also learn rules for initiating and sustaining conversations.
- When two languages are learned simultaneously, three stages of language acquisition can be identified. Bilingual children may be more advanced than monolinguals in certain aspects of congitive development. Debate rages over how best to educate children whose native language isn't English.
- Piaget, Kohlberg, Freud, and Erikson have each studied the development of moral reasoning, or the ability to distinguish right from wrong.

● Observational Exercise

During the preschool years, the child becomes more and more adept at using thought, language, memory, and reasoning to help solve problems and relate to the world. However, these mental processes are limited by preschoolers' egocentrism—their tendency to experience every event in relation to themselves. Demonstrate this egocentrism by using a facsimile of Piaget and Inhelder's Three-Mountain Task to test a 5 year old. Compare his or her responses with those of an 8 to 9 year old.

Procedure: Set three containers close together on a card table, coffee table, or other small table. (Large, medium, and small soft drink containers work nicely. Or you might use a coffee can, soup can, and tuna can. Paint the containers or wrap them with different colored construction paper to make them easily distinguishable.)

Place four chairs around the table. Now take a photograph or make a sketch of the three-object configuration from each of the four positions.

Invite the children, one at a time, to sit at the table. Arrange the pictures in front of the child. Now ask the child to perform the following tasks and record the responses of each child for comparison.

	5 year old Correct?		8 year old Correct?	
	Yes	*No*	*Yes*	*No*
1. "Look at the 'mountains' (the colored cans). Select the picture of the mountains that is the same as what you see."				

	5 year old Correct?		8 year old Correct?	
(continued from previous page)	*Yes*	*No*	*Yes*	*No*

2. Have the doll sit in the chair to the child's right. Ask, "What picture of the mountains matches what the doll sees?"

3. Have the doll sit in the chair to the child's left. Ask, "What picture of the mountains matches what the doll sees?"

4. Seat the doll across from the child and ask, "What picture of the mountains matches what the doll sees?"

Now have the child sit across from his or her original position. Give the child one of the photos to hold and ask him or her to sit at the seat that would show the mountains just as they are in the picture. Repeat this procedure with each of the pictures.

	5 year old Correct?		8 year old Correct?	
	Yes	*No*	*Yes*	*No*
a. Picture 1				
b. Picture 2				
c. Picture 3				
d. Picture 4				

1. Describe the differences in the performances of the 5 and the 8 year old.
2. In each case, does the child's accuracy improve in moving from chair to chair? Explain why or why not.

● **Recommended Readings**

Bissex, G. L. (1980). *Gnys at wrk: A child learns to write and read.* Cambridge, MA: Harvard Univ. Press.

Chukovsky, K. (1963). *From two to five* (original Russian text translated by Miriam Morton). Berkeley: Univ. of California Press.

Curtiss, S. (1977). *Genie: A psycholinguistic study of a modern day wild child.* New York: Academic Press.

deVilliers, P. A. & deVilliers, J. G. (1979). *Early language.* Cambridge, MA: Harvard Univ. Press.

Formanek, R., & Gurian, A. (1980). *Why? Children's questions.* Boston: Houghton-Mifflin.

Hakuta, M. (1986). *Mirror of language: The debate on bilingualism.* New York: Basic Books.

Iwamura, S. G. (1980). *The verbal games of preschool children.* New York: St. Martin's.

Schulman, M., & Mekler, E. (1985). *Bringing up a moral child: A new approach for teaching your child to be kind, just and responsible.* Reading, MA: Addison-Wesley.

Social and Emotional Development During the Preschool Years

● The Changing Face of the American Family

When Ward and June Cleaver were raising Wally and "The Beaver" in the 1960s, the nuclear family had one model: a stay-home mother, a working father, and two children (preferably one boy and one girl). Divorce was a disgrace; living together (called "shacking up") was shameful; and children born out of wedlock had their birth certificates stamped ILLEGITIMATE. Things have changed somewhat since then. As we approach the year 2000, alternative family styles are the rule rather than the exception. Today's family may consist of working mothers, single parents, older parents, surrogate parents, caretaker fathers, same-sex couples, unmarried parents, extended stepfamilies, or extended nuclear families (grandparents, uncles, cousins, and whoever). Which configuration is best? The best family for any child continues to be the one that will meet the child's physical needs while nurturing his psychological needs. Families don't have to be traditional to be functional.

Socialization Within the Family

The family plays a central role in socializing the child by training him to be a productive member of society. Socialization is accomplished by relating the values of the culture to the child, reacting to the child's behavior, and serving as a model for imitation (Maccoby & Martin, 1983). Cultural expectations are transmitted in the parent's verbalizations to the child as well as in the stories he reads and the games he plays. "Don't slurp your soup," "Sit up straight," "Do your homework," "Don't talk back to your grandmother" are common messages. Parents then assess how well the child's behavior conforms to their active teaching. Children who comply are rewarded; children who deviate are punished. Values can be communicated nonverbally, too. When father runs from a spider or mother kisses grandmother's cheek each time she sees her, the child can learn that spiders are to be avoided at all costs and older relatives deserve affection.

Adults' investment in parenting has more of an impact on their socialization practices than their degree of investment in work. Parents who are committed to their role of caregiver demand more mature behavior from their children and describe their children more favorably than mothers or fathers who were strongly committed to their role as provider or worker (Greenberger & Goldberg, 1989).

The emotional tone of the family—warm vs. hostile—makes the child more or less responsive to parental guidance (Maccoby, 1980). A warm parent is affectionate, enthusiastic about the child's accomplishments, enjoys time spent with the child, is sensitive to the child's needs and moods, and genuinely cares for the child. The hostile parent is just the opposite—rejecting, emotionally distant, disappointed in the child, and unfulfilled by parenting. The warm parent is a far more effective agent of socialization than the hostile parent for several reasons. First, a child who disobeys the warm parent stands to lose the powerfully rewarding love, attention, and companionship received from that parent. The child who disobeys a hostile parent has little to lose since the relationship is less than positive. Second, warm parents are far more likely than hostile parents to detail their expectations and to explain the reasons for them. It's a lot easier to follow the "rules" when you know what they are and why they exist (Maccoby & Martin, 1983). Third, warm parents make a child feel good about themselves and their abilities. The secure, self-confident child feels less anxious and learns more efficiently than the child who feels high stress and low self-esteem as a consequence of parent hostility. Fourth, since warm parents understand their child's developing capacities, they adjust their expectations to fit the child's developmental level. When children are offered behavioral strategies that they can successfully apply, they feel competent and motivated to obey. Finally, even preschoolers are interested in fairness. If warm parents control behavior in ways that seem reasonable and predictable, the child is more likely to comply (Kuczynski et al., 1987).

Interactions with Mother

During the preschool years, the nature of the mother/child relationship changes. Both mother and child stop relying on the physical closeness that characterizes infancy, for preschoolers can communicate through words and gestures, not solely by cries that demand physical attention. It's not that the preschoolers need or love their mother any less than they did previously; it's only that they now have a variety of ways of expressing love and seeking approval. Their newly acquired ability to use symbolic thought permits preschoolers to represent their relation-

■ **Figure 10–1**

The family is the central force in the preschooler's life.

ship with their parents mentally. The emotional bond between parents and children thus becomes more enduring, because the child can maintain it even when the parents are not present.

Rather than clinging to their mothers as infants do, preschool children venture off a ways, often glancing at, smiling at, talking to, or showing their mothers toys from a distance (Clarke-Stewart & Hevey, 1981). Children of this age seem to feel comfortable and willing to explore as long as they can see or hear their mothers. As children grow older, they venture farther away. Early research by Rheingold and Eckerman (1973) found that preschoolers between the ages of 2 and 4 went a third of a meter farther from their mothers each year during 15 minutes of outdoor free play. Children seem to establish their own boundaries in play areas such as parks and to stay within those boundaries without being reminded. In another expression of children's independence, besides increasing the distance between themselves and their mothers, preschoolers tend to play apart from them for longer periods of time without becoming bored or feeling the need to check back.

During the preschool years, children learn to tolerate brief but complete separations from their mothers. Between the ages of 1 and 4 children show less and less emotional upset at separation, and by age 4 such distress is quite rare (Sroufe et al., 1983). But in times of mild stress—for example, when they are left in the presence of strangers—even 3 year olds want physical comfort and reassurance from their mothers.

While children are gradually putting more distance between themselves and their mothers and displaying more interest in autonomy, mothers are finding their own ways of facilitating their children's independence. First, the mother tends to reduce the amount of physical contact between herself and the child. Next she relaxes the level of surveillance and attention she gives, and finally she reduces the number of interactions she initiates, moving toward a *partnership* in which both she and the child contribute equally to the exchange (Clarke-Stewart & Hevey, 1981). This in no way suggests that mothering becomes passive. On the contrary, sensitive mothers foster optimal development in the cognitive, emotional, and social domains by being attentive, warm, stimulating, responsive, and nonrestrictive in interacting with their young children (Field et al., 1987). During this period, too, sensitive mothers promote their child's skill in problem solving and competence in interacting with peers by using a combination of authoritarian (direct commands, physical punishment, reprimands) and authoritative styles (suggestions and positive incentives) (Kochanska et al., 1989).

Depressed mothers inhibit parent–child interaction, however, by offering fewer verbal exchanges and fewer positive statements than nondepressed mothers. Sons are less compliant when their mothers are in negative moods (Jouriles et al., 1989). Similarly, 4–7 year olds have difficulty comprehending their mother's anger when it stems from a complex combination of factors or from past events. When maternal anger results from marital conflict, preschoolers tend to blame themselves (Covell & Abramovich, 1988).

It is clearly possible for mothers to establish a parent–child partnership when the mother is consistently available, but what happens when the mother works outside the home? In a study on the impact of day care on social development, L. W. Hoffman (1989) reported that rather than becoming clingier and more dependent, children of working mothers become self-sufficient and independent sooner than children whose mothers are not employed. Later these same children displayed higher achievement motivation and competence.

Interactions with Father

In two-adult families, as the mother's caretaking role declines and she begins to establish a partnership with the child, the father's role becomes more prominent. Preschoolers, especially boys, prefer to play with their fathers and to work with them in solving tasks (Clarke-Stewart, 1980). The more time fathers spend playing with their children, the more positive the father–child relationship tends to be—and the more likely the mother is to talk and play with the child as well. One of the most important aspects of fathering during the preschool years seems to be the general level of the father's involvement in the child's life. Involved fathers tend to have children who progress well both in their cognitive–motivational development and their social–emotional relations (Belsky, 1980). Fathers who are present but uninvolved may be a source of stress for the child.

Child development and parenting are influenced by the quality of the marital relationship (Belsky, 1981). When marital relationships are positive, fathers are highly involved with their children and mothers are both more positively oriented toward the children and more competent in childcare tasks. On the other hand, when marriages are marked by tension and conflict, the level of parental involvement with children either increases or decreases. The more husbands blame or criticize their wives, the more negatively oriented these mothers are toward their children (Clarke-Stewart, 1980). Similarly, parents may invest themselves in the parenting role in ways that compensate for negative aspects of the marriage—for instance, by being overprotective when the marriage is dissatisfying. Along these lines Gath (1989) has found that the presence of a child with special needs doesn't mar a good marriage so much as it disrupts the balance of a moderate or a vulnerable one.

The Consequences of Parent Treatment: Aggression, Competence, Dependence/Independence

Aggression

In 1953 Robert Sears and colleagues found that children who are physically punished by their parents display more aggressive behavior at school than children whose parents use nonviolent discipline. Today 40 years later, the conclusion remains unchanged: Aggressive parents usually have aggressive children (Parke & Slaby, 1983). Because it is unacceptable for children to retaliate and hit their parents, they lash out at peers, pets, objects and siblings instead. In addition to the use of physical punishment, other child-rearing strategies and parent characteristics have been found to contribute to aggressiveness in preschoolers (Larzelere, 1986):

1. Indifference to the true needs of the child
2. Inconsistent discipline

■ **Figure 10–2**

Aggressive behavior is common during the preschool period.

3. Impulsive and harsh discipline
4. Rejecting the child as a person; active dislike of the child
5. Being overly critical of the child's behavior or of the child as a person
6. Lack of emotional support for the child
7. Vague or unclear rules and expectations for the child as a member of the family
8. Not providing reasons or explanations for the child's punishment nor suggestions for alternative behaviors
9. Heavy TV viewing (especially action-adventure programs)

Competence

Competent children are friendly, cooperative, and achievement oriented (Baumrind, 1971, 1980). Parents who provide their children with stimulating toys, games, and social interaction encourage the development of good cognitive skills. Children with such high-level skills are better problem solvers and have higher self-esteem, both of which lead to greater competence.

Competent children are also better at controlling and predicting outcomes than less competent children. When parents use reason and explanation as they discipline, children can better understand household rules and behavioral expectations and can *choose* to obey, thereby reducing the anxiety associated with arbitrary punishment.

Another aspect of competence involves *social competence,* or the ability to use the environment and one's personal resources to make the most of any situation (Waters & Sroufe, 1983). Both Sroufe (1983) and Erik Erikson (1963) assume that the development of social competence is cumulative, with each stage building on the one that precedes it (Tables 10–1 and 10–2). Prior to the preschool period, the child has had to acquire psychological regulation, or what Erikson calls "basic trust." The competent infant can adjust to the environment, anticipate that his needs will be met, and establish an attachment to an individual who will serve as a safe base for exploration. When the infant can derive comfort from the attachment figure but also be free enough to leave the caregiver to explore the environment, the child has acquired what Erikson calls "autonomy." Now that he's a preschooler, the child must learn to develop a measure of self-control, to adapt to social/sex roles, and to acquire a sense of purpose and self-direction, or "initiative" in Erikson's terms.

Dependence/Independence

Diana Baumrind's (1980) *parenting styles*—permissive, authoritarian, and authoritative—are associated with independence/dependence in children. *Permissive* parents are warm and loving but nondemanding and make little attempt to control their child's behavior. Children of permissive parents are the least self-reliant, self-controlled and curious of all children studied. *Authoritarian* parents are emotionally cool, restric-

social competence
the ability to adapt successfully to social situations

permissive
a parenting style that is responsive and nurturant, but exerts little control and makes few demands. The permissive parent is overly tolerant and rarely restrictive

authoritarian
a parenting style that is controlling and demanding and pays little attention to the needs of the child. Obedience is valued over communication and negotiation and physical punishment is used to make the child obey.

■ **Table 10–1** *Phases in the Development of Social Competence*

PHASE	AGE	ISSUE	ROLE FOR CAREGIVER
1	0–3 mos.	Physiological regulation	Smooth routines.
2	3–6 mos.	Management of tension	Sensitive, cooperative interaction
3	6-12 mos.	Establishing an effective attachment relationship	Responsive availability
4	12–18 mos.	Exploration and mastery	Secure base
5	1½–2½ yrs.	Individuation	Firm support
6	2½–4½ yrs.	Management of impulses, sex-role identification, peer relations	Clear roles and values, flexible control

Source: Based on Sroufe, 1983.

■ **Table 10–2** *Erikson's Stages of Psychosocial Development*

AGE (YEARS)	ISSUE	POSSIBLE OUTCOMES
1	Trust vs. mistrust	Infant learns to trust, or mistrust, that needs will be met by mother or others.
2	Autonomy vs. shame and doubt	Toddler learns to exercise will, make own choices, and control himself—or becomes doubtful and uncertain that he can do things on his own.
3–5	Initiative vs. guilt	Preschooler acquires direction and purpose, learns to initiate activities and enjoys accomplishments—or feels guilty about attempts at independence.

Source: Based on Erikson, 1963.

tive, controlling, and punitive. They demand unquestioned obedience. As a result, their children are more withdrawn, aggressive, unhappy, and distrustful than others. *Authoritative* parents are confident, warm, rational, and self-correcting. They reason with their children and encourage children's autonomy, comments, and questions but also enforce rules firmly and expect high levels of achievement. The children of authoritative parents tend to be more independent than the children of authoritarian or permissive parents because

1. The parent also values the child's individuality and self-expression
2. Parents define limits for the child's behavior, but the child is free to make his own decisions within those limits

It is important to point out that parent–child interactions have a reciprocal quality. The parent may adopt a certain parenting style, but that style is changed to fit the parent's mood and the behavior in question. Likewise, a child who is consistently happy or pleasant elicits a different response pattern from parents than a child who usual temperament is more angry, fearful, or depressed (Hall, 1984).

authoritative
a parenting style that balances control and demands with warmth and responsiveness. A democratic approach is used and the child's needs and rights are recognized and respected.

Consequences of Parent Maltreatment: Psychological Abuse

Children can be mistreated physically (Chapter 7), sexually Chapter 14), or psychologically. While infants may not understand the words, "I hate

psychological abuse/psychological maltreatment
verbal and nonverbal behavior that assaults the child's sense of self worth: insults, ridicule, lack of confidence directed toward the child

In Touch

NATIONAL INSTITUTE OF MENTAL HEALTH
PUBLIC INQUIRIES BRANCH
5600 Fishers Lane
Room 15C–05
Rockville, MD 20857
301–443–4517

Federal agency that answers questions about psychological disturbance

you! I wish you were never born!'', those same words can profoundly affect a preschooler who understands language and can be deeply scarred by ridicule, rejection, degradation, humiliation, or terrorization (Hart & Brassard, 1987). The accompanying feature discusses several things parents should avoid saying to their kids—ever.

Psychological maltreatment takes the form of an attack on the emotional competence of the child, systematic belittling of his character and achievements, and consistent indifference to the child's needs for attention, praise, or affection. Such abuse undermines the child's need to receive and give love and to feel worthwhile as a human being. Maltreated children react by having more difficulty regulating their emotions and controlling negative impulses than children who are well treated (Rieder & Cicchetti, 1989).

Mental Health workers and the legal profession focus on the frequency and intensity of the maltreatment and whether harm is intentionally or unintentionally afflicted (Gelles & Cornell, 1983). Yet regardless of the circumstances, maltreatment is associated with serious learning and adjustment problems. Maltreated children are more likely to tell lies, steal, have low self-esteem, underachieve, exhibit dependency, be depressed, and be aggressive, both against themselves (self-destructive behavior and suicide) and others (assault and homicide) than children who were not maltreated (Hart & Brassard, 1987). Psychological maltreatment occurs in families, schools, childcare centers, hospitals, recreational sites, juvenile justice programs—anywhere where adults and children interact (Rosenberg, 1987).

The incidence of child maltreatment is based on parent's willingness to admit to emotionally abusive encounters with their children or on children's retrospective recollections as adults. As a consequence, accurate figures do not exist, but all estimates are high (Starr, 1979). If 2 million American children are physically abused each year, perhaps 10–20 million children are psychologically maltreated (Johnson & Showers, 1985). If our society weren't quite so accepting of force and violence, fewer children would be victimized (Belsky, 1980).

PREVENTING MALTREATMENT Prevention efforts must be directed toward both families and society if the incidence of child maltreatment is to decline (Rosenberg & Reppucci, 1985; Melton & Thompson, 1987). Families can be helped by:

- Educating people about children before they become parents
- Teaching parents nonviolent disciplinary strategies
- Providing more job and job-related training for financially needy families
- Funding organizations like Parents Anonymous that support and rehabilitate abusive parents

A Closer Look

Things Parents Should Avoid Saying to Their Children

Even the best parents occasionally lose control and say the wrong thing to their child. The parent might be temporarily relieved, but some real damage can be done to the child's self-esteem when adults speak out of frustration, anger, or fatigue. Here are some phrases to avoid—along with some suggestions as to more useful strategies.

1. *Why can't you be more like. . .?*

A child who is compared unfavorably with a sibling or friend feels devalued and comes to resent the highlighted child for being "better" and putting pressure on her. Instead of making general comparisons, target a specific behavior you want changed. If you say, "Why can't you be like Heather? She always does her homework," help the child focus on her homework and be more successful in following through. Then, in essence, you are still valuing the child (they don't need to be like Heather to be good; they already are) while correcting a problem behavior (homework completion).

2. *How could you be so stupid?*

Children (people) do behave in foolish ways and say silly things. But calling a child's words or actions "stupid" only helps erode his fragile self-confidence. When people feel stupid, they feel inadequate and inept. When parents tell children they are stupid, children are likely to believe them, and such beliefs undermine self-worth. If the condemnation was prompted by the child playing with matches, focus on improving the behavior rather than making demoralizing statements. The reason playing with matches is stupid is that fire can destroy life and property. Tell the child *why* he needs to stop what he is doing and not repeat the activity; don't just label the behavior as stupid.

3. *Sometimes I wish I had never had kids.*

When children hear this, they feel unloved, unwanted, and rejected. This is such a powerful statement that sometimes it is internalized and stays with the child into adulthood. Raising children is a difficult and frustrating job, but one obligation parents have to children is to make sure they always feel loved and secure. Instead of saying, "I hate you. I wish you were never born," express anger and frustration by saying, "Sometimes I wish you would just start listening to what I say." or say "Sometimes your behavior makes me very angry." Those are legitimate expressions of feeling that don't destroy the child in the process. If parents do say hurtful things to their children, go back and try to heal the relationship by hugging the child and saying, "I said something cruel to you. I'm sorry. When I get angry sometimes I say things I don't mean. I have to work on not saying those things."

4. *You're the smart one/the funny one/the athletic one/the lazy one. . .*

All of these labels, whether positive or negative, are confining and can prevent a child from ever seeing her real self. The "smart one" may feel pressure never to fail; the "smart one" may overlook her artistic or social talents because, after all, they're not artistic or social, *they're smart.* The label also makes a statement about what the parent *thinks* is important, and this perception may conflict with what the child values about herself.

Negative labels are particularly damaging because they can become self-fulling prophecies for behavior. It's hard to care about weight loss when people call you "fat" (even affectionate terms, like *gordita,* can be harmful); it's hard to feel a sense of self-control when everyone expects you will get into a fight. Compliment the child, but don't confine them in the description.

(continued on next page)

(continued from previous page)

5. *Do it—or else.*

Non specific threats don't motivate behavior. Or else *what?* Sometimes out-of-control parents offer specific threats that are also inappropriate—"If you ever do that again, I'll kill you," or "Do that once more and you'll be grounded for the rest of your life." These are foolish and irresponsible statements that just undercut rather than elevate the parent's authority. A better strategy would be to choose a punishment that is appropriate and that you can and will implement. "If you don't get your chores done, you won't get to watch TV tonight." "The next time you hit your brother, you'll have to stop playing and come in and sit down." The effective parent carries through on the consequence since that's the only way the child will take the discipline seriously.

6. *If you don't come with me now, I'll leave without you.*

This statement is designed to frighten children into hurrying along. However, it uses a very real fear children already have—the fear of abandonment or being left by their parents—to control the child's behavior. Children need to have the security of knowing that their parents will *never* abandon them. Rather than making children anxious and insecure, parents can encourage timely compliance by reminding children of time lines and by offering them options. "You can walk out the door by yourself or I can pick you up and carry you out, which will it be?" "We have five minutes more to play. I'll set the timer and then we'll clean up."

Adapted from: Van Der Meer, Antonia. "The 10 Worst Things You Can Say to Your Kids (and How to Stop Saying Them)." *Redbook*, November 1989, p. 32. Used with permission.

In addition our society needs to become less tolerant of violence, especially as used against children. Our laws must be changed to become more responsive to the needs of children and our courts must act with more speed and conviction to assure safe and psychologically healthy environments for its most vulnerable citizens.

■ **Figure 10–3**

Ads like these appear on billboards and in magazines. Their aim is to educate people and to tell them where they can seek help.

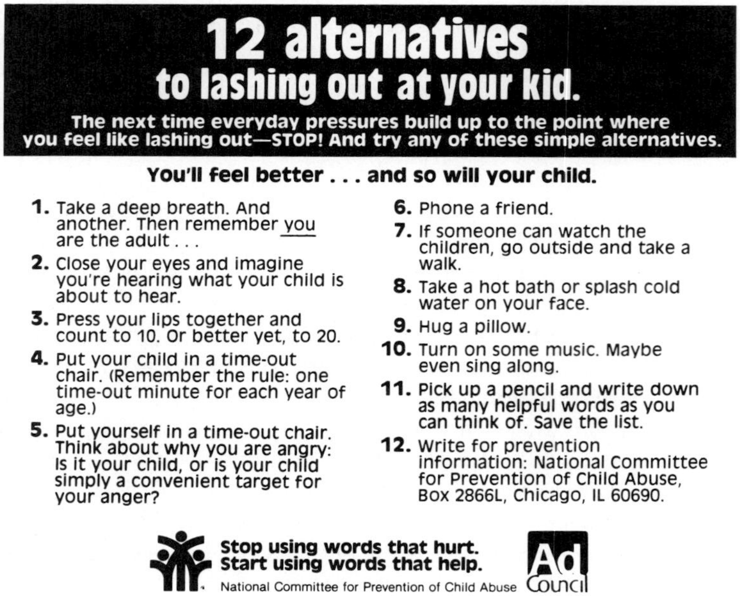

Interactions with Siblings

Interactions with siblings are often the preschooler's first social experience with other children close in age. Eighty-seven percent of American families have more than one child (J. Dunn, 1985). Sibling relationships during the preschool years have unparalleled power and intimacy because of the nearly constant and close contact brothers and sisters maintain (J. Dunn, 1988). In most cases, younger children watch and imitate the behavior of older siblings, especially in same-sex pairs. Older siblings, especially older sisters, will most often assume the role of teacher, helper, or manager (Stoneman et al., 1986; G. H. Brody et al., 1985). This pattern becomes more prevalent with age. Older children tend to assume the dominant role while playing with their younger brothers and sisters, offering positive behavior (toys, talking to them, giving directions) as well as more antagonistic behavior (hitting, tattling, and insulting) (Abramovitch et al., 1986). They also tend to comfort younger siblings when the mother is absent. Older firstborns are less competitive and show more positive attitudes toward their siblings than younger firstborns (Stocker et al., 1989). Younger siblings are more helpful and less antagonistic within the family when their parents' level of marital stress is low (G. H. Brody et al., 1987).

The quality of sibling exchanges ranges from almost all positive to almost all negative. Sibling interactions are more positive when the older sibling has been interested in helping with or entertaining the baby from the beginning and when both siblings are the same sex. These siblings play together happily and the older sibling tends to help, smile, and structure activities to accommodate the younger child's abilities (Dunn & Kendrick, 1982). But *sibling rivalry,* or feelings of antagonism or resentment toward a brother or sister, is also a possibility. Most commonly, sibling rivalry develops in response to a marked decrease in warmth and attention on the parent's part toward the older child after the baby's birth and an increase in the number of prohibitions they impose (Kendrick & Dunn, 1983). Older siblings may feel deprived of their parents' attention and affection and those feelings are often intensified if they have to give up a private room for the "intruder" or if their mothers become more distant and less sensitive to their needs.

sibling rivalry
feelings of jealousy, hostility, or anger that may develop between brothers and/or sisters

Here's an account of a typical response to a younger sibling's presence:

> As a firstborn child I remember feeling quite threatened by my second sister. It wasn't that I felt unloved or displaced by her birth. I just thought that as an infant she was getting more than her fair share of laughs and compliments from my parents. To divert some of that attention to me, I devised a strategy I thought would work: I started to tell jokes! Needless to say, it wasn't terribly effective. The jokes a 4 year old can make up (I couldn't even get material from a joke book because I couldn't read yet) weren't that funny, except maybe to another 4 year old. So aside from an occasional laugh, I got mostly groans and concerned looks from my par-

■ Figure 10–4

Sometimes preschoolers feel like being an only child once again.

ents. (Of course, their responses made me try all the more). Old habits die hard, though. Even now when I become a little tense or need attention, I've been known to tell a joke or two. I don't use any of the material I made up as a child, so I'm more likely to draw a favorable response. Interestingly, I don't tell many jokes to my parents. I still don't think they fully appreciate my sense of humor! (Author's files)

Rivalry is most likely among certain kinds of children: same-sex children, children who are between 1.5 and 3 years apart in age, tense and relatively nonadaptive children, and children whose parents are inconsistent with respect to discipline (Kendrick & Dunn, 1983). Moreover, sibling rivalry and hostility are often increased when one of the brothers or sisters has a chronic disability or a health problem (McKeever, 1983). Poor sibling relationships during the preschool years predict more peer hostility and trouble with teachers when children are in elementary school (N. Richman et al., 1982). Even siblings whose relationships are basically positive engage in more conflict, crying, and aggression during the preschool years because the period is a particularly difficult one for children.

Sibling rivalry is not inevitable, but it may be intensified during the preschool period because of the egocentrism and cognitive constraints of the preoperational period. Also, such rivalry might have more to do with the parents than the children (where there is favoritism, for example, or where parents see rivalry when none exists). In any case, certain strategies are effective in preventing or minimizing negative sibling reactions to a new baby (Table 10–3).

ONLY CHILDREN What do Elvis Presley, FDR, and Leonardo da Vinci have in common? Each grew up as an only child (Lipsitt, 1989b). Ten percent of American families limit their family size to just one child. Only children are incorrectly assumed to be spoiled, lonely, selfish, and maladjusted. In reality, only children fare just as well as children from two-child families. Compared to children with siblings, only children get better grades, go farther in school, are expected to behave more maturely, and have more positive and affectionate relationships with their parents (Falbo & Polit, 1986). Only children do not seem to be disadvantaged socially, having as many close friends, and exhibiting more social behavior (positive and negative) than children with siblings. While only children report as much life satisfaction as others, both they and their parents see advantages and disadvantages to one-child families (Blake, 1981) (Table 10–4).

If any child is at a disadvantage in families, it seems to be the second born. Compared to both firstborn and only children, second borns are less socially advanced, are praised less often, receive less of the parents' time, seek less comfort from others in times of stress, and are less mature and less achievement oriented (Snow et al., 1981).

■ **Table 10–3** *Managing Sibling Rivalry*

Sibling rivalry is not inevitable. How parents prepare the child for the birth of a sibling and the strategies they use to facilitate sibling interaction after birth are important in minimizing or eliminating negative reactions.

1. Prepare the child for the sibling's birth. The timing of information about the expected sibling depends on the firstborn's age and degree of maturity. Toddlers have no real understanding of the passage of time. "In six months" or "on September 23" has little meaning because it is too abstract. Also, toddlers want things "right now" and can't understand the mother's refusal to produce the baby on demand. Tell the child about the new baby when the mother begins to get large and noticeable changes take place in the house to prepare for the new arrival. A month or two is ample time for the young child; older children should be told sooner, since they often become aware of the expected sibling by overhearing adult conversation.

2. Give older children realistic expectations about the sibling. Telling them you're bringing home a playmate is unfair because it's untrue. (One disappointed child was overheard to say, "How can she play school with me? She won't answer any questions and she can't even color!") Let them know what babies are like, how dependent they are, and what habits and behaviors they usually display. Help older children understand infancy and familiarize them with newborn appearance and behavior by showing them pictures of themselves and other family members, introducing them to other new babies, or visiting the local hospital's newborn nursery.

3. Maintain stability by avoiding abrupt change. Don't have children give up their room or their crib for the new baby. The child may react with resentment and hostility. Good planning will minimize the stress of transition. If the new baby needs the existing crib in the nursery, for example, the older child should get a "big bed" (a twin or infant bed) in advance of the baby's arrival. If the child is made to feel grown-up and special in the new bed, he or she is likely to cooperate. The parents need to express continuing affection for the first child. Let the child know that he or she will always be a valued and important member of the family. Praise the child's positive behavior.

4. Include the child in social visits after the baby is born. Visitors may inadvertently cause problems when they shower the new baby with attention and all but ignore the first child. Involve older children in social visits as much as possible by including them in conversation and praising them publicly to the guests. It's nice when the visitors bring gifts for both children, but in case they don't, have a small present that might be given to the toddler to open at this time or let the big brother or big sister be in charge of the gift opening.

5. Help children become involved with the baby. Before the birth, the mother can involve children by letting them feel the baby move and letting them help make preparations for the baby's arrival. Help the child identify with the new baby by calling it "our baby" rather than Mommy's or Daddy's baby. After birth, toddlers can be helped to participate in childcare activities if they wish. Forcing contact or giving older children too much responsibility may make them resent the baby and the extra burden of work it produces.

6. Avoid overprotecting the baby. Rather than scolding children for being clumsy and inadvertently "hurting" the baby, mothers can teach skills to toddlers to increase their level of competence. Instructing children about the baby's soft spot, the need to support the neck, and so on, and then actively supervising and praising their efforts should produce positive results.

7. Avoid being overly restrictive and judgmental. If the baby is sleeping, for example, and you want to keep the noise level down, let toddlers play in a more distant portion of the house. If the baby cries in the presence of older children and you weren't there to see the cause, don't assume that the older children were necessarily to blame.

8. Try to understand expressions of jealousy or resentment. Children may indicate dislike for the baby or they may seek attention by displaying regressive behavior (like wetting or indulging in baby talk) or by becoming aggressive and assaultive. Punishment will only increase the child's level of frustration and the incidence of this undesirable behavior. In all these cases, children are trying to communicate their dissatisfaction; take time to observe their behavior and talk with them. Also examine your own behavior to make sure you're treating all children fairly. Because of its harmful potential, redirect physical aggression into other types of activities.

9. Provide plenty of loving attention. Older children will benefit from extra special attention from parents. Reinforce their sense of security and belongingness. Allow them to "try on" the baby's role by laying on the changing table or having a bottle, if they wish, to let them see how it feels to be a baby. They can return to their "older child role" after a reasonable period of time. Make a special effort to be responsive and considerate.

■ **Table 10–4** *Advantages and Disadvantages of Living in a One-child Family*

ADVANTAGES		DISADVANTAGES	
MENTIONED BY CHILDREN	MENTIONED BY PARENTS	MENTIONED BY CHILDREN	MENTIONED BY PARENTS
Avoiding sibling rivalry	Having time to pursue one's own interests and career	Not getting to experience the closeness of a sibling relationship	Walking a "tightrope" between healthy attention and overindulgence
Having more privacy	Less financial pressure	Feeling too much pressure from parents to succeed	Having only one chance to "make good" as a parent
Enjoying greater affluence	Not having to worry about "playing favorites" among children	Having no one to help care for parents when they get old	Being left childless in case of the child's death
Closer parent-child relationship			

Source: Hawke & Knox, "The One-Child Family: A New Life Style." *The Family Coordinator, 27,* 1978, p. 215–219. Used with permission from the National Council on Family Relations.

FIRSTBORN AND LATER-BORN CHILDREN The oldest (firstborn) child enjoys a special position in the family. The first birth may be the most anxiously anticipated by parents and grandparents because of its novelty and excitement. Firstborn children (especially males) are most likely to receive names that tie them to the family lineage—for example, James Jr., or William Edward III. Such names confer special honor upon the child and sometimes special responsibility, too. In addition, eldest children bask in the complete and undivided attention of their parents without pressure to share them or their possessions with anyone else.

Eldest children are born into an adult world and remain more adult-oriented, mature, self-controlled, conforming, and responsible than their siblings (Falbo, 1981). Parents often have higher expectations for their firstborn than for later-born children. Parental approval is a powerful motivator. During the school years, parents are the child's chief social influence and may be the reason firstborns typically do better in school and in business and are more likely to attend college and graduate school, even though they are frequently no smarter than their later-born siblings.

To their disadvantage, firstborns have to endure the relative inexperience of their parents and to serve as "test cases" for later siblings. Although some firstborns are overprotected and indulged by their parents, many report harsher treatment than their siblings, who seem to receive more consideration and leniency as the parents mellow with age and experience (Abramovitch et al., 1982). Furthermore, the oldest child is frequently encouraged to set a good example for the other children and may be required to help care for younger siblings, sometimes before they are ready for such responsibility.

With all this pressure, it is not surprising that many firstborns are also more anxious, less self-assured, and have a greater fear of failure and guilt than later-born children. Firstborns are also more apprehensive about pain and may be less able to cope with some anxiety-producing situations than later borns. All siblings have their share of problems, however. Although more firstborns are oversensitive and have sleep disorders, later borns are more likely to be diagnosed as aggressive or hyperactive.

The child in the "middle" is often caught between two intense relationships. On the one hand, the parent's concern and involvement with the firstborn remains strong throughout childhood and beyond. On the other hand, the baby of the family, or last-born child, is often affectionately indulged by parents and held emotionally close. Perhaps as a result of family interaction patterns, the middle child frequently seeks the friendship and affection of people outside the immediate family. Although middle children tend to be extroverted and pleasure-seeking, they are not terribly effective or successful in their social encounters. By their own report, middle borns indicated they felt less supported by their families but do not feel hostile toward or alienated from their parents or siblings (G. E. Kennedy, 1989). Boys bracketed by two girls or girls by two brothers may fare better than other combinations since they receive more special attention as a function of their sex.

By the time the last child arrives, the family has usually evolved considerably. Not only are there other siblings to influence the last child, but the parents may feel confident as caregivers. Often, too, the family is more financially secure. In short, some of the pressure that was present when the family was young may now have dissipated, freeing the last child from some of the constraints experienced by his siblings. While the last-born child tends to be achievement-oriented, striving, and popular, like the firstborn, he has little of the insecurity and self-doubt that may plague big brother or big sister. Since family size is directly related to socioeconomic level (larger families having generally lower incomes), differences in parent–child interactions in large and small families are never completely separate from the family financial status. When large families are better off financially, many of the disadvantages associated with increased family size are more or less neutralized.

What is responsible for birth-order effects in families? Size is one factor. Compared with smaller families, larger families may be more likely to assign tasks on the basis of the age and sex of the sibling. Linda Musun Baskett (1984) feels that parent's stereotypic expectations of their first, middle, and last child's behavior are more influential than the child's actual behavior in bringing about birth-order effects. Regardless of the explanation, parents can compensate for the effects of birth order by modifying their orientation and expectations toward the child. For example, they can reduce some of the pressure placed on the firstborn and include the middle child in special one-to-one activities with parents. Each child would then be loved and valued for his own good qualities and unique talents.

● Family Life

A mutual relationship exists in two-parent families: The emotional quality of the marriage impacts children and the presence of children and their personalities affect the marital relationship. When parents get along and support each other, they become more competent and responsive to their children (S. S. Feldman et al., 1983). The stress produced by arguing, fighting, and family discord affects everyone negatively. The emotional ties between the quarreling parents disintegrate; moreover, the parent–child relationship is damaged as parents direct negativity toward the children. Both boys and girls display more behavior problems by age 4 if they experienced family conflict during infancy. In a study of more than 20,000 children in England and the United States, Andrew Cherlin and colleagues (1991) concluded that more long-term behavioral and psychological problems are attributable to marital strife and dysfunction than to actual divorces. Marital unhappiness and family conflict have negative implications for the emotional quality of the mother–daughter relationship (Stoneman et al., 1989). Conflict and negativity at home predict delinquency and poor peer relations, especially for boys (Emery, 1982). Mavis Hetherington and colleagues (1982) suggest this is because parents quarrel more in the presence of boys than girls, thus protecting their daughters from the ill effects of family discord.

Children have a profound impact on the parent's relationship with each other. The birth of the first child produces a shift toward more traditional adult roles, even in egalitarian marriages (Antill et al., 1983). When children are even-tempered, nondemanding, compliant, and healthy, mothers and fathers have more positive energy left over to invest in each other. However, a child with a difficult temperament at age 2 is more likely to exhibit disruptive behavior problems with parents by age 4 (Pettit and Bates, 1989).

Disruptions in Family Life

Divorce

The divorce rate in the United States has been increasing steadily over the last 2 decades. It is now estimated that two-thirds of the children born in the 1990s will be faced with their parents' divorce or separation (Moody, 1990). One million American children under age 18 experience the divorce of their parents each year, some for the second time (Glick

A Closer Look

China's One-Child Policy

In 1979 the People's Republic of China undertook a massive social experiment to ensure abundance for all by limiting their burgeoning population. The "one-child" policy was adopted, based on a Chinese slogan: "One is best, at most two, never a third." For the most part, Chinese women and their partners are following the guidelines. Chinese women have, on the average, 2.25 children (WuDunn, 1991). But what kind of social and emotional impact does this policy have on the people of China and on the only children born out of compliance with the law?

Families who comply with the one-child policy are offered financial incentives—monthly subsidies, higher pensions, priority housing and health care, and free education for the child (Crooks & Baur, 1990). Punishments may be meted out to those who have more than two children—they may lose their education and health benefits and have reduced opportunities for housing. There have also been reports of forced sterilizations and nonconsentual abortions.

The most common reason for couples to want additional children is to have a son to continue the family name and ancestry. By Chinese tradition, daughters are married out of the family, while sons remain in the family to care for their aging parents. Parents sometimes kill female infants or abort female fetuses so they can try again without being penalized by the state.

Besides placing severe restrictions on people's right to plan their own family, China's one-child policy may be changing the way Chinese parents relate to their children. There is a growing tendency for parents to overindulge their children—to create a generation of "little emperors." "Chubby" children exist in China

today, an occurrence unheard of in earlier years (Landers, 1990). Four to 10 year old only children in China were rated by their peers as less cooperative and more selfish than children with siblings. Not surprisingly, only children were not sought out as friends, looked up to as leaders, or asked for advice as much as children with siblings. Only children did get along well with teachers, however. In a country like China, each person's satisfaction is supposed to come from serving the country, not from serving oneself. Indulged, self-serving children may undercut that focus. Toni Falbo, a social psychologist at the University of Texas, will return to China to conduct further research on whether strict family planning programs help or hinder a child's development.

Chinese policy encourages only one child.

■ ● ▲   CONCEPT SUMMARY

Helping Children Cope with Imminent Divorce

- Speak honestly in language they can understand.
- Assure them they are not the cause.
- Emphasize the finality of the decision.
- Assure them they will continue to be loved and cared for.
- Don't express hostility toward each other in front of the children.
- Don't use the children as go-betweens in personal disagreements.
- Don't engage in long and drawn out custody cases.
- Provide opportunities for open discussion.
- Express your emotions (depression, anger, and the like) but don't overwhelm the children with your feelings.
- Make realistic promises to the child and keep all promises made.
- Look for changes in the child's behavior that might indicate stress (e.g., changes in personal habits, school behavior).

and Lin, 1987). Divorce is thus the norm rather than the exception in most families. While no other country in the world rivals the divorce rate experienced in the United States, most children from divorced families end up reasonably well (Bronfenbrenner, 1986).

Eighty-nine percent of the children of divorce live with their mothers. Since 1980, the number of fathers granted sole custody of dependent children increased from 9 to 11% (U.S. Bureau of the Census, 1987). Noncustodial parents visit frequently at first but as time passes, noncustodial fathers see their children less than noncustodial mothers (Kurdek, 1988). Visiting parents are often indulgent and permissive, encouraging custodial parents to be harsh and restrictive in order to regain control.

Predicting the impact of divorce on the child is a complex undertaking since many different factors are involved. Families vary greatly—in the amount of tension and hostility between parents, the resulting financial strain, and the disruption of routine the divorce entails. In the majority of cases, the woman's standard of living after divorce drops an average of 73%, while the man's rises by 42% (National Film Board of Canada, The Feminization of Poverty, 1990). Other variables influencing the impact on the children are their ages at the time of the divorce and their sensitivity and ability to adapt to change (Hetherington et al., 1989). Almost all children, however, experience divorce and the events that precede and follow it as stressful.

CUSTODIAL PARENTS' IMMEDIATE REACTIONS TO DIVORCE The emotional turmoil related to divorce might render the parents less able to care for their children than they were in less troubled times. Caregivers who are depressed, preoccupied, or hostile may spend less time interacting with their young children than usual (Vaughn, Gove, & Egeland, 1980). Predictable mealtimes, bedtimes, and other household routines usually disintegrate and parents vacillate between being detached and laissez-faire to being punitive, strict, and demanding.

CHILDREN'S IMMEDIATE REACTIONS TO DIVORCE Preschoolers and young elementary school children are generally considered to be the most vulnerable to inconsistencies in the quality of their care, owing to their continued need to identify with the parents and their inability to understand their parents' problems and the consequences of them (Wallerstein & Kelly, 1980). The negative effects of divorce also have the most lasting consequences for this age group (Allison and Furstenberg, 1989).

Two and a half to 3½ year olds might react to the atmosphere engendered by divorce by whining, crying, and clinging more than usual. They may also have trouble eating, sleeping, and staying dry at night. Four year olds, on the other hand, might whine, cry, and hit other children, while 5 and 6 year olds become more anxious, aggressive, and clingy. It's not uncommon for all children of divorce to feel angry, afraid, depressed, guilty, and divided about loyalties to their parents, regardless of their age (Hetherington et al., 1989). The stress of divorce can interfere with children's level of play, their ability to get along with their peers, and even their physical health (Gottman & Katz, 1989).

Preschoolers' egocentrism is a special factor for them with regard to divorce, for it makes them more likely to feel guilty or responsible for their parents' problems. In addition, magical thinking can complicate their reactions, misleading children into believing that they have more control over family events than they actually do. For example, a child might wish in anger that a parent would disappear and, when the parent actually does leave, conclude through transductive reasoning that the wishing made it happen (Flavell, 1985).

Besides age, sex is another factor that affects a child's vulnerability to the impact of a divorce. Boys seem to have a particularly difficult time adjusting, experiencing more cognitive, social, and emotional problems than girls while the breakup is in progress (Zaslow, 1989). Moreover, as long as 2 years after their parents' divorce, boys tend to have more trouble concentrating, do less well in school, and are more aggressive and demanding than girls from divorced families. Girls are more likely to internalize their grief and frustration. Rather than acting out, girls cry, withdraw, and blame themselves. Several explanations have been proposed to explain these sex differences. Emery (1982) suggests that preschool-age boys from divorce families are exposed to more stress and receive less support and nurturance from mothers, teachers, and peers than preschool-age girls. Thus, their reactions are more extreme because their distress level is higher. Also, parents react differently to the stress reactions of sons and daughters. It's easier for parents to sympathize with the controlled reactions of girls and to provide additional calming support. Parents tend to be impatient and unsympathetic with boys, however. Ironically, this reaction generally amplifies boys' aggression and leads to more parental rebuke and rejection as part of a negative response cycle.

As one might expect, the first year following a divorce is the most difficult for both parents and children (Hetherington et al., 1982). During this time, children may feel that they have little or no control over their lives because of changes in residence, socioeconomic status, and household responsibilities—not to mention the changes in the attitudes and availability of both parents. Preschool children in this period are less mature and less imaginative than normal. They seek help, attention, and physical proximity to adults more often than they did prior to the divorce and tend to smile less and to pout and scowl more (Hetherington et al., 1982). On a more positive side, younger children may experience more consistent and regular parenting in the postdivorce period once one parent moves out and the other no longer needs to confront or anticipate confronting the departed spouse on a daily basis (Wallerstein & Kelly, 1980).

CHILDRENS' LONG-TERM REACTIONS TO DIVORCE Both parents and children show significant improvements in adjustment by 2 years after the divorce unless special circumstances exist. Children who were maladjusted prior to divorce are particularly likely to experience long-lasting emotional problems following divorce (Hetherington, 1979). If poor parent–child relations are prolonged, the child's self-esteem and emotional stability may suffer. Boys may continue to be more vulnerable than girls years after the initial breakup. If inconsistent discipline continues, children are more likely to develop behavior problems than when parents respond to conflict or issues consistently (F. E. Gardner, 1989). The child's own personality and response style can exacerbate or insulate her from the negative effects of divorce. Childrens' long-term adjustment typically takes one of three forms: aggressive-insecure, opportunistic-competent, or caring-competent (Hetherington, 1989).

The single most important step parents can take to assure the stability and happiness of their children following divorce is to put aside their differences and support each other in their new roles (Wallerstein & Kelly, 1980). If such support is not possible, the child's adjustment to divorce can be improved by structured school environments run by warm, mature, predictable teachers and by the loving attention of extended family members and friends (Hetherington et al., 1982). Sibling relationships are much more positive when spouse/ex-spouse relationships are more congenial (MacKinnon, 1989). Other factors that can help ease the postdivorce transition for children include:

1. Economic stability in the home
2. Maintaining/establishing a positive relationship with the noncustodial parent
3. Staying in the same home or school or having as few residence/school changes as possible
4. Living with an emotionally stable parent

While a productive, stable relationship with both parents would be ideal, it is particularly important that children maintain or establish a good relationship with the same-sex parent. Girls adjust best when they reside in households headed by the mother and boys' adjustment is facilitated by *regular* contact with their fathers (J. S. Wallerstein, 1984). When boys live with their fathers, they are less demanding and more mature than boys who live with their mothers (Santrock & Warshak, 1979). Fathers are more effective in encouraging compliance and cooperation from their sons than mothers perhaps because fathers are seen as more powerful and authoritative and because fathers offer more praise for following instructions—and less praise for being disruptive—than mothers do (Hetherington et al., 1982).

Blended/Reconstituted Families

Single-parent families are usually transitional units, given the high rate of remarriage, usually to new partners. Five out of six divorced men and three out of four women in the United States remarry within 3 years of their divorces (Glick, 1984). In the 1990s some 12 million adults and 6.5 million children will live in "blended" or reconstituted families. Remarriage often seems like the perfect solution to the crisis of divorce, because it offers a ready-made family. Unfortunately, the stresses associated with remarriage are second only to those encountered around divorce (Lutz, 1983). The strains of trying to establish affectionate ties, make disciplinary policies, assign household chores, organize sleeping arrangements, and juggle finances in a family structure that sometimes looks like the organizational chart of a multinational corporation lead to an even higher divorce rate in second than in first marriages.

reconstituted/blended families when the parents and children of two divorced families come together as a unit after remarriage

One of the greatest challenges for children in blended families is adjusting to a new live-in parent. Many children associate the word *stepmother* with *wicked* thanks to stories like Cinderella, Snow White, and Hansel and Gretel. Oddly, our society has few negative stereotypes about stepfathers. At any rate, the emotional bond that develops between children and their birth parents, both male and female, does not exist between children and stepparents. Thus, reciprocal affection has to be forged, though doing so is fraught with difficulty. For example, a child might feel jealous of the new adult with whom she must share the natural parent. And the child may feel powerless since she had no choice in forming a life with the new adult. In fact, the child can wind up feeling defeated on many counts: in failing to prevent the divorce or to reunite the parents or to stop the remarriage. Finally, the child might unconsciously redirect any hostility she feels toward the estranged parent at the new stepparent.

The most common reconfiguration is the mother–stepfather family since more mothers retain custody of their children than fathers. Boys adapt well to this arrangement, generally welcoming contact with a stepfather who helps relieve the mother of the coercive act-out/get-punished cycle shared by divorced women and their sons (Wallerstein & Kelly, 1980). Girls adapt less favorably perhaps because their mother becomes less dependent on them for emotional support and affection (Clingempeel & Segal, 1986). Apparently, the best circumstances for girls is to live in nondivorced families or to live with divorced mothers who do not remarry (J. S. Wallerstein, 1984). Girls have a particularly difficult time getting along with stepmothers probably because girls in father–stepmother families are usually emotionally close to their fathers and the stepmother threatens that bond (Hobart & Brown, 1988). Nevertheless, remarried mothers are just as involved, nurturant, and available to their children as mothers from intact marriages (Santrock et al., 1988).

Once the new family is established, trying to please all the adults can place an exhausting burden on the children. If a child gets into trouble, for instance, she might now have to answer to three people instead of just two. And the child might feel some pressure to protect the absent parent—or the stepparent—by withholding news on special trips or good times with the present adult. Often, however, the child will do just the opposite—magnifying the fun and importance of special times and activities in reports to the absent parent, possibly in an effort to manipulate that adult into doing as much or more. On the other side of the coin, of course, is the possibility that the child might find herself loved, cared for, and appreciated by three adults instead of just two. Parents can try to minimize problems by being sensitive and fair in dealing with *all* their children, both stepchildren and natural offspring, and by maintaining positive relationships with each other. A useful book on stepparenting is *Stepfamilies (Good Answers to Tough Questions)* by Joy Berry, Childrens Press, 1990.

Death

Preschool children are unprepared to deal realistically with death due to the limits of their cognitive abilities. Children between the ages of 3 and 5 are simply unable to acknowledge the finality of death. They see death as a temporary state like sleep. The child conceives of the dead person as existing somewhere (e.g., in heaven or under the ground) and as able to eat, hear, and think, though not very well. As far as the preschool child is concerned, dead things can be brought back to life if you "treat them right," "give them food," or "talk to them" (Berzonsky, 1987).

When preschool children are confronted with the death of others, they may display a variety of reactions. For one, they may become angry with family members or medical personnel for failing to revive or maintain the person. They find no comfort in statements like "the doctor did everything possible." Magical thinking leads preschoolers to believe that they or others are all-powerful and can bring about any outcome just by wishing it so or by doing the right things. Thus, children comprehend disease, illness, and accident only within the context of the egocentrism that dominates their perceptions (Atwood, 1984). When asked why Grandpa died, a child might say "He swallowed a bug that ate up his insides," or "He never liked peas."

■ **Figure 10–5**

It's difficult to know what everything means when you're still so young.

Children might manifest certain fears for the first time after a death experience. They might begin to fear ghosts, for instance, because they believe the dead person to be alive somewhere. Or they may fear sleep, especially if death has been explained in such terms ("Grandma is taking a long sleep" or "Uncle Ben died in his sleep"). Children may also fear abandonment, anticipating that other loved ones will mysteriously disappear and fail to return as the dead person did.

Sometimes children begin to fear their own deaths after experiencing the death of someone else. One parent recalls her child's reaction:

> We had been driving in New England and had stopped at a lot of historic sites—churches, town halls, and homes of famous people. We were talking about how fascinating it was to see the artifacts and old grave markers when I noticed our 6 year old was uncharacteristically quiet.
>
> What's the matter, honey?" I asked. "Didn't you like the church and the old cemetery?"
>
> "Remember the one that said 'Beth Anne our Baby'?" she said solemnly. "I never knew kids could die."

Although children become depressed when a parent dies, young children's grief reactions are generally less prolonged and less severe than those of older children. Changes in family patterns—moving, uncertain financial arrangements, or exposure to the grief of others—may be more difficult for the child to cope with than the death itself.

HELPING CHILDREN COPE WITH DEATH It is tempting to try to shelter children from death and other harsh realities. Our society views death-related topics as "morbid" and "inappropriate for discussion." But to avoid the subject of death and keep children away from those who are dying is to deny them the opportunity to express their feelings and discover healthy outlets for their sadness, grief, and anger (Weber &

■ **Table 10–5**   *Helping Children Cope with the Imminent Death of Another*

1. Tell the truth in a sympathetic, straightforward way.

2. Avoid euphemisms such as "He will pass away" and statements such as "The angels are coming to get her" if the family is not religious. Misleading statements can have a lasting impact on a child's life. In one example, a boy was told that his father was on an extended business trip and would not return, when the father had in fact died. Since the child was not allowed to see his father's body or even go to the funeral, he had no way of knowing that what he was told was not true. Even after he was an adult and had been told the truth, he reported continuing to look wistfully at airplanes and trains, "hoping to get a glimpse of (his) father" (Author's files).

3. Reassure the child that she will continue to be loved and cared for by those who remain. Make every effort not to separate siblings.

4. If the child is to visit the dying person, be specific in explaining what the child should expect—for example, "He's lost some weight," "He might not talk much," or "A machine helps her breathe".

5. It is not necessary to suggest that the visit may be the child's last.

6. Give children a choice. They shouldn't be forced to visit a dying relative or to view the dead body or go to the funeral if they don't want to. Children who attend a parent's funeral are no more likely to experience long-term anxiety or depression than those who don't (Weller et al., 1988).

7. Encourage children to express their feelings. There's no need to counsel a child to be a "stout fellow and don't cry." Crying can provide a much needed emotional release. Also, encourage the child to ask questions even if the answer is "I don't know" or is emotionally difficult.

8. Don't hide your own grief from the child. It is all right for children to see that others are sad as long as they aren't overwhelmed by the emotions of others. Children feel more a part of the family when they share in the grieving process.

Fournier, 1985). Ignoring a death during the preschool period when children have confused notions about what dying really means often increases their fears and exacerbates their fantasies about being responsible for the event. Suggestions to help prepare children for the imminent death of another are given in Table 10–5.

CHILDREN'S OWN DEATHS As unfair as it seems, sometimes children too become ill and die. Children as young as 5 or 6 can usually sense when they are seriously ill (Gordon & Klass, 1979). These children need to know what is happening to them and to know that someone will be there and comfort them when they are in pain since they feel particularly afraid and isolated when they are in the hospital (Clunies-Ross & Lansdown, 1988). They also need simple, honest answers to their questions. The worst thing a parent can do is lie to a sick child or pretend that "nothing is wrong." Parents and doctors sometimes adopt this strategy because they underestimate children's understanding of the concept of death (Vianello & Lucamante, 1988). Lying for any reason can cause children to stop trusting the parent and can increase their feelings of loneliness and abandonment at a time when they need extra support and affection. Organizations like the "Make-A-Wish Foundation" try to grant the last requests of the dying child (meetings with famous people, a dream vacation).

In Touch

THE COMPASSIONATE FRIENDS
PO Box 3696
Oak Brook, IL 60522–3696
312–323–5010

Support for bereaved families

● Interactions with Peers

Peers, or age mates, along with the family, are important agents of socialization during the preschool years. Compared with parent–child interactions, peer interactions during early childhood tend to be more physical and playful, less predictable (more positive *and* more negative elements), and more likely to involve objects (Hartup et al., 1988). Peer interactions increase in frequency between the ages of 2 and 5, and the nature of social behavior changes with development. While peer interactions during infancy amount to observing and touching others, a dramatic change in peer relations takes place during the preschool years. Some of the one-way, solitary activities are gradually replaced by reciprocal associations. As a result, true social play emerges. Children spend so much time practicing play behavior that the preschool period is called "the play years" (K. H. Rubin et al., 1983). Play enhances the social, emotional, physical, and cognitive development of the child (see Table 10–6).

Patterns of Play

In a classic study of peer interaction, Mildred Parten (1932, 1933) described five ways children play in the presence of others:

■ Table 10–6 *The Value of Play*

---

1. *Reframing.* Events are reframed—that is, given different connotations. A child may grimace and roll around on the floor pretending to be hurt. This is socially acceptable as play rather than proper behavior.

2. *Reversals.* There are many examples of reversal behavior in children's play—reversal of roles (pretending to be a fire chief, a monster, or an animal), reversal of rules (trying out different ways of sharing), and reversal of tactics (learning a more flexible approach to routine behavior by playfully changing the routine).

3. *Abstraction of prototypes.* When a child plays a different role, such as being a doctor or a monster, actions that are used in play are abstracted from the object being represented—the child acts like a doctor or like a monster.

4. *Theme and variation.* We can often see a child in play focusing on some central action or object—for example, making a "horrible" face and growling or pushing an object along and making "car-engine noises." The child may then produce variations on these themes—the monster waves its long arms, stomps its feet, or becomes another form of monster; the object is a car, a firetruck, an airplane, and the engine noises vary accordingly.

5. *Boundaried space-time.* Objects set limits on play and children set limits on their play by some frame of reference. A toy fire truck cannot really function like the real thing, nor can the child actually do the job of a real doctor; and the monster must not be too frightening and is not capable of injuring or biting playmates. Similarly, there are times for playful behavior and times for proper behavior.

6. *Modulation of excitement.* When children play they are aroused by the activity and excited by the pleasure they get from play. During the preschool years children learn to control the tempo of excitement. In playing games excitement must be modulated, and if the game is also a task there is likely to be a cumulative or growing sense of excitement until a climax when the task is completed.

Source: Adapted with permission from Sutton-Smith, 1979, pp. 15–22.

solitary play
Parten's term for play that a child engages in alone, without involving other children

onlooker
Parten's term for play that involves watching another person's activities but not participating in them

parallel play
play in which two or more children engage in activities next to each other without interacting

associative play
Parten's term for play in which children interact but are each involved in their separate activities. These children do not cooperate during play

cooperative play
Parten's term for play involving two or more children focused on a particular game or activity that has specific rules

1. *Solitary play.* The child plays alone and independently with toys, sometimes within speaking distance of other children but appearing not to notice them and making no effort to communicate or share with them.
2. *Onlooker play.* The child spends most of the time watching other children play. He often talks to the others, asking questions and giving suggestions, but does not participate.
3. *Parallel play.* The child plays beside but not with another child. Both children play with similar toys though their activities are unrelated.
4. *Associative play.* The child plays with another child. The two talk about common activities and borrow and loan toys. Each child acts alone, however, since the two do not share a goal.
5. *Cooperative play.* The children play together and help each other in an activity that produces some material product or achieves some goal. There is a division of labor and shared goals.

Table 10–7 summarizes the amount of time preschool and kindergarten children are engaged in each of Parten's play types. Parallel and solitary play predominate during infancy, but 3 and 4 year olds may still exhibit these forms of play. The percentage of time preschoolers choose these activities remains stable between the ages of 3 and 6. Children engaging in parallel play may actually be imitating each other, making this play form more social and interactive than previously believed (Uzgiris, 1981).

Contrary to popular belief, children who spend a lot of time in solitary play activities are not necessarily socially maladjusted. Working on an art project, putting something together, or doing a puzzle are solitary

■ **Table 10–7** *Changes in Occurrence of Parten's Social Play Types from Preschool to Kindergarten Age*

	PRESCHOOL 3–4 YEARS	KINDERGARTEN 5–6 YEARS
Total nonsocial activity	41%	34%
Uninvolved and onlooker behavior	19%	14%
Solitary play	22%	20%
Parallel play	22%	23%
Cooperative play	37%	43%

Source: Laura E. Berk, *Child Development*, 2d Ed. © 1991 Allyn & Bacon. Reprinted with permission.

activities usually chosen by bright children who want the challenge of accomplishing something on their own (K. H. Rubin, 1982).

As children grow and their thinking moves beyond self-focus, cooperative play begins to dominate and children become more social. In cooperative play, children cooperate with each other to play a formal game, perform a service, create a material product, or dramatize a real-life situation. The play is goal-directed and the children assume specific roles and functions such as leader, mother, or fire chief. They have a feeling of belonging to the group and establish rules for play. For example, they might organize themselves to clean up a section of a playroom, going on to cooperate with each other in assigning duties and completing tasks. Frequently, one or two children will assume supervisory roles and direct the efforts of others, which sometimes results in greater efficiency. The social behavior of only children in group settings is not distinguishable from that of children with siblings (Zheng & Colombo, 1989).

■ **Figure 10–7**

(left) Preschoolers engaging in parallel play. (center) Associative play among preschoolers. (right) Cooperative play among preschoolers.

A child who feels uncertain about joining a group or who perhaps is just tired may become an *onlooker*, only indirectly involved in the play activities of the group. Onlookers often talk to the children they are observing, asking questions and giving suggestions, but this is the extent of their participation. Since they are close enough to hear and see everything that takes place, onlookers often learn by watching others. Watching TV is a variation of onlooker play.

Although onlooker play is both normal and common, the child who never or rarely participates in group play might need some help in overcoming shyness or becoming more self-confident or assertive. Onlooker behavior is different from withdrawal. The withdrawn child shows little interest in what is going on and rarely associates with others in any context.

There is evidence to suggest that social play gives children more than just enjoyment and physical exercise. Some research indicates, for instance, that children who are deprived of social play with preschool-age peers have more difficulty understanding other people's points of view and getting along with their age mates than children who play with others during the preschool years (K. H. Rubin et al., 1984). This finding has particular significance for children with special needs such as physically handicapped, mentally handicapped, or gifted children.

dramatic play
play that involves the use of the imagination (i.e., pretending or using make believe); also called pretend play or make-believe play

social pretend play
where two or more children play pretend together

Dramatic Play

Preschoolers exhibit *dramatic play*, in which they use their imaginations and pretend to have different identities in different situations (Bretherton, 1989). Children as young as 12 months of age engage in make-believe or pretend play, first directing their pretense toward themselves before extending it to others (Howes, 1988). By age 2 or 3, play becomes more complex and involves other people. Among the most common themes in children's dramatic play are domestic scenes involving husbands and wives, scenarios with parents and children, and fantasy (reenacting a story they have heard or an idea they have). Dramatic play that involves at least two children who communicate verbally about the play is called *social pretend play*. Compared with other patterns of play, children's interactions during social pretend play were more enjoyable, lasted longer, were more involved, and involved greater reciprocity (Connolly et al., 1988). Compared with boys, girls use more turn taking and conversational exchange in social pretend play. Boys engage in solitary pretence more often than girls (Black, 1989).

Dramatic play not only helps children learn social rules, understand the world, and practice the roles of adulthood; it may also be an important aid to emotional development. Through play, children can deal with fears or stresses that arise in real life situations—for example, death, divorce, illness, or hospitalization. By copying the behavior of the adults around them, they can learn successful (or unsuccessful) strategies for understanding situations and resolving crisis. Interest-

■ **Figure 10–8**

Dramatic play.

■ **Table 10–8** *Play Activities and Equipment Suitable for the Preschool-Age Child*

	3 YEARS	4 YEARS	5 YEARS	PURPOSE

Gross motor play	Swings
	Slides
	Tricycles
	Sandbox
	Wading Pool
	Wagons
		Rope ladders
		Jungle gym
		Swimming
		Trapeze
			Roller skates
			Ball playing
			Bicycle with training
			  wheels
				Develop and refine gross
				  motor skills

Creative play	Sand play
	Water play
	Play dough and clay
	Finger painting
	Large blocks
	Musical toys
		Crayons and chalk
		  drawing
		Easel painting
		Rhythm band
		Simple puzzles
			Cutting pictures
			Carpentry tools
			Simple sewing and
			  handcraft
			Puzzles
				Promote motor
				  coordination; encourage
				  self-expression

Dramatic play	Farm animal toys
	Dolls
	Dollhouses
	Trucks, cars, planes
	Toy phones
		Dolls
		Dress-up clothes
		Group play
		Housekeeping toys
		Store play toys
		Nurse and doctor kits
		Wooden boxes
			Toy carpenter kits
			Paper puppets
			Handkerchief puppets
			Large wooden and
			  cardboard boxes
			Pedal cars and trucks
			Dolls
				Encourage use of
				  imagination; teach
				  children about social
				  roles

Language Readiness	Color-coded
	  xylophone
		Musical and story
		  tapes
		Electronic learning toys (like Texas Instruments
		  Words . . . To GO!)
			Playing with puppets	Can enhance beginning
				  speaking, naming, and
				  listening skills

Arithmetic Readiness	Building blocks	Picture and number
		  lotto
			Simple board games
			  (like *Chutes &*
			  Ladders)
				Practice in classifying,
				  quantifying, turn
				  taking, and following
				  directions.

Quiet play	Books—fairy tales
	Nursery rhymes and
	  stories
	Children's records
		Books—fairy tales and
		  adventures
			Books about real
			  adventures of
			  people and animals
			Selected television
			  programs
				Limit activity or involve
				  the child passively

Games	Where is Thumbkin? Mulberry bush Clapping games Eentsy-weentsy spider	Simon says Dog and bone Two little blackbirds	Bean bag throw Skip tag Ball play Hide and seek	

Source: Adapted with permission from Sutton-Smith, 1979.

ingly, dramatic play begins to decline during the school years (ages 6–12). Perhaps the child becomes more interested in other activities than in fantasy, or perhaps the imagination is expressed through other channels such as daydreaming, creative writing, or art (K. H. Rubin et al., 1983). Table 10–8 lists play activities and equipment suitable for preschool-age children.

Other Influences on Preschooler's Play

The sex of the children, their experience, the setting, the materials, and the size of the play group all have effects on peer interaction. For example, preschool children are consistently more sociable toward same-sex playmates than toward those of the other sex (Maccoby, 1988). Preschool boys tend to be more vigorous and physical in their play, while preschool girls are more orderly, quiet, and cooperative (DiPietro, 1981). When boys and girls play in mixed-sex groups, boys tend to be less destructive than at other times and girls become more independent.

Having no toys is actually preferable to having too few toys to go around. Where there are no toys, more contacting, smiling, gesturing, and imitating takes play among young children, while conflicts are more likely where there are few toys (Levitt & Weber, 1989). The presence of an adult may encourage children to suppress vigorous, aggressive play or to increase the level of cooperative play (Pellegrini, 1984). Finally, because of their tendency to centrate, preschoolers younger than 4 or 5 can play in a sustained manner, no matter what type of play, with only one other partner at a time. Children are usually more cooperative and competent in interaction during their first meeting with others if they have had previous experience with peers, and if the meeting takes place in a familiar setting such as their own homes (Rubin & Sloman, 1984).

Parents influence their children's play by choosing neighborhoods where contact with peers is easy and frequent or, where children feel isolated and secluded, by providing models of social interaction and by scheduling contact with their agemates. Older children can arrange their own peer experiences, but preschoolers must rely on their parents.

Peer Relations

The preschool child relates to his peers in an egalitarian fashion. Unlike adult-child interactions at this age, two peers have the same status, same authority, and same physical skills and intellectual capacities (Hartup, 1983). A child can choose his friends, but children are chosen by adults to complete tasks, make apologies to others, and help out.

Preschoolers not only distinguish adults from peers, they also interact differently with children younger or older than themselves. Willard Hartup (1983) found that children act dependently toward older children, are nurturant toward younger children, and are playful—even aggressive—with children their own age. Among young children, interaction with peers is often initiated when one child copies the nonverbal actions of another (Eckerman et al., 1989). Children tend to remain together after a conflict if they were interacting before it. Younger children are more likely to walk away from a fight than older children (Laursen & Hartup, 1989).

Early Friendships

Affectionate bonds underlie early friendships. Three to 4 year old children who are "friends" seek each other out, play with each other often, resolve conflicts well, are more responsive and communicate well (clear messages and coherent conversation), and generally have more positive than negative exchanges (Hinde et al., 1985). Compared to able-bodied children, disabled children tend to be less responsive to peers, make irrelevant comments, and act less socially mature (Black & Hazen, 1990; Howes, 1988). Children who are securely attached to the mother get along better, are happier, and are less controlling than children who are insecurely attached (Park & Waters, 1989). They are also perceived as more competent by teachers and are liked better by them (Cohn, 1990). Preschool-age boys and girls are equally likely to have "friends."

Most early friendships form quickly and end quickly, however. Friendships among preschoolers can be ended by hitting, arguing, insulting, refusing to share, or even being absent or unavailable when the partner wants to play (Selman, 1980; Laursen & Hartup, 1989).

preschools/child-care centers
sites staffed by professionals who care for and instruct children while the parent(s) work

● Socialization Outside the Family

Interactions with Other Adults

Between the ages of 1 and 3, children rarely interact with strangers unless their parent is present. But by about age 3, children begin to socialize with unfamiliar adults even when their parents are not around. Preschoolers typically display interest and excitement in the presence of adult strangers and model their affect and demeanor. Friendly strangers usually provoke friendly responses, and gruff, distant strangers prompt fear and avoidance (Clarke-Stewart, 1978).

Preschools and Child-Care Centers

In the 1950s, only 12% of married women with preschool-age children worked outside the home. By 1986, that number had grown to 55 percent (U.S. Department of Labor, 1987). Care can be provided by "centers" or private homes. "Good" day care not only provides adequate physical care and supervision but offers learning experiences as well. While middle class children may not demonstrate intellectual gains as a result of their day-care experience, they don't show deficits, either. Underclass children from less stimulating environments stand to gain the most from high quality day care (Caldwell, 1986; Burchinal et al., 1989). Even 4 years after their day-care experiences, children from better quality day-care programs had more friendly interactions with peers,

■ **Figure 10–9**

Dancing at day care.

and were seen as happier, less shy, and more socially competent by their age mates (Vandell et al., 1988). *Who* is in charge and *how many* other children are present continue to be important factors in assessing the impact of day care on children. Parents should visit the site and talk with the parents of enrolled children to find the program best suited for their individual child. Other guidelines for selecting high quality child care are given in the Toward Effective Parenting feature at the end of Chapter 7.

Some child-care centers offer formal academic instruction for preschool children while others simply offer supervised free play. The National Association for the Education of Young Children (NAEYC) offers guidelines for creating developmentally appropriate preschool curricula that take into account the child's age and developmental level. Examples of developmentally appropriate and inappropriate expectations/activities for 3–5 year olds include:

FOR 3 YEAR OLDS:
Appropriate:
- providing many opportunities for children to play (by themselves, beside other children, with other children)
- allowing children to enter and leave small groups at will (3 year olds are not comfortable with much group participation)

Inappropriate
- expecting young children to all sit and listen quietly during whole group activities

FOR 4–5 YEAR OLDS:
Appropriate:
- providing many opportunities to see how reading and writing are *useful*
    listening to stories
    "reading" stories
    seeing print in use
    participating in "plays" and "storytelling"
    experimenting with drawing and writing

Inappropriate
- instruction in reading or writing that involves recognizing single letters
- reciting the alphabet
- coloring within the lines
- being instructed in the correct formation of letters on the printed line

The 32-page booklet is available from NAEYC, 1834 Connecticut Ave. NW, Washington, DC, 20009–5786.

Children at child-care centers usually have opportunities to develop large- and small-muscle skills plus eye/hand coordination as they play

A Closer Look

The Building Blocks of Social Skills

According to French ethologist Hubert Montagner, five types of actions, when combined into certain sequences, can make or break social relations in nursery school and possibly beyond.

1. *Actions that pacify others or produce attachment:*

   Offering another child toys or candy

   Lightly touching or caressing the other child

   Jumping in place, clapping one's hands

   Smiling

   Extending one's hand as if begging

   Taking the other child's chin in one's hand

   Cocking one's head over one shoulder, leaning sideways, rocking from left to right

   Vocalizing in a nonthreatening way

2. *Threatening actions that generally produce fear, flight, or tears in the target child:*

   Loud vocalizations

   Frowning

   Showing clenched teeth

   Opening one's mouth wide

   Pointing one's index finger toward the other child

   Clenching one's fist

   Raising one's arm

   Leaning one's head forward

   Leaning one's whole trunk forward or shadowboxing

3. *Aggressive actions*

   Hitting with hands or feet

   Scratching

   Pinching

   Pulling the other child's hair or clothes

   Shaking the other child

   Knocking the other child down

   Grabbing something that belongs to the other child

   Throwing something that belongs to the other child

4. *Gestures of fear and retreat*

   Widening one's eyes

   Blinking

   Protecting one's face with bent arms

   Moving one's head backwards

   Moving one's trunk or one's whole body backward

   Running away

   Crying after an encounter with another child

According to Montagner, the secret of preschool social success is to use many gestures from the pacifying/attaching category. Perhaps the most effective sequence within this category is a tilt of the head over one shoulder combined with a smile. Sometimes it includes extending one hand toward the other child, as if to shake hands. Either way, this sequence triggers a friendly response more than 80% of the time. Children on the receiving end seem to melt—they often calm down, show affection, and some will give up cherished objects of their own free will.

(continued on next page)

(continued from previous page)

His observations show that children who will be the real leaders by age 10 or so emerge from the pacifying/attaching group *rather than* from the aggressive group. Dominant/aggressive children cannot make lasting coalitions. They are generally disliked by others and any groups that form around them disintegrate because of the chaos produced by their aggression. The *real leaders* use pacifying/attaching behaviors as often as others but, in addition, they participate in many competitions (for desired toys, preferred space) and they generally win. Their signals are clear—they do not start fights but will stand their ground if attacked. Leaders also start new activities for the whole group more than 75% of the time.

Adapted from: Pines, Maya (1984). "Children's Winning Ways." *Psychology Today*, 18 (12), 58–65. Used with permission.

on playground equipment, ride bikes, paint, draw, or play catch. They are usually allowed to make their own choices to some extent while still receiving guidance. Preschool also offers children opportunities to use their imagination, curiosity, and creativity while they learn to appreciate the needs of others and gain skill in social interaction. Children typically attend preschool 3–5 days a week for 2–3 hours a day. Isolated children or those with no siblings or siblings quite different in age stand to profit most from opportunities to socialize with others.

Day-care center teachers are usually female but an increasing number of males are beginning to be involved in preschool teaching. Most male teachers report that they chose their occupation out of a love for pre-school-age children and a desire to make a special contribution to the children's lives (Robinson, 1981). Male preschool teachers can serve as a consistent, nurturing male model for children from father-absent homes, teaching by example that caring for young children is appropriate work for men as well as women.

Preparing Children for Kindergarten

Not all children attend preschool or child-care centers, but most enroll in kindergarten at about age 5. Many new experiences await the child: riding a bus, taking a lunch or eating in the cafeteria, being away from home, being surrounded by a large number of children, accepting guidance from the teacher, and finding her way around a new environment. The child needs help in adjusting to the new experiences that make up entry into school, and mothers are more likely than fathers to offer that help (Harris & Knudsen, 1988). Children typically do better in school if they are developmentally ready and know what to expect. Instead of pushing and pressuring the child, parents should simply begin to foster a positive attitude about education while allowing their children to be the best and fullest they can be for their age. Some other skills and experiences may be helpful:

1. Enthusiastic about learning
2. Able to follow more than one direction at a time without having instructions repeated
3. Able to express themselves clearly enough to be understood
4. Listen carefully
5. Able to think about themselves and the world around them
6. Understand simple concepts like hot/cold, full/empty
7. Give-and-take experiences with children their own age and size
8. Able to take responsibility for doing some things on their own
9. Some experience with simple memory tasks (numbers, recognizing objects, and the like)
10. Practice in tasks involving eye–hand coordination, scanning, small-muscle skills and visual discrimination (puzzles, cutting with scissors)
11. Mature enough to benefit from the social and intellectual stimulation. Sometimes older is better in kindergarten, particularly for boys who are less neurologically mature than their female counterparts or for children who come from late-maturing families. In the later grades, 23% of the children whose birthdays were between June and October and who were among the youngest in their kindergarten classes made up 75% of one school's failure population (Libman, 1987).

● Television and the Young Viewer

In our electronic age, young viewers face an external influence surely as great as, if not greater than, school has ever been. That force, of course, is television. Virtually every family in the United States owns or has access to a television set and even children in the first year of life are exposed to TV in varying degrees. Television attracts the attention of children under the age of 1 and can influence their thoughts and behavior even if they don't understand what they are seeing (D. G. Singer, 1983). By the time children graduate from high school, they will have spent 11,000 hours in school but over 15,000 hours in front of the TV set (Murray, 1989).

The amount of viewing varies among households, but the average preschooler watches 2–4 hours of television per day. Some children watch as little as 5 hours per week, but some watch for as long as 100 hours per week (D. R. Anderson et al., 1986). The heaviest TV viewing comes from children who are from lower socioeconomic class families, or are brighter than their peers, or are from larger families, or have younger siblings, or are in preschool or daycare and whose parents watch a lot of TV (Pinon et al., 1989). Even given these variations, the amount of TV viewing time increases steadily throughout the preschool period. Before long, in the average household television watching occupies more of the child's time than any other single activity except sleeping (Murray & Solamon, 1984).

Program Comprehension

Preschooler's comprehension of television programs is limited by the same factors that limit their understanding of real world events—sequencing difficulties, difficulty taking the perspective of others, and trouble distinguishing reality from fantasy. When preschool children watch a program, they typically focus on a specific character or characters and on a certain behavior or activity, but they are unable to follow the details of a single concrete story until they are between 5 and 9 (Collins and Duncan, 1984). To the young preschooler, everything on TV is "real," even things he has never seen before, like talking animals, monsters, and kids who fly. Four to 6 year olds are more sophisticated: They recognize that cartoons are make-believe but accept everything else as real (Downs, 1990). Also, since children 5 and under are not following the plot, the story is over when the program goes off.

TV and Social Interaction

In an early study on the effects of television watching on children's behavior, Lyle (1971) found that the more time families spend together watching TV, the less time they spend involved in other family activities. TV watching accounts for about one-fourth of the total time family members spend together each week. It is also the most common recreational pursuit shared by parents and children (Fischman, 1986). Often parents of young children use television as a babysitter—a means of keeping children quiet and occupied—and in some instances they may feel that the presence of the TV reduces the pressure to provide specific educational experiences for their children (Huston et al., 1990). When family tension is high, the television may actually help control the level of violence and hostility among family members. Rather than focusing on each other, they can watch TV instead. In fact, children whose parents are less empathic and sensitive toward them show a preference for fantasy-oriented TV content (Tangney, 1988).

TV Watching and Academic Achievement

A relationship has also been found between large amounts of television watching and low school grades. The children who spend the most time watching TV generally spend less time on their homework and less time practicing reading than others (Gunter, 1982). One study showed that when the television viewing time of first graders was restricted, school performance and developmental test scores improved (Gadberry, 1980).

However, while watching commercial television is associated with poor schoolwork, watching educational program such as *Sesame Street* and *3–2–1 Contact* is related to higher grades in school, especially if children were from families where parents were better educated (Henderson & Rankin, 1986). And television can actually be integrated with the educational process, as when school-age children are given old TV scripts to read while watching videotaped presentations of the show in an effort to encourage reading (Gunter, 1982).

Some investigators argue that TV robs children of valuable play time. They see children as missing out on exercising their muscles and interacting creatively with their peers, arguing that TV encourages children to be nonverbal, nonsocial and inactive (Singer & Singer, 1983). Television has also been accused of undermining critical thinking since the information on TV programs is more nearly complete than that presented on the radio or in books, magazines, or newspapers (Peterson et al., 1983).

■ **Figure 10–10**

Mesmerized . . . the electronic babysitter.

Advertisements

Programs are only one element of the television-viewing experience. Advertisements intended to sell products are another, and ads made for children are a controversial subgroup of these. Because preschoolers accept information uncritically and have no way of judging the relative worth of products, they are deeply affected by televised advertisements. Studies show that preschoolers remember product attributes and sing commercial jingles and that nine out of ten preschoolers ask for food items and toys they see advertised on TV (Taras et al., 1989). Apparently, preschoolers believe that all advertised food products are desirable. For example, children who see commercials for snacks and breakfast cereals high in sugar content ask for those products, while those who see public service advertisements advocating more nutritional foods understand the content of the message but ask for the sugary snacks anyway (P. E. Peterson et al., 1984). Even though children's recall of specific ads lessens over time, the ethics of advertisers are being questioned by those who feel that child-directed commercials take unfair advantage of a vulnerable population (Singer and Singer, 1983; Silverman et al., 1988).

TV Stereotypes

Ethnic and gender role stereotypes are so frequently displayed on television programs that as early as the first grade, children have formed attitudes about racial and ethnic groups and know whether TV commercials are intended for boys or for girls (Huston et al., 1984). When gender role portrayals are nontraditional, however, kindergarteners and

gender role stereotype
generalized expectations about appropriate behaviors for males and females

second graders seem to notice (Rosen-Wasser et al., 1989). But for the most part, children learn its a boy's world since most of the TV stars (human or otherwise) are male and those who aren't (Minnie Mouse, Prarie Dawn, Meryl Sheep, Daisy Duck, Lois Lane, and the like) are lackluster and tiresome (Rabicoff, 1989).

Aggressive and Antisocial Behavior

Violence on television causes concern because children repeat what they see or hear on TV even though they may not understand what it means (Bandura, 1973). Preschoolers give us particular concern in this regard, for they have difficulty distinguishing reality from fantasy, and are therefore more vulnerable to the influence of TV violence than older children. On the average, there are 9 acts of physical aggression and 7.8 acts of verbal aggression per hour on North American television programming, and 69% of these instances are incidental to the plot (Williams et al., 1982). Even more disturbing is that the rate of violence depicted in cartoons such as "Roadrunner," "Popeye," and "Teenage Mutant Ninja Turtles" is even higher than for standard programming (21 violent acts per hour) and the violent actions are often exaggerated for effect. Children have even been known to jump from windows trying to fly like their television heroes.

Research corroborated by two Surgeon General's reports (1972, 1982) substantiates four conclusions regarding the effects of TV violence on children's behavior (Liebert and Sprafkin, 1988):

1. *Children who watch televised violence are more likely to act aggressively than those who do not.* This conclusion holds for both boys and girls, across all socioeconomic levels, and within all geographic areas (NIMH, 1982). Violence is particularly likely to be imitated when it is initiated by someone likeable for the justifiable purpose of achieving some noble goal (Hearold, 1986). Increases in systolic blood pressure are found to accompany watching televised violence (Bushman & Geen, 1990).

   In one of the few controlled experiments on the effects of TV violence, Tannis MacBeth Williams (1985) studied isolated Canadian towns where residents had no television reception at all (Notel), received a single TV channel (Unitel) or four different channels (Multitel). By the end of the study a year later, Notel was receiving one TV channel and Unitel was receiving two. The levels of both verbal and physical aggression rose in Notel after children in the town began watching TV (Figure 10.1).

2. *The impact of televised violence is both cumulative and long-lasting.* The most violent preschoolers, those with a reputation for aggression, have a steady diet of televised violence. They are more likely to attack another child, attack property, disobey rules, and have less frustration tolerance than peers who watch less TV violence.

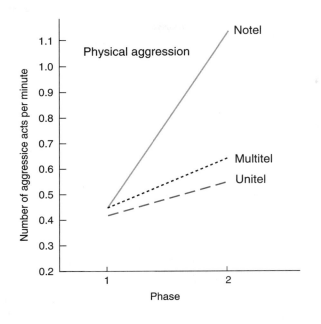

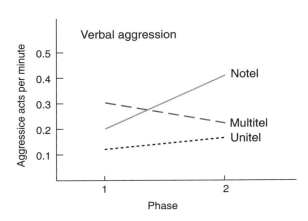

■ **Figure 10–11**

Findings from the Canadian study of the effects of TV violence on violent behavior. Phase 1 measurements were taken prior to the introduction of television to Notel. In Phase 2, measurements were drawn one year after television was available in Notel.

Longitudinal studies lasting from 11 to 22 years found that the single best predictor of aggressiveness at age 19 was the amount of violence children had watched at age 8 (Eron, 1982). A second follow-up at age 30 revealed the continued impact of early violent TV viewing assessed in terms of serious criminal involvement (Huesmann, 1986).

3. *Children who watch more televised aggression have a different attitude about violence from those who watch less aggression on TV.* They are more likely to advocate the use of violence for solving problems and resolving disputes and to assume that the world is a dangerous place that requires the application of counterforce (Collins and Korac, 1982).

4. *Televised violence hardens children to the suffering of others and encourages "kicking someone when he's down" rather than "helping him back on his feet".* Five to 9 year olds had an opportunity to help a child-partner win a game by pushing a button labelled "help" or to prevent a child from winning by pushing a button labelled "hurt." The "hurt" button increased the temperature of the child-partner's game stick so much that it would burn him if touched. Robert Liebert (1986) found that children who watch more violence on TV are much more likely to hurt than help the unseen child partner. Thus, TV violence not only makes aggressive responses more likely but also more appropriate than nonaggressive responses in the eyes of children.

Supporters of media violence insist that aggression is part of life and that it is actually beneficial, helping viewers discharge hostility vicariously rather than acting it out (Lorenz, 1966). But the overwhelming majority of studies conducted over the last 25 years indicate that children who watch televised violence are not calmed but aroused by violent programs and are more, not less, likely to aggress in the future. In the words of one investigator,

> Although for some children under some conditions, viewing televised violence may enable the child to discharge some of his or her aggressive feelings, for many children under many circumstances, viewing aggression on television leads to an increase in aggressive feelings, attitudes and behavior (Murray, 1980, p. 38)

Minimizing the Negative Impact of TV

For some parents who are concerned about the TV viewing habits of their children, one solution is simply to remove the TV set. Others find it possible to set limits and establish guidelines about viewing time and program content, thus permitting TV to influence but not monopolize the child's time. For other suggestions on controlling children's TV viewing, see Table 10–9.

The Positive Consequences of TV Viewing

Television, School Readiness and Prosocial Behavior

Although television has its disadvantages, there is some evidence that programming designed for young children can have positive consequences as well. An example is *Sesame Street,* which premiered in 1962 and represented a major innovation in children's television. Using a mixed cast of human and Muppet characters who today are recognized internationally, the program was directed at disadvantaged inner-city preschool children and focused on exposing its young viewers to reading, counting, and social and emotional skills. Currently, *Sesame Street* is seen in more than 50 countries worldwide (Cook & Curtin, 1985).

Most evaluations of *Sesame Street* have been positive. Children who watch often and in the presence of a parent tend to improve on the skills the program teaches compared with children who watch infrequently. Three to 5 year olds tend to gain more vocabulary skills than 5–7 year olds (Rice et al., 1990). Children who watch *Sesame Street* frequently may be more interested in reading than nonwatchers (Salzer, 1984). And, contrary to the expectations of some critics, viewers do not find school boring and mundane compared with *Sesame Street*. In fact,

■ **Table 10–9** *Suggestions for Controlling Children's Television Viewing*

1. *Know what your children watch and when.*
   A log of how much time children spend in front of the tube will often speak for itself about whether TV is playing too large a role in their lives. Be alert to the content, of course, including commercials.

2. *Notice how TV viewing affects your child.*
   Do they become transfixed after watching a while? Do some shows make them tense and lead to fighting or quarreling? What effects does TV have on family communication and interaction when all are watching together?

3. *Choose what to watch. Don't leave program selection to chance.*
   You wouldn't put a refrigerator in a young child's room and allow him to eat whatever he wanted. Why should you use any less control in guiding TV program selection? By making a choice, you gain control over the television rather than having the television control you. If you have cable, hook it up to a set the child doesn't have access to in case he views when you are not there to set the channel.

4. *Learn to turn the set off.*
   The television doesn't need to run constantly. Turn it off once the program you choose to watch is over. If the programming is unappealing, purchase a VCR and rent videos instead.
   A ban on dinner in front of the TV isn't a bad idea, for parents as well as children. Some parents may have rules about TV viewing when playmates are over.

5. *Set limits on viewing.*
   Even when there *is* something on to watch, children needn't just vegetate in front of the TV. Perhaps TV time is a reward for schoolwork completed or a confirmation of cooperative behavior for the day. Maybe it occurs *after* reading or sharing in the home. Prioritize activities. Sometimes television isn't the first priority (even though it's the easiest).

6. *Watch programs with your child.*
   Make sure the child can distinguish reality from fantasy. Talk about troubling outcomes or events. Interpret the storyline for the child so he understands the reason for the actions.

7. *Offer clear support or disapproval of TV characters, actions, values.*
   When something is presented on TV that is offensive or violates the family's value system, let your child know by expressing your disapproval—even booing and hissing. When something on TV supports the family's views, verbalize your approval, cheer, or even applaud. Let your child know that TV presents material to think about and weigh, not just material to passively accept as fact.

8. *Use time spent watching TV for maximum benefit.*
   Television can provide a resource for new words. Parents can list television terms like "mutant" and "enterprise" and help children look them up. Games can be played with the words and they can be used in conversation. Television programs can also serve as a springboard for discussions on sensitive topics like death, abuse, and drug involvement.

as early as 1971 Bogatz and Ball found that children who watch the show often like school more and do better than those who rarely watch it.

Another series for preschoolers, *Mister Rogers' Neighborhood* is designed to stimulate creativity and imagination and to reinforce children's sense of personal worth. Fred Rogers, the program's creator, writer, and star, closes each show by telling his TV friends, "I like you just the way you are." Many parents report that after watching *Mister Rogers' Neighborhood*, nursery school children are more likely to tolerate delays, observe rules, and show friendliness and cooperation during play than those who watch neutral films (Murray and Solamon, 1984).

■●▲   CONCEPT SUMMARY

Socialization During the Preschool Years

● *The Family*
  - The family plays the most central role in socialization.
  - The emotional tone of the family, parenting style, and the quality of the child's interactions with the parents affect child responsiveness to guidance and the development of specific competencies.
  - Maltreatment affects child self-esteem, parent-child interactions, and child behavior.
  - Children establish a partnership with their parents, showing less physical dependency and a greater ability to give and take in social interactions.
  - In general, fathers have more positive and more frequent interactions with their preschoolers than with their infants.
  - Sibling relationships are generally the first peer contact children have. They are sustained and often influential.
  - Children experience differential treatment and expectations due to birth order and the presence or absence of siblings.
  - Compared with other age groups, the loss of a parent through divorce or death is particularly traumatic for the preschooler.
  - Stepfamilies can provide both positive and negative opportunities and interactions for children

● *Peers*
  - Preschool play tends to be more physical, playful, interactive, egalitarian, and unpredictable than infant play.
  - Dramatic (or social pretend) play allows the preschooler to use imagination.
  - Friendships are formed.

● *Other adults*
  - Most of the sustained contact children will have with adult strangers will be through school, church, or alternative care.

● *Television*
  - Almost all preschoolers watch some television, and some watch extensively. Play time may be abandoned for TV viewing.
  - Program comprehension is limited, although preschoolers can focus on the actions of a particular character.
  - They are limited in distinguishing real from make-believe (most 4–6 year olds know cartoons are not "real").

- Watching TV programs may be the main source of social interaction between parents and their preschool-age children.
- Preschoolers can imitate what they see on TV and remember messages and information.
- Preschooler imitation of antisocial behavior seen on TV is a long-standing concern.

● The Self

Self-Concept and Self-Esteem

During the preschool years, children begin to piece together a picture of themselves as individuals. They know their own names, can recognize pictures of themselves, and are beginning to understand the ways in which people differ and are similar (Harter, 1983). As children become more self-aware, they also become more self-evaluative. Three year olds make frequent comments about their own abilities ("I can ride by myself" or "I'm wearing a pretty dress"). By the age of 3.5 or 4, children do less boasting and show more concern about being liked and performing competently. Some typical statements include, "Are you my friend?" and "Is this right?"

Children under age 6 severely overestimate their own abilities (Dweck and Elliot, 1983). They predict perfect scores for themselves on *all* tests, rank themselves at the top of their classes, and generally believe their behavior is flawless (Stipek, 1981). Why? Because their magical thinking allows them to presume they can do anything they wish. In the preschooler's mind, Descartes' "I think therefore I am" becomes "I am therefore I will." Parents and authority figures can exert a crushing influence on the preschooler's self-evaluation. Even young, bright-eyed optimists will revise their self-assessments downward when ridiculed, criticized, or devalued by adults (Stipek et al., 1984).

Preschool-age children are aware of racial and ethnic differences, particularly skin color and hair style. Direct answers to questions about such differences help children understand that skin color differences exist and help them identify themselves as members of particular racial or religious groups. The best answer to give 3 or 4 year olds when they ask, "Am I black?" (or "Am I Jewish?" is to say "Yes, you are, just like Mommy and Daddy" (or some other authority figure). Because children of this age have positive feelings about their parents and other adults, they see it as desirable to resemble them, especially if the parents are enthusiastic about their identity. An answer like, "Yes, you're (black/

self-esteem
an evaluation of the self concept on good-bad, worthy-unworthy, capable-incapable dimensions

■ Figure 10–12

Moving away from sex-role stereotypes.

gender identity
the realization that one is either a
male or a female

sex role identity
an individual's perception of
themselves as relatively masculine or
relatively feminine

Jewish) and that won't ever change" conveys an entirely different meaning and a less positive message about cultural and ethnic identity.

Owing to the weight our society gives to physical appearance, children who wear leg braces, use wheelchairs, or have visible disabilities are often viewed with pity and sadness. To promote positive self-regard, adults must evaluate *all* children in terms of what they *can* do, not in terms of their liabilities and limitations.

Gender Identity, Gender Constancy, Sex Stereotypes and Sex Roles

Part of all children's social-emotional development involves identifying themselves as males or females, or forming a *gender identity*. By age 2 or 3, a boy may be able to tell you he is a boy and may become upset if someone makes a mistake about his sex (Ruble, 1988). As young children are coming to grips with their own sexual identity, they are also implicitly learning about *sex stereotypes* or beliefs that identify culturally appropriate behavior for females and males (Fagot et al., 1986). Children as young as age 2.5 believe

boys . . . like to help father
            say, "I can hit you"
            will "be boss"
            and "mow the lawn"
girls . . . like to play with dolls
            talk a lot
            never hit
            say, "I need some help"
            "clean the house"
            and later will "be a nurse"
        (Kuhn et al., 1978).

Despite the political activism in the area of women's rights in the 1970s and 1980s, adult men and women have deviated little from traditional sex stereotypes suggesting that notions of masculine and feminine and their accompanying behaviors are deeply ingrained and stable over time (Table 10–10).

Furthermore, the behavior of preschoolers is strongly influenced by their stereotypic beliefs. Thus, they consistently and inflexibly select sex-typed activities for themselves (toys, games, clothing, hairstyles) and demand that others do the same. In this way, a *sex role identity* is formed—a concept of oneself as relatively masculine or relatively feminine. Until the 5–7 year old cognitive shift that takes place during middle childhood, preschoolers will regard sex-stereotyped behavior as a corequisite of one's gender and not as something freely chosen or even modified to fit one's personality or needs.

■ **Table 10–10** *Stereotypically Masculine and Feminine Traits**

	MASCULINE	FEMININE
Physical characteristics	Strong	Soft
	Tall	Small
	Sturdy	Graceful
Personality characteristics	Independent	Emotional
	Aggressive	Kind
	Outspoken	Tactful
	Dominant	Gentle
	Ambitious	Considerate
	Self-confident	Gets feelings hurt
	Stands up under pressure	Cries easily
	Takes a stand	Excitable in major
	Active	crises
	Competitive	Understanding
	Adventurous	
Interactions with others	Acts as a leader	Devotes self to others
	Not easily influenced	Needs approval
		Aware of other's
		feelings
		Expresses tender
		feelings
Preferences/aptitudes	Likes math and science	Likes children
	Mechanical aptitude	Enjoys art and music
	Skilled in business	Home-oriented
	Makes decisions easily	Creative
	Doesn't give up easily	Neat
Acceptable occupations	Truck driver	Telephone operator
	Insurance agent	Elementary school
	Chemist	teacher
		Nurse

*As judged by college students in the 1980s (Ruble, 1983). Adapted with permission.

Biological and Environmental Factors that Influence the Development of Sex Role Identity

BIOLOGICAL FACTORS Do children's genes and hormones set the tone for their sex role identity? Do females act more nurturant and males more aggressive because they *cannot* do otherwise? Cross-cultural studies suggest considerable diversity among males and females of the world regarding sex-stereotyped behavior. In the 1930s anthropologist Margaret Mead (1935/1963) reported sex role reversals in the three New Guinea tribal societies she studied. Arapesh men and women were feminine (cooperative and helpful); Mundugumore men and women were masculine (aggressive and ruthless); while Tchambuli men were dependent and easy going and Tchambuli women were dominant, cold, and assertive. Since this research does not conclusively negate biological factors in sex role development, more penetrating studies have been conducted (Sigmon, 1987).

John Money and Anke Ehrhardt (1972) and other researchers (Hines, 1982; Reinisch, 1981) have studied boys and girls exposed to abnormal levels of prenatal sex hormones. Boys whose bodies could not make full use of the androgens in their bloodstreams prior to birth identified themselves as males but were quieter and less ready to engage in competitive sports than other boys (Money & Ehrhardt, 1974). In another example, some girls whose mothers took a synthetic hormone similar to androgen to prevent miscarriage during pregnancy were born with ambiguous genitals. Although surgery gave them a normal female appearance, these girls were decidedly more masculine in their tastes and preferences than a comparable group of females. These girls accepted their gender identity but preferred vigorous sports, preferred slacks and shorts to dresses and skirts, and showed little interest in jewelry, cosmetics, or hairstyles. Interestingly, follow-up studies showed that these girls made successful mothers as adults (Money, 1978). Apparently, biological factors have an organizing effect on later sex role behavior. While there are overall sex differences in the brain, there is disagreement in the literature as to whether certain parts of the corpus callosum (the band of tissue that connects the two hemispheres) are responsible for sex differences in interhemispheric transfer of information and visual attention (Potter & Graves, 1988; Byne et al., 1988).

ENVIRONMENTAL INFLUENCES A considerable body of research has been collected to document the powerful effect people and information in the environment have on sex role behavior. Parents are strongly predisposed to regard their newborns in a sex-stereotyped manner. At 24 hours old, sons were seen as larger, firmer, better coordinated, more alert, stronger, and hardier; daughters were viewed as softer, weaker, more delicate, finer featured, more inattentive, and more awkward even though all babies rated were the same weight, height and had the same APGAR scores (J. Z. Rubin et al., 1974). Despite the women's rights movement of the 1970s and early 1980s, parents' expectations for their sons and daughters have changed very little in 20 years (Brooks-Gunn, 1986). Fathers' stereotyped expectations were found to be more extreme than mothers', however (Fagot, 1981).

Because of their expectations, parents judge a child's behavior as appropriate or inappropriate for their sex and reinforce or punish accordingly (Block, 1983). Parents provide sex-appropriate toys for their youngsters. They also expect more independent problem solving and self-initiated behavior from their boys than their girls, while providing more help and encouraging more dependency from their girls than their boys. Interestingly, fathers are more concerned about the appropriateness of their children's sex role behavior than are mothers. Mothers treat both boys and girls with nurturance and support, while the fathers are actively involved in training traditional sex-typed responses (Langlois & Downs, 1980). Most parents do make a special effort to provide sex role socialization activities for children who are the same sex as they: fathers take sons fishing and to the "game," mothers bake cookies and shop with their daughters. It's no wonder that children from parent-absent or divorced families are less sex stereotyped in their play than children from two-parent families (Stevenson & Block, 1988).

In addition to specific sex role training, parents and other adults also model sex-typed behavior for children to imitate. Media portrayals of males and females are highly stereotypic (Huston, 1983). Depictions in picture books, story books, and school texts parallel television (Scott & Schau, 1985). Children who observe their parents acting in a non-stereotyped way on a daily basis (mothers repairing broken items and fathers cooking) tend to hold less stereotypic views of men and women and report more nontraditional choices themselves (Weinraub et al., 1984).

sex role socialization
encouraging males and females to behave in sex stereotyped ways

Teachers as agents of sex role socialization Teachers encourage their students to adopt behaviors that conform to the "feminine" environment of the school. Quiet, passive behavior in males and females is encouraged while loud, assertive behavior is rebuked by both male and female teachers (Fagot, 1985). At the same time, teachers support traditional home-based socialization by calling on boys to demonstrate "masculine" sex-typed items while reinforcing "lady-like" behavior in girls (Serbin et al., 1979). When teachers move out of "feminine activities" (like arts and crafts) and into male-preferred contexts, children follow their lead, but without a model to imitate, children quickly and completely revert back to traditional sex-typed activities within the classroom (Serbin et al., 1981).

sex typed activities
behaviors considered appropriate for males but inappropriate for females and vice versa

Peers and Siblings as Agents of Sex Role Socialization Eleanor Maccoby (1990) suggests that the peer group provides the primary setting for the differential socialization of girls and boys. By age 3, same-sex peers reinforce each other for sex-appropriate behavior and reject or ignore those whose play activities cross gender lines (Langlois and Downs, 1980). Boys are more harshly criticized for sex-inappropriate play than girls (Serbin et al., 1979). As a consequence, boys play with boys and girls with girls in a social system that promotes and strengthens sex stereotypes. Because of the preschooler's level of cognitive development, they are even *more* rigid and extreme in their sex stereotypes than adults. Mixed-sex play can be encouraged by teachers or promoted by the physical design of the classroom, but children won't choose mixed-sex activities on their own until puberty (Hartup, 1983).

Sibling influence on sex typing is similar to peers but is much more complex because sibling effects exist within the larger context of the family. In particular, family size influences sex typing. Same-sex children in two-child families display more sex-typed behavior than same-sex children in large families (Stoneman et al., 1986). Apparently, children from larger families strive to be different from one another in order to distinguish themselves from the crowd. As a result, same-sex siblings from large families may engage in *either* cross-sex or sex-typed activities.

Acquiring Gender and Sex Role Identities:
Theoretical Explanations

PSYCHOANALYTIC THEORY Freud felt that around age 4 boys became intuitively aware of their mother's sexuality, unconsciously felt erotic desire for their mothers, but feared their father's revenge (the Oedipal conflict). (A similar process, the Electra complex, was hypothesized by Freud for girls, whereby mothers and daughters were rivals for the father's love). Realizing their power disadvantage, boys and girls learn to *identify* with their rival parent, matching their behavior to his or her image as a way of reducing conflict. Thus, through identification, boys come to act like their fathers and girls learn to emulate their mothers. Psychoanalytic theory is difficult to test scientifically and when tested, the findings do not support the predictions; i.e., boys and girls are found to be more similar to their *mothers* than to same-sex parents; children adopt sex-typed behavior 1–2 years before the Oedipus/Electra complex is predicted to occur (Stangor & Ruble, 1987). Consequently, psychoanalytic theory is not terribly useful in explaining gender/sex role identity.

SOCIAL LEARNING THEORY Social learning theory postulates that gender roles are learned in the same way as other behaviors, through imitation, reward, and punishment. Boys and girls are rewarded for sex-appropriate behaviors and punished for sex-inappropriate ones (Siegal, 1987). The theory also assumes girls look to female role models to imitate behaviors acceptable for their gender while boys look more to men as imitative models.

While social learning theory makes sense on an intuitive level, it can't account for the facts from research. First, children do not necessarily imitate the behavior of same-sex adults more than that of opposite-sex adults. Little girls will try to apply make-up like their mommies, but so will little boys. Children imitate same-sex adults more consistently after age 5 or 6, but by that time the child has already acquired a strong gender/sex role identity. And second, boys and girls are differentially sensitive to reinforcement about sex-typed behavior (Fagot, 1985). Girls change their behavior when they receive feedback from either peers or the teacher; boys are much more responsive to sex role recommendations made by peers.

COGNITIVE-DEVELOPMENTAL THEORY Lawrence Kohlberg (1966) suggested that gender/sex role identity required an understanding of gender related concepts. The child must first learn sex-linked labels (boy,

Oedipal conflict
according to Freud, a series of events that occur in the phallic stage of psychosexual growth that encourage the development of a superego or conscience in a boy as well as the identification of the boy with his father

Electra conflict
according to Freud, a series of events that occur in the phallic stage of psychosexual growth that encourage the development of a superego or conscience in a girl as well as the identification of the girl with her mother

social learning theory
a theory of behavior that stresses the role of observing and imitating others in the acquisition of new responses

man, girl, woman) and apply them correctly to themselves (occurs between age 2 and 3.5). They must then acquire *gender consistency or gender constancy*, an appreciation that their gender is stable and permanently assigned (occurs between age 4 and 7). When children understand that genital differences are responsible for gender constancy, they can understand that perceptual transformations do not affect gender assignment (Bem, 1989).

Research suggests that children who understand gender consistency usually watch same-sex models more than other-sex models (Ruble et al., 1981). But the biggest weakness in the theory is that 2 and 3 year olds consistently display sex-typed behavior long before the concept of gender consistency is in place (Fagot et al., 1986, Leonard & Archer, 1989).

gender constancy/gender consistency
the realization that one's sex assignment (male or female) is permanent and unaffected by one's behavior or dress

GENDER SCHEMA THEORY Sandra Bem (1983, 1985) feels that children socialize themselves into gender roles. First, they learn about society's perceptions of traditional masculinity and femininity, organizing that knowledge into cognitive categories called *gender schemas*. They then identify behaviors in their society's gender schema that apply to them as males or females and adapt their attitudes and behaviors accordingly. Gender schema theory predicts that children ignore sex-inappropriate activities because they conclude the behavior is "not for me" (Signorella & Liben, 1983). Consequently, the child gathers a significant body of knowledge about sex-appropriate behavior but learns much less about other-sex activities and behaviors. It also explains why young children reject *androgyny* for themselves. Androgynous people possess both masculine and feminine characteristics and can manifest them as the situation demands (boys can be both tough and tender; girls both assertive and passive). Preschoolers can't be androgynous until they can reject or reevaluate their gender schemas (Bem, 1985).

gender schema theory
a theory that combines the social learning perspectives with the cognitive developmental approach to explain the acquisition of sex-stereotyped behavior and knowledge

androgyny
involves a combination of masculine and feminine behaviors

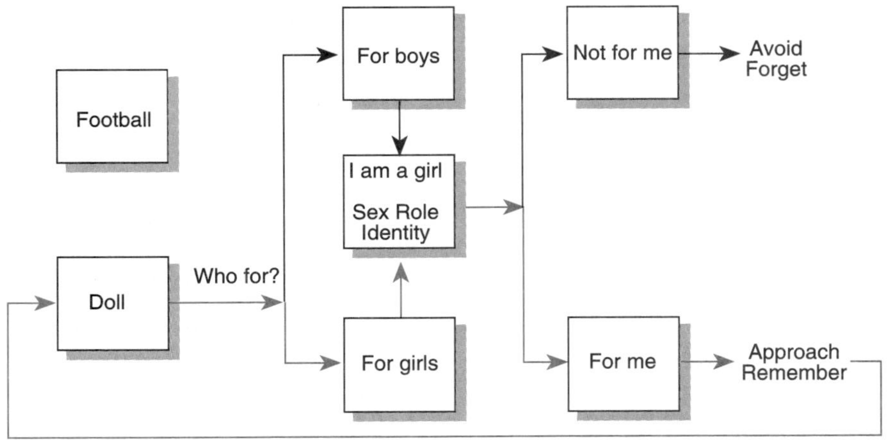

■ **Figure 10–13**

A gender schema model for organizing stimuli/events into sex-typed preferences and sex-appropriate behavior.

■ **Table 10–11** *Sex Similarities and Differences*

CATEGORY	FINDINGS	CATEGORY	FINDINGS
Physical Attributes		Creativity	Females excel on verbal creativity tests, but otherwise no difference.
Strength	Males taller, heavier, more muscular after puberty.	Cognitive style	Males excel on spatial-visual disembedding tests starting at adolescence, but no general differences in cognitive style.
Health	Females less vulnerable to illness and disease, live longer.		
Activity level	Some evidence that preschool boys more active during play in same-sex groups; school-age boys and girls are active in different ways.		
		Personality Characteristics	
Manual dexterity	Women excel when speed is important; findings hard to interpret.	Sociability	No consistent findings on infants' responsiveness to social cues; school-age boys play in larger groups; women fantasize more about affiliation themes, but there is no evidence that one sex wants or needs friends more.
Abilities			
General intelligence	No difference on most tests.		
Verbal ability	Some evidence that females acquire language slightly earlier; males more often diagnosed as having reading problems; females excel on various verbal tests after age 10 or 11.*	Empathy	Conflicting evidence; probably depends on situation and sex of participants in an interaction.
Quantitative ability	Males excel on tests of mathematical reasoning from the start of adolescence.*	Emotionality	Self-reports and observations conflict; no convincing evidence that females feel more emotional, but they may express certain emotions more freely.
Spatial-visual ability	Males excel starting in 10th grade, but not on all tests or in all studies.*		

Sex Differences

Sex roles and stereotypes suggest vast differences in the behavior of boys and girls, so much so that each refers to the other as the "opposite sex." But what types of differences actually exist? In 1974 Eleanor Maccoby and Carol Jacklin published *The Psychology of Sex Differences*, a review of over 1600 studies on sex differences and similarities. While their original work *did* underestimate the extent to which males and females differ on some traits, recent research supports two of Maccoby's and Jacklin's conclusions: (a) that similarities between the sexes far outweigh the differences, and (b) if differences do exist, their magnitude is generally small. Table 10–11 summarizes the research findings in the area of sex differences.

■ **Table 10–11** *(continued)*

CATEGORY	FINDINGS	CATEGORY	FINDINGS
Dependence	Conflicting findings; dependence appears not to be a unitary concept or stable trait.	Aggressiveness	Males more aggressive from preschool age on; men more violent, more likely to be aggressive in public, more likely to be physically aggressive in situations not involving anger.
Susceptibility to influence	Preschool girls more obedient to parents; boys may be more susceptible to peer pressure; no overall difference in adult susceptibility to persuasion across different settings in laboratory studies.	*Values and Moral Perceptions*	Some controversial evidence that males and females approach choice and conflict somewhat differently. Males seem more likely to emphasize abstract standards of justice, fairness, balancing of individual rights. Females seem more likely to emphasize the ethics of care, human attachments, balancing of conflicting responsibilities.
Self-esteem and confidence	No self-reported differences in self-esteem, but males more confident about task performance; males more likely to take credit for success, less likely to blame selves for failure.		
Nurturance	No overall differences in altruism; girls more helpful and responsive to infants, small children; some evidence that fathers are responsive to newborns as mothers are, but issue of maternal versus paternal behavior remains open.		

Source: Table from *The Longest War: Sex Differences in Perspective,* Second Edition by Carol Tavris and Carole Wade, copyright © 1984 by Harcourt Brace Jovanovich, Inc., reprinted by permission of the publisher.

*Differences statistically reliable but quite small.

● Emotional Development

Up to now in the chapter we have concentrated on the external forces that work on preschool children as they emerge out of infancy and enter the world at large. Now we turn to the internal landscape, looking at the inner forces called emotions.

Autism

Autism is a serious emotional disturbance diagnosed by the time the child is 3 years old (Short & Schopler, 1988). The earlier autism is diagnosed, the more severe it tends to be (76% of cases are identified by parents at 24 months). The autistic child displays four major symptoms (Rutter & Garmezy, 1983):

■ **Figure 10–14**

Autistic children in school.

1. *Lack of social interaction.* Autistic children actively avoid people, do not respond to affection or verbal stimulation, and do not make normal eye contact.
2. *Prolonged involvement in repetitive behaviors.* The child may spend hours sitting, gazing at his hands, or twirling an object, usually in a way that has nothing to do with its intended purpose. As a consequence, most parents find autistic children to be "good babies," requiring little attention and demanding nothing but predictability.
3. *Reacts with intense displeasure to any change in familiar surroundings or routine.* Difficult to manage—passive or irritable. Frequent temper tantrums and/or self-destructive behavior.
4. *Displays severe communication problems.* If the child learns words, he uses them inappropriately, runs words together (Iwantthatthing), or simply just repeats what others say (a behavior called *echolalia*). Some autistic children can learn to use sign language.

It's difficult to know what the autistic child's cognitive or sensory capabilities are since these children are so unresponsive. Many are retarded; many have epilepsy and experience seizures (Deykin & MacMahon, 1980). When the disorder was first identified in the 1940s, the autistic child's aloof behavior was thought to be caused by parents who were cold and avoidant. Mothers were held primarily responsible (Kanner, 1943). Subsequent studies have found no particular family pattern or parent personality to be responsible for autism (Achenbach, 1984). Instead, the brain damage associated with autism is thought to be caused by developmental interference after conception or by a recessive gene (Courchesne et al., 1988). Ten percent of autistic children have fragile-X syndrome, a chromosomal abnormality (Rutter & Garmezy, 1983). The brains of autistic children seem to overproduce serotonin, a neurotransmitter, and chemicals called opiods, responsible for decreased pain perception and lower levels of motivation. The medication Fenfluramine, designed to reduce serotonin levels, has had mixed results (Barthelemy et al., 1989). Naltrexone, a drug designed to block opiod receptors, has enjoyed more success, particularly in reducing the incidence of self-injurious behavior among autistic children (Vandershaf, 1987).

The incidence of autism in the United States is 3 per 10,000 live births. While intensive training in language and social skills can help some autistic individuals, only one-third make a good-to-fair adjustment to life as adults (Geller et al., 1982). At UCLA, Ivar Lovaas' program of intensive behavioral treatment for the autistic child has recorded particularly positive results (Landers, 1987).

Fear

Fear is characterized by the anticipation of pain or great distress and is associated with a specific object or event. During the first 2 years of life, fear is a common response to unpredictable environmental stimuli. Infants are frightened by unfamiliar people and places, being left alone, the loss of physical support (falling), and flashes of light. By the time children are 2 or 3, their imagination is a significant source of fear. Since preschoolers can imagine beasts, sounds, and intruders, their fantasy images sometimes frighten them as much as the real thing since they have trouble distinguishing reality from fantasy. And because they are constrained by the illogic of preoperational thought, preschoolers feel a very profound sense of vulnerability and dependence since they don't know what to do to stop from being afraid (Dibrell & Yamamoto, 1988).

Both genetics and learning may account for the acquisition of fear. Fear responses to certain potentially dangerous stimuli such as heights, strangers, loud noises, and the dark may be inborn since avoidance of these circumstances has survival value. Fear responses can also be learned. A child who is knocked down by a dog, hit by a car, locked in a small room, or lost may learn to avoid the object, situation, and/or person associated with the fright. Television provides an endless stream of potentially frightening images. And parents may pass on their own fears to their children by providing a behavioral model or by being overprotective and conveying the belief that the world is a dangerous place.

Agoraphobia, or fear of public places, and *childhood panic disorder* may be more common among preschoolers than previously believed (Ballenger et al., 1989). Avoidant behavior, one of the primary symptoms, may be overlooked, since it is acceptable for preschoolers to act dependent and solicit protection. Children whose mothers died before they were 10 are almost 7 times more likely to be diagnosed as having agoraphobia than those whose mothers remain alive (Tweed et al., 1989).

Behaviorally, preschool children express fear by crying, clinging, or trying to escape, and they exhibit characteristic facial expressions and body postures when they are frightened. Often, they stare wide-eyed and open-mouthed, orient themselves away from the fear source, and assume flight posture. In contrast to preschoolers, frightened 6–12 year olds cry very little or not at all (Murphy, 1985).

Most of the fears expressed by 3–6 year olds are unrealistic, involving nearly impossible events, like attacks by exotic animals or imaginary creatures. Children in this age group mention snakes more often than any other animal as an object of fear but also identify lions, tigers, bears, ghosts, witches, and monsters as scary. Preschool children may be equally troubled when they see people who are missing a limb or a facial feature. They might stare and ask probing questions in part because the unfamiliar sight attracts their attention and in part because their sense of wholeness has been violated. It takes time for children to realize that a person with a disability is still a person and can function quite well despite missing body parts (B. A. Wright, 1983).

Fearfulness is influenced by age, gender, socioeconomic status, and society. As children grow older, new fears develop to take place of objects and situations that have become more tolerable (Table 10–12). The more children know about their world, the more they discover there are genuine reasons to be afraid. As children learn about the increasing levels of violence in our society, they worry about abduction, personal injury, and someone getting into their homes (Zill, 1983). Although girls report more fears than boys, it is not clear whether girls are actually more fearful. The difference might lie in the willingness to report since it's less socially acceptable for a boy to admit he's afraid. On the other hand, boys are greater risk takers than girls (Ginsberg & Miller, 1982). At the zoo, boys take more risks than girls do, riding elephants and camels and feeding, touching, and patting other animals. Fear may be present for both genders but boys may be activated and excited by fear while fear may cause girls to withdraw.

Poor children tend to be more fearful than middle or upper class children perhaps because they are exposed to outcomes (such as murder, illness, starvation, assault, and robbery) that other children are sheltered from. As society evolves, children's fears change accordingly. Children growing up in the 1940s were afraid of Hitler; in the 1950s, of communism; in the 1960s and 70s, of nuclear war, and in the 1990s, of becoming homeless or victimized by crime. Changes in our own society

---

■ **Table 10–12** *Childhood Fears*

AGE	FEARS
0–6 months	Loss of support, loud noises
7–12 months	Strangers; heights; sudden, unexpected, and looming objects
1 year	Separation from parent, toilet, injury, strangers
2 years	A multitude of stimuli, including loud noises (vacuum cleaners, sirens and alarms, trucks, and thunder), animals, dark rooms, separation from parent, large objects or machines, changes in personal environment, strange peers
3 years	Masks, dark, animals, separation from parent
4 years	Separation from parent, animals, dark, noises (including noises at night)
5 years	Animals, "bad" people, dark, separation from parent, bodily harm
6 years	Supernatural beings (e.g., ghosts, witches, Darth Vader), bodily injury, thunder and lightning, dark, sleeping or staying alone, separation from parent
7–8 years	Supernatural beings, dark, media events (e.g., news on the threat of nuclear war or child kidnapping), staying alone, bodily injury
9–12 years	Tests and examinations in school, school performances, bodily injury, physical appearance, thunder and lightning, death, dark
Teens	Social performance, sexuality

Source: Papalia & Olds, *A Child's World,* Fifth Ed. (McGraw-Hill, 1990) (after Morris & Kralochwill). Used with permission.

and in the nations of the world will in part determine the fears of the next generation.

Helping Children Cope with Fear

Preschoolers are limited in their ability to accept explanations or other points of view, to understand logic, and to distinguish reality from fantasy. For all these reasons, no other period of development is laden so heavily with fears. The lamp cord looks like a snake, the shadows on the wall look like spiders, and all kinds of gruesome things are known to lurk behind doors, under beds, and in darkened closets. A man who came to this country at age 6 told me that as a child, he was afraid to return to his kindergarten classroom after his first experience with Halloween. His native country had no such customs, and preoperational thought had led him to believe that his classmates had been kidnapped or transformed into hideous beasts.

How can caregivers help children cope with their fears? In dealing with a child who is afraid of bears lurking in the dark, for example, it's tempting to force confrontation ("You turn on the light yourself"), shame the child ("Don't be such a baby!"), use logic ("Bears are more afraid of us than we are of them"), or ignore the problem entirely. Unfortunately, all these strategies only make things worse (DuPont, 1983). Not only do children have their fear to contend with, but they also have to worry about losing their parent's support. Probably the best way to help children manage their fears is to provide emotional support while aiding the child in gradually gaining control over the environment. Some of the most effective solutions are also the simplest (e.g., providing a night light, modeling controlled behavior, accompanying the child or giving them help when they ask, or reading books to them like *Goodnight, Moon* and *There's a Nightmare in My Closet*). Most irrational fears subside once the child reaches age 5 or 6.

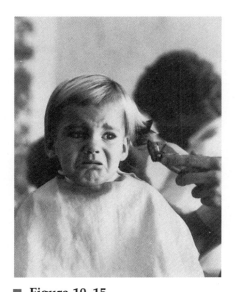

■ **Figure 10–15**

Benjamin Smith is not too happy about his first haircut.

Anger and Aggression

Researchers have been interested in studying children's antisocial behavior for more than half a century (Jersild & Markey, 1935). Prior to age 3, children usually express anger through undirected temper tantrums, hitting, and angry cries. In this age group, anger is most often provoked by parents' attempts to establish eating, sleeping, playing, and bathing routines and to help the child learn bowel and bladder control. After age 3, disputes with playmates rather than parents are the primary causes of angry outbursts. Usually, such quarrels have to do with possessions or objects (Laursen & Hartup, 1989). Aggression directed at retrieving an object, territory, or privilege is called *instrumental aggression*. Older children are more likely to engage in *hostile aggression,* where another person, not an object, is the target of the attack. Until children

instrumental aggression
using aggression to obtain an object, territory, or privilege

hostile aggression
attacking another person where the focus of the attack is the person him- or herself (i.e., calling someone names to hurt their feelings)

dominance hierarchies
organizing persons from least
dominant to most dominant, where
the most dominant person has a
controlling interest over the others

can use words effectively, they rely on physical aggression to intimidate others.

Dominance hierarchies are established as children become winners and losers in aggressive confrontations. The dominance hierarchy actually reduces the number of fights among peers since they already know what the outcome will be. But since the hierarchy is based on competitive outcomes, children at the end of the "pecking order" may come to feel inferior and submissive (Rosen et al., 1988).

Between the ages of 3 and 5, children begin to express their anger verbally by scolding, insulting, or threatening others (Hartup, 1983). To be able to hurt someone using words requires considerable thought (Parke & Slaby, 1983). The child has to use what she knows about self-esteem and self-concept to select the most upsetting insults. Attacks on competence, physical appearance or personality cut deep ("Stupid id-iot!" "Ugly fatso!" "Nerd-wierdo!" "Crybaby!"). In this way cognitive development transforms physical aggression into a subtler and more complex behavior. Hurting someone's feelings requires a lot more intellectual skill than just hitting.

At all ages, boys are more aggressive than girls (Maccoby and Jacklin, 1980). This difference is noticeable in the early play of 2–3 year olds and persists into adulthood. Both genetic and learned factors may influence the outcome. Paralleling primate species, human boys are more active, play in larger groups, and involve more rough and tumble elements in their play. Girls are more sedate, stay closer to their mothers, and prefer smaller groups to larger ones. These behaviors could also be attributed to differences in the way boys and girls are socialized. Our society tells boys not to hit girls and tells girls not to hit anyone (Tavris & Wade, 1984). Since aggressive behavior can be learned by observing a model, sex differences in aggression aren't necessarily genetic (Patterson, 1982). Preschool children may also react to frustration by becoming aggressive since frustration arouses negative emotions (Berkowitz, 1989).

The Development of Self-Control

self-control
being able to resist temptation; to
recognize and redirect behavior that
has negative moral implications

Preschoolers must work to learn to control anger and to find acceptable outlets for their emotions (Dodge, 1989). The capacity for self-control and restraint are in place by the third year of life (Weisz, 1978). Adults' responses to children's aggression can strongly influence the way children control aggressive acts. Adults who are more tolerant of aggression influence children to maintain aggressive response patterns, whereas adults who reject aggression are more likely to encourage self-control. By the end of the preschool period, children know that some type of control is necessary to avoid embarrassment and ridicule when aggression is inappropriate. There is considerable variation in the amount of control they actually achieve, however.

Prosocial Behavior

Prosocial behavior is behavior that benefits another. When that behavior is performed at some cost or risk to self, it is called *altruism* (Radke-Yarrow et al., 1983). Giving is an action initiated as young as 2 or 3 years. Children will give "gifts" to others (a pencil, a bit of food, a drawing) as a way of initiating contact (Radke-Yarrow et al., 1983). Often, preschoolers will offer their effort and time as when an adult is sweeping the patio and they want to help, too. When 4–5 year old children have more chores and household responsibilities, they tend to offer more help and comfort. Black preschool males from single-mother families demonstrated more prosocial behavior than either white males or white females or children from smaller families (Richman et al., 1988; Rehberg & Richman, 1989).

Recognizing Emotions

Prosocial behavior often depends on recognizing emotions in others so help can be tailored to fit their needs. Mothers encourage their children, especially girls, to discuss their feelings by the time they are 18 months old. By age 3, mothers and children can have meaningful conversations about emotional states (Dunn & Munn, 1987). In an early study, Borke (1971) showed 3–8 year old children expressive drawings of happy, sad, frightened, and angry faces and then read them stories about a child eating a favorite snack, losing a toy, or getting lost in the woods. Even the youngest children could identify the emotions on the four faces, and some could even identify the emotion depicted in the story. Happy stories were the easiest to identify (60% of the 3 year olds answered correctly), followed by stories about fear. By age 5.5, children would usually identify stories about happy or sad events. Stories involving anger weren't identified correctly until still later and the emotions "surprise" and "disgust" were the most difficult of all (Robordy et al., 1988).

Because of their inability to decenter and to focus on multiple aspects of a situation, preschool children cannot imagine feeling two emotions at the same time (Whitesell & Harter, 1989). For example, preschoolers don't believe they can feel excited about Santa Claus but grumpy about having to go to bed on Christmas Eve. Even though they attempt deception by age 3, preschoolers also have difficulty understanding that people sometimes hide the way they really feel, pretending to be happy when they're sad or acting surprised when they weren't surprised at all (Gross & Harris, 1988). Boys are more likely to admit trying to deceive than girls (Lewis et al., 1989).

Limited by their egocentric perspective, preschool children assume that other people are made happy or sad by the events that affect them. For example, Mom or Dad would be happy "if they got a new toy" and sad "if they lost their blanket." By age 6 children realize their parents

■ **Figure 10–16**

Most preschoolers love to "help."

altruism
an unselfish concern for or devotion to others; selfless helping

decenter
the ability to focus on more than one aspect of a situation simultaneously; opposed to *centration*

have a different perspective from their own, but their egocentricity persists and they continue to include themselves in their explanations of others' emotions. Thus, in the preschooler's opinion, mothers would get mad if "I got lost" and would be angry "If I told a lie" (Harter, 1979).

The Development of Empathy

sympathy
to feel pity, compassion, or sorry for
another person

The development of empathy parallels that of emotional recognition. Toddlers can feel sympathetic distress when another person is sad, angry, or upset but they do not have the ability to assume another person's perspective. Preschoolers are beginning to understand that others have feelings that may be different from their own, and they use this knowledge when they react to others. They empathize more with children who have acceptable reasons for their behavior (happy to have a friend to play with) than children who give unacceptable reasons (happy to

---

■●▲   CONCEPT SUMMARY

The Self

- Preschoolers can understand who they are and (to an extent) the classes or groups to which they belong.

- Because of their egocentrism, many of the preschooler's statements involve themselves or make reference to themselves.

- Most preschoolers are overly self-confident because they have an imperfect understanding of the skill it takes to complete a task and the amount of such skill they possess.

- By age 2 or 3, boys and girls can correctly identify their own sex (gender identity) and are learning about sex-typed activities and expectations. Culture/environment seems to play the biggest role in both gender identity and sex role transmission.

- Psychoanalytic theory, social learning theory, cognitive developmental theory, and gender schema theory all attempt to account for why children are able to acquire behaviors considered appropriate to their gender.

- Fears are more common and more intense during the preschool period because of the child's active imagination and inability to reason logically.

- Preschoolers are sensitive to the emotions of others and may display empathy.

---

have hurt another child) (Barnett & McMinimy, 1988). A preschool-age child may offer toys or physical comfort like a hug when they sense another person is distressed. They can also be verbally supportive and sympathetic, saying "That's OK, James, don't cry." Thus, the ability to empathize predicts prosocial behavior (Stayer & Roberts, 1989).

Prosocial/empathic behavior may be spontaneous or it may result from learning. Some children are simply more compassionate than others, helping when the need presents itself or because "they want to" (Zahn-Waxler & Radke-Yarrow, 1982). While recognizing temperament differences among children, parents can expect their children to be honest and helpful and reward them for doing so (Barnett et al., 1980). Children can also learn to help and care when they come from families where much household responsibility is shared or from close-knit communities where neighbors are mutually supportive or when they feel similar to the person needing help or support (Gibbs & Woll, 1985).

Nonsexist Childrearing

TOWARD EFFECTIVE PARENTING

One of the greatest burdens boys or girls can feel is to be trapped by sex stereotypes and behavioral expectations that allow some behaviors but prohibit others. All children, whether male or female, need love and consistent guidelines from their parents rather than double standards based on stereotypic beliefs. Even though the Constitution says, "All *men* are created equal," we can treat all our *children* equally by applying nonsexist guidelines to child rearing:

nonsexist
without bias or discrimination on the basis of a person's sex

1. *Spend for the individual, not the stereotype.* If you buy your son an $80 baseball glove but only spend $19.95 on your daughter's glove because she probably won't play as much, your actions are unjustified, particularly if you don't yet know who really likes baseball/softball and who doesn't. Everyone needs to feel good about the way they look: Daughters aren't the only ones who need braces, medication for acne, clothing, and hair products. Everyone needs spending money: Girls shouldn't be encouraged to become dependent on boys for the things they need. Independent people can take care of themselves.

2. *Don't let your children use sex role rationales to get what they want.* Your daughter might claim she needs you to watch every practice/session/lesson because "That's what mommies do." Your son may claim he has to do all the work around the house "because he's a boy." No matter what pressures are placed on parents by their children, each child deserves an *equal* share of time, attention, and affection. Divide your time equally among your children's activities. If it's important to your child for you to be there, make every effort to do so, whether the child is a boy or a girl. Offer equal praise and have equal expectations—boys don't necessarily excel at "boy things" and girls don't necessarily excel at "girl things."

(continued on next page)

3. *Don't be doctrinaire about equal pay.* Is it alright to pay for gymnastics lessons for the gifted athlete but not the child who has trouble doing a forward roll? Let your child's *interests* (and not their apparent talent or their sex) dictate their involvement and your support. Children need equal opportunities to see if they like something or not and if they are any good at it. Praise the child who struggles as sincerely as the child who excels. Guide, don't push.

4. *Saving and opportunity should be sexless.* If the boy has a college tuition fund, the girl should have one also. Saving for one child's education and not another's is cruel and restrictive. Allowance should be based on age-related responsibilities, not on whether one is a male or female. Make sure everyone has jobs and the compensation rate is the same no matter who does them. Avoid stereotyping home chores—boys always taking out the trash and mowing the lawn; girls always doing the dishes and the laundry. Because *everyone* needs to learn to take care of themselves, jobs should be rotated. Girls need to take out the trash and mow the lawn and surely as boys need to do the dishes and the laundry.

Source: Pogrebin, Letty Cottin. (1980). *Growing up Free.* New York: McGraw-Hill. Reprinted with the permission of the author.

● Chapter Summary

● Successful families come in a variety of forms, but all have a common goal: to meet the needs of their children. During the preschool years, the family is the most influential agent of socialization.

● Mother–child relationships enter a partnership phase where each contributes equally to the interaction. Mothers (in the role of primary caregiver) also facilitate reasonable independence during this time. Fathers (generally secondary caregivers) spend more time with their preschoolers than with their infants and the exchanges are more positive.

● Parents set the tone for the development of behaviors such as aggression, competence, and dependence/independence in their children. Psychological maltreatment leads to dysfunctional, maladaptive behavior. Abuse prevention rather than treatment is the key.

● Most American children have siblings. Depending on their age, birth order, and sex, siblings may adopt stereotypic roles in dealing with each other (teacher, boss, and so forth). The quality of sibling interactions varies considerably from household to household and sibling pair to sibling pair. Compared with children who have siblings, most only children are advantaged and well-adjusted.

● Marital harmony facilitates the parent-child relationship, while marital discord disrupts it. Today, the majority of children experience the divorce or separation of their parents. Children display some fairly predictable short- and long-term reactions to divorce. Post-separa-

tion/divorce congeniality among the parents is the most significant aid to child adjustment. Remarriage has both advantages and disadvantages for children.
- Cognitive limitations prevent the preschool from a full understanding of death and its consequences.
- Compared to infants, the play of preschool age children is more social, interactive, and imaginative. Friendships form easily among this age group and may end readily, too.
- The majority of American children have some contact with alternative caregivers. Day care may include anything from formal instruction to supervised free play. Great care should be taken when selecting day-care providers and alternative care settings.
- Preschool age children are interested in watching television, have some understanding of program content (although they can't follow a plot), and may watch TV rather than playing, exercising, or interacting with others. Children are exposed to both desirable and undesirable information through television, and they have the capability to imitate what they see.
- During the preschool years, children develop a sense of their own race/ethnicity, appearance, identity, and abilities. Environmental factors seem more influential in sex role identity than the child's genes and hormones. Reliable differences that exist in the behavior of boys and girls are called sex differences.
- Autism is a severe emotional disturbance that is usually diagnosed by the time the child is 3 years old. Four specific behavioral criteria confirm the diagnosis.
- Preschoolers are more fearful than infants because they have active imaginations and more fearful than school-age children because they can't distinguish reality from fantasy.
- Anger and aggression are two common antisocial behaviors expressed by preschoolers. Helping, cooperation, and empathy are common prosocial behaviors.

● Observational Exercise

Children acquire a great deal of information about the world through play. Play also provides an opportunity for the preschooler to practice and consolidate some important social and motor skills. One way to understand more about the preschooler's play is to observe the child in a free-play situation in a preschool, nursery school, or daycare center.

Procedure: Contact the director of a nursery school, preschool, or daycare center in your area to ask permission to visit the facility and observe children at play. During your visit, try to observe at least four or five children who are participating in activities of their choosing.

1. Did you observe examples of the following types of play? If so, describe the behavior of the children involved.

Descriptions of Play Activities

a. Solitary play
b. Onlooker play
c. Parallel play
d. Associative play
e. Cooperative play
f. Dramatic play

2. What were the ages of the children involved? Did many younger children (age 3 or so) engage in cooperative play? Why not?
3. Describe the composition of the playgroups. Were same-sex children or children of both sexes involved?
4. Describe the roles the children adopted during their play activities. Would you describe the roles as traditional (sex-stereotyped) or nontraditional? Explain.

● Recommended Readings

Adams, P. L., Milner, J. R., & Schrepf, N. A. (1984). *Fatherless children.* New York: Wiley.

Adcock, D., & Segal, M. (1983). *Making friends: Ways of encouraging social development in young children.* Englewood Cliffs, NJ: Prentice-Hall.

Comer, J., & Poussaint, A. (1976). *Black child care: A guide to emotional and psychological development.* New York: Pocket Books.

Dobson, J. (1988). *The strong willed child: Birth through adolescence.* Wheaton, II: Tyndale House.

Faber, A., & Mazlish, E. (1988). *Siblings without rivalry.* New York: Avon.

Fraiberg, S. (1984). *The magic years: Understanding and handling the problems of early childhood.* New York: Scribners.

Galinsky, E., & David, J. (1989). *The preschool years: Family strategies that work—from experts and parents.* New York: Times Books. (This book deals with reducing sibling rivalry, etc.)

Morgan, S. M. (1981). *The unreachable child.* Memphis, TN: Memphis State Univ. Press. (Deals with the subject of autism.)

Pogrebin, L. C. (1980). *Growing up free: Raising your child in the 80s.* New York: Bantam.

Reit, S. (1985). *Sibling rivalry.* New York: Ballentine Books.

Tavris, C., & Wade, C. (1984). *The longest war: Sex differences in perspective* (2nd ed.). San Diego, CA: Harcourt Brace Jovanovich.

Whiting, B. B., & Whiting, J. W. M. (1975). *Children of sex cultures.* Cambridge MA: Harvard Univ. Press.

PART 4
The School Years

483

Physical Development During the School Years

● **Physical Development**

General Characteristics

The middle years of childhood, between the ages of 6 and 12, are most often referred to as the *school years*. This period is characterized by slow but steady physical growth, the perfection of motor abilities, and the rapid development of cognitive and social skills. Individual differences are great during these years as each child follows her own unique timetable of growth. If children continued to grow in this period at the rate they grew during infancy, they would be 100 feet tall and would weigh about 480 million pounds (McCall, 1979)! However, growth rate declines in the school years; it will accelerate again when the child enters adolescence. Patterns of physical growth are similar for males and females during the early school years. Toward the end of this period, girls will be taller and heavier than boys, since they begin their adolescent growth spurt first.

Height and Weight

Increases in height and weight are gradual and steady in this phase compared with those in the early years, and, again, in adolescence. Between the ages of 6 and 12, the average child will grow 2–2.5 inches and gain 3–6 pounds (Tanner, 1978). The average 6 year old child is almost 3.5 feet tall and weighs about 40 pounds; the average 12 year old child is almost 5 feet tall and weighs about 80 pounds. Thus, within this period, it takes children 6 years to double their weight and to increase their height by one-third, 12 times as long as it takes the infant to grow a proportional amount.

■ **Figure 11–1**

Size variations among same-age boys and girls.

As always, however, there is considerable individual variation in matters of growth. When children get enough to eat and are reasonably healthy, genetics accounts for individual differences. When children live in poverty and illness, socioeconomic class and urban–rural differences in growth appear. Height more than weight reflects a child's nutritional history. Undernourished children are shorter in stature than well-nourished children (Pollitt et al., 1982). Not surprisingly, under all circumstances physically abused children grow less well than nonabused children (Karp et al., 1989).

The size and growth rates of boys and girls are comparable until age 9, and then girls begin to grow more rapidly than boys. For both boys and girls, the initial indication of the growth spurt is a sudden increase in foot length and shoe size (Tanner, 1978). Adult height can be estimated from the child's height at a particular chronological age. At age 6, a boy's height will be about 65% of his eventual adult height, while a girl's height then will be about 70% of her full size. By age 12, boys and girls will have reached 84 and 93% of their height, respectively. By age 12, the average girl is an inch taller than the average boy and two pounds heavier. Boys typically do not begin their adolescent growth spurt until they are 12–14 years old (Tanner, 1978).

Body Proportions

Although the school years are a time of steady overall growth, the growth rate is not constant, and some body parts, such as the legs, grow faster than others. Leg growth accounts for 66% of the height increases that occur from age 1 to the onset of adolescence. Both boys and girls

primary teeth
the 20 deciduous teeth or baby teeth

are long-legged. Their clothes become too short during the school years, not too tight around the middle as during the play years.

Compared with the preschool period, school-age children have a marked improvement in posture. The rounded shoulders, slight spinal curvature, and prominent abdomen of the early years are replaced by a more erect bearing. Consequently, school-age children gain efficiency in using their arms, legs, and trunk and in moving from place to place.

Besides having a lean and leggy look, the school age child begins to have a more elongated face with more adult proportions. During the first 6 years of life, the upper part of the head grew rapidly to accommodate brain development. Now the lower face and jaw begin to catch up to make room for the permanent teeth. As the jaw lengthens, the eustachian tubes are pulled from a horizontal to a vertical position. Because drainage is improved, middle ear infections are less common in middle childhood than during the preschool years.

School-age children usually have a tooth either coming or going, so toothless smiles are common among this age group. By age 11 or 12, both boys and girls have all their permanent teeth except the second and third molars. Girls are 1–6 months ahead of same-age boys in the eruption of permanent teeth.

Internal Systems and Tissues

The Brain

One of the most striking indications of the child's increasing maturity is the dramatic slowdown in the rate of head growth. Brain growth has essentially finished by age 10 or 12. After age 5, head circumference increases by only half an inch every 5 years until maturity (Whaley & Wong, 1988).

The Skeleton

Throughout childhood, bone growth is concentrated in the face, arms, and legs. Children are more flexible than adults because their ligaments are less firmly attached and there is more space between the bones at the joints. But since the ossification process is still incomplete, children are less resistant to breaks, fractures, and muscle pulls than mature adults. Toe-dancing before 13 can damage the child's growing foot. Since children are generally active and are often daring during this period, skateboarding, doing "wheelies," and generally taking risks, the likelihood that they will be injured is high.

Scoliosis, or curvature of the spine, may cause loss of flexibility or deformity. The cause may be genetic or be associated with other diseases or deformities. It can appear at any age but is most frequent in adolescent or preadolescent girls (Schwartz et al., 1990). Early detection during this time is important for later growth and posture.

■ **Figure 11–2**

The "toothless grin" is a common sight during the school years.

■ **Figure 11–3**

Average age in year and month of the emergence of permanent teeth for boys and girls.

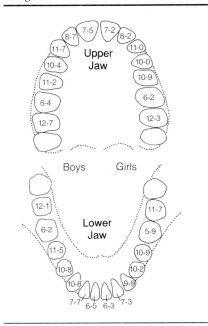

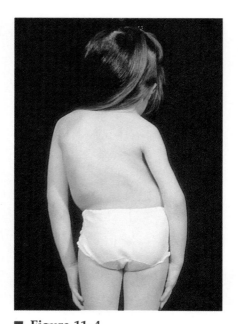

■ Figure 11–4

Scoliosis, or curvature of the spine.

scoliosis
curvature of the spine

tendonitis
inflammation of the tendon, the band
of tissue that connects muscle to bone

Osgood-Schlatter syndrome
a collection of symptoms due to
overuse of the knee joints

hypertension
high blood pressure

Muscle and Fat

Owing to higher levels of male sex hormone, school-age boys have more muscle tissue than school-age girls. In both sexes during this time muscles increase in size and consequently in strength, although the number of muscle fibers remains about the same. Thus, both males and females double their strength during the school years. Males make impressive strength improvements as they approach adolescence.

It is important to note, however, that the muscles of the 6–12 year old are still functionally immature when compared with those of an adolescent. Activities such as sports, dance, skating, and bike riding help develop muscle tissue while improving coordination. Care must be taken not to overuse muscle groups. Playing too hard in competitive sports can lead to tendinitis, "tennis elbow," Osgood-Schlatter syndrome, and stress fractures (Whaley & Wong, 1988).

The body's most important muscle, the heart, grows more slowly during the school years and is proportionally smaller now than at any other period of life (Schwartz et al., 1990). Therefore, activities that involve prolonged, intense physical exertion may not be advised for some. Blood pressure slowly increases during the school years as the heart becomes more efficient in pumping blood. Boys and girls have essentially the same blood pressure readings until the onset of puberty. The blood pressure readings of black and white children do not differ significantly, even though blacks have a higher rate of adult hypertension, or high blood pressure.

A collection of personality characteristics known as Type A behavior has been associated with high blood pressure and increased risk of heart attack in adulthood. The roots of Type A behavior seem to be established in childhood. Children who are firstborn, adapt poorly, have low tolerance for frustration, are usually in a bad mood, and, especially for boys, are achievement oriented and competitive, are most likely to become Type A adults (Steinberg, 1986; Ivanovich et al., 1987). Perhaps children with Type A tendencies could be taught less reactive ways of responding in order to lower health risks later on.

OBESITY Body fat accounts for about 15% of the average school-age child's total body weight. Girls tend to retain more fat than boys at age 6, but, unless their eating habits differ, both sexes accumulate body fat at an even rate from age 7 to adolescence. Today more than 25% of school-age children are obese (Gortmaker et al., 1987). Judgments of obesity are influenced by cultural standards. Scientists in the United States measure the thickness of the skin behind the upper arm, pinched between two fingers, as one indication of obesity. The amount of fat deposited under the skin of obese children is 2 to 3 times that of normal children.

Over the past 25 years, the number of obese children has increased from 18% (1965) to 26%. Sometimes obesity is strictly genetic—80% of all obese children are born to large parents (Epstein et al., 1990). But frequently, children gain excessive weight because they are physically inactive and they eat too much of the wrong types of foods. Personality may influence these choices. Children with "difficult" temperaments (lower in predictability, attention-span, and persistance) are more likely to become obese than "easier" children (Carey et al., 1988). Television watching is also implicated in obesity. Every hour of television a child watches increases her likelihood of becoming overweight (Dietz & Gortmaker, 1985).

Obesity can be a serious social problem for school-age children. By age 6 or 7 children have adopted the cultural notion that thin is beautiful and begin to "worry" about their weight (W. Feldman, 1988). By age 9, 50% of girls have dieted to lose weight. That number increases to 80% by the time girls are 10 or 11 (Hill et al., 1992). Fat children are often teased, ridiculed, and rejected by their peers, learning to resent their own size and ultimately themselves. Heavy children are also at risk for high blood pressure, diabetes, and orthopedic conditions of the hips, legs, and feet. For any treatment program to be successful, the child must be motivated to participate, the family must be involved, and a health professional should guide the process. For the most part, the family will be encouraged to lose weight themselves, praise the child's positive efforts, and change their eating, buying, and food preparation habits, including snacking and using food as a reward or incentive. The child will be trained to select healthier snacks, to take smaller portions of some foods, to increase her activity level, and to relinquish any psychological or emotional ties to food (e.g., food is my only friend) (Epstein et al., 1990). Crash diets, fad diets, and programs that encourage dependency rather than stressing education and independent maintenance can be hazardous to the child's health (Graves et al., 1988).

Reproductive System

Puberty is a transitional period between childhood and adulthood beginning at age 10–12 for girls and 12–14 for boys. Children start to grow rapidly during this phase as their bodies become ready for sexual maturity. Both the primary sex characteristics (those structures essential to reproduction) and the secondary sex characteristics (those characteristics like body hair and breast tissue that are associated with the mature form but are not required for reproduction) develop during puberty (Table 11–1). As you can see, a wide range of variability and unevenness in physical growth exists during this time. For example, some children mature much earlier than others and development is asymmetrical (it's normal for one breast to be larger than the other, for example). Although expected, developmental variability is a source of great concern for the preadolescent. Among girls, height and breast development but not pubic hair growth is associated with a positive body image, positive peer relationships, and superior adjustment (Brooks-Gunn & Warren, 1988).

■ **Figure 11–5**

Obesity affects more than 25% of the school age population, boys and girls alike.

orthopedic
pertaining to diseases, injuries, or disorders of the joints, tendons, ligaments, muscles or bones

puberty
the period of development characterized by rapid physical growth and the maturation of sexual and reproductive functions

primary sex characteristics
male or female structures essential to reproduction

secondary sex characteristics
physical characteristics that develop during puberty that help distinguish the sexes but are not necessary for sexual reproduction

■ **Table 11–1** *The Normal Maturational Sequence of Primary and Secondary Sex Characteristics*

CHARACTERISTIC	BOYS Average Age	BOYS Age Span	GIRLS Average Age	GIRLS Age Span
Beginning breast development (nipples and breasts elevated to form "bud stage"); rounding of hips			11	8–13
Appearance of pubic hair		10–15	11–12	
Appearance of axillary (armpit) hair		12–17	12–13	
Onset of menstruation			12.66	9–18
Beginning growth of scrotum and testes	11½–13	10–15		
Beginning growth of penis	13			
First ejaculation		11–15		
Voice begins to deepen	13–16	11–18		

Sources: Tanner, 1982.

menstruation
in mature females, the monthly shedding of the uterine lining

menarche
the female's first menstrual period

The average age of the onset of menstruation is 12.5, but some girls begin their monthly periods as early as age 10 or 11. In order for girls to anticipate and understand the events that accompany that first period (menarche), it is important that they know some basic information about menstruation by age 10. A girl who is unprepared for menarche may be frightened or unduly concerned about the unexpected bleeding. She might also feel embarrassed and isolated if she lacks the clarifying information about physical maturation or change—too embarrassed or too isolated to ask about what she needs to know.

Although there is no event corresponding to menarche that signals the onset of adolescence in boys, boys also need information to prepare them for the maturational changes that they will experience during puberty. Many parents wait too long to begin conversations about sexual topics. Now that sex can have life-threatening consequences through AIDS transmission, timely, noncontentious discussions are crucial. It's never too early to let children know that they have options and that the behavioral choices they make will shape their own futures (Lipsitt, 1988a). Parents need to set aside their own discomforts and anxieties about sexual conversations with their children so they can be effective educators and moral guides. A newspaper article, TV program, pamphlet from the doctor's office, or book can provide a comfortable starting point for a first-time or follow-up discussion. No matter how people feel about the appropriateness of sex education, there is no delaying the progress of normal development and the emergence of puberty.

Other Systems

The gastrointestinal system is quite mature by the time the child is in school. School-age children experience fewer stomach upsets, steadier blood sugar levels, and a greater stomach capacity than younger ones. Though children at this stage do not need to be fed as carefully or as frequently as preschoolers, caregivers still need to be vigilant in minimizing the child's junk food intake. (Diet and nutrition are considered more fully below.)

The lungs continue to grow until about age 8, though the respiratory airways grow well into adolescence. Breathing becomes increasingly less abdominal and more efficient, with the child breathing out less oxygen and more carbon dioxide than ever before. Also, lung capacity increases and the respiratory rate, or number of breaths per minute, slowly decreases throughout the school-age period. Respiratory rate averages the same for males and females.

Bowel and bladder control are usually well established by the school years. Bladder capacity is generally greater in school-age girls than in boys, but individual differences are great (Schwartz et al., 1990). As in the preschool period, temporary lapses in control may be caused by stress or illness.

Perceptual Development

Vision

The normal farsightedness of the preschool child becomes 20/20 vision between the ages of 9 and 11. Binocular vision (in which both eyes work together) is usually well established by age 6. The slow development of the eyes is one reason why reading is best delayed until approximately 6 years of age.

Color vision deficiency (color blindness) occurs in 3.8% of all school-age children in the United States. This is a genetic sex-linked problem 13 times more common in males than in females. While there is no cure, parents and teachers who are aware of children's color deficiencies can avoid overreliance on color coding and other such mistakes.

Hearing

The ear and sense of hearing are well developed by school age and auditory sensitivity continues to improve. Maximum sensitivity to mid-range tones is established first, followed by high-range improvements and then low-range improvement. After age 10, auditory sensitivity declines to adult levels (Trehub et al., 1988).

color vision deficiency (color blindness)
a sex-linked genetic disorder involving the ability to perceive color groups because of absent or dysfunctional cones; red-green and yellow-blue color blindness exist; some persons lack the ability to perceive any color

genetic sex-linked disorder
see X-linked inheritance

■ ● ▲   CONCEPT SUMMARY

Growth During the School Years

- Growth is slow and steady until puberty, when girls tend to mature first.

- The average child grows 2–2.5 inches taller and weighs 3–6 pounds more each year during the school years.

- Generally, girls are slightly taller and heavier than boys.

- Growth is concentrated in the legs, arms, and face.

- Baby teeth are replaced by permanent teeth (the wisdom teeth usually erupt during adolescence and the so-called 12 year molars might be "late").

- Brain growth is essentially complete by age 10 or 12.

- Boys have more muscle tissue than girls; strength is similar until puberty, however.

- Genetics, personality, TV watching/inactivity, and poor diet have been implicated in obesity.

- Puberty involves the development of both primary and secondary sex characteristics.

- The heart and lungs continue to mature.

- Sensory systems are mature.

serous otitis media
middle ear infection

Although mild hearing losses usually do not create communication problems for the school-age child, 3–5% of children in this age group have hearing deficits that interfere with learning (Hathaway, 1991). Kindergarten and primary-age children with hearing losses have trouble learning phonics. The most common cause of hearing loss among kindergarten and first grade children is serous otitis media, a middle-ear infection in which the eustachian tubes become blocked and a serum-like fluid collects in the middle ear. Impaired hearing results from loss of movement of the otic bones—the hammer, anvil and stirrup—which transmit sound vibrations. Untreated ear infections can result in permanent hearing loss.

● Motor Development

During the school years, motor skills are refined and expanded. Through play and endless practice, children perfect six basic motor behaviors: running, jumping, sequencing foot movements, balancing, throwing, and catching. Some school-age children seem to be transformed into cartwheel machines or compulsive free-throw shooters as they concentrate on improving their skills. Richard Engelhorn (1988) found that improvement in motor skills keeps pace with maturation although practice affects the performance of some skills, such as learning to kick a ball. *Reaction time*, the speed with which a child reacts to a stimulus, also improves with age. For example, most school-age children find it easier to kick a ball than to catch it. Accuracy in kicking and throwing improve with maturity and practice.

Motor activity is vital for the development of muscle tone, balance, coordination, strength, and endurance, as well as for stimulating body functions and improving metabolism. Most school-age children need little encouragement to participate in physical activity. These children organize games, play on playground equipment, and are skilled in riding bikes, using skateboards, jumping rope, and skating.

■ Figure 11–6

Playing hop-scotch.

Competitive Sports

Throughout this period, children channel more and more energy into controlled, goal-directed activities such as sports and cooperative play. Also, children, especially boys, become more competitive and tend to form larger, more complex groups when they play. Each year 20 million American girls and boys 6–12 years of age participate in team sports (American Academy of Pediatrics, 1989). Little league baseball is the most popular, followed by football, soccer, and other programs such as swimming, track, and gymnastics. The benefits of team sport participation include social contact with peers, the exhilaration of self-improvement, learning the value of teamwork, the fun of the sport, and the importance of physical fitness. Further, children whose parents are distant or absent can often benefit from contact with supportive, caring coaches. And, if team sports involvement promotes regular exercise and a commitment to fitness, child athletes may have a better chance of avoiding or minimizing the health problems common to mature Americans—heart disease, obesity, and high blood pressure.

While children can be helped by team sports, they can be hurt by them, too. Common sports-related injuries range from bumps, scrapes, and bruises, to such catastrophic conditions as paralysis and head injuries. Although there is no completely safe sport, some activities involve greater risk of injury than others (Table 11–2). Statistically, the risk of injury is greatest in football and smallest in swimming and soccer. However, the safety of *all* organized sports is improved by the proper use of safety equipment such as padding and shin guards, preseason conditioning, the availability of someone trained to recognize serious injury, established first aid procedures, a preparticipation physical, well-maintained facilities, strict enforcement of safety rules, and adequate warm-up and stretching.

reaction time
the speed with which an individual can respond to a particular stimulus

■ **Table 11–2** *Risks and Injuries Associated with Six Major Team Sports*

SPORT	ASSOCIATED INJURIES	STRATEGIES TO PREVENT INJURY

1. Baseball (contact sport)
Comment: Most injuries are caused by the ball, which may be traveling as fast as 70 mph.
	Frequency of injury:
	(8–15 years)
	  Head 38%
	  Arms 39%
	  Trunk 4%
	  Legs 19%
	Proportion of injuries per position:
	  Pitcher 5%
	  Catcher 16%
	  1st Base 5%
	  2nd Base 6%
	  3rd Base 5%
	  Shortstop 5%
	  Outfield 14%
	  Runners 17%
	  Batters 22%
	  On-deck hitters 7%
	  Miscellaneous 3%
		Restrict number of innings child can pitch.
		Discourage prolonged practice and excessive throwing.
		Eliminate steel spikes (use soccer-type cleats instead).
		Eliminate sliding or use breakaway base.
		Eliminate on-deck circle and keep players in dugout.
		Use face protectors (attached to batting helmets).
		Conditioning:
		Lightweight training.
		Wind sprints (running full out for 10–15 yards; stop; repeat).
		Side-stepping exercises.
		Backward and forward running exercises.

2. Basketball (contact sport)	Lower extremity (especially ankle) because of prolonged running. Rate for injury for boys 16/100; girls are more often injured but are also in poorer condition at the beginning of the season.	Preseason conditioning. Warm-up and stretching exercises.
3. Football (collision sport) *Comment:* Football has a high injury rate compared with other contact and noncontact sports.	Two hundred and thirty thousand persons receive emergency room treatment each year for football related injuries. In eight years (1971–1979), there were 1129 serious football injuries (high school and college teams). Average injury rate: 15% The most serious injuries involve the head and neck.	Helmet and facemask protection. As per National Federation of State High School Associations, 1976: use of head blocking and face tackling prohibited. Mouthpieces. Soccer-type cleats. Pads (hip, kidney, shoulder, rib, tailbone, knee, and thigh). Preseason conditioning, warm-up, and stretching exercises.
4. Gymnastics (noncontact sport) *Comment:* Gymnastics has a high rate of injury compared with other noncontact sports, but the injuries tend to be less serious.	Trampolines are the major source of injury (especially head and neck trauma). Nineteen thousand persons receive emergency room treatment each year for trampoline injuries.	Avoid the trampoline. Proper conditioning, warm-up, and stretching exercises.

■ **Table 11–2** *(continued)*

SPORT	ASSOCIATED INJURIES	STRATEGIES TO PREVENT INJURY
5. Soccer (contact sport) *Comment:* Soccer has a low injury rate; it also doesn't favor any sex, body type, or age.	Type of injury: 39% blisters, skin abrasions 36% bruises 20% sprains, strains 5% fractures	Appropriate shoes. Proper conditioning, warm-up, and stretching exercises.
6. Swimming (noncontact sport) *Comment:* Swimming has a low injury rate. Children with handicaps can be involved (especially some asthmatic children). Better than tennis, basketball, and bicycling for developing stamina, muscle endurance, strength, and flexibility. An overweight child is not necessarily penalized in swimming.	Occasional muscle pulls, mild shoulder and knee injuries.	Proper conditioning warm-up, and stretching exercises.

Source: Galton, 1981.

Psychological damage may ensue for children who feel humiliated or degraded if pressured to participate. Such children literally have no way to win—if they play, they are blamed for their mistakes; if they quit, they are accused of giving up, being a disappointment, and letting others down. Children should have some say about whether or not they play sports and about what sport, if any, they participate in. Motives for participation change with age. Older children value having fun with friends on a team more than younger children, while younger children value winning and becoming popular on the team more than older athletes (H. P. Stern et al., 1990).

Some critics of organized sports for children cite the emphasis on competition and winning as a distinctly negative aspect. Too often, beating the opponent is stressed over learning sports fundamentals, involving everyone, and improving skills. Children learn that winning, setting records, and striving for first place are all that matter. Parents sometimes get carried away as much as coaches in competitive situations, often viewing their children's victories as their personal successes and their children's failures as indications of their own shortcomings. Sensitive parents can encourage striving, improvement, and a drive for excellence without creating an obsession for perfection.

Girls and Sports

How do 6–12 year old girls and boys "measure up" when it comes to sports involvement? In a comparison between the athletic performances

■ **Figure 11–7**

Trying out for Little League. If Jeffrey's catch is anything like his yell, he'll have a place on the team.

■ **Figure 11–8**

In the 90s, girls can lead the cheers **and** *score the goals.*

■ **Figure 11–9**

Let go of your stereotypes, here comes 6-year-old Sammy Markowitz, racer-to-be (all 35 pounds of him!) Determination comes in all shapes and sizes.

of young males and females, Wilmore (1982) came to the following conclusions:

1. *Body build:* 8–12 year old girls are about 2 years ahead of boys in physical, bone, and hormonal development.
2. *Forearm strength:* Mature men are 30–40% stronger than mature women, but sex differences in the 7–17 year old age group are much smaller. Boys do outdistance girls in throwing.
3. *Endurance:* Males and females are similar in their capacity for endurance.
4. *Flexibility:* Girls excel in tasks that require rhythm and agility.
5. *Running speed:* Boys and girls are equivalent until age 12.
6. *Injury rate:* The rate of injury is no greater for girls than for boys in badminton, basketball, cross-country, gymnastics, softball, swimming, tennis, track and field, and volleyball. Most injuries that do occur are minor. Sports with the highest rates of serious injuries for girls are basketball, field hockey, softball, and gymnastics.
7. *Implication of injuries:* The girl's bony pelvis provides excellent protection for the reproductive organs of the nonpregnant female. There is no evidence that trauma to the breasts increases the incidence of cancer later in life (Galton, 1981). In general, sports participation among school-age girls has no unfavorable influence on future pregnancy and childbirth.

Between the ages of 13 and 18, girls' participation in sports drops off markedly and physical ability declines. Do girls drop out just because they don't see themselves becoming more skilled? Perhaps. But other factors such as fear of injury, lack of motivation, interest in boys, and a more traditionally feminine sex role orientation may be more influential (Butcher, 1989). Society would do well to encourage physical fitness in young women as a hedge against later obesity, heart disease, osteoporosis, and certain types of joint diseases.

Sports Participation by the Physically Limited

Children with heart problems, high blood pressure, asthma, convulsive disorders, poor vision, or skeletal abnormalities need not automatically be excluded from sports participation. Generally, if conditions like diabetes or seizure activity are controlled and if the physician judges the child fit, no activity is necessarily barred. The American Academy of Pediatrics has recognized the need for mentally retarded children to engage in physical activities where competition is deemphasized and coordination and involvement are stressed. Wheelchair sports programs in track, basketball, and tennis are growing in size and popularity. Although most wheelchair sports involve adult participants, many have children's divisions.

Other Motor Skills

Most children can discriminate left from right on their own bodies by age 7 (Schwartz et al., 1990). The discrimination of left and right on others develops soon after that. However, the ability to imitate the movements of a person who is standing and facing them poses quite a challenge to the school-age child. This particular skill may not be acquired until adolescence.

Handedness is well established by age 6, and small-muscle ability and artistic skill improve steadily from then until 12. Thus, children make great strides in writing and drawing during the school years. With practice, school-age children can learn to play a musical instrument and to master a variety of handicraft skills such as ceramics, needlework, painting, and model building. In this regard, girls continue to have greater hand and finger dexterity than boys. They also perform fine motor tasks more quickly and accurately than boys.

In addition to dexterity, eye–hand coordination improves substantially during the school years. Two developments take place that facilitate intercepting a moving target. By age 8, the child is better able to plan a movement and by age 10, there is an increase in the child's ability to control the speed and direction of their grasp (Bairstow, 1989). Ac-

■ **Figure 11–10**

School age children, particularly girls, have the dexterity to master a complex instrument like the violin.

■ ● ▲ CONCEPT SUMMARY

Motor Development

- Children improve in running, jumping, sequencing foot movements, balancing, throwing, and catching.

- Children add skilled movements associated with sports, games, music, hobbies, etc.

- Reaction time improves.

- Eye-hand coordination improves.

- Most school-age children are physically active.

- Competitive sports participation is common during these years.

- Many girls drop out of sports after puberty.

- Left–right discrimination improves.

- Handedness is well established.

- Fine motor skills improve, with girls having greater dexterity than boys.

handedness
see hand preference
dexterity
see manual dexterity

tivities like hitting a volleyball, catching a softball, and even netting a butterfly will be much easier for the older school-age child than for the younger one.

Interestingly, despite the steady progress in fine motor and eye–hand skills, school-age children become noticeably more clumsy and less well coordinated during their growth spurt years. Children may be more distractible when they are growing; they are also unused to maneuvering larger feet and a taller frame. Daydreaming and other preoccupations may also lead to the appearance of clumsiness.

● Health and Safety

Typically, physical health is very good during the school years. As a group, school-age children are healthier than preschoolers, infants, or adolescents. Older children get sick less frequently than younger ones because their immunological resistance is stronger, the transmission of infection from one part of the internal system is less likely within their bodies, and particular structures, such as the middle ear, are more fully developed than before. Children who began receiving inoculations against childhood diseases as young infants are scheduled to complete the series between the ages of 4 and 6, just before they enter kindergarten. Between ages 10 and 12, children should receive a final rubella inoculation. Beyond that, adult tetanus and diphtheria shots are called for every 10 years.

immunological resistance
the body's ability to fight off disease due to natural or artificial immunity

Statistically, children between the ages of 5 and 12 have the lowest mortality and illness rates of any age group. The U.S. Census Bureau has reported that 95% of the individuals within this age group are in good or excellent physical health (U.S. Census Bureau, 1990). However, certain conditions—such as tooth decay, asthma, and appendicitis—are more likely now than in other developmental periods.

Tooth Decay

Tooth decay is the most common health problem of the school years. The ages of greatest vulnerability for cavities are 4 to 8 years for the primary teeth and 12 to 18 years for the permanent teeth. Dietary, health, and hereditary factors all seem to play a role in susceptibility to cavities. Children who eat a lot of sweets between meals, who are in poor health, or who have inherited structural defects in the surface of their teeth may have more cavities than those who limit sweets, are in good health, and inherit a dental structure that resists decay. Natural or refined sugars, like those in "gummy" candies, caramels, and raisins, pose the greatest threat since they adhere to the teeth for long periods of time, attracting decay-causing bacteria. Brushing regularly and especially after sugary snacks, regular checkups, and the use of fluoride and painted sealants on the teeth all reduce the likelihood of cavities in school-age children.

Asthma

Asthma is a chronic allergic reaction that causes mild-to-severe episodes of respiratory illness marked by wheezing, coughing, and shortness of breath. Most childhood asthmatics are males who have a history of frequent upper respiratory tract infections during early childhood (Avery, 1988). Asthma accounts for a large percentage of school absence due to chronic illness. Physical exercise and emotional stress can provoke an *asthma attack*. During the attack, the airways of the lungs become blocked, trapping air within the lungs and interfering with breathing. A severe asthma attack is a medical emergency.

Children with asthma and their families need to learn to use the prescribed drugs and to identify factors that precipitate asthma attacks. Rather than overcautiously limiting the child's normal life experiences, they can learn to maximize the child's participation in everyday activities while minimizing the likelihood of attack.

In Touch

ASTHMA AND ALLERGY
 FOUNDATION OF AMERICA
 (AAFA)
1717 Massachusetts Ave., NW
Suite 305
Washington, DC 20036

Appendicitis

Although rare in infancy, appendicitis—inflammation of the fingerlike projection of the large intestine called the appendix—is one of the most common illnesses requiring surgery in childhood. The first symptom of appendicitis is stomachache. The aching increases in intensity and localizes in the right portion of the lower abdomen. Nausea and vomiting are common signs; fever may or may not be present. Surgery to remove the appendix is required. Males are more likely to be affected than females; the incidence of appendicitis rises in the spring, since inflammation of the stomach and intestinal tract is higher during this time of the year (Whaley & Wong, 1988).

appendicitis
inflammation of the appendix

Appendicitis is caused by a bowel mass that develops just before the valve that separates the large and small intestines. As infection develops, the appendix becomes inflamed, and as the infection progresses, blood flow becomes restricted. The pressure within the appendix may cause it to burst, which could result in abdominal infection. A child whose appendix has ruptured is sicker and requires more time to recover, but the loss of the appendix itself is inconsequential since this organ has no known function.

Nutrition and Eating Habits

Although young school-age children are growing slowly and require proportionately fewer calories than infants or preschoolers, they are accumulating some nutrients to support the increased growth needs of

■ Figure 11–11

Some pretty magical things can happen when you're eating lunch with your friends in the school cafeteria.

the later school years and early adolescence. They also need good nutrition to sustain their generally active lifestyle and to provide the energy needed to learn in school. Thus, nutrition continues to be highly important throughout the school years, with growth and good health both resting on a balanced diet. When 5–11 year old children classify foods into groups, four dimensions appear: (a) sweets vs. nonsweets, (b) meal entrees, (c) drinks, and (d) breakfast foods (Michaela & Contento, 1984). These categories do not reflect much nutritional understanding. If the focus is on the four traditional food groups, the recommended daily diet for children includes:

3 servings of milk or milk products
2 servings of meat or meat substitutes (such as peanut butter)
4 servings of fruits and vegetables
4 or more servings of bread and cereals
   (Whitney and Cataldo, 1987)

For meats, fruits, and vegetables, a serving is loosely defined as 1 tablespoon (T) per year of age. Thus, at 8 years of age, one serving of any of these foods would be 8T or ½ cup.

In 1991 the nutritional emphasis moved away from fats, oils, and meat, and toward cereals, grains, vegetables, and fruits when the Pyramid Approach to Daily Food Choices was adopted by the U.S. Department of Agriculture. Even growing children who *need* fats and cholesterols should be careful not to overindulge. Children with elevated cholesterol levels should be pinpointed so they can be taught to safely lower their cholesterol intake.

cholesterol
fatty material present in the body tissues required for the metabolism of fat, and the production of vitamin D and certain hormones

A Closer Look

A Sound Mind in an Unsound Body

Children with chronic illnesses make up about 2% of the total school population. Illnesses like diabetes, muscular dystrophy, cancer, chronic asthma, and sickle cell anemia might take their toll on these children physically, but their minds, their judgments, their personalities, and their intellect are not directly touched by the disease.

We've come a long way from believing the myth that severe chronic illnesses leave indelible psychological scars on all their victims. Research also permits us to reject the notion that each illness affects children in a unique way, creating a "cancer personality" or a "diabetic personality." For the most part, chronically ill children are normal children who just have to operate under different circumstances.

Ralfie Diaz, age 16, has a rare and fatal spinal-muscular atrophy called Werdnig-Hoffman disease. It has wasted his body down to 50 pounds, leaving him almost literally skin and bones. "When I take a bath and look at myself naked," explains Ralfie, "I think 'God Jesus.' I'm disappointed when it comes to my body. But when it comes to my inside, my personality, my sense of humor, I'm proud of the way I am. I think I'm a nicer person. The girls always tell me, 'You're special. You're different than the other guys.' "

The mental health of the chronically ill child is influenced by several factors: the stability of the family, the previous psychological health of the child, the age at which the illness began, its visibility to other people, and the amount of time missed from school. Kids who aren't socially or emotionally behind their peers can adapt well to the hospital environment and well to the outside world.

Ralfie Diaz and his nurse practitioner, Sunni Levine.

Two levels of care are required by most children with severe illnesses. First, they need good, disease-specific medical care. Second, they and their families need help uncomplicating the special circumstances of day-to-day living. They need help finding child-care workers who understand the child's problems, finding teachers who can respond to the child's needs, dealing with the economic burden of treatment and care, and handling their own worries, guilt, depression, and anxiety. The earlier a child and her family are told about the diagnosis, the more likely they are to be well adjusted. Openness and directness in all matters associated with chronic illness seems to facilitate adaptation and coping.

Adapted from: Hurley, Dan (1987) "A Sound Mind in an Unsound Body." *Psychology Today*, 21 (8), 34–38, 42, 43.

Several factors may influence the child's eating habits as they enter school. First, weekday mornings are no longer leisurely—there are busses to catch and classes to attend. The new deadlines and time pressures might lead to relying on foods that are quick and easy to prepare, only some of which may have high nutritional value. Second, parents' buying behavior is often influenced by the child's food preferences. Parents have a tendency to buy the foods their child likes to avoid fussing at meal and snack times, rather than the foods they need. Third, parents and other role models may exhibit poor eating habits. Fourth, school-age children have more freedom from parental supervision. They can eat their lunch, throw it away, or sell it to the highest bidder. They also tend to have money to spend on treats. Although junk food tastes good and is filling, even fortified snacks can't take the place of nutritious meals. Overall, the child's eating habits and the quality of his diet continue to be influenced by the family's eating patterns.

Eating Disorders

low thyroid output
see hypothyroidism

Eating disorders like anorexia and bulimia are most common during adolescence but may manifest as early as the school years. Sometimes organic conditions such as anemia, hypoalbuminemia, and low thyroid function are responsible for weight loss (K. Wright et al., 1990). Biological factors like picky eating and digestive problems may make anorexia nervosa more likely, while pica (eating nonfood substances) and other self-control problems may predict later bulimia (Marchi & Cohen, 1990). In addition, fully 50% of anorexia and/or bulimia sufferers have had a history of sexual abuse (R. C. Hall et al., 1989). Finally, young women who engage in strenuous exercise like gymnastics, distance running, or ballet where the emphasis is on a thin physique may be more likely than other young women to try to adapt their bodies to the sport by self-starvation or gorging and purging (Garner et al., 1987).

Sleep

The amount of sleep required during the school years gradually diminishes with age. A normal, active, and healthy 6 year old will sleep an average of 11 or 12 hours a night; by age 12, 9 or 10 hours of nighttime sleep is usually sufficient. Regular naps are strongly resisted during this time; fortunately, they are generally unnecessary. If sleep problems do exist, they typically involve nightmares and bladder control (enuresis) (Fisher & McGuire, 1990).

Drug Use

Drug and alcohol use during the school years involves more than just sharing a cigarette out by the barn or finishing an abandoned bottle of beer. The findings of a 1990 survey of over 6,000 students in the Los Angeles area are both encouraging and depressing (Kollars, 1990). The good news is: The drug prevention ads have paid off. Drug experimentation among seventh graders has declined somewhat since 1988. The bad news is: A substantial number of kids are both *using and abusing drugs by the time they reach high school*. According to the LA area findings, one child in five has been drunk or high on drugs (such as beer, wine, cocaine, or marijuana) at least once by the time they reach the seventh grade, and fully half have used alcohol within the last 6 months. Three percent of all seventh graders are seriously involved with beer or marijuana, drinking or smoking at least once a week. Many of these students have serious problems at home (like abuse or neglect) and turn to drugs and alcohol to escape, elevate mood, and relieve pressure. Peer pressure and the disappearance of childhood from the life cycle (pushing kids toward more and more sophisticated behaviors) are also contributing factors (Norwood, 1985). Once school-age children start using substances on a regular basis, they develop both physical and psychological dependencies that make it difficult to "just say no" and risk later health complications (National Council on Alcoholism, 1988).

School-age children's drug involvement is not limited to experimentation and abuse. Some 6–12 year olds are also dealers. Enticed by the profits, drug dealing seems like a lucrative enterprise to the aspiring young yuppie or the child from the inner city (Barnes, 1990). Of course, the real bottom line for drug-dealing children is addiction, school dropout, incarceration, physical injury, and/or death.

Apparently, anti-drug ads and educational campaigns aimed at the nonuser can help keep children away from drugs. Students in some school districts learn "smoking is gross" by examining lifelike models of diseased tongues, ulcerated mouths, and cancer-infested lungs. Drug-

■ **Figure 11–12**

An anti-drug ad targeting the parents of school age children.

■ **Figure 11–13**

"Ooo, that's gross!" Children at a school Health Fair get a look at a model of a lung with cancer and emphysema from smoking. Such presentations give kids concrete reasons not to start smoking.

A Closer Look

Of Books and Bulletproof Vests

Bulletproof back-to-school clothing is the latest thing for big city children in the 90s. Some children in New York City, Chicago, and Los Angeles wear protective clothes to school as a deterrent to injury or death by random gunfire and drive-by shootings. The clothing, including vests, windbreakers, and jackets, is made of Kevlar, synthetic material 5 times stronger than steel and relatively lightweight. It is used in police bulletproof vests and as vehicle armor.

Protection bears a high price tag, however. The clothes range from $250 to $600. Also joining the back-to-school line are bulletproof clipboards and book bags. And when these children are ready to enter the business world, they can turn in their Kevlar vests for lined coats, business suits, briefcases, and umbrellas.

When one 8 year old child was asked about his Kevlar denim jacket, he said, "It feels only slightly

Two New York schoolchildren (ages 5 and 4) wear bullet-resistant clothing to class.

heavier than a normal jacket." "It feels good," he said, patting the hidden panels. "It feels like you have good protection and nobody even knows you have it on." Another satisfied customer.

Source: Associated Press, September 9, 1990. Adapted with permission.

free pledges are being taken by kindergarten students in some areas. Students also need to learn stress management strategies, to see that education, not drugs, offers the way out of poverty and family chaos, and to have access to effective treatment programs if they're already drug-involved.

Accidents

While it is true that school-age children are involved in fewer accidents than children in younger age groups, accidents (especially motor vehicle accidents) continue to be the leading cause of death and injury among 6–12 year olds, followed by drowning and burns. Normal, physically active school children sustain a high incidence of cuts, scrapes, and bruises. A fairly large proportion also incur fractures and sprains. The incidence of all injuries is significantly higher for boys than girls, and most injuries occur in or near the home or school. A government survey found bicycles, glass, swings, skateboards, all-terrain vehicles, and nails most frequently involved in accidents and injuries to 6–12 year olds (U.S. Bureau of the Census, 1991).

Some children appear to be accident prone, suffering significantly more accidental injuries than their peers. Accident proneness may be linked to personality, perceptual, and situational factors. Clumsy children process spatial information differently from kids who aren't clumsy. It's not that they can't see the chair in the hallway, for example (visual acuity isn't a problem), it's just that they *misperceive* the distance, size, and shape of the chair, making collision more likely (Lord & Hume, 1987). Visual-spatial therapy can help the child improve his judgments of objects.

visual-spatial therapy
a treatment approach involving training visual-search strategies

In addition, children who have many accidents may also be overactive, restless, and impulsive; hostile and resentful; or immature and attempting to compete beyond their capacity. It is also possible that the parents of accident-prone children offer less supervision, are emotionally distant in their relationships with children, or display a nonchalant attitude toward injury. Of course, some children simply live in more dangerous environments, but children who experience considerable stress due to change, disruption, or loss may be particularly susceptible to accidents. Children can be self-injurious because they are depressed, distraught, and unhappy. For them, injuries result from unsuccessful suicide attempts. Although most of us associate suicide in youngsters with adolescence, not with younger groups, a growing percentage of school-age children are making suicide attempts.

Child Molestation and Incest

Two of the most horrible and revolting crimes against children involve sexual assault. *Child molestation* involves sexual contact between a child under age 12 and someone outside the family. The person who commits *incest* is a relative by blood or marriage. Incest is more likely to actually involve intercourse than molestation, which usually involves touching and fondling. Compared to molestation, sexual abuse involving relatives is more likely to be repeated because of easy access—the child is a captive in a home where the incestor sees the child on a daily basis or even shares a room with her.

child molestation
a sexual assault on a child made by a nonrelative
incest
a sexual assault on a child made by a relative

Most of the victims are school-age girls and most perpetrators are males. Boys are also sexually abused but our society has a double standard regarding child sexual contact: It pities a girl who has been sexually assaulted by a male, but it judges a boy "lucky" to be involved with an older woman (Crooks & Baur, 1990). Western society also does not encourage boys to be vulnerable or powerless. This attitude mitigates against boys coming forward when they are actually victimized. Statistics indicate that 1 in every 9 or 10 boys and 1 in every 4 or 5 girls will be sexually victimized before age 18 (Crooks & Baur, 1990).

Even though these numbers are alarming, they grossly underestimate the frequency of sexual crimes against children in American society. Police and agency records reflect only *reported* crimes. Most of these crimes go unreported for several reasons. First, the child may not realize that anything "wrong" took place since they cannot distinguish between appropriate and inappropriate physical affection. The fact that the offender is often a friend or relative may add to the child's confusion. Second, because concealment is the key to child sexual abuse, the child is often sworn to secrecy and implicitly or explicitly threatened if she tells. Often the child voluntarily protects the incestors since she doesn't want to "get Uncle or Grandpa into trouble" and then be blamed for the uproar. Third, ironically, when children do complain about sexual improprieties, parents often assume the child is lying or making things up. Often, they don't want to believe such an attack happened, and if they know the perpetrator, they may have difficulty imagining that a respectable person could do such a thing. Most experts agree, however, that children almost never lie about sexual abuse, since it goes beyond anything they can imagine or have seen on TV (Gordon et al., 1990). And finally, if parents do acknowledge the assault, they may be reluctant to confront the offender or involve the authorities. In some of these cases, it seems that potential harm to the offender's reputation (as a church member, family man, professional) is a higher priority than the physical and emotional damage incurred by the child. Since 1981 professionals who come in contact with children (teachers, day-care worker, dentists, and so on) have been mandated by law to report any type of suspected abuse.

Incest and molestation are illegal in every state. Virtually every society on earth abhors incest (the "incest taboo"). Seen in this light, who commits these crimes and why do they continue? People who molest children are often lonely, shy, and feel socially inadequate and inferior. For an adult who feels uncomfortable in an adult world, children offer a safer, less threatening opportunity for a relationship. People who commit incest, on the other hand, are reasonably normal, well-adjusted individuals whose *attitude* about child sexual contact justifies their behavior to their own minds. They are generally aloof and emotionally distant from the child (Trotter, 1985). And although they will often apologize to the child for anything the child thinks has happened, many incestors *truly feel they have done nothing wrong.* Guilty siblings say they were just having fun or were curious. Guilty parents or other authoritative adults feel they have the right to teach their child about sex in any manner they choose ("It's better for her to have it with me than with some rough young punk in the back seat of a car"). In their eyes, they were just being a good parent and often contend that the child enjoyed it, too, otherwise they would have reported it.

Other factions of our society support this attitude by trivializing the impact of incest on children. Kiddie porn groups encourage parents and

contempt of court
the charge made by a judge that an individual is not cooperating with the instructions of the court

A Closer Look

Protecting Children from the People Who "Love" Them

All parents fear something unspeakable happening to their children. But when it does, at least one can take comfort that the legal system will settle the score, right? Not necessarily. First, struck by tragedy and then let down by the courts, the following people are taking steps to make sure disaster doesn't strike twice for others.

—

When Elizabeth Morgan and Eric Foretich married, theirs seemed like the perfect union: two physicians with compatible interests fueled by a lifetime commitment to each other.

But over time, strife and discord replaced happiness and compatibility and divorce proceedings ensued. Although Morgan accused her husband of sexually assaulting their daughter Hilary from about the age of 2 on, the divorce judge dismissed her claims and granted the couple joint custody of Hilary. To protest that decision, Morgan refused to divulge Hilary's whereabouts so as to prevent Foretich from having contact with her daughter and carrying out the joint custody accord. The judge then ordered Elizabeth Morgan jailed for civil contempt of court until she would specify her daughter's location. Determined to keep her daughter hidden to stop the alleged incest, Morgan spent *more than 2 years (759 days)* in incarceration before the authorities intervened on her behalf. Proving that she would not relent until her daughter's custody dispute was resolved to her satisfaction, an appeals court determined that her confinement was designed to coerce her, not to punish her, and that she must be freed so she could receive a trial and due process of law. In September of 1989 Congress passed a bill that was

signed into law that would limit contempt of court confinements to 1 year.

Even with Morgan's release, the case was far from over. Morgan vowed to leave Hilary in hiding as long as she remained unsatisfied that the law will protect Hilary from further abuse. Upon retrial, Elizabeth Morgan was granted sole custody of her daughter; Foretich did not contest the decision.

—

Rosealyce Thayer of Springfield, Vermont, reports that the authorities didn't act quickly enough to save the life of her 11 year old daughter Caty.

In 1983 while Caty and friend Rachel Zeitz were out walking, a stranger forced Caty into his car at gunpoint. Terrified, Rachel darted into a neighbor's house to report the kidnapping. Minutes later Rosealyce arrived at the police station and asked police for a land and air search for the car (Rachel had given an excellent description of the vehicle). No search was initiated. When the Thayers began searching on their own, the chief of police (who has since left Springfield), stationed a police cruiser to block their driveway and another officer in their home to prevent them from placing calls.

From Rachel's description, the police *knew* who the kidnapper was. The next morning they arrested Gary Schaefer, 31, a mechanic. Then they found Caty's body just 1 1/2 miles from the abduction site. Schaefer confessed to Caty's rape and murder and to the rape and murder of a 12 year old Springfield girl 9 years earlier. He is serving 30 years to life.

Rosealyce Thayer has channelled her rage into legislative action. She testified before the Vermont legislature for a bill requiring immediate police

(continued on next page)

(continued from previous page)

searches when a child is reported missing. It became the law. She is now working with the National Victim's Center to pass other pieces of legislation in other states.

—

Denice Reich of Denver felt confident that she had hired the perfect nanny in Carolyn Lewis to care for her 9 month old son, Andrew. But late one night, Denice and her husband were jolted awake when Lewis screamed, "The baby's dead!"

Andrew was taken to the hospital, where he experienced seizures, a racing heart, and lapses of unconsciousness. The toxicology report indicated a near-lethal dose of Elavil, an adult antidepressant. It was thought that Lewis had given the drug to the infant to prevent him from crying.

When Andrew finally stabilized, it was clear that he just wasn't the same child he was before the drug overdose.

The police agreed that all the evidence pointed to the nanny, but privacy laws prevented the police from checking her medical history, and the district attorney said there wasn't enough evidence to prosecute. Other authorities told Denice that "this was an isolated incident" and that "she was a hysterical mother."

Finally, other women whose children had been injured by caregivers came forward. Lewis pleaded guilty to felonious assault and misdemeanor child abuse, avoided trial, and was given 2 years deferred judgment—after which time the case would be reevaluated. Denice Reich and her colleagues went on to found Public Awareness About Child Care (PAACC), an organization that collects information about children killed or hurt by careproviders and pushes for legislation to protect children and their families from such abuses.

"The law is still full of ironies," says Denice. "We can trace a stolen car but not a child abuser."

Some excerpts from *Parade* magazine, March 18, 1990. Reprinted with permission from *Parade*, © 1990.

toxicology
the branch of medical science that deals with the effects of poisons and the treatment of poisoning

In Touch

PARENTS UNITED
7120 Franklin Ave.
Los Angeles, CA 90046
1–800–421–0353
Self-help for sexually abusing parents and families

children to share their sexuality to strengthen the family unit ("The family that *plays* together stays together"). A regular feature of Hustler magazine is the cartoon "Chester the Molester," a character who enjoys sex with children. Even our elected officials make cavalier and completely ill-informed statements on why there is no need to permit abortion when pregnancy results from incest. Louisiana State Representative Carl Gunter explains, "The way we get thoroughbred horses is through inbreeding. With incest, you could get super-smart kids." (*The Progressive,* September, 1990, p. 11). Not even a dose of old-fashioned religion can reverse these attitudes since most sexual offenders are already conservative, very moralistic, and devoutly religious (Stark, 1984). (See the accompanying Issue: Protecting Children from the People Who "Love" Them.)

It is increasingly evident that sexual victimization is extremely traumatic for children and has long-term consequences that can permanently alter the course of the child's life. Many female victims have difficulty trusting others, forming intimate relationships, and within relationships, feeling comfortable with their sexuality and their partner's needs (Harter et al., 1988). Many of these victims cannot tell the difference between being loved and being raped. Other difficulties for both males and females include low self-esteem, feelings of guilt and shame, and more depression, anger, drug and alcohol use, sleep disturbance,

■ **Table 11-3** *How to Prevent a Child from Being Molested (or Worse)*

TEACH YOUR CHILDREN:

1. No one has the right to touch the private parts of their body or make them feel uncomfortable. They have the right to say "no."
2. How to deal with bribes and threats, as well as the possibility of physical force.
3. About sexual assault when you are teaching them about safety. Provide specific definitions and examples of sexual assault.
4. To tell you if anyone asks to take or has taken their picture.
5. Adults do not come to children for help. Adults ask adults for help.
6. To never go near a car with someone in it. To never get into anyone's car without your permission.
7. To trust the arrangements you made for pick-up and delivery; if someone approaches them about an apparent "change in plans," tell your child to wait to hear directly from you first before going with someone else.
8. To tell you if anyone has made any unusual requests of them.
9. To tell you if someone has given them gifts of money.
10. To never go into someone's home without your permission.
11. When they are away from home, scared, or uncomfortable, they have the right to use the telephone without asking anyone's permission.
12. To tell you of any situation where someone has made a statement about sex or love to them.
13. To never answer the door when they are alone.
14. To never admit to anyone over the telephone that they are home alone. (They can answer truthfully that "My mother/father can't come to the phone right now.")
15. That you will always believe them about molestation/incest and will protect them from further harm (NOTE: Children almost never lie about sexual assault because nothing that they have learned about compares to that experience).

PARENTS/CAREGIVERS:

1. Back up your child's right to say "no."
2. *Report all instances of molestation/incest.* Recognize that offenders do not change without intervention.
3. Encourage communicating by taking what your child says seriously.

4. Eliminate secrets between yourself and your child.
5. Model self-protective and limit-setting behavior for your child.
6. Question any money or gifts your child brings home—you want to know the source and the purpose, you don't just want to take something away from the child.
7. Know who your child spends time with and what activities they engage in.
8. Be watchful about any bond that might develop between your child and an adult in her life (including teachers, clergymen, coaches, friends, etc.).
9. Avoid letting your child go on overnight trips where just one adult is in charge.
10. Never leave your child unattended, day or night.
11. Tell your child that you will not schedule any repairs or deliveries when you are not there; if a repair person, delivery person, or even a police officer comes to the door, answer questions with the door closed. Never open the door and let them inside.
12. Never leave your child unattended in the car. Molestation/abduction only takes a minute.
13. Be involved in all your child's sports and activities.
14. Be watchful of coaches/leaders who do not have a child of their own in the same group.
15. Listen to your child when they tell you they don't want to go with someone. There may be a reason why.
16. Never make your child submit to physical contact (hugs, kisses, sitting on people's laps) if they do not want to. Children have the right to say "no" even if that person is the parent's parent, favorite aunt, etc.
17. No one should want to be with your child more than you. When someone is showing your child too much attention, ask yourself why.
18. Be sensitive to any changes in your child's behavior or attitudes.
19. Never belittle any fear or concern your child may express to you.
20. Never compromise any private or confidential matter your child may share with you unless someone's life is in imminent danger.

and suicide than the general population (Stark, 1984; Briere et al., 1988). Some individuals become sexual abusers themselves in an attempt to hurt others the way they've been hurt. Fully 50% of all victims end up with serious psychological problems and many females end up being victimized *again* in adulthood (Lipsitt, 1988a).

■ Figure 11–14

Reading material to help prevent child abuse and child sexual assault.

In Touch

MARVEL COMICS GROUP
Spider Man and Power Pack
P.O. Box 94283
Chicago, IL 60690

---

posttraumatic stress disorder (PTSD)
a condition characterized by periodic episodes of anxiety, depression, or panic provoked by reminders of past traumas

Although there is no panacea for child sexual abuse, children can be taught what to look for and which touches are "good" and "bad" (Table 11–3). The National Committee for the Prevention of Child Abuse has issued a comic book in which Spider Man and Power Pack communicate important messages to kids that might be ignored from other sources. Endorsed by the National Education Association, the comic is available for a tax-free donation of $1.

Incest-molestation survivors benefit from group and individual therapy designed to help them resolve emotional issues associated with the trauma. Removing the perpetrator from the home or obtaining a restraining order can help the child feel safer until family therapy can be initiated (Wodarski & Johnson, 1988). Children also need the daily love and support that comes from others who truly believe in them and value them as people. If children continue to feel threatened or unsafe, they will often run away from home and take their chances on the streets.

Reactions to Trauma: Posttraumatic Stress Disorder (PTSD)

Children generally disclose their efforts to cope with stress by changing their behavior: acting out, withdrawing, becoming depressed, or rebelling. Delayed reactions to stress, called *posttraumatic stress disorder (PTSD)*, were first identified in the Viet Nam era war veterans. However, PTSD seems to result from a variety of circumstances (sexual abuse/assault, surviving a catastrophic accident, witnessing injury and death) and has been identified in children (Yule & Williams, 1990).

When PTSD manifests itself, the child acts as though the trauma were recurring. The *Diagnostic and Statistical Manual of Mental Disorders*, 3rd edition, revised (DSM-III-R) associates insomnia, hypervigilance, nightmares, exaggerated startle, and generalized agitation with PTSD (Famularo et al., 1990). Early detection speeds treatment (Pynoos & Nader, 1988).

■●▲   CONCEPT SUMMARY

Promoting and Maintaining Development

● *Immunizations*
  – These should be completed by age 10 or 12 for those who began inoculations as infants.

- *Illness*
  - School age children are rarely sick.
  - Tooth decay is the most common health related problem.
  - Asthma and appendicitis are more common now than in other age periods.

- *Nutrition*
  - School-age children have a poor understanding of nutrition and require guidance for nutritious snack and meal selection.
  - Good nutrition sets the stage for rapid growth during puberty.
  - A minority of school age children (mostly girls) will develop eating disorders.

- *Sleep*
  - 9–12 hours of nighttime sleep are required by most school age children.
  - Nightmares and enuresis are the most common sleep problems.

- *Drug use*
  - A substantial number of children are using or abusing drugs by the time they enter high school.
  - Drug experimentation has declined in recent years.
  - Alcohol, cigarettes, marijuana, and cocaine tend to be the drugs of choice.
  - Drug use can lead to health complications and drug dependence, as well as school dropout, incarceration, and injury/death.

- *Accidents*
  - The accident rate is lower for school-age children than for any other age group.
  - Motor vehicle accidents are still the most common cause of accidental death and injury.
  - Boys are still more likely to be involved in accidents than girls.
  - Home and school are the most common sites of accidents.

- *Sexual assault*
  - School-age children (particularly girls) are at highest risk for molestation/incest.
  - Victimization can permanently alter the course of the child's life (e.g., PTSD can develop).
  - Perpetrators may acknowledge involvement but often deny wrongdoing.
  - Boys who are victimized are discouraged from reporting sexual assault and are often assumed to require no treatment.

- *Posttraumatic stress disorder (PTSD)*
  - This syndrome involves a delayed and often personally debilitating reaction to extreme trauma.

● Handicapping Conditions

Attention-Deficit Disorder (with or without Hyperactivity)

attention deficit hyperactivity disorder (ADHD)
a disorder of childhood involving inattention, distractibility, impulsiveness, and hyperactivity

Attention-deficit hyperactivity disorder, or ADHD, is the term used to describe children whose ability to learn and profit from new experience is impaired by their distractability, impulsiveness, lack of concentration, restlessness, inappropriate talking, and lack of regard for dangerous consequences (DSM-III-R, 1987). ADHD is diagnosed before the age of 7 (Schworm & Birnbaum, 1989).

Different groups of people give different estimates of the incidence of ADHD. Professional psychologists estimate that 5–10% of the school-age population is attention-deficit disordered; teachers give slightly higher estimates, but parents' estimates were highest of all. Half of all parents of school-age boys were very concerned about their child's activity level (Lord, 1982). Even though boys are more likely than girls to be labeled hyperactive, the behavior of ADHD girls is strikingly similar to that of ADHD boys (W. F. Horn et al., 1989). Whatever the diagnostic source, attention-deficit hyperactive disorder is the most common behavioral disorder seen by child psychiatrists in the United States.

Many different factors seem implicated in causing hyperactivity. There may be a genetic foundation to ADHD since hyperactivity runs in families (J. A. Johnson, 1981). Trauma during delivery, prenatal alcohol and cocaine exposure, lead poisoning, radiation exposure, family and school stress, overreaction to a rigid, inflexible environment, neurotransmitter deficiencies, low levels of arousal (overcome by high levels of activity), vitamin B deficiency, food allergies, and food additives (preservatives, colorants) are all possibilities, but none accounts for the majority of cases (Hadley, 1984). Brain damage and abnormal EEGs are *not* necessarily associated with attention-deficit disorder. Also, the diets of ADHD boys are *not* significantly different from the diets of non-ADHD boys (B. J. Kaplan et al., 1989). Regardless of diet (high sugar intake or not), hyperactive children have elevated blood sugar levels (Connors, 1987).

behavior modification
see modification

Because the causes of attention-deficit hyperactive disorder are varied, the treatment must be varied, too. Dietary changes, like those suggested by Dr. Ben Feingold (1975), behavior modification programs, drug treatment, and play therapy each help some ADHD children but not others. Drug treatment needs to be carefully considered because of its potentially serious side-effects, such as decreased alertness, speech impairment, insomnia, loss of appetite, temporary growth suppression, and drug dependence (Sprague & Ullman, 1981). A priority in the treatment of ADHD is providing help to parents in managing their hyperactive children. Parents of affected children may be critical, punitive, and disapproving. Techniques have been developed for improving parent–child relationships, helping ADHD children manage their behavior around their peers, and improving self-esteem (Barkley, 1989).

Learning Disabilities

Learning disabilities also tend to be diagnosed during the school years because they, like attention-deficit hyperactive disorder, have an adverse effect on educational achievement. About 5% of all children with apparently normal vision, hearing, motor skills, emotional development, intelligence, and motivation have difficulty learning particular school skills like reading, writing, and calculating (Grant & Snyder, 1984). Their senses transmit the information properly but learning disabled children have trouble *processing* the material their brain receives (Hammill, 1990). For example, a child may be able to pronounce the word *bag* but doesn't know what the word means when he reads it. For some children, the word *bag* looks like another word (*grab*, for example) or like a nonsense syllable (*arg, bgr,* for example). Even if children can recognize all the letters of the alphabet by sight, they may not be able to spell words, sound them out, or name the individual letters that comprise a word *even when they are looking directly at them.* Numbers and number relationships are processed in much the same way as words by the child with a learning disability. Despite a widespread belief to the contrary, girls are just as likely as boys to have the reading impairment dyslexia (Shaywitz et al., 1990).

What causes these specific perceptual disorders? Most professionals suspect some type of brain dysfunction that interferes with the synthesis and integration of perceptual information or with the child's ability to concentrate, or both (Gladstone et al., 1989). The particular cause of the dysfunction is unknown at this time, but birth trauma, low birth weight, malnutrition in infancy, and certain genetic factors (learning disabilities run in families) are suspected (DeFries et al., 1987; Farnham-Diggory, 1978). Chapter 12 will address the school-based strategies for helping learning disabled children compensate for their learning differences and cope with the self-consciousness they feel in the classroom.

In Touch

ASSOCIATION FOR CHILDREN
AND ADULTS WITH LEARNING
DISABILITIES
4156 Library Road
Pittsburgh, PA 15234

Prenatal Drug Exposure

Although their behaviors aren't new, their label is: drug babies. About 10–15% of babies born in the United States in 1989 were exposed to drugs or alcohol while still in their mother's womb (Associated Press, November 25, 1990). That number has been steadily increasing since the beginning of the crack epidemic in 1984 and has produced wave after wave of prenatally exposed children in the school systems.

Some of these children are mentally retarded. Many more of them have normal intelligence but engage in behaviors that interfere with learning. Irritability, unwillingness to make eye contact, inability to bond with parents or teachers, chronic forgetfulness, clumsiness, a dislike of touching, and poor language development are common symptoms of drug-exposed children. These children may play next to other classmates but seldom interact. They don't like distractions, such as school bells, too many bright lights or colors, or people coming in and out of the classroom. They prefer predictable routines and have trouble making the transition from one activity to another. Some of these same behaviors are displayed by children born to mothers who had little or no prenatal care or who experience poor nutrition, neglect, or poverty.

Special day classes, tutors, and coping skills can help children prenatally exposed to drugs experience more school success and less frustration.

■ **Table 11–4** *Summary of Growth and Development During School-Age Years*

AGE	PHYSICAL	COGNITIVE	SOCIAL/EMOTIONAL
6	Slower growth rate Weight range is between 35.5 and 58 lbs. Height ranges between 42 and 48 inches Active and busy Improved eye-hand coordination Improved manual dexterity Uses hands as tools	Identifies common objects by their use Likes to draw and color Can cut, fold and paste paper Can sew crudely if the needle is threaded Can make simple clay figures Likes playing table games and simple card games Can evaluate objects in a collection (i.e., nicest; most colorful, etc.) Uses more descriptive phrases in speech Knows right and left on own body Can orient to time of day (knows its morning, afternoon, etc.) Can carry out a command that involves three separate activities Tests their own skills Is usually in the first grade	Takes a bath without supervision Can perform bedtime activities alone May have temper tantrums Enjoys peers Sometimes takes things that aren't theirs Has difficulty admitting misdeeds Likes to do things "their way" Frequent imitation of adult models May be giggly May be boastful May cheat to win More independent
7	Weight ranges between 39 and 66.5 lbs. Height ranges between 44 and 51 inches Average height increase per year: 2 inches Can brush and comb hair acceptably without help Can use a knife to cut meat; still needs some help More caution with new activities Practices activities to improve skills Less fidgety	Repeats three numbers backwards Can copy a diamond Can read a clock correctly to the nearest quarter hour Reads mechanically; may skip words Notices parts missing from pictures Is usually in the 2nd grade	Does not require constant companionship—can spend productive time alone Engages in same-sex play almost exclusively Plays easily in groups Likes to have a choice when helping Less inclined to steal Less resistant and stubborn

■ **Table 11–4**   *(continued)*

AGE	PHYSICAL	COGNITIVE	SOCIAL/EMOTIONAL
8–9	Weight ranges between 43 and 87 lbs. Height ranges between 46–56 inches Height increase remains at about 2 inches per year Movement is graceful, fluid Motor task performance is smoother, quicker Can use household tools like a hammer or screwdriver Always on the go: jumps, chases, climbs Hard to quiet down after recess Dresses self completely	Can count backwards from 20 to 1 Can repeat the days of the week; months of the year in order Knows the date Can give change for a quarter Exercises good judgment when buying objects (doesn't always buy "junk") More time conscious; concerned about getting to places on time Describes objects in detail; doesn't just focus on use Is a more proficient reader; begins to enjoy reading for its own sake Attends the 3rd or 4th grade	More self critical Enjoys school Likes to give the "right answer" Afraid of school failure Feels shame if they do something wrong Can perform household chores (dusting, taking out trash, etc.) Can take care of their own needs at the table Likes to compete when playing games Easier to get along with at home (more cooperative; better behaved) Can be dramatic and entertaining Responds well to reward Plays mostly with own sex but is beginning to mix Indicates preference in friends, groups Interested in boy-girl relationships but won't admit it
10–12	Slower growth in height, more rapid in weight Weight ranges from 54 to 128 lbs. Height ranges from 50–64 inches Posture more nearly adult-like Physical changes that accompany puberty may begin to appear Girls' bodies become less angular and more rounded Child may become obese in this period Full set of teeth present (except wisdom teeth) Can produce some simple drawings or paintings	Reads for information and enjoyment Writes short stories Writes letter to friends, relatives Does easy repair work Makes useful articles Is in grade 5, 6, or 7	Uses the telephone, mostly for practical purposes Enjoys conversation Responds to magazine, TV or other advertising by mailing in coupons, calling numbers Friend-focused Chooses friends more selectively Enjoys friends—talks about them constantly Beginning interest in boy-girl relationships Enjoys the family; wants to please mom and dad More diplomatic More affectionate More responsible Can care for others left in their charge Can wash and dry own hair (may need to be reminded to do so) Can take responsibility for raising pets Can be left alone for an hour or two Can do some cooking and some sewing

**TOWARD
EFFECTIVE
PARENTING**

Anticipatory Coping:
Make Every Minute Count

The death of a child is one of the most tragic events that can strike a family. Only the death of a parent or spouse carries equal grief. Sometimes children are ill and death is anticipated; sometimes it strikes suddenly and without warning. In either case, it is a devastating blow in terms of loss of hopes, future relationships, and experiences that have not yet been shared. Parents who have lost a child share many commonalities (Knapp, 1987). They all want desperately to remember the child, they need to talk about their loss, and they try to find a logical reason for the death.

Parents who have lost children, especially through sudden death, often feel guilty and remorseful about their child's experiences and their time together. "I was always promising to take her to the game and I never did." "I didn't even say, 'I love you' that last day. I wonder if they knew how much I cared." These statements are tragic reminders that one needs a sense of closure to accept the finality of the situation. Books need to be finished; ends need to be tied.

Rather than spending time longing for the things we cannot have with those who are no longer here, make the most of *each moment* you share with your living child. Try to organize your life so there will be no regrets and no loose ends.

1. *Remember that humans are mortals; unfortunately that includes children, too.* If you have a sense that time together is uncertain, you will structure your life and your priorities differently. Live each day to its fullest. Really allow yourself to enjoy your children and to get to know them as people. Be grateful for each minute of time you spend together, but be balanced in your approach rather than indulgent, smothering, and emotional.

2. *Focus on the positive.* Try to see things in a positive light; practice looking at the glass as half full rather than half empty; try to make lemonade out of life's lemons. You'll learn some valuable lessons in the process *and* you'll be a lot happier.

3. *Take care of your baggage from the past.* In order to live a psychologically unconstrained life, you will need to resolve conflicts from the past. Unburden yourself by confronting things that have been troubling you and work them through. Substance abuse, dysfunctional childhoods, unloving parents, low self-esteem, and sexual victimization are just a few examples of the emotional baggage we carry. A good therapist can greatly facilitate the process.

4. *Try to resolve difficulties and challenges quickly and effectively.* Everyone has disagreements and shares some bad feeling from time to time. Carrying grudges and hanging on to problems stand in the way of a positive, productive focus. In the scheme of things, is the issue at question really *that* important that you stop talking to someone you love, disown a child or a parent, or otherwise take some rash step that may be irrevocable? Perhaps, but maybe not. *Communication* is the key to all relationships, personal and professional. *Talk* about what's bothering you; share feelings and then you will be able to work out a compromise that places things back on even ground.

5. *Learn to give and accept love.* As funny as this sounds, some people have never learned how to give and take in this area. Practice giving compliments and praise rather than criticism and condemnation. Look for the good. You'd be surprised how good it feels both to you and the recipient. Learn to accept praise and compliments from others—just say "Thank you" instead of stammering and trying to undo the statement. Furthermore, people don't know you care until you *tell* them. Practice saying, "I love you." If you can't use the "L" word, use other phrases like "You're really special to me," "I don't know what I'd do without you," and "You mean so much to me."

● Chapter Summary

● The school years extend from about age 6 to about age 12. During this time, the growth rate is slow and steady and motor skills are perfected. Developments in cognition and social skills are the most dramatic.

● Poverty, illness, and abuse have the most significant impact on growth. Most school-age children look taller, thinner, and leggier than they did as preschoolers since the skeletal system grows most rapidly during this time. Twenty-five percent of all school children are obese.

● Until age 9, boys and girls are of comparable size and strength. Girls begin to experience accelerated growth between age 10 and 12 and boys between age 12 and 14 as they ready for puberty. The average American girl menstruates by the time she is 12.5 years old.

● All the child's sensory systems are functioning at adult levels. Ear infections are rare since the eustachian tube is more vertical now, but the residual effects of hearing loss may affect learning.

● Children refine their gross and fine motor skills and eye-hand coordination by learning games, playing sports, developing artistic talents, learning to play a musical instrument, or taking on hobbies. Handedness is well established by age 6.

● School-age children have the lowest illness and mortality rates of any age group. Tooth decay is the most common health problem.

● Good nutrition continues to be important to support development. Since school-age children are more independent, they may eat less well and less predictably than preschoolers. Eating disorders may manifest as early as the school years, particularly in females who feel the need to remain thin or who are serious athletes.

● Drugs and alcohol are not unknown to school-age children. Children from dysfunctional families are at particular risk. Drug experimentation has declined somewhat since 1988, however.

● While school-age children are involved in fewer accidents than other age groups, motor vehicle accidents continue to be the leading cause of death and injury. Accident proneness, impulsiveness, hostility, and poor judgment contribute to the accident rate.

- School-age children are more likely targets for sexual assault (molestation or incest) than other age groups. More girls than boys tend to be victims; more males than females tend to be perpetrators. While most of these crimes go unreported and most of the victims untreated, the incidence of reporting and receiving treatment has been increasing steadily.
- Posttraumatic stress disorder (PTSD) has recently been recognized as occurring in children.
- Attention-deficit hyperactive disorder (ADHD) and learning disabilities may prevent children from having as much control as they would like over their behavior or its outcomes. More boys than girls experience both conditions and both conditions appear to have genetic and environmental components.

● Observational Exercise

Tasks involving the use of mirrors make interesting tests of the school-age child's eye/hand coordination and left/right discrimination.

Procedure: Test a 6 year old and a 10 year old of the same sex, one at a time, and record their performances.

1. Have the child stand in front of a full-length mirror and touch the reflection to answer the following questions:

	6 year old			*10 year old*		
	Yes	*No*	*Time Elapsed*	*Yes*	*No*	*Time Elapsed*

   a. Point to your nose.
   b. Point to your left leg.
   c. Point to your right ear.
   d. Use your left hand to point to your left shoulder.
   e. Use your right hand to point to your left knee.
   f. Tie a bow around your neck using only the mirror image to guide you.

2. Seat the child at a table that has a mirror propped up perpendicular to the writing surface. Place a piece of paper in front of the mirror and instruct the child to:

   a. Write the number 18 so it will appear correctly in the mirror's reflection.
   b. Print the word *BOOM* so it will appear correctly in the mirror's reflection.
   c. Print his or her name so it will appear correctly in the mirror's reflection.
   d. Draw a circle while looking only at the mirror image.
   e. Draw a triangle while looking only at the mirror image.
   f. Draw a star while looking only at the mirror image.

g. Trace the number 5 while looking only at the mirror image.

h. Trace the number 8 while looking only at the mirror image.

i. Trace the patch of a simple maze while looking only at the mirror image.

To compare the performance of the two children, note the amount of time it takes each to complete each task and if the task can be solved. Also, note the number of errors, retracings, false starts, and times when the pencil goes out of the line or maze.

3. Describe the similarities and differences in the two children's performances.

● Recommended Readings

Collipp, P. J. (Ed.). (1980). *Childhood obesity* (2nd ed.). Littleton, MA: PSG Publishing.

Epstein, L., & Squires, M. S. (1988). *The stoplight diet for children: An eight-week program for parents and children.* Boston: Little, Brown.

Pomeranz, V. E., & Schultz, D. (1984). *The mothers' and fathers' medical encyclopedia* (rev. ed.) New York: New American Library.

Saunders, A., & Remsberg, B. (1986). *The stress-proof child.* New York: The New American Library.

Turecki, S., & Tonner, L. (1985). *The difficult child.* New York: Bantam Books. (Discusses hyperactivity.)

Cognitive Development During the School Years

● Cognitive Development

Between the ages of 5 and 7, children's thought processes change dramatically. During this time, the confusions, distractions, and inconsistencies of preoperational thought are gradually replaced by a rudimentary form of logic. Many cultures have noticed that the 6–7 year old is a more competent thinker and assign them new responsibilities. In the Middle Ages, a child was assigned adult status at age 7 when he was considered to be capable of being without his mother or his nanny (Aries, 1962). The Catholic Church has long maintained that a 7 year old can tell the differences between right and wrong and can begin the ritual of confession. Western scientists have labelled this change the *5-to-7 shift* since it marks a transition from the use of intuition and conjecture to reliance on a more logical problem solving style (Kenny, 1983).

Impressive changes in brain development set the stage of the 5-to-7 shift (Fishbein, 1984). Beginning around age 2, cross-modal zones are established to connect parts of the brain with each other. These interconnections tie together different sensory events or modalities. For example, a child might associate an orange with its colorful skin. Later on, associations will also be formed between the orange and its distinctive smell, sweet flavor, the arrangement of letters in its spelling, and the sound of the spoken word. Between the ages of 5 and 6, the major development of all cross-modal zones has been completed (Fishbein, 1984). It's not surprising, then, that the 7–8 year old begins to think more like an adult than a child. Throughout development a reciprocal relationship forms between cognition and brain maturation: Brain maturation may support cognitive changes but cognitive activity can also accelerate brain activity.

5-to-7 shift
the time during which the child makes a cognitive transition from the preoperational stage to the stage of concrete operations (Piaget's terms) or from intuition to logic

cross-modal zones
nerve networks that permit information flow from one part of the brain to another

521

Piaget's Theory of Cognitive Development: Concrete Operations

For Inhelder and Piaget (1964) the hallmark of cognitive development during the stage of concrete operations is the ability to think logically about concrete, or real-world, events and experiences. Concrete logic becomes possible when the child can understand the *operations,* or set of powerful rules, that can transform information from one form to another. Such rules include mathematical operations (identity, addition, division, and so on) and relations among categories (e.g., class inclusion, seriation). With these rules at his disposal, the school-age child can actively control his thought processes, shifting his mind into reverse to retrace mental steps or shifting away from personal experiences and immediate perceptions toward other salient variables.

Decentration

One of the most significant operations mastered by the school age child is *decentration.* Children in the concrete operations stage can decenter their thinking, taking into account several aspects of an object or event at the same time. They recognize that there may be more than one way of arriving at a conclusion and they are able to delay action until they have evaluated alternative responses. They can now solve conservation tasks designed to measure the child's ability to understand apparent transformations. Concrete operational children are no longer fooled into thinking, for instance, that a flattened two-ounce ball of clay is larger than the comparison ball, because they understand that the shape of the clay is irrelevant to its weight.

There appears to be a developmental sequence in the child's ability to conserve. Children can usually conserve numbers by about 6 or 7, mass and length by 7 or 8, weight around 9 or 10, and volume by 14 or 15 (R. Gold, 1983). Inhelder and Piaget (1955/1958) called the developmental lag in conservation abilities *horizontal decálàge,* from the French *decáler* meaning "to displace." Cowan (1978) suggests that the explanation for decálàge lies in the number of dimensions to be isolated in each task and treated as conceptually different. The conservation of amount, for instance, involves two dimensions: units of measurement have to be separated from the location of the units. The conservation of mass involves separating weight from number and location. Volume conservation involves even more complex operations, which children cannot perform until they enter the period of formal operations, at about age 12. When they have mastered the concepts of identity (the amount remains constant even if the shape changes), reversibility (reversing the transformation brings the object back to its original shape), and reciprocity (a change in one dimension compensates for a change in the other when one considers both dimensions simultaneously), children can conserve along any physical dimension. As noted earlier, however,

---

concrete operations
the third stage in Piaget's cognitive theory where reasoning becomes more logical and children can understand some "rules of operation". Children still need to focus on concrete objects; abstract thought is lacking or very limited

conservation tasks
in Piaget's terms, tasks that test the child's knowledge of the identity of matter; if the child can solve the conservation tasks, he/she knows that the physical characteristics of the entity can change but certain other properties stay the same

horizontal decálàge
In Piaget's terms, the sequential mastery of concepts within a single developmental stage

identity
the notion that form can change, but if nothing has been added or taken away, the amount is still the same

reversibility
the notion that something that has been changed can be returned to its original state by reversing the process that lead to the change

reciprocity
if the mass remains constant, a change in one dimension necessitates a change in another (i.e., if a mass becomes flattened, it will become wider as it becomes thinner)

TYPE OF CONSERVATION	DIMENSION	CHANGE IN PHYSICAL APPEARANCE	CHILD IS ASKED THE CONSERVATION QUESTION	AGE AT WHICH TASK CAN BE SOLVED
NUMBER	Number of elements in a collection	Rearranging or dislocating elements in a collection	*Which line has more marbles? Preconserving child will say longer line has more. Conserving child will say both have same number.	6-7
SUBSTANCE (MASS) (CONTINUOUS QUANTITY)	Amount of a malleable substance (e.g., clay or liquid)	Altering its shape	*Do the two pieces have the same amount of clay? Preconserving child will say no. Conserving child will say yes.	7-8
LENGTH	Two sticks of equal length	Move one stick over	*Which stick is longer? Preconserving child will say one is longer. Conserving child will say both are the same length.	7-8
AREA	Two identical pieces of cardboad with same number of blocks	Rearrange blocks on one cardboard	*Do the two pieces of cardboard have the same amount of open space? Preconserving child will say no. Conserving child will say yes.	8-9
WEIGHT	Weight of an object	Altering shape	*Which object weighs more? Preconserving child will say vertical shape weighs more. Conserving child will say both weigh the same.	9-10
VOLUME	Two identical balls of clay in two identical glasses	Change the shape of one of the balls	*Do the two pieces of clay displace the same amount of water? Preconserving child will say no. Conserving child will say yes.	14-15

■ **Figure 12–1**

Children's interpretations of traditional Piagetian conservation tasks.

the refinement of the ability to conserve may also be accelerated through training and practice (Gelman & Baillargeon, 1983). When the verbal rules are given to explain how to solve each conservation problem (e.g., no matter where you put them, the number of pennies is just the same), children solve the problems more efficiently and remember the principles over time. Children in societies where concrete operational skills have little relevance develop these skills much later than their more urbanized peers (Heron & Dowel, 1974).

School-age children are also capable of applying their new logic to understanding real-life transformations. When caterpillars go through metamorphosis to become butterflies, preschoolers assume that the caterpillars crawled away and some butterflies took their place. But the child in the concrete operations stage can focus both on the steps in the process and on the beginning and end and can therefore understand that the caterpillars have changed, not disappeared. The school-age child can readily appreciate that while butterflies can't become caterpillars again, a cardboard and block fort can be disassembled into its component parts, and mathematical calculations such as addition can be reversed by means of subtraction.

The ability to conserve provides the child in concrete operations with a new sense of stability and security. The child now knows that certain aspects of the environment are permanent and unchanging despite changes in their appearance. For example, children's life savings don't shrink or grow arbitrarily depending on whether the coins are spread or stacked. By the same token, having a small, thick piece of cake is as good as having a thin, wide one. Their new cognitive tools can also give school-age children confidence in their own judgments. Because they can rely on what they *know* rather than on what they *perceive*, the concrete operational child not only understands that conservation can and does take place but believes it *must* (Moshman & Timmons, 1982). This feeling of the inevitability of outcomes makes children feel sure enough about their own interpretations of reality to resist counter suggestions from adults. For example, Piaget tried to dissuade a 7 year old girl from insisting (correctly) that the amount of water in a tall glass equaled that in a shorter glass. He argued:

> But a girl your age was here yesterday and she said there was more water (in the glass) because (the water level was) higher.
> "She's just silly, that's all," was the 7 year old girl's reply (Cowan, 1978, p. 188)

Further, school-age children are shocked and dismayed that their parents and other adults don't follow rules completely and fully since they are convinced that negative consequences will surely follow:

> When 10 year old Heather saw that her mother was driving at 27 miles per house in a 25 mile zone, she became indignant. "Either slow down or let me out. I'm not going to be here when the police come."

A New Egocentrism

We saw in the preceding chapters that preschool children are unable to take the viewpoint of others and that they have difficulty understanding that other people can reach conclusions different from their own. This preoperational egocentrism is replaced in the school years by a different

THE FAMILY CIRCUS   by Bil Keane

"Hold it, Mommy! You've got 12 things here!"

kind of egocentrism, one that permits more flexibility, logic, and objectivity. School-age children realize that their way of thinking is not the only way, and they are now able to appreciate situations and circumstances from the point of view of other people. Evidence of this ability is the relatively consistent success of children at this stage at solving Piaget and Inhelder's Three-Mountain Task (Piaget & Inhelder, 1969). When asked what a doll seated to the left, right, and front of the subjects might see, young school-age children can occasionally select the correct drawing, but the accuracy of perspective taking significantly improves by the time the child is 11 or 12.

It is when concrete operational children attempt to solve difficult tasks that their new egocentrism is revealed. Once school-age children have formed a hypothesis about how or why things work, they tend to force contradictory facts into their hypotheses rather than changing the hypotheses to fit the facts. In short, school-age children want to feel they are right, whether or not the evidence actually bears them out. In a classic study of this type of thinking, Weir (1964) set preschoolers, school-age children, and adolescents to the task of figuring out how a three-knobbed machine operated. Success was rewarded with candy from a machine. Since one knob never paid off, one paid off one-third of the time, and one knob paid off two-thirds of the time, getting the most candy depended on figuring out which knob did what. Preschoolers solved the problem by using trial and error. They learned to press only the two-thirds knob to get the most candy. Adolescents formed several hypotheses and tested them systematically to determine how the machine worked. Of the three groups, school-age children had the most difficulty. Their concrete orientation usually encouraged them to form a single hypothesis, such as "If I win, I'll stay with the knob; if I lose, I'll try another." Of course, using this strategy did not maximize the candy payoff (even with the two-thirds knob, they'd get only 66 percent of the candy they could if they alternated between the two-thirds and the one-third knob). Frustrated concrete thinkers continued to believe their hypothesis was correct, blaming the machine for failing to pay off as they thought it should. Children tend to apply strategies that favor their particular theories through age 12 (Schauble, 1984).

Logical Reasoning

According to Piaget, the school-age child develops the ability to use inductive reasoning. Induction involves reasoning from a specific experience or observation to a general principle. Children must apply this reasoning when they learn rules and operations. For example, when the child's hamster had babies, he now had more hamsters. Thus, the child could reason, adding something to any preexisting amount increases that amount. Exploratory strategies for generating evidence do improve with age (Schauble, 1990). On an interpersonal level, inductive reasoning forms the foundation for empathy. If I felt bad after Sam made fun

inductive reasoning
a type of reasoning whereby general laws are inferred from specific examples

of my report, then everyone must feel bad when other people humiliate them. Between the third and fifth grade, great advances are made in the ability of the child to understand "if-then" conditions. Additional improvement in reasoning skills occurs between the eighth grade and college in distinguishing "if-then" conditions from "if and only if" statements (Byrnes & Overton, 1988).

The counterpart to inductive reasoning, deductive logic, does not appear until the stage of formal operations (12 to adult). Deductive reasoning is more challenging than induction since it requires going from general principles to specific behaviors. To be able to assert, for example, that since all people deserve respect, discrimination against blacks, gays, or women is wrong requires understanding concepts that the child may have never experienced. Since school-age children are bound by *concrete* examples, deduction won't appear until they can reason beyond what is and consider what can be.

Concept Formation

NUMBER By age 6 or 7, children's understanding of one-to-one correspondence is complete. School-age children realize, for example, that six remains six whether it is represented as $5 + 1$, $9 - 3$, six stars, or six dreams. They also understand that some variables are irrelevant to number—for example, a long row of six bottles is not equal to a compressed row of twelve glasses (see Figure 9–3 from Chapter 9).

TIME As noted earlier, preschoolers in the preoperational period of cognitive development have no sense of time. They usually think of their parents as old, for example, and assume that they've always been old (disconcerting to the age-conscious adult, to say the least). In this stage, *past*, *present* and *future* are generalized concepts—like *before*, *during*, and *after*. For example, both Columbus' discovery of North America and Mother's birth occurred in the past and as far as the preoperational preschooler is concerned, they could have taken place in any temporal sequence! Preschoolers also have difficulty conceptualizing time as independent of activities. They assume that time passes slowly when they are waiting for a friend to come and quickly when they're having fun.

Along these same lines, until age 8, children have difficulty placing events in their appropriate time sequence, because units of time (minutes, years, and so on) have little meaning to them. After age 8, children have a more precise understanding of time passage. Because they are more logical, they understand that time "flows" and that units of time are consistent intervals of measurement independent of any activity that occurs within them. They are usually able to classify past and future events according to how recently they occurred, and are increasingly able to understand time-related concepts like next June, last summer, and so on. While even 4–6 year olds can use language to indicate some future action ("We can play later"), generally only children 10 years and older include the word *promise* to reassure the hearer of their commitment (Astington, 1988).

SPATIAL OPERATIONS Before they reach school age, children also have difficulty understanding distance, because they don't comprehend the basic units of measurement (miles, blocks, feet). Even the terms *far away* and *close* have little meaning except as they relate to the child personally. Young children might even interpret the statement that New York is a "long way" from California as meaning "around the block" or "by the school." The ability to understand distance improves through the school years.

Children frequently confuse time, distance, and speed, often assuming that the longer the trip, the greater the distance. Thus, preschool children may assume that they went farther during an hour's stop-and-go shopping trip around town than they did on an hour-long plane.flight to Grandma's. Also, children have little appreciation of the time it takes to travel from place to place. A 6 year old child from the Midwest approached his parents early one morning to ask about their taking a drive to Disney World in Orlando, Florida. "Are you kidding?" the father replied, "That's about 700 miles worth of driving!" "Well," said the child sincerely, "we could pack a lunch."

The ability to navigate within a new environment, even with the help of a map, is a skill that develops slowly during the school years. Young school-age children lose their spatial bearings easily in unfamiliar and complex spaces (like shopping malls or new schools). Six to 12 year olds are helped to find their way when landmarks are pointed out at decision points ("It's just past that green sign.") (Cornell et al., 1989). Older children can draw a map of an area if they have had a chance to thoroughly explore the space, but even 10 year olds have trouble creating a cognitive map or a mental representation of an environmental space in order to give directions or locate an object (A. W. Siegel, 1981).

CLASSIFICATION Concrete operational children understand the relationship between a whole and its parts. If an 8 year old is shown three collies and seven beagles and is asked if there are more beagles or more dogs, the child will say there are more dogs. The 4–5 year old child, in contrast, would say more beagles. Younger children cannot solve the collies-beagles-dogs problem correctly because they cannot hold both the class (dogs) and the subclass elements (beagles and collies) in mind simultaneously and move between them. The skill of moving between classes is called *class inclusion* or the *addition of classes*.

By applying their class inclusion skills, school-age children are able to form class hierarchies and to understand that all things have multiple identities. They themselves are sons or daughters, children, human

■ Figure 12–2

School-age children can correctly sort objects on the basis of two dimensions (such as shape and color), demonstrating that they can decenter and take more than one aspect of a situation into consideration.

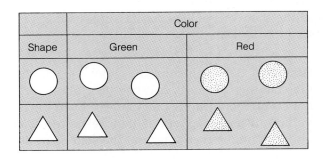

beings, grandchildren, and students. Dogs are animals but also living creatures, wild or domesticated animals, and so forth.

A more complex classification task involves sorting objects with respect to two or more attributes that vary systematically. For example, classes of animals (cats and bears) and classes of sizes (large and small) can be cross-multiplied to form combined classes of large bears, large cats, small bears, and small cats. Four or 5 year olds can sort according to some of these crossed categories (respond to "Give me all the pictures of small cats," for example). But when the items begin to vary in other ways (cats lying down and sitting; brown bears and black bears), it takes a few more years of practice and maturation to be able to ignore the irrelevant cues. By age 6 or 7 most children can understand multiplication of classes. A 7–8 year old child in the stage of concrete operations can sort cutouts in two shapes and two colors into their appropriate groups, constructing a four-cell color-by-shape matrix.

Six to 12 year olds love to classify and are notorious for having myriad collections of objects, animals, and friends. Parents often complain that their school-age child's room has been transformed into a museum and that every shelf is a display case for anything from coins and dolls to baseball cards and bugs. Collections require knowledge of the addition and multiplication of classes, but so do school work and games. A child who understands football knows you can score by a pass or a run that creates a touchdown. A point-after conversion, a safety, or a field goal also increases the score. In football, different players can be involved and different plays run (a handoff, QB sneak or keeper, forward pass, lateral, and so on), but they all could lead to a single outcome: points on the scoreboard, or yardage gained. In the classroom, classification skills are required before the child can understand the intricate relationship between city, county, state and federal government in the United States.

SERIATION In addition to classifying and grouping objects, school-age children are capable of sequencing or ordering items according to some measurable dimension, such as weight or size. This process is called *seriation*. They might arrange their crayons from lightest to darkest, their friends from nicest to meanest, and the items in their lunch from yummiest to yukkiest. In order to solve such tasks, the child must be able to consider two aspects of the relationship between objects at the same time. When sorting sticks of different lengths, for example, they have to select the stick that is longer than the last one but shorter than the rest. Children don't master this complex task until they are 6 or 7 years old.

One of the first series that children become familiar with is that of numbers. Preschool children, especially those who watch television programs such as *Sesame Street*, can often count from 1 to 20 without error. But not until age 7 or 8 do children begin to realize that numbers correspond to specific quantities and have specific "place values." They learn that 9 is greater than 5 and that 9 in 942 has a higher place value that the 9 in 97 even though both numbers are represented by the same symbol. Number concepts introduced to school-age children should be reinforced by concrete examples. The child comprehends the word *nine* more easily if he is urged to count out nine beans, nine shells, or nine buttons.

■●▲ CONCEPT SUMMARY

Characteristics of Thought During the School Years (Stage of Concrete Operations)

- Can understand the rules that account for specific outcomes
- Can take into account several aspects of a situation or an object at once (decentration)
- Can understand reversibility and transformation (e.g., is more effective in solving conservation tasks than the preschooler)
- Can use the rules learned solving concrete problems to solve real-life tasks
- Are able to rely on what they know rather than on what they perceive
- Are more logical (can use inductive reasoning)
- Can take the viewpoint of others
- Change the facts to fit their hypotheses rather than changing their hypotheses to fit the facts (a *new* egocentrism)

The Information Processing Approach to Cognitive Development

While Piaget claims that school-age children think better than younger children because they can better understand logical operations, information processing theorists suggest that concrete logic is a consequence of improved attention, perception, memory, and problem solving skills (Siegler & Richards, 1982).

Attention

The ability to focus on relevant information while ignoring distraction or irrelevant cues improves during the school years. In an early study Hagan and Hale (1973) measured central learning (memory of task-relevant items) and incidental learning in fourth, sixth, and eighth graders by having students focus on cards that contained pictures of household items and animals. Results indicated that when children were asked to recall all the animals they saw (central learning), their memories improved with age. However, beyond age 11 or 12, memory for incidental items (housewares) declines, demonstrating that older children are able to concentrate more efficiently on the task at hand while blocking out extraneous information (Tipper et al., 1989).

Interest is a high attention-getter for children. Children remember interesting sentences, even though allocating less attention to them than to less interesting passages (Shirley & Reynolds, 1988). Thus, children must engage in some strategy other than attention to learn high-interest material. Children who were exposed to alcohol prenatally demonstrate continued attentional decrements at age 7 (Streissguth et al., 1986).

Perception

Concrete operational logic also influences the way children organize and interpret sensory information. In a study of children's perception of visual illusions, Elkind (1978, 1981) found that children can't spontaneously alternate figure and ground in Figure 12–3 to see both the duck and the tree until they are 10 or 11 years old. Apparently, children need to master the logical concept of reversibility before they are able, perceptually, to reverse their impressions of an illusion.

The Embedded Figures Test (Witkin et al., 1971) also requires that the child be able to see a figure in a number of ways. In order to discover the hidden figure, the child must be able to shift from whole to part while blocking out other distracting lines and shapes. Four and 5 year olds can locate the "easy" embedded figures; the more "difficult" figures are not found until age 6 or 7 (Vurpillot, 1976). Older children are more capable of searching their visual environment thoroughly and sys-

central learning
the ability to recall task-relevant items and to ignore task-irrelevant items

incidental learning
memory for items other than those one was directed to learn

Embedded Figures Task
a perceptual test requiring that the individual identify specific stimuli within a complex visual field

■ **Figure 12–3**

In this figure-ground illusion, younger children see only the tree while older children can see the duck figure as well as the tree.

tematically. When children are under the age of 6 or 7, they look quickly and randomly at the figures, thus missing the embedded portions.

Memory Capacity and Memory Strategies

School-age children are able to hold more information in memory and, because of their improved classification skills, are better at mentally organizing that material than younger children (A. L. Brown et al., 1983). *Rehearsal* occurs more spontaneously during the school years and is more efficiently applied. Five year olds can rehearse when taught to repeat the information they must remember, but unless they are cued, they forget to use rehearsal (Hitch et al., 1989). By the time children are in the second grade, they automatically repeat information to themselves to improve memorizing. When asked to remember a list of 18 items, 8 year olds rehearse by simply repeating the last thing they see or the last word they hear *(desk, desk, desk).* Eleven and 13 year olds rehearsed the complete list, adding each new word/item to the end of the list (desk. . .desk, hat. . .desk, hat, tie. . .etc.) (Hitch et al., 1989). Thus, the rehearsal strategy of the older child is far superior to that of the younger child, who remembers a much smaller percentage of items.

Memory is improved by categorizing or organizing items on a list into related groups. When 10–11 year olds work with this list of words *(bread, pants, milk, stamps, eggs, postcards, dress, butter),* they would probably organize it like a shopping list: *grocery store* (bread, milk, eggs, butter), *post office* (stamps, postcards), *dry cleaners* (pants, dress). The categories themselves become retrieval cues for the individual items. Younger children organize material differently, using the sound of the word or obvious associations to form categories (e.g., *bread* and *butter;* *pants* and *postcards*) (Lindberg, 1989). Younger children remember far fewer items than older children and although 4 and 5 year olds can be taught to categorize, they forget to use it unless reminded (Chance & Fischman, 1987). When asked to sort one-color pictorial stimuli, second to sixth graders focus more on what the pictures *mean* than on how they look (Bernt, 1989).

Older children are also more likely to use *elaboration,* a memory aid that relies on visual imagery, and verbal aids (like acronyms) to enhance memory (Pressley, 1982). To remember the name of the points on the compass, for example, the school-age child can remember the word NEWS, where the letters stand for north, east, west, and south. Grade school children can also make up their own stories or acronyms to help them remember better. Younger children have trouble remembering the acronym, let alone the items each letter represents.

Metamemory, or *metacognition,* is an awareness of memory and an understanding of how it works; it develops during the school years (Flavell, 1977). By the time children are in kindergarten, they understand a great deal more about memory than they did as preschoolers.

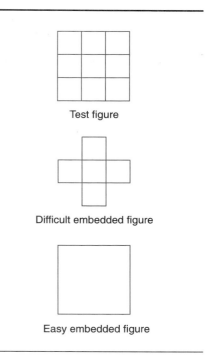

Test figure

Difficult embedded figure

Easy embedded figure

■ Figure 12–4

In the Embedded Figures Test, children are asked to find the examples in the test figure. Such a test involves good spatial perception as well as the ability to ignore irrelevant cues.

categorization
organizing information to be remembered into groups of related objects

elaboration
strategies for facilitating recall that involve working with the information to be remembered to change its form (i.e., to create a visual stimulus, to make a meaningful sentence from the words on a list, etc.)

Lange and Guttentag (1990) found that kindergartners and first graders knew what it meant to learn, remember, and forget. They understood that remembering things that happened a long time ago was more difficult than remembering things that occurred recently. And they realized that it was more difficult to remember a large number of items than just a few and that studying something made remembering it easier. In another study, third and fifth graders reported that time affects memory and that meaningful objects such as antonyms are easier to remember than unrelated words. They also could cite a number of useful memory strategies, such as writing notes to themselves and leaving objects to be remembered close to their lunch boxes or next to the front door. School-age children grow progressively more confident in the "feeling of knowing" probably because they are more accurate and leave fewer answers blank (Butterfield et al., 1988).

Perhaps the biggest difference between preschoolers and school-age children is that preschoolers *think* they are more adept at remembering than they really are (Lange & Guttentag, 1990). Memory tasks look easy to them (it's just a list of words, for heaven's sake) and because they are perception bound, preschoolers are fooled into thinking they have memorized the "easy" list when in fact, they have not. Concrete, reality-oriented school children *know* what a challenging task memorizing can be. As a consequence, they use whatever aids they can think of to make the process easier. The more self-confidence they have in their metamemory strategies, the better their memory performance (Bandura 1989). Also, once children understand the central role that memory plays in information processing, they gain more insight into metamemory strategies (Fabricius et al., 1989).

After age 7, children also tend to tie their own performance to feelings of self-worth. Younger children don't seem to care if they make a mistake; they don't seem to believe a mistake reflects on them personally. Older children are bothered by their poor performance and try to maximize positive outcomes to avoid appearing "stupid" or "incompetent" (Jovanovic et al., 1989). One implication of this research is that we can't depend on young children to tell us whether or not they understand a concept. They may truly not know if they do or don't. Rather than asking children if they have any questions or asking for a verbal assessment, educators and parents should probably "test" the child's level of competence behaviorally (J. J. Moore et al., 1986).

Knowledge Base

What a child already knows about an area or subject influences both what he can learn and what he can remember. More complex knowledge can't be acquired until basic foundations are laid. So children have to build on what they know rather than trying to acquire random bits of disjointed information on a topic. Thus, some school-age children may acquire an expertise in certain fields (coin collecting, Mars, computer programming) that surpasses the knowledge level of most adults. It's not that these children are intellectually precocious, it's just that they're motivated to acquire, organize, and store information about their specialty area and have the cognitive hardware to do so (Chi, 1982).

Problem Solving Strategies

The school-age child is a more successful problem solver than the preschooler since the older child can use language to generate rules to help solve problems. In the transposition paradigm (see Figure 12–5), the child is trained to select a certain response (in this case, the larger circle). If, in the next phase, the smaller circle is replaced by a circle larger than B, which circle will the child choose? Three to 4 year olds do not seem to learn a general rule ("Select the larger circle") during the training phase. Instead, they consistently continue with whatever answer was "correct" in the training trials, in this case, selecting B. Older children can apparently recognize a relationship between the two circles, can verbalize a relationship ("Look for the larger circle"), and will select C on the test trial. When children can use a language concept to formulate rules about solving problems, they are said to be employing a *verbal mediation response* (Kendler & Kendler, 1962, 1970).

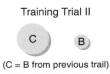

Training Trial I

Child is conditioned to pick the larger circle, B

Training Trial II

(C = B from previous trail)

■ Figure 12–5

The transposition paradigm.

■●▲ CONCEPT SUMMARY

Changes in Information Processing Capacities

- More efficient in ignoring distracting, irrelevant cues
- Are best at remembering things that *interest* them
- Use more thorough and systematic visual search strategies
- Spontaneously use rehearsal strategies to improve memory
- Organize material for understanding/remembering in a more efficient way
- More likely to use elaboration to improve memory
- Have a better understanding of how memory works (metamemory)
- Make more realistic assessments regarding task difficulty
- Tie problem solving abilities to feelings of self-worth
- Can use verbal mediation responses to improve problem solving

transpositional paradigm
a method of assessing whether children can learn problem solving rules through training trials

verbal mediation response
using inner speech to relate one's thoughts and actions in order to control one's behavior or improve comprehension

The Psychometric Approach: Using Intelligence Tests to Measure Cognitive Development

Within the field of psychology, there is still considerable debate about the definition of the term *intelligence* and the utility of IQ test scores. Some psychologists (we'll call them generalists) define intelligence as a general capacity for acquiring knowledge and applying that knowledge to solve problems. This general capacity is referred to as *g* (Sternberg & Davidson, 1985). While some people may know more or less about specific areas (like math or science), people are generally considered bright or dull depending on how much *g* factor they possess. Thus, generalists feel it is appropriate to use a single IQ score to represent *g*.

g
a single, common intelligence representing abstract reasoning and the *general* capacity for acquiring knowledge

Other psychologists, the separatists, believe that intelligence is a collection of separate skills that are basically independent of one another. A person who is good at doing crossword puzzles, for example, won't necessarily also be good at fixing things, and vice versa. Both persons, however, could be considered intelligent. The number of individual mental abilities has been estimated to range from 3 (Sternberg, 1986) to 6 or 7 (Thurstone, 1938; Gardner, 1983) to 120 (Guilford, 1985) and include such diverse talents as bodily-kinesthetic intelligence, creative abilities, and perceptual speed. Most intelligence tests provide individual scores for subtests (supporting the notion of specialized skills) as well as a general IQ score (supporting the notion of *g*). It's also likely that *g* coexists with specific mental abilities providing a foundation for their expression and correlating them with other skills (Vernon, 1977, 1989). This is the interactionist perspective.

Each of the foregoing groups, the generalists, the separatists, and the interactionists led by Vernon, would recognize both a genetic and an environmental component to intelligence. While each person inherits a specific intellectual potential, the environment can influence the expression of that potential. The relative contributions of genetics and the environment have been hotly debated and portend some interesting consequences. If intelligence is mainly inherited, the collective IQ of society can be enhanced by having its brightest citizens conceive and bear children (Jensen, 1990). If intelligence is primarily determined by the environment, then the quality of the child's home and school environment can have a profound impact (Scarr & Kidd, 1983).

Taken as a whole, the psychometric approach to cognitive development raises some important and interesting issues, but it has been criticized for relying too heavily on test scores and academic skills and for failing to explain *how* individuals learn intelligent behaviors.

Yet despite these concerns intelligence testing is common during the school years. In most schools, children take group achievement and aptitude tests every few years. *Achievement tests* measure the individual's present level of knowledge or skill, while *aptitude tests* measure one's capacity to perform certain tasks. As with the original intelligence tests,

achievement tests
a test that measures how much an individual knows about a specific content area

aptitude test
a test that measures one's ability to engage in certain tasks

contemporary IQ instruments are used to predict school performance and to highlight specific learning skills and deficits.

The most widely used test of intelligence of 7 to 13 year olds is the Wechsler Intelligence Scale for Children, Revised (WISC-R). This test was originally developed in 1959 by David Wechsler, the same medical school professor who devised the WPPSI (Wechsler Preschool and Primary Scale of Intelligence) for preschool age children and the WAIS-R (Wechsler Adult Intelligence Scale, Revised) for adults. This WISC-R is divided into two scales, verbal and performance. The verbal section contains the following subtests (each is followed here by a sample question or questions):

1. *General knowledge:* How many minutes are in an hour?
2. *Reasoning ability:* How are an apple and a pear alike? What would you do if you found a wallet lying on the sidewalk and no one was around the claim it?
3. *Number skills and computational ability:* What is 2 + 17 − 3? If it takes 3 men 5 hours to row across the river, how long will it take 2 men?
4. *Memory:* Repeat these numbers in order: 3874; repeat these numbers backwards: 209548.
5. *Vocabulary:* What does *to procrastinate* mean? What does the word *rapport* mean?

The performance section contains the following subtests (with sample tasks for each—see also Fig. 12–6.

1. *Logical thought:* The child must put pictures in a sequence to make them tell a story.
2. *Part/whole relations:* The child must tell what is missing from a picture.
3. *Spatial relations:* The child must assemble puzzles and arrange small blocks to copy a design.
4. *Memory:* The child must learn symbol codes for numbers and fill in the proper code for number sequences.

spatial relations
the connection between objects in three-dimensional space

Items within each subtest are presented in order of increasing difficulty. Speed of completion is an important factor, since many of the subtests are timed. The WISC-R yields a *verbal IQ* (based on scores from the verbal subtests), a *performance IQ* (based on scores on the performance subtests), and a *full-scale IQ* (based on all subtest scores). The child's scores are compared with those obtained by large numbers of children of the same age. An IQ score of 100 is considered average; IQ scores above or below 100 indicate that the child scores better or worse than the average child in his age group. About two-thirds of all children tested score within the average range of intelligence (Sattler, 1982). The rest of the scores cluster around this average, with about 3% of the population scoring in the gifted range and about 3% in the mentally retarded range.

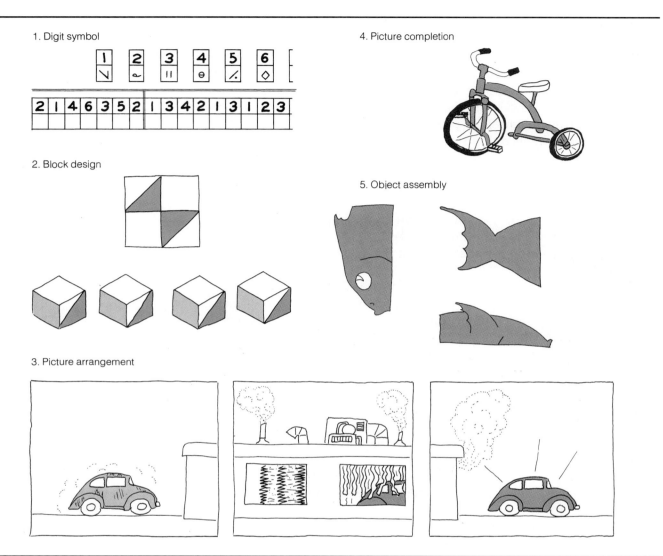

1. Digit symbol

4. Picture completion

2. Block design

5. Object assembly

3. Picture arrangement

■ **Figure 12–6**

Examples of items like those on the performance subscales of the WISC-R.

Interpreting and Using IQ Test Scores

The results of such intelligence test scores as those from the WISC-R are taken to indicate the child's ability to comprehend ideas or instructions, analyze problems, and find solutions. The Wechsler test appears to specifically assess memory, verbal and perceptual-spatial skills (Anastasi, 1982).

Psychologists use IQ test scores to help predict present and future school grades. About 60% of the time children with higher IQs are the top achievers in school while those with lower IQs get lower grades (Sattler, 1982). Some consistency in scores is also maintained over time since children who get better grades in elementary school tend to get better grades in high school as well.

IQ is related to school retention and years of school completed (Pellegrini et al., 1987). More than half of the children who drop out of school have relatively lower grades and lower IQs than those who stay. Thus, IQ and school performance can be helpful in targeting a population of students at risk for academic failure and dropout.

IQ scores may be used to help diagnose specific learning skills and deficits and to identify students for special program placement. An IQ test may be given to assess school readiness in a child who wishes to enter kindergarten before age 5. Along with other measures, IQ scores may be used to determine the advisability of skipping or retaining a student, placing him in a program for the gifted and talented, or recommending remediation.

IQ has some relationship to later job selection. When jobs have academic entrance requirements (medicine, law), people with higher IQs are more likely to apply and be qualified. IQ has little or no relationship with job success, however. High IQ pilots don't necessarily have better safety records than lower IQ pilots. Similarly, high IQ seamstresses don't sew any straighter than lower IQ seamstresses. IQ and job satisfaction are also unrelated. Just because your IQ is high doesn't mean you'll necessarily like what you do.

Test Score Accuracy

How accurately IQ test scores reflect children's true abilities is a matter of some debate. In addition to an inherited potential, a number of other factors, such as familiarity with or membership in the culture devising the test, can influence the outcome of an IQ test (McCall, 1983). Table 12–1 shows a classic example.

THE DEVELOPMENTAL ENVIRONMENT

General Health Children in good health have had the developmental advantage of good nutrition, proper rest, exercise, and freedom from illness. A child in poor health may not have the physical or psychological energy to learn or grow as his genes dictate.

Quality of the Home Environment Robert Bradley and Bettye Caldwell (1984) found that children who score high in IQ tests come from families who

1. provide appropriate play materials
2. are involved with their child and emotionally responsive
3. talk to their child
4. give the child an opportunity to learn and explore
5. expect their child to learn and achieve

■ **Table 12–1**   *Excerpts from the Chitling Test*

1. A "handkerchief head" is:
   a. a cool cat
   b. a porter
   c. an uncle Tom
   d. a hoddi
   e. a preacher

2. Which word is most out of place here?
   a. splib
   b. blood
   c. gray
   d. spook
   e. black

3. A "gas head" is a person who has a:
   a. fast moving car
   b. stable of "lace"
   c. "process"
   d. habit of stealing cars
   e. long jail record for arson

4. "Down-home" (the South today), for the average "soul brother" who is picking cotton from sunup until sundown, what is the average earning (take home) for one full day?
   a. $.75   b. $1.65   c. $3.50   d. $5   e. $12

5. "Bo Diddley" is a:
   a. game for children
   b. down-home cheap wine
   c. down-home singer
   d. new dance
   e. Moejoe call

6. If a pimp is up tight with a woman who gets state aid, what does he mean when he talks about "Mother's Day"?
   a. second Sunday in May
   b. third Sunday in June
   c. first of every month
   d. none of these
   e. first and fifteenth of every month

7. "Hully Gully" came from:
   a. East Oakland
   b. Fillmore
   c. Watts
   d. Harlem
   e. Motor City

8. If a man is called a "blood," then he is a:
   a. fighter
   b. Mexican-American
   c. Negro
   d. hungry hemophile
   e. Redman or Indian

9. Cheap chitlings (not the kind you purchase at a frozen food counter) will taste rubbery unless they are cooked long enough. How soon can you quit cooking them to eat and enjoy them?
   a. 45 minutes
   b. two hours
   c. 24 hours
   d. one week (on a low flame)
   e. one hour

10. What are the "Dixie Hummingbirds"?
    a. part of the KKK
    b. a swamp disease
    c. a modern gospel group
    d. a Mississippi Negro paramilitary group
    e. Deacons

11. If you throw the dice and seven is showing on the top, what is facing down?
    a. seven
    b. snake eyes
    c. boxcars
    d. little Joes
    e. 11

12. "Jet" is:
    a. an East Oakland motorcycle club
    b. one of the gangs in "West Side Story"
    c. a news and gossip magazine
    d. a way of life for the very rich

13. T-Bone Walker got famous for playing what?
    a. a trombone
    b. piano
    c. "T-flute"
    d. guitar
    e. "Hambone"

Those who are not "culturally deprived" will recognize the correct answers are:
1. c **2.** c **3.** c **4.** d **5.** c **6.** e **7.** c **8.** c
9. c **10.** c **11.** a **12.** c **13.** d

Source: Dove, A. "The Chitling Test."

Family Size Robert Zajonc's (1975, 1983) confluence model suggests that if children are closely spaced and come from large families, IQs will decline a point or two for each child as you go down the birth order. Zajonc suggests the confluence effect is due to the "diluted" intellectual environment that results from parents having less and less time to give to each child as an individual as family size increases. While birth order may influence IQ, it doesn't have to. Spacing births 5 years apart, having older children tutor younger ones, and providing special parent time for each child can neutralize the "dumber by the dozen" effect Zajonc predicts. If any child is disadvantaged, it is the last born who has no younger sibling to tutor or teach.

Test Experience Being "test wise" can be as important as knowing the right answers when taking a test. A child who marks a fill-in bubble with an X or answers in the booklet and not on the answer sheet will not get credit for his work even if he is correct. Since most intelligence tests are timed, valuable time will be spent figuring out the testing procedure rather than working on the test questions.

Formal Training (Education) Since standardized IQ tests such as the WISC-R predict school grades, they are at least in part a measure of academic training. High absenteeism on the child's part, poor quality teaching, or a poor curriculum could lower test scores. Poverty or homelessness could have a significant impact on the type of educational experience available to the child. When poor children attend preschool or special day care, they score significantly higher on IQ tests and function better in school than poor children without such enrichment (Ramey and Campbell, 1987; Lazar & Darlington, 1982; Garber & Heber, 1982).

standardized
a test that is administered according to a specific, consistent set of rules and whose scores are interpreted in a prescribed manner

Cultural Background The values and traditions of one's culture can influence IQ test scores. The WISC-R and other widely used IQ tests were written by white middle-class males and reflect white middle-class language and values. If a child has not had a certain experience common to the middle class (e.g., going on vacation), he may not be able to correctly answer a test item dealing with that experience. Not only do culturally diverse children get penalized for not knowing about the mainstream culture, but they receive no IQ test credit for their own unique experiences. Creating a culture-fair or culture-free test is not an easy task. When blacks, Latinos, Asians, or Native Americans write IQ tests, the language, values, and experiences of *their* particular cultures are incorporated, too, placing test-takers from the mainstream culture at a disadvantage.

PERSONALITY FACTORS

Achievement Motivation A child who has a high need to achieve is constantly striving toward excellence and better performance on any task encountered. Children low in the need to achieve do not feel as pressed to do their best and try their hardest on an IQ test or anything else. If children can be helped to exert personal control over school/test success by using effective strategies and feeling confident in their application, achievement motivation should improve (E. A. Skinner et al., 1990).

achievement motivation
the tendency to display persistence and striving when faced with a task to solve

Interest in the Test Some children feel that tests are important measures of performance. While such children may not feel compelled to be high achievers under all circumstances (homework, group work in class, assigned projects), they are motivated to do their best "when it counts."

Test Anxiety The opportunity to perform can motivate the child to succeed or it can create test anxiety—a debilitating level of tension that interferes with the child's ability to concentrate on the test items or even prepare for the exam. Test anxiety is tied into fear of failure, performance anxiety, and a perception of little personal control (learned helplessness). Without intervention, levels of learned helplessness and test anxiety remain stable over time (Fincham et al., 1989).

self-efficacy
the perception that one is capable of successfully performing a task

Self-Confidence/Self-Efficacy Increased self-confidence and feelings of personal effectiveness enhance task concentration and test performance (Pintrich & deGroot, 1990).

cognitive style
the tendency to focus on the entire problem (field dependent) or to separate the problem into its component parts and examine each part (field independent)

Cognitive Style Some children focus on the whole problem at hand (field dependency) while others can take the problem apart and examine each part (field independent). While field-dependence/independence aren't the only cognitive styles, they do affect problem solving. Not surprisingly, field-independent children are better at intellectual tasks than field-dependent children (Kagan, 1983).

cognitive tempo
the tendency to have a reflective or impulsive style

Cognitive Tempo Impulsive children answer quickly, valuing speed more than accuracy. Reflective children take more time when they solve problems, pay more attention to detail, and are concerned about being correct. Reflective/impulsive styles can be assessed by the Matching Familiar Figures test (Kagan et al., 1964). Reflective children have an advantage on IQ tests when time limits don't interfere.

■ **Figure 12–7**

Impulsive and reflecting problem-solving styles can be identified by noting children's responses to items similar to these on the Matching Familiar Figures Test. The impulsive child sees no differences between the bears; the reflective child notes differences.

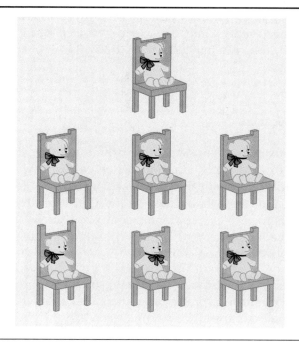

SITUATIONAL FACTORS

Perceived Importance of the Test If a child is motivated to perceive the test at hand as important, he will try harder to succeed than if he thought the test results were trivial or the test invalid.

Confidence about the Test The better prepared and competent the child feels at test time, the better he will perform. It's highly reinforcing to take a test and know that some if not most of your answers are correct.

Physical Condition at Test Time A child who is rested, well-nourished, relaxed, and healthy is much more likely to maximize his potential on an IQ test than the child who is tired, hungry, tense, or sick.

External Interference The environment needs to be free from distractions that can divert attention and break concentration. Sometimes the interference is external (dogs barking, train or traffic sounds, sirens); sometimes the test-taking situation has built-in distractions (clock ticking, desks spaced too close, someone constantly coughing or sneezing). Minimizing distractions can maximize test performance.

Effects of the Examiner Even in a group testing situation, rapport needs to be established between the test taker and the examiner. The examiner should be nonjudgmental, encouraging, friendly, and patient. In this way, the test-taker can feel relaxed and confident about his responses.

TEST CHARACTERISTICS

Kinds of Learning or Abilities Required Obviously, children can perform best on tests that ask questions about things they've learned or test skills they've acquired.

Bad Test Items Some test items are poorly worded, ambiguous, vague, or even insoluable. Bad test items lower students' scores through no fault of their own.

Speed Requirements Timed tests penalize the child who has a reflective style, becomes anxious when he has to go fast, or has poor coordination or motor skills.

RANDOM INFLUENCES

Guessing Guessing can spuriously raise or lower scores.

Clerical Error Scoring/recording errors can affect the accuracy of the test results.

■ **Figure 12–8**

Over time, an IQ can decline (A), increase (B), or stay relatively the same (C).

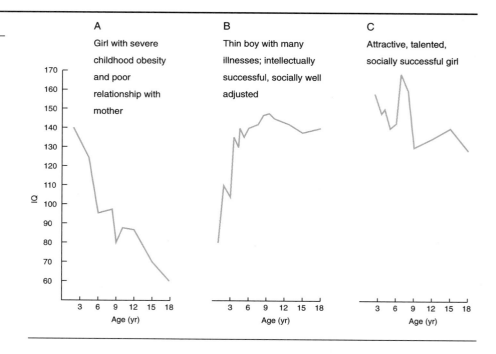

A

Girl with severe childhood obesity and poor relationship with mother

B

Thin boy with many illnesses; intellectually successful, socially well adjusted

C

Attractive, talented, socially successful girl

Not only can these factors affect the accuracy of individual test scores, but they can also affect test-retest reliability. As early as 1948 Honzik and his colleagues found that the scores of more than half of the children they tested varied dramatically over time. The first child in Figure 12–7 scored in the superior range as a young child but in the borderline retarded range as an adolescent. How can the same person be both intellectually superior and retarded? A similar fluctuation is seen for Child 2 but in the opposite direction. Obviously, an IQ score isn't something you have, like long fingers or dark skin; it is something you can access, where accessibility is enhanced or impeded by the child's past and present life circumstances. Generally, the older the child, the more stable the IQ (McCall, 1984). Still, the older child's IQ can fluctuate between 10 and 20 points in either direction.

Alternatives to Traditional IQ Testing

Psychologists disillusioned with the narrow academic focus and poor reliability of current IQ tests have devised instruments of their own with a broader focus. Howard Gardner (1983) identifies six different intelligences that each follow a separate developmental path:

1. Linguistic intelligence (skill with words and word meanings)
2. Musical intelligence (sensitivity to tone and pitch)

■●▲ CONCEPT SUMMARY

Factors that Affect IQ Test Scores
(In Addition to Inherited Potential)

GENERAL	PERSONALITY	SITUATIONAL AND TEST-SPECIFIC	RANDOM
General health	Achievement motivation	Perceived importance of the test	Guessing
Quality of the home environment	Interest in the test	Confidence about the test	Clerical error
Family size	Test anxiety	Physical condition at test time	
Test experience	Self-confidence/ self-efficacy	External interference	
Formal training (education)	Cognitive style	Effects of the examiner	
Cultural background	Cognitive tempo	Bad test items	
		Speed requirements	

3. Logical–mathematical intelligence (math skills and abstract reasoning)
4. Spatial intelligence (understanding the physical world and being able to represent and modify that world artistically or structurally)
5. Bodily–kinesthetic intelligence (body control and coordination)
6. Personal intelligence (understanding feelings and motivations)

Only two of Gardner's intelligences (1 and 3) are measured on traditional IQ tests.

Yet another view is proposed by Robert Sternberg (1986). Sternberg postulates three aspects of intelligence:

1. Componential intelligence—the type of analysis and problem solving skills assessed by standing IQ tests and achievement tests
2. Experiential intelligence—corresponds to creativity and insightfulness
3. Contextual intelligence—involves being able to relate to one's environment (also known as "street smarts")

kinesthetic
a sensation of movement, weight, resistance and position of the muscles and joints of the body; a sense of body movement and position

Sternberg (1988) also suggests that people develop intellectual styles to help integrate their own personality into any specific intellectual task.

Both Sternberg and Gardner would assert that standard IQ tests can assess standing and progress in school, but in the outside world, personal intelligence, creativity, body control and coordination, and street smarts may be just as important as academic knowledge.

Schools are gradually abandoning the exclusive use of the standard intelligence test as a measure of a child's worth and potential in favor of a battery of broad-ranging tests. Sandra Scarr (1981) suggests that schools should encourage social competence by educating the whole child, not just the child's mind. While the cognitive abilities measured by IQ tests are one aspect of social competence, other aspects include the child's self-esteem, physical health, motivation, adaptive behavior, and social skills. In order to see what a child *can* learn, a new approach called dynamic assessment offers the child as many clues as he needs to complete the task. The child is then asked to solve a similar problem to see if he can transfer learning from one task to another (Campione et al., 1982). By counterbalancing for culture and family background, the SOMPA (System of Multicultural Pluralistic Assessment, Mercer & Lewis 1978) tries to retain children in regular classrooms. Proponents claim that without the SOMPA adjustment, many ESL (English as a Second Language) and poor children would score in the retarded range because their English skills are poor and their school exposure minimal. However, others suggest that SOMPA's diagnostic outcomes are the same as other standardized measures, such as the full-scale IQ from the WISC-R (Heflinger et al., 1987).

Achievement Tests

While intelligence tests are intended to give some indication of a child's learning potential, achievement tests are designed to measure how much a child knows. Achievement tests are administered in most American schools every year or on a fixed schedule, for example, third, fifth and eighth grades. Achievement test items are similar to those in Table 12–2. The results are usually reported as percentile scores, where the average child scores at the 50th percentile. Scores above or below the 50th percentile indicate relatively higher or lower scores (respectively) when compared to the norms of the child's grade or age.

Teachers can use achievement test scores to give students work that is reasonably challenging but not overwhelming. Communities and school boards use achievement test scores as one measure of accountability in education. When scores compare favorably to national or state averages, schools and teachers are congratulated. When scores are low, there may be pressure on schools and individual teachers to improve.

■ **Table 12–2**   *Some Sample Items from a Fourth-Grade Achievement Test*

COMPREHENSION

Bill took out some bread and made toast. He spread peanut butter on it. Then he took out a glass and poured himself some milk.

What did Bill do first?
- ○ poured some milk
- ○ took out a glass
- ○ took out some bread
- ○ spread peanut butter

SPELLING

This _____ is fun to play.
- ○ gaym
- ○ game
- ○ gaime
- ○ gamme

LANGUAGE MECHANICS

Choose the best punctuation:

That cloud is very fluffy
- ○ fluffy?
- ○ fluffy,
- ○ fluffy.
- ○ Correct as it is

LANGUAGE EXPRESSION

Which sentence best combines the two underlined sentences into one?

The old house is big. The old house is yellow.
- ○ The old house is big and yellow.
- ○ The house is old and big and yellow.
- ○ The house is bigger than the old, yellow house.
- ○ The old house is a big house and a yellow house.

MATHEMATICS COMPUTATION

Subtract. 12 − 11 =
- ○ 1   ○ 12   ○ 23   ○ 2
- ○ None of these

MATHEMATICS CONCEPTS

What number is missing from this number sequence? 1, 2, 3, ___ , 5
- ○ 2   ○ 3   ○ 4   ○ 6

SCIENCE

Which of these comes from a plant?
- ○ egg   ○ milk
- ○ meat   ○ apple

SOCIAL STUDIES

What is a large body of salt water called?
- ○ a pond   ○ a river
- ○ an ocean   ○ an island

Source: From Comprehensive Tests of Basic Skills, 4th Edition. Copyright © 1989 by McGraw-Hill Inc. Published by CTB Macmillan/McGraw-Hill. Used by permission.

One of the challenges in constructing achievement tests involves grouping math and verbal abilities according to grade level. Should a first grader, for example, be able to multiply single-digit numbers? if so, when—after 2 months of instruction? Should first graders know the meaning of words such as *exhibit* and *conflict?* Yet another challenge is constructing a test that does not inadvertently penalize children who are poor readers, who have trouble following directions, or who have not had the experiences discussed in the test items (e.g., going to a summer camp). Even though achievement test items have been carefully selected and worded, the student's performance may still be negatively affected by the same factors that introduce variability into IQ testing. Conversely, achievement test scores can be enhanced if teachers give students plenty of practice in taking tests and familiarize students with the kinds of material that will appear in the test. Like intelligence test scores, the results of achievement tests may provide useful information but should be interpreted with caution.

Creativity

creativity
the ability to develop new and socially valued solutions, products, etc.

divergent thinking
trying to think of many solutions to a particular problem

convergent
trying to find the one, right answer to a problem

Even though creativity has been mentioned already as an aspect of intelligence, the concept of creativity bears a closer look. Although both intelligence and creativity involve analyzing and solving problems, a highly creative person may not score well on tests of intelligence. Why? Some say because creativity requires divergent thinking while intelligence tests assess convergent thinking (Guilford, 1967). Convergent thought involves eliminating many alternatives to a single correct answer—*the* solution to the problem. Divergent thinking involves not a narrowing but an expanding of possible alternatives. Thus divergent thought is the ability to solve problems in new and original ways. This type of thinking is usually measured by creativity tests that may require verbal responses or drawing.

Like intelligence, the notion of creativity and its assessment raises considerable controversy. Is creativity a general capacity that exists within people (*c* instead of *g*)? Or is creativity something that can be developed by anyone with sufficient motivation and direction? (Dacey, 1989) If creativity is a personality trait, then creative people should differ from less creative ones in important ways. Indeed, 4 decades ago Barron (1955) found that creative adults tended to be enthusiastic, ambitious, independent, open-minded, introspective, exhibitionistic, and self-centered. This perspective also assumes creativity is an irrepressible force: Evidence of the individual's creativity would surface in any task or profession the individual undertakes.

And yet there is evidence that creative individuals are made, not born. Studies of achievements of precocious children (scientific discoveries, athletic accomplishments, musical compositions, inventions, and the like) all reveal extensive training by talented teachers and exceptional parental support (D. H. Feldman, 1980). According to this point of view, you don't necessarily need to be a creative person to ensure a creative outcome. Being an innovative person can be entertaining and interesting. But to be useful, creativity must be tied back to the real world. A creative solution isn't just novel or different, it is also appropriate, parsimonious, and challenging to the status quo. High scores on tests of creativity are not strongly associated with actual creative accomplishments (Wallach, 1985). Having a lot of ideas doesn't necessarily mean that any of the ideas have merit.

While some amount of raw talent underlies creative achievement, creativity can be encouraged. Carl Rogers (Harrington et al., 1987) and others suggest the following suggestions play an important role in the development of constructive creativity:

1. Encourage children to feel free to express their feelings or opinions.
2. Help them manipulate and evaluate ideas (Rogers, 1954).
3. Avoid punitive discipline.
4. Tolerate/accept children's creative ideas.

5. Support children who risk being different.
6. Be open to experience (Rogers, 1954).
7. Have confidence in the child's ability to behave appropriately.
8. Model creative, fluent information processing.
9. Expose the child to other creative thinkers.
10. Discourage conformity, especially among girls. No sex differences are found until the third grade, when girls' creativity scores begin to decline (Tegano & Moran, 1989).
11. Provide systematic training beyond mastery in an area of the child's interest.
12. Provide direct instruction in problem finding (not just problem solving) (Cliatt et al., 1980).
13. Encourage make-believe or imaginative play.
14. Help children be original and entertain more than one solution to a problem (Haylock, 1987).
15. Eliminate time constraints from enjoyable tasks.

● Variation in Learning Ability

Every child in the United States, citizen or noncitizen, is entitled to free education from kindergarten through high school in the public school system. Teaching to meet the educational needs of all students requires flexibility and an understanding of factors that account for variation in the ability to learn. The special needs of the learning disabled, handicapped, attention deficit disordered (ADD), mentally retarded, and gifted and talented will be examined here.

Gifted and Talented

> I was standing in front of the (3rd grade) classroom explaining how the earth revolves around and how, because of its huge size, it is difficult for us to realize that it is actually round. All of a sudden, Spencer blurted out, "The earth isn't round." I curtly replied, "Ha, do you think it's flat?" He matter-of-factly said, "No, it's a truncated sphere." I quickly changed the subject. Spencer said the darndest things (Payne et al., 1974, p. 94)

In a classic study on the development of intelligence, Lewis Terman (Terman, 1925) followed the development of more than 1500 children who scored in the genius range of intelligence between 1925 and 1959. From his findings and others, an agreed-on definition of *giftedness* has evolved—gifted children are those with demonstrated achievement and/or potential in any of the following areas, singly or in combination:

1. General intellectual ability (high IQ or achievement test scores)
2. Specific academic aptitude (excellence in certain subject areas, such as mathematics or science)

productive thinking
In Terman's terms, using thought to discover new things and generate solutions to problems

3. Creative or productive thinking (the ability to discover new things and find new alternatives; the ability to look at life in new ways; Torrance, 1972)
4. Leadership ability (the ability to help solve problems)
5. Visual and performing arts (talents in art, music, dance, drama, and related disciplines)
6. Psychomotor ability (excellence in sports)

The following are more specific characteristics of gifted and talented children:

1. Talking before other children their age
2. The ability to categorize objects
3. An interest in mathematics (can count objects, tell time, subtract or divide)
4. The ability to use imagination (e.g., devise costumes, have imaginary friends)
5. The ability to concentrate, working on tasks longer than other children their same age
6. An interest in collecting things
7. An early interest in music, art, mechanics, writing
8. A good sense of humor
9. A tendency to be self-critical

Three to 5% of all U.S. school children are judged to be gifted or talented on the basis of test results or teacher/parent nominations (Horowitz & O'Brien, 1986). Gifted children come from all levels of society, all races, and all ethnic groups. Gifted children process information differently from the nongifted. Rather than relying on step-by-step processing, they are particularly skilled at organizing and interpreting large amounts of information at one time, even when focusing on detail (Schofield & Ashman, 1987). Options for educating gifted children include early admission to school, acceleration, and enrichment.

Early admission involves starting a child in school before the traditional age of 5 or 6. While a small percentage of emotionally mature precocious children could benefit from instruction at age 4, most young children still need to play and explore and develop social competencies before they are ready for the rigors of formal education (Zigler, 1987). Enrichment may be provided within the regular classroom in the form of extra work and special projects, through self-contained classes for the gifted, or through pull-out programs where gifted children are gathered together. Unfortunately, unless all children have special opportunities the gifted can come to feel isolated by being set apart. Extra/different assignments can be seen as a welcome opportunity to explore something new or as punishment for being "different."

Of all the approaches, acceleration is the most controversial and the most promising. A younger child might suffer emotionally when placed with older students (Who would go to the senior prom with a 10 year

A Closer Look

No Boys Allowed: A Solution to Bolster Female Academic Achievement?

Are there significant differences in the educational experiences of girls attending private coed schools vs. single-sex schools? Dr. Valerie Lee thinks so. She and an associate have studied girls' elementary and high school achievement and have found several advantages associated with girls-only settings (Lee & Bryk, 1987).

1. Starting at about the sophomore year in high school, students in girls' schools surpassed the academic achievement of their coed peers by their senior year in reading, writing, and science.
2. Girls in single-sex institutions feel more positively about school.
3. Girls in single-sex institutions have greater educational aspirations.

4. Girls in single-sex institutions do more homework and watch less television.
5. Girls in single-sex institutions have fewer absences.
6. Girls in single-sex institutions have fewer discipline problems.
7. Girls in single-sex institutions have less traditional views of men's and women's proper roles.

It's possible that some of these differences are caused by the schools themselves. Single-sex high schools tended to be smaller and had fewer students per teacher than private coed schools and provided more support, more individual attention, and a sense of common purpose. It's also possible that in single-sex schools, girls get the attention they deserve because boys aren't there to dominate the math and science classes. The girls don't get to compete with the boys, but they aren't distracted by them, either.

old "senior"?), but for the child who is both intellectually capable *and* socially mature, acceleration can provide the challenge and stimulation the child needs with the regular curriculum for that grade level (Stanley, 1978).

Sometimes children are so exceptional that their behavior is seen as surreal or disturbing;

> When Michael was 2 years and 3 months olds, the family visited our laboratory. At that time, they described a youngster who had begun speaking at 5 months and by 6 months had exhibited a vocabulary of more than 50 words. He started to read English when he was 13 months old. In our laboratory he spoke five languages and could read in three of them. He understood addition, subtraction, multiplication, division, and square root, and he was fascinated by a broad range of scientific constructs. He loved to make puns, frequently bilingual ones (B. E. Robinson, 1981, p. 63).

coed schools
schools enrolling both males and females

■ Figure 12–9

Like other children, gifted children benefit from a stimulating learning environment.

Tested 2 years later when he was 4.5, Michael functioned intellectually like a 12 year old.

Children like Michael have trouble fitting in and being accepted. Some exceptionally gifted children also show high rates of emotional disturbance (Janos & Robinson, 1985). It is possible that precocious learners also experience precocious emotional development. Instead of being afraid of dogs and lightning like their peers, they have worked through these fears and are frightened by more complex issues like the possibility of being kidnapped or the humiliation of making a mistake. Their behavior might be interpreted as weird because it's not expected from their age group (Chance, 1989). In general, however, gifted children have a positive self-concept and do well socially in elementary school, but generally less well in high school (Grossberg & Cornell, 1988).

Although some school districts provide educational opportunities for gifted and talented children, many do not. Federal expenditures for the handicapped are generally many times higher than those for the gifted. One explanation for the funding discrepancy might be that the needs of the handicapped are perceived to be more immediate and serious than those of the gifted. Unfortunately, however, children with exceptional abilities can't necessarily make it on their own. Just like other children, they need nurturance, guidance, and stimulation to develop to their full potential.

Mental Retardation

To be considered mentally retarded, a child must score below 70 on a standardized IQ test (language barriers and cultural bias removed) *and* have significant difficulties *adapting* to his environment (adjusting to school, communicating, making friends, self-care skills, and so forth). To distinguish mental retardation from later brain damage, the low IQ scores and adaptive behavior problems must appear before age 18 (Diagnostic and Statistical Manual of Mental Disorders, DSM-III-R, 1987).

Between 2 and 3% of all children are diagnosed as retarded, with the rate slightly lower for girls than for boys (2 girls for every 3 boys) Gearhart & Weishahn, 1984). Classification is based on severity—mild, moderate, severe, and profound. Causes are divided into two broad categories: physical and cultural/familial causes. Physical causes of retardation account for 25% of all cases and include genetic and chromosomal disorders and brain damage that occurred prenatally (due to disease, malnutrition, drug exposure, and such problems), during birth, or postnatally (due to accident or illness). Almost all cases of severe and profound mental retardation have physical causes. For the most part, physical causes can be prevented by:

1. Providing proper nutrition to pregnant women and young children
2. Encouraging adolescent girls to avoid pregnancy

3. Providing adequate prenatal care for pregnant women
4. Consulting genetic counselors regarding the statistical chances of having a mentally retarded child so the risks are known prior to conception
5. Providing good supervision and a safe play area for the child

Cultural-familial causes are more insidious. The child with cultural-familial retardation shows no brain damage per se but may come from deprived, unstimulating environments or from environments that have dysfunctional elements. Often, children from these families can develop normally when placed in special enrichment programs as young infants (Haskins, 1986).

The vast majority of mild and moderately retarded children can benefit from training in adaptive skills and a basic academic education (up to about sixth grade). Helping retarded children learn involves:

1. Giving them more time to process information and respond
2. Providing very complete and detailed instructions
3. Valuing their contributions and respecting them as people
4. Repeating information/instructions frequently
5. Offering immediate feedback
6. Breaking complex tasks into achievable components
7. Providing clear, concrete examples
8. Realizing that the child may not be able to learn general rules or strategies to apply to future situations. Thus, each problem is brand new to the child even though it may be very similar to ones they have encountered before.

Myths abound about mental retardation (Table 12–3). Today we know that enrichment, pull-out programs, and programs involving the child's parent(s) can all help the retarded child live with purpose, a degree of independence, and a feeling of self-worth (Spitz, 1986).

■ **Figure 12–10**

An educable mentally retarded child stringing beads in school.

In Touch

ASSOCIATION OF RETARDED CITIZENS
2501 Avenue J
Arlington, TX 76006

■ **Table 12–3** *Common Misconceptions about Mental Retardation*

1. *Myth: All mentally retarded people are children.*
Despite their often youthful appearance and sometimes immature behavior, mentally retarded persons grow up just like nonretarded persons. Those between the chronological ages of zero and 12 or 13 are children, 13 to 18 year olds are adolescents, and by the age of 19 or 20, these individuals are adults.

2. *Myth: People who are mentally retarded are also mentally ill.*
Mental illness occurs in people of all levels of intelligence, including those of average and above average intelligence.

3. *Myth: Mentally retarded persons can't be helped.*
Many mentally retarded people can be helped with appropriate training and guidance.

4. *Myth: Mentally retarded people are often criminals.*
Mentally retarded people are much less likely than those of average or above average intelligence to be involved in crime. However, a disproportionate number of mentally retarded people are in penal institutions for a variety of reasons, not the least of which is that they're more likely than others to get caught or blamed.

5. *Myth: Mentally retarded people can "pollute the gene pool" if they are allowed to have children.*
Most causes of mental retardation are not genetic, and much retardation can be prevented with adequate prenatal care and good health practices.

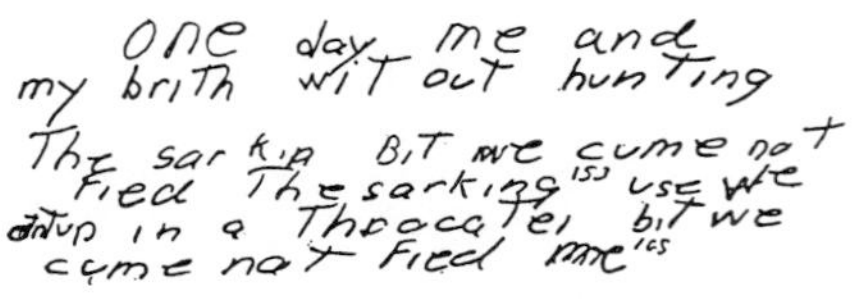

■ Figure 12–11

Farnham-Diggory (1978) reported this story written by a 13-year old boy with a significant learning disability. The story reads: One day me and my brother went out hunding the Sark. But we could not find the Sark. So we went up in a helicopter but we could not find him. The story was to be 200 words in length; the little numbers next to the words are indications that the child is keeping track of the length of his story.

Learning Disabilities

"He could not talk until age 4. He did not learn to read until he was 9. His teacher felt that he was mentally slow, unsociable, and absent-minded. He failed the entrance exams to college, passing only after he had studied for them one full year. He lost three teaching positions.

Who was he?

. . .he later went on to formulate the theory of relativity.

Albert Einstein

Some children exhibit behaviors that interfere with their ability to learn or seem to have difficulty acquiring a specific skill, like reading, writing or calculating. Interference may be due to perceptual problems, motor deficiencies, hyperactivity, or attention deficits. Taken together, these types of problems are called *learning disabilities*. In general, a child may be classified as learning disabled (LD) if he has trouble listening, thinking, speaking, reading, copying, writing, spelling, calculating, *and* those difficulties are not a consequence of low IQ (mental retardation), sensory deficits, or emotional disturbance (PL94–142; L. S. Siegel, 1989). Between 2 and 8% of the school-age population is seriously affected by learning disabilities; another 14–15% experience moderate difficulties (Farnham-Diggory, 1986). Compared to girls, boys are more frequently diagnosed as being learning disabled. Examples of perceptual–motor and writing/spelling deficits may be found in Figure 12–11.

The specific causes of learning disability are still unclear. While specific brain damage has been ruled out for lack of evidence, some researchers suspect the brains of learning disabled children simply do not function in the same way as the brains of non–learning disabled students. For example, learning disabled children have been found to recognize words by how they look, not how they sound. The "shape" of the word, not the word itself, is perceived so *grab* may be read as *grub* and *check* as *chalk*. This leads to embarrassment on the part of the students and strange behavior if they give someone chalk instead of a check. Not surprisingly, LD students display considerably more anger than non-LD students, especially if they perceive their ability to control their environment is poor (Heavey et al., 1989).

While the specific causes of the dysfunction are being debated, practitioners have devised strategies for helping the LD child learn in the classroom setting. Second, fourth, and fifth grade children prefer that help be given by their regular classroom teacher rather than by a specialist (Jenkins & Heinen, 1989). Since a learning disability is not something that is outgrown, the following strategies help some, but not all, children:

1. Summarize and repeat information.
2. Use diverse examples to convey meaning.
3. Give assignments both orally and in written form to avoid confusion.

4. If necessary, allow students to demonstrate their knowledge by non-conventional methods (oral exams with a reader, extended time limits).

5. Be sure to include time for questions and discussion.

6. Read aloud any information on the board or on transparencies. Verbally describe charts, diagrams, maps, and illustrations.

7. Explain slowly and in a step-by-step fashion.

8. Permit the use of calculators or spelling dictionaries when the limitations are severe.

9. Give less weight to spelling errors in written work when that disability is severe (perhaps give two grades—content and mechanics).

10. Computer-scored answer sheets can create serious perceptual dilemmas for some students. Provide alternative answer sheets.

11. Let the students dictate their written work to a scribe.

12. Front, middle classroom placement may facilitate attention and understanding.

13. Avoid unduly complex language structures (double negatives, the passive voice, and the like).

Children with Hearing or Vision Problems

A small percentage of schoolchildren do not hear or see well. Some children are born blind or deaf while other children sustain injuries or illness/infections that affect their vision or hearing. The detection of mild to moderate sensory impairment is challenging. A child may be able to compensate for her problem or may be misdiagnosed as mentally retarded or emotionally disturbed because she doesn't pay attention (Mollick & Etra, 1981). Deafness and visual impairment each occur at the rate of 1 child per 1000 in the United States. Hearing loss is much more common than blindness. Thousands of school children are permanently hard of hearing but not deaf. In the majority of cases, hearing aids, special classes, teletypewriters, interpreters, readers, preferred classroom seating (front and center), and eyeglasses make a substantial difference in the child's ability to learn.

Children with Physical Disabilities

Physical limitations may result from total or partial paralysis or some other chronic condition that requires the use of a wheelchair, crutches, braces, prostheses, canes, or walkers for mobility. The child may have been born with the disability or left disabled as a consequence of an illness/infection or accident. Many physically disabled children have normal intellectual and sensory skills. Their biggest barrier to learning involves accessibility to classrooms, libraries, museums, and laboratories that are guarded by stairs or undersized doors.

■ **Figure 12–12**

A visually impaired child reciting the Pledge of Allegiance.

■ ● ▲   CONCEPT SUMMARY

Characteristics of Children with Special Educational Needs

● *Gifted and talented*
  - Have the ability to go beyond the information at hand
  - Already have a substantial knowledge base, making some information too basic
  - Benefit from intellectual challenge

● *Mentally retarded*
  - Have limited memory and problem solving skills
  - Have limited comprehension
  - Have difficulty adapting to their environment
  - Need to go at a slower pace than other students

● *Learning disabled*
  - Have difficulty reading, writing, calculating, or acquiring other specific skills
  - Need flexibility in instruction (nonconventional methods)
  - Are *not* retarded

● *Children with sensory handicaps*
  - Need special accommodations like typewriters, preferred seating (close to the front), tape recorders, and the like to facilitate learning
  - May require more time for assignments
  - May benefit from mainstreaming

● *Children with physical disabilities*
  - Need accessible learning environments
  - May benefit from mainstreaming
  - May need special accommodations to facilitate learning

---

mainstreaming
the Federally mandated practice of assigning handicapped children to regular classrooms instead of segregating them in special classrooms

In 1975 the right of physically, socially, and mentally handicapped children to equal educational opportunity was specifically acknowledged and guaranteed by the passage of Public Law (PL) 94–142. PL 94–142 states that separate education may not always be the best answer for children with special needs and that for them "equal educational experience" might be schooling in regular classrooms.

From this legislation the concept of *mainstreaming* evolved. Mainstreaming involves integrating handicapped children with nonhandicapped students in regular classrooms whenever possible. The law states that handicapped children are to be placed in the "least restrictive environment." The meaning of this stipulation varies with the individual and the type and degree of disability. Proponents of mainstreaming argue that the younger the handicapped child is when placed in a regular classroom and the more time she spends there, the better is the educational outcome (Peck and Cooke, 1983). And while the educational benefits of mainstreaming have materialized, the process has failed to neutralize the negative attitudes toward some students whose learning abilities vary. Gifted adolescents (particularly females) are devalued by their high school peers both intellectually and socially (Austin & Draper, 1981). Retarded students receive the most rejection of all groups, even after lengthy mainstreaming (Brewer & Smith, 1989). Students who are retarded react by developing a negative self-concept and working at levels below their capabilities (Kirk & Gallagher, 1983). Of all the groups, the physically handicapped fare the best when mainstreamed and adjust to their peers and classrooms just as well as their nonhandicapped counterparts (Lewandowski & Cruickshank, 1980).

Helping All Children Learn at School

Regardless of what happens at school, parents can play a significant role in helping children maximize their intellectual potential. Parents can stimulate their children's curiosity, creativity, and intellectual achievement by the following means:

1. Reading to their children
2. Trying to find playmates who will stimulate the children's thinking and with whom their children can communicate
3. Taking their children to museums, historical sites, and concerts
4. Answering the children's questions rather than insisting on quiet all the time. If parents do not know the answer to a child's question, they can research the question themselves or help the child find the answer
5. Taking care not to push the children too much or force them to perform for company or friends
6. Taking care not to suppress the children's fantasy lives or overstructure their lives
7. Allowing children to make decisions
8. Showing interest in the child's schoolwork and getting involved at school (attending school functions, participating in parent/teacher nights, and so forth)
9. Providing writing materials—chalk, paper, pencils
10. Discussing events with their children; talk about what they see, read, observe in others, watch on TV. Inviting their comments
11. Giving children help when they need it but not "overhelping" them
12. Putting some limits on TV watching

A Closer Look

Can School Wait?

A growing number of parents are choosing to educate their children at home. Disenchanted with public schools because of drug problems, low academic standards, inadequate discipline, or moral or religious conflicts, parents have decided their children will get a better education at home than in school. Nobody yet keeps a precise count, but the U.S. Department of Education estimates about 260,000 children are being taught at home each year. States vary in their regulation of home schools. North Dakota, Michigan, and Iowa allow children to be schooled at home only if a certified teacher (a parent or someone else) does the teaching. A few states require that home-school educators meet minimum standards in key subjects like reading, science, math, and history. Many states require that home-schooled children be tested each year.

Opponents of home schooling doubt that most parents are adequately trained to teach their children. They also warn that children who are taught at home run the risk of being isolated, becoming too dependent on parents, and having inadequate social skills. But advocates tell a different story. A 1987 survey of 591 home-schooled children by the Home School Legal Defense Association of Washington, D.C., found that 88% scored at or above their grade level on standardized tests. Aware of the risks of isolation, many home-school advocates make sure their children are involved in non-school activities with other children.

No one—least of all the parents who have tried it—says that teaching at home is easy. Parents have to have confidence in themselves and have to learn to trust their judgments. They also have to acknowledge that they cannot be an expert on every subject. Questions without easy answers can be researched so both the parent and the child know more than when they started. Many home-school advocates enlist teachers, museums, and other home schoolers to help with curriculum. Each year, the state of California holds a home-school convention offering lectures, materials and contact with other home-school advocates.

There is very little information on how home-taught individuals fare as adults. One thing is certain—some children and some parents are better suited to home schooling than others.

Source: Hull, Victor "For Some, Schooling's a Family Job." *Los Angeles Times*, April 15, 1987, Pt. 1, 1,16–17. © 1987 Los Angeles Times. Adapted with permission.

13. Paying attention to signs of poor health, fatigue, and stress in their child
14. Expecting good things from children and highlighting the positive things they do
15. Have a close, warm relationship with the child
16. Buy them books or take them to the library
17. Know your child's teacher; attend open house and parent–teacher conferences; know what's happening at school board meetings and PTA meetings

● Language Development

The dramatic changes in cognitive ability during the school years are paralleled by equally profound progress in language development. Children's ability to communicate improves primarily because children become less concrete, less literal, less egocentric, and because they focus attention for sustained periods of time (K. E. Johnson, 1989). They also receive and profit from instruction in language related skills (Romaine, 1984). Young children who are retarded or learning disabled seem to benefit from the simultaneous use of signing with spoken language (Gines et al., 1988).

Vocabulary Size and Word Meaning

Six to 12 year old children continue to expand their reading vocabularies and to improve their understanding of words and word meaning. A typical vocabulary list for a first grader includes basal words (such as *pet*, *ball*, and *pencil*) as well as words from the literary readers. By the time the child is in the sixth grade, she is expected to know the definition and spelling of such words as *intimidate, segregation*, and *facilitate*. School-age children who are helped to see the relationship between words and who notice common word structures develop more extensive vocabularies than those without such training. For example, if a child knows that the word *beauty* describes something attractive, she will easily recognize that *to beautify* means to make something more attractive. A knowledge of root words, prefixes, and suffixes is also helpful.

It's not easy to use words correctly, however, and children in this age group often make mistakes. An 8 year old child asked a salesclerk for a book called *How to Captivate Men*. Looking dubious, the salesclerk said, "Is this for you?" "No, it's for my dad," the child replied. "For your dad! Why would he want something like that?" "That's easy," said the child. "He's a policeman!" As children become older they are able to give more abstract and less egocentric definitions of words (Holtzman, 1983). For example, a 6 year old might define the word *sucker* as "I like it. It tastes good," while a 12 year old would be more likely to produce the conventional definition, "Candy on a stick" and may even know that *sucker* is slang for a person who is easily fooled. Also, as the child's class inclusion skills improve, a child can understand that many words have similar if not identical meanings (e.g., *petite, dainty*, and *tiny*).

Like their younger counterparts, school-age children like words and enjoy using them. Six to 12 year olds readily learn chants, poems, and song lyrics. Children make decisions by reciting "Eeny, meeny, miney, mo"; jump rope to "Not last night, but the night before. . ." and rebuff insults with "Sticks and stones may break my bones but words can never hurt me!" Groups of children often use secret languages, such as Pig Latin or Double Dutch, to keep their communications private. Nicknames are also common during the school years; children sometimes even welcome the attention that insulting or offensive nicknames bring. Teasing and name-calling are often signs of affection among elementary school children. For example, I called my kindergarten paramour Carl the Carrot and he called me Anna Banana. Although we both hated those names, we liked each other.

Using Grammar

School-age children continue to refine their understanding of the structure of the language and the way words are organized into sentences. Six and 7 year olds tend to be confused by irrelevant information, complex constructions, and the implied meaning of certain words. Carol Chomsky (1969) presented 5–10 year old children with a blindfolded doll and asked if the doll was "easy to see" or "hard to see." Most of the younger children misinterpreted the sentence and were misled by the blindfold; they answered "hard to see." Six, 7, and 8 year olds showed intermediate levels of understanding in this task, but by age 9 and 10 none of the children were confused by the irrelevant blindfold. They all said the doll was easy to see because she was in plain sight and not hidden. Carol Chomsky (1969) found that by the age of 9, almost all children can identify the subject and meaning of these complex sentences as well:

John promised Bill to go. (Who is going?)
The car was bumped by the truck. (What did the bumping?)

A construction like "John asked Bill what to do" is more difficult and its meaning may not be understood until the child is 10 or 11.

Just because children don't use proper grammar in their personal speech doesn't mean they are unable to understand correct usage. Provided they have had plenty of opportunity to learn, a child who says, "He don't want that" knows the grammatically correct form is "He doesn't want that" but just chooses not to use it. Using different forms of speech in different circumstances or with different people is called *code-switching* (Bernstein, 1973).

code switching
situation-specific and person-specific language

Children who have language difficulties are also more likely to exhibit aggressive behavior. Apparently, the child has a need to express herself if not verbally then physically (Burke et al., 1989).

Communication Effectiveness

As I mentioned earlier, young children may not know that they don't understand or that directions are incomplete and unclear. Instead, they just nod and go forward without asking questions or looking for more information. An older child is more likely to realize that something is unclear, to stop and look puzzled, and to identify the source of the confusion, and suggest an appropriate revision (Beal, 1987).

If children have articulation problems during the school years, these letter combinations are most likely involved: *thr, shr, sk, sh, ch, s, j* and *z*. Articulation difficulties that persist past age 7 or 8 may be due to cleft palate, hearing loss, malocclusion, or imitation of imperfect speech models. A lisp or consistent speech omission can be carried into adulthood but not always recognized or considered a problem by the general public.

As they decenter, children are increasingly able to take another person's perspective and to use persuasion. After they hear a story, 6 year olds cannot tell you what the people in the story were told and what they now know. The ability to keep story details straight improves dramatically by age 12 or 13 (Edelstein et al., 1984).

Improvement also takes place in the child's ability to persuade someone to do something for them. The best persuasive arguments don't just express a need but also take into account the experiences and personality of the listener. John Flavell and colleagues (1968) asked children to show how they would talk their dad into buying them a TV set for their room. Six and 7 year olds express the need ("Dad, I really want a TV in my room"), and spend the rest of their time begging and trying to look deserving ("Please, daddy, please, please. . ." [big smile, hug daddy]). Eleven and 12 year olds, on the other hand, use arguments that demonstrate an understanding of the household budget ("I know we have to spend our money carefully"), the benefit of the purchase ("I could spend a lot more time watching the educational shows my teacher talks about"), and offer an insight into the past ("When you were a kid, I bet you wanted your own TV, too"). By the fourth grade, children are more sensitive to the listener's needs than younger children (Sonnenschein, 1986).

Just being able to understand word meaning makes a huge difference in communication effectiveness. For example, children under 8 respond to the sentences "Ask me your name" and "Tell me you name" in the same way: They give the questioner their name. And, because an understanding of cause and effect develops throughout the school years, children may use conjunctions such as *because* and *then* to express time, not causality. Another troublesome area is connectives such as *but* and *although*: school-age children do use them occasionally, but even sixth graders have an easier time recognizing when these words are used appropriately than actually using them in their own speech.

The 6–12 year old also has difficulty using certain relational terms. The following adjective pairs are listed in order of their difficulty, from easiest to hardest: *big/little, tall/short, long/short, high/low, wide/narrow, thin/thick,* and *deep/shallow* (deVilliers & DeVilliers, 1978). Also, children often understand such concepts as *left of,* and *sister of,* or *more important than* as absolute attributes rather than relationships among existing ob-

■●▲ CONCEPT SUMMARY

Language Development During the School Years

- Continuously expanding vocabulary
- Display less literalness and concreteness in interpreting word meaning
- More sophisticated use of grammar
- May still use some words incorrectly, especially in personal speech
- Are quicker to acknowledge that they don't understand something
- More skilled in the art of persuasion
- Still experience some difficulty using relational terms
- Can appreciate humor because of expanded cognitive abilities

jects. On the side of improvement, however, school-age children can see relationships in terms of reciprocal roles—for example, in order to be a sister, one must have a sibling. This represents a considerable advance over the younger child's ability to think in terms of relationships. The preschooler typically refers to any adult female in a family as "your mother"—even when talking with that female's husband!

Dialects/Nonstandard English

Versions of a language characterized by minor variations on the standard form are called dialects. Dialects can be regional (Southern—*y'all* for *you all*), or associated with social groups (*bad* for *good/cool*) or professions (baseball talk—"Don't throw that cheese in here," and the like). Black English is perhaps the most familiar dialect spoken in the United States. This dialect is spoken mostly by blacks living in low-income areas but is readily understood by most blacks and some nonblacks as well. Here are some examples of black English phrases:

- You ain't goin' to no store, y'unnerstan'?
- They be saying if you smart, you go to work.
- I ax Alvin do he know how to play.
- Nobody didn't know he didn't.

Black English is not just a corruption of standard English but a dialect with its own complex structure and complete and consistent set of rules (Labov, 1972). Once one understands the grammatical rules that govern the production of black speech, some of which originated in African linguistic patterns, black English becomes logical and comprehensible to nonspeakers. For example, consider the sentence, "Nobody didn't know he didn't." If we apply the rules for constructing sentences using negatives, this sentence translates into "Nobody knew he did".

A child who speaks black English at home may be at a disadvantage in a school system that recognizes only standard English (Wiener et al., 1983). When the teacher corrects the child's speech, the child may not understand because she didn't feel she made an error (Romaine, 1984). Furthermore, if teachers adopt the attitude that black English is wrong or inferior, the black child may develop feelings of inadequacy and eventually drop out of a system that is punitive and nonsupportive. It is important that teachers give instruction in standard English to black students while simultaneously recognizing the legitimacy of their nonstandard speech and protecting their self-esteem.

Humor

School-age children appreciate more sophisticated forms of humor than their preschool counterparts. While silliness and "bathroom humor" are the mainstays of the 3–6 year olds, 6–12 year olds are more likely to enjoy riddles, jokes, and rhymes that focus on unexpected or incongruous events (McCauley et al., 1983). Here are some representative samples:

- How can you double your money?
  Fold it.

- How many months have 28 days?
  All of them.

- Where do sheep get their hair cut?
  At the baa-baa shop.

- How do you keep a skunk from smelling?
  Hold its nose.

- What did the dog say when it sat on sandpaper?
  Ruff! Ruff!

- Why did the elephant wear green sneakers?
  So it could hide in the grass.

- What's big, purple, and lives in the ocean?
  Moby Grape.

- *Patient:* Doctor, I have a problem. Everyone seems to be turning into owls.
  Doctor: How did it start?
  Patient: It started with my best friend.
  Doctor: Who?
  Patient: Oh, no! You've got it, too!

- At the restaurant they met,
  Romeo and Juliet.
  When neither one could pay the debt,
  Rom-e-owed what Juli-et.

To understand jokes and riddles of this sort, school-age children must have acquired considerable knowledge about the world. They must recognize, too, that the same word can have different meanings and words that sound the same aren't necessarily the same words. And they must know the characteristics of certain animals and even have some familiarity with classical literature. The preschool child is incapable of understanding the logic (or logical illogic) that forms the basis of these jokes and riddles. Their language skills aren't extensive enough and they haven't gathered enough concrete information about their surroundings to understand the concepts of the ideas presented. If preschool children laugh at this humor, they are probably modeling the amusement displayed by others or are laughing because the situation demands that response. We can often assess a young child's understanding of a joke by judging his or her ability to repeat it to another person. After laughing loudly at a story told by his older brother, one 6 year old was encouraged to tell the joke to his mother. Although the child posed the right question, "What did the mayonnaise say to the refrigerator?" he ruined the punch line by saying, "Shut the door, I'm getting dressed." (Actually, it's "Shut the door, I'm dressing—get it?") For the preschooler, the punchline doesn't really matter. Both versions are equally funny because they don't have the cognitive ability to interpret the play on words (McGhee, 1979).

Most of the jokes and riddles that fourth and fifth graders tell involve puns or some form of language ambiguity. This type of humor is challenging but comprehensible for school-age children unaffected by learning disabilities (Bruno et al., 1987). By the time the child is an adolescent, puns are more obvious and less startling than they were during the middle years. The older child tends to think that absurdity (as in "elephant jokes"), humor with aggressive themes, and humor that pokes fun at adults are funnier than plays on words (Pinderhughes & Zigler, 1985). For example,

- *First student:* What would you tell the teacher if you had to miss school because you lost your voice?
  Second student: Nothing.

- How many teachers does it take to change a lightbulb?
  Student's version: Five. One to hold the light bulb and four to rotate the table.
  Teacher's version: None. Teacher's aren't afraid of the dark.

- *Parent:* What did you learn in school today, dear?
  Child: I don't have to educate you all over again, do I?

Tongue twisters amuse language-competent children who enjoy challenges to their speaking skills and delight when others misspeak themselves. Some common tongue twisters include "she sells seashells by the seashore" and "rubber baby buggy bumpers." (If the fascination of these examples isn't apparent at first glance, try saying each phrase three times fast.)

By the time children are 9 or 10, they have gained enough control over some of their early fears to joke about them. They judge ghost stories and horror films to be entertaining, as they do jokes about darkness, death, burial, and other tragedies. Laughter discharges some of the child's anxiety about these topics, even though the apparent preoccupation with the grisly and macabre may be disturbing to adults.

Masten (1986) found that the most competent children in school tend to have the best sense of humor. Teachers judged these children as cooperative, productive, and attentive, while the child's peers found them to be happy, fun to be with, and good leaders. Children who lack a sense of humor may find themselves more isolated from their peers (Sherman, 1985).

● Moral Development

As children's brains develop, their ability to reason and perceive matures and their world view changes. The cognitively based 5-to-7 shift affects moral reasoning in the same way it affects general intellectual growth: As children begin to understand logical rules, they also come to understand that laws, rules, and social expectations exist to guide behavior. We will examine the theories of Jean Piaget and Lawrence Kohlberg to explain moral development during the school years.

Piaget's Ideas about Moral Development

**heteronomous morality
(moral realism)**
in Piaget's theory of moral development, the stage in which rules are regarded as unchangeable, absolute and imposed by an external authority

Piaget (1935/1965) felt that when the child enters the stage of concrete operations at age 6 or 7, he also enters a new stage of moral development. He called it the *stage of heteronomous morality* or *moral realism* (heteronomous means under an outside authority). During the preschool years, children play for the sheer pleasure of the activity, with little concern over outcomes or rules. When they pass into the stage of moral realism, however, they not only become aware of rules, they believe the rules are sacred, unchangeable, are developed by God or adults, and should be obeyed under all circumstances. According to one 6 year old, "You can't play (the game) any other way...it would be cheating" (Piaget, 1935/1965, p. 59, 63).

The lingering egocentrism of young children encourages them to adhere to three beliefs. First, they believe in *imminent justice,* wherein wrongdoing invariably leads to punishment. Second, the morality of an act is judged by its *objective consequences,* not the objective intentions of the person. In other words, the bigger the mess or loss, the greater the crime. And, finally, young school-age children believe in the *absolutism* of moral perspectives, the idea that there is only one correct moral conclusion per circumstance and everyone automatically agrees with that conclusion. Perspective taking is limited.

**autonomous morality/morality
of cooperation**
the most advanced of Piaget's stages of moral reasoning in which rules are viewed as flexible, purposeful, and developing out of cooperative social agreement

By age 10 or so, Piaget noted a shift in the child's moral reasoning. He called this new stage the *stage of autonomous morality* or the *morality of cooperation.* As children become less egocentric and more flexible by age 9 or 10, they are also able to realize that rules are not fixed but arbitrary, can change when players agree, and that it is possible to make personal decisions about obeying rules. Since the older child can consider the feelings and viewpoints of others while assessing his own behavior, his moral decision making shows more leniency and flexibility than that of younger children. And, as peer group solidarity develops, the moral authority of adults is replaced in part by a morality based on cooperation and mutual understanding. At this stage it's not always wrong to break the rules or to disobey authority; rather, the motives, the rules, the specific situation are all brought to bear in making a judgment. Children now understand the reciprocity expressed in the Golden Rule and can apply it and similar principles to their own behavior. Conversely, the 9 to 11 year old child's sense of fairness is shaken by inequality. Children now argue over who got the largest piece of cake and object when they feel they're doing more than their share of work. The operative principle is that punishment should fit the crime. And since they feel praise and punishment should be distributed in a non-arbitrary, even-handed way, it is hard for children at this stage to understand that the same behavior might evoke different responses from different people. For example, a marginal student who gets a report card filled with Cs might receive lavish praise, while a more capable student with the same grades in the same subjects might be encouraged to develop more efficient study habits. When the reasons for differentiating the performances are given, however, most children understand the disparity. Genuine objectivity and the ability to reason abstractly are not achieved until adolescence and beyond.

Kohlberg's Theory of Moral Development

Lawrence Kohlberg sought to refine and extend the ideas of Piaget (1935/1965) and the pioneering work of James M. Baldwin (1894) by creating a comprehensive three-stage theory.

In Chapter 9 we said that the moral reasoning of preschool children was influenced by a concern for obedience and punishment and for satisfying personal needs. Kohlberg refers to this orientation as the *preconventional level of morality*. Preconventional moral reasoning coincides with the preoperational stage of cognitive development (Kitchener, 1983). When children enter the stage of concrete operations, they are able to turn away from their egocentric thinking, growing more concerned about appearing "good" and "fair" and looking to others to approve their moral acts. According to Kohlberg (1969, 1976) this shift in focus is characteristic of what he called the *conventional level (level 2) of moral reasoning*. When confronted with the ethical dilemma involving Heinz, his dying wife, and the druggist (given in Chapter 9), the conventional thinker is likely to argue this way:

conventional moral reasoning
Kohlberg's second stage of moral development in which social reactions to moral dilemmas affect the decision-making process; the moral motivation is to conform to rules and to please people in positions of power and authority

> PRO: Heinz was not really wrong to steal because he was trying to save his wife's life.
> PRO: Heinz should steal the drug because it is his responsibility if his wife died. He can pay the druggist later.
> CON: It's against the law to steal. Heinz should find some other way to get the drug.
> CON: Heinz should not steal because it's not nice to steal and people won't like you when you take things that don't belong to you.

Concern with law and order is an important aspect of conventional reasoning. Children (and many adults) who reason at this level strive to uphold society's standards of right and wrong, and they have rigid ideas and rules. Rules/laws are seen to have an absolute purpose: to maintain the social order and protect people. Thus, rule infraction/law breaking is considered to be inherently immoral because it creates chaos in a stable, agreed-upon social framework.

The child at the conventional stage can assume another's perspective, a particularly important achievement for understanding different motives. Speeding, for example, is against the law and would be judged to be bad at this level. But if the person didn't intend to speed (if their accelerator was sticking or the speedometer was faulty), then the speeding is excusable. Children age 6 and older also take into account the emotional reactions of the wrongdoer when evaluating the transgression, judging a "happy" wrongdoer to be worse than a "sorry" one (Nunner-Winkler & Sodian, 1988).

The next stage of Kohlberg's scheme, level 3, is called *postconventional moral reasoning*, and this is the orientation more typical of adolescents than school-age children.

Moral Judgments and Moral Behavior

In a classic study of 10,000 school children, Hugh Hartshorn and Mark May (1928-1930) found that students who endorse rigid moral standards or who display mature moral reasoning don't necessarily behave in ethical or desirable ways. Nine to 11 year old children are quick to find excuses to justify their own rule infractions ("I took that dollar because I. . ."). Although older children may know when they've done something wrong, they may still be unable to rely on reason to guide their behavior in emotionally trying circumstances. Why the inconsistency? Solving moral dilemmas involves trying to coordinate several sets of conflicting needs and motives, including the laws/rules of the culture, the morality of their peers, the guidelines enforced by their parents and teachers, and their own self-interest (Turiel & Smetana, 1984). In addition, the third or fourth grade child who has read a story may be able to identify its moral ("It's about being nice") but may not necessarily be able to apply what they've learned to actual situations and circumstances (Johnson & Goldman, 1987). Thus, moral decision making benefits from practice and maturity and from specific instruction on how to generalize moral principles to real life.

Cheating

Dishonest behavior is influenced by a variety of factors, and certain specific situations might compromise the honesty of even the most strong-willed, temptation-resistant child. Contrary to popular belief, boys are not more willing to cheat than girls. Teachers rate girls as more trustworthy than boys, and girls are less likely to admit cheating, but the actual frequency of cheating tends to be much the same for both sexes (Coady & Sawyer, 1986). Moreover, cheating is by no means a rare phenomenon: Between 50 and 80% of elementary, high school, and college students said they would cheat under certain circumstances. Children who fear failure or have high needs to achieve have to weigh the risks of being discovered against the potential benefits of being dishonest. When the likelihood of getting caught is high, high-need achievers usually won't risk discovery, but when the stakes are high and the risk of being caught is low the frequency of cheating increases. Students who feel they must receive high grades to qualify for programs, meet their parents' expectations, or live up to personal standards, are more likely to cheat than those who have less to lose by failure.

The frequency of lying decreased with age when fourth, seventh, and tenth grade boys were compared (Stouthamer-Loeber & Loeber, 1986). Boys who tell lies were also more likely to engage in other problem behaviors like delinquency, theft, and fighting. Parental conflict and parental rejection are correlated with lie telling (Stouthamer-Loeber & Loeber, 1986).

■ Figure 12–14

Cheating at school is becoming increasingly common.

Encouraging the Development of Moral Reasoning

Adults can stimulate complex moral thinking in children by discussing right and wrong with them and exposing them to people who are at slightly more advanced levels of moral reasoning than the children themselves (Nicholls & Thorkildsen, 1988). Children who live with dictated moral rules often reason at low levels, since they have few chances to think about the principles involved in the rules they follow. Children who are encouraged to practice communication patterns and to consider such issues as the value of fairness and the merits of individual freedom reach higher levels of moral thinking than those who do not discuss such topics (Lapsley & Quintana, 1985). Parents whose discipline strategies consistently involve reasoning and explanation and an emphasis on feelings ("We don't hit because . . ." or "How would you feel if. . .?") are more likely to encourage complex moral judgments and highly self-controlled behavior in their children than parents who use other disciplinary techniques and who don't encourage emotional empathy (Kohlberg et al., 1983).

The Development of Ideas Regarding Fairness and Justice

As early as 1977 William Damon found that Kohlberg's moral dilemmas may be too abstract and unrealistic to accurately measure the moral reasoning of younger children. Using a task that involves allocating rewards among group members, Damon identified six developmental levels of *distributive justice reasoning*, three of which apply to the school-age child (Table 12–4). When younger children were asked to divide up 10 candy bars among 4 children as appreciation for work completed (making bracelets), 5 and 6 year olds want everyone to have an absolutely equal share regardless of special circumstances (2.5 candy bars each). Older children (8 and 10 years of age) tend to consider productivity, group solidarity, responsibility, age, and other factors in their notions of distributive justice, taking each situation as a special case

distributive justice reasoning
a concept of fairness concerning the allocation of rewards among group members

■ **Table 12–4**   *Damon's Levels of Children's Distributive Justice Reasoning*

LEVEL	APPROXIMATE AGE	DESCRIPTION
0-A	4	Fair allocation of rewards is confused with the child's momentary desires. Children of this level believe that they themselves should get more simply because they want more.
0-B	4–5	Children cite an objective attribute as a fair basis for distribution, but it is arbitrary and irrelevant to the situation. A child should get more for being the oldest, a fast runner, or having the most friends.
1-A	5	There is recognition that each participant has a stake in the rewards, but children of this level think the only way competing claims can be resolved is by strictly equal distribution. Special considerations like merit or need are not taken into account.
1-B	6–7	Fair distribution is equated with deservingness and concrete reciprocity. There is recognition that some people may have a greater claim to rewards for having worked harder.
2-A	8	Children recognize a variety of conflicting claims to justice, including equal treatment, merit, and need. Each claim is weighed, and parties with special needs, such as a younger child who cannot produce as much or a child who does not get any allowance, are given consideration.
2-B	8 and older	As in 2-A, all claims are considered. In addition, a fair distribution of rewards is seen as one that furthers the social goals of the group—for example, by encouraging future productivity or promoting friendship and group solidarity.

Source: Damon, *The Social World of the Child*, 1977. Reprinted with permission.

(Thorkildsen, 1989). For example, if one child completed 3 bracelets and the rest only 2 each, then older children would consider giving the more productive member more candy. Like moral reasoning, concepts of distributive justice are related to Piaget's stages of cognitive development and perspective-taking skills (Blotner & Beareson, 1984).

The Development of Prosocial and Altruistic Reasoning

In Kohlberg's dilemmas, the motive to help is always contrasted with legal prohibitions or the dictates of an authority figure. Nancy Eisenberg and her colleagues (1982, 1986) wondered what children would decide to do if a prosocial action was pitted against the child's own self-interest. For example, children are asked to consider the following:

> One day a girl named Mary was going to a friend's birthday party. On her way she saw a girl who had fallen down and hurt her leg. The girl asked Mary to go to her house and get her parents so the parents could come and take her to the doctor. But if Mary did run and get the child's parents, she would be late for the birthday party and miss the ice cream, cake, and all the games. What should Mary do? Why? (Eisenberg, 1982, p. 231)

On the basis of interviews with children ages 4 to 10, Eisenberg was able to identify five age-related levels of prosocial reasoning (Table 12–5). Paralleling Kohlberg's stages, children move from an egocentric

---

■ **Table 12–5** *Eisenberg's Levels of Prosocial Moral Reasoning*

LEVEL	APPROXIMATE AGE	DESCRIPTION
1. Hedonistic, pragmatic orientation	Preschool, early elementary school	"Doing right" satisfies one's own needs. Reasons for helping or not helping another refer to gains for the self, e.g., "I wouldn't help because I might get too hungry."
2. "Needs of others" orientation	Preschool, elementary school	Concern for the physical, material, and psychological needs of others is expressed in simple terms, without clear evidence of perspective-taking or empathic feeling, e.g., "He needs it."
3. Stereotyped, approval-focused orientation	Elementary school and high school	Stereotyped images of good and bad persons and concern for approval justify behavior, e.g., "He'd like him more if he helped."
4. Empathic orientation	Older elementary school and high school	Reasoning reflects an emphasis on perspective-taking and empathic feeling for the other person, e.g., "I'd feel bad if I didn't help because he'd be in pain."
5. Internalized values orientation	Small minority of high school students, no elementary school pupils	Justifications for moral choice are based on internalized values, norms, desire to maintain contractual obligations, and belief in the dignity, rights, and equality of all individuals, e.g., "I would feel bad if I didn't help because I'd know that I didn't live up to my values."

Source: Eisenberg, *The Development of Prosocial Behavior* (Academic Press, 1982). Adapted with permission.

focus, to trying to win the approval of others, to an internalized standard of what is right and good. Children who are caring, sympathetic, and understanding as preschoolers are likely to remain so during the school years, but some variables continue to shape the child's prosocial tendencies. For example, the family has considerable impact on the likelihood that the child will be helpful. And parents who are empathic, model positive behavior, reward their children for cooperation, and assign age-appropriate responsibilities within the family are more likely to encourage cooperation and helping among their children than parents who do not (Eisenberg et al., 1983; Koestner et al., 1990).

Altruistic actions speak louder than words in affecting the behavior of children. When parents don't practice the benevolencies they preach, their children are less likely to exhibit helpful behavior than when parents are consistent in word and deed (Eisenberg et al., 1983). Parents who exhort others to do good deeds but who act selfishly themselves are even more negatively influential. Their children overlook their verbal messages in favor of the more obvious behavioral ones. Thus, children avoid doing what their hypocritical parent says they must do, simply modeling their behavior instead.

As with other forms of moral behavior, the development of helping and cooperative behavior is enhanced by well-developed role-taking skills and a capacity for empathy. Victor Battistich and his colleagues (1989) instituted a school-based program for children in grades K-4 designed to enhance prosocial development. They found the program helped children make substantial gains in conflict resolution and problem solving. Since empathic children can take the perspective of the other person more readily, they know what it feels like to need help. They can also reduce their own vicarious suffering and guilt by being altruistic. Furthermore, children with higher social skills are more competent help-seekers and help-givers than children with weak social skills (Tyler & Varma, 1988). True altruism becomes more possible with age. High school students are more likely than elementary school students to help when the cost of helping is high (Eisenberg & Shell, 1986).

The Development of Self-Control

Helping, being fair, caring, and doing the right thing all involve proactive behaviors planned and initiated by the child. Another aspect of moral development involves *inhibiting* behaviors that conflict with moral outcomes and acquiring *self-control*. While preschoolers find it difficult to delay gratification and resist temptation, by the time children are in the first or second grade, they can think up strategies on their own to help them maintain control (Mischel, 1974). In one study, children played a game where pieces of candy were placed in front of them in such a way that the longer they waited, the more candy they got (Toner & Smith, 1977). The children who were able to wait the longest diverted their attention by counting to themselves, looking at the wall, playing a game, or repeating a moral prohibition to themselves ("It's better if I wait"). As they grow older, children seem to understand that some delay strategies are more effective than others. Focusing on the reward of eating ("The candy will be yummy and sweet") is less helpful than concentrating on the waiting itself ("I just have 10 more minutes to go") (Mischel & Mischel, 1983).

Personality factors also play a role. Children who are less able to delay gratification are described as rebellious, unpredictable, self-indulgent, or hostile. Those displaying the most delay of gratification tended to be responsible, productive, consistent, and interested in intellectual matters and controlled (Funder & Block, 1989).

■●▲   CONCEPT SUMMARY

Moral Development During the School Years

- Realize it's not always wrong to break the rules
- Can consider others' motives and intentions in assessing their actions
- Reciprocity and fair exchange are important principles
- Make moral decisions that reflect the need for social approval
- Emotional reactions of the wrongdoer influence the evaluation of the infraction ("being sorry" helps the school-age child feel more forgiving)
- May be able to apply moral principles if allowed to practice communication patterns, to understand the reasons for the "rules," and to role-play outcomes
- May cheat during the school years if the risk is low and the situation compelling
- Cooperation and helping can be encouraged if those behaviors are modeled by the parents and if children are taught to be empathic and are given age-appropriate responsibilities
- When hypocrisy is involved, actions speak louder than words—children will model adults' behavior and ignore their admonition
- Are better able to delay gratification than younger children

---

● Basic School Skills—The 3 Rs and a C

In the United States, formal education officially begins in the first grade. The current back-to-basics movement in education stresses literacy in reading, writing, mathematics, and computer skills.

Learning to Read

Reading is fundamental to school achievement because it is implicated in practically everything the child does. Almost all assignments are preceded by written instructions. If the child can't read and comprehend the assignment, even high-level math and composition skills won't help her successfully complete the assignment. The first step in teaching children to read involves helping them become familiar with the alphabet and letter–sound associations. Next, children must begin to learn how to pronounce common letter groups, especially those pronounced differently from the letters themselves (*ee* vs. *e* vs. *ey* [which sounds like *a* and *e* together]). At this point, children begin processing letters, sounds, words, and meanings all at the same time (Paris & Lindauer, 1982). Because of this multi-level processing, beginning reading programs should probably teach *both* phonics (word attack) and whole-word recognition rather than one or the other (Baron, 1979).

Children who are poor readers in the first grade have an 88% likelihood of being poor readers and poor writers in the fourth grade (Juel, 1988). Poor readers demonstrate poor word decoding skills and practice reading less than good readers. Reading comprehension can be improved by instructing children to look for "clue" words (Yuill & Joscelyne, 1988).

Learning to Write

Writing skills, like reading, are developed by practice and an organized plan of attack. Specific suggestions from research for encouraging good writing include the following (Laine & Schultz, 1985; S. Graham & Harris, 1988):

1. Early writing should come from personal experience or from something going on in the classroom. (Write an ending to the story we just read, compose an ad for a lost dog, or write about what you like to do with your free time.)
2. Let children know that writing has different purposes and takes different forms: to persuade, to ask for information, to record ideas, to express something new/imaginative, to have fun, and on and on.
3. Discuss the objectives of the assignment and help the children generate ideas before the actual writing begins.
4. Once the writing begins, let it flow uninterrupted.

5. Always allow time for revision. Each child can be helped to reorganize and reevaluate the piece. Help children correct grammar, punctuation, capitalization, and spelling. Work until a good draft emerges. Deemphasize mistakes.

6. Not every child's work is a masterpiece. Avoid relying on just the "top" student to read her work—it's disheartening to the less polished writers. Display or "publish" all papers.

7. Strengthen the child's writing skills by planning reading and oral exercises around the writing activity.

8. Have children write often under pleasant, supportive circumstances.

Developing Math Skills

"Hands on" mathematics ("Math Their Way") is the current focus, involving manipulating concrete objects in order to discover or understand math principles. Rote memorization is deemphasized, but once the "math facts" are learned, drill and practice in the basic skills is critical. More stress is typically placed on the reasoning skills involved than on just attaining the right answer (Lawson & Bealer, 1984). When teachers have a positive attitude toward mathematics, children will, too (Schofield, 1981). Also, math problems that use simple, concrete language are easier for children to solve than those using abstract ambiguous language (Cummins et al., 1988).

Computer Skills

Computer literacy, skill in operating and utilizing computers, has joined reading, writing, and arithmetic as a desired product of the school experience. While computers don't replace teachers, they do serve as valuable learning aids. Computers can tutor children in various subjects, giving them practice answering specific questions, as well as instant feedback. The child can check her knowledge of math facts, the parts of a flower, or the voyages of Columbus by using computers instead of workbooks. Reading comprehension on the screen is the same as for the printed page (Gambrell et al., 1987). Computers can be used in place of calculators and typewriters. Word-processing programs allow children to compose on the computer, learning keyboard skills and having the ability to add, delete, or rearrange text without redoing the entire assignment. Computer games can be both educational and fun. The program entitled *Oregon Trail* tests the child's ability to understand the hazards faced by the pioneers and to plan effectively enough to make it from Independence, Missouri, to the West Coast without starving, falling prey to hostile Indians, or breaking down. Computer simulations, like those used in the sciences, can help children conduct on-the-spot experiments that would be too costly, dangerous, or lengthy to do in

■ **Figure 12–15**

In a computerized world, the students need an Apple as much as the teacher used to.

■ Figure 12–16

Leaving elementary school and entering middle school or junior high is an important transition in a child's life.

class. For example, children can see what effect the destruction of the world's forests can have on the world's oxygen supply or how increasing levels of pollution can affect the wildlife in and around a lake. Finally, children can learn the logic of programming by creating and refining their own software.

While computers certainly reinforce learning and provide opportunities to explore, they don't seem to accelerate the acquisition of knowledge (Greenfield, 1984). Even though children don't seem to learn any *faster* using computers, they do seem to enjoy the process. Children voluntarily come early, stay late, and donate recess time to "play" with the computer. In addition to stimulating interest and increasing motivation, computers also increase rather than decrease social interaction among students. Children working on computers talk about their work more, collaborate more and seek the advice and counsel of others more frequently than students working on more traditional classroom tasks (Hawkins et al., 1982). Computers can also offer an alternative way of learning for handicapped students (who can't hold a pencil or pen in their hands, for example), for deaf students (who benefit from immediate, understandable feedback), or for learning disabled students (who can correct their spelling instantly on the word processor and create "literate" compositions just like their non-LD peers) (Prinz & Nelson, 1985; Glazer & Curry, 1988–1989). Girls may find computing less approachable or appropriate when programs are gender biased (Spelling Baseball or Demolition Division), when computer labs are closely allied with mathematics departments, when the "atmosphere" of the lab creates discomfort (noisy, competitive, and the like), or when girls are less successful than boys in persuading their parents to invest in a home computer (Lepper, 1985).

Encouraging School Success

School success can be facilitated in a multitude of ways by teachers, principals, and school staff. Here are only a few suggestions:

1. Hire teachers who are knowledgeable, well trained, dedicated, responsible, and who love their work. Teachers must also be warm, caring, supportive individuals who truly enjoy and respect children.
2. Children may do better in school when they have teachers who are excellent models for diversity in gender, race, ethnic background, or physical status.
3. Institute breakfast programs for poor/disadvantaged students who may come to school hungry.
4. Establish a homework hotline where children and parents can call in to check homework assignments.
5. Provide tutors and organize study groups for children whose parents cannot help with homework.

►► ISSUE ◄◄

Rating the School Systems: America—2, Japan—10

Since the mid 1980s, concern has been growing that Americans are falling behind students from other countries in educational achievement (B. F. Skinner, 1984; Spence, 1985). While the United States boasts more Nobel laureates than any other nation, the prospects for the future look increasingly dim as our students' math and science scores continue to trail those of students in Asian countries such as Japan and Korea. The motivation to "do something" to reestablish quality in the American school is even coming from major corporations like Texas Instruments (*Newsweek*, Special Edition, Fall/Winter, 1990):

> "Today the competition isn't just the student in the next row or the next town. The competition is sitting in classrooms all over the world."

So what should be done? Let's start by looking at the similarities and differences between the children and schools in America and Japan, this country's main competitor.

People-centered differences. One possibility is that Japanese children outperform Americans because they are simply more capable, have superior brains or some other inborn advantage. A comparison of the top 10% of American and Japanese students show virtually identical achievement (Flynn, 1987) as does a comparison of the cognitive development of first and fifth graders in Japan, Taiwan, and the United States (Uttal et al., 1988). According to these data, Asians do not appear to be genetically superior in intelligence.

Although most students share the same goals (happiness, success), Japanese and American students differ in their expectation of success. Basically, Americans have a more pessimistic attitude about "making it," and those doubts may operate as a self-fulfilling prophecy. Low expectations can contribute to lower levels of achievement (Goleman, 1990). The Japanese also tend to believe that if you do not do well in school, you are doomed to a poor job. American

students see a far more tenuous link between academic achievement and job/income. Many of America's heroes and highest paid individuals are self-made people for whom education was lacking or made little or no difference (Elvis Presley, Babe Ruth, Michael Jackson, Henry Ford).

Cultural differences. Both American and Japanese cultures attempt to instill a strong work ethic. While Americans have traditionally worked hard to achieve, Japanese work harder. Compared to Americans, Japanese and Chinese students have more positive views of homework (Chen & Stevenson, 1989). In a study of almost 8,000 high school students in the San Francisco area, Asian-Americans spent about 40% more time doing homework and studying than did their non-Asian counterparts and, as a consequence, got better grades (Dornbusch et al., 1987).

Asians are socialized to respect and obey their parents' wishes. Most Asian parents value academic success in part because high status brings the family honor and in part because of centuries

(continued on next page)

A Japanese classroom.

(continued from previous page)

of tradition that witnesses the rise of the intellectual elite into positions of power in their homelands (H. W. Stevenson et al., 1990). Asian parents coax their child to work harder in school and may even give them extra schoolwork themselves and extra help (Chen & Stevenson, 1989). There is a significant difference between most Asian parents and other parents in how they react to a child's poor performance. Most Americans accept occasional failures, emphasizing the child's strengths. The Japanese tend to believe that if you're not doing well, you're not working hard enough. They feel anyone can succeed if they really try (Dornbusch et al., 1987).

Differences in the school systems themselves. In general, Japanese students spend more time in school than American students. Saturday is a regular schoolday in Japan and Korea. The school day itself is also longer. Each year American children spend more hours in front of the television than they do in the classroom. Asian children spend most of their free time doing homework (1/2 hour of homework assigned—U.S. average; 3 hours of homework assigned—Japanese average).

Self-discipline is also rigorous and absolute in Japan, so behavior problems and other disruptions rarely impede the progress of education. One might expect more instruction, more time on task, and more homework to have a beneficial effect on academic performance.

In order to improve educational achievement in the United States and remain competitive on a global level, we don't have to change the whole structure of our society. Americans *do* need to relearn the value of education and hard work. And they must provide support for their school systems, both financially and emotionally.

6. Provide bilingual education to help children make the transition into the educational mainstream.
7. Help teachers identify children who may be anxious, apathetic, alienated, or troubled. Provide support services for such children and their families.
8. Children often act as others expect them to. Have confidence in each child's ability to succeed.
9. Be aware of any biases that exist in your treatment of children. Treat all children equally at all times.
10. Motivate children by providing sincere praise, attention and approval for their effort and commitment in academics, athletics, and social arenas.
11. Help children conquer test anxiety and performance fears by reassuring children (tell them "don't worry if you miss some") and by removing time limits when possible.
12. Encourage a sense of pride and self-worth in all children.
13. Be intolerant of prejudice and teasing displayed by children toward other children.
14. Reduce interpersonal tensions by giving all children the chance to interact positively and on an equal footing with those perceived to be different.
15. Use elaborate verbal instructions and prompts to improve performance (Warton & Bussey, 1988).

Setting the Tone for Schoolwork at Home

TOWARD EFFECTIVE PARENTING

Parents and their children are educational partners. Parents can help their children get their homework done in a timely and accurate fashion by establishing some guidelines in the home:

1. *Teach and model self-discipline.* The basic maxim of homework is: Work comes before play. Children have a difficult time accepting that order until they understand that they actually get rewarded for their work by the free time or play that follows. Let your children see you working before you play, also, by verbalizing, "I need to do these bills before I can watch that program" or "Let's get this kitchen cleaned up before we go shoot baskets."

2. *Create a place for your child to do homework.* The child usually needs a quiet setting free of television, conversation, or other noise distraction. Doing homework in the same place every night also builds "the homework habit"—an association between a place and its function. It's OK for kids to occasionally study around others or with the radio on provided they can get the work done in a quality way.

3. *Know your child's schedule.* Especially by the fourth grade or so, the child should have homework almost nightly. Be in touch with your child's teacher so you know her philosophy of homework (Back to School Night or open house is a good time to do this). Be suspicious if your child never or rarely has homework. Losing homework or forgetting books or assignments is no excuse for not getting it done.

4. *Have good resources on hand.* It's easier for a child to check facts if he has access to a dictionary, encyclopedia, atlas, or almanac. The library is an obvious resource, but may be less convenient in terms of time.

5. *Moderate your child's homework anxiety.* A little anxiety might be motivating, but a lot can be debilitating. Try not to let your child get too relaxed or too uptight about her homework. Offer support and encouragement when she's down and offer direction if she's stuck. If she is too overwhelmed, she may just give up.

6. *Don't do your child's homework for him.* I know it's tempting. After all, you're so much smarter now than when you were young and it does end the battle over coaxing a reluctant child to work. But think about it. Your child isn't going to learn the assignment, he's going to become overly dependent on you to solve his problems, and he'll be overwhelmed when he is finally on his own because the level of the homework has surpassed your level of expertise. Urge him to at least *try.* Many teachers give out their home phone numbers or have a "homework hot line" number that can be called when kids get stuck.

7. *Praise your child's efforts.* No child will get all her homework problems right all the time. Acknowledge your child's effort to learn, especially if she tried hard on the assignment. Mistakes are human; everyone makes them. Use performance feedback as a learning opportunity rather than as an opportunity to criticize.

8. *Show an interest in the completed work that comes home, too.* Look through your child's folders and read his stories and reports. Showing an interest

in *all* his work, not just the homework, reinforces the idea that school is important and worthy of everyone's attention. Be generous with praise for achievement and improvement. Tell him how proud you are of his hard work no matter what the score or grade.

● Chapter Summary

● The 5-to-7 shift marks a cognitive transition between what Piaget calls preoperational thought and the stage of concrete operations. Compared with preschoolers, children in the stage of concrete operations are more logical and flexible in their thinking. School-age children can understand transformations, decenter their thinking, use inductive reasoning to solve problems, and are more objective than younger children.

● From an information processing perspective, school-age children's attention, memory, perception, and problem solving skills improve significantly. They can ignore distractions and irrelevant information better. They spontaneously use efficient organizational strategies to understand and remember material. They can also formulate rules to help them solve problems.

● Intelligence, achievement, and aptitude testing is common during the school years. The definition of *intelligence* has generated considerable debate within the field of developmental psychology. The issues include a consideration of whether intelligence is a broad (nontraditional) or narrow (academically focused) concept and whether intelligence is a collection of separate skills or is a generalized ability. Although the scores obtained from standardized intelligence tests may have some predictive value (academic performance, academic retention, and learning skills deficits), test score outcome may be influenced by a myriad of factors and thus should be interpreted with caution.

● Creativity involves divergent thinking and the production of new, useful solutions. While creativity may have some genetic basis, creative thinking can be encouraged to develop.

● School children who are gifted and talented, mentally retarded, learning disabled, or have sensory or physical handicaps/challenges require special accommodations to meet their educational needs.

● Language skills improve dramatically during the school years as vocabulary expands, grammar improves, and children come to appreciate some of the subtleties of word meaning and the communication process. School-age children enjoy using secret languages and telling jokes and riddles.

- Rules and regulations guide not only school-age children's cognition but their moral orientation as well. Toward the end of this age period, children see rules as more flexible and arbitrary, focus on "fairness," are interested in making moral judgments that please others, and can understand the motivation or intentions that underlie an action. Moral decision making can benefit from practice, understanding the reasons behind the actions, and role playing. Still, school-age children may be tempted to cheat or be dishonest if the situation compels them to compromise their values.
- Formal education focuses on the acquisition of reading, writing skills, computation, and computer skills.

● Observational Exercise

The child's ability to use his or her memory improves markedly during the school years because of maturation and practice. Both short- and long-term memory capacity can be demonstrated through the use of simple recall tasks.

Procedure: Compare the memory performance of a 7 year old and an 11 year old on the following tasks. Work with each child separately in an area with few distractions.

Short-Term Memory

1. I am going to say some numbers and I want you to say them back to me in order. Listen carefully.
   1. 3 5 9 7
   2. 4 1 6 2 5
   3. 8 5 2 1 6 3
   4. 6 9 1 7 3 8 4
   5. 2 6 8 5 4 9 1 3

2. Now repeat the numbers I say in reverse order. For example, if I say 3 7 you would say 7 3. Okay. Listen carefully and then repeat these numbers in reverse order.
   1. 8 5
   2. 3 7 2
   3. 4 5 6 8
   4. 5 2 1 9 7
   5. 7 8 5 2 3

Long-Term Memory

1. I'm going to ask you some questions and I want you to try to answer them as best you can.
   a. What was your teacher's name last year?
   b. What is your telephone number?

    c. Who is the president of the United States?

    d. Name the months of the year in their proper order. Begin with January.

    e. Name the colors of the rainbow.

    f. Name five ways people can get from place to place (i.e., modes of transportation).

    g. Name seven jobs adults can do to earn money.

    h. Name as many words as you can that begin with the letter *R.*

    i. Name as many words as you can that begin with the *ST* sound.

2. What are your conclusions about the memory-performance differences between the 7 and 11 year old child?

● Recommended Readings

Albert, R. S. (1983). *Genius and eminence.* Oxford, England: Pergamon.

Bloom, B. S. (1985). *Developing talent in young people.* New York: Ballantine.

Cox, N. D., & Boston, B. O. (1985). *Educating able learners: Programs and promising practices.* Austin: Univ. of Texas Press.

Feldman, D. H. (1980). *Beyond universals in cognitive development.* Norwood, NJ: Ablex. (On the development of prodigies and creative persons.)

Feldman, D. H., & Goldsmith, L. T. (1986). *Nature's gambit: Child prodigies and the development of human potential.* New York: Basic Books.

Gardner, H. (1985). *Frames of mind: The theory of multiple intelligences.* New York: Basic Books.

Lickona, T. (1985). *Raising good children.* New York: Bantam.

Simon, S. B., & Olds, S. W. (1977). *Helping your child learn right from wrong.* New York: McGraw-Hill.

Social and Emotional Development During the School Years

● Developmental Tasks of the Family

Parent/child involvement changes in nature when children enter school. Rather than actively doing things for their children, parents' new role is to provide guidelines to help the children do things for themselves. The basic developmental tasks facing the family of the school-age child are adapting to the child's expanding world, letting the child go, recognizing the child's readiness for greater responsibility and independent decision making, helping the child maintain values, and encouraging a positive self-concept.

The Child's Expanding World

As children grow through the school years, they want to spend proportionally more time with their friends and less time with their families. They may even seem anxious to leave the house and reluctant to return. This behavior can be highly disturbing to parents if they interpret it as rejection. Parent–child relations can be further strained as fifth or sixth grade children begin to question the authority and knowledge of parents who they previously considered all-knowing and all-powerful. The mother is often particularly affected since she is usually the primary caregiver.

To cope with the child's changing attitudes and behavior, some parents are tempted to assume the role of "pal" or "friend" to their children. In so doing, they hope to recapture some of the love and esteem that they see being directed outside the family. But this strategy is seldom successful. Children need the stable security provided by mature adults to whom they can turn for comfort and advice. To be effective, parents must maintain some control while simultaneously letting their children think and act more for themselves. They must also begin to interact in more mature, friendly ways with their children, refraining from the effusive displays of affection that preschoolers respond to. With the guidance and support of a loving family, children can develop the self-confidence and maturity they need to function independently and effectively (Amato, 1989).

Parents of school-age children also need to adjust to the presence of other legitimate adult authority figures in their child's life, namely principals, teachers, and coaches. Some insecure parents feel threatened by the affection and regard their children feel toward certain teachers, for example. Children are not replacing their parents with other adults, they are merely expanding their list of significant others.

Conflicts between home and school may appear in this stage, centering on disagreements on disciplinary practices, values, grades, level placement, and work load. To ease the problem, parents can work with the school to help their children make the necessary transition to self-responsibility. Cooperation among parents, teachers, and other school personnel can facilitate the child's adaptation to and progress in school.

Letting Children Go

Letting go, bit by bit, is part of the inevitable process of preparing children for independent living. It involves allowing youngsters to take progressively more responsibility for themselves and their actions. This task is one of the hardest that parents of school-age children face. At the heart of the conflict is the necessity to let children learn from their mistakes. Sometimes the child's choices are appropriate and lead to positive outcomes; at other times, they are unwise and shortsighted. The challenge to parents is to provide guidance without being overprotective. In general, children experience fewer failures and recover more quickly when they do fail if they know their parents are proud of them as people and have faith in their competence and resilience. Children whose parents belittle them and communicate doubt as to their abilities usually experience more failure and less achievement in school and a greater loss of self-esteem than those with more supportive parents (Grolnick & Ryan, 1989).

Letting go does not mean that parents must step out of their children's lives abruptly or completely. Parents of school-age children can continue to participate in their children's activities, but on a different level from before. For example, instead of playing baseball with children who now prefer to spend some of their time with their peers, parents can provide transportation, volunteer time as a coach, or watch from the sidelines. And, for their own sake, they can establish contact with other families who are having the same experiences with their school-age children. Such contact provides support and encouragement for those parents who are having trouble adjusting to their child's changing needs.

By making their own adjustments, parents will discover that interacting with the school-age child can be just as satisfying as when the child was young.

Encouraging Greater Responsibility

School age children are ready for more responsibility both at home and away. With some initial instruction and supervision, young children can care for their rooms, make their beds, and help with some household tasks, such as meal preparation and clean-up, vacuuming and dusting, and some gardening chores. By age 8, most children are responsible enough to run short-distance errands alone, take full charge of pet care, help wash the car, entertain younger siblings, and perform other moderately demanding jobs. By age 10, the child may be interested in a paper route or summer job to provide spending money. Some parents give their children a regular allowance that may or may not be tied to the completion of certain tasks. And parents can help their children learn the value of money and develop shopping skills by limiting the amount of money they are allowed to spend—on school clothes, for example.

Parents will see a gain in autonomy in their children during this period. The 10 year old will want to go places alone or with friends—for example, to the movies, sports events, or after-school activities. Even checking out library books alone becomes an important issue. Ten year olds can usually handle themselves adequately in public. Often, they display better behavior away than at home, much to their parents' frustration! Doing things on their own can give children in this age range a sense of accomplishment and exhilaration.

Children's involvement in household chores, pet and sibling care, and outside activities plays an important role in their development of useful skills, self-confidence, and the appreciation of the tasks involved in daily living. Furthermore, research shows that children with household responsibilities behave in more nurturing, helpful, and mature ways than those who have no such demands upon them (Baumrind, 1971).

Once it is agreed that children will participate in the housework, parents need to give feedback to support and guide each child's performance. The following guidelines can help in minimizing conflict and facilitating the child's independence:

1. Encouraging the child's independent efforts; do not condemn or criticize poor results. If poor results are due to a lack of knowledge, teach the child the necessary process or skills.
2. Avoid labeling tasks with respect to sex, and rotate jobs among family members to prevent monotony and improve job performance.
3. Allow children some choice in what they do so they can pursue their interests and practice decision making.

■ **Figure 13–1**

School age children can take responsibility for helping with the care of younger siblings.

4. Flexibility is important. If the children have other demands on their time (such as homework), help with the task or temporarily take it over to allow the child to concentrate on priorities. Help the child plan ahead, anticipating the duration of each task and blocking out the available time.

5. Do not tolerate poor performance or redo the task for the child if the child is capable of repeating and improving the performance.

Maintaining Values

Parents transmit their values and beliefs to their children throughout the child-rearing years. During the middle years, children have the opportunity to apply these values in making independent decisions and to test them against other alternatives. For example, children must make value decisions regarding such areas as truth telling, personal habits (for instance, deciding whether to smoke), religion, and interpersonal relationships. When parents and peer values conflict in such matters, school-age children often side with their peers. In one study where parents strongly approved of a specific behavior but peers strongly disapproved, only 31% of the children went along with their parents. When both parents and peers approved of a behavior, the children selected the approved behavior 88% of the time (Vils, 1980).

The values children inherit are more resistant to change when children know the reasons for or the justification behind the beliefs. Simply telling children not to smoke because cigarette smoking is "wrong" gives them very little ammunition to use in defending their belief against challenge. Conversely, understanding the pros and cons of an issue and gaining practice in countering opposing arguments helps children identify with and commit themselves to their particular personal beliefs. Also, with respect to value choices, where children are involved in healthy activities with adults and peers that satisfy some of their needs for adventure, excitement, and challenge, they may not be as highly motivated to try more risky activities such as smoking, drinking, or drug use. A final strategy is for families to share activities with other families, so that their children can develop relationships among groups that the parents themselves select.

Encouraging High Self-Esteem

Perhaps the most important predictor of personal happiness and effective functioning is high *self-esteem*. Self-esteem refers to an individual's positive feelings about herself and her abilities and competencies in specific areas. In a classic study Stanley Coopersmith (1967) found that children with high self-esteem feel confident, self-assured, and comfortable in their relationships with adults and peers. They expect to be successful in the tasks they undertake and assert themselves even at the risk of disapproval. Because children with low self-esteem are preoccupied with themselves, they can devote less time to outside activities. Uncertain about their own abilities, children with low self-esteem withdraw rather than attempt a task. They tend to be quiet and unobtrusive and are characteristically filled with self-doubt. Because such children expect to fail, they do not try very hard and indeed often do not succeed. This pattern is part of a destructive cycle in which failure further reduces self-esteem, making future failure more likely.

For the most part, self-esteem is a consequent of the child's home and school experience. The parents of children with high self-esteem are usually high in self-esteem themselves, reasonable and fair in discipline, emotionally stable, warm and nurturant, and compatible with one another. High self-esteem children also tend to have good relationships with their same-sex parents and tend to be involved in family discussions and decision making. Self-esteem can be enhanced in boys by providing them with dispositional praise after they help someone or share (e.g., "You're such a thoughtful person, Ryan" (Mills & Grusec, 1989). If children's opinions are sought and their ideas respected, they are more likely to gain confidence and self-respect. Contrary to popular belief, height, physical attractiveness, and membership in a stigmatized group (racial, ethnic, physically limited) do not significantly affect children's judgments of their own self-worth (Crocker & Major, 1989).

In contrast, the parents of children lacking in self-confidence tend to have low self-esteen, tease (even innocently), label their children negatively, consider their children burdens, and are inconsistent and erratic in discipline, alternating between harsh and permissive treatment. Self-esteen tends to increase if at least one of the child's parent displays warmth and acceptance. Having a domineering father lowers self-esteem for boys but not for girls, and boys with dominant mothers have higher self-esteem than those whose mothers are more passive. The children of parents who fight with each other are also predictably low in self-esteem.

Adults can help children gain in self-esteem by

1. Helping them feel *powerful* (children need a sense that they can influence their lives and the lives of others)
2. Helping them feel *competent* (successfully performing tasks they feel are important)
3. Helping them feel *virtuous* (understanding moral guidelines so they can distinguish between right and wrong)
4. Helping them feel *significant* (people important to the child need to express their love, respect, and approval of her)

Teaching children specific skills also helps improve their self-esteem. Children who are good artists or skillful on a skateboard can feel special, and good about their accomplishments.

■ ●▲   CONCEPT SUMMARY

Developmental Tasks of the Family

● *The child's expanding world*
 - Children spend proportionately more time with friends and less with their families
 - Adults other than parents are increasingly important

● *Letting children go*
 - Children want to make more and more of their own decisions
 - Parents are challenged to provide guidance without being overly restrictive or protective

● *Encouraging greater responsibility*
 - Help children take responsibility for some household chores and personal items

● *Maintaining values*
 - Children will be challenged either to maintain or abandon the value system stressed by parents. When children know the reasons for their beliefs, their value systems are more resistant to change

● *Encouraging high self-esteem*
 - Self-esteem is influenced by the child's self-perception and her home and school experiences. Adults can help children gain/maintain self-esteem by helping them feel powerful, competent, virtuous, and significant.

● The Schoolchild and the Family

Like preschoolers, 6–12 year olds thrive in families that offer warmth, encouragement, and understanding. Although school-age children become increasingly independent as they mature, they still need reasonable, consistent guidelines to direct their behavior. They might complain about restrictions long and loudly but, in the end, controls make children feel secure and are seen as expressions of their parent's concern and love (Whaley & Wong, 1988). For children of this age, their families are their safe harbors, their anchors. Parents may enforce restrictions but they are also there to care for children when they are hurt—physically or emotionally.

Support in times of emotional pain requires that lines of communication remain open. But free-flowing communication is important in other areas of life, too, not just where comfort is needed. Parents who remain accessible serve as "sounding boards" for new jokes, listen to tales of achievement, interact with teachers when there are problems at school, give advice, and guide children in their relationships. In short, they relate to their children in many ways that change and adapt as the children grow.

Interactions with Parents

We have seen that as children become gradually more involved in seeking independence and securing their own identities, they detach somewhat from their parents. As a consequence, parent–child relations change significantly. During the preschool years, parents and their children establish a partnership (Chapter 10), where constant supervision is coupled with teaching self-help skills, perfecting language, and playing with the child. In contrast, parents spend half as much time entertaining, supervising, and taking care of a school-age child as they do preschoolers (Hill & Stafford, 1980). Parents spend time reminding children to do things ("It's homework time," "Time to get dressed"), rather than doing those things with them or for them. Consequently, the parents' role changes from that of a partner to that of a consultant or coregulator during the school years (Maccoby, 1984). The child needs food and transportation, informs parents of his plans, and the parents try to invoke methods of controlling the child's behavior as they shuttle the child to and fro. Honesty and cooperation are essential for coregulation. When parents need to correct or control school-age children, the use of physical punishment decreases while reasoning withdrawing privileges, and appealing to their sense of self ("Were you proud of yourself when you did that?") are common. School-age children are less likely to tantrum, yell, or hit when they don't get what they want. Instead, they often try to negotiate. If the outcome still isn't acceptable, the school-age child might react by pouting, holding grudges, and not speaking to the offending parties.

Children don't want to marry their mommies and daddies any longer. They want to hang out with their friends. "Spending the night" is an important age ritual for both boys and girls. Kindergarten children who told their parents everything may be more guarded and secretive by the time they are in the second grade, since they now also have peers as confidants. Much whispering takes place when school-age friends come to play—secrets are gigglingly exchanged. Furthermore, school-age children can be expected to defend their peers when Mom or Dad criticizes their appearance or behavior.

But there's a positive side to this detachment, too. When children loosen emotional ties with their parents and begin to affiliate more with peers, they gain a different perspective on their parents' roles. School-age children's decreasing egocentricity helps them understand both some of the privileges and some of the obligations of parenthood. While it is true that parents set their own hours and decide for themselves

HERMAN®

"We only do dogs."

what to eat or wear, they also spend a great deal of time worrying, planning for the future, solving problems, arranging schedules, and providing support. Consider this particularly sensitive description written by an 8 year old rural French boy about his mother:

> Mommy.
> Mommy, I see you with your blue apron and your pale face,
> Mommy, I see you, I always see you when you have a minute,
> You sit by the fire, mending our clothes.
> Mommy, I see you cooking, the steaming soup for all of us.
> Poor Mommy, you work to help your children.
> Mommy, I see you when you're very tired you close your blue eyes.
>
> Claude, age 8 (Lepman, 1971, p. 9)

Children from middle class families tend to view their fathers more positively during the school years than during their preschool years. Typically they feel their fathers have become more nurturant and boys especially want to spend time with their fathers. Most children rate their mothers higher than their fathers as companions, however (Furman & Buhrmester, 1985). Father's and mother's role perceptions differ when their children enter school (Power & Shanks, 1989). Fathers feel their task is to actively encourage independence and assertiveness and to use forceful discipline. Fathers who work in jobs that require flexibility and self-direction tend to be more flexible and place less emphasis on obedience from their children (Kohn & Schooler, 1983). Mothers see themselves as more involved in training their children in interpersonal skills like manners and politeness. In general, parents use more punishment and less reward with their same-sex children. Parents of girls stress prosocial behavior, while parents of boys stress the importance of behaviors related to self-care. Generally, personal–social competence among elementary school children is associated with high levels of support from parents, a high allocation of household responsibilities, a high level of parental control, and a low level of parental punishment (Amato, 1989).

Parents of underclass children, especially fathers, are traditionally more distant, more punitive, and more rigid with their children than their middle class counterparts, although this orientation may be changing. When fathers have stressful jobs (law enforcement, military), they tend to bring some of the stress home. Such families tend to be more violent and dysfunctional than others whose fathers are under less pressure (M. L. Hoffman, 1984).

Regardless of social class, boys who have warm, loving relationships with their fathers are more likely to do well in school and less likely to become delinquents than boys whose fathers are more emotionally distant. Strong father–son relationships are related to high self-confidence, peer approval, and a positive masculine self-image in school-age boys. Girls also benefit from strong nurturant relationships with their fathers,

alcoholic
a person who has a compulsive need to drink alcohol and whose behavior and judgment are impaired as a result of alcohol abuse

In Touch

CHILDREN OF ALCOHOLICS
  FOUNDATION
P.O. Box 4185
Grand Central Station
New York, NY 10163–4185
1-800-359-COAF
(in NY 212-754-0656)

Education, prevention and support for
  children and adults.

A Closer Look

Nonadult Children of Alcoholics

Overshadowed by the problems of their parents and the dysfunctionality of their families, approximately 7 million children in this country under the age of 18 live with an alcoholic parent or parents. Their existence is an uncertain one. Never knowing if their parent will be drunk or sober, unable to predict the affected parent's behavior and moods, these children live in an atmosphere of confusion, denial, and insecurity.

Family isolation further increases their anxiety. The goings-on of the alcoholic household are almost always kept from outsiders at almost any cost. Children accept their parents' warning that "what happens in our family is nobody's business." Desperate to keep the silence, children will lie to teachers about bruises and tardies; they avoid any activities that will involve their parents and are afraid to bring children to their homes for fear of embarrassment or later punishment.

Children living in alcoholic families adopt a variety of coping mechanisms to survive. Denial is one of the most common. If it isn't happening, you don't have to cope with it. Others simply pretend a different reality. Some children split their alcoholic parent into two people—a good parent and a bad parent. And still others become numb to life and their whole existence.

There's no easy way to predict adult outcomes for these children. Some children are very resilient; others crack under the pressure and have lifelong adjustment problems. Other factors, like the severity of the parent's drinking, the amount of marital conflict in the home, the presence of

(continued from previous page)

Artwork provides theraputic benefits for children of alcoholics and also educates others about this problem. (right) An anonymous child aged 7–12 depicts the situation as "Drink, mad, sad." (left) A 12 year old girl expresses her feelings as the oldest child in an alcoholic family. These drawings are from "The Images Within: A Child's View of Parental Alcoholism," an education and prevention program to help all school age children learn about family alcoholism and ways to give help to their friends or get help for themselves.

(continued from previous page)

siblings, the sex of the alcoholic parent, and the child's relationship to that parent all influence the child's reaction and adaptation. Research has found that girls tend to be more resilient than boys. Having an alcoholic mother is much more damaging than having an alcoholic father. Most children with alcoholic mothers have serious psychosocial problems by the age of 18 because of the effects of fetal alcohol syndrome or because her nurturance and love are inaccessible to the child. Furthermore, the more disruptive the household, the worse the children fared.

Just having one caring outsider can make a world of difference for these children. Teachers, coaches, therapists, or the parents of friends can provide some stability and a hedge against their chaotic world. The biggest challenge comes in identifying these children early enough. Guilt and shame usually prevent the children of alcoholics from coming forward on their own. Usually, unless the parent is in treatment, the children get bypassed. There are some behavioral signs, however: Children from alcoholic homes are often dressed inappropriately; they fail to return permission slips, absence slips, or homework; they become tense if they sense that the teacher needs to talk with or meet the parent; and they are consistently late for school or stranded without a ride after school.

Adapted with permission from Stark, E. "Forgotten Victims." *Psychology Today*, January 1987, pp. 58–62. © 1987 Sussex Publishers, Inc.

but not as much as boys do. It's not clear whether parental warmth determines the child's behavior or whether the child's behavior affects parental warmth, or both (Russell & Russell, 1989).

Parents' Moods and Emotions

DEPRESSION Sometimes parents' depression is tied to family events and sometimes it manifests itself independently. Parents of special-needs children (hyperactive, autistic, retarded, and so on) may find themselves depressed and demoralized by the daily challenges of coping with a static condition, and that resignation may cause their children to suffer high rates of depression (R. T. Brown et al., 1988).

When children and parents feel less worthy as people and less self-efficacious, they become vulnerable to depression (Hammen, 1988). Vulnerability to depression seems to expose mothers to more life stress, housing and financial problems, and sometimes a poorer choice of new spouses and living partners, which exacerbate the existing depression (Puckering, 1989). Some children of depressed mothers are themselves depressed; others show good resilience and temperament. Depressed mothers don't necessarily have distorted perceptions of their child's abilities/problems. John Richters and David Pellegrini (1989) found that teachers' and depressed mothers' ratings of children's behavior problems yielded substantially similar portraits. However, moderately (but not severely) depressed mothers may be at risk for child abuse and physical aggression compared to nondepressed mothers (Zuravin, 1989).

ANGER Children can recognize when their mothers are angry, but they may have trouble explaining its cause or understanding why it is directed toward them after their parents fight (Covell & Abramovich, 1988).

● Lifestyle Differences Among Two-Parent Families and Single-Parent Families

Schoolchildren are able to tolerate separations from parents for hours or days with little or no insecurity (Skeen & McKenry, 1980). But more permanent changes in the structure of the family, such as death or divorce, may have a profound impact on the child's development and ability to function.

Divorce

Divorce continues to be a common occurrence in the lives of American children. In the 1990s the *majority* of school children in the United States will experience the breakup of their parent's marriage. In some ways, school-age children are better equipped than preschoolers to deal with the impact of divorce. Because they can shift perspectives, school-age children can understand the reasons for divorce (although they may not accept them) and are less likely to blame themselves for the outcome. These older children are also more aware of their own feelings and more open about admitting their sadness than younger children (J. S. Wallerstein, 1984). While divorce may threaten the preschooler's self-concept and the trust she has in others, school-age children tend to react to divorce with despondency, fear of abandonment, anger, and feelings of being deprived. They may also feel loneliness and a loss of identity. Some children who are having family problems show specific kinds of behavioral symptoms associated with stress, particularly at school. Absent-mindedness, nervousness, lethargy, moodiness, withdrawal, declining grades, and physical complaints may show up in children whose families are in turmoil. Teachers report more acting out by boys whose parents fight a lot or are separated, while separation and remarriage increases the level of girls' acting out in school (Zill, 1983). Also characteristic is a sudden shift toward extreme behavior: a normally well-behaved child may suddenly become restless or agitated or may act out by fidgeting, talking back, or destroying school property. Each of these problem behaviors may be present in children prior to the actual divorce, especially if the parents are in conflict and inaccessible (Block et al., 1986). Although almost all children have some type of difficulty adjusting to divorce, children of newly employed mothers may be particularly overwhelmed. Not only has this child's family been reconfi-

■ **Figure 13–2**

Dad and daughter prepare Sunday breakfast for themselves. In single-parent families, children often share more responsibility since there are fewer adults to fill-in.

joint custody
where both divorced parents share the responsibility for dependent children

gured, but they also have to cope with their mother's transition from stay-home caregiver to breadwinner.

Regarding the aftermath of divorce, when parents remain supportive of each other and mutually cooperative and when children maintain a good relationship with both parents, the children display fewer negative effects (Camara & Resnick, 1989; Wierson et al., 1989). When children feel they have to divide their loyalties, they risk alienating the other parent. Sometimes parents have differing sets of policies about staying up late, using the phone, eating certain foods (like candy) or TV watching, for example. If the child gets to watch an R-rated video with one parent, but the other parent expressly forbids such films, the child is in a dilemma. Not only is it unclear whether watching R-rated films is really OK or not but the child will certainly displease one parent no matter what they choose ("You watched an R-rated video! You know I don't allow that" vs. "Come on! What's the big deal? Your mom is such a prude. This is a good movie.")

Lengthy battles over child custody have a long-lasting impact. Families whose disputes lasted an average of 4.5 years and who were finally awarded joint custody had children who were more emotionally troubled and behaviorally disturbed than those families where a parent was granted sole custody (J. R. Johnston et al., 1989). In the absence of lengthy custody disputes, there is no difference between joint- and sole-custody arrangements on children's postdivorce adjustment (Kline et al., 1989). Warshak & Santrock (1979) found it was better for the self-esteem and social relations of school-age boys to be in their father's custody, while girls tended to do better with their mothers. Girls tend to be more independent, more achievement motivated, and less demanding when raised by their mothers. Only about 10% of the children of divorced parents live with their fathers (Hetherington, 1989).

Both boys and girls can grow well in homes where mothers are single parents. When divorced mothers encourage independent, mature, masculine behaviors from their sons and hold positive attitudes toward their ex-husbands and men in general, boys' levels of masculinity are comparable to those of males from intact families (Hetherington, 1989). Ten years after the divorce of their middle class parents, girls were found to feel anxiety in their relationships with men and to experience a temporary drop in their social self-confidence (Wallerstein & Corbin, 1989).

Although families run by single mothers often have fewer financial resources than when the marriage was intact, the level of stress is high in both father- and mother-headed single-parent families. These single parents are more likely to use abusive violence toward their children than parents in dual-caretaker households (Gelles, 1989).

Some single-parent families exist because the mother has never married. Most involve young, low-income, poorly educated women for whom pregnancy was a surprise, but some are headed by highly educated, self-sufficient women who planned their pregnancies carefully. The women can be heterosexual or homosexual in orientation. For an insight into families run by lesbian mothers, see the accompanying feature.

Stepfamilies

The reason that boys and girls display so much acting out at school after their parents have remarried is that second marriages fail at an even higher rate than first marriages do (Bumpas, 1984). Preschool children are most concerned about attaching to their stepparent and "sharing" their biological parent. School-age children want to know what the "rules" are, what they should call their stepparent (Mom or Sue?) and how many new "siblings" might fit into the picture. Parental remarriage is most difficult for prepubertal boys (E. R. Anderson et al., 1989). Much of the time, remarriage leads to a better standard of living for the family despite the other adjustments. Children tolerate mother–stepfather families best (Hetherington et al., 1985). Boys in mother–stepfather homes do almost as well as boys from nondivorced families. Girls experience a little more stress, perhaps because they have less frequent and less intimate access to their mothers (Clingempeel & Segal, 1986).

Father–stepmother families may begin with more problems (custody out of necessity, not choice) and so experience more confusion and interaction difficulties (Ihinger-Tallman & Pasley, 1987). Even if custodial fathers were more closely tied to their children prior to the marriage, the marriage strains the attachment. Interestingly, girls may fare better than boys in these arrangements *if* they can get along with their stepmothers. Noncustodial mothers maintain more regular contact with their children than noncustodial fathers. Apparently, the third time is the charm with regard to marriage in American society. Although third marriages tend to be stable, they may occur after all the children have grown and left home.

Married Couples with Absent Partners

Sometimes children can be separated from one parent or the other because of the parent's profession. Such parents are those who are frequent fliers (travel extensively due to business), are in the military, or who live away from their families to be closer to their jobs. The parent who is gone creates what professionals call an "ambiguous loss" for the child: They are part of an intact family, but in reality the mother/father isn't there at bedtime, for their birthday parties, or their rehearsals. Over the long term, children may stop counting on the absent parent and may develop and ambivalent relationship toward him or her (Libman, 1987).

In Touch

> **MILITARY FAMILY RESOURCE CENTER**
> Ballston Towers #3, Suite 903
> 4015 Wilson Blvd.
> Arlington, VA 22203
>
> Provides help for military families

A Closer Look

Lesbian Mothers

The label *lesbian mother* seems like a contradiction in terms since homosexual procreation is not possible (Falk, 1989). Lesbian women have always raised children in our society, becoming parents by adoption, artificial insemination, or heterosexual intercourse (Basile, 1974). It's only been in the last 10 years that civil rights and liberation movements have given lesbian mothers the courage to identify themselves. Between 1.5 and 5 million lesbian women reside with their children in the United States today (Davies, 1979). Most lesbian mothers come to our attention because they are involved in court cases over custody rights.

By law, the courts are supposed to use "the best interests of the child" standard in deciding custody. Once the issue of lesbianism is raised, however, the judge seems more influenced by the attitudes and stereotypes held about homosexuality than by any facts in the case relative to the child's best interests ("Burdens on Gay Litigants," 1984). The biased assumptions the courts hold about lesbian mothers include:

1. All homosexuals are mentally ill. Therefore, lesbian women are incapable of being good parents.
2. Lesbian mothers are less maternal than heterosexual mothers since the lesbian's chief priority is her relationship with another adult, not her relationship with her children.
3. In lesbian families, children are more likely to be sexually molested by the parent or the parent's partner or acquaintances.
4. The sex role development of the child will be significantly impaired in lesbian families.
5. Children are more likely to become homosexual themselves when raised by a lesbian parent.

6. Children of lesbian mothers are more likely to be traumatized or stigmatized by society or by their peers.

Research has been conducted to test each of these assumptions. There is no evidence to suggest that lesbian mothers or their children are more disturbed than heterosexual mothers or their children. To summarize from Falk (1989):

1. Compared to matched heterosexual controls, lesbian mothers have the same or lower incidence of psychiatric disorders.
2. Lesbian mothers and heterosexual mothers are more alike than they are different in their maternal attitudes and self-concepts. Some studies indicate lesbian mothers may actually be *more* child-oriented than heterosexual mothers.
3. Although the children of lesbian mothers were not without their problems, the extent and frequency of problems is consistent with those of single heterosexual mothers. Marital discord and divorce are more consistently correlated with a child's poor adjustment than the mother's sexual orientation.
4. There is no evidence that homosexual parents are more likely to seduce or allow their children to be seduced than their heterosexual counterparts or that homosexuals are more likely than heterosexuals to molest children or have incestuous relationships.
5. Even using the most conservative measures, studies found that lesbian mothers do not exert a detrimental influence on their children's sex role development.
6. Lesbianism is not "contagious." The sexual orientation of the children raised in heterosexual or lesbian homes does not seem to be influenced by the sexual orientation of their parents.

7. The children of lesbian mothers may be affected by social stigma and may fear being ostracized and teased. However, children know it is society and not their mothers who are responsible for the prejudice and almost without exception, children were proud of their lesbian mother for standing up for her beliefs.

Thus, the mother's sexual orientation has no detrimental effect on her child's behavior or adjustment. Further, heterosexual and homosexual women are far more alike than different in their child-rearing practices and ability to nurture. As a consequence, the best interests of the child lay with a loving parents, not with a homosexual parent or a heterosexual parent (Basile, 1974).

Of particular importance is how the remaining parent copes. If the left-behind parent is OK, the child will be OK. If the parent is anxious and depressed, her or his mood and apprehensiveness will affect the child.

Schoolchildren with Employed Mothers or Unemployed Fathers

More than half of all American schoolchildren have mothers who work outside the home. Because they are involved with school and social activities during the day, their parents' absence is less of a problem for school-age children than for preschoolers or infants (Piotrkowski & Stark, 1987). School-age children are better able to find companionship and stimulation with peers and other adults. They are also more capable of understanding their mother's need for outside work and of appreciating the satisfaction their mothers may derive from work outside the home (Scarr, 1984). L. Hoffman (1984) found that the school-age children of working mothers tended to take more responsibility for themselves and for household chores and to have a more positive attitude toward women and women's abilities. Girls whose mothers work outside the home tended to be more independent and to express more admiration for their mothers than girls of mothers without outside jobs (Bronfenbrenner & Couter, 1982). Rules governing children's behavior are more consistent in the homes of working mothers, perhaps to make sure things function as smoothly as possible in her absence. All things considered, the best-adjusted schoolchildren live with satisfied mothers who are happy either staying home or working an outside job (Zimmerman & Bernstein, 1983). Scarr and colleagues (1989) reiterate that the school achievement, IQ test scores, and emotional and social development of the children of employed mothers are every bit as good as those of children whose mothers are not employed.

lesbian
a female homosexual

Civil Rights Movement
a social movement that gained national attention in the 1960s and 1970s to grant equal rights to women, minorities, the handicapped and homosexuals

homosexuality
a person whose sexual orientation is toward persons of the same sex

psychiatric disorders
serious psychological disturbance that requires hospitalization and/or medication

■ **Figure 13–3**

This young leukemia patient has time to pose with his masterpiece while he battles his illness.

Children whose parents work usually, however, need supervision before and after school, and they may not receive it. Those at particular risk when left unsupervised are physically limited, unprepared for the demands of school, hurried into premature adulthood, or disconnected from the social worlds around them (J. B. Erikson, 1988). On-site before-and-after-school programs have the potential of helping thousands of children cope and stay safe and out of trouble until their parents can pick them up.

Children have to make adjustments when a parent enters the job market for the first time. They also have to adjust when an employed parent loses a job. Most studies have focused on unemployed fathers and found them to be self-conscious, depressed, anxious, and more prone to violence than employed fathers (Moen et al., 1981). The stress of unemployment is not unique to men and may be particularly hard on single-parent females who lack a network of emotional support.

Death

The child acquires a more realistic understanding of death during middle childhood. By age 9 or 10, children understand that death is permanent and irreversible, involving cessation of bodily functions (Kubler-Ross, 1983). Their decreasing egocentricity also helps school-age children realize that death is universal and will happen to them. Losing a parent through death is a profound and long-lasting emotional trauma for the school-age child. Even 5 or as long as 20 years after the loss, both boys and girls who experienced the death of a parent were more submissive and introverted and less aggressive than other children, including those who experienced loss through divorce (Berlinsky & Biller, 1982).

Children who are terminally ill themselves gather information about their illness and come to realize that death is imminent (Bluebone-Langner, 1989). The well siblings of ill children are confronted with many problems, among them unpredictable family schedules, financial strain, lack of attention, and emotional confusion, guilt, and ambivalence. Siblings in families with higher cohesion and a stronger religious and recreational emphasis experienced fewer behavioral problems after the loss of a brother or a sister to cancer (B. Davies, 1988).

In specific circumstances, caregivers can tailor information about death to the child's level of cognitive awareness. Those who draw from familiar experiences, such as the death of a pet, can best help the child relate to the experience. Education about death for kindergarten and first grade children that focuses on dead leaves in the fall and on the food chain helps children see that death is actually a normal and natural part of life. Older children can focus on adjusting to the loss and coping with fears for the future (Masterman & Reams, 1988).

Adoption

About 6% of all children in the United States (some 5 million individuals) are adopted. Adoption caseworkers estimate that for every child who is adopted, an average of 70 people come to know about the adoption. Those people include aunts, uncles, in-laws, and neighbors who have never seen the mother pregnant but suddenly see her come home with a child. Thus, it is almost impossible to keep adoptions a secret and to prevent adopted children from learning that they are adopted. Thus, the issue is not *whether* to but *how* to tell children they are adopted so they understand the message (Brodzinsky, 1984).

Most professionals suggest that caregivers answer a child's questions as completely as possible and in a truthful and loving manner. Telling children they were "chosen," "found," or "a gift from God" may be fine for preschoolers who may not pursue the matter, but school-age children will request more specific details and may become impatient if the parents attempt to be evasive. Adoptive parents need to be reassured that the child's curiosity is natural and predictable. Just because children want to know more about their birthparents and background to understand their identity doesn't mean they are rejecting the parents who raised them or indicating dissatisfaction with their lives. They just need to know who they are and where they came from.

Similar identity issues are faced by children conceived by artificial insemination and other birth technologies. Artificial insemination is usually a secretive undertaking because of the guilt and shame attributed to infertility. Parents who are artificially inseminated are often reluctant to be forthright about their child's origins, opting instead to avoid such discussions altogether or to "invent" a "proper" past for their child. This "lethal secret" approach to birth origins is designed to protect or spare the child but actually does just the opposite—the child feels betrayed by the lies and ashamed of her "second class citizenship." As with adoption, children conceived by artificial insemination have the right to know the truth about themselves and their background. Such information can be provided in a timely and loving way so as to make the child feel "special" rather than "subhuman."

Adoption placement personnel are increasingly concerned about the adopted child's ethnic or racial identity. In the best of all circumstances, adoptees and their adopted families would share a similar racial or ethnic heritage. In this way, the parents could be positive role models and the adopted child could more closely identify with her found family and her own ethnicity or race (P. R. Johnson et al., 1987).

In Touch

> NORTH AMERICAN COUNCIL ON
> ADOPTABLE CHILDREN (NACAC)
> 2001 S Street, NW
> Washington, DC 20009
>
> Offers support for adoptive parents

Homelessness and Poverty

Homeless children have to face the daily stress of not having a permanent place to live, moving frequently, not having enough to eat or sufficient medical care (Bassuk & Gallagher, 1990). School-age homeless children are severely anxious and depressed. In many ways, they are robbed of the essential elements of childhood—safe and predictable routines, privacy, stability, and a sense of belonging (Landers, 1989). Some homeless children can't remember what it's like to open a refrigerator door for a glass of milk. They have to live under desperate and often revolting conditions just to survive. "It's a terrible thing to be a garbage picker just to have enough to eat," said the mother of one child. Finding shelter in burned out or condemned buildings, children tolerate no gas, light, or heat and the incessant patter of rats. "Everyday, I go to the fire hydrant to fill plastic jugs with water for cooking, cleaning, and washing up for school," said one 15 year old Bronx child. "I got no choice." (Drogin, 1985).

Overburdened parents are often stressed beyond their limits:

> "The stress of feeling guilty. Maybe I did something wrong (to cause the layoff). I couldn't eat. I couldn't sleep. I lost 42 pounds in 3 weeks. I was afraid to eat for fear I'd be taking it out of my kid's mouth. I got to the point of trying to commit suicide. I had pills. I thought of cutting my wrists. I thought I had no right to be here because I couldn't support my kids." (Drogin, 1985).

When homeless children do attend school, they may find they have fallen behind their age-mates in reading and math skills. Their academic and social progress is also impeded by emotional problems, frequent illness, poor nutrition, developmental delays, and frequent movement during the school year (Rafferty & Shinn, 1991). Statistics on New York's homeless show the two-thirds of these children have switched schools at least once since becoming homeless, and one-third have transferred 2–6 times (Lipsitt, 1989a).

In Touch

> **NATIONAL COALITION FOR THE HOMELESS**
> 1621 Connecticut Ave., NW
> Department P, Suite 400
> Washington, DC 20009
>
> **THE NATIONAL ALLIANCE TO END HOMELESSNESS**
> 1518 K Street, NW
> Department P. Suite 206
> Washington, DC 20005

■ ● ▲   CONCEPT SUMMARY

Lifestyle Changes During the School Years

● *Divorce*
  – Affects the majority of school children
  – They are better equipped than preschoolers to deal with the impact of divorce
  – The stress of divorce may produce changes in the school-age child's behavior
  – Children of newly employed mothers are the most overwhelmed by divorce
  – Child adjustment can be facilitated if parents remain cooperative and don't wage difficult custody battles

- Children, especially girls, do better in the custody of same-sex parents
- Both boys and girls can grow well in single-parent homes

- *Stepfamilies*
  - Second-time marriages have a higher divorce rate than first-time marriages
  - School-age children want to understand the new family rules
  - Remarriage, especially mother–stepfather, may lead to a higher standard of living for the family
  - Boys get along with stepfather or stepmother; girls may have trouble relating to stepmother

- *Work-related parental absence*
  - Early separation from the father can adversely effect both boys and girls

- *Parental Employment/Unemployment*
  - The majority of schoolchildren have mothers who work outside the home
  - School-age children cope with maternal employment better than preschoolers
  - Children of employed parents take more responsibility for themselves and the household
  - Lack of proper supervision placed children at risk for mishap and misbehavior
  - The stress of unemployment affects family relationships

- *Death*
  - School-age children have a more realistic understanding of death

- *Adoption*
  - It is unwise to keep adoption a secret

- *Homelessness*
  - Creates severe anxiety and depression in children
  - Homeless children fall behind in school, if they attend at all

Abduction

The pictures of missing children on shopping bags, posters, and milk cartons remind us that this is not a safe world for children. Stranger abductions account for 200–300 of the 350,000 children taken each year (Freiberg, 1990). Ironically, most (over 90%) of the missing children are abducted by family members, mostly men, involved in child custody disputes.

stranger abductions
where a person unknown to the child kidnaps that child

■ **Figure 13–4**

Two brothers, ages 4 and 7, reading together.

In an effort to reduce the incidence of child abduction and the trauma involved for the child and the family, parents need to know where their children are at all times. Never leave a child alone or unattended, even for a minute. Children also need to be told to check with the custodial parent before going *anywhere* or doing *anything* with anyone, even relatives and estranged parents. Finally, teach children to use the telephone. Make sure they know their home phone number by heart. Teach them how to communicate to the operator that they need to make a collect call. And urge them to call at *any time* of the day or night.

● **Interactions with Siblings**

Siblings' relationships tend to be particularly significant during middle childhood. School-age children may be more skilled at understanding their younger siblings' needs and wants because they can now view situations from different perspectives. Moreover, they may also be able to play the role of helper, teacher, boss, or friend to younger family members because they understand the behaviors that define the roles.

Through interactions with their siblings, boys and girls begin to learn how people respond and react to the things they do and say. Siblings practice eliciting certain behaviors from their brothers or sisters (gratitude, annoyance, surprise, fear) and then go about the task of dealing with others outside the family. Poor sibling relationships—particularly during the preschool years—have been found to predict poorer relationships with others outside the family, such as teachers and peers (Richman et al., 1982). For the most part, how well their parents get along (whether they are divorced or not) is the best predictor of the quality of sibling relationships (MacKinnon, 1989).

Older siblings frequently complain that the younger ones are pests and copycats. Little ones want to watch, follow, and imitate their older brothers and sisters. "Get a life" is the older child's frequent reaction. Just as children learn from their parents, they also learn from their siblings (J. Dunn, 1983). Interestingly, older children don't mimic the activities of the younger ones, although they may insist siblings stop or move what they are doing because it's interfering or inconveniencing them to some extent.

Teacher is a common role for older siblings to play, particularly after they start school. An early study suggests children are most likely to accept help and guidance from older sisters than from older brothers (Cicirelli, 1976). Older sisters tend to be effective teachers because they talk more, use more examples, and give more feedback than brothers do. When met with resistance, older sisters are more likely to reason with their siblings, while older brothers are more likely to use force. Little sisters are particularly responsive to the teachings of their older female siblings.

■ ● ▲ CONCEPT SUMMARY

Family Interaction Patterns During the School Years

● *Interactions with Parents*
  – Children detach somewhat from the family, but still need guidance
  – Parent's role changes from partnership to consultant/coregulator
  – Children tend to negotiate for what they want, rather than having emotional outbursts
  – Detachment may give children a more realistic impression of a parent's roles and responsibilities
  – Mothers are the preferred companions
  – Fathers viewed more positively by middle class children
  – Fathers tend to encourage independence and assertiveness; mothers tend to train interpersonal skills
  – A boy's warm relationship with father insulates them against delinquency and school failure
  – Parental stress and depression can affect children

● *Interactions with Siblings*
  – Siblings teach and help each other more now
  – Siblings practice social skills by interacting with each other
  – Younger siblings emulate older ones
  – Other-sex siblings have the most harmonious relationships; same-sex siblings, especially brothers, tend to bicker
  – Siblings of handicapped/terminally ill children are at no greater risk of adjustment problems than siblings of nonhandicapped/healthy children

---

Although children typically learn more from their sisters, the most harmonious interpersonal relationships tend to develop between other-sex siblings. Same-sex siblings tend to bicker; two brothers argue more than any other sibling combination, and the presence of an older brother may make post divorce siblings dyads more negative and less harmonious than the presence of an older sister (MacKinnon, 1989). Boys generally get along better with girls and vice versa, possibly because they are striving for different goals and parents have different expectations of their behavior. Thus, it may be that they compete less with each other than other sibling combinations and that each individual feels less jealous of any love and attention the other might receive.

With age, siblings become more equal in power and status. Over time, helping decreases and conflict increases, but positivity in the relationship increases (Vandell et al., 1987). Siblings who can develop a true feeling of trust, friendship and respect for each other may be able to

■ Figure 13–5

Big sister as make-up artist.

chronically ill
an illness which lasts over a long
time (as distinguished from *acute*)

communicate more effectively than child–parent or child–peer pairs (Cicirelli, 1976).

How do sibling relationships fare when a brother or sister is ill, disabled, or impaired? Popular belief assumes that siblings of handicapped and ill children experience more frequent stress, neglect, behavioral problems, and psychological disturbance, but such is not necessarily the case (Howlin, 1988; Lobato et al., 1988). Children are more likely to "tease" or "bug" retarded siblings than nonretarded siblings (Gamble & Mettale, 1989). But most often unaffected siblings feel depressed, angry, mad, or worried when their impaired brother or sister gets hurt or sick (Cadman et al., 1988). In a massive study of over 2,300 siblings of chronically ill children in 1,896 families, David Cadman and colleagues (1988) found no increased risk of adjustment problems. Compared to other children, siblings of ill children were no more likely to be socially isolated, avoid participation, or lack competence in school, play, or leisure activities.

● Interactions with Peers

Throughout development, children's behavior is influenced by their peers. Babies as young as a few days old will listen to and imitate the cries of other infants (Simner, 1971). Year old children placed together will approach and explore each other, if only briefly. Between 2 and 6 years of age, children become less dependent on adults and more dependent on other children. If 2 or 3 year olds are accompanied by a familiar peer, they do not need their mothers to be present to feel comfortable and free to explore in a strange setting (Maccoby & Feldman, 1972). Also, the amount of time the child spends away from home increases gradually throughout the school years. School-age children devote more time each day to playing with friends than they do to watching television, reading, playing alone, or working.

The Peer Group

Same-age, same-sex children may assemble into informal peer groups during the school years. Between the ages of 6 and 9, these groups are rather small, loosely organized groups whose membership changes frequently. Few formal rules are in place and common interests or a common goal are usually the basis for the groups (O'Brien & Bierman, 1988). School-age children are interested in fan clubs, setting and studying world records, and forming collections.

By the time children are in the fifth or sixth grade, however, their groups have become more structured, more formalized, more exclusive, and more cohesive. All peer groups develop a status hierarchy among their members. "Knowing one's place" in the group tends to facilitate cooperation and actually diminishes disagreements. Leaders emerge in both male and female groups and are maintained until the group goals change (Savin-Williams, 1979). Elaborate rules and rituals as well as special membership requirements are characteristic of peer groups in later childhood. In order to gain entrance to the fort or clubhouse, for example, all members might have to wear a blue T-shirt. Those who do not comply will be turned away. Secret passwords are other examples of the rituals of middle childhood (Elkind, 1979).

Most of the rules that govern the behavior of peer group members emphasize independence from adults and emotional control. Strong disapproval is expressed for "crybabies," "teacher's pets," and "tattletales." Given the context of peer scrutiny and criticism, children may feel mortified if they are made to dress as their parents dictate or to participate in public displays of family affection. One of the most damaging insults a young schoolchild can deliver is to call a peer a "baby." On the other hand, being called "big" or "grown up" is among the most satisfying compliments.

School-age children expect each other to follow social norms that promote courtesy, fair play, and respect for others (Hartup, 1983). Cooperation is a frequently chosen conflict-resolution strategy among girls, while boys favor competition (Crick & Ladd, 1990). When working in groups, waiting one's turn, doing one's part, asking for advice, and graciously giving and receiving compliments are all examples of acceptable behavior.

conflict resolution strategy
an approach for working through disagreement or difficulty

The Function of Peers

Like the family, the child's peers are agents of socialization. Peers transmit information about attitudes and values and influence each other's behavior through modeling and reinforcement. By age 4, children provide much more positive social reinforcement to their peers than they did at age 2 or 3 (Hartup et al., 1988). Praise, attention, approval, smiles, affection, sharing, and cooperation are most often given to same-sex peers who, in turn, reciprocate the positive treatment. Peers also reinforce socially appropriate behavior, help refine values, and provide comfort and support. Children learn a wide variety of responses by observing their peers' behavior. They imitate everything from hairstyle, voice inflection, and reasoning skills to selfishness, disobedience, and dishonesty. But children do not copy the behavior of just anyone. They are most likely to imitate peers whom they perceive as warm, rewarding, powerful, high in status (e.g., older), in control of resources, and similar to themselves (Hartup, et al., 1988).

Conformity is the mainstay of the peer group structure. Children are more likely to conform during the school years than any other time of life, even if doing so means giving the wrong answer or risking being in trouble (C. C. Wilson et al., 1989). If the child's moral reasoning leads

■ **Figure 13–6**

Can you guess what constitutes appropriate beachwear for this group of school age girls?

antisocial
opposed to the general good or acting contrary to the basic principles of society

him to be conscious of rules and to be viewed as "good," schoolchildren conform to the group because they value their peers' opinions even more than those of adults. Not until after age 12 or so do children react more on an individual basis. By this time, they have internalized standards of conduct so they feel less of a need to conform to peer behavior or misbehavior. Although children's peers might persuade them to engage in antisocial behavior (shoplifting, sneaking a peek at adult magazines, smoking), the child who is headed for serious trouble later on is the one who doesn't get along with peers and is seen as an outcast (Hartup, 1984). Furthermore, peer pressure also sometimes reinforces behaviors supported by adults such as getting good grades, being responsible, and respecting elders (B. B. Brown et al., 1986).

Peer Acceptance and Popularity

Peer group acceptance is facilitated by a variety of personality factors and skills. All children want to "fit in," and all children need the recognition and support of their peers. While the ease with which relationships are established and maintained varies considerably from child to child, once established, the child's status or standing in the group changes little over time (Coie & Dodge, 1983). A star remains a star, rejected children are actively disliked, and neglected children are ignored. By the time they're in the third grade, children can accurately describe their own reputation among their peers (Krantz & Burton, 1986). Higher levels of cooperative play at the beginning of the year predict gains in peer acceptance by the end of the year (Ladd et al., 1988).

Physical Appearance

Adults tend to like people who are physically attractive, and as early as age 3–5, children come to value physical attractiveness in others (Adams & Crane, 1980). Children like clean, cute kids more and judge them to have more positive personality characteristics than children they consider less attractive (Langlois, 1985).

Children's assessments of physical attractiveness encompass such factors as physique and maturational rate in addition to particular physical features. The most popular boys tend to be those who have medium builds and good muscle development and who mature early. While girls admire athletic-looking boys, they tend to favor the "thin" look for themselves and their female friends. Early maturing girls tend to be more popular in Grades 7–9 with both males and females. Before that time, later maturing girls have more prestige and recognition in their peer groups.

Children judge physically disabled children to be less attractive than their nonhandicapped peers. Further, they perceive peers who are retarded or who use crutches, braces, or wheelchairs and those having amputations, burns, or facial disfigurements as dissimilar to themselves and less desirable as friends (Parish et al., 1980). These results suggest that the early impact of mainstreaming has had fewer positive effects than hoped on changing children's attitudes towards their disabled peers. It's ironic that most disabled children can adjust to their limitations but that nondisabled children still have difficulty accepting others with variations in physique (Tarnowski et al., 1989).

■ **Figure 13–7**

Everyone wants to capture the attention of the cutest girl in class.

Of all the variations in childhood physique, obesity is most likely to result in peer rejection (Harris & Smith, 1982). Children who are overweight have more behavior problems, fewer friends, and are twice as likely to be thought of in negative terms (e.g., as forgetful, cheating, lying, sloppy, mean, ugly, dirty, or stupid) as their thin or muscular peers. Sadly, obese children tend to select more negative than positive adjectives to describe themselves, too (Banis et al., 1988). Why is obesity so universally devalued? Probably because we tend to hold obese people or their parents responsible for their condition (Harris & Smith, 1982). Because obesity is associated with overeating, eating the wrong food, or lack of exercise, we often insist that overweight children have little self-control and have "let themselves get fat." Although this assessment may be correct in some cases, obesity may also stem from other factors out of the child's control. Whatever its cause, obesity has serious physical and psychological implications and obese children need to be helped, not ridiculed.

Similarity

Children who share common attributes tend to affiliate with each other. Gender is an important factor. Same-sex play preferences established during the preschool years become even more pronounced once the child is in school. Boys and girls develop different styles of social interaction, each suited to their own particular psychological needs. Other-sex friendships do develop during the school years, but are typically short-lived, probably because at this age males and females have few common interests or behaviors.

Interracial friendships are more likely to be established and maintained during the school years if children have had equal-status contact with other racial groups through integrated housing or educational systems. Similarities in lifestyle, interests, attitudes, and educational level also facilitate interracial acceptance. In junior high school, whites have more in-school contact and blacks more out-of-school contact with their friends (Clark & Ayers, 1988).

Most children prefer to interact with same-age peers since their interests and skills are more compatible. Younger children often want to play with those who are older because their play appears more exciting and fun and because affiliation with the "big kids" increases their prestige. Older children do not voluntarily initiate play with younger ones unless they're bored, are babysitting, or are socially immature and feel safer in the company of those who are less likely to ridicule and criticize them (D. C. French, 1984).

Personality and Social Skills

Sometimes group acceptance is predicated on the expression of certain personality traits. Some peer groups value toughness, intellectualism, or creativity. The child who possesses these traits is more likely to be

■ **Table 13–1** *The Social Processes of Friendship Formation*

PROCESS	DEFINITION	EXAMPLE
1. Communication clarity and connectedness	Request for message clarification followed by appropriate clarification of the message.	**Child A:** Give it to me. **Child B:** Which one? **Child A:** The purple one with yellow ears.
2. Information exchange	Asking questions and eliciting relevant information.	Where do you live? What color is your crayon?
3. Establishing common ground	Finding something to do together and/or exploring their similarities and differences	Let's play trucks. I like tea parties, do you?
4. Self-disclosure of feelings	Questions about feelings by one child are followed by expression of feeling by the partner.	I'm really scared of the dark and snakes, too.
5. Positive reciprocity	One partner responds to another's positive behavior or serves to extend or lengthen a positive exchange; usually involves joking, gossip, or fantasy.	**Child A:** Did you hear what happened to Mary's sister? **Child B:** No, tell me and then I'll tell you another thing about Mary.
6. Conflict resolution	The extent to which play partners resolve disputes and disagreements successfully.	**Child A:** I want the blue truck. **Child B:** No, I'm playing with it. **Child A:** I want it. **Child B:** O.K. let's play with it together.

Source: Hetherington & Parke, *Child Psychology,* Third Edition (1986, McGraw-Hill). Reproduced with permission.

accepted than the child who does not. But there also seems to be a collection of characteristics and behaviors that facilitate popularity and acceptance in *most* groups. Children who are friendly, outgoing, kind, low in anxiety, cooperative, reasonably self-assured, well adjusted, quick to offer praise, and sensitive and responsive to others' needs tend to be well liked by both peers and adults (Ladd & Price, 1987). The most popular children also tend to communicate easily, interact comfortably and appropriately with new acquaintances and old friends, and possess a sense of humor (Masten, 1986). Prosocial behavior is a prerequisite for high social status and popularity (J. C. Wright et al., 1986) (see Table 13–1).

■ **Figure 13–8**

Two young friends swapping lunch-box goodies.

Peer-rejected children tend to be argumentative, nonverbally hostile, aggressive, distractible, withdrawn, hyperactive, immature, and misinterpret the behaviors of others (usually assuming a negative motive when there was none) (Shantz, 1987; Nowicki & Oxenford, 1989). Aggressive peers ("bullies") are judged socially undesirable from Grade 1 on. Withdrawn peers are seen as increasingly less likeable as children progress through elementary school (Younger & Piccinin, 1989). Children who are neglected by their peers are regarded as shy loners (Carlson et al., 1984). Except for those who are extremely withdrawn, neglected children simply prefer solitary activities even though they have good social skills (Zimbardo & Redl, 1981).

Friendships

Within their peer groups, children often value certain associations more highly than others. Girls are more likely to have a single best friend and to play in smaller groups and at more sedate activities (dolls, art, handicrafts) than boys. Boys, on the other hand, maintain more friendships and are more likely than girls to engage in rough-and-tumble play or large-scale games (Hartup, 1983). Friendships among elementary school children are more reciprocal and mutually satisfying than they were during the preschool years. By the time the child is 7, common interest and mutual helping are important attributes of friends (Rubin, 1980). In the words of one young child, "Kristen is my best friend. She likes to dance and so do I. We give each other presents."

Sharing is often the hallmark of a true friendship among 6 to 9 year olds, particularly if it involves providing something unique or special or giving more than was expected. A 9 year old explains:

> One day I forgot my lunch and did not have enough money for the cafeteria. Jeff shared his lunch with me. Not just the bad stuff, but everything, including his dessert. He really did a special thing that day. Nobody made him. He is my best friend because he is always thinking of others.

Nine and 10 year olds come to appreciate the fact that not everyone can become friends. They know that just because you ride the bus with four kids from your neighborhood, you won't necessarily become best friends with one of them. Children this age realize that friends share common interests, feelings, and beliefs; if they like each other, they spend a lot of time together by choice and they *don't fight* (Berndt, 1981).

At some time between 9 and 15, however, children begin demanding more of their friends than shared interests and reciprocated behaviors. Friendship takes on an emotional intensity and intimacy that goes beyond just "doing things for each other" (Selman, 1980). Children consider their friends to be special people and often desire an exclusive relationship with peers they feel closest to. They realize that it takes a long time to cultivate a friendship and that friends enjoy a unique level

■ **Table 13–2** *Onset Grades for Friendship Expectations*

GRADE 2	GRADE 3	GRADE 4	GRADE 5	GRADE 6	GRADE 7
Friend as help-giver* Share common activities*	Propinquity* Stimulation value Organized play Demographic similarity Evaluation*	Acceptance* Admiration* Increasing prior interaction*	Loyalty and commitment*	Genuineness* Friend as receiver of help	Intimacy potential* Common interest* Similarity in attitudes and values

*These friendship expectations tend to increase with age.

Source: Hetherington & Parke, *Child Psychology*, Third Edition (1986, McGraw-Hill). Reproduced with permission.

of understanding, trust, reciprocity, and self-disclosure (Kahn & Turiel, 1988). In the words of one 12 year old:

> Trust is everything in a friendship. You tell each other things that you don't tell anyone else; how you really feel about personal things. It takes a long time to make a close friend, so you feel really bad if you find out that he is trying to make other close friends, too. (Selman & Selman, 1979, p. 74)

Female and androgynous males experience more intimate friendships than sex-typed males (Jones & Dembo, 1989). It is at this stage that petty jealousies can develop between friends who become overly possessive or protective. A friend who simply talks with someone else or fails to spend a designated lunch break with the other may cause the latter to question the friend's emotional commitment (Berndt, 1981). For a grade-by-grade summary of friendship expectations see Table 13–2. Gottman (1983) has studied the process by which children become friends. As children communicate more and receive more information about each other, they simultaneously discover differences and commonalities, learn to resolve conflict, and exchange more personal data. The extent to which a sense of trust, mutuality, and good feeling develops influences the strength of the friendship.

Children without Friends

As unfortunate as it seems, some children have no friends, best or otherwise. Unpopular among their peers, these children are often excluded from sports or games (or chosen last), ignored during lunch and recess, and never invited to birthday parties or after-school functions. Rejected, friendless children report being lonely and depressed and having little confidence in their abilities. The older they get, the worse the rejection feels. They are also more likely to experience serious adjustment problems later in life, including a higher than average rate of delinquency,

■ ● ▲ CONCEPT SUMMARY

Interactions with Peers

- Children spend the majority of their day playing with friends
- Peer groups have a status hierarchy among the members
- Most peer groups have formalized rules and expectations to which members are expected to conform
- Peers are influential agents of socialization
- Children who are attractive, thin, nonhandicapped, similar to others, and affable are more readily accepted
- Friendships are important to both boys and girls during the school years
- Most friendships involve same-sex persons

■ **Figure 13–9**

Every once in a while, school age children have one of those sit-on-the hood-of-the-car-with-towel-on-my-head days

school dropout, and mental health complications (Parker & Asher, 1987). It's not clear whether rejection leads to the development of depression or whether depressed children are more likely to be rejected (E. Kennedy et al., 1989).

Although physique and appearance can influence peer acceptance, most children without friends lack the social skills needed to initiate and sustain interactions with others. Immaturity, silliness, withdrawal, argumentativeness, grumpiness, high anxiety, or unprovoked hostility may be perceived as odd or annoying by peers (French, 1988). Children with adjustment problems and a high need for attention also tend to be unpopular. Children who whine, beg, or cry are usually ignored by peers, while those who are demanding or aggressive may be hit, shoved, or verbally threatened. About 10% of rejected children are subjected to extreme levels of direct physical and verbal abuse by their peers (Perry et al., 1988).

Socially incompetent children drive others away. In a sense, children without friends are their own worst enemies. Since they often fail to understand why other children are rejecting them and how to interpret social cues, their behavior remains unchanged and they often have poor self-concepts (Asher et al., 1982; Dozier, 1988). Peer hostility and isolation escalate as other children become increasingly impatient with the deviant behavior, and a negative cycle of exclusion and avoidance is established.

Fifty to 60% of unpopular children have been found to benefit from instruction in social skills (learning to take turns, get involved, initiate conversation, give attention to others, cooperate, and so forth). Outcome effectiveness is enhanced if children believe they can exert control over the outcomes of social situations and expect interpersonal success (Lepore et al., 1989; Rabiner & Coie, 1989).

Peer Group Focus: Cooperation vs. Competition

Whether on the playground, in the classroom, in sports, or—later—in business, competition is considered good, proper, and even essential for American children, especially boys. As early as kindergarten, children find a task more interesting if it has a competitive focus (Butler, 1989). Even when they play team sports, everyone knows who the best players are.

The competitive motive is so thoroughly ingrained in American children that they sometimes compete even when competition will *hurt* rather than help them. Kagan and Madsen (1972) set up a game of 24 moves where children could choose either to block or free another player's path toward a goal. Reaching the goal let you win a toy. When children cooperate and move out of each other's way, they could win four toys apiece within the allotted moves. American children usually spend so much of their time blocking their opponent that *no one* wins any toys.

The competitive motive can be relinquished when children must work together to achieve a *shared* goal. In the classic Robber's Cave Experiment, Muzafer Sherif and colleagues (1961) demonstrated that just putting two groups together is not enough to encourage cooperation. Even special occasions like movies and goodwill dinners fostered competition. However, when there is a valued goal (keeping the summer camp open) and the goal can only be attained by working together, even rival competitive factions can cooperate. Age also adds flexibility. When 6–13 year olds were tested, older children were more likely to adapt their strategy (cooperative vs. competitive) to the social goal than younger children (Schmidt et al., 1988).

● Play

The vigor of children's play increases during the school years when both boys and girls engage their favorite friends in rough-and-tumble play (Humphreys & Smith, 1987). Girls play games of chase and tag while boys wad themselves together in good natured fights and wrestling matches. Through it all, everyone is smiling and laughing. Popular boys enjoy rough-and-tumble play with their parents as well while rejected boys become overstimulated (MacDonald, 1987). When a rejected child tries to join a rough-and-tumble play group, his behavior often evolves into real aggression and causes further rejection (Pellegrini, 1988). Chil-

rough-and-tumble play
play that involves elements of physical interaction (chasing, tackling, wrestling, etc.)

dren are more tolerant of unpopular children during competitive than cooperative play (Gelb & Jacobson, 1988).

In the early grades, children spend most of their time outside school playing formal and informal games with peers. Games like hopscotch, Red Rover, tag, jumprope, and Simon Says are popular in this age group. These games have many functions, allowing children to expend some of their energy, develop coordination and physical prowess, refine social skills, understand concepts such as cooperation and competition, and feel challenged. As children advance to the later primary grades, favorite games have more requirements for cooperation, contain less make believe, and are more organized and highly structured (Baumeister & Senders, 1989). This was overheard during play: "When we play (Monopoly) we have a rule that we can't buy property or houses" "What's the point of going around the board then?" That's just the rule. That's how we play." Board games such as checkers and Monopoly are popular, although computerized or video games have replaced much spontaneous play during the school years. Outdoor sports like baseball, soccer, football, and basketball still involve millions of boys and girls each year.

● The School Experience

The school is second only to the family in influence during middle childhood. Entering school at age 5 or 6 marks a sharp change in routine. School children are separated from parents and siblings for at least half of their waking hours. In addition, they must adjust to a new set of interpersonal contacts, including peers and other adult authority figures. Most children want to go to school, and most adapt well to the new environment. Still, variations within the school setting can have an important impact on children's educational experiences and social and emotional development. Both children's academic achievement and the quality of their relationships with their teachers and classmates can have profound effects on their later career choices and social behavior patterns. Let's look at some of the specific factors that can have an impact.

Teacher/Student Interactions

The teacher is the architect of the child's learning environment. Within the guidelines established by the principal, the classroom teacher sets the pace, designs the curriculum, and determines how learning materials will be presented to the students. The teacher evaluates the child's performance while providing emotional support, transmitting values, encouraging appropriate behavior, and discouraging inappropriate behavior. Since the elementary school teacher acts as a parent in many ways, teachers in the early primary grades are selected on the basis of their abilities to nurture and comfort young children as well as on their academic qualifications.

Just as parents adopt certain styles in dealing with children, so do teachers adopt certain styles in regulating their classrooms. Three types of teaching styles can be identified: authoritative, permissive, and democratic (Rutter et al., 1979). *Authoritarian* teachers make all the decisions, permit no student choice or input, praise good work, but are otherwise impersonal. *Democratic* teachers encourage group decisions, let children choose, and often join in activities with the children. *Permissive* teachers do not interfere, shifting control to the children and responding only when specific requests are made. Democratic teachers encourage the most productivity, the most self-direction, and the fewest arguments. Authoritarian teachers have children who vacillate between passivity and rebellion, while permissive teachers foster boredom, hostility, and inactivity.

Students like certain teachers more than others. Research shows that their assessments are based on the personal qualities of the teachers and the way they interact with their students (Brophy & Good, 1986). Not surprisingly, the best-liked teachers are kind, considerate, sympathetic, interested in students as people, fair, flexible, tolerant, consistent in discipline, concerned, enthusiastic, and attractive. Children also cite the ability to make information clear and interesting and to explain things in a way that helps them learn as qualities of well-liked teachers. Conversely, disliked teachers are usually perceived to be strict and unfair. Explosive teachers, who react angrily or who lose their tempers easily, create tension and anxiety in students.

Popular, well-liked teachers seem to bring out the best in their students. Many of the qualities that students like in teachers also encourage students to participate more in class, to assume a greater responsibility and participate more in decision making, to behave more independently, to express their feelings more freely, and to be more creative. And of course, students are more likely to try to please and cooperate with liked rather than disliked teachers. Because children often emulate the behavior of their teachers, impulsive children can develop more reflective response styles and do better in school if their teachers model and reward reflective behavior (Kagan et al., 1964).

Although most teachers try to treat all their students in an unbiased way, teachers generally develop one of four attitudes toward their pupils—attachment, concern, indifference, and/or rejection—and these attitudes can affect the nature of student–teacher classroom interactions (Minuchin & Shapiro, 1983). Interestingly, the teacher's personal preference for a student is relatively independent of the child's reputation in her peer group (Taylor, 1989). Teachers may feel attached to students who give them pleasure, fulfill their needs, or make few demands on their time, and may thus share these students' suggestions or ideas with the class, crediting and praising them publicly.

Punishments
	Lashes
1. Boys and Girls Playing Together	4
2. Fighting at School	5
3. Quareling at School	5
4. Gambleing or Betting at School	4
5. Playing at Cards at School	10
6. Climbing for Every Foot Over Three Feet Up a Tree	1
7. Telling Lies	7
8. Telling Tales Out of School	8
9. Giving Each Other Ill Names	3
10. Swaring at School	8
11. For Misbehaving to Girls	10
12. For Drinking Spiritous Liquors at School	8
13. Making Swings and Swinging on Them	7
14. For Waring Long Finger Nails	2
15. Misbehaving Persons on the Road	4
16. For Going to Girls Play Places	3
17. Girls Going to Boys Play Places	3
18. Coming to School With Dirty Faces and Hands	2
19. For Calling Each Other Liars	4
20. For Wrestling at School	4
21. For Weting Each Other Washing at Playtime	2
22. Scuffling at School	4
23. For Going and Playing about the Mill or Creek	6
24. For Going about the Barn or doing any Mischief about the Place	7

(10 November 1848)

■ **Figure 13–10**

Children who went to school during the 1849 Gold Rush in Sacramento, California had to abide by these rules or suffer the consequences.

Teachers may show concern, too, for students who require considerable time and attention. Many children have trouble spelling, low self-esteem, frantic schedules (due to single parenting or some other challenge), insufficiently warm or cool clothing, or lack money for lunch. More and more children display severe problems and are markedly dysfunctional, needing immediate counseling and other special services. One teacher reports:

> Al (not his real name) was a thin boy with an expression that could convey open hatred but with a smile that brought sunshine into the classroom. He had asthma, and would often come in from recess wheezing and violently coughing. Once, he was so sick, I took him to the office to go home. Actually, I had to drag him because he kept saying, "I don't want to go home. I don't want to go home." His sister met us halfway up the hall and joined the chorus, "Mom says you can't go home. Mom says you can't go home."
>
> Al had trouble writing coherently. His stories were out of sequence and rambling. But there was one main exception—a story Al wrote about how he had killed a man. Someone had broken into the family's apartment and began attacking Al's mother. She screamed to Al to go get the gun. He did and shot the man in the head. The police came and took him to juvenile hall for a couple of days. When asked about how he felt about it, he said, "I felt nothing."
>
> Needless to say, I was shocked and reported the whole story to my principal. There had been no mention of this in any of Al's records or by his mother. The principal called Al's home and spoke with Al's aunt. She said Al had made up the whole thing. She said he was an only child who was looking for attention because his mother was pregnant. However, Al had two sisters registered at the school.
>
> The next day Al tore up the story and said his mother had told him not to write about it any more. I told him his aunt had said he made it up. He replied, "She wasn't there." I believe Al.
>
> . . . .
>
> I have prayed and cried and spent family time in deep agitation over my troubled students like Al. I am not alone. My principal keeps a list of students by her bed to pray for them and admits to many a sleepless night. Teaching is a bittersweet career with soaring highs and heart-wrenching lows. I feel guilty when the school year ends because there is so much I wanted to do. It's not for lack of trying: I haven't given up. I just ran out of time.
>
> Stephanie Sachs
> Elementary school teacher
> Fresno, California
> (Excerpted from the Sacramento Bee, May 26, 1991)

In contrast, some teachers are indifferent to students who do not make much of an impression on them, passing over both their abilities and their misbehavior. Such students are often passive and participate little in class discussions. And some teachers reject difficult students outright.

Unresponsive, overly demanding children who also behave inappropriately or disruptively in class cannot seem to do anything right in the opinion of some teachers. Such children might receive little or no positive attention, even when their behavior is appropriate (Coie & Dodge, 1988). Consider this exchange, a typical expression of indifference:

STUDENT: What should I write about?
TEACHER: Oh, you'll think of something, or is that asking too much?

These teachers may be burned out, overworked, or burdened by their own personal stresses and conflicts. Attention and assistance are needed by the minority of teachers who are indifferent or rejecting.

Teacher's Expectations

Can a teacher's attitude affect the student's behavior? Despite its methodological flaws, Robert Rosenthal and Lenore Jacobsen's classic work (1966) on the *self-fulfilling prophecy* suggests that people often act as others expect them to. Thus, the expectations teachers form about a child's school performance may influence that child's academic achievement. Rosenthal and Jacobsen told a number of elementary school teachers that some of their pupils showed a potential for marked intellectual growth during the academic year, though the children identified as the potential "bloomers" were actually chosen at random. After several months, children were tested, and those who were expected to show impressive intellectual gains did in fact score higher on standardized IQ tests than the remaining students. They also outperformed their peers in reading and were rated as more intellectually curious in the classroom. The younger the child, the more pronounced the effect.

How can we account for the self-fulfilling prophecy? Teachers who expect high performance from children may provide them with more feedback, may spend more time with them than with other children, and may demand more output from them as well (Good, 1980). Teachers may provide little encouragement for mastering complex tasks to children they perceive as low achieving; they may also be surprised, rather than congratulatory, when such a child actually does achieve (Brophy, 1983). Apparently, the amount of attention a child receives is partly a function of how likely she is to benefit from that attention. Teachers, like others, need to relinquish the stereotype that male achievement is more important (or even more likely) than female achievement. A girl's academic self-concept is closely tied to her parent's and teacher's estimates of her potential (Eccles, Science Weekend Address, APA, August, 1991).

Two circumstances in particular seem to promote the development of self-fulfilling prophecies. First, when students are ability grouped or tracked, teachers develop certain fixed ways of interacting with the different groups (Evertson, 1982). The "low" groups go slowly, get more

self-fulfilling prophesy
the idea that people often behave as they are expected to; also, that the interpretation of a particular behavior often reflects the biases and expectations of the interpreter

ability grouping or tracking
an educational philosophy that suggests children can benefit more from instruction when their peers are all at about the same level of achievement

basic skills instructions, and spend less time applying what they know. Stigmatized by their peers as "dumb," children in the low-ability groups have low self-esteem, low motivation, and as a consequence, lose academic ground as time goes on, widening rather than closing the performance gap between themselves and the high-ability group. Second, teachers who have strong fears about losing control of their class will promote negative self-fulfilling prophecies as a way of manipulating student behavior (Cooper, 1979). When students are treated inconsistently, receive high levels of criticism, have their requests denied, and are seldom called on, they lose their motivation to achieve as well as their motivation to disrupt, and simply withdraw.

The self-fulfilling prophecy has important implications for minority group, poor, and handicapped students. Teachers who consider these students to have little intellectual potential are probably not surprised when their achievement is low (Minuchin & Shapiro, 1983). Sadly, as early as the preschool years, teachers provide less verbal stimulation to classes of lower-income students than to classes of middle-income students (Quay & Jarritt, 1986). Teachers may misinterpret cultural communication practices and draw faulty conclusions about the child's attitude or skills. For example, some cultures avert their eyes to show respect while middle class Americans may expect eye contact as a sign of attention and deference. However, teachers who understand their students and have confidence in their student's ability to achieve may be gratified by their level of effort, commitment, and overall success. It's important to point out that teachers who are self-confident and experienced tend to reject expectancy information if it disagrees with their firsthand observations of the child's behavior (Carter et al., 1987).

Peer Teachers and Cooperative Learning

Some children receive instruction not only from adults but also from peers serving as tutors or assistant teachers. For example, older elementary school students may be selected to help tutor younger students in classroom fundamentals. In this arrangement, cross-age tutors usually meet with the child's teacher to formulate an instructional plan that will meet the child's needs and last for as long as necessary. The results indicate that such tutorial programs benefit all involved. Both tutors and students make progress in the tutorial subject. In a study of low-achieving fifth graders who tutored third graders, the tutors reported that in addition to improving academically, their pupils showed increased self-confidence and commitment to their work. Both tutors and their students grew less tense, became better at expressing themselves, and showed improved attendance records (Allen & Feldman, 1973). Of equal important is the great sense of accomplishment and pride the tutors experienced in helping younger children.

cooperative learning
learning as groups or units where individuals within each group tutor each other

Cooperative learning involves assigning tasks to groups, not individuals, where every member of the group plays a role in problem solving.

Getting to know others by working together.

Minority students respond most positively to the cooperative learning situation when the emphasis of the group remains noncompetitive (Johnson & Johnson, 1985). A noncompetitive group approach to learning may also foster more peer acceptance of learning disabled students (M. A. Anderson, 1985).

The Physical Environment of the Classroom

The arrangement and size of the classroom may affect the child's tendency to participate and learn. Regardless of the child's age, sex, grade level, or subject matter, or the age or sex of the teacher, children who sit in the front row or near the center of the room with a row and column arrangement of desks interact more with the teacher than students who sit elsewhere. Eye contact and close proximity encourage communication. But it is not clear whether more interested students sit in the front-center region of the class or whether students who occupy these seats become more interested and participate more in class proceedings as a function of their location. To encourage more equal participation, elementary school teachers can vary the seating arrangement of their classrooms so that everyone has a chance to sit in the front row or toward the center at least once during the school year.

Another option (and one that might be more considerate of the child who is uncomfortable "up front") is to vary the arrangement of the desks, not just the child's position among them. The effectiveness of three arrangements—small clusters of desks, a large circle of desks, and the row and column—has been assessed (Rosenfield et al., 1985). Children participated more in class and were more attentive in the large circle; desk clusters ranked second. The most off-task behavior, disruption, and nonparticipation came from the row and column configuration.

Research shows that as class size increases, four things happen: The teacher and the demonstrations become more difficult to see, aggression increases, class participation decreases, and individualized attention decreases (McAfee, 1987). Fewer students ask fewer questions and less discussion is generated overall (Smith & Connolly, 1980). Also, grade. school teachers often spend much teaching time disciplining students who behave inappropriately. The ideal class size for fostering academic achievement is 15–20 students. Beyond 20 students, class size seems unrelated to learning outcomes (Educational Research Service, 1980). Since active participation and individual attention aids the learning process, students are better served by smaller, less crowded classes.

Textbooks and Readers

stereotype
oversimplified, generalized characteristics ascribed to a person because of their group membership (i.e., assuming that all blondes are dumb)

Both the themes and content of textbooks and readers influence children's perceptions of everyday life in American society and color their own behavior. For example, when kindergarten children in a research project were read stories in which males and females were portrayed in narrow, stereotyped ways, they were more likely to choose a sex-stereotyped toy (dolls for girls; cars for boys) than children who heard stories with less stereotyped characters (Ashton, 1983). Similarly, when nontraditional multicultural readers are used, children develop more positive attitudes about their diverse classmates.

The portrayal of the female protagonist in stories has changed over the last decade. In the 1950s and 1960s she was depicted as selfish and narcissistic. In the 1980s and 1990s, she is more likely to display practical knowledge and intellectual prowess and is guided by a system of values and ethics (D'Angelo, 1989). However, male characters continue to outnumber female characters and are given most of the central roles and offered more variety in the roles they portrayed (S. M. McDonald, 1989).

Children seem to prefer stories that feature characters they can relate to and activities they are interested in. Boys tend to like stories with male characters; females, stories with female characters (Kropp & Halverson, 1983). Childrens' second choices in stories relate to a preference for a particular activity, not the sex of the main character. The reading scores of boys in particular are affected by the interest value of the stories they read. When boys had a chance to read stories about astronauts and airplanes, they read better and understood more than when they were given a low-interest story to read. Girls' average reading scores were less strongly affected by content and interest level (Asher & Markell, 1974).

Still another problem with readers and textbooks seems to be in the accuracy of the information presented. Don Lessem (1991) argues for

■ ● ▲   CONCEPT SUMMARY

Facilitating Learning

During the school years, learning is facilitated by:

- Democratic teachers who love their jobs and have positive characteristics and positive expectations for student success
- Cooperative learning
- Placement in the center front of the classroom
- Arranging desks in a circle or in clusters
- Reading assignments that provoke interest and are easy to relate to

example, that most of what passes for facts about dinosaurs is fiction: The art is inaccurate, the timeframe is off by sometimes millions of years, and little is mentioned about the conduct of science itself. If our children are going to be in touch with science, history, or whatever, then the books they read should be in touch with these subjects, too.

Putting It All Together: Effective Schools

Some schools simply do a better job of educating their students than other schools. Successful schools have more than just skilled teachers, good textbooks, or up-to-date equipment. Successful schools create a total learning environment where all factions of the school—teachers, parents, students, and administrators—work together to accomplish shared goals of academic excellence. Rutter (1983) summarizes the characteristics of consistently effective schools:

Administration

- Clearly stated values shared by all school personnel
- Strong teacher support
- High expectations and standards of excellence
- Give children real responsibilities
- The entire focus of the school (activities, funding, time allocation, and the like) is on high academic standards

The Physical Environment

- Well maintained (age doesn't matter)
- Clean
- Attractive

The Teaching Staff
- Well trained *and* experienced
- Praise students frequently and sincerely
- High expectations conveyed to all students
- Skilled in classroom management, prevent problems rather than discipline after the fact; constantly monitor students' behavior*
- Are warm and caring
- Treat all children equally
- Love their jobs—teaching is their first-choice activity

*The strongest predictor of student achievement

The School Day
- Structured and well planned
- More complex, high-interest exercises than simple, rote memorization or factual exercises
- Most of the day is spent on task with few distractions
- Homework is assigned regularly (more rather than less homework is given)

The Students
- Heterogeneous rather than homogeneous in background
- Fair to good academic skills
- Responsive to instructor
- Generally enjoy school, like their teachers
- Have supportive parents

● Emotional Development

Fear

By the time children reach 5 or 6, most of their early fears have subsided. For example, school-age children are more likely than preschoolers to understand that alligators live in zoos and swamps and not under beds, that spooky things on television are just make believe, and that people who wear Halloween costumes are little children and not monsters. And although concerns about the dark, exotic animals, and imaginary creatures like ghosts decrease in middle childhood as children become better able to separate reality from fantasy, fears about school and social relationships increase. In middle childhood, irrational and fantasy fears are replaced by more realistic concerns about everyday life. For example, school-age children may share their parents' worries about finances or health. Fear of death, of school failure, of rejection by teachers, par-

A Closer Look

How Did Children Weather the (Desert) Storm?

It was the leaving that was hard. The tears, the fears, the uncertainty of return. Mature-looking children clinging to their parents as though they were still toddlers. And feeling no shame.

The Gulf War touched everyone but none so keenly as the children. It was one of the first wars where public attention was focused on mothers, not just fathers, leaving behind families. It was one of the first wars that offered continuous coverage, almost as events were occurring. And, unlike the last war, we could watch without being too horrified because the military censors kindly cut and pasted what the American public would view.

For children touched by the war, it was more than a new vocabulary, a new enemy, and waving flags. The war was a threat to their future, their security, and their parent's life. What children could not say with words, they displayed in their actions: unprovoked crying, inattention, withdrawal, acting out, starting fights, stomachaches, clinginess, nightmares, depression, moodiness, and insomnia.

Most of the 400,000 children whose parents served were reunited with their mothers and fathers. For them, their symptoms and memories should fade with time. But some lives will be forever changed by the war. Roger Lee Haws of Fresno, California, was 3 years old when his father was reported killed in an Iraqi artillery barrage. Too young to understand that his father was gone, he reportedly touched the tears as they streamed down his mother's and grandmother's face during the funeral. "Why cry?" he asked.

Some Desert Storm children and their families will be strengthened by loss. People learn new coping skills and may vow not to take each other for granted again. Many others will be devastated by the stress of conflict, loss, separation, and repatriation. Only time will reveal the true number of Desert Storm casualties.

Jenifer and Jessica at their school's Welcome Home ceremony for parents who served in Desert Storm. Their father is an Air Force sergeant.

ents, or peers, of getting hurt by bullies are all concerns that begin to emerge in the elementary school years.

Children around the world share remarkably similar concerns (Yamamoto et al., 1987). School-age girls express more fears than boys and rural children are more fearful than urban children (Davidson et al., 1989). Interestingly, children in America and in other countries rated the birth of a sibling as the least worrisome of all. Apparently, school-age children are much more afraid of losing their parents altogether than of having to do something as minor as share them with a new brother or sister.

War, especially one so televised as the Persian Gulf War of 1991, provoked considerable fear and misgiving from school-age children in Israel, the Middle East, and the United States.

Gulf War
another name for the Persian Gulf War

Fear is a normal reaction in some situations, and everyone has a few fears. But fear that is irrational, out of proportion to the extent of the perceived threat, and so intense that it interferes with the child's daily functioning may require professional attention. These exaggerated fears are called *phobias*. An example of a phobia might be a fear of snakes. The fear becomes irrational when it includes avoidance of certifiably harmless snakes, pictures of snakes, and rubber "play" snakes. The fear is classified as intense when it involves extreme reactions such as wild climbing or running, heart palpitations, or fainting, and it is judged debilitating or limiting when the phobic individual spends most of his time avoiding situations and circumstances where he imagines snakes might be lurking. Phobias are particularly common during the school years.

School Phobia/School Refusal

school phobia/school refusal
intense anxiety associated with school attendance

Of particular concern with regard to school-age children is the fear known as *school phobia*. It is common and normal for the beginning student to feel some anxiety and trepidation about attending school for the first time. But anxiety about school attendance that verges on panic and is accompanied by physical symptoms such as vomiting, diarrhea, dizziness, and headache is a full-blown phobia. What is striking about school phobia is that the symptoms subside within a few hours once the child has been allowed to stay home. Also, no such symptoms are evidence on weekends or holidays. School phobia occurs in about 5% of the school-age population. The incidence is about the same for boys and girls (Utter, 1987).

secondary gain
benefits that are sometimes associated with an adverse circumstance (for example, a person who is handicapped might qualify for more financial aid at a college than a nonhandicapped person)

School phobia can be anxiety related or prompted by a wish to obtain secondary gains. A school-related incident may trigger an anxiety-related phobic reaction. For example, the child may feel that her teacher is overly critical or may fear failing an important exam or giving an oral presentation. Discrimination based on race, dress, physique, ethnicity, or a fear of gangs or a school bully may also prompt anxiety-related reaction. Such school phobic children are usually girls and often have an intensely dependent relationship with their parents, usually their mothers. For this reason, school phobia may be a form of separation anxiety (DSM-III-R, 1987). These children are reluctant to be separated from their mothers and the mothers may be equally reluctant to see their children go. These highly dependent children are not afraid to go to school; they are afraid to leave home, sometimes fearing that their mothers will be injured while they are away. Parents who are weak, insecure, inconsistent, and have difficulty making decisions in the child's presence produce children who worry a lot about them and may contribute to their child's fear of school (Bernstein & Garfinkel, 1988).

Finally, some children who become school phobic do so not to escape school but to receive the pleasures and attention involved in staying home. This secondary-gains orientation is adopted primarily by boys who have parents who don't attach much importance to school (Utter, 1987).

The treatment of school phobia depends on its cause. The source of the anxiety should be identified (teacher–child relations, parent–child dependency, threatening school situation, or whatever). When the child is helped to understand and cope with fear, the symptoms usually disappear. Most professionals agree that the school phobic child should not be allowed to stay home from school. In severe cases where returning to school is unsuccessful, professional help is advised.

Emotional Turmoil

Since few school-age children voluntarily talk about personal distress, adults often have to "discover" children's emotional problems by examining their behavior. Antisocial behavior like stealing, lying, or aggression is called *acting out* if it masks emotional trauma. Children who witness or experience violence may develop rage that is expressed by acting out and perhaps symbolically or vicariously hurting the aggressor. Traumatized children also withdraw and fail to learn even though they are capable. Depression or anxiety that stem from loss, rejection, coping with violence, or coping with conflict may manifest itself as school failure. Children who act out are also frequently rejected by their peers, who don't understand the sudden, inappropriate displays (Taylor, 1989). Some parents use their children as pawns in the game of mutual hostility. When children receive conflicting messages they have nowhere to turn (*Mom:* "Study hard. I'm paying a lot of money to send you to that school," vs. *Dad:* "You flunked English? That's great! Your mother should never have sent you there in the first place.") Some lash out, others withdraw. Until someone identifies the emotional trauma and intervenes to help the child, the interpersonal problems and learning difficulties will persist.

acting out
behavior that is disruptive, aggressive, or otherwise incongruous

■ Figure 13–12

Hostile aggression knows no gender limitations.

Aggression

In the absence of emotional disturbance, aggressive behavior can be used by school-age children to attract attention, to get their way, to establish power/dominance, seize property, and hurt others (Boldizar et al., 1989). Verbal insults and playground fights that involve pushing, kicking, and hitting are more common during the school years than during the preschool period (Hay & Ross, 1982). Many teachers blame the Teenage Mutant Ninja Turtles for bringing violence to the classroom (Associated Press, March 19, 1991). While the "Turtles" cartoons often have a moralistic message, children ignore the message and model the aggressive behavior. Apparently, parents focus on the message—as a justification for letting their children watch!

Aggressive children are generally unpopular, are targets of aggressive retaliation, and are disruptive in class. However, aggressive children may also be named as best friends if their aggression is protective or secures resources and power (Cairns et al., 1988). Contrary to popular opinion, children don't grow out of their aggression (Olweus, 1982). Aggressive behavior is stable over time because it is a well-established, learned behavior.

For reasons still not entirely clear, boys continue to be more aggressive than girls, as they were in the preschool period. Until the fifth grade, girls and boys display no differences in verbal aggression. Verbally aggressive children also tend to be physically aggressive (McCabe & Lipscomb, 1988). Normative shifts in patterns of aggression occur with development. Over time, boys become more likely to use direct confrontation and physical attacks; girls become more likely to use social aggression and ostracism (Cairns et al., 1989). Girls tend to be less tolerant of aggression in others than boys are (Lancelotta & Vaughn, 1989).

Children learn to be aggressive by viewing violence, either live or on TV, or by being rewarded for aggressive acts (Singer & Singer, 1985). When aggression "pays off" it is more likely to be used in the future. Parents and teachers can have an effect in reducing the level of aggression school-age children display by modeling and rewarding nonaggressive solutions to problems and by explaining behavior on the part of others that might otherwise provoke an outburst. Aggressive children expect less guilt and parental disapproval for responses to provoked aggression than to unprovoked aggression. Each sex disapproves of aggression directed towards its members (Perry et al., 1989). When possible, aggressive behavior should be ignored. If it cannot be safely ignored, then the aggressive child should be dealt with by a warm, positive adult. Social isolation and deprivation of privileges are nonviolent control strategies. The aggressive child also needs to be exposed to those children who model and are rewarded for positive, nonhostile interpersonal contacts and conflict resolution strategies.

■●▲   CONCEPT SUMMARY

Emotional Development

- The strongest fears that school-age children have are reality-based and could actually happen

- Irrational fears, called phobias, are particularly common. One example is school phobia, or school refusal.

- Acting out is one indication of emotional distress

- Aggressive behavior can be motivated by a variety of causes

- Boys tend to be more aggressive during the school years than girls

- Siblings and physical assault are likely to provoke anger

- Anger may explode into aggression

Anger

Angry feelings may or may not explode into aggressive behavior, but when children watch adults express anger, they tend to feel angry and distressed themselves, particularly if they have parents who are physically aggressive toward each other (Cummings et al., 1989). Two common causes of anger in school-age children are siblings and being physically assaulted (Rotenberg, 1985). The combination of verbal and physical anger made children more upset and angry than other nonverbal anger or verbal anger alone. With increasing age, children retaliate more frequently with verbal insults than physical assault (Rotenberg, 1985). In boys, high levels of anger, aggression, impatience, and mood negativity may indicate a Type A behavior pattern that may persist into adulthood (Whalen et al., 1989).

● Individual Differences

According to Erik Erikson (1963), boys and girls become gradually more peer and society oriented during the middle years of childhood. Turning their attention from play to work, 6 to 12 year olds learn the skills of their culture in order to become productive members of society. American children learn to read, write, and count; children from some other cultures may learn to care for animals and work in the fields, weave cloth and make rope, or grind corn and other grain. Erikson defines the challenge faced by the school-age child as involving *industry vs. inferiority*. The goal in this period, according to Erikson, is to establish oneself as a skilled and competent worker. The danger is that children of this age will develop a sense of inferiority after trying but failing to accomplish tasks, or that they will come to value work so highly that they will neglect relationships with people or become excessively competitive.

Like Erikson, Sigmund Freud (1938/1973) considered the school years to be a time when cognitive growth takes precedence over physical and sexual development. Compared to the physiological upheaval that takes place during adolescence, middle childhood is a period of relative calm and stability—a period of *latency*. Freud hypothesized that latency occurs because the conscience, or superego, is strong enough to keep unacceptable urges under control. However, sexual latency does not imply an absence of sexuality. Six to 12 year olds continue to explore themselves sexually and to think, talk, and joke about sexual matters. Nor does latency imply an absence of anxiety. Freud suggested that school-age children may develop *defense mechanisms* (denial, repression) to cope with anxiety that threatens their fragile self-concepts. Defense mechanisms may be used (or overused) throughout adulthood to allay anxiety and protect self-esteem.

latency
in Freud's theory, the psychosexual stage spanning the school years. During this time, sexual development takes a backseat to intellectual development

superego
Freud's term for the conscience

defense mechanisms
in Freud's theory, those behaviors engaged in subconsciously or unconsciously to ward off anxiety

---

TOWARD EFFECTIVE PARENTING

Promoting Children's Mental Health

Researchers in the emerging field of developmental psychopathology have begun to address two data needs. They are (a) identifying the factors most predictive of serious maladjustment in children, and (b) studying children who show normal development even when exposed to known risk factors for psychological or behavioral disturbance (Peters & Orley, 1987). The goal of this research is to balance the current mental health care delivery system for children with a strong emphasis on prevention.

Health promotion or *positive health* concentrates on establishing positive behaviors and attitudes rather than on symptom reduction. It is aimed at the entire population of children, not just at children at risk, since many emotional problems that children encounter can be seen as responses to specific situations and circumstances. In so doing, health promotion can help children *stay* mentally healthy and resilient and can help the 10–20% of moderate to severely disturbed children learn to cope with new stresses in an effort to *reestablish* their positive functioning.

Children who are mentally healthy are socially competent, have a source of social support, utilize problem solving skills, and are able to cope with stress.

1. *Social competence.* Socially competent children relate appropriately to people in the environment. Children should be taught to:

- initiate conversation
- take turns and cooperate

positive health
focusing on prevention rather than treatment

- help others
- recognize emotions in others
- express their needs
- understand the needs of others
- resist negative peer pressure
- resolve disputes

2. *Social support.* Children need to know that others care, are interested, and are there for them. Parents, extended family members, siblings, peers, teachers, and coaches are among those who can provide social support for the child. One source is not necessarily better than the other if parents cannot provide the caring and interest the child needs.

3. *Problem solving skills.* Children need to be able to recognize the existence of a problem and then to generate possible solutions and evaluate their potential effectiveness before they take action. When children learn a general approach to problem solving, they can apply the outcome to any situation that arises (home, school, job, interpersonal).

4. *Coping with stress.* The child needs to learn how to identify and reduce the impact of stress while simultaneously bolstering himself. The child can be taught to

- recognize stress
- utilize social support
- reduce the level of stress (e.g., through relaxation, thought blocking)
- identify his personal strengths/skills
- enhance feelings of self-worth
- be persistent—don't give up
- move from trying to change the situation to adjusting to the situation the way it is, if nothing can be changed (Band & Weisz, 1988)

If one views mental illness as the absence of behaviors and attitudes that promote adjustment, then training children to cope with stress, solve problems, be socially competent, and identify social support should help prevent mental distress.

● Chapter Summary

- Children gain more independence from their families during the school years while still depending on the family for guidance and support. The developmental tasks faced by the family of the school-age child include adapting to the child's expanding world, letting him or her go, encouraging greater responsibility, helping the child maintain values, and encouraging high self-esteem.
- School-age children develop closer ties to their peers as they detach somewhat from their parents. Fathers from middle class families are viewed more positively, while fathers from underclass families are

generally more distant, especially if they experience considerable pressure and stress. Parents' moods can affect child behavior.

- The majority of school-age children in the 1990s will experience the divorce or separation of their parents. Unlike preschoolers, school-age children can understand the reasons for divorce and are less likely to blame themselves. Behavioral symptoms like acting out and withdrawal are displayed when children are distressed. The negative impact of divorce can be minimized when parents remain supportive and mutually cooperative and when lengthy custody battles are avoided. Remarriage is most stressful for prepubertal boys. Girls can cope with remarriage provided they remain close to their mothers (in mother–stepfather arrangements) or develop a positive relationship with their stepmothers if their father remarries. Other challenges involve adjusting to parents' extended absences (travel/job related), parental employment or unemployment, or the loss of a parent through death.
- Children practice their social skills and social roles with their siblings. The quality of sibling relationships is predictive of relationships with peers.
- School-age children spend considerable time socializing with their peers. Within each peer group, children play particular roles and are expected to conform to established rules and norms. In return, children receive acceptance, information, praise, and direction. Popular, well-liked children are physically attractive, not overweight, similar to others, easy to get along with, adept at modeling prosocial skills, and the same sex and same age as their peers.
- During the school years, friendship involves sharing and later, emotional intimacy and mutual trust. Girls tend to have fewer and more intense friendships than boys. For both boys and girls, play can be vigorous, spontaneous, and involve formal and informal games.
- Formal schooling takes up much of the school-age child's day and is vitally influential in directing the child's attention from play to work. The teacher is the most important component of the child's school experience and teacher's expectations, curriculum and assignments, and arrangement of the classroom can have either a positive or negative effect on the child's ability to learn.
- School-age children are troubled more by realistic concerns (like death, personal failure, and finances) than by fantasy or make believe. About 5% of the school age population develop school phobia, or school refusal. Others may express their emotional distress by acting out or becoming aggressive.

● Observational Exercise

The influence of school and peers grows increasingly important the longer children are in school. During this period, children identify their age-mates as likeable or not and choose to form friendships or keep their distance. One way to study the nature of social relationships among children is to interview them about their classmates. In so doing, one can come to understand the social structure—including the power and influence hierarchies—in the classroom and to examine children's self-perceptions in the group.

Procedure: Interview five same-sex children from a fifth- or sixth-grade classroom about their same-sex peers. Assure them that what they tell you will remain confidential and ask them not to talk about the interview with their friends until the study has been completed. Ask the following questions in the interview:

1. Among the boys/girls in your class

   a. Whom would you call the smartest? Is this person fairly well liked? Why or why not?
   b. Whom would you call the cutest boy or girl? Is this person fairly well liked? Why or why not?
   c. Whom would you call the best athlete? Is this person fairly well liked? Why or why not?
   d. Whom would you call the nicest? Is this person fairly well liked? Why or why not?
   e. Is there any student whom almost everyone likes? Why is that person so popular?
   f. Is there any student whom almost everyone dislikes? Why is that person so unpopular?
   g. Which boy or girl would you consider your best friend in class? What is it about that person that you particularly like?

2. Summarize the information from the five interviews as follows, inserting the appropriate student names in the spaces below.

	Smartest	Cutest	Best Athlete	Nicest	Most Popular	Least Popular
1.						
2.						
3.						
4.						
5.						

● Recommended Readings

Burns, C. (1986). *Stepmotherhood: How to survive without feeling frustrated, left out or wicked.* New York: Perennial Library.

Cherlin, A. J., & Furstenberg, F. F., Jr. (1986). *The new American grandparent: A place in the family, a life apart.* New York: Basic Books.

Dolmetsch, P., & Shih, A. (Eds.). (1985). *The kids' book about single parent families.* New York: Doubleday.

Dunn, J. (1985). *Brothers and sisters.* Cambridge, MA: Harvard Univ. Press.

Elkind, D. (1988). *The hurried child.* New York: Addison-Wesley.

Faber, A., & Mazlich, E. (1982). *How to talk so your kids will listen and listen so your kids will talk.* New York: Avon books.

Gibbs, J. T., & Huang, L. N. et al., (1989). *Children of color: Psychological interventions with minority youth.* San Francisco: Jossey-Bass.

Lifton, B. J. (1979). *Lost and found: The adoption experience.* New York: Dial Press.

Osman, B., & Blinder, H. (1986). *No one to play with.* New York: Warner Books.

Paris, E. (1984). *Stepfamilies: Making them work.* New York: Avon.

Pogrebin, L. C. (1983). *Family politics.* New York: McGraw-Hill.

Rubin, Z. (1980). *Children's friendships.* Cambridge, MA: Harvard Univ. Press.

Schaefer, C. E. (1984). *How to talk to your children about really important things.* New York: Harper & Row.

Shreve, A. (1987). *Remaking motherhood: How working mothers are shaping our childrens' futures.* New York: Viking.

Shure, M. B., & Spivak, J. (1978). *Problem-solving techniques in child rearing.* San Francisco: Jossey-Bass.

Sorosky, A. D., Baran, A., & Pannor, R. (1978). *The adoption triangle: The effects of sealed records on adoptees, birth parents, and adoptive parents.* New York: Anchor Press.

Zimbardo, P. G., & Radl, S. (1982). *The shy child.* Garden City, NJ: Doubleday.

PART 5
Adolescence

633

Physical Development During Adolescence

CHAPTER

14

Adolescence is the period of transition from childhood to adulthood. Changes in physical appearance, sexual development, and rapid growth are the most obvious signs of this period. Although frequently confused, the terms *adolescence* and *puberty* refer to two distinct but related processes. Puberty is the period of adolescence that ends with sexual maturity. Adolescence is usually defined as the span of time from the beginning of puberty to the beginning of adulthood.

The precise boundaries of adolescence are difficult to identify. Physiologically, adolescence is generally thought to begin at age 11 or 12, with the gradual appearance of secondary sex characteristics, and to end at age 18 or 22, when the body stops growing. Adolescence tends to begin and end earlier in girls than in boys. But individual variation is greater during adolescence than during any other age period, because not all children begin, progress through, and end adolescence at the same time. Thus, chronological age tells us almost nothing about a child except perhaps his grade level in school (Lipsitz, 1979). Likewise, cultural variation during this period is also great, because cultures themselves vary with respect to the rituals and customs related to adolescence.

Hormonal Factors in Development

The growth and change that accompany adolescence are not due to a single dramatic event but are parts of a slowly unfolding process beginning with conception. When the child reaches approximately 8 or 9 and the cells of the hypothalamus are mature, the brain signals the body to increase the hormone output from the growth-regulating glands in the following sequence. First, the hypothalamus causes the pituitary gland to increase its production of growth hormones and other activat-

adolescence
the period between childhood and adulthood that begins with puberty and ends with the cessation of growth

hypothalamus
a gland that influences temperature regulation, hunger and thirst regulation, sexual behavior and other important functions

635

ing hormones. Then these pituitary hormones stimulate the release of other growth-related and sex-related hormones by the thyroid gland, adrenal glands, testes, and ovaries. Over time, these hormones plus others interact in complex ways to stimulate an orderly sequence of physical changes. These changes usually start to manifest themselves by the time the child is 10 or 11 years old (Susman et al., 1985).

The Timing of Puberty

Exactly when puberty begins depends on a variety of factors. Genetics plays an important role. The onset of puberty and such events as menstruation occur more closely in time among identical (monozygotic) twins than among dizygotic twin girls or female siblings (Tanner, 1978). Nutrition and general health also influence the timing of puberty, since deprived children mature later than those who are well cared for. Higham (1980) suggests that a critical metabolic rate must be reached before puberty can begin. There is also some evidence that the proportion of body fat in females must equal or exceed 17% of their total body weight for menstruation to begin or continue (Higham, 1980). These findings may explain why in adolescents with eating disorders and among dancers and female athletes in rigorous training *menarche* is often delayed and menstrual periods are irregular (Frisch, 1983). Anorexia nervosa may also cause general growth retardation in adolescents (Root & Powers, 1983).

Since the first immigrants settled this country, American children have been growing larger and maturing earlier than before (Petersen, 1979). The average Pilgrim male measured under 5 feet tall in 1620.

menarche
the first menstrual period

■ Figure 14–1

The age of first menstruation has dropped significantly since 1900.

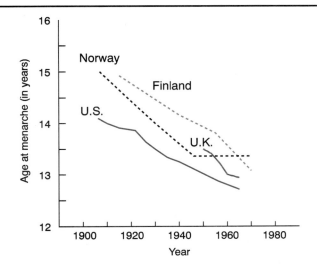

Today, the average male stands about 5'8" and at about 5'4" even the modern American woman would tower over a Colonist. In 1900, the average age of the first menstruation for females in the United States was 14 years, 2 months. Today that average is between 12 and 13 years (Petersen, 1979). These generational differences, collectively called the *secular trend in growth*, are probably due to health and nutrition factors and their favorable impact on genetics. It is predicted that once some optimum level of health and nutrition is reached, the secular trend in growth will show little variation from generation to generation. Among American middle class women over the last 30 years, the average age of onset of menstruation has stabilized at 12.8 years (Warren, 1983). Other cultures are still making secular gains as health conditions improve.

secular trend in growth
growth and maturational rate differences noted between the generations

The Adolescent Growth Spurt

The term *adolescent growth spurt* refers to changes in height, weight, and body proportions that occur with the onset of adolescence. Growth and change are more dramatic and apparent during adolescence than at any other stage in development after age 2 (Thornberg & Aras, 1986). All children experience a growth spurt in adolescence, but the timing, duration, and intensity of the surge varies from child to child. It is important for parents and children to keep in mind that *normal* (within the range of normal growth) does not necessarily mean average during the growth-spurt years.

For both boys and girls, the growth spurt lasts about 4½ years (Chumlea, 1982). Girls tend to start rapid growth earlier than boys, however, probably because girls are more neurologically mature than boys from birth on. The typical girl begins her adolescent growth spurt between ages 7.5 and 11.5 years; the average age of onset is 9.5. Girls' growth rate peaks at about 11 years, 8 months (Lipsitz, 1979). Boys begin their spurt about 2 years later, between the ages of 10.5 and 16 (the average age being 13), and reach a peak at about age 14 (Chumlea, 1982).

Ultimate height is a concern for both adolescents and their parents. Despite a relaxation of traditional sex-role expectations, today's boys are still worried about being "too short" and girls about growing "too tall." Most such fears are unfounded, though, since boys and girls who were taller or shorter than their peers in childhood are likely to remain so during adolescence. However, girls who start their growth spurts early are shorter at the beginning of puberty but have a longer period of rapid growth and tend to grow more than girls who mature later (Slap, 1986). Later-maturing girls are somewhat taller at the onset, but have a shorter and less intense period of growth.

Growth in height has been continuous throughout development, so by adolescence the average boy has attained 78% of his adult height, and the average girl, 84% (Thornberg & Aras, 1986). During the peak years, the average boy will grow 4–5 inches in height per year, while the average girl will growth about 3.5 inches per year (Slap, 1986). The extremities, neck, and nose grow first. The hands and feet appear large in relation to the rest of the body. Next, the hips, trunk and spinal cord lengthen. Girls usually achieve their full height by age 19, and boys by age 21 or 22. Boys require more growing time than girls because they start later, usually attain greater height, and generally have larger muscles, heart, lungs, and frames than most of their female counterparts.

As adolescents grow taller they also grow heavier. Both boys and girls just about double their weight between the ages of 10 and 18, with boys adding between 15 and 65 pounds and girls between 15 and 55 pounds during the growth-spurt years (Beal, 1980). During early adolescence, girls tend to outweigh boys, but by about age 14, boys tend to surpass girls in weight as they do in height.

Much of the weight increase during adolescence is due to skeletal growth and the development of lean (primarily muscle) body mass. Because muscle development is influenced by male sex hormones, boys develop far more muscle mass than girls (Slap, 1986). Male muscles increase both in cell number and size during puberty, while female muscles increase only in size. Girls average a 45% increase in muscle strength during adolescence, while the average boys gains 64% in muscle strength. Girls still demonstrate more finger dexterity than boys, a sex difference that has existed since the preschool years.

Both boys and girls show a decline in fat development during the growth-spurt years. Males become leaner and more angular during puberty. Females become smoother and more rounded as fat is redistributed over their entire bodies, concentrating in the thighs, hips, buttocks, and around the breast tissue. At physical maturity, females average twice as much body fat as males. Skeletally, boys have greater overall height, longer arms and legs, and more shoulder width than girls, while girls have broader hips than boys.

Other Aspects of Adolescent Growth

Besides increases in height and weight, less apparent but equally important changes take place in the growth-spurt years. The brain undergoes its last growth spurt between 14 and 16 years (Harmon, 1984). The lungs grow in size and capacity, especially in males, who have broader shoulders and a larger chest cavity than females (Tanner, 1978). The heart increases in size and strength, doubling its weight during the adolescent years. Boys typically have larger hearts and lungs and higher blood pressure than females because of their greater size. Endurance seems to be influenced more by training than sex. Female distance runners have more endurance than male nonrunners of the same age, but by age 10, most girls become less physically active than most boys, resulting in endurance differences that favor males (Wilmore, 1982).

The liver, stomach, spleen, kidneys, pancreas, thyroid gland, and digestive tract all reach adult size during puberty. In contrast, lymphatic system tissues (tonsils, adenoids, and so forth) decrease in size.

The skin of females becomes softer, smoother, and thicker due to the increased production of estrogen during this period. In both males and females, oil-bearing glands just under the surface of the skin, especially on the face, neck, upper back, shoulders, and chest, become extremely active during adolescence. *Acne* is an inflammatory condition of the hair follicles and the oil-bearing glands of the skin. Although not limited to the adolescent age group, it occurs most frequently in 16–20 year olds as increased levels of hormones (especially male sex hormone) stimulate gland growth and increase secretions. Ninety percent of all teenage boys and 80% of girls are affected in varying degrees (Hathaway, 1991). The appearance of acne precedes the onset of menstruation by 1 to 2 years in girls.

Acne can be aggravated by emotional stress, winter weather, some stimulant drugs, and the hormone flux that takes place prior to menstruction. Specific foods such as chocolate and greasy food, once thought to exacerbate the condition, do not seem to influence its severity. Treatment usually does not shorten the duration of the acne but it can control its severity, reduce scarring, and improve appearance at a time when children are especially sensitive about their looks. Self-treatment is extremely common and may do more to aggravate the condition than control it.

Sweat glands which respond to both high temperatures and emotional stimulation become fully functional during puberty. Heavy sweating appears to be more common in boys than in girls and in athletic teens than in sedentary ones, and body odors become more noticeable now in both sexes. The adolescent's brain and sensory systems have reached adult size and capacity by puberty (Tanner, 1978). (While the teen can clearly hear and understand messages, compliance is another issue!)

Sexual Maturation

In both boys and girls, the adolescent growth spurt is accompanied by sexual maturation. The increased quantity of sex hormones released by the ovaries and testes during adolescence is responsible for the development of both primary and secondary sexual characteristics. *Primary sex characteristics* are involved in reproduction. Fertility is achieved when the ovaries, fallopian tubes, uterus, and vagina in the female, and the penis, testes, ejaculatory ducts, vas deferens, prostate gland, seminiferous tubules, and seminal vesicles in the male mature. The *secondary*

■ **Table 14–1** *Stages of Female Maturation*

STAGE	BREAST	PUBIC HAIR	OTHER	APPROXIMATE AGE IN YEARS
1	Only the nipple shows elevation.	None	None	10–11
2	Breast bud appears as a small mound formed by the elevation of the breast and nipple. Pigmented area increases in diameter.	Sparse, long, slightly pigmented, downy. It is straight or only slightly curly, primarily along the labia.	Height spurt begins. Total body fat increases. Hips widen.	11–12
3	Further enlargement of breast and areola with no separation of their contours	More widespread, darker, coarser, curlier.	Vaginal enlargement. Height spurt peaks late in this period. Menarche late in this stage or early stage 4.	12–13
4	Pigmented area and nipple may rise to form a secondary mound above the level of the breast.	Adult in type but not as widespread.	Axillary (armpit) hair appears just before or after menarche.	13–14
5	Pigmented area has recessed to general breast contour. Breast is now mature.	Adult in type, quantity, and distribution pattern.	None	14–15+

Source: Tanner, 1962.

axillary
relating to or located near the arm pit

sex characteristics help differentiate mature males from females but are not necessary for reproduction. Secondary sex characteristics include voice changes, breast development, the appearance of body and facial hair, the broadening of the shoulders, and increased width and depth of the pelvis (see Tables 14–1 and 14–2).

In adolescent males, the testes produce large quantities of masculinizing hormones, or androgens. The androgens stimulate the growth of the larynx (associated with voice changes) and the appearance of pubic, facial, and axillary hair. They also accelerate skeletal growth and development, increase the number and size of muscle cells, and broaden the shoulders, enlarge the chest, and narrow the hips (of men). Along with growth hormones, androgens are responsible for the initiation of the adolescent growth spurt.

The female's ovaries increase their secretion of feminizing hormone, or estrogen, and progestins (pregnancy hormones) during puberty. Estrogen and progestins cause the girls' hips to grow wider and fatty tissue to be redistributed over the body. They also stimulate uterine and vaginal growth, encourage skeletal maturation, and inhibit height increases.

Because estrogens and androgens are produced by the adrenal glands of both sexes in varying amounts, males display some increases in fat

■ **Table 14–2** *Stages of Male Maturation*

STAGE	GENITALIA	PUBIC HAIR	FACIAL HAIR	OTHER	APPROXIMATE AGE IN YEARS
1	Penis, testes, and scrotum are of childhood size.	None	Like that in childhood.	Growth spurt begins. Body fat increases.	11.5–11.8
2	Scrotum and testes enlarge, but not penis. Scrotal skin reddens.	Sparse, long, slightly pigmented, downy. It is straight or slightly curly, primarily at the base of penis.	Little change.	Male physique begins to appear.	11.5–13.5
3	Continued growth of scrotum and testes. Penis grows mainly in length	Darker, coarser, curlier, spreading sparsely over the junction of the pubes.	About 50% of males show a small amount of short, lightly pigmented hair at corners of upper lip and on sides of face in front of ears.	Shoulders broaden, muscle mass increases; voice begins to deepen.	13–14
4	Continued growth of scrotum and testes. Penis grows mainly in width.	Adult in type but not as widespread.	Moderate amount of short, lightly pigmented, coarse down on upper lip; also long, fine, unpigmented hair on cheeks and occasionally along borders of the chin.	Axillary (armpit) hair appears. Voice deepens. Ejaculation may occur. Slight enlargement of breasts.	14–15
5	Adult in size.	Adult in type, quantity, and distribution pattern.	Conspicuous growth on upper lip. Longer, more pigmented hair on sides of face.	Breast enlargement ends after hormonal balance is established.	15+

Source: Tanner, 1982.

distribution and some transient breast-tissue development during adolescence due to estrogen, while females grow taller, somewhat more muscular, experience a deepening of the voice, and develop body hair in response to androgens. Testosterone, an androgen, is also responsible for the development of the labia majora and the clitoris in females.

Sexual maturity is reached when the adolescent boy or girl can reproduce themselves. Although boys may experience orgasms throughout childhood, ejaculation is not possible until age 13 or 14 when the prostate and seminal vesicles are mature enough to produce semen

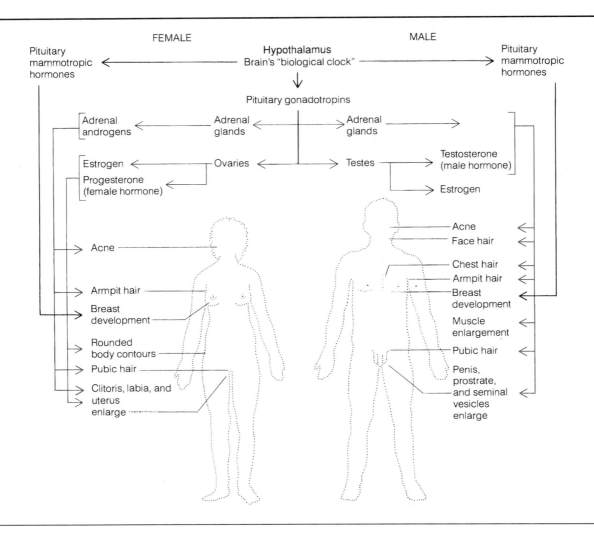

FEMALE   Hypothalamus   MALE

Pituitary   Brain's "biological clock"   Pituitary
mammotropic ←——————————————————————————→ mammotropic
hormones   hormones

                                        ↓

                                Pituitary gonadotropins

Adrenal   ←—— Adrenal ←——   ——→ Adrenal
androgens   glands   glands

Estrogen   ←—— Ovaries ←——   ——→ Testes   ——→ Testosterone
Progesterone   (male hormone)
(female hormone)   ——→ Estrogen

                                                            ——— Acne
                                                            ——— Face hair
                                                            ——— Chest hair
→ Acne   ——— Armpit hair
                                                            ——Breast
→ Armpit hair   development
  Breast   Muscle
→ development   enlargement
  Rounded   ——Pubic hair
→ body contours
→ Pubic hair   Penis,
→ Clitoris, labia, and   prostrate,
  uterus   and seminal
  enlarge   vesicles
                                                            enlarge

■ Figure 14–2

The effects of hormones on development at puberty.

wet dreams (nocturnal emissions) an involuntary ejaculation that occurs during sleep

(Crooks & Baur, 1990). Viable sperm won't be present in the ejaculate until age 14 (Kulin et al., 1989). In 1948 Alfred Kinsey reported that most males experience their first ejaculation while masturbating. Adolescent boys may also have wet dreams, or nocturnal emissions, an involuntary release of semen while sleeping. The associated dream content may or may not be sexual in nature. Even though the sperm count may be variable during the first ejaculation, fertility should be presumed and sexually active boys should weigh the pros and cons of parenthood occurring before they graduate from the eighth grade.

The first menstruation is called menarche and typically occurs between age 12 and 14 for American girls. Initial periods are usually irregular and may or may not be accompanied by ovulation. The variability of ovulation does not mean a girl can have sex without worrying

A Closer Look

The Funny Pages and the Facts of Life

The comic strips are starting to catch up with television. In May, 1991, Greg Evans, creator of "Luann," decided that his character had matured past braces, pierced ears, and first dates. It was now time for her to have her period.

But in the middle of the funny pages? Controversy isn't new to the comics.

"Doonsbury," "Pogo," and "Cathy" have been poking fun at politics and the status quo for years. But until "Luann," more serious and more private issues involved in "coming of age" hadn't surfaced.

Of the 250 newspapers that run "Luann" only 4 declined to run the "Luann Becomes a Woman" series. Interestingly, the "M" word (menstruation) was never mentioned. Are the comics the proper forum for these issues? Decide for yourself:

about pregnancy for 1–1.5 years after her initial period. 31 percent of girls age 15 to 19 had babies in 1988 (U.S. Census Bureau, 1991).

In other cultures, menstruating women are regarded as unclean, impure and even dangerous. Contact with menstrual blood is thought to kill cattle (in parts of Africa) and render men infertile. Likewise, our own Western culture treats menstruation as an unspeakable hygienic crisis. Since American women are encouraged to disguise, deodorize, and medicate their periods, it's no wonder that adolescent women feel less than positive about menarche and their initiation into womanhood. Generally, adolescents who reach menarche later have reasonable expectations about menstruation and are better prepared, more knowledgeable, and tend to react more positively (Koff et al., 1982).

■●▲ CONCEPT SUMMARY

Physical Changes During Adolescence

- Changes may begin to appear as early as age 10 or 11.
- Extremities, neck, and nose grow first.
- Full height is attained by age 19 for girls, by age 21–22 for boys.
- The average male is taller and heavier than the average female.
- Weight gain accelerates.
- The body achieves adult proportions.
- Muscle mass and strength increase, especially for boys.
- Girls continue to demonstrate more finger dexterity than boys.
- Fat development slows for males and females.
- Fat is redistributed in females.
- The brain's last growth spurt is between 14 and 16 years of age.
- Lung size and capacity increase.
- The size and strength of the heart increase.
- While the majority of the internal organs reach their mature size, the tissues in the lymphatic system decrease in size.
- Oil-bearing glands in the skin become active.
- Texture changes in the skin occur in females.
- Sweat glands become fully functional.
- All sensory systems have reached adult size and capacity.
- Primary sex characteristics appear.
- Secondary sex characteristics appear.
- Sexual reproduction becomes possible.

Menstrual Disturbances

Menstrual disturbances are more common among adolescent females than adult females, creating even more negative feelings towards menstruation among young people (Woods, 1986). Menstruation with accompanying pain or discomfort is called *dysmenorrhea* and is usually caused by an overproduction of prostaglandins, chemicals that cause the uterus to contract (Owen, 1984). Dysmenorrhea becomes increasingly common in the first 5 years after the onset of adolescence. Girls

dysmenorrhea
pain or discomfort before or during menstruation

prostaglandins
hormones that cause uterine contractions

may experience cramping, abdominal pain, backache, or leg ache during the first few days of their periods, but only *14%* would describe the pain as "severe." Adolescent girls who experience dysmenorrhea are sometimes accused of using it as an excuse to avoid undesirable activities. Although this may occur, for many young women dysmenorrhea is a very real and incapacitating problem (Klein & Litt, 1983).

Amenorrhea refers to delayed menstruation or an absence of menstruation for 3 months or longer in a nonpregnant female. Amenorrhea is common as the young woman's cycle is becoming more regular. Intensive exercise, low body fat, physical or emotional stress, hormonal problems, and poor health are associated with amenorrhea. Anorexic women frequently stop menstruating as they become more emaciated (J. Falk et al., 1983). Thirty percent of a sample of American women training for the Olympics reported missed menstrual periods (Loucks & Horvath, 1985).

Premenstrual syndrome, PMS, involves a collection of physical and psychological symptoms that occur prior to menstruation and may continue throughout the cycle. Some of the uncomfortable physical symptoms include weight gain, nausea, breast tenderness, headaches, dizziness, increased appetite and a craving for sweets (especially chocolate). Negative moods, anxiety, depression, irritability, confusion, tearfulness, anger, social withdrawal, and insomnia are the psychological states that may be experienced. Symptoms are labelled PMS when they are severe enough to have a disruptive effect on a woman's life (York et al., 1989). Thus, not all women who have symptoms have PMS, and not all women with PMS experience all the symptoms. Fluctuations in sex steroids and hormones may be responsible for PMS making adolescent females particularly vulnerable as their bodies try to stabilize hormonally (Hammarback et al., 1989).

amenorrhea
the absence or cessation of menstruation in a mature, nonpregnant female

anorexic
a person who has anorexia nervosa, an eating disorder that results in self-starvation

premenstrual syndrome (PMS)
uncomfortable physical and emotional symptoms that occur 2–12 days prior to the onset of menstruation

● Normal Variations in Development

While the sequence of maturational events is basically the same for all persons, healthy children can begin developing at any time from age 8 or age 16 and beyond. Also, the sequence of events may vary somewhat from person to person. For example, in females, unpigmented pubic hair may appear before breast changes occur (Crooks & Baur, 1990). While the maturation of the penis may be complete in some boys by age 13.5, for others it may not be complete until age 17 or even older. In females, breast development may begin as early as age 8 or as late as age 13. These dramatic variations in development are illustrated in Figure 14–3 which compares the growth rates of normal same-age boys and normal same-age girls.

In addition, once into adolescence, some children develop more rapidly than others. For example, it takes between 1.5 and 6 years for a

■ **Figure 14–3**

Variations in development among males and females at the same chronological age.

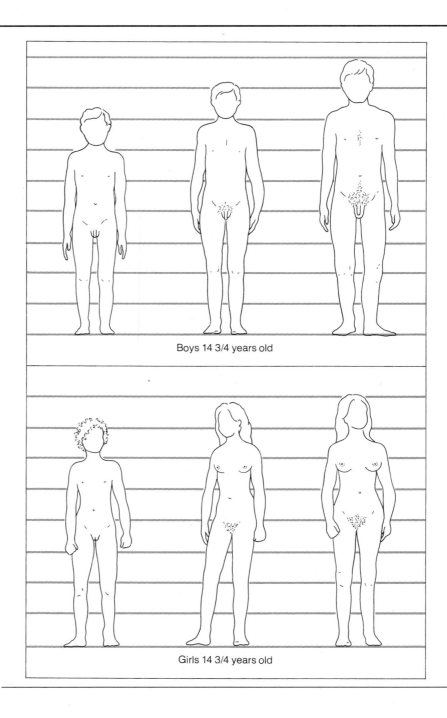

Boys 14 3/4 years old

Girls 14 3/4 years old

girl's breasts to reach maturity. Male genitalia may require 2–5 years to reach adult size (Tanner, 1978). Children who desperately wished to begin adolescence may now wonder if their bodies will ever complete the maturational process.

● **Psychological Aspects of Adolescence**

Adolescents are acutely aware of the range and variety of physical changes taking place in themselves and their peers. Any discrepancies from the norm that they perceive in themselves can elicit strong feelings—ranging from pride and elation to discomfort, embarrassment, and anxiety. Such discrepancies can influence the way adolescents view themselves and the way they are viewed by others. Studies of early and late maturing males and females suggest the sexes may be differentially affected by the timing of puberty (Brooks-Gunn & Warren, 1985).

Early and Late Maturation in Boys

Early maturing boys tend to be treated more like adults than children both by their peers and other adults. More mature behavior is expected from early maturing males than from physically less developed boys of the same age. Early maturing boys tend to be respected and admired socially. And owing to the earlier growth spurt in girls, early maturing boys may not feel much of a discrepancy between themselves and the girls their age. Thus, they may become involved with girls sooner and have more confidence in boy–girl relations than late maturing boys (Duncan et al., 1985). Although the early maturing boy differs from his peers, he is not likely to feel insecure about those differences. His greater strength and sexual maturity and his more manly physique are consistent with society's expectations of older males.

In contrast, late maturing boys often feel left behind, first by the girls and then by most of their friends. Their bodies may seem painfully inadequate and childish when compared with those of more mature boys, and they may fear that no cute girls will be left by the time they are "ready". Late maturing boys are more likely to be treated like children than like young adults. They are also more likely to have difficulty achieving recognition in athletics and becoming popular with the girls.

Extensive data from the Berkeley Growth Study (Livson & Peskin, 1980) suggest that the male's maturational rate may have an impact on his personality and self-esteem. Early maturing boys were found to be more relaxed, poised, controlled, and self-confident than late maturers. They also proved more popular and more likely to be chosen as leaders. Conversely, late maturing boys try hard to be accepted socially but their attempts are often perceived as inappropriate and insecure. As a result, late maturing boys tend to feel inadequate and rejected, to have lower self-esteem, and to display more aggression, perhaps because of their insecurities.

Even as adults in their early thirties, many late maturers still emerge as less self-controlled, less responsible, and less dominant in relations with others and are more likely to ask for help than early maturing counterparts. Early maturers, on the other hand, tend to be conforming,

■ **Figure 14–4**

School dances are fun, but they also highlight the maturational differences between boys and girls.

dominant, conventional, and concerned about making a good impression. By age 38, however, most differences between early and late maturers have disappeared (Livson & Peskin, 1980).

Despite the obvious difficulties, all is not lost for the young later maturing male. Parents, teachers, and others can help minimize the anxiety that often surrounds late maturation by making an effort not to treat the individual as younger than he really is and encouraging participation in tasks where physical size and strength do not affect performance, such as music, art, theater, or academics. In some sports, such as gymnastics, diving, and horseback riding, the slighter, smaller male has a distinct advantage over the male who is heavier and bulkier. And in many hobbies, such as model building and videogame playing, size and strength have no influence whatsoever.

Early and Late Maturation in Girls

The effects of early and late maturation in girls are less clear-cut and more variable than for boys. While early maturation is generally advantageous to boys, early maturation tends to have negative psychosocial effects for girls (Brooks-Gunn, 1988).

Early maturing girls who are taller and more physically developed than their peers may feel they have little in common with other females their age, and their peers may feel the same about them. Early maturing females tend to be the most dissatisfied with their weight (69% want to be thinner) (Duncan et al., 1985). The interests and concerns of these more developed girls may differ from those of others and they might attract teasing or ridicule out of interest or envy. Fortunately for early maturing girls, their social problems are relatively short lived. By the time most of their age-mates enter puberty themselves (by the seventh or eighth grade), they are more likely to be liked and respected by their peers than later maturing females (Conger & Petersen, 1984).

Tobin-Richards and colleagues (1983) found that seventh-grade girls who perceive themselves to be "on time" in comparison with their peers had the most positive views about themselves and their bodies, while late maturing girls had the next most variable self-evaluations. Of course, slow maturing girls need to be emotionally supported and reassured that they are not abnormal while they are waiting for their bodies to grow. As trivial as these physical concerns may seem to adults, they are very real and disturbing to the child who desperately wants to be grown up but whose body will not cooperate, as the following quote most poignantly suggests:

> Are you there, God? It's me, Margaret. Gretchen, my best friend got her period. I'm so jealous, God. I hate myself for being so jealous, but I am. I wish you'd help me just a little. Nancy's sure she's going to get it soon,

■●▲   CONCEPT SUMMARY

Characteristics of Early and Late Maturing Adolescents

	GIRLS	BOYS
Early maturers	Feel different from their peers	Treated more like adults
	Usually dissatisified with their weight	Mature behavior expected
	May be teased/ridiculed by peers until they themselves mature	Respected by peers
		Admired socially; popular
		Likely to be chosen as a leader
	Ultimately liked better than later maturers	May be involved sooner with girls
	Receive mixed messages about whether sex is good or bad	Feel fairly secure about body image
		More relaxed, poised, self-confident
Late maturers	May need reassurance while they are waiting to grow	Feel left behind
		Less secure about body image
		Treated more like children
		May be less popular with the girls
		May struggle to compete in traditional sports
		Less relaxed, poised, self-confident
		Behavior judged inappropriate by peers
		Feel rejected; unpopular
		More aggressive
		Can achieve success in areas where size and strength do not affect performance

too. And if I'm late, I don't know what I'll do. Oh, please, God, I just want to be normal. (Blume, 1970, p. 100)

Western culture's views of early maturing males and females differ. For boys, the strength, physical prowess and sexual maturity of adolescence bring them more in line with traditional conceptions of masculinity. Girls achieve sexual maturity in adolescence, too, but they may receive mixed messages about whether early sexual activities are "good" or "bad." On the one hand, it may be exciting to date older boys and to become involved in mature male/female relationships. On the other hand, heterosexual involvement can limit a girl's ability to develop relations with other girls her own age and to grow as an individual in her own right. The parents of early maturing girls are often more restrictive and more disapproving than the parents of later maturing girls (Crockett & Peterson, 1987). In the final analysis, a girl's adjustment to the changes of puberty probably depends more on her own personality, the kind of support, encouragement, and guidance she receives from her parents, and the values and expectations of her peer group than on whether she matures early, on time, or late (Conger & Petersen, 1984).

Measuring Up

Both boys' and girls' self-perceptions can be affected not only by the timing of maturation but also by their own evaluations of the physical changes taking place in their bodies. Many adolescents are at least temporarily dissatisfied with how they look (Siegel, 1982). Research shows that teenagers cite physical concerns such as skin problems, dissatisfactions with body height and body weight, and the desire for a better figure or a more athletic build more frequently than intellectual or social problems. Because society places greater emphasis on the physical appearance of women, teenage girls tend to be less satisfied with the way they look than most teenage boys. Reassuringly, adolescents see themselves in a progressively more favorable light as they make the transition from junior high school to high school and from high school to college.

When adolescents fear that their physical characteristics are not comparable to those of their peers or that their appearance departs from accepted norms, their self-concepts may suffer. Boys with slim, athletic builds tend to have higher self-esteem than boys who see themselves as either too heavy or too thin (Conger & Petersen, 1984). Adolescent males and females who consider themselves attractive tend to be happier and have higher self-esteem into their forties than those who see themselves as plain or homely during their teen years.

As mentioned previously, compared with adolescent boys, girls display even more concern about their appearance and physical development (Duncan et al., 1985). Western society has clear-cut ideas about the characteristics that define feminine beauty, and those standards are difficult to achieve. Beauty pageants exist by the score for teenage contestants. A "Mr. Teen USA" competition has never been staged. Why? Because we value men more for their ability and we value women more for their appearance (Matlin, 1987). Moreover, compared with that of boys, an adolescent girl's self-esteem is more directly tied to her relationships with others and to subjective remarks about her appearance. For example, girls are more likely than boys to interpret the remark "You look awful" to mean "You are awful."

Support for the adolescent's fragile self-esteem can begin at home. Rather than belittling their appearance and ridiculing their hair styles, parents can make a special effort to compliment their teens on a regular basis. Something sincere and positive can always be noted: "You look cute today," "Your hair is so shiny," or "I love those colors." By experimenting with different styles, the adolescent can gain peer acceptance while discovering what's best for her personally. When parents are more tolerant and less critical of their son's or daughter's appearance (after all, it's just a fad), teens will experience less stress and will have more positive energy to apply toward developing a stable self-concept (Jourard & Landsman, 1980).

● Adolescent Sexuality

Sexual Attitudes

The body changes that occur during puberty and the emotional responses that accompany these changes encourage adolescents to focus on their emerging sexuality. External influences are significant, too: peer pressure, increased permissiveness regarding sexual behavior, and society's expectations of teenagers all propel adolescents toward sexual activity at increasingly earlier ages. Teens have to make six important sexual decisions: to have sex, to have children, to use birth control, to have an abortion, to give up a baby for adoption, and to marry (Juhasz et al., 1986).

Parents' sexual attitudes are typically more conservative than teens' attitudes. Parents would prefer that their children wait until they are adults or married to have sex and then, only with someone they love (Chilman, 1983). In contrast, three-fourths of all adolescents thought premarital sex involving love was acceptable for their age group. Adolescents who rely heavily on television for information about sexuality have high standards for female beauty and believe that premarital, extramarital, and promiscuous sex are acceptable (J. D. Brown et al., 1990). A sexual double standard affects males and females throughout their lives. Males are encouraged to assert their sexuality, while females are pressed to deny their sexuality or risk being labeled "loose" or "easy." Parents may be secretly proud of their son's sexual activity but shocked and humiliated when they find out about their daughter's. The regressive features of the double standard may extend far beyond sexual encounters. Females may learn that men deserve more latitude in their behavior and that "good women" always let men take the lead.

Sexual messages surround adolescents. Billboards, teen radio stations, TV, and peers encourage if not pressure children into sexual activity. Teens who resist are labeled uptight, out of it, or even gay. Some cope by becoming expert storytellers; others feel confused, guilty, and inadequate as they succumb to encounters they neither want nor are psychologically prepared to handle.

double standard
a behavior that is evaluated positively when engaged in by members of one group but negatively evaluated when initiated by others

■ **Figure 14–5**

Couple pairing begins to occur during adolescence.

Sexual Behavior

Masturbation

Masturbation is a common sexual expression in childhood and even more common among adolescents. By the end of adolescence, almost all males and three-fourths of the females have masturbated to orgasm (Sorensen, 1973; Reiss, 1986). Even though masturbation is a normal, healthy behavior, most adolescents still feel ashamed and anxious about doing so and are uncomfortable talking about it. Sex educators suggest masturbation can serve as an outlet for sexual tension, can provide valuable self-knowledge, and helps the teen avoid unwanted pregnancy and sexually transmitted disease (Crooks & Baur, 1990).

Petting

petting
physical contact including kissing, touching, and genital stimulation but excluding intercourse

Petting refers to any noncoital sexual contact like touching, kissing, holding, or rubbing. Petting is also known as necking, messing around, and making out. "Heavy petting" is common among teens. Even in the 70s, half of the girls and two-thirds of the boys had experienced petting to the point of orgasm (Hunt, 1974). Petting offers a shared sexual activity without the risk of pregnancy.

Sexual Orientation

sexual orientation
feeling attracted to members of your own sex or other-sex persons

Most teens are biologically and psychologically organized toward heterosexuality. They select other-sex people to "go with," date, and develop intimate relations with. While 6% of females and 11% of males have same-sex contact during adolescence, a much smaller percentage identify themselves as exclusively homosexual (Remafedi, 1987). Most homosexuals become aware of their orientation during adolescence and most realize that "coming out" can have devastating consequences (D. Anderson, 1987). Emotionally it's difficult not to be "part of the crowd." Widespread homophobia and hate crimes make gay and lesbian teens the targets of abuse and maliciousness even by those who used to call them friends. Those who are willing to befriend the adolescent homosexual can offer sympathy and support but little in the way of guidance. Therapists hired by the parents will often try to "change the teenager back" despite the fact that the American Psychological Association views encouraging change against a person's will unethical (American Psychological Association, Press Release, 24 January 1975). High suicide rates are a disastrous consequence of teen homosexuality (Coleman & Remafedi, 1989). Ironically, organizations that provide support for adult homosexuals are reluctant to help those who are still "under age" (i.e., younger than the age of consent—usually 18). Parents have successfully sued such agencies "for contributing to the delinquency of a minor."

"coming out"
the process of becoming aware of and disclosing your own homosexuality; may be used more generally to indicate a person acknowledging *any* challenging life circumstance

homophobia
an irrational fear of homosexuality, homosexual persons, or of one's own homosexuality

■ **Table 14–3** *Percentage of Adolescents Who Reported Having Premarital Intercourse by Age 19*

	FEMALES	MALES
Kinsey (1948, 1953)	20%	45%
Sorenson (1973)	45%	59%
Zelnick and Kantner (1977)	55%	No males in survey
Zelnick and Kantner (1980)	69%	77%
Mott and Haurin (1988)	68%	78%

Source: Crooks & Baur, 1990, p. 465.

Intercourse

Since Alfred Kinsey and his associates completed their study of American women in 1953, we have had information on the incidence of premarital sex among adolescents (Table 14–3). Even though at least 6 million teenagers are sexually active by age 15, for both males and females the figures have been increasing steadily until the 1980s, when the rates leveled off. The increases have been considerably larger for females than males even though among every sample, fewer women than men engage in premarital sex.

It is unlikely that the fear of AIDS is responsible for keeping the numbers constant in the 1980s. Most teens do not feel they are at risk for the disease and even if teens do change their behavior, only one in five alter it in effective ways (Strunin & Hingson, 1987). In May, 1988 1% of all reported AIDS cases involved adolescents. That number doubles each year (Brooks-Gunn et al., 1988).

Ironically, despite their attitudes, love has very little to do with having intercourse during the teen years. Here are the reasons boys and girls gave in response to a Planned Parenthood poll (The Facts of Life Team, 1989).

	Girls	*Boys*
Peer pressure	34%	26%
Pressure from boys	17%	—
Curiosity	14%	16%
"Everyone is doing it"	14%	10%
Sexual gratification	—	11%
Love	11%	6%

The age of first intercourse differs for boys and girls. Boys become sexually active sooner than girls. By age 16, half of all males surveyed

■ **Table 14–4** *Contraceptive Effectiveness*

Norplant implant	99.7%
Tubal ligation	99.6
IUD	99.2
Oral contraceptives	97.0
Condom	88.0
Diaphragm	82.0
Vaginal sponge	72.0

Source: *Studies in Family Planning* magazine, p. 5.

withdrawal
having intercourse but ejaculating outside the partner's body; an ineffective birth control method
birth control pill
oral contraceptive

had had sex, compared to just over 25% of the girls (The Facts of Life Team, 1989). The timing of the transition from virgin to nonvirgin depends on a number of variables. Younger siblings have consistently higher levels of sexual activity at a given age than older siblings (Rodgers & Rowe, 1988). Both males and females will have sex relatively earlier if they are more independent, place a lower value on academic achievement, are more critical about society, tolerate deviance, are less compatible with their parents, are less religious, and have friends that both approve of and engage in premarital sex (Jessor et al., 1983). In contrast, teens who initiate sexual intercourse later are more conventional, more conservative, avoid drug and alcohol use, are more involved with religion, are marriage oriented, feel less capable in cross-sex relationships, feel relatively less attractive, and set and achieve educational and occupational goals. It should be noted that the latter group is not "maladjusted" in any way: They have as many friends as nonvirgins, no less life satisfaction, and no more stress (Jessor et al., 1983).

About half of all teenagers do not use contraception the first time they have sex (Beck & Davies, 1987). Younger teens may delay practicing safe sex up to a year even if they are having sex regularly; 18–19 year old white adolescents seldom wait longer than a month or two to begin using some type of contraception (Hofferth & Hayes, 1987). Ten percent of teens choose condoms; ineffective methods like withdrawal are popular. Effective methods like birth control pill use are rare (Table 14–4). Ignorance about contraceptive methods and their effectiveness is a widespread consequence of poor or nonexistent sex education (Scales, 1987). Even if adolescents know about contraceptives, they may not use them because they're not easily available and they don't want to appear to be planning intercourse. In terms of the teenager's moral world view, if sex just happens, it's more acceptable than if it is planned and birth control is used. Sadly, that fact brings us to a major complication of adolescent sexuality: unplanned pregnancy.

Adolescent Pregnancy

While births to females in most other age groups are declining, the number of pregnancies in the adolescent population, particularly among girls 15 and under, has been increasing (U.S. Census Bureau 1991). Each year over 1 million American teenage girls ages 15–19 become pregnant, four-fifths of them by mistake. Little is known of teens' pregnancy motivations. Teen pregnancy rates are higher among Latinos and blacks, and lowest among Asians. Of these pregnancies, 50% will give birth, 10% miscarry, and 40% choose abortion (Trussel, 1988). Only 7% of unmarried teen mothers relinquish their children for adoption. Couples wanting to adopt outnumber available babies by 40 to 1.

There are far more health risks for mother and child associated with having babies during the teen years than becoming pregnant during middle age. Inadequate prenatal care, not the mother's biological immaturity, accounts for the majority of pregnancy complications. During the first trimester of pregnancy 7 out of 10 teens do not see a doctor. Denial encourages pregnant teens to maintain their life-style, which often includes poor nutrition, inadequate sleep and exercise, and the continued use of drugs, alcohol, and tobacco (Moss & Hensleigh, 1988). As a consequence, the babies born to adolescent mothers suffer greatly. The infant mortality rate is 200 times higher than for babies born to older mothers because of the high percentage of low birth weight (Bright, 1987). Babies born to poor teenage mothers are at particular risk (R. A. Davis, 1988). Infants who survive experience more than their share of birth defects, mental retardation, learning disabilities, emotional disorders, abuse, and neglect.

Pregnancy is hard on the teenager herself. A girl who is 10 to 13 years old and still actively growing may compromise her final physical stature by becoming pregnant. If the girl has not reached physical maturity, she and the fetus compete for available nutrition to supply their growth needs (Leppart, 1984). The death rate from pregnancy complications is much higher among girls under age 15 than among older girls. Teenage mothers can have healthy babies and uncomplicated pregnancies if they receive early and regular prenatal care, are well nourished, receive supplemental dietary iron, are disease free, drug free, and avoid exposure to sexually transmitted diseases (Petersen & Boxer, 1982).

The most far-reaching consequence of teenage pregnancy is that statistically the young parent(s) can expect to forego a high school diploma, live below the poverty line, and become dependent on social services. Although it is no longer legal to prevent pregnant teens or teen mothers from attending public school, 80% drop out anyway and don't return (Felsman et al., 1987). Faced with the financial responsibility of raising a child and supporting themselves, teens need to find employment but lack the skills and experience to qualify for high paying jobs. Teens who marry to try to provide a family for their child and share the economic and emotional burdens of parenthood struggle against odds that often prove insurmountable. Seventy to 80% of teen marriages that occur when a child is on the way or already born end in divorce. Males find themselves liable for child support when they may not even have a job that enables them to be self-supporting. Ironically, history often repeats itself. Forty-three percent of fathers age 17 and under and 22% of teenage mothers 17 and under had teenage parents themselves (Alan Guttmacher Institute, 1981). Chances are that many of the babies of today's teen pregnancies will become parents during adolescence themselves in a cycle that perpetuates itself from generation to generation. Adolescent mothers benefit from the support of their partners and parents (Unger & Wandersman, 1988).

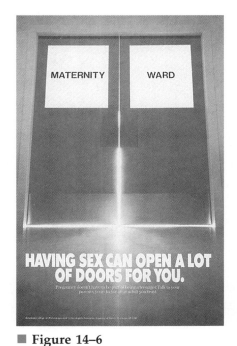

■ **Figure 14–6**

A poster designed to discourage unplanned teenage pregnancy.

■ ● ▲   CONCEPT SUMMARY

Complications of Teenage Pregnancy

- *Physical*
  - Higher miscarriage rate than for the general population
  - Infant mortality rate is 200 times higher than babies born to older mothers
  - High percentage of low birth weight
  - Babies have more birth defects, mental retardation, and learning disabilities
  - Babies experience more emotional disorders, abuse, and neglect
  - Pregnant teen may compromise her own final adult stature
  - Death rate from childbirth complications greater than for older women

- *Social/Psychological*
  - 80% drop out of school
  - Usually live in poverty
  - The majority become dependent on social services
  - Lack the skills/education to qualify for high-paying jobs
  - If teen parents marry, their chances of getting a divorce hover between 70 and 80%.

Preventing Teenage Pregnancy

Changes in parent–child relations, in the adolescent's world view, and in society can help teens prevent unwanted pregnancy. Here are a few suggestions:

1. Encourage high self-esteem so the teen will have the courage to express her point of view and the conviction that her opinion is as valid as anyone else's.
2. Following the lead of the Scandinavian nations, institute compulsory sex education at every grade level.
3. Repeal "Snitch Laws" that require parents to be notified before medical examinations, contraceptive prescriptions, or abortions can be performed.
4. Offer free or low-cost confidential contraceptive services to adolescents.
5. Help adolescent boys understand that birth control isn't just their partner's responsibility.

6. Increase the availability of condoms and other devices by placing them in pharmacies, supermarkets, and vending machines.
7. Encourage TV programming to stop portraying unwanted pregnancy as something that happens only to prostitutes and drug abusers. Stop glamorizing sex.
8. Encourage adolescents to place academic achievement and career goals as high life priorities. Reward their efforts.
9. Encourage more positive dialogue between the adolescent and her parent.
10. Help teens understand that sex without birth control isn't romantic—it's stupid.
11. Help teens understand that having sex is *never* a test of love ("If you love me, you'll. . .")
12. If teenage girls can't say no to sex, help them say "Not now."
13. Institute programs that help teens avoid unwanted pregnancy that parallel the Smoking/Alcohol Abuse Prevention programs.
14. The Planned Parenthood Federation projects that for each $1 spent to prevent teen pregnancy $13 will be saved in future medical and welfare costs. Successful pilot programs have been initiated to help high-risk adolescents remain child-free by paying them an allowance for each week they avoid pregnancy.

In Touch

> PLANNED PARENTHOOD
>   FEDERATION OF AMERICA, INC.
> 810 Seventh Ave.
> New York, NY 10019
>
> SIECUS (Sex Information and
>   Education Council of the United
>   States)
> Fifth Avenue, Suite 801-2
> New York, NY 10011

Sex Education

The cultural norm in America is for parents to withhold sexual information from their children. Even at the high school level, information about sexuality is considered to be premature and likely to lead to experimentation or indiscriminate promiscuity (Richardson & Cranston, 1981). Given the statistics on the incidence of premarital sex, it is difficult to see how sex education during adolescence could be viewed as premature. And when studies were conducted to see if sexual information promotes early sexual activity, just the opposite was found to be true. Only 17% of 15 and 16 year olds who took sex education reported having sex, compared with 26% of those who did not (Brooks-Gunn and Furstenberg, 1986). Furthermore, even if educated teens do become sexually active, they are more likely to use contraception than uneducated teens (S. Baker et al., 1988).

Parents, especially fathers, seem to have difficulty talking freely with their teenagers about sex (Tucker, 1989). If parents are questioned, they tend to respond to sex-related questions from teens with denial, avoidance, teasing, and disapproval. As a consequence, friends become the principal source of information about sex in the United States (Papini et al., 1988). Such "information" can have serious consequences if teens hear that they can't get pregnant if they only have sex once in a while, for example. The challenge facing parents is how to get actively in-

A Closer Look

Getting Pregnant in Class

If there's one thing that health education classes lack, it's realism. Well, not anymore. First, it was "Flour Sack" or "Egg" babies that students had to care for (or get babysat) during the entirety of the course. Now the "Empathy Belly" is here.

Invented by Seattle childbirth educator Linda Ware to enlighten expectant fathers, the "Belly" has made its way into high school classes and Pregnancy Prevention Programs. Here it helps males and females simulate the physical experiences of the last 3 months of pregnancy and shatters some of the romantic illusions of teenage pregnancy.

Completely external, the Belly consists of a canvas-and-velcro vest with a pregnant belly (water-filled vinyl bag), a lung constrictor (rib belt), breasts, and fetal limbs and head (simulated by 3 strategically placed lead weights). The 30-pound Belly presses in on the wearer as well as protrudes outward and simulates 20 of the third-trimester discomforts of pregnancy ("everything but the morning sickness and the varicose veins—and, of course, the baby!").

A boy models the Empathy Belly in class.

When wearers are asked to tie their shoes, pick up a load of laundry, stoop down to pick something up, or get up quickly from a standing or lying position, it becomes immediately clear that pregnancy is no picnic. The idea is not to degrade the condition of pregnancy per se, but to help students see that it takes a lot of effort, commitment, resilience, and maturity to see a pregnancy through on a physical level, let alone on an emotional or social level.

volved in their child's sex education in order to avoid some of the complications incurred by deferring to the child's peers. The Toward Effective Parenting section at the end of the chapter can help parents get started.

In response to the frequent lack of information from the home and misinformation given by peers, some public school systems are offering sex education courses. Unfortunately, many of these courses are incomplete and important topics are omitted because of pressure from vocal parent groups. One adolescent in 10 felt their school sex education program taught them what they wanted to know. The topics adolescents want to learn about most, in order of importance, are (Ostrov et al., 1985):

1. Feelings about the other sex
2. Birth control
3. Pregnancy and parenthood
4. Abortion
5. How to decide about sex

Public sex education—like private, home-based sex education—does not lead to promiscuity and experimentation. Instead, it is associated with delaying the age of first intercourse and using contraceptives effectively (Eisen & Zellman, 1987).

● Health and Safety Issues in Adolescence

Disease and Illness

Adolescents are considered to be the healthiest segment of the population. Acute disease and illness are rare in this age group. And the effects of habits and practices that may compromise the adolescent's health (such as poor nutrition, cigarette, alcohol and other drug use, and sexual practices that lead to infection) may not become apparent for several years. Two medical problems, gynecomastia and varicocele, are relatively common in boys. Varicocele (varicose veins of the scrotum) can lead to low sperm production and permanent infertility if not treated; gynecomastia (breast-like fatty pads on the chest) can cause embarrassment and concern about one's masculinity (Silber, 1985). In general, however, there are five conditions that deserve attention: hypertension, ulcerative colitis, hepatitis, infectious mononucleosis, and sexually transmitted disease.

gynecomastia
a condition where fatty tissue is laid down in a male's chest giving the appearance of female breasts

Hypertension

Hypertension, or high blood pressure, affects 15–20% of the adult population in the United States, and researchers are becoming convinced that hypertension in adults may have its origins during the school years or adolescence. Between 1–2% of 6–12 year olds and 11–12% of all adolescents are estimated to be hypertensive (Schwartz et al., 1990). Increased blood pressure can be caused by excessive weight, excessive dietary salt, kidney disorders, or genetics (a family history of high blood pressure or cardiovascular disease). Some drugs, toxins, and chemicals also elevate blood pressure.

Hypertension is a difficult condition to detect. There are no behavioral symptoms associated with it. In very severe cases, the child might manifest blurred vision, severe headaches, irritability, or seizures. Blood pressure can be monitored in regular physical checkups. The treatment of childhood hypertension includes exercise, reducing calorie and salt intake, and discontinuing or altering any medications or compounds that might elevate blood pressure.

Ulcerative Colitis

ulcerative colitis
a medical condition where the intestines bleed and become inflamed

Ulcerative colitis involves inflammation and bleeding in the intestinal tract. The initial symptom is the painless passage of a bloody stool, often in the early morning. Later symptoms include severe diarrhea, abdominal pain, dehydration, and malnutrition due to malabsorption of food.

Ulcerative colitis generally occurs between the ages of 10 and 19. The incidence is highest among whites and people in upper socioeconomic groups. Although a child can inherit a genetic predisposition for ulcerative colitis, environmental factors, especially those that cause stress and emotional disturbance, can exacerbate the symptoms. Affected children tend to be emotionally dependent and fragile (Hathaway, 1991). Dietary management and medications provide some relief from symptoms. Psychotherapy may also influence the success of the treatment.

Viral Hepatitis

Viral hepatitis is a disease which impairs the liver. The different forms of the virus can be spread by poor sanitation practices (not washing after using the bathroom, since the virus is present in fecal material), IV needle sharing, and sexual transmission (blood, semen, vaginal secretions, and saliva all contain the virus). Once a person is infected, the disease must run its course since there is no effective treatment. A vaccine does exist to protect against Hepatitis B. High risk groups like health care workers, IV drug users, and homosexual men and prostitutes are encouraged to be vaccinated (Centers for Disease Control, 1988).

Infectious Mononucleosis

infectious mononucleosis ("mono")
a viral disease that causes malaise, lack of energy, and flu like symptoms

chronic fatigue syndrome
a collection of symptoms caused by a virus that weakens one's immune system and leads to lethargy and lack of energy

Adolescents are more susceptible to infectious mononucleosis ("MONO") since their resistance is lowered by poor diet, lack of sleep, and frequent exposure to the virus. Its flu-like symptoms generally last about a week. Long-term complications of the spleen that can lead to hepatitis are possible. There's also some suggestion that mononucleosis makes one more susceptible to the virus associated with Chronic Fatigue Syndrome later in life (Avery, 1988).

Sexually Transmitted Disease (STD)

Diseases like chlamydia, herpes, genital warts, AIDS, syphilis, and gonorrhea are spread by sexual contact and are epidemic in the United States. A disproportionately high number of adolescents develop these diseases because large numbers of modern teenagers are sexually active, don't use protection, assume an "it won't happen to me" attitude about risk, and begin having sex at young ages with multiple partners (Crooks & Baur, 1990). The incidence of STDs is higher in males than in females, and many are incurable. Table 14–5 outlines the mode of transmission, symptoms, treatment, and complications of the most common STDs.

To curb the rising tide of STD transmission, emphasis must be placed on prevention through education and behavior change. Perfectly safe sex involves *no* sexual contact whatsoever, so abstinence is the most effective means of avoiding contact with a sexually transmitted disease. If adolescents are going to take preventive measures, they must feel "at risk." This attitude is difficult for them to adopt when they don't see any immediate consequences, when an incubation period exists for some diseases before symptoms manifest themselves (for AIDS it is 5–10 years!), and when they maintain an "it can't happen to me" attitude (Flora & Thoresen, 1988).

If the adolescent is sexually active, the following considerations and practices can lead to "safer" sex (Crooks & Baur, 1990):

In Touch

AIDS HOTLINE FOR
   ADOLESCENTS
1-800-234-TEEN

1. Rethink your need to have sex with multiple partners.
2. Avoid sex with people who you know or suspect have had multiple partners.
3. Avoid sex with anyone who has sores, blisters, warts, rashes, discharge, odor or anything out of the ordinary around or near their genitals.
4. Use *latex* condoms. (Animal skin condoms have "pores" through which microorganisms can pass. They also break more easily.)
5. Use a spermicidal foam, cream, or jelly that contains nonoxynol-9, the most effective agent against the AIDS virus. (Condoms and spermicides used together offer the best protection.)
6. Avoid all contact with the partner's anus.
7. Avoid all contact with the male partner's semen.
8. Do not share any implements that could become contaminated with blood (IV needles, syringes, razor blades, toothbrushes).
9. Wash your genitals (and the surrounding area) with soap and water both before and after sexual contact.
10. If symptoms are discovered in the partner during or after sex, consult with your physician or clinic immediately. The antibiotic tetracycline reduces the possibility of developing a variety of STDs after high-risk exposure. Routine self-medication is not advisable.
11. If you notice any itching, burning, discharge, pain, odor, bumps, or sores in or around your genitals, consult with your physician immediately. Prompt treatment is best. Also, be prepared to identify your partner(s) for treatment, also. For a teenager, sex may be worth living for but it's not worth dying for.

Nutritional Needs of Adolescents

During the growth-spurt years, the adolescent's nutrient and kcalorie needs increase to support the dramatic changes in height, weight, body build, and physiological functioning. Because boys typically develop a

■ **Table 14–5** *Common Sexually Transmitted Diseases*

DISEASE	TRANSMISSION	SYMPTOMS	TREATMENT	COMPLICATIONS
AIDS (Acquired Immune Deficiency Syndrome)	Usually passed through sexual contact or IV needle sharing Can be transmitted to the newborn if the breast milk contains the HIV virus	Vary with the type of cancer or opportunistic disease that infects the person Fever, night sweats, weight loss, loss of appetite, fatigue, atypical bruising/bleeding, chronic cough, etc. are common symptoms	No known treatment Antiviral drugs (AZT, DDC) slow the progression of the disease but do not cure Opportunistic diseases/tumors are treated	Fatal Men pass the AIDS virus more readily than women; thus women are more likely to receive than transmit the virus
Chlamydia	Usually sexual contact It can be spread by the fingers from one body part to another	(Women) Inflammation of the urethra or cervix (pain on urination; mild irritation or itching of the genitals; slight discharge) May also be expressed as pelvic inflammatory disease (PID) (abdominal pain, nausea, vomiting, headache, elevated temperature, disrupted menstrual periods) (Men) Burning on urination and penile discharge Pain, swelling, "heavy feeling" in affected testes	Nonpenicillin antibiotic	Few or no early symptoms present for women May coexist with gonorrhea Major cause of infertility and ectopic pregnancy Contributes to pregnancy complications (premature labor, postpartum endometriosis) 10 times more stillbirth or infant death with infected mother Most common cause of eye infections in newborns Newborns may also develop chlamydial pneumonia
Genital Herpes	Transmitted by genital contact Can spread the virus from one part of one's body to another Virus may survive 2–4 hours on toilet seats; spa benches; towels; gloves; speculums	Small, red painful bumps called *papules*	No known cure Some treatments reduce symptoms	Person is highly contagious when sores are present Infected women more likely to develop cancer of the cervix Infection passed to the newborn can lead to severe complications or death of the baby

■ **Table 14–5** *Common Sexually Transmitted Diseases*

DISEASE	TRANSMISSION	SYMPTOMS	TREATMENT	COMPLICATIONS
Genital Herpes *(continued)*				Virus, when not active, is dormant and may remain with infected persons for life There is some risk of transmission *even when the person is asymptomatic* and the disease is dormant
Genital Warts	Spread through genital or anal contact	May grow outside or inside genitals May be hard and yellow-gray or soft, pink, and cauliflower-like	Topical medication, freezing, cauterization, surgical removal	Warts may grow inside urethra and cause obstruction and bleeding Warts often progress to cancerous states in both men and women (usually cervical cancer) Can spread to other sites
Gonorrhea	Genital contact	(Women) May be expressed as pelvic inflammatory disease (PID) (Men) Foul-smelling, cloudy discharge from penis Burning sensations with urination	Penicillin sensitive and penicillin-resistant strains of gonorrhea exist	Few or no early symptoms in 40% of men; 80% of women Early symptoms clear up without treatment but disease is still present and can seriously affect major organs and systems Newborn can develop a gonococcal eye infection May coexist in women with vaginitis (trichomoniasis)
Syphilis	Spread through genital contact May be spread through contact with open lesions	(Primary stage) painless sore called a chancre; (secondary stage) chancre disappears and a skin rash develops; (latent stage) no observable symptoms; (tertiary stage) involvement of major organ systems; death may result	Antibiotic treatment must be repeated if syphilis infection has existed for longer than one year	Primary and secondary stage symptoms disappear without treatment but disease process is still present and doing its damage May be transmitted by a pregnant woman to her unborn child through the placenta

Source: Crooks & Baur, 1990.

larger frame and more muscle mass, their kcalorie needs are greater than the average girl's. Activity level also influences nutrient needs. An active 15 year old boy who is growing rapidly may require 4,000 kcalories per day just to maintain his body weight. An inactive 15 year old girl who has essentially completed her growth may need fewer than 2,000 kcalories per day to avoid gaining unwanted weight (Whitney & Cataldo, 1987). Male and female athletes need additional nutrients plus adequate fluid intake for optimal performance (Morgan, 1984).

About one-fourth of the teen's total daily kcalorie intake comes from snacks. Fast-food restaurants, vending machines, and stores may provide breakfast, lunch, and/or dinner to active teens on the go. The hamburger-and-milk-shake lunch is actually a very nutritious choice, supplying about 45% of needed protein and calcium, and 21% of the daily required allowance of iron. Adolescents have the easiest time complying with guidelines to "eat a variety of goods" and "eat foods with adequate fiber and starch." They have the most difficulty reducing sugar, fat, saturated fat, and cholesterol in their diets. Boys have trouble eliminating excess salt from their diets (Read et al., 1988). Table 14–6 lists other best- and worst-choice menu items from popular fast-food restaurants.

Iron is the nutrient most commonly lacking in the adolescent's diet. To prevent anemia, adolescent girls need extra iron in their diets once they begin menstruating. They also need sufficient calcium to prevent later osteoporosis (Morgan, 1984). For adolescent boys, iron supports muscle growth and development. The National Academy of Sciences (1977) suggests that the best dietary source of absorbable iron is meats of all varieties. When adolescents do eat at home, parents can fix nutritious meals and offer nutritious snacks. Other nutrient deficits are most often associated with exotic diets (trying to exist solely on french fries, for example), strict vegetarianism, and simply not eating.

osteoporosis
demineralization of the bone tissue causing bone loss and bone weakness

Eating Disorders

OBESITY Healthy weight is calculated as a function of age and frame size (small, medium, large). If for her age and frame a teenager's ideal weight is between 110–122 pounds and she weighs over 20% more than that (between 140 and 152 or more), she is considered to be obese. Obesity affects roughly 25% of all U.S. teenagers, primarily because of overeating, lack of exercise, low physical activity, poor food choice or selection, and a predisposition toward gaining weight carried forward from childhood (Gortmaker et al., 1987). When adolescents overeat compulsively, they frequently perceive their life quality and relationships as less positive than the nonrisk group, use overeating to defend against insecurity, worry and day dream, and have parents who engage in addictive behavior (overeating, substance abuse, gambling, and the like)

■ **Table 14–6**   *Best and Worst Nutrition Bites from the Fast-Food Restaurants*

McDonald's
(708) 575-FOOD

Best: Hamburger, frozen yogurt, orange sorbet, chunky chicken salad, low-fat shake.

Worst: Double cheeseburger, Big Mac with cheese, sausage McMuffin, fries.

Burger King
(800) YES-1800

Best: BK broiler without sauce, light Italian dressing, chicken specialty sandwich without mayo, regular hamburger.

Worst: Whopper, sausage croissan'wich, fries.

Wendy's
(800) 443-7266

Best: Chili, junior hamburger, fish fillet, plain baked potato, some salad bar selections with reduced-calorie Italian dressing.

Worst: Double cheeseburger, taco salad, pasta salad, potato salad, coleslaw, fries.

Pizza Hut
(316) 687-8450

Best: Hand-tossed thin and crispy pepperoni pizza, hold the pepperoni; regular pizza without cheese, or with half the cheese and lots of vegetables.

Worst: Thick and chewy pizza with lots of cheese and meat.

Kentucky Fried Chicken
No consumer hotline

Best: Chicken with skin removed, corn on the cob without butter.

Worst: Extra crispy chicken, french fries.

Taco Bell
(800) 735-8226

Best: Bean burrito, pintos and cheese, chicken fajita, steak fajita, taco, soft chicken taco.

Worst: Nachos, double beef supreme burrito, Mexican pizza.

Arby's
(800) 2-ADVISE

Best: French dip roast beef sandwich, grilled chicken barbecue, turkey deluxe without the mayo, plain baked potato, side salad with light Italian dressing, blueberry muffin.

Worst: Regular roast beef sandwich, roast chicken club, chicken cordon bleu, steak deluxe, apple turnover.

Source: © 1990 Center for Science in the Public Interest. Adapted from *Nutrition Action Healthletter* (1875 Connecticut Avenue, N.W., Suite 300, Washington, D.C. 20009-5728. $20.00 for 10 issues).

(Marston et al., 1988). The parents of obese adolescents are often overprotective (Brone & Fisher, 1988).

Even for young people obesity poses a health problem by straining the skeletal system and putting too much stress on the heart, lungs and kidneys. Socially and emotionally, obesity can be devastating for the teen who is already struggling for self-acceptance and peer approval.

Fat is hard to lose no matter when or how it was gained. Adolescents are particularly vulnerable to fad diets and other "quick fixes" for weight gain. To avoid permanent physical damage, any weight loss program should be supervised by a nutritionist and/or a physician.

ANOREXIA NERVOSA Anorexia nervosa is a psychological disturbance characterized by food obsessions, a distorted body image, low self-esteem, and self-starvation. One of the most consistent findings is that anorexic women have trouble establishing a sense of identity that is

body image
one's evaluation of one's physique

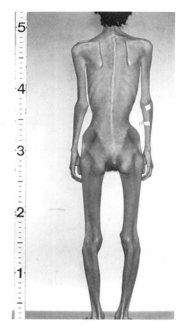

■ Figure 14–7

A photo of an anorexic woman facing away from the camera. She is so thin that her tailbone literally looks like a tail.

bulimia nervosa (bulimia)
an eating disorder characterized by episodic overeating to excess and dieting or voluntary vomiting or laxative use

independent from their parents and from others who wish to control their lives (Goldstein, 1981). Society can also be implicated in anorexia nervosa for putting pressure on women to be slender in order to be accepted. Girls who felt most negatively about their bodies early in adolescence were also most likely to develop eating disorders (Attie & Brooks-Gunn, 1989). Ninety-six percent of all anorexics are affluent, well-educated girls between the ages of 12 and 23 (American Academy of Pediatrics, 1987). Anorexia affects 1 woman out of every 100.

Anorexia is often preceded by a normal diet in response to a crisis (changing schools, being teased about "being fat," the onset of menstruation, coping with parental divorce, leaving for college). At some point the dieting becomes compulsive. Losses of 70–80 pounds or up to 30% of original body weight are not uncommon. Weight loss is often accompanied by intense overactivity and compulsive exercising. One anorexic patient even jogged while hospitalized "to keep up her muscle tone" (Minuchin et al., 1978).

The irony of anorexia nervosa is that in trying to establish control over their bodies and their environments, anorexics actually lose control as they become more and more involved in weight loss. While 30% of all anorexics get better on their own, 10–20% die from the effects of chronic starvation. Prevention and early detection are crucial if young lives are to be saved. The following symptoms require treatment (Bruch, 1979):

1. Denial of hunger. The person insists she feels full even after eating a minute amount of food
2. Cessation of menstruation
3. Distorted body image. The individual might insist that a severely emaciated person looks "really attractive. . .maybe a little heavy"
4. Increased social isolation. The illness becomes so all-encompassing that it takes all one's energy to starve oneself
5. Bizarre rituals surrounding eating and food handling—for example, increasing dietary restrictions, establishment of rigid eating schedules, hoarding or throwing food away, stretching meals out for hours
6. Severe overreaction to weight gain (severe depression, rage, or suicidal threats)
7. No known illness that would account for the weight loss
8. The appearance of fine hairs (lanugo) all over the body; dry skin and brittle nails
9. Cold intolerance
10. Drastic weight loss that continues even after an ideal weight is reached

BULIMIA NERVOSA (BULIMIA) Bulimia nervosa is sometimes referred to as the gorging/purging syndrome. Bulimics often feel they have discovered the perfect solution for controlling their weight: If they feel they have overeaten, they simply purge their systems at least twice a week by vomiting, excessive exercise, strict dieting, and/or using laxatives and diuretics. Sadly, this "solution" becomes a compulsive trap for the bulimic who becomes so extreme that she may consume as many as 55,000 calories in one sitting and suffer tooth decay, gastric irritation, electrolyte imbalance, and ulcers from vomiting and laxative use. A bulimic food binge is usually inconspicuous, lasts an hour or two, and is focused on high-calorie, soft, sweet foods.

Bulimia affects 1–2% of the female population. Most bulimics are young women (between age 15 and 30) who feel overweight during adolescence but in actuality are generally of normal weight or slightly underweight. Two percent of all bulimics started gorging and purging in junior high school (Stein & Brinza, 1989). Eighty percent of all high school and college bulimics are white, 16% are black, and 3% are Hispanic or Asian (Howat & Sexton, 1988). Depression may place women at greater risk for bulimia (McDaniel, 1986). Women with bulimia frequently report feeling deprived of the love and attention of their parents (Humphrey, 1986). Yet another line of research has discovered a relationship between bulimia and levels of cholecystokinin (CCK), a hormone found in the intestines, blood plasma, and brain that plays a role in satiety. Apparently, bulimics have much lower levels of CCK after eating than nonbulimic women. As a result, bulimic women may feel more hungry sooner and may not feel full even after consuming thousands of calories (Rosenfield, 1989). CCK adjustment is being tested. Antidepressant drugs and psychotherapy have been helpful in the treatment of bulimia, particularly if the bulimic's irrational beliefs about food are addressed (Thornton & DeBlassic, 1989).

As a hedge against the development of eating disorders, women are encouraged to learn to like the way they look rather than longing for the looks they don't have. Gloria Steinem's *Revolution from Within* (Little, Brown & Co., 1992) focuses on this issue. Her premise: When people dislike their bodies, it is difficult to like themselves.

In Touch

AMERICAN ANOREXIA AND
  BULIMIA ASSOCIATION
133 Cedar Lane
Teaneck, NJ 07666

JOHNS HOPKINS EATING AND
  WEIGHT DISORDERS CLINIC
Medical Meyer Building
600 North Wolfe St.
Baltimore, MD 21205

Accidents

Although the incidence of disease-related death is lower during adolescence than at any other time during the lifespan, the rate of injury and death due to accidents increases dramatically among 15–25 year olds, especially for males. Motor vehicle accidents involving cars, motorcycles, boats, all-terrain vehicles, and riding lawn mowers are responsible for about 40% of the deaths in this age group (U.S. Census Bureau UD). Very often the adolescent is driving too fast for the existing conditions or loses control due to inexperience, overconfidence, or the influence of alcohol or other drugs (Summala, 1987). Seat belts are seldom used.

Teens who won't or can't abstain from drugs and alcohol are encouraged to "designate" a driver who can be relied on for safe, substance-free transport.

Offering a chilling comment about the harsh realities of teen life, murder and suicide are ranked as the second and third major causes of adolescent death. The availability of weapons, drug involvement, the increasing acceptance of violence, hate crimes, and the influence of street gangs are all partially responsible for killing thousands of teens annually. Teens are both murder victims and murderers (D. G. Cornell et al., 1987). The black adolescent male is particularly likely to be victimized: 1 black male out of every 34 will be murdered before he reaches his 30th birthday. The comparable homicide rate for white males is 1 out of 218 (Centers for Disease Control, 1991).

Between 1960 and 1980 the suicide rate for 15–19 year olds *tripled* (American Academy of Pediatrics, Committee on Adolescence, 1988). As shocking as this statistic is, the actual suicide rate is probably much higher. Some drug overdose cases, accidental shootings, drownings, and car accidents are reported as unintentional for insurance purposes or to protect the privacy of the individual or the family when, in fact, a suicide was involved. David Elkind (1984) feels that today's teens experience higher levels of debilitating stress due to increased family, peer, and social conflicts. Suicide risk factors and suicide prevention are discussed in Chapter 16.

Drug Use

Drug use in adolescence encompasses a variety of substances ranging from tobacco and alcohol to illicit drugs such as marijuana, narcotics (primarily heroin), and stimulants such as cocaine, crack and amphetamines (like crank). The use of marijuana, tobacco, and alcohol is widespread among adolescents. By the time adolescents are seniors in high school, 92% have tried alcohol, 67% have smoked cigarettes, 50% have used marijuana, 21% have tried stimulants (crank and other amphetamines), 15% have used cocaine in some form, and 11% have taken tranquilizers (L. D. Johnston et al., 1988).

Although these figures seem alarmingly high, they actually represent a *decline* in the pattern of drug use and abuse that began in the late 1970s. Among adolescents who remain in school, white high school seniors are more likely to use drugs than black seniors (Associated Press, 1989). Thus, contrary to the stereotype, teenage drug use in the United States is not necessarily a black problem, it's an American problem. With the exception of cigarette smoking, girls use less drugs than boys.

Parents' drug use is an important precursor to teen drug use in many cases. However, kids who use drugs are influenced more by the approval and use patterns of their peers and teen idols (sports figures, rock stars) than their parents. High fear tactics to persuade teens to stop

In Touch

PARENTS OF MURDERED
  CHILDREN
100 E. 8th Street, B41
Cincinnati, OH 45202

are ignored because the long-term consequences often don't manifest themselves for years. When teens see their friends using drugs and suffering no harmful effects, the credibility of programs that emphasize health dangers and legal risks is negated. If adolescents reject getting drunk or trying illegal drugs, they often do so because their peers disapprove and they fear it will make them less attractive (bad breath and other disagreeable odors). Teens who abstain have decided "that's not the kind of person I want to be," and are able to delay gratification (Shedler & Black, 1980; Vicary & Lerner, 1983). Academic achievement, good mental and physical health, and a low rate of drug abuse among their parents further insulate teens against substance use (Marston et al., 1988). Successful education/prevention programs generally have these components in common (Flay, 1985):

1. Peer pressure resistance training
2. Information on *immediate* rather than long-term effects
3. Making a public commitment to behave in particular ways
4. Altering misperceptions
5. Discussing family influences
6. Inoculation against mass media ads (for smoking, and alcohol use)
7. Use of high-status peer leaders

Teens at highest risk for drug use appear to be creative, independent, unconventional, and assertive (Chassin et al., 1989). More than half of all teenage chronic drug users are faced with severe problems including physical and sexual abuse, school failure due to learning disabilities, arrests and other run-ins with the law, and depression and suicide (Associated Press, December 19, 1989). (Casual drug use may signal adjustment problems; it also could be due to normal adolescent exploration). Thus, the most effective programs for teens would combine drug abuse prevention/treatment with treatment for personal problems.

Parents and teens frequently come into conflict about drug use. A controversy surrounding drug detection is highlighted in the accompanying Issue.

In Touch

NATIONAL FEDERATION OF
 PARENTS OF DRUG-FREE
 YOUTH
1-800-554-KIDS
301-585-5437 in Maryland

Cocaine

The epidemic of cocaine use in America has spurred concern about teen cocaine involvement. With some 2 million people using cocaine daily in the United States, estimates are that at least 10% of that number (200,000) are 12–18 year olds (Brooks-Gunn et al., 1988). Crack cocaine users appear to be a particularly vulnerable population of children who begin drug use younger, have poorer grades, are more depressed, and more alienated from friends and family than other cocaine users (Ringwalt & Palmer, 1989). Environmentally exposed children—those living with cocaine-using parents who usually are nonnurturant and don't supervise their children's activities—exhibit almost twice as many

▶ ▶ I S S U E ◀ ◀

Home Drug Tests—Is Spying a Parental Right?

In August of 1990, DrugAlert became available. DrugAlert is a spray kit that lets parents test their children's rooms from drugs. It has touched off a wave of controversy about the parent's right to know vs. the child's right to privacy.

The kit is designed to test for the presence of marijuana and cocaine. Parents are instructed to wipe a special piece of paper on a surface the drugs may have touched and then to spray the paper with the chemicals contained in the kit. Two different chemical sprays are needed to test for marijuana; only one is needed for the cocaine test. Traces of cocaine turn the paper turquoise, while marijuana turns it brick red.

Why go to all that trouble? Why not just ask your child if he's using drugs? Denial is a large part of drug abuse. Some teens would rather risk telling a lie than admitting to drug involvement. Also, the adolescent may be addicted to the substance and afraid of drug withdrawal or even public exposure if his friends don't happen to know he is using or using heavily. Ironically, family stress and poor communication may have contributed to the adolescent's substance use in the first place.

Pharmacologists and toxicologists are skeptical about the validity of DrugAlert. Many different substances besides the drugs in question might produce positive results. For example, over-the-counter antihistamines and preparations like Anbesol would probably react like cocaine. Thus, parents would conclude their child was using cocaine when in fact he was merely treating a head cold!

Such false conclusions would be unfortunate but not as unfortunate as the betrayal of trust the child would feel knowing the parent snuck into his room to test the desk top or clothing. Invasion of privacy is a serious charge, but where do the child's rights end and the parent's rights begin? Does the adolescent have a right to keep drugs in the parents' home, and nothing be said about it?

While the experts continue the debate, one can only hope that the results from kits like DrugAlert will not be used as an end but as a means to opening up honest and straightforward discussions between parents and children about the serious implications of illicit drug involvement.

---

conduct disorder
behaviors that are legal *except* when performed by underage individuals

negative behaviors (severe emotional disturbances, conduct disorders, and behavior problems) as children prenatally exposed to cocaine (Youngstrom, 1991). The risk of AIDS is present when injectable forms of cocaine are used and needles are shared.

Cigarette Use

About 26% of the teenage population will try smoking. Those who stick with it light up for the first time around age 12. Although the percentage of adults who smoke is declining, the number of adolescents who smoke is holding constant at 18.7%. Young women smokers now outnumber young male smokers (L. D. Johnston et al., 1988). Cigarette smoking can severely complicate any existing respiratory ailments, such as asthma and bronchitis. Athletic endurance declines among teens who smoke.

The use of smokeless tobacco has increased significantly among adolescents. Sixty percent of adolescent males try smokeless tobacco by age 11 or 12, and 7% use it daily (Ary et al., 1987). The average reported use (3–5 dips of moist pouch tobacco per day) contains as much nicotine as 10–13 cigarettes. Adolescents who smoke cigarettes and have friends who use smokeless tobacco are most likely to "chew". Interestingly, parent tobacco use is not an accurate predictor of teen smokeless tobacco use. Smokeless users are also more likely to be white, to come from rural areas, to be less assertive, and to use alcohol, smoke cigarettes, and use marijuana (Elder et al., 1988; Botvin et al., 1989). Smokeless tobacco use is associated with oral cancer, tooth abrasion, tooth loss, and nicotine dependence.

Since most people become addicted to smoking once they have started, prevention may be the best approach to decreasing tobacco use in society. Indeed, the goal of health care professionals in the United States is to achieve a smoke-free society by the year 2000. The most effective programs, which are directed at fifth and sixth graders, avoid preaching and help young people develop strategies to handle pressures to smoke, whether from peers, the media, or adults. Smoking is most likely to be turned down by adolescents when their peers feel it "isn't cool" and when smoking threatens their personal appearance. Smoking prevention programs that focus on long-term health consequences (emphysema, lung cancer, heart disease) are ineffective because 11–15 year olds do not plan far into the future (Murray et al., 1985). Generally, people who avoid smoking during adolescence are much less likely to smoke as adults than those who begin as teenagers.

Another approach to reducing cigarette use among adolescents is to enforce the laws that restrict the sale of cigarette and other tobacco products to minors. Only 10 states (Colorado, Georgia, Kentucky, Louisiana, Montana, New Hampshire, New Mexico, Virginia, Wisconsin, and Wyoming) do not regulate the sale and distribution of tobacco products. In most states a minor is anyone under the age of 18. But the range of definitions for minors among individual states varies from age 15 in Hawaii to age 19 in Utah. Community education, enforcement of the sales laws by fine, imprisonment, or both, and the elimination of cigarette vending machines should cause cigarette use by teens to decline (USDHHS, 1988).

Alcohol Use

Although parents don't usually give their children cigarettes, many allow them to drink alcohol, beginning with "sips" when the children are young and then offering children and their friends drinks with dinner and to celebrate social occasions. Of all drugs, alcohol is most likely to be used and abused by teens. Most children have had their first taste of alcohol before reaching high school. The National Institute on Drug

Cigarette smoking can help you look older.

If you think smoking adds years to your appearance, remember that it also takes years off your life.
AMERICAN ✝ LUNG ASSOCIATION of Minnesota

■ **Figure 14–8**

An anti-smoking ad from the American Lung Association. Every day, 3000 more teens become smokers in the U.S.

smokeless tobacco
products that release nicotine through chewing not smoking

emphysema
a chronic disease that impairs breathing by enlarging the air sacs of the lungs

Abuse (1987) reports that among 12–17 year olds, 52% have used alcohol in the past year and 31% in the past month. The number of first-time alcohol users among teens is declining (Associated Press, February 6, 1991).

Unlike cigarette use, children tend to follow the drinking patterns of their parents. Children who come from homes where one or both parents are moderate to heavy drinkers will usually become moderate to heavy drinkers themselves. Dysfunctional families and alcoholic parents account for high rates of drinking among teens. Alcoholism has a genetic component that "improves" a child's chances of alcoholism by a factor of 4. Boys who drink tend to do so more heavily than girls, and beer and wine coolers are the favorite teenage drinks. In addition, teenagers who drink tend to have friends who drink. They are also more likely to smoke cigarettes or use marijuana than nondrinkers and to get low grades in school and to forego college (Johnston et al., 1988).

Most teenagers start drinking because they want to appear older or because their peers encourage drinking. In Sweden both early and late maturing teenage males begin drinking sooner than their normally-maturing, same-age peers (Anderson & Magnusson, 1990). In their early 20s, more late maturers (36%) than early (8%) or normal maturers (14%) register for alcohol abuse. The other reasons teenagers give are the same ones expressed by adults: to relax and unwind, to reduce anxiety, to make them feel more comfortable in social situations, and to allow them to temporarily escape their problems.

As previously mentioned, driving under the influence (DUI) is a significant cause of motor vehicle injuries and fatalities. Figure 14–9 pro-

■ **Figure 14–9**

The relationship between alcohol consumption and legal intoxication at the blood-alcohol level of .08%. While it takes more alcohol for the heavier person to become legally intoxicated, the more a person drinks, the more impaired their driving becomes.

Your weight	Number of drinks							
90 - 109 lbs	1	2	3	4	5	6	7	8
110 - 129 lbs	1	2	3	4	5	6	7	8
130 - 149 lbs	1	2	3	4	5	6	7	8
150 - 169 lbs	1	2	3	4	5	6	7	8
170 - 189 lbs	1	2	3	4	5	6	7	8
190 - 209 lbs	1	2	3	4	5	6	7	8
210 - 229 lbs	1	2	3	4	5	6	7	8
230 lbs & up	1	2	3	4	5	6	7	8

☐ (.01% - .04%) May be DUI (Driving Under the Influence)
☐ (.05% - .07%) Likely DUI
■ (.08% & up) Definitely DUI

vides a chart for determining blood alcohol level by body weight and alcohol consumption. SADD (Students Against Driving Drunk) provides a contract that requires a reciprocal agreement between parent and child. Students promise to call home if they need safe transportation and parents promise to respond without hassling the child that night. Parents also promise not to drink and drive themselves. Many students and their parents are signing such contracts. Designating a driver or (for special occasions) sharing the cost of a limousine will also cut down on fatalities. Parents can discourage adolescents from using alcohol by modeling abstinence or moderation in drinking, encouraging assertiveness, fostering high self-esteem, and helping teens solve their problems or meet their needs through more productive, positive means.

Marijuana Use

Marijuana is the most widely used illicit drug in the United States. Many adolescents use marijuana for the same reasons their parents use alcohol—to relax, unwind, and improve mood. The results of the two drugs are much the same physiologically because both substances are central nervous system depressants and disinhibitors. Marijuana, though, is also technically classified as an hallucinogen in higher doses.

About 20% of teens age 12–17 have had some experience with marijuana; 12% of that age group have used marijuana in the past month (Johnston et al., 1988). Most of the time, a child's first exposure to marijuana comes during high school. Sometimes, however, children's own parents "turn them on" to the drug. Marijuana use among adolescents is declining.

Of all the illicit drugs, marijuana is considered to be the safest by users and nonusers alike (American Academy of Pediatrics, 1980). Marijuana is nonnarcotic and not physically addicting, though psychological dependence may develop with repeated use. Contrary to early warnings, marijuana use is not necessarily a stepping-stone to more serious drugs. Its short-term effects for normal dosage levels include increased appetite, slowed reaction time, and moodiness. Chronic marijuana smoking, on the other hand, is associated with heart and lung problems, slow reaction time, impaired memory and impaired learning. In addition, lethargy and general fatigue may undermine the motivation of adolescents who smoke at least twice a week. Regular marijuana use in males and females is associated with increased tolerance for deviance, greater rebelliousness, and dissociation from the parents (Mayer & Ligman, 1989).

About 5–10% of all young people are chronic heavy users of marijuana. Much of the motivation for marijuana use at whatever level comes from peer pressure, curiosity, and the desire to exert independence from adults and to defy authority. Most marijuana users have friends who smoke the drug. Since marijuana use may impair driving ability, smokers need to know that driving under the influence may increase the likelihood of accidents.

Sexual Victimization

Date or Acquaintance Rape

In a date rape situation, a date or friend is used for sexual gratification against his or her wishes. Usually, but not always, the female is the victim. Date rape often results from sexual misunderstandings (Abbey, 1982): Just because a person is friendly doesn't mean they want to engage in sex. In Western culture, sex role socialization may encourage some men to assert their masculinity by being sexually forceful. A litany of rape mythology continues to exist to support such aggression (women like to be forced; when women say no they mean yes; women can avoid rape if they really want to; once women get men aroused, men can't stop; women are sexual teases who ask for it, and so on and on) (Crooks & Baur, 1990). Of course, all these statements are false.

Date/acquaintance rape is a grossly underreported crime, since our stereotypes about male and female sexuality interfere with our percep-

date/acquaintance rape
forced sexual activity with a nonstranger

■ **Figure 14–11**

Good looks mean a young woman takes pride in her appearance . . . it doesn't mean "she's asking for it."

■ **Table 14–7** *Suggestions for Avoiding Date Rape*

To avoid date rape, avoid people who:
- Get hostile when you say "no"
- Ignore your wishes
- Try to make you feel guilty, prudish, or "uptight"
- Are jealous or possessive
- Ignore personal space boundaries
- Are agggressive or anger easily

---

tion of the rape (Koss & Siebel, 1988). Since we don't believe men can be raped (they can by both men and women), and we assume men welcome any sexual contact they can get, even forced (they don't), we tend to dismiss the claims of male rape victims. Similarly, we hold females responsible for date rape by impugning their judgment and carriage (with such words as "Why did you ask him into your house?", "What did you *think* would happen?", and "Why did you wear *that* outfit? Weren't you really advertising for sex?"). Contrary to popular belief, date rape doesn't occur on a first or second date among relative strangers. The couple usually knows each other fairly well (Muehlenhard & Linton, 1987).

Date rape can be prevented by encouraging high self-esteem, re-evaluating traditional sex role stereotypes, and training teens to be assertive and to be able to defend against force (Parrott, 1989). Table 14–7 offers some guildelines for evaluating dating companions.

Abuse and Neglect

Neglect and physical, sexual, and emotional abuse are experienced by teens in all socioeconomic classes. Neglect is more common than abuse and involves ignoring teens and not providing for their care, health, or safety. Physically abused adolescents have usually been "beaten up" by their parent(s), who often claims the child has disobeyed (Blum, 1987). Emotional abuse is far more difficult to detect since harsh criticism, humiliation, and demeaning remarks leave no visible scars (Garbarino et al., 1986).

Like other sexual crimes, incest or sexual contact between relatives is vastly underreported. In one early retrospective study, 19% of women and 9% of men acknowledged they had been sexually exploited by an adult relative before they were 17 (Finkelhor, 1979). The adult usually relies on his position of authority or his emotional closeness to the child rather than physical force to pressure compliance. Male adults who commit incest are often emotionally immature, devoutly religious, very conservative, very insecure, and heavy drinkers (Doueck et al., 1987).

In Touch

DAUGHTERS AND SONS UNITED
PO Box 952
San Jose, CA 95108
408-280-5055

Self-help for physically abused
  children

■ ● ▲   CONCEPT SUMMARY

Health Concerns of Adolescence

Compared to younger children, adolescents have higher rates of:

- hypertension
- ulcerative colitis
- viral hepatitis
- infectious mononucleosis
- sexually transmitted disease
- iron deficient diets (although this is true of infants, too)
- eating disorders (overeating, anorexia nervosa, bulimia)
- motor vehicle accidents
- victimization through homicide
- suicide
- drug use
- sexual victimization

Adolescent-age children do not enjoy, encourage, or initiate this type of activity.

Abuse and neglect represent a profound betrayal of trust between child and parent. Physical, sexual, and psychological maltreatment of adolescents accounts for much of the runaway, drug abuse, violent criminal behavior, psychological disturbance, youth prostitution, hyperactivity, eating disorders, and suicide among this age group (Wisdom, Annual Meeting, AAAs, February 16, 1991). HIV infection is another life-threatening consequence of child sexual abuse (Gellert & Durfee, 1989).

**TOWARD
EFFECTIVE
PARENTING**

Talking to Your Children about Sex

Just getting a dialogue started on the topic of sexuality is important, since ignorance will be the child's greatest liability:

Question: When should parents start telling kids about sex?

Answer: Probably when the child begins to ask questions, and that's usually by the age of 4. Use simple straightforward language. Be brief.

Question: How can parents avoid feeling awkward and embarrassed?

Answer: It takes practice to overcome discomfort. Try taking a college level course in human sexuality. Check out some age-appropriate books from your local library (the reference librarians are a great help). In short, if parents educate themselves, they'll feel more comfortable with the material. Be honest about your feelings. Admit that you're uncomfortable, that you may never have had the advantage of talking with your own parents about sex, but that it's important to talk and find out anyway.

Don't hesitate to convey your values and feelings but give your children the freedom to develop their own values. ("I know many of your friends are having sex but there are big responsibilities associated with sexual activity. You have to guard against getting pregnant and getting diseases like herpes or chlamydia. You also risk feeling hurt and used. I'd like to help you delay your sexual activity until you're really ready to cope with all this.")

Question: How do I bring up the topic of sexuality?

Answer: Sometimes a TV program, movie, someone's pregnancy, or a newspaper article can provide an entry to an interesting and far-ranging discussion. A program on date rape can help you encourage your child not to force or be forced. *Any* accurate information is better than none. If parents can't say the words, perhaps they could buy the child a recommended book (not *Playboy, Playgirl,* or *Penthouse*).

It's never too late to start talking to your teen about sex.

Teens' curiosity about sex is not necessarily an admission that they are sexually active. Parents who want to keep the lines of communication open should provide information rather than interrogating and should avoid violating their child's privacy.

At the very least, information about first menstruation or the potential for ejaculation during masturbation or wet dreams should be conveyed. Otherwise, the events come as quite a shock to the unprepared (Crooks & Baur, 1990). The bottom line for parents is that if they want their children to come to them, they have to provide an open, safe, and nonjudgmental atmosphere for discussion. The pros and cons of different choices can be examined. Ultimately, the child will have to make his or her own decision. Most of the time, those decisions are prudent.

Sometimes, however, teens still get pregnant, raped, or infected with a disease. Instead of anger, saying "I told you so," and disenfranchisement of the teen, adolescents need their parents' support in coping with these new challenges and knowing what choices and options are still available.

● Chapter Summary

● Adolescence is the transitional period between childhood and adulthood. Accelerated growth, referred to as the *growth spurt,* is the first observable sign of adolescence. Increased hormone output stimulates the onset of the growth spurt. During adolescence, final stature is achieved, internal organs and systems attain adult size and functioning, and sexual maturity is reached.

- The timing and outcome of puberty are affected by the sex of the individual, genetics, fat-to-lean ratio (for girls), nutrition, and general health. The range of normal variation is considerable, and early and late maturation have psychological consequences for both sexes.

- Reproductive capacity is reached when the primary sex characteristics are mature. When girls begin their menstrual periods (age 12–14) and boys ejaculate viable sperm (age 14–15), fertility should be presumed. Menstrual disturbances like dysmenorrhea, amenorrhea, and PMS are more common among adolescents than adults.

- Sexual messages abound in American society, but many are confusing and contradictory for the teen. Once adolescents discover their sexual orientation, they may keep their sexuality in reserve or may express it through petting, self-stimulation, or intercourse. Since most sexually active teens shun contraceptive use, pregnancy and STD transmission are common consequences of teen sexuality. Teenage pregnancy poses health-related challenges for both the adolescent and her baby; poverty, school dropout and unemployment/underemployment are frequently associated with pregnancy during adolescence.

- Adolescents tend to receive little information on sexuality from their parents, since many parents falsely believe the such information encourages promiscuity and experimentation. Peers are the most common source of sex-related information, followed by the schools. There is considerable debate about the content of sex education classes/seminars in the public schools.

- Adolescents are ranked as the healthiest segment of the population because of their low disease and illness rate. However, sexually transmitted disease, hypertension, ulcerative colitis, viral hepatitis, and infectious mononucleosis are more common in this age group than in others.

- Teens' nutrient needs are highest when they are growing most rapidly. Balanced nutrition can be attained, but most diets are low in iron and calcium and too high in fats and refined sugars. Adolescents, particularly females, are vulnerable to developing eating disorders.

- While the disease rate is low, the injury rate is high, particularly among adolescent males. Motor vehicle accidents, where the adolescent is the operator, account for the majority of deaths and complications. Homicide and suicide are ranked second and third.

- Drug use among adolescents may be on the decline, but the numbers are still disturbingly high. Alcohol, tobacco products, and marijuana (respectively) are the drugs of choice.

- Teens may be sexually victimized by peers (acquaintance rape) or by relatives (incest). Sadly, neglect and emotional abuse are also common.

● Observational Exercise

Adolescence is a time of great individual variation in development. One might perceive one's own personal growth as accelerated, normal, or slow relative to peers, and such perceptions may affect self-confidence and peer-group status.

Procedure: Interview two male and two female adults (i.e., college age or older) regarding their rate of physical development during adolescence. Record each person's responses for purposes of comparison. Ask these questions:

1. Would you classify yourself as an early or late maturer during adolescence?
2. Was it uncomfortable for you to be (ahead of/behind) your peers in development? If so, in what ways?
3. Do you think it is harder for boys or for girls to be (early/late) as you were? Why?
4. Rate yourself on these attributes as they pertained to you during your adolescent years.

   a. How self-confident were you?　/_____/ _____/ _____/ _____/
   Very　　　　　　　　　　　　　　　Not at all

   b. How popular were you?　/_____/ _____/ _____/ _____/
   Very　　　　　　　　　　　　　　　Not at all

   c. Were you respected by your peers?　/_____/ _____/ _____/ _____/
   Highly　　　　　　　　　　　　　　Not at all

   d. Were you respected by adults?　/_____/ _____/ _____/ _____/
   Highly　　　　　　　　　　　　　　Not at all

   e. Were you treated as a mature person?　/_____/ _____/ _____/ _____/
   All the time　　　　　　　　　　　Never

5. Did you excel in any particular area, such as sports or academics?
6. If you could do things over again and had control over your own maturational rate, would you want to develop at a faster or slower pace than you did? Why?

● Recommended Readings

The Boston Women's Health Collective. (1984). *The new our bodies, ourselves: A book by and for women.* New York: Simon & Schuster.

Cassell, C. (1988). *Straight talk from the heart: How to talk to your teenagers about love and sex.* New York: Simon & Schuster.

Elkind, D. (1984). *All grown up and no place to go: Teenagers in crisis.* Reading, MA: Addison-Wesley.

Madaras, L., & Madaras, A. (1986). *Lynda Madaras' growing up guide for girls.* New York: New Market.

Madaras, L., & Madaras, A. (1986). *What's happening to my body? book for girls: A growing up guide for parents and daughters* (rev. ed.) New York: New Market.

Madaras, L., & Saavedra, D. (1987). *What's happening to my body? book for boys: A growing up guide for parents and sons* (2nd, revised ed.). New York: New Market.

McGuire, P. (1983). *It won't happen to me.* New York: Delacorte. (A book about pregnancy)

Planned Parenthood Federation of America. (1986). *How to talk with your child about sexuality.* New York: Doubleday.

Simon, N. (1982). *Don't worry, you're normal: A teenager's guide to self-health.* New York: Thomas Y. Crowell Junior Books.

Warshaw, R. (1988). *I never called it rape.* New York: Harper & Row. (On the topic of date/acquaintance rape)

Cognitive Development During Adolescence

CHAPTER

15

● **Piaget's Theory of Cognitive Development:
The Stage of Formal Operational Thought**

The stage of formal operational thought is the fourth and last stage of
cognitive development described by Jean Piaget (Piaget, 1936/1963;
Inhelder & Piaget, 1958, 1964). Beginning around age 10 or 11, becoming
fully functional around age 15, and continuing throughout adolescence,
the stage of formal operations includes:

1. the use of abstract concepts
2. the ability to consider real and hypothetical events
3. the ability to solve problems systematically
4. the use of logic

formal operational thought
according to Piaget, the fifth and final
stage of cognitive development,
characterized by abstract thinking and
the ability to systematically test
hypotheses. This stage is not reached
until adolescence, if at all.

Thinking Abstractly

The ability to understand the intangible characteristics of concepts is the
hallmark of abstract thought. The ability to think abstractly first appears
between the ages of 10 and 12 (Martarano, 1977). Children in the stage
of concrete operations have difficulty understanding concepts like loyalty, freedom, and courage because they tend to focus on specifics and
away from general principles. Here are the responses of four boys when
asked, "What is the purpose of laws?" (Adelson et al., 1969):

abstract thought
thinking that is not tied to material
objects or particular examples

11 year old: Well, so everybody won't fight, and they have certain laws
so they won't go around breaking windows and stuff and
getting away with it.

13 year old: To keep people from doing things they're not supposed
to, like killing people and . . . if you're in the city, like
speeding and things like that.

683

■ Figure 15–1

Formal operational thought permits adolescents to learn and master complex tasks involving logic, deduction, and skill.

15 year old: To keep us safe and free.

18 year old: Well, the main purpose would be just to set up a standard of behavior for people, for society living together so they can live peacefully and in harmony with one another.

The 11 and 13 year old cited specific laws while the 15 and 18 year olds were able to move beyond specifics in their descriptions to reason *why* laws in general were important.

Exploring New Possibilities

Abstract thought helps adolescents think about what can be in addition to what is. School-age children in concrete operations are bound by a concrete, practical-minded approach to solving problems. They can relate best to things they can experience or observe. When solving problems, for example, school-age children typically accept the first explanation they think of as the only possible solution (Inhelder & Piaget, 1958). In contrast, adolescents, using formal operations, can break through the bonds of the here and now to explore possibility in addition to reality. Thus, they can speculate about, say, what life would be like on a distant planet or what might happen if the world's water supply were polluted. Older children are more likely than school-age children to see these hypothetical questions as complex and involving many interrelated factors. Further, they can envision a whole spectrum of possible solutions and outcomes. Younger children, on the other hand, may have difficulty getting beyond the fact that our water supply isn't actually polluted, for example. They often simply dismiss such questions with a simple reply like, "We could just get water some other place," that both betrays their naivete and highlights the limitations of their thinking.

Adolescents' well-known tendency to be critical of people and existing political, social, and religious systems may stem from their new capacity for formal operational thought (McKinney & Moore, 1982). Since adolescents can imagine alternatives and hypothetical possibilities, the discrepancies between the real world and their ideal states become painfully apparent to them. For example, they might begin to see inconsistencies between their parents' professed attitudes and their actions. Teenage sons and daughters may suddenly wonder aloud how their parents can live in a country that tolerates poverty or racism, or why parents continue to lecture about the dangers of smoking while continuing to smoke themselves. These young people might also begin to question the status quo in the country, entertaining elaborate and grandiose strategies for "eliminating crime" or "stopping environmental pollution." And because adolescents have the capacity to consider many possible explanations or solutions, they may be hesitant to commit themselves to a single point of view, as younger children might, before carefully weighing the evidence for and against each alternative.

Parents might find adolescents' critical orientation and political hedging tiresome or irritating. It might help if they understood that their child's new concern with the world's deficiencies is probably more apparent than real. When adolescents are observing discrepancies and considering alternative systems and behaviors, they are actually exercising their newfound cognitive abilities rather than seriously remaking the world.

Systematic Problem Solving

Another important feature of formal operational thought is the development of a systematic methodical approach to problem solving. Barbel Inhelder and Piaget (1958) called this problem solving orientation *hypothetico-deductive reasoning* since the child first identifies all possible *hypotheses* or solutions to a problem before *deducing* ways to systematically test each hypothesis.

hypothetico-deductive reasoning the process of generating hypotheses and then systematically testing each to find the solution

To demonstrate the existence of hypothetico-deductive reasoning, Inhelder and Piaget (1958) presented tasks based on the physical sciences to children of various ages. One of the most famous of these is the pendulum problem. Nine to 15 year olds were given the materials to construct a pendulum and shown how to vary the length of the string, attach different weights, push with varying amounts of force, and release the weight from various heights (Ginsberg & Opper, 1979). They were then asked to determine which factor or factors affect how fast the pendulum swings. Younger children tended to try variables in combination:

1. Long string, high release, hard push, light weight—slow swing
2. Short string, high release, easy push, heavy weight—fast swing

When they got differences in outcomes (as with the above example), they didn't know which of the three factors was responsible since only the release height was held constant. Younger children tend to look for evidence to support their particular hypothesis, not for evidence to refute it. If these children felt the weight was the most significant feature, they might point to the above as confirmation.

The older children in the study varied one factor systematically while holding all others constant:

	Heavy vs. Light Weight	*Hi vs. Low Release*
HARD PUSH	no difference	no difference
EASY PUSH	no difference	no difference
LONG STRING	no difference	no difference
SHORT STRING	no difference	no difference

■ Figure 15–2

The pendulum problem. Is the speed of the pendulum swing controlled by the length of the string, the speed of the push, or the amount of weight, or some combination?

length of the string?   speed of the push?   amount of weight?

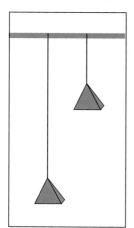 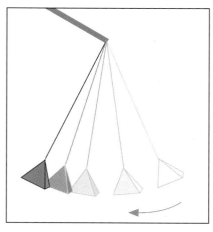 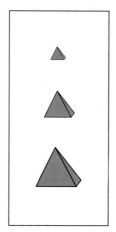

...or a combination of each?

	Hard vs. Easy Push	*Long vs. Short String*
HEAVY WEIGHT	no difference	slower vs. faster
LIGHT WEIGHT	no difference	slower vs. faster
HIGH RELEASE	no difference	slower vs. faster
LOW RELEASE	no difference	slower vs. faster

After testing was complete, the older child was able to correctly deduce that only string length affects the speed of the pendulum's swing, the other factors (weight, height of release, and force of release) being irrelevant to that outcome.

The same hypothetico-deductive strategy used in the pendulum problem can be applied to problems of daily living (Baker, 1982). If students are not doing as well in a class as they expect to, they can systematically search out an answer after formulating hypotheses. If the suspected causes are:

1. too much TV watching
2. not enough study time
3. not enough sleep

then the possible solutions involve:

1. TV
2. study

3. sleep
1. & 2. (TV and study)
1. & 3. (TV and sleep)
2. & 3. (study and sleep)
1., 2., & 3. (TV, study, and sleep)
0. none of the above

With three different hypotheses, there are 7 combinations that could account for the poor academic achievement. There's also the possibility that all three hypotheses may be wrong and that some other factor or factors (stress, failing eyesight) may be responsible.

Sometimes definite answers are not possible. When factors are merely related to a behavior but are not necessarily causal, a *correlation* is said to exist. For example, all convicted criminals drank milk at some point in their lives. Does drinking milk *cause* people to break laws or is it just one factor that criminals have in common? This type of reasoning is very difficult for even the older adolescent to comprehend. It's difficult enough to actually find the right answer, but when there is no right answer, the adolescent must devise an estimate based on possibilities. The nuances of multiple factors, estimates, and differential influence that underlie correlational thinking are not mastered until later adulthood, if then (Chance & Fischman, 1987).

The Use of Logic

Other forms of logic besides any involving in hypothetico-deductive reasoning develop during the stage of formal operations. Adolescents are able to integrate what they have learned from the past with their present knowledge, and they can combine information from a variety of sources. Another cognitive tool available to adolescents is *propositional logic* which enables them to judge the truth of logical relationships. Consider the following statements:

propositional logic
the ability to judge the truth of logical relationships; the ability to assess the appropriateness of reasoning strategies before applying them

PROPOSITION 1: All sheep are animals.
PROPOSITION 2: All animals are brown.
PROPOSITION 3: All sheep are brown.

When school-age children are faced with such statements, they tend to consider each proposition in isolation. The younger child focuses on the factual relationship among the statements. They reason that because some sheep are not brown, the conclusion is false. Adolescents in the stage of formal operations understand that logic can be manipulated independently of factual content. It is clear to adolescents that all sheep are not brown, but they can still understand that *if* sheep are animals, and *if* all animals are brown, *then* it follows logically that all sheep are brown (Flavell, 1985).

■●▲   CONCEPT SUMMARY

Characteristics of Formal Operational Thought

- The ability to think abstractly
- The ability to think about possibility in addition to reality
- The systematic exploration of cause and effect through the hypothetico-deductive method
- The ability to judge the truth of logical relationships (propositional logic)
- The ability to use deductive reasoning
- The ability to acquire expertise within a particular content area

When statements cannot be verified because they're not factual, younger children have trouble coordinating the variables. Solve this problem:

Sam is shorter than Joe.
Sam is taller than Bill.
Who is the tallest of the three?

Concrete thinkers find it difficult to deal with opposite terms (taller and shorter) within the context of relational statements. Thus, they often are led to incorrect conclusions. The logic of formal operations helps adolescents transform the first statement into terms consistent with the other two, and the conclusion becomes obvious:

Joe is taller than Sam.
Sam is taller than Bill.
Who is the tallest of the three?
(Answer: Joe)

● Acquiring Formal Operational Thinking

Formal operational thought provides the individual with flexibility, an appreciation of complexity, a theoretical orientation, and hypothesis-generating and testing capabilities that are nonexistent in the stage of concrete operations during childhood. Still, it is important to note that although adolescents are maturationally ready to understand the logic of formal operations, some use formal operational thought more effectively than others, and some never seem to achieve this level of reasoning at all, not even as mature adults.

In 1972 Diane Papalia tested 265 people between the ages of 10 and 50 on the pendulum task described above and noted who was successful in solving the task:

Age Group	% Solving the Problem
10–15	45%
16–20	53%
21–30	65%
45–50	57%

One-third to one-half of Papalia's subjects did not use formal operations when asked to solve the pendulum problem. Why not? Apparently, the development of formal operations is not as natural or inevitable as Piaget assumed. While all normal individuals pass through the sensori-motor stage and display evidence of preoperational and concrete operational thought, the stage of formal operations permits more individual variability and is less predictable (Chance & Fischman, 1987).

Training and experience affect the development of formal operational thought. Because Inhelder and Piaget's tasks (1958, 1964) are based on the physical sciences, it is not surprising that children who have taken math, chemistry, physics, or biology do better than students who have had no such coursework (McClosky et al, 1980). And even though many adults may not succeed in solving scientific problems or problems involving logic, they frequently use formal operations to solve meaningful problems that interest them. Thus, a mechanic may separate and control variables when troubleshooting a piece of faulty machinery but fail to use this approach when buying a home computer or trying to settle disagreement with his wife (Flavell, 1977).

Culture may be another variable that influences the development of formal operational thought. Formal operational thought may be superfluous in some cultures or among some people. On the other hand, formal operational reasoning may exist in all the world's cultures if we just know where to look. Although the Kalahari Bushmen of Africa may be unable to identify any of the variables that influence the speed of the pendulum's swing, they demonstrate high levels of formal operational thought when discussing the hunting and tracking of game animals (Tulkin & Konner, 1973). They develop hypotheses about the animals' movements, their timing, and whether or not they're wounded, and then test these hypotheses against new information, rejecting or altering them until they make the catch. The Neo-Piagetians would assert that the capacity to develop formal operational reasoning exists among all normal humans (Flavell, 1977). Whether people in individual cultures use formal operations, however, seems to depend on their individual needs and the culture's willingness to provide the training.

● The Information Processing Approach to Cognitive Development

Information processing theorists focus on the quantitative changes in memory and learning strategies to explain the qualitative changes that take place in adolescent cognition. In general, adolescents are more organized, systematic, self-correcting, and thus more efficient in solving problems than younger children. The following summarizes the significant differences in information processing between children and adolescents.

Changes in Processing Capacity and Speed

The adolescent seems able to handle or process more information at one time than the younger child. The differences could be due to a maturational change in the brain that permits an increase in the capacity of short-term memory (Dempster, 1981). Experience would also account for such differences since older children have had more practice than younger ones in retaining and combining information (Siegler, 1983). Either way, processing capacity increases with age. Speed of processing improves as well for visual and memory search functions. Apparently, the central mechanism that limits speed of performance changes with age (Kail, 1988).

Changes in Processing Strategies

Processing strategies help children sort, organize, and store information more efficiently. Three such strategies are rehearsal, organization, and elaboration. They are discussed next.

Rehearsal

Compared to younger children, older children are more likely to rehearse or repeat to themselves the information they are trying to memorize. Not only do younger children need prompting and instruction to rehearse, but they have difficulty implementing the strategy even when it is used (Ornstein et al., 1985). Apparently, it takes time and practice for rehearsal to become more automatic and efficient and useful as a memory aid (Baker-Ward et al., 1984).

Organization

Organization involves grouping related items together to aid memorization. In organizing the following list of items,

DOG	BONE	CAT	MOUSE	HAT
SOCK	SHOE	HORSE	HAY	COAT

younger children divide their lists into large numbers of categories, leaving many isolated items (Frankel & Rolling, 1985):

DOG–CAT

SOCK–SHOE

HAT–HAY

COAT

BONE

HORSE

MOUSE

Younger children are also likely to recategorize on subsequent trials, giving the impression that they have no consistent plan for organizing (Bjorkland & Zeman, 1983).

CAT–MOUSE

DOG–BONE

HORSE–SHOE

SOCK–COAT

HAT

HAY

In contrast, adults are less likely to organize the information into associative pairs than into broad categories of animals, clothing items, and foods that are less automatic and more consciously considered.

DOG	SOCK	BONE
CAT	SHOE	HAY
MOUSE	HAT	
HORSE	COAT	

When presented with a list of items (helicopter, bee, penguin, and angels) that have few obvious characteristics in common, younger children show little if any organization (Bjorklund & Hock, 1982). Adolescents might see a common category, however: items with wings.

Elaboration

Elaboration involves creating a relationship between two objects when no natural relationship exists. Elaborating often involves the use of mental images or the development of an acronym to facilitate learning. For example, if you need to remember the difference between port and starboard on a ship, you can remember the phrase, "I left port" to cue the association between port and the left side. *Roy G. Biv* is the acronym for the colors of the visual spectrum in their correct sequence (red–orange–yellow–green–blue–indigo–violet).

Because elaboration requires more imagination and a more systematic search for meaning, it does not appear until after age 11 and continues to develop into young adulthood (Pressley, 1982). In fact, elaboration is such an effective memory aid that it tends to replace other memory strategies over time. However, individual differences among adolescents and young adults is great. While virtually everyone uses rehearsal and organization, elaboration is a far less universally applied memory strategy (Pressley, 1982). Exactly why some people never think of using elaboration as a memory aid is unclear at this time.

Changes in Problem Solving Strategies

One of the most useful problem solving strategies available to adolescents is deductive reasoning. An individual who can deduce the correct answer can reason from general to specific, progressively narrowing the range of possibilities. The game of Twenty Questions provides an example of a strategy shift. When young children have to guess what you are thinking of, they tend to make specific guesses, like "Is it a cow?", "Is it a car?" and so on. The adolescent, on the other hand, imposes a strategy to eliminate categories of answers: "Is it alive?", "Is it a plant?", "Is it an animal?", and so on. This approach makes guessing the right answer far more likely than the school-age child's approach of asking random specific questions.

Robert Siegler (1981, 1983a, 1983b) suggests that cognitive development involves acquiring a set of four rules that can be applied to solve problems. The rules are learned in order and each rule predicts a particular response pattern. Rule 1 (acquired by age 5) roughly corresponds to preoperational thought, where only one feature of the situation can be taken into account. Rule 2 (acquired by age 9) marks a transition between Rules 1 and 3. Rule 3 (acquired by age 9) is a concrete operational rule where two aspects of a situation can be considered, just not systematically. Rule 4 (acquired by age 13) reflects formal operational thought and a systematic relational strategy. As the rules are acquired by training and feedback, they can be applied in increasingly more sophisticated ways. Until children can adopt new ways of thinking, how-

deductive reasoning
a type of reasoning whereby general laws suggest conclusions about specific cases

Calvin and Hobbes   by Bill Watterson

ever, advanced rules cannot be learned (Shaklee et al., 1988). While most of Siegler's work has focused on solving well-structured problems, his rule-assessment approach to cognitive development can also be applied to less structured problems as well.

The acquisition of knowledge within a specific content area seems to improve the child's use of memory and problem solving strategies. Children who excel in a particular field (the LA Dodgers, chess, coin collecting, rock music) know more about problem solving in their field of expertise than less knowledgeable peers or even adults (Chi, 1978, 1982). Experts not only gather more knowledge within their particular domain but the sheer quantity of knowledge may accelerate the way the information is organized.

Children vary not only in how much they know but in how they use the knowledge they have accumulated (A. L. Brown et al., 1983). Bransford and colleagues (1981) found that one difference between academically successful and unsuccessful fifth graders was the extent to which they would use their existing knowledge base to understand new information. Over the long run, then, if the child can't use what she knows, she can't understand something new, and if she can't understand new information, she can't add to her existing knowledge base.

● The Psychometric Approach

Psychometricians have found that the concept of "intelligence" seems to change with age. Adolescents can demonstrate a broader array of cognitive skills and abilities than younger children (Sternberg & Powell, 1983). So while a child might be described as intelligent in a relatively general way, the adolescent's abilities are sharper, more defined, and easier to distinguish (e.g., reading comprehension, vocabulary, memory). Psychologists have never agreed on the number of factors that ultimately comprise mature human intelligence.

An alternate point of view is that factors or abilities that emerge in childhood don't change but remain constant over time. The only thing that changes with time is the acquisition of *more* of that same skill: more memory, more comprehension, and so on (Bayley, 1968). According to this perspective, adolescents aren't more intelligent than younger children, they simply *have* more intelligence.

Measuring individual differences in intelligence among adolescents is inherently difficult (Sternberg, 1984). Besides motivational issues and variances in health, well being, intellectual style, and the adequacy of the testing environment, the very real possibility exists that a specific question on a specific IQ test may or may not assess the ability it was designed to measure (Sternberg, 1988). Thus, intelligence tests *may* test cognitive ability, but imperfectly at best.

intellectual style
whether one is a reflective vs. an impulsive thinker (also called cognitive style)

When you're an adolescent, something as small as a blemish can ruin your whole day.

imaginary audience
an assembled group of listeners or
spectators assumed to be present

● Social Cognition

Although cognitive abilities can expand dramatically during adolescence, all stages of cognitive development are limited by some form of egocentricity, and adolescence is no exception. The egocentrism of adolescence manifests itself in the great amount of time these young people spend in thinking about themselves and comparing themselves with others. *Am I normal?* they wonder. *What do I mean to others? Why do I exist?* Adolescents often ponder such questions as they try to establish their identities for themselves apart from their families and friends.

Owing to the great amount of time adolescents generally spend preoccupied with thoughts about themselves, they often have trouble realizing that the people they associate with are not thinking about them as well. Adolescents seem to assume that their every move and nuance will be evaluated by an "imaginary audience" of their peers, as a stage performer is judged by a theatre critic (Elkin, 1978). With this orientation, a facial blemish can be a catastrophe *(What will everyone say?),* while a new outfit might be expected to provoke universal acclaim *(They'll love it!).* Meanwhile, of course, adolescents' teenage peers are equally self-involved (Buis & Thompson, 1989). Rather than critically evaluating the traits and characteristics of others, they are often so self-absorbed that they hardly notice their peers.

Egocentrism also prevents adolescents from distinguishing the unique from the universal. A young woman overwhelmed by first love may believe that no one knows how she feels (with special reference to her parents). Similarly, although adolescents are often capable of accurately assessing other people's thoughts, feelings, and intentions, they may fail to do so because they permit their egocentrism to interfere with their perceptions. For example, adolescents frequently misattribute their feelings to others, assuming that a peer who performs poorly on a biology exam dislikes biology because they themselves do.

In another example of egocentrism, teenagers often see their lives as fables, with themselves as heroes dedicated to some great purpose (Inhelder & Piaget, 1958). They may feel they are destined to solve problems that others have been unable to correct, or to leave behind a legacy in the area of art, science, or athletics. This sense of elevated purpose may motivate some adolescents to strive toward perfection and to adopt an idealistic orientation toward the world. It may further lead them to believe that they are not subject to the laws of probability affecting ordinary people. One teen may assume she can't get pregnant; another that he won't be involved in an automobile accident or become addicted to drugs. These conclusions are rooted not in precautions taken against pregnancy, drug addiction, or automobile accidents, but rather in the egocentricity that misleads the teenager into feeling invulnerable to adversity (Blum, 1985).

■●▲ CONCEPT SUMMARY

Characteristics of Adolescent Egocentrism

- The tendency to think about themselves and their own ideas a great deal

- The assumption that others are constantly thinking about them, too, and evaluating their behavior (imaginary audience)

- The assumption that no one knows how they feel

- The assumption that their experiences are unique compared with others

- A sense of elevated purpose and importance (personal fable)

- A feeling of invulnerability

- Idealism

Adolescents gradually relinquish their egocentricity and idealism as they are forced to confront the world as it is, not as they would like it to be. After some setbacks and disillusionments, by late adolescence most have come to terms with the way things are and have adjusted their needs and aspirations to fit society (Newman, 1985). Inhelder and Piaget (1958) wrote that adolescents' first real jobs play a significant role in helping them orient to others in a realistic manner. Adolescents can learn about other people's feelings, reactions, and tendencies as they learn to deal with the demands of their employers, coworkers, and patrons (Sternberg et al., 1982).

● Language Development

Changes in cognitive functioning continue through adolescence to influence the way children use and understand language. Formal operational thought encourages adolescents to add to their vocabulary, use more sophisticated words, and communicate in more complex sentences. The ability to construct general hypotheses and consider alternative explanations may lead to the use of "if/then" constructions and phrases that involve conditional words such as *therefore* and *however*.

While preschoolers and school-age children interpret most phrases in a literal or concrete fashion, adolescents develop the ability to understand several levels of meaning, from obvious to subtle. Consider these differences in the interpretation of proverbs among children ages 4.5 to 11 (Saltz, 1979, p. 511):

1. *Never go into deep water until you can swim.*

    Intended meaning: Don't attempt things you don't have the skills for.

    Age 5: Because you'll drown if you don't know how to swim.
    Age 7: Cause you'll drown.
    Age 9: Learn how to swim first.
    Age 10: Wait till you're older.
    Age 11: Only do what you know you can do.

2. *People who live in glass houses shouldn't throw stones.*

    Intended meaning: Don't' criticize others unless you're invulnerable to criticism yourself.

    Age 5: Because it breaks that glass.
    Age 7: Never throw stones at a house.
    Age 9: You know people don't live in glass houses. I don't see no glass houses.
    Age 11: If you hurt people, you may get hurt yourself.

3. *When the cat's away the mice will play.*

    Intended meaning: When the person in charge is absent, people will do what they shouldn't.

    Age 5: Cause the mouse scares the cat.
    Age 6: When the cat goes away, the mice stay.
    Age 7: Because the cat would eat the mice so they play when the cat is gone.
    Age 10: When parents are away, children will wreck the house.

satire
writing that exposes or ridicules human shortcomings in a witty or ironic way

metaphorical expressions
a figure of speech in which one object or idea is compared with another in order to suggest a similarity between the two (i.e., She was a pillar of strength)

dysfluent speech
speech that is choppy, halting, and produced with great effort

Abstract thought also enables the adolescent to understand satire, political and social messages in cartoons and literature, and metaphorical expressions, such as "He threw caution to the wind."

As in middle childhood, adolescents' peers and social contacts have considerable influence over their language. High school cliques often develop special words and phrases to reflect their feelings ("He's soooo cute!" or "What's your problem?"), their impressions of others (*nerd, geek*) or a group identity (Danesi, 1989). Talking "like all their friends do" helps exclude outsiders and prevents adults from understanding adolescent conversation and builds cohesiveness and a sense of belonging among group members.

Sometimes stuttering or dysfluent speech follows children into adolescence. The Speech Foundation of America (Fraser & Perkins, 1988)

Thinking about Society

The stage of formal operations also helps adolescents organize a more sophisticated, more consistent set of principles to guide their social and political thinking. Older adolescents tend to formulate more general principles, while younger adolescents are more concrete. More than 30 years ago Adelson & O'Neil (1966) asked fifth through twelfth graders about devising laws in a new island society. They found that children and young adolescents emphasize self-interest, individual rights, and immediate consequences (what's mine is mine), while older adolescents look more to the future and emphasize community needs (everybody must give up a portion of their land to build a school). Gallatin (1980) asked sixth and twelfth graders about their concepts of poverty and if poverty can ever be eliminated. Here are examples of two types of answers:

> 6TH GRADER: Maybe in the future, if they could enforce the law that all lazy people should work.

> 12TH GRADER: Yes, because this is the most highly advanced, richest country in the world. And the world knows we're putting money over here, overseas there, or we're putting money there. Money in Africa, putting a hell of a lot of money in Asia [and] the Southwest. I don't see why we should be putting money there while we still have poor here. (Gallatin, 1980, p. 350–351)

■ **Figure 15–5**

Consciousness-raising experiences help adolescents identify important belief systems.

The younger child is content simply to blame the individual for his economic condition; the older child sees other elements, namely the importance of the government and its citizens working together to identify the poor and give them the resources to move out of poverty and into self-sufficiency. True to formal operations, the 16 year old sees poverty as multidetermined while the sixth grader identifies only one causal factor to the exclusion of all others.

Adolescent Values

While conflict does arise between parents and children, the tension does not typically arise because of conflicting goals or values. For the most part, teens eventually adopt the values, beliefs, and goals of their parents, their social class, and their culture. Adolescents, especially those from immigrant families, can help socialize their own parents by explaining or interpreting the values and life-styles of the new culture.

Almost 35 years have passed since the "youth revolution" of the 1960s. Although the political climate of today is vastly different from that of 30 years ago, have adolescents' values changed or remained

values
principles or standards of an individual or a group; ideals

▶▶ I S S U E ◀◀

Adolescent Skinheads and Hate-Motivated Violence

Germany, 1942. Adolf Hitler moves to create the Nazi image of utopia—all one, all pure, and all white. The Aryan Race. Reaching that goal involved implementing the Final Solution—ridding German society (and eventually the world) of all "undesirables." The death camps, torture, and unspeakable horror became the outcome of Nazi hate.

Many Americans feel smugly self-removed from the World War II Nazi atrocities. *That* could *never* happen here, they assert. But it can and *is* happening here. Racial thinking has reemerged in the United States to a point where it can once again energize action. Acting alone or led by bands of 16–25 year old youth called Skinheads or Neo-Nazis, the perpetrators of hate crimes strike again and again. Hate crime in America is a rising phenomenon fueled by a conservatism among adolescents that hasn't been felt in the United States since the early 1960s. (Most national organizations prefer not to quantify the number of incidents, believing that the reporting may be tied to increases in violence).

As a youth gang movement, Skinheads are the fastest growing component of a white supremacist movement that is both widespread and diffuse. On November 11, 1988, ABC aired the infamous *Geraldo* program that contained some of the ugliest dialogue ever broadcast about blacks and Jews and ended in a fight provoked by the Skinheads on the panel in which Geraldo Rivera's nose was broken. Other incidents of racially-motivated violence have included drive-by shootings, knives and firearms on campus, and wilding in the Skinhead tradition of the "Boys Night Out," where Skinheads take to the street in search of victims.

Even the younger child is not exempt from the influence of the right-wing white supremacists. Distributed by underground software companies with names like "Adolf Hitler Software, LTD", some 140 Aryan or Nazi computer games are being circulated in Europe and the United States. The games test the player's skill in advancing through the Nazi SS by successfully gassing "inferiors" and being resourceful enough to sell the gold teeth of the dead to buy more poison and build more gas chambers. According to one poll in Austria, 39% of high school students were familiar with the games and 22% actually played them (Associated Press, May 1, 1991).

As we pass through a period of declining national authority and a worsening economy, the hate movement attempts to explain America's fall readily and easily. People are starting to listen. Some children and teens are listening, too.

Source: Excerpt is from an essay published in *The Nation*, "The American Neo-Nazi Movement Today" by Elinor Langer. Research for the essay was supported, in part, by grants from the Fund for Investigative Journalism and the Dick Coldensohn Fund. Copyright © 1990 by Elinor Langer. Reprinted by permission of Georges Borchardt, Inc. for the author.

An adolescent skinhead.

constant over time? Research indicates that compared with individuals who were teenagers in the 1960s, today's youth:

1. Are more concerned about themselves and less concerned about others and about society in general
2. Are more materialistic and concerned with financial security; "making more money" is an important factor in deciding to attend college (American Council on Education, 1989)
3. Are more politically conservative
4. Are less politically tolerant (Corbett, 1988)
5. Are more concerned about the realistic possibility of war. Males and adolescents from higher socioeconomic backgrounds had more positive views of war than females and individuals from lower socioeconomic backgrounds (B. W. Stevenson et al., 1988)
6. Are more skeptical about the fallibility of major social institutions such as Congress, big business, big labor, the courts, the schools, the president, and law enforcement agencies
7. Are more accepting of pornography, homosexuality, and premarital sex, with the liberal trend in sexual attitudes slowing, however, in the early 1980s (T. W. Smith, 1990)
8. Are more likely to consider childbearing as a matter of individual choice rather than as a duty to society
9. Consider self-expression and self-fulfillment important goals and continue to view nutrition, general health, self-improvement, and psychological or spiritual well-being as significant concerns

The attitudes of adolescents in the South are becoming similar to those of the North (Corbett, 1988). Adolescent values can have some influence on risk taking and peer choice (Millstein & Irwin, 1988). When young adolescents endorse parental values oriented toward altruism, they are less likely to report friendships with peers who had been involved in deviant activities (Whitbeck et al., 1989).

● The Search for Self

Ego Identity

Before puberty, school-age children generally have a well-developed sense of self. In the 10 or 11 years since their birth, they have developed their sex role identities, their moral standards, and their roles in their families, neighborhoods, peer groups, and schools. They have come to understand how people feel about them and how others judge their abilities. They may even respond when others say, "Hey, gorgeous!", "Hey, brain!", "Hey, jock!", or even, "Hey, dummy!" Good or bad, popular or not, school-age children know where they stand. They are

politically conservative
in the United States, a person who is politically cautious, opposed to government intervention, and supportive of a market-based economy

pornography
spoken, written, or visual materials designed to be sexually arousing

Skinheads
a NeoNazi youth group composed of young (teen/young adult) white males who engage in racially motivated violence and shave their heads to symbolize their beliefs

Nazi
a member or follower of the party that controlled Germany under the leadership of Adolf Hitler. Among other things, Nazis believe in white supremacy and the destruction of other races and peoples (i.e., Blacks, Jews, homosexuals, the disabled, etc.)

ego identity
having a sense of oneself as a person

personal identity
knowing "who you are" as a person

fully familiar with their bodies and their brains, their capabilities and their limitations.

But in adolescence something happens to disrupt the comfortable stability of childhood. The dramatic changes in this period require an extensive reevaluation of the self. Adolescents must make some satisfactory adaptation to their new sexual maturity, for instance. They must develop their own standards of behavior and reorient their lives with an eye to leaving school and making their way in work and in the social world. Thus, the main developmental task of adolescence is to build a new sense of personal identity by modifying existing self-perceptions, goals, and values and adopting new ones (Hamburg & Takanishi, 1989). To accomplish this task, the adolescent must achieve physical maturity, and make decisions about independence from parents, marriage, military service, and occupation (Shannon, 1982). This process begins at about age 11–13 when many children are experiencing the adolescent growth spurt. Eighty-one percent of preteen girls report being happy as they begin their search for self. Sixteen percent hope that nothing about them changes. Among those who wish they could change something about themselves, 13% aren't satisfied with their intelligence, 44% aren't satisfied with their looks, and 45% would alter their weight (Stark, 1989).

It takes 4 to 8 years to complete the growth cycle and reach physiological maturity. Adolescents require approximately an equal amount of time to reattain emotional and social stability and an enduring sense of personal identity. As suggested by M. L. Hoffman (1975), there is a relationship between the child's experiences and behavior in the elementary years and the child's behavior as an adolescent.

> The search for personal identity is not an easy one. Adolescents enter the threshold of personhood seeking an image they do not know, in a world they rarely understand, with a body that they are just discovering. They have a mixed desire to be an individual who wants to assert him or herself while, at the same time, fearing to lose the little security and reassurance that only family can offer. (E. T. Jones, 1969, p. 332)

It is important to understand that identity is not attained all at once. The adolescent vacillates considerably between childhood and maturity, at times seeming highly sophisticated and objective and at times lapsing into baby talk and tantrums. Erik Erikson (1956, 1963) devoted much of his professional life to studying the development of self-identity. He believed that the major crisis to be resolved during adolescence was that of *identity vs. role confusion*. According to Erikson, an individual's sense of identity maintains continuity with the past and corresponds with other people's appraisals of him as a person. Thus, someone with a firmly established sense of identity behaves in a fairly predictable, consistent manner. One who has not achieved self-identity is said to suffer from role confusion. People in this state exhibit aimless behavior

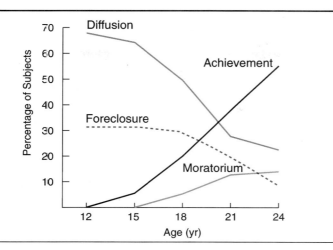

■ **Figure 15–7**

Percentage of adolescents and young adults in each of Marcia's (1980) four identity statuses.

fluctuations, since they have no consistent set of values, beliefs, goals, or procedures to guide their behavior.

Erikson believed that adolescents struggled with the two alternatives, identity achievement versus role confusion, until some satisfactory resolution occurred. According to James Marcia (1980), adolescents experiencing role confusion may go through one of four phases—foreclosure, alienated achievement, identity diffusion, and moratorium—in their search for a personal identity.

Foreclosure implies that the adolescent tends to adopt earlier roles or accedes to parental wishes without considering alternatives that may better suit his own needs and personality. For example, an adolescent may study medicine because his mother "always wanted a doctor in the family" or may become a teacher because "the family thinks teaching is an honorable profession." When children accept other people's plans prematurely and uncritically, they may discover what they really want to do or be only after years of medical school or college.

Some adolescents may consciously reject the roles their parents and society consider appropriate, and *alienated achievement* may evolve: The child takes on the role that is essentially the opposite of one he is expected to select. Some examples of alienated achievement are extreme— the son of a police captain that becomes a drug dealer, or the daughter of a conservative senator becomes involved in left-wing political activities. More often, alienated achievement is far less dramatic. For example, the son of a devoutly religious couple simply stops going to church with his parents, or a firstborn daughter who is expected to produce grandchildren may choose to remain childless.

Adolescents who undergo *identity diffusion* are apathetic about finding an identity. They have few commitments, values, or goals—whether

identity achievement
in Marcia's scheme, having acquired a sense of the roles one will play

foreclosure
in Marcia's scheme, premature identity formation, often occurring before alternatives more suitable to the person's own needs and characteristics are considered

alienated achievement
in Marcia's scheme, assuming an identity opposite to that expected

identity diffusion
in Marcia's scheme, a lack of clarity that arises when the person is not motivated to find an identity

■●▲ CONCEPT SUMMARY

Marcia's Identity Statuses

● *Foreclosure*
  – Adopt earlier roles
  – Accede to parent's wishes
  – Don't consider alternatives

● *Alienated achievement*
  – Select an identity in opposition to their expected identity

● *Identity diffusion*
  – Apathetic about identity search

● *Moratorium*
  – Experimenting with several roles
  – A stage of conflict/crisis

their own or their parents—and they typically appear unmotivated and uncaring:

> I'd like to be involved and busy but most of the time it's too much trouble. I just don't have the drive. I figure I can work at my dad's place if I need to or there's always welfare or unemployment if I need it. My parents get uptight with me and my teachers say they don't like my attitude. But I just think: tomorrow's another day. I guess I do care what happens to me, just not enough to do anything about it right now.

identity moratorium
in Marcia's scheme, experimenting with different roles during the process of identity formation

An *identity moratorium*—or temporary halt—may take place before the process of identity formation is complete. An individual may want to experiment with several roles before committing himself to just one. Moratorium is a state of identity limbo filled with conflict and crisis over unresolved questions about the future. This turmoil, which can be exaggerated by the physiological changes taking place during adolescence, may account for some of the anxiety, depression, and lack of commitment experienced by teens.

identity status
in Marcia's scheme, the phases an individual can pass through in search of a personal identity

Adolescents may pass from one identity status to another in their search for a stable sense of self. Philip Meilman (1979) found that 12 and 13 year olds start as identity diffused or foreclosed, with the majority shifting toward identity achievement by late adolescence or early adulthood. The percentage of individuals in moratorium increases to about 12% between 18 and 21 years of age and stays at that level

A Closer Look

(Bumpersticker) Hire an Adolescent While They Still Know Everything

For most other cultures, school *is* the adolescent's work. In American culture, however, 40% of 16 and 17 year olds have jobs during the school year and 80% of all high school seniors have had some work experience by the time they graduate (Steinberg et al., 1982). Most work simply to have more spending money, not because their parents or families are economically needy. And most are employed at minimum wage in retail sales, food service, or clerical positions.

   While working can help reinforce the American value of productivity, and can help teens learn how to manage money, people, time, and responsibility, there are some drawbacks associated with work. Adolescents who work 15–20 hours a week get lower grades, have higher absentee rates at school, and are less involved in school than their nonworking peers (Greenberg & Steinberg, 1986). And while working adolescents can afford nicer clothing and newer cars, they also are more likely to spend their earnings on drugs and alcohol, to spend less time with their families, and to drop

Stocking and retail work are common first jobs for teens.

out of school altogether. Adolescents who cannot delay gratification will have trouble reducing their hours at work to take college classes that only promise to build them a more solid financial future. Such adolescents may be inclined to quit school in order to work full time and realize short-term gains while ignoring the very real possibility that they are simultaneously limiting (perhaps for a lifetime) their ability for advancement and upward mobility.

through age 24. Moratorium is considered a healthy stage while identity diffusion and foreclosure are considered maladaptive since they are frequently associated with lower self-esteem, less-responsible behavior and more self-preoccupation (Marcia, 1980).

Vocational Identity

Career choice is a highly significant aspect of adult identity. Children as young as 5 or 6 think and talk about "what they want to be when

vocational identity
choosing a career or professional path for oneself

■ Figure 15–8

Entering the world of work: Welcome to McDonalds.

they grow up." Their choices tend to be unrealistic and impractical, of course, but they are also fun and exciting. For example, a young child is more likely to want to grow up to be an astronaut or a rock star than a postal clerk or a telephone operator. As children approach adolescence, their career choices become more realistic, but many still find it difficult to decide which profession or vocation is best for them (Mitchell, 1988). Final career choice is guided by several factors, including one's parents, peers, and personality.

Influences on Vocational Choice

In earlier times, children grew up to do the work their parents did. Girls became housekeepers and mothers, and boys learned their fathers' trades or became a partner in their fathers' businesses. Parents' occupations continue to influence their children's career choices, but not as directly as before. Fathers' occupations seem to have more influence on their sons' career choices; mothers' work tends to influence their daughters' career decision (Conger & Peterson, 1984). However, parents can have an effect in encouraging their children to be upwardly mobile by rewarding them for good schoolwork and supporting their plans to go to college or tradeschool. When parents have high ambitions for their children, the children generally aspire to occupations higher than their parents'. Peers play a role in recognizing a vocation as appropriate and attainable for a particular person; they also provide models for imitation. Children may not consider certain professions, for example, until they talk to age-mates who hope to become computer programmers, fashion designers, filmmakers, or geneticists.

Since 1988, more females than males select career options that require a college education. In 1988, 46% of white females and 6% of black females enrolled in college compared with 39% of white males and 4% of black males (National Center for Health Statistics, 1990). And more and more women are selecting nontraditional careers (carpentry, fire science, commercial fishing) even though high school based vocational counselors may advise a more traditional choice (Matlin, 1987). The slight differences that exist between males' and females' verbal and spatial achievement scores have no significant impact on their ability to succeed at the career of their choice.

TOWARD EFFECTIVE PARENTING

Helping Your Child Develop Critical Thinking Skills

In the decision-laced world of the adolescent, it's as important to know *how* to think as it is to know *what* to think. *Critical thinking* involves the ability to be skeptical about assertions and claims until they are objectively examined. The critical thinker demands that arguments be supported by facts before she accepts them. Thus, critical thinkers suspend judgment until they have had a chance to think about what was said or what is being asserted.

Since critical thinking helps individuals avoid errors of judgment, impulsive decisions, and intellectual malaise, it is a skill well worth developing. Here are some of the steps involved:

1. *Identify the issue.* What problem or assertion is involved? State the problem precisely so you can understand the issue at stake.
2. *Gather information about both sides of the issue.* Don't rely on what you've heard or what you think you know about something. Find out the facts from reputable sources.
3. *Evaluate the evidence and the reasoning behind it.* Carefully consider all the arguments on both sides and the assumptions that underlie them. Weigh the validity of all arguments so you will be able to decide what to believe.
4. *Draw a conclusion.* Considering all the variables, what is the best conclusion to draw at this time? Simple answers or solutions may be misleading.

critical thinking
skills that allow for analyzing and evaluating information

● Chapter Summary

● The fourth and last stage in Piaget's cognitive theory is the stage of formal operations. It involves the ability to think abstractly, to explore new possibilities, to solve problems systematically, to understand logic, and to use deductive reasoning.

● From an information processing perspective, the adolescent can hold more information in short-term memory and can process that information faster and more efficiently than the younger child. Processing strategies include rehearsal, organization, and elaboration.

● Psychometricians debate whether adolescents acquire new intellectual skills or whether they refine the intellectual skills they already possess (or some combination of the two).

● Egocentrism is present among all age groups and adolescence is no exception. Adolescent egocentrism is manifested in the great amount of time teens spend being self-absorbed and self-critical. Teens frequently assume that no one understands them and no one has had experiences like they have had. Their egocentric self-focus may also give them a false sense of invulnerability, making them think they are exempt from harm when, actually, they are not.

● Adolescents can use language in more complex and sophisticated ways because their thinking is less literal and more abstract. The language teens use to communicate with their peers may have a structure and meaning all its own. Speech dysfluencies create challenges to communication.

- In their moral decision making, adolescents have the capacity to take intentions into account, to look to the future, and to understand that one must behave as one's conscience dictates, even if this means breaking the rules. Men's and women's moral judgments may have a different focus.
- While there may be value differences between one generation of adolescents and another, adolescents typically embrace the values, goals, and ideals of their parents.
- Adolescents are faced with two identity attainment tasks: to achieve a stable sense of self (ego identity) and to establish oneself in the workforce (vocational identity).

● Observational Exercise

Formal operational thought provides adolescents with the ability to hypothesize, experiment, and reject or accept the assumptions they formulate. You can demonstrate these aspects of formal operational reasoning by replicating the pendulum problem devised by Piaget and Inhelder (1958).

Procedure: Test two same-sex adolescents, one 11–13 years old and one 15–18 years old. Show them how to use the pendulum and how to vary the swing, the length of the string, and the weight of the object suspended. Vary the weights by using a cup, pair of pliers, spoon, and comb (see the figure). Ask each student these questions:

1. What do you think is the most important factor in determining the speed of the pendulum's swing—string length, weight, force of the push, or some combination?
2. How would you go about testing your answer?

Observe and record the adolescent's problem-solving attempts. Does the subject approach the problem systematically, testing one assumption

Replicating the pendulum problem using household objects.

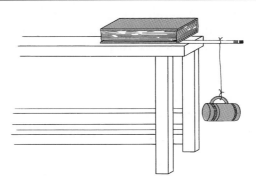

and then another? Does the subject arrive at the correct solution (that the length of the string is the factor affecting the speed of the swing)?

How does the approach of the younger child differ from that of the older one?

Note: Be sure the pendulum is working before the testing begins.

● **Recommended Readings**

Gilligan, C. (1983). *In a different voice: Psychological theory and women's development.* Cambridge, MA: Harvard University Press.

Hummell, D. L., & McDaniels, C. (1979). *How to help your child plan a career.* Washington, D.C.: Acropolis.

Social and Emotional Development During Adolescence

● **Adolescents and Their Families**

Adolescent/Parent Relationships

> My parents were so dumb when I was 17 and so smart when I was 21. I can't believe how much they learned in 4 years! (Paraphrase of original statement by Mark Twain)

Contrary to popular belief, parents continue to play an important role in the lives of their adolescents and, for the most part, adolescents and their parents love and value each other (J. P. Hill, 1987). This is not to say that occasional conflicts don't arise as parents and teens sort through their new roles and new expectations. For example, most parents acknowledge their teenage children's right as maturing preadults, to new privileges and increasing responsibilities. But they may also feel uneasy about relinquishing their roles of protector and advisor to children so inexperienced, who may be rash and unpredictable at times. And the adolescents themselves may feel ambivalence about such transitions. While they may protest any hint of parental intervention, calling it "interference," they may still be expecting their parents to do certain things for them and to provide guidance in certain situations (Siegel, 1982).

When adolescents do have a conflict with their parents, it is usually focused on a day-to-day behavior and not a deep-rooted value. For example, parents are much more likely to have an objection about homework or chores, dates, or the latest hairstyles than over political candidates, the place of religion in the family, or the family budget (Montemayor, 1983).

A small portion of teenagers say they can't stand to be around their parents and may try to escape their predicament by running away from home or becoming delinquent. As you look at Table 16–1 and compare

runaway
a dependent child who escapes their parent's control by leaving home without consent

delinquent
criminal acts committed by minors such as homicide, robbery, and rape as well as truancy, underage drinking, and running away

713

■ **Table 16–1** *Three Most Common Causes of Arguments with Parents*
According to Adolescents (Selected Studies, 1929–1982)

STUDY	SAMPLE	CAUSES OF ARGUMENTS
Lynd & Lynd (1929)	348 males, 382 females: grades 10–12	1 Time I get in at night 2 Number of times I go out during school nights 3 Grades at school
Punke (1943)	989 males, 1721 females: high school students	1 Social life and friends 2 Work and spending money 3 Clothes
Remmers (1957)	15,000 males and females: high school students	1 I'm afraid to tell parents when I've done wrong 2 Parents are too strict about my going out at night 3 Parents are too strict about the family car
Johnstone (1975)	1261 males and females: ages 13–20	1 Studying 2 Use of spare time 3 School
Rosenthal (1982)	630 males and females: ages 13–16	1 Drinking or smoking 2 Time and frequency of going out 3 Doing jobs around the house

Source: Papalia & Olds, *A Child's World*, Fifth Edition (McGraw-Hill, 1990) (after Montemayor, 1983). Used with permission.

the types of arguments that parents and teens have had over the last 60 years, you can see that the focus of adolescent–parent conflict has changed very little over time. Adolescents clash more frequently with their mothers than their fathers and girls report more quarrels than boys. Interestingly, both boys and girls identify their mothers as the person who has the greatest influence over their lives (Amato, 1989).

Margaret Matlin (1987) reports that a double standard exists among many parents. Parents seem to have an easier time granting freedom to their sons than to their daughters. Parents tend to worry more about their daughters' safety and sexual behavior, citing particular anxiety over possible pregnancy. When they argue with their children, instances involving girls tend to pertain to emotional issues such as the nature of the disagreements instead of the issue at hand (e.g., "You always ask when I'm tired") and who they date, while those involving boys tend to focus more on objective issues such as the use of the care and church attendance. Thus, it might be said that overall a daughter's adolescence causes parents more concern and tension than a son's.

Regarding attitudes about the family, sex differences appear among the children themselves. Perhaps as a consequence of differential socialization and the cultural tendency to hold female children emotionally close, girls are more ambivalent about their approaching autonomy

■ **Figure 16–1**

Parents continue to play an important role in the lives of their adolescent children.

than boys. While boys tend to seek freedom from the constraints of the family, girls look for ways to have freedom within it, striving for independence of thought and feeling within the family unit.

Although adolescents may protest limitations on their behavior, reasonable guidelines and school and household reponsibility still represent parental love and concern to them, and in the final analysis a fair use of control makes adolescence easier for everyone (Amato, 1989). In the face of the adaptations necessary as children become adolescents, parents can help their children grow into competent adults by demonstrating their interest; keeping the lines of communication open; providing independence within limits; exhibiting a low level of control and punishment; remaining loving, accepting, firm, flexible, reasonable, consistent, and trusting; setting a good example; and being democratic (J. P. Hill, 1987).

By late adolescence, much of the readjustment has been accomplished and parent/child relationships have usually improved considerably (Montemayor, 1983). Both adolescents and parents have gained confidence in the teenager's decision-making abilities. Moreover, parents are usually more comfortable with their children's independence and choices than at first and may even have come to think of the children as friends or colleagues. Although behavior and personalities will continue to evolve throughout the lifespan, it is during the late teens and early twenties that the adolescent's real and final liberation from parental domination takes place.

social competence
the degree to which individuals feel capable and adequate around others

■ **Table 16–2** *Negative Parent/Child Interaction Patterns*

PARENTING STYLE	ADOLESCENT'S REACTION
Overcoercive Parents are rigid, demanding, perfectionistic. High unattainable standards are set for the child. Parents often punish and belittle.	Models parent's behavior—becomes extremely self-critical or driving ("workaholic"). Rebellion or resistance. Withdrawal, regression; self-deprecation, poor self-esteem, depression, or other somatic symptoms.
Overpermissive Parents are indulgent and unable to set limits. Children are rarely punished or denied gratification.	Expects immediate gratification without effort or responsibility. Often unimpressed, bored with life; seeks out new thrills; poor self-control.
Overprotective Adolescent is shielded from the ordinary or imaginary hazards of living.	Adolescent models parent's behavior and becomes fearful; curiosity is stifled; self-esteem is low. Angry and rebellious toward parents, who restrict their experiences and promote their fears; poor self-esteem.
Rejecting Parents subtly or openly convey feelings of not wanting or loving the child. Adolescent may be belittled, scapegoated, or neglected.	Child feels unwanted, unloved, and worthless. May retaliate and provoke further rejection. This adolescent often has a great need for acceptance and approval, but the defense mechanisms used to cope with parental rejection (clowning, aggrandizement, and withdrawal) all interfere with the development of interpersonal relationships.
Distrustful Parents have little faith in the adolescent and assume the child has the same weaknesses they do.	The adolescent tends to confirm the parent's distrust.
Symbiotic One parent (usually the mother) has an abnormally close relationship with the teen. Normal contact with peers and society is restricted. The parent often has a "you and me against the world" attitude.	The adolescent may not develop an independent personality and may feel inadequate when separated from the parent. Curiosity and peer relationships are suppressed. Anger and hostility may develop toward the involved parent.
Vicarious Parents live through the child and pressure him or her to excel in areas important to the parents.	Initially, adolescents may try to comply with parents' wishes. Later, they may become anxious, rebellious, and/or withdrawn, since they never quite live up to their parent's expectations. Contact with peers may suffer because of their narrowed interests.

■ **Table 16–2** *(continued)*

PARENTING STYLE	ADOLESCENT'S REACTION
Inconsistent	
Parent's reactions and expectations are unpredictable. Often there is marital conflict and drug or alcohol abuse.	Adolescents in these situations feel frustrated and anxious, and may withdraw or rebel.
Neglectful	
These parents ignore their responsibilities to the adolescent. The child may be emotionally or physically abused.	Adolescents in such cases usually have poor self-esteem and cannot trust or rely on others. They may seek out individuals or groups to substitute for the parent. Often the adolescent is angry.

Source: Excerpted from Comerci et al., 1979.

Sibling Relationships During Adolescence

Positive sibling relationships seem to strengthen the adolescent's social competence (Amato, 1989). Adolescents who are more sociable feel closer to their siblings and are more popular with their peers than adolescents who report less sociability (Daniels, 1986). Conflicts still arise between siblings, however, over borrowed clothing, favors, space, privacy, and other such issues.

Divorce and Single-Parent Homes

In some families, adolescents have to cope with family stress in addition to their own developmental challenges. Sometimes the issues causing conflict are resolved, and sometimes they lead to divorce. Although adolescents may be better equipped to cope with divorce than younger children because they are more self-reliant, they are also more likely to become angry and blame the parents for spoiling *everything*. Divorce can pose a special problem for teenagers if their parents become regressive, compete with them for dates, or flaunt their sexuality (E. R. Anderson et al., 1989). Practical concerns can become burdensome, too, if the custodial parent forces the adolescent to assume too much responsibility—for example, the complete care of younger siblings or the total emotional support of the parent.

Adolescents who do not live with their biological fathers appear to be at special risk for truancy, running away, smoking, and getting into trouble with the law and at school (Dornsbusch et al., 1985). The pres-

truancy
being absent from school without permission or a valid excuse

In Touch

TOUGH LOVE
PO Box 70
Sellersville, PA 18960

Crisis intervention strategies with adolescents and their families

A Closer Look

Committed Teens: The Coming of Age of Private Mental Hospitals

Difficult, disruptive, disobedient adolescents—kids who once might have been sent to military schools or even juvenile-detention centers—are now being locked up in mental hospitals. Overall, inpatient hospitalization for children under 18 has increased from 82,000 in 1980 to more than 112,000 in 1986, the last year for which statistics are available. Most of that increase was in admissions to private hospitals; roughly 43,000 children were admitted to free-standing private psychiatric hospitals in 1986, compared to 17,000 in 1980 and 6,452 in 1970. These young people, four out of five whom are white and most of whom are middle or upper class, are frequently sent away by anxious or exasperated parents looking for help. Sometimes the adolescents are seriously disturbed; many have drug or alcohol problems. But in other cases they may be simply rebellious teenagers struggling with their parents over anything from the music they play to the boyfriend or girlfriend they choose.

Whatever the reason, they are often held behind locked doors, virtually without civil rights. In the name of therapy they are subjected to a strict regimen of reward and punishment—an application of behavioristic principles that may include stretches in solitary confinement (a small unfurnished white cubicle called "the quiet room") and physical restraint.

Despite the dramatic increase in admissions, the practice of hospitalizing difficult kids is not new. Patient-advocacy groups have been calling it a national disgrace for years.

Some hospitals have even set up employee-incentive programs to stir up new business.

Insurance companies, too, have had a hand in the growth of private hospitals, however inadvertently. Some policies cover up to 100 percent of inpatient costs, which can run from $12,000 to $27,000 a month. Therefore it's often less of a financial burden—and usually more convenient—for parents to commit their children than to get them effective counseling.

Making the right decision isn't easy, and many working parents, particularly single parents, are

Is your teenager running away without leaving home?

You see him but you can't touch him. Or talk to him. Or even get him to look you in the eye.

At first you thought it was only a phase, but it's not. He's stopped seeing old friends. He's lost interest in sports. He skips school.

You know his new crowd not only drinks but is using drugs, too.

After trying every kind of reward and punishment, you feel like there's absolutely nothing left to do.

But there's still one thing you can do. Call the Adolescent CareUnit.

The Adolescent CareUnit is a short-term, inpatient treatment program for youngsters who abuse alcohol and drugs. It's a professional, medically supervised program that's successfully treated thousands of adolescents across the country.

At the Adolescent CareUnit your child can learn how to cope with his problems instead of running away from them with alcohol. Or drugs. Or excuses.

But before he can help himself, you have to help him.

Call the Adolescent CareUnit and talk to one of our counselors. And give your child a chance to become part of your home again, instead of just living there.

ADOLESCENT CAREUNIT
Nobody cares the way we do.

A dramatic ad designed to encourage parents to place their troubled teen in a residential treatment center (the 90s term for a mental hospital for youth).

easily overwhelmed by their teenagers' growing pains.

The best hope for the future is to learn from the system's mistakes. Many patients' advocates believe that all teenage psychiatric admissions should be subject to stricter criteria and mandatory outside review. They urge parents to get second opinions if hospitalization is recommended for their children.

The problem is urgent. "Adolescence is tough," says Dr. Mary Jane England, a Prudential Insurance executive. "We remember ourselves—the foolish things we did. Thank God our parents didn't put us in hospitals for them."

Source: Darnton, N. "Committed Youth." *Newsweek.* July 31, 1989, pp. 66–72. © 1989 Newsweek, Inc. All rights reserved. Excerpted with permission.

ence of another adult in the home—a grandmother, uncle, mother's friend but not a stepfather—can insulate children, especially boys, from peer pressure to be antisocial. Apparently, a woman's parenting style is different when she is a single mother or a remarried parent than when she simply shares her home with another adult. Parental remarriage is most difficult for white prepubescent boys (E. R. Anderson et al., 1989). In 2 years, however, almost everyone makes a good adjustment and begins to feel more stable and satisfied with their lives (Enos & Handel, 86; Levin, 1988–1989).

● Peer Relationships

As we have seen, popular belief aside, parental influence does not necessarily diminish as peers come to play a greater role in the adolescent's life. Nor are the values of the adolescent peer group and of the teen's parents mutually exclusive. First, parent and peer values in middle class homes are usually more similar than different, since a person's family and friends usually share the same background (J. P. Hill, 1987). In fact, since peers and parents usually come from the same socioeconomic group, peers may actually reinforce the parents' values in the areas of education, sex, politics, vocation, and society. Second, neither parents nor peers have an impact on all areas of adolescent decision making (Hartup, 1983). Rather, their reach is limited to different areas. Peer values tend to have their effect in matters of music, fashion, entertainment, language, friends, and dates, while parents' influence is stronger on their children's decisions involving moral and social values and their understanding of the adult world. Concern about peer evaluation can encourage adolescents to make more responsible choices, however (Ford et al., 1989). Finally, there is considerable variation among individual adolescents. Highly self-confident, independent adolescents can profit

oppositional defiant behavior
being argumentative; disobedient

adolescent adjustment reaction
behavior problems some think are related to the process of making the transition from adolescence to adulthood

institutionalization
to place in an institution for care and treatment

residential care
care received while hospitalized or institutionalized

from the viewpoints of both parents and peers without being excessively dependent on either (Hartup, 1983). Interestingly, the most self-confident, independent, individualistic adolescents who are relatively unconcerned with being popular may find that peers flock around *them*.

Urie Bronfenbrenner (1974) has suggested that very peer-oriented children affiliate strongly with their same-age friends more because of parental disregard than the inherent attractiveness of the group. Such adolescents are forced to seek attention and approval from their peers because of the passive neglect and relative lack of concern they feel at home. These adolescents are also more likely than more independent children to hold negative views of themselves, to be less interested and less effective in school, to be involved in activities such as teasing, skipping school, listening to music, gossiping, or doing something illegal. And they are less likely to be involved in making or doing something, playing musical instruments, watching sports, or helping someone.

Still, there's no doubt at all that peers play an important role in adolescent development. The functions of adolescent middle class peer groups are the same as they were in childhood. Peers interact together, develop skills and interests appropriate for their age group, and share similar problems and feelings (Fasick, 1984). When German children are rejected, it's usually because they get into trouble, socialize with deviant peers, and engage in self-derogation (Silbereisen et al., 1989). Parental support can protect the child from experiencing all three of those reasons for rejection.

To find out about a typical day in the life of an adolescent, Csikszentmihalyi and Larson (1984) asked 2,734 high school students to write down what they were doing and with whom when the beeper they carried sounded at random. The results indicate that they spend about as much time engaged in productive activity as they do relaxing and having fun. Teens also spend more time with friends or alone than they spend with their families and tend to rate peer time more enjoyable than other time (Corsaro & Eder, 1990).

As you can see from Figure 16–2, when teens and peers get together, they are either in *groups* or with other-sex or same-sex *friends*. In the United States, high school freshmen like to spend time in same-sex groups; sophomores hang more with same-sex friends; juniors prefer mixed sex-groups, while seniors prefer to be with their boyfriends or girlfriends (Czikszentmihalyi & Larson, 1984). Thus, teen groups facilitate the transition from crowd to dyad and from friend to couple. Just "hanging" with the group and talking or passing the time is a favorite teen activity. Hanging provides a chance for like-minded teens to band together with friends, to "escape" parents, and to try out new ways of dressing and behaving. It also offers males and females a chance to initiate interaction in the relative security of a group situation (B. B. Brown et al., 1986). Other favorite passtimes include shopping, cruising, and partying.

self-derogation
actions or words designed to lessen one's self-importance

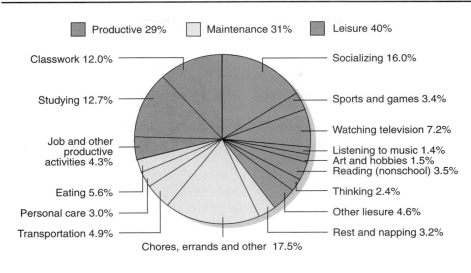

Productive 29%   Maintenance 31%   Leisure 40%

Classwork 12.0%

Studying 12.7%

Job and other productive activities 4.3%

Eating 5.6%

Personal care 3.0%

Transportation 4.9%

Chores, errands and other 17.5%

Socializing 16.0%

Sports and games 3.4%

Watching television 7.2%

Listening to music 1.4%
Art and hobbies 1.5%
Reading (nonschool) 3.5%

Thinking 2.4%

Other liesure 4.6%

Rest and napping 3.2%

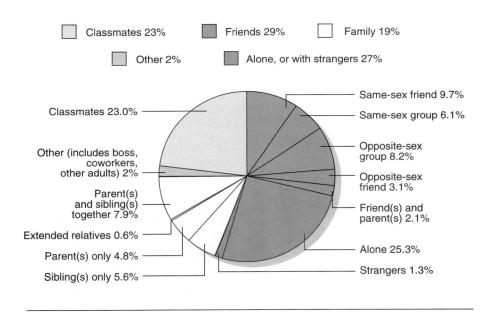

Classmates 23%   Friends 29%   Family 19%

Other 2%   Alone, or with strangers 27%

Classmates 23.0%

Other (includes boss, coworkers, other adults) 2%

Parent(s) and sibling(s) together 7.9%

Extended relatives 0.6%

Parent(s) only 4.8%

Sibling(s) only 5.6%

Same-sex friend 9.7%

Same-sex group 6.1%

Opposite-sex group 8.2%

Opposite-sex friend 3.1%

Friend(s) and parent(s) 2.1%

Alone 25.3%

Strangers 1.3%

Best Friends

Although adolescents spend considerable time in groups, most teenagers want to have one or two best friends. Best friends usually share a number of obvious characteristics, such as age, school grade, sex, socioeconomic status, and ethnic background (Hartup, 1983). Similarities in behavior, values, and interests in friends may also be apparent. The percentage of close friends who are members of the other sex increases with age, but even in later adolescence, same-sex friendships predominate, especially where best friends are concerned. Girls' friendships are typically more frequent, deeper, and more interdependent than those of boys. Girls reveal greater needs for nurturance, a greater desire to sustain intimate relationships, and more concern about losing friends. In contrast, boys tend to place more emphasis on the results of the friendship, such as having a congenial companion with whom to share common activities and having someone who will help you when you are in trouble (B. B. Brown et al., 1986).

The nature of friendship changes throughout adolescence. In a classic study, Douvan and Adelson (1966) identified three phases of friendship: the shared activity phase (11–13 years), the shared identity phase (14–16 years), and the individuality phase (17 and older). In early adolescence, friends need to be fun, easy to get along with, and unselfish. Best friends do things together. By the time children are 14 or so, their needs change: They don't need a playmate as much as a confidant. With an emphasis on sharing secrets, a friend is someone who must be supportive, understanding, sensitive, and trustworthy. By sharing their feelings and explaining themselves to each other, adolescent friends learn to understand themselves. Loyalty is an essential component of friendship during middle adolescence. As adolescents grow more confident and secure, friends are valued for their individuality and for what they can add to the relationship. As petty jealousy subsides, friends can appreciate each other's talents and abilities. Compatibility becomes the hallmark of good friends (Crockett et al., 1984).

■ **Figure 16–3**

A group of girls "hanging" after class.

■●▲ CONCEPT SUMMARY

Social Relations During Adolescence

● *Family*
- Most parents and teens have positive relationships.
- Conflict occurs because of role transition (the adolescent desires more mature treatment and the parent has difficulty thinking of her as more than a large child).
- Conflicts are usually focused on daily routine issues, biased expectations, and culture.
- The quality of the relationship improves steadily throughout adolescence.
- Popular, socially competent adolescents tend to get along with their siblings.
- Divorce can be a major disruption in the teen's life.

● *Peers*
- Peers hold values congruent to the teen's and the teen's parents.
- They are more influential on superficial aspects of living (fashion, choice of music) than on substantial issues.
- Because of problems at home, some teens are peer-dependent.
- Younger adolescents congregate in groups; older adolescents in pairs.
- Best friends are compatible, supportive, trustworthy, and confidential.

Special problems arise when the adolescent has to move and, as a consequence, changes schools. As a group, children who move lose touch with their friends and peer groups, and report less intimacy with their best friends. Boys who relocate have more difficulty coping than girls, experiencing more rejection among their new peers than residentially stable boys (Vernberg, 1990).

● Adolescents and the Schools

In the United States, approximately 95% of those individuals between the ages of 14 and 17 are enrolled in high school or remedial classes (U.S. Census Bureau, 1983). Less than 10% of this group attend private or parochial school, and fewer still attend so-called alternative schools or are taught at home. Higher levels of reading, math, and writing skills will be required of today's high school graduates to interact with infor-

parochial school
a school maintained and controlled by the church or some other religious group

alternative school
home schooling or some similar out-of-school education

mation systems, currently the fastest growing sector of the economy, and to compete in the global marketplace. There is also a growing need to attain conversation skills in languages other than English.

High school offers students an opportunity to excel academically and/or socially. Some environments are more encouraging than others and some students more highly motivated than their peers. Let's look at these two dimensions individually: the school environment and achievement motivation.

The School Environment

Perception of School Size

Adolescents may perceive their high schools to be either "large" or "small." Compared with students in larger schools, a greater proportion of students at smaller schools participate in school activities. Students at smaller schools feel more of an obligation and responsibility to participate directly and to play an active role; students in larger schools feel more comfortable as bystanders, obtaining vicarious enjoyment from the efforts of others.

When asked to evaluate their school experience, students from small schools indicated that the satisfaction they derived from school focused more on improving their capacity, feeling challenged, or closely cooperating with their peers. Students from larger schools, on the other hand, reported deriving pleasure from other people's activities ("I enjoyed listening to the arguments of both debaters") and from belonging to something "big." Academically or socially marginal students often feel like outsiders in the school system, overlooked and irrelevant. It is more difficult for the marginal student to "get lost" in small schools than in large schools, because everyone is easily accounted for and few people are left out of activities and projects. As a result, marginal students are less likely to drop out of small schools, despite their grades, IQ test scores, and family backgrounds. In larger schools, the dropout rate is considerably higher. The main advantage of large schools is the diversity of experiences they offer.

The Teachers

As with younger children, teachers play an influential role in adolescent development. The right teachers may help adolescents to overcome limitations and make the most of their talents and interests, whereas teachers who are ill-suited for working with young people generally, or with particular kinds of young people, may have serious—sometimes disastrous—effects on their students. School success is facilitated by teachers who take education seriously, care for students as people, treat them as responsible, capable humans, and expect success (J. S. Coleman et al., 1981). Students also cite good organization and actively involving stu-

■ **Figure 16–4**

(left) In class and on-task in a high school classroom. (right) High school graduation is a proud moment for everyone.

dents in the learning process as important factors. Teachers who are hostile or dominating tend to have a negative effect on student adjustment.

Achievement Motivation

Achievement motivation, or the tendency to persist when challenged or the need to accomplish certain goals, can be an important predictor of school success (Dweck & Elliot, 1983). Teens, especially boys, who are high in academic self-esteem attribute success to dependable personality characteristics such as high ability and attribute failure to overlooking something controllable like task difficulty or making insufficient effort (Talwar et al., 1989). Some girls, on the other hand, are credited with effort and ability when they succeed but may receive negative personal feedback from parents or teachers when they fail (hearing "I guess you really aren't good at math after all" or "If you'd stay off the phone, you could apply yourself to your work"). When girls' abilities get blamed for failure, they may develop learned helplessness or lower achievement expectancy and the tendency to give up rather than persist or even try (Parsons, 1983). Hyperactive adolescents may continue to be poor achievers if they retain the qualities of poor impulse control and inattention into high school (Lambert, 1988; Fischer et al, 1990). Ideally, reshaping expectations and attributions should take place prior to adolescence, but it's never too late to undercut learned helplessness by:

academic self-esteem
how school performance figures into one's evaluation of oneself

1. Reinterpreting failure by stating, "You can do it if you try harder/ get a tutor" or something similar
2. Exposing such adolescents to other teens who demonstrate persistence and initiative
3. Encouraging crediting ability and effort, not luck or the easiness of the task, as the reason for success
4. Underscoring success by saying, "You really studied hard," "You're really good at this," or "You're really smart"

5. Avoiding destructive criticism ("Your baby brother could do better") or unreasonably high expectations
6. Providing additional assistance for students who are hyperactive or learning disabled

Does the high-achieving academic star want to be remembered as a brilliant student? Usually not. While mainstream adult society values academic success, social success in adolescent society is measured more in terms of popularity, athletic prowess, and leadership. Although 80% of adolescents polled saw academic achievement as important in shaping their future, being remembered as a brilliant high school student is one of the last things on most of their minds (Fasick, 1984). Academic success in adolescence is related to higher social responsibility involving social commitment, openness to sociopolitical change, and tolerance of individual and culture differences (Greenberger, 1984). As students grow toward adulthood, the hallmarks of adolescent culture become less and less important as more adult values and long-term goals surface.

sociopolitical change
modification of the existing social and governmental power structures

● Emotional Development

The emotional focus is different for boys and girls during their teen years. For adolescent girls, the most frequent, intense, and long-lasting emotions involve relationships and experiences with others. For boys, activities and situations where performance is assessed is more emotionally charged (Stapley & Haviland, 1989). Boys are more likely than girls to deny having emotional experiences. (The only emotion they didn't deny in their retrospective reports was *joy*. Interest, surprise, shyness, guilt, sadness, fear, anger, disgust, contempt, shame, and self-hostility were assessed). Joy is the most salient positive emotion for boys and girls; anger is the most salient negative emotion.

self-hostility
antagonism directed at the self

The source of emotional experiences changes with the age of the adolescent (Stapley & Haviland, 1989). Prior to puberty, the most memorable emotional experiences occurred in the context of the child's family; after puberty, their most salient emotional experiences were with their peers rather than with their families or alone. Adolescent boys don't report having emotional experiences when they are with a girl, on a date, or simply talking. Girls, on the other hand, frequently report feeling emotions when they are with a boy in the same context.

Anger is one emotion that parents may mistakenly encourage their teens to suppress or deny. The nondestructive *expression* of anger is highlighted in the accompanying feature.

Self-Esteem

A large-scale study of 2,400 girls and 600 boys at 36 public schools in 12 communities commissioned by the American Association of Univer-

A Closer Look

Acknowledging Anger

Some parents' philosophy of family happiness involves denying or mislabeling unhappy emotions. They reason that if people don't *act* angry, they won't *feel* angry; and if family members don't *feel* angry, then everyone will get along and be happy.

There's just one problem. Emotions don't work that way.

When people aren't allowed to acknowledge their anger, they become confused about this emotion. If the rule is "No angry people here," then when feelings of real anger start to well up inside, the feelings are feared, evaded, or spirited away. Denial and avoidance of emotions leave people poorly equipped to deal with their own anger or the anger of others.

Rather than being held captive by negative emotions, psychologists recommend a procedure for understanding and accepting our emotions.

1. *Acknowledge your anger.* Call it what it is. If you feel irritated, annoyed, or displeased, you're probably angry. Labeling your emotions correctly will help you understand what you're feeling in any particular circumstance. Avoid shying away from a label because you're not "supposed" to feel angry or disappointed with a child because you are a woman, because you are a parent, or because you are a professional.

2. *Accept your anger.* Anger is a natural part of one's emotional life. It's OK to feel angry. Everyone does now and then. Angry feelings don't go away if you don't accept them, they just go underground and may be transformed into depression, powerlessness, or over-control. When a person says to herself, "I'm angry and I have every right to feel this way," it validates her reaction, provides a focus, and then encourages the person to take control of the situation.

3. *Channel your anger.* While angry feelings are normal and understandable, anger is not a license to discharge negative emotions in unacceptable ways. Hurting another person when one is angry should not be tolerated. Neither should destroying the property of others. The angry person needs to stay in control as much as possible. Time and distance can often help reestablish control. Saying, "I'm much too angry now to talk to you about what you did. I need some time to cool down" is a fine solution. Buy some time, take a walk, sleep on your feelings, count to 10—whatever works for you. Then anger has a two-fold positive purpose— to help vent some nasty feelings and to open a channel of communication about why the circumstance/exchange provoked anger in the first place. The goal is not to avoid becoming angry, but to avoid losing control while angry.

Source: Israeloff, R. "Anger." *The Sacramento Bee*, 1992. Used with permission.

sity Women and released in 1991 found that the self-esteem gender gap widens during adolescence. Girls emerge from adolescence with a poor self-image, relatively low expectations from life, and much less confidence in themselves and their abilities than boys. When elementary school boys were asked how often they felt "happy the way I am," 67% answered "always". By high school, 46 percent still felt that way, but for girls the figures dropped from 60% to 29%.

self-image
like self-perception, the person's idea of him or herself as an individual with specific characteristics and behaviors

Why does girls' self-esteem plummet? If it were hormonal, then all girls would lose comparable degrees of self-worth at roughly the same time. Apparently, girls' self-confidence is not sabotaged by their own genes. Sometimes between the ages of 11 and 16 girls become aware that people hold unequal expectations for males and females. After finding out that people believe males can do things, boys end up with higher self-esteem as they progress through adolescence. In contrast, when females discover that adults, including their teachers, believe that most females *cannot* do things, they begin to lose self-confidence and correspondingly lose interest in subjects like math and science.

Just how are these expectations conveyed? Whether consciously or unconsciously, teachers treat boys and girls differently in the classroom. Because boys are expected to achieve, they are given more attention and better-quality attention by adults. In the classroom, they are asked more questions and given more feedback than girls. The result is that boys end up feeling pretty good at a lot of things, are more willing to speak up in class, to argue with their teacher or an authority figure if they think they're right, and to believe that they can achieve their career dreams. Adolescent girls, on the other hand, are much likely to feel "they are not that smart" or "not smart enough to achieve their career goals." African-American girls were much more likely to retain their self-esteem in high school than white or Hispanic girls, but they felt less positively about their teachers and schoolwork as time went on. Obviously, teachers and parents have a great opportunity to reverse the trend of declining self-esteem for their female children and students by acknowledging their abilities and conveying their confidence in them as women.

Issues in Identity Formation

School Dropout

school dropout
a student who voluntarily leaves school before completing their training or receiving their degree

Today, 15–20% of all United States high school students leave school before earning their diplomas (U.S. Census Bureau, 1991). Most of these adolescents are nonwhite students from poor families. Asian-American students are the *least* likely to drop out; Native Americans are most likely to leave school without graduating. When the impact of poverty is eliminated, the educational attainment among whites, blacks, and Hispanics disappears (Center for Educational Statistics, 1987).

"pushout"
adolescents who are forced from the school system because of pressure, hostility, or indifference

Reasons for leaving high school are many are varied. Some students are *pushouts*, forced from the educational system by subtle pressures or indifference to their needs. Students with learning disabilities or behavioral disorders may fall into this category. Some students' parents force them to leave home. In these cases, the child must quit school to get a job to support themselves. Other students are pushed out of the educational system because the school facilities available to them are too dangerous to attend. Despite laws in each state making school attendance mandatory until age 16, some adolescents never attended school, either because their parents avoided enrolling them or because no school is available to meet their special needs.

Dropouts, on the other hand, are those students who voluntarily leave the system before completing their education. Some of these students become alienated from school and simply don't want to attend classes any longer. Others fail to see the relevance of the courses being offered and are frustrated and bored by the low marks they earn, the lack of interest of their teachers, and the discrimination they experience from peers and teachers. Usually, these students lack ambition, are addicted to drugs, are pressured by friends who dropped out, want to start working, or have other personal reasons for dropping out.

Besides an adolescent's personal motivations for quitting school, his family has a marked influence on school success. School dropouts typically receive less encouragement from their parents about school activities and vocational plans than school graduates. When parents are indifferent about school and don't value education, it's hard for their children to maintain a positive attitude and to remain in the educational system. In general, parents who accept and understand their children as people are more likely to foster school success—and success in other life areas as well—than parents who don't recognize their adolescent's positive attributes. In this same vein, dropouts are more likely than graduates to have low self-esteem, feelings of inferiority, negativism, and feelings of hostility and resentment. As we have seen, low self-esteem and accompanying negative feelings can result from poor parent–child relationships.

Peers often have a major influence on adolescents' decisions on whether or not to stay in school. Most adolescents want to do what their friends are doing. Students whose peers dislike school or are eager to have full-time jobs may drop out because they strongly identify with the others. Lack of peer acceptance and resulting social isolation can also contribute to an adolescent's decision to leave school.

Dropping out of high school is likely to result in serious vocational and social problems. High school prepares adolescents to compete in the job market by providing instruction in basic skills, increasing knowledge, and certifying general competence. Many employers simply will not hire an applicant who is not a high school graduate. And this trend is growing as our society becomes increasingly involved in high technology.

When dropouts do find work, only about 15% have jobs that require technical skills. Most wait tables, work in retail stores and offices, babysit, or work in factories, on labor crews, or on farms. More than half of the dropouts surveyed regretted leaving school (Center for Educational Statistics, 1987).

The private sector as well as the government has developed programs to help teens at risk for dropping out stay in school. Entrepreneurs have offered to pay for certain youths' college education if they would graduate from high school. Government programs like Upward Bound have helped low-income parents and their teens work within the system to achieve success in high school and then go on to college. A toll-free national hotline has been established to offer advice for helping students facing academic penalties because of school absence (1–800–NET-WORK). In addition, parents, teachers, and school boards have been working on modifying the curriculum to be more responsive to student's training needs.

Runaway/Homeless Youth

The myth is that they're adventurous teens—they hang out all the time because they chose fun and friends over work and responsibility. The truth is that they don't want to be on the streets. But their parents don't want them, and society can't offer them legitimate work because they're too young and don't have a high school diploma. The street is the only place left.

Accurate numbers are hard to come by, but an estimated 1 to 1.3 million teens are homeless because they've run away from home or been pushed out ("thrown away") by their parents. Eight-sex percent of runaways report some form of physical or sexual abuse; 13% have been hurt seriously enough by their parents to require a trip to the hospital emergency room (Chance, 1989). Overlapping that, 44% of runaways report escaping long-term crises involving drug or alcohol abusing parents or stepfamily problems, while 20% are running away from short-term crises like divorce, illness, death, or school problems (Hersch, 1988). Close to half of the kids are encouraged to leave home or get thrown out of the house because their parents can't afford to support them, think they're a burden, actively dislike/reject them, or because their behavior is considered offensive/unacceptable (they're pregnant, "incorrigible," *not* on the football team, are homosexual, or whatever). Only half of the runaways/throwaways have a realistic hope of returning home, usually because home continues to be a dysfunctional place where parents remain abusive or uncaring (Hersch, 1988).

What are teens who hit the streets looking for? Safety, security, and someone to love them. Unfortunately, it is not the social workers and the psychologists who meet runaways on street corners and in the train and bus stations, but the drug dealers, pimps, and pornographers. Soon teens find themselves swapping one type of grim existence for another. Over half of the teens who have been on the streets for a month or longer becomes involved in prostitution. Their involvement may range from pimping to turning 8–12 "tricks" in a 24-hour period depending on what they need to "survive." They may become drug involved/

addicted either at their pimp's urgings or because it dulls the pain. Neurophysiological damage from drug use may impair their memory, attention, ability to learn, and ability to cope either temporarily or permanently. Homeless teens may experience abuse at the hands of their peers, their "johns," or their pimps. Emotional disturbance is widespread in the form of depression, antisocial behavior, suicidal thoughts, and self-destructive behavior.

In addition to the exploitation, abuse, and psychological trauma of runaway and throwaway youth, perhaps the biggest threat to longterm well-being is the risk of AIDS. Sexual involvement, more than anything else, increases the likelihood of exposure. Because homeless teens are desperate for money, there's hardly anyone they won't sleep with. Health professionals believe homeless teens know about AIDS but ignore the risk. If the teen is a prostitute, customers pay more if they don't have to use condoms. In addition, runaway teens may live with hustlers, sex-show performers, or IV drug users who may infect them even if they *aren't* prostitutes themselves. There is also the risk of rape and sexual assault. Maybe teens are willing to take risks because they think death from AIDS (or anything else) would not be a catastrophe but a blessing. Mostly, there are so many ways to die every day on the street that they cannot focus on something that may kill them years from now (Hersch, 1988). It's unlikely that the United States will experience an AIDS epidemic among adolescents because of the latency period between the onset of the infection and the appearance of symptoms. But there is an epidemic of *exposure,* where over 50% of homeless teens who hustle every night will test HIV positive within 10 years (Hersch, 1988).

Many of these youth need ongoing intensive therapy and health care but seldom get it. Shelters are designed to keep homeless teens for no more than 15 days. In that time, it's difficult to perform an adequate diagnosis for their myriad problems, let alone offer effective treatment. *Covenant House* in New York and *Children of the Night* in Los Angeles offer food, shelter, medical care, and support for street teens. For all their good work, money is always tight, space is in short supply, and volunteers are always needed.

Juvenile Delinquency

Juvenile delinquency involves more than just petty misbehavior. Is the teen who shoplifts, cuts school, or defaces property a juvenile delinquent? Not unless shoplifting, truancy, or vandalism is part of a *pattern* of illegal or destructive behavior. If the truancy, underage drinking, running away, or disobedience is chronic or habitual, then the teen will be charged with a *status offense*—a behavior that is legal *except* when it is committed by a minor (a person under 16 or 18 years of age, depending on the state) (Gold & Petronio, 1980). Murder, rape, and robbery are considered criminal acts no matter who commits them. Some-

---

In Touch

COVENANT HOUSE
"NineLine"
1-800-999-9999

A runaway hotline that offers counseling, shelter, and other referral information

NATIONAL RUNAWAY SWITCHBOARD
1-800-621-4000

Helps parents locate runaway youth and encourages teens to contact their families

juvenile delinquent
a lawbreaker under the age of 16 or 18 (depending on the state)
shoplifting
stealing merchandise from a store while pretending to be a customer
vandalism
willful or malicious damage to public or private property
status offense
an act that breaks the law only because it is performed by an underage person (i.e., running away, truancy)

A Closer Look

Wilding: Hurting Others Just for the Fun of It

We've heard it before. Oh, those impetuous youths! Out for a good time. Usually that means something innocuous like tying up traffic downtown by "cruising," playing car stereos loud enough to "share the sounds," or converging *en mass* at a favorite fast-food establishment for some "eats."

Well, no more. The innocence of youth has been shattered by a new word in our vocabularies, *wilding.* Wilding describes the behavior of groups of teens who have fun by hurting others. They commit atrocious crimes against others in the name of "having a good time." Generally, these are kids who are not gang members and who are without criminal records.

Wilding was responsible for the fate of the Central Park Jogger, a 28 year old female investment banker who was brutally beaten, knifed, and raped by males age 14–17. She was found on an isolated road, covered with mud, and almost dead from brain damage, loss of blood, and exposure. Why did they do it? "It was fun!" said one of her suspected attackers in lockup as he and

his compatriots nonchalantly whistled at policewomen and sang a popular song of the time, "Wild Thing." In 1987 three Brooklyn teens set fire to a homeless couple. When the rubbing alcohol they poured on them wouldn't ignite, they went to a local station for gasoline instead. That worked. A year later in rural Missouri, three teens killed a friend just to know what it would feel like to kill somebody! What could they possibly be thinking as they attacked the teen victim over and over again with baseball bats? "This is fun!"

There are many complex reasons for wilding. But one of the most compelling is the glorification of violence in the movies, on television, and in music. The message seems to be: it's OK to enjoy brutality and suffering as long as you find it entertaining. Parents need to teach their children to make wise choices about what they see and what they do. But the entertainment industry also must assume some responsibility. Is it reasonable for them to claim they have the right to distribute anything they choose under the protections afforded by the First Amendment? Or is it important for society to remind the entertainment business that making a buck at any moral cost is a decision that ultimately costs us all.

Data source: *Newsweek,* May 29, 1989.

"wilding"
lawbreaking (malicious vandalism or assaults) perpetrated by adolescents and young adults for the purposes of self-entertainment and pleasure

times (depending on the state) the courts treat teenage criminals differently from adult criminals; sometimes, however, minors may be tried as adults no matter what their age. Some states (like Florida) even permit granting minors the death penalty for serious or violent crimes.

SEX DIFFERENCES Eighteen year olds, especially 18 year old males, are the most violent faction of our society. More than 90% of all juveniles in correctional facilities in the United States are males (U.S. Department of Justice, 1988). In the United States, about 3 or 4 juvenile males are arrested for each minor female. Why do these sex differences exist? By the time boys are 13 or 14 years old, they are bigger and stronger than before and violence is more effective against both male and female foes. Also, peer society condones (even encourages) aggression among boys but discourages it among girls. For example, in some parts of this country, if you're male and don't play football in high school or you've never been in "trouble," you're considered to be a wimp. Similarly, the girl "who can beat up all the boys" might be very popular in the fourth or fifth grade, but by the time she's in the eighth or ninth grade, she's probably more of a flirt than a pugilist. (If older girls have black eyes, it's most likely because they were struck by their boyfriends or parents and *not* because they got into a fight at school.) In addition, the juvenile crime statistics may favor males because they commit more crimes against outsiders and hence are more likely to be reported. Females are more likely to be involved in status offenses that involve the immediate family (running away, drug use, truancy) or that involve consenting males (prostitution). Thus, many crimes committed by female juveniles remain undiscovered, or if discovered, unreported or unprosecuted.

■ **Figure 16–5**

Just because you're young doesn't mean you can get away with murder—or any other crime.

CAUSES OF DELINQUENCY Delinquency is not a social class phenomenon. It exists at all levels of society. Poor or underclass delinquents are more likely to come to public attention because their parents can't keep them out of the criminal justice system—they can't afford to "settle" with the authorities or the victims or to pay to have their sons or daughters placed in rehabilitation or psychiatric care. The single most predictive indicator of adolescent delinquency is the child's relationship with his parents (Patterson & Stouthamer-Loeber, 1984). In general, the better children get along with their parents, especially their fathers, the less likely it is that they will engage in delinquent behavior. Mutual hostility, neglect, abuse, excessive permissiveness, rejection, and a lack of cohesiveness typify relationships between parents and delinquent teens (Steinberg, 1987). Frequently, the parents of adolescent offenders just don't care or can't keep track of their child's whereabouts. When problems are brought to the parent's attention, they are apathetic about rule breaking and tend to forego effective discipline in favor of lecturing or threatening. When parents make time for their children and make a commitment to parenting, they can teach their children to behave responsibly within the context of the law.

It should come as no surprise that poor parent–child relations also affect delinquents' views of themselves. Juvenile offenders almost always have low self-esteem and a negative self-image, tending not to like or value themselves and to picture themselves as "lazy," bad, or ignorant or inadequate. Early lying and stealing may predict future crime (Loeber & Dishion, 1983). As young children, chronic delinquents engaged in a *variety* of antisocial acts in a *variety* of settings—home, school, neighborhood. In these cases, the behavior is not just a "phase" to be outgrown because it's unbecoming as an adult. Once antisocial or

rehabilitation
the act of restoring an individual to a state of useful activity by helping them turn away from or cope with events that lead to inefficient or ineffective behavior

law-breaking behavior is established, it is rarely relinquished (Farrington, 1982).

HELPING DELINQUENTS According to the Center for the Study of Social Policy (1991), the juvenile incarceration rate for the state of California went up 82% between 1979 and 1987. Similar, though less dramatic, increases in juvenile crime have been felt all over the nation. Even though incarceration is commonplace, sending adolescent offenders to prison is the *worst* way to rehabilitate them. Very few adolescents are hardcore incorrigibles or sociopaths with no regard for the well-being of others and no remorse for the harm they do (Mulvey & LaRose, 1986). With the exception of first degree murder and kidnapping, California youths serve longer terms for first-time offences than adults for the same crimes (Associated Press, June 2, 1991). Most juvenile offenders refer to the juvenile justice system as a "merry-go-round"—the recitivism rate is 80%. Two-thirds of them are stoned or drunk at the time of their crime, and they rarely receive treatment for substance abuse. Some metropolitan cities are experimenting with "Teen Courts" where juvenile offenders committing "lesser" crimes are judged by their peers and the sentences that are handed down are legally binding. The hope is not only to lighten the load on the system but to help teens take their crime and punishment more seriously.

Unlikely the stereotype, many of the youth in prisons are passive-dependent adolescents who got into trouble trying to conform to their peer groups' expectations. Typically these youngsters have had no adequate parental supervision in their lives, have had considerable time on their hands—usually as unemployed dropouts with no plans for the future—and are easily bullied by others. About one-third of the juvenile offenders were child victims themselves. Abused or neglected by their parents, living in an atmosphere of violence or economic chaos, these kids don't care about other people because people don't care about them.

The best treatment for delinquency is probably prevention. Specifically, we can encourage positive parent–child interactions, intervene to halt abuse, monitor children's social and cognitive development, and provide early detection and treatment of problems with self-esteem, school, and family. Cessation of delinquency is part of a broader change in the adolescent's behavior. Job-training programs and drug treatment centers are desperately needed. When delinquent adolescents' drug abuse declines, they usually change social networks and experience improved relationships with their families. In this way, they are less likely to continue their delinquent patterns (Mulvey & LaRosa, 1986).

Gangs

In big cities and small towns, groups of adolescents are banding together into gangs to establish power, territory, and influence. Gangs represent most racial and ethnic groups. Gang members from one generation may be succeeded by their children. Sometimes gang members are recent arrivals from other nations who haven't successfully assimilated into American culture. Feeling alienated or disenfranchised from the status quo, these teens drop out of school, have trouble finding employment, and feel that their traditional ways aren't respected.

Violence is the mainstay of the gang structure. Generally, the targets of violence are rival gang members, but many times innocent individuals get caught in the cross fire or are victimized by drive-by (even *bike-by*) shootings. Helping youths stay out of gangs involves developing support networks around high-risk kids that provide them with someplace to go, something productive to do, and someone who genuinely cares about them (Bazar, 1990).

Common Psychological Disturbances

Some degree of anxiety, stress, and conflict arise in all developmental phases. However, there is evidence that psychological problems are more common at certain ages than others. For children, referrals to psychological and psychiatric clinics tends to peak between 4–7 years, 9–11 years, and 14–16 years (Berg, 1984). Each of these age ranges represent a transitional period in which physical, cognitive, or social developments or changes in parent–child interactions may temporarily disrupt the child's psychological equilibrium. During adolescence, these changes are at work simultaneously. Aggressiveness in childhood is a significant predictor of maladjustment in adolescence (Lerner et al., 1988).

psychiatric care
treatment received under a psychiatrist's care in a hospital setting

Mental disorders are experienced by 18–22% of the nation's adolescents (Office of Technology Assessment Study, 1991). Comprehensive descriptions of the treatment of mental disturbances in adolescents may be found elsewhere. Here we will discuss the most significant forms of adolescent emotional disturbance: anxiety reactions, depression, suicide, and adolescent schizophrenia. (Eating disorders are discussed in Chapter 14).

Anxiety Reactions

Anxiety is a normal reaction to some life situations. However, anxiety that is excessively strong and debilitating or that appears to be chronic may be a sign of a clinically significant disturbance. Anxiety reactions are more common in adolescence than in middle childhood, and their frequency appears to increase particularly in the period between the onset of puberty and early adulthood.

anxiety reaction—(also called an anxiety disorder)
a psychological disturbance marked by a combination of fear, anxiety, and attempts to avoid the anxiety

The psychological symptoms of an acute anxiety reaction are a sense of impending doom, restlessness, agitation, and tearfulness. Physical symptoms are nausea, vomiting, dizziness, headache, sweatiness, trembling, and respiratory disturbance. Fear of failure, poor social adjustment, poor physical health (e.g., cancer, heart disease), and disturbed parent–child relations are all examples of problems that can trigger anxiety reactions (Bowen, 1985).

Consider this description of a classic anxiety reaction:

> John, a boy of sixteen, who made straight *A*s in grade 10 and *D*s and *F*s in grade 11 was referred to a psychiatrist because he missed 120 class periods in one semester. He said, "I know my parents want me to do well and last year that was enough, but now I hassle with them all the time, particularly my mother. I want to go into a profession, but this worries me, and I can't get my head together enough to do any work." (L. C. Miller, 1974, p. 345).

What John doesn't mention here is that he lost two teachers he especially liked when he entered the eleventh grade and that he neither knew nor liked his other teachers. Pressures from home, his own insecurities, and the need to cope with changes in his classroom situation combined to create enough anxiety to encourage John to deliberately miss school. Although class absence helped him avoid the stress of changing teachers, it did nothing to minimize the conflicts and pressures at home or ease his own self-doubts.

In contrast to anxiety in most adults, adolescents' anxiety reactions are usually tied to specific and apparent causal factors, as in John's case. Thus, clinical intervention techniques that can be focused quickly with adolescents are generally more successful than with adults. And intervention is highly recommended where adolescents experience long-term anxiety, for such reactions can become chronic and actually solidify into a way of life.

Depression

depression
a psychological disturbance ranging from mild to severe characterized by feelings of worthlessness, unhappiness, powerlessness, and guilt.

Though usually temporary, depression is fairly common among adolescents. Depression generally manifests itself in one of two ways in adolescents: in feelings of emptiness, loneliness, and isolation, or in trouble concentrating in school (Herskowitz, 1988). Often the problem centers around the difficulty of finding a suitable adult identity. Where this is the case, the depression has a high likelihood of being eliminated through treatment.

A second type of depression, and one more difficult to treat, stems from a series of disappointments or tragedies. Where this is the case, a fairly insignificant event such as a poor exam grade or a broken date can be the "last straw" that triggers the depression. Encouraging the adolescent to "snap out of it" is not a viable option under these circumstances, since people in this state feel they have no alternatives left to try and nowhere else to turn (Hodgman, 1983). Young people who have reached this level of despair are likely suicide risks.

Depression seems to manifest itself differently for adolescent-aged boys and girls. Self-hostility is an important predictor of depression for girls, while anger is a more important predictor for boys (Stapley & Haviland, 1989). Adolescent boys tend to blame their depression on concerns about not performing well, while girls tend to cite interpersonal problems. Common symptoms of depression in boys and girls also differ. Boys tend to become irritable, have sleep disturbances, and display social withdrawal and work inhibition when they are depressed. Depressed girls display their depression by body image distortion, weight loss, and feelings of lack of personal satisfaction.

■ Figure 16–6

Depression and despair are fairly common feelings during adolescence.

SUICIDE Beginning at about age 11 or 12, when children begin to develop an image of a mature self, the rate of attempted suicide increases dramatically (U.S. Census Bureau, 1991). In the United States, one adolescent attempts suicide *each minute*. Each day, 14 suicide attempts result in death (D. A. Brent, 1989). Sex differences also emerge: girls make more attempts, while boys' attempts are more often "successful" (American Academy of Pediatrics, 1988). Although there may be other reasons, one explanation is that males tend to use more lethal methods, such as firearms, hanging, and explosives. Females, on the other hand, tend to use methods that allow time for rescue, such as drug or poison ingestion, and that "don't make a mess." Interestingly, the drugs used in adolescent suicide are usually medications prescribed for parents, such as barbiturates or antidepressants, or those intended for household use, such as aspirin (Whaley & Wong, 1988). The choice of method may be a function of socialization. It's more acceptable for girls to ask for and receive help. Traditionally, girls are perceived as vulnerable and dependent. Boys, on the other hand, are supposed to be tough and independent. They're also supposed to win. In the case of suicide, "winning" costs them their life.

Although the attempt itself often seems rash and impulsive, the problems that underlie the unhappiness and create a context for suicide have generally existed for some time. In the words of one 17 year old boy who died in 1987 due to carbon monoxide asphyxiation:

> I am a terrible son. I haven't been able to communicate with you although you have tried . . . I was not doing anything right in school, in swimming or socially. Please do not blame yourselves for what I did.

Jacobs (1971) has identified four stages in the development of suicidal behavior:

1. A long-standing history of problems (from childhood to the onset of adolescence)
2. A period of escalation of problems (since the onset of adolescence and in excess of those normally associated with adolescence)
3. The progressive failure of available adaptive techniques for coping with old and new problems, which leads the adolescent to a progressive social isolation from meaningful social relationships

4. The final stage, characterized by the chain-reaction dissolution of any remaining meaningful social relationships in the weeks and days preceding the suicide attempt

The adolescent suicide attempter is overwhelmed with anxiety and/or disappointment due to problems at home (47%), depression (23%), problems with friends and social relations (22%), low self-esteem (18%), boy–girl relationships (16%), and feelings that no one cared (13%) (Gallup Poll, 1991). Suicide attempters often report receiving excessive criticism, little positive feedback, and little affection from their parents. Many adolescent suicide victims are firstborns who have experienced considerable pressure to be successful and to set a good example (American Academy of Pediatrics, 1988). Since their problems seem insoluable and they have lost sight of other options and the energy to enact change, they simply want to do something "to stop the pain." Suicide becomes that something.

Sensationalizing suicide through the media is probably irresponsible. Berman (1988) suggests that while the incidence of suicide itself does not rise appreciably after a news story or media presentation that focuses on suicide, people may copy the *method* of suicide described in the story. Dedicating a yearbook to a student who committed suicide or calling school off in honor of these deaths certainly acknowledges the individual but may provide notoreity for the method of choice and inadvertently encourage others who need attention to get it by taking their own life.

Most adolescents who attempt suicide don't want to die. If we are alert to the warning signs of suicide, we can intervene to prevent tragic and needless loss of life. Most potential suicides let at least one other person know they are considering suicide before they attempt it. Other warning signs include:

1. Changes in sleeping or eating habits
2. A sudden change in school performance (bad grades from a good student, or the like)
3. A breakup of a love relationship
4. Sudden substance abuse or other antisocial behavior
5. Giving away prized possessions
6. Talking about death or suicide; reference to their own death
7. No more interest in social relations
8. Sudden neglect of appearance and hygiene
9. Complaining about physical problems when no physical problems exist
10. Marked persistent depression; looks and sounds sad and unhappy

There's even some evidence that elevated levels of the hormone *cortisol* may be linked both with depression and suicide risk in children (Pfeffer, Annual Meeting of the American Psychiatric Association, 1991). To pre-

In Touch

AMERICAN ASSOCIATION OF
  SUICIDOLOGY
2459 Ash
Denver, CO 80222
1-303-692-0985

Information about suicide prevention

■ ● ▲   CONCEPT SUMMARY

Common Disturbances and Problems

- *School Dropout*
  - Involves 15% of all high school students
  - Most are from non-Asian or poor families
  - School may not serve the adolescent's needs or may be too dangerous; teens also may see no value in school
  - Family and peers have the most influence on school attendance decisions
  - Lowers employability; lowers salary

- *Juvenile Delinquency*
  - Involves a pattern of behavior
  - Teen may be charged with a status offense or other criminal act
  - Males are more likely to be involved than females
  - Exists at all levels of society
  - More likely in children who have poor relations with their parents
  - Delinquent teens frequently have poor self-esteem
  - May have begun with a variety of antisocial acts while young
  - Prison hardens rather than rehabilitates the juvenile offender
  - Prevention is the best approach

- *Psychological Disturbance*
  - Often predicted by aggressiveness in childhood
  - Disrupts/interferes with the adolescent's life
  - Anxiety disorders and depression are the most common conditions
  - Depression may place the teen at risk for suicide
  - Most suicides involve warning signs
  - Schizophrenia is the most frequently occurring serious disorder of adolescence
  - Teens who are vulnerable to stress, exposed to considerable stress, or who inherit genetic predispositions to these conditions are at most risk

vent death through suicide, those who become aware of these symptoms should take them as indications of a serious problem (Steinberg & Levine, 1990). Professional intervention can help both adolescents and their families work through immediate crises and longstanding conflicts.

Schizophrenia

Sometimes withdrawal and escape are reasonable ways of coping with life's problems. Changing jobs, spending some time alone, or affiliating with a different crowd can provide troubled adolescents with new contacts, new directions, and time to refocus their energies and reestablish their equilibrium. However, escape so extreme that it involves withdrawal from reality into an imaginary world can signal a serious psychological disturbance called *schizophrenia*. Schizophrenia is the most frequently occurring psychotic disorder among adolescents, increasing from age 15 and leveling off by the late 30s. Characteristics of schizophrenia include decreased energy, poor emotional control, obsessive preoccupations, hostile and impulsive behavior, depersonalization, hallucinations, disordered thinking, language difficulties, and/or difficulty establishing meaningful relationships with others (Crow, 1985). The young person afflicted with this condition often appears distracted, withdrawn, and confused.

Two factors that seem to play a role in the development of schizophrenia in adolescence are an extreme vulnerability to stress (such vulnerability may be an inherited trait) plus exposure to an extreme amount of physical or psychological stress. A genetic predisposition toward schizophrenia also seems to run in families. Positive outcomes with treatment are most likely when the sufferer is an older adolescent with a history of good academic and social adjustment, one whose early response to treatment is positive, and one in whom the onset of the difficulty was sudden rather than gradual. Even then, the prognosis is not that good: Only one-third of the persons labelled schizophrenic/autistic improve; one-third stabilize and stay the same; and one-third worsen (Wolf & Goldberg, 1986).

obsessive
a person affected by a repetitive, intrusive thought or thought pattern

depersonalization
not acknowledging individuals personally or providing person-specific approaches to interaction

hallucinations
a sensory experience that does not correspond to reality, i.e., hearing or seeing things that aren't present or failing to hear or see things that are present

---

TOWARD EFFECTIVE PARENTING

The Positive Attributes of Adolescents

Although the teen years pose some challenges for adolescents and their parents, these years also offer some of life's most exciting opportunities. Adolescents stand on the threshold of adult life and work. They are establishing friendships that may last a lifetime; learning to relate to their parents and siblings on a deeper, more meaningful basis; and coming to appreciate their own unique blend of talents, skills, abilities, and limitations. Adolescents are able to formulate realistic goals and plan their accomplishments—for example, making preparations for marriage, education, or a career. And because of their youth and adaptability, adolescents have enough energy and resilience to withstand almost any crisis.

Adolescents are not always cognizant of their many strengths, and the parents of adolescents sometimes look past those strengths. In 1966 Otto and Healy identified 15 positive attributes of adolescents. They are as true of teens today as then. Teens are

1. energetic, full of life
2. idealistic, genuinely concerned for the future of the country and the world
3. intellectually curious; they question contemporary values, philosophies, ideologies, institutions
4. perceptive
5. courageous, willing to take risks, to "stick their necks out"
6. independent
7. fair, intolerant of injustice or wrongdoing
8. reliable, responsible
9. honest, open, straightforward
10. loyal and supportive
11. possessors of a good sense of humor
12. flexible, responsive to change
13. optimistic, positive outlook on life
14. inclined to take things seriously
15. sensitive to and aware of other people's needs
(Otto & Healy, 1966, p. 296)

By focusing on adolescents' strengths rather than their weaknesses, by treating them as individuals rather than as a group, and by dispelling some of the myths associated with the teen years, we can help adolescents maximize their changes for success, happiness, and personal growth throughout the teen years and beyond.

● Chapter Summary

● Although adolescents' needs and roles have changed within the family, their parents continue to play an important role in their lives. Reasonable guidelines are still essential. If conflicts do arise, they tend to focus more on daily issues like homework and chores and are waged more frequently with mothers than with fathers and with daughters more than sons. Parents may maintain a double standard by treating sons and daughters differently, and teenage children may engage in sex-stereotyped behavior themselves. By late adolescence, the quality of adolescent-parent interactions has usually improved.

● Adolescents who get along with their siblings tend to have more social competence outside the home.

● To judge its effects on all the age groups discussed, parental divorce or separation is probably most challenging for the teen and the preschooler.

● Peers play a vital role in adolescent development. Teens tend to select peers who are similar to themselves and thus support the family's value system. Neglected/rejected adolescents may turn to peers for guidance if they don't receive appropriate love and attention at home. Contrary to the stereotypes, teens spend as much time engaged in productive activity as they do relaxing and having fun.

- Close friendships are valued by the adolescent for the support, trust, and togetherness they offer.

- Ninety-five percent of 14–17 year olds attend public or private high schools. The school environment and personnel influence school satisfaction and school achievement. System indifference, school failure, pregnancy, lack of peer acceptance, boredom, discrimination, substance abuse, and lack of encouragement can prompt school dropout.

- Juvenile delinquency, involving a pattern of law-breaking or destructive behavior, is most likely among males around the age of 18. Females are more likely to be involved in status offenses, and those adolescents who live in poverty are more likely to enter the system for their delinquent offenses.

- Anxiety reactions and depression (sometimes with the potential for self-destructive behavior) are common among adolescents. Schizophrenia is a severe form of psychological disturbance that is more common among teens and young adults than other age groups of the population.

● Observational Exercise

One of the tasks of adolescence is to form a personal identity. Perceptions of the self that relate to appearance, skills, social and school performance, and family role are evaluated either positively, negatively, or neutrally. Taken as a whole, these impressions form the adolescent's self-concept.

Procedure: Compare the self-concepts of three adolescents, ages 15 to 18, by having them write statements in answer to the question "Who am I?" Provide a sheet of lined paper and a pencil and then say,

1. "Please number from 1 to 10 down the left margin of the page. In the spaces beside the numbers, write down statements that describe you and that answer the question 'Who am I?' as that statement refers to you. For example, a person could write down 'I am a good athlete' or 'I am one of five children.' "

   "Try to think of as many statements as you can up to ten that would describe you and your perceptions of your abilities. Remember to be honest, and be assured that your answers will be kept confidential."

   Score each statement by putting a + by those that indicate a positive or favorable self-evaluation ("I am a good student"), a 0 by those that are neutral ("I go to school"), and a − by statements that indicate that the person feels negatively about the particular trait or characteristic mentioned ("I am a poor speller"). Total the number of +, 0, and − statements.

2. What is your overall impression of each adolescent's self-concept? What areas do they perceive as strengths? What areas do they feel they are weak in? Do the older children you tested have more positive or more negative feelings about themselves? To what extent are peers and parents mentioned in the statements?

● Recommended Readings

Baker, R. (1984). *Growing up.* New York: New American Library.

Bell, R. et al. (1988). *Changing bodies, changing lives.* New York: Vintage.

Elder, G. H., Jr. (1974). *Children of the Great Depression.* Chicago, IL: Univ. of Chicago Press.

Erikson, E. (1968). *Identity: Youth and crisis.* New York: Norton.

Glenbard East Echo (compilers). (1984). *Being adolescent: Conflict and growth in the teenage years.* New York: Basic Books.

Kolehmainen, J., & Handwerk, S. (1988). *Teen suicide.* Minneapolis, MN: Lerner.

York, P., York, D., & Wachtel, D. (1983). *Toughlove.* New York: Bantam.

Youniss, J. (1980). *Parents and peers in social development: A Sullivan-Piaget Perspective.* Chicago: Univ. of Chicago Press.

Glossary

A, not B, phenomenon according to Piaget, when a child in stage 4 of the sensorimotor period searches for an object only in the first hiding place (A) even if it has subsequently been moved to a different location (B)

ability grouping or tracking an educational philosophy that suggests children can benefit more from instruction when their peers are all at about the same level of achievement

able-bodied children children without physical limitations to their activities

absolutism the belief that all people agree there is only one morally correct interpretation for each situation

absorption the extent to which one possesses an imagination or takes an imaginative perspective

abstract thought thinking that is not tied to material objects or particular examples

academic self-esteem how school performance figures into one's evaluation of oneself

acceleration the practice of skipping advanced children to higher grades

accident proneness an inclination or disposition to sustain accidental injury

accommodation Piaget's term for the process of shifting or enlarging mental categories or modes of thinking to encompass new information

accutane an anti-acne medication with serious teratogenic potential

acetylcholine a neurotransmitter that plays a role in memory and muscle function

achievement motivation the tendency to display persistence and striving when faced with a task to solve

achievement tests a test that measures how much an individual knows about a specific content area

acinar cells milk-producing cells of the mammary glands

acne a skin disorder in which skin pores become clogged and inflamed

acting out behavior that is disruptive, aggressive, or otherwise incongruous

active hand the preferred or dominant hand

active (REM) sleep the cycle of sleep characterized by the presence of rapid eye movements, internal body activity, active brain waves, and dreaming.

activity level the extent of one's energy output (busy, energetic vs. quiet, sedate)

adaptability the extent to which the individual can cope with change

adaptation Piaget's term for the cognitive process of adjusting one's thinking to accept ideas or information; adaptation takes two forms, accommodation and assimilation

adenine (A) one of the 4 essential bases that make up DNA and RNA

adenoids an overgrowth of glandular tissue behind the nose in the upper part of the throat

adolescence the period between childhood and adulthood that begins with puberty and ends with the cessation of growth

adolescent adjustment reaction behavior problems some think are related to the process of making the transition from adolescence to adulthood

adolescent growth spurt rapid acceleration in height, weight, and physical proportions that accompanies adolescence

adoptee an individual who is adopted

adoptive family the family into which the adopted child is placed

adoptive parent an adult who is a child's legal guardian but who is not that child's birth parent

adrenal glands glands located on the top of each kidney that secrete adrenal hormones and become active in times of stress

adrenal hormones hormones like adrenalin and nonadrenalin secreted by the adrenal glands

afterbirth the placenta and other membranes present in the uterus to support the baby; delivered during the third stage of labor

age norms normal or expected for a particular chronological age

aggressive/insecure one longterm adjustment to divorce where children feel unsettled and act out

agoraphobia a irrational fear of open spaces and/or public places

AIDS (acquired immunodeficiency syndrome)   an illness where a virus invades the body and destroys the ability of the immune system to fight disease

albinism   a disease characterized by the congenital lack of pigmentation

alcoholic   a person who has a compulsive need to drink alcohol and whose behavior and judgment are impaired as a result of alcohol abuse

alienated achievement   in Marcia's scheme, assuming an identity opposite to that expected

alignment   a term used to describe the appearance of the chromosomes just before cell division

allele   each gene in a gene pair; has a dominant or a recessive form

allergic reaction   a hypersensitivity of the body to a specific substance

alpha fetoprotein   a protein present in the mother's bloodstream during pregnancy; used as a marker in the prenatal diagnosis of Down's syndrome

alternating speech   dialogue where each speaker adds new information or direction to the conversation

alternative birth centers (ABCs)   centers dedicated to the delivery of babies; usually affiliated with a hospital or medical clinic

alternative care   child care provided by someone other than the child's parents

alternative school   home schooling or some similar out-of-school education

altruism   an unselfish concern for or devotion to others; selfless helping

ambiguous genitals   external genitals that do not identify clearly at birth as either male or female

ambivalent attachment   in Ainsworth's scheme, children who display a blend of contact-seeking and contact-resisting behavior

amenorrhea   the absence or cessation of menstruation in a mature, nonpregnant female

American Academy of Pediatrics (AAP)   the governing body for pediatricians in America

American Psychological Association   the governing body for professional psychologists in the United States

amniocentesis   a prenatal diagnostic procedure whereby amniotic fluid is withdrawn from the womb so the fetal cells can be examined for specified genetic, metabolic, and chromosomal abnormalities.

amnion (or bag of waters; also amniotic sac)   the membrane that contains the amniotic fluid that cushions the developing child

amniotic fluid   the liquid that surrounds and protects the developing child

amniotic sac   see amnion

amphetamines   a stimulant drug called an ''upper''

amputation   a body appendage lost due to surgery or trauma

analgesic   a medication that controls pain without the loss of consciousness

anal sphincter   the round muscle that closes the anus

anal stage   Freud's second stage of psychosexual development where the child receives gratification from the expulsion and retention of his/her feces

anal type personality   Sigmund Freud's notion of the development of the personality of the individual who becomes fixated at the anal stage of psychosexual development

androgens   those hormones (including testosterone) secreted by the testes of the male and the adrenal glands of the female; called male sex hormones

androgyny   involves a combination of masculine and feminine behaviors

anemia   a deficiency in the number of red-blood cells in the blood leading to weakness and fatigue

anencephaly   the congenital absence of the forebrain and midbrain

animism   the belief that inanimate objects are alive and therefore have emotions, feelings and motives. A characteristic of preoperational thought

anorexic   a person who has anorexia nervosa, an eating disorder that results in self-starvation

antibiotics   the group of medicines produced by molds, bacteria and other microorganisms developed to kill or slow the growth of disease-causing bacteria

antibodies   proteins in the blood that destroy or neutralize disease-causing antigens

antidepressant   a drug used to counteract feelings of worthlessness, despair, negativity, and hopelessness

antisocial behavior   actions that contradict the basic principles of society or that oppose the general good

antisocial   opposed to the general good or acting contrary to the basic principles of society

anus   the end of the large intestine

anvil, hammer, stirrup   the otic bones; the three smallest bones in the human body

anxiety reaction—(also called an anxiety disorder)   a psychological disturbance marked by a combination of fear, anxiety, and attempts to avoid the anxiety

Apgar scale   an assessment device used to evaluate the health-status of the just born baby

appendicitis   inflammation of the appendix

applied research   research designed to solve practical problems

aptitude test   a test that measures one's ability to engage in certain tasks

artificial insemination   a birth technology where sperm are introduced into the vagina by a medical procedure rather than by sexual intercourse

Aryan Race   In Nazi terminology, racial stock of non-Jewish, caucasian, and Nordic descent

aspartame   a substance contained in artificial sweeteners

assimilation   Piaget's term for the inclusion of new information into already existing mental categories or schema

association areas   areas in the cortex that are not affiliated with specific lobes; thought to process and store information

associative play   Parten's term for play in which children interact but are each involved in their separate activities. These children do not cooperate during play

asthma   a chronic or recurring allergic condition characterized by problems with breathing and feelings of suffocation

asynchrony (disengagement)   when infant/person interactions become disjointed and do not coincide

attachment   During prenatal development, attachment refers to the burrowing of the embryo into the uterine wall

attachment (bond)   an affectionate emotional tie between two people, a person and an animal, or a person and an object that endures over time

attention   focusing or concentrating on a particular task or circumstance

attention deficit disorders (ADD) a childhood disorder involving inattention and impulsiveness

attention deficit hyperactivity disorder (ADHD) a disorder of childhood involving inattention, distractibility, impulsiveness, and hyperactivity

attention span the amount of time one can remain focused on a particular task

attrition a decrease in the original number of subjects due to factors beyond the investigator's control, such as illness, relocation, or lack of motivation

auditory cortex the portion of the brain that is involved in interpreting auditory inputs; located in the temporal lobe

authoritarian a parenting style that is controlling and demanding and pays little attention to the needs of the child. Obedience is valued over communication and negotiation and physical punishment is used to make the child obey.

authoritative a parenting style that balances control and demands with warmth and responsiveness. A democratic approach is used and the child's needs and rights are recognized and respected.

autism a schizophrenic-like condition beginning in infancy or early childhood marked by social isolation, repetitive movements, and communication difficulties.

autobiographical memory one's memory for events that occur in one's own life

autonomous morality/morality of cooperation the most advanced of Piaget's stages of moral reasoning in which rules are viewed as flexible, purposeful, and developing out of cooperative social agreement

autopsy examination of the tissues of a dead body to determine the cause of death

autosomes twenty two pairs of chromosomes in the nucleus of the cell that do not include the sex chromosomes

auxiliary verb a verb used in addition to the main verb to express tense, mood or voice: i.e., she *will* stay

axillary relating to or located near the arm pit

babbling an early stage of language development during which the infant repeats a combination of sounds such as *bebebe*

babyness Lorenz's term for the collection of endearing physical characteristics of infants that persuade people to care for them because "they're so cute"

baby biographies records kept by laypersons about the growth and development of their children

baby bottle tooth decay (BBTD) tooth decay that occurs in some bottlefed infants

Baby M case the famous case of surrogacy that forced the Supreme Court to decide if the contract made between the surrogate and the infertile couple is binding

basic research research designed to accumulate information about a particular behavior or issue

battered child syndrome the cycle of abuse that leads ⅓ of those who were abused to abuse others

battered woman a female who has been assaulted by someone in a marriage or marriage-like relationship

Bayley Scales of Infant Development a test of infant mental capacity and psychomotor development

bedtime ritual/routine a specific pattern of events repeated prior to bedtime

behavioral states the sleep-wake orientation of the newborn

behavior modification see modification

bendectin an antinausea medication now counterindicated during pregnancy

Berkeley Growth Study a longitudinal study initiated during the 1940s to study patterns of physical development

"bikini" incision a transverse rather than lengthwise incision made in the mother's abdomen during cesarean section

bilirubin a substance that is present in elevated quantities in newborns with immature liver function

Binet-Simon scale the first intelligence test; designed to determine who could best benefit from public education

binocular vision visual perception that depends on inputs from both eyes

biochemical dealing with the chemical structure of living things

biological maturation theory Gesell's theory which suggests that development proceeds as the nervous system matures

bipolar disorder (formerly called manic-depressive behavior) a mood disorder marked by an alteration between two emotional extremes, depression and mania

birth control pill oral contraceptive

bi/multilingualism fluency in two (bi) or more than 2 (multi) languages

black English an English dialect with its own structure and rules of grammar

blastocyst multicelled organism formed from the union of the egg and the sperm that implants on the uterine wall

bloody show the loss of the mucous plug usually during labor

blood (Rh) incompatibility a condition that exists when the mother's blood contains the protein substance, Rh, and the baby's blood does not and vice versa

body image one's evaluation of one's physique

bone cancer abnormal cell changes that take place in the bony tissue

bone marrow donor an individual from whom bone marrow is taken for transplant purposes

botulism an often fatal poisoning caused by a bacteria that grows in improperly stored food

Boy's Night Out In NeoNazi terminology, a time frame targeted for hate-motivated violence

brain stem see hindbrain

Brain stem auditory evoked response test a test of newborn hearing acuity that studies the activity of the auditory nerves in response to stimulation

Braxton-Hicks contractions uterine contractions that may persist through the pregnancy without dilating the cervix; also called false labor pains or false labor

Brazelton newborn assessment scale (BNAS) an evaluation device used to assess aspects of newborn behavior

breast cancer abnormal cell changes in the breast tissue that have a destructive potential for the breast tissue itself or for the woman's body

breech (breech presentation) a position in the mother's uterus where the baby lies with its bottom and/or feet toward the cervix rather than with its head down

bronchitis inflammation of the bronchial tubes

bubbling burping; urging air bubbles out of the baby's esophagus

bulimia nervosa (bulimia)   an eating disorder characterized by episodic overeating to excess and dieting or voluntary vomiting or laxative use

burnout   emotional exhaustion

caffeine   a stimulant found in coffee, tea, cola, and chocolate

calcium   a metallic element that is essential for the growth of the bones and teeth

capillaries   the tiniest of blood vessels; red blood cells have to pass in single file to get through the capillaries which connect the arteries to the veins

cardiopulmonary resuscitation (CPR)   a lifesaving technique involving the administration of artificial breathing and heart stimulation

caring/competent   one longterm adjustment to divorce where children display interpersonal warmth and good coping skills

carrier   individuals who possess recessive genes for particular traits but who do not manifest the traits themselves

cartilage   the soft, mineral-laden tissue that hardens into bone

case study research   a research method in which a single subject or a small number of cases is studied extensively

cataract surgery   medical procedure to correct a cloudy or opaque condition in the lens of the eye

catch-up growth   development that "makes up for" existing deficiencies in growth

categorization   organizing information to be remembered into groups of related objects

caudal block   regional anesthesia that numbs the pelvic floor

CCK (cholecystokinin)   a hormone that may play a central role in feeling full after a meal

(cell) differentiation   see cell specialization

cell division   the process of chromosome duplication that produces new cells

cell specialization   the process whereby body cells assume responsibility for the development of specific organs and systems

central learning   the ability to recall task-relevant items and to ignore task-irrelevant items

central nervous system   the nervous system tissue encased in bone: the brain and spinal cord

centration   the tendency of the preoperational child to focus attention on one aspect of a situation or object while excluding all others

cephalocaudal principle   a pattern of growth that proceeds from the head downward (literally, "from head to tail")

cerebral palsy   damage to the brain before or during birth that results in voluntary muscular control problems

certainty   being sure; feeling confident about one's judgments

cervix   the mouth or opening of the uterus

cesarean section (C-section)   a surgical procedure in which a baby is delivered through an incision in the abdominal and uterine walls.

chickenpox   an infectious disease commonly contracted during childhood

childcare center   alternative care provided in a specialized facility; also called daycare or nursery school

childhood panic disorder   a psychological condition in which the child frequently experiences attacks of severe anxiety which can involve sweating, fainting/feeling faint, increased heart rate, chest pain, and/or difficulty breathing

child development   the scientific study of how and why growth and change occur in the preadult years

child molestation   a sexual assault on a child made by a nonrelative

child welfare advocates   professionals or private citizens who safeguard children's rights

chlamydia   a sexually transmitted disease caused by a bacterial infection

cholesterol   fatty material present in the body tissues required for the metabolism of fat, and the production of vitamin D and certain hormones

chorion   protective tissue that lines the placenta

chromosomal damage   breakage or framentation of the chromosomes

chromosomes   thread-like microscopic bodies found in the nucleus of every human cell. Chromosomes carry the genes transmitted from parents to offspring that determine an individual's inherited characteristics

chromosome abnormalities   developmental problems caused by missing, additional, or malformed chromosomes

chronically ill   an illness which lasts over a long time (as distinguished from *acute*)

chronic fatigue syndrome   a collection of symptoms caused by a virus that weakens one's immune system and leads to lethargy and lack of energy

chronic illness   an illness that recurs or lasts a long time

chronic miscarriage   repeatedly unable to carry a pregnancy to term

chronological age   a person's age in years

"chunk"   a meaningful group of letters or digits

cilia   hairlike projections that permit movement

circumcision   the surgical removal of the foreskin of the penis

civil disobedience   refusing to obey existing laws as a means of passively resisting and upholding one's personal convictions

Civil Rights Movement   a social movement that gained national attention in the 1960s and 1970s to grant equal rights to women, minorities, the handicapped and homosexuals

classical conditioning   the process by which a subject learns to associate a neutral stimulus (such as a tone) with a meaningful stimulus that evokes a reflex response (such as food). After the subject receives training, the neutral stimulus alone will evoke the same response as the meaningful stimulus

classification   sorting objects into categories or classes

class inclusion   the concept that one item can belong to several subsets or classes

clavicle   collarbone

cleft palate   a complete or partial split along the length of the palate of the mouth due to faulty prenatal development

clitoris   a highly sensitive structure of the external female genitals; plays a central role in orgasm

cocaine   a white, crystalline alkaloid obtained from coca leaves

code switching   situation-specific and person-specific language

coed schools   schools enrolling both males and females

cognitive development   age-related changes in the child's ability to think, remember, solve problems, and make decisions

cognitive map   a mental representation of a physical location

cognitive style   the tendency to focus on the entire problem (field dependent) or to separate the problem into its component parts and examine each part (field independent)

cognitive tempo the tendency to have a reflective or impulsive style

cohort effect differences between groups of individuals that are attributable to differential socialization (also called the historical context of development)

coitus sexual intercourse

cojoined (Siamese) twins monozygotic twins that do not separate fully when the zygote from which they are formed spontaneously duplicates

colic a sudden severe attack of abdominal pain

color constancy the realization that the actual color of an object is not affected by distance or lighting

color vision deficiency (color blindness) a sex-linked genetic disorder involving the ability to perceive color groups because of absent or dysfunctional cones; red-green and yellow-blue color blindness exists; some persons lack the ability to perceive any color

colostrum the first fluid produced by the breasts before actual milk production begins; also called first milk

"coming out" the process of becoming aware of and disclosing your own homosexuality; may be used more generally to indicate a person acknowledging *any* challenging life circumstance

componential intelligence In Sternberg's view, the assessment of intelligence and achievement by using standardized tests

comprehension understanding

computer literacy facility in computer usage and, to a lesser extent, computer programming

concatenative thinking thinking characteristic of the preoperational period whereby the child assumes, wrongly, that a causal relationship exists between certain objects and situations

conception see fertilization

concepts an abstract idea(s) based on grouping objects according to a common theme

concordance the degree of similarity shared by twins on certain measurable traits

concreteness a characteristic of preoperational thought whereby children can understand specific examples and situations they can observe and experience but have difficulty with the abstract

concrete operations the third stage in Piaget's cognitive theory where reasoning becomes more logical and children can understand some "rules of operation". Children still need to focus on concrete objects; abstract thought is lacking or very limited

conduct disorder behaviors that are legal *except* when performed by underage individuals

confidentiality to maintain documents/information in strict secrecy; nondisclosure of personally identifying information

conflict resolution strategy an approach for working through disagreement or difficulty

conformity maintaining or changing one's behavior to be consistent with group standards

congenital present at birth

congenital malformations physical abnormalities present at birth

conscience a mental faculty which encourages one to distinguish right from wrong and to choose to do right

consciousness the state of being alert, awake and aware

conservation tasks tasks originally devised by Piaget to assess children's skill in understanding apparent transformations

contact comfort Harry Harlow's term for the security and satisfaction derived from stimuli that satisfy the infant's tactile needs

contact seeking the extent to which one enjoys/is soothed by physical contact

contempt of court the charge made by a judge that an individual is not cooperating with the instructions of the court

contextual intelligence In Sternberg's view, the assessment of intelligence and achievement by an examination of one's ability to adapt to one's environment

contraception birth control

control in experimental research, the ability to exclude potentially confounding variables from influencing the outcome of the study

conventionalism the degree to which individuals conform to accepted, traditional standards or practices

conventional moral reasoning Kohlberg's second stage of moral development in which social reactions to moral dilemmas affect the decision-making process; the moral motivation is to conform to rules and to please people in positions of power and authority

convergent thinking trying to find the one, right answer to a problem

convulsions an involuntary, sometimes violent, series of muscle contractions

cooperative learning learning in groups or units where individuals within each group tutor each other

cooperative play Parten's term for play involving two or more children focused on a particular game or activity that has specific rules

coordinate sentence any sentence where a conjunction (and, but, etc.) ties together two ideas

coos/cooing the infant's first noncry vocalizations

coroner an official whose chief duty is to determine the cause of suspicious death

corporeal punishment physical punishment

correlational research a research method that indicates whether two variables are related to one another

correlation the degree of relatedness between two variables

cortex the outer layer of matter covering the brain

cortisol a hormone which in high levels is linked with suicide and/or depression

crack street-slang for cocaine that is smoked rather than injected or sniffed

craniofacial pertaining to the head and face

crank street-slang for methamphetamines (addictive synthetic stimulants)

cravings an intense desire or longing

creativity the ability to develop new and socially valued solutions, products, etc.

criminal justice system the country's courts of law

critical period a specific time in an organism's life when it is susceptible to the influence of certain stimuli and after which those same stimuli have little or no effect

critical thinking skills that allow for analyzing and evaluating information

cross-cultural research a research method that attempts to compare the activities/behaviors of one culture with others

cross-modal zones   nerve networks that permit information flow from one part of the brain to another

cross sectional research   research that involves comparing the behavior of groups of individuals of various ages to determine whether age-related differences exist

crowning   the appearance of the baby's scalp at the vaginal opening

CS (conditioned stimulus)   in classical conditioning, the stimulus that was paired with the unconditioned stimulus which now, through training, evokes the conditioned response

cultural-familial   causes of retardation found within the culture or family practices

culture   the beliefs, behaviors, and accomplishments of a group of people transmitted from one generation to the next

curds   lumps formed by coagulated milk

CVS (chorionic villus sampling)   a prenatal diagnostic procedure where a small piece of the chorion is removed for analysis

cystic fibrosis   a genetic disease characterized by inadequate functioning of the pancreas and chronic infection of the respiratory system

cytomaglovirus   the virus that causes cytomegalic inclusion disease

cytomegalic inclusion disease   an infectious disease that has serious (and sometimes fatal) teratogenic potential

cytosine (C)   one of the 4 essential bases that make up DNA and RNA

date/acquaintance rape   forced sexual activity with a nonstranger

daydreaming   shifting attention away from the task at hand while awake to thinking of something usually unrelated

death penalty   to execute a lawbreaker as punishment for their crime

decenter   the ability to focus on more than one aspect of a situation simultaneously; opposed to *centration*

decibel(s)   a unit of measuring sound intensity

deciduous teeth   the child's first set of teeth (20 in total); also called milk teeth, falling teeth, or baby teeth

deductive reasoning   a type of reasoning whereby general laws suggest conclusions about specific cases

deer tick   the insect that spreads Lyme disease to humans

defense mechanisms   in Freud's theory, those behaviors engaged in subconsciously or unconsciously to ward off anxiety

deferred imitation   copying a behavior sometime after it was observed

dehydration   to lose water

delinquent   a minor who commits criminal acts such as homicide, robbery, and rape as well as truancy, underage drinking, and running away

dental displacement   unnatural shifting of the position of the teeth

Denver Developmental Screening Test   updates the Shirley (1933) data in providing norms for infant motor development

dependent variables   the subject's responses to the independent variables

depersonalization   not acknowledging individuals personally or providing person-specific approaches to interaction

depression   a psychological disturbance ranging from mild to severe characterized by feelings of worthlessness, unhappiness, powerlessness, and guilt.

depth perception   an awareness of the distance between oneself and an object

design stage   the stage of drawing development entered when the child begins to use geometric shapes to form designs

despair   John Bowlby's second stage of separation, where the infant is quiet and withdrawn

detachment   John Bowlby's last stage of separation where the infant seems to recover their positive affect but not their affectionate tie to their estranged parent

developmentalists   developmental psychologists

developmental psychologists   scientists who study changes in growth and behavior in the preadult years

dexterity   see manual dexterity

diabetes   a genetic metabolic disorder characterized by insulin deficiency and excess sugar in the blood

dialect   a minor variation of a standard language due to such factors as geographical location and usage

diaphragm   the membrane between the chest cavity and the abdominal cavity used in inhaling and exhaling

difficult child   the child who is generally negative and intense

digital thermometer   a device for assessing body temperature with a numeric readout

dilatation (dilation)   the opening or dilating of the cervix to allow the baby to pass into the birth canal

diphtheria   an infectious disease inoculated against in the DPT vaccine

disabled children   a child with some degree of incapacity; physically or mentally challenged

discipline   socializing the child by setting and enforcing limits on his or her behavior

discrepancy theory   the view that the child's emotional response to a novel stimulus is determined by the degree of similarity between the new stimulus and an internal representation of a stimulus to which the new one is compared

disorganized/disoriented attachment   children that use either contradictory approach-avoidance strategies or lack a consistent attachment strategy with their parent

distributive justice reasoning   a concept of fairness concerning the allocation of rewards among group members

diuretic   a drug that increases the secretin of body fluids by the kidneys

divergent thinking   trying to think of many solutions to a particular problem

divorce   the legal dissolution of marriage

dizygotic twins   fraternal twins

DNA (deoxyribonucleic acid)   the chemical molecule that makes up the genes

dominance hierarchies   organizing persons from least dominant to most dominant, where the most dominant person has a controlling interest over the others

dominant trait   inherited characteristics that are expressed with relative frequency in the general population

double helix   the molecular shape of DNA described by Watson and Crick in 1953

double standard   a behavior that is evaluated positively when engaged in by members of one group but negatively when initiated by others

Down's syndrome   a chromosomal abnormality caused by the presence of an extra (47th) chromosome; formerly called Mongolism

dramatic play play that involves the use of the imagination (i.e., pretending or using make believe); also called pretend play or make-believe play

DrugAlert a chemical compound that identifies the presence of certain controlled substances on certain surfaces

drug babies the term used to refer to newborns with traces of addictive drugs in their bloodstream due to maternal transfer

drug withdrawal the physical reaction that accompanies the cessation or interruption of drug use by a drug addicted person

DSM-III-R the diagnostic and statistical manual developed by psychiatrists and used to classify psychological disturbance

due date the estimate of the baby's date of birth, based on the woman's last menstrual cycle and a 266 day human gestational period

dynamic assessment using many pieces of information in addition to the standardized intelligence test scores to assess the level of intellectual functioning

dysfluent speech speech that is choppy, halting, and produced with great effort

dysfunctional childhood a childhood marred by some type of impairment or abnormality

dysmenorrhea pain or discomfort before or during menstruation

easy child the child who is generally happy and adaptive

eating ritual a specific pattern of events repeated at each mealtime

echolalia the intentional imitation of another's speech sounds

eclampsia formerly called toxemia of pregnancy; a condition characterized by high blood pressure, water retention, and excess protein in the urine

ectoderm the embryonic tissue layer primarily responsible for the development of the nervous system and the skin

EEG electroencephalograph—an instrument that detects and records electrical activity in the brain

egalitarian marriage a marriage in which both members are equal partners

egocentric stage (moral realism or heteronomous morality) According to Piaget, the first stage of moral development in the preschool period in which children believe rules are set by an outside authority and are unchangeable. Since the rules are usually incomprehensible, preschoolers *often* change them to suit their purposes

egocentrism the orientation that takes into account one's own point of view and excludes other's perspectives

ego identity having a sense of oneself as a person

ejaculation the process whereby semen is expelled through the penis

ejaculatory ducts ducts located within the prostate gland that store semen

ejection (let down reflex) an automatic action that releases milk from the milk storage sites in the breast; caused by the release of oxytocin in a woman's body

elaboration strategies for facilitating recall that involve working with the information to be remembered to change its form (i.e., to create a visual stimulus, to make a meaningful sentence from the words on a list, etc.)

elavil a drug classified as an antidepressant or mood elevator

Electra conflict according to Freud, a series of events that occur in the phallic stage of psychosexual growth that encourage the development of a superego or conscience in a girl as well as the identification of the girl with her mother

Embedded Figures Task a perceptual test requiring that the individual identify specific stimuli within a complex visual field

embedding inserting a relative clause into a sentence with a main clause

embryologist a biologist who is an expert in understanding the formation and development of embryos

embryology the branch of biology that focuses on change and development during the prenatal period

embryo the developing child 2–8 weeks after conception. Basic body structures and systems are formed during this period.

embryo transfer a birth technology where an embryo is transferred from one organism to another as a remedy for infertility

emergency room the portion of the hospital that treats sudden or severe illness or injury

emotional display rules learned guidelines for the expression of emotion

empathy sharing emotions with another by imagining what they must be feeling or going through

emphysema a chronic disease that impairs breathing by enlarging the air sacs of the lungs

endoderm the embryonic tissue layer primarily responsible for forming the gastrointestinal tract, lungs, and major glands.

endometriosis a condition in which uterine tissue grows outside the uterus in various parts of the abdominal cavity

enrichment the practice of providing advanced work and special projects for the advanced student

epidural anesthesia regional anesthesia given during delivery to numb the lower pelvis

epidural block see epidural anesthesia

episiotomy a surgical incision made at the base of the vagina during childbirth to prevent tearing

equilibration Piaget's term for the mental balance achieved through the assimilation and accommodation of conflicting experiences and perceptions

estriol a hormone present in the mother's bloodstream during pregnancy used as a marker in the prenatal diagnosis of Down's syndrome

estrogen a class of hormones that develop female's reproductive and body structures; also called female sex hormones

ethics acceptable standards of conduct or a code of responsible behavior

ethnicity people sharing a common language, national origin, culture, history or race.

ethnic stereotype a generalized belief (usually false) about a person's race or background

ethological theory a theory interested in understanding the evolutionary origins of behavior and its adaptive value or significance for survival

etiquette good manners; proper or polite behavior

Eustachian tube the canal that connects the pharynx with the middle ear

exhibitionistic demonstrative; not shy or inhibited

experiential intelligence In Sternberg's view, the assessment of intelligence and achievement by an examination of creativity and insight

expressive jargon   the apparently meaningless sounds infants make that sound like meaningful words and sentences

extroverted   socially outgoing

eye-hand coordination   visually directed manual activities

facial interest   the child's tendency to be preoccupied with the human face as a stimulus

Fallopian tubes   tubes providing a conduit between each ovary and the uterus

farsighted   the ability to see distant objects clearly, while close objects are less clear

fasting   to eat little food or only certain types of food usually as part of a religious observance

fearfulness   the extent to which one feels personal misfortune is imminent

fear of strangers (stranger anxiety)   a fear of unfamiliar others or changes in familiar settings and people; first displayed by infants around 7–8 months of age

feature encoding   remembering significant aspects of stimuli

fecal material   waste products from the bowel

"female semen"   according to Galen, the repository of the preformed human

fenfluramine   a drug used in the treatment of autism designed to reduce serotonin levels in the brain

feral children   children who were lost in the wild and survived but did not learn the ways of civilization

fertility   reproductive capability

fertilization   when the genetic material from the egg and sperm merge to form a zygote; also called conception

fetal alcohol effects (FAE)   a less severe form of FAS

fetal alcohol syndrome (FAS)   a congenital disorder in the infant associated with maternal ingestion of alcohol during pregnancy

fetal surgery   operating on the developing child prior to birth to correct conditions that could result in serious impairment or even death

fetoscopy   a prenatal diagnostic procedure where fiberoptic imaging is used to view the developing child within the uterus

field dependent   in problem solving, the tendency to focus on the entire problem

field experiment   a research method in which subjects are assigned to treatment or control groups in the natural environment instead of in the laboratory setting

field independent   in problem solving, the tendency to break a problem into its component parts before attempting a solution

fifth disease (erythemia infectiosum)   has the potential for producing a serious form of anemia in unborn children

finalism   a preoperational notion that all movement is purposeful or is performed for some function

fine motor skills   physical skills that require small muscle coordination such as drawing, sewing, or playing a musical instrument

finger dexterity   see manual dexterity

5-to-7 shift   the time during which the child makes a cognitive transition from the preoperational stage to the stage of concrete operations (Piaget's terms) or from intuition to logic

fixation   an abnormal preoccupation

fontanels/soft spots   areas of cartilage between the bones of the baby's skull

food additives   anything added to food to enhance color, freshness, shelf life, nutritional value, resistance to spoilage etc.

forceps   curved metal instruments designed to fit around the baby's head to assist with the birth; the use of forceps is largely outdated

foreclosure   in Marcia's scheme, premature identity formation, often occurring before alternatives more suitable to the person's own needs and characteristics are considered

foreskin   the skin that sheaths the penis glans

formal operational thought   according to Piaget, the fifth and final stage of cognitive development, characterized by abstract thinking and the ability to systematically test hypotheses. This stage is not reached until adolescence, if at all.

form discrimination   the ability to tell one shape or object from another

Foundling Home   an orphanage

fovea   the portion of the retina where cones are concentrated; provides the sharpest visual image when light is focused on it

fragile-X syndrome   a sex chromosome disorder in which the X-sex chromosome contains a gap or break; associated with mental retardation and autism

fraternal twins   twins formed from two separate zygotes; also called dizygotic twins

freestanding birth clinic   a medical center dedicated to the delivery of babies

free choice   a decision made without coercion or constraint

frontal lobes   located in the anterior portion of each hemisphere, areas of tissue in the brain that play a role in directing muscle movement and in higher order mental processes such as reasoning, problem solving and the acquisition of knowledge

frozen embryo   the process of lowering the temperature of an embryo so it can be preserved until it is time to be implanted

full scale IQ   an IQ estimate based on the combined verbal and performance subscale scores

g   a single, common intelligence representing abstract reasoning and the *general* capacity for acquiring knowledge

galactosemia   an inherited metabolic intolerance to the sugar found in milk

gametes   male and female reproductive cells. Each carries half the number of chromosomes found in the other cells of the human body

gangs   see street gangs

gastric   of or pertaining to the stomach

gastrointestinal   relating to the stomach and intestines

gazing   to look steadily; to fix one's attention

gender constancy/gender consistency   the realization that one's sex assignment (male or female) is permanent and unaffected by one's behavior or dress

gender identity   the realization that one is either a male or a female

gender role stereotype   generalized expectations about appropriate behaviors for males and females

gender schema theory   a theory that combines the social learning perspectives with the cognitive developmental approach to explain the acquisition of sex-stereotyped behavior and knowledge

generalists those who believe it is more appropriate to represent intelligence as a single, general capacity (*g*) than as a collection of separate skills

geneticist an expert in genetics

(genetic) predispositions a tendency to inherit the traits, characteristics or behaviors of one's ancestors

genetics the passing of genes and the inherited characteristics they specify from one generation to the next

genetic code the biochemical message created by the arrangement of the 4 bases of the DNA molecule

genetic counseling advice to potential parents based on principles of human genetics regarding the probability of genetic problems in offspring; conducted by a professional called a genetic counselor

genetic engineering the intentional manipulation of genes to produce specific outcomes

genetic sex-linked disorder see X-linked inheritance

genetic transmission the passing of genes and the inherited characteristics they specify from one generation to the next

gene (s) the basic units of heredity carried by the chromosomes; each gene is a section of the genetic code

genitalia (also genitals) female or male sex organs

genitals the sex organs of males and females

genital herpes a sexually transmitted disease characterized by blisters on or near the genitals

genotype the characteristics that an individual has inherited, as prescribed by his or her genes, that may or may not be expressed

gentle birth procedures (Leboyer method) a birth designed to accommodate the newborn's needs rather than the needs of the medical staff (i.e., higher room temperature, no harsh lighting, etc.)

germinal stage/period of the ovum the first period of prenatal development, extending from conception to implantation (about 10–14 days)

Gesell Developmental Schedules an evaluation of the young infant's motor, adaptation, language, and social behavior

gestational diabetes diabetes that develops during pregnancy

gestational week a 7-day span of time during the prenatal period

GIFT (gamete intra-Fallopian transfer) a birth technology in which the sex cells or gametes are introduced into the woman's Fallopian tubes instead of her vagina

gifted/talented an individual with exceptional and/or precocious talent or potential in a particular area (academics, music, athletics, etc.)

Golden Rule the moral principle that one "do unto others as you would have them do unto you"

gonorrhea a sexually transmitted disease that causes inflammation of the mucous membranes

grammar a language skill concerned with the rules by which words are arranged (syntax) as well as the meanings of the words (number, person, case, gender, and tense)

greeting response a characteristic pattern of facial expressions that infants display when they are pleased to see someone they know

gross motor skills physical skills that require large-muscle movement such as running, climbing and jumping

growth retardation preventing the organism from growing or developing to their genetic potential

growth suppression when an individual is prevented from growing normally (any number of factors can be responsible)

guanine (G) one of the 4 essential bases that make up DNA and RNA

guilt feeling remorseful for a real or imagined wrongdoing

Gulf War another name for the Persian Gulf War

gynecomastia a condition where fatty tissue is laid down in a male's chest giving the appearance of female breasts

habituation a simple type of learning whereby a particular stimulus becomes so familiar to the organism that it ceases to elicit any physiological response

hallucinations a sensory experience that does not correspond to reality, i.e., hearing or seeing things that aren't present or failing to hear or see things that are present

handedness the tendency to prefer to perform activities with either the left or right hands

hand grasp grasping using the whole hand as a unit

hand preference see handedness

"hands on" mathematics teaching math concepts using manipulatives rather than lecture and example

hate-motivated violence crimes against individuals or groups of individuals

hCG (human chorionic gonadotropin) the hormone secreted soon after implantation; it is detected in pregnancy tests to confirm conception

head circumference the distance around the head at the eyebrows

heat stroke/hyperthermia a condition in which the body temperature is higher than normal

hemangioma (birthmark) patches of discolored skin caused by the overaccumulation of blood vessels in the skin's surface

hemisphere lateralization see lateralization

hemophilia (also called "bleeder's disease") an inherited disease that prevents the blood from clotting normally

hepatitis B a viral infection that impairs liver function

heredity the tendency of individuals to develop the traits and characteristics possessed by their ancestors

hernia a condition where part of an organ bulged through the wall of its body cavity

heteronomous morality (moral realism) in Piaget's theory of moral development, the stage in which rules are regarded as unchangeable, absolute and imposed by an external authority

heterosexual (heterosexuality) a person whose sexual orientation is toward persons of the other sex

heterozygous the condition that exists when the alleles of a gene pair differ from one another

high risk pregnancies pregnancies that require close medical supervision to safeguard the health of the mother and/or the baby

hindbrain the brain stem; the part of the brain that includes the pons, medulla and the cerebellum

hippocampus the portion of the brain that plays an important role in the formation of new memories

HIV positive a test result that confirms the presence of human immunodeficiency virus

Hodgkin's disease a disease characterized by progressive enlargement of the lymph glands

holophrase the use of a single word to convey a complete thought; a single-word sentence

homebirth   giving birth at home or in familiar surroundings rather than in a medical facility

homecare   alternative care provided in someone's home

HOME inventory   Bradley and Caldwell's test of the social, cognitive and emotional aspects of the infant's home environment

homelessness   being without a permanent place of residence

home pregnancy tests   an over-the-counter kit that tests the woman's urine for the presence of hCG

home-school educators   individuals dedicated to teaching their children at home

homicide   taking the life of another

homophobia   an irrational fear of homosexuality, homosexual persons, or of one's own homosexuality

homosexuality   a person whose sexual orientation is toward persons of the same sex

homozygous   the condition that exists when the alleles of a gene pair are identical

Homunculists   A group that was formed during the Middle Ages to support the notion that the preformed human resided in the male sperm, not the female ovum

horizontal decálàge   In Piaget's terms, the sequential mastery of concepts within a single developmental stage

horoscope   a prediction of one's personal fate based on the position of the planets

hospital maternity ward   a specialized area within a hospital dedicated to the delivery of babies and the aftercare of new mothers

hostile aggression   attacking another person where the focus of the attack is the person him- or herself (i.e., calling someone names to hurt their feelings)

HPL (human placental lactogen)   a substance released during pregnancy; used as a marker in estimating risk for FAS/FAE

humerus   the long born of the upper arm

hunger cries   specific cries produced by the baby to indicate they need to be fed

"hurried babies"   babies pushed to excel; may be susceptible to the superbaby syndrome

Hyaline membrane disease   a specific cause of respiratory distress syndrome in newborns

hydatiform mole   a grape-like cluster of cells that occasionally grows in the uterus

hypertension   a medical condition commonly called high blood pressure; stresses the heart and blood vessels

hyperthermia   a condition that causes an increase in body temperature

hypervigilance   a state of intense alertness and watchfulness

hypoalbumenia   a condition caused by too little albumin, a water-soluble protein, in the system

hypothalamus   a gland that influences temperature regulation, hunger and thirst regulation, sexual behavior and other important functions

hypothesis   predicted outcomes of experiments based on the results of related studies, theories, and real-life experiences

hypothetico-deductive reasoning   the process of generating hypotheses and then systematically testing each to find the solution

hypothyroidism   a condition where the thyroid gland is underproducing

hysterectomy   surgical removal of the uterus

identical twins   twins formed from a single zygote that spontaneously duplicates itself and separates; also called monozygotic twins

identification   in Freud's terms, to associate closely enough with another person to be influenced by that person

identity achievement   in Marcia's scheme, having acquired a sense of the roles one will play

identity   the notion that form can change, but if nothing has been added or taken away, the amount is still the same

identity diffusion   in Marcia's scheme, a lack of clarity that arises when the person is not motivated to find an identity

identity moratorium   in Marcia's scheme, experimenting with different roles during the process of identity formation

identity status   in Marcia's scheme, the phases an individual can pass through in search of a personal identity

illegitimate   a term that has largely fallen from use indicating the child's parents were not married when they were born

illicit drugs   illegal drugs like cocaine and heroin

imaginary audience   an assembled group of listeners or spectators assumed to be present

imitation   copying, modeling

immigrant   leaving one's native country and coming to another to make permanent residence there

imminent justice   the belief that doing wrong inevitably leads to punishment; this belief is held by children in Piaget's stage of moral realism (heteronomous morality)

immune globulin (VZIG)   a substance that counters the severity of chickenpox in an exposed individual

immune system   the system that protects the organism from disease or infection

immunization   an inoculation to add to the body's immune protection

immunoglobulin/IgG   cow antibodies present in human breastmilk if the mother eats dairy products

immunological resistance   the body's ability to fight off disease due to natural or artificial immunity

implantation   occurs when the zygote burrows into the lining of the uterus where it can be nourished and protected until birth

impulsive   in problem solving, the tendency to answer questions quickly, but sometimes not accurately

incest   a sexual assault on a child made by a relative

incest taboo   a society-wide prohibition against sexual relations between relatives

incidental learning   memory for items other than those one was directed to learn

incipient cooperation stage of moral development   according to Piaget, the stage of moral development in which 5–9 year old children define a set of rules each time they play together. The rules may vary slightly each time even though the same game may be involved

incompetent cervix   a medical term for a cervix that doesn't remain closed during pregnancy

incomplete dominance   a condition where the heterozygous form does not express the dominant trait but an intermediate condition, part way between dominant and recessive expression

incubator   a box-like apparatus that provides a controlled environment for the newborn

independent variables   the factors in an experiment that are manipulated by the experimenter

induced birth   an artificially initiated birth

inductive reasoning　a type of reasoning whereby general laws are inferred from specific examples

infancy　the period of development between birth and about age 3

infantile amnesia　Freud's term for the apparent "forgetting" of experiences that occurred during infancy

infant mortality　likelihood of a baby dying in the first year of life

infectious mononucleosis ("mono")　a viral disease that causes malaise, lack of energy, and flu like symptoms

inflection　change or variation in the tone or pitch of one's voice

information processing approach　a general theoretical approach to the study of cognition that views the human mind as a complex, symbol manipulating system through which information flows, is processed/examined, and then is utilized, dismissed, or stored as memory

informed consent　a full disclosure of the research aims and procedures prior to agreeing to participate

inoculation　see immunization

insecure/avoidance attachment　according to Ainsworth, children who do not miss parents when they leave and actually avoid them when they return

insomnia　difficulty falling asleep or staying asleep

institutionalization　to place in an institution for care and treatment

instrumental aggression　using aggression to obtain an object, territory, or privilege

intellectual style　whether one is a reflective vs. an impulsive thinker (also called cognitive style)

intelligence　measurable abilities that represent accumulated knowledge or experience (i.e., the ability to cope with the environment, to judge, comprehend and reason, to understand and deal with people, symbols and objects, to act with purpose and effectiveness)

intensity of reaction　the extent to which vocalizations are loud or soft

interactionists　those who believe it is more accurate to combine the theories of intelligence and conceptualize intellectual functioning as a series of independent skills *in addition to* some general capacity for thinking and acquiring knowledge

***in vitro* fertilization**　a technology to improve the chances of fertilization by having the ovum and sperm meet in a *petri* (laboratory dish); the conceptus (if formed) is then implanted back into the host mother

intercourse　penile/vaginal sex

intercranial hemorrhage　bleeding inside the cranium

interdisciplinary　between or among different disciplines

internal or autonomous morality　in Piaget's theory of moral development, the last stage of moral reasoning. Children in this stage realize that rules can be broken in good conscience, changed when everyone agrees, and that one's intentions are as important as the outcome of a situation.

interventricular hemorrhage　bleeding into the spaces or the ventricles of the brain

interview　a research method in which the investigator asks specific questions pertaining to a particular hypothesis

intonation　see inflection

intrauterine growth retardation　see growth retardation

introspective　tending to examine one's own feelings and thoughts

IQ (intelligence quotient)　a formula originally based on measured mental age divided by chronological age times 100 (MA/CA × 100 = IQ)

iron deficiency anemia　weakness and fatigue caused by low levels of iron ingestion

irreversibility　the inability of the preoperational child to reverse their thinking to undo transformations

IV needle　a needle used to inject substances *intra*venously

jaundice　a condition caused by the build up of bilirubin in the baby's bloodstream

jaw misalignment　when the upper and/or lower jaws are out of their proper position

job market　the current status of employment opportunity and business enterprise

joint custody　where both divorced parents share the responsibility for dependent children

juvenile delinquent　a lawbreaker under the age of 16 or 18 (depending on the state)

juvenile detention centers　the part of the penal system that houses juvenile lawbreakers

kcalories (pronounced calorie)　a unit of food energy; stands for kilocalorie

kegel exercises　exercises to strengthen the pubococcygeal muscles of the pelvic floor.

Kevlar　a synthetic material that is designed to deflect bullets

kibbutz　a collective farm or settlement in modern Israel

kiddie porn　sexually explicit visual erotica involving children

kidneys　two organs lying against the back in the abdominal cavity that filter waste out of the bloodstream

kinesthetic　a sensation of movement, weight, resistance and position of the muscles and joints of the body; a sense of body movement and position

kwashiorkor　a serious nutritional disease in children caused by protein deficiency

labia majora　the outer lips of the vulva

laboratory experiment　a research method in which subjects are studied in a controlled environment

labor coach　an individual present during the birth who attends to, assists, and supports the laboring woman

lactation　milk production

lallation　the accidental imitation of another's vocalizations

language acquisition　the process of learning one's native language

language acquisition device (LAD)　Chomsky's term for the hypothetical mechanism that accounts for the infant's inborn ability to learn language

language dance　the tendency of the baby to synchronize his or her movements to the sound and pattern of human speech directed toward them

language production　the ability to produce spoken words

language switching　when the bilingual child intersperses words from one language into a sentence in the other language

lanugo　temporary downy hair found on the shoulders, forehead, and neck of some newborns

large-for-gestational age (LGA)　a baby who is larger than expected for their chronological age

large muscle skills　see gross motor skills

larynx　the "voice box"; it contains the vocal cords and is the organ of speech

latency　in Freud's theory, the psychosexual stage spanning the school years. During this time, sexual development takes a backseat to intellectual development

latex condoms   a latex sheath that fits over the penis as a contraceptive device and as protection against sexually transmitted disease

laws of heredity   the principles that govern the transmission of inherited characteristics

laxative   a drug that promotes the discharge of fecal material from the bowel

leadership   the degree to which one influences or directs others

lead exposure   the inadvertent intake (usually ingestion or transdermal exposure) of lead, a potentially toxic heavy-metal

learned helplessness   the notion that depression may result when people perceive they have no control over the major events that affect them

learning   changes in behavior resulting from specific experiences and/or instruction rather than from genetics or inherited characteristics

learning disability   perceptual or nervous system problems that prevent the child with normal intelligence from learning easily

learning theory/behaviorism   a theoretical perspective founded by John B. Watson that maintains that most behavior is learned or conditioned rather than inborn

left hemisphere   the half of the brain on the left hand side of the person's body that influences speech and right side body movement, among other things

lesbian   a female homosexual

lethal   likely to result in death

lethargy   sluggishness, inactivity, lack of energy

leukemia   a disease characterized by the existence of abnormal numbers of white blood cells

lidocaine   a topical pain killer similar to novocaine

lightening (also called settling, dropping)   the settling of the fetus into the mother's pelvis in preparation for birth

limbic system   a collection of brain structures involved in attention, memory, motivation, and emotion

linguist   a scientist who studies languages

"little scientist"   Piaget's term for the active "hypothesis testing" during the trial-and-error experimentation stage

locomotion   movement from place to place

longitudinal research   long-term studies of an individual or group of individuals designed to monitor changes that take place over time

long-chain polyunsaturated fatty acids   a hydrocarbon compound

long-term memory store (LTM)   the third and final stage in Atkinson and Shiffrin's memory model; LTM can retain information in permanent memory

low birth weight   either a premature or small-for-date designation that is associated with a weight at birth of less than 7 pounds

low risk pregnancy   a pregnancy that can progress satisfactorily without intensive medical supervision

low thyroid output   see hypothyroidism

lung capacity   the amount of oxygen that can be contained by the lungs

Lyme disease   a tick-borne disease that has serious teratogenic potential

lymphatic system   the tissues in the body that screen out harmful substances and produce lymphocytes to aid in infection control

lymphoma   cancer of the blood stream

magical thinking   the preoperational belief that reality can be altered by thoughts or wishes

mainstreaming   the Federally mandated practice of assigning handicapped children to regular classrooms instead of segregating them in special classrooms

Make-A-Wish Foundation   an organization dedicated to granting the ''last wishes'' of terminally ill children

malformations   pertaining to abnormal or atypical development, usually physical

malnutrition   a condition resulting from a lack of nutrients in the body tissues

mammary glands   specialized milk-producing glands within the woman's breasts

mammary gland tissue   milk glands in the female breasts

mania   an agitated depression marked by constant, nonproductive activity and a lack of inhibitions

manual dexterity   skill in using the hands

marijuana   a drug obtained from the dried flowers of the hemp plant

masturbation   self-stimulation of the genitals

maternal AFP screening   a test conducted to determine the amount of AFP in the mother's blood stream (see alpha fetoprotein)

maternal depression   see postpartum depression; postpartum psychosis

maturation   growing to reach full potential or development

measles   an infectious disease of childhood that one can be inoculated against

meconium aspiration syndrome   a collection of symptoms associated with the fetus's inhalation of meconium present in the amniotic fluid at birth

meconium   fetal waste material present in the baby's bowel at birth

media   means of expression or communication, like newspapers or television

meiosis   the special process of chromosome duplication and cell division that produces ova and sperm, each containing different combinations of genetic material on 23 chromosomes

melanin   the pigment present in the body that helps pigment the hair, skin and eyes

melatonin   a substance secreted by the pineal gland that plays a role in sexual maturation

memory   the system which permits recall or reconstruction of past experiences

menarche   the female's first menstrual period

meningitis   a serious illness characterized by the inflammation of the membranes that surround the spinal cord

menopause   the cessation of menstruation due to aging or the surgical removal of the ovaries

menstrual cycle   the period during which the lining of the uterus us sloughed off if conception and implantation have not occurred

menstruation   in mature females, the monthly shedding of the uterine lining

mentally retarded   a child who scores below 70 on a standardized scale of intelligence and has significant difficulty making changes and adjusting to changing environments

mental development index   an index from Bayley scale that measures nonmotor behaviors

mental representation   to picture or symbolize something in one's mind

mesoderm   the embryonic tissue layer that develops into the muscles, bones, and circulatory system

metabolic rate   the rate at which the body converts food into energy

metamemory   an awareness and understanding of one's own thought processes; also called metacognition

metaphorical expressions   a figure of speech in which one object or idea is compared with another in order to suggest a similarity between the two (i.e., She was a pillar of strength)

methadone   a synthetic narcotic drug used as a substitute for heroin in the treatment of heroin addiction

methylmercury poisoning   a toxic accumulation of mercury in the body tissues and/or fluids

microwaving   heating in a microwave oven

midbrain   the portion of the brain that acts as a relay station, routing information from the brain stem to higher brain regions

Middle Ages   the period of European history between the Fall of the Roman Empire and the beginning of the Renaissance (5th C BC—15th C BC)

middle childhood   the period of development between ages 6 and 12 (roughly); also called the school years

midwife   (also called a certified nurse-midwife) a nurse with special training and licensing who monitors pregnancy and oversees delivery, often in a home setting

minimum distance principle (MDP)   the idea that children make mistakes in inferring causality from sentence constructions because they assume that a phrase that follows a subject is somehow related to it

miscarriage (miscarry)   (also called a spontaneous abortion)—the spontaneous termination of pregnancy by natural causes such as the failure of the embryo to develop properly

Mister Rogers' Neighborhood   a long running PBS program for preschoolers starring Fred Rogers

mitosis   the process of chromosome duplication and cell division that creates new cells, each containing the same 46 chromosomes

mixed or cross lateral preference   the case where one is right handed, for example, but left eyed, left footed, etc.

modeling   imitating, copying

molded head   a newborn head that is temporarily misshapen due to pressures on the fetal skull during birth

monolinguals   individuals who speak one language

monozygotic twins   identical twins

mood disorders   psychological disturbances that affect emotional states

mood quality   characterization of emotional tone ranging from positive to negative

morality of cooperation   see autonomous morality

moral development   the development of attitudes and beliefs that help children determine whether behaviors are right or wrong

moral realism   see heteronomous morality

morphogenesis   the development of the body systems and organs during the period of the embryo (also called organogenesis)

mortality   likelihood of death

motor cortex   the portion of the brain involved in sending messages out to the muscles of the body to initiate movement; located in the frontal lobes

motor pathways   systems of nerve cells that transmit information from the brain to the muscles and glands

mouthing   examining objects by mouth

mucous plug   mucous secretions and blood vessels that accumulate at the mouth of the cervix to help protect the uterus from contamination

multicultural/multinational learning   focusing on diversity within American society by highlighting the various cultural backgrounds and origins of the population

multiple ovulation   releasing more than one ovum during a cycle thus allowing for the possibility of twins or multiple conception

multiple sclerosis   a disease characterized by the abnormal hardening of tissues within the body

mumps   an infectious disease of childhood that one can be inoculated against

murder   the unlawful and intentional killing of another human being

muscular dystrophy   a genetic disease that is characterized by the progressive weakening or wasting of the skeletal muscles

myelagenetic cycles   a series of changes in the myelination of specific brain structures

myelinate/myelinization   the process of coating nerve fibers with a fatty covering called the myelin sheath that speeds up nervous system transmission

naltrexone   a drug used in the treatment of autism designed to block opium receptor sites

naturalistic observation   a research method in which subjects' naturally occurring behavior is observed in their usual surroundings and subjects are unaware of the presence of the investigator

nature/nurture controversy   the debate within psychology over the relative influence on behavior of nature (genetics) and nurture (the environment)

Nazi   a member or follower of the party that controlled Germany under the leadership of Adolf Hitler. Among other things, Nazis believe in white supremacy and the destruction of other races and peoples (i.e., Blacks, Jews, homosexuals, etc.)

Nazi SS   A corp of troops organized by Hitler as his personal bodyguard and later put in charge of exterminations and massacres (abbreviated from the German *Schutzstaffel*, literally, protection staff)

need to achieve   striving to accomplish success in a competitive situation

negatives   the use of "no" and its derivatives

neglect   failure to provide proper attention or support

neonatal intensive care unit (NICU)   a specialized hospital facility providing medical care for sick or premature infants

NeoNazis   A present day movement to restore the beliefs of Hitler's Nazi (National Socialism) Party

Neopiagetian theories   theories put forth to extend and clarify Piaget's work in cognitive development

neural tube closure defects   malformations in the development of the spinal column that lead to congenital defects like anencephaly or spina bifida

neurofibromatosis   a genetic disorder where usually benign tumors grow under the surface of the skin; also known as Elephant Man's syndrome

neurologically mature   the end of nervous system growth

neurological impairment   dysfunction of the nervous system

neuron(s)   nerve cells

neurosensory impairment   nervous system damage that affects sensation

neurotransmitter   a chemical released by a neuron in the brain; plays an important role in nerve cell transmission

neutral stimulus   in classical conditioning, the stimulus which, prior to training, elicits no particular reaction

nicotine   a stimulant drug contained in tobacco and tobacco products

nightmare   an unpleasant, anxiety-provoking dream

night terrors   nightmares that usually take place during NREM sleep

Nobel laureate   an individual who has received a Nobel prize

"noble savage"   Jean-Jacques Rousseau's notion of the child-as-uncivilized-potential

noncoital sexual contact   see petting

noncustodial parents   after divorce, the parent who was not granted custody of the child or children

nonorganic failure to thrive (NOFTT)   a collection of symptoms associated with significantly delayed growth in children caused by emotional deprivation and neglect rather than direct physical abuse

nonoxynol-9   a specific spermicide found to be effective in killing microorganisms that carry sexually transmitted diseases

nonsexist   without bias or discrimination on the basis of a person's sex

nonstandard English   see dialect

nontraditional conception   any technology that scientifically assists conception among infertile persons

nonviolent discipline   training that corrects a child's behavior without the use of physical punishment like spanking or slapping

norms   standards of behavior considered "normal" or average for a group

Norplant   a subdermal contraceptive device

obesity   a condition where a person becomes extremely fat

objectivity   impartiality, lack of bias

object constancy   the realization that the actual size, shape, or color of an object is not affected by viewing angle, lighting, or distance.

object permanence   the knowledge that objects in the environment have a permanent existence independent of one's interaction with them

obsessive   a person affected by a repetitive, intrusive thought or thought pattern

obstetric chair   an alternative to positioning a laboring woman on a gurney

octoxynol-9   like nonoxynol-9 a spermicide effective against some sexually transmitted disease organisms

Oedipal conflict   according to Freud, a series of events that occur in the phallic stage of psychosexual growth that encourage the development of a superego or conscience in a boy as well as the identification of the boy with his father

olfactory   of or pertaining to the sense of smell

one-to-one correspondence   matching each number with a single item when counting

onlooker   Parten's term for play that involves watching another person's activities but not participating in them

only children   children without brothers or sisters

oocytes   immature egg cells in the ovaries

operant conditioning   Skinner's term for learning that results from past reinforcement or punishment

operating principles   rules for improving the comprehension of oral language

opiods   drugs derived from opium and opium-containing compounds

opportunistic/competent   one longterm adjustment to divorce where children function relatively well, making sure their own needs are met

oppositional defiant behavior   being argumentative; disobedient

oral contraceptives   birth control medications taken by mouth (commonly known as "the pill")

oral stage   Freud's first stage of psychosexual development where the child receives gratification primarily through sucking and other oral stimulating

organic   relating to a physical or physiological cause

organizational theories   an approach that suggests that emotions play a central role in behavior by influencing cognition and encouraging exploration, attachment, and withdrawal from harm.

organization   Piaget's term for the process of synthesizing and analyzing perceptions and thoughts

organogenesis   see morphogenesis

orgasm   a series of involuntary muscular contractions occurring during the peak of sexual arousal

orthopedic   pertaining to diseases, injuries, or disorders of the joints, tendons, ligaments, muscles or bones

Osgood-Schlatter syndrome   a collection of symptoms due to overuse of the knee joints

ossification   the process of replacing cartilage with bony tissue

osteoporosis   demineralization of the bone tissue causing bone loss and bone weakness

otic bones   the three, small bones that transmit auditory impulses through the hearing system

otitis media   middle ear infection

otoscope   an instrument for examining the health of the ear canal and ear drum

outercourse   noncoital sexual behavior

ovary (ovaries, pl.)   female gonad in the pelvis that produces ova and female sex hormones

overextension   the overuse of a given word used to describe several objects that share a particular characteristic

overgeneralization   the inappropriate application of grammatical rules

overlapping speech   where a dialogue involved repetition of the speakers words rather than a novel addition or response (i.e., Mother: "Do you like that?" Child: "Like that?")

overnourishment   overfeeding; providing more nutrition that one needs to support growth or maintain weight

Ovists   A group that was formed during the Middle Ages to support the notion that the preformed human resided in the female ovum

ovulate   release of a mature ovum from the ovary

ovum (ova, pl.)   female gamete or reproductive cell

oxytocin   a hormone that causes the milk storage glands in the breasts to release their milk; it also causes the uterus to contract and heal after childbirth

pacifier a rubber nipple or similar object given to babies to suck on

pain cry a specific cry that the baby emits indicating severe distress

palmar grasp grasping using the palm and fingers as a unit

pancreas a gland below the stomach that secretes enzymes into the small intestine to aid digestion and produces insulin

parallel play play in which two or more children play next to each other without interacting

parochial school a school maintained and controlled by the church or some other religious group

partial immersion where terms in the speaker's native language are occasionally referenced even though the nonnative language predominates

partnership a term characterizing a more coequal, symbiotic relationship between the child and his/her parents

passive hand the nondominant hand

passive smoking inhaling tobacco smoke as a function of being in a smoke-filled environment

passive voice designating that the subject is receiving the action rather than committing the action (The boy was bit by the spider)

paternal engrossment the father's fascination with and commitment to his infant

pattern perception the ability to visually recognize designs or arrangements

PCP an hallucinogenic drug also known as "angel dust"

pediatrician a physician specializing in the medical care of babies and children

peers/agemates a person who is equal to another in age, social class, skill, or so forth.

Pendulum Problem A task concocted by Inhelder and Piaget to test hypothetico-deductive reasoning

penis specialized male tissue through which sperm and urine pass

percentile any value found by dividing the group into a hundred equal parts

perception bound making judgments based on one's perception of an object or situation while ignoring other relevant cues. A characteristic of preoperational thought

perception the process of interpreting sensory input

perceptual disorder difficulties in interpreting sensory input

perceptual preference the sensory system that the child relies on most for information about the world

perceptual-spatial skills skills in interpreting sensory information and relating that information to a three-dimensional world

performance IQ an IQ estimate based on the scores for the performance subscales of the Wechsler tests

perineal of or pertaining to the perineum (the tissue between the end of the vagina and the anus)

period of the embryo the second period of prenatal development during which immature versions of all major body organs and systems develop; extends from the second gestational week to the end of the 8th gestational week

period of the fetus the period of prenatal development that extends from the 9th gestational week until birth. During this time, the child prepares for life outside the womb

permanent teeth the 32 teeth that will eventually replace the deciduous teeth

permissive a parenting style that is responsive and nurturant, but exerts little control and makes few demands. The permissive parent is overly tolerant and rarely restrictive

persistence the degree of tenacity one possesses

personality (also called temperament) distinctive traits, characteristics and behaviors of an individual

personal identity knowing "who you are" as a person

petting physical contact including kissing, touching, and genital stimulation but excluding intercourse

pharmacologist a scientist who deals with the sources, qualities, preparations, and uses of drugs

phenotype the observable characteristics an individual has inherited

phobia an irrational, extreme fear out of proportion to the extent of the threat

phonemes the smallest unit of speech sounds that can be discerned auditorally

phosphorus a nonmetallic element that interacts with calcium to provide for bone and tooth development

physical development age-related changes in the organs, tissues, and systems of the body

Physician's Desk Reference a helpful source of information about American pharmaceuticals (updated each year)

pica craving for or compulsive eating of nonfood items

pictoral stage the last stage of drawing development in which the child can produce recognizable pictures of familiar objects

pincer grasp grasping involving the thumb and forefinger opposed

pineal gland the gland within the brain that may influence sleep and wakefulness

pitocin a synthetic hormone introduced intravenously to initiate labor

pituitary gland an endocrine gland located at the base of the brain which secretes hormones that regulate the functions of the body organs

pivot words words used repeatedly by children in combinations with various other words called X-words

PKU (phenylketonuria) a genetic disease that affects protein metabolism; if untreated, can lead to severe mental retardation

PL 94-142 the Public Law which, among other things, is the legal mandate for mainstreaming

placement stage the stage in the development of drawing characterized by scribbling confined to a particular region of a page

placenta the organ that develops at the site of implantation; the mother's blood circulates through the placenta and passes oxygen and nutrients to the baby

play exercise done for recreation or pleasure

pneumonia an infection that causes inflammation of the lungs

Poison Control Center any of several regionalized offices specializing in prompt information about the toxicity of specific substances and in the treatment of poison ingestion

polio a viral disease that attacks the neuromuscular system leaving one paralyzed or with reduced motor movement; can impair breathing; can be fatal. Routinely vaccinated against

politically conservative in the United States, a person who is politically cautious, opposed to government intervention, and supportive of competitive enterprise

polygenic traits   traits produced by the interaction of several genes

pornography   spoken, written, or visual materials designed to be sexually arousing

port-wine stain   a flat, purplish birthmark or hemangiona

positive health   focusing on prevention rather than treatment

positive reinforcement   giving the organism something they enjoy/desire after they perform a desired behavior

postconventional moral reasoning   the third and last stage of moral development in Kohlberg's theory. In this stage (much like in Piaget's stage of autonomous morality), one's conscience and consensus takes precedence over arbitrary rules.

postmaturity   an infant born weighing more than 3800 grams and more than 2 weeks past due

postpartum contractions (afterpains)   uterine contractions that persist after the baby is born

postpartum depression   hormonally influenced feelings of loss and sadness after the delivery; also called the baby blues

postpartum hemorrhage (third stage bleeding)   bleeding that occurs after the delivery of a baby if fragments of the placenta remain in the uterus

postpartum psychosis   a serious form of postpartum depression

posttraumatic stress disorder (PTSD)   a condition characterized by periodic episodes of anxiety, depression, or panic provoked by reminders of past traumas

pragmatics   rules for language usage

preconventional level of morality   Kohlberg's term for the first stage of moral development where the child focuses on avoiding punishment and satisfying personal needs

prehension   skills involved in grasping or holding objects

prelinguistic   nonlanguage communication

premarital sex   having sexual intercourse prior to marriage

premature (preterm)   a baby born who has developed for less than 37 gestational weeks and weighs less than 5½ lbs.

premenstrual syndrome (PMS)   uncomfortable physical and emotional symptoms that occur 2–12 days prior to the onset of menstruation

prenatal   the period of development prior to birth

prenatal sex hormones   circulating hormones that help develop the reproductive organs and the external genitals

prenatal syphilis   fetal syphilitic infection from maternal transmission

preoperational stage   the stage of cognitive development that follows the sensorimotor stage in Piaget's scheme. The preoperational child has some mental concepts but hasn't acquired the means or operations by which to manipulate and transform them

prepared childbirth   a term coined by Grantly Dick-Read to refer to instruction given to prospective parents about the birth process and about pain management

prepubescent   in the period prior to puberty

preschools/child-care centers   sites staffed by professionals who care for and instruct children while their parent(s) work

preschool   the period of development between ages 3 and 6 (roughly); also called early childhood

pretend play   play in which imagination or creativity is displayed; make-believe play

primacy effect   in memory tasks, a better memory for items at the beginning of the list than at the middle or the end

primary circular reactions   according to Piaget, simple repetitive acts that involve the child's body such as kicking or thumb sucking; these behaviors are characteristics of Piaget's second stage of the sensorimotor period

primary infertility   where the couple has never been able to conceive

primary sex characteristics   male or female structures essential to reproduction

primary teeth   see deciduous teeth

principles of dominant and recessive inheritance   laws of heredity governing dominant and recessive traits discovered by Gregor Mendel in 1865

private speech   speech that is uttered but not directed to anyone in particular; common among preschool age children

processing capacity   the amount of information that can be examined or considered at one time

processing speed   the amount of time it takes to identify, understand, and act on information

productive thinking   In Terman's terms, using thought to discover new things and generate solutions to problems

profanity   disrespectful or vulgar language

progestins   female sex hormones that are crucial to the establishment and maintenance of pregnancy

prolactin   a hormone released by the woman's body after childbirth that stimulates milk production

pronatalist   literally, "in favor of birth"; an attitude that supports parenthood

propositional logic   the ability to judge the truth of logical relationships reflecting thinking; the ability to assess the appropriateness of reasoning strategies before applying them

propped bottle   a babybottle that is being supported by an object rather than by a person

prosocial behavior   actions that involve helping or cooperating which support the basic principles of society and uphold the general good

prostaglandins   hormones that cause uterine contractions

prostate gland   a gland located at the base of the bladder that produces a portion of the semen released during ejaculation

prosthesis   an artificial appliance, like an eye or limb

prostitute   a person who offers sex in exchange for something of value (usually money or drugs)

protest   John Bowlby's first stage of separation, where the infant is distressed and actively searches for the parent

protodirective   telling a person to do something they are already doing

proximodistal principle   growth that proceeds from the spine to the extremities (literally, "from near to far")

pseudodialogue   a prompted dialogue where the speaker responds to looks and other nonverbal signals as though they were words

pseudoimitation   an adult interrupts the child's vocal play to imitate its sound and the baby continues its vocalizations in turn after the adult

psychiatric care   treatment received under a psychiatrist's care in a hospital setting

psychiatric disorders   serious psychological disturbance that requires hospitalization and/or medication

psychoanalytic theory   a theoretical position originated by

Sigmund Freud that emphasizes the role of unconscious motives and of early childhood experience

psychological abuse/psychological maltreatment verbal and nonverbal behavior that assaults the child's sense of self worth: insults, ridicule, lack of confidence directed toward the child

psychometrics using tests or assessment devices to measure behavior

psychomotor abilities In Terman's terms, sports aptitude

psychomotor development index an index from the Bayley scale that measures large and fine muscle skills

psychosocial theory a stage level approach to development advanced by Erik Erikson that emphasizes the importance of social interaction and the environment in shaping behavior

psychosomatic illness an illness that is influenced by a person's experiences or reactions to experiences

psychotic disorder a serious psychological disturbance; schizophrenia, affective disorders, and paranoia are examples of psychotic disturbances

puberty the transition from childhood to adulthood during which the reproductive structures mature

pubic hair pigmented hair that covers the area around the pubic bone

PUBS—(percutaneous umbilical blood sampling) a prenatal diagnostic procedure for sampling and testing the baby's blood for abnormalities

pull-out programs the practice of providing special coursework for children in a classroom outside their own

punishment an unpleasant or aversive event that reduces the likelihood that the response that preceded it will be repeated

"pushout" adolescents who are forced from the school system because of pressure, hostility, or indifference

quadruplet one of four offspring born at one birth

qualitative change variation in type

quantitative change variation in amount

quickening when fetal movements can be felt by the mother

quiet (NREM) sleep the cycle of sleep in which brain and body activity are reduced and no rapid eye movements are displayed

race people sharing a common ancestry, history, nationality, country, or origin

radiation emission of radiant energy by xrays or other sources

rads a measure of radiation intensity

random assignment using random procedures such as flipping a coin to assign subjects to a particular group in an experiment, thereby eliminating a source of potential bias

rape intercourse or other sexual penetration forced on an individual who sincerely resists

rapid eye movements (REMs) darting movements made by the eyes during sleep, but especially during dreaming

reaction time the speed with which an individual can respond to a particular stimulus

reactivity a measure of emotional stability ranging from calm to irritable

readiness Arnold Gesell's term describing the physical maturation that prepares the child to make advances in motor development

recall to remember without cues or prompts

recessive trait inherited characteristics that are rarely expressed in the general population

reciprocity if the mass remains constant, a change in one dimension necessitates a change in another (i.e., if a mass becomes flattened, it will become wider as it becomes thinner)

recognition noticing that a stimulus is familiar

reconstituted/blended families when the parents and children of two divorced families come together as a unit after remarriage

red measles see measles

reflective in problem solving, the tendency to answer questions slowly and thoughtfully, demonstrating a concern for accuracy

reflexes automatic, inborn behaviors that generally have survival value

reflex smiles automatic smiling rather than purposeful, voluntary smiling

regional anesthetics a substance that produces the loss of physical sensation in certain body regions without the accompanying loss of consciousness

rehabilitation the act of restoring an individual to a state of useful activity by helping them turn away from or cope with events that lead to inefficient or ineffective behavior

rehearsal repeating or going-over material in an effort to retain or remember it

reinforcement in operant conditioning, any event that increases the likelihood that a given response will occur again (for example, giving a child a stick of chewing gum every time they go potty on the toilet will increase their chances of toileting correctly in the future)

relative size the size of one object in reference to another

remarriage marriage after divorce

replication repeating an experiment to verify its results

representative sample a research sample in which every individual in the total population in question has an equal chance of being included in the study.

residential care care received while hospitalized or institutionalized

respiratory distress/respiratory distress syndrome (RDS) breathing complications experienced by newborns

respiratory monitors specialized devices used to check for interruptions in breathing

respiratory rate generally a measure of breathing rate (breaths-per-minute)

restraining order a court order that legally restricts one person from having access or contacting another person

retina the portion of the inside of the eye containing the photoreceptor cells, the rods and cones

retinopathy of prematurity (ROP) permanent damage to the immature retina of the newborn eye by prolonged exposure to intense light or oxygen

reversibility the notion that something that has been changed can be returned to its original state by reversing the process that lead to the change

rhythmicity the extent to which behavior is predictable and patterned vs. unpredictable and lacking pattern

robbery unlawfully seizing another person's property; if the property is taken in the owner's presence, violence or the threat of violence is used

rooming-in the practice of keeping the mother and the baby in a single room after delivery

rough-and-tumble play play that involves elements of physical interaction (chasing, tackling, wrestling, etc)

rubella formerly called German measles; an infection that is particularly teratogenic to the unborn

runaway a dependent child who escapes their parent's control by leaving home without consent

salivation secreting saliva

satiety feeling full after a meal

satire writing that exposes or ridicules human shortcomings in a witty or ironic way

saturated fat fats that don't break down easily in our systems, coating our arteries or being stored in our tissues as weight gain

scanning to visually search with a slow, sweeping movement of the eyes

scheme(s) (also schema) Piaget's term for general ways of thinking about, interacting with, or comprehending different aspects of the environment. Piaget believed children develop specific schemes or mental categories of information about specific objects or experiences and that these schemes are retained in memory

schizophrenia a serious psychological disturbance marked by fluctuations in mood, unusual behavior, and disordered thinking and social reactions

school dropout a student who voluntarily leaves school before completing their training or receiving their degree

school phobia/school refusal intense anxiety associated with school attendance

school retention maintaining a child's status as a full-time student

school years the period of development called middle childhood

scientific method specific procedures and assumptions that guide the conduct of scientific investigations

scoliosis curvature of the spine

scrotum the external pouch of skin in males that contains the testes

secondary circular reactions behaviors characteristic of the third sensorimotor stage, whereby the infant repeats an action to produce responses from objects or people (i.e., squeezing a toy to hear it squeak or laughing with an adult during play)

secondary gain benefits that are sometimes associated with an adverse circumstance (for example, a person who is handicapped might qualify for more financial aid at a college than a nonhandicapped person)

secondary infertility where the couple has been able to conceive, but is unsuccessful in subsequent attempts

secondary sex characteristics physical characteristics that develop during puberty that help distinguish the sexes but are not necessary for sexual reproduction

secular trend in growth growth and maturational rate differences noted between the generations

secure attachment according to Ainsworth, the most common form of attachment, whereby the child feels comfort when the parent is present, experiences moderate levels of stress when the parent leaves, and quickly and happily reestablishes contact when the parent returns

seizure a neuromuscular event characterized by spasms and loss of consciousness

selective attention concentrating on some features of the environment while excluding others

self-awareness recognizing the existence of the self

self-concept a person's perception of him or herself as an individual with specific characteristics and behaviors

self-control being able to resist temptation; to recognize and redirect behavior that has negative moral implications

self-derogation actions or words designed to lessen one's self-importance

self-efficacy the perception that one is capable of successfully performing a task

self-esteem an evaluation of the self concept on good-bad, worthy-unworthy, capable-incapable dimensions

self-fulfilling prophesy the idea that people often behave as they are expected to; also, that the interpretation of a particular behavior often reflects the biases and expectations of the interpreter

self-hostility antagonism directed at the self

self-image like self-perception, the person's idea of him or herself as an individual with specific characteristics and behaviors

self-perception interpretations of one's own behavior

self regulation/self control socializing oneself by setting limits on one's own behavior

semantics the language skill involved with learning word meaning

semen a fluid ejaculated through the penis that contains sperm and other secretions

semilingualism being somewhat proficient in a language

seminal vesicles a small gland located at the end of each vas deferens that secretes an alkaline fluid that becomes part of the ejaculate

seminiferous tubules thin, coiled structures with each testis in which sperm are produced

sensitive period see critical period

sensorimotor development/sensorimotor period Piaget's first stage of cognitive development (extending from birth to age 2) during which children rely on their senses and motor behavior to explore the world

sensorimotor play play activities during the sensorimotor period of cognitive development

separation protest (separation anxiety) a child's verbal or nonverbal expression of distress at the departure of his or her attachment figure

separatists those who believe it is more appropriate to represent intelligence as a collection of separate, independent skills than as a single general capacity

seriation arranging items in a logical sequence (i.e., tallest to shortest; lightest to darkest)

serotonin a brain neurotransmitter that plays an important role in sleep and mood changes

serous otitis media middle ear infection

Sesame Street a groundbreaking PBS television program originally designed to provide enrichment for disadvantaged children

sexually transmitted disease (STD) diseases that are spread by sexual contact; traditionally called veneral disease (VD)

sexual abstinence noninvolvement in sexual activity

sexual exploitation to take advantage of someone sexually

sexual maturity after puberty, when one is able to reproduce

sexual orientation feeling attracted to members of your own sex or other-sex persons

References

Abbey A. (1982). Sex differences in attributions for friendly behavior: Do males misperceive females' friendliness? *Journal of Personality and Social Psychology, 42,* 830–838.

Abel, D. l. (1988). Fetal alcohol effects in families. *Neurotoxicological Teratology, 10*(1), 1–2.

Abramovitch, R., Corter, C., Pepler, D. J., & Stanhope, L. (1986). Sibling and peer interaction: A final follow-up and comparison. *Child Development, 57,* 217–229.

Abramovitch, R., Pepler, D., & Corter, C. (1982). Patterns of sibling interaction among preschool-age children. In M.E. Lamb & B. Sutton-Smith (Eds.) *Sibling Relationships.* Hillsdale, New Jersey: Erlbaum.

Abrams, G. (1986, September 12). Turning in parents for using drugs: The great debate. *Los Angeles Times,* Part V, pp. 1, 6–7.

Achenbach, T. M. (1984). *The status of research related to psychopathology.* In W.A. Collins (Ed.) Research on school-age children: A report of the panel to review the status of basic research on school-age children. Washington, D.C.: National Academy of Sciences.

Acredolo, L. & Goodwyn, S. (1988). Symbolic gesturing in normal infants. *Child Development, 59,* 450–466.

Adams, G. R., & Crane, P. (1980). An assessment of parents' and teachers' expectations of preschool children's social preference for attractive or unattractive children and adults. *Child Development, 51,* 224–231.

Adams, R. E., & Passman, R. H. (1981). The effects of preparing two-year-olds for brief separation from their mothers. *Journal of Personality and Social Psychology, 52,* 1068–1070.

Adams, R. J. (1989). Newborns' discrimination among medium and long-wavelength stimuli. *Journal of Experimental Child Psychology, 47*(1), 130–141.

Adelson, J., Green, B., & O'Neil, R. P. (1969). The growth of the idea of law in adolescence. *Developmental Psychology, 1,* 327–332.

Adelson, J., & O'Neil, R. P. (1966). Growth of political ideas in adolescence: The sense of community. *Journal of Personality and Social Psychology, 4,* 295–306.

Adler, T. (1989a, July). Cocaine babies face behavior deficits. *APA Monitor,* p. 14.

Adler, T. (1989b, June). Social cues alter kids' likes, dislikes. *APA Monitor,* p. 22.

Affonso, D. D., & Domino, G. (1984). Postpartum depression: A review. *Birth Issues in Perinatal Care & Education, 11*(4), 231–235.

Ainsworth, M. D. S. (1973). The development of infant-mother attachment. In B. M. Caldwell & H. M. Ricciuti (Eds.), *Review of child development and research: Vol. 3. Child development and social policy.* Chicago: University of Chicago Press.

Ainsworth, M. D. S. (1982). Attachment: Retrospect and prospect. In C. M. Parkes & J. Stevenson-Hinde (Eds.). *The place of attachment in human behavior.* New York: Basic Books.

Ainsworth, M. D. S. (1985). Patterns of attachment. *Clinical Psychologist, 38*(2), 27–29.

Ainsworth, M. D. S., & Bell, S. M. (1970). Attachment, exploration and separation: Illustrated by the behavior of one-year-olds in a strange situation. *Child Development, 41,* 49–67.

Ainsworth, M. D. S., Blehar, M., Waters, E., & Wall, S. (1978). *Patterns of attachment.* Hillsdale, New Jersey: Erlbaum.

Ainsworth, M. D. S. & Wittig, B. A. (1969). Attachment and exploratory behavior of one-year-olds in a strange situation. In B. M. Foss (Ed.), *Determinants of infant behavior* (Vol. 4.) London: Methuen.

Alexander, T. M., & Ehns, J. T. (1988). Age changes in the boundaries of fuzzy categories. *Child Development, 59*(5), 1372–1386.

Allen, D. A., Raprin, I., & Niznitzer, M. (1988). Communication disorders of preschool children: The physician's responsibility. *Journal of Developmental and Behavioral Pediatrics, 9*(3), 164–170.

Allen, V. L., & Feldman, R. S. (1973). Learning through tutoring: Low achieving children as tutors. *Journal of Educational Psychology, 42,* 1–5.

Alley, J. M. et al. (1988). Dietary flouride supplements: The role of the physician. *Journal of the Medical Association of Georgia, 70*(9), 829–832.

Allison, P. D., & Furstenberg, F. F. (1989). How marital dissolution affects children: Variations by age and sex. *Developmental Psychology, 25*(4), 540–549.

Altemeir, W. A., O'Connor, S. M., Sherrod, K. B., & Vietze, P. M. (1985). Prospective study of antecedents for nonorganic failure to thrive. *Journal of Pediatrics, 106,* 360–365.

Amato, P. (1989). Family processes and the competence of adolescents and primary school children. *Journal of Youth and Adolescence, 18*(1), 39–53.

American Academy of Pediatriçs, Committee on Adolescence. (1988). Suicide and suicide attempts in adolescents and young adults. *Pediatrics, 81*(2), 322–324.

American Academy of Pediatrics. Committee on Drugs. (1980). Marijuana. *Pediatrics, 65*(3), 652–656.

American Academy of Pediatrics, Committee on Drugs. Transfer of drugs and other chemicals into human milk. *Pediatrics, 84*(5), 924–936.

American Academy of Pediatrics, Committee on Fetus and Newborn. (1987). Neonatal anesthesia. *Pediatrics, 80*(3), 446.

American Academy of Pediatrics, Committee on Genetics. (1989). Prenatal diagnosis for pediatricians. *Pediatrics, 84*(4), 741–744.

American Academy of Pediatrics, Committee on Infectious Diseases. (1989). Haemophilus influenzal type B conjugate vaccine: Update. *Pediatrics, 84*(2), 386–387.

American Academy of Pediatrics, Committee on Nutrition. (1989). Iron fortified infant formulas. *Pediatrics, 84*(6), 1114–1115.

American Academy of Pediatrics, Committee on Sports Medicine and Committee on School Health. (1989). Organized athletics for preadolescent children. *Pediatrics, 84*(3), 583–584.

American Academy of Pediatrics. (1989). Report of the task force on circumcision. *Pediatrics, 84*(4), 388–391.

American Academy of Pediatrics, Task Force on Infant Mortality (1986). Statement on infant mortality. *Pediatrics, 78*(6), 1155–1160.

American Cancer Society (1985). Cancer statistics, 1988. *Cancer Journal of Clinicians, 38*(1), 21.

American Council on Education. (1989). College freshmen's attitudes. Brown University. *Child Behavior & Development Letter*, January 1989, p. 7.

American Psychiatric Association, Diagnostic and Statistical Manual, 3rd ed. rev. (DSM-III-R). (1983). Washington, D.C.: *American Pyschiatric Association.*

American Psychological Association, Division on Developmental Psychology. (1968). Ethical standards for research with children. *Newsletter*, 1–3.

American Pyschological Association. (1975, January 24). Press Release.

Anand, K. J. S., & Hickey, P. R. (1987). Pain and its effect in the human neonate and fetus. *New England Journal of Medicine, 317*(21), 1321–1329.

Anastasi, A. (1982). *Psychological Testing* (5th ed.). New York: Macmillan.

Anderson, D. (1987). Family and peer relations of gay adolescents. *Adolescent Psychiatry. 14*, 162–178.

Anderson, D. R., Lorch, E. P., Field, D. E., Collins, P. A., & Nathan, J. G. (1986). Television viewing at home: Age trends in visual attention and time with TV. *Child Development, 57*, 1024–1033.

Anderson, D. R., Lorch, E. P., Field, D. E., & Sanders, J. (1981). The effects of TV program comprehension on children's visual attention to television. *Child Development, 52*, 151–157.

Anderson, E. R., Hetherington, E. M., & Clingempeel, W. G. (1989). Transformations in family relations at puberty: Effects of family context. Special issue: Early adolescent transitions: Longitudinal analyses of biological, psychological and social interactions. *Journal of Early Adolescence, 9*(3), 310–334.

Anderson, J. R., & Milson, R. (1989). Human memory: An adaptive perspective. *Psychological Review, 96*(4), 703–719.

Anderson, M. A. (1985). Cooperative group tasks and their relationship to peer acceptance and cooperation. *Journal of Learning Disabilities, 18*(2), 83–86.

Anderson, T., & Magnusson, D. (1990). Biological maturation in adolescence and the development of drinking habits and alcohol abuse among young males: A prospective longitudinal study. *Journal of Youth & Adolescence, 19*(1), 33–41.

Andolsek, D. M. (1990). *Obstetric care: Standards of prenatal, intrapartum and postpartum management*. Philadelphia: Lea & Febiger.

Antill, J. K., Cotton, S., & Tindale, S. (1983). Egalitarian or traditional: Correlates of the perception of an ideal marriage. *Australian Journal of Psychology, 35*(2), 245–257.

Apgar, V. (1953). A proposal for a new method of evaluation in the newborn infant. *Current Research in Anesthesia and Analgesia, 32*, 260–267.

Apgar, V., & Beck, J. (1973). *Is my baby alright?* New York: Trident.

Appelbaum, M. I., & McCall, R. B. (1983). Design and analysis in developmental psychology. In P. H. Mussen (Ed.), *Handbook of Child Psychology* (4th ed.), Vol. 1. New York: Wiley.

Aries, P. (1962). *Centuries of childhood: A social history of family life.* New York: Vintage, 1962.

Arnott, N. (1990, May). How to conquer crying and colic. *American Baby*, pp. 71, 73, 75.

Ary, D. B., Lichtenstein, E., & Severnsen, H. H. (1987). Smokeless tobacco use among male adolescents: Patterns, correlates, predictions and the use of other drugs. *Preventive Medicine, 16*(3) 385–401.

Asch, R. H., Asch, B., Asch, M., Bray, R., & Rojas F. J. (1988). Performance and sensitivity of modern home pregnancy tests. *International Journal of Fertility, 33*(3), 154, 157–8, 161.

Ascher, J. (1987, April). Born to be shy. *Psychology Today*, pp. 56–59, 62–64.

Asher, S. R., & Markell, K. A. (1974). Sex differences in comprehension of high and low interest reading material. *Journal of Educational Psychology, 66*, 680–687.

Asher, S. R., Renshaw, P. D., & Hymel, S. (1982). Peer relations and the development of social skills. In S. G. Moore & C. K. Copper (Eds.). *The young child: Review of Research* (Vol. 3). Washington, D.C.: National Association for the Education of Young Children.

Ashmead, D. H., & Perlmutter, M. (1980). Infant memory in everyday life. In M. Perlmutter (Ed.), *New directions in child development, 10: Childrens' memory*, San Francisco: Jossey-Bass.

Ashton, E. (1983). Measures of play behavior: The influences of sex role stereotyped children's books. *Sex Roles, 9*(1), 43–47.

Associated Press. (1989, August 17). Unwed moms now have one in four births. U.S. Reports, *Sacramento Bee*, p. A20.

Associated Press. (1989, December 19). Survey: White teens more apt to use drugs. *Sacramento Bee*, p. A14.

Astbury, J. et al. (1990). Neurodevelopmental outcome, growth, and health of extremely low birth weight survivors: How soon can we tell? *Developmental Medicine and Child Neurology, 32*(7), 582–589.

Astington, J. W. (1988). Children's production of commissive speech acts. *Journal of Child Language, 15*(2), 411–423.

Atkin, C. (1978). Observation of parent-child interaction in supermarket decision making. *Journal of Marketing, 42*, 41–45.

Atkinson, R. C., & Shiffrin, R. M. (1968). Human memory: A proposed system and its control processes. In K. W. Spence and J. T. Spence (Eds.) *Advances in the psychology of learning and motivation* (Vol. 2). New York: Academic Press.

Attie, I., & Brooks-Gunn, J. (1989). Development of eating problems in adolescent girls: A longitudinal study. *Developmental Psychology, 25*(1), 70–79.

Atwood, V. A. (1984). Children's concepts of death: A descriptive study. *Child Study Journal, 14*(1), 11–29.

Austin, A. B., & Draper, D. C. (1981). Peer relationships of the academically gifted: A review. *Gifted Child Quarterly, 25* (3, summer), 129–133.

Austin, A. M., Salehi, M. T., & Leffler, A. (1987). Gender and developmental differences in children's conversations. *Sex Roles, 16*(9–10), 497–510.

Avery, M. E. (1988). Pediatric medicine. Baltimore, MD: Williams & Wilkins.

Azrin, N., & Foxx, R. (1980). *Toilet training in less than a day.* New York: Simon & Schuster.

Babow, I., & Kridle, R. (1972). Problems and encounters of a suicidal adolescent girl. *Adolescence, 7*, 459–478.

Badzinski, D. M., Contor. J., & Hoffner, C. (1989). Children's understanding of quantifiers. *Child Study Journal, 19*(4), 241–258.

Bahrick, L. E., & Pickens, J. N. (1988). Classification of bimodal English and Spanish language passages by infants. *Infant Behavior & Development, 11*(3), 277–296.

Baillargeon, R., & Graber, M. (1988). Evidence of location memory in 8-month-old infants in a nonsearch AB task. *Developmental Psychology, 24*, 502–511.

Bains, W. (1987). *Genetic engineering for almost everybody.* London: Penguin Books.

Bainum, C. K., Lounsbury, K. R., & Pollio, H. R. (1984). The development of laughing and smiling in nursery school children. *Child Development, 55*, 1946–1957.

Bairstow, P. J. (1989). Development of planning and control of hand movement to moving targets. *British Journal of Developmental Psychology, 7*(1), 29–42.

Baker, C. D. (1982). The adolescent as theorist: An interpretive view. *Journal of Youth & Adolescence, 11*(3), 167–181.

Baker, S., Thalberg, S., & Morrison, D. (1988). Parents' behavioral norms as predictors of adolescent sexual activity andcontraceptive use. *Adolescence, 23*, 278–281.

Baker-Ward, L., Ornstein, P. A.,& Holden, D. J. (1984). The expression of memorization in early childhood. *Journal of Experimental Child Psychology, 37*, 555–575.

Baldwin, A. (1968). *Theories of child development.* New York: Wiley.

Baldwin, J. M. (1894). *Mental development in the child and the race.* New York: MacMillan.

Ballenger, J. C., Carek, D. J., Steele, J. J., & Cornish-McTighe, D. (1989). Three cases of panic disorder with agoraphobia in children. *American Journal of Psychiatry, 146*, 922–924.

Band, E. B., & Weisz, J. R. (1988). How to feel better when it feels bad: Children's perspectives on coping with everyday stress. *Developmental Psychology, 24*, 247–253.

Bandura, A. (1969). *Principles of behavior modification.* New York: Holt.

Bandura, A. (1973). *Aggression: A social learning analysis.* Englewood Cliffs, NJ: Prentice-Hall.

Bandura, A. (1977). *Social learning theory.* Englewood Cliffs, NJ: Prentice-Hall.

Bandura, A. (1989). Regulation of cognitive processes through perceived self-efficacy. *Developmental Psychology, 25*(5), 729–735.

Banis, H. T., Varni, J. W., Wallander, J. L., Korsch, B. M. et al. (1988). Psychological and social adjustment of obese children and their families. *Child Care, Health & Development, 14*(3), 157–173.

Banks, M. S., & Bennett, P. J. (1988). Optical & photoreceptor immaturities limit the spatial and chromatic vision of human neonates. *Journal of the Optical Society of America. Part A. Optics & Image Science, 5*(12), 2059–2079.

Banks, M. S., & Salapatck, P. (1983). Infant visual perception. In P. H. Mussen (Ed.), *Handbook of child psychology* (4th ed.), Vol. 2, 435–571. New York: Wiley.

Banks, S. P., & Kahn, M. D. (1982). *The sibling bond.* New York: Basic Books.

Baranowski, T. et al. (1983). Social support, social influence, ethnicity and the breastfeeding decision. *Social Science & Medicine, 17*, 1599–1611.

Barden, R. et al. (1989). Effects of cranoacial deformity in infancy on the quality of mother-infant interactions. *Child Development, 60*(4), 819–824.

Barkley, R. A. (1989). Hyperactive girls and boys: Stimulant drug effects on mother-child interactions. *Journal of Child Psychology, Psychiatry & Allied Disciplines, 30*(3), 379–390.

Barnard, K. E., & Bee, H. L. (1983). The impact of temporally patterned stimulation on the development of preterm infants. *Child Development, 54*, 1156–1167.

Barnes, E. (1990, June). Children of the damned. *Life Magazine*, pp. 31–41.

Barnett, M., Howard, J., King, L., & Dino, G. (1980). Antecedents of empathy: Retrospective accounts of early socialization. *Personality & Social Psychology Bulletin, 6*, 361–365.

Barnett, M. A., & McMinimy, V. (1988). Influence of the reason for the other's effect on preschooler's empathetic response. *Journal of Genetic Psychology, 149*(2), 153–162.

Baron, J. (1979). Orthographic and word-specific mechanisms in children's reading of words. *Child Development, 50*, 60–72.

Barron, F. (1955). The disposition toward originality. *Journal of Personality and Social Psychology, 51*, 478–485.

Barthelemy, C. et al. (1989). Urinary dopamine metabolites as indications of the responsiveness to tenfluramine treatment in children with autistic behavior. *Journal of Autism & Developmental Disorders, 19*(2), 241–254.

Bartsch, K., & Wellman, H. M. (1988). Young children's conception of distance. *Developmental Psychology, 24*(4), 532–541.

Basile, R. A. (1974). Lesbian mothers I. *Women's Law Reporter, 2*(2), 3–18.

Baskett, L. M. (1984). Ordinal position differences in children's family interactions. *Developmental Psychology, 20*(6), 1026–1031.

Bassuk, E. L., & Gallagher, E. M. (1990). The impact of homelessness on children. *Child & Youth Services, 14*(1), 19–33.

Bates, E. (1976). Pragmatics and sociolinguistics in child language. In D. Morehead and A. Morehead (Eds.). *Language deficiency in children: Selected readings.* Baltimore, MD: University Park Press.

Battistich, V., Solomon, D., Watson, M., & Solomon, J. et al. (1989). Effects of an elementary school program to enhance prosocial behavior on children's cognitive-social problem-solving skills and strategies. *Journal of Applied Developmental Psychology, 10*(2), 147–169.

Baughman, M. D. (1963). *Educator's handbook of stories, quotes, and humor.* Englewood Cliffs, NJ: Prentice-Hall.

Baumeister, R. F., & Senders, P. S. (1989). Identity development and the role structure of children's games. *Journal of Genetic Psychology, 150*(1), 19–37.

Baumrind, D. (1971). Harmonious parents and their preschool children. *Developmental Psychology, 4*, 99–102.

Baumrind, D. (1980). New directions in socialization research. *American Psychology, 35*, 639–652.

Bayley, N. (1935). The development of motor abilities during the first three years. *Monographs of the Society for Research in Child Development, 1*, 1–26.

Bayley, N. (1949). Consistency and variability in the growth of intelligence from birth to eighteen years. *Journal of Genetic Psychology, 75*, 165–196.

Bayley, N. (1965). Research in child development: A longitudinal perspective. *M-P Quarterly, 11*, 183–208.

Bayley, N. (1968). Behavioral correlate of mental growth: Birth to thirty-six years. *American Psychologist, 23*, 1–17.

Bayley, N. (1970). The development of mental abilities. In P. Mussen (Ed.), *Carmichael's manual of child psychology* (3rd ed.) Vol. 1, 1163–1209. New York: Wiley.

Bazar, J. (1990, July). Psychologists can help youths stay out of gangs. *APA Monitor*, p. 39.

Beal, C. R. (1987). Repairing the message: Children's monitoring and tension skills. *Child Development, 58*(2), 401–408.

Beal, V. A. (1980). *Nutrition in the life span.* New York: Wiley.

Beardslee, W. R. et al. (1982). The effects of infantile malnutrition on behavioral development: A follow up study. *American Journal of CLinical Nutrition, 35*(6), 1437–1441.

Beck, J. G., & Davies, D. K. (1987). Teen contraception: A review of perspectives on compliance. *Archives of Sexual Behavior, 16*(4), 337–368.

Beck, M., & Quade, V. (1989, July 3). Baby blues, the sequel. *Newsweek*, p. 62.

Becker, J. A. (1988a). The success of parents' indirect techniques for teaching their preschoolers pragmatic skills. *First Language, 8*(23, Pt. 2), 173–181.

Becker, J. A. (1988b). "I can't talk, I'm dead": Preschooler's spontaneous metapragmatic comments. *Discourse Processes, 11*(4), 457–467.

Bee, H. L. (1989). *The developing child* (5th ed.). New York: Harper & Row.

Bee, H. L. et al. (1982). Prediction of IQ and language skill from neonatal status, child performance, family characteristics and mother-infant interaction. *Child Development, 53,* 1134–1156.

Begley, S., & Robins, K. (1989, February 27). Erasing port-wine stains, *Newsweek,* p. 65.

Bell, R. Q. (1974). Contribution of human infants to caregiving and social interaction. In M. Lewis & L. A. Rosenblum (Eds.), *Effect of the infant on its caregiver.* New York: Wiley.

Bellugi, U. (1970). Learning the language. *Psychology Today, 3,* 33–66.

Belskey, J. (1980). A family analysis of parental influence on infant exploratory competence. In F. Petersen (Ed.), *The father-infant relationship: Observational studies in a family context.* New York: Praeger Special Studies.

Belsky, J. (1981). Early human experience: A family perspective. *Development Psychology, 17*(1), 3–23.

Belsky, J. (1985). Exploring individual differences in marital change across the transition to parenthood: The role of violated expectations. *Journal of Marriage & The Family, 47,* 1037–1044.

Belsky, J. (1988). Infant day care and socioemotional development: The United States. *Journal of Child Psychology & Psychiatry and Allied Disciplines, 29*(4), 397–406.

Belsky, J. & Rovine, M. (1987). Temperament and attachment security in the Strange Situation: An empirical rapproachment. *Child Development, 58,* 787–795.

Bem, S. L. (1983). Gender schema theory and its implications for child development: Raising gender aschematic children in a gender schematic society. *Signs, 8,* 598–616.

Bem, S. L. (1985). Androgyny and gender schema theory: A conceptual and empirical integration. In T. B. Sonderegger (Ed.),Nebraska Symposium on Motivation, 1984, *Psychology and gender.* Lincoln: University of Nebraska Press.

Bem, S. L. (1989). Genital knowledge of gender constancy in preschool children. *Child Development, 60*(3), 649–662.

Benedetto, C. (1989). Eicostanoids in primary dysmenorrhea, endometriosis, and menstrual migraine. *Gynecological Endocrinology, 3*(1), 71–94.

Berg, I. (1984). Adolescence. *British Journal of Psychiatry, 144,* 94–97.

Berg, K., & Berg, K. (1979). Psychosociological development in infancy: Stat, sensory function, and attention. In J. Osofsky (Ed.), *Handbook of infant development.* New York: Wiley.

Berk, L. E. (1986). Private speech: Learning out loud. *Psychology Today, 20*(5), 34–42.

Berk, L. E. (1989). *Child development,* New York: Allyn & Bacon.

Berkowitz, L. (1989). Frustration-aggression hypothesis: Examination and reformulation. *Psychology Bulletin, 106*(1), 59–73.

Berlinsky, E., & Biller, H. (1982). *Parental death and psychological development.* Lexington, MA: Lexington Books.

Berman, A. L. (1988). Fictional depictions of suicide in television films and imitation effects. *American Journal of Psychiatry, 145,* 982–986.

Berman, R. (1984). From nonanalysis to productivity: Interim schemata in child language. In I. Levin (Ed.), *Stage & structure.* Norwood, NJ: Ablex.

Berndt, T. J. (1981). Relations between social cognition, nonsocial cognition and social behavior: The case of friendship. In J. H., Flavell & L. D. Ross (Eds.), *Cambridge studies of social and emotional development: Frontiers and possible futures.* New York: Cambridge University Press.

Bernstein, B. (1973). *Class, codes and controls* (Vols. 1 & 2). London: Routledge & Kegan Paul.

Bernstein G. A., & Garfinkel, B. D. (1988). Pedigrees, functioning and psychopathology in families of school phobic children. *American Journal of Psychiatry, 145,* 70–74.

Bernt, F. M. (1989). Children's use of schematic concepts in free classification tasks: A closer look. *Journal of Genetic Psychology, 150*(2), 187–195.

Bertenthal, B. I., & Campos, J. J. (1987). New directions in the study of early experience. *Child Development, 58,* 560–567.

Berzonsky, M. D. (1987). A preliminary investigation of children's conceptions of life and death. *Merrill-Palmer Quarterly, 33*(4), 505–513.

Bettes, B. A. (1988). Maternal depression and motherese: Temporal and intonational features. *Child Development, 59*(4), 1089–1096.

Bialystok, R. (1986). Children's concept of word. *Journal of Psycholinguistic Research, 15*(1), 13–32.

Bierman, K. L., & Furman, W. (1984). The effects of social skills training and peer involvement on the social adjustment of preadolescents. *Child Development, 55,* 151–162.

Bigelow, A., MacLean, J., Wood, C., & Smith, J. (1990). Infants' responses to child and adult strangers: An investigation of height and facial configuration variables. *Infant Behavior & Development, 13*(1), 21–32.

Binkin, N., Yip, R., Fleshood, L., & Trowbridge, F. (1988). Birthweight and childhood growth. *Pediatrics, 82,* 828–834.

Bird, H. R. (1980). Stranger reaction versus stranger anxiety. *Journal of the American Academy of Psychoanalysis, 8*(4), 555–563.

Bird, J. E. (1988). Optimism in parental predictions of children's future behavior. *Early Child Development & Care, 35,* 29–38.

Bishop, D., & Bowine, E. (1985). Do young children understand comparatives? *British Journal of Developmental Psychology, 3*(2), 123–131.

Bjorklund, D. F., & Hack, H. S. (1982). Age differences in the temporal locus of memory organization in children's recall. *Journal of Experimental Child Psychology, 32,* 347–362.

Bjorklund, D. F., & Zeman, B. R. (1983). The development of organizational strategies in children's recall of familiar information: Using social organization to recall the names of classmates. *International Journal of Behavioral Development, 6,* 341–353.

Black, Betty. (1989). Interactive pretense: Social and symbolic skills in preschool play groups. *Merrill-Palmer Quarterly, 35*(4), 379–397.

Black, B. & Hazen, N. L. (1990). Social status and patterns of communication in acquainted and unacquainted preschool children. *Developmental Psychology, 26*(3), 379–387.

Blake, J. (1981). The only child in America: Prejudice vs. performance. *Population and Development Review, 1,* 43–54.

Blanchard, J., & Meyers, C. E. (1983). A review of attachment formation and disorders of handicapped children. *American Journal of Mental Deficiency, 87*(4), 359–371.

Blass, E. M., & Hoffmeyer, L. B. (1991). Sucrose as an analgesic for newborn infants. *Pediatrics, 87*(2), 215–218.

Blau, Z. S. (1981). *Black children/white children: Competence, socialization and social structure.* New York: The Free Press.

Blevins-Knabe, B. (1987). Development of the ability to insert into a series. *Journal of Genetic Psychology, 148*(4), 427–441.

Bliss, L. S. (1987). "I can't talk anymore, my mouth doesn't want to": The development and clinical applications of modal auxiliaries, language, speech and hearing services in schools, *18*(1), 72–79.

Block, J. H. (1983). Differential premises arising from differential socialization of the sexes: Some conjectures. *Child Development, 54,* 1335–1354.

Block, J. H., Block, J., & Gjerde, P. F. (1986). The personality of children prior to divorce: A prospective study. *Child Development, 57*(4), 827–840.

Blomberg, S. (1980). Influences of maternal distress during pregnancy on complications in labor and delivery. *Acta Psychiatria Scandanaria, 62*(5), 399–404.

Blotner, R., & Bearison, D. J. (1984). Developmental consistencies in sociomoral knowledge: Justic reasoning and altruistic behavior. *Merrill-Palmer Quarterly, 30*, 349–367.

Bluebond-Langner, M. (1989). Worlds of dying children and their well siblings. *Death Studies, 13*(1), 1–16.

Blum, R. W. (1985). The adolescent dialectic: A developmental perspective on social decision-making. *Psychiatric Annals, 15*(10), 614–618.

Blum, R. (1987). Contemporary threats to adolescent health in the United States. *Journal of American Medical Association, 257*(24), 3390–3395.

Blume, J. (1970). *Are you there, God? It's me, Margaret.* Scarsdale, New York: Bradbury Press.

Boccia, M., & Campos, J. (1983, April). Maternal emotional signaling. Its effect on infants' reaction to strangers. Paper presented at the meeting of the Society for Research in Child Development, Detroit, MI.

Bogin, B. (1988). *Patterns of human growth.* Cambridge: Cambridge University Press.

Boldizar, J. P., Perry, D. G., & Perry, L. C. (1989). Outcome values and aggression. *Child Development, 60*(3), 571–579.

Bolsmier, J. (1977). Visual stimulation and the wake-sleep behavior in human neonates. *Developmental Psychology, 10*, 219–227.

Bolton, V. N., Wren, M. E., & Parsons, J. H. (1991). Pregnancies after in vitro fertilization and transfer of human blastocysts. *Fertility & Sterility, 55*(4), 830–832.

Bonnelykke, B. (1990). Maternal age and parity as predictions of human twinning. *Acta Geneticae Medicae et Gemellologiae, 39*(3), 329–334.

Booth, W. (1991, April). Mating call—human eggs may beckon sperm. *Sacramento Bee,* pp. A1-A12.

Borke, H. (1971). Interpersonal perception of young children: Egocentrism or empathy? *Developmental Psychology, 5*, 263–269.

Bornstein, M. H. (1985). How infant and mother jointly contribute to developing cognitive competencies in the child. *Proceedings of the National Academy of Science, 82*, 7470–7473.

Bornstein, M. H. (1989). Sensitive periods in development, structural characteristics and causal interpretations. *Psychological Bulletin, 105*(2), 179–197.

Bornstein, M. H., & Sigman, M. D. (1986). Continuity in mental development from infancy. *Child Development, 57*, 251–274.

Botta, R. M., Salvo, C., & Galluzzo, G. (1990). Fetal macrosomia in children of diabetic mothers: Relationship with excess weight in early years. *Minerva Endocrinologica, 15*(3), 215–8.

Botvin, G. J., Baker, E., Tortu, S., Dusenbury, L. et al. Smokeless tobacco use among adolescents: Correlates and concurrent predictions. *Journal of Developmental & Behavioral Pediatrics, 10*(4), 181–186.

Bounchard, C. (1991). Current understanding of the etiology of obesity: Genetic and nongenetic factors. *American Journal of Clinical Nutrition, 53* (G Supplement), 15819–15859.

Bounchard, T. J., Jr. (1981). A study of mental ability using twin and adoption designs. *Progress in Clinical Biological Research, Pt. B*, 21–23.

Boulot, P. et al. (1990). Obstetrical results after embryonic reductions performed in 34 multiple pregnancies. *Human Reproduction, 5*(8), 1009–1013.

Bowen, J. (1985). Helping children and their families cope with congenital heart disease. *Critical Care Quarterly, 8*(3), 65–74.

Bower, B. (27 April, 1985). Caution: Emotions at play. *Science News, 127*, 266–267.

Bower, T. G. R. (1981). *Development in infancy* (2nd Ed.). San Francisco: W. H. Freeman.

Bowlby, J. (1958). The nature of the child's tie to his mother. *International Journal of Psychoanalysis, 39*, 350–373.

Bowlby, J. (1973). *Separation and loss.* New York: Basic Books.

Bowlby, J. (1980). *Attachment and loss* (Vol. 3.) Loss. New York: Basic Books.

Bowman, J. A., Sanson-Fisher, R. W., & Webb, G. R. (1987). Interventions in preschools to increase the use of safety restraints by preschool chil-

dren. *Pediatrics, 79*(1), 103–109.

Brackbill, Y. L. (1958). Extinction of the smiling response in infants as a function of reinforcement schedule. *Child Development, 29*, 115–124.

Bradley, R. H., & Caldwell, B. M. (1980). The relation of home environment, cognitive competence and IQ among males and females. *Child Development, 51*, 1140–1148.

Bradley, R. H., & Caldwell, B. M. (1984). 174 children: A study of the relationship between home environment and cognitive development during the first 5 years. In A. W. Gottfried (Ed.), *Home environment and early cognitive development: Longitudinal research.* New York: Academic Press.

Brake, S. C., Fifer, Wm. P., Alfasi, G., & Fleischman, A. (1988). The first nutritive sucking responses of premature newborns. *Infant Behavior & Development, 11*(1), 1–19.

Bransford, J. D., Stein, B. S., Shelton, T. S., & Owings, R. A. (1981). Cognitive and adaptation: The importance of learning to learn. In J. Harvey (Ed.), *Cognition, social behavior and the environment.* Hillsdale, NJ: Erlbaum.

Brazelton, T. B. (1973). *Neonatal behavioral assessment scale.* Philadelphia, Lippincott.

Bredemeier, B. J. et al. (1986). Promoting moral growth in a summer sport camp: The implementation of theoretically grounded instructional strategies. *Journal of Moral Education, 15*(3), 212–220.

Bremner, J. C. (1989). Perceptual and intellectual development in infancy. *Science Progress, 73*(202, Pt. 4), 443–456.

Brent, D. A. (1989). Suicide and suicidal behavior in children and adolescents. *Pediatrics in Review, 10*, 269–275.

Brent, R. L. (1989). The effect of embryonic and fetal exposure to x-ray, microwaves, and ultrasound: Counseling the pregnant and nonpregnant patient about these risks. *Seminars in Oncology, 16*(5), 347–368.

Brent, R. L., & Beckman, D. A. (1990). Environmental teratogens. *Bulletin of the New York Academy of Medicine, 66*(1), 123–163.

Bretherton, I. (1989). Pretense: The form and function of make-believe play. *Developmental Review, 9*(4), 383–401.

Brewer, N., & Smith, J. M. (1989). Social acceptance of mentally retarded children in regular schools in relation to years mainstreamed. *Psychology Reports, 64*(2), 375–380.

Breznitz, Z., & Friedman, S. L. (1988). Toddler's concentration: Does maternal depression make a difference? *Journal of Child Psychology & Psychiatry & Allied Disciplines, 29*(3), 267–279.

Briere, J., Evans, D., Runtz, M., & Wall, T. (1988). Symptomology in men who were molested as children: A comparison study. *American Journal of Orthopsychiatry, 58*(3), 457–461.

Bright, P. (1987). Adolescent pregnancy and loss. *Maternal-Child Nursing Journal, 16*, 1–2.

Brody, G. H., Stoneman, Z., & Burke, M. (1987). Family system and individual child correlates of sibling behavior. *American Journal of Orthopsychiatry, 57*(4), 561–569.

Brody, G. H., Stoneman, Z., Mackinnon, C. E., & Mackinnon, R. (1985). Role relationships and behavior between preschool-aged and school-aged sibling pairs. *Developmental Psychology, 21*(1), 124–129.

Brody, L. R., Zelazo, P. R., & Chaika, H. (1984). Habituation-dishabituation to speech in a neonate. *Developmental Psychology, 20*, 114–119.

Brody, R. (1989, March). Stop, look and listen. *American Baby,* pp. 66–68.

Brodzinsky, D. M. (1984). New perspectives on adoption revelation. *Adoption & Fostering, 8*(2), 27–32.

Brone, R. J., & Fisher, C. B. (1988). Determinants of adolescent obesity: A comparison with anorexia nervosa. *Adolescence, 23*(89), 155–169.

Bronfenbrenner, U. (1974, August). The origins of alienation. *Scientific American, 231*, 53–61.

Bronfenbrenner, U. (1986). Alienation and four worlds of childhood. *Phi Delta Kappan, 67*, 430–436.

Bronfenbrenner, U., & Couter, A. C. (1982). Work and family through time and space. In S. B. Kamerman & C. D. Hayes (Eds.), *Families that work: Children in a changing world*. Washington, D.C.: National Academy Press.

Bronson, G. W. (1990). Changes in infants' visual scanning across the 2- to 14-week age period. *Journal of Experimental Child Psychology, 49*(1), 101–125.

Bronzaft, A. L. (1989). Noise is hazardous to child's health and well being. *The Brown University Child Behavior & Development Letter, 5*(10), Oct., 1–3.

Brook, J. S., Gordon, A. S., Brook, A., & Brook, D. W. (1989). The consequences of marijuana use on intrapersonal and interpersonal functioning in black and white adolescents. *Genetic, Social & General Psychology Monographs, 115*(3), 349–369.

Brooks, J., & Weintraub, M. (1976). A history of infant intelligence testing. In M. Lewis (Ed.), *Origins of intelligence: Infancy & early childhood*. New York: Plenum.

Brooks-Gunn, J. (1986). The relationship of maternal beliefs about sex typing to maternal and young children's behavior. *Sex Roles, 14*, 21–35.

Brooks-Gunn, J. (1988). Antecedents and consequences of variations in girls' maturational timing. *Journal of Adolescent Health Care, 9*(5), 365–373.

Brooks-Gunn, J., Boyer, C. B., & Hein, K. (1988). Preventing HIV infection and AIDS in children and adolescents. *American Psychologist, 43*(11), 958–964.

Brooks-Gunn, J., & Furstenberg, F. (1986). The children of adolescent mothers: Physical, academic, and psychological outcomes. *Developmental Review, 6*(3), 224–251.

Brooks-Gunn, J., & Warren, M. P. (1985). Measuring physical status and timing in early adolescence: A developmental perspective special issue: Time of maturation and psychosocial functioning in adolescence: I. *Journal of Youth & Adolescence, 14*(3), 163–189.

Brooks-Gunn, J., & Warren, M. P. (1988). The psychological significance of secondary sexual characteristics in nine- to eleven-year-old girls. *Child Development, 1988, 59*(4), 1061–1069.

Brophy, J. E. (1983). Research on the self-fulfilling prophecy and teacher expectations. *Journal of Educational Psychology, 75*, 631–661.

Brophy, J. E., & Good, T. L. (1986). Teacher behavior and student achievement. In M. C. Wittrock (Ed.), *Handbook of research on teaching*. New York: MacMillan.

Brown, A. L., Bransford, J. D., Ferrara, R. A., & Campione, J. C. (1983). Learning, remembering and understanding. In P. H. Mussen (Ed.) *Handbook of child psychology* (4th ed.), Vol. 3. New York: Wiley.

Brown, A. L., & Kane, M. J. (1988). Preschool children can learn to transfer: Learning to learn and learning from example. *Cognitive Psychology, 20*(4), 493–523.

Brown, B. B., Eicher, S. A., & Petrie, S. (1986). The importance of peer group ("crowd") affiliation in adolescence. *Journal of Adolescence, 9*(1), 73–96.

Brown, B. B., Lohr, M. J., & McClenaham, E. L. (1986). Early adolescents' perceptions of peer pressure. *Journal of Early Adolescence, 6*, 139–154.

Brown, E. V. (1990). Developmental characteristics of figure drawings made by boys and girls ages 5 through 11. *Perceptual and Motor Skills, 70*(1), 279–288.

Brown, J. D. et al. (1990). Television and adolescent sexuality. Conference: Teens and television. *Journal of Adolescent Health Care, 11*(1), 62–70.

Brown, R. (1973). *A first language: The early stages*. Cambridge, MA: Harvard University Press.

Brown, R., Cazden, C., & Bellugi-Klima, U. (1969). The child's grammar from 1 to 3. In J. P. Hill (Ed.), *Minnesota Symposia on child psychology* (Vol. 2). Minneapolis: University of Minnesota Press.

Brown, R. T., Borden, K. A., Clingerman, S. R., & Jenkins, P. (1988). Depression in attention deficit–disordered and normal children and their parents. *Child Psychiatry & Human Development, 18*(3), 119–132.

Bruce, V. & Green, P. R. (1990). *Visual perception: Physiology, psychology, and ecology*, 2nd ed. Hillsdale, N.J.: Erlbaum Associates.

Bruch, H. (1979). *The golden cage: The enigma of anorexia nervosa*. New York: Vintage.

Bruner, J. S. (1973). *Beyond the information given: Studies in the psychology of knowing*. New York: Norton.

Bruner, J. S. (1977). Early social interaction and language acquisition. In H. R. Schaffer (Ed.), *Studies in mother-infant interaction*. London: Academic Press.

Bruno, R. M., Johnson, J. M., & Simm, J. (1987). Perception of humor by regular class students and students with learning disabilities. *Journal of Learning Disabilities, 20*(9), 568–570.

Bryer, J. B., Nelson, B. A., Miller J. B., & Krol, P. A. (1987). Childhood sexual and physical abuse are factors in adult psychiatric illness. *American Journal of Psychiatry, 144*(11), 1426–1430.

Buis, J. M., & Thompson, D. N. (1989). Imaginary audience and personal fable: A brief review. *Adolescence, 24*(96), 773–781.

Bumpas, L. L. (1984). Children and marital disruption: A replication and update. *Demography, 21*, 71–82.

Burdens on gay litigants and bias in the court system: Homosexual panic, child custody, and anonymous parties [Note]. (1984). *Harvard Civil Rights and Civil Liberties Law Review, 19*, 497–559.

Bureau of Labor Statistics (1987, November 25). As coded in the *New York Times*, p. 89.

Burke, A., Crenshaw, D., Green, J., Schlosser, M., & Strocchia-Rivera, L. (1989). Influence of verbal ability on the expression of aggression in physically abused children. *Journal of the American Academy of Child & Adolescent Psychiatry, 28*, 215–218.

Burnham, D. K., Vignes, G., & Ihsen, E. (1988). The effect of movement on infant's memory for visual compounds. *British Journal of Developmental Psychiatry, 6*(4), 351–360.

Burton, R. V. (1976). Honesty and dishonesty. In T. Lickona (Ed.), *Moral Development & Behavior*. New York: Holt, Rinehart & Winston.

Bushman, B. J., & Geen, K. G. (1990). Role of cognitive-emotional mediators and individual differences in the effects of media violence on aggression. *Journal of Personality and Psychology, 58*(1), 156–163.

Bushnell, I. W., Sai, F., & Mullin, J. T. (1989). Neonatal recognition of the mother's face. *British Journal of Developmental Psychology, 7*(1), 3–15.

Burchinal, M., Lee, M., Ramey, C. T. (1989). Type of day-care and preschool intellectual development in disadvantaged children. *Child Development, 60*(1), 128–137.

Butcher, J. E. (1989). Adolescent girls' sex role development: Relationship with sports participation, self-esteem and age of menarche. *Sex Roles, 20*(9–10), 575–593.

Butler, R. (1989). Interest in the task and interest in peers' work in competitive and noncompetitive conditions: A developmental study. *Child Development, 60*(3), 562–570.

Butler, R. J. (1989). Maternal attributions and tolerance for nocturnal enuresis. *Behaviour Research & Therapy, 24*(3), 307–312.

Butterfield, E. C., Nelson, T. O., & Peck, V. (1988). Developmental aspects of the feeling of knowing. *Developmental Psychology, 24*(5), 654–663.

Butterfield, E., & Siperstein, G. (1972). Influence of contingent auditory stimulation upon non-nutritional suckle. In J. Bosma (Ed.), *Oral sensation and perception: The mouth of the infant*. Springfield, IL: Charles C. Thomas.

Byne, W., Bleier, R., & Houston, L. (1988). Variations in human corpus callosum do not predict gender: A study using magnetic resonance imaging. *Behavioral Neuroscience, 102*(2), 222–227.

Byrd, K., & Cooper, E. B. (1989). Expressive and receptive language skills in stuttering children. *Journal of Fluency Disorders, 14*(2), 121–126.

Byrnes, J. P., & Duff, M. A. (1988). Young children's comprehension and production of causal expressions. *Child Study Journal, 18*(2), 101–119.

Byrnes, J. P., & Overton, W. F. (1988). Reasoning about logical connectives:

A developmental analysis. *Journal of Experimental Child Psychology, 46*(2), 194–218.

Cadman, D., Boyle, M., & Offord, D. R. (1988). The Ontario Child Health Study: Social adjustment and mental health of siblings of children with chronic health problems. *Journal of Developmental & Behavioral Pediatrics, 9*(3), 117–121.

Cairns, R. B., Cairns, B. D., Neckerman, H. J., Ferguson, L. L. et al. (1989). Growth and aggression: I. Childhood to early adolescence. *Developmental Psychology, 25*(2), 320–330.

Cairns, R. B., Cairns, B. D., Neckerman, H. J., Gest, S. D. et al. (1988). Social networks and aggressive behavior: Peer support or peer rejection? *Developmental Psychology 24*(6), 815–823.

Caldwell, B. M. (1986). Daycare and early environmental adequacy. In W. Fowler (Ed.), *Early experience and the development of competence. New Directions for Child Development, 32,* 11–30.

Callanan, M. A. (1989). Development of object categories and conclusion relations: Preschooler's hypotheses about word meaning. *Developmental Psychology, 25*(2), 207–216.

Camara, K. A., & Resnick, G. (1989). Styles of conflict resolution and co-operation between divorced parents: Effects on child behavior and adjustment. *American Journal of Orthopsychiatry, 59*(4), 560–575.

Cameron, P. A., & Gallup, G. G. (1988). Shadow recognition in human infants. *Infant Behavior & Development, 11*(4), 465–471.

Campbell, D. M. (1991). Multiple births: Too often a disaster. *British Medical Journal, 302* (6779), 740–741.

Campione, J. C., Brown, A. L., & Ferrara, R. A. (1982). Mental retardation and intelligence. In R. J. Sternberg (Ed.), *Handbook of human intelligence.* New York: Cambridge University Press.

Campos, J. J., Caplovitz, K. B., Lamb, M. E., Goldsmith, H. H., & Stenberg, C. (1983). Socioemotional development. In M. M. Harth & J. J. Campos (Eds.), *Handbook of child psychology: Vol. 2, Infancy & developmental psychoanalogy,* (4th ed.). New York: Wiley.

Campos, J. J., Langer, A., & Krowitz, A. (1970). Cardiac responses on the visual cliff in prelocomotor human infants. *Science, 170,* 196–197.

Canick, J. A., Knight, G. J., Palomaki, G. E. et al. (1988). Low second trimester maternal serum unconjugated oestriol in pregnancies with Down's syndrome. *British Journal of Obstetrics and Gynecology, 95*(4), 330–333.

Carey, W. B., Hegvik, R. L., & McDeritt, S. C. (1988). Temperamental factors associated with rapid weight gain and obesity in middle childhood. *Journal of Developmental and Behavioral Pediatrics, 9*(4), 194–198.

Carlan, S. J., Angel, J. L., & Knuppel, R. A. (1991). Soulder dystocia. *American Family Physician, 43*(4), 1307–1311.

Carlson, C. L., Lahey, B. B., & Veeper, R. (1984). Peer assessment of the social behavior of accepted, rejected and neglected children. *Journal of Abused Child Psychology, 12,* 189–198.

Carter, K., Sabers, D., Cushing, K., Pinnegar, S., & Berliner, D. C. (1987). Processing and using information about students: A study of expert, novice and postulant teachers. *Teaching & Teacher Education, 3,* 147–157.

Casey, P. H., Bradley, R., & Wortham, B. (1984). Social and nonsocial home environment of infants with nonorganic failure-to-thrive. *Pediatrics, 73*(3), 348–353.

Centers for Disease Control (1978). Honey exposure and infant botulism. *Morbidity and Mortality Weekly Report, 27*(29), 249.

Centers for Disease Control (1988). Changing patterns of groups at high risk for hepatitis B in the United States. *Morbidity & Mortality Weekly Report, 37,* 429–437.

Centers for Disease Control (1991, July 26). Life expectancy (as reported in the *Sacramento Bee,* p. A4).

Center for Educational Statistics (1987). Who drops out of high school? From high school and beyond. Washington, D.C.: Office of Educational Research and Improvement, U.S. Department of Education.

Centerwall, B. S., & Robinette, C. D. (1989). Twin concordance for dishonorable discharge from the military: With a review of genetics of antisocial behavior. *Comprehensive Psychiatry, 30*(5), 442–446.

Chalmers, B. (1982). Psychological aspects of pregnancy: Some thoughts for the 80s. *Social science and medicine, 16*(3), 323–331.

Chance, P. (1989, April). Precocious fears in the gifted. *Psychology Today,* p. 20.

Chance, P. (1989). Running away from home—and danger. *Psychology Today, 23*(9), 10.

Chance, P., & Fischman, J. (1987). The magic of childhood. *Psychology Today, 21*(5), 48–58.

Chaney, C. (1989). I pledge a legiance tothe flag: Three studies on word segmentation. *Applied Psycholinguistics, 10*(3), 261–281.

Chapman, M., & Lendenberger, U. (1989). Concrete operations and attentional capacity. *Journal of Experimental Child Psychology, 47*(2), 236–258.

Chasnoff, I. J. (1991). Cocaine and pregnancy: Clinical and methodolic issues. *Clinics in Perinatology, 18*(1), 113–123.

Chasnoff, I. J., Chisum, G. M., & Kaplan, W. E. (1988). Maternal cocaine use and genitourinary tract malformation. *Teratology, 37*(3), 201–204.

Chassin, L., Presson, C. C., & Sherman, S. J. (1989). ''Constructive'' vs. ''destructive'' deviance in adolescent health-related behaviors. *Journal of Youth & Adolescence, 18*(3), 245–262.

Chatoor, I. (1989). Infantile anorexia nervosa: A developmental disorder of separation and individuation. Special issue: Psychoanalysis and eating disorders. *Journal of the American Academy of Psychoanalysis, 17*(1), 43–64.

Chatterjee, M. S., Abdel-Rahmen, M., Bhandal, A., Klein, P., & Bogden, J. (1988). Amniotic fluid cadmium and thiocyanate in pregnant women who smoke. *Journal of Reproductive Medicine, 33*(5), 417–420.

Chen, C., & Stevenson, H. W. (1989). Homework: A cross-cultural examination. *Child Development, 60*(3), 551–561.

Cherlin, A. J. et al. (1991, June 7). Longitudinal studies of effects of divorce in children in Great Britain and the United States. *Science,* Vol. 252, pp. 1386–1389.

Cherry, R. S. (1981). Development of selective auditory attention skills in children. *Perceptual and Motor Skills, 52,* 379–385.

Cherukuri, R., Minkoff, H., Feldman, J., Parekh, A., & Glass, L. (1988). A cohort study of alkaloidal cocaine (''crack'') in pregnancy. *Journal of Obstetrics & Gynecology, 72,* 2, 147–151.

Chi, M. T. H. (1978). Knowledge structures and memory development. In R. S. Siegler (Ed.), *Children's thinking: What develops?* Hillsdale, NJ: Erlbaum.

Chi, M. T. H. (1982). Knowledge development and memory performance. In M. Friedman, J. P. Das, & N. O'Connor (Eds.). *Intelligence and learning.* New York: Plenum.

Chilman, C. S. (1983). *Adolescent sexuality in a changing American society* (2nd ed.). New York: Wiley.

Chomsky, C. S. (1969). *The acquisition of syntax in children from five to ten.* Cambridge, MA: Massachusetts Institute of Technology (MIT).

Chomsky, C. (1969). *The acquisition of syntax in children from 5–10.* (Research Monograph No. 57). Cambridge, MA: M.I.T. Press.

Chomsky, N. (1968). *Language and the mind.* New York: Harcourt, Brace and World.

Chomsky, N. (1986). Some observations in language and language learning: Reply to Macnamara, Arbib, Moore & Furrow. *New Ideas in Psychology, 4*(3), 363–377.

Christensen, A. P., & Matthew, R. S. (1987). Habit reversal and differential reintroducement of other behavior in the treatment of thumbsucking: An analysis of generalization and side-effects. *Journal of Child Psychology & Psychiatry, 28,* 281–295.

Chumlea, W. C. (1982). Physical growth in adolescence. In B. B. Wolman (Ed.). *Handbook of developmental psychology.* Englewood Cliffs, NJ: Prentice-Hall.

Church, M. W., & Gerkin, K. P. (1988). Hearing disorders in children with fetal alcohol syndrome: Findings from case reports. *Pediatrics, 82*(2), 147–154.

Cicirelli, V. G. (1976). Siblings teaching siblings. In V. L. Allen (Ed.), *Children as teachers: Theory and research in tutoring.* New York: Academic Press.

Clapp, J. F. (1989). The effects of maternal exercise on early pregnancy outcome. *American Journal of Obstetrics & Gynecology, 161* (6, Pt. 1), 1453–1457.

Clark, E. V., & Hecht, B. F. (1983). Comprehension, production, and language acquisition. *Annual Review of Psychology, 34,* 325–349.

Clark, H. H., & Clark, E. V. (1977). *Psychology & language: An introduction to psycholinguistics.* New York: Harcourt Brace Jovanovich.

Clark, J. C., Whitall, J., & Phillips, S. J. (1988). Human interlimb coordination: The first 6 months of independent walking. *Developmental Psychobiology, 21*(5), 445–450.

Clark, M. L., & Ayers, M. (1988). The role of reciprocity and proximity in junior high school friendship. *Journal of Youth & Adolescence, 17*(5), 403–407.

Clarkson, R. L. (1989). Early identification and intervention for hearing loss. *The Brown University Child Psychology & Development Letter, 5*(10) 1, 3.

Clarke-Stewart, K. A. (1977). *Child care in the family: A review of research and some propositions for policy.* New York: Academic Press.

Clarke-Stewart, K. A. (1978). Recasting the lone stranger. In J. Glick & K. A. Clarke-Stewart (Eds.), *The development of social understanding.* New York: Gardner Press.

Clarke-Stewart, K. A. (1980). The father's contribution to child development. In F. A. Pedersen (Ed.), *The father-infant relationship: Observational studies in a family context.* New York: Praeger Special Studies.

Clarke-Stewart, K. A. (1988). The "effect" of infancy day care reconsidered. Risks for parents, children, and researchers. Special issue: Infant day care. *Early Childhood Research Quarterly, 3*(3), 293–318.

Clarke-Stewart, K. A. (1989). Infant daycare: Maligned or malignant? Special issue: Children and their development: Knowledge base, research agenda, and social policy application. *American Psychology 44*(2), 266–273.

Clarke-Stewart, K. A., & Hevey, C. M. (1981). Longitudinal relations in repeated observations of mother-child interactions from 1 to 2½ years. *Developmental Psychology, 17,* 127–145.

Cliatt, M. J. P., Shaw, J. M., & Sherwood, J. M. (1980). Effects of training in the emergent thinking abilities of kindergarten children. *Child Development, 51,* 1061–1064.

Clifton, R. K., Clarkson, M. G., Gwiazda, H., Bauer, J. A., & Held, R. M. (1988). Growth in head size during infancy: Implications for sound localization. *Developmental Psychology, 24*(4), 477–483.

Clingempeel, W. G., & Segal, S. (1986). Stepparent-stepchild relationship and the psychological adjustment of children in stepmother and stepfather families. *Child Development, 57,* 474–484.

Clunies-Ross, C., & Landsown, R. (1988). Concepts of death, illness and isolation found in children with leukaemia. *Child Care, Health & Development, 14*(6), 373–386.

Coady, H., & Sawyer, D. (1986). Moral judgment, sex and the level of temptation as determinants of resistance to temptation. *Journal of Psychology, 120*(2), 177–181.

Cohn, D. A. (1990). Child-mother attachment of six-year-olds and social competence at school. *Child Development, 61*(1), 152–162.

Coie, J. D., & Dodge, K. A. (1983). Continuities and changes in children's social status: A five-year longitudinal study. *Merrill-Palmer Quarterly, 29,* 261–282.

Coie, J. D., & Dodge, K. A. (1988). Multiple sources of data on social behavior and social status in the school: A cross-age comparison. *Child Development, 59*(3), 815–829.

Colby, A., Kohlberg, L., Gibbs, J., & Lieberman, M. (1983). A longitudinal study of moral judgment. *Monographs of the Society for Research in Child Development, 48* (Serial No. 200).

Coleman, E., & Remafedi, G. (1989). Gay, lesbian and bisexual adolescents: A critical challenge to counselors. Special issue: Gay, lesbian and bisexual issues in counseling. *Journal of Counseling & Development, 68*(1), 36–40.

Coleman, J. S., Hoffer, T., & Kilgore, S. (1981). *Public & private schools: Report submitted to the National Center for Education Statistics.* Chicago: National Opinion Research Center.

Collins, W. A., & Duncan, S. W. (1984). Out-of-school settings in middle childhood. In W. A. Collins (Ed.), *Research on school-age children: Report of the panel to review the status of basic research on school-age children.* Washington, D.C.: National Academy of Sciences Press.

Collins, W. A. & Korac, N. (1982). Recent progress in the study of the effects of television viewing on social development. *International Journal of Behavioral Development, 5*(2), 171–193.

Combs, C. A., Robertson, P. A., & Laros, R. K., Jr. (1990). Risk factors for third-degree and fourth-degree perineal lacerations in forceps and vacuum deliveries. *American Journal of Obstetrics & Gynecology, 163*(1 Pt. 1), 100–104.

Condon, J. T., & Hilton, C. A. (1988). A comparison of smoking and drinking behaviors in pregnant women: Who abstains and why. *Medical Journal of Australia, 148*(8), 381–385.

Conger, J. J., & Petersen, A. C. (1984). *Adolescence & Youth: Psychological development in a changing world* (3rd ed.). New York: Harper & Row.

Conners, C. K. (1988). Does diet affect behavior and learning in hyperactive children? *Harvard Medical School Mental Health Letter, 5*(5), 7–8.

Connolly, J. A., Doyle, A. B., & Reznick, E. (1988). Social pretend play and social interaction in preschoolers. *Journal of Applied Developmental Psychology, 9*(3), 301–313.

Cook, T. D., & Curtin, T. R. (1985). Evaluating the CTW model for producing educational television. *Educational Communications & Technology Journal, 33*(2), 91–112.

Cooper, H. M. (1979). Pygmalion grows up: A model for teacher expectation communication and performance. *Review of Educational Research, 48,* 389–410.

Cooper, R. P., & Aslin, R. N. (1990). Preference for infant-directed speech in the first month after birth. *Child Development, 61*(5), 1584–95.

Coopersmith, S. *The antecedents of self esteem.* San Francisco: Freeman.

Corbett, M. (1988). Changes in noneconomic political attitudes of Southern and Northern youth, 1970s to 1980s. *Journal of Youth & Adolescence, 17*(3), 197–210.

Cornell, D. G., Benedek, E. P., & Benedek, D. M. (1987). Juvenile homicide: Prior adjustment and a proposed typology. *American Journal of Orthopsychiatry, 57*(3), 383–393.

Cornell, E. H., Heth, C. D., & Broda, L. S. (1989). Children's way finding: response to instructions to use environmental landmarks. *Developmental Psychology, 25*(5), 755–764.

Corrigan, R. (1983). The development of representational skills. In *Levels and transitions in children's development* (New directions for child development, No. 21). San Francisco: Jossey-Bass.

Corsaro, W. A., & Eder, D. (1990). Children's peer cultures. *Annual Review of Sociology, 16,* 197–220.

Coster, W. J., Gersten, M. S., Beeghly, M., & Cicchetti, D. (1989). Communicative functioning in maltreated toddlers. *Developmental Psychology, 25*(6), 1020–1029.

Courchesne, E., Yeung-Courchesne, R., Press, G. A., Hesselink, J. K., & Jernigan, T. L. (1988). Hypoplasia of cerebellar vermae lobules VI & VII in autism. *New England Journal of Medicine, 318,* 1349–1354.

Covell, K., & Abramovitch, R. (1988). Children's understanding of internal anger: Age and source of anger differences. *Merrill-Palmer Quarterly, 34*(4), 353–368.

Cowan, P. A. (1978). *Piaget with feeling: Cognitive, social and emotional dimensions.* New York: Holt, Rinehart & Winston.

Cowan, W. M. (1979). The development of the brain. *Scientific American, 241,* 112–133.

Cox, M. J., Owen, M. T., Lewis J. M., & Henderson, V. K. (1989). Marriage, adult adjustment and early parenting. *Child Development, 60*(5), 1015–1024.

Cratty, B. J. (1979). *Perceptual and motor development in infants and children* (2nd ed.). New York: MacMillan.

Crick, N. R., & Ladd, G. W. (1990). Children's perceptions of the outcome of social strategies. *Developmental Psychology, 26*(4), 612–620.

Crocker, J., & Major, B. (1989). Social stigma and self-esteem: The self-protective properties of stigma. *Psychology Review, 96*(4), 608–630.

Crockett, L., Losoff, M., & Petersen, A. C. (1984). Perceptions of the peer group and friendship in early adolescence. *Journal of Early Adolescence, 4*(2), 155–181.

Crockett, L. J., & Peterson, A. C. (1987). Pubertal status and psychosocial development. Findings from the Early Adolescent Study. In R. M. Lerner & T. T. Foch (Eds.), *Biological-psychosocial interactions in early adolescence: A lifespan perspective.* Hillsdale, New Jersey: Erlbaum.

Crooks, R., & Baur, K. (1990). *Our sexuality* (4th ed.). Redwood City, CA: Benjamin Cummings.

Crow, T. K. (1985). The two-syndrome concept: Origins and current status. *Schizophrenia Bulletin, 11,* 471–486.

Crowe, T. K., Deitz, J. C., Bennett, F. C., & Tekolste, K. (1988). Preschool motor skills of children born prematurely and not diagnosed as having cerebral palsy. *Journal of Developmental and Behavioral Pediatrics, 9*(4), 189–193.

Crowley, G., Hagar, M., & Marshall, R. (1990, June 25). AIDS: The next ten years, *Newsweek,* pp. 20–27.

Cruikshank, B. M., Eliason, M., & Merrifield, B. (1988). Long-term sequelae of cold-water near-drowning. *Journal of Pediatric Psychology, 13*(3), 379–388.

Csikszentmihalyi, M., & Larson, R. (1984). *Being adolescent: Conflict and growth in the teenage years.* New York: Basic Books.

Cummings, E. M., Vagel, D., Cummings, J. S., & El-sheikh, M. (1989). Children's responses to different forms of expression of anger between adults. *Child Development 60*(6), 1392–1404.

Cummins, D. D., Kintsch, W., Reusser, K., & Weimer, R. (1988). The role of understanding in solving word problems. *Cognitive Psychology, 20*(4), 405–438.

Cuneo, D. O. (1980). A general strategy for quantity judgments: The height and width rule. *Child Development, 50,* 170–179.

Curtiss, S. (1977). *Genie: A psycholinguistic study of a modern-day "wild child."* New York: Academic Press.

The custody case that went up in smoke. (1990, August 27). *Newsweek,* p. 66.

Dacey, J. S. (1989). Discriminating characteristics of families of highly creative adolescents. *Journal of Creative Behavior, 23*(4), 263–271.

Damon, W. (1977). *The social world of the child.* San Francisco: Jossey-Bass.

Danesi, M. (1989). Adolescent language as affectively coded behavior: Findings of an observational research project. *Adolescence, 24*(94), 311–319.

D'Angelo, D. A. (1989). Developmental tasks in the literature for adolescents: Has the adolescent female protagonist changed? *Child Study Journal, 19*(3), 219–238.

Daniels, D. (1986). Differential experiences of siblings in the same family as predictors of adolescent sibling personality differences. *Journal of Personality and Social Psychology, 51*(2), 339–346.

Daniels, D., Plomin, R., & Greenhaigh, J. (1984). Correlates of difficult temperament in infancy. *Child Development, 55*(4), 1184–1194.

Danis, R. P., Newton, N. & Keith, L. (1981). Pregnancy and alcohol. In J. M. Leventhal (Ed.), *Current problems in obstetrics and gynecology.* New York: Textbook Medical Publishers.

Danremiller, J. L. (1989). A test of color constancy in 9- and 20-week-old human infants following stimulated illuminant changes. *Development Psychology, 25*(2), 171–184.

Dannemiller, J. L., & Stephens, B. R. (1988). A critical test of infant pattern preference models. *Child Development, 59*(1), 210–216.

Darwin, C. (1872/1965). *The expression of emotions in man and animals.* Chicago, University of Chicago Press.

Dasen, P., & Herm, A. (1981). Cross-cultural tests of Piaget's theory. In H. C. Traindis & A. Hern (Eds.) *Developmental Psychology: Vol. 4. Handbook of cross-cultural psychology.* Boston: Allyn & Bacon.

das Gupta, P., & Bryant, P. E. (1989). Young children's causal inferences. *Child Development, 60*(5), 1138–1146.

Davidson, P. M., White, P. N., Smith, D. J., & Poppen, W. A. (1989). Content and intensity of fears in middle childhood among rural and urban boys and girls. *Journal of Genetic Psychology, 150*(1), 51–58.

Davies, B. (1988). The family environment in bereaved families and its relationship to surviving sibling behavior. *Children's Health Care, 17*(1), 22–31.

Davies, R. C. (1979). Representing the lesbian mother. *Family Advocate, 1*(3), 21–23, 36.

Davis, D. L. (1989, November). Bunking with baby. *American Baby,* pp. 116, 120.

Davis, R. A. (1988). Adolescent pregnancy and infant mortality: Isolating the effects of race. *Adolescence, 23*(92), 899–908.

Davison, G. C., & Neale, J. M. (1982). *Abnormal psychology: An experimental clinical approach.* (3rd ed.). New York: Wiley.

Day, N. L. et al. (1990). Effect of prenatal alcohol exposure on growth and morphology of offspring at 8 months of age. *Pediatrics, 85*(5), 748–752.

Deaux, K. (1985). Sex & gender. In M. R. Rosenzweig & L. W. Porter (Eds.), *Annual review of psychology,* (Vol. 36). Palo Alto, CA: Annual Reviews, Inc.

DeCasper, A., & Fifer, W. (1989). Newborns prefer their mother's voices. *Science, 208,* 1174–1176.

DeFries, D. C., Fulker, D. W., & LaBuda, M. C. (1987). Evidence for a genetic etiology in reading disability of twins. *Nature, 329,* 537–539.

Dempster, F. N. (1981). Memory span: Sources of individual and developmental differences. *Psychology Bulletin, 89,* 63–100.

Dennis, W. (1935). The effect of restricted practice upon the reaching, sitting and standing of two infants. *Journal of Genetic Psychology, 47,* 17–32.

Denny, F. W., & Clyde, W. A. (1983). Acute respiratory tract infections: An overview. In W. A. Clyde & F. W. Denny (Eds.), Workshop on acute respiratory diseases among children of the world. *Pediatric Research, 17,* 1026–1029.

deVilliers, J. G., & deVilliers, P. A. (1978). *Language acquisition.* Cambridge, MA: Harvard University Press.

DeVries, R. (1969). Constancy of gender identity in the years three to six. *Monographs of the Society for Research in Child Development, 34*(3, Serial No. 127).

Deykin, E. Y., & MacMahon, B. (1980). The incidence of seizures among children with autistic symptoms. In S. Chess & A. Thomas (Eds.), *Annual progress in child psychiatry and child development.* New York: Brunner/Mazel.

Diaz, R. M. (1983). Thought and two languages: The impact of bilingualism in cognitive development. *Review of research in education, 10,* 23–54.

Dibrell, L. L., & Yamamoto, K. (1988). In their own minds: Concerns of young children. *Child Psychiatry and Human Development, 19*(1), 14–25.

Dien, D. S. F. (1982). A Chinese perspective on Kahlberg's theory of moral development. *Developmental Review, 2,* 331–341.

Dietrich, K. N. et al. (1991). Lead exposure and the cognitive development of urban preschool children: The Cincinnati lead study cohort at age

4 years. *Neurotoxicology & Teratology, 13*(2), 203–211.

Dietz, W. H., & Gortmaker, S. L. (1985). Do we fatten our children at the television set? Obesity and television viewing in children and adolescents. *Pediatrics, 75,* 807–812.

DiPietro, J. (1981). Rough and tumble play: A function of gender. *Developmental Psychology, 17,* 50–58.

Dodge, K. A. (1989). Coordinating responses to aversive stimuli: Introduction to a special section on the development of emotion regulation. *Developmental Psychology, 25*(3), 339–342.

Dolgin, K. G., & Behrend, D. A. (1984). Children's knowledge about animates and inanimates. *Child Development, 55,* 1646–1650.

Donaldson, M., & Balfour, G. (1968). Less vs. more: A study of language comprehension in children. *British Journal of Psychology, 59,* 461–472.

Dornbusch, S. M., Carlsmith, J. M., Bushwall, S. J., Ritter, P. L., Leiderman, H. et al. (1985). Single parents, extended households, and the control of adolescents. *Child Development, 56,* 326–341.

Dornbusch, S. M., Ritter, P. L., Leiderman, P. H., Roberts, D. F., and Fraleigh, M. J. (1987). The relation of parenting style to adolescent school performance. *Child Development, 55,* 1244–1257.

Doueck, H. J., Ishisaka, A. H., Sweany, S. L., & Gilchrist, L. D. (1987). Adolescent maltreatment: Themes from the empirical literature. *Journal of Interpersonal Violence, 2*(2), 139–153.

Douvan, E., & Adelson, J. (1966). *The adolescent experience.* New York: Wiley.

Downs, A. C. (1990). Children's judgments of televised events: The real versus pretend destruction. *Perceptual and Motor Skills, 70*(3), Pt. 1, 779–782.

Dozier, M. (1988). Rejected children's processing of interpersonal information. *Journal of Abnormal Child Psychology, 16*(2), 141–149.

Drogin, B. (1985, June 3). True victims of poverty: The children, *Los Angeles Times,* Pt. 1, 1, 10, 11.

Dromi, E. (1984). The one word period as a stage in language development. Quantitative and qualitative accounts. In I. Levin (Ed.), *Stage & structure.* Norwood, New Jersey: Ablex.

Druerd, B., Kinney, M. B., & Bothwell, C. (1989). Preventing baby bottle tooth decay in American Indian and Alaskan native communities. A model for planning. *Public Health Reports, 104,* 31–40.

DSM-III-R (1983). (*Diagnostic and statistical manual of mental disorders,* 3rd ed., revised). Washington, D.C.: American Psychological Association.

Duncan, P. D. et al. (1985). The effects of pubertal timing on body image, school behavior, and deviance. Special issue: Time of maturation and psychosocial functioning in adolescence: I. *Journal of Youth & Adolescence, 14*(3), 227–235.

Dunn, J. (1983). Sibling relationships in early childhood. *Child Development, 54,* 787–811.

Dunn, J. (1985). *Brothers & sisters.* Cambridge, MA: Harvard University Press.

Dunn, J. F. (1988). Sibling influences on childhood development. *Journal of Child Psychology & Psychiatry. Allied Disciplines, 29*(2), 119–127.

Dunn, J., & Kendrick, C. (1982). *Siblings: Love, envy, and understanding.* Cambridge, MA: Harvard University Press.

Dunn, J., & Munn, P. (1987). Conversations about feeling states between mothers and their young children. *Developmental Psychology, 23,* 132–139.

Dunn, J., & Shatz, M. (1989). Becoming a conversationalist despite (or because of) having an older sibling. *Child Development, 60*(2), 399–410.

Dunn, M. S. et al. (1991). Bovine surfactant replacement therapy in neonates of less than 30 weeks gestation. A randomized controlled trial of prophylaxis versus treatment. *Pediatrics, 87*(3), 377–386.

DuPont, R. L. (1983). Phobias in children. *Journal of Pediatrics, 102*(6), 999–1002.

Dweck, C. S., & Elliott, E. S. (1983). Achievement maturation. In P. H. Mussen. (Ed.), *Handbook of child psychology* (Vol. 4.) New York: Wiley.

Dykes, L. J. (1986). The whiplash shaken infant syndrome: What has been learned? *Child Abuse & Neglect, 10*(2), 211–221.

Eaton, W. O., Chipperfield, J. G., & Singbeil, C. E. (1989). Birth order and activity level in children. *Developmental Psychology, 25*(4), 668–672.

Eckerman, C. O., Davis, C. C., and Didow, S. M. (1989). Toddler's emerging way of achieving social coordinations with a peer. *Child Development, 60*(2), 440–453.

Eckerman, C. O., & Stein, M. R. (1990). How imitation begets imitation and toddlers' generation of games. *Developmental Psychology, 26*(3), 370–378.

Edelstein, W., Keller, M. & Wahlen, K. (1984). Structure and content in social cognition: Conceptual and empirical analyses. *Child Development, 55,* 1514–1526.

Eden, A. N. (1989). Infant allergies. *American Baby, 51*(4), 99.

Edlin, G. (1990). *Human genetics: A modern synthesis.* Boston: Jones & Bartlett Publishers.

Edmonds, L. D. et al. (1982). Cojoined twins in the United States: 1970–1977. *Teratology, 25*(3), 301–308.

Educational Research Service (1980). *Class size: A critique of recent metaanalyses.* Arlington, VA: Educational Research Service.

Edwards, R. G., & Craft, I. (1990). Development of assisted conception. *British Medical Bulletin, 46*(3), 565–579.

Eiger, M. S., & Olds, S. W. (1987). *The complete book of breastfeeding.* New York: Workman Press.

Einspieler, C., Widder, J., Holzer, A., & Kenner, T. (1988). The predictive value of behavioral risk factors for sudden infant death. *Early Human Development, 18,* 101–109.

Eisen, M., & Zellman, G. (1987). Changes in incidence of sexual intercourse of unmarried teenagers following a community-based sex education program. *The Journal of Sex Research, 23,* 527–544.

Eisenberg, N. (1982). The development of reasoning regarding prosocial behavior. In N. Eisenberg (Ed.), *The development of prosocial behavior.* New York: Academic Press.

Eisenberg, N., Lennon, R., & Pasternack, J. F. (1986). Altruistic values and moral judgment. In N. Eisenberg (Ed.), *Altruistic emotion cognition and behavior.* Hillsdale, NJ: Erlbaum.

Eisenberg, N., Lennon, R., Roth, K. (1983). Prosocial development: A longitudinal study. *Developmental Psychology, 19*(6), 846–855.

Eisenberg, N., & Shell, R. (1986). Prosocial moral judgment and behavior in children: The mediating role of cost. *Personality & Social Psychology Bulletin, 12*(4), 426–433.

Eisenberg, N., Shell, R., Pasternack, J., Lennon, R., Beller, R., & Mathy, R. M. (1987). Prosocial development in middle childhood: A longitudinal study. *Developmental Psychology, 23,* 712–718.

Elder, J. P., Molgaard, C. A., & Gresham, L. (1988). Predictions of chewing tobacco and cigarette use in a multiethnic public school population. *Adolescence, 23*(91), 689–702.

Elias, G., Hayes, A., & Broerse, J. (1988). Aspects of structure and content of maternal talk with infants. *Journal of Child Psychology & Psychiatry & Allied Disciplines, 29*(4), 523–531.

Elkind, D. (1971). *A sympathetic understanding of the child 6 to 16.* Boston: Allyn & Bacon.

Elkind, D. (1978). Understanding the young adolescent. *Adolescence, 13,* 127–134.

Elkind, D. (1979). *Child development and education: A Piagetian perspective.* New York: Oxford University Press.

Elkind, D. (1981). Recent research in cognitive and language development. *G. Stanley Hall Lecture Series, 1,* 61–80.

Elkind, D. (1984). *All grown up and no place to go.* Reading, MA: Addison-Wesley.

El-Sheikh, M., Cummings, E. M., & Goetsch, V. L. (1989). Coping with adults' angry behavior: Behavioral, physiological and verbal responses in preschoolers. *Developmental Psychology, 25,* 490–498.

Emde, R. N. (1980). Toward a psychoanalytic theory of affect. I. The organizational model and its propositions. In S. Greenspan & G. Pollock (Eds.), *The course of life: Psychoanalytic contributions toward understanding personality development.* Washington, D.C.: U.S. Government Printing Office.

Emde, R. N., Gaensbauer, T. J., & Harmon, R. J. (1976). Emotional expression in infancy. A behavioral study. *Psychological Issues, 10*(37), New York: International Universities Press.

Emery, R. E. (1982). Interparental conflict and the children of discord and divorce. *Psychology Bulletin, 92,* 310–330.

Eminson, C. et al. (1986). Repetition of accidents in young children. *Journal of Epidemiology & Community Health, 40*(2), 170–173.

Engelhorn, R. (1988). EMG and motor performance changes with practice of a forearm movement by children. *Perceptual & Motor Skills, 67*(2), 523–529.

Enos, D. M., & Handal, P. J. (1986). The relation of parental marital status and perceived family conflict to adjustment in white adolescents. *Journal of Consulting & Clinical Psychology, 54*(6), 820–824.

Epstein, L. H. et al. (1990). Five-year follow up of family based behavioral treatments for childhood obesity. *Journal of Counseling & Clinical Psychology, 58*(5), 661–664.

Erikson, E. H. (1956). The problem of ego identity. *Journal of the American Psychoanalytic Association, 4,* 56–121.

Erikson, E. H. (1963). *Childhood and society,* (2nd ed.). New York: Norton.

Erickson, J. B. (1988). Real American children: The challenge for after-school programs. *Child and Youth Care Quarterly. 17*(2), 86–103.

Erlenmeyer-Kimling, L., & Jarvik, L. F. (1963). Genetics and intelligence. *Science, 142,* 1477–1479.

Ernhart, C. B. et al. (1987). Alcohol teratogenicity in the human: A detailed assessment of specificity, critical period and threshold. *American Journal of Obstetrics & Gynecology, 156*(1), 33–39.

Elzel, B. C., & Gewirtz, J. L. (1967). Experimental modification of care-taker-maintained high rate operant crying in a 6- and a 20-week old infant (Infans tyrannotearus): Extinction of crying with reinforcement of eye contact and smiling. *Journal of Experimental Child Psychology, 5,* 303–317.

Eron, L. D. (1982). Parent-child interaction, televised violence, and aggression in children. *American Psychology, 37*(2), 244–252.

Evertson, C. (1982). Differences in constructional activities in higher- and lower-achieving junior high English and math classes. *Elementary School Journal, 82,* 329–350.

Fabricius, W. V., Schwanenflugel, P. G., Kyllonem, P. C., Barclay, C. R. et al. (1989). Developing theories of the mind: Children's and adults' concepts of mental activities. *Child Development, 60*(6), 1278–1290.

The Facts of Life Team. (1989, May). Teen sex: not for love. *Psychology Today,* pp. 10–12.

Fagan, J. F. (1977). An attention model of infant recognition. *Child Development, 48,* 345–359.

Fagan, J. F. (1985). A new look at infant intelligence. *Current Topics in Human Intelligence, 1,* 223–246.

Fagot, B. I. (1981). Stereotypes versus behavioral judgments of sex differences in young children. *Sex Roles, 7,* 1093–1096.

Fagot, B. I. (1985). Beyond the reinforcement principle: Another step toward understanding sex role development. *Developmental Psychology, 21,* 1097–1104.

Fagot, B. I., Leinbach, M. D., & Hagan, R. (1986). Gender labeling and the adoption of sex typed behaviors. *Developmental Psychology, 22,* 440–443.

Falbo, T. (1981). Relationship between birth category, achievement, and interpersonal orientation. *Journal of Personality and Social Psychology, 4*(1), 121–131.

Falbo, T., & Polit, D. (1986). A quantitative review of the only child literature: Research evidence and theory development. *Psychology Bulletin, 100,* 176–189.

Falk, J., Halmi, D., Eckert, E., & Caspar, R. (1983). Primary and secondary amenorrhea in anorexia nervosa. In S. Golub (Ed.), *Menarche.* Lexington, MA: Lexington Books.

Falk, P. J. (1989). Lesbian mothers: Psychosocial assumptions in family law. *American Psychology, 44*(6), 941–947.

Famularo, R., Kinscherff, R., & Fenton, T. (1990). Symptom differences in acute and chronic presentation of childhood past-traumatic stress disorder. *Child Abuse & Neglect, 14*(3), 439–444.

Fantz, R. L. (1964). Visual experience in infants: Decreased attention to familiar patterns relative to novel ones. *Science, 146,* 668–670.

Fantz, R. L., Fagan, J., & Miranda, S. B. (1975). Early visual selectivity. In L. Cohen & P. Salapatek (Eds.), *Infant perception: From sensation to cognition* (Vol. 1). New York: Academic Press.

Farmer, A. E., McGuffin, P., & Gottesman, I. I. (1987). Twin concordance for DMS-III schizophrenia: Scrutinizing the validity of the definition. *Archives of General Psychiatry, 44*(7) 634–641.

Farnham-Diggory, S. (1978). *Learning disabilities.* Cambridge, MA: Harvard University Press.

Farnham-Diggory, S. (1986). Time, now, for a little serious complexity. In S. J. Ceci (Ed.). *Handbook of cognitive, social and neuropsychological aspects of learning disability* (Vol. 1). Hillsdale, NJ: Erlbaum.

Farrington, D. P., Biron, L., & LeBlanc, M. (1982). Personal and delinquency in London and Montreal. In J. C. Gunn & D. P. Farrington (Eds.) *Abnormal offenders: Delinquency and the criminal justice system.* New York: Wiley.

Fasick, F. A. (1984). Parents, peers, youth culture, and autonomy in adolescence. *Adolescence, 19*(73), 143–157.

Faust, M. S. (1977). Somatic development of adolescent girls. Monographs of the Society for Research in Child Development, 42(No. 1), 1–90.

Fava, G. A. et al. (1982). Psychological reactions to amniocentesis: A controlled study. *American Journal of Obstetrics & Gynecology, 143*(5), 509–513.

Feingold, B. F. (1975). *Why your child is hyperactive.* New York: Random House.

Feldman, D. H. (1980). *Beyond universals in cognitive development.* Norwood, NJ: Ablex.

Feldman, H. (1981). A comparison of intentional parents and intentionally childless couples. *Journal of Marriage & the Family, 43*(3), 593–600.

Feldman, S. S., Nash, S. C., & Aschenbrenner, B. G. (1983). Antecedents of fathering. *Child Development, 54,* 1628–1636.

Feldman, W. (1988). Culture versus biology: Children's attitudes toward thinness and fatness. *Pediatrics, 81,* 190–194.

Felsman, D., Brannigan, G., & Yellin, P. (1987). Control theory in dealing with adolescent sexuality and pregnancy. *Journal of Sex Education and Therapy, 13,* 15–16.

Ferber, R. A. (1987). Behavioral "insomnia" in the child. *Psychiatric Clinics of North America, 10*(4), 41–53.

Ferguson, T. J., & Rule, B. G. (1982). Influence of inferential set, outcome intent and outcome severity on children's moral judgments. *Developmental Psychology, 18,* 843–851.

Ferketich, S. L. & Mercer, R. T. (1989). Men's health status during pregnancy and early fatherhood. *Research in Nursing and Health, 12*(3), 137–48.

Fernald, A., (1989). Intonation and communicative intent in mothers' speech to infants: Is the melody the message? *Child Development, 60*(6), 1497–1510.

Fernald, A., & Simon, T. (1984). Expanded intonation contours in mothers' speech to newborns. *Developmental Psychology, 70,* 104–113.

Field, D. (1981). Can preschool children really learn to conserve? *Child Development, 52,* 326–334.

Field, T., Healy, B., Goldstein, S., & Guthertz, M. (1990). Behavior-state matching and synchrony in mother-infant interactions of nondepressed versus depressed dyads. *Developmental Psychology, 26*(1), 7–14.

Field, T. M., Schanberg, S. M., Scafidi, F., Bauer, C. R. et al. (1986). Effects of tactile/kinesthetic stimulation on preterm neonates. *Pediatrics, 77,* 654–658.

Field, T. M., Woodson, R. Greenberg, R., & Cohen, D. (1982). Discrimination and imitation of facial expressions by neonates. *Science, 218,* 179–181.

Field, T. et al. (1985). Pregnancy problems, postpartum depression and early mother-infant interactions. *Developmental Psychology, 21*(6), 1152–1156.

Field, T. et al. (1987). Face-to-face interaction behavior across early infancy. *Infant Behavior & Development, 10*(1), 111–116.

Field, T. et al. (1987). Working mother-infant interaction across the second year of life. *Infant Mental Health Journal, 8*(1), 19–27.

Fincham, F. D., Hokoda, A., & Sanders, R. (1989). Learned helplessness, test anxiety and academic achievement: A longitudinal analysis. *Child Development, 60*(1), 138–145.

Fingarette, H. (1988). *Heavy drinking: The myth of alcoholism as a disease.* Santa Barbara, CA: University of California Press.

Finke, N. (1987, December 4). A matter of death and life. *Los Angeles Times,* Pt. V, pp. 1, 24.

Finkelhor, D. (1979). *Sexually victimized children.* New York: Free Press.

Fischer, K. W., & Pipp, S. L. (1984). Processes of cognitive development: Optimal level and skill acquisition. In R. J. Sternberg (Ed.), *Mechanisms of Cognitive Development.* San Francisco: W. H. Freemen & Co.

Fischer, M. et al. (1990). The adolescent outcome of hyperactive children diagnosed by research criteria: II. Academic, attentional, and neuropsychological status. *Journal of Consulting & Clinical Psychology, 58*(5), 580–588.

Fischman, J. (1986). The children's hours. *Psychology Today, 20*(10), 16–17.

Fishbein, H. D. (1984). *The psychology of infancy and childhood: Evolutionary and cross-cultural perspectives.* Hillsdale, NJ: Erlbaum.

Fisher, B. I., & McGuire, K. (1990). Do diagnostic patterns exist in the sleep behaviors of normal children? *Journal of Abnormal Child Psychology, 18*(2), 179–186.

Fisher, S., & Greenberg, R. P. (1977). *The scientific credibility of Freud's theories and therapy.* New York: Basic Books.

Fivush, R., & Hammond, N. R. (1989). Time and again: Effects of repetition and retention interval on 2 year olds' event recall. *Journal of Experimental Child Psychology, 47*(2), 259–273.

Fivush, R., Hudson, J., & Nelson, K. (1983). Children's long term memory for a novel event: An exploratory study. *Merrill-Palmer Quarterly, 30,* 303–316.

Flanagan, G. L. (1962). *The first nine months of life.* New York: Simon & Schuster.

Flavell, J. H. (1968). *The development of role-taking and communication skills in children.* New York: Wiley.

Flavell, J. H. (1985). *Cognitive development* (2nd ed.). Englewood Cliffs, NJ: Prentice-Hall.

Flavell, J. H. (1977). *Cognitive development.* Englewood Cliffs, NJ: Prentice Hall.

Flay, B. R. (1985). Psychosocial approaches to smoking prevention: A review of the findings. *Health Psychology, 4,* 449–488.

Flora, J. A., & Thoresen, C. E., (1988). Reducing the risk of AIDS in adolescents. *American Psychologist, 43*(11), 965–970.

Flynn, J. R. (1987). The rise and fall of Japanese IQ. *Bulletin of the British Psychological Society, 40,* 459–464.

Fontaine, P., & Toffler, W. L. (1991). Dorsal penile nerve block for newborn circumcision. *American Family Physician, 43*(4), 1327–1333.

Fontaine, R., & le Bonniec, G. P., (1988). Postural evolution and integration of the prehension gesture in children aged 4–10 months. *British Journal of Developmental Psychology, 6*(3), 223–233.

Ford, M. E. et al. (1989). Processes associated with integrative social competence: Emotional and contextual influence on adolescent social responsibility. *Journal of Adolescent Research, 4*(4), 405–425.

Frankel, M. T., & Rollins, H. A. (1985). Associative and categorical hypotheses of organization in free recall of adults and children. *Journal of Experimental Child Psychology, 40,* 304–318.

Frankel, S. A., & Wise, M. J. (1982). A view of delayed parenting: Some implications of a new trend. *Psychiatry, 45*(3), 220–225.

Frankenburg, W. K., Dodds, J. B., Fandal, A. W., Kazuk, E., & Cohrs, M. (1975). *Denver developmental screening test: Reference manual.* Denver: University of Colorado Medical Center.

Fraser, J., & Perkins, W. H. (Eds.). (1988). Do you stutter?: A guide for teens, (Publication No. 21) *Foundation of America,* Memphis, TN:

Freeman, J. M., & Nelson, K. B. (1988). Intrapartum asphyxia and cerebral palsy. *Pediatrics, 82*(2), 240–249.

Freeman, N. (1980). *Strategies of representation in young children.* London: Academic Press.

Freiberg, P. (1990, August). Most missing children taken by family members. *APA Monitor,* p. 23.

French, D. C. (1984). Children's knowledge of the social functions of younger, older and same-age peers. *Child Development, 55,* 1429–1433.

French, D. C. (1988). Heterogeneity of peer-rejected boys: Aggressive and nonaggressive subtypes. *Child Development, 59*(4), 976–985.

French, L. A. (1989). Young children's responses to "When" questions: Issues of directionality. *Child Development, 60*(1), 225–236.

Frenkel, J. K. (1990). Toxoplasmosis in human beings. *Journal of the American Veterinary Medical Association, 196*(2), 204–248.

Freud, A., & Dann, S. (1951). An experiment in group upbringing. *Psychoanalytic Study of the Child, 6,* 127–168.

Freud, S. (1905/1953). Three essays on the theory of sexuality. In J. Strachey (Ed.), *The standard edition of the complete psychological works of Sigmund Freud* (Vol. 7). London: Hogarth Press.

Freud, S. (1961). Some psychical consequences of the anatomical distinction between the sexes. In J. Strachey (Ed.), *Standard edition of the complete works of Sigmund Freud* (Vol. 19). London: Hogarth Press. (Original work published in 1925).

Freud, S. (1973). *An outline of psychoanalysis.* London: Hogarth Press. (Original work published in 1938).

Fried, P. A. (1989). Cigarettes and marajuana: are there measurable long-term neurobehavioral teratogenic effects? *Neurotoxicology, 10*(3), 577–583.

Friend, T. (1988, May 5). Preventing stillbirths by counting kicks. *USA Today,* Sect. D1.

Frisch, R. E. (1983). Fatness, puberty, and fertility. In J. Brooks-Gunn & A. C. Petersen (Eds.), *Girls at puberty: Biological, psychological and social perspectives.* New York: Plenum.

Fullard, W., & Reiling, A. M. (1976). An investigation of Lorenz's "babyness." *Child Development, 47,* 1191–1193.

Funder, D. C., & Block, J. (1989). The role of ego-control, ego-resiliency and IQ in delay of gratification in adolescence. *Journal of Personality and Social Psychology, 57*(6), 1041–1050.

Furmen, W., & Buhrmester, D. (1985). Children's perceptions of the personal relationship in their social networks. *Developmental Psychology, 21*(6), 1016–1024.

Furth, H. G. (1964). Research with the deaf: Implications for language and cognition. *Psychology Bulletin, 62,* 145–164.

Gadberry, S. (1980). Effects of restricting first graders' TV viewing on leisure time use, IQ change, and cognitive style. *Journal of Applied Developmental Psychology, 1,* 45–57.

Gaensbauer, T. J. (1980). Anaclitic depression in a three-and-one-half-month-old child. *American Journal of Psychiatry, 137,* 841–842.

Gallatin, J. (1980). Political thinking in adolescence. In J. Adelson (Ed.),

Handbook of adolescent development. New York: Wiley.

Galton, L. (1981, March 26). Playing games is great for kids–if it's just play. *Los Angeles Times*, Pt. III, 1, 10–11.

Gamble, W. C., & Mettale, S. M. (1989). Coping with stress in sibling relationships: A comparison of children with disabled and nondisabled siblings. *Journal of Applied Developmental Psychology, 10*(3), 353–373.

Gambrell, L. B. et al. (1987). Young children's comprehension and recall of computer screen displayed texts. *Journal of Research in Reading, 10*(2), 156–163.

Garbarino, J., Guttman, E., & Seeley, J. (1986). *The psychologically battered child: Strategies for identification, assessment, and intervention.* San Francisco: Jossey-Bass.

Garber, H., & Heber, R. (1982). Modification of predicted cognitive development in high-risk children through early intervention. In D. K. Detterman & R. J. Sternberg (Eds.), *How and how much can intelligence be increased?* Norwood, NJ: Ablex.

Garcia, E. E. (1983). Becoming bilingual during early childhood. *International Journal of Behavioral Development, 6*(4), 375–404.

Gardner, F. E. (1989). Inconsistent parenting: Is there evidence for a link with children's conduct problems? *Journal of Abnormal Child Psychology, 17*(2), 223–233.

Gardner, H. (1980). *Artful scribbles: The significance of children's drawings.* New York: Basic Books.

Gardner, H. (1983). *Frames of mind: The theory of multiple intelligences.* New York: Basic Books.

Gardner, L. I. Deprivation dwarfism. (1972). *Scientific American, 227,* 76–82.

Garner, D. M. et al. (1987). A prospective study of eating disturbances in the ballet. *9th World Congress of the International College of Psychosomatic Medicine, 48*(1–4), 170–175.

Gath, A. (1989). Parental reactions to loss and disappointment: The diagnosis of Down's syndrome. *Developmental Medicine and Child Neurology, 27*(3), 392–400.

Gause, R. W. (1988, February). Chickenpox during pregnancy. *American Baby*, pp. 38, 53.

Gearhart, B. R., & Weishahn, M. W. (1984). *The exceptional student in the regular classroom* (3rd ed.). St. Louis: Times Mirror/Mosby.

Gelb, R., & Jacobson, J. L. (1988). Popular and unpopular children's interactions during cooperative & competitive peer group activities. *Journal of American Child Psychology, 16*(3), 247–261.

Geller, E., Ritvo, E. R., Freeman, B. J., & Yuwiler, A. (1982). Preliminary observations of the effect of senfluramine on blood serotonin and symptoms in 3 autistic boys. *New England Journal of Medicine, 307*(3), 165–169.

Gellert, G. A., & Durfee, M. J. (1989). HIV infection and child abuse. *New England Journal of Medicine, 321*(10), 685.

Gelles, R. J. (1989). Child abuse and violence in single-parent families: Parent absence and economic deprivation. *American Journal of Orthopsychiatry, 59*(4), 492–501.

Gelles, R. J., & Cornell, C. P. (1983). International perspectives on child abuse. *Child Abuse & Neglect, 7,* 375–386.

Gelman, R., & Baillargeon, R. (1983). A review of some Piagetian concepts. In P. H. Mussen (Ed.), *Handbook of child psychology* (4th ed.), Vol. 3. New York: Wiley.

Gelman, R., Bullock, M., & Meck, E. (1980). Preschoolers' understanding of simple object transformations. *Child Development, 51,* 691–699.

Genesee, F. (1989). Early bilingual development: One language or two? *Journal of Child Language, 16*(1), 161–179.

Gesell, A., & Ames, L. B. (1937). Early evidence of individuality in the human infant. *Scientific Monthly, 45,* 217–255.

Gesell, A., Ames, L. B., & Ilg, F. L. (1974). *Infant and child in the culture of today: The guidance of development in home and nursery school* (rev. ed.), New York: Harper & Row.

Gesell, A., & Thompson, H. (1934). *Infant behavior: Its genesis and growth.*

New York: McGraw-Hill.

Gewirtz, J. L. (1969). Mechanisms of social learning: Some roles of stimulation and behavior in early human development. In D. A. Goslen (Ed.), *Handbook of socialization theory and research.* New York: Rand McNally.

Ghazi, H. A., Spielberger, C., Kallen, B. (1991). Delivery outcome after infertility—a registry study. *Fertility & Sterility, 55*(4), 726–732.

Gibbs, J. G., & Woll, S. B. (1985). Mechanisms used by young children in the making of empathic judgments. *Journal of Personality, 54*(4), 575–585.

Giblin, P. T., Poland, M. L., Waller, J. B., & Ager, J. W. (1988). Correlates of neonatal morbidity: Maternal characteristics and family resources. *Journal of Genetic Psychology, 149*(4), 527–533.

Gibson, E. J., & Walk, R. R. (1960). The "visual cliff." *Scientific American, 202,* 2–9.

Gilligan, C. (1977). In a different voice: Women's conception of the self and of morality. *Harvard Educational Review, 47,* 481–517.

Gilligan, C. (1982a). *In a different voice: Psychological theory and women's development.* Cambridge, MA: Harvard University Press.

Gilligan, C. (1982b). New maps of development: New visions of maturity. *American Journal of Orthopsychiatry, 52,* 199–212.

Gilroy, F. D. & Steinbacher, R. (1991). Sex selection technology utilization: Further implications for sex ratio imbalance. *Social Biology, 38* (3–4 Fall–Winter), 285–8.

Gines, R., Leaper, C., Monahan, C., & Weickgenant, A. (1988). Language learning and retention in young language-disordered children. *Journal of Autism & Developmental Disorders, 18,* 281–294.

Gingras, J. L., O'Donnell, K. J., & Hume, R. F. (1990). Maternal cocaine addiction and fetal behavioral state. I: A human model for the study of sudden infant death syndrome. *Medical Hypotheses, 33*(4), 227–230.

Ginsburg, G. P., & Kilbourne, B. N. (1988). Emergence of vocal alteration in mother-infant interchanges. *Journal of Child Language, 15*(2), 221–235.

Ginsberg, H., & Opper, S. (1979). *Piaget's theory of intellectual development* (2nd ed.). Englewood Cliffs, NJ: Prentice-Hall.

Ginsberg, H. J., & Miller, S. M. (1982). Sex differences in children's risk taking behavior. *Child Development, 53,* 426–428.

Gitterman, D., & Johnston, J. K. (1983). Talking about comparisons: A study of young children's comparative adjective usage. *Journal of Child Language, 10*(3), 605–621.

Gladstone, M., Best, C. T., & Davidson, R. J. (1989). Anomalous bimanual coordination among dyslexic boys. *Developmental Psychology, 25*(2) 236–246.

Glasier, A., & McNeilly, A. S. (1990). Physiology of lactation. *Baillieres Clinical Endocrinology and Metabolism, 4*(2), 379–395.

Glass, P. (1990). Light and the developing retina. *Documenta Ophthalmologica, 74*(3), 195–203.

Glazer, S. M., & Curry, D. (1988–89). Word processing programs: Survival tools for children with writing problems. *Journal of Reading, Writing, & Learning Disabilities International, 4*(3), 187–199.

Glick, P. C. (1984). American household structure in transition. *Family Planning Perspectives, 16*(5), 205–211.

Glick, P. C., & Lin, S. (1987). Remarriage after divorce. Recent changes and demographic variations. *Sociological Perspectives, 30,* 162–179.

Gold, M., & Petronio, R. J. (1980). Delinquent behavior in adolescence. In I. Adelson (Ed.), *Handbook of Adolescent Psychology.* New York: Wiley.

Gold, R. (1983). Inappropriate conservation judgments in the concrete operations period. *Genetic Psychology Monographs, 107*(2), 189–210.

Goldberg, S., Perlmutter, M., & Myers, N. (1974). Recall of related and unrelated lists by 2-year-olds. *Journal of Experimental Child Psychology, 18,* 1–8.

Goldhaber, M. K., Polen, M. R., & Hiatt, R. A. (1988). The risk of miscarriage and birth defects among women who use video display terminals during pregnancy. *American Journal of Industrial Medicine, 13*(6),

695–706.

Goldsmith, H. H. (1983). Genetic influences on personality from infancy to adulthood. *Child Development, 54*(2), 331–355.

Goldsmith, M. F. (1985). Possible herpes virus role in abortion studies. *Journal of American Medical Association, 251,* 3067–3070.

Goldstein, M. J. (1981). Family factors associated with schizophrenia and anorexia nervosa. *Journal of Youth and Adolescence, 10,* 385–405.

Goldstein, D. J., & Bracey, R. J. (1988). Temperament characteristics of toddlers born prematurely. *Child: Care, Health & Development, 14*(2), 105–109.

Goleman, D. (1990, September 17). Asian-American students' academic success probed. *Sacramento Bee,* p. B16.

Golinkoff, R. M. (1983). The preverbal negotiation of failed messages: Insights into the transition period. In R. M. Golinkoff (Ed.), *The transition of prelinquistic to linguistic communication.* Hillsdale, NJ: Erlbaum.

Gollin, E. S., & Sharps, M. J. (1987). Visual perspective-taking in young children: Reduction of egocentric errors by induction of strategy. *Bulletin of the psychometric society, 25*(6), 435–437.

Good, T. L. (1980). *Teacher expectations, teacher behavior, student perception and student behavior: A decade of research.* Paper presented at a meeting of the American Educational Research Association.

Gopnik, A., & Graf, P. (1988). Knowing how you know. Young children's ability to identify and remember the sources of their beliefs. *Child Development, 59*(5), 1366–1371.

Gordon, A. K., & Klass, D. (1979). *They need to know.* Englewood Cliffs, NJ: Prentice-Hall.

Gordon, B. N., Schroeder, C. S., & Abrams, J. M. (1990). Children's knowledge of sexuality: A comparison of sexually abused and nonabused children. *American Journal of Orthopsychiatry, 60*(2), 250–257.

Gorga, D. et al. (1991). The neuromotor behavior of preterm and full term children by three years of age: Quality of movement and variability. *Journal of Developmental & Behavioral Pediatrics, 12*(2), 102–107.

Gortmaker, S. L., Dietz, W. H., Sobol, A. M., & Welher, C. (1987). Increasing pediatric obesity in the United States. *American Journal of Diseases of Children, 141,* 535–540.

Gotlib, I. N. et al. (1991). Prospective investigation of postpartum depression: factors involved in onset and recovery. *Journal of Abnormal Psychology, 100*(2), 122–132.

Gottesman, I. (1978). Schizophrenia and genetics. In L. Wynne (Ed.), *The nature of schizophrenia.* New York: Wiley.

Gottfried, A. W., & Gilman, G. (1985). Visual skills and intellectual development: A relationship in young children. *Journal of the American Optometric Association, 56*(7), 550–555.

Gottfried, A. W., & Rose, S. A. (1980). Tactile recognition memory in infants. *Child Development, 51,* 69–74.

Gottman, J. M. (1983). How children become friends. *Monographs of the Society for Research in Child Development, 48,* (Serial No. 201).

Gottman, J. M., & Katz, L. F. (1989). Effects of marital discord on young children's peer interaction and health. *Developmental Psychology, 25*(3), 373–381.

Graham, J. M., Jr., Hanson, J. W., Darby, B. L., Barr, H. M., and Streissguth, A. P. (1988). Independent dysmorphology evaluations at birth and 4 years of age for children exposed to varying amounts of alcohol in utero. *Pediatrics, 81*(6), 772–778.

Graham, S., & Harris, K. R. (1988). Instructional recommendations for teaching writing to exceptional students. *Exceptional Children, 54,* 506–512.

Grant, W. V., & Snyder, T. (1984). *Digest of educational statistics, 1983–84.* Washington, D.C.: National Center for Educational Statistics.

Graves, T., Meyers, A. W., and Clark, L. (1988). An evaluation of parental problem solving training in the behavioral treatment of obesity. *Journal of Consulting & Clinical Psychology, 56,* 245–250.

Greenberg, M., & Morris, N. (1974). Engrossment: The newborn's impact upon the father. *American Journal of Orthopsychiatry, 44*(4), 520–531.

Greenberger, E. (1984). Defining psychosocial maturity in adolescence. *Advances in Child Behavioral Analysis & Therapy, 3,* 1–37.

Greenberger, E., & Goldberg, W. A. (1989). Work, parenting and the socialization of children. *Developmental Psychology, 25*(1), 22–35.

Greenberger, E., & Steinberg, L. (1986). *When teenagers work.* New York: Basic Books.

Greenfield, P. M. (1984). *Mind and media: The effects of television video games and computers.* Cambridge, MA: Harvard University Press.

Grolnick, W. S., & Ryan, R. M. (1989). Parent styles associated with children's self-regulation and competence in school. *Journal of Educational Psychology, 81*(2), 143–154.

Gross, D., & Harris, P. L. (1988). False beliefs about emotion: Children's understanding of misleading emotional displays. *International Journal of Behavioral Development, 11*(4), 475–488.

Grossberg, I. N., & Cornell, D. G. (1988). Relationship between personality adjustment and high intelligence: Terman versus Hallingworth. *Exceptional Children, 55*(3), 266–272.

Guilford, J. P. (1967). *The nature of human intelligence.* New York: McGraw-Hill.

Guilford, J. P. (1985). The structure-of-intellect model. In B. B. Wolman (Ed.), *Handbook of Intelligence.* New York: Wiley.

The Guiness Book of World Records (1991). New York: Bantam Books.

Gulko, J., Doyal, A., Serbin, L. A., & White, D. R. (1988). Conservation skills: A replicated study of order of acquisitions across tasks. *Journal of Genetic Psychology, 149*(4), 425–439.

Gullo, D. (1988). A comparative study of adolescent and older mother's knowledge of infant abilities. *Child Study Journal, 18*(3), 223–231.

Gunter, B. (1982). Does television interfere with reading development? *Bulletin of British Psychological Society, 35,* 232–235.

Gustafson, G. E., & Harris, K. L. (1990). Women's responses to young infants' cries. *Developmental Psychology, 26*(1), 144–152.

Alan Guttmacher Institute (1981). *Teenage pregnancy: The problem that hasn't gone away.* New York: Viking.

Hack, M. et al. (1989). Outcomes of extremely low birth weight infants between 1982 and 1988. *New England Journal of Medicine, 321,* (24), 1642–1647.

Hadley, J. (1984, July–August). Facts about childhood hyperactivity. *Children Today,* pp. 8–13.

Hagen, J. W., & Hale, G. A. (1973). The development of attention in children. In A. D. Pick (Ed.) *Minnesota symposium on child psychology, vol.* 7, pp. 117–140. Minneapolis: University of Minnesota Press.

Haith, M. M. (1980). *Rules newborns look by.* Hillsdale, NJ: Erlbaum.

Haith, M. M. (1986). Sensory and perceptual processes in early infancy. *Journal of Pediatrics, 109*(1), 158–171.

Hakuta, K. (1986). *Mirror of language.* New York: Basic Books.

Halford, G. S. (1989). Reflections on 25 years of Piagetian cognitive developmental psychology: 1963–1988. *Human Development, 32*(6), 325–357.

Halford, G. S., & Boyle, F. M. (1985). Do young children understand conservation of number? *Child Development, 56,* 165–176.

Hall, E. (1984). Sandra Scarr: What's a parent to do? *Psychology Today, 18*(5), 59–63.

Hall, R. C. et al. (1989). Sexual abuse in patients with anorexia nervosa and bulimia. *Psychosomatics, 30*(1), 73–79.

Halmesmaki, E. et al. (1987). Prediction of fetal alcohol syndrome by maternal alpha fetoprotein, human placental lactogen and pregnancy specific beta 1-glycoprotein. *Alcohol & Alcoholism, Suppl. 1,* 473–476.

Hamburg, D. A., & Takanishi, R. (1989). Preparing for life. *American Psychologist, 44*(5), 825–827.

Hamilton, E. M. N., Whitney, E. N., & Sizer, F. S. (1985). *Nutrition: Concepts and controversies* (3rd ed.). St. Paul, MN: West Publishing.

Hammarback, S., Damber, J., & Backstrom, T. (1989). Relationship between symptom severity and hormone change in women with premenstrual syndrome. *Journal of Clinical Endocrinology & Metabolism, 68*, 125–130.

Hammen, C. (1988). Self-cognitives, stressful events, and the prediction of depression in children of depressed mothers. *Journal of Abnormal Child Psychology, 16*(3), 347–360.

Hammill, D. D. (1990). On defining learning disabilities: An emerging consensus. *Journal of Learning Disabilities, 23*(2), 74–84.

Hanigan, W. C. et al. (1990). Tentorial hemorrhage associated with vacuum extraction. *Pediatrics, 85*(4), 534–539.

Hans, S., & Marcus, J. (1987). A process model for the development of schizophrenia. *Psychiatry, 50*(4), 361–370.

Harlow, H. F., & Zimmerman, R. R. (1959). Affectional responses in the infant monkey. *Science, 130*, 431–432.

Harmon, D. S. (1984). Brain growth theory and educational psychology. *Psychology Reports, 55*(1), 59–66.

Harrington, D. M., Block, J. H., & Block, J. (1987). Testing aspects of Carl Rogers' theory of creative environments: Child rearing antecedents of creative potential in young adolescents. *Journal of Personality and Social Psychology, 52*, 851–856.

Harris, K., & Knudson, S. L. (1988). Parental and teacher priorities for kindergarten preparation. *Child Study Journal, 18*(2), 61–73.

Harris, M. B., & Smith, S. D. (1982). Beliefs about obesity: Effects of age, ethnicity, sex and weight. *Psychology Reports, 51*(3), 1047–1055.

Harris, P. L. (1983). Infant cognition. In J. H. Flavell & E. M. Markman (Eds.), *Handbook of child psychology: Vol. 2. Infancy & developmental psychobiology* (4th ed.). New York: Wiley.

Harris, W. H., Durkin, H., & Flores, A. (1980). Choosing to be child-free. *Journal of School Health, 49*(7), 379–382.

Harrison, E. R. (1990). The emergence of childrens' ability to classify paintings: A developmental study using computer manipulated images. *Visual Arts Research, 16*(1, Issue 31), 48–57.

Hart, C. H., Ladd, G. W., & Burleson, B. R. (1990). Children's expectations of the outcome of social strategies: Relations with sociometric status and maternal disciplinary styles. *Child Development, 61*(1), 127–137.

Hart, D. (1988). A longitudinal study of adolescents' socialization and identification as predictors of adult moral judgment development. *Merrill-Palmer Quarterly, 34*(3), 245–260.

Hart, S. N., & Brassard, M. R. (1987). A major threat to children's mental health: Psychological maltreatment. *American Psychology, 42*, 160–165.

Harter, S. (1979, May 31–June 2). *Children's understanding of multiple emotions: A cognitive developmental approach.* Invited address presented to the Ninth Annual Symposium of the Jean Piaget Society, Philadelphia, PA.

Harter, S. (1983). Developmental perspectives on the self-system. In P. H. Mussen (Ed.), *Handbook of child psychology*, (Vol. 4). New York: Wiley.

Harter, S., Alexander, P., and Neimeyer, R. (1988). Long term effects of incestuous child abuse in college women: Social adjustment, social cognition and family characteristics. *Journal of Consulting and Clinical Psychology, 56*, 5–8.

Hartshorne, H. & May, M. S. (1928 to 1930). *Moral studies in the nature of character: Vol. 1. Studies in deceit., Vol. 2. Studies in self-control, Vol. 3. Studies in the organization of character.* New York: Macmillan.

Hartup, W. W. (1983). Peer relations. In P. H. Mussen (Ed.), *Handbook of child psychology* (4th ed.), Vol. 4. New York: Wiley.

Hartup, W. W., Laursen, B., Stewart, M. I., & Eastenson, A. (1988). Conflict and the friendship relations of young children. *Child Development, 59*(6), 1590–1600.

Harvey, D. et al. (1982). Abilities of children who were small-for-gestational-age babies. *Pediatrics, 69*(3), 296–300.

Harvey, E. B., Boice, J. D., Honeyman, M., & Flannery, J. T. (1985). Prenatal x-ray exposure and childhood cancer in twins. *New England Journal of Medicine, 312*, 541–545.

Haskins, R. (1986). Social and cultural factors in risk assessment and mild mental retardation. In D. C. Farren & J. D. McKinney (Eds.), *Risk in intellectual and psychosocial development.* Orlando, FL: Academic Press.

Hatcher, R. (1988). *Contraceptive technology 1989–1989.* New York: Irvington.

Hathaway, W. E. (1991). Current pediatric diagnosis and treatment. Norwalk, CT: Appleton.

Hauck, M. R. (1991). Mothers' descriptions of the toilet training process; A phenomenologic study. *Journal of Pediatric Nursing, 8*(2), 1–6.

Hawke, S., & Knox, D. (1978). The one-child family: A new lifestyle. *The Family Coordinator, 27*, 215–219.

Hawkins, J., Sheingold, K., Gearhart, M., & Berger, C. (1982). Microcomputers in schools: Impact on the social life of elementary classrooms. *Applied Developmental Psychology, 3*, 361–373.

Hay, D. F. (1985). Learning to form relationships in infancy: Parallel attainments with parents and peers. *Developmental Review, 5*(2), 122–161.

Hay, D. F., & Ross, H. S. (1982). The social nature of early conflict. *Child Development, 53*, 105–113.

Hayes, D. P., & Ahrens, M. G. (1988). Vocabulary simplification for children: A special case of "motherese"? *Journal of Child Language, 15*(2), 395–410.

Hayes, D. S., Chemelski, B. E., & Birnbaum, D. W. (1981). Young children's incidental and intentional retention of televised events. *Developmental Psychology, 17*, 230–232.

Haylock, D. W. (1987). Mathematical creativity in school children. *Journal of Creative Behavior, 21*, 48–60.

Hays, D. P. (1981). Teratogenesis: A review of the basic principles with a discussion of selected agents: Part III. *Drug Intelligence and Clinical Pharmacy, 15*(9), 639–640.

Hearold, S. (1986). A synthesis of 1043 effects of television on social behavior. In G. Comstock (Ed.), *Public communications and behavior* (Vol. 1). New York: Academic Press.

Heavey, C. L., Adelman, H. S., Nelson, P., & Smith, D. C. (1989). Learning problems, anger, perceived control and misbehavior. *Journal of Learning Disabilities, 22*(1), 46–50.

Hebb, D. O. (1946). On the nature of fear. *Psychology Review, 53*, 259–276.

Hebb, D. O. (1949). *The organization of behavior.* New York: Wiley.

Heckhausen, J. (1988). Becoming aware of one's competence in the second year: Developmental progression within the mother-child dyad. *International Journal of Behavioral Development, 11*(3), 305–326.

Heflinger, C. A., Cook, V. J., & Thackrey, M. (1987). Identification of mental retardation by the system of multicultural pluralistic assessment: Nondiscriminatory or nonresistant? *Journal of School Psychology, 25*(2), 177–183.

Hegsted, D. M. (1990). Trends in food consumption: Implications for infant feeding. *Journal of Pediatrics, 117* (2, Pt. 2), 580–3.

Heinbuck, C. L., & Hershberger, W. A. (1989). Development of visual attention: A stereoscopic view. *Perception and Psychophysics, 45*(5), 404–410.

Henderson, R. W., & Rankin, R. J. (1986). Preschoolers' viewing of instructional television. *Journal of Educational Psychology, 78*(1), 44–51.

Henrion, R. (1988). Pregnancy and AIDS. *Human Reproduction, 3*(2), 257–262.

Hepper, P. G. (1989). Foetal learning: Implications for psychiatry? *British Journal of Psychiatry, (155*, Sept.), 289–293.

Heron, A., & Dowel, W. (1974). The questionable entity of the concrete operations stage. *International Journal of Psychology, 9*(1), 1–9.

Hersch, P. (1988). Coming of age on the streets. *Psychology Today, 22*(1), 28, 30–37.

Herskowitz, J. (1988). *Is your child depressed?* New York: Pharos Books.

Heslin, J. (1983/84, winter). Third-trimester nutrition. *Childbirth Educator,* pp. 38–39.

Hetherington, E. M. (1979). Divorce: A child's perspective. *American Psy-*

chologist, 34(10), 851–858.

Hetherington, E. M. (1989). Coping with family transitions: Winners, losers and survivors. Meetings of the Society for Research in Child Development. *Child Development, 60*(1), 1–14.

Hetherington, E. M., Cox, M, & Cox, R. (1982). Effects of divorce on parents and children. In M. Lamb (Ed.), *Nontraditional families.* Hillsdale, NJ: Erlbaum.

Hetherington, E. M., Cox, M., & Cox, R. (1985). Long-term effects of divorce and remarriage on the adjustment of children. *Journal of the American Academy of Child Psychiatry, 24,* 518–530.

Hetherington, E. M., Stanley-Hagan, M., & Anderson, E. R. (1989). Marital transitions: A child's perspective. Special Issue: Children and their development. *American Psychologist, 44*(2), 303–312.

Hewson, P., Oberklaid, F., & Menahem, S. (1987). Infant colic, distress and crying. *Clinical Pediatrics, 26*(2), 69–76.

Hibbard, B. M. (1988). *Principles of obstetrics.* Stoneham, MA: Butterworth.

Higgins, A. T., & Turnure, J. E. (1984). Distractability and concentration of attention in children's development. *Child Development, 55,* 1799–1810.

Higham, E. (1980). Variations in adolescent psychohormonal development. In J. Adelson (ed). *Handbook of adolescent psychology.* New York: Wiley.

Hill, A. J., Oliver, S., & Rogers, P. J. (1992). Eating in the adult world: The rise in dieting in childhood and adolescence. *British Journal of Clinical Psychology, 31* (Pt. 1), 95–105.

Hill, C. R., & Stafford, F. P. (1980). Parental care of children: Time diary estimates of quantity, predictability and variety. *Journal of Human Resources, 15,* 219–239.

Hill, J. P. (1987). Research on adolescents and their families: Past and prospect. In C. E. Irwin (Ed.), *Adolescent social behavior and health.* San Francisco: Jossey-Bass.

Hill, W. L., Borovsky, D., & Rovee-Collier, C. (1988). Continuities in infant memory development. *Developmental Psychobiology, 21*(1), 43–62.

Hinde, R. A., Titonus, G., Easton, D., & Tamplin, A. (1985). Incidence of "friendship" and behavior toward strong associates versus nonassociates in preschool. *Child Development, 56,* 234–235.

Hines, M. (1982). Prenatal gonodal hormones and sex differences in human behavior. *Psychology Bulletin, 92,* 56–80.

Hitch, G. T. et al. (1989). Development of rehearsal in short-term memory: Differences between pictorial and spoken stimuli. *British Journal of Developmental Psychology, 7*(4), 347–362.

Hobart, C., & Brown, D. (1988). Effects of prior marriage children on adjustment in remarriages: A Canadian study. *Journal of Comparative Family Studies, 19,* 381–396.

Hoble, J. (1982). Premature birth: Spotting the risks. *Contemporary Obstetrics/Gynecology, 19,* 209–232.

Hobson, R. P. (1990). On acquiring knowledge about people and the capacity to pretend: Response to Leslie (1987). *Psychology Review, 97*(1), 114–121.

Hodgman, C. H. (1983). Current issues in adolescent psychiatry. *Hospital and Community Psychiatry, 34*(6), 514–521.

Hofferth, S. L., & Hayes, C. D. (Eds.). (1987). *Adolescent sexuality, pregnancy and childbearing: Vol. 2. Risking the future.* Working papers and statistical appendixes. Washington, D.C.: National Academy of Sciences.

Hoffman, L. (1984). Work, family and the socialization of the child. In R. Park (Ed.), *Review of child development research,* (Vol. 7). Chicago: University of Chicago Press.

Hoffman, L. W. (1989). Effects of maternal employment in the two-parent family: A review of the research. *American Psychology, 44*(2), 283–292.

Hoffman, M. L. (1975). Moral internalization, parental power, and the nature of the parent-child interaction. *Developmental Psychology, 11,* 228–239.

Hoffman, M. L. (1979). Development of moral thought, feeling and behavior. *American Psychology, 34,* 958–966.

Hoffman, M. L. (1984). Interaction of affect and cognition in empathy. In C. E. Izard, J. Kagan and R. B. Zajonc (Eds.). *Emotions, cognition and behavior.* Cambridge, MA: Cambridge University Press.

Hohlstein, R. R. (1982). The development of pretension in normal infants. *American Journal of Occupational Therapy, 36*(3), 170–176.

Hojat, M. (1987). A psychodynamic view of loneliness and mother-child relationships: A review of theoretical perspectives and empirical findings. Special issue: Loneliness: Theory, research and applications. *Journal of Social Behavior and Personality, 2*(2, Pt. 2), 89–104.

Holden, C. (1980). Identical twins reared apart. *Science, 21,* 1323–1327.

Hollenbeck, A. R., & Slaby, R. G. (1979). Infant visual and vocal responses to television. *Child Development, 50,* 41–45.

Holtzman, M. (1983). *The language of children: Development in home and in school.* Englewood Cliffs, NJ: Prentice-Hall.

Homzie, M. J., & Lindsay, J. S. (1984). Language and the young stutterer: A new look at old theories or findings. *Brain and Language, 22*(2), 232–252.

Honzik, M. P. (1983). Measuring mental abilities in infancy: The value and limitations. In M. Lewis (Ed.), *Origins of intelligence: Infancy and early childhood* (2nd ed). New York: Plenum.

Honzik, M. P., MacFarlane, J. W., & Allen, L. (1984). The stability of mental test performance between 2 and 18 years. *Journal of Experimental Education, 17,* 309–329.

Horn, J. (1983). The Texas Adoption Project: Adopted children and their intellectual resemblance to biological and adoptive parents. *Child Development, 54,* 268–275.

Horn, W. F., Wagner, A. E., & Ialongo, N. (1989). Sex differences in school-aged children with pervasive attention deficit hyperactivity disorder. *Journal of Abnormal Child Psychology, 17*(1), 109–125.

Hornik, R., & Gunnar, M. R. (1988). A descriptive analysis of infant social referencing. *Child Development, 59*(3), 626–634.

Horowitz, F. D., & O'Brien, M. (1986). Gifted and talented children: State of knowledge and directions for research. *American Psychology, 41*(10); 1147–1152.

Horvard, L., & Carlo, G. (1991, April 1). Millions of hungry kids. *Newsweek,* Periscope.

Howat, P. M., & Saxton, A. M. (1988). The incidence of bulimic behavior in a secondary and university school population. *Journal of Youth and Adolescence, 17*(3), 221–231.

Howes, C. (1988). Peer interaction of young children. *Monographs of the Society for Research in Child Development, 53*(1).

Howes, C. (1990). Can the age of entry into child care and the quality of child care predict adjustment in kindergarten? *Developmental Psychology, 26*(2S), 292–303.

Howes, P., & Markman, H. J. (1989). Marital quality and child functioning: A longitudinal investigation. *Child Development, 60*(5), 1044–1051.

Howlin, P. (1988). Living with impairment: The effect on children of having an autistic sibling. *Child: Care, Health & Development, 14*(6), 395–408.

Hubert, N. C. (1989). Parental subjective reactions to perceived temperament behaviors in their 6- and 24-month-old children. *Infant Behavior and Development, 12*(2), 185–198.

Hubley, P., & Trevarthen, C. (1979). Sharing a task in infancy. In. I. Uzgiris (Ed.). *Social interaction and communication during infancy.* (New directions for child development. No. 4). San Francisco: Jossey-Bass.

Hudson, B., Pepperell, R., & Wood, C. (1987). The problem of infertility. In R. Pepperell, B. Hudson, & C. Wood (Eds.), *The infertile couple,* Edinburgh: Churchill-Livingstone.

Hudson, J. A. (1990). Constructive processing in children's event memory. *Developmental Psychology, 26*(2), 180–187.

Huesmann, L. R. (1986). Psychological processes promoting the relation between exposure to media violence and aggressive behavior by the viewer. *Journal of Social Issues, 42,* 125–139.

Humphrey, L. L. (1986). Structural analysis of parent-child relationships in eating disorders. *Journal of Abnormal Psychology, 95*(4), 395–402.

Humphreys, A. D., & Smith, P. K. (1984). Rough and tumble in preschool and playground. In P. K. Smith (Ed.), *Play in animals and humans.* Oxford, England: Basil Blackwell.

Humphreys, A. D., & Smith, P. K. (1987). Rough and tumble, friendship, and dominance in school children and evidence for continuity and change with age. *Child Development, 58,* 201–212.

Hunt, C. E., & Brouillette, R. T. (1987). Sudden infant death syndrome: 1987 perspective. *Journal of Pediatrics, 110*(5), 669–678.

Hunt, M. (1974). *Sexual behavior in the 1970s.* Chicago: Playboy Press.

Hurley, D. (1987). A sound mind in an unsound body. *Psychology Today, 21*(8), 34–38, 42, 43.

Huston, A. C. (1983). Sex typing. In P. A. Mussen (Ed.), *Handbook of child psychology,* (4th ed.) Vol. 4. New York: Wiley.

Huston, A. C., Greer, D., Wright, J. C., Welch, R., & Ross R. (1984). Children's comprehension of televised formal features with masculine and feminine connotations. *Developmental Psychology, 20,* 707–716.

Huston, A. C. et al. (1990). Development of television viewing patterns in early childhood: A longitudinal investigation. *Developmental Psychology, 26*(3), 409–420.

Huttenlocher, J. (1974). The origins of language comprehension. In R. L. Solso (Ed.), *Theories in cognitive psychology.* Potomac, MD: Lawrence Erlbaum Associates.

Huttenlocher, J., & Smiley P. (1987). Early word meaning: The case of object names. *Cognitive Psychology, 19*(1), 63–89.

Hwang, C. P. (1986). Behavior of Swedish primary and secondary caretaking fathers in relation to mother's presence. *Developmental Psychology, 22,* 749–751.

Ihinger-Tallman, B., & Pasley, K. (1987). *Remarriage.* Newbury Park, CA: Sage.

Ingram, N., & Butterworth, G. (1989). The young child's representation of depth in drawing: Process and product. *Journal of Experimental Child Psychology, 47*(3), 356–369.

Inhelder, B. (1960). Criteria of stages in mental development. In J. M. Tanner & B. Inhelder (Eds.), *Discussions on child development.* New York: International Universities Press.

Inhelder, B., & Piaget, J. (1958). *The growth of logical thinking from childhood to adolescence* (trans. A. Parsons & S. Seagrim). New York: Basic Books (originally published in 1955).

Inhelder, B., & Piaget, J. (1964). *The early growth of logic in the child* (trans. G. A. Lunzer & D. Papert). New York: Harper & Row (originally published in 1959).

Isabella, R. A., Belsky, J., & von Eye, A. (1989). Origins of infant-mother attachment: An examination of interactional synchrony during the infant's first year. *Developmental Psychology, 75*(1), 12–21.

Isaksen, J. G. (1986). *Watching and wondering: Observing and recording child behavior.* Palo Alto, CA: Mayfield Publishing Co.

Ivan, L. V. et al. (1983). Head injuries in childhood. A two-year survey. *Canadian Medical Association Journal, 128*(3), 281–284.

Ivanovich, J. M., Matteson, M. T. & Gamble, G. O. (1987). Birth order and type A coronary behavior pattern. *Individual Psychology, 43,* 42–49.

Izard, C. E. (1982). *Measuring emotions in infants and children.* New York: Cambridge University Press.

Izard, C. E. (1990). Facial expressions and the regulation of emotions. *Journal of Personality and Social Psychology, 58*(3), 487–498.

Izard, C. E., Hembree, E. A., Dougherty, L. M., & Coss, C. L. (1983). Changes in two- to nineteen-month-old infants' facial expressions following acute pain. *Developmental Psychology, 19,* 418–426.

Izard, C. E. Hembree, E. A., & Huebner, R. R. (1987). Infants' emotion expressions to acute pain. *Developmental Psychology, 23,* 105–113.

Jackson, K. A., & Gibson, R. A. (1989). Weaning foods cannot replace breast milk as sources of long chain polyunsaturated fatty acids. *American Journal of Clinical Nutrition, 50*(5), 980–982.

Jacobs, J. (1971). *Adolescent suicide.* New York: Wiley.

James, W. H. (1987). The human sex ratio, Part 2: A hypothesis and a program of research. *Human Biology, 59*(6), 873–900.

Janerich, D. T., Thompson, W. D., Varela, L. R. et al. (1990). Lung cancer and exposure to tobacco smoke in the household. *New England Journal of Medicine, 323*(10), 632–6.

Janos, P. M., & Robinson, N. M. (1985). Psychosocial development in intellectually gifted children. In F. D. Horowitz, & M. O'Brien (Eds.). *The gifted and talented: Developmental perspectives.* Washington, D.C.: American Psychology Association.

Jarski, R. W., & Trippett, D. L. (1990). The risks and benefits of exercise during pregnancy. *Journal of Family Practice, 30*(2), 185–189.

Jenkins, J. R., & Heinen, A. (1989). Student's preferences for special delivery: Pull-out, in-class or integrated model. *Exceptional Children, 55*(6), 516–523.

Jersild, A. T. & Markey F. V. (1935). Conflicts between preschool children. *Child Development Monographs, No. 21.* New York: Teacher's College Press, Columbia University.

Jessor, R., Costa, F., Jessor, L., & Donovan, J. E. (1983). Time of first intercourse: A prospective study. *Journal of Personality and Social Psychology, 44*(3), 608–626.

Jimenez, S. L. M. (1989, September). Will it hurt my baby? *American Baby,* pp. 74, 76, 78.

Joffe, L. S., & Vaughn, B. E. (1982). Infant-mother attachment: Theory, assessment and implications for development. In B. B. Wolman (Ed.), *Handbook of developmental psychology,* Englewood Cliffs, NJ: Prentice-Hall.

Johnson, C. F. & Showers, J. (1985). Injury variables in child abuse. *Child Abuse and Neglect, 9,* 209–215.

Johnson, D. F., & Goldman, S. (1987). Children's recognition and use of rules of moral conduct in stores. *American Journal of Psychology, 100,* 205–224.

Johnson, D. W., & Johnson, R. T. (1985). Relationships between black and white students in intergroup cooperation and competition. *Journal of Social Psychology, 125*(4), 421–428.

Johnson, J. A. (1981). The etiology of hyperactivity. *Exceptional Children, 47,* 348–354.

Johnson, J. Fabian, V., & Pascual-Leone, J. (1989). Quantitative hardware changes that constrain language development. *Human Development, 32*(5), 245–271.

Johnson, K. E. (1989). *Human developmental anatomy.* New York: Wiley: Harwal Publishing Company.

Johnson, P. R., Shireman, J. F., & Watson, K. W. (1987). Transracial adoption and the development of black identity at age eight. *Child welfare, 66*(1), 45–55.

Johnson, W. F. et al. (1983). Maternal perception of infant emotion from birth through 18 months. *Annual Progress in Child Psychiatry and Child Development, 1983,* 144–155.

Johnston, J. R., Kline, M., & Tschann, J. M. (1989). Ongoing postdivorce conflict: Effect on children of joint custody and frequent access. *American Journal of Orthopsychiatry, 59*(4), 593–604.

Johnston, L. D., O'Malley, P. M., & Bachman, J. G. (1988). National trends in drug use and related factors among American high school students and young adults. *National trends through 1987.* Rockville, MD: National Institute of Drug Abuse.

Jones, D. C., Swift, D. J., & Johnson, M. A. (1988). Nondeliberate memory for a novel event among preschoolers. *Developmental Psychology, 24*(5), 641–645.

Jones, E. T. (1969). Needs of negro youth. In D. G. Winter and E. M. Nuss (Eds.). *The young adult: Identity and awareness.* Glenview, IL: Scott, Foresman.

Jones, G. P., & Dembo, M. H. (1989). Age and sex role differences in intimate friendships during childhood and adolescence. *Merrill-Palmer Quarterly, 35*(4), 445–462.

Jones, K. L. (1991). Developmental pathogenesis of defects associated with prenatal cocaine exposure: fetal vascular disruption. *Clinics in Perenatology, 18*(1), 139–146.

Jones, K. L. et al. (1973). Patterns of malformation in offspring of chronic alcoholic women. *Lancet, 1*, 1267.

Jones, S. S., & Raag, T. (1989). Smile production in older infants: The importance of a social recipient for the facial signal. *Child Development, 60*(4), 811–818.

Jourard, S. M., & Landsman, T. (1980). *Healthy personality* (4th ed.). New York: MacMillan.

Jouriles, E. N., Murphy, C. M., & O'Leary, K. D. (1989). Effects of maternal mood on mother-son interaction patterns. *Journal of Abnormal Child Psychology, 17*(5), 513–525.

Jovanovic, J., Lerner, R. M., & Lerner, J. V. (1989). Objective and subjective attractiveness and early adolescent adjustment. *Journal of Adolescence, 12*(2), 225–229.

Juel, C. (1988). Learning to read and write: A longitudinal study of 54 children from first through 4th grades. *Journal of Educational Psychology, 80*(4), 437–447.

Juhasz, A. M., Kaufman, B., & Meyer, H. (1986). Adolescent attitudes and beliefs about sexual behavior. *Child and Adolescent Social Work Journal, 3*(3), 177–193.

Kagan, J. (1971). *Change and continuity in infancy.* New York: Wiley.

Kagan, J. (1974). Discrepancy, temperament, and infant distress. In M. Lewis & L. Rosenblum (Eds.). *The origins of fear.* New York: Wiley.

Kagan, J. (1979). Overview: Perspectives on human infancy. In J. Osofsky (Ed.), *Handbook on infant development.* New York: Wiley.

Kagan, J. (1982). *Psychological research on the human infant: An evaluative summary.* New York: W. T. Grant Foundation.

Kagan, J., Kearsley, R. B., & Zelazo, P. R. (1978). *Infancy: Its place in human development.* Cambridge, MA: Harvard University Press, 1978.

Kagan, J., Reznick, J. S., & Snidman, N. (1987). The physiology and psychology of behavioral inhibition in children. *Child Development, 58*, 1459–1473.

Kagan, J., Reznick, J. S. and Snidman, N. (1988). Biological bases of childhood shyness. *Science, 240*, 167–171.

Kagan, J., Rosman, B. L., Day, D., Albert, J., & Phillips, W. (1964). Information processing in the child: Significance of analytic and reflective attitudes. *Psychological Monographs, 79* (No. 578).

Kagan, S., & Madsen, M. C. (1972). Rivalry in anglo-American and Mexican children of two ages. *Journal of Personality and Social Psychology, 24*, 214–220.

Kahn, P. H., & Turiel, E. (1988). Children's conceptions of trust in the context of social expectations. *Merrill-Palmer Quarterly, 34*(4), 403–419.

Kail, R. (1984). *The development of memory in children.* San Francisco: W. H. Freeman.

Kail, R. (1988). Developmental functions for speeds of cognitive process. *Journal of Experimental Child Psychology, 45*(3), 339–364.

Kalat, J. W. (1981). *Biological Psychology.* Belmont, CA: Wadsworth Press.

Kanner, L. (1943). Autistic disturbance of affective contact. *Nervous Child, 2*, 217–250.

Kaplan, B. J., McNicol, J., Conte, R. A., & Moghadam, H. K. (1989). Overall nutrient intake of preschool hyperactive and normal boys. *Journal of Abnormal Child Psychology, 17*(2), 127–132.

Kaplan, P. S., Werner, J. S., & Rudy, J. W. (1990). Habituation, sensitization and infant visual attention. *Advances in Infancy Research, 6*, 61–109.

Karmiloff-Smith, A. (1984). Structure versus process in comparing linguistic and cognitive development. In I. Levin (Ed.), *Stage and structure.* Norwood, NJ: Ablex.

Karp, R. J. et al. (1989). Growth of abused children. Contrasted with the non-abused in an urban poor community. *Clinical Pediatrics, 28*(7), 317–320.

Kataria, S., Frutiger, A. D., Lanford, B., & Swanson, M. S. (1988). Anterior fontanel closure in healthy term infants. *Infant Behavior and Development, 11*(2), 229–233.

Katz, S., & Kravetz, S. (1989). Facial plastic surgery for persons with Down Syndrome: Research findings and their professional and social implications. *American Journal on Mental Retardation, 94*(2), 101–110.

Kaufman, J., & Zigler, E. (1987). Do abused children become abusive parents? *American Journal of Orthopsychiatry, 57*(2), 186–192.

Kavanaugh, R. D. (1979). Observations on the role of logically constrained sentences in the comprehension of "before" and "after." *Journal of Child Language, 6*, 353–357.

Kaye, K. (1982). *The social and mental life of babies.* Chicago: University of Chicago Press.

Kee, D. W., & Bell, T. S. (1981). The development of organizational strategies on the storage and retrieval of categorical items in free-recall learning. *Child Development, 52*, 1163–1171.

Kempe, C. H., & Helfer, R. E. (1980). *The battered child* (3rd ed.). Chicago: University of Chicago Press.

Kempe, R. S., & Kempe, C. H. (1978). *Child abuse.* Cambridge, MA: Harvard University Press.

Kendler, H. H., & Kendler, T. S. (1962). Vertical and horizontal processes in problem solving. *Psychological Review, 69*, 1–16.

Kendler, H. H., & Kendler, T. S. (1970). Developmental processes in discrimination learning. *Human Development, 13*, 65–89.

Kendrick, C., & Dunn, J. (1983). Sibling quarrels and maternal responses. *Developmental Psychology, 19*(1), 62–70.

Kennedy, E., Spence, S. H., & Hensley, R. (1989). An examination of the relationship between childhood depression and social competence amongst primary school children. *Journal of Child Psychology & Psychiatry & Allied Disciplines, 30*(4), 561–573.

Kennedy, G. E. (1989). Middleborn perceptions of family relationships. *Psychological Reports, 64*, 755–760.

Kent, S. E., & Jones, R. (1988). Pseudomonas vaccination in chronic ear disease. *Journal of Laryngology and Otology, 102*(7), 579–81.

Kenny, S. L. (1983). Developmental discontinuities in childhood and adolescence. In *Levels and transitions in children's development* (New directions for child development, No. 21). San Francisco: Jossey-Bass.

Kermolan, R., & Campos, J. J. (1988). Locomotor experience: A facilitator of spatial cognitive development. *Child Development, 59*(4), 908–917.

Kirk, S. A., & Gallagher, J. J. (1983). *Educating exceptional children* (4th ed.). Boston: Houghton Mifflin.

Kisbourne, M. (1982). Hemispheric specialization and the growth of human understanding. *American Psychologist, 37*(4), 411–420.

Kiser, L. J., Bates, J. E., Maslin, C. A., & Bayles, K. (1986). Mother-infant play at six months as a predictor of attachment security at thirteen months. *Journal of the American Academy of Child Psychiatry, 25*, 68–75.

Kitchener, K. S. (1983). Human development and the college campus: Sequences and tasks. In *Assessing student development* (New directions for student services). San Francisco: Jossey-Bass.

Kitzinger, S. (1981). *The complete book of pregnancy and childbirth.* New York: Knopf.

Kizer, K. W. et al. (1990). Vitamin A—a pregnancy hazard alert. *Western Journal of Medicine, 152*(1), 78–81.

Kjersgaard, A., Thranov, I., Rasmussen, O., & Hortz, J. Male or female sterilization: A comparative study. *American Fertility Society, 51*, 439–443.

Klapper, Z. S. (1968). Psycho-educational aspects of reading disabilities. In G. Nachez (ed.) *Children with reading problems.* New York: Basic Books.

Klaus, M. H., & Kennell, J. H. (1976). *Maternal-infant bonding.* St. Louis: C. V. Mosby.

Klein, J. R., & Litt, I. F. (1983). Menarche and dysmenorrhea. In J. Brooks-Gunn & A. C. Petersen (Eds.), *Girls at puberty: Biological, psychological and social perspectives.* New York: Plenum.

Kleinman, R. L. (1980). *Family planning handbook for doctors.* International Planned Parenthood Medical Publications. New York: New York.

Kline, M. S., Tshann, J. M., Johnston, J. K., & Wallerstein, J. S. (1989). Children's adjustment in joint and sole physical custody families. *Developmental Psychology, 25*(3), 430–438.

Knopp, R. J. (1987). When a child dies. *Psychology Today, 21*(7), 60–67.

Kocaard, V. C. (1991). The physiological role of the pineal gland as the masterswitch of life, turning on at birth breathing and geared to it the function of the autonomic nervous system. The cause of SIDS examined in this context. *Medical Hypotheses, 34*(2), 122–126.

Kochanska, G., Kuczynski, L. & Radke-Yarrow, M. (1989). Correspondence between mothers' self-reported and observed child-rearing practices. *Child Development, 60*(1), 56–63.

Koestner, R., Franz, C., & Weinberger, J. (1990). The family origins of empathic concern: A 26-year longitudinal study. *Journal of Personality and Social Psychology, 58*(4), 709–717.

Koff, E., Rierdan, J., & Sheingold, K. (1982). Memories of menarche: Age, preparation and prior knowledge as determinants of initial menstrual experience. *Journal of Youth and Adolescence, 11*, 1–9.

Kogan, N. (1983). Stylistic variation in childhood and adolescence. Creativity, metaphor and cognitive style. In P. H. Mussen (Ed.), *Handbook of child psychology* (4th ed.). Vol. 3. New York: Wiley.

Kohlberg, L. (1966). A cognitive-developmental analysis of children's sex role concepts and attitudes. In E. E. Maccoby (Ed.). *The development of sex differences.* Palo Alto, CA: Stanford University Press.

Kohlberg, L. (1969). Stage and sequence: The cognitive-developmental approach to socialization. In D. A. Goslin (Ed.), *Handbook of socialization theory and research.* Chicago: Rand McNally.

Kohlberg, L. (1971). From is to ought: How to commit the naturalistic fallacy and get away with it in the study of moral development. In T. Mischel (Ed.), *Cognitive Development and epistemology.* New York: Academic Press.

Kohlberg, L. (1976). Moral stages and moralization: The cognitive-developmental approach. In T. Lickona (Ed.), *Moral development and behavior: Theory, research and social issues.* New York: Holt, Rinehart & Winston.

Kohlberg, L., & Gilligan, C. (1971). The adolescent as philosopher: The discovery of the self in a postconventional world. *Daedalus, 100*, 1051–1086.

Kohlberg, L., Levine, C., & Heiver, A. (1983). *Moral stages: A current formulation and a response to critics.* Basel, Switzerland: Karger.

Kohn, M. L., & Schooler, C. (1983). *Work and personality: An inquiry into the impact of social stratification.* Norwood, NJ: Ablex Press.

Kolb, B. (1989). Brain development, plasticity and behavior. *American Psychologist, 44*(9), 1203–1212.

Kollars, D. (1990, May 25). More kids just say no: Drug use down in state schools. *Sacramento Bee*, pp. B1, B3.

Koniak-Griffin, D., & Rummell, M. (1988). Temperament in infancy: Stability, change and correlates. *Maternal-Child Nursing Journal, 17*(1), 25–40.

Koops, B. L., Morgan, L. J., & Battaglia, F. C. (1982). Neonatal mortality risk in relation to birth weight and gestational age: Update. *Journal of Pediatrics, 101*, 969–977.

Kopp, C. B. (1982). Antecedents of self-regulation: A developmental perspective. *Developmental Psychology, 18*(2), 199–214.

Kopp, C. B. (1983). Risk factors in development. In P. H. Mussen (Ed.) *Handbook of Developmental Psychology* (4th ed.) Vol. 2. New York: Wiley.

Korones, S. B. (1981). *High risk newborn infants: The basis for intensive nursing care.* St. Louis: C. V. Mosby.

Koss, L., & Seibel, C. (1988). Stranger and acquaintance rape. *Psychology of Women Quarterly, 12*, 1–24.

Krantz, M., & Burton, C. (1986). The development of the social cognition of social status. *Journal of Genetic Psychology, 147*, 89–95.

Kreek, M. J. (1982). Opiod's disposition and effects during chronic exposure in the prenatal period in man. *Advances in Alcohol and Substance Abuse, 1*(3–4), 21–53.

Kreminitzer, J. D., Vaughn, H. G., Kurtzberg, D., & Dowling, K. (1979). Smooth pursuit eye movements in the newborn infant. *Child Development, 50*, 442–448.

Kretschmer, K., & Wright, J. (1990, April 1). Babyproofing basics. *American Baby*, pp. A18, 20, 22.

Kropp, J. J., & Halverson, C. F. (1983). Preschool children's preferences and recall for stereotyped and nonstereotyped stories. *Sex Roles, 9*(2), 261–272.

Kropp, J. P., & Haynes, O. M. (1987). Abusive and nonabusive mothers' ability to identify general and specific emotional signals of infants. *Child Development, 58*, 187–190.

Kubler-Ross, E. (1983). *On children and death.* New York: MacMillan.

Kuczynski, L., Zahn-Waxler, C., Radke-Yarrow, M. (1987). Development and context of imitation in the second and third year of life: A socialization perspective. *Developmental Psychology, 23*, 276–282.

Kuhn, D., Nash, S. C., & Brucken, L. (1978). Sex role concepts and two- and three-year-olds. *Child Development, 49*, 445–451.

Kulin, H., Frontera, M., Demers, L., Bartholomew, M., & Lloyd, T. (1989). The onset of sperm production in pubertal boys. *American Journal of Diseases of Children, 143*, 190–193.

Kumar, R., & Robson, K. M. (1984). A prospective study of emotional disorders in childbearing women. *British Journal of Psychiatry, 144*, 35–47.

Kurdek, L. A. (1988). A one-year follow-up study of children's divorce adjustment and postdivorce parenting. *Journal of Applied Developmental Psychology, 9*(3), 315–328.

Kurinij, N., Shiono, P. H., & Rhoads, G. G. (1988). Breastfeeding incidence and duration in black and white women. *Pediatrics, 81*(3), 365–370.

Kurtines, W., & Grief, E. B. (1974). The development of moral thought: Review and evaluation of Kohlberg's approach. *Psychology Bulletin, 81*, 453–470.

Labov, W. (1972). *Language in the inner city: Studies in the black English vernacular.* Philadelphia: University of Pennsylvania Press.

Ladd, G. W., & Price, J. M. (1987). Predicting children's social and school adjustment following the transition from preschool to kindergarten. *Child Development, 58*, 1168–1189.

Ladd, G. W., Price, J. M., & Hart, C. H. (1988). Predicting preschoolers' peer status from their playground behaviors. *Child Development, 59*(4), 986–992.

Laine, C. & Schultz, L. (1985). Composition theory and practice: The paradigm shift. *Volta Review, 87*(5), 9–20.

Lamb, M. E., (1977). Father-infant and mother-infant interaction in the first year of life. *Child Development, 48*, 167–181.

Lamb, M. E. (Ed.) (1978). *Social and personality development.* New York: Holt, Rinehart, & Winston.

Lamb, M. E. (1982, April). Second thoughts on first touch. *Psychology Today*, pp. 9–11.

Lamb, M. E. (1984–85). A comparison of "second order effects" involving parents and siblings. *Research and clinical center for child development*, 1984–85, No. 8 (Annual Report), 1–7.

Lambert, N. M. (1988). Adolescent outcome for hyperactive children: Perspectives on general and specific patterns of childhood risk for adolescent educational, social and mental health problems. *American Psychology, 43*(10), 786–799.

Lancelotta, G. X., & Vaughn, S. (1989). Relation between types of aggression and sociometric status: Peer and teacher perceptions. *Journal of Educational Psychology, 81*, 86–90.

Landers, S. (1987). Autism turns a corner. *APA Monitor, 18*(6), 26.

Landers, S. (1989). Homeless children lose childhood. *APA Monitor, 20*(12), 1, 33.

Landers, S. (1990, February). China's one child push studied by psychologist. *APA Monitor*, p. 35.

Landry, S. H., Chapieski, L., Fletcher, J. M., & Denson, S. (1988). Three-year outcome for low birth weight in infants: Differential effects of early complications. *Journal of Pediatric Psychology, 13*(3), 317–327.

Landry, S. H., Schmidt, M., & Richardson, M. A. (1989). The effects of intraventricular hemorrhage on functional communication skills in preterm toddlers. *Journal of Developmental and Behavioral Pediatrics, 10*(6), 299–306.

Lange, G., & Guttentag, R. E. (1990). Relationships between study organization, retrieval organization, and general and strategic-specific memory knowledge in young children. *Journal of Experimental Child Psychology, 49*(1), 126–146.

Langlois, J. H. (1985). From the eye of the beholder to behavioral reality: The development of social behaviors and social relations as a function of physical attractiveness. In C. P. Herman (Ed.), *Physical appearance, stigma and social behavior*. Hillsdale, NJ: Erlbaum.

Langlois, J. H., & Downs, A. C. (1980). Mothers, fathers and peers as socialization agents of sex-typed play behaviors in young children. *Child Development, 51*, 1237–1247.

Langlois, J. H., Roggman, L. A., & Riesner-Danner, L. A. (1990). Infants' differential social responses to attractive and unattractive faces. *Developmental Psychology, 26*(1), 153–159.

Lapsley, D. K., & Quintana, S. M. (1985). Recent approaches to the moral and social education of children. *Elementary School Guidance and Counseling, 19*(4), 246–259.

Larin, H. M. (1982). Drug and obstetric medication effects on infant behavior as measured by the Brazelton Neonatal Behavioral Assessment Scale. *Physical and Occupational Therapy in Pediatrics, 2*(1), 75–84.

Larzelere, R. E., (1986). Moderate spanking: Model or deterrent of children's aggression in the family? *Journal of Family Violence, 1*(1), 27–36.

Laursen, B., & Hartup, W. W. (1989). The dynamics of preschool children's conflicts. *Merrill-Palmer Quarterly, 35*(3), 281–297.

Lawson, A. E. & Bealer, J. M. (1984). The acquisition of basic quantitative reasoning skills during adolescence: Learning or development? *Journal of Research on Science Teaching, 21*(4), 417–423.

Lazar, I., & Darlington, R. (1982). Lasting effects of early education: A report from the consortium for longitudinal studies. *Monographs of the Society for Research in Child Development, 47* (Whole No. 195).

Leader, A., Wong, K. H., & Dietel, M. (1981). Maternal nutrition in pregnancy. Part 1: A review. *Canadian Medical Association Journal, 125*(6), 545–549.

Leboyer, F. (1975). *Birth without violence*. New York: Knopf.

Lee, V. E., & Bryk, A. S. (1987). Effects of single sex secondary schools on student achievement and attitudes. *Journal of Educational Psychology, 78*, 381–395.

Lefebvre, F. et al. (1988). Outcome at school age of children with birthweights of 1000 grams or less. *Developmental Medicine and Child Neurology, 30*(2), 170–180.

Lefton, L. A. & Valvatne, L. (1988). *Mastering psychology, 3rd ed.* Boston: Allyn & Bacon.

Lempert, H. (1984). Topic as starting point for syntax. *Monographs of the Society for Research in Child Development, 49*(5), 1–73.

Leonard, B. E., (1990). Psychoneuro-immunology: An area of interest for the psychopharmacologist? *Journal of Psychopharmacology, 4*(1), 1–6.

Leonard, S. P., & Archer, J. (1989). A naturalistic investigation of gender constancy in three- to four-year old children. *International Journal of Developmental Psychology, 7*(4), 341–346.

Lenneberg, E. H. (1967). *Biological foundations of language*. New York: Wiley.

Lepman, J. (Ed.) (1971). *How children see our world*. New York: Avon.

Lepore, S. J., Kiely, M. C., Bempechat, J., & London, P. (1989). Children's perceptions of social abilities. Social cognitions and behavioral outcomes in the face of social rejection. *Child Study Journal, 19*(4), 259–271.

Lepper, M. R. (1985). Microcomputers in education: Maturation and social issues. *American Psychology, 40*, 1–18.

Leppart, P. C. (1984). The effect of pregnancy on adolescent growth and development. *Women and Health, 9*(2–3), 65–79.

Lerner, J. V. et al. (1988). A longitudinal study of negative emotional states and adjustment from early childhood through adolescence. *Child Development, 59*(2), 356–366.

Lerner, R., Jovanovic, J., & Lerner, J. (1989). Objective and subjective attractiveness and early adolescent adjustment. *Journal of Adolescence, 12,* 225–229.

Lessem, D. (1991, June 2). An awful scandal—dinosaurs. *Sacramento Bee*, Forum p. 1.

Levin, M. L. (1988–89). Sequelae to marital disruption in children. Special issue: Children of divorce: Developmental and clinical issues. *Journal of Divorce, 12*(2–3), 25–80.

Levine, S. C., & Carey, S. (1982). Up front: The acquisition of a concept and a word. *Journal of Child Language, 9*(3), 645–657.

Levitt, M. J., & Weber, R. A. (1989). Social involvement with peers in 2½ year old toddlers: Environmental influences. *Environment and Behavior, 2*(1), 82–98.

Lewandowski, L. J., & Cruickshank, W. M. (1980). Psychological development of crippled children and youth. In W. M. Cruchshank (Ed.), *Psychology of exceptional children and youth* (4th ed.). Englewood Cliffs, NJ: Prentice Hall.

Lewis, M. (1971). Individual differences in the measurement of early cognitive growth. In J. Hellmuth (Ed.), *Exceptional infant: Vol. 2, Studies in abnormalities*. New York: Brunner/Mazel.

Lewis, M. & Brooks-Gunn, J. (1979). *Social cognition and the acquisition of self*. New York: Plenum.

Lewis, M., & Michalson, L. (1983). *Children's emotions and moods*. New York: Plenum.

Lewis, M., Stanger, C., & Sullivan, M. W. (1989). Deception in 3-year-olds. *Developmental Psychology, 25*(3), 439–443.

Lewis, M., Sullivan, M. W., & Michalson, L. (1984). The cognitive-emotional fugue. In C. E. Izard, F. Kagan, & R. B. Zajonc (Eds.), *Emotions, cognition and behavior*. New York: Cambridge University Press.

Libman, J. (1987, April 29). In kindergarten, sometimes older is better. *Los Angeles Times*, Pt. V, p. 1, 4.

Libman, J. (1987, August 29). The frequent flier's kids: *Los Angeles Times*, Pt. V, p. 1–2.

Lieberman, A. B. (1989, February). Episiotomy. *American Baby*, pp. 30, 34–35.

Lieberman, A. B. (1990, May). Pitocen: Forced labor. *American Baby*, pp. 56, 58–59, 93–94.

Liebert, R. M. (1986). Effects of television on children and adolescents. *Journal of Developmental and Behavioral Pediatrics, 7*(1), 43–48.

Liebert, R. M., & Sprafkin, J. (1988). *The early window: Effects of television on children and youth* (3rd ed.). New York: Pergamon.

Lindberg, M. A. (1989). The development of attribute dominance in the knowledge base. *Journal of Genetic Psychology, 150*(3), 269–280.

Lindner, K. J. (1988). Age changes in assembly performance: A component analysis. *Perceptual and Motor Skills, 67*(3), 955–959.

Linkletter, A. (1957). *Kids say the darndest things!* Englewood Cliffs, NJ: Prentice-Hall.

Lipsitt, L. P. (1987). Trends on corporeal punishment. *The Brown University Child Behavior and Development Letter, 3*(10), 6.

Lipsitt, L. P. (1987b). Consensus on infant/toddler day-care reached by researchers. *The Brown University Child Behavior and Development Letter, 3*(11), 7.

Lipsitt, L. P. (1988c). When lost innocence is good for children: Using Dr.

Koop's pamphlet. *The Brown University Child Behavior and Development Letter, 4*(6), 1–2.

Lipsitt, L. B. (1988b). Latchkey kids at risk? New studies give mixed answers. *The Brown University Child Behavior and Development Letter, 4*(10), 7.

Lipsitt, L. P. (1988a). Effects of incestuous childhood experiences on later behavior. *The Brown University Child Behavior and Development Letter, 4*(12), 1–2.

Lipsitt, L. P. (1989b). Research debunks myths of only children. *The Brown University Child Behavior and Development Letter, 5*(7), 5–6.

Lipsitt, L. P. (1989a). Homeless children in school. *The Brown University Child Behavior and Development Letter, 5*(9), 5.

Lipsitz, J. S. (1979, October). Adolescent development: Myths and realities. *Children Today,* pp. 2–7.

Little, A. H., Lipsitt, L. P., & Rovee-Collier, C. (1984). Classical conditioning and retention of the infant's eyelid response: Effects of age and interstimulus interval. *Journal of Experimental Child Psychology, 37,* 512–524.

Little, B. B. et al. (1991). Is hyperthermia teratogenic in the human? *American Journal of Perinatology, 8*(3), 185–189.

Livson, N., & Peskin, H. (1980). Perspectives on adolescence from longitudinal research. In J. Adelson (Ed.), *Handbook of Adolescent Psychology.* New York: Wiley.

Lobato, D., Faust, D., & Spirito, A. (1988). Examining the effects of chronic disease and disability on children's sibling relationships. *Journal of Pediatric Psychology, 13*(3), 389–407.

Loche, J. T., & Pearson, D. M. (1990). Linguistic significance of babbling: Evidence from a tracheostomized infant. *Journal of Child Language, 17*(1), 1–16.

Locke, J. L. & Pearson, D. M. (1990). Linguistic significance of babbling: evidence from a tracheotomized infant. *Journal of Child Language, 17*(1), 1–16.

Loeber, R., & Dishion, T. (1983). Early predictions of male delinquency: A review. *Psychology Bulletin, 94,* 68–99.

Londerville, S., & Main, M. (1981). Security of attachment, compliance and maternal training methods in the second year of life. *Developmental Psychology, 17,* 289–299.

Long, P. (1986, December). Growing up military. *Psychology Today,* pp. 31–37.

Lord, C. (1982). Psychopathology in early development. In S. Moore and C. Cooper (Eds.), *The young child: Reviews of research* (Vol. 3). Washington, D.C.: National Association for the Education of Young Children.

Lord, R., & Hume, C. (1987). Perceptual judgments of normal and clumsy children. *Developmental Medicine and Child Neurology, 29,* 250–257.

Lorenz, K. (1966). *On aggression.* New York: Harcourt, Brace, & World.

Lorenz, K. Z. (1971). *Studies in animal and human behaviors* (Robert Martin, Trans.). Cambridge, MA: Harvard University Press.

Lou, H. O. C. (1982). *Developmental neurology.* New York: Raven.

Loucks, A., & Horvath, S. (1985). Athletic amenorrhea: A review. *Medicine and science in sports and exercise, 17,* 56–72.

Lovaas, O., & Simmons, J. A. (1969). Manipulation of self-destruction in three retarded children. *Journal of Applied Behavioral Analysis, 2,* 143–157.

Lowrey, G. H. (1978). *Growth and development of children* (7th ed.). Chicago: Year Book.

Lunde, D. T., & Lunde, M. R. (1980). *The next generation: A book on parenting.* New York: Holt, Rinehart and Winston.

Lutz, P. (1983). The stepfamily: An adolescent perspective. *Family Relations, 32,* 367–375.

Lyle, J. (1971). Television in daily life: Patterns of use (overuse). In *Television and Social Behavior,* Vol. 4. Washington, D.C.: U.S. Government Printing Office.

Lynch, G., & Gall, C. (1979). Organization and reorganization in the central nervous system. In F. Falkner & J. Tanner (Eds.), *Human growth.* New York: Plenum.

Lyons-Ruth, K. (1977). Binocular perception in infancy: Response to auditory-visual incongruity. *Child Development, 48,* 820–827.

Mabry, M. & Evans, T. (May 18, 1992). Crime: A conspiracy of silence. *Newsweek,* 37.

MacArthur, C., & Knox, E. G. (1988). Smoking in pregnancy: Effects of stopping at different stages. *British Journal of Obstetrics and Gynaecology, 95*(6), 551–555.

Maccoby, E. E. (1980). *Social development,* Psychological growth and the parent-child relationship. New York: Harcourt Brace Jovanovich.

Maccoby, E. E. (1984). Middle childhood in the context of the family. In W. A. Collins (Ed.), *Developing during middle childhood: The years from six to twelve.* Washington, D.C.: National Academy Press.

Maccoby, E. E. (1988). Gender as a social category. *Developmental Psychology, 24*(6), 755–765.

Maccoby, E. E. (1990). Gender and relationships: A developmental account. *American Psychology, 45,* 513–520.

Maccoby, E. E., & Feldman, S. S. (1972). Mother-attachment and stranger reactions in the third year of life. *Monographs of the Society for Research in Child Development, 37*(1, Serial No. 146).

Maccoby, E. E., & Jacklin, C. N. (1974). *The psychology of sex differences.* Stanford, CA: Stanford University Press.

Maccoby, E. E., & Jacklin, C. N. (1980). Sex differences in aggression: A rejoinder and reprise. *Child Development, 51,* 964–980.

Maccoby, E. E., & Martin, J. A. (1983). Socialization in the context of the family: Parent-child interaction. In P. H. Munsen (Ed.), *Handbook of child psychology* (Vol. 4). New York: Wiley.

MacDonald, K. (1987). Parent-child play with rejected, neglected and popular boys. *Developmental Psychology, 23,* 705–711.

MacEnvoy, B. et al. (1988). Early affective antecedents of adult Type A behavior. *Journal of Personality and Social Psychology, 54*(1), 108–116.

Macey, J. C. (1986). Innovations in family and community health. *Family and Community Health, 8*(4), 84–88.

Macfarlane, J. A. (1975). Olfaction in the development of social preferences in the human neonate. In M. A. Hofer (Ed.), *Parent-infant interaction.* Amsterdam: Elsevier.

Mackinnon, C. E. (1989). An observational investigation of sibling interactions in married and divorced families. *Developmental Psychology, 25*(1), 36–44.

Mahalski, P. A. (1983). The incidence of attachment objects and oral habits at bedtime in two longitudinal samples of children aged 1½–7 years. *Journal of Child Psychology and Psychiatry, 24*(2), 283–295.

Mahoney, G. (1988). Maternal communication style with mentally retarded children. *American Journal on Mental Retardation, 92*(4), 352–359.

Main, M., & Cassidy, J. (1988). Categories of responses to reunion with the parent at age 6: Predictable from infant attachment classifications and stable over a 1-month period. *Developmental Psychology, 24*(3), 415–426.

Main, M., Kaplan, N., & Cassidy, J. (1985). Security in infancy, childhood, and adulthood: A move to the level of representation. *Monographs of the Society for Research in Child Development, 50*(1–2), 66–104.

Main, M., & Solomon, J. (1989). Procedures for identifying infants as disorganized/disoriented during the Ainsworth Strange Situation. In M. Greenberg et al. (Eds.), *Attachment during the preschool years.* Chicago: University of Chicago Press.

Makin, J. W., & Porter, R. H. (1989). Attractiveness of lactating females' breast odors to neonates. *Child Development, 60*(4), 803–810.

Malatesta, C. Z., Culver, C., Tesman, J. R., & Shepard, B. (1989). The development of emotion expression during the first two years of life.

Monographs of the Society for Research in Child Development, 54(1–2), 1–104.

Malatesta, C. Z., Grigoryev, P., Lamb, C., Albin, M., & Culver, C. (1986). Emotional socialization and expressive development in preterm and full term infants. *Child Development, 57*, 316–330.

Malatesta, C. Z., & Haviland, J. M. (1982). Learning display rules: The socialization of emotion expression in infancy. *Child Development, 53*, 991–1003.

Malina, R. (1982). Motor developments in the early years. In S. Moore & C. Cooper (Eds.), *The young child: Reviews of research* (Vol. 3). Washington, D.C.: National Association for the Education of Young Children.

Malloy, M. H., Kleinman, J. C., Land, G. H., & Schramm, W. F. (1988). The association of maternal smoking with age and cause of infant death. *American Journal of Epidemiology, 128*(1), 46–55.

Mandler, J. M. (1988). How to build a baby: On the development of an accessible representational system. *Cognitive Development, 3*(2), 113–136.

Mange, A. P. (1990). *Genetics: Human aspects* (2nd ed.). Sunderland, MA: Sinauer Associates.

March of Dimes (1988). Protocol of care for the battered woman. *Professional Materials Department*. White Plains, NY: 10605.

Marchi, M., & Cohen, P. (1990). Early childhood eating behaviors and adolescent eating disorders. *Journal of the American Academy of Child and Adolescent Psychiatry, 29*(1), 112–117.

Marcia, J. E. (1980). Identity in adolescence. In J. Adelson (Ed.), *Handbook of adolescent psychology*. New York: Wiley.

Markman, E. M. (1977). Realizing that you don't understand: A preliminary investigation. *Child Development, 48*, 986–992.

Markman, E. M. (1979). Classes and collections: Conceptual organization and numerical abilities. *Cognitive Psychology, 11*, 395–411.

Marks, I. M. (1987). The development of normal fear: A review. *Journal of Child Psychology and Psychiatry and Allied Disciplines, 28*(2), 667–697.

Marshall, W. A. & Tanner, J. M. (1969). Variations in the pattern on pubertal changes in girls. *Archives of Disease in Childhood, 44*, 291–303.

Marston, A. R. et al. (1988). Characteristics of adolescents at risk for compulsive overeating on a brief screening test. *Adolescence, 23*(89), 59–65.

Martarano, S. C. (1977). A developmental analysis on Piaget's formal operations tasks. *Developmental Psychology, 13*, 666–672.

Martin, D. L. (1989). Children's use of gender-related information in making social judgments. *Developmental Psychology, 25*(1), 80–88.

Martorell, R. (1989). Body size, adaptation and function. *Human Organization, 48*(1), 15–20.

Mason, D. (1986, November). Buying time. *American Baby*, pp. 54, 78–79, 81–83.

Massarik, F. (1981). *Genetic disease control: A social psychological approach*. Beverly Hills: Sage Publications.

Masten, A. S. (1986). Humor and competence in school-aged children. *Child Development, 57*, 461–473.

Masterman, S. H., & Reams, R. (1988). Support groups for bereaved preschool and school-age children. *American Journal of Orthopsychiatry, 58*(4), 562–570.

Matera, C. et al. (1990). Prevalence of use of cocaine and other substances in an obstetric population. *American Journal of Obstetrics and Gynecology, 163*(3), 797–801.

Matlin, M. W. (1987). *The psychology of women*. New York: Holt, Rinehart and Winston.

Mattis, N. G. (1988). AIDS education should be geared to the age of the child. *The Brown University Child Behavior and Development Letter, 4*(3), 5–7.

Maugh, T. H., II (1991, March 27). Research links colic to cow antibodies. *Los Angeles Times*, p. A19.

May, K. (1989, winter). Is it time to fire the coach? *Childbirth Educator*, pp. 30–35.

Mayer, J. (1975). Obesity during childhood. In M. Winick (Ed.), *Childhood obesity*. New York: Wiley.

Mayer, J. E. & Ligman, J. D. (1989). Personality characteristics of adolescent marijuana users. *Adolescence, 24*(96), 965–976.

Mazur, B., Piper, M. C., & Ramsay, M. (1988). Developmental outcomes in very low birth weight infants 6 to 36 months old. *Journal of Developmental and Behavioral Pediatrics, 9*(5), 293–297.

Maziade, M., Boudreault, M., Cote, R., & ThiVierge, J. (1986). Influence of gentle birth delivery procedures and other perinatal circumstances on infant temperament: Developmental and social implications. *Journal of Pediatrics, 8*(1), 134–136.

McAfee, J. K. (1987). Classroom density and the aggressive behavior of handicapped children. *Education and Treatment of Children, 10*(2), 134–145.

McCabe, A., & Lipscomb, T. J. (1988). Sex differences in children's verbal aggression. *Merrill-Palmer Quarterly, 34*(4), 389–401.

McCall, R. B. (1979). *Infants*. Cambridge, MA: Harvard University Press.

McCall, R. B. (1983). Exploring developmental transitions in mental performance. In *Levels and transitions in children's development*. (New Directions for child development, No. 21). San Francisco: Jossey-Bass.

McCall, R. B. (1984). Environmental effects on intelligence: The forgotten role of discontinuous nonshared within-family factors. *Annual Progress in Child Psychiatry and Child Development, 1984*, pp. 119–132.

McCall, R. B., & McGhee, P. E. (1977). The discrepancy hypothesis of attention and affect in infants. In F. Weizmann & I. Uzigiris (Eds.), *The structuring of experience*. New York: Plenum.

McCall, R. B., Parke, R. D., & Kavanaugh, R. (1977). Imitation of live and televised models in children 1–3 years of age. *Monographs of the Society for Research in Child Development, 42* (Serial No. 173).

McCarthy, P. (1987). Sterilization and its discontents. *Psychology Today, 21*(10), 10–13.

McCauley, C., Woods, K., Coolidge, C., & Kulick, W. (1983). More aggressive cartoons are funnier. *Journal of Personality and Social Psychology, 44*, 817–823.

McClain, C. S. (1990). The making of a medical tradition: vaginal birth after cesarean. *Social Science and Medicine, 31*(2), 203–210.

McClosky, M., Caramazza, A., & Green, B. (1980). Curvalinear motion in the absence of external forces: Naive beliefs about the motion of objects. *Science, 210*, 1139–1141.

McCormick, C. M., & Maurer, D. M. (1988). Unimanual hand preferences in 6-month-olds. Consistency and relation to familial handedness. *Infant Behavior and Development, 11*(1), 21–29.

McDaniel, K. D. (1986). Pharmacological treatment of psychiatric and neuro-developmental disorders in children and adolescents. (Part 1–3). *Clinical Pediatrics, 25*(2, 3, 4), 65–71, 198–224.

McDonald, A. D., McDonald, J. C., Armstrong, B., Cherry, N. M., Cote, R., Lavoie, J. (1988). Fetal death and work in pregnancy. *British Journal of Industrial Medicine, 45*(3), 148–157.

McDonald, S. M. (1989). Sex bias in the representation of male and female characters in children's picture books. *Journal of Genetic Psychology, 150*(4), 389–401.

McGhee, P. E. (1979). *Humor: Its origin and development*. San Francisco: Freeman.

McGowan, J. D., Attman, R. E., & Kanto, W. P., Jr. (1988). Neonatal withdrawal symptoms after chronic maternal ingestion of caffeine. *South Journal of Medicine, 81*(9), 1092–1094.

McKeever, P. (1983). Siblings of chronically ill children: A literature review with implications for research and practice. *American Journal of Orthopsychiatry, 53*(2), 209–218.

McKenna, J. J. et al. (1990). Sleep and arousal patterns of co-sleeping human mother/infant pairs: A preliminary physiological study with implications for the study of sudden infant death syndrome (SIDS). *Amer-

ican Journal of Physical Anthropology, 3(3), 331–347.

McKenzie, B. E., Toctell, H. E., & Day, R. H. (1980). Development of visual constancy during the first year of human infancy. *Developmental Psychology, 16*, 163–174.

McKinney, J. P., & Moore, D. (1982). Attitudes and values during adolescence. In B. B. Wolman (Ed.), *Handbook of Human Development*. Englewood Cliffs, NJ: Prentice-Hall.

McLaughlin, B., White, D., McDevitt, T., & Raskin, R. (1983). Mothers' and fathers' speech to their young children: Similar or different? *Journal of Child Language, 10*(1), 245–252.

McLean, F. H. et al. (1991). Postterm infants: Too big or too small. *American Journal of Obstetrics and Gynecology, 104*(2), 10–24.

McManus, I. C., Sik, G., Cole, D. R., Mellon, A. F. et al. (1988). The development of handedness in children. *Journal of Developmental Psychology, 6*(3), 257–273.

McMurray, R. G., & Katz, V. L. (1990). Thermoregulation in pregnancy: Implications for exercise. *Sports Medicine, 10*(3), 146–158.

Mead, M. (1963). *Sex and temperament in three primitive societies*. New York: Morrow (originally published in 1935).

Meehan, F. P. et al. (1989). Update on delivery following prior ceseren section: A 15-year review 1972–1987. *International Journal of Gynecology and Obstetrics, 30*(3), 205–212.

Mehler, J., Bertoncini, J., Barrière, M., & Jassick-Gerschenfeld, D. (1978). Infant recognition of mother's voice, *Perception, 7*, 491–497.

Meilman, P. W. (1979). Cross-sectional age changes in ego identity status during adolescence. *Developmental Psychology, 15*, 230–231.

Melton, G. G., & Thompson, R. A., (1987). Legislative approaches to psychological maltreatment: A social policy analysis. In M. R. Brassard, R. Germain, & S. N. Hart (Eds.), *Psychological maltreatment of children and youth*. New York: Pergamon Press.

Meltzoff, A. N. (1988). Infant imitation after a 1-week delay: Long term memory for novel acts and multiple stimuli. *Developmental Psychology, 24*(4), 470–476.

Meltzoff, A., & Moore, M. K. (1977). Imitation of facial and manual gestures by human neonates. *Science, 198*, 75–78.

Meltzoff, A. N., & Moore, M. K. (1983). Newborn infants imitate adult facial gestures. *Child Development, 54*, 702–709.

Meltzoff, A. N., & Moore, M. K. (1989). Imitation in newborn infants: Exploring the range of gestures imitated and the underlying mechanisms. *Developmental Psychology, 25*(6), 954–962.

Menyuk, P. (1977). *Language and maturation*. Cambridge, MA: M.I.T. Press.

Menyuk, P. (1984). *Prescriptive manual for parents and teachers of language impaired children*. Washington, D.C.: U.S. Office of Special Education and Rehabilitative Services.

Mercer, J. R., & Lewis, J. F. (1978). *System of multicultural pluralistic assessment*. New York: Psychological Corporation.

Meredith, H. V. (1978). *Human body growth in the first 10 years of life*. Columbia, SC: The State Printing Co.

Merriman, W. E., Azmitia, M., & Perlmutter, M. (1988). Rate of forgetting in early childhood. *International Journal of Behavioral Development, 11*(4), 467–474.

Mervis, C. B., & Mervis, C. A. (1988). Role of adult input in young children's category evolution: I. An observational study. *Journal of Child Language, 15*(2), 257–272.

Mervus, C. (1983). Acquisition of a lexicon. *Contemporary Educational Psychology, 8*(3), 210–236.

Messer, D. J., & Vietze, P. M. (1988). Does mutual influence occur during mother-infant social gaze? *Infant Behavior and Development, 11*(1), 97–110.

Michaela, J. L., & Cortento, I. R. (1984). Spontaneous classification of foods by elementary schoolaged children. *Health Education Quarterly, 11*(1), 57–76.

Miller, C. A. (1987). *Maternal Health and Infant Survival*. Washington, D.C.:

National Center for Clinical Infant Programs.

Miller, J. F., & Chapman, R. S. (1981). Collecting and recording speech samples. In J. F. Miller (Ed.), *Assessing language production in children: Experimental procedures*. Baltimore: University Park Press.

Miller, L. C., Barrett, C. L., & Hampe, E. (1974). Phobia of childhood in a prescientific era. In A. Davids (Ed.), *Child personality and psychopathology: Current topics*. New York: Wiley.

Miller, P. H., & Aloise, P. A. (1989). Young children's understanding of the psychological causes of behavior: A review. *Child Development, 60*(2), 286–297.

Miller, V., Onotera, R. T., & Deinard, A. S. (1984). Denver developmental screening test: Cultural variations in southeast Asian children. *Journal of Pediatrics, 104*(3), 481–482.

Mills, A. F. (1990). Surveillance for anemia: Risk factors and patterns of milk intake. *Archives of Disease in Children, 65*(4), 420–31.

Mills, J. L., Harlap, S., & Harley, E. E. (1981). Should coitus late in pregnancy be discouraged? *Lancet, 2* (8328), 135–138.

Mills, R. S., & Grusec, J. E. (1989). Cognitive, affective, and behavioral consequences of praising altruism. *Merrill-Palmer Quarterly, 35*(3), 299–329.

Millstein, S. G., & Irwin, C. E. (1988). Accident-related behaviors in adolescents: A biopsychosocial view. *Alcohol, Drugs and Driving, 4*(1), 21–29.

Minuchin, P. P., & Shapiro, E. K. (1983). The school as a context for social development. In P. H. Mussen (Ed.), *Handbook of child psychology* (4th ed.), Vol. 4. New York: Wiley.

Minuchin, S., Rosman, B. L., & Baker, L. (1978). *Psychosomatic families: Anorexia nervosa in context*. Cambridge, MA: Harvard University Press.

Mischel, H. N., & Mischel, W. (1983). The development of children's knowledge of self-control strategies. *Child Development, 54*, 603–619.

Mischel, W. (1974). Procession delay of gratification. In L. Berkowitz (Ed.), *Advances in experimental social psychology* (Vol. 7). New York: Academic Press.

Mitchell, C. E. (1988). Preparing for vocational choice. *Adolescence, 23*(90), 331–334.

Mobray, C. T., Lanir, S., & Halce, M. (1982). Stress, mental health and motherhood. *Birth Psychology Bulletin, 3*(2), 10–33.

Moen, P., Kain, E., & Elder, G. (1981). *Economic conditions and family life*. Washington, D.C.: National Academy of Sciences Committee on Child Development and Public Policy.

Mollick, L. B., & Etra, K. S. (1981). Poor learning ability . . . or poor hearing? *Teacher, 98*, 42–43.

Money, J. (1978). *Sex determination and sex stereotyping: Aristotle to H–Y antigen*. Address to the Western Psychology Association, San Francisco, CA, April, 1978.

Money, J., & Ehrhardt, A. A., (1972). *Man and woman, boy and girl*. Baltimore, MD: Johns Hopkins University Press.

Money, J., & Ehrhardt, A. A. (1974). *Man and woman, boy and girl*. New York: New American Library.

Montemayor, R. (1983). Parents and adolescents in conflict: All families some of the time and some families all of the time. *Journal of Early Adolescence, 3*, 83–103.

Moody, F. (1990, October 28). The real costs of no fault divorce. *Sacramento Bee*, pp. F1–F2.

Moore, C., Bryant, D., & Furrow, D. (1989). Mental terms and the development of certainty. *Child Development, 60*(1), 167–171.

Moore, C., & Davidge, J. (1989). The development of mental terms: Pragmatics or semantics? *Journal of Child Language, 16*(3), 633–641.

Moore, J. J., Mullis, R. L., & Mullis, A. K., (1986). Examining metamemory within the context of parent-child interactions. *Psychology Reports, 59*(1), 39–47.

Moore, K. L. (1988). *The developing human: clinically oriented embryology* (4th ed.). Philadelphia: Saunders.

Moore, K. L. (1989). *Before we are born: Basic embryology and birth defects*.

Philadelphia: Saunders.

Moran, G., Krupka, A., Tutton, A., & Symons, D. (1987). Patterns of maternal and infant imitation during play. *Infant Behavior and Development, 10,* 477–491.

Moran, N. C. et al. (1989). Congenital malformations and psychosocial development in children conceived by in vitro fertilization. *Journal of Pediatrics, 115*(2), 222–227.

Morgan, B. L. (1984). Nutritional needs of the female adolescent. *Women and Health, 9*(2–3), 15–28.

Morley, R. et al. (1988). Mother's choice to provide breast milk and developmental outcome. *Archives of Disease in Childhood, 83*(11), 1302–1305.

Morton, R. F. (1989a, January). Alpha-fetoprotein screening. *American Baby,* pp. 41–42.

Morton, R. F. (1989b, April). Infectious disease in pregnancy. *American Baby,* pp. 74, 76–77.

Moses, S. (1989, November). Studies explore issues of insecure attachment. *APA Monitor,* p. 34.

Moshman, D. & Timmons, M. (1982). The construction of logical necessity. *Human Development, 25*(5), 309–323.

Moss, N., & Hensleigh, P. A. (1988). Substance use by Hispanic and white non-Hispanic pregnant adolescents: A preliminary study. *Journal of Youth and Adolescence, 17*(6), 531–541.

Muehlenhard, C., & Linton, M. (1987). Date rape and sexual aggression in dating situations: Incidence and risk factors. *Jouranl of Consulting Psychology, 34,* 186–196.

Mulvey, E. P., & LaRosa, J. F. (1986). Delinquency cessation and adolescent development: Preliminary data. *American Journal of Orthopsychiatry, 56*(2), 212–224.

Murphy, D. M. (1985). Fears in preschool age children. *Child Care Quarterly, 14*(3), 171–189.

Murray, D. M. et al. (1984). The prevention of cigarette smoking in children: A comparison of four strategies. *Journal of Applied Social Psychology, 14*(3), 274–288.

Murray, J. L., & Bernfield, M. (1988). The differential effect of prenatal care on the incidence of low birth weight among blacks and whites in a prepaid health care plan. *New England Journal of Medicine, 319,* 1385–1391.

Murray, J. P. (1980). *Television and youth: Twenty five years of research and controversy.* Boys Town, NB: The Boys Town Center for the Study of Youth Development.

Murray, J. P. (1989). Using TV sensibly. *The Brown University Child Behavior and Development Letter, 5*(9), 1, 4.

Murray, J. P., & Solamon, G. (Eds.) (1984). The future of children's television: Results of the Markle Foundation/Boys Town Conference. Boys Town, NE: Boys Town Center for the Study of Youth Development.

Murray, P. L., & Mayer, R. E. (1988). Preschool children's judgments of number magnitude. *Journal of Educational Psychology, 80*(2), 206–209.

Myers, B. J. (1984). Mother-infant bonding: The status of this critical period hypothesis. *Developmental Review, 4*(3), 240–274.

Myers, N., & Perlmutter, M. (1978). Memory in the years from 2 to 5. In P. Ornstein (Ed.), *Memory development in children.* Hillsdale, NJ: Erlbaum.

Myslivecek, J. et al. (1987). Some features of early-conditioning dynamics shown by instrumental toy activation in infants. *22nd Conference in Higher Nervous Functions, Activitas Nervosa Superior, 29*(2), 127–129.

NAEYC position statement on standardized testing of young children 3 through 8 years of age. (1988, March) *Young Children,* pp. 42–47.

Naeye, R. L. (1981). Nutritional/nonnutritional interactions that affect the outcome of pregnancy. *American Journal of Clinical Nutrition, 34* (Supp. 4), 727–731.

Naeye, R. L., & Peters, E. C. (1984). Mental development of children whose mothers smoked during pregnancy. *Journal of Obstetrics and Gynecology, 64,* 601.

Narod, S. A., DeSanjose, S., & Victora, C. (1991). Coffee during pregnancy: A reproductive hazard? *American Journal of Obstetrics and Gynecology, 164*(4), 1009–1114.

National Academy of Sciences, Committee on the Nutrition of the Mother and Preschool Child. (1977). *Iron Nutrition in Adolescence.* Washington, D.C.: Government Printing Office.

National Bureau of the Census, Center for Health Statistics (1990). Washington, D.C.: U.S. Government Printing Office.

National Institute of Mental Health (NIMH) (1982). *Summary Report: Vol. 1. Television and behavior: Ten years of scientific progress and implications for the eighties.* (DHHS Publication No. ADM 82-1195). Washington, D.C.: U.S. Government Printing Office.

National Institute on Drug Abuse (1987). Cocaine use remains steady, other drug use declines among high school seniors. *NIDA Notes, 2*(2), 1.

Naus, M. J. (1982). Memory development in the young reader: The combined effects of knowledge base and memory processing. In W. O. Ho and S. White (Eds.), *Reading expository text.* New York: Academic Press.

Needham, J. (1934). *A history of embryology.* London: Cambridge University Press.

Nelson, K. (1973). Structure and strategy in learning to talk. *Monographs of the Society for Research in Child Development, 38* (1–2, Serial No. 149).

Nelson, K. (1981). Individual differences in language development: Implications for development and language. *Developmental Psychology, 17*(2), 170–187.

Nelson, K. (1989). Remembering: A functional developmental perspective. In P. R. Solomon, G. K. Goethels, C. M. Kelley, & B. R. Stephens (Eds.). *Memory: An interdisciplinary approach.* New York: Springer-Verlag.

Nelson, L. B., Erlich, S., Calhoun, J. H., Matteucci, T., & Finnegan, L. P. (1987). Occurrence of strabismia in infants born to drug-dependent women. *American Journal of Diseases of Children, 141,* 175–178.

Nelson-Le Gay, S., DeCooke, P., & Jones, E. (1989). Children's self-perceptions of competence and help seeking. *Journal of Genetic Psychology, 150*(4), 457–459.

Newman, J. (1985). Adolescents: Why they can be so obnoxious. *Adolescence, 20*(79), 635–646.

Newman, J. (1990). Breastfeeding problems associated with the early introduction of bottles and pacifiers. *Journal of Human Lactation, 8*(2), 59–63.

Newton, L. D. (1983). Helping parents cope with infant crying. *JOGN Nursing, 12*(3), 199–204.

Nicholls, J. G., & Thorkoldsen, T. A. (1988). Children's distinctions among matters of intellectual convention, logic, fact and personal preference. *Child Development, 59*(4), 939–949.

Ninio, A., & Rinott, N. (1988). Fathers involvement in the care of their infants and their attributions of cognitive competence to infants. *Child Development, 59,* 652–663.

Nisan, M., & Kohlberg, L. (1982). Universality and variation in moral judgment: A longitudinal and cross-sectional study in Turkey. *Child Development, 53,* 865–876.

Norwood, G. R. (1985). A society that promotes drug abuse: The effects on pre-adolescence. Special issue: Emerging adolescents: Their needs and concerns. *Childhood Education, 61*(4), 267–271.

Nowicki, S., & Oxenford, C. (1989). The relation of hostile nonverbal communication styles to popularity in preadolescent children. *Journal of Genetic Psychology, 150*(1), 39–44.

Nunner-Winkler, G., & Sodian, B. (1988). Children's understanding of moral emotions. *Child Development, 59*(5), 1323–1328.

Nyman, G. (1987). Infant temperament, childhood accidents and hospitalization. *Clinical Pediatrics, 26*(8), 398–404.

O'Brien, S. F., & Bierman, K. L. (1988). Conceptions and perceived influence of peer groups: Interviews with preadolescents and adolescents. *Child Development, 59*(5), 1360–1365.

Ogra, P. L. et al. (1982). Human milk and breastfeeding: An update on the state of the art. *Pediatrics Research, 16*(4 Pt. 1), 266–271.

Ohlendorf-Moffat, P. (1991, February). Surgery before birth. *Discover,* pp. 59–66.

Oller, D. K., & Siebert, J. M. (1988). Babbling of prelinguistic mentally retarded children. *American Journal on Mental Retardation, 92*(4), 369–375.

Olson, C. L. et al. (1991). Intrapartum intervention and delivery outcome in low-risk pregnancy. *Journal of the American Board of Family Practice, 4*(2), 83–88.

Olson, R., Olson, C., & Cox, N. S. (1990). Maternal birthing positions and perineal injury. *Journal of Family Practice, 30*(5), 553–557.

Olson, S. L., Bayles, K., & Bates, J. E. (1986). Mother-child interaction and children's speech progress: A longitudinal study of the 1st 2 years. *Merrill-Palmer Quarterly, 32*(1), 1–20.

O'Malley, J. M. (1982). *Children's English and sciences study.* Language minority children with limited English proficiency. Rosslyn, VA: InterAmerica Research Associates.

Olweus, D. (1982). Development of stable aggressive reaction patterns in males. In R. Blanchard & C. Blanchard (Eds.), *Advances in the study of aggression* (Vol. 1). New York: Academic Press.

O'Rahilly, R. & Muller, F. (1987). *Developmental stages in human embryos.* Washington, D.C.: Carnegie Institution of Washington.

Ornstein, P. A. Medlin, R. G., Stone, B. P., & Naus, M. J. (1985). Retrieving for rehearsal: An analysis of active rehearsal in children's memory. *Developmental Psychology, 21,* 633–641.

Oro, A. S., & Dixon, S. D. (1988). Waterbed care of narcotic-exposed infants. *American Journal of the Diseases of Children, 142,* 186–188.

Ostrov, E., Offer, D., Howard, K., Kaufman, B., & Meyer, H. (1985). Adolescent sexual behavior. *Medical Aspects of Human Sexuality, 19,* 28–31, 34–36.

Otto, H., & Healy, S. (1966). Adolescent's self perception of personality strengths. *Journal of Human Relations, 14*(3), 483–490.

Owen, P. (1984). Prostaglandin synthetase inhibitors in the treatment of primary dysmenorrhea: Outcome trials reviewed. *American Journal of Obstetrics and Gynecology, 148,* 96–103.

Page, E. B., & Grandon, G. M. (1979). Family configuration and mental ability. Two theories contrasted with U.S. data. *American Educational Research Journal, 16,* 257–272.

Page, H. (1989). Estimation of the prevalence and incidence of infertility in a population: A pilot study. *American Fertility Society, 51,* 571–577.

Pairano, P. et al. (1988). Effects of early human malnutrition on working and sleep organization. *Early Human Development, 20*(1), 67–76.

Pantell, R. H., Fries, J. F., & Vickery, D. M. (1977). *Taking care of your child: A parents' guide to medical care.* Reading, MA: Addison-Wesley.

Papalia, D. (1972). The status of several conservation abilities across the life-span. *Human Development, 15,* 229–243.

Papalia, D. E. & Olds, S. W. (1982). *A child's world: Infancy through adolescence,* 3rd ed. New York: McGraw-Hill.

Papini, D., Farmer, F., Clark, S., & Snell, W. (1988). An evaluation of adolescent patterns of sexual self-disclosure to parents and friends. *Journal of Adolescent Research, 3,* 387–401.

Paris, S. G., & Lindauer, B. K. (1982). The development of cognitive skills during childhood. In B. B. Wolman (Ed.), *Handbook of developmental psychology.* Englewood Cliffs, NJ: Prentice-Hall.

Parish, J. S. et al. (1980). Normal and exceptional children's attitudes toward themselves and one another. *Journal of Psychology, 104*(2), 249–253.

Park, K. A., & Waters, E. (1989). Security of attachment and preschool friendships. *Child Development, 60*(5), 1076–1081.

Parke, R. D. (1981). *Fathers.* Cambridge, MA: Harvard University Press.

Parke, R. D., & Slaby, R. G. (1983). The development of aggression. In P. H. Murren (Ed.), *Handbook of child psychology* (4th ed.), Vol. 4. New York: Wiley.

Parke, R. D., & Tinsley, B. R. (1981). The father's role in infancy. Determinants of involvement in caregiving and play. In M. E. Lamb (Ed.), *The role of the father in child development.* New York: Wiley.

Parker, J. G., & Asher, S. R. (1987). Peer relations and later personal adjustment: Are low-accepted children at risk? *Psychology Bulletin, 102*(3), 357–389.

Parkinson, C. E. et al. (1986). Behavioral differences of school age children who were small-for-dates babies. *Developmental Medicine and Child Neurology, 28*(4), 498–505.

Parmelee, A. H., & Sigman, M. D. (1983). Perenatal brain development and behavior. In P. H. Mussen (Ed.), *Handbook of child development* (4th ed.), Vol. 2. New York: Wiley.

Parmelee, A., & Stern, E. (1972). The development of states in infants. In C. Clement, D. Purpura & F. Mayer (Eds.), *Sleep and the maturing nervous system.* New York: Academic Press.

Parrott, A. (1989). Acquaintance rape among adolescents: Identifying risk groups and intervention strategies. Special issue: Adolescent sexuality: New challenges for social work. *Journal of Social Work and Human Sexuality, 8*(1), 47–61.

Parsons, J. E. (1983). Expectancies, values, and academic behaviors. In J. T. Spence (Ed.), *Achievement and achievement motives. Psychological and sociological approaches.* San Francisco: W. H. Freeman.

Parten, M. B. (1932). Social participation among preschool children. *Journal of Abnormal Social Psychology, 27,* 243–269.

Parten, M. B. (1933). Social play among preschool children. *Journal of Abnormal and Social Psychology, 28,* 136–147.

Pascual-Leone, J. (1980). Constructive problems for constructive theories. In R. H. Kluwe & H. Spada (Eds.), *Developmental models of thinking.* New York: Academic Press.

Passman, R. H., & Weisberg, P. (1975). Mothers and blankets as agents for promoting play and exploration by young children in a novel environment: The effects of social and nonsocial attachment objects. *Developmental Psychology, 11,* 170–177.

Patterson, G. R. (1982). *A social learning approach to family intervention: Vol. 1. Coercive family processes.* Eugene, OR: Castalia Press.

Patterson, G. R. & Stouthamer-Loeber, M. (1984). The correlation of family management practices and delinquency. *Child Development, 55,* 1299–1307.

Paul, M., & Himmelstein, J. (1988). Reproductive hazards in the workplace: What the practitioner needs to know about chemical exposures. *Obstetrics and Gynecology, 71*(5 Pt. 1), 921–938.

Payne, J. S., Kauffman, J. M., Brown, G. B., & DeMott, R. M. (1974). *Exceptional children in focus.* Columbus, OH: Merrill.

Pêcheux, M. G., & Lecuyer, R. (1983). Habituation rate and free exploration tempo in 4-month old infants. *International Journal of Behavioral Development, 6*(1), 37–50.

Pêcheux, M. G., Lepecq, J-C, & Salzaralo, P. (1988). Oral activity and exploration in 1–2 month-old infants. *British Journal of Developmental Psychology, 6*(3), 245–256.

Peck, C. A., & Cooke, T. P. (1983). Benefits of mainstreaming at the early childhood level: How much can we expect? *Analysis and Intervention in Developmental Disabilities, 3*(1), 1–22.

Pellegrini, A. D. (1984). The social cognitive ecology of preschool classrooms: Contextual relations revisited. *International Journal of Behavioral Development, 7*(3), 321–332.

Pellegrini, A. D. (1988). Elementary-school children's rough-and-tumble play and social competence. *Developmental Psychology, 24*(6), 802–806.

Pellegrini, D. S. et al. (1987). Correlates of social and academic competence in middle childhood. *Journal of Child Psychology and Psychiatry and Al-*

lied Disciplines, 28(5), 699–714.

Penman, R. et al. (1983a). Mothers' speech to prelinguistic infants: A pragmatic analysis. *Journal of Child Language, 10*(1), 17–34.

Penman, R. et al. (1983b). Synchrony in mother-infant interaction: A possible neurophysiological base. *British Journal of Medical Psychology, 56*(1), 1–7.

Perez-Reyes, M., & Wall, M. E. (1982). Presence of tetrahydrocannabinol in human milk. *New England Journal of Medicine, 307*, 819–820.

Perris, E. E., & Clifton, R. K. (1988). Reaching in the dark toward sound as a measure of auditory localization in infants. *Infant Behavior and Development, 11*(4), 473–491.

Perry, D. G., Kasel, S. J., & Perry, L. C. (1988). Victims of peer aggression. *Developmental Psychology, 24*(6), 807–814.

Perry, D. G., Perry, L. C., Weiss, R. J. (1989). Sex differences in the consequences that children anticipate for aggression. *Developmental Psychology, 25*(2), 312–319.

Pershagen, G. (1989). Childhood cancer and malignancies other than lung cancer related to passive smoking. *Mutation Research, 222*(2), 129–135.

Peters, R. DeV., & Orley, J. (1987). Promotion of children's mental health: A beginning. *The Brown University Child Behavior and Development Letter, 3*(6), 1–4.

Petersen, A. C. (1979). Female pubertal development. In M. Sugar (Ed.), *Female adolescent development.* New York: Brunner/Mazel.

Petersen, A. C., & Boxer, A. (1982). Adolescent sexuality. In T. Coates, A. C. Petersen, & C. Perry (Eds.), *Adolescent health: Crossing the barriers.* New York: Academic Press.

Peterson, C. C., Peterson, J. L., & Carroll, J. (1983). Television viewing and imaginative problem solving during preadolescence. *Journal of Genetic Psychology, 147*, 61–67.

Peterson, P. E. et al. (1984). How pronutrition television programming affects children's dietary habits. *Developmental Psychology, 20*(1), 55–63.

Pettit, G. S., & Bates, J. E. (1989). Family interaction patterns and children's behavior problems from infancy to 4 years. *Developmental Psychology, 25*(3), 413–420.

Petitto, L. A. & Marentette, P. F. (1991). Babbling in the manual mode: Evidence for the ontogeny of language. (Science, 251) (5000), 1493–1496.

Pfiffner, L. J., & O'Leary, S. G. (1989). Effects of maternal discipline and nurturance on toddler's behavior and affect. *Journal of Abnormal Child Psychology, 17*(5), 527–540.

Philipps, L. H., & O'Hara, M. W. (1991). Prospective study of postpartum depression: 4½ year follow up of women and children. *Journal of Abnormal Psychology, 100*(2), 151–155.

Phillips, E. J. (1969). Characteristics essential for the emergence of problem solving behavior. *Psychology, 6*(1), 19–29.

Phipps, S., Drotar, D., Joseph, C., Geiss, C. et al. (1989). Psychological impact of home apnea monitoring: Temporal effects, family resources and maternal coping style. *Journal of Developmental and Behavioral Pediatrics, 10*(1), 7–12.

Phipps, W., Cramer, D., Schiff, I., Belisle, S., Stillman, R. Albrecht, B., Gibson, M., Berger, M., & Wilson, E. (1987). The association between smoking and female infertility as influenced by the cause of infertility. *Fertility and Sterility, 48*, 377–382.

Piaget (1924/1964). *Judgment and reasoning in the child.* Paterson, NJ: Littlefield, Adams & Co. (originally published in 1924).

Piaget, J. (1926). *The language and thought of the child.* New York: Harcourt and Brace.

Piaget, J. (1951). *Play, dreams and imitation in childhood.* New York: Norton (originally published in 1945).

Piaget, J. (1952). Biography: In C. A. Murcheson (Ed.), *A history of psychology in automography* (Vol. 4). Worchester, MA: Clark University Press.

Piaget, J. (1937/1954). *The construction of reality in the child.* New York:

Basic Books (originally published in 1937).

Piaget, J. (1936/1963). *The origins of intelligence in children* (Trans. M. C. Cook). New York: Norton (originally published in 1936).

Piaget, J. (1959/1969). *The early growth of logic in the child.* New York: Basic Books.

Piaget, J. (1965). *The moral judgment of the child* (trans. M. Gabain). New York: Free Press (first published in English in 1935).

Piaget, J. (1970). Piaget's theory. In P. H. Mussen (Ed.), *Carmichael's manual of child psychology* (3rd ed.). New York: Wiley.

Piaget, J. (1976). *The child's conception of the world.* New York: Harcourt and Brace (originally published in 1929).

Piaget, J., & Inhelder, B. (1948/1956). *The child's conception of space.* London: Routledge and Kegan Paul (originally published in 1948).

Piaget, J., & Inhelder, B. (1969). *The psychology of the child.* New York: Basic Books.

Pinderhughes, E. E., & Zigler, E. (1985). Cognitive and motivational determinants of children's humor responses. *Journal of Responses in Personality, 19*(2), 185–196.

Pinon, M. F., Huston, A. C., & Wright, J. C. (1989). Family ecology and child characteristics that predict young children's educational television viewing. *Child Development, 60*(4), 846–856.

Pintrich, P. R., & deGroot, E. V. (1990). Motivational and self-regulated learning components of classroom academic performance. *Journal of Educational Psychology, 82*(1), 33–40.

Piotrkowski, C. S., & Stark, E. (1987). Children and adolescents look at their parents' jobs. *New Directions for Child Development, 35*, 3–19.

Polakoff, P. L. (1990). Prevention of reproductive disorders requires more research, vigilance. *Occupational Health and Safety, 59*(8), 37, 51,

Pollitt, E., Mueller, W., & Leibel, R. L. (1982). The relation of growth to cognition in a well-nourished preschool population. *Child Development, 53*(5), 1157–1163.

Popper, B. K., & Culley, C. K. (1989). Breastfeeding makes a comeback— for good reason. *The Brown University Child Behavior and Development Letter, 5*(2), p. 1–4.

Post, E. M. et al. (1981). A condensed table for predicting adult stature. *Journal of Pediatrics, 98*(3), 440–442.

Potera, C. (1986, spring). Update: Exercising for two. *Childbirth Educator*, p. 11.

Potter, S. M., & Graves, R. E. (1988). Is interhemispheric transfer related to handedness and gender? *Neuropsychologia, 26*(2), 319–325.

Power, T. G., & Chapieski, M. L. (1986). Childrearing and impulse control in toddlers: A naturalistic investigation. *Developmental Psychology, 22*(2), 271–275.

Power, T. G., & Shanks, J. A. (1989). Parents as socializers: Maternal and paternal views. *Journal of Youth and Adolescence, 18*(2), 203–220.

Pratt, D. E., Bieber, E., Barners, R. et al. (1991). Transvaginal intratubal insemination by tactile sensation: A preliminary report. *Fertility and Sterility, 56*(5), 984–986.

Pratt, M. W., Kerig, P., Corvan, P. A., & Cowan, C. P. (1988). Mothers and fathers teaching 3-year-olds: Authoritative parenting and adult scaffolding of young children's learning. *Developmental Psychology, 24*(6), 832–839.

Prechtl, H. (1974). The behavioral states of the newborn infant: A review. *Brain Research, 76*, 185–212.

Pressley, M. (1982). Elaboration and memory development. *Child Development, 53*, 296–309.

Prinz, P. M., & Nelson, K. E. (1985). ''Alligator eats cookie'': Acquisition of writing and reading skills by deaf children using the microcomputer. Special issue: The psycholinguistics of writing. *Applied Psycholinguistics, 6*(3), 283–306.

Prior, M., Leonard, A., & Woods, G. (1983). A comparison study of preschool children diagnosed as hyperactive. *Journal of Pediatric Psychology, 8*(2), 191–207.

Puckering, C. (1989). Annotation: Maternal depression. *Journal of Child Psychology and Psychiatry and Allied Disciplines, 30*(6), 807–817.

Pulkkinen, L. (1982). Self-control and continuity from childhood to late adolescence. In P. B. Baltes & O. G. Brim, Jr. (Eds.), *Life-span development and behavior* (Vol. 4). New York: Academic Press.

Pullen, I. M. (1984). *Psychological aspects of genetic counseling.* London: Academic Press.

Purtillo, D. F., & Sullivan, J. L. (1979). Immunological basis for superior survival of females. *American Journal of Diseases of Children, 133,* 1251–1253.

Pynoos, R. S., & Nader, K. (1988). Psychological first aid and treatment approach to children exposed to community violence: Research implications. *Journal of Traumatic Stress, 1*(4), 445–447.

Quay, L. C. & Jarrett, O. S. (1986). Teachers' interactions with middle- and lower-SES preschool boys and girls. *Journal of Educational Psychology, 78,* 495–498.

Rabicoff, R. (1989, September 30). Kids' TV: Where girls learn its a boys' world. *Sacramento Bee,* pp. 1, 4.

Rabiner, D., & Coie, J. (1989). Effect of expectancy indications on rejected children's acceptance by unfamiliar peers. *Developmental Psychology, 25*(3), 450–457.

Radin, M. (1981). The role of the father in cognitive, academic and intellectual development. In M. E. Lamb (Ed.), *The role of the father in child development.* New York: Wiley.

Radke-Yarrow, M. R., Zahn-Waxler, C., & Chapman, M. (1983). Children's prosocial dispositions and behavior. In P. A. Mussen (Ed.), *Handbook of child psychology* (4th ed.), Vol. 4. New York: Wiley.

Rafferty, Y., & Shinn, M. (1991). The impact of homelessness on children. *American Psychology, 46*(11), 1170–1179.

Rakic, P. (1988). Specification of cerebral cortical areas. *Science, 241,* 170–176.

Ramey, C. T., & Campbell, F. A. (1987). The Carolina Abecedarian Project. An educational experiment concerning human malleability. In J. J. Gallagher & C. T. Ramey (Eds.), *The malleability of children.* Baltimore, MD: Paul H. Brookes.

Read, M. H., Harveywebster, M. & Usinger-Lesquereux, J. (1988). Adolescent compliance with dietary guidelines: Health and education implications. *Adolescence, 23*(91), 567–575.

Reardon, P., & Bushnell, E. W. (1988). Infants' sensitivity to arbitrary pairings of color and taste. *Infant Behavior and Development, 11,* 245–250.

Redei, G. P. (1982). *Genetics.* New York: MacMillan.

Rehberg, H. R., & Richman, C. L. (1989). Prosocial behavior in preschool children: A look at the interaction of race, gender, and family composition. *International Journal of Behavioral Development, 12*(3), 385–401.

Reich, P. A. (1986). *Language development.* Englewood Cliffs, NJ: Prentice-Hall.

Reinisch, J. M. (1981). Prenatal exposure to synthetic progestins increases potential for aggression in humans. *Science, 211,* 1171–1173.

Reiss, I. L. (1986). *Journey into sexuality: An exploratory voyage.* Englewood Cliffs, NJ: Prentice-Hall.

Remafedi, G. (1987). Adolescent homosexuality: Psychosocial and medical implications. *Pediatrics, 79,* 331–337.

Rescorla, L. A. (1984). Individual differences in early language development and their predictive significance. *Acta Paedologica, 1*(2), 97–116.

Rest, J. (1983). Morality. In P. Mussen (Ed.), *Handbook of child psychology* (Vol. 4). New York: Wiley.

Rheingold, H. L., & Eckerman, E. D. (1973). Fear of the stranger: A critical examination. In H. W. Reese (Ed.), *Advances in child development and behavior* (Vol. 8). New York: Academic Press.

Ribordy, S. C., Camras, L. A., Stefani, R., & Spaccarelli, S. (1988). Vignettes for emotion recognition research and affective therapy with children. *Journal of Clinical Child Psychology, 17*(4), 322–325.

Ricciuti, H. N., & Breitmayer, B. J. (1988). Observational assessments of infant temperament in the natural setting of the newborn nursery: Stability and relationship to perinatal status. *Merrill-Palmer Quarterly, 34*(3), 281–299.

Rice, M. (1983). The role of television in language acquisition. *Developmental Review, 3*(2), 211–224.

Rice, M. L. et al. (1990). Words from "Sesame Street": Learning vocabulary while viewing. *Developmental Psychology, 26*(3), 521–428.

Rice, M. L., Huston, A. C., Truglio, R., & Wright, J. C. (1990). Words from "Sesame Street": Learning vocabulary while viewing. *Developmental Psychology, 26*(3), 421–428.

Riese, M. L., (1988). Size for gestational age and neonatal temperament in full term and preterm AGA-SGA twin pairs. *Journal of Pediatric Psychology, 13*(4), 521–530.

Richardson, J. G., & Cranston, J. E. (1981). Social change, parental values and the salience of sex education. *Journal of Marriage and the Family, 43*(3), 547–558.

Richman, C. L., Berry, C., Bittle, M., & Himan, K. (1988). Factors related to helping behavior in preschool-age children. *Journal of Applied Developmental Psychology, 9*(2), 151–165.

Richman, N., Graham, P., & Stevenson, J. (1982). *Preschool to school: A behavioral study.* London: Academic Press.

Richters, J., & Pellegrini, D. S. (1989). Depressed mothers judgments about their children: An examination of the depression-distortion hypothesis. *Child Development, 60*(5), 1068–1075.

Ridenour, M. V. (1982). Infant walkers: Developmental tool or inherent danger? *Perceptual Motor Skills, 55*(3 Pt. 2), 1201–1202.

Rieder, C., & Cicchetti, D. (1989). Organizational perspective on cognitive control functioning and cognitive-affective balance in maltreated children. *Development Psychology, 25*(3), 382–393.

Riesner, J., Yonas, A., & Wilkner, K. (1976). Radial localization of odors by human newborns. *Child Development, 47,* 856–859.

Ringwalt, C. L., & Palmer J. H. (1989). Cocaine and crack users compared. *Adolescence, 24*(96), 851–859.

Rinich, E., Drotar, D., & Brinish, P. (1989). Security of attachment and outcome of preschoolers with histories of nonorganic failure to thrive. *Journal of Clinical Child Psychology, 18*(2), 142–152.

Roberts, K. (1983). Comprehension and production of word order in Stage 1. *Child Development, 54*(2), 443–449.

Roberts, K., & Cuff, M. D. (1989). Categorization studies of 9- to 15-month old infants: Evidence for superordinate categorization? *Infant Behavior and Development, 12*(3), 265–288.

Roberts, M. (1987). No language but a cry. *Psychology Today, 21*(6), 57–58.

Roberts, M. C., Broadbent, M. H. (1989). Increasing preschooler's use of car safety devices: An effective program for day care staff. *Children's Health Care, 18,* 157–162.

Robinson, B. E. (1981). Changing views on male early childhood teachers. *Young Children, 36,* 27–32.

Robinson, D. (1989, May 28). Who should receive medical aid? *Parade Magazine,* p. 4–5.

Robinson, H. B. (1981). The uncommonly bright child. In M. Lewis & L. A. Rosenblum (Eds.), *The uncommon child.* New York: Plenum.

Rochat, P. (1987). Mouthing and grasping in neonates: Evidence for the early detection of what hard or soft substances afford for action. *Infant Behavior and Development, 10,* 435–449.

Rode, S. S. et al. (1982). Attachment patterns of infants separated at birth. *Annual Progress in Child Psychiatry and Child Development, 1982,* pp. 182–187.

Rode, S., Change, P., Fisch, R., & Sroufe, L. A. (1981). Attachment patterns of infants separated at birth. *Developmental Psychology, 17,* 188–191.

Rodgers, J. L., & Rowe, C. (1988). Influence of siblings on adolescent sexual behavior. *Developmental Psychology, 24*(5), 722–728.

Rodis, J. F. et al. (1990). Management and outcomes of pregnancies complicated by human B19 parvovirus infection: A prospective study. *American Journal of Obstetrics and Gynecology, 163*(4 Pt. 1), 1168–1171.

Rogers, C. K. (1954). Towards a theory of creativity. *ETC: A Review of General Semantics, 11,* 249–260.

Rogers, D. L., Perrin, M. S., & Waller, C. B. (1987). Enhancing the development of language and thought through conversations with young children. *Journal of Research in Childhood Education, 2*(1), 17–29.

Rogers, M. F. (1989, July). Testing newborns for HIV. *The Brown University Child Behavior and Development Letter,* p. 7.

Rogers, S. J. (1988). Characteristics of social interactions between mothers and their disabled infants: A review. *Child: Care, Health and Development, 14*(5), 301–317.

Roggman, L. A., & Peery, J. C. (1989). Parent-infant social play in brief encounters: Early gender differences. *Child Study Journal, 19*(1), 65–79.

Romaine, S. (1984). *The language of children and adolescents: The acquisition of communication competence.* Oxford: Blackwell.

Root, A. W., & Powers, P. S. (1983). Anorexia nervosa presenting as growth retardation in adolescents. *Journal of Adolescent Health Care, 4*(1), 25–30.

Rose, R. J., & Ditto, W. B. (1983). A development-genetic analysis of common fears from early adolescence to early adulthood. *Child Development, 54,* 361–368.

Rose, S. A. (1988). Shape recognition in infancy: Visual integration of sequential information. *Child Development, 59*(5), 1161–1176.

Rose, S. A., Feldman, J. F., McCarton, C. M., & Wolfson, J. (1988). Information processing in seven-month-old infants as a function of risk status. *Child Development, 59*(3), 589–603.

Rose, S. A., & Wallace, I. F. (1985). Visual recognition memory: A predictor of later cognitive functioning in preterms. *Child Development, 56,* 843–852.

Rosen, L. A., Furman, W., & Hartup, W. W. (1988). Positive, negative and neutral peer interaction as indications of children's social competency. The issue of concurrent validity. *Journal of Genetic Psychology, 149*(4), 441–446.

Rosenberg, M. S. (1987). New directions for research on the psychological maltreatment of children. *American Psychology, 42*(2), 166–171.

Rosenberg, M. S., & Reppucci, N. D. (1985). Primary prevention of child abuse. *Journal of Counsulting and Clinical Psychology, 53,* 576–585.

Rosenfeld, A. H. (1989, March). New treatment for bulima. *Pyschology Today,* p. 28.

Rosenfield, A. (1982). The pill: A review of recent studies. *Johns Hopkins Medical Journal, 150*(5), 177–180.

Rosenfield, P., Lambert, N. M., & Black, A. (1985). Desk arrangement effects on pupil classroom behavior. *Journal of Educational Psychology, 77,* 101–108.

Rosenkoetter, L. I., Huston, A. C., & Wright, J. C. (1990). Television and the moral judgment of the young child. *Journal of Applied Developmental Psychology, 11*(1), 123–137.

Rosenstein, D., & Oster, H. (1988). Differential facial responses to four basic tastes in newborns. *Child Development, 59*(6), 1555–1568.

Rosenthal, P. et al. (1989). Jaundice in infancy. *Pediatric Review, 11*(3), 79–86.

Rosenthal, R., & Jacobsen, L. (1966). Teacher's expectancies: Determinants of pupil's IQ gains. *Psychology Reports, 19,* 115–118.

Rosen-Wasser, S. M., Lingfelter, M., & Harrington, A. F. (1989). Nontraditional gender role portrayals on television and children's gender role perceptions. *Journal of Applied Developmental Psychology, 10*(1), 97–105.

Roshon, M. S., & Hagen, R. L. (1989). Sugar consumption, locomotion, task orientation and learning in preschool children. *Journal of Abnormal Child Psychology, 17*(3), 349–357.

Ross, G. (1989). Some thoughts on the value of infant tests for assessing and predicting mental ability. *Journal of Developmental and Behavioral Pediatrics, 10*(1), 44–47.

Ross, H. S. (1982). Establishment of social games among toddlers. *Developmental Psychology, 18,* 509–518.

Rotenberg, K. J. (1985). Causes, intensity, motives, and consequences of children's anger from self reports. *Journal of Genetic Psychology, 146*(1), 101–106.

Rothblum, E. (1988). Introduction: Lesbianism as a model of a positive lifestyle for women. *Women and Therapy, 8,* 1–12.

Rothstein-Fisch, C., & Howes, C. (1988). Toddler peer interaction in mixed-age groups. *Journal of Applied Developmental Psychology, 9*(2), 213–219.

Rovee-Collier, C. K. (1984). The ontogeny of learning and memory in human infancy. In R. Kail & N. E. Spear (Eds.), *Comparative perspectives on the development of memory.* Hillsdale, NJ: Erlbaum.

Rovee-Collier, C., Earley, L., & Stafford, S. (1989). Ontageny of early event memory: III. Attentional determinants of retrieval at 2 and 3 months. *Infant Behavior and Development, 12*(2), 147–161.

Rubin, K. H. (1982). Nonsocial play in preschoolers: Necessary evil? *Child Development, 53,* 651–657.

Rubin, K. H., Daniels-Beirness, T., & Bream, L. (1984). Social isolation and social problem solving: A longitudinal study. *Journal of Consulting and Clinical Psychology, 52*(1), 17–25.

Rubin, K. H., Fein, G. G., & Vandenberg, B. (1983). Play. In P. A. Mussen (Ed.), *Handbook of Child Psychology* (4th ed.), Vol. 1. New York: Wiley.

Rubin, J. Z., Provenzano, F. J., & Lurid, Z. (1974). The eye of the beholder: Parents' views on sex of newborns. *American Journal of Orthopsychiatry, 44,* 512–519.

Rubin, Z. (1980). *Children's friendships.* Cambridge, MA: Harvard University Press.

Rubin, Z., & Sloman, J. (1984). How parents influence their children's friendship. In M. Lewis (Ed.), *Beyond the dyad.* New York: Plenum.

Ruble, D. N. (1988). Sex role development. In M. H. Bornstein & M. E. Lamb (Eds.), *Developmental psychology: An advanced textbook* (2nd ed.). Hillsdale, NJ: Erlbaum.

Ruble, D. N., Balaban, T., & Cooper, J. (1981). Gender constancy and the effects of sex-typed televised toy commercials. *Child Development, 52,* 667–673.

Ruff, H. A., & Lawson, K. R. (1990). Development of sustained, focused attention in young children during free play. *Developmental Psychology, 26*(1), 85–93.

Ruffman, T. K., & Olson, D. R. (1989). Children's ascriptions of knowledge to others. *Developmental Psychology, 25*(4), 601–606.

Rush, D. et al. (1988). The National WIC Evaluation: Evaluation of the special supplemental food program for women, infants and children. V. Longitudinal study of pregnant women. *American Journal of Clinical Nutrition, 48*(2 Suppl.), 439–483.

Russell, P. J. (1990). *Genetics,* 2nd ed. Glenview, IL: Scott-Foresman.

Russell, J., Mills, I., & Reiff-Musgrove, P. (1990). The role of symmetrical and asymmetrical social conflict in cognitive change. *Journal of Experimental Child Psychology, 49*(1), 58–78.

Russell, A., & Russell, G. (1989). Warmth in mother-child and father-child relationships in middle childhood. *British Journal of Developmental Psychology, 7*(3), 219–235.

Rutter, M. (1983). Stress, coping and development: Some issues and some questions. In N. Garmezy & M. Rutter (Eds.), *Stress, coping and development in children.* New York: McGraw-Hill.

Rutter, M. (1983). School effects on pupil progress: Research findings and policy implications. *Child Development, 54,* 1–29.

Rutter, M., & Garmezy, N. (1983). Developmental psychopathology. In P. H. Mussen (Ed.), *Handbook of Child Psychology* (4th ed.), Vol. 4. New York: Wiley.

Rutter, M., Maughan, B., Mortimore, P., & Ouston, J. (1979). *Fifteen thousand hours: Secondary schools and their effects on children.* Cambridge, MA: Harvard University Press.

Sachs, J. (1985). Prelinguistic development. In J. B. Gleason (Ed.), *The development of language*. Columbus, OH: Merrill.

Saltz, R. (1979). Children's interpretation of proverbs. *Language Arts, 56*, 508–514.

Salzer, R. I. (1984). Early reading and giftedness; Some observations and questions. *Gifted Child Quarterly, 28*(2), 95–96.

Sameroff, A. J., & Zax, M. (1973). Perinatal characteristics of the offspring of schizophrenic women. *Journal of Nervous and Mental Diseases, 46*, 178–185.

Sandberg, E. C. (1978). *Synopsis of obstetrics* (10th ed.). St. Louis: C. V. Mosby.

Sanders-Phillips, K., Strauss, M. E., & Gutberlet, R. L. (1988). The effect of obstetric medication on newborn infant feeding behavior. *Infant Behavior and Development, 11*(3), 251–263.

San Francisco AIDS Foundation. (1988). *Pregnancy and AIDS*. 333 Valencea St., 4th Floor, San Francisco, CA, 94103.

Santrock, J. W., Sitterle, K. A., & Warshak (1988). Parent-child relationships in stepfather families. In P. Bronstein & C. P. Cowan (Eds.), *Fatherhood today: Men's changing role in the family*. New York: Wiley.

Santrock, J. W., & Warshak, R. A. (1979). Father custody and social development in boys and girls. *Journal of Social Issues, 35*, 112–125.

Sattler, J. M. (1982). *Assessment of children's intelligence and special abilities* (2nd ed.). Boston: Allyn and Bacon.

Saunders, E. J. & Saunders, J. A. (1990). Drug therapy in pregnancy: The lessons of diethylstilbestrol, thalidomide, and bendectin. *Health Care of Women International, 11*(4), 423–32.

Savin-Williams, S. R. (1979). Dominance hierarchies in groups of early adolescents. *Child Development, 50*, 142–151.

Sawin, D. B., Parke, R. D., Harrison, A. N., & Kreling, B. (1975, September). *The child's role in sparing the rod*. Paper presented at the Annual Convention of the American Psychological Association, Chicago, IL.

Scales, P. C. (1987). How we can prevent teen pregnancy (and why it's not the real problem). *Journal of Sex Education and Therapy, 13*(1), 12–15.

Scarr, S. (1968). Environmental bias in twin studies. *Eugenics Quarterly, 25*, 34–40.

Scarr, S. (1981). Testing for children: Assessment and the many determinants of intellectual competence. *American Psychology, 36*, 1159–1166.

Scarr, S. (1984). *Mother care, other care*. New York: Basic Books.

Scarr, S., & Kidd, K. K. (1983). Developmental behavior genetics. In M. M. Harth & J. J. Campos (Eds.), *Handbook of child psychology: Infancy and developmental psychobiology* (Vol. 2). New York: Wiley.

Scarr, S., Phillips, D., & McCartney, K. (1989). Working mothers and their families. *American Psychology, 44*(11), 1402–1409.

Scarr, S. & Salapatek, P. (1970). Patterns of fear development during infancy. *Merrill-Palmer Quarterly, 16*, 53–90.

Scarr, S., & Weinberg, R. (1983). IQ performance of black children adopted by white families. *American Psychology, 31*(10), 726–739.

Schacter, D. L., & Moscovitch, M. (1984). Infants, amnesiacs and dissociable memory systems. In M. M. Oscovitch (Ed.), *Infant memory: Its relation to normal and pathological memory in humans and other animals*. New York: Plenum.

Schaffer, H. R. (1978). Acquiring the concept of the dialogue. In M. H. Bornstein & W. Kessen (Eds.), *Psychological development from infancy: Image to intention*. Hillsdale, NJ: Erlbaum.

Schaffir, J. (1991). What are little boys made of? The never-ending search for sex selection techniques. *Perspectives in Biology and Medicine, 34*(4), 516–525.

Schauble, L. (1990). Belief revision in children: The role of prior knowledge and strategies for generating evidence. *Journal of Experimental Child Psychology, 49*(1), 31–57.

Scher, M. S., Richardson, G. A., Coble, P. A., Day, N. L., & Stoffer, D. S. (1988). The effects of prenatal alcohol and marijuana exposure: Disturbances in neonatal sleep cycling and arousal. *Pediatric Research,*

24(1), 101–105.

Schiedt, P. C. et al. (1991). Intelligence at 6 years in relation to neonatal bilirubin levels: Follow up of the National Institute of Child Health and Human Development Clinical Trial of Phototherapy. *Pediatrics, 87*(9), 797–805.

Schieffelin, B. B., & Ochs, E. (1983). A cultural perspective on the transition from prelinguistic to linguistic communication. In R. M. Golinkoff (Ed.), *The transition from prelinguistic to linguistic communication*. Hillsdale, NJ: Erlbaum.

Schlesinger, H. S., & Meadow, K. P. (1972). *Sound and sign: Childhood deafness and mental health*. Berkeley, CA: University of California Press.

Schmeck, H. M. (1984, January). As scoffing fades, pineal gland gets its due. *The New York Times*, pp. C1–2.

Schmidt, E. & Eldridge, A. (1986). The attachment relationship and child maltreatment. *Infant Mental Health Journal, 7*(4), 264–273.

Schmidt, C. R., Ollendick, T. H., & Stasnowicz, L. B. (1988). Developmental changes in the influence of assigned goals on cooperation and competition. *Developmental Psychology, 24*(4), 574–579.

Schneider-Rosen, K., Braunwald, K. G., Carlson, V., & Cicchetti, D. (1985). Current perspective in attachment theory: Illustrations from the study of maltreated infants. In I. Boetherton & E. Waters (Eds.), Growing points of attachment theory and research. *Monographs of the Society for Research in Child Development, 50*(1–2, Serial No. 209).

Schofield, H. L. (1981). Teacher effects on cognitive and affective pupil outcomes in elementary school mathematics. *Journal of Educational Psychology, 73*(4), 462–471.

Schofield, N., & Ashman, A. (1987). The cognitive processing of gifted, high average and low average ability students. *British Journal of Educational Psychology, 57*, 9–20.

Schuckit, M. A. (1987). Biological vulnerability to alcoholism. *Journal of Consulting and Clinical Psychology, 55*(3), 301–309.

Schwartz, D. et al. (1981). On the relationship between the number of spermatozoa and the probability of conception. *Reproduction, Nutrition and Development, 21*(64), 979–988.

Schwartz, M. W. et al. (1990). *Pediatric primary care*. New York: Year Book Med.

Schwartz-Bickenbach, D. et al. (1987). Smoking and passive smoking during pregnancy and early infancy: Effects on birth weight, lactation period and cotinine concentrations in mother's milk and infant's urine. *Toxicology Letters, 35*(1), 73–81.

Schworm, R. W., & Birnbaum, R. (1989). Symptom expression in hyperactive children: An analysis of observations. *Journal of Hearing Disabilities, 22*(1), 35–40.

Scott, J. R. et al. (1990). *Danforth's obstetrics and gynecology* (6th ed.). Philadelphia: J. B. Lippincott.

Scott, K. P., & Schau, C. G. (1985). Sex equity and sex bias in instructional materials. In S. S. Klein (Ed.), *Handbook for achieving sex equity through education*. Baltimore, MD: Johns Hopkins University Press.

Seal, K. (1987, November 20). Superchildren—pushed too far for their own good? *Los Angeles Times*, Pt. V; pp. 1, 8.

Sears, R. R., Whitney, J. W. M., Nowlis, V., & Sears, P. S. (1953). Some child-rearing antecedents of aggression and dependency in young children. *Genetic Psychology Monographs. 47*, 135–234.

Seaward, P. G., & Sonnedecker, E. W. (1990). Natural childbirth—the Johannesburg Hospital Experience 1983–1989. *South African Medical Journal, 78*(11), 677–680.

Seder, J. I. (1980). Infant's shoes: Attitudes of podiatrists and pediatricians. *Journal of the American Podiatry Association, 70*(5), 244–246.

Sedvall, G. (1981). Neurotransmitter disturbances and predisposition to depressive illness. *Advances in Biological Research, 7*, 26–33.

Segal, N. L. (1989). Origins and implications of handedness and relative birth weight for IQ in monozygotic twin pairs. *Neuropsychologia, 27*(4), 549–561.

Selikowitz, M. (1990). *Down syndrome: The facts*. Oxford, England: Oxford University Press.

Selman, R. L. (1980). *The growth of interpersonal understanding*. New York: Academic Press.

Selman, R. L., & Selman, A. D. (1979). Children's ideas about friendship: A new theory. *Psychology Today, 13*(4), 71–80, 114.

Seo, I. S., Gillim, S. E., & Mirkin, L. D. (1990). Hyaline membranes in postmature infants. *Pediatric Pathology, 10*(4), 530–540.

Sera, M. D., Troyer, D., & Smith, L. B. (1988). What do two-year-olds know about the sizes of things? *Child Development, 59*(6), 1489–1496.

Serbin, L. A., Connor, J. M., & Citron, C. C.(1981). Sex-differentiated free play behavior: Effects of teacher modeling, location and gender. *Developmental Psychology, 17*, 640–646.

Serbin, L. A., Connor, J. M., & Iler, I. (1979). Sex stereotyped and nonstereotyped introductions of new toys in the preschool classroom: An observational study of teacher behavior and its effects. *Psychology of Women Quarterly, 4*, 261–265.

Shaklee, H., Holt, P., Elek, S., & Hall, Laurie (1988). Covariation judgment: Improving rule use among children, adolescents and adults. *Child Development, 59*(3), 755–768.

Shannon, L. W. (1982). *Assessing the relationship of adult criminal careers to juvenile careers*. Iowa City: University of Iowa, Iowa Urban Community Research Center.

Shantz, C. M. (1987). Conflicts between children. *Child Development, 58*, 283–305.

Shapiro, L. R. et al. (1984). Obesity prognosis: A longitudinal study of children from the age of 6 months to 9 years. *American Journal of Public Health, 74*, 968–972.

Shaywitz, S. et al. (1990, August 22). Prevalence of reading disability in boys and girls. Results of the Connecticut Longitudinal study. *Journal of the American Medical Association, 264*(8), 998–1002.

Shedler, J., & Block, J. (1980). Adolescent drug use and psychological health: A longitudinal inquiry. *American Psychologist, 45*(5), 612–630.

Shelov, S. (1989, November). SIDS. *American Baby*, pp. 113–114, 126.

Sherif, M. et al. (1961). *Intergroup conflict and cooperation: The Robbers Cave experiment*. Norman, Oklahoma: Institute of Group Relations.

Sherman, L. W. (1985). Humor and social distance. *Perceptual and Motor Skills, 61*(3, Pt. 2), 1274.

Shettles, L., & Rorvik, D. (1989). How to choose the sex of your baby, rev. ed. NY: Doubleday.

Shiono, P. H., & Klebanoff, M. A. (1989). Bendectin and human congenital malformations. *Teratology, 40*(2), 151–155.

Shirley, L. L., & Reynolds, R. E. (1988). Effects of interest on attention and learning. *Journal of Educational Psychology, 80*(2), 159–166.

Shirley, M. M. (1933). The first two years: A study of 25 babies. Vol. 1. Postural and locomotor development. *Institute of Child Welfare Monographs* (No. 6). Minneapolis: University of Minnesota Press.

Short, A. B., & Schopler, E. (1988). Factors relating to age of onset in autism. *Journal of Autism and Developmental Disorders, 18*(2), 207–216.

Shukat, E. M., & Haines, A. (1986). The colicky baby. *American Baby, 48*(4), 64–65, 71–73.

Siegal, M. (1987). Are sons and daughters treated more differently by fathers than by mothers? *Developmental Review, 7*, 183–209.

Siegel, A. W. (1981). The externalization of cognitive maps by children and adults: In search of ways to ask better questions. In L. S. Liben, A. H. Patterson & N. Newcombe (Eds.), *Spatial representation and behavior across the life span*. New York: Academic Press.

Siegel, L. S. (1989). IQ is irrelevant to the definition of learning disabilities. *Journal of Learning Disabilities, 22*(8), 469–478.

Siegel, O. (1982). Personal development in adolescence. In B. B. Wolman (Ed.) *Handbook of developmental psychology*. Englewood Cliffs, NJ: Prentice Hall.

Siegler, R. S. (1981). Developmental sequences within and between concepts. *Monographs of the Society for Research in Child Development, 46*, (2 Serial No. 189).

Siegler, R. (1983a). Information processing approaches to cognitive development. In P. Mussen (Ed.), *Manual of Child Psychology* (4th ed.), Vol. 1. New York: Wiley.

Siegler, R. S. (1983b). Fine generalizations about cognitive development. *American Psychologist, 38*, 263–277.

Siegler, R. S., & Richards, D. D. (1982). The development of intelligence. In M. Lewis (Ed.), *Origins of intelligence: Infancy and early childhood*. New York: Plenum.

Sigman, M. et al. (1989). Effects of microwaving human milk: Changes in IgA content and bacterial count. *Journal of the American Dietetic Association, 89*(5), 1–2.

Sigmon, S. B. (1987). Sex roles: Their relationship to cultural and biological determinants. *Sexual and Marital Therapy, 2*(1), 29–33.

Signorella, M. L., & Liben, L. S. (1984). Recall and reconstruction of gender-related pictures: Effects of attitude, task difficulty and age. *Child Development, 55*, 393–405.

Silber, T. J. (1985). Some medical problems common in adolescence. *Medical Aspects of Human Sexuality, 19*(2), 79–85.

Silbereisen, R. K. et al. (1989). Maturational timing and the development of problem behavior: Longitudinal studies in adolescence. Special issue: Early adolescent transitions. *Journal of Early Adolescence, 9*(3), 247–268.

Silk, A. M., & Thomas, G. V. (1988). The development of size scaling and children's figure drawings. *British Journal of Developmental Psychology, 6*(3), 285–299.

Silverman, W. K., Jaccard, J., & Burke, A. E. (1988). Children's attitudes toward products and recall of product information over time. *Journal of Experimental Child Psychology, 45*, 365–381.

Simner, M. L. (1971). Newborns' response to the cry of another infant. *Developmental Psychology, 5*, 136–150.

Sinclair, D. C. (1989). *Human growth after birth* (5th ed.). Oxford: Oxford University Press.

Singer, D. G. (1983). A time to reexamine the role of television in our lives. *American Psychology, 38*, 815–816.

Singer, J. L., & Singer, D. G. (1983). Psychologists look at television. *American Psychology, 38*, 826–834.

Singer, J. L., & Singer, D. G. (1985). Television-viewing and family communication style as predictors of children's emotional behavior. *Journal of Children in Contemporary Society, 17*(4), 75–91.

Singer, L. (1986). Long-term hospitalization of failure to thrive infants: Developmental outcome at 3 years. *Child Abuse and Neglect, 10*(4), 479–486.

Siqueland, E. R., & Lipsitt, L. D. (1966). Conditioned head-turning behavior in newborns. *Journal of Experimental Child Psychology, 3*, 356–376.

Skeels, H. M. (1942). A study of the effects of differential stimulation on mentally retarded children: A follow-up report. *American Journal of Mental Deficiency, 46*, 340–350.

Skeels, H. M. (1966). Adult status of children with contrasting early life experiences: A follow-up study. *Monographs of the Society for Research in Child Development, 31*(3, Serial No. 105).

Skeen, P., & McKeny P. (1980). The teacher's role in facilitating a child's adjustment to divorce. *Young Children, 35*, 3–12.

Skinner, B. F. (1957). *Verbal behavior*. New York: Appleton-Century-Crofts.

Skinner, B. F. (1984). The shame of American education. *American Psychology, 39*, 947–955.

Skinner, E. A., Wellborn, J. G., & Connell, J. P. (1990). What it takes to do well in school and whether I've got it: A process model of perceived control and children's engagement in school. *Journal of Educational Psychology, 82*(1), 22–32.

Slap, G. B. (1986). Normal physiological and psychosocial growth in the adolescent. *Journal of Adolescent Health Care, 7*(6, Suppl.), 13–23.

Slater, A., Cooper, R., Rose, D., & Morison, V. (1989). Prediction of cognitive performance from infancy to early childhood. *Human Development, 32*(3–4), 137–147.

Slobin, D. I. (1975). On the nature of talk to children. In E. H. Lenneberg & E. Lenneberg (Eds.), *Foundations of language development* (Vol. 1). New York: Academic Press.

Slobin, D. I. (1981). The origins of grammatical encoding of events. *Behavioral Development—A Series of Monographs*, pp. 185–199.

Smart, M. S. & Smart, R. C. (1978). *Infants: Development and relationships,* 2nd ed. New York: Macmillan.

Smith, C., Carey, S., & Wiser, M. (1985). On differentiation: A case study of the development of the concepts of size, weight and density. *Cognition, 21*(3), 177–237.

Smith, G. F., & Warren, S. T. (1985). The biology of Down syndrome. *Annals of the New York Academy of Sciences, 450*, 1–9.

Smith, L. (1990, May 2). A sound education. *Sacramento Bee*, pp. 51, 53.

Smith, P. B., & Pederson, D. R. (1988). Maternal sensitivity and patterns of infant-mother attachment. *Child Development, 59*(4), 1097–1101.

Smith, P. K., & Connolly, K. J. (1980). *The ecology of preschool behavior.* Cambridge, England: Cambridge University Press.

Smith, T. W. (1990). A report: The sexual revolution? *Public Opinion Quarterly, 54*(3), 415–435.

Snow, M. E., Jacklin, C. N., & Maccoby, E. E. (1981). Birth order differences in peer sociability at thirty-three months. *Child Development, 52,* 589–596.

Snow, M. E., Jacklin, C. N., & Maccoby, E. E. (1983). Sex-of-child differences in father-child interaction at one year of age. *Child Development, 54*(1), 227–232.

Society for Research on Child Development, Ethical Interest Group (1975). *Ethical standards for research with children.* Chicago, IL: Society for Research in Child Development.

Socol, M. L. et al. (1982). Maternal smoking causes fetal hypoxia: Experimental evidence. *American Journal of Obstetrics and Gynecology, 124*(2), 214–218.

Sonnenschein, S. (1986). Development of referential communication skills: How familiarity with a listener affects a speaker's production of redundant messages. *Developmental Psychology, 22*(4), 549–552.

Sophian, C. (1988). Early developments in children's understanding of numbers: Inferences about numerosity and 1-to-1 correspondence. *Child Development, 59*(5), 1397–1414.

Sorensen, R. C. (1973). *Adolescent sexuality in contemporary America: Personal values and sexual behavior ages 13–19.* New York: Abrams.

Sosa, R. J., Kennell, J., Klaus, M. et al. (1980). Effect of a supportive companion on perinatal problems, length of labor and mother-infant interaction. *New England Journal of Medicine, 303*, 597–600.

Spence, J. T. (1985). Achievement American style: The rewards and costs of individualism. *American Psychology, 40*, 1285–1295.

Sperling, D. (1987, November 3). Needless surgery. *USA Today*, p. 2D.

Spitz, H. H. (1986). Preventing and curing mental retardation by behavioral intervention: An evaluation of some claims. *Intelligence, 10*, 197–207.

Spitzer, W. O. et al. (1990). Links between passive smoking and disease: A best-evidence synthesis. *Clinical and Investigative Medicine, 13*(1), 17–42; discussion, 43–46.

Sprague, R., & Ullman, R. (1981). Psychoactive drugs and child management. In J. Kaufman and D. Hallahan (Eds.), *Handbook of special education,* Englewood Cliffs, NJ: Prentice-Hall.

Sroufe, L. A. (1979). Socioemotional development. In J. D. Osofsky (Ed.) *Handbook of infant development.* New York: Wiley.

Sroufe, L. A. (1983). Individual patterns of adaptation from infancy to preschool. In M. Perlmutter (Ed.) *Proceedings of the Minnesota Symposium on Child Psychology.* Hillsdale, NJ: Erlbaum.

Sroufe, L. A. (1985). Attachment classification from the perspective of infant-caregiver relationships and infant temperament. *Child Development 56*, 1–14.

Sroufe, L. A. (1986). Appraisal: Bowlby's contribution to psychoanalytic theory and the developmental psychology—attachment, separation, loss. *Special issue: 30th anniversary of Association for Child Psychology and Psychiatry and Allied Disciplines, 27*(6), 841–849.

Sroufe, L. A. (1988). A developmental perspective on day care. Special issue: Infant day care. *Early Childhood Research Quarterly, 3*(3), 283–291.

Sroufe, L. A., Fox, N., & Pancake, V. (1983). Attachment and dependency in developmental perspective. *Child Development, 54*, 1615–1627.

Sroufe, L. A., Waters, & Matas, L. (1974). Contextual determinants of infant affective response. In M. Lewis & L. Rosenblum (Eds.), *The emergence of fear.* New York: Wiley.

St. James-Roberts, I. (1989). Persistent crying in infancy. *Journal of Child Psychology and Psychiatry and Allied Disciplines, 30*(2), 189–195.

Stangor, C., & Ruble, D. N. (1987). Development of gender role knowledge and gender constancy. In S. Liben & M. L. Signorella (Eds). *Children's gender schemata.* San Francisco: Jossey-Bass.

Stanley, J. C. (1978). Radical acceleration: Recent educational innovation of Johns Hopkins University. *Gifted Child Quarterly, 22*, 63–67.

Stapley, J., & Haviland, J. M. (1989). Beyond depression: Gender differences in normal adolescents' emotional experiences. *Sex Roles, 20*(5/6), 295–308.

Stark, E. (1984, May). The unspeakable family secret. *Psychology Today,* 42–46.

Stark, E. (1989, June). Girls happy with themselves. *Psychology Today,* p. 10.

Starr, R. H., Jr. (1979). Child abuse. *American Psychology, 34*, 872–878.

Steihm, E. R., & Vink, P. (1990). Transmission of human immunodeficiency virus infection by breastfeeding. *Journal of Pediatrics, 118*(3), 410–412.

Stein, D. M., & Brinza, S. R. (1989). Bulimia: Prevalence estimates in female junior high and high school students. *Journal of Clinical Child Psychology, 18*(3), 206–213.

Steinbacher, R. (1986, August 15). The hidden agenda is fewer female babies. *USA Today*, p. 8A.

Steinberg, L. (1986). Stability (and instability) of Type A behavior from childhood to young adulthood. *Developmental Psychology, 23*(3), 451–460.

Steinberg, L. (1987). Familial factors in delinquency: A developmental perspective. *Journal of Adolescent Research, 2*(3), 255–268.

Steinberg, L., & Levine, A. (1990). *You and your adolescent: A parent's guide to development from 10 to 20.* New York: Harper and Row.

Steinberg, L. D., Greenberger, E., Garduque, L., Ruggiero, M., & Vaux, A. (1982). Effects of working on adolescent development. *Developmental Psychology, 18*, 385–395.

Stenberg, C., Campos, J., & Emde, R. (1983). The facial expression of anger in seven-month old infants. *Child Development, 54*, 178–184.

Stene, J. et al. (1981). Paternal age and Down's syndrome: Data from prenatal diagnoses. *Human Genetics, 59*(2), 119–124.

Stern, D. (1977). *The first relationship: Mother and infant.* Cambridge, MA: Harvard University Press.

Stern, H. P. et al. (1990). Young children in recreational sports: Participation maturation. *Clinical Pediatrics, 29*(2), 89–94.

Sternberg, R. I. (1982). Who's intelligent? *Psychology Today, 16*(4), 30–39.

Sternberg, R. (Ed.) (1984). *Mechanisms of cognitive development.* San Francisco: Freeman.

Sternberg, R. J. (1986). *Intelligence applied.* New York: Harcourt Brace Jovanovich.

Sternberg, R. J. (1988). Mental self-government: A theory of intellectual styles and their development. *Human Development, 31*(4), 197–221.

Sternberg, R., & Davidson, R. (1985). Cognitive development in the gifted and talented. In F. Horowitz & M. O'Brien (Eds.), *The gifted and talented: Developmental perspectives.* Washington, D.C.: American Psychiatric Association.

Sternberg, R., & Powell, J. (1983). The development of intelligence. In P. Mussen (Ed.), *Handbook of Child Psychology*, (3rd ed.), Vol. 3. New York: Wiley.

Stevens, J. H., & Bakeman, R. (1985). A factor analytic study of the HOME scale for infants. *Developmental Psychology, 21*(6), 1196–1203.

Stevenson, B. W., Roscoe, B., & Kennedy, D. (1988). Perceptions of conventional war: Late adolescents' views. *Adolescence, 23*(91), 613–627.

Stevenson, H. W., Lee, S., Chuansheng, C., Stigler, J. W. et al. (1990). Contexts of achievement: A study of American, Chinese and Japanese children. *Monographs of the Society for Research in Child Development, 55*(1–2)[221]. 1–123.

Stevenson, M. R., & Block, K. N. (1988). Paternal absence and sex role development. *Child Development, 59*, 793–814.

Stewart, P., & Spiby, H. (1989). A randomized study of the sitting position for delivery using a newly designed obstetric chair. *British Journal of Obstetrics and Gynecology, 96*(3), 327–333.

Stinnett, N., Farris, J., & Walters, J. (1974). Parent-child relationships of male and female high school students. *Journal of Genetic Psychology, 125*, 99–106.

Stipek, D. J. (1981). Children's perceptions of their own and their classmate's ability. *Journal of Educational Psychology, 73*, 404–410.

Stipek, D. J., Gralinski, J. H., & Kopp, C. B. (1990). Self-concept development in the toddler years. *Developmental Psychology, 26*(6), 972–977.

Stipek, D. J., Roberts, T. A., Daubarn, M. E. (1984). Preschool-age children's performance expectations for themselves and another child as a function of the incentive value of success and the salience of past performances. *Child Development, 55*, 1983–1989.

Stjernfeldt, M., Berglund, K., Lindsten, J., & Ludvigsson, J. (1986, June 14). Maternal smoking during pregnancy and risk of childhood cancer. *The Lancet*, pp. 1350–1352.

Stocker, C., Dunn, J., & Plomin, R. (1989). Sibling relationships: Links with child temperament, maternal behavior and family structure. *Child Development, 60*, 715–727.

Stone, L. J., & Church, J. (1984). *Childhood and adolescence* (5th ed.). New York: Random House.

Stoneman, Z., Brody, G. H., & Burke, M. (1989). Marital quality, depression, and inconsistent parenting: Relationship with observed mother-child conflict. *American Journal of Orthopsychiatry, 59*(1), 105–117.

Stoneman, Z., Brody, G. H., & Mackinnon, C. E. (1986). Same sex and cross-sex siblings: Activity choices, roles, behavior and gender stereotypes. *Sex Roles, 15*, 495–511.

Stouthamer-Loeber, M., & Loeber, R. (1986). Boys who lie. *Journal of Abnormal Child Psychology, 14*(4), 551–564.

Straus, M. A., & Gelles, R. J. (1986). Societal change and change in family violence from 1975 to 1985 as revealed by two national surveys. *Journal of Marriage and the Family, 48*(3), 465–479.

Strayer, J., & Roberts, W. (1989). Children's empathy and role taking: Child and parental factors, and relations to prosocial behavior. *Journal of Applied Developmental Psychology, 10*(2), 227–239.

Strayer, J. & Schroeder, M. (1989). Children's helping strategies: Influence of emotion, empathy, and age. *New Directions for Child Development,* Sum. No., *44*, 85–105.

Streissguth, A. P. et al. (1986). Attention, distraction, and reaction time at age 7 years and prenatal alcohol exposure. *Neurobehavioral Toxicology and Teratology, 8*(6), 717–725.

Streissguth, A. P., Barr, H. M., Sampson, P. D., & Darby, B. L. et al. (1989). IQ at age 4 in relation to maternal alcohol use and smoking during pregnancy. *Developmental Psychology, 25*(1), 3–11.

Strichartz, A. F., & Burton, R. V. (1990). Lies and truth: A study of the development of the concept. *Child Development, 61*(1), 211–220.

Strunin, L., & Hingson, R. (1987). Acquired immuno-deficiency syndrome and adolescents: Knowledge, beliefs, attitudes and behaviors. *Pediat-*

rics, *79*, 825–882.

Stunkard, A. J., Foch, T. T., & Hrubek, Z. (1986). A twin study of human obesity. *Journal of American Medical Association, 256*, 51–54.

Stutts, M. A., & Hunnicutt, G. G., (1987). Can young children understand disclaimers in television commercials? *Journal of Advertising, 18*(1), 41–46.

Sullivan, M. W., & Lewis, M. (1988). Facial expressions during learning in 1 year old infants. *Infant Behavior and Development, 11*(3), 369–373.

Summala, H. (1987). Young driver accidents: Risk taking or failure of skills? *Alcohol, Drugs and Driving, 3*(3–4), 79–91.

Super, C. M. (1981). Cross-cultured research on infants. In H. C. Triandes and A. Herm (Eds.), *Handbook of Cross Cultured Psychology* (Vol. 4). Boston: Allyn and Bacon.

Susman, E. J. et al. (1985). The relation of relative hormone levels and physical development and social-emotional behavior in young adolescents. Special issue: Time of maturation and psychosocial functioning in adolescence: I. *Journal of Youth and Adolescence, 14*(3), 245–264.

Sutton-Smith, B. (1979). *Play and learning.* New York: Gardner Press.

Suzuki, S. (1969). *Nurtured by love.* New York: Exposition Press.

Svedja, M., & Campos, J. (1982). *The mother's voice as a regulation of the infant's behavior.* Paper presented at the meeting of the International Conference on Infant Studies, Austin, Texas.

Svedja, M. J., Campos, J. J. & Emde, R. N. (1980). Mother-infant "bonding": Failure to generalize. *Child Development, 51*, 775–779.

Swick, K. J. & Hassell, T. (1990). Parental efficacy and the development of social competence in young children. *Journal of Instructional Psychology, 17*(1), 24–32.

Talwar, R., Schwab, J., & Lerner, R. M. (1989). Early adolescent temperament and academic competence: Tests of "direct effects" and developmental contextual models. Special issue: Early adolescent transitions. *Journal of Early Adolescence, 9*(3), 291–309.

Tangney, J. P. (1988). Aspects of the family and children's television viewing content preferences. *Child Development, 59*(4), 1070–1079.

Tanner, J. M. (1978). *Education and physical growth* (2nd ed.). New York: International Universities Press.

Tanner, J. M. (1982). *Growth at adolescence,* 2nd ed. Oxford, England: Scientific Publications.

Taras, H. L., Sallis, J. F., Patterson, T. L., Nadar, P. R. et al. (1989). Television's influence on children's diet and physical activity. *Journal of Developmental and Behavioral Pediatrics, 10*(4), 176–180.

Tarnowski, K. J., Rasnake, L. K., Linschied, T. R., & Mulick, J. A. (1989). Behavioral adjustment of pediatric burn victims. *Journal of Pediatric Psychology, 14*(4), 607–615.

Tarr, P. (1990). More than movement: Scribbling reassessed. *Visual Arts Research, 16*(1, Issue 31), 83–90.

Tavris, C., & Wade, C. (1984). *The longest war: Sex differences in perspective* (2nd ed.). San Diego, CA: Harcourt Brace Jovanovich.

Taskinen, H. K., (1990). Effect of parental occupational exposures on spontaneous abortion and congenital malformation. *Scandanavian Journal of Work Environment and Health, 16*(5), 297–314.

Taylor, A. R. (1989). Predictions of peer rejection in early elementary grades: Roles of problem behavior, academic achievement and teacher preference. *Journal of Clinical Child Psychology, 18*(4), 360–365.

Tedder, J. L. (1991). Using the Brazelton Neonatal Assessment Scale to facilitate the parent-infant relationship in a primary care facility. *Nurse Practitioner, 18*(3), 20–30, 35.

Tegano, D. W., & Moran, J. D. (1989). Sex differences in the original thinking of preschool and elementary school children. *Creativity Research Journal, 2*(1–2), 102–110.

Tellegen et al. (1988). Personality similarity in twins reared apart and together. *Journal of Personality and Social Psychology, 54*(6), 1031–1039.

Teller, D. Y., & Bornstein, M. H. (1987). Infant color vision and color perception. In P. Salapatek & L. B. Cohen (Eds.), *Handbook of infant perception* (Vol. 1). From sensation to perception. Orlando, Fla: Academic Press.

Tenovuo, A. H. et al. (1988). Risk factors associated with severely small for gestational age neonates. *American Journal of Perinatology, 5*(3), 267–271.

Terman, L. M. (1925). *Genetic studies of genius: Vol. 1. The mental and physical traits of a thousand gifted children.* Stanford, CA: Stanford University Press.

Terman, L. M. (1954). Scientists and nonscientists in a group of 800 gifted men. *Psychology Monographs, 68*(7), 1–44.

Terman, L. M., & Oden, M. H. (1959). *Genetic studies of genius: Vol. 5. The gifted group at mid-life: Thirty five years' follow up of the superior child.* Stanford, CA: Stanford University Press.

Termine, N. T., & Izard, C. E. (1988). Infants' responses to their mothers' expressions of joy and sadness. *Developmental Psychology, 24,* 223–229.

Teti, D. M., & Ablard, K. E. (1989). Security of attachment and infant-sibling relationships: A laboratory study. *Child Development, 60*(6), 1519–1528.

Tew, M. (1985). Place of birth and perinetal mortality. *Journal of the Royal College of General Practitioners, 35,* 390–394.

Thatcher, R. W., Walker, R. A., Guidice, S. (1987). Human cerebral hemispheres develop at different rates and ages. *Science, 236* (4805), 1110–1113.

Thoman, E. B., & Whitney, M. D. (1989). Sleep states of infants monitored in the home: Individual differences, developmental trends, and origins of diurnal cyclicity. *Infant Behavior and Development, 12*(1), 59–75.

Thomas, A., & Chess, S. (1977). *Temperament and development.* New York: Brunner/Mazel.

Thomas, A., Chess, S., & Birch, H. G. (1970). The origins of personality. *Scientific American, 223*(2), 102–109.

Thomas, A., Chess, S., & Korn, S. J. (1982). The reality of difficult temperament. *Merrill-Palmer Quarterly, 28,* 1–20.

Thomas, G. V., Chaigne, E., & Fox, T. J. (1989). Children's drawings of topics differing in significance: Effects on size of drawing. *British Journal of Developmental Psychology, 7*(4), 321–331.

Thompson, L. A., & Massaro, D. W. (1989). Before you see it, you see its parts: Evidence for feature encoding and integration in preschool children and adults. *Cognitive Psychology, 21*(3), 334–362.

Thompson, R. A. (1987). Empathy and emotional understanding: The early development of empathy. In N. Eisenberg & J. Strayer (Eds.), *Empathy and its development.* San Francisco: Jossey-Bass.

Thompson, R. A. (1990). Vulnerability in research: A developmental perspective on research risk. *Child Development, 61*(1), 1–16.

Thompson, R. A., & Lamb, M. E. (1984). Assessing qualitative dimensions of emotional responsivness in infants: Separation reactions in the strange situation. *Infant Behavior and Development, 7*(4), 423–445.

Thorkildsen, T. A. (1989). Pluralism in children's reasoning about social justice. *Child Development, 60*(4), 965–972.

Thornberg, H. D., & Aras, Z. (1986). Physical characteristics of developing adolescents. *Journal of Adolescent Research, 1*(1), 47–78.

Thornton, L. P., & DeBlassie, R. R. (1989). Treating bulimia. *Adolescence, 24*(95), 631–637.

Thurstone, L. L. (1938). Primary mental abilities. *Psychometric Monographs (No. 1).* Chicago: University of Chicago Press.

Times Wire Service (1987, November 26). Tests to help spot Down's Syndrome in fetus reported. *Los Angeles Times,* Pt. 1, p. 38.

Tipper, S. P. et al. (1989). Mechanisms of attention: A devlopmental study. *Journal of Experimental Child Psychology, 48*(3), 353–378.

Tittmar, H. G. (1990). What's the harm in just a drink? *Alcohol and Alcoholism, 26*(2–3), 287–291.

Tobin-Richards, M., Boxer, A., & Petersen, A. C. (1983). The psychological impact of pubertal change: Sex differences in perceptions of self during

early adolescence. In Brooks-Gunn & A. C. Petersen (Eds.), *Girls at puberty: Biological, psychological and social perspectives.* New York: Plenum.

Tolman, E. C. (1948). Cognitive maps in rats and men. *Psychology Review, 55,* 189–208.

Tomasello, M., Conti-Ransden, G., & Ewert, B. (1990). Young children's conversations with their mothers and fathers: Differences in breakdown and repair. *Journal of Child Language, 17*(1), 115–130.

Toner, I. J., & Smith, R. A. (1977). Age and overt verbalization in delay maintenance behavior in children. *Journal of Experimental Child Psychology, 24,* 123–128.

Toney, L. (1983). The effects of holding the newborn at delivery on paternal bonding. *Nursing Research, 32*(1), 16–19.

Torrence, E. P. (1972). Characteristics of creatively gifted children and youth. In E. P. Trapp & P. Himelstein (Eds.), *The exceptional child.* New York: Appelton-Century-Crofts.

Trautner, H. M. et al. (1989). Age-graded judgments of children's drawings by children and adults. *International Journal of Behavior Development, 12*(4), 421–431.

Trehub, S. E., Schneider, B. A., Morrongiello, B. A., & Thorpe, L. A. (1988). Auditory sensitivity in school-age children. *Journal of Experimental Child Psychology, 46*(2), 273–285.

Treichel, R. S. (1987). Immunogenetic studies of maternal-fetal relationships: A review. *Genetica, 73*(1–2), 69–79.

Trotter, R. J. (1985). Fathers and daughters: The broken bond. *Psychology Today,* p. 10.

Trussel, J. (1988). Teenage pregnancy in the United States. *Family Planning Perspectives, 20,* 262–273.

Tucker, S. K. (1989). Adolescent patterns of communication about sexually related topics. *Adolescence, 24*(94), 269–278.

Tulkin, S. R., & Konner, M. J. (1973). Alternative conceptions of intellectual functioning. *Human Development, 16,* 33–52.

Turiel, E. (1978). Social regulations and domains of social concept. *New Directions for Child Development, 1,* 45–74.

Turiel, E., & Smetana, J. G. (1984). Social knowledge and action: The co-ordination of domains. In W. M. Kurtines & J. L. Gewirtz (Eds.), *Morality, moral behavior and moral development.* New York: Wiley.

Turkheimer, M., Bakeman, R., & Adamson, L. B. (1989). Do mothers support and peers inhibit skilled object play in infancy? *Infant Behavior and Development, 12*(1), 37–44.

Tweed, J. L., Schoenbach, V. J., George, L. K., & Blazer, D. G. (1989). The effects of childhood parental death and divorce on six-month history of anxiety disorders. *British Journal of Psychiatry, 154,* 823–828.

Tyler, F. B., & Varma, M. (1988). Help-seeking and helping behavior in children as a function of social competence. *Journal of Applied Developmental Psychology, 9*(2), 219–231.

Unger, D. G. & Wandersman, L. P. (1988). The relation of family and partner support to the adjustment of adolescent mothers. *Child Development, 59*(4), 1056–1060.

Urberg, K. A., & Kaplan, M. G. (1989). An observational study of race-, age-, and sex-heterogeneous interaction in preschoolers. *Developmental Psychology, 10*(3), 299–311.

U.S. Bureau of the Census (1984). *Statistical abstract of the United States: 1984 (104th edition).* Washington, D.C.: U.S. Government Printing Office.

U.S. Bureau of the Census, (1987). *Current population reports. Series P-20.* Washington, D.C.: Government Printing Office.

U.S. Bureau of the Census (1991). *Statistical abstract of the United States: 1991 (111th ed.).* Washington, D.C.: U.S. Government Printing Office.

U.S. Department of Health and Human Services (1988). Campaign cuts illegal sale of tobacco to minors in half. *Tobacco and Youth Reporter, 3*(1), 1–2.

U.S. Department of Justice (1988). *Statistics*. Washington, D.C.: U.S. Government Printing Office.

U.S. Department of Labor, Bureau of Labor Statistics (1987, August 12). *News*. Washington, D.C.: U.S. Government Printing Office.

Uttal, D. H., Lummis, M., & Stevenson, H. W. (1988). Low and high mathematics achievement in Japanese, Chinese and American elementary-school children. *Developmental Psychology, 24*, 335–342.

Uttal, D. H., & Wellman, H. M. (1989). Young children's representation of spatial information acquired from maps. *Developmental Psychology, 25*(1), 128–138.

Utter, W. F. (1987). School refusal more than just a stomach ache. *The Brown University Child Behavior and Development Letter, 3*(4), 1–3.

Uzgiris, I. C. (1981). Two functions of imitation in infancy. *International Journal of Behavior and Development, 4*, 1–12.

Vandell, D. L., Henderson, V. K., & Wilson, K. S. (1988). A longitudinal study of children with day-care experiences of varying quality. *Child Development, 59*(5), 1286–1292.

Vandell, D., Minnett, A., & Santrock, J. (1987). Age difference in sibling relationships during middle childhood. *Journal of Applied Developmental Psychology, 8*, 247–257.

Vandershaf, S. (1987). Autism: A chemical excess? *Psychology Today, 21*(3), 15–16.

Vaughan, B. E., Gove, F. L., & Egeland, B. (1980). The relationship between out-of-home care and the quality of infant-mother attachment in an economically deprived population. *Child Development, 51*(4), 1203–1214.

Vaughn, B. E. et al. (1989). Attachment behavior, attachment security, and temperament during infancy. *Child Development, 60*(3), 728–737.

Vernberg, E. M. (1990). Experiences with peers following relocation during early adolescence. *American Journal of Orthopsychiatry, 60*(3), 466–472.

Vernon, P. A. (1989). The generality of *g*. *Personality and Individual Differences, 10*(7), 803–804.

Vernon, P. E. (1971). *The structure of human abilities*. London: Methuen.

Vernon, P. E. (1979). Intelligence testing and the nature/nurture debate, 1928–1978: What's next? *British Journal of Educational Psychology, 49*(1), 1–14.

Vianello, R., & Lucamante, M. (1988). Children's understanding of death according to parents and pediatricians. *Journal of Genetic Psychology, 149*(3), 305–316.

Vicary, J. R. & Lerner, J. V. (1983). Longitudinal perspectives on drug use: Analysis from the New York Longitudinal Study. *Journal of Drug Education, 13*(3), 275–285.

Vils, U. (1980, February 2). What other kids think rates no. 1. *Los Angeles Times*, Pt. 5, pp. 1, 5.

vonHofsten, C. (1983). Catching skills in infancy. *Journal of Experimental Psychology (Human Perception), 9*(1), 75–85.

Vurpillot, E. (1968). The development of scanning strategies and their relation to visual differentiation. *Journal of Experimental Child Psychology, 6*, 623–650.

Vurpillot, E. (1976). *The visual world of the child*. (Transcribed by W. E. C. Gilham). New York: International Universities Press (originally published in 1972).

Vygotsky, L. S. (1962). *Thought and language*. New York: Wiley.

Wadsworth, J. (1983). Family type and accidents in preschool children. *Journal of Epidemiology and Community Health, 37*(2), 100–104.

Wagner, M. E., Schubert, J. H. P., & Schubert, D. S. P. (1985). Family size effects: A review. *Journal of Genetic Psychology, 146*, 65–78.

Wahler, R. G., & Dumas, J. E. (1989). Attentional problems in dysfunctional mother-child interactions. An interbehavioral model. *Psychology Bulletin, 105*(1), 116–130.

Walden, T. A., & Ogan, T. A. (1988). The development of social referenc-ing. *Child Development, 59*(5), 1230–1240.

Walker, L. J. (1989). A longitudinal study of moral reasoning. *Child Development, 60*(1), 157–166.

Walker-Andrews, A. S. (1986). Intermodal perception of expressive behaviors: Relation of eye and voice? *Developmental Psychology, 22*, 373–377.

Wallach, M. A. (1985). Creativity testing and giftedness. In G. P., Wallach & K. G. Butler (Eds.), *Language and learning disabilities in schoolage children*. Baltimore: Williams and Wilkins.

Wallerstein, E. (1980). *Circumcision: An American health fallacy*. New York: Springer.

Wallerstein, J. S. (1984). Children of divorce: Preliminary report of a ten-year follow up of young children. *American Journal of Orthopsychiatry, 54*, 444–458.

Wallerstein, J. S., & Corbin, S. B. (1989). Daughters of divorce: Report from a ten-year follow-up. *American Journal of Orthopsychiatry, 59*(4), 593–604.

Wallerstein, J. S. & Kelly, J. B. (1980, January). California's children of divorce. *Psychology Today, 14*, 67–76.

Ward, T. B. (1989). What makes a vibble a vibble? A developmental study of category generalization. *Child Development, 60*(1), 214–224.

Warren, M. P. (1983). Physical and biological aspects of puberty. In J. Brooks-Gunn & A. C. Petersen (Eds.), *Girls at puberty: Biological and psychosocial perspectives*. New York: Plenum.

Warren-Leubecher, A., & Carter, B. W. (1988). Reading and growth in metalinguistic awareness: Relations to socioeconomic status and reading readiness skills. *Child Development, 59*(3), 728–742.

Warshak, R. & Santrock, J. W. (1979). *The effects of father and mother custody on children's social development*. Paper presented at the meeting of the Society for Research in Child Development, San Francisco.

Warton, P., & Bussey, K. (1988). Assisted learning: Levels of support. *British Journal of Developmental Psychology, 6*(2), 113–123.

Waters, E., & Sroufe, L. A. (1983). Social competence as a developmental construct. *Developmental Review, 3*, 79–97.

Waters, E., Vaughn, B. E., & Egeland, B. (1980). Individual differences in infant-mother attachment relationships at age one: Antecedents in neonatal behavior in an urban, economically disadvantaged sample. *Child Development, 51*, 208–216.

Watson, J. B., & Raynor, R. (1920). Conditioned emotional reactions. *Journal of Experimental Psychology, 3*, 1–14.

Watson, J. S., & Ramey, C. (1972). Reactions to response-contingent stimulation in infancy. *Merrill-Palmer Quarterly, 18*(3), 219–227.

Watson, M. W. (1981). The development of social roles: A sequence of social-cognitive development. In K. W. Fischer (Ed.), *Cognitive development (New directions for child development, No. 12)*. San Francisco: Jossey-Bass.

Weathersbee, P. S. (1980). Early reproductive loss and the factors that may influence its occurrence. *Journal of Reproductive Medicine, 25*(6), 315–318.

Weaver, K. A. & Anderson, G. C. (1988). Relationship between integrated sucking pressures and first bottlefeeding scores in premature infants. *Journal of Obstetric, Gynecologic, and Neonatal Nursing, 17*(2), 113–20.

Weber, J. A., & Fournier, D. G. (1985). Family support and a child's adjustment to death. Special issue: The family and health care. *Family relations. Journal of Applied Family and Child Studies, 34*(1), 43–49.

Wegman, M. E. (1990). Annual summary of vital statistics—1989. *Pediatrics, 86*(6), 835–847.

Weinberg, C. R., Wilcox, A. J., & Baird, D. D. (1989). Reduced fecundability in women with prenatal exposure to cigarette smoking. *American Journal of Epidemiology, 129*(5), 1072–1078.

Weinraub, M., Clemens, L. P., Sockloff, A., Ethridge, T., Gracely, E., & Myers, B. (1984). The development of sex role stereotypes in the third year: Relationship to gender labeling, gender identity, sex-typed toy preference and family characteristics. *Child Development, 55*, 1493–1503.

Weir, M. W. (1964). Development changes in problem-solving strategies.

Psychology Review, 71, 473–490.

Weissbluth, M., & Liu, K. (1983). Sleep patterns, attention span, and infant temperament. *Journal of Developmental and Behavioral Pediatrics, 4*(1), 34–36.

Weisz, J. R. (1978). Choosing problem-solving rewards and Halloween prizes: Delay of gratification and preference for symbolic reward as a function of development, maturation and personal investment. *Developmental Psychology, 14*, 66–78.

Weller, E. B., Weller, R. A., Fristad, M. A., Cain, S. E., & Bowes, J. M. (1988). Should children attend their parents' funeral? *Journal of American Academy of Child and Adolescent Psychiatry, 27*, 559–562.

Werner, H. (1948). *Comparative psychology of mental development.* New York: Science Editions.

Werner, J. S., & Siqueland, E. K. (1978). Visual recognition memory in the preterm infant. *Infant Behavior and Development, 1*, 79–94.

West, M. J., & Rheingold, H. L. (1978). Infant simulation of maternal instruction. *Infant Behaviors and Development, 1*, 205–215.

Westover, K. M., DiLoreto, M. K. and Shearer, T. R. (1989). The relationship of breastfeeding to oral development and dental concerns. *ASDC Journal of Dentistry for Children, 56*(2), 140–143.

Whalen, C. K., Henker, B., Hinshaw, S. P., & Granger, D. A. (1989). *Externalizing behavior disorders, situational generality.*

Whaley, L. F., & Wong, D. L. (1988). *Essentials of pediatric nursing* (3rd ed.). St. Louis: C. V. Mosby.

Whelan, E. M. (1975). *A baby? . . . Maybe: A guide to making the most fateful decision in your life.* New York: Bobbs-Merrill.

Whitbeck, L. B. et al. (1989). Value socialization and peer group affiliation among early adolescence. *Journal of Early Adolescence, 9*(4), 436–453.

White, P. A. (1988). Causal processing: Origins and development. *Psychology Bulletin. 104*(1), 36–52.

White, S. H., & Pollemor, D. B. (1979). Childhood amnesia and the development of a socially accessible memory system. In J. F. Kihlstrom & F. J. Evans (Eds.), *Feral disorders of memory.* Hillsdale, NJ: Erlbaum.

Whitehurst, G. J., Falco, F. L., Lonigan, C. J., & Fischel, J. E. (1988). Accelerating language development through picture book reading. *Developmental Psychology, 24*(4), 552–559.

Whitelaw, A. et al. (1988). Skin-to-skin contact for very low birthweight infants and their mothers. *Archives of Disease in Childhood, 63*, 1377–1381.

Whitesell, N. R., & Harter, S. (1989). Children's reports of conflict between simultaneous opposite-valence emotions. *Child Development, 60*(3), 673–682.

Whitney, E. N., & Cataldo, C. B. (1987). *Understanding Normal and Clinical Nutrition* (2nd ed.). St. Paul: West Publishing.

Wickstrom, R. (1977). *Fundamental Motor Patterns* (2nd ed.). Philadelphia: Lea and Febiger.

Wiener, F. D., Lewnau, L. E., & Erway, E. (1983). Measuring language competency in speakers of Black American English. *Journal of Speech and Hearing Disorders, 48*(1), 76–84.

Wierson, M., Forehand, R., Fauber, R., & McCombs, A. (1989). Buffering young male adolescents against negative parental divorce influences: The role of good parent-adolescent relations. *Child Study Journal, 19*(2), 101–115.

Williams, H. G. (1983). *Perceptual and motor development.* Englewood Cliffs, NJ: Prentice-Hall.

Williams, T. M. (Ed.) (1985). *The impact of television: A natural experiment involving three towns.* New York: Academic Press.

Williams, T. M., Zabrack, M. L. & Joy, L. A. (1982). The portrayal of aggression on North American television. *Journal of Applied Social Psychology, 12*(5), 360–380.

Willson, J. R. et al. (1991). *Obstetrics and gynecology* (9th ed.). St. Louis, C. V. Mosby.

Wilmore, J. H. (1982). The female athlete. In R. A. Magill, M. J. Ash, & F. L.

Small (Eds.), *Children in sports.* Champaign, IL: Human Kinetics Publishers.

Wilson, C. C., Lazarre, J. A., & Tingstrom, D. H. (1989). Children's resistance to deviation: Multiple behavioral models. *Journal of Genetic Psychology, 150*(1), 75–83.

Wilson, M. N. (1986). The black extended family: An analytical consideration. *Developmental Psychology, 22*, 246–258.

Wilson, R. S. (1972). Early mental development. *Science, 175*, 914–917.

Winchester, A. M. & Mertens, T. R. (1983). *Human Genetics,* 4th ed. Glenview, IL: Scott Foresman.

Winner, E. (1986). Where pelicans kiss seals. *Psychology Today, 20,* pp. 25–26, 30–35.

Wiswell, T. E. et al. (1990). Meconium aspiration syndrome: Have we made a difference? *Pediatrics, 85*(5), 715–721.

Witkin, H. A., Oltman, P. K., Raskin, E. & Karp, S. A. (1971). A manual for the embedded figures test. Palo Alto, CA: Consulting Psychologists Press.

Wodarski, J. S., & Johnson, S. R. (1988). Child sexual abuse: Contributing factors, effects and relevant practice issues. *Family Therapy, 15*(2), 157–173.

Wolf, L., & Goldberg, B. (1986). Autistic children grow up: An 8–20 year follow up study. *Canadian Journal of Psychiatry, 31*, 550–556.

Wolff, P. H. (1959). State and neonatal activity. *Psychosomatic Medicine, 21*, 110–118.

Wolff, P. H. (1969). The natural history of crying and other vocalizations in early infancy. In B. M. Foss (Ed.), *The determinants of infant behavior* (Vol. 4). London: Methuen.

Wolock, I., & Horowitz, B. (1984). Child maltreatment as a social problem: The neglect of neglect. *American Journal of Orthopsychiatry, 54*, 530–543.

Woods, N. (1986). Socialization and social context: Influences on perimenstrual symptoms disability and menstrual attitudes. In V. Olesen & N. Woods (Eds.), *Culture, society, and menstruation.* Washington, D.C.: Hemisphere.

Worobey, J., & Blajda, V. M. (1989). Temperament rating at 2 weeks, 2 months and 1 year: Differential stability of activity and emotionality. *Developmental Psychology, 25*, 257–263.

Wride, N. (1986, August 15). Parents turned in by daughter charged. *Los Angeles Times,* Pt. 3, p. 3.

Wright, B. A. (1983). *Physical disability: A psychological approach* (2nd ed.). NY: Harper & Row.

Wright, J. C., Giammarino, M., & Parad, H. W. (1986). Social status in small groups: Individual-group similarity and the social "misfit." *Journal of Personality and Social Psychology, 50*(3), 523–536.

Wright, K., Smith M. S., & Mitchell, J. (1990). Organic diseases mimicking atypical eating disorders. *Clinical Pediatrics, 29*(6), 325–328.

WuDunn, S. (1991, June 16). China's one-child policy breeds many broken hearts. *Sacramento Bee,* p. A22.

Xeromeritou, A. (1989). Verbal abilities of left- and right-handed children. *The Journal of Psychology, 123*, 121–132.

Yakovlev, P. I., & Lecours, A. R. (1967). The myelogenetic cycles of regional maturation of the brain. In A. Minkowski (Ed.), *Regional development of the brain in early life.* Oxford: Blackwell.

Yamamoto, K., Soliman, A., Parsons, J., & Davies, O. L. (1987). Voices in unison: Stressful events in the lives of children in six countries. *Journal of Child Psychology and Psychiatry, 28*(6), 855–864.

Yamauchi, Y., & Yamanouchi, I. (1990). The relationship between rooming in/not rooming in and breastfeeding variables. *Acta Paediatrica Scandinavica, 79*(11), 1017–1022.

Yanchinski, S. (Ed.). (1989). *Biotechnology: A brave new world?* Cambridge, MA: Lutherworth.

Yap, J. N-K (1988). The effects of hospitalization and surgery on children:

A critical review. *Journal of Applied Developmental Psychology, 9,* 349–358.

York, R., Freeman, E., Lowrey, B., & Strauss, J. (1989). Characteristics of premenstrual syndrome. *American College of Obsetricians and Gynecologists, 73,* 601–605.

Younger, A. J., & Piccinin A. M. (1989). Children's recall of aggressive and withdrawn behaviors: Recognition memory and likeability judgments. *Child Development, 60*(3), 580–590.

Youngstrom, N. (1991, September). Drug exposure in home elicits worst behaviors. *APA Monitor,* p. 23.

Yuill, N., & Joscelyne, T. (1988). Effect of organizational cues and strategies on good and poor comprehenders' story understanding. *Journal of Educational Psychology, 80*(2), 152–158.

Yule, W., & Williams, R. M. (1990). Post-traumatic stress reactions in children. *Journal of Traumatic Stress, 3*(2), 279–295.

Zahn-Waxler, C., & Radke-Yarrow, M. (1982). The development of altruism: Alternative research strategies. In N. Eisenberg-Berg (Ed.), *The development of prosocial behavior.* New York: Academic Press.

Zajonc, R. B. (1983). Validating the confluence model. *Psychology Bulletin, 93,* 457–480.

Zajonc, R. B., & Marcus, G. B. (1975). Birth order and intellectual development. *Psychology Review, 82,* 74–88.

Zaslow, M. J. (1989). Sex differences in children's response to parental divorce: II. Samples, variables, ages and sources. *American Journal of Orthopsychiatry, 59*(1), 118–141.

Zaslow, M. J., Robinovich, B. A., Suwalsky, J. T., & Skein, R. P. (1988). The role of social context in the prediction of secure and insecure/avoidant infant-mother attachment. *Journal of Applied Developmental Psychology, 9*(3), 287–299.

Zeanah, C. H. et al. (1985). Prenatal perception of infant personality: A preliminary investigation. *Journal of American Academy of Child Psychiatry, 24*(2), 204–210.

Zelazo, P. R., & Kearsley, R. (1980). The emergence of functional play in infants: Evidence for a major cognitive transition. *Journal of Applied Developmental Psychology, 1*(2), 95–117.

Zelazo, P. R., & Leonard, E. L. (1983). The dawn of active thought. *New Directions for Child Development, No. 21,* 37–50.

Zheng, S-Y. & Colombo, J. (1989). Sibling configuration and gender differences in preschool social participation. *Journal of Genetic Psychology, 150*(1), 45–50.

Ziemer, M. M., & George, C. (1990). Breastfeeding and the low birthweight infant. *Neonatal Network, 9*(4), 33–38.

Zigler, E. F. (1987). Formal schooling for 4-year-olds? No. *American Psychology, 42,* 254–260.

Zill, N. (1983). *Healthy, happy and insecure.* New York: Doubleday.

Zimbardo, P. & Redl, S. L. (1981). *The shy child: A parents' guide to preventing and overcoming shyness from infancy to adulthood.* New York: McGraw-Hill.

Zimmerman, I. L., & Bernstein, M. (1983). Parental work patterns in alternative families: Influences on child development. *American Journal of Orthopsychiatry, 53*(3), 418–425.

Zinober, B., & Martlew, M. (1985). Developmental changes in four types of gestures in relation to acts and vocalizations from 10 to 21 months. Special issue: Infancy. *British Journal of Developmental Psychology, 3*(3), 293–306.

Zuravin, S. J. (1989). Severity of maternal depression and three types of mother-to-child aggression. *American Journal of Orthopsychiatry, 59*(3), 377–389.

Credits

Index